GW01459378

THE BUILDINGS OF ENGLAND

FOUNDING EDITOR: NIKOLAUS PEVSNER

HAMPSHIRE:
WINCHESTER AND THE NORTH

MICHAEL BULLEN, JOHN CROOK, RODNEY HUBBUCK
AND NIKOLAUS PEVSNER

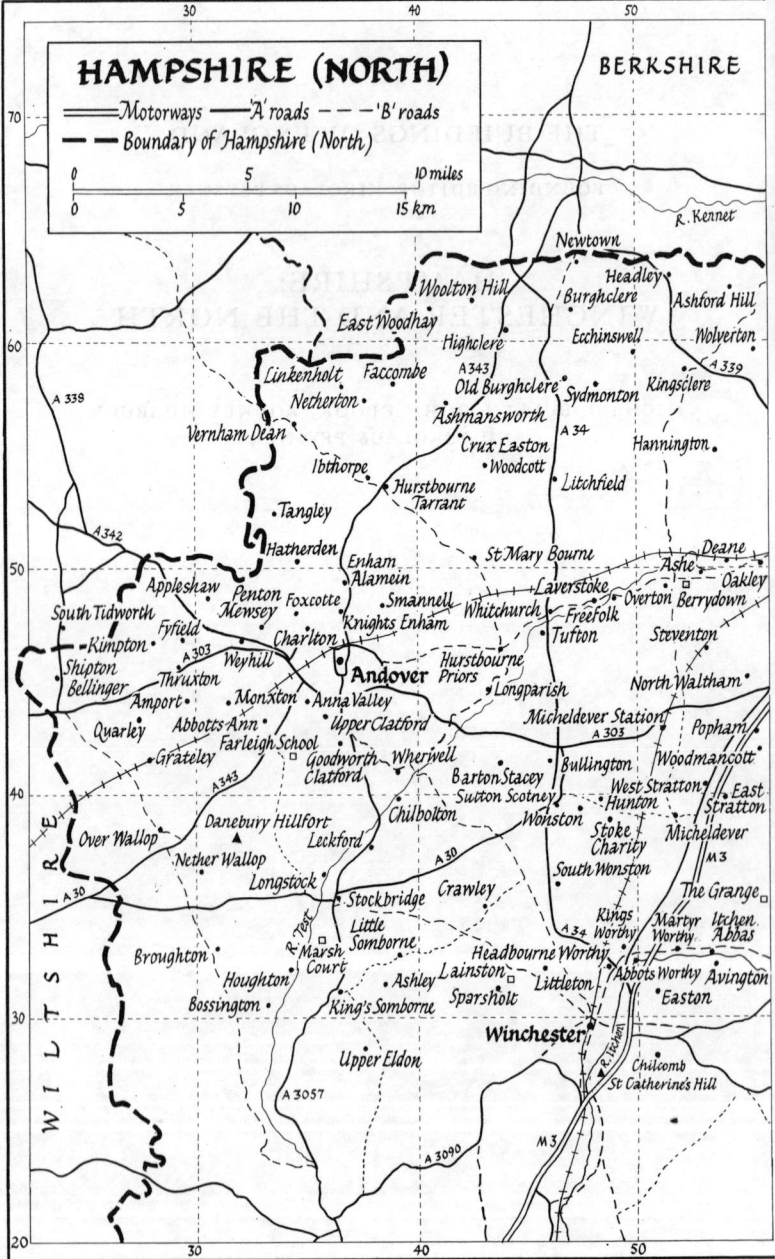

HAMPSHIRE (NORTH)

BERKSHIRE

Motorways   'A' roads   - - - 'B' roads

Boundary of Hampshire (North)

0   5   10 miles

0   5   10   15 km

R. Kennet

Newtown

Woolton Hill   Headley   Ashford Hill
East Woodhay   Burghclere   Wolverton
Highclere   Ecchinswell
A 339   Linkenholt   Faccombe   *A 343*   Old Burghclere   Sydmonton   Kingsclere
Netherton   Ashmansworth   *A 34*   Hannington
Vernham Dean   Crux Easton   Litchfield
    Ibthorpe   Woodcott
  Tangley   Hurstbourne
A 342   Tarrant
   Hatherden   St Mary Bourne   Deane
Appleshaw   Enham   Ashe   Oakley
South Tidworth   Penton   Alamein   Laverstoke   Overton   Berrydown
Kimpton   Mewsey   Foxcotte   Smannell   Whitchurch   FreeFolk
Fyfield   *A 303*   Knights Enham   Tufton   Steventon
Shipton   Weyhill   Charlton   Hurstbourne   North Waltham
Bellinger   Thruxton   **Andover**   Priors
Amport   Monxton   Anna Valley   Longparish
Quarley   Abbotts Ann   Upper Clatford   Micheldever Station   Popham
Grateley   Farleigh School   Wherwell   *A 303*   Woodmancott
A 343   Goodworth   Barton Stacey   West Stratton   East
   Clatford   Chilbolton   Sutton Scotney   Hunton   Stratton
Over Wallop   Danebury Hillfort   Wonston   Stoke   Micheldever
  Nether Wallop   Leckford   Charity   *M 3*
A 30   Longstock   *A 30*   South Wonston
   Crawley   The Grange
  Stockbridge   Kings   Martyr   Itchen
Broughton   Little   *A 34*   Worthy   Worthy   Abbas
  R. Test   Somborne   Headbourne Worthy   Avington
  Marsh   Ashley   Lainston   Abbots Worthy
Houghton   Court   Littleton   Easton
Bossington   King's Somborne   Sparsholt
    Upper Eldon   **Winchester**
   A 3057   Chilcomb
    R. Itchen   St Catherine's Hill
WILTSHIRE   *A 3090*   *M 3*

60   70   80

N

A33
M4

BERKSHIRE

70

A327

Mortimer
West End
Silchester

Eversley

Yateley

Baughurst   Tadley   Stratfield Saye   Heckfield   Bramshill

A340   Stratfield Turgis   Hartley   House   Hartford   Minley   Hawley

Pamber   Bramley   Wespall   Mattingley   Bridge   Manor

Ramsdell

Monk   Sherfield   Rotherwick   West Green   Elvetham   Cove

Ewhurst   Sherborne   on-Loddon   Hartley

A339   The Vyne   Hook   Wintney   Farnborough

Wootton   Sherborne   Nately Scures   Winchfield

St Lawrence   St John   A33   Fleet

Worting   Old Basing   Newnham   Dogmersfield

Basingstoke   Andwell   Up Nately   North Warnborough   Church   Aldershot

Crookham

Mapledurwell   Greywell   Odiham   Ewshot

Cliddesden   Hackwood Park   Upton Grey   Crondall

Winslade   Tunworth   South Warnborough   SURREY

M3   Farleigh Wallop   Weston Patrick   Long Sutton

Dummer   Herriard   A31

Ellisfield   A339

Nutley   Moundsmere   Lasham   Bentley

Manor

Chilton   Bradley   Shalden   Froyle   Isington

Candover   Preston Candover   Alton   Holybourne   Binsted

Bentworth

Brown Candover   Beech   East Worldham   Kingsley

Northington   Wield   Medstead   Chawton   West Worldham   Headley

Bighton   Hartley Maudit   Oakhanger   Bordon   Passfield   Grayshott

Abbotstone   Old Alresford   Four Marks   Farringdon   A325   Bramshott

Itchen   A31   Selborne   Blackmoor

Stoke   New Alresford   Ropley   Newton   Greatham   A3   Liphook

Ovington   Bishop's Sutton   East Tisted   Valence   Empshott

Tichborne   A32   Colemore

Cheriton   West Tisted   Hawkley   Liss

Bramdean   Privett   High Cross   SUSSEX

A272   Hinton Ampner   Steep   Hill Brow

Kilmeston   Froxfield   Bedales   Sheet

West Meon   A272   Langrish   Petersfield   A272

East Meon   A3   Buriton

60   70   80   20

PEVSNER ARCHITECTURAL GUIDES

The Buildings of England series was created and largely
written by Sir Nikolaus Pevsner (1902–83). First editions of the
county volumes were published by Penguin Books
between 1951 and 1974. The continuing programme of
revisions and new volumes has been supported by research
financed through the Buildings Books Trust since 1994

THE PEVSNER BOOKS TRUST

formerly the Buildings Books Trust,
an independent registered charity, number 1042101.
It promotes the appreciation and understanding of
architecture by supporting and financing
the research needed to sustain new and revised volumes of
The Buildings of England, Ireland, Scotland and *Wales*

The Trust gratefully acknowledges
major grants towards the cost of research
and writing from

Walter Guinness Charitable Trust
Lady Anne Scott
Charlotte Bonham Carter Charitable Trust
Ellis Campbell Charitable Trust
Hampshire County Council
The Open Churches Trust
and
Laurence Kinney

assistance with photography from

ENGLISH HERITAGE

Hampshire: Winchester and the North

BY

MICHAEL BULLEN

JOHN CROOK

RODNEY HUBBUCK

AND

NIKOLAUS PEVSNER

WITH CONTRIBUTIONS FROM

SIMON BRADLEY

CHARLES O'BRIEN

AND

EDWARD ROBERTS

THE BUILDINGS OF ENGLAND

YALE UNIVERSITY PRESS
NEW HAVEN AND LONDON

YALE UNIVERSITY PRESS
NEW HAVEN AND LONDON
302 Temple Street, New Haven CT 06511
47 Bedford Square, London WC1B 3DP
www.pevsner.co.uk
www.lookingatbuildings.org.uk
www.yalebooks.co.uk
www.yalebooks.com
for
THE PEVSNER BOOKS TRUST

Published by Yale University Press 2010
2 4 6 8 10 9 7 5 3 1

ISBN 978 0 300 12084 4

Copyright © Nikolaus Pevsner and David Lloyd, 1968
Copyright © Michael Bullen, John Crook and
Rodney Hubbuck, 2010

Printed in China
through World Print
Set in Monotype Plantin

All rights reserved.
This book may not be reproduced
in whole or in part, in any form (beyond that
copying permitted by Sections 107 and 108 of the
U.S. Copyright Law and except by reviewers
for the public press), without written
permission from the publishers

The 1967 edition of
Hampshire and the Isle of Wight
was dedicated to
'the Ministry of Housing and Local Government,
whose lists of buildings of architectural or historic interest are
one of the finest tools we have'

2010 dedication

to the Hampshire Buildings Preservation Trust and all
architects, buildings craftspeople and specialist conservationists
employed on Historic Buildings repair and rescue
in Hampshire

CONTENTS

LIST OF TEXT FIGURES AND MAPS

Every effort has been made to contact or trace all copyright holders. The publishers will be glad to make good any errors or omissions brought to our attention in future editions.

MAPS

PHOTOGRAPHIC ACKNOWLEDGEMENTS

We are grateful to English Heritage and its photographer Nigel Corrie for taking many of the photographs in this volume (© English Heritage Photo Library) and also to the sources of the remaining photographs as shown below. We are grateful for permission to reproduce them as appropriate.

Michael Bullen: 80, 85, 121
Hugh Chevallier: 84
John Crook: 2, 6, 7, 8, 9, 10, 11, 12, 13, 14, 18, 19, 20, 21, 23, 24, 25, 26, 27, 31, 33, 34, 35, 36, 37, 38, 39, 40, 41, 43, 44, 45, 50, 52, 53, 71, 73, 95, 105, 109
Elvetham Hall Hotel: 103
English Heritage (NMR): 3, 64
English Heritage (Photo Library): 62
Angelo Hornak: 107, 110, 122
Rodney Hubbuck: 4, 47, 116
John Hunt: 114
Peter Inskip Architects: 115
National Trust Photo Library/A.C. Cooper and The Estate of Stanley Spencer 2010. All rights reserved DACS: 117
National Trust/Richard Holttum: 58
National Trust Photo Library/Andrea Jones: 62, 65
National Trust Photo Library/James Mortimer: 56, 81
National Trust Photo Library/Derrick E. Witty: 54
Stratfield Saye Preservation Trust: 70
Winchester College: 42

MAP REFERENCES

The numbers printed in italic type in the margin against the place names in the gazetteer of the book indicate the position of the place in question on the index map (pp. ii–iii), which is divided into sections by the 10-kilometre reference lines of the National Grid. The reference given here omits the two initial letters which in a full grid reference refer to the 100-kilometre squares into which the county is divided. The first two numbers indicate the *western* boundary, and the last two the *southern* boundary, of the 10-kilometre square in which the place in question is situated. For example, Basingstoke (reference 6050) will be found in the 10-kilometre square bounded by grid lines 60 (on the *west*) and 70, and 50 (on the *south*) and 60; Winchester (reference 4020) in the square bounded by the grid lines 40 (on the *west*) and 50, and 20 (on the *south*) and 30.

The map contains all those places, whether towns, villages, or isolated buildings, which are the subject of separate entries in the text.

ACKNOWLEDGEMENTS

The *Buildings of England* guide to *Hampshire and the Isle of Wight* was published in 1967 and was written jointly by Nikolaus Pevsner and David W. Lloyd. In its revised form the guide is now divided into three, one volume for the Isle of Wight (2006, revised by David W. Lloyd) and two for the mainland, of which this, covering Winchester and the northern half of the county is the first to be published. The other, covering the s of the county, including Portsmouth, Southampton, Bournemouth and the New Forest is in preparation. Although gathering of research for a new edition of Hampshire began many years ago, work in the northern county commenced properly in 2002. All of the entries for this area were written originally by Nikolaus Pevsner and in the task of revision the division of labour has been as follows: Rodney Hubbuck, who also undertook a great deal of preparatory research for the whole of the northern area, has updated all the church entries. Winchester, including the Cathedral and St Cross Hospital, has been revised by John Crook. For the secular buildings in most of the villages and hamlets and smaller towns the author is Michael Bullen. He has also written all of the entries for the country houses except The Vyne and Hinton Ampner House, which are by Charles O'Brien, who also revised the entries for several villages: Ashley, Bossington, Broughton, Froxfield, Greatham, High Cross, Houghton, King's Somborne, Nether Wallop, Over Wallop, Privett, Sheet, Steep, Upper Eldon and West Meon. The accounts of the buildings of the major towns, other than churches, have been revised by Simon Bradley (Aldershot, Andover and Farnborough) and Charles O'Brien (Basingstoke and Petersfield). Much information has been shared between the authors in the course of the work and the complete text was edited by Charles O'Brien.

In common with all the revised editions of Pevsner's work the aim has been to preserve at the very least the spirit of his style and wherever possible to preserve his descriptions and opinions. But the extent of new research available to revisers and improved understanding of many buildings has frequently made it necessary to start afresh, especially in the major settlements. Moreover, the aim of the revisers has been to include significant buildings which either escaped Pevsner's attention or whose interest, half a century on, is now appreciated. While there is no attempt to be comprehensive, and revisers bring with them their own prejudices, readers of this edition will not only find a greater selection of Victorian, Edwardian and twentieth century architecture but also more on vernacular buildings, in which Hampshire is so rich.

Foremost acknowledgement and thanks must be given to our contributors: Edward Roberts not only wrote the section on vernacular buildings in the introduction to the Middle Ages but his research and scholarship on Hampshire houses before 1700 has also ensured the accurate description of numerous timber-framed and other buildings included in the gazetteer. In addition we are grateful for the specialist chapters in the Introduction by Michael Barker (Geology and Building Materials) and Barry Cunliffe (Prehistoric and Roman), who also revised and updated his original gazetteer entries for the 1967 edition of *Hampshire and the Isle of Wight*. David W. Lloyd has given constant advice and encouragement over many years, including loans of research material and writing innumerable letters conveying valuable information and observations. Other readers have also written in since 1967 to point out errors, omissions and to suggest items for inclusion in the revised edition, notably the late Sir Howard Colvin, Peter Cormack, Patrick Farman, Geoffrey Fisher, the late Andor Gomme, Peter Howell, George McHardy, Thomas Merriam, Nicholas Riall, Barry Shurlock, Nicholas Taylor, Simon Watney and Roger White.

In the course of revision many people have generously shared their knowledge of various buildings and assisted with enquiries on specific subjects. At the top of this list come the County and District Council Conservation Officers and the staff of the County Architects Department and its successors. Several individuals have also given much-needed advice. In addition to those acknowledged elsewhere, they are James Abson, Peter Atkinson, Louise Bainbridge, Denise Baker, Keith Barrett, John Barton, Keith and Corinne Bennett, Jennifer Berry and Bob Wallbridge (Winchester schools), Marcus Binney, Peter Bird, David Blissett, Geoff Brandwood, Marion Brinton, Sarah Brown, Mary Callé, Mike Clark, Steve Clow, Brian Collins, Jonathan Croad, Mr and Mrs G. Dawson, Geoffrey Denford, Caroline Edwards, David Esterley, Jim Ewing, Richard Falconer, Matthew and Vicky Feldwick (Winchester University chapel), Bill Fergie, Andy Foster, Jane Geddes, Claire Gapper (plasterwork), Alec Gillies, Chris Gotto, Alastair Graham, Frank Green, Martin Gregory, Pat Grover, Dennis Hadley, Gavin Haig, Helen Harvey, Dom Cuthbert Brogan OSB and Dom Thomas Harper OSB at Farnborough Abbey, Roland Harris, Hugh Harrison, Chris Higgins, Toby Huitson, Tony Humphrys, Michael Jackson, Paul Jeffery, David Trevor-Jones, Brenda Kipling, Jeremy Lake, Elizabeth Lewis, Phillip Lindley, Simon Mays, Elizabeth McKellar, Dan Miles and Martin Bridge (dendrochronology), John Minnis, Linda Monckton, Martin Morris, Richard K. Morris, Kathryn Morrison, Christopher Norton, Karen Parker, Alexandra Parry, Gordon Pearson, Pamela Peskett, Fay Poulter, Alan Powers, Ken Qualmann, Mary Ray (Petersfield), Gill Rushton, Andrew Rutter, Andrew Saint, Nigel Saul, Matthew Saunders, Barbara Selby,

David Sermon, Martin Smith, Pete Smith, Graham Soffe, Tim Tatton-Brown, Mike Taylor, Sir Bryan Thwaites, Charles Tracy, Ross Turle, Michael Underwood, Parthe Ward, Nigel Westbrook, Eva White and Professor Barbara Yorke. The following also made available their knowledge and research on individual architects, Paul Bradley (William Burn), Steven Astley (Thomas Chawner), Sally Jeffery (John James) and Judith Patrick (Walter Cave).

Clergy and private owners who have granted access to buildings throughout the northern county are too numerous to mention individually. However, we are especially grateful to Sandra de Laslo at Pelham Place, John Hervey Bathurst at Somborne Park and Lord Inchyra at Rookley Manor, and to the archivists at Rotherfield Park (Lou Elderton) and Highclere (Jennifer Thorp and latterly John Rymill). It would have been impossible to revise some of the entries without access to research by, and advice from, David Blissett (Highclere), David Brock (The Grange and Highclere Castle), Alison Deveson (Hurstbourne Park and Hackwood House, with Martin Smith, and Whitchurch), Richard Garnier (Laverstoke Park), Anthony Geraghty (Farnborough Abbey), Roger Harris (the churches at Old Basing and Stoke Charity), Elain Harwood (Hook, C20 schools, and Hill House, Headley), Maurice Howard and Edward Wilson (The Vyne), Peter Inskip (Berrydown), Laurie Kinney (Lord Wandsworth College), John Martin Robinson (Old Alresford House), Kenneth Parry (Pelham Place), Brenda Poole (C19 church restorations and the work of John Colson), Ken Qualdman (Wield church, among others), Michael B. Readhead (Houghton Lodge), John Redmill (The Grange), Edward Roberts and Bill Fergie (Sydmonton House), Richard Tanner (Steventon) and Tom Stuart Smith (Hurstbourne Park landscape). Those with special knowledge of specific places and their buildings are Desmond Graves (Quarley), Laurence Giles (Bramshott, Liphook, Liss and area), Jane Hurst (Alton and area), Richard Johnston (Yateley), Sheila Millard (Odiham), Robert Parr (Broughton) and Richard Tanner (Steventon).

In addition, we must record thanks to John Wells, Simon Goddard, Dr Geoffrey Day and Suzanne Foster at Winchester College, and Anne Archer, librarian at Bedales, who helped supply information that was denied to Pevsner in 1967 by the Bursar, for whom 'Neither time nor clerical assistance make it possible . . .'

The authors have relied extensively on the resources of archives and libraries for their research and in this task have been further assisted by Karen Evans, who pursued enquiries at the RIBA library and National Archives. Special acknowledgement must be made of the staff of local libraries and in Winchester, above all to the Hampshire Record Office (notably Sarah Lewin), the City Museum and the Local Studies Library, where the late Philippa Stevens helped with references to churches from the Winchester Diocesan Chronicle. At the Cathedral Library, much assistance was given by successive canon librarians and their assistants: The Revd Keith Walker, the Revd Roly Riem, John Hardare, Jo Bartholomew. The various research libraries in London, in particular the RIBA, have offered valuable advice and assistance. Outside the county and London, thanks is owed to the staff of English Heritage's National Monuments Record Centre at Swindon and Cambridge University Library. Among other librarians and archivists we are especially grateful to Derek Hammond (Royal Bank of Scotland), Tina Staples (HSBC), Laura Taylor (Lloyds TSB) and Sally Day (Aldershot Military Museum).

A special debt of gratitude is owed to Julia King, who checked the entries for churches in the Guildford Diocese and pursued further research on them. Several other people kindly read draft texts for Winchester. They are Professor Martin Biddle and the late Mag. Birthe Kjølbye-Biddle, Michael Carden (St Cross), Bridget Cherry, Dr Geoffrey Day, Suzanne Foster, Dr John Hare, Robin Freeman, Professor Tom Beaumont James, and Michael St John Parker (Winchester College). In the rest of the area John Newman offered valuable advice on the text for Bramshill House and Maurice Howard provided the same for The Vyne.

For assistance in the preparation of the final manuscript for publication, Michael Bullen would like to thank Bronwen Edwards for her support and forbearance, while Rodney Hubbuck and the editor are greatly indebted to Maureen Gale, Henry Challender, Lilly Englebrecht and Daniel Hand for the accuracy of their typing. A thank you from the revisers is due to Sophie Kullmann, who as Production Editor was a splendid and patient superintendent of the final stages of publication.

As ever, the authors will be grateful to receive details of errors and omissions through the offices of the publisher.

INTRODUCTION*

Hampshire with the Isle of Wight is eighth in size among English counties. It has two large cities: Southampton and Portsmouth, but they belong to the south of the county; in the northern area covered by this volume the greatest city architecturally is Winchester but in terms of population Aldershot, Farnborough, Basingstoke and Andover (the last two due to London overspill) are greater. They account for the increasingly urban or suburban character of parts of the E and N of the county, but the rest is still predominantly rural and zealously guarded by the planning authorities. It has some of the finest and least spoilt scenery in the south of England: the famous valleys of the Meon, Itchen and Test are a haven of small villages, while a more varied area extends from the heights of the South Downs at the westernmost edge of the Western Weald, where the great rolling hangars of the chalk scarp close to Petersfield and Selborne flank a borderland landcape of remarkable contrasts, to the mixed heath and woodland gently rising to the high ground around Grayshott. Further N, beyond a fragment of the Anglo-Saxon Royal forest of Alice Holt are the flat sandy heaths of the Surrey border around Aldershot. In this NE corner of the county are the most strikingly impressive landscape features of Hampshire: the majestic single conifers and groups of conifers ones sees in so many places, enormous yew trees, and the introduced cedar trees, macrocarpa, Scotch firs – the first planted in England at Bramshill – and especially Wellingtonias, most extensive in great estates at Elvetham, Stratfield Saye and Tylney Hall. The dependence of this aspect of the flora of Hampshire on the geology of the county needs no emphasis and it is that subject to which one must first turn.

GEOLOGY AND BUILDING STONES
by
Michael Barker

The geographic area of the county of Hampshire comprises the major part of the larger geological structure known as the

* Unless otherwise stated the introduction has been written by Michael Bullen, Rodney Hubbuck, Charles O'Brien and Edward Roberts.

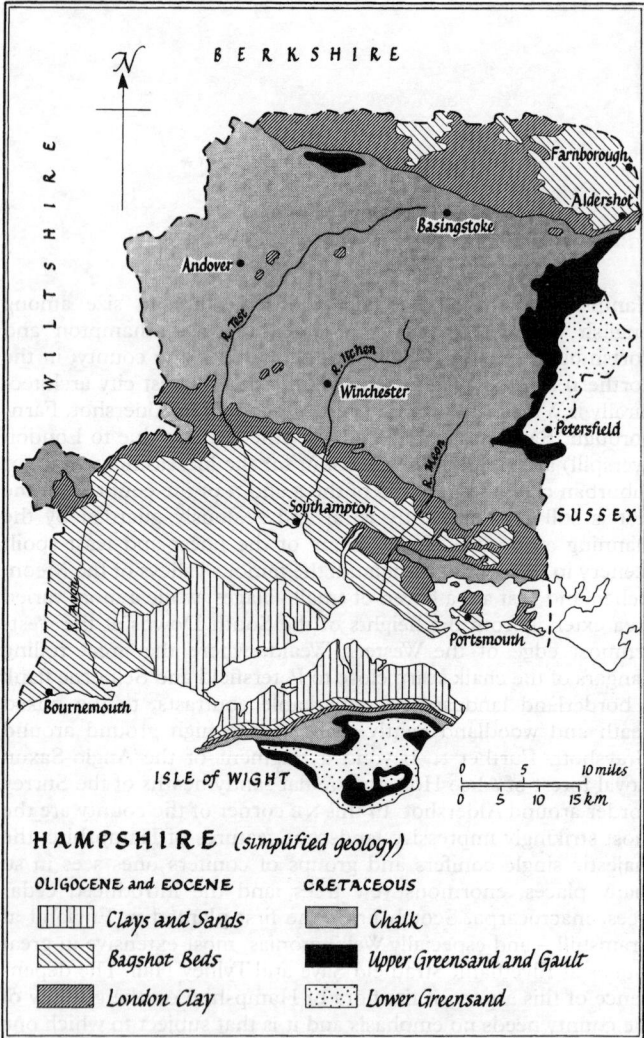

Geological map of Hampshire

HAMPSHIRE BASIN, which extends w into parts of Dorset and Wiltshire and e into West Sussex. The surface geology of the basin is dominated by the CHALK FORMATION and overlying sand and clay sediments of younger age. The chalk country is a SE continuation of Salisbury Plain and extends across Hampshire in a large rectangle lying N of a line running approximately from West Tytherley in the W as far as the rolling grasslands of the South Downs at Rowlands Castle in the SE. At its N edge between Highclere and Farnham (Surrey) it reaches and exceeds 270 ft (250

metres; maximum 322 ft, 297 metres) at Walbury Hill in Berkshire in the North Downs. Overlying this large area is a covering
of flinty soil, which was formed under periglacial conditions.
Over much of the chalk, this soil is very thin but it is thicker in
depressions and local hollows. Older rocks are exposed only in
the E and NE of the county, where the UPPER AND LOWER
GREENSANDS, with the Gault Clay sandwiched in between,
come to the surface. These are the oldest exposed rocks of the
region, deposited approximately 120 million years ago, and
extend in an arcuate belt from Midhurst (W Sussex) through
Petersfield and Bordon NE to Farnham (Surrey). There is also a
small area of Upper Greensand exposed around Sydmonton in
the NW.

In the N, from Highclere E to Aldershot, and S to the coast, in
a line from Lockerley to Cowplain, the chalk area is overlain by
the younger sands and CLAYS of Tertiary sediments. These form
a landscape characterized by forests of oak and pine (in contrast
with the shallow-rooted beeches on chalk soils) and flat expanses
of sandy heaths, reflecting the soils derived from the underlying
geology. In the S, the heathlands extend from the Forest of
Bere via Hursley Forest into the New Forest and beyond to
Christchurch and Bournemouth. Crossing through this landscape are the famous Hampshire rivers of the Test, Itchen,
Hamble and Meon, which drain S and SE from the Chalk before
reaching the sea. Their drainage pattern cuts across the underlying geology because it is an inherited (post-glacial) superimposed
drainage on a landscape where the rivers discharged into an
easterly flowing Palaeo-Solent.

The distribution of the basin's rocks and its underlying basement structure was determined by mountain-building events
during earlier DEVONIAN AND CARBONIFEROUS times
(between 320 and 290 million years ago (mya)). In the south-
west of England, the eroded roots of these mountains are exposed
as granites and slates. Similar rocks probably lie deep under the
Hampshire Basin but in Hampshire these roots (with an E–W
fault system in the fabric of the rocks) subsided during
MESOZOIC (261–65 mya) and TERTIARY times to form a
sedimentary basin. More than 3 kilometres (almost 2 miles) of
sediments were deposited, beginning with continental sediments
of TRIASSIC age (251–200 mya) followed by marine sediments
of the JURASSIC (200–145 mya) and CRETACEOUS (145–65 mya
– including Chalk at the top), followed in turn by the
mixed marine/freshwater deposits of the Tertiary (mostly
EOCENE/OLIGOCENE, 65–30 mya). The changing nature of
these deposits in general mirrors the prevailing worldwide sea-
level changes over the last 200 million years, and Chalk deposition occurred when sea level was at an all-time high and little
land would have been visible. Later, in the MIOCENE (23–5
mya), the basin became land when it was uplifted (inverted) as
part of global plate movements. As a consequence, the deep
underlying fault systems were reactivated and movements on
these produced an E–W distribution of folds and faults within the

basin that defines the outcrop patterns seen in the countryside today. In the s of the county, we find evidence of this uplift as large *en-échelon* folds such as the Isle of Wight monocline. A mixture of permafrost conditions and heavy rains associated with the last Ice Age achieved the final sculpting of the topography. During this final phase, not only were the valleys and slopes defined but also larger features such as the Palaeo-Solent river and the English Channel were cut. Finally, around 8,500 to 7,500 years ago, the offshore barrier islands of Portsea and Hayling islands were formed and the Isle of Wight was separated from the mainland.

The essential character and structure of the Hampshire Basin may be seen if we follow the disposition of the Chalk in a line of section from the great E–W chalk spine of the Isle of Wight,* through Portsmouth to the South Downs, into the Weald and eventually the North Downs. All the various strata form a series of major fold structures that are asymmetric in cross-section and have steeply dipping northern limbs and gently dipping southern limbs. From Culver Down, the northern limb of the chalk anticline on the Isle of Wight actually dips vertically beneath the island's surface, gradually decreasing its angle of descent as it extends underneath the northern part of the island, the Solent and Portsea Island before re-appearing N of Portsmouth as the white hills that form the Portsdown Anticline. The Chalk then descends once more beneath a wide valley, floored by younger early Tertiary sands and clays, in which we find the Forest of Bere, Bishop's Waltham and Bishopstoke, before re-emerging to the N as the extensive incline leading up to the magnificent South Downs (highest point Butser Hill, near Buriton, 294 ft, 271 metres). The South Downs and its thinner-ridged counterpart, the North Downs, form a more open anticline than Portsdown, and this anticline has been eroded to expose in its core the older Lower Cretaceous Upper and Lower Greensands and Gault Clays.

Because of the predominance of chalk over most of the county, few good natural BUILDING STONES were readily available. Considerations of cost and accessibility meant that local materials had to be used wherever possible, so Hampshire's vernacular buildings up to the C18 are predominantly characterized by the use of timber framing and, later, brick construction. For the most part, CHALK is too soft to use for load-bearing construction although it has been extensively employed in the form of chalk pisé, or puddled chalk, for example in the thatched and rendered boundary walls still much in evidence in the Test Valley; its light weight also made it suitable for the webs of medieval roof vaults, e.g. the Deanery porch, Winchester. At certain levels, however, when deposition slowed or even halted in the Chalk seas, cementation of the sediment took place on the sea bed, producing a band of 'hard' chalk generally known as CLUNCH. Its development over the area of the basin is sporadic and there-

* For a fuller description of the geology of the Isle of Wight see *The Buildings of England: Isle of Wight*, by David W. Lloyd and Nikolaus Pevsner.

fore its use in building is not as widespread in Hampshire as in other chalk areas, such as East Anglia. But it can be found in several medieval buildings, notably the churches at Bentley, Ashley, Bishops Sutton and Long Sutton. Its use is mainly for carved work, e.g. the doors at Winchfield and Hartley Mauditt or the arcades at St Michael, Basingstoke, and especially Binsted and Empshott. It can be used as an inferior stone for external quoins.

51

The most widely used local stone is FLINT, whose distribution across Hampshire results from three separate processes that each provide localized deposits of usable materials. Between the Chalk and the overlying sediments of Tertiary age lies a distinctive layer of sticky 'Clay-with-Flints' (known as the Reading Beds – and which later were also the source of raw materials for brickmaking in Hampshire). This layer developed after the sea retreated at the end of the Cretaceous (65 mya) and exposed the chalk to weathering by acid rain for millions of years. As the chalk dissolved it left insoluble flints on the surface together with small amounts of clay. Other deposits of flint were concentrated in river terraces during the Ice Age, particularly during periods of heavy rainfall and high sea levels. Remnants of these terraces have been found throughout the area, as in the Meon valley. In other areas, the flints have been redistributed into Plateau Gravels that can still be seen as thin gravel spreads on the Chalk of the South Downs. Finally, coastal processes and storms at the end of the Ice Age concentrated flints as huge offshore submarine bars, which eventually accreted and allowed the islands of Portsea and Hayling to be constructed in the more sheltered waters behind them. Most of the flint found here must have originated from the floor of what is now the English Channel (which still retains a carpet of flint over much of its area) but is also partly derived from the river systems draining the Hampshire Basin.

Some buildings of outstanding architectural significance have been constructed entirely in flint, notably the Roman walls of Portchester Castle (South Hants), but its irregularity requires extensive use of mortar and its natural hardness necessitated considerable manual working. So the use of flint for construction is strictly limited and mostly used either to supplement scarce availability of building stone or more often in combination with timber and, later, brick. The Normans used flint for the core work of their buildings, as can be seen at Winchester Cathedral where the core of the Romanesque W massif is still standing. Picturesque use of knapped flint, in which the surface of the nodule is chipped away (knapped) to produce a flattened, smooth grey-black surface, is very widespread and this is a distinctive feature of older cottages and walls in Hampshire's villages. The name flint is restricted to the forms of non-crystalline silica (as distinct from crystalline forms such as amethyst) that develop within the Chalk. The same material found in other limestones is called CHERT but has not been as extensively used as flint because these same limestones generally make better building stone, e.g. Portland stone.

The most valuable source of local building stone was provided by quarries in the E of the county which exposed a hard band within the Upper Greensand (sometimes called MALMSTONE). This was a marine sand containing glauconite, which provides the green colour of the rock (on the Isle of Wight it is known as 'Green Ventnor' and was much used at Winchester College, St Cross, and elsewhere in the C14). Where these sands are patchily lithified by cements, they can be used for building. But even this stone is weak and generally weathers very badly when exposed to atmospheric pollution and acid rain. The difficulty and expense of transporting stone means that for the medieval period at least, its use and distribution is concentrated close to the Greensand areas centred on Selborne where the stone is often as white as chalk. Most domestic buildings have used it only for dressings, and in ecclesiastical architecture for interior tracery and carvings, for example in Binsted and Titchfield (South Hampshire) churches. The other type of sandstone which occurs in the same Wealden edge is darkly coloured and sometimes known as IRONSTONE. In rough chunks, it is suitable for masonry walling, e.g. Tankerdale Farm, Steep, and the Manor House, Greatham, and the church towers of St Michael, Aldershot, Buriton and Liss. PUDDINGSTONE, a conglomerate found in the sandy heaths of E Berkshire and NW Surrey is used in the Late Saxon chancel of Hartley Wintney and as late as *c.* 1500 at Heckfield (W tower).

In the S of the county, Greensand stone could be obtained from the Isle of Wight, which also provided a source for good freshwater LIMESTONES, notably the hard QUARR STONE which was much used for the Romanesque cathedral at Winchester later supplemented by reused Combe Down OOLITIC LIMESTONE from Old Minster, and BINSTEAD STONE found, for example, at Winchester College and the church at Nately Scures. But from an early date there was a need for higher-quality IMPORTED STONE. French stone can often be found in Hampshire buildings of all ages. The Norman keep of Portchester Castle, for example, is made of CAEN STONE of Middle Jurassic age, and it was popular for fine carving in the best buildings, notably in the details of the church at St Cross, and sculpture at Wolvesey Palace in the C12 but also on a grand scale at Winchester Cathedral, where it was extensively used in the C13 retrochoir and for the late C15 Great Screen. Also at the C13 chancel at Buriton.

After the Great Fire of London, counties and boroughs throughout England wanted to model their public buildings on those of London, for which white Upper Jurassic Portland limestone had been used. In South Hampshire PORTLAND STONE was easily imported by sea barges from Dorset to the coastal ports. A significant early use in North Hampshire are the bases, though not the columns themselves, of *John Webb*'s portico at The Vyne (1650s) and School at Winchester College (1683–7). These are quintessential buildings of this period, with Portland stone dressings and quoins contrasting with red brick in the manner of the best new buildings in London and very much in Wren's style. But extensive use of this stone belongs to the late C19 and C20, e.g the refronting of Tedworth House, South Tidworth (1878–80), and the finest examples of its use, the Portsmouth Guildhall (1885–6) and Southampton's Civic Centre (1929–30). The great quarries on the Isle of Portland are testimony to the vast amounts of stone hewn and sawn. On top of the Dorset Portland limestones lay another group of rocks that are widely used not only as walling stones, for example in the naval defences of Portsmouth, but also decoratively. These are the thinly bedded Purbeck limestones with their quaint names like Hard and Soft Cap, Hard Cockle, Shelly Weatherstones and, most famously, the Purbeck marble. These limestones are usually fossil-rich and were deposited in thinner beds than the underlying Portland stones. PURBECK MARBLE is widely distributed in Hampshire churches where it was used from the C12 for decorative piers (e.g the clustered shafts of Winchester Cathedral retrochoir), fonts and tomb carvings, e.g. Barton Stacey and Brockenhurst (St Peter) as well as doorways; in its structural form it is found in the arcades of the Great Hall at Winchester Castle Purbeck marble is not a true marble but a highly fossiliferous lake limestone containing vast numbers of the freshwater snail *Viviparus purbeckensis*. In North-West Hampshire, it was often easier and cheaper to obtain from Somerset the golden-coloured Middle Jurassic stone (either the Inferior Oolite – e.g. DOULTING AND HAM STONE – or Great Oolites such as BATH STONE), although significant use of these is associated with improvements in transport in the C19 that enhanced access to a variety of stones from around Britain, e.g., at Holy Trinity Privett, but even into this period, however, much of Hampshire derived its building materials from within the county. The excellent clays yielded enormous quantities of BRICK of varying hues, depending (in part) on the area, from the rich reds of Fareham derived from the Reading Beds to the pale bricks of the Gault Clay areas in North-East Hampshire, the creamy yellows from Beaulieu (Exbury) and the more yellow-brown bricks from the London Clay found over much of the county. The last was the most heavily exploited and there is no discernible local colour variation except where individual manufacturers used distinctive surface dressings or fired at different temperatures. Other pale-coloured bricks are produced from recent localized deposits of fine-grained wind-blown sediment called brick-earth. These were formed during periglacial conditions. Most of the clay pits have been utilized as landfill sites or for building developments: Ocean Park (Portsmouth) and the site of the air traffic control centre at Swanwick are two examples. Close to the latter the late C19 buildings of the Bursledon (London Clay) brickworks have been gradually restored, and a reminder of the artistic skill of the brickmaker is *Lutyens*'s office for the Daneshill tile works at Basingstoke. The relatively abundant sand, limestone and gravels in the Hampshire Basin have been combined for the easy production of cement and concrete. From the C20 and into the present, steel and concrete-framed buildings have used cladding of veneers of distinctive decorative stone from many parts of the world, e.g. larvikite (also known as pubstone) from Norway

31

and swirling garnet-rich gneisses from India – to see these exotic rocks, one need only walk down the High Street of any Hampshire town and look at the newer buildings.

PREHISTORIC AND ROMAN NORTH HAMPSHIRE
by
Professor Barry Cunliffe

Of the earliest millennia of human history – the PALAEOLITHIC period – North Hampshire has comparatively little to offer and certainly nothing that can be graced with the term 'building'. At best we have a scatter of flint tools, mainly handaxes, found in the river gravels or on patches of clay-with-flints on higher parts of the chalk downs. After about 10,000 BC, following the last cold spell of the Ice Age, the temperature improved and woodland developed over the land, providing cover for a variety of animals – and rich hunting grounds for the foraging groups who now began to multiply. These MESOLITHIC communities are best known from their many camp sites on the Upper Greensand ridge of the E Weald. By the fifth millennium they were prolific. At Oakhanger near Selborne a long-occupied camp has been excavated producing thousands of flint artefacts, axes, saws, scrapers and, most characteristically, the small microlith flints used to tip arrows and fish spears. The settlements favoured glades in the woodland, river valleys and lakesides (e.g. Woolmer, Bramshott).

The fourth and third millennia were a time of rapid change on the Hampshire downland as foraging gave way to cultivation and husbandry regimes that were to characterize the NEOLITHIC period. Perhaps the most significant discovery of recent years has been just how prolific are the scatters of flints, representing Neolithic activity, over the chalkland. Where collection has been systematic flint scatters are found to be less than ½ m. apart. The implication is that the downland was being extensively opened up for settlement and for agriculture.

One characteristic monument of the Neolithic period – the causewayed camp – a type found in Wiltshire and along the Sussex Downs – appears to be absent from Hampshire, which is surprising unless it occupied a marginal position between the core zones on either side. The other characteristic monument – the LONG BARROW – is, however, very well represented by the well-preserved examples at Barton Stacey, Hinton Ampner and the Wallops. The thorough excavation of the long barrow of Nutbane, Penton Mewsey, has provided valuable evidence of the complex rituals involved. Before the barrow was built the site was occupied by a wooden enclosure in which the dead bodies appear to have been exposed. Mortuary houses of this kind are known elsewhere and imply that the *rite de passage* of death involved a long period when the bodies, presumably of members of a lineage, lay in the open until the process of death was considered to have been completed, at which point flanking ditches were dug and the rubble derived from them was piled up to form a highly visible long mound. Once created, these memorials to ancestors would have formed the focus of oral histories passed from one generation to the next.

By the beginning of the second millennium the burial rite had changed, the emphasis now being on individual burial in ROUND BARROWS of various forms and sizes arranged in groups. Impressive clusters in North Hampshire are to be found at Broughton, dominated by a large bell barrow, Laverstoke, Petersfield Heath, Stockbridge Down and Litchfield. The last group, on Lower Woodcott Down – the famous Seven Barrows (but actually ten) – form an impressive line dominating the insignificant A34 which weaves between them. Linear arrangements of this kind are quite common and hint that there may have been some structured progression in the burial sequence. If so, then the barrows might have been 'time-lines' giving the community an immediate visual sense of its own antiquity rooted in the place, each barrow representing an individual biography.

Barrows covered burials, cremated or inhumed, rich or poor, for most of the second millennium. More than a thousand are known in North Hampshire but even allowing that many have been ploughed out, there are far too few to reflect accurately the size of population. What we are presently seeing are the burials of the elite, the rest of the population having been disposed of in ways that leave little obvious trace. By the end of the second millennium (the LATE BRONZE AGE) barrows were a thing of the past. The dead were now cremated and their ashes buried in flat urnfields like the thoroughly excavated example at Kimpton which was still in use in the C7 BC.

Apart from burial monuments there is little visible sign of human activity on the Hampshire chalkland until about 1400 BC (MIDDLE BRONZE AGE) when the impact of settlement and agriculture began to make a lasting physical impression. Until then a comparatively low density of population meant that there was little pressure on land and it may be that ploughed fields came and went as cultivation zones shifted, but after about 1400 BC communities began to apportion the landscape in a more permanent way. Long linear boundary ditches were dug, like the ditch that runs along the chalk ridge parallel with the River Bourne (upon the line of which Quarley hill-fort was later built). Another – still a prominent earthwork – divides Stockbridge Down eastwards from Woolbury. These early 'linears' were Hampshire's first land boundaries and in the two cases mentioned were clearly intended to separate arable land from pasture. The Stockbridge Down linear is remarkable in that, give or take a few yards, it has remained the boundary between arable and pasture ever since.

Many of the FIELD SYSTEMS laid out at this time can still be seen, at least on aerial photographs. These 'Celtic fields' as they are usually called, were regularly laid out plots, squarish in plan, covering about an acre. Each represents the area that could be ploughed in a day by a single plough team assuming that each field was cross-ploughed. The regularity with which they were set out suggests that large tracts of land were divided up at the same time; it may even be possible to recognize in the planning the holdings of particular lineage groups.

A few centuries later, between 1000 and 700 BC, parts of the chalkland were subject to another phase of land division which hints at a major agrarian reorientation. Now large acreages of arable were put out of commission by new systems of linear ditches which cut through them, dividing the land into massive tracts dependent upon the river valleys. The implication is that considerable acreages, once farmed for cereals, were given over to pasture. At the same time a number of hilltops were enclosed with banks and ditches. Examples include Balksbury (now largely beneath Andover), Danebury (the Outer Earthwork) and Walbury. Such archaeological evidence as there is is consistent with these enclosures serving as places where livestock could be corralled for culling, castration, and redistribution at the appropriate season.

By about 700 BC we enter what is still conventionally called the IRON AGE – a period during which iron begins to replace bronze as the principal metal for tools and weapons. The territoriality and land apportionment, which had begun six or seven centuries earlier, continued with the appearance of a rash of hill-forts built at various times during the period c. 700–500 BC. These 'early hill-forts' as they are known (to be distinguished from the earlier hilltop enclosures) are very well represented on the Hampshire chalkland. Ladle Hill (see Litchfield) is a rare example of an unfinished HILL-FORT the earthworks of which show the actual process of construction, the activities of the individual work gangs being easily recognizable. Quarley Hill is a fine example of a completed fort as are Woolbury and the earlier Bury Hill (see Upper Clatford). Other hill-forts, like St Catherine's Hill, Winklebury (Basingstoke), and Beacon Hill (Old Burghclere), have features which suggest later modifications in the C4–C3 BC. This is even clearer at Danebury where its massively rebuilt entrance is typical of C3–C2 BC developments.

Most of these forts have been subject to some excavation, allowing a broad sequence of change to be sketched. It seems that probably all the North Hampshire hill-forts began in the period 700–500 but that very few – and Danebury is a prime example – continued in use after C4 BC to become 'developed hill-forts'. Bury Hill is a rare example of a massively defended fort built anew about C2 BC on an earlier, long-abandoned site. What it all means is hotly debated but most will agree that the forts were multi-purpose, reflecting a growing sense of community and territoriality. The C4–C3 seems to have been a time of unrest. It was after this that Danebury was strongly redefended and a large resident population moved into the enclosure. It may be that social stress, breaking out into bouts of open hostility, characterized the C3–C2, culminating in the early CI BC when Danebury was violently destroyed.

The period from about 70 BC to the Roman invasion in AD 43 was a time of rapid change in Hampshire. Trade with the Continent intensified through the port of Hengistbury Head in South Hampshire and it is possible that immigrant groups from the Belgic region of N Gaul may have entered Hampshire through the Solent ports, setting up their main market at Winchester – a town which the Romans were to call *Venta Belgarum* (the 'market of the Belgae'). In the wake of Caesar's rampaging through Gaul in 58–51 BC more Belgae from the tribe of the Atrebates, led by Commius, arrived to set up a kingdom in the N of the county with its capital at *Calleva* (Silchester). Insofar as one can judge from the evidence of locally minted coins and from scraps of historical evidence, this Atrebatic polity rose to dominate the region, though by the time of the Roman invasion in AD 43 the unity may have begun to fragment in the new phase of political unrest that provided the Emperor Claudius with an excuse to invade.

The Roman period

In AD 43 the Roman army under the command of Aulus Plautius landed in Britain to begin the subjugation of the tribes of the south-east. Their initial objective seems to have been to control the more economically advanced regions up to and including the Cotswolds ridge, and to this end they established a temporary frontier running from Exeter to Lincoln linked by the Fosse Way. Crucial to their strategy in the difficult initial moments of the invasion were two friendly enclaves, the Iceni of Norfolk under their king Prasutagus and the Regni of West Sussex and South Hampshire ruled by King Togidubnus, whose centre of power lay in the Chichester–Fishbourne area. Both rulers became client-kings under Roman authority and governed semi-independently for two or three decades before their fiefdoms were absorbed into the province.

It is quite possible that Fishbourne in West Sussex was chosen for one of the military landings in the summer of AD 43. The archaeological evidence shows that a military base was established there, and it was probably from Fishbourne that Vespasian, then commander of the *Legio II Augusta*, set out to conquer the Isle of Wight before facing the hostile tribes of the south-west, most particularly the Durotriges of Dorset. Fishbourne, in the safety of Togidubnus's kingdom, was a convenient base from which to launch an attack. It is highly likely that ancillary bases were established along the coast. Bitterne is one contender. Another is Hamworthy in Poole Harbour where military remains have been recovered. The army seems to have passed quickly through Hampshire within the first months of the campaign, leaving no lasting military installations behind, and it may be that all or most of the county passed under the control of the pro-Roman Togidubnus to whom, according to Tacitus, additional territories were given as a reward for his support.

The legacy of the brief military phase was a network of supply roads which soon became the commercial arteries of the region linking the harbours and the already flourishing urban centres of Chichester (West Sussex), Winchester and Silchester. This greatly improved system of communications provided the infrastructure which underpinned the steady economic development providing the basis for three centuries of peace and prosperity.

Hampshire came briefly into mainstream history in the closing decades of the C3 when in 286 Carausius, previously a naval commander, proclaimed himself Emperor of Britain. To protect his territory he strengthened the coastal fortifications of the SE, and it was probably under his authority that a new fort was built at Portchester. The breakaway empire did not last long and in 296 the imperial authorities, who had established themselves in Boulogne, launched an invasion force which slipped into a Solent port (probably Bitterne) under cover of a thick fog, avoiding the British fleet which had been patrolling near the Isle of Wight. Then followed a rapid march through Hampshire to London. The rebels capitulated and Britain was restored to the empire.

The two coastal forts of Bitterne and Portchester continued to be maintained throughout the C4 but Portchester was eventually abandoned about 370, by which time the province was suffering increasingly from raids from Ireland, Scotland and from across the North Sea. In the uncertainty of the times the imperial infrastructure collapsed. Appeals from the province for help went unanswered until finally, in AD 410, the central authorities told the towns of Britain to look to their own defence. The brief Roman interlude was at an end.

North Hampshire, dominated by the rolling chalkland of the Hampshire Downs and watered by the fast-flowing rivers Test and Itchen, is archetypal rural Roman Britain – a countryside of farms served by the two market towns of *Venta* (Winchester) and *Calleva* (Silchester) with minor local markets at road stations like East Anton, at a crossroads now in the suburbs of Andover, and at Neatham on the road from Chichester to Silchester.

The main TOWNS were not particularly large, 100–140 acres, with a resident population of a few thousand each, but they provided the market and administrative services needed to maintain a system of prosperous agricultural production and to keep the farmer well supplied with the small luxuries that made life agreeable.

The Hampshire downland presents one of the densest villa-landscapes in Britain, with a particular concentration around the Andover crossroads where the upper valley of the Test offers a rich variety of well-watered soils. Excavations have shown that most, if not all, of the VILLAS developed on sites which were already long established by the end of the Iron Age, the implication being of a continuity of land ownership spanning generations. Many of the establishments were timber-built until the late C2 or early C3 when masonry construction began to become more common. Some installed small bath suites and a few could afford patterned mosaic floors, but few became really affluent. One that did was the villa at Fullerton in the Anton valley. Here a new corridor villa with integral bath suite and floored throughout with mosaics was built in the early C4. The new-found prosperity probably came from the profits of a water mill installed some generations before when the farm was far more modest. Another villa with an elaborate mosaic was Thruxton, but there is some suggestion here that the mosaic was only installed late in the C4 when the old farm was turned into a shrine for ancestors.

On the E side of the county the W end of the Weald provided an excellent potting clay which was exploited by generations of potters throughout the Roman period. The numerous kilns and waster heaps are widely distributed throughout Alice Holt Forest and must represent a major local industry serving not only the Hampshire villas but also the surrounding towns including London.

To a farmer, a potter or a town trader living in the early decades of the C4 life was good and the future of their offspring assured, yet within the span of a single lifetime it was all over – the *pax Romana* was at an end.

THE MIDDLE AGES

For the purpose of this account the Middle Ages runs from the Anglo-Saxon period to the Dissolution. In architectural terms this takes us from the mid-C7 foundation of the Old Minster at Winchester to the Renaissance of the early C16. Hampshire had several royal estates in the possession of the Saxon kings and Winchester, having been in continuous occupation from the end of the Roman period, became a royal seat, a cathedral and see. Its pre-eminence was confirmed immediately after the Norman Conquest by the occupation and enlargement of the Anglo-Saxon palace as the Conqueror's principal residence, the building of the castle and, in time, the creation of a new cathedral. After the Conquest the best land in the county was predominantly in the hands of the Church, partly the consequence of grants made to the leading monastic establishments by the Anglo-Saxon kings: in the north of Hampshire the major landholders after the Bishop were St Swithun's Priory, St Mary's Abbey and New Minster (Hyde Abbey from *c.* 1110), all in Winchester, and Wherwell Priory. The Bishop's pre-eminence is reflected in the number of high-status buildings associated with his holdings. Right up to the mid C16, however, there were hardly any significant secular lords, although two of them probably created the towns at Odiham and Petersfield (charter granted 1184). New towns were also founded by the bishops of Winchester: New Alresford in 1200, and Overton and Newtown which were in existence by 1218. The first two were reasonably successful but Newtown, after initial prosperity, had more or less failed by the C17. Whitchurch was established by the Priory of St Swithun in 1284. It was a centre for cloth making like Alton, Andover and Basingstoke. Several of these smaller towns had been granted rights to markets by the early C13. The event of greatest commercial significance in North Hampshire was the annual St Giles Fair in Winchester, which drew international traders. A settled picture is disrupted from the early C14 by agricultural depression and the Black Death, which appeared early in Hampshire. In recent years dating of timber buildings has given a slightly fuller picture of survival of structures from before this period. The population of Winchester was cut from over 11,000 in 1300 to just 3–5,000 by 1377, and yet the mid to later C14 until the mid C15 was a period of resurgence for the city, in the reconstruction of the cathedral, the building of residences in The Close for the senior monastic officials, the establishment of the College and the enlargement of the Hospital of St Cross.

Anglo-Saxon churches

Quantitatively Hampshire, compared with some other counties, has not much to contribute, despite the cultural importance of Winchester, but qualitatively the excavations at Winchester establish the north of the county as an area not to be left out of an Anglo-Saxon pilgrimage. The story should begin with
p. 564   FOUNDATIONS, beginning with the 'Old Minster' at Winchester, established in 648 by Cenwealh, king of Wessex, possibly as the church of the royal palace but which became the cathedral in the 660s. Excavations have established its unexpected and thrilling form. Originally a nave with N, S and E *porticus* and sometime later with a detached W entrance tower, it evolved by stages to become one of the largest churches in England.

The 'New Minster', built alongside the cathedral in 901 and coinciding with the revival of Winchester under Alfred, was a transeptal basilica of virtually the same size and plan as Charlemagne's Saint-Denis. No doubt provoked by its impressive appearance and scale, the cathedral in the mid to late C10 was given a remarkable structure at its W end, filling the space between the nave and the tower and sheltering the now empty tomb of St Swithun. Its purpose appears to have combined ceremonial and liturgical functions, including a gallery for the king to see the high altar. There followed an addition at the E end and an outer crypt, evidence of increased numbers of altars in the church. The beautification of the church is hinted at by some fragments of coloured glass, sculpture, a stone grave marker and wall painting excavated in the 1960s.

The wealth of C10 and C11 fragments excavated at Winchester show that both Old Minster and New Minster were richly decorated externally with narrative friezes of stone figures and groups. This tells us a good deal about SCULPTURE and the 'Winchester style' of the C10, with its strong emphasis on figural work.

Although nothing may be seen intact in Winchester, the county
has a group of external stone figures of outstanding importance
in the famous rood at Romsey (South Hampshire), and the larger
than life-sized Crucifixion groups with the Virgin and St John at
Headbourne Worthy and Breamore (South Hampshire). They
belong to the first half of the CII and the latter two alas exist as
shadows only, since all that was relief was hacked off by fanatics.
The unusually robust example at Headbourne Worthy is of a
piece with the church, i.e. c. 1030, and was erected over a
coeval w door. At Whitchurch is a very interesting gravestone to   6
Frithburh showing continuity with Roman traditions by taking
the form of a Roman altar with the demi-figure of Christ, a form
apparently unique in Anglo-Saxon art. At Weyhill a grave-slab is
re-set externally into the N vestry. Its top half has been defaced
but the lower half has a typically Saxon cross of c. 1000. Part of
a late C9 cross-shaft is at Steventon. Another from Prior's Barton
(now in Winchester Museum) was perhaps associated with the
lost church of St Faith, one face having beasts' heads, the other
interlace. It belongs to a group of crosses found in south-west
England in the late C8 and early C9. At Wherwell a fragment of
cross-shaft (perhaps CIO–CII) is reworked as a CI3 corbel. It
probably came from the nunnery established there c. 986. Also
of the CIO–CII are sundials at All Saints, Hannington, and St
Maurice in Winchester.

CHURCHES, especially those held by the bishop and the
monasteries of Winchester, were of stone, mostly of flint, many
with Binstead stone dressings. DEDICATIONS to St Swithun are
quite common among the pre-Conquest churches, e.g. Headbourne Worthy, Martyr Worthy, Nately Scures, and St Swithun-
upon-Kingsgate, in Winchester, which was held by the Cathedral
Priory. Other early churches are known from documents, e.g.
Micheldever (903) and Wonston (901), but this rarely means the
survival of visible Anglo-Saxon fabric. The typical motifs of long-
and-short quoins and lesenes (or pilaster strips) do occur in a
few places and the majority are close to the city at Headbourne
Worthy (c. 1030), which marked the northern boundary of the
monastic estate of St Swithun's Priory, Hinton Ampner and
Little Somborne. Of these Headbourne Worthy is the largest and
most interesting. Hinton Ampner, on a smaller scale, is also of
the two-cell type but Little Somborne has an even simpler single-
cell plan, although over-restored (its chancel was added c. 1200
and subsequently removed). Other churches with pre-Conquest
evidence include Crondall, where foundations excavated below
the nave are of a major flint church, and its dependent chapel at
Yateley, also Hannington and Hartley Wintney (St Mary, chancel
only). Elsewhere, e.g. at Barton Stacey, Chilbolton, Farnborough
etc., one must rely on the thin walls, overall scale or setting to
suggest the presence of early fabric. At Nether Wallop, on the
other hand, the evidence of the early CII church is proved alone
by the WALL PAINTING (revealed in 1971) of two angels above   5
the chancel arch, which is the oldest in situ in England and is by
an artist of the Winchester School. The church was in a royal

demesne manor later held by Countess Gueda of Earl Godwin. The N door, re-set from its original position, may be of the same Late Saxon date but if so its features are among the earliest examples of motifs that became routine in the Norman phase, e.g. nook-shafts with simple cushion capitals.

Norman and Transitional churches

The scale of activity is impressive. About 100 churches in the area have CII–CI2 features and the evidence points to a quickening of building during the episcopate of Henry of Blois (1129–71) and especially in his last decade, following the civil war and unrest of his brother Stephen's reign (1135–54), during which time there was some considerable damage in Winchester itself. There was an even more pronounced surge of new work in the decades either side of 1200. It goes without saying that an overlap existed between the Anglo-Saxon and the decades after the Conquest. Of this so-called SAXO-NORMAN phase there is the nave of Quarley and the chancel of Tichborne where in the details of windows and buttressing the outgoing and incoming traditions co-exist. For NORMAN architecture proper the beginning is of course Walkelin's work at the CATHEDRAL, begun in 1079. He was a former canon of Rouen, and what he began at Winchester is strongly influenced by the traditions of Upper Normandy, but in its scale surpassing anything there and without equal in Norman England. It was carried on quickly as a prestige project as important as the Conqueror's White Tower at the Tower of London. Much survives and is the most impressive display in England of architecture of the first generation after the Conquest. The sources for its cruciform plan with at its E end an apse, ambulatory and Lady Chapel comes from Normandy, but Winchester was also surprisingly independent from Norman precedent in having square-ended chapels at the E end of the aisles rather than the radial arrangement favoured on the Continent, and transepts with aisles not only on the E and W sides but also around the ends. The apsidal choir with projecting axial chapel (also apsidal) is not preserved, although the plan is seen in the groin-vaulted crypt beneath (and a bench from the chapel has now been identified). This and the transepts and also the surviving entrance to the chapter house can safely be assumed to date from before Walkelin's death in 1098. The piers are sturdy, capitals confined to the block shape or large single, double, or triple scallops, vaulting to groin-vaults.* Arches are unmoulded, and inside at least there is no ornament whatever. Outside, the windows have just a thin band of chip carving and hoodmoulds of billet. That is all.

---

*The rib-vaults of a very simple CII profile (half-roll between half-hollows) are a replacement of after 1107. The same profile was still used in the sacristy at St Cross Hospital, Winchester, the one room there which dates from, or even before, the foundation in 1136.

The local influence of the cathedral seems to have been minimal, perhaps confined to a few lesser monastic churches, but not enough survives to be certain. There were NEW FOUNDA-TIONS in the early C12 at Pamber (Benedictine), just one among a large number of alien priories in Hampshire as a whole. A century later comes the Augustinian foundation at Selborne. The priory church at Pamber is one of a small number in the N of the county that have major Early Norman elements, here in the form of the low crossing tower, the only part surviving of an unaisled cruciform-plan church consecrated, perhaps unfinished, in 1129, with four noble roll-moulded arches below blank tripartite arcading.

A cruciform plan with a crossing tower is a form shared by several LARGER PARISH CHURCHES. The earliest is Alton, perhaps built c. 1072–90 when Walkelin's cathedral was rising at Winchester, but it has remaining only the ambitious central tower. Its internal arches have animate capitals, very rare for a parish church at such an early date. East Meon was begun on a bold scale c. 1090 and finished c. 1150, with the specially fine ashlar crossing tower financed by Henry of Blois which is among the most splendid towers of its date. At Petersfield, begun c. 1120, is an amazing fragment, the E wall of a more ambitious central tower with exceptionally ornately patterned internal wall surfaces of typical Anglo-Norman fashion, clearly financed by a wealthy founder, here perhaps Robert, Earl of Gloucester. Its upper stage is a miniature reproduction of the internal arcading of the cathe-dral's lantern tower (hidden since 1635 by a timber vault) that was newly rebuilt after the fall of its predecessor in 1107. Old Basing, begun c. 1120 on an estate of Hugh de Port, the greatest of Hampshire's lay landowners, was also once cruciform with a crossing tower (of which the lower stages survive with lateral arches in a mutilated state) and seems to have followed a Late Saxon plan with transepts narrower than the nave. The dimen-sions of the tower at Old Basing are repeated at Kingsclere, where there is much more to see of a large work of c. 1135, perhaps due to St Mary's Abbey, Rouen. Inside and out it is austere, the plain interior relieved only by low-relief patterning around the w arch of the low central tower, which unusually has a stair-turret orig-inally for access above the lantern stage (cf. St John, Devizes, Wilts.). At Crondall c. 1170 the nave was planned around the Saxon footings already referred to, and to a much richer format at the E end, formerly below an axial tower (destroyed in the mid C17) of which the lower stage of the coeval stair-turret survives.

Among the SMALLER CHURCHES, one interesting item is Chilton Candover, where the tunnel-vaulted Early Norman crypt is preserved and evidently belonged to an apsidal-ended two-cell church. Although everything there above the crypt level has been lost, elsewhere quite a few small churches remain unenlarged, e.g. the simple two-cell churches at Ashley, Ashmansworth and Upper Eldon. Customary evidence of Early Norman date is CHANCEL ARCHES and DOORWAYS. The chancel arch of Upton Grey (c. 1125) has billet moulding but such features are just as

Winchfield, south entrance.
Drawing by J.D. Coleridge, 1931

likely to be unelaborate in their details. Even churches held by
Bishop Henry of Blois at Wield and Bishops Sutton (both
c. 1150) are less ambitious than one might expect. Wield is of
flints laid in lines (like the E hall at Wolvesey, the chancel at
Broughton and nave at Cliddesden). Bishops Sutton, like its
neighbour Bramdean, is unusual in having a pointed chancel
arch. Nately Scures (c. 1130) is another rare survival, a single-cell
plan of nave and apsidal chancel in one and with an unusual
trefoil-headed S doorway.

   In light of the major role usually played by CARVED DECORA-
TION in Norman architecture there really is remarkably little
except the tympana of the door at Old Burghclere (c. 1130),
which is content with an overall pattern of fish-scales, and Monk
Sherborne (c. 1140) which is even more introverted with just an

incised lattice pattern. Both are surpassed by Winchfield, another complete small church of *c.* 1150, which despite its size has a 16 carved chancel arch with elaborate soffit rolls of Moorish design and a s doorway in similar style with foliated capitals. The decorative details are so raw and ferocious that one would place them without hesitation in the first third of the century, yet the context is one not possible before 1150. The best architectural sculpture beyond any doubt is the capitals from Hyde Abbey, now in St 11 Bartholomew, Hyde and Winchester Museum, with their animals in roundels and their stylized foliage. Similar ones including a remarkable small capital with acrobats of *c.* 1130–40 are among the display of sculpture in the Triforium Gallery, the cathedral's museum. They date from around 1130–55 and like so much of this period in n Hampshire must be associated with the explosion of artistic activity associated with Bishop Henry, of which some indication can be taken from the treasury that he built in the s transept of his cathedral and the Holy Sepulchre Chapel.

If you want to see the highest level of SCULPTURE in the style the Normans brought in and favoured, you must examine the richness of the TOURNAI FONTS, of which Hampshire has four. All but one are in the N: Winchester Cathedral, East Meon and St Mary Bourne, possibly introduced under the aegis of Henry of Blois. In the whole country there are ten. They seem to date from about 1140 or 1160, and their style of ornamental decoration, and even more their figurework, especially the scenes from the legend of St Nicholas at Winchester Cathedral, is resolutely 12 organized and leaves nothing to accident. The choice of subject is evidence of the bishop's command; perhaps further evidence of Henry of Blois as donor. Tournai marble (in fact a limestone that takes a polish) had a short fashion in England. From about 1170 it was replaced by a local material, the shelly limestone known as Purbeck marble (*see* also Geology, above). This is greyer or more greenish, and much of what was produced was just turned shafts. In other fields also the Purbeck marblers tended to prefer the standardized product to individual initiative. The prime proof of that is the PURBECK FONTS, of table-top type, as the Tournai ones had been, but decorated with nothing but very shallow blank arches or simple, if sometimes impressive, flat leaves, circles, rosettes etc. The latter especially at Kingsclere. Only at Bramley are there scenes – an *Agnus Dei* (cf. Warnford, South Hampshire). Of these fonts – which are mostly in the N part of the county – there are over twenty, and in addition six octagonal ones. Among the finest is the large one at Littleton, provided by St Swithun's Priory, Winchester.

The peak of architectural activity in Hampshire was the years between about 1170 and about 1230. No one has yet explained why. Possibilities are the economic and political significance of Winchester, the wealth of the see, the newly established monasteries, the presence of a few major nobles as landowners. To find an arcade of these years in a church is almost a standard experience. The years are those of the TRANSITION from Norman to E.E., and often in Hampshire not of an organic transition, but

of elements of the old style standing side by side with elements
of the new. St Cross, Winchester, is the principal representative
of this situation. The dates are considered to be: choir by 1171;
transept arms and E bay of nave by c. 1200; remainder of nave
c. 1225–50. The start is with exuberant zigzag, but pointed arches
enter into the design soon and the vault, even of the E end, is
entirely French Gothic.

After St Cross the other important, although lesser, churches
are connected with the bishops of Winchester and the monks of
St Swithun's Priory. The details of the development cannot
here be summarized. Round bell-openings, a Norfolk motif
(Norwich), occur at Pamber Priory. Otherwise there are lancet
windows and pointed arches, with only slight chamfers. This is a
leitmotif of the group of churches of the Transition. Others are
round PIERS, often still with the archaic square abacus with
nicked corner or an octagonal abacus, and with base spurs (e.g.
St Leonard Oakley, c. 1200), CAPITALS first with many small
scallops, then very often with trumpet scallops, and occasionally
waterleaf or flat plain or fluted upright leaves, changing gradually to stiff-leaf and crockets. Those of the chancel arch at
Wonston are especially unusual. ARCHES range in morphologi-
cal order from round and single-step to round with slight
chamfers and pointed. But early and late features are found in
any kind of combination. Churches in which to see these
situations particularly well are Bentworth, Bighton, Binsted (with
an aisled chancel), Crondall, Easton, Herriard, Nether Wallop
and Selborne. Of these Crondall is outstanding with a nave of
c. 1170–75. It also has a rib-vaulted chancel, like Easton which
also has an apse. This is a complete church of c. 1170–1200,
unaisled but elaborately finished, especially the remarkable S
doorway. There is another sumptuous doorway at Hartley
Mauditt of about the same time. St Mary Bourne is interesting,
for it has a remarkably long, aisled nave. The nave was for the
Cathedral Priory, c. 1175. At Buriton the arcades seems to have
been begun c. 1170–80. Here the N arcade E respond capital is of
a rare type. At Buriton also are base mouldings of waterholding
type, i.e. c. 1180. They appear in the W responds.

Churches: Early English to Late Gothic

The EARLY ENGLISH style appears for the first time without any
transitional hangover in the complete remodelling of the E end
of Winchester Cathedral, including the retrochoir, instigated by
Bishop Godfrey de Lucy (1189–1204) before 1202, but not long
before. This has three parallel aisles and tall lancet windows, wonderfully slender Purbeck piers, and finely detailed ribs. The original intention was probably to create a structure with a clerestory,
and presumably an E window and gable, stepping down to a lower
Lady Chapel, also clerestoried, flanked by single-storey chapels.
Subsidence problems during construction modified the project,
and the retrochoir ended up as a hall church (*see* p. 582). The

Lady Chapel was completed well after de Lucy's death (1204) and the change in design. It has elaborate PLATE TRACERY in the openings below the vault, and that cannot be attributed to before *c.* 1225–30. For the dating of plate tracery in Hampshire Henry III's Great Hall in Winchester Castle (1222–36, *see* p. 32) is invaluable. The windows of the Hall (some restored faithfully in the mid C19) are tall with a quatrefoil in the head and have a transom. The design, on a smaller scale, can be found repeated in the lowside window of St Swithun, Headbourne Worthy. But in the wider area, the incidence of the new style in the PARISH CHURCHES is relatively rare and relates to remodellings or enlargements for new chancels and aisles rather than completely new buildings; only East Worldham is completely early C13 and still with earlier motifs as well as a heavily Victorianized appearance. The rib-vaulted early C13 chancel of Crondall, with dog- tooth and crocket capitals, perhaps influenced by the choir of Canterbury Cathedral, is a uniquely ambitious scheme for a parish church but there are also the chancels of Bramshott (*c.* 1220), Bentworth (probably before 1248), Kimpton (early C13) to consider. Longparish, which was held by Wherwell Abbey, has an early C13 nave and aisles, still with some Transitional elements. The W end of the nave of the church of St Cross belongs to the C13. In the N porch can be traced E.E. at its most mature. The arches of the chancel and unusual transeptal chancel chapels at Barton Stacey, of *c.* 1220 are impressive spacially. Among smaller incidences is the tower arch at Buriton, in appearance similar to the chancel arcade at East Meon, the nave S wall and chancel at Headbourne Worthy, arcades at Hurstbourne Tarrant (both), Nether Wallop (N) and St Mary, Silchester (N aisle and S arcade). [17]

It is astonishing how scarce the GEOMETRICAL and DECO- RATED STYLE, from *c.* 1250 to *c.* 1350, is in Hampshire.* The replacement of the cathedral presbytery, W of Bishop de Lucy's retrochoir, with Dec work occurred before 1316, by *Thomas of Witney*, but only the piers and arches remain. The clerestorey was also complete but the window tracery had to wait until at least a generation later, or even later still, so in its general character it is Early Perp and the same is true of the W front, where after 1346 Bishop Edington began the remodelling but seems to have completed only the porch before there was a hiatus (possibly caused by the Black Death). When building resumed at the very end of his life, in the mid 1360s, it was in an Early Perp style (*see* below). Edington's Chantry Chapel in the cathedral is also instructive of the transition from Dec to Perp in the mid C14. It may have been ready as early as 1350 and also has a few Perp elements, the doorway mouldings in particular, and they derive from the Gloucester S transept of the 1330s, which is the first complete piece of Perp architecture we have but has also minor Dec features still. At Edington in Wiltshire, where the bishop founded a chantry and rebuilt the church in 1351–61, there are also Dec and Perp features side by side with more emphasis on Dec than on Perp. [40] [38]

*A fine early example is a remarkable window at St John the Baptist, Winchester of *c.* 1260.

Among PARISH CHURCHES there are few examples of extensive building work. The two new churches are both due to wealthy
holders of their advowsons: Amport (earlier C14 for the Dean and
Chapter of Chichester Cathedral) is Dec throughout. Although
in its present form largely by *Slater & Carpenter*, the original parts
have characteristic Kentish window tracery and ballflower (a rare
if not unique feature in Hampshire). The Bishop of Bath and
Wells may have paid for the extraordinary timber-framed church
at Hartley Wespall, *c*. 1330; it is Dec in the sense that its massive
timbers have cusped profiles making a showpiece on the w wall.
It is perhaps among the earliest timber-framed churches in
England. Even ENLARGEMENTS of parish churches are relatively
uncommon. St Mary Bourne was given a new chancel *c*. 1300,
that at Froyle was also rebuilt but a little later, *c*. 1330, and a
small number of churches also had chantry chapels added for
local families in the earlier C14 at Binsted (de la Bere), Selborne
(de Gurdon) and St Mary Bourne (des Andeleys). Of these St
Mary Bourne is unusual for being a widening of the existing s
aisle. There are one or two large WINDOWS (St Cross, Winchester, W, and the cathedral) but hardly any really enterprising
flowing tracery. A number of churches have trefoil-headed lancets
(e.g. Long Sutton, s chapel E). Binsted also has windows with
pointed-trefoiled lights and bar tracery suggesting such a date,
yet the chantry to which they belong was established only in 1332.
At Buriton the rebuilt chancel has bar tracery with an uncusped
circle at its head, consistent with the date of *c*. 1270. Characteristic of the Geometrical phase are the spherical triangles in the
tracery of the rebuilt chancel at Froyle, and the same motif is
found elaborated in the s transept E aisle of the cathedral with
ogee-headed lights. Perhaps the most beautiful Geometrical
tracery in North Hampshire, however, is that of the s window of
St John the Baptist, also in Winchester, *c*. 1260. There is the characteristic Early Dec type of Y-tracery (cusped or uncusped) in
several places, e.g. Bishops Sutton (w), Old Burghclere, Over
Wallop and others, and of *c*. 1300 is a window with intersecting
tracery at Hannington, and the type with an encircled quatrefoil
at Ashe (cf. Amport). At St Cross, the church's five-light w
window (*c*. 1335) again has a circle in the head but also incorporates curvilinear forms (the clerestory is of the same period).
The more typical manner of the mature phases of Dec is reticulated tracery, the best example of which is the E window at Froyle
(*c*. 1320), the pattern standard but with an exceptional moulded
frame. Late Dec, very late perhaps, can be found at Penton
Mewsey (1360s), where the windows have some of the fancier
flowing details, e.g. mouchettes in a wheel at the head of the E
window, and some splendid details in the s door. The priest's
door has a Berkeley arch and the church's stone bellcote is
unique in Hampshire. Goodworth Clatford tower shows the style
reappearing as late as 1540.
    If Dec is poor in Hampshire, PERPENDICULAR is rich but
not in the parish churches by comparison with Dorset or Wiltshire, and there is nothing like the grandeur of East Anglia or

30

p. 29

20

Somerset or the Cotswolds. One must begin again in Winchester, for at Winchester Perp is richer and more instructive than perhaps anywhere else in England. This is due to three causes: the rebuilding of large parts of the cathedral, the six major chantry chapels in the cathedral, and the foundation and early development of the College. Together they present us with a chronological framework as firm as any scholar might desire. Yet owing to the relative immutability of Perp, the lesson is not as valuable as one might expect. It begins fully with the episcopate of William of Wykeham. He was appointed bishop in 1367 but was not fully active in building until the 1390s when, with his master mason *William Wynford*, he completed the remodelling of the Norman nave. This included the completion of the w front 40 left unfinished by Bishop Edington. As noted above, this was already displaying Early Perp characteristics in its design before Edington's death, and while the differences between his and Wykeham's work can easily be seen they are not stylistically a development at all. Wykeham's Perp is essentially the same (panel tracery, blank panelling round the windows, lierne-vaulting). Inside, the high lierne vault is one of the most convincing in 37 England. During the same period Wykeham laid the foundation stone of Winchester College and consecration of the chapel and cloisters took place in 1395. Wynford was again his architect. The two men had met first at Windsor Castle where Wykeham was clerk of works and Wynford the chief mason, and he collaborated on Wykeham's other foundation of New College, Oxford. The chapel has a seven-light E window of characteristic Wynford type and a roof with timber vault by *Hugh Herland*. This is a curious design, essentially a lierne vault but in its form appearing to anticipate the coming vogue for fan-vaulting. Wykeham died in 1404 but his chantry chapel in the nave may well have been under way in the previous decade. It is much higher than Edington's 39 and started the scale of the Winchester chantry chapels to come. In the retrochoir, Cardinal Beaufort's Chantry, erected 1450–76, is far more ornate than Wykeham's had been but shares the motif of an open upper stage. It has a fan-vault (the first in Hampshire) and ends in a thicket of closely detailed canopies. This motif was taken up and simplified in the chantry chapel built opposite for Bishop Waynflete (†1486, the chapel by then already complete), but the fan-vaulting here is reduced to springers at the corners for a vault of intricate patterns of blind tracery, including rose and star patterns. At the end of the century Bishop Courtenay (†1493) partly rebuilt and partly remodelled the Lady Chapel, and his successor, Bishop Langton (†1501), reconstructed the early C13 SE chapel as a chantry for himself. Both have fine woodwork screens and complex lierne-vaults. Bishop Fox rebuilt the E choir gable, and rebuilt the presbytery roof in preparation for the insertion of a wooden lierne vault, sumptuous work, and exceptionally richly studded with figures bosses. Then, before 1509, he remodelled the presbytery aisles, and finally in 1525 he inserted screens between the Dec piers. This is again sumptuous work, and although the vault is of wood it is exceptionally richly

Basingstoke, St Michael, exterior from the south.
Engraving by Owen Browne Carter, C19

studded with figured bosses. Bishop Fox's chantry chapel was
completed *c.* 1513–18, before his death, and may have been
53   designed by *William Vertue*. Thus it is still Late Perp, like Beaufort's and Waynflete's. To the chantry chapels at the cathedral
must be added those at Winchester College, which were almost
certainly undertaken by the cathedral's chief masons and follow
on from the construction of the principal buildings. First is that
42   for John Fromond, the College steward, built *c.* 1425–45 in
Cloisters, probably by *Robert Hulle*. It is a fully formed building,
like a two-storey house with a library on the upper floor and has
a complex lierne vault with bosses. The same is true of the
chantry of Warden Thurbern (†1450), which was mostly built
1473–85 at the base of the chapel bell-tower, no doubt by Hulle's
successor *William Graver*, who might also have been responsible
for Waynflete's chapel.

The sum tally of anything of major interest outside Winchester is very small. The Perp works in the PARISH CHURCHES are
no more than the enlargement of Alton (*c.* 1400), Old Basing
(early C15 and early C16) and Basingstoke (*c.* 1464–5 (chancel)
and 1510–25), the last of which is North Hampshire's only
example of a proper Perp town church, with a characteristically
lofty interior of satisfying spaciousness, due to the patronage of
local merchants. Odiham also has tall arcades of the type
expected for the Late Perp decades, though one set was probably reconstructed in the C17. The chancel of St Michael, Aldershot, can be dated to 1399–1400 and is one of a number of repairs
and restorations, especially *c.* 1398–1404, coinciding with the last
years of William of Wykeham's episcopate when, having recommenced the major remodelling of the cathedral, he was anxious
to improve the churches.

Of this activity there is evidence, especially in WINDOWS. Early
Perp is represented by the E window of Herriard, three lights with
cusped heads and vertical mullions between the upper lights. It
may have been paid for by Hartley Wintney Priory after 1333.
Towards the end of the century is Bentley's chancel, very unusually with a clerestory, and with a classic three-light panel-
traceried window; also Farringdon (windows of 1370–1400),
Headbourne Worthy (roof also) and the former E window of
Sherborne St John, probably c. 1395. The influence of the late
C14 court style can be found in the N doorway of New Alresford
and window tracery at Headley, c. 1380 (both following the traditions of *Henry Yevele*), and windows of the complexity associated with *William Wynford* at Winchester are at Heckfield
(c. 1383), St Michael, Aldershot (chancel 1399–1400) and Alton
(c. 1400). Continuation of Wynford's influence can be seen at
Old Basing, where the windows of the early C15 aisles are direct   50
descendants of the windows at Winchester College Hall. In the
same church is mid-C16 tracery of a thoroughly up-to-date kind,
whose outline design is still inscribed on the plaster of the S
chapel wall. The straight-headed types of window associated with
the late C15 are at Stoke Charity, Hannington and Bramshott,
while East Meon has the distinctive Winchester type of four lights
under a wide segmental arch, dated to 1493–1500 by the rebus
of Bishop Langton.

Perp in most counties usually means TOWERS but in N Hampshire there are only a few: Headley (c. 1380), Bramshott (c. 1400,
contemporary with addition of transepts), Heckfield (c. 1500),
the monumental W tower of Barton Stacey (probably early C16),
and the reconstruction at Old Basing. SPIRES are not common
but notable wood-framed early C15 examples are at Alton,
Bramshott and Liss (St Peter). Yateley, late C15, is of special interest for its tower is timber-framed with aisles like one finds in
Essex (such an arrangement probably originally existed at
Hartley Wespall). This is one of a number of churches, mostly   28
near the Berkshire border, that boast some bold and impressive
TIMBERWORK. A few are entirely timber-framed; early C14
Hartley Wespall has already been mentioned but there is also
Mattingley. It is probably of two phases, traditionally the third
quarter of the C15 and probably the early C16, close-studded with
brick-nogging. It now has a single roof covering nave and aisles
(the latter added by *Butterfield*) and, like a number of other
Hampshire churches, a bell-turret. At Rotherwick, the early C16
nave was also originally entirely timber-framed. Of churches
partly timber-framed the best is Crawley, with nave and aisles
dated to the 1370s when Wykeham held the advowson. Wooden
posts supporting BELFRIES are also quite a North Hampshire
feature and there are examples at Binsted (C13? inside the stone
tower), Bishops Sutton (C14), Farnborough (the timbers reused
for the present tower c. 1700), Long Sutton and importantly
Ropley (late C14? unusually lofting above a stone transept). South
Warnborough (late C14), Houghton (C15), Hurstbourne Tarrant
(C15) and Monk Sherborne (C15?). Timber ROOFS survive in a

number of churches: Mapledurwell (C14, nave roof in unusual pointed barrel form, with plain tie-beams, braced collars and purlins); Overton (chancel *c.* 1300, with two well-carved bosses); Holybourne is early C15, reconstructed after a fire and with tie-beams similar to Alton. From the later period and into the early C16 the numbers increase: Cliddesden, Easton, Hurstbourne Tarrant, Greywell, Newnham, Weyhill, Whitchurch and Wolverton. The early C16 roofs at Rotherwick and Old Basing are of near identical design. Of special interest is the roof of the chancel chapel at Stoke Charity, built *c.* 1475 which has a huge wall plate frieze of Somerset type, unique in Hampshire.

Decoration, furnishings and monuments: c13, c14 and c15

WALL and VAULT PAINTING must have first place, for the Holy Sepulchre Chapel in Winchester Cathedral possesses what David Park has called 'the finest of all late Romanesque wall paintings in England', a deposition and entombment that until the 1960s was mostly concealed by a repainting of the chapel *c.* 1230 that, together with the roundels with angel busts painted some ten year later on the vault of the cathedral's Guardian Angels Chapel, is some of the best C13 work in England. Both show strong Byzantine influence. Some other end-of-the-C12 wall painting is at Farnborough with three female saints, some early C13 painting at Stoke Charity (St Gregory), some at Bramley including one scene identified as the murder of Becket (the subject also appears at St Cross *c.* 1275), and substantial remains of a complete scheme at Silchester, also *c.* 1230, with fictive masonry patterns. Of the next century the best paintings are at Hurstbourne Tarrant (The Four Living and the Four Dead and a very fragmentary Wheel of Sins now almost obliterated), and the Seven Deadly Sins feature in the paintings at Hartley Wintney (mid-C14). The best mid to late C14 ones are the Doom paintings at Farringdon (now hidden). For the early C15 the paintings at Nether Wallop, of St George and the Dragon and figures of a king and queen in a tower, a large figure of Christ with trade emblems and St Nicholas, all stand out. The wall paintings in the Lady Chapel of Winchester Cathedral date from *c.* 1510–20 and are strongly influenced by those of Eton College Chapel. There is, as at Eton, a whole cycle on the N and S walls of the chapel, and the style is wholly dependent on that of Flanders. In addition, St Christophers of the familiar size and type, both C15, at Bramley and Tufton, the latter with mysterious incised patterns of circles.

STAINED GLASS of the C13 in north Hampshire is rare, and what there is is not local, but it is all of exquisite beauty: at Grateley (from Salisbury Cathedral), and a small panel at Headley. At Winchester College, in the former Headmaster's house, is an imported C13 panel from St Germain des Prés, Paris. There is nothing else until the beginning of the C14 with the superb heraldic glass at Froyle, in the tracery lights of the large

E window, and also two small early C14 figures at Tichborne. The most important are the parts left in their original state of the glass made for the E window of the Winchester College Chapel as part of a major scheme by Master *Thomas of Oxford* in 1393. They are among the most characteristic of their date in England. From the C15 and earlier C16 there is less of interest (St Cross Winchester, Basingstoke, Sherborne St John, and Stoke Charity with emblems of Edward IV). But the best glass is at The Vyne and for that *see* below.

Of FURNISHINGS no more can be reported for the late C12 and early C13 than two items in Winchester Cathedral: the Pilgrims' Gates which incorporate exquisite late C12 work, the 12-ft bench in the S transept, and the curved bench whose radius suggests it comes from the apse of the Romanesque axial chapel. PISCINAS are particularly common in the first half of the C13, often with trefoil or ogee arches. They range from the simple to the elaborate of one, two (Bighton, Buriton, Hinton Ampner, St Cross Winchester, and St Mary Bourne, a specially ornate example) or even three drains (Bishops Sutton). The piscina is accompanied by sedilia at Buriton and Headbourne Worthy, a shelf at Penton Mewsey and at Froyle combined with the Perp window. Among the pillar types special note should be made of the Perp one at Broughton with its playful figures. FONTS are notable only by their absence, just those of the table type continuing into the C13 at Bentworth and Empshott, the typical C13 octagonal one at Bramshott, one with a tiled surround at Hurstbourne Tarrant, one with heads at Sherborne St John, a mysterious one at All Saints, Odiham, with a bracket. C14 Dec tracery on that at Kings Worthy, and octagonal Perp ones with quatrefoils at Crawley, Hartley Mauditt (with heraldry like Over Wallop), Heckfield, Liss, etc. Of Dec furnishings the Winchester Cathedral STALLS (*c.* 1308) are the finest, with their slim detached shafts and their foliage in the spandrels, already knobbly in the C14 way. The misericords of the seats are varied and of high quality too and matched in excellence by the late C14 misericords at the College. Of SCREENS, a wooden one of Dec details is in St John the Baptist, Winchester, another was taken from St Maurice in the same city and is now at the barracks at Flowerdown, Littleton. It is likely to be *c.* 1310 and its small size and quality suggest it might have originated as a tomb screen in the cathedral. But far finer than this is the blank screen or blank arcading, also *c.* 1310 at the foot of the cathedral feretory facing the retrochoir. By *Thomas of Witney*. This, with its ogee arches and ample crocketing, is the most ornate piece of Dec in the county but sadly spoiled by the insertion of icons in the late C20. The cathedral also has several Perp stone screens. Perp wooden screens in the parish churches are rare; that at Basingstoke (chancel S arcade) might be contemporary with the restoration of the chancel in the 1460s, and the ROOD SCREEN with five-light divisions at Bramley is a rare survival. Others are at St John Winchester, Chilbolton, Freefolk and Silchester (with the emblem of Katharine of Aragon). In the Lady Chapel at

Winchester and at South Warnborough ROOD LOFTS or their parapets are preserved but nowhere are screen and loft found together. Parts of the rood may be preserved in the belfry at Hurstbourne Tarrant. Dummer has a rood canopy, a rarity, as well as a pulpit. REREDOSES are an integral part of the chantry chapels in the cathedral, from Edington's onwards. The large reredos in Winchester College Chapel dates from *c.* 1470, but the largest and most important of all is that in the cathedral presbytery, the Great Screen, dated to 1450–75. For PANELLING there is that in the Langton Chapel, very sumptuous. TILES in the cathedral retrochoir form one of the largest *in situ* pavements, dated to 1250–1360 and of more than one style and maker, the earlier ones characteristic of the Wessex style, which occur also at St Cross in combination with late C14 tiles by *William Tyler* of Otterbourne. Other C13 tiles are at Barton Stacey, Farringdon and Selborne.

The Winchester *Ecclesia* is the finest SCULPTURE of its date (*c.* 1230) in England, and closely dependent on (and worthy of) Chartres. It very likely occupied one of the niches in the Deanery porch and was probably ornamented with rich metalwork. Indeed there is extremely fine carving of every date in the cathedral although a good deal of this is *ex situ* and hard to date. Elsewhere, from the end of the medieval period there is the Mass of St Gregory, *c.* 1500, at Stoke Charity which was rediscovered in the C19, and there is also an interesting survival at Old Basing of a Virgin and Child, probably commissioned by Sir John Paulet before 1525 but re-set into the gable of the nave when it was rebuilt in 1551–6.

If FUNERARY MONUMENTS are included, the mid-C13 Purbeck relief in Winchester Cathedral to mark the heart-burial of Bishop Aymer de Valence (†1260) is up to the best standard. Of Purbeck marble also are the effigy of Bishop Peter des Roches with a low tiara and a short stylized beard, and the interesting coffin-lid with a foliated cross at Pamber Priory. The earliest effigy of a knight is at Thruxton (possibly Sir John Cormeilles †1200) and may well go back to the late C12 or early C13 if the design of his helmet is to be taken as evidence. Of the early C14 is the recumbent effigy of a lady at East Worldham, perhaps Margery de Venuz, of which only her bust is carved, and the vicar of King's Somborne, set under a Dec arch. The best monument of the C14 is in the cathedral, that of Arnaud de Gaveston, of which the front of the tomb-chest is in one place, the Purbeck marble effigy with the usual crossed legs in another. The effigy is at least equalled in quality by the effigy of a lady at Silchester. Other CROSS-LEGGED KNIGHTS are at Binsted, St Mary Bourne, and Pamber Priory (7 ft (2.2 metres) long), the last of oak. Four C14 monuments are of the type with the coffin-lid kept as a plain lid except for a sunk shape at the top, where the head or bust of the deceased appears. They are at Silchester (two), East Worldham and East Tisted. The latter has a dog at the feet of the effigy.

EFFIGY.
(March 1861)
IN THE CHURCH OF ST MARY BOURNE,
HANTS.

Supposed to Represent one of the
Family of D'aundele of
WYKE MANOR.

St Mary Bourne, St Peter, effigy of Sir Roger des Andeleys, c14.
Lithograph, c. 1861

Later Gothic monuments deserve a little more attention. We
start with BRASSES, of which there are in Hampshire relatively
few but relatively significant. The earliest are at Sherborne St
John (Raulin Brocas and wife) c. 1360, demi-figures with Norman
French inscription, also King's Somborne, with two figures,
probably brothers, of 1380, and at Crondall, also 1380s, the Rev.
Kaerwent in his vestments. The finest is at St Cross, John de
Campeden, the master of the hospital and Canon of Southwell,
with the date of death 1410, nearly 6 ft (1.8 metres) long. At
Thruxton also a splendid large figure of Sir John Lisle: he died
†1407, the brass made c. 1425 and showing him in armour under
a canopy. At Nether Wallop is a rare early c15 brass of Dame
Mary Gore, Prioress of Amesbury, and from later in the century,
c. 1490, the touching figures of a civilian and his lady at Brown

Candover. Of about the same time and taking us up to the end of the reign of Henry VIII is the group of brasses at Sherborne St John, all for the Brocas family. Of the fashion for ALABASTER EFFIGIES, the earliest in Hampshire are the recumbent effigies in the cathedral for Bishops Edington (†1366 but his monument perhaps even earlier) and Wykeham (†1404, his much repainted and repaired). But they are not great in number by any calculation. Apart from the couple of *c.* 1520 at Oakley, alabaster is more routinely associated with C17 monuments in Hampshire. More generally the effigies of the bishops in their chantries are nothing special, including Beaufort (†1447), who is a C17 copy. Cadavers or corpses in decomposition instead of, or in addition to, effigies were originally a conception of France of about 1400. They appeared in England some twenty or thirty years later (Lincoln, Bishop Fleming †1435) and then soon became a favourite theme (*see* the Brocas brass †1488 at Sherborne St John). In Hampshire we have only two cases, both very late: Bishop Fox †1528 and Bishop Gardiner †1555, both in the cathedral.

A quite large type of Early Tudor monument and elaborate in decoration is one issuing from Purbeck and sent to many English counties. They stand against the wall and have a TOMB-CHEST and above it an arch, panelled inside and on the side pieces, and a top cresting. The arches always are flat and can even be replaced by a horizontal on curved springers. Such monuments we have in North Hampshire are at Stoke Charity (John Waller †1527) and Crondall (Sir George Paulet †1532 and also Sir John Gyfford †1563). The type occurs even later yet at South Warnborough (Sir Thomas Whyte †1570).

Discussion of Early Tudor monuments brings us neatly to the EARLY RENAISSANCE in North Hampshire. The story might begin as early as 1510 on the evidence of a stone cornice with some crude classicizing detail (now in the cathedral's Triforium Gallery) which may have come from the chantry chapel for Bishop Langton. There is also the intriguing incorporation of classical volutes in the side walls of Bishop Fox's chantry chapel, completed in 1518, but these are most likely later ornaments to an otherwise undiluted Late Gothic structure. We are on firmer ground with the embellishment of the presbytery by Bishop Fox. The works associated with him usually show evidence of advanced taste, no doubt influenced by his close relations with court circles. The screens N and S of the presbytery are a side by side of purely Gothic and purely Renaissance motifs. The date is 1525. The structural parts such as the four-light windows are purely Gothic, but friezes and inscription tablets and the tomb-chests along the tops of the screens are Renaissance. Of these the latter might even be slightly later additions. Of about the same time, or a little before, are the canopied seats now in the S transept which have the initials of Prior Silkstede (†1524). They are still in the Late Gothic mode but incorporate pilasters with candelabra and arabesque ornament. Fox also donated the stalls

---

*But the chest for Silkstede (1498–1524) at Shanklin, Isle of Wight, is in a fully Renaissance style dated 1512.

at St Cross, Winchester. Although broken up, one may see that these had typical profile heads in medallions, and in the details emphatically show the influence of French styles.

Of the full scheme of stained glass commissioned by Fox for the cathedral presbytery aisles only fragments are preserved but they are especially interesting. For what is left seems to be closely related to the scheme commissioned for the Holy Ghost Chapel at Basingstoke, where in the early 1520s William Sandys, a powerful courtier, began construction of a family burial chapel (dedicated to the Holy Trinity). Although now ruinous a series of statue tabernacles show Continental influences. Sandys, through his government positions, had direct contact with the Low Countries and not only commissioned work through agents but imported foreign craftsmen to work for him. The stained glass commissioned for the chapel (and now in the chapel at The Vyne)   54 is datable to c. 1522–4, possibly designed by *Bernard van Orley* and almost certainly made abroad. Side by side with the glass of King's College Chapel it is the most important in the country. It is Netherlandish and Early Renaissance, and hence much more opulent in its architectural features than anything made in England would be (other fragments are at St Michael, Basingstoke, and the Holy Ghost (R.C.) church in Basingstoke). The stained glass of Sherborne St John (Brocas Chapel) is at least as opulent. Before his death Sandys also commissioned, c. 1536, a pair of Tournai marble tombs for himself and his wife from *Arnold Hermanzone* of Aire-en-Artois. They survive but are sadly uninformative of their original appearance. Sandys's private chapel at The Vyne is contemporary with his great rebuilding there in 1524–6 (for which *see* below) and remains one of the best-preserved of its kind in England. The stalls are of English make, it looks, and they too are Early Renaissance but in a conventional way.

Of special interest for this period are some of the most ambitious stone monuments in the parish churches, which Dr Nicholas Riall has attributed to *Thomas Bertie*. These are the two Paulet monuments at Old Basing in Gothic style c. 1525, the de Lisle monument at Thruxton of about 1524 (with details similar to the tomb-chest for Bishop Pontoise in the cathedral presbytery screens), East Tisted of c. 1530 which began as an Easter Sepul-   55 chre, and the Pexall monument at Sherborne St John, c. 1535, where again Renaissance and Gothic motifs are mixed. All of this type are, or were, placed between chancel and a chancel chapel and open to both. The pattern is followed for the two mid-C16 Paulet monuments at Old Basing, with Renaissance details of unique character, erected in the S chapel. This is also of interest because it was built during Queen Mary's brief reign. At Sherborne St John is the brick porch, dated 1533 and also Renaissance in a few bits, e.g. small volutes to blind panelling. With the chapel dedicated to Bishop Gardiner (†1555) in the   52 cathedral we are on the border between the first and second phase of the Renaissance, and in particular the High Renaissance manner as it emerged in England in the decoration of Nonsuch

Palace for Henry VIII. While the Gothic screen windows and
vaulting and the Early Renaissance crestings are as they had been
for the last thirty years in the bishops' chantries, the base,
pilasters and friezes are all derived from the Italo-French
Cinquecento and the reredos inside has – admittedly on a very
small scale – columns instead of pilasters, shell niches and also
two statuettes.

Major secular buildings

The street pattern of much of Winchester dates from the Saxon
burh of Alfred but by comparison with the minsters we know relatively little of the royal palace. The Conqueror appears to have
retained it and enlarged it as his principal residence. Building of
the CASTLE at Winchester began within a year of the Conquest.
Of the CII fabric nothing remains visible above ground. The earliest standing remains are associated with mid-CI3 reconstruction of its defences but otherwise there is only the aisled Great
Hall, known from documents to have been built between 1222
and 1236, of Henry III's castle to provide a clue to its medieval
appearance, the rest deliberately slighted in the Civil War. It is,
next to Westminster Hall, the finest medieval hall in England,
with powerful clustered Purbeck piers, doorways in the end bay,
as was the English custom, a raised dais platform, and close to
it an ornate doorway to the solar and queen's lodgings. It is in
its dimensions a double cube: 110 by 55 by 55 ft (35 by 17.5 by
17.5 metres).

In the wider county the church was the principal landowner,
so little is to be found in the way either of Crown properties or
seats of local magnates except for MOTTE-AND-BAILEY earthworks at Old Basing, erected for Hugh de Port, the only minor
lord with significant holdings in Hampshire, and Gains Castle,
Ashley, seat of William Briwere, where the outline of the ringwork and bailey are very clear. Of King John's Odiham Castle,
all that survives is the octagonal keep, the only one of its kind in
England (but cf. Chilham Castle, Kent, of the late CI2), built
soon after 1216. But little of its architectural detail is preserved.

Instead the most important class of secular buildings in the
medieval period are the stone-built EPISCOPAL RESIDENCES.
The bishops of Winchester were amongst the wealthiest in northern Europe and could afford to build without much concern for
costs, but restricted themselves to a small number of houses of
varying status from which to manage their estates. At the head
was the Norman palace at Wolvesey in Winchester, which was
fortified during the early CI2 civil war between Stephen and
Matilda. The ruins consist of a N range, a keep, and another tower
of *c.* 1130–40, and the traces of a tremendous great hall of *c.* 1170,
i.e. of Henry of Blois – 140 ft (44 metres) long and on the upper
floor. Unfortunately nothing survives of the other great houses
at Bishops Sutton (Henry of Blois) or Highclere (rebuilt by
William of Wykeham in the late CI4), each of which provided a

major residence at the heart of extensive manorial holdings in
the NW and E of the county. The Court House, East Meon, is the   29
substantial remains of one of the smaller country houses
designed for more temporary residence. It was built in 1395–7
for William of Wykeham, the work overseen by his master mason,
William Wynford. What is left is the hall lit by square-headed
windows and with an unadorned crown-post roof, typical for late
C14 Hampshire. Over the buttery and pantry is a chamber with
a garderobe block attached, but the chamber block at the upper
end, along with the former oriel, has alas gone, along with the
numerous ancillary buildings which would have served it. There
was something similar at Overton although this was little used
and replaced by a farmhouse in the early C16.

Also significant for the history of domestic architecture in the
county are the COMMUNAL FOUNDATIONS established by the
bishops: Winchester College and the enlargement of the Hospital of St Cross. Both are major building enterprises following the
Black Death. In 1387 Wykeham laid the foundation stone of Winchester College, the largest and most consistently and intelli-
gently planned school or college of the time anywhere in Europe.
Building went on very quickly, and in 1394 the school and the
foundation (with its warden, fellows, chaplains, etc.) began to
function. It consists of an outer court and then Chamber Court
with the sets and dormitories and hall and chapel. The inner and
outer gatehouses are both on a monumental scale, and hall and
chapel lie in the S range of Chamber Court and in line, though   41
the chapel is of course on the ground floor, whereas the hall is
on the upper floor. S of Chamber Court and not axial is the cloister, built as the college graveyard. During his last years Cardinal
Beaufort, Bishop of Winchester (†1447), stimulated no doubt by
the College, established a new foundation at St Cross Hospital
with accommodation (of a higher class than before) for its
brethren. It too closely follows the character of large domestic
buildings of the late Middle Ages in the adoption of a courtyard
format, with services, an outer court, and the lodgings around a
larger inner one. Here again a hall was provided but on this occasion simply adapted from the existing, C14, hall. The kitchen lies
in the same relation to it as at the College, and the gatehouse is
almost a copy of the College's Inner Gate. The most interesting
part of the buildings is the range for the brethren, two-storeyed   34, 36
and planned so that there is access to four apartments from one
staircase, and each two apartments have one chimney.

The Priory of St Swithun, like the bishops, also had extensive
landholdings in the county. The Prior's Lodging in The Close at
Winchester survives only in part but what remains is impressive.
Its C13 porch has ribs exactly like those of the cathedral retro-   23
choir central aisle and tracery almost exactly like the Lady
Chapel arcading. The prior's great chamber also survives but not
of the same period as the porch, its roof timbers dated to
1459. Nearby, and also associated with the vanished monastic
buildings, is the Guest Hall (now incorporated into The Pilgrims'   35
School) with its remarkable hammerbeam roof of *c.* 1310

attributed to *Thomas of Witney*, who was then at work in the cathedral, and the stables of 1479, both of which attest to the high status of the Priory. The prior also stretched to country houses, of which the only evidence in the northern county now may be a range of the Court House, West Meon. The country residence kept by the Abbess of St Mary's Winchester at Lyss Place, Liss, is also partly preserved. Of several other MONASTERIES the most interesting survival is at Wherwell Priory. Here a large part of an impressive sturdy timber-framed roof remains intact. Of aisle construction, dateable to 1250–1280, it is of six bays and perhaps belonged to the infirmary.

More survives of substantial RECTORIES, which like the larger houses are also generally of stone or brick. The earliest survival is at Old Burghclere (now the Manor House), a manor of the Bishops of Winchester. At its core is a two-bay hall with a roof of raised aisle construction and stone outer walls with coeval windows. Another early stone-built example at Buriton has a late C13 hall block with a C14 cross-wing, and the Old House, Wonston, of *c.* 1400, has a hall with gabled cross-wings. Although altered in 1740 much of the medieval house survives, including a timber-framed former detached kitchen. The Chancellors of Salisbury were the rectors of Odiham, which explains the ambitious flint and stone-built chamber block of 1448–9 at The Priory, the former rectory, in that town. The hall, probably timber-framed, has gone but there is a charming early C16 miniature brick porch with polygonal corner buttresses and oriel window. The mid-C15 lodging range at Kimpton Manor is a fragment of another medieval rectory, its status reflected in its continuous jetty and early C16 brick chimney with chequerboard decoration. Two modest timber-framed rectories also survive. That at Headbourne Worthy probably dates to the late C15 while the other at Littleton (1500/1) – now called Monk's Rest – extends to only three bays but what is presumably the rector's bay has a stone fireplace and a garderobe to the room above.

SECULAR MANOR HOUSES of comparable status are rarer: best is Hall Place, Bentworth, a stone-built house with former aisled hall and porch of *c.* 1300 and later cross-wings and, close by, an early C14 chapel. The remarkable group of three stone and timber-framed chamber blocks, from the C14 to the C16, at Bramshott Manor should be mentioned here too, one with a good crown-post roof. From the second half of the C15 date some large MANOR FARMHOUSES. They are of special interest, for they were built and occupied by men who took permanent leases of large areas of land from the Church and in time came to consider themselves gentlemen. Two good representatives are the former farmhouse, now called Littleton Manor (1485) and Court Farm, Overton (1505–7), the latter of which was actually rebuilt for the tenant at the bishop's expense. Other landowners did the same thing, e.g. Goleigh Manor Farm, Priors Dean (owned by Winchester College and built 1466), and Manor Farm House, King's Somborne (1504–8), which was owned and built by Magdalen College, Oxford, and doubled as an occasional residence for their representative.

Old Basing, the siege of Basing House.
Engraving by Wenceslaus Hollar, *c.* 1645

By the very end of the period there were a number of other large manor houses, e.g. at Beaurepaire, Bramley (Brocas), Thruxton (de Lisle) and Dogmersfield (Bishop of Bath and Wells and later the Earls of Southampton), but only two might be classed as GREAT HOUSES: The Vyne and Basing House and of these only The Vyne has survived to any significant extent. In its present form, however, it is still only a fraction of the considerable house erected by William Sandys between 1524 and 1526; he was created Lord Sandys in 1533 and became Henry VIII's Lord Chamberlain (*see* also p. 531). The house was brick-built, with diapered walls, and comprised buildings arranged around at least three courtyards. Apartments were provided for the King and Queen, and in the Oak Gallery (though slightly altered) are still significant survivals of linenfold panelling with heraldry, and in the chapel gallery also remains of painted decoration imitating striped hangings. In spite of its scale and ambition, within a decade Sandys was also beginning conversion of Mottisfont Abbey (South Hampshire), his reward from the Dissolution, and evidently intended to make that his principal residence but he died in 1540 while work was still going on. At The Vyne also there is that one mysterious large roundel with the representation of the Emperor Probus which is terracotta, purely Tuscan, and in all probability the work of *Giovanni da Maiano*, who did the Hampton Court roundels and others as well. It may not have come to The Vyne until the C18, in which case it may have been salvaged from the destruction of Whitehall Palace. However, a similar carved bust in a tondo, of stone, found nearby on the site of Basing House (Old Basing) no doubt originated at that house. This was the other great mansion of the earlier C16, erected by Sir William Paulet, one of the most powerful courtiers of his day, and from 1551 the 1st Marquess of Winchester. But there has been even more destruction here than at The Vyne. Paulet was granted a licence to crenellate in 1531, building a large new house alongside the earlier one, but unfortunately we know little more about the building history other than that it appears to have still been under construction in 1569 when we have workmen's accounts. However, to what part of this rambling and complex

pp. 531, 534

56

58

57

p. 432

house the work related we have no idea. Its final extent, although not its plan, is evident from Hollar's engraving but, after its initial destruction in the Civil War and the subsequent robbing of materials, the surviving fabric is rather pathetic: a few walls with towers, a turret and a gateway and some excavated walls. The Vyne and Basing were houses of brick, the usual choice for the most fashionable at this time and attesting to that taste is also the slender octagonal brick stair-tower at Malshanger (*see* Oakley), all that remains of the house of William Warham, the Archbishop of Canterbury, which he inherited in 1507.

Smaller rural and urban buildings

Enough has been said of the residences of the elite and gentry. So to the houses constructed in the regional, or VERNACULAR style, occupied by those who worked for a living, either on the land or as craftsmen and traders, as distinct from those who owned property and lived on rents. The standard vernacular form until the middle of the C17 was the TIMBER-FRAMED HOUSE.* The earliest survivors in North Hampshire date to the late C13 and C14. They can be box-framed, aisled or of cruck construction. The frame is generally infilled with wattle and daub. Chalk cob was used in medieval Winchester for the hovels of the poor but all surviving cottages and farm buildings built of cob seem to post-date 1700. Flint commonly formed the low, foundation walls for the frame but did not appear combined with brick in external walls until the early C17 and did not become a common feature until the late C17. Knapped flints might be used as nogging between close studs of timber, e.g. at Monk's Rest, Littleton (1500/1), as was ironstone at Tankerdale Farm, Steep (1622), and brick laid in herringbone pattern at Church Cottage, Basingstoke (*c.* 1541).

Aisled or aisle-derivative houses are rare: the latest dated example being the base-cruck hall at Trees Cottage, Froxfield (1359). True CRUCK HOUSES form a significant part of the surviving stock of medieval rural houses, especially in the W and N of the county. Their numbers thin out towards the SE and they are absent entirely E of the Weald edge. They are generally low buildings whose cramped first-floor space came to be seen as inconvenient, and this may explain why dated examples are confined to the C14, C15 and early C16. The earliest BOX-FRAMED HOUSES are in towns, e.g. No. 42 Chesil Street, Winchester (1292), and Monk's Cottage, Odiham (1300), and rare in rural areas before 1400. Box framing came to predominate in both town and country during the early C16 and was universally accepted for framed houses thereafter. LARGE-PANEL FRAMING, in which there is no mid rail at half-storey height, was universal until the mid C15. Then for a century both large and small-panel framing were common, but after the mid C16 the latter became

* The dates given in brackets are the felling dates for the timbers, established by dendrochronology.

the norm. Long, straight braces, almost square in section, are occasionally found in late C13 and C14 houses but, in general, curved braces were used from the early C14 through to the mid C16. Straight braces became common thereafter and are the only known form in the C17. Ogee braces were occasionally used as display features on the fronts of buildings during the years in and around the early C16, and close studs, also used for display, occur in larger houses from the late C15 to the mid C17. Tension, or down-swinging, braces are unusual, especially in C16 houses. JETTIES are generally confined to larger houses in rural areas, e.g. Kimpton Manor (1445) and Bramley Manor (1545/6), but were more common in towns. Numerous medieval town houses have the hall range parallel to the street with a single, jettied cross-wing. These jetties have generally been underbuilt with a masonry wall at a later date and the C15 Old Farm House at St Cross near Winchester gives a good idea of the original form. Jettied cross-wings at both ends of the central range are decidedly rare, e.g. Goleigh Manor (formerly a farmhouse) at Priors Dean (1466). Most cross-wings were simply jettied towards the front of the house, and houses jettied on both the front and one adjacent side are restricted to urban commercial centres. Only one house – Nos. 31–35 High Street, Overton (1541/2) – is known with jetties on opposite sides.

46

47

Fewer than ten WEALDEN HOUSES (hall houses without cross-wings but with jettied end bays) have been found in North Hampshire, but No. 35 High Street, Winchester (1340), is the earliest known Wealden anywhere. All other dated Wealdens belong to the C15, although it is likely that some were built in the early C16. Rarer still are continuously jettied houses with open halls. These are something of a Hampshire speciality of which Shillingbury Cottage, formerly The Crease, at Micheldever (1463–83), is an outstanding example. As open halls ceased to be built, continuous jetties became commoner – apparently as a form of display in rural or suburban houses: in the C16 at Tudor Cottages, King Street, Odiham (1540), and in the C17 at The Old Post Office, Tichborne (1608/9).

On some larger houses and on cross-wings the gable-end was the general form for ROOFS for most of the period. With this exception, it may be said that the fully hipped roof seems to have been common throughout Hampshire in the C14, e.g. at The Old Blue Boar, St John's Street, Winchester, and remained common E of the Weald edge until the early C16. It was superseded by the half-hipped roof, which became the standard form in Hampshire until the end of the C17 when fully hipped roofs on brick houses were in vogue again. ROOF TRUSSES show a fairly clear line of development, starting with the KINGPOST TRUSS of which only two are known to survive in the county, both dating to the late C13: one is at No. 42 Chesil Street, Winchester (1292). The CROWN-POST TRUSS, as seen at East Meon Court House, was the dominant form in the C14 and a few survive from the early C15. The picture differs only to the E of the Weald edge where the crown-post remained common throughout the C15 and probably

29

into the early C16. In the rest of North Hampshire, the SIDE-PURLIN TRUSS was dominant from the early C15 onwards. The clasped side-purlin truss came first – e.g. Manisty Cottage, Odiham (1400). At first this had a single crown strut between tie- and collar-beams and often, on either side of this strut, two braces curving out from the tie-beam to the principal rafter. The mid C15 saw two innovations: the early form of clasped side-purlin roof was superseded by a form with queen struts, and the tenoned side-purlin roof was introduced; although it is only found in high-status buildings until the late C16. Open roof trusses generally take the form of arch-braced collars, sometimes combined with arch-braced tie-beams. In the C17 a variety of ways were found to clear attic space of intrusive beams: with upper crucks at Grange Farm, Old Basing, and with a combination of stub and dropped tie-beams at Conford House, Bramshott.

Medieval STAIRS seem to have been little more than a ladder rising to a hatch in the ceiling. A framed staircase first appears at Abbotts Barton Farmhouse, Winchester (1545–77). WINDOWS generally comprised wooden mullions without glazing and were closed with wooden shutters. Glazed windows survive from the parlour end of Sevington Manor, Tichborne, built in c. 1600. Glazing appeared in houses further down the social scale during the C17, although lower-status rooms were still given wooden mullions.

Most framed houses have a linear, rectangular PLAN, and cross-wings are uncommon except in towns where they have often been disguised by later remodelling in brick. Except in large town centres, nearly all surviving medieval houses conformed to a tripartite plan with an OPEN HALL, often only of one bay, between end bays. At the 'high', i.e. parlour, end of the hall was often a bench fixed to the partition, where mortices for fixing can sometimes still be detected. At the 'low', i.e service, end of the hall, there was a cross-passage that separated the hall from a service bay. Early attempts to restrict the smoky area within the hall occasionally involved the flooring-over of the 'high-end' bay and leaving the 'low-end' as a smoke bay. Few such 'half-floored halls' have been found but Fardells at Micheldever (1572) is a good example, and at Beechcroft, Tunworth (1601–2), only part of the smoke bay was open while the other part accommodated a gallery between first-floor chambers. Smoke-hoods, made like timber-framed funnels, survive in a few smaller houses: that at Nos. 56–58 Winchester Street, Overton (post-dating 1533 but probably pre-dating 1600), gives some idea of their period of popularity.

The earliest dated, completely FLOORED HALL is at Nos. 67–69 High Street, Odiham (1476/7). Introduced in large town houses and rural manor farmhouses, the innovation had spread to smaller cottages by the late C16. It was a plan that generally required a masonry chimneystack. This was only rarely attached to the side of the hall, e.g. at Abbotts Barton Farm, Winchester (1491–6). It was much more often placed towards the low end of the hall backing on to the cross-passage, thus producing the

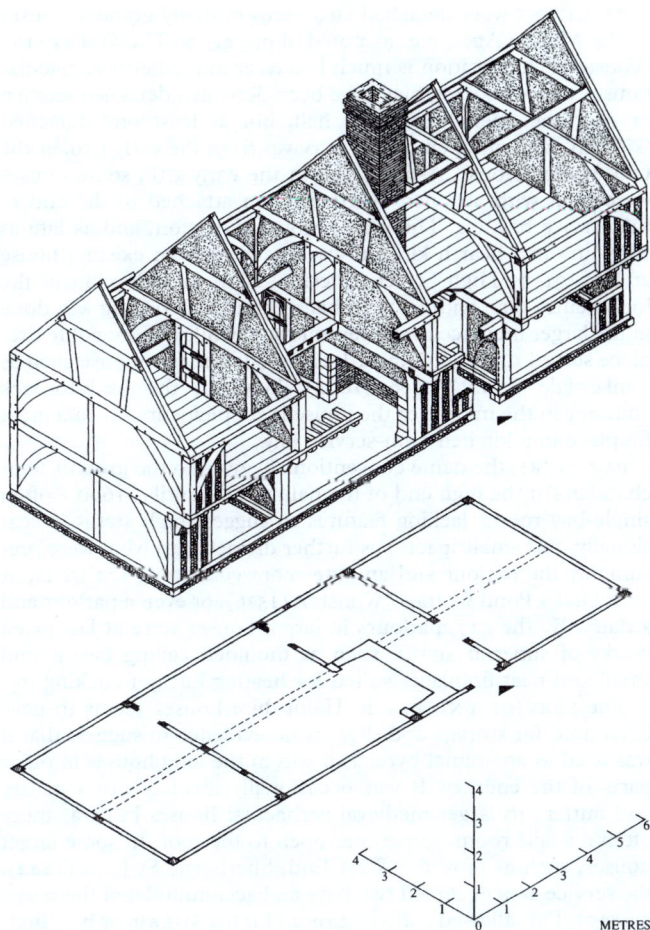

Petersfield, Nos. 1–2, The Square, reconstruction.
Axonometric drawing by Jonathan Snowdon, 2003

HEARTH-PASSAGE PLAN. This plan was very common in larger houses in the early C16, e.g. No. 1 The Square, Petersfield (1532–3), and Tudor Cottages, King Street, Odiham (1540). The LOBBY-ENTRY PLAN, in which the house was entered via a lobby next to the chimney, had been introduced by 1579/80 at No. 15 The Spain, Petersfield. It was the dominant plan in vernacular houses for the first sixty years of the C17 and it is very occasionally found in the early C18, e.g. Cole Henley Cottage, Whitchurch (dated 1715 by inscription). In the second half of the C17, a symmetrical front became fashionable and entrance was generally made through a centrally placed front door: into a hall with a staircase in larger houses and directly into the larger front room in smaller houses.

KITCHENS were detached structures in many grander houses in the Middle Ages, e.g. as noted above at the The Old House, Wonston. The position is much less clear in medieval vernacular houses where cooking may have been done in a detached kitchen or over the open fire in the hall, but at least one detached 'kitchen' with an open hearth survives from the early C16, at the Old Manor House, Ashley. Also in the early C16, some houses were built with an open-hearth kitchen attached to the end of the service bay, e.g. The White House, Littleton, and as late as 1625 an open-hearth kitchen was attached to an existing house at Nos. 31–35 High Street, Overton. With the adoption of the lobby-entry plan with back-to-back chimneys, cooking was done in the larger fireplace in the central room while a more polite fireplace served the adjoining parlour. In a larger farmhouse such as Tankerdale Farm, Steep (1622), however, the back-to-back chimney in the middle of the house is supplemented with a great fireplace in a kitchen-cum-service bay.

PARLOURS, the name conventionally given to the ground-floor chambers at the high end of the hall, were – until *c.* 1600 – often single-bay rooms lacking features to suggest high status. Occasionally, this small space was further divided into what were presumably the parlour and an ante-room containing the stairs, as at St Olaf's Pond Cottage, Wonston (1536), or even a parlour and a dairy. By the C17, parlours in larger houses were at last given marks of superior status, such as moulded ceiling beams and small and neat fireplaces suited for heating but not cooking.

The SERVICE-END BAY in Hampshire houses seems to have been used for storage and there is no evidence to suggest that it was used as an animal byre, as it was in the long houses in other parts of the country. It was occasionally divided into a pantry and buttery in larger medieval vernacular houses but was more often a single room, sometimes open to the roof. In some larger houses, such as Nos. 6–8 West End, Sherborne St John (1444), the service area occupied two bays and accommodated the cross-passage. This allowed sufficient room for the SOLAR, or best first-floor chamber, to be placed over the service end. Indeed, in houses with in-line plans this is more common than a position over the parlour. It is only when solars were placed in cross-wings that they are found as frequently at the high as at the low end of the house. Solars had two or more bays and their open trusses took a similar form to open trusses in halls. By the C17, two-bay solars are rarely found but first-floor rooms in larger farmhouses were often heated.

Most medieval TOWN HOUSES resemble rural houses, except that the hall with cross-wing is a commoner form in towns. In the commercial heart of Winchester, and in other large towns throughout England where street frontage was at a premium, there are peculiarly urban forms. Some, like No. 42 High Street (1312–52?) and No. 43 High Street, Winchester (1508), are three-storey houses, jettied on both upper floors. These are essentially large single rooms stacked one on another and, in the former case, built over a contemporary cellar. Others, like Nos. 33–34

High Street (1463/4), are entirely aligned at a right angle to the street. Here, narrow frontages are jettied out over a pavement walkway. Notable, too, is Godebegot, Nos. 101–102 High Street, Winchester (1462/3), which has a three-storey range parallel to the street and ranges of two-storey shops forming a courtyard behind.

Outside Winchester, there are town houses that appear to have been post-medieval shops, e.g. Nos. 17–19 High Street, Petersfield, whose rather showy front has a central pediment and three pendants inscribed with the date 1613. Probably the most remarkable semi-urban houses in the county are Castle Bridge Cottages, North Warnborough (1477/8 and 1534/5), a development on the outskirts of Odiham but obviously related in some way to urban trade or industry. Although interrupted by a Victorian rebuilding of one house, this was originally a continuous row of jettied houses, nine bays in length. Finally, large COURTYARD INNS seem to be an exclusively urban form in Hampshire. A fine example is The Angel Inn, Andover (1445–53), built by Winchester College. The great hall with scissor-braced hall truss, the gatehouse and a wing with superior lodging and inferior lodgings over stables still survive. The former George Inn at Alton p. 125 (1501) retains part of a similar lodging range with evidence of garderobes projecting over the River Wey and, from the early C17, The White Hart, Overton, has a gatehouse and a suite of rooms with a stair-tower.

The earliest surviving AGRICULTURAL BUILDINGS are BARNS. These were principally used to store corn, although some served subsidiary functions such as sheltering livestock. Two of the earliest barns are of cruck construction: at Breach Farm, Sherfield-on-Loddon (1391), and at Summers Farm, Long 48 Sutton (1441). Just as the demise of cruck construction occurred at about the same time in houses and in agricultural buildings, so changes in the form of roof trusses and bracing were similarly matched. Close parallels include the introduction of the clasped-purlin, queen-strut truss in the mid C15 and the change to small-panel framing and straight braces in the second half of the C16. Even the use of trusses to clear attic headroom is paralleled by the upper crucks in the C17 barn at The Manor House, Vernham Dean. But there were also differences: notably the persistence and predominance of AISLED BARNS until the end of the medieval period and beyond, and the continuance of timber framing in barns for at least a hundred years after the framed tradition had ended in domestic buildings. Barns attached to the manor farmhouses were, like the houses, at the very upper limit of the vernacular threshold: e.g. at Manor Farm, Old Burghclere (1451), where the barn is eight bays in length, and at Court Farm, Overton (1496), whose barn originally comprised nine bays. By the early C16, fine barns and stables of brick were associated with aristocratic residences, e.g. Basing House barn (1535). 49 Vernacular barns, however, were exclusively timber-framed until the late C17, some earlier ones having wattle-and-daub infill to the panels but most being clad in weatherboards. Few have

decorative features. Surviving granaries, cartsheds, cattle sheds
and hop kilns apparently post-date 1700, although all but the last
are known from medieval documentary sources. Except for the
STABLES of the elite – e.g. Chawton House (1593) – pre-1700
stables for working horses are rare, although a probable C17
example survives at Grange Farm, Tichborne. It seems possible
that, as in the S of the county, they occupied an end bay of
a barn. This arrangement is found at the splendid barn built
of malmstone at Mill Court, Binsted (dated by inscription to
1667).

ELIZABETHAN AND THE
SEVENTEENTH CENTURY

By now we have reached beyond the DISSOLUTION. A total of
fifteen Hampshire monasteries were dissolved between 1536 and
1539, including in the N St Swithun's Priory and Hyde Abbey,
Winchester. Some establishments were closed well before, e.g.
Selborne Priory was shut by Bishop Waynflete in 1486 and its
endowments used for his foundation of Magdalen College,
Oxford. The Bishop of Winchester kept hold of most of his estates
until the mid C19 but the lands of the monasteries passed first to
the Crown and then were sold to men prominent in national and
local government. Leading royal ministers Sir William Paulet
(from 1551 the 1st Marquess of Winchester) and Thomas Wriothesley (later Earl of Southampton) built up large estates in the
county, Paulet adding to those inherited from the de Ports and
Wriothesley helping himself liberally to the stones of Hyde
Abbey. It was also the moment for local gentry to advance
their position in the county by acquiring land and building. Winchester Cathedral remained in use, and although the priory was
dissolved, several of its residential buildings were simply adapted
to the new requirements. There was some reuse of monastic
buildings elsewhere, at e.g Wherwell where the abbess's lodging
p. 550 was retained, although nothing other than part of the infirmary
(later stables) seems to have survived. At Lyss Place, Liss, the
C19 house incorporates a medieval stone range of the house
belonging to St Mary's Abbey, Winchester, which seems to have
been converted to a hall in 1542. But many redundant buildings
were simply plundered for their stone and the streets of Winchester still bear testament to the myriad ways in which fine
masonry could be reused. In the wider countryside there is good
evidence of the extent of rebuilding of smaller houses, much less
so of churches. The Civil War saw Winchester briefly occupied,
the cathedral ransacked and the city surrendered to Cromwell
in 1645, and also the famous siege and eventual destruction
in that year of Basing House. By the end of the period the
restoration of Charles II promised, briefly, to restore Winchester

as a centre of regal power with Wren's plan to build a palace – the King's House – at the high sw corner of Winchester town above the remains of the medieval castle and to clear all the buildings and streets which lay between this and the cathedral. The palace was completed only in part, before the death of the King in 1685, and abandoned within a few years of the Hanoverian succession.

Churches, chapels and church furnishings

Generous medieval provision means that new ecclesiastical building was almost absent (East Stratton of 1677, Northington of 1675 and Highclere of 1688, all on old sites, excepted, but all dem.) right down to the later C17, and what there is in Hampshire is Gothic Survival, i.e. an unselfconscious carrying on in the late medieval style, e.g. at Odiham where there was a major restoration and refurbishment in the 1630s. Similarly in our part of the county the whole development from Jones and Webb to Wren is unrepresented, especially following the destruction of *Jones*'s choir screen at the cathedral. All that can be found in the north of the county is brick TOWERS, or parts of towers, at Upper Clatford, whose brick top is dated 1578 and has inside an arch with characteristic Elizabethan mouldings. St Mary Bourne is also Elizabethan, and rather plain. St Michael, Aldershot, has a tower of *c.* 1600, an engaging combination of brick and ironstone, and of later date the towers at Bramley (1636–40), the superior brick upper stages at Odiham (1649), Crondall, built in 1659 of brick, a surprisingly monumental work from the last year of the Cromwellian Interregnum, and modelled on the tower of St Mary, Battersea, and finally New Alresford (1689, brick top stage after a fire) and Upton Grey (1690). But they do not change materially, even between the C17 and the C18. A small number of churches had minor repairs and additions in the Jacobean and Carolean years, e.g. new windows, porches etc., but much has been lost to the activities of the Victorians. Sparsholt has a classical doorway of 1631 with coeval door with fine low-relief strapwork. Old Basing needed more thorough treatment after 1660, following the attentions of Cromwellian soldiery engaged in the siege of Basing House, but even there the evidence is only in the existence of a mid-C17 doorway and restoration of the Paulet tombs. The best exemplar of the late C17 is now the interior of the chapel at Wolvesey, Winchester, remodelled in the 1670s by Bishop Morley.

50

There is little architecturally to indicate the strength of NONCONFORMITY until the C18 and C19, although there was one of the earliest Baptist chapels at Broughton (altered 1818 and 1926) and a Quaker meeting house at Tadley from 1662. The second oldest meeting house in England survives at Alton, built in 1672 and in a typically domestic style unexpressive of its purpose.

Among CHURCH FURNISHINGS there is nothing much until one comes to the Jacobean years and the Laudian years, to use the most appropriate term. Then they proliferated, especially during the episcopate of Bishop Walter Curle from 1632 to 1647, although there are no complete ensembles. At Winchester a variety of works were instigated after a visit by the King in 1636.

p. 613 Of *Inigo Jones*'s classical screen of 1638 only fragments remain in the cathedral's lapidarium;* the two rare bronze statues of James I and Charles I by *Le Sueur* are at the W end of the nave. Most of what survives from the C17 is new WOODWORK. To start with there are several dated PULPITS (required by law after 1603) between 1620 and 1660 (Basing 1622, the spectacular piece at Alton 1625, Odiham 1634, Sherborne St John 1634, Winchfield 1634, Silchester (with tester) 1639, Tadley 1650 and Monk Sherborne 1651) and quite a number of undated ones. There are also LECTERNS at St Mary Bourne and Sherborne St John. Of dated SCREENS there are two: Empshott 1624 with strapwork and Herriard 1635 (originally part of the Jervoise family pew), and at Steventon a screened Jacobean family pew survives, although relocated. Among the undated ones is St Peter, Farnborough, which is of *c.* 1630. The most interesting COMMUNION RAILS are those of the Lady Chapel (formerly in the presbytery) in the cathedral and St Cross at Winchester, both not with the usual balusters but with openwork ovals and spurs arranged in a cruciform way. They must date from the 1660s but in a style of thirty years before. The communion rail now in the presbytery at Winchester Cathedral is another example of retrospective styling, probably executed *c.* 1700 but in the manner of Edward Pearce, with scrolling openwork and putti. It was *Edward Pearce* himself,

73 with *Valentine Housman*, who supplied the single most impressive
45 set of woodwork in Hampshire: the screen, reredos and wall panelling of the Winchester College Chapel, provided by Warden Nicholas in 1680–3 (re-set in the College's New Hall of the 1950s). The communion rail with lush openwork acanthus and putti at Brown Candover is probably Flemish, and in any case not English. It came from Northington. Of FONTS, the most interesting one is that at Tangley, of the early C17, because it is made of lead. All the stone fonts are unremarkable. One has a date, Upper Clatford of 1629, with octagonal baluster stem and chalice-like bowl. Also a number of ROYAL ARMS of above average interest, notably the Elizabethan arms at Basingstoke and Jacobean ones at Old Basing and Bramley, both of which have arms set against perspective interiors with black-and-white chequer floors. The charming COMMANDMENTS BOARD at All Hallows, Whitchurch, is dated 1604.

We have already described the early C16 MONUMENTS. Monuments between the mid C16 and the late C17 are far more copious, and also more spectacular – a change of mind noticeable all over England. The Elizabethan age was the first age of

---

*Although much of it has been reassembled in the Museum of Archaeology and Anthropology, Cambridge.

monster monuments, e.g. in Westminster Abbey. Hampshire has none of these, but even so, plenty show ambition and pride. The evidence is best arranged by types. Two new types appeared about the middle of the C16. One has no figures at all, but CLASSICAL ORNAMENT and strapwork, usually rather large and often very good. This type is represented in Hampshire by Wherwell (†1551), Winchester Cathedral (Mason †1559), and – a latecomer – Easton (1595). The Mason tomb is interesting, for its ornamental details link it with Bishop Gardiner's Chapel in the cathedral.

The other new type is that with detached KNEELING FIGURES (kneeling brass effigies had of course been quite usual). This is first seen at East Tisted (†before 1564) and Highclere (†1600. By *Isaac James* and *Bartholomew Atye*) and – again a latecomer – Andover (†1621) and some minor ones (e.g. Bentworth, with a kneeler). At Andover something significant is taking place. The effigy of the husband (†1611) is seated frontally, and only the others kneel. At Priors Dean †1631 (probably by *William Wright*) the kneeling figure is usual but her infants in swaddling clothes (or shrouds) stand vertical. This inventiveness, the wish to get away from old-established types and to produce something ingenious as a conceit, is characteristic of the Nicholas Stone period and especially the second quarter of the C17. We can see the same happen in the most conventional of all types of monuments, that with a RECUMBENT EFFIGY. This now usually occurs with flanking columns, perhaps a back arch, often strapwork on the back wall, and as a rule a top achievement with some strapwork. All this is entirely of Flemish origin, and the craftsmen were often Netherlanders. Examples of the type in our area are Hurstbourne Priors (†1574), Wield (†1617, his effigy behind and above hers), Tichborne (alabaster, †1621; sculpturally very good), and Greatham Old Church (†1632). An oddity of the type is a Lady at Thruxton, because she is of oak, a material then right out of use for monuments. Variants of the Elizabethan standard are at Freefolk (†1614), where the effigy is recumbent but awkwardly rolled on its side, and at Stratfield Saye, where in 1640 the *Christmas* brothers made two semi-reclining alabaster effigies, he behind and above her, and then two grilles in the tomb-chest with the gruesome sight of crowded bones behind them.

The styles of the Italian Mannerists were communicated to English monumental sculpture by sculptors of Netherlandish or French origin in the early C17. Foremost among them was *Le Sueur* who designed the figures of James I and Charles I for Inigo Jones's screen at Winchester Cathedral. But there were others active in court circles, notably *Isaac Besnier*, whose strikingly classical monument to Richard Weston, Earl of Portland and Lord Treasurer, is in the Guardian Angels' Chapel at the cathedral. The memorial, approved by the Earl in 1631, is worthy of the Italian princes of the early C16, complete with an outstanding bronze effigy, probably by *Francesco Fanelli*, the first Italian sculptor to have been active in England since Torrigiano in the Early Tudor period. It is a singular work for its date in England and

69

68

p. 591

that such an advance in funerary sculpture appears first at Winchester rather than Westminster is explained by Weston's appointment as Lord Lieutenant, captain of the Isle of Wight and Vice-Admiral for the county in the early 1630s. That to Sir Henry and Lady Bridget Kingsmill at Kingsclere is by *William Stanton*, one of the major London tomb sculptors. A semi-reclining figure in armour is used for the monument to Sir Thomas Hooke †1677 at Wootton St Lawrence, almost certainly by *Abraham Storey*, and at Chawton for Sir Richard Knight, †1679. The latter, attributed to *Jasper Latham*, has an up-to-date, rather Dutch representation (Knight was exiled in Holland). From the earlier C17 the chief innovation is the introduction of BUSTS, which are first encountered in the Portland monument at Winchester set in niches and presiding over the effigy of the deceased. Elsewhere, busts are usually placed in an oval recess. Sherborne St John, Richard Atkins †1635 appears to have been directly influenced by the work of Le Sueur and is attributed to *John Colt* the younger. Others are Upton Grey, Lady Dorothy Eyre †1650, probably by *Edward Marshall*, and Priors Dean, Sir John Compton, and Compton Tichborne †1653 and †1657, attributed to the *Marshall* workshop and *Thomas Burman*. At Hinton Ampner (Lady Stewkeley †1679, attributed to *John Bushnell*) the bust is accompanied by curtains. Elsewhere it is just once at the top of a composition with an open scrolly pediment, e.g. Hartley Wespall (Lady Stawell †1692), which also has a demi-skeleton. These monuments are of a more distinctly Baroque character and that becomes the predominant mode for the tablets and cartouches from now until the early C18; a good example is at Upton Grey by *Richard Wood* of Oxford. But before the century is out we also have an early example of a STANDING FIGURE on a funerary monument. This is of Sir John Clobery †1687 in Winchester Cathedral, attributed to *Sir William Wilson*, and it is decidedly clumsy. One monument stands entirely outside these traditions: Humphry May †1657, in the cloister of Winchester College, which takes the form of a free-standing classical pedestal with an urn, possibly by *Jasper Latham*.

Country houses

Even taking into account the redistribution of land in the years after 1540 and the C17 as whole, the period is not remembered by great houses, and this is only partly explained by losses to rebuilding in the C18–C20. The destruction of large houses that existed in the early C16 has been noted. Looking further into the century the roll call is sobering: Wield (William Wallop, *c.* 1580); Steventon (Sir Richard Pexall, *c.* 1570); Berry Court (near Nether Wallop, also a Paulet house, *c.* 1580); Hurstbourne Park and Farleigh House (respectively the principal and subsidiary seats of the Wallops, Earls of Portsmouth), Elvetham (1591, 1st Earl of Hertford). Of Abbotstone, another of William Paulet's houses, the only trace may be the substantial timber-framed range

incorporated into an c18 farmhouse. It has been tree-ring dated
to 1562 and is probably part of a lodging range. However, what
survives has little architectural pretension. Of those who were in
the ascendancy at this time, Sir John Kingsmill, magistrate and
associate of Thomas Cromwell and Thomas Wriothesley,
embarked c. 1540 on the construction of Sydmonton Court. This
is an early example of an E-plan house, but unfortunately, apart
from a couple of stepped gables, substantial c18 and c19 alterations have left few of its c16 features. The LATER C16 is not
much richer. Chawton House is the best offering and an inter-   59
esting example of a manor house rebuilt on an aristocratic scale
by John Knight, whose family had leased the manor before they
purchased in 1583. It is notable also for what appears to have
been a change of plan before completion – begun as an E-plan,
the service end was rebuilt as a parlour wing in the 1590s and
the plan of the house turned around. The stables of 1593, on a
shallow U-plan with gabled wings, are an important survival too
(there is a similar but smaller early c17 stable at Ludshott Manor
and a large, but architecturally less sophisticated, stable range at
Hartley Court Farmhouse, Hartley Wespall). Avington Park, the   74, p. 150
manor of which was obtained by the Clerk family shortly after
the Dissolution, has probable late c16 origins too, although little
of that may now be seen. The little brick gatehouse at Bramshott   p. 204
Place must be mentioned here, for it is all that remains of the
Mervyn house which may also date from the 1580s. It has circular corner buttresses with ball finials, ogee gables and oriel
windows. Probably formerly a gateway in a courtyard wall, its
upper room may have served as a banqueting house.

With the JACOBEAN years things change somewhat: the county
has one 'prodigy' house in Bramshill, built for Edward, the 11th   60, p. 199
Lord Zouche, and begun no doubt soon after his acquisition of
the property in 1605. It was not completely new, however, but
incorporated parts of an existing house on a hilltop site, factors
that must have dictated its peculiarly narrow courtyard plan. So
behind the stately façade the building extends in depth much
beyond its width. The front appears to have the usual E-plan but
that is the consequence of the removal of two long wings which
originally projected around an entrance court. Their loss also
means that the façade is a combination of almost blunt plainness
with a fantastic display of the de Vries and Dietterlin kind in the
porch, i.e. the middle frontispiece, derived from the contemporary frontispiece at Northumberland House, London, and one of
the most fanciful pieces of design of its date anywhere. This combination, even though here it is something of an accident, is typically Jacobean. We find it in the façade of Charlton House,
Greenwich, and in the contrast between the two façades at Hatfield. The frontispiece also served originally to mask externally
the fact that the entrance was off-centre, leading into the cross-
passage of the asymmetrically placed hall.

Lord Zouche also laid out gardens at Bramshill and it seems
likely that such formal gardens may have existed at The Vyne in
the early c17, but of these the only evidence is the famous brick

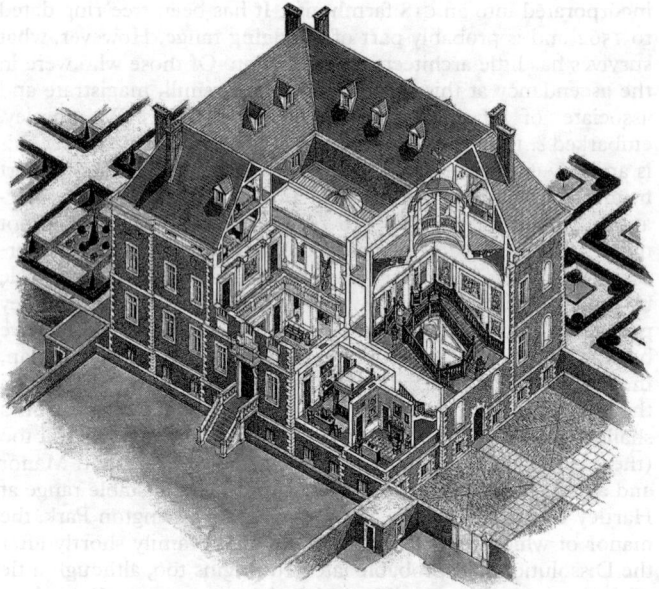

The Grange.
Cutaway drawing by Stephen Conlin, 2009

62   domed summerhouse of Greek-cross plan, now dated to *c.* 1632.
It may therefore have been built for Alathea Sandys who had
contacts in the court circles and perhaps therefore with the world
of Inigo Jones, Isaac de Caus and early C17 CLASSICISM.
Although Jones himself is unrepresented by any buildings in
Hampshire, his closest assistant and follower *John Webb* was the
65   architect for the remodelling of The Vyne between 1653 and 1659
p. 534 for Chaloner Chute. The house was reduced to an E-plan, two
rooms deep, and to its principal front was added the monumental four-column Corinthian portico, the earliest actually realized
for a domestic purpose in England and which through its association with Venetian precedent may well have been considered
singularly appropriate for houses of the new republic.
      What one typically considers to be the legacy of the Jones inno-
vation, however, is the plain, sensible, unornamented house with
a hipped roof, typified by Chevening, Coleshill and other mid-
C17 houses. This tradition is, or rather was, represented in North
Hampshire by the original house at The Grange, built in 1664–73
for Sir Robert Henley by *William Samwell* and which lies at the
core of the building remodelled by *Wilkins* in the early 1800s. It
was brick, with Portland stone dressings, and had two storeys
over a raised basement with two floors of attic rooms in its, by
all accounts, rather overbearing hipped roof – the w elevation up
to eaves level has been reconstructed. The house also had court-

yards front and back flanked by pavilions. The mansion at
Hackwood Park, built for Charles Paulet, the 6th Marquess of   p. 305
Winchester, in 1683–8 seems to have been in the same mode but
was evidently quite modest, just a single pile with pavilions at
right angles connected to it by quadrant links – the form still discernible despite extensive remodellings in the C18 and C19. At
Abbotstone, Paulet also erected a new house close to the site of
the old, 'in the Italian manner', between 1685–95; Gibbons-style
carvings, salvaged at its demolition in 1762, were reused at Hackwood. Its appearance is unrecorded. The INTERIORS of greatest
significance for the large houses are at Bramshill, especially the
state rooms that run along the E side on the first floor and
culminate in the long gallery along the N front. They have spectacular but austere marble chimneypieces with polychromatic   61
geometrical decoration. The plaster ceilings are particularly fine,
mostly broad-ribbed, with hanging pendants of obelisk and spiral
form. In the hall the stone screen is another piece of fantastic
Jacobean design, covered with painted shields and with carvings
of the Cardinal Virtues in the spandrels of the arches. At Chawton
House, the plain hall screen of the early 1580s contrasts with the
sumptuous joinery associated with the alterations of the 1650s,
particularly the staircase with its large turned balusters and a
doorcase with Ionic pilasters and pediment. A tantalizing loss
from The Vyne is the staircase erected by *Webb*, and little survives
of his work inside the house to indicate its mid-C17 character,
but to him are attributed a number of fireplaces, and they are
not classical but a sign of a curiously capricious playing with classical materials typical of the C17 outside the immediate court
circle. Another such fireplace is at Farleigh House.

Lesser houses in town and country

The house of a wealthy yeoman or gentleman in mid-C16 Hampshire might have had a PLAN with a central hall range and flanking cross-wings. This is a medieval form, although by this date
and at this social level the hall would no longer be open to the
roof. An example is Bramley Manor House of *c.* 1545, which has   46
a hearth backing on to the cross-passage at the lower end of the
hall, a typical arrangement by that date. However, by about 1600
the usual plan of houses of this status would be the lobby entry,
and Sevington Manor, Tichborne, of *c.* 1600, is one of the largest
examples. Nevertheless the hall and cross-wings plan also survived, as seen in the early C17 Moor Place (Bramshill) where it
is combined with side chimneystacks and, originally, a central
two-storey bay window, suppressing the essential asymmetry of
the passage entrance. The lobby-entry plan was generally more
suited to the smaller house; those of more middling status, like
their aristocratic counterparts, seem to have held on to the hall-
with-cross-wings plan for longer, their larger size allowing
the combination of a central entrance and an asymmetrically
placed hall. Examples include the much altered Bordean House,

Langrish, of 1611, the similarly altered Froyle Place of *c.* 1600
and the early C17 Vernham Manor, Vernham Dean, with its excessively long central range. As with the great house, by the middle
of the century more compact plans are seen in the houses of the
wealthier farmers and lesser gentry. Two early examples are the
Manor House, West Worldham, and Polhampton House,
Overton, with double-pile square plans, of brick with hipped
roofs, mullioned windows, and retaining vestigial halls to one side
of a central entrance passage. Both have fine staircases with symmetrical double balusters. This type is common by the turn of
the century and examples abound: single, sometimes double pile,
of brick with cross-windows and moulded or modillion eaves
cornice to a hipped roof, e.g. Blounce House, South Warnbor-
72   ough, 1699 and Glenthorne, East Meon, 1697. The adoption
of BRICK or MASONRY CONSTRUCTION in place of timber
framing occurs after *c.* 1660 e.g. Polhampton, above, and Goleigh
Farmhouse, Greatham (*c.* 1675–85), built predominantly of the
local ironstone, and this contributes to the difficulty over the
course of the C17 in distinguishing between the houses of the
prosperous yeomen and minor gentry described above.

In terms of DETAILS, several mid-C17 houses of medium rank
belong to the trend that Sir John Summerson called 'Artisan
Mannerism' to characterize buildings with classical features but
without the scholarly purity associated with Jones and the court
circle. Typically such houses have raised brick quoins, moulded
brick friezes, superimposed or giant brick pilasters with terracotta capitals, sometimes shaped or Dutch gables, often raised
brick window surrounds, and brick door surrounds, again with
70   pilasters. Good examples are the oldest parts of Stratfield Saye
House (*c.* 1630), with superimposed pilasters and Dutch gables
imposing control on a very long façade. Its influence is seen
among a later and lower class of house at Dummer Grange,
which is one of a group around Basingstoke with pilasters and
other classicizing details, e.g. at Pamber, Wyeford Farm and
Pamber Place (part dated 1665); Bulls Down Farmhouse,
Bramley (1670) and in Basingstoke itself No. 8 Church Street,
one of the most valuable survivals in that architecturally lean
town. Similar rustic classicism appears at Kilmeston Manor, at
Brook House, Church Crookham, Bighton Manor (*c.* 1675), and
may well have been the original character of Tangier House built
in 1662 by Sir Thomas Hooke near Wootton St Lawrence. At
Winchester the same trend can be seen in the Deanery's Long
Gallery (1673), at Hyde House (which belonged to the Paulets)
and in the terraced houses in Dome Alley in the Cathedral Close
built in 1662–5. These last are especially interesting also for their
terraced urban form and distinctive interior planning.

The type is also in evidence in the towns, especially at Winchester where there was not only activity in reconstructing
canonry houses in The Close following the depredations of the
Commonwealth (notably the partial destruction of the Deanery)
but also aristocratic house-building in the suburbs (e.g. Hyde
Abbey House). In small towns too: the great fire of 1689 that
destroyed New Alresford is still clearly remembered by the

number of good large brick houses of the characteristic late C17 type, e.g. No. 47 Broad Street, with near-symmetrical front, fine brickwork and heavy modillion cornice and hipped roof.

Finally, a note on domestic FITTINGS AND DECORATION in the smaller houses. A good indicator of status here is the STAIR-CASE. In the early C17, winding stairs were generally squeezed into the space between the chimney and the back wall of the house, but larger farmhouses had separate stair-towers, often rising to the attic floor, e.g. Tankerdale Farm, Steep (1622) and Goodyers, Petersfield (the brick tower surviving, the stair replaced). In the towns Nos. 5–8 The Close, Winchester (1662–5 as already mentioned), have good splat balusters. The most remarkable Jacobean fitting is the fireplace in the Warden's Lodgings at Winchester College of 1615, and in the same building is 1680s panelling by *Edward Pearce* (contemporary with his fittings for the College chapel). Nearby, at No. 3 The Close (now The Pilgrims' School) the former canonry house has a fine staircase, and panelling by *Valentine Housman*, one of Wren's chief joiners, who may have been employed at this time on the King's palace at Winchester. To the earlier period belongs the set of WALL PAINTINGS in one room at Pittleworth Manor, Bossington, datable to 1540, 1580 and 1600. Also late C16 panels at Baigens, Chawton, with wildlife, and of *c.* 1600 also the amusing 'parliament of the fowls' at The George Hotel at Odiham. Summers Farm, Long Sutton, has imitation panelling with strapwork patterns acknowledging indirectly the superseding of painted decoration by wainscoting in the late C17. PLASTERWORK is much rarer. Hyde Abbey House, Winchester (*c.* 1620), has an imported panel of the Five Senses, there is a ceiling at Hill Place, Empshott (*c.* 1680), and rustic late C17 strapwork at The White Hart, Whitchurch, but the best work is that in School at Winchester College and similar work over the stair at No. 3 The Close, both associated with Warden John Nicholas.

64

63

79

Public buildings

There is not much to note other than a handful of institutions provided as benefactions, notably ALMSHOUSES in the towns, the best of which are at Winchester (Peter Symonds' Almshouses, 1605–7), and others are at Basingstoke (Deane Almshouses *c.* 1608), Odiham (1623, accompanied by the Pest (or Poor) House of 1622); Alton (Geales' Almshouses, 1656) and Andover (Pollen's Almshouses, 1686). SCHOOLS, another building type that began to proliferate from the second half of the C17, adopt the standard domestic plans of the period, albeit using materials which reflect their relatively high status, e.g. Eggar's School, Alton, of 1642, and the more modest school at Cliddesden, of 1656, both with usual lobby-entry plan of the period and both brick. But the outstanding item is School at Winchester College of 1683–7, in the style of Hooke and beautifully embellished with tall arched windows along the flanks and a large room inside with seating around the walls.

GEORGIAN AND REGENCY

An underlying theme of the period *c.* 1700–1840 is agricultural improvement and the gradual enclosure of the land for this purpose, mostly for growing corn and raising sheep in the down-land areas. The houses of gentlemen farmers, who controlled large landholdings, now take precedence over the older class of yeomen farmers. At the same time there was also growth in the county's towns, although this was much less pronounced in the N than in the S, other than in Winchester which became a centre for entertainments among the society of which Jane Austen, who was born at Steventon, lived at Chawton and died at Winchester, was the keenest observer.

Country houses

BAROQUE country houses are not plentiful in the N of the county. The principal example was the great house at Hurstbourne Park (Hurstbourne Priors) for the 1st Earl of Portsmouth, possibly designed by *Thomas Archer c.* 1712, but this was demolished in the late C18. The best surviving large house of this date is instead Avington Park, built *c.* 1713, a very substantial remodelling of a late C16/early C17 house that dictated its plan and proportions. The wings were doubled in width in the later C18, faithfully following the original pattern. The principal feature is a giant Doric portico, largely filling the recessed centre. *John James* has been suggested as the architect, without evidence, but he certainly designed Herriard House (1703–6, dem.), which a surviving model shows was a two-and-a-half-storey block of nine bays with a giant order of Doric pilasters. *James*'s own house, Warbrook House, Eversley, was built in 1724. It is a villa, originally a cube, with three-bay temple fronts front and back, articulated by pilaster strips, and with Venetian windows in the tympana: naturally a very personal design. James may also have

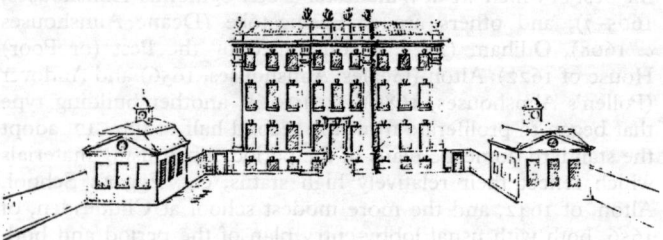

Herriard House.
Drawing, 1703–6

been responsible for the rebuilding of Firgrove Manor, nearby, about ten years later, with its full-height canted bays flanking a pedimented centre. Among the smaller houses Lainston House has an H-plan betraying its C17 origins, but it is now a creation of the years around 1700. It has the modillion cornice and hipped roof of the period and some very fine brickwork in its side elevations, of probably twenty years later. Farleigh House (1731) for John Wallop, Viscount Lymington, incorporates part of an older house belonging to his family. It is characterized by the use of flint, and in the centre of the garden front is a full-height canted bay, a popular motif in the earlier C18, its arched windows with Gibbs surrounds.

No large PALLADIAN houses survive in the county: *John Sanderson*'s Stratton Park of 1731 (*see* East Stratton) for the 4th Duke of Bedford was reduced and remodelled by *Dance* in 1806 and *Vardy*'s reconstruction of the s front of Hackwood, as late as 1761–3, for the 3rd Duke of Bolton has also gone. While we have no record of the remodelling of Highclere for Robert Herbert in the early C18, a Palladian pleasure pavilion (Milford Lake House) of *c.* 1743 is preserved in its park. This is attributed to Robert's brother, *Henry Herbert*, the 9th Earl of Pembroke, and since the 1830s has incorporated fittings from the old house that are in a markedly Kentian style. West Green House is a much   75 more modest house, enlarged, probably in the 1730s or 40s, for General Hawley; and notable for its garden front which has busts in roundels above the ground-floor windows, behind which is a Palladian saloon. Hawley's membership of the Charlton Hunt raises intriguing possibilities of connection with the Duke of Richmond and Roger Morris. A late, and anonymous, example of the style is Winchfield House of *c.* 1770: a villa, with canted bays front and back and short towers with pyramidal roofs in the centre of each side.

Generally speaking, the major styles of the C18 are represented in the country houses by INTERIOR DECORATION. Of the earlier C18 there were good plaster ceilings in the 1740s wing at Dogmersfield Park in the style of Artari and Bagutti but they were destroyed by fire. Of the Palladian phase Stratfield Saye has a   p. 507 double-height hall created *c.* 1755, its Ionic screen giving it a very Neoclassical feel that evidently still suited the Duke of Wellington after he received the house in 1817. There are also two ceilings based on plates in Robert Wood's *The Ruins of Palmyra* (1753) and, of about the same time, plasterwork ceilings in a ROCOCO style. This is especially prevalent in houses of *c.* 1750 (and more common in the towns than in the major houses) and appears in one superb ceiling at Old Alresford House (1749–51 by *William Jones*). The ceilings at Stratfield Saye are stylistically similar to those in the suite of drawing rooms at The Vyne, fitted out for John Chute in the 1760s. Here are the most important mid to later C18 interiors in North Hampshire, including the remarkable staircase hall designed by *Chute* himself. It is Palladian but must   81 be considered primarily as a most ingenious and imaginative exercise by a gifted amateur rather than as an ideologically pure expression in the Burlington mode. Chute was a dreamer and experimenter but without the wealth or inclinations of his friend Horace Walpole, himself a generation younger, to always act upon them. Chute's membership of the Committee of Taste made him one of the pioneers of the GOTHIC REVIVAL in its playful unlearned phase, and he designed in this style at Strawberry Hill, but it makes only a limited appearance in his own home. In the later C18 the NEOCLASSICAL style of Robert Adam is not well represented, especially if one discounts the fittings salvaged in the late 1930s from the Adelphi for a room at Hinton Ampner House and in the same house the copy of his ceiling for a house in Berkeley Square. The closest contemporary expression of Adam's aesthetic is the charming painted decoration at Avington Park of the 1790s (contemporary with the less-accomplished additions to the house by *James Darley* for James Brydges, later the 3rd Duke of Chandos) with grotesque and Pompeian ornament. It is light and gay and not too solemn, in contrast with the earnest Baroque exterior. The most serious note is struck by the grisaille figures in the saloon, attributed to *Vicenzo Valdrè*, who worked at Stowe.

The later C18 was not a particularly productive time for major country house building in the northern part of Hampshire. The only complete house of the period is Laverstoke House, 1796–8, by *Joseph Bonomi*. Of seven bays with a portico of attenuated Ionic columns, it is handsome but a pale shadow of Bonomi's more radical design exhibited at the Royal Academy in 1797. This is of three storeys with an Ionic portico *in antis* and a porte cochère at the rear linking to a semicircular range of domestic

p. 332

offices. Highclere Castle was improved in the late 1770s by the 1st Earl of Carnarvon, including the addition of the N front, possibly by *Capability Brown*, but this has been lost, like everything else before it, under *Barry*'s total mid-C19 transformation. *James Wyatt* rebuilt Hurstbourne Park in 1778 for the 2nd Earl of Portsmouth in a Late Palladian manner but it too was replaced in the C19 and Wyatt is otherwise unrepresented in the N of the county. From 1805 his nephew *Samuel Wyatt* enlarged and

p. 305

remodelled Hackwood Park (already altered in the 1760s by *Vardy*) in a smooth classical style for Thomas Orde-Powlett. At his death two years later, the work was taken over by *Lewis Wyatt*. The respect for the earlier house is strikingly revealed in the Carolean Revival style for the interiors, one of the earliest instances of its use in a country house. The design and workmanship are of the highest quality and the result utterly convincing, due in a great part, no doubt, to his stuccoist, *Francis Bernasconi*, woodcarver, *Edward Wyatt* and stone carver, *Richard Wyatt*.

Moving into the early C19 North Hampshire suddenly comes to the forefront of Neoclassical design with two great GREEK

94

REVIVAL country houses: Stratton Park and The Grange. *George Dance the Younger* radically reduced and remodelled the 4th Duke of Bedford's Palladian mansion at East Stratton *c.* 1803, for the banker Sir Francis Baring, whose family had acquired much

of the Paulet estates during the C18. The externally plain and stuccoed house was dominated by a great Doric portico, which [93] mercifully survived the house's demolition in 1960. Modelled on the temple at Paestum, filtered through Ledoux, it was the first portico inspired by Antique precedent on an English country house. Baring's neighbour at The Grange, Henry Drummond, also a banker, was not to be outdone. For him c. 1809–10 *William Wilkins* completely transformed William Samwell's mid-C17 house, creating a Greek temple in the Hampshire countryside; [94, p. 296] the hexastyle Parthenon portico, two columns deep, dominates one end of the house but perversely does not mark the entrance. Additions (since removed) were made by *Smirke* and the *Cockerells*, of which *C. R. Cockerell*'s conservatory (1824), in the form of a subsidiary temple, is partly preserved. Smirke also designed the compact Neoclassical house at Worthy Park near Winchester (*see* Abbots Worthy) in 1816–20, and Cockerell was among the architects, *C. H. Tatham* included, who with their eye on the main chance submitted designs for palaces for the Duke of Wellington even before the victory at Waterloo. The grandest plan of all was that of the Duke's own architect, *Benjamin Deane Wyatt*, but when Stratfield Saye was bought by a grateful nation in 1817 Wellington satisfied himself by tinkering with the old house.

Among the smaller early C19 country houses, the Grecian is used with ambition at Tichborne House, c. 1802, notable for its fine Greek Doric portico. It is a creditable effort, particularly if it is, as recorded, by the Tichborne family's steward, *Joseph Hodgkinson*. A very smooth and august design is Redenham House, near Appleshaw, also early C19 with a porch of paired Ionic columns. The same motif appears at Highfield Park, Heckfield, which was the dower house for Stratfield Saye from c. 1817 and has has a pair of full-height elliptical bows, a feature very characteristic of the Regency and which appears also on the slightly earlier Malshanger House, Oakley Hall, and any number of lesser early C19 houses.

The chief monument to the PICTURESQUE among the larger country houses of North Hampshire is Rotherfield Park (*see* East [101, p. 249] Tisted), *J. Parkinson*'s castle-style house for James Scott of 1815–24. Although much refaced it remains original in outline and forms the centrepiece of the wider landscape created by *W. S. Gilpin* after 1818. This leads inevitably into a discussion of GARDENS, PARKS and their buildings.

Of the period in which the fashion was for formal gardens, it is known that the Royal gardener *George London* was employed at Herriard in the laying out of parterres, there were parterres also at Bramshill c. 1715 and Griffier in the 1740s depicts the [p. 348] extensive formal gardens at Hurstbourne Park, with canals, cascades and garden buildings, the most significant remnant of which is the so-called Bee House, probably designed as a banqueting house and just possibly by *Thomas Archer*. *John James*'s interest in garden design is evident in his Le Nôtre-influenced garden of c. 1724 at Warbrook (*see* Eversley), with radial alleys

and canals converging on the centre of the w front of the house.
Of similar inspiration and of about the same date, but on an even
p. 307 grander scale, is *Bridgeman*'s Spring Wood Garden at Hackwood
for the 3rd Duke of Bolton, radially planned with alleys meeting
at a central *rond-point* and with a raised terrace around the
perimeter. It was furnished with buildings by *Gibbs*, of which the
Menagerie pavilion of 1724 survives. Also at Hackwood is an
p. 305 equestrian statue in lead of George I of 1722 by *John van Nost
II*, given by the king to the 2nd Duke. A show of retrospective
loyalty to the pre-Hanoverian monarchy is the equestrian lead
89 statue of William III at Petersfield, by *John Cheere*, 1757, set up
by the sons of Sir William Jolliffe, the town's Whig M.P.

Of the informal Rococo gardens of the mid C18 the evidence
is restricted to surviving ornamental structures, chief among
84 them the Hunting Lodge, Odiham; all that remains of a fantastic group of eyecatchers built in his park at Dogmersfield by
Paulet St John around 1740, its front is a piece of Early Jacobean
Revival (but with Gothic openings) with three excessively tall
shaped gables. At Highclere, Robert Herbert's pleasure grounds
of the 1730s are remembered by a roofless temple (reusing
Corinthian columns from *Hugh May*'s Berkeley House) and
Heaven's Gate, a great arch on the hillside s of the house. But
the style of landscaping to which such buildings belonged was
swept away by *Capability Brown* and his followers. Brown was
involved directly in the remodelling of the park at Highclere
c. 1770, with winding drives through wooded belts and a com-
96 plement of garden buildings including a circular Ionic temple and
a gatehouse in the form of a triumphal arch, to mark Henry
Herbert's creation as Earl of Carnarvon in 1793. Similar revisions
were made at Dogmersfield by *William Emes*, who also oversaw
the erasing of the Elizabethan landscaping at Elvetham. *Repton*
was at work at Herriard House in 1792–3 and in a minor way,
perhaps, at Stratton Park. The climax is the setting for The
Grange, as evocative now of Arcadia as it was always intended to
be, but its designer is unknown.

Of estate buildings not already mentioned, the most important
are STABLE BLOCKS. Early and mid-C18 examples are the best,
usually arranged around three sides of a courtyard. At Avington
Park they have a particularly fine show front with pediments and
blind arcading; at Dogmersfield Park and Hawley Park (1743)
they are low and have pedimented central pavilions with cupolas;
they may be by the same hand. The stables at Wolverton follow
a similar pattern, but at nearby Ewhurst the courtyard ranges are
treated as pavilions originally linked by short walls. From the end
of the period is Hackwood's stables/riding school by *Lewis Wyatt*
of 1818–19, more typical of the aristocratic scale of such buildings found in other counties but rare in Hampshire. Wyatt's also
is the lodge of triumphal arch form, and *Dance* provided the
equally memorable classical-cum-castellated entrance to Stratton
92 Park. With these can be mentioned some ESTATE COTTAGES at
Herriard, East Stratton by *Dance* and East Tisted.

Housing in the villages and towns

The advancing prosperity of Hampshire from the late C17 derived from the land and from the development in the towns of businesses and industries (brewing, malting, silk milling etc.). This is reflected in the number of good houses that proliferate from the beginning of the C18 and which dominate so much of one's impression of the generality of domestic buildings in the county. While the direction of influence was no doubt from town to country the appearance of the houses of the landed elite will also have played its part in the encouragement of polite architecture among the wealthier classes in the parishes. As far as the TOWNS are concerned one can see a rapid trend towards rebuilding, or refronting. Winchester has the most to offer, although New Alresford has the most consistently rewarding C18 townscape in the whole of North Hampshire and at Alton too the effect of the Georgian rebuilding sets the tone for much of the High Street. Even the smaller towns, or large villages, such as Stockbridge, Overton and Kingsclere strike one as predominantly Georgian even if it is no more than skin-deep. TOWN HOUSES after 1700 continue a trend begun in the later C17 for brick houses with symmetrical fronts and hipped roofs. Timber framing is replaced by brick, and in the period up to *c.* 1725 the most recognizable characteristic is the use of blue or grey vitrified bricks, with rubbed or gauged dressings of red brick (e.g. Dragon House, Petersfield). Segment-headed windows are another early C18 feature as are brick parapets instead of the wooden eaves cornices, following London where such features had been proscribed since 1707. The best examples of this kind are in Winchester in the streets S of the High Street and uphill of the cathedral, especially St Thomas Street, Kingsgate Street and Southgate Street. The most important house of this period, however, is a departure from this norm: Serle's House, which may well be the work of *Thomas Archer* and belongs to the Baroque tradition. The Palladian influence is evident from the mid C18 in the incorporation of Venetian windows and lunettes and, e.g., in the intriguing aedicular framed gateways at Wickham House, Winchester. The highlight at Alton is Westbrooke House of the middle of the century, with some lively plasterwork inside. Of about the same date at Petersfield, another town of increasing prosperity in the C18, is the house (now Lloyds TSB Bank) of 1759 which has a window above its entrance with a voluted surround. New Alresford and Alton have a high proportion of late C18 refrontings, many with finely detailed doorcases etc. The crossover between town house and suburban villa is Goldings, Basingstoke, a refronting *c.* 1765 of a C17 house, further aggrandized *c.* 1800. It had a sizeable landscaped park and is one of the few houses in the towns to retain significant interior decoration.

In the VILLAGES, the trends seen in the towns are followed in the new, or remodelled, houses built by the clergy and squirearchy. Later in the period come villas or rural retreats,

especially in the areas close to the coaching roads or where sport
in the form of hunting, racing (at Winchester and Stockbridge)
or fishing (on the Itchen and Test) was the attraction. They are
frequently not much less than small country houses, sometimes
with substantial grounds. The Manor House, Froyle, and
Clanville House, near Weyhill, are very characteristic of the late
C17/early C18 type, symmetrical with timber modillion cornices
and hipped roofs and (at the latter) segmental windows. The Old
Rectory at Abbotts Ann (*c.* 1716) is similar. Smaller but very
attractive square versions of the same, with raised brick quoins,
are the rectories at Cheriton, Chilbolton and Hinton Ampner, all
of before 1715, and Netherton House of *c.* 1720. Then in the years
around 1730–40 come handsome taller houses with raised base-
ments: the Old Vicarage, King's Somborne, the Old Rectory,
Houghton, and Bramdean Manor House. Also of this date,
Ropley House and the (stone-built) Old Rectory at Headley, both
with straight panelled parapets. Old Alresford House, built
c. 1740 for Dr John Hoadly, son of Bishop Hoadly, is of the type
seen in Winchester with vestigial pilasters of blue brick infilling
between the windows. One enigmatic survival is the garden
gateway at Itchen Stoke House which may survive from the
rectory of *c.* 1720. Pediments over central projections are a
common feature in the later C18, e.g. Cliddesden Down House,
Chilton House, Crux Easton House.

Around 1800 small stuccoed houses become fairly common,
e.g. Steventon House built for Jane Austen's brother, but the
most enchanting development of these years is the enthusiasm
for the Picturesque. This is very evident in the Test and Itchen
valleys where the vernacular of cob or flint walls and thatched
roofs provides a cue. Of the small number of *cottages ornés*
in Hampshire, the N has one of the best and most ambitious:
Houghton Lodge of *c.* 1790. Its estate was large enough, however,
to consider it as a *ferme ornée*. The architect just might be *John
Plaw*, who lived in Hampshire. Aspects of the design are very
striking, in particular the resemblance of its Gothic windows to
those at Sezincote (Glos.), which it predates by about five years.
Inside is much original decoration. A little later, again in a waterside setting, is Swan Cottage at Old Alresford with a rustic
veranda. Proximity to the river seems to inspire playful detailing,
see e.g. the Fishing Cottage at Leckford and Woodbury House,
Longparish, both probably 1820s.

The general form of new FARMHOUSES in the C18 and early
C19 is pretty modest (three bays, two storeys etc.) and so numerous that only a selection are described in the gazetteer, but the
following are at the more ambitious end of the type, sometimes
with outbuildings (granaries, barns etc.) more impressive than
the house itself: Hare's Farmhouse, Hartley Wintney, of *c.* 1700
is the characteristic Queen Anne type already noted; Will Hall
Farm, Alton, has a mid-C18 house with a pedimented front and
good contemporary interiors; at Old Ditcham Farm is the stu-
pendous barn constructed of diaphragm arches; something so
unusual that it is hard to credit either the late C17 or mid-C18

dates given for it. Also astonishing and perplexing as to its original purpose is the brick and malmstone barn at Buriton Manor
House of the early c18. Around the 1760s there is a small vogue
for Gothic, notably at Rookley Manor, Little Somborne, and with
less sophistication but still a lot of charm at Lythe Farm, near
Steep. A good example of the adoption of the forms of larger
early c19 houses is Down Grange Farm, outside Basingstoke:
classic Regency with double bows on the front. A few houses have
DOVECOTES of which the best examples are at Broughton (1684),
a tall brick cylinder with a cone roof, and Compton Manor,
King's Somborne (1726), with chalk nesting boxes inside.

Churches and chapels

In the ecclesiastical field there is much less to say than in the
secular and hardly any names of note. In the emergence of a new
style a telling comparison of two village churches may be made
between Wolverton and Quarley. Wolverton of 1717 has a remark- 87
ably powerful W tower and shaped and stepped gables as a
'revivalist' feature in the Vanbrugh–Hawksmoor sense, and inside
arched screens between centre and transepts in a rhythm small-
large-small, but with the second small bent at an angle to allow
for diagonal doorways to pulpit and lectern; this also a Van-
brughian conceit. Quarley, on the other hand, in 1723 has a
purely Palladian or Inigo-Jonesian E window of the Venetian type,
and this is inscribed as a present from two squires on adjoining
Wiltshire estates who were connected with the earliest Palladi-
anism or Jonesism in England: William Benson of Wilbury,
whose own house of 1710 starts the Jones Revival, and Henry
Hoare, Lord of the Manor of Quarley and son of Henry Hoare
of Stourhead, who employed Colen Campbell there as early as
1721. *John James* is a local architect but with a national reputation. He was the eldest son of the vicar of Basingstoke and after
he had established himself returned to live at Eversley, to whose

Winchester, St Peter, Milner Hall
Engraving, 1798

church he contributed a new tower in 1735. He almost certainly
had a hand in the design of the church at Abbotts Ann *c.* 1716.
Old Alresford was also rebuilt in the mid C18, the body in 1753,
the tower in 1769. C18 towers are also at Buriton, Froyle, Nether
Wallop and Thruxton. The only church to be remembered for
architectural reasons is Stratfield Saye of 1754–8 by *John Pitt*,
which is on a Greek-cross plan. Two others up to 1775, Avington
of 1768–71 and Crux Easton of 1775, are worth a visit, but primarily for their interiors, the former especially well preserved.

There are some other minor items of interest. An enthusiasm
for GOTHIC can be found very early (or *very* late) at Farleigh
Wallop in the rebuilding *c.* 1733 by *Viscount Lymington* with Perp
motifs, and for the mid century there is the chapel at The Vyne
with its illusionistic paintings of fantastical tracery and vaulting
commissioned from *Spiridione Roma*, which go with the tomb
chamber specially designed by *John Chute* to receive the monument to his ancestor, Speaker Chute (*see* below); both date
from the 1760s. Towards the end of the century the Roman
Catholic chapel at Winchester (now Milner Hall) of 1792 (Relief
Act passed 1791) is by *John Carter*, like Chute a passionate and
early exponent of the Gothic Revival in England. Also notionally
Gothic is the audacious intervention at Micheldever in 1806–8
by *George Dance the Younger* for the Barings, his patrons at Stratton Park. This is memorable less for its beauty than the exceptionally interesting replanning of the nave as an octagon, with
stellar vault, for centralized worship. A slightly earlier, minor,
medievalizing job is that by *Soane* for the Brocas Chapel at
Bramley, dated 1801. The plaster vault, four-centred, is decorated
with thin Gothic arches across and thinner fancy ribs, innocent
of archaeology. Of whole new churches the style can be seen
superficially applied to the typical Georgian preaching box in the
old church at Dogmersfield by *John Eads*, a Headley bricklayer.
The best Gothick church in Hampshire is as late as 1818: Deane,
with its pointed plaster vault, remarkable *Coade* stone details in
its thin chancel screen, and its elaborate altar surround. To the
small number of new churches before 1840 when the story of
church building becomes interesting once more, one can add
East Woodhay, of 1822–3 by *Billing & Son* and Appleshaw of
1830–1 by *T.M. Shurmer*.

Among the buildings of NONCONFORMIST worship* only two
need singling out and they are typically very small, modest and
domestic: the Meeting House at Tadley, 1718–19, the Old Chapel
at Long Sutton, built for the Countess of Huntingdon's Connexion, and best of all, that at Mortimer West End of 1798 and
1805, with its simple barn-like interior.

The general rule in Hampshire is that what distinguishes many
of the C18 churches is their FURNISHINGS. A small number
have a complete ensemble of Georgian appurtenances – box
pews, galleries, pulpit and reading desk, and hatchments and
monuments – the outstanding examples being Abbotts Ann

---

*It has been noted that during the episcopate of Bishop Hoadly, the diocese of
Winchester earned a reputation as one hospitable to Dissenters.

(which in addition has the splendid set of maidens' garlands), Avington, Freefolk, Hartley Wintney St Mary (old church) and Wolverton. Among individual items, brass CHANDELIERS should be singled out. There are ten dated ones in North Hampshire, either of the type with a ball as the centre, or with a more Baroquely shaped centre. There is no development from the early to the late C18. The examples are Winchester St John (1700, imported from Thetford), Wolvesey Palace chapel (1709, from Dorchester), Kingsclere (given in 1713), Froyle (1716), Winchester College (1729), Yateley (1738), Winchester Cathedral (1756, two), Avington (1771), Alton (1780) and Knights Enham (1798). There is a little C18 STAINED GLASS at Eastrop (Basingstoke) and especially at The Vyne where are preserved two important early to mid-C18 pieces by *William Price Jun.* and *John Rowell* (his glass at Newnham has gone). From the first decades of the C19 there is a panel at Deane of the Crucifixion, *c.* 1820, in the Late Georgian pictorial tradition, possibly after *Van Dyck*, painted in enamels upon a large sheet of glass and part of a rare surviving coeval scheme of ornamental glazing, apparently in the national colours of Belgium – chosen as appropriate for a Waterloo memorial church. Of greater importance are the Winchester College Chapel windows of 1821–8 by *Betton & Evans* (*David Evans*) of Shrewsbury, reproducing the original scheme of *c.* 1390–3, which ushered in a more architectonic and correct ecclesiological style. Regardless of their hard, acerbic quality, as historical replicas they are a sentinel landmark in the early C19 revival of traditional glass painting. Also at Winchester College, in the entrance staircase of Warden's Lodging, a Gothic window of 1833 by *J. H. Russell* of Oxford (fl. 1813–26) is still Late Georgian though more advanced in canopy work, with a figure of William of Wykeham. A small heraldic panel at Bramdean church, brought from Hinton Ampner church, is a rare surviving work of 1828 by *James Edwards,* part of a large but now depleted mostly heraldic scheme.

MONUMENTS of the lesser kind follow a familiar sequence from Baroque to Neoclassical over the course of a century, emulating the standards set by the London makers and with the familiar motifs of urns against pyramids, pilastered aedicules, inverted torches and into the early C19 mourning figures, military trophies, weeping willows and broken columns. Some compositions are evergreen, e.g the cartouche with putto and drapery for Hugh Stewkeley †1719 (at Hinton Ampner) which derives from the mid-C17 Banks monument at Christ Church, Oxford. Of Early Georgian monuments, the makers who take us from the traditions of the late C17 to the second decade of the C18 include *James Hardy*, who was Jasper Latham's assistant until 1676. Monuments at Buriton (1695) and Highclere (1692) are attributed to him and the latter, for Sir Robert Sawyer, is specially fine. Works known to be by him, however, are of twenty years later at Silchester (1712) and Elvetham (1714), and are more typical of early C18 Baroque fashions in wall monuments, the former with putti, the latter with busts. Among the grander early C18 pieces is the reredos type, with standing figures, very unemotional on a monument at East Woodhay (†1724; the wife †1732 by *Francis*

Bird). The major sculptors of the early c18 do not make much of a showing in the funerary monuments of North Hampshire but among the best are those by *Sir Henry Cheere*. That to Bishop Willis †1734, in Winchester Cathedral is particularly noteworthy. He is shown reclining against a reredos background. Lady Rodney †1757 at Old Alresford, is splendidly done in various marbles and with two seated allegorical figures. Cheere may well have executed also the monument to Thomas Cheyney (†1760) in the cathedral, with its elaborate symbolism and figures of Hope and Truth. His influence carries on for some years, e.g. the Jolliffe memorial †1771 at Petersfield. Cheere's pupil *Roubiliac* is represented by an extremely early work of 1733 at Wootton St Lawrence with a free-standing bust against an obelisk, and in a minor way at Highclere (†1740 designed by the amateur architect *Sir Charles Frederick*).

In the later period the essential change is that from Baroque and Rococo to classicism, from *Roubiliac* to *Wilton* and then *Flaxman*. But Wilton in Hampshire is not the classicist at once. The monument in Winchester Cathedral to Bishop Hoadly who died in 1761 is a Rococo composition with a profile bust in drapery surrounds but at the same time adorned with a cluster of secular motifs, including the Phrygian cap, symbolic of Hoadly's controversial liberalism. The two outstanding funerary monuments of the last quarter of the c18 – one of them really a memorial, not a funerary monument – are also still close to the Baroque: Speaker Chute at The Vyne (made *c.* 1775–81) by *Thomas Carter Jun.*, and Bernard Brocas †1777 at Bramley, probably by the same sculptor. Both are entirely free-standing without any back wall. Speaker Chute is represented semi-reclining in a wonderfully easy posture, Bernard Brocas is sinking back into the arms of a young woman. The latter has fine panel reliefs to the tomb-chest, the former shields and Ionic columns. Carter started as a carver of chimneypieces (one was commissioned for The Vyne, but never executed) and was well established by the 1750s as a statuary. Of the familiar later Georgian sculptors represented in Hampshire, next in order of birth is *Nollekens*, born in 1737, but what there is of his (Dogmersfield †1808) is not of particular value. *Richard Hayward* signs a monument at Northington and then – at an interval of ten to fifteen years – follows *Flaxman*. He was certainly successful in Hampshire. Thirteen of his monuments are in Hampshire churches and of these six are in the N of the county. Of the greatest beauty is the Dr Warton in Winchester Cathedral (1801–4), an exquisitely set-out composition, with figures in contemporary dress, the poet's lyre as a crest and herm portraits of Aristotle and Homer. At the same time it is full of that tender sympathy Flaxman had for children, in this case Winchester College boys. His most interesting work is at Micheldever, executed between 1801 and 1813, where Flaxman did three reliefs of intricate, crowded composition; strangely Baroque for their date and designed for a setting conceived by Dance. His works at Old Basing (1794), Petersfield (1801) and Stratfield Saye (1804) have mourning figures by an urn, a type which was repeated *ad nauseam* down to 1830 and beyond by provincial sculptors (see e.g. *Gibbs* at Hurstbourne Tarrant and *Cooke* at Farleigh Wallop for the 2nd Earl of Portsmouth). *Sir Richard Westmacott*, again twenty years younger than Flaxman, is represented by the fine monument at Weyhill (†1803) with two youths contemplating a broken column (also soon widely adopted as a cliché of the genre). Westmacott's son *Richard West-macott Jun.* has his magnum opus at Northington, with two seated angels above an elaborately portrayed entry to a vault. The conception goes back to Canova, but the date is 1848 and in it one detects the sentimental strain common to the Victorians (*see* also his monument at Bramshott). To return to the date order of birth of the sculptors for the few remaining notes, *John Bacon Jun.* has three monuments (Heckfield, Winchester Cathedral (Morgan and Littlehales)); none noteworthy but one with military trophies, another with a weeping willow, motifs much in vogue among other unnamed funerary sculptors. *Humphrey Hopper* is represented by a Gothic monument to the Rev. Austen at Steventon †1819 and Elizabeth Chute at Sherborne St John †1842. And so we come to Chantrey and Theed, both in their works entirely of the C19. *Chantrey*'s Bishop North of 1825 in Winchester Cathedral is a dignified portrait. He kneels in profile, a composition Chantrey used for other bishops as well. *Theed* maintained many Late Georgian conventions see, e.g., his monument to Canon Williams at Winchester and the memorial at Newton Valence.

Memorials in the form of LEDGER STONES set into the floor of a church become quite common from the late C17 (an early example is Ann Tylney †1681, at Rotherwick) and proliferate after 1700. The best have finely lettered inscriptions, occasionally witty (e.g. Thomas Welstead †1617 at Winchester College), and armorial roundels in shallow relief. There are many at Winchester Cathedral but perhaps the best groups are those at Amport, to the Paulets and to the Wither family at Wootton St Lawrence. Nice individual items are at Yateley. CHURCHYARD MONUMENTS of the more ambitious kind are uncommon in North Hampshire, even at Winchester, but a particular interesting item is the Egyptian pyramid at Nether Wallop, specially designed in 1748 by *John Blake* of Winchester as an impregnable mausoleum for Dr Douce and wife. For sheer entertainment there is the engaging inscribed gravestone of John Buckett †1804 at Old St Peter, Stockbridge.

Public, commercial and industrial buildings

No GUILDHALLS, TOWN HALLS or MARKET HOUSES survive in North Hampshire from before the C18 (with the possible exception of the Beehive in Whitchurch), so the sequence begins with Winchester's Old Guildhall of 1712–13 but then leaps forward to Whitchurch's Town Hall of 1786–7, and the humbler Stockbridge Town Hall of 1790, and on to Alton's plain free-standing Town

Hall of 1813 and finally Basingstoke's Town Hall, a simple stuccoed building of 1832–4 by *Lewis Wyatt* (altered 1864), at the end
of this tradition. What they share across a century is a basic
pattern of an arcaded, open but usually later enclosed, ground
floor and meeting room above. Of similar form, but otherwise
in a different league, is *John Langdon*'s Guildhall at Andover of
1825–6: a striking free-standing stone building, Palladian in form
but with Grecian details. Perhaps the finest building of this ilk is
O. B. Carter's Corn Exchange in Winchester (now the Discovery
Centre) of 1835–8 with its Tuscan portico '. . . a first-class
example to show the step from severe Classical to Italianate'
(Pevsner).

Many of the early market houses and town halls no doubt
included lock-ups, but the first surviving purpose-built PRISON
is the former bridewell at Odiham (now police station and
library), a simple building of 1743, with ranges either side of a
courtyard. *George Moneypenny*'s gaol in Winchester (*c.* 1805) is
among the most impressive of the kind in the country, even
though it survives in façade fragments; like Dance's Newgate it
has vermiculated rustication to show how impregnable it is. The
C17 WORKHOUSE in Old Basing was largely indistinguishable
from any lobby-entry house of the period, and while Froyle
Parish Workhouse (now Brecklands) of *c.* 1800 is clearly a more
specialized building it remains essentially domestic in character.
Larger examples, with similar long narrow plans, include Alton
(1793, now Adams House) and Headley (1795, now Headley
Grange).

SCHOOLS of the earlier C18 still retain the lobby-entry
plan-form of the C17 – i.e. later than in conventional domestic
buildings – appearing in Hatherden in 1725 and at Sherfield-on-
Loddon in 1737–8. Usually one side was the schoolroom and the
other the master's accommodation. Several examples (Andrews
School, Holybourne, *c.* 1721–30, the old Churcher's College,
Petersfield, 1729–30 and Love's Charity School, Froxfield,
1733–4) have the end chimneys typical of contemporary houses,
but generally retain the two functions split between the ground-
floor rooms. By 1815, however, Thomas Sheppard's school at
Amport is a specialized building, no longer based on a domestic
plan and form, although both the schoolroom and master's
accommodation are still under a single roof. Varying from this
pattern is the former schoolroom of Dr Charles Richards's
Academy in Hyde Close, Winchester, of 1795 by *Soane*.

Related to the civic and commercial activity of the Georgian
town were INNS AND HOTELS, nowhere more clearly demonstrated than at the Grosvenor Hotel in Stockbridge of *c.* 1820,
built as a means of gaining political influence in this notorious
rotten borough. It has a large two-storey porch on Doric columns
spanning the pavement, a characteristic feature of Late Georgian
coaching inns (see e.g. the White Hart, also in Stockbridge, and
the White Hart at Hook). Other notable early C19 inns include
the White Hart at Whitchurch, the Star and Garter at Andover
and the Red Lion at Petersfield.

Anna Valley, Abbotts Ann, ironworks.
Engraving, 1813

There were the usual rural INDUSTRIES. The most important
BREWING centre was, and is, Alton and there are many examples of HOP KILNS in the villages around. A few old brewery
buildings survive in the town, notably a remarkable mid-C19
maltings with a particularly complex wooden roof structure. In
common with other rural counties with fast-flowing rivers, from
the mid C17 there is also a preponderance of WATER MILLS
(many converted to residential use in the C20). The best example
architecturally is Bossington Mill (1767) with its dignified pedimented façade and cast-iron Gothic windows, but typically the
buildings are less ambitious, with a picturesque vernacular
mixture of brick, tile and weatherboarding. Good, well-preserved
C18 and early C19 groups are at Gailey Mill, Kingsclere, Bere
Mill, Laverstoke, Upper Mill, Longparish and Headley Mill
(still operating commercially). The most impressive examples,
however, are the mills at Winchester (rebuilt 1743–4 for tanning)
and Whitchurch (1815, rebuilt in 1817 for silk milling), both of   85, p. 554
which retain their machinery in working order. A site also associated with the textile industry is the old TANNERY in Marlborough Street, Andover, which includes an exceptionally large chalk
cob structure of the early C19. Another important manufacture
was, and remains, PAPER. The most important mill was that
belonging to Henri Portal at Laverstoke, where the paper for the
Bank of England was made. The most important IRONWORKS
was that established in 1813 at Anna Valley by the Taskers, which
produced architectural ironwork from bridges to columns and
windows. Of the works, there remain some associated cottages
and houses.

Of CANALS, the Andover Canal, linking that town with Southampton from 1794, and the Basingstoke Canal, an offshoot from the Wey Navigation, built 1778–94, were moderately successful, providing improved trade with these market towns and their rural hinterland. The former was rebuilt as a railway in the C19 and little evidence remains. The latter declined through the C20 and was largely infilled at its w end but the rest was revitalized after 1974 between the Wey and Greywell Tunnel, the finest piece of canal engineering in the county, 1200 yds long. The Salisbury Canal, connecting with the Andover Canal and just outside the area of this volume, never reached its intended destination.

VICTORIAN AND EDWARDIAN

'A bumper period' in Hampshire, thought Pevsner. While the county remained predominantly agricultural, and increasingly wealthy on the back of it, from the very beginning of Victoria's reign the railways placed the towns and villages of the north within easy reach of London. This led to some mild urban expansion but also enabled men who had made money in business and trade to move into the country, some taking over and improving existing country estates. As the century progressed middle-class city dwellers moved out as well, building the Arts and Crafts houses in which this part of the county is particularly rich. The railways also brought the army to Aldershot and that is an event of major significance for North Hampshire.

Houses in the countryside

Of MAJOR COUNTRY HOUSES, the only one of national importance in North Hampshire is Highclere Castle; *Charles Barry*'s great remodelling of the 3rd Earl of Carnarvon's house after 1842. But what a house it is. Contemporary with the Palace of Westminster, its style is the Elizabethan of Wollaton Hall (Barry called it Anglo Italian). Unfinished at the Earl's death in 1849, much of the interior is the work of *Thomas Allom* and others of the 1860s. Other EARLY TO MID-VICTORIAN houses of the period are considerably smaller. Bossington House is straightforward Jacobean Revival by *John Davies* of 1834 but in an excellent setting by the Test. Adhurst St Mary, Sheet, by *P. C. Hardwick* (1857–9) for J. Bonham-Carter is also in a fairly conventional Tudor Gothic. Again amid a fine landscaped setting with remarkably varied trees. Hardwick's most rewarding designs in North Hampshire are the garden buildings at Laverstoke House.* The remodelling of Red Rice House (now Farleigh School) by

Especially the Gothic Gardner's Cottage of c. 1854.

margin notes: 100, p. 334; 102; p. 371

William Burn in 1844–5 is a cool classical composition, with French-inspired banded rustication, and contrasts favourably with the more routine Elizabethan of Burn's Amport House (1855–7) for the 14th Marquess of Winchester. Burn worked also at Dogmersfield Park (1861–2, his staircase has survived the destruction) and his thin Jacobean remodelling of Hartley Grange, Hartley Wintney (1861), does him less justice. We have rushed on to the 1860s so we must go back and pick up the thread from the 1850s. Penton Lodge is respectable Italianate, with an impressive cantilevered stone staircase, but is mainly notable as *William Cubitt*'s country house, remodelled by him in 1852. Presumably he was his own architect. This is also the place to mention the home of that other great Victorian building contractor, Sir John Kelk, for whom *John Johnson* recast Tedworth House (*see* South Tidworth) in Baroque style in 1878–80.

At the end of the 1850s come three remarkable HIGH VICTORIAN houses, each impressive but to some degree hard to love: Minley Manor, Elvetham Hall and Farnborough Hill. The first, p. 397 1858–62 by *Clutton* for the banker Raikes Currie, is one of the earliest country houses inspired by French Renaissance architecture, a red brick and stone chateau in the North Hampshire heathland. It was enlarged by *Devey* in 1885–6, who wisely stuck to the same style, but allowed himself more freedom in the garden buildings. Equally remarkable, not to say challenging, is *Teulon*'s Elvetham for the 4th Lord Calthorpe, of 1859–62, one 103, p. 258 of the architect's four great houses (a fragment of another Teulon house, no more than a tower, survives at Hawkley Hurst). The style is hard to define, Pevsner's description of it as 'Frenchy' is about right, but there are other things in there too and it is insistently polychromatic. The interior is notable for its decorative scheme, including glass by *Lavers* & *Barraud*, stone-carving by *Earp* and *Skidmore* metalwork. Farnborough Hill, built for the publisher Thomas Longman 1860–3, is equally awkward: a Burgundian fantasy, with a highly ornamented timber frame and steep-pitched roofs with Rhenish gables. Quite what inspired *H. E. Kendall* to adopt this style is not known. Perhaps it reflects an interest in this period, shared by Clutton at Minley, in experimenting with 'exotic' styles. Unlike Minley, however, Farnborough Hill was a stylistic dead end. Blackmoor House (1868–73 and 1882–3) for Sir Roundell Palmer is one of *Waterhouse*'s major domestic works. It is respectable Tudor with a touch of Gothic, a hangover from his earlier design, and with more than a hint of Shaw's contemporary Old English houses. His other Hampshire house, Coldhayes, near Steep, of 1869–73 and 1875–82 for Palmer's brother, is wild by comparison, in a mixed Franco-English style, curious for so disciplined an architect. *Shaw* himself doesn't feature highly in North Hampshire but his seamless Queen Anne style additions to Yateley Hall, a true Queen Anne house, in 1871–2, are quite worthy of him.

LATE VICTORIAN houses enter their stride in the 1890s: of the previous decade one need only single out *Destailleur*'s additions to Farnborough Hill for the Empress Eugénie, with French-inspired details adding to the already fantastic appearance, and interiors remodelled in Second Empire style, incorporating some fittings from the Tuileries. Near Basingstoke are two houses for South African expatriates: Sherfield Manor and Tylney Hall. The first is a thorough remodelling, in a Wrenaissance-cum-Jacobean, of a mid-C19 house for James Taylor, a retired mining financier, in 1898–99. The architects were *Wade & Frankiss*. Between 1898 and 1901 Taylor's friend and neighbour, the gold and diamond millionaire Lionel Phillips, employed *R. S. Wornum* to remodel Tylney Hall (Rotherwick). The Baroque water tower aside, it is conventionally Jacobethan; more interesting is *Weir Schultz*'s banqueting hall, his completion of the interior and work in the garden. EDWARDIAN country houses include Hollington House, Elizabethan by *A. C. Blomfield* (1903–4), and Moundsmere Manor by *Reginald Blomfield* of 1908–09, the latter (despite reduction) perhaps still the epitome of the period in the fashionable Wrenaissance and with a formal garden.

p. 371

Associated with some of the larger houses (e.g. Laverstoke and Elvetham) are good contemporary ESTATE COTTAGES and other buildings. Of MODEL FARMS, the best and largest examples are those erected over a wide area of the Meon valley by William Nicholson, who purchased the Basing Park estate near Privett in 1863 and invested heavily in the erection of integrated complexes of cattle sheds, grain stores, sawmills etc., built of knapped flint with brick trim (e.g. Home Farm at Basing House but also Venthams Farm, Froxfield).

The archetypal small Victorian house is the PARSONAGE, and the style of the parsonage in Hampshire as we enter the Victorian age is typically Tudor. Numerous examples abound in the N of the county: Abbots Worthy House, *c.* 1834 by *J. C. Buckler*, Nether Wallop, 1838 by *O. B. Carter* and East Tisted, 1839–41 by *T. E. Owen*. It is still going strong in the 1850s, e.g. Dummer, 1850 by *W. J. Donthorn*, and *Hellyer*'s first design for Kingsclere was Tudor too. By this date of course, Gothic is the style of choice, but few of the big names are represented, with nothing by Pugin, Scott, Butterfield or Street. *Woodyer* is represented by the former rectory at Winchfield (1849–50), actually a remodelling of an earlier building, which is emphatically Gothic, and *Teulon* by Elvetham, 1857. Of the second-tier figures, we have *R. J. Withers* at West Liss (1863), *T. H. Wyatt* at Weston Patrick (*c.* 1868) and *Ferrey* at Overton (1851). Most obscure is *F. T. Digweed* and his vicarage at Ecchinswell (1853). *William White*'s parsonage at Hatherden (now Michaelmas House) of *c.* 1865 has no specifically Gothic motifs, and is moving towards a simpler Vernacular Revival style. The move away from Gothic is nowhere more clearly shown than in the rectory at Woolton Hill (now Wellbrook House) of 1875–7 by *G. G. Scott Jun.*, a very early example of the Georgian Revival (though the rejected scheme with Dutch gables was more in tune with the contemporary Queen Anne of Shaw). *Granville Streatfeild*'s 1907 Neo-Georgian vicarage at Ashmansworth is a direct descendant.

Parsonage design might have been the laboratory of stylistic development, certainly through the middle years of the Victorian

period, but a similar progression can be seen from the middle of
the century onwards in the increasing number of SMALLER
HOUSES IN THE COUNTRY, which is a mix of those with and
without associated estates. Many of these are within striking distance of the railways and were built with money made in London.
One of the earliest, and one important architecturally, is Tile
Barn at Woolton Hill of c. 1850–60, one of *George Gilbert Scott*'s
rare domestic works, for John Winterbottom, a City businessman.
It is assertively Gothic with Ruskinian structural polychromy.
Nearby East Woodhay has the peculiar Tudor/Scottish Baronial
of Stargrove and the more acceptable Italianate of Malverleys
by *T. H. Wyatt*, both of c. 1860–60. Neo-Jacobean appears at
Redfields, Church Crookham, by *Alfred Eggar* for a London
barrister (1877–9), and Finkley House, Smannell (c. 1860). It is
still in evidence, loosely, for *Sir Banister Fletcher*'s Abbess Grange,
Leckford (1900–1). *T. E. Collcutt*'s Winchfield Lodge (1885) is in   p. 727
a version of Shaw's Old English, as is *W. D. Caröe*'s Testcombe,
Chilbolton (1887 93). *Matthew Wyatt*'s own Corner House at
Weston Patrick (c. 1886–8) is Queen Anne and, as befits its location, the Surrey Style appears in *J. H. Christian*'s Grayshott
Hall (1886–7). Close by at Headley, Benifold, by *A. C. Blomfield*   p. 323
(1898–1900) is in roughcast Shavian Queen Anne at the front
and a more sober Georgian at the back. The revival of the style
of William and Mary also appears at the turn of the century, e.g.
Downsland House, Crondall (1899) and Westbury House, East
Meon (1906). Woodcott House by *Crickmay & Sons* (1909–10)
and Buriton House by *J. H. Ball* (1912) are inspired by English
architecture of the years around 1700. This style was also readily
adopted by the architects of the Arts and Crafts Movement and
in Hampshire that subject deserves to be looked at separately.

The Arts and Crafts Movement

The N of the county has two centres associated with the movement, one around Hartley Wintney in the NE and the other to
the E around Steep on the Weald edge. Their importance is comparable to contemporary centres in the Cotswolds and, as there,
the Hampshire architects and designers were inspired by the previous generation of Morris and Philip Webb. At Liphook is
Webb's Goldenfields, a late work of 1890–92. But it is not typical,
having been intended originally as a gate lodge (1890–2) to a larger
(unbuilt) house and its local influence was probably minimal.
   The Hartley Wintney story starts in 1897 with *Ernest Newton*
acquiring a timber-framed cottage at Hazeley Heath, near Mattingley, and enlarging it for himself in his C18 cottage style.
Newton had a number of Hampshire commissions, including one
of his earliest, an estate cottage at West Stratton of 1888, the
delectable Four Acre House at West Green, near Hartley Wintney   116
(1901–2), Newbies, Baughurst (1902), Dawn House, Winchester
(1907) and the Manor House, Upton Grey for Charles Holme,   p. 528
editor of *The Studio* (1907), a complete Arts and Crafts ensemble with plasterwork by *Bankart* and garden by *Jekyll*. In 1898–9

Robert Weir Schultz, probably introduced to the area by Newton, altered West Green House in a sympathetic Georgian style, and began an association with Hartley Wintney which lasted to his death in 1951. In 1899 he bought land at Phoenix Green, with C. R. Seymour, son of the local rector, and A. W. Pearce, and converted some old barns on the site as his own house: The Barn (now Weir's Barn) was built in two phases, *c*. 1901 and 1911–12 around which he developed a charming garden. As well as designing houses nearby for his associates, the vernacular-inspired Croft for Pearce and at West Green, the Neo-Georgian Inholmes for Seymour, he built a couple of houses on the site as a speculation *c*. 1907–9 and went on to develop a significant practice in North Hampshire, from Winchester to Petersfield, including, in his later years, houses on a speculative development in Hartley Wintney for the local builders, *Pool & Son*. His work at Tylney Hall for Lionel Phillips (*see* above) was an exception to the generally modest scale of these projects. In 1918 Schultz's friend, *W. R. Lethaby*, came to live at Hartley Wintney and both he and Schultz are buried in the churchyard there.

At Steep, the decisive influence was the establishment in 1900 of Bedales School with a progressive curriculum that included a strong emphasis on practical handicrafts. In 1901 *Alfred Powell* designed Little Hawstead, Steep, for his brother, Oswald, second master at the school, and in 1906 designed The Red House at Froxfield, for the poet Edward Thomas whose sons attended the school. His collaborator, as builder, was *Geoffrey Lupton*, an old Bedalian who worked with Ernest Gimson at Sapperton, Gloucestershire, before returning to Hampshire, where he built himself a house and workshop close to the Red House (he also built a study for the poet, separate from the house itself). Gimson was also connected with Bedales through his nephews Humphrey and Basil, who were pupils; Basil subsequently joined the staff and *Humphrey Gimson* designed him a house, Five Oaks, in 1912, p. 496   built, again, by Lupton. *Ernest Gimson* designed the cruck-built school hall of 1910. But perhaps his finest work is the school 113   library, one of the great monuments of the Arts and Crafts movement. It was built posthumously in 1919–21, *Sydney Barnsley* overseeing its construction by Lupton and Sydney's son, *Edward Barnsley*, another former pupil, who worked with Lupton and eventually took over his workshop.

Several other architects associated with the Arts and Crafts Movement and the Art Workers' Guild carried out domestic commissions in North Hampshire. *Mervyn Macartney* remodelled a p. 482   country cottage for himself near Silchester, Rosebank (now Macartneys), in 1898, and obtained several commissions on the Hampshire/Berkshire border. *M. H. Baillie Scott* designed Pyotts, Winchester (1907), Green Place, Stockbridge (1906–7 and 1913), and *Halsey Ricardo* was the architect of Barn Close House, Itchen Abbas (1910–11). *Gerald Horsley* was behind several buildings, including stables, cottages and an extraordinary walled garden, on the Cholderton Lodge estate near Amport *c*. 1900. However, his great house there, published in *The Builder* in 1898, remained unrealized. *Herbert Austin* of *Paley & Austin* remodelled

Kingsworthy Court (now House) for himself in an Arts and Crafts Georgian in 1905–6, and this also has a wonderfully rich interior. Although *Voysey* built nothing in Hampshire (his 1914 design for a house at Ashmansworth was unrealized) he died in a cottage in Abbots Worthy in 1941, presumably when his son, C. Cowles-Voysey, was working on the County Council building in Winchester. The Voysey style, however, is very explicit in the design of Buckmore House, Petersfield, by *Walter Cave*, 1897. Cave's more usual style is strongly represented by his addition to the Tile Barn, Wootton Hill. *Detmar Blow* began as an architect-craftsman but after 1906 he was in partnership with *Ferdinand Billery*, a Beaux-Arts-schooled Parisian, and while there is no trace of the self-denying rigour of the Arts and Crafts in their remodelling of Beenham Court (now Cheam School), Headley, in 1912–13, the sumptuous and eclectic classical C17 and C18 interiors have the movement's attention to detail and quality.

Lutyens requires a special mention, with three houses in North Hampshire. All are Tudor in character, before his switch to classicism. First the little-known Berrydown (1897–8), for Archibald ¹¹⁵ Grove, editor of the *New Review*, mysterious behind its walled courtyards, and Voysey-like with its roughcast walls and sweeping roofs. Daneshill, Basingstoke (1903), is the most conventional of the three, but in beautifully detailed brick. Its owner, Walter Hoare, was the proprietor of Daneshill Brickworks. And lastly, surely one of Lutyens's finest houses, Marsh Court (1901–4) for ¹¹⁴, p. 389 Herbert Johnson, all of chalk, high above the Test. The garden, with *Gertrude Jekyll*, makes the most of its sloping site, playing games with levels worthy of Escher, the moat of the entrance front becoming a terrace on the garden side, stepping down to a sunken pool. Jekyll appears in several other places, e.g. Amport House, again with Lutyens, and Tylney Hall with *Weir Schultz*. Three of Lutyens's former assistants feature in North Hampshire too. *Horace Farquharson* extended and re-fitted Adhurst St Mary, Sheet, for the Bonham-Carters in 1902–3, while *Norman Evill* designed a pair of good houses in Silchester: New Timber (now Romans Hotel, 1908–9) and The Grange (1909), and *J. D. Coleridge* built Darby Green House, Yateley (1911, for himself), Hawley village hall (1921), and was possibly responsible for the rather overblown Waterside, Bramshott (1921–3). Their master's early influence is clearly evident.

An important and accomplished local practice in the years before 1914 was the Petersfield-based firm of *Unsworth & Unsworth* (from *c.* 1909, *Unsworth, Son & Triggs*); their style usually stays close to a Wealden vernacular (tile-hanging, timber framing etc.) but always avoiding cliché, see e.g. The Platts, Sheet (1907–8); Hailie, Liphook; Durford Court, Hill Brow; and Ashford Chace, Steep (all 1912). *W. F. Unsworth* adapted a C17 house, Restalls, Steep, for himself in 1905 and *H. Inigo Triggs* altered farm buildings at Liphook (Little Boarhunt) for his home in 1910–11. Triggs was also a specialist in garden design and several examples of the firm's work are accompanied by his superb layouts and plantings. Other Hampshire practices had partners who could work in this style, notably *Henry Hill* of

Cancellor & Hill of Winchester, *H. G. Courtney* and *Norman Nisbett* of *Colson & Nisbett*. The pre-war tradition runs well into the 1920s. A late exponent is *Ernest Barrow*, who designed Chilbolton Cottage for himself in 1921, incorporating two existing old cottages, and developed a modest local practice which included Lower Mill, Longparish, a butterfly-plan house of 1922. The other person of interest is *G. H. Kitchin*, son of the Dean of Winchester. He did much minor ecclesiastical and domestic work from the 1890s until the 1920s, distinguished by high-quality carving and woodwork (by his company *Thomas & Co.*, a partnership with *James Thomas* (later known as *J. T. Laverty*); see e.g. their former premises at Chesil Rectory, Winchester). Kitchin's own house is at Compton, s of Winchester, just outside the area covered by this volume.

Churches

By the early 1840s church building and restoration in the area was faster paced than it had been in the Late Georgian years. The briefly favoured NEO-NORMAN Revival is represented at Cove (1842–4, with Enmore Green, Dorset, one of two near-identical cruciform churches by *G. Alexander*), Elvetham (1840–1 by *Henry Rhodes*) and Newnham (1847 by *Benjamin Thorne*), of which the latter two were remodellings of partly original Norman fabrics. SECOND POINTED was recommended in the same years by *The Ecclesiologist*, and means the period of Gothic from about 1250 to the early C14 with plate tracery and bar tracery and details freeing themselves gradually from the standard Geometrical motifs, but stopping short of the ogee arch and flowing tracery. The earliest examples of this turn in North Hampshire belong to the years 1843–5. Of these, Andover, by the little-known *Augustus Frederick Livesay* (1807–79) of Portsmouth,* has an outstanding interior, arguably the most important C19 church in the county. Livesay had more than co-operation with the re-founder, the Rev. Dr W. S. Goddard, former headmaster of Winchester College. It is grandly and majestically E.E., like the best Commissioners' churches but learned too, inspired by details of Salisbury Cathedral. Andover is indeed a church one does not forget, lofty with an apse two-storied to the outside and screened inside against the chancel by a screen of slender shafts. Here, though in different forms, the respect of the architectural past, as it really was, is as patent as in the four churches from which this necessary digression has led us. They are Dogmersfield (1842–3) and Baughurst (1845–6) by *Ferrey*, St Thomas, Winchester (1845–7, completed with an elaborate spire in 1856–7), a surprisingly ambitious Scott-like church by *E. W. Elmshie* of London (and later of Malvern), and West Meon of 1843–6 by *Scott*.

99

* Livesay had earlier designed the church at Newtown, Isle of Wight, which is more correct in its details.

Itchen Stoke, St Mary.
Engraving by G. Smith, 1868

Scott is the first of the big High Victorian LONDON ARCHI-
TECTS to appear in this survey; he did only one other church in
the area: Highclere of 1869–70. But many of the major metropolitan names do appear in North Hampshire. They can be
divided into conformers and individualists. Among the latter
William Burges is represented with a small, beautifully detailed
church in Fleet (1860–2), in a Continental Early Gothic in brick,

yet as Pevsner says, 'remarkably restrained and yet very powerful with its transverse brick arches'. It is a fine, simple, indeed
important, example of the increasingly acceptable fashion for
foreign Gothic *c.* 1858–68 allowed by *The Ecclesiologist. S. S.
Teulon*, at his most inventive an adventurous rogue architect,
appears with a strikingly unusual church at Hawkley (1864–5) in
a robust mixed foreign Romanesque style, with original sculptured details. *Henry Conybeare*, a little-known architect, at Itchen
Stoke (1865–6) provided an excitable, essentially First Pointed
church of mixed English and French detail (clearly inspired a
little by Sainte Chapelle). The colourful polychromy of the quite
impressive interior seems straight out of a chromolithograph.
John Johnson, although not in the top flight, produced his *chef
d'oeuvre* at South Tidworth (1879–80), a deceptively large and
richly finished estate church for Sir John Kelk with a wilful E.E.
exterior, partly of Yorkshire derivation (e.g. Skelton in the West
Riding) and partly of his own invention. *Butterfield* is seen in
restorations of local churches, but none as good or interesting as
his Winchester Hospital. Heckfield of 1876–7 is almost a rebuilding in which the only 'rogue' element is in the strongly exposed
ironstone rubble on his new N aisle. His major restoration at
Sparsholt of 1883 is equally extensive with a timber-framed top
stage to the tower and a muscular S porch. At St Michael, Winchester, his planned rebuilding of 1881–90 was only half realized
and his major internal restoration of St Cross Hospital Church,
Winchester (1860–5),* involved only refurnishing and some powerful chancel decoration executed by *Harland & Fisher* (*c.* 1865),
now removed. Butterfield at his best and most surprisingly
sensitive appears at Mattingley in 1867–9 with the repair
and enlargement of the early C16 timber-framed chapel. *Street*
provided only two characteristically drastic but respectful
restorations at Headbourne Worthy (1865–6) and South Warnborough (1869–70), but with limited intervention. *William White*,
great-nephew of the naturalist Gilbert White of Selborne, did
several jobs in North Hampshire, perhaps thanks to his native
connections. Most interesting among them are two idiosyncratic
small churches: Smannell and Hatherden, near Andover, both of
1856–7; Smannell has quirky detail. His Linkenholt of 1870–1 is
more conventional but neatly finished. Tangley of 1875, with a
Frenchy spired W tower of 1897–8, is essentially a reconstruction
after the medieval nave collapsed during the restoration work,
and Longstock (planned 1877 and built 1879–80) was given a
new N aisle and NW steeple. Equally important among ecclesiological architects, *R. J. Withers* did one exemplary restoration in
Hampshire at Shipton Bellinger 1877–9 with a highly original
font.

    A. W. Blomfield, arguably not in the front rank of Victorian
church architects, was busy in North Hampshire, and at Privett
(1876–8) excelled himself in the service of William Nicholson,
distiller and local M.P. The church is lavish with commanding

---

*Butterfield was engaged in restoration over a longer period, 1858–93 (accounts).

spire and particularly good nave roof. Even more prolific was
Henry Woodyer, based near Guildford, Surrey, and thus particularly active in the south-eastern counties. His North Hampshire
churches collectively provide a good broad sample of his inventive yet learned style. New churches, in a correct ecclesiological
Middle Pointed are at: Worting (1847–53), with characteristic
belfry timbers exposed; Holy Trinity, Winchester (1851–4, a large
inexpensive town church of Anglo-Catholic tradition); Monxton
(1852–3); Wherwell (1854–8) and, best of all, Newtown (1864–5),
whose beautiful foliate carved details are proto-Art Nouveau and
show Woodyer's marked propensity for original and thoughtful
design ahead of his time. His well-detailed and sometimes muscular woodwork is 'advanced' almost of the Arts and Crafts
Movement (e.g. the porch at Lasham 1866). His most interesting restorations at Winchfield (1849–50), Longparish (1851–2),
Easton (1868 and 1872) and Litchfield (1874–5) were drastic
interventions, but with respectful detail.

Pearson, a major architect so widely patronized across the
country, is thinly represented in the area. His best work is the
confident, essentially High Victorian E.E. chancel at Over Wallop
(1866), apparently replacing a genuine C13 predecessor with
characteristic ruthlessness; in 1875 he restored the nave and
raised a Frenchy saddleback roofed upper stage to the low C13
W tower in an equally direct and uncompromising spirit. His two
new churches, Laverstoke (1892–6) and All Saints, Winchester,
(1885–9), are lower-voltage but deftly detailed minor works
without his impressive vaulting. An equally prolific London
name, though not among the best, is *T. H. Wyatt*. Wyatt was lord
of the manor of Weston Patrick, and rebuilt the church (1866–8)
in a crisp E.E. above his usual standard. His early church at
Woolton Hill, with *Brandon* (1849), is unremarkable except for
its bizarre arcade. But his major inspiration at Oakley (1868–70)
is interestingly mostly Perp, then a rare choice, but here relating
to the partial rebuilding of c. 1509. Wyatt's Perp here came
remarkably early in Hampshire; it was followed a few years later
by *T. G. Jackson* in his two churches for the Barings: East
Stratton (1878) and the much bigger and more elaborate
Northington (1887–90) with its superb flint exterior dominated
by a soaring W tower of Somerset type.

Up to 1870, RESTORATIONS throughout North Hampshire
were usually thorough interventions. The most interesting of
them, Thruxton, in two phases, 1849 and 1869, is little known
and the architects involved have not been traced. The restorer of
1869 remains, as Pevsner says, 'an anonymous rogue'. He added
a boldly canopied priest's doorway *à la* Bishopstone, South
Wiltshire around an immured chantry tomb, an act which
Pevsner appreciated as 'outrageous but full of pluck'. *Blomfield's*
restoration of Petersfield was a major intervention for its date,
1874, and for the later jobs *Comper's* restoration and reordering
of East Meon stands out as the finest example.

Of LOCAL ARCHITECTS the only figure to make an impression is *John Colson* (1820–1895) of Winchester and his son of the same name. None of Colson senior's works in North Hampshire are specially remarkable. His love of naturalistic carving is well seen in the best of them, Stockbridge of 1865–6, executed by *Harry Hems*, and in his major restoration at St Lawrence, Wootton (1863–4), executed by *Mr Plumley*. The influence perhaps of J. P. Harrison's church at Hursley (South Hampshire) for Keble is clear in many of his conventional correctly Middle Pointed churches even as late as 1872 at St Paul's, Winchester (it was begun in that year, but greatly enlarged and completed in stages and finished in 1910, the style by then impossibly *retardataire*). Colson was a pupil of *Owen Browne Carter*, also of Winchester, who was Street's master. On his own account he restored Fyfield and Grateley churches (of 1846–7 and 1851 respectively), built churches and restored others in the county.

The cusp from High to LATE VICTORIAN in ecclesiastical architecture, comes *c.* 1870 with a change from the fashion for First Pointed and a move away from Continental Gothic. Anti-High Victorian are several churches. *Bodley & Garner*'s fine and quiet Ecchinswell of 1885–7 is learnedly Dec. Bodley of course, in his attitude, belongs with Pearson and the aggressive innova-tors. While at Ecchinswell he is Dec in order not to be Second Pointed and he was, like *G. G. Scott Jun.* (represented by Ashe, 1877–8), also instrumental in bringing about a new appreciation of Perp, which, immediately after the Palace of Westminster and after Pugin in his writings had branded it decadent, had lost all support. In connection with the popularity of the LATE GOTHIC in these years, a completely exceptional building might here find its place: the mausoleum church for Napoleon III that Eugénie built by her house at Farnborough in French Flamboyant style, though with a dome and crypt that are both conceits distant from that style. It is a marvellous one-off, standing outside the main narrative of church building in England. So the account here should conclude just before the First World War with three good churches: St Laurence (R.C.), Petersfield, by *John Kelly* of Leeds, completed 1909, providing an unlikely addition to the townscape of an Italian Baroque dome with a lantern; the unforgettable Romanesque of St Joseph (R.C.), Aldershot, by *Drysdale*, 1911–13; and the free Gothic of *Temple Moore*'s All Saints, Bas-ingstoke, 1915–17, one of the highlights of that town.

Church furnishings, stained glass and monuments

It can be taken for granted that the new or restored churches by the big names (*Bodley & Garner*, the *Scotts*, *White*, *Woodyer*, *Pearson*, *Blomfield* and *T. G. Jackson*) are often accompanied by good furnishings and decoration, by the best-known practition-ers of the period (e.g. carving by *Farmer & Brindley*, *Earp & Hobbs* and *Thomas Nicholls*, mosaic work by *Powells*, tiles by *Minton* or *Maw*). Special mention can be made of South

Tidworth, where the influence of Butterfield's All Saints, Margaret Street, can be discerned in details. Also of note are the outstanding sculptural repopulation of the niches of the Great Screen in the cathedral in the 1880s supervised by *Sedding*, *White*'s remarkable furnishings at Andover of 1871 with a specially bold font, Laverstoke with its German Gothic reredos derived from St Jackob Rothenburg ob der Tauber, Bavaria, the fittings at Blackmoor (*Herbert Baker* and *Pearson*), the chancel fittings at Cliddesden by *W. S. Hicks* and the contributions at the very end of the period (and in the mid C20) by *Comper* at East Meon (1905–12) and *Sir Charles Nicholson* at Aldershot, St Michael (1926).

The major Victorian revival of ecclesiastical STAINED GLASS after 1838 is well seen in North Hampshire. For the 1840s there is perhaps a more than usually large representation of non-figural grisaille pattern-work schemes, possibly due to the influence of the evangelical Charles Sumner, Bishop of Winchester 1827–69. Best of these are at Andover *c.* 1843, and Kingsclere 1848 by *Wailes*. A once even fuller scheme by *Ward* in Scott's church at West Meon of 1843–6 has largely disappeared, but a good heraldic W window remains a fine example of its now rare kind. An equally choice example of the period is at Brown Candover of 1845 by *William Miller*, perhaps designed by *T. H. Wyatt*. It has in addition pictorial medallions. Best of Early Victorian pictorial glass is at Thruxton, 1843, in correctly medievalizing windows by *Willement* at his most convincingly archaic. Willement worked briefly for *Pugin*, who is represented by a single but not specially remarkable window of *c.* 1850 at East Woodhay, made by *J. Hardman & Co.* The dense, even febrile colours favoured by the cognoscenti of the Ecclesiological Society, seen at Thruxton, are in full play at St Thomas and St Clement, Winchester, in a powerful E window of 1847 by *William Warrington*, with details in an *altdeutscher* manner, and in more conventional chancel schemes at Goodworth Clatford and Wherwell by *Wailes* of 1858 for the Iremonger family. Even more strident are the windows by *David Evans* of Shrewsbury at Winchester Cathedral (N and S nave aisles of *c.* 1850) and Thruxton of 1857 with dramatic figures still showing early C19 Renaissance 'tendencies'.

More scholarly High Victorian Gothic is more extensive in the region with the revival in full swing, a creative wave in which the major national firms (some newly established in the late 1850s) are all represented: e.g. *O'Connor* at Aldershot Royal Garrison Church (1863), and *Hardman*, again specially to the fore at Dogmersfield (1863), East Worldham (1865), Eversley (1863; designed by *John Hardman Powell*), Farringdon (*c.* 1860), Lasham (1866), Newtown (1865) and Easton (1870) of which the last three were for Henry Woodyer. At Winchester in the Great Hall of Winchester Castle, Hardman's mainly heraldic scheme of 1871 is successful, architecturally allied to the building. The long-standing and prolific *Powells* are best seen from the 1860s in a large scheme at Amport (*c.* 1866) and St Thomas and St Clement, Winchester (1858 and 1861), with panels by several

of the firm's 'in-house' designers (e.g. *Casolani* and *Henry Holiday*
at Amport). Holiday also worked for *Heaton, Butler & Bayne*, who
with *Lavers & Barraud* and *Clayton & Bell* are very prominent.
Clayton & Bell's best early work is seen at Buriton (*c.* 1862), Over
Wallop (1866), Dogmersfield (*c.* 1867) and Hawley (1867–8): all
with the firm's characteristically thoughtful arrangement of reds
and blues as backgrounds to small figure panels. *Heaton, Butler
& Bayne*'s finest early work can be seen at the Royal Garrison
Church, Aldershot, in two windows, the later of 1869, Froxfield
High Cross (1871), and Blackmoor (1868), the last successful
architectonic grisaille pattern-work with figure panels by *Henry
Holiday*. The ubiquitous *Lavers & Barraud* (*Lavers Barraud &
Westlake* from 1868) are best seen at Old Burghclere (*c.* 1861),
Longparish (*c.* 1860), Petersfield (1875) and Weston Patrick
(1868). *Burlison & Grylls* and *Kempe*, patronized by Bodley, the
Scotts and others, produced elaborate highly finished works in
the newly favoured C15 style. Most important is the scheme at
Hartley Wespall of 1868 by *Burlison & Grylls*, under *George Gilbert
Scott Jun.*'s control, and the outstanding Jesse Tree window at
Froyle (1892). Early work by *Kempe* is at Highclere (*c.* 1876) and
Froyle (1874 and 1878). His firm's most highly finished later
works in Hampshire are the three great windows of Winchester
Cathedral Lady Chapel (1897), by their chief designer *J. W. Lisle*.
   The most renowned and arguably the most freely artistic of
Victorian glass painters, *Morris & Co.*, appear in their mature
middle and later years at Minley (by *Philip Webb*, *Morris*,
Ford Madox Brown and *Burne-Jones*, 1870) and Heckfield (1885,
again by *Burne-Jones*) and in the C20 by the four large windows
of the Epiphany Chapel, all of 1910 by *J. H. Dearle* (1859–1932)
with panels from designs by *Burne-Jones* of 1872,* in exquisite
foliate pattern settings clearly by *Morris*. The Aesthetic Movement produced one oddly outré window (*c.* 1882) at Aldershot,
Holy Trinity by *J. G. Sowerby* of Gateshead with figures by *Arthur
Hardwick Marsh* in foliate settings by the architect designer
T. R. Spence. Also artistic and free from conventions is the glass
by *Heywood Sumner* at Church Crookham – progressive for
its date, 1900, showing a refreshing clarity of line and simplicity
of colour – where he had previously decorated the church
in sgrafitto, a technique he had helped to revive (*see* also No. 1
The Close, Winchester). He is essentially of the Arts and Crafts
Movement, whose greatest and most influential glass painter
is *Christopher Whall* (Dogmersfield, 1898; Tichborne House
Chapel; Bossington; and Winchester Cathedral). Whall's
influence extends far into the C20, chiefly through his brilliant
pupils including his daughter, *Veronica Whall* and *Louis Davis*
whose E window at East Woodhay, represents a good example of
the style. Other Whall-influenced windows at Winchfield by
Herbert Hendrie, 1910, and St Michael the Archangel, Aldershot,
by *Arnold Robinson* of Bristol, 1919, are of the same good tradition.

108

* First used for the chapel of Castle Howard, Yorkshire.

FUNERARY MONUMENTS of the Early Victorian period have been noted above. Bishop Wilberforce's monument by *Sir G. G. Scott*, 1873, at Winchester Cathedral is the finest of the Gothic Revival, continuing the tradition of reclining effigies for episcopal monuments (although the trend for effigies can also be seen at Eversley (with tomb-chest by *William Slater*) and All Saints, Fleet (Lefroy, carved by *Thomas Nicholls*) in the 1850s). Of the Goths there is also *Butterfield*'s Crimean War Memorial of 1858 at Winchester College with coloured marbles. From the 1870s there is a greater degree of realism, see e.g. *J. E. Boehm*'s monuments at Aldershot, Micheldever and Northington (the last for members of the Baring family), and in the next generation comes the more expressive manner of the 'New Sculpture' movement, which is represented by some minor works and also by the finest Edwardian monument, *Sir Bertram Mackennal*'s reclining bronze of Sir Redvers Buller, 1910, at Winchester Cathedral. *Hamo Thornycroft*'s memorial to Paul Springman †1913 at Crondall, in the churchyard, also deserves a place here.

Urban and rural developments: housing, public buildings etc.

There are no PLANNED DEVELOPMENTS to speak of. The closest one gets is in Winchester, where a new suburb was laid out on the high ground at the W end of the town with a mixture of VILLAS and TERRACES, but this was carried out piecemeal. The architectural character is predominantly Late Georgian, with Nashian stuccoed finishes but taking on the more Italianate character so typical of the Early Victorian. The architect for at least part of this was *Owen Browne Carter*, the most prolific of the local architects of this period.

As a predominantly rural area, North Hampshire also cannot show much in the way of significant Victorian CIVIC ARCHITECTURE. The highlight is Winchester Guildhall, of 1871–3 by *Jeffery & Skiller*, modelled on a northern French cloth hall of the C13 and clearly influenced by Godwin's Northampton Town Hall of ten years earlier, and its extension in a contrasting E.E. for the Art School in 1876 by *Thomas Stopher*. County administration remained on the site of Winchester Castle and incorporated the medieval Great Hall, which was first restored as a courtroom by *Owen Browne Carter* in the 1840s and altered by *T. H. Wyatt* and *Matthew Wyatt III*, contemporary with the addition of Assize Courts (1873–4, dem.). But the surrounding Council offices date from the major expansion of county authorities in the late C19 and early C20 and are in a uniform flint-faced Tudor style. Of the more minor works, Winchester's Market House, a late piece of Greek Revival of 1857, and the Assembly Rooms in Odiham, of 1865, are both squarely in the Georgian tradition. Others trace the familiar development in Victorian styles from the Italianate corn exchange at Basingstoke (1864–5) to the Gothic ensemble of Alton's Assembly Rooms, Museum and

Hospital etc. of 1879–80 by *Charles Edward Barry*, and the Free
Style of Farnborough by *George Sherrin*, 1896–7, and Aldershot
Town Hall, 1904 by *C. E. Hutchinson*.

Victorian reform of public order and public health produces
large institutions. There is the PRISON at Winchester, of 1846–50,
a panopticon-plan with a suitably imposing gatehouse. This type
of plan, for easy surveillance of inmates, was also the standard
layout for the purpose-built WORKHOUSES spawned by the
New Poor Law in 1834. Buildings at Andover and Winchester
(partially preserved) arose in 1835–7, the former by *Sampson
Kempthorne*, the Poor Law Commission's architect, the latter executed to his plans by the City Surveyor, *William Coles*. Radial
plans were employed also at New Alresford and Petersfield (both
by *Edward Hunt*, 1835–6) but fell from favour, and Whitchurch
of 1847 by *S. O. Foden* has the more usual linear T-plan arrangement of the mid-century, and Winchfield, an ambitious Italianate
design by *Edmund Woodthorpe* (the elder) of 1871, is of the much
larger kind which became the norm with several separate blocks
for different functions. Progressive planning in institutional
buildings is also represented by the Royal Hampshire County
HOSPITAL by *Butterfield*, 1863–8. It has a standard linear plan
but with a relatively novel emphasis on improved sanitation (separate wards in each wing, with sanitary towers at the corners)
that Butterfield develops into an ingenious asymmetry. It is also
the best Gothic Revival secular building in the county.

Small Early Victorian SCHOOLS, built by the Anglican
National Society and British & Foreign Schools Society (Nonconformist) survive in large quantities. The style from 1840 to
c. 1855 is, more often than not, Neo-Tudor and heavily dominated in this period by *John Colson*. Gothic is more common in
the schools of the late 1850s and 60s when there is also a sprin-
kling of big names, very frequently because of associated church
work: *William White* at Smannell, Andover and Linkenholt; *Street*
at Laverstoke; *Butterfield* at Northington; *Burges* at Winchfield;
Devey at North Farnborough, *Waterhouse* at Blackmoor; and
A. W. Blomfield at High Cross and Privett. BOARD SCHOOLS, the
non-denominational schools established under the 1870 Education Act, appear quite late in North Hampshire, are a phenom-
enon of the towns and are neither numerous nor specially
memorable: the best are at Petersfield by *H. T. Keates* (1894–5),
a single storey with shaped gables and open turrets, and Fairfields School, Basingstoke, by *Charles Bell* of London (1887–8),
which alone of all the schools in the northern county adopts the
two-storey format and secular style associated with the London
schools. Among the older FREE SCHOOLS that were rebuilt at
this time variations of Gothic are the norm: May's School (now
Mayhill Junior) at Odiham, 1876 by *Edmund Woodthorpe*, is a
mixture of Tudor and Gothic, while Churcher's College,
Petersfield, 1879–81 by *G. R. Crickmay*, is all Butterfieldian
Gothic. *Butterfield* was himself engaged in the remodelling and
extension of Winchester College in 1868–71, replacing some of
the Early Victorian work by *G. S. Repton*, but this is not the best
of him.

The Winchester Diocesan Training School (now the core of the University of Winchester campus) is also in an appropriately churchy collegiate Gothic with, originally, a very lively roof-line, by *Colson Sen.* of 1859–69, and Gothic also is the former West Downs School, Winchester (now part of the University), by *Thomas Stopher Jun.* of *c.* 1880. This has Arts and Crafts additions by *John Simpson*, 1905–6, and other late C19 and early C20 educational buildings also adopt freer secular styles. Sometimes it is one appropriate to the period of their original foundation: Tudor style for Peter Symonds College, Winchester, by *B. D. Cancellor*, 1899, and late C17 domestic for Perin's School, New Alresford, of 1909–10. The best of these more liberated years is the Old Museum at Winchester College by *Champneys* of 1894–7 in an enterprising, resourceful, and jolly English Baroque, and *E. S. Prior*'s extraordinarily eclectic Music School, 1903–4.

Among the other types of new civic buildings typical of the Victorian age there is surprisingly little to be found, indicative of how small many of North Hampshire's towns were until the C20. Mid-Victorian POLICE STATIONS (Petersfield, 1858 and Whitchurch, 1862, one by *Thomas Stopher Sen.*, the other by his son) are very modest indeed, still essentially houses rather than assertive symbols of law and order, and the FIRE STATION at New Alresford (1881 by the town's architect *William Hunt*) is little more than a shed. Winchester has a MUSEUM, a nice flint job by *Colson, Farrow & Nisbett*, 1902–3, on a site previously occupied by the Mechanics' Institute and Reading Room, but individual PUBLIC LIBRARIES, as opposed to those integrated with civic schemes such as that at Alton, are entirely unrepresented until the C20 unless one counts the plain brick shed for the Prince Consort Library at Aldershot. Some villages have INSTITUTES or VILLAGE HALLS for public gatherings, and these are a particular feature of the turn of the C20 when they are executed in appropriately rural Arts and Crafts styles, e.g. at Hartley Wintney by *T. E. Collcutt*, the Voysey-ish halls at Grayshott and Binsted, Lutyens style at Sheet and the ambitious conversion of farm buildings at Crawley as part of the Edwardian estate improvements there by the Scots firm of *Fryers & Penman*. The manner established before the war still held currency well into the 1920s.

PUBLIC SCULPTURE is rare but of great interest. At Aldershot is the gargantuan equestrian statue of the Duke of Wellington by *Matthew Cotes Wyatt*, 1838–46. Unliked by the Duke and much derided, it originally stood on top of Constitution Arch, Hyde Park Corner, until that was moved in 1883. Also by the same artist is the uncompleted sculpture of St George and the Dragon at Stratfield Saye, originally intended for George IV at Windsor. The designer of the memorial to the Duke himself, a soaring column carrying his statue at the entrance to Stratfield Saye, is *Marochetti*, 1863 (whose earlier monuments to the Duke are at Leeds and Glasgow). Another equestrian monument not in its original location, and an example of the 'New Sculpture' movement of the late C19, is that to Field Marshal Lord Strathnairn, 1891 by *E. Onslow Ford*, now at Foley Manor, Liphook. However, the two most original pieces of late C19 sculpture are in

109 Winchester: *Alfred Gilbert*'s seated bronze of Queen Victoria of 1887, described by Susan Beattie as 'the triumph of the spiritual and secret over the physical and mundane', now in the Great Hall, and *Hamo Thornycroft*'s King Alfred of 1901, in the Broadway.

Victorian and Edwardian COMMERCIAL BUILDINGS are not as memorable in North Hampshire as one might expect. There are some good HOTELS from the earlier period, notably the Market Hotel, Winchester (1840s, possibly by *O. B. Carter*, now the Theatre Royal), and The White Hart at Andover, still in the Georgian tradition. PUBS are more interesting and more plentiful. There is a group in Winchester of the 1870s and 80s, e.g. the former County Arms and the former Dolphin in the High Street. These are by *Thomas Stopher*, who with his son *Thomas Jun.* is the most prolific of the Winchester architects in the commercial field (but largely unrepresented in the wider county). There are a number of improved pubs in the villages, especially *c.* 1900, of which the former King's Arms, Binsted (*c.* 1895–6), probably by *Gilbert Ogilvy*, is a particularly fine example in the Old English style, but the stand out is the Arts and Crafts-style Fox and Pelican at Grayshott, a reformed public house of 1899 by *Read & MacDonald*, originally with a sign by *Walter Crane* (now lost).

The earliest surviving Victorian BANKS date from the 1860s and are exclusively Italianate: *Robert Critchlow*'s Capital & Counties Bank in Winchester, *c.* 1863, and a triumvirate for the London & County Bank by *Frederic Chancellor* in Winchester (1863–4), Basingstoke (1865) and Petersfield (1865). Lloyds TSB Bank in Farnborough, of the 1890s, is a rare example of Gothic and also of interest are *Stopher*'s remodelling of the Winchester Guildhall for Lloyds Bank in 1915 and *Edward Maufe*'s Lloyds Bank in South Tidworth, 1914–15, a forerunner of so much interwar Banker's Georgian.

Laverstoke Mill.
Engraving, 1854

John Colson & Son, that other prolific Winchester practice, also did a lot of SHOPS, including the best late C19 shopfront in the city: Wells Bookshop, College Street (1891). The national chains tended to employ their own architects, and Boots' exaggerated Neo-Tudor in the High Street, 1905 by *M. V. Treleaven*, is the most memorable. In the same Tudor Revival is the front of the former Picture House, Winchester, *c.* 1912 by *Greenwood*. There is another early CINEMA in Aldershot (1913 by *J. P. Briggs*) with French-inspired detailing, but the more lavish style of theatre interiors is the fine Baroque Revival interior by *F. G. M. Chancellor* at the Theatre Royal, Winchester.

Transport and industry

Mainline RAILWAYS came early to Hampshire. The pioneering London & Southampton Railway opened 1834–40, passing through the sparsely populated uplands to Basingstoke and Winchester on the way to the docks. The effort required to build these early lines (*Joseph Locke*, engineer, and *Thomas Brassey*, contractor) is testified to by spoil heaps close to Litchfield Tunnel (one of four on the central section of the line), where the tracks of the navvies' wheelbarrows are still evident. The architect for the line was *William Tite*; his compact classical STATIONS between London and Basingstoke were rebuilt with the widening of this section *c.* 1900, but those at Micheldever and Winchester remain. The similar stations at Whitchurch and Andover on the Salisbury branch, opened in 1854 and which has a fine viaduct at Hurstbourne Priors, are probably his too. At Petersfield, on the London–Portsmouth line opened in 1859, *Tite*'s station is stuccoed Neo-Tudor, a style popular with the early railways. From the 1860s onward other railways filled in the gaps between the main lines. Architecturally, the most interesting are the simple, consistent, arch-windowed brick designs of the Mid-Hants, opened 1865 (New Alresford is the most ambitious), the Queen Anne Revival of the Hurstbourne–Fullerton Junction branch (1884, Wherwell and Longparish) and the pretty Arts and Crafts of the Meon Valley stations (East Tisted, Privett) by *T. P. Figgis*, *c.* 1903.

Of other INDUSTRIAL BUILDINGS there is hardly anything of note other than the pumping station associated with the improvements in sanitation at Winchester in the 1870s, and the former paper mill at Laverstoke which was extensively remodelled for the Portals in the mid C19 by *Thomas Hellyer* to integrate manufacture and printing of banknotes; the new buildings are appropriately fronted by a formidable gatehouse.

Military buildings

Hampshire contains the spiritual homes of all three armed services: the Navy at Portsmouth, the Army at Aldershot, and the Air Force at Farnborough.

Aldershot was established as part of the military reforms after the Duke of Wellington's death in 1852 and to answer the demands presented by the Crimean War. *Clutton*, of all people, provided the plan, and the buildings were designed by the *Royal Engineers*. Some brick and stone barracks were built in 1854–9 and in the 1880s and 90s the original wooden huts were replaced with brick barrack blocks. Although not great architecture, the overall effect must have been impressive; however, very little has survived the modernizations of the 1960s, and only a few fragments of the barracks remain, a screen here, and carved pediment there. What do survive are some important individual buildings, such as the lodge to the former Royal Pavilion, *Fowke*'s Prince Consort Library, funded and endowed by Prince Albert, and the Beaumont Riding School, all of the 1850s, the gargantuan Cambridge Military Hospital of 1875–9 and of course the garrison churches. Until recent demolitions, Tidworth Camp, at South Tidworth, was the best example of a Late Victorian army camp in North Hampshire. In 1897, under the Military Works Act of that year, the War Office began acquiring land on and around Salisbury Plain to develop it as a permanent army training area. A second act in 1899 provided monies for barrack building, and Tidworth Camp, on the edge of the Plain, was one of the principal results, built 1902–5 at an estimated cost of £1.6 million to model designs and layout developed by the Design Branch of the War Office. The planning is clear, with the eight barracks treated as handed pairs, and the layout spacious and well treed. The buildings are, however, extremely utilitarian, with the only application of style a nod to the Baroque, visible in the officers' messes and houses. Other buildings of a few years later, e.g. the Wesleyan Soldiers Home and the senior officers' housing outside the main site, are Arts and Crafts-influenced. Some of the standard designs seen at South Tidworth also appear at Aldershot and Bordon Camp (the Louisburg Barracks of c. 1904). Architecturally superior to any other army buildings in North Hampshire, however, are the former Peninsula Barracks, Winchester. From 1796 Wren's unfinished palace for Charles II, the 'King's House', had been used as barracks. These important buildings were destroyed by fire in 1894 and were rebuilt in 1899–1905 to the designs of *Edward Ingress Bell* in a lavish Neo-Wren style, recalling the originals.

The origins of the Royal Air Force are to be found close to the home of the army, at Farnborough, the Royal Engineers' Balloon Depot moving here from Aldershot in 1905. The Royal Flying Corps was founded here in 1912 and the Royal Aircraft Factory established, but inevitably little survives architecturally from this early period. A demountable airship hangar of 1910–11 has been reconstructed as part of the early C21 office developments on the site, and there is an early wind tunnel of 1916, the first in a remarkable sequence of such structures. More substantial is the housing at Rafborough built for workers at the Royal Aircraft Factory in 1917–18, designed by the *Office of Works* and clearly influenced by the Unwinian garden suburb.

NORTH HAMPSHIRE SINCE 1914

The interwar period

Of the WAR MEMORIALS the greatest architecturally is *Sir Herbert Baker*'s serene Cloister at Winchester College of 1922–4 (Kipling thought it 'as near perfection . . . as human work can be'), which he echoed in a rustic manner at Blackmoor for Lord Selborne (something similar was planned by Ernest Gimson for Bedales but unrealized). Baker also provided the county memorial at the W front of Winchester Cathedral – one of his crosses. Nearby is the Rifle Corps Memorial, by *John Tweed*, one of the only ones in the area to have a figure of an infantryman, something quite common elsewhere. Rather surprisingly there is no single major memorial at Aldershot. Of the other towns, *Triggs*'s subtle, academic memorial at Petersfield is probably the best, and in the villages, *Lutyens*'s crosses at Stockbridge and King's Somborne stand out, along with Longstock and Sutton Scotney (by *T. D. Atkinson*), the unusually substantial pedestal monument at Wherwell by *W. H. Ward*, and *Maurice Adams*'s curious wooden plaque at Holybourne. But superior to all of these artistically is the Sandham Memorial Chapel, Burghclere, and its cycle of paintings by *Stanley Spencer* of 1926–1932. As Pevsner [117] wrote, 'They are not a war memorial in any conventional sense. There is no fighting here, nor any showy heroism. It is nearly all everyday scenes, and much is hospital routine, but seen and rendered with a deep sense of human fate and mute endurance.' Their originality is outstanding in early C20 English painting.

There are few new CHURCHES to speak of and what there is still essentially in the Gothic tradition, either explicitly so as in *Sir Charles Nicholson*'s chapel for St Michael, Basingstoke (1919–20), with its Perp flushwork, or in a stripped form (*Maufe*'s additions to St Mary, Liss and his church at Hook, 1937–8), or reduced to its barest details at St Christopher, Cove, by *Curtis Green* (1934–5) where secular architectural motifs are prominent. The chapel at Farnborough Hill School by *Adrian Gilbert Scott* (1931–2) is very economical but impressive Early Gothic, all in light brick. The habit persists even into the 1950s at the Good Shepherd church, Four Marks, by *Felix Lander*. Liss also has a triptych by *Martin Travers* in his personal interpretation of Baroque (otherwise he appears in Hampshire as a designer of glass) and sculpture by *Eric Gill*. Among early C20 church monuments, a tablet at Mortimer West End, of 1928, by *Henry Pegram*, is notable.

The story of HOUSES is mostly one of continuity with before 1914, in which the dominant idiom, as already noted, remained the Arts and Crafts. By the 1930s, however, the move to a more strait-laced Neo-Georgian is evident, for example, in Stonerwood Park, Steep, by *Baillie Scott & Beresford*, 1931, The Dower House, Weston Corbett, by *Braddell, Deane & Bird* of 1936, with Art Deco staircase, and two works reflecting a more scholarly appreciation of the C18: Upton Manor, Vernham Dean and Hinton

Ampner House, both by *Wellesley & Wills*, 1937. Contemporary with these are *Goodhart-Rendel*'s more eclectic additions to Farleigh House. Some houses display modernistic tendencies (e.g. High Hurlands, Bramshott, by *Curtis Green & Partners*, 1934, and Rake Holt, Hill Brow, by *Unsworth, Goulder & Bostock*, 1936) but strict Modernism, of the Continental variety, is scarce – for that one looks to the southern coastal belt – and the one (early) example in the N, *Colin Lucas*'s Silver Birches at Burghclere of 1927, has been altered out of all recognition. A perhaps more important aspect of the interwar period in Hampshire are some early examples of the rescue and restoration of old buildings, e.g. Sherfield Court by *Wellesley & Wills* (for Gerald Wellesley) *c.* 1922; the Court House, East Meon, by *P. Morley Horder* for himself in 1927, and Southington Mill by *Oliver Hill*, 1939–40.

The chief PUBLIC HOUSING is the Stanmore Estate, Winchester, of the early 1920s, laid out for the City Council by *William Dunn* with attractive cottages by *Curtis Green*. Like most housing of this period, it follows the principles of the low-density garden suburb, and this is true also of the contemporary village at Enham Alamein, developed for the treatment and training of disabled ex-servicemen. Its architect was *William Harding Thompson*.

Interwar PUBLIC BUILDINGS are almost as scarce as the churches. *Baker* added to the Neo-Tudor County Council buildings in Winchester (1930–1) but the major county project, new buildings by *C. Cowles-Voysey* in that city, was delayed by the next war. Petersfield Town Hall, of 1935–6 by *Seely & Paget*, modernistic with a degree of streamlining, is the principal example of the period but pretty minor at that. Much better are the neat brick fire stations by the County Architect, *A. Simpson Low*, in Winchester (1935) and New Alresford (1939–40).

Of the interwar SCHOOLS, the most interesting is Lord Wandsworth College, Long Sutton, which was conceived before the War as an agricultural college for orphans. *Guy Dawber*'s prize-winning scheme of 1914 was completed to a less ambitious design after 1925. His buildings are Neo-Georgian, but quite free and with Art Deco details. A contemporary interest in Y-plan buildings is displayed here and in the sanatorium at the former Clayesmore School, Crawley, by *J. J. Joass* (1923). Also of note is *Baker*'s conversion of the Winchester College brewhouse for the Moberly Library, 1932–4. The most ambitious 1930s scheme is *Mitchell & Bridgewater*'s Neo-Georgian St Swithun's School, Winchester, of 1931–4.

Banks provide one of the richer seams of COMMERCIAL ARCHITECTURE. Baroque is still alive in *T. B. Whinney*'s former London, City & Midland at Petersfield of 1918–20 (probably a pre-war design) and *Musselwhite & Son*'s Lloyds in Basingstoke of 1925, but a plainer Georgian is soon the norm. There is a group of erudite designs by *Horace Field*, including Lloyds at Andover, 1919–21, and Hartley Wintney, 1927–8, both Palladian Revival. Typically inventive of the architect is *Walter Holden*'s appropriately martial National Provincial Bank at Aldershot of 1925.

W. H. Smith in Winchester High Street, by *G. L. Blount &*
F. C. Bayliss of 1925, is quite serious Late Arts and Crafts outside
but with a Merrie England interior (see also their W. H. Smith,
Salisbury). At the other end of the stylistic scale are *A. G. Porri*'s
modernistic offices for Eli Lilly in Basingstoke of 1939. The best
cinemas are both in Aldershot: the Empire of 1930 by *Harold S.*
Scott and the Ritz by *Verity & Beverley*. Both are of the 'super'
variety, no doubt to cope with the large military audience. One
pub worth singling out, displaying the influence of Dutch Modernism, is the Anton Arms, Andover, of 1937.

From 1945 to the present

The most significant aspect is the pace of URBAN DEVELOP-
MENTS which hitherto, Winchester excepted, had been very
modest. Now, like other south-eastern counties, Hampshire came
under pressure to accommodate overspill population from
London and businesses relocating from the capital. Hook,
between Fleet and Basingstoke, was proposed in 1958 as the site
of a New Town for 100,000 people. The design eschewed the dispersed low density neighbourhood unit ideas of earlier new
towns in favour of a concentrated, high-density linear form. But
following local opposition and concerns about its financial via-
bility, in May 1960 it was agreed that the housing need should
be absorbed by expansion of Basingstoke, Andover and Tadley.
Of these, Basingstoke had been identified for expansion as early
as 1944, in the *Greater London Plan*, and the first development
followed in the early 1950s. However, the major increase there
and in Andover after 1963 resulted from joint development plans
between the *London County Council* and *Hampshire County*
Council. *John Craig*, who had overseen the Hook proposals,
headed the LCC at Andover and at Basingstoke, where the shopping centre spans the Loddon valley with road and servicing
underneath, the influence of the aborted scheme at Hook can be
seen. The general planning principles are of a commercial centre
surrounded by satellite neighbourhoods and industrial estates
connected by pedestrian routes and a ring road, i.e. closer to the
classic New Town plan than Hook would have been. Both towns
have prospered, but Basingstoke has been the more successful,
despite the destruction of much of the pre-1960 town centre,
which Andover avoided. Tadley and Farnborough also had some
overspill estates, much of the latter after 1965 under the *Greater*
London Council Architects Department, and at Aldershot there was
considerable post-war rebuilding of the army camp, somewhat in
the spirit of the New Towns, with an ambitious masterplan for
major reconstruction after 1965. In the rural areas there are two
examples of innovative District Council housing at Baughurst
and Bishop's Green (Ecchinswell) by *Eric Chick* with *Powell &*
Moya.

The M3 MOTORWAY (the first part constructed 1968–71
between Camberley, Farnborough, Fleet and Basingstoke)

stimulated the growth of towns and villages close to the Surrey
border, forging an almost continuous conurbation from Aldershot to Yateley, where earlier housing had also been encouraged
by the establishment of Blackbushe Airport on Yateley Common.
Here one finds a concentration of new CHURCHES but in total
they do not amount to much. One might single out early 1960s
designs by *Roger Pinckney* at Andover, Tadley and Winchester as
representative of national trends in traditional church architecture, while a more radical approach can be seen in St Gregory
(R.C.), New Alresford, by *Melhuish Wright & Evans*, 1967–8.
Among individual items there is stained glass by *Reyntiens*
(Hinton Ampner, 1969; Odiham 1969; All Saints, Basingstoke,
1985), etched glass by *Laurence Whistler* (Ashmansworth, Hannington and Steep) and furnishings at Ashford Hill by *David
Wynne* and *Alan Caiger-Smith*, Fleet by *Michael Murray* and by
Edward Barnsley at Bramley and Hinton Ampner. The fashion for
auditoria-style churches is a feature of recent years, e.g. St Mary,
Eastrop, and St Bede, Popley, both in Basingstoke, the latter with
advice from *Robert Maguire*, one of the post-war pioneers in the
Liturgical Movement.

The 1960s also produced a small but significant number of
new COUNTRY HOUSES. They fall into two camps: traditional
and progressive. Of the former, among others, are Weston Patrick
House by *Sir Albert Richardson*, Hinton Ampner House, by *Trenwith Wills & Wills*, after a fire in 1960, Basing House (Privett) by
Claud Phillimore and the additions by *Raymond Erith* at Netherton and Hunton Manor. Even *Yorke Rosenberg & Mardall* can be
found working in a Neo-Georgian manner at The Burrow, Longstock. A radical alternative was Stratton Park by *Stephen Gardiner
& Christopher Knight*, 1963–5, a glazed Miesian box, but one
whose significance has to be weighed against the sacrifice of
Dance's mansion to realize it, and, also for Lord Ashburton, the
Lake House at The Grange, by *Francis Pollen*, 1971–6. Both of
these houses are relatively compact alternatives to their monster
predecessors but the magnum opus is Hill House, Headley, by
Denys Lasdun, 1969, a grand Corbusian conception of a white-
walled villa in parkland. The diminutive and experimental Studio
House, a weekend cottage by *Edward Cullinan*, at Ashford Chace,
Steep, ought to be cherished but like other minor private
Modernist houses has not fared well.

The single most important achievement of the later C20 has
been the work of the *Hampshire County Architects' Department* and
in particular its SCHOOLS. As part of the Southern Consortium
of Local Authorities (SCOLA) the post-war county adopted an
anonymous prefabricated system (Eggar's Secondary, Holybourne, 1967, is typical) but after the appointment of *Colin Stansfield-Smith* as County Architect (famously cancelling a massive
order for chain-link fencing as his first act) it has produced the
most consistently progressive and imaginative designs of any
local authority in England, enjoying a golden period in 1982–5
of experimenting with open-plan classrooms and shared social
spaces in informal, fun, envelopes for the primary schools (at

Ashford Hill, at Four Lanes and Hatch Warren schools, Basingstoke, and at Burnham Copse Infants, Tadley) as well as   p. 515
working in a more serious High-Tech mode (appropriately) at
Farnborough College of Technology. This tradition of quality
and innovation continued up to and beyond Stansfield-Smith's
retirement in the provision of special needs schools, libraries,
public buildings etc., notably Woodlea School, Bordon (1991),
the County Record Office, Winchester (1992–3), Milestones   121
Museum, Basingstoke (1996–8), Alton Library (2004), Lanterns
Children's Centre, Winchester (2005) and Burnham Copse
Primary School, Tadley (2008). Contemporary works in educational buildings by independent architects are also of interest,
especially the refurbishing of schools at Church Crookham
(1984) and Fleet (1987) by *Edward Cullinan*, Fleet Infants'   120
School by *Michael Hopkins & Partners* (1986), and the superb
Olivier Theatre at Bedales by *Feilden Clegg Architects*, 1994–6.

By the early 1980s, there had also been some significant new
OFFICE BUILDINGS, the most innovative of which are by *Arup
Associates*: Mountbatten House (1974–6) and Belvedere (1981) at
Basingstoke, and Briarcliffe House (1984), Farnborough. In their
frank exposure of services and structure they display some of the
characteristics associated with the High-Tech tradition, of which
there is one other example, the Intec Business Centre at
Basingstoke by *Gebler Associates* with *Brian Taggart Associates*,
c. 1984. Regrettably they remain the exception in towns over-
burdened by the banal.

In counterpoint to these there has also been the REVIVAL OF
HISTORIC STYLES, or rather the continuation of traditions well
established in Hampshire, notably the local vernacular, refracted
through the lens of the C19 Arts and Crafts Movement. As we
have noted, the vogue for Georgian or Late Georgian was prevalent in many country houses well into the 1960s, and one would
also count in the County Council offices (Queen Elizabeth
II Court) at Winchester, whose design, by *C. Cowles-Voysey*, was   118
held over from before the war and then modified with extremely
successful results by *John Brandon-Jones*. It is not Neo-Georgian
as such but informed by English and Northern European architecture of the C17 and C18. The key exponent of the classical tradition has been *Robert Adam*, whose career begins in North
Hampshire. His work encompasses varied types and styles (principally, but not exclusively, English classicism) from offices
(Sheridan House, Jewry Street, Winchester of 1982–4, Dogmersfield Park, 1986), urban housing (Broad Street, New Alresford)
and village housing (Bradley), to public buildings (library,
Bordon) as well as additions to many country houses, culminating in the first entirely new country house in decades: Ashley Park
of 2001–5.

A very significant development of the later C20, again for
offices, is that in the High Street, Winchester, by *Donald Insall &
Associates*, a pioneering work of 1972–6 in which the novel
element was the CONSERVATION AND REUSE of several historic
buildings. The legacy of this approach is represented by two very

different early C21 examples in North Hampshire. One is the
revival of The Grange, rescued from total destruction by the
Barings through the timely intervention of the state in 1975,
prompted by the activism of, among others, the architect John
Redmill. Since then it has been imaginatively reused through the
extension of its former conservatory as an opera house (by *Studio
E Architects*). Even in its ruinous state the house represents a
victory for the conservationists. The Hampshire Buildings Preservation Trust, established 1977, has also played a central role in
saving many fine buildings, notably the Whitchurch Silk Mill.
Bringing the story up to date is the former Royal Aircraft Establishment at Farnborough, where the successful lobbying for the
protection of the pioneering aeronautical structures, including
the beautiful concrete wind tunnels and an airship hangar of
1910–11, secured them as the set piece of a business park, nicely
complemented by *Allies & Morrison*'s office buildings. Nearby,
also making use of land vacated by the RAE, are the new buildings of Farnborough Airport, a small but impressive group of
control tower, hangar and terminal building begun by *Reid Architecture* in 2001. Changes at Farnborough belong to the wider
story of REGENERATION in some of the towns since the mid-
1990s. In Basingstoke, in common with numerous English towns
and cities in the early C21, this has been 'retail-led' resulting in
the town centre's comprehensive reconstruction for the second
time in half a century, but also reintroducing a residential
element. Aldershot, with the considerable reduction of the Army,
presents a bigger challenge for replanning, again for the second
time since the 1960s, and reuse of a large number of buildings
now falling redundant. At the time of writing, the future of the
masterplan for its reconstruction looks uncertain. Some of the
regeneration has been accompanied by the pressure for new
housing in the south-east, and at Basingstoke there has been the
commendable reconstruction of social housing at Oakfield and
at Andover, the small but highly progressive scheme of 'eco-
housing' at Hockney Green by *Zedfactory*, 2005–7, developing the
concepts for energy-efficient mass housing pioneered by *Bill
Dunster* in Sutton, South London.

FURTHER READING

There is no early COUNTY HISTORY. The first comprehensive
account is R. Mudie, *Hampshire* (3 vols, 1839) followed by
another trilogy, B. Woodward, T. C. Wilks and C. Lockart's
General History of Hampshire (1861–9). Lastly in the C19, there is
T. W. Shore's *History of Hampshire* (1892). A good modern
history is B. Carpenter Turner: *History of Hampshire* (1963, 2nd
edn, 1978) and P. Brandon, *The North Downs* (2005) includes
part of the northern county. However, by far the most useful
general work is the Victoria County History (5 vols, 1900–12);

a revised edn commenced 2007. This can be supplemented usefully by *The Little Guide to Hampshire* 1904, revised 1948. Also helpful are *Kelly's Directories* and some earlier short-lived directories (*Pigots, White's* etc). The *Shell Guide to Hampshire* by J. Rayner (1937) is early in the series and the gazetteer is not comprehensive. J. Draper, *Hampshire: The Complete Guide* (1990) is a worthy substitute. The *Proceedings of the Hampshire Field Club and Archaeological Society* (*HFC*) have been published annually since 1885 (renamed *Hampshire Studies* from 1996) 1 and invaluable small articles appear in the twice-yearly Newsletter. Since 1991, the *Hampshire Papers* series has published nearly thirty individual studies on aspects of the county's history.

WINCHESTER has received more attention than any other place in the northern county. Antiquarian interest began with the cathedral, with Clarendon and Gale's *History and Antiquities of the Cathedral Church of Winchester* (1715) (drawing on Clarendon's MS notes of 1683). Other buildings had to await the mid-century, with the anonymous (actually Thomas Warton's) *Description of the City, College and Cathedral of Winchester* (1760) and his expanded *History* of 1773 based on the same work, both eclipsed within four decades by Bishop John Milner's seminal *History and Survey of the Antiquities of Winchester* (1798–9). c18 and c19 scholars concentrated on major historical monuments; study of domestic buildings had to wait until had to wait until T. D. Atkinson, *Winchester Street Architecture* (1934). Of modern resources, the primary one is *Winchester Studies* (general editor Martin Biddle), which includes Derek Keene's magisterial analysis of properties and property-holders (vol. 2, 1985). The best recent general outline history is T. Beaumont James's *Winchester: From Prehistory to the Present* (2007). It includes an up-to-date bibliography. For the city's architectural heritage, A. Rutter, *Winchester, Heart of a City* (2009) is perceptive and well illustrated, including R. Whinney on the archaeological development of Winchester. An excellent series of booklets published by Winchester City Museums deals with specific periods in the city's history. For the cathedral (Robert Willis's masterly account of the cathedral is still of some value), *Winchester Cathedral 900 Years*, ed. J. Crook (1993) contains many scholarly articles on aspects of the church and its contents, including a full bibliography. Individual parts of the cathedral are also analysed in John Crook's 'East arm and crypt of Winchester Cathedral', *Journal of the British Archaeological Association*, 142 (1989); his joint paper with Yoshio K. Kusaba, 'The Transepts of Winchester Cathedral in the *Journal of the Society of Architectural Historians*, 50 (1991); and a chapter in the *Festschrift for Martin and Birthe Biddle* (2010) entitled *The Romanesque West Front of Winchester Cathedral*. The same author has also studied the tomb of Henry of Blois in his paper 'The Rufus tomb in Winchester Cathedral' (*Antiquaries Journal*, 79, 1999). The story of William Walker's work is chronicled in Ian T. Henderson and John Crook's *The Winchester Diver* (1984). Other aspects of the cathedral are studied in booklets published by Friends of Winchester Cathedral, notably Mary Callé,

Winchester Cathedral Stained Glass (2008).The houses of the Close are studied in J. Crook, *The Wainscot Book* (Hampshire Record Series, 1984), and the same author's paper on 'Winchester Cathedral Deanery' was published in the Hampshire Field Club's *Proceedings*, 43 (1987). Another article, 'The Pilgrims' Hall, Winchester: hammerbeams, base crucks and aisle-derivative roof structures', in *Archaeologia* 109 (1991) places this important building in the wider context of early C14 halls. For the Hospital of St Cross, Peter Hopewell, *Saint Cross: England's oldest Almshouse* (Phillimore, 1995) provided useful historical background, but the latest history, which takes into account much new archaeological and historical research is John Crook's *The Hospital of St Cross and Almshouse of Noble Poverty* (Trustees of St Cross Hospital, 2010). The architectural development of the College is admirably summarized by J. Harvey in a chapter in *Winchester College Sixth Centenary Essays* (ed. R. Custance, 1982), building on his earlier paper in the *Journal of the British Archaeological Association* xxviii (1965). The Castle is chronicled in H. M. Colvin et al., *The History of the King's Works*, Vols. I and II (1963), and the construction of Winchester Palace for Charles II in vol. V (1977). Most recent is *The Castle Winchester, Great Hall & Round Table*, by M. Biddle and B. Clayre (Hampshire County Council, 2nd edn, 2006) and these authors' Winchester Studies vol. 6.i, *Winchester Castle* is eagerly awaited. The Westgate has its own booklet in the City Museum's series by G. Denford and K. Parker (2005). Two significant domestic buildings are discussed in E. Lewis and others, *Medieval Hall Houses of the Winchester Area* (1988). For archaeology and history of Winchester churches there is a detailed study: *Churches of Medieval Winchester* by Barbara Carpenter Turner, a collation of articles from The Hampshire Chronicle (1957), and later studies by Derek Keene. Also, B. Patten, *Catholicism and the Gothic Revival: John Milner and St Peter's Chapel, Winchester* (Hampshire Papers 21, 2001).

The most accessible account of the TOWNS is David W. Lloyd's *Historic Towns of Hampshire and Surrey* (1993). Alton has a thorough history in W. Curtis, *A Short History and Description of the Town of Alton in the County of Southampton* (1896) and aspects of the town have been covered since 1997 in the *Alton Papers*. At Aldershot, Douet, *British Barracks 1600–1914* offers the comparative picture for the military town and more generally useful is Lt-Col. H. N. Cole, *The Story of Aldershot* (1951; new edn 1980). Andover is covered by M.T.H. Child, *Andover in Hampshire: Life in the town before 1720* (1969); E. Mathews, *History of Andover* (1971); Dacre and Earney, *Andover, the last 4000 years* (1975); J. E. H. Spaul, *Andover, an historical portrait* (1977); A. C. Raper, *Andover Past* (2001). D. K. Coldicott's, *Elizabethan Andover*, 2004 is particularly useful for C16 and C17 buildings. Also see *Look back at Andover*, the journal of the Andover History and Archaeology Society. R. Warmington, *Timber Framed Buildings in Andover* (1970) is still useful, though now inevitably a little out of date. A. Hawker, *The Story of Basingstoke*, 1984 (rev. edn 1999) fills in the history since the 1960s expansion. For Farnborough, there is Rev. A. E. Kinch, *Chapters of the History of Farnborough* (1911). Of the smaller towns, Odiham is perhaps the most fully studied, for example in *The Odiham Society's Journal*, S. Millard, *The Parish of Odiham, an historical guide* (1993), and *Odiham High Street: an itinerary.* New Alresford has A. J. Robertson, *History of Alresford* (1937; derived from notes by Robert Boyle of 1774, and perpetuating the myth of the canalized Itchen) and more recently I. Sanderson's *Alresford Displayed. Some Account of the History of Petersfield* by E. Arden Minty (1923) is an attractive guide to the town, but much useful research can be found also in *High Street, Petersfield* (Petersfield Area Historical Society, 1984). Also a detailed study of *The Square, Petersfield* and a monograph on the town by D. Jeffrey and Mary Ray (2009). Stockbridge has H. Saxton's brief *A Portrait of Stockbridge* (2001) and articles by Rosemary Hill (HFC, 1976 and 1977).

For most VILLAGES the Victoria County History is still the main source but part of the county is covered by B. Edwards, *Historic rural settlement in Basingstoke and Deane and Test Valley* (1995). There are many individual village histories. Older examples include Rev. R. H. Clutterbuck, *Notes on the parishes of Fyfield, Kimpton, Penton Mewsey, Weyhill and Wherwell* (1898); W. Eyre, *Brief history of the Parishes of Swarraton and Northington* (1890); S. Warner, *An account of . . . Newton Valence* (1928). Of the modern accounts it is worth mentioning Rev. R. C. Toogood, *A History of Bramley* (1993); J. H. Smith, *Grayshott* (1978); M. Routh, *Amport* (1986); J. G. Wathen, *Beech and Beyond* (1996); E. Roberts and E. Crockford, *A History of Tichborne* (n.d.). Also V. Perks, *Enham Village centre* (*c.* 1988). Of the slew of millennium publications, the best include *A History of the Parish of East Woodhay*, (2000); R. Parr, *The Hampshire Broughton* (2002); D. S. Dunbar, *A history of the parish of Crawley . . .* (2000) *Farringdon and Chawton, The Last Hundred Years 1900–2000* (2000).

For CHURCHES M. Green, *Hampshire Churches* (1967) has good lists, particularly of fittings. Other studies have focused on smaller areas, e.g. Beggs, *Churches of the Test Valley* or are cross-county studies, e.g. The Churches of the Wessex Heartlands by P. H. Hase in *The Medieval Landscape of Wessex* (1994, ed. M. Aston and C. Lewis). For Roman Catholic churches the literature is sparse: there is the centennial history *Portsmouth Diocese Past and Present* by Gerard Dwyer (1981). Otherwise there is only C. Stell, *Nonconformist Chapels and Meeting Houses in South-West England* (RCHME, 1991). By period there is for the earlier churches, 'The Mother Churches of Hampshire' by P. H. Hase in *Minsters & Parish Churches, 950 1200* (1988, ed. J. Blair), A. R. and P. M. Green, *Saxon Architecture and Sculpture* (1951) and Taylor and Taylor, *Anglo-Saxon Churches* (1965). For Anglo-Saxon sculpture there is the *Corpus of Anglo-Saxon Stone Sculpture*, vol 4 (ed. D. Tweddle et al., 1995) E. Fernie, *Architecture of Norman England* (2002) is generally useful. For individual churches and ecclesiastical buildings there are papers in the HFC proceedings (*see* above). D. K. Coldicott, *Hampshire Nunneries* (1989) and J. Hare, *The Dissolution of the Monasteries in Hampshire* (Hampshire Papers 16, 1999) give essential background. Pamber Priory is the subject of a detailed study by Moira Grant (2000) following the well-illustrated 'An account of West Sherbourne (Pamber) Priory Church' by C. E. Keyser, HFC 8. Basingstoke, St Michael is dealt with by John Hare in a detailed historical study, *Church Building and Urban Prosperity on the Eve of the Reformation: Basingstoke and its Parish Church*, HFC 2007). Church guidebooks are of variable quality. Among the best are those for Alton and Eversley (2004). An earlier study of Headbourne Worthy by its restoring rector the Rev J. H. Slessor (1883) is still useful. For other C19 and later churches, the periodicals are a good source – *The Builder, Building News* and *The Ecclesiologist* – as are contemporary newspapers, especially *The Hampshire Chronicle*, and the more informative annuals of the *Winchester Diocesan Chronicle* from 1862 to 1914. The records of the Incorporated Church Building Society are online at *www.churchplansonline.org*. A comprehensive collection of early mid-C19 drawings, collated *c.* 1864 for Bishop Charles Sumner, are at Winchester Cathedral Library. Almost as extensive is the series of sketchy watercolours by R. Ubsdell of Portsmouth *c.* 1840–50 in Portsmouth City Museum and Art Gallery.

For CHURCH FURNISHINGS there is a Diocesan Survey – *The Treasures of Hampshire Churches* (1935) – and NADFAS church recordings, in Hampshire Record Office. On individual furnishings there is *The Mediaeval Paving Tiles of the Alton area of NE Hampshire*, by the Rev. G. Knapp (HFC, 18, 1953). For medieval STAINED GLASS, the best and fullest source is still J. D. Le Couteur, *Ancient Glass in Winchester* (1920). For early C16 stained glass in Winchester Cathedral and The Vyne, A. Smith in *The Journal of Stained Glass* vol. XXXI (2007). The *Corpus Vitrearum Medii Aevi* website (*www.cvma.ac.uk*) has good images of glass at Froyle, Grateley, Selborne and Winchester. C19 and C20 glass is comprehensively covered in the*www.stainedglassrecords.org* website. BRASSES are covered by W. Lack, *The Monumental Brasses of Hampshire and the Isle of Wight* (2007). On MONUMENTS, the Renaissance monuments and tombs so richly represented in North Hampshire churches and Winchester Cathedral are described and analysed in several papers by Nicholas Riall, e.g.: on the tomb of Sir John and Mary Lisle at Thruxton Church (*Architectural History*, vol. 50, 2007) and the Pexall monument at Sherborne St John (*Hampshire Studies*, vol. 62, 2007, pp. 143–67) and also the Paulet monuments at Old Basing (Hampshire Studies, vol. 64, 2009, pp. 147–71).

Among the larger SECULAR BUILDINGS, Odiham Castle is described in *The History of the King's Works, Volumes 1 and 2, The Middle Ages* (1963). Then for COUNTRY HOUSES, there are two well-illustrated early general works: J. Hewetson, *Architectural and Picturesque Views of Noble Mansions in Hampshire* (1830) and G. F. Prosser, *Select Illustrations of Hampshire comprising picturesque views of the seats of the nobility and gentry* (1833). The standard works for the C19 and C20 are M. Girouard, *The Victorian*

Country House (1979); J. Franklin, *The Gentleman's Country House and its Plan 1835–1914* (1981); C. Aslet, *The Last Country Houses* (1982); J. M. Robertson, *The Latest Country Houses* (1984). Accounts of individual houses are: Sir William Cope, *Bramshill: Its History and Architecture* (c. 1886); C. W. Chute, *A History of The Vyne* (1888); and W. Austen-Leigh and M. Knight, *Chawton Manor* (1911). Modern examples include B. Myers's pamphlet on *The Manor of Minley* (1984); D. J. Croman, *A History of Tidworth and Tedworth House* (1991); L. Jebb, *Preston House: A History* (1991); D. A. Mostyn, *The Story of a House: a History of Farnborough Hill* (1999); K. S. Parry, *Pelham Place: A History* (2001); E. Roberts and B. Fergie, *Sydmonton House: An Architectural Appraisal* (unpublished, 2004); J. M. Robinson, *Alresford House, Old Alresford* (also unpublished, 2004). New research on major houses has been published in *Basing House Hampshire Excavations 1978–1991* (HFC Monograph 10, 1999) and M. Howard and E. Wilson, *The Vyne: A Tudor House Transformed* (2003). For the latter see also in C. Rowell in *Burlington Magazine* (CLXV, 2003) and articles by R. Bowdler and J. Harris in *Apollo* (155, April 2002). The most studied house is The Grange, noyably essays by J. Mordaunt Crook and E. Mercer, in H. Colvin and J. Harris (eds) *The Country Seat* (1970) and J. Geddes in *Architectural History* (vol. 26, 1983) and *Furniture History* (vol. XXII, 1986); Hackwood is the subject of an unpublished report of 2000 by A. Deveson and M. Smith but see also A. Coleridge, *Lord Camrose, The Dukes of Bolton and Hackwood* (Christies' Sale Catalogue, 1998). Hinton Ampner House is detailed by R. Dutton, *A Hampshire Manor* (1968), supplemented by the National Trust guidebook and C. O'Brien in *Apollo* (no. 422, 1997).

Country Life has illustrated articles on most of the major, and some minor, country houses and there are many articles and references in the leading architectural journals *Architects' Journal, Architectural Review, Builder, The Building News* etc.) from the mid-C19 to the present. The one good source on ARTS AND CRAFTS houses in the Petersfield area is K. M. Blackwood, *In Search of Utopia* (unpublished dissertation, 1993) and there is more useful material in A. Carruthers, *Edward Barnsley and his Workshop: Arts and Crafts in the Twentieth Century* (1992).

An essential source for Hampshire PARKS AND GARDENS is the register produced by the Hampshire Gardens Trust. A good overview is G. Hedley and A. Rance, *Pleasure Grounds: The Gardens and Landscapes of Hampshire* (1987). Useful general works include P. Henderson, *The Tudor House and Garden* (2005), D. Ottewill, *The Edwardian Garden* (1989) and J. Brown, *Gardens of a Golden Afternoon* (1982). Inigo Triggs's garden design is described in *Country Life* (6 October 1995) and the gardens at Upton Grey Manor House and West Green House in Rosamund Wallinger, *Gertrude Jekyll's Lost Garden: the Restoration of an Edwardian Masterpiece* (2000) and C. Aslet, *Quinlan Terry, The Revival of Architecture* (1986).

The most important source on VERNACULAR BUILDINGS is Edward Roberts's comprehensive *Hampshire Houses 1250–1700* (2003) which includes a full bibliography of primary and secondary sources. Also E. Lewis, E. Roberts and K. Roberts, *Medieval Hall Houses of the Winchester Area* (1988). One local study is G. Meirion-Jones's 'The Domestic Buildings of Selborne' (HFC 29, 1974). The modern vernacular of plotland development, in which North Hampshire is so rich, is discussed in Dennis Hardy and Colin Ward, *Arcadia for All: The Legacy of a Makeshift Landscape* (1984). For FARMS useful work is E. Course and P. Moore, 'Victorian Farm Buildings in Hampshire' in *Proceedings of the Hampshire Field Club*, 40 (1984) which covers the model farms built by the Basing Estate.

For SCHOOLS, see P. J. Holmes, *A History of Robert May's Schools at Odiham* (1991). Bedales School is described in R. Wake and P. Denton, *Bedales School. The First Hundred Years*, 1993 and the Arts and Crafts architecture is described by R. Holder, "The Work of Each for the Weal of All': Bedales School and its early buildings", in *Architecture 1900* (ed. P. Burman, 1998). Lord Wandsworth College, Long Sutton, is described by L. Kinney in *The Edwardian Great House* (ed. Malcolm Airs, 2000). The progressive work of the later C20 County Architect's Department is described in *Hampshire Architecture* (Academy Editions 1974–84, 1985) and R. Weston, *Schools of Thought: Hampshire Architecture 1974–1991* (1991), as well as the contemporary journal.

General works for INDUSTRIAL ARCHAEOLOGY in Hampshire include M. Ellis (ed.), *Hampshire Industrial Archaeology: A Guide*, 1975 and R. Riley (ed.), *A Short guide to the Industrial Archaeology of Hampshire* (1994). For canals there is C. Hadfield, *The Canals of Southern England* (1955, 1969) and for railways H. P. White, *A Regional history of the Railways of Great Britain, Volume 2 Southern England* (1961, 5th ed. 1992). There is a useful gazetteer *Water and Wind Mills in Hampshire and the Isle of Wight* (1978) and J. Reynolds, *Windmills and Watermills* (1970). *Bridges in Hampshire of Historic Interest* (2000). The Taskers' Foundry is described in L. T. C. Rolt, *Waterloo Ironworks* (1969). Gazetteers of brickworks and breweries, by M. F. Tighe and W. C. F. White respectively, appear in the Proceedings of the Hampshire Field Club in 1970 and 1971. MILITARY BUILDINGS at Aldershot and South Tidworth are described in J. Douet, *British Barracks 1600–1914: their Architecture and Role in Society*, 1998. For the Royal Aeronautical Establishment site at Farnborough, see the report by Adam Wilkinson for SAVE Britain's Heritage, 2001.

Information on ARCHITECTS who worked in Hampshire can be found in H. M. Colvin, *A Biographical Dictionary of British Architects 1600–1840* (4th edn, 2008), the RIBA's *Directory of British Architects 1834–1914* (2 vols., 2001), A. S. Gray, *Edwardian Architecture: A Biographical Dictionary* (1985) and Sidney Gold, *Biographical Dictionary of Architects in Reading* (1999), which is good for buildings on the northern edge of the county. Relevant studies of architects are P. Meadows, *Joseph Bonomi Architect 1739–1808*, 1988; R. Freeman, *The Art and Architecture of Owen*

Browne Carter 1806–1859 (1991, Hampshire Papers 1); B. Poole, *John Colson: a Hampshire Architect of the Victorian Age*, 2000, Hampshire Papers 20); M. Drury, *Wandering Architects* (2000) on Geoffrey Lupton; K. Powell, *Edward Cullinan Architects* (1995); J. Lever, *Catalogue of the Drawings of George Dance the Younger and George Dance the Elder* (2003); M. Saunders on S. S. Teulon and R. Morrice on Ernest Newton in R. Brown, ed., *The Architectural Outsiders* (1985); J. Allibone, *George Devey* (1991); W. Whyte, *Oxford Jackson* (2006); W. G. Newton, *The Work of Ernest Newton* (1925); D. Ottewill, 'Robert Weir Schultz (1860–1951): An Arts and Crafts Architect', *Architectural History*, vol. 22 (1979); C. Cunningham and P. Waterhouse, *Alfred Waterhouse* (1992); J. Elliott and J. Pritchard, *Henry Woodyer* 2002; J. M. Robinson, *The Wyatts* 1999, A. Powers, *Francis Pollen* (1999), and *Classical Design in the late Twentieth Century: Recent Work by Robert Adam* (1990).

The standard works on post-reformation SCULPTURE are *Sculpture in Britain: 1530–1830*, by Margaret Whinney, 1968 (rev. John Physick, 1988) and I. Roscoe, *A Biographical Dictionary of British Sculptures 1660–1851* (2009). For particular periods the following are essential: *A Biographical Dictionary of London Tomb Sculptors c. 1560–1660* by Adam White (Walpole Society 61, 1999); B. Read, *Victorian Sculpture* (1982), and S. Beattie, *The New Sculpture* (1983). The latter is especially valuable for the Victoria monument at Winchester.

Among the extensive literature on ARCHAEOLOGY, the HFC have published *The Millennium Publication: A Review of Archaeology in Hampshire 1980–2000*. On individual sites the most important works are: B. Cunliffe, *Danebury Hillfort* (6 vols, 1984–95), G. C. Boon, *Silchester, the Roman Town of Calleva* (1974) and *Long Barrows in Hampshire and the Isle of Wight* (RCHM, 1979). Detailed analysis of excavations at Silchester are by M. G. Fulford, published between 1989 and 2006. Most recent is A. Payne, M. Corney and B. Cunliffe, *The Wessex Hillforts Project* (2006).

The best collection of Hampshire books and primary sources is in the Hampshire Record Office at Winchester *www. hants.gov.uk/archives*; there is also a good collection for Winchester in the City Museum. Much useful material can be found in other town libraries. Other sources not already mentioned include the Red Boxes of photographs at the National Monuments Record in Swindon, the on-line listings of buildings in *www.imagesofengland.org.uk* and the collection of resources on the Heritage Gateway website (www.heritagegateway.org.uk). A full general bibliography, including further sources for individual architects and artists, can be found at the reference section of the Pevsner Architectural Guides' website, *www. lookingatbuildings.org.uk*.

GAZETTEER

ABBOTSTONE
Itchen Stoke

A deserted settlement on high ground by a tributary of the River Arle. Earthworks mark the location of the village and church (ruinous by 1589).

ABBOTSTONE FARMHOUSE. C18 brick but incorporating remains of the Tudor mansion of William Paulet, the 1st Marquess of Winchester: three and a half timber-framed bays of 1562 (dendrochronology), probably part of a lodging range. Attached to the E end, where the frame is truncated, is a fragment of a grand late C17 brick building with moulded stone set-back and quoins. This must relate to the subsequent house, built for the 6th Marquess in 1685–95 and demolished in 1762 (*see* Old Alresford church). Substantial earthworks of two terraces are probably associated with the gardens described by Defoe in 1724.

ABBOTS WORTHY
Kings Worthy

The manor was in the possession of Hyde Abbey, Winchester, and was the site of a mill and a crossing point of the Itchen.

ABBOTS WORTHY MILL, Mill Lane. C18 chequer brickwork with big hipped roof. Enchanting setting with an C18 three-arched BRIDGE carrying a footpath across the river.

ABBOTS WORTHY HOUSE. One wing of *c.* 1834 by *J. C. Buckler*; the rest of 1950 by *Phillimore & Jenkins*, part of an uncompleted Neo-Georgian transformation for Esmond Baring. Opposite the former SCHOOL, Gothic, of 1857–8 by *P. C. Hardwick*. Further W, KINGSWORTHY GROVE, a gabled gault brick villa, *c.* 1840 with Neo-Tudor details and cast-iron veranda. Pedimented coachhouse. THE OLD RECTORY is 1880s Queen Anne with behind, DENIM of *c.* 2000, built of concrete blockwork, with low hipped metal roof and windows in vertical bands.

WORTHY PARK (Prince's Mead School), ¼ m. ENE overlooking the Itchen valley. Crisp, compact Neoclassical house of 1816–20 by *Robert Smirke* for Sir Charles Ogle. Lovely pale honey-coloured gault brick, sparingly detailed with Portland stone. The principal elevations have two-storey three-bay centres, on the S side with blank round arches over the ground-floor windows, and slightly projecting flanking three-storey towers. One-storey three-bay wings with parapets, balustraded (S) and plain (N). The porte cochère of four fluted Ionic columns was added 1825 'in accordance with the original design of the architect' (Prosser). Plain entrance hall with severe marble chimneypiece and mutule cornice. Cantilevered stone staircase with fluted cast-iron balusters and wreathed mahogany handrail; oval roof-light. The drawing room less restrained, with a richly decorated cornice and a shallow-coffered ceiling with patera. Large white marble chimneypiece.

Former STABLES, presumably by *Smirke*. In the centre a projecting pavilion with Doric colonnade and cupola with four Ionic columns supporting a shallow dome; urn finial. At the original entrance from the Basingstoke Road is a former LODGE, by *Smirke*. – SPORTS HALL. 2003; a design-and-build project, the original concept by *Clive Houghton* of *Architecture plb*. Long and low, sunk in to the ground.

ABBOTTS ANN

ST MARY. 1715–16; convincingly attributed to *John James*. Built by Thomas 'Diamond' Pitt, East India merchant, Lord Chatham's grandfather, and a commissioner of Queen Anne's Fund for New Churches. Light brick and stone. Battlemented W tower of Gothic outline with Victorian pinnacles. The easternmost of the round-arched windows have Lombardic tracery of 1868. Classical stone W doorway with a bold segmental hood. W window and bell-openings segment-headed. Delightfully complete interior, with coved ceilings and plenty of original furnishings: – COMMUNION RAILS. – FONT. Polygonal wooden baluster and bowl with wooden cover. Paid for in 1725 but it looks like a chalice; i.e. more *c.* 1800. – PULPIT, renewed in 1931, original tester removed. – BOX PEWS. – WEST GALLERY. 1716, later enlarged. Sturdy Tuscan columns. PANELLING above the gallery. Late Elizabethan. – CHANDELIER. *c.* 1830 (Sherlock). – ROYAL ARMS dated 1718, in the tower. – STAINED GLASS. E window, one of several by *A. Gibbs*, 1868, a testimonial to the Rev. and Hon. Samuel Best, rector. – MONUMENT. Rev. James Wendey †1727, Governor Pitt's chaplain at Fort St George, 1667–1707. A nice cartouche. – MAIDEN GARLANDS, funerary tributes to virtuous unmarried parishioners, more than in any other church. Forty fine crowns of hazel, with white gloves of parchment, set up between 1740 and 1973.

THE OLD MANOR, in a walled enclosure by the church, rebuilt in the C18 as a farmhouse. S is THE MANOR, its early C19 stuccoed front with curved porch. E of the church, THE OLD RECTORY. Early C18. Two storeys, chequered brick with stone string course and coved plaster eaves. Five widely spaced bays with narrow windows flanking the entrance, typical of the Queen Anne style. Originally L-plan with the staircase in the rear angle, infilled *c.* 1847 for the Rev. Best. Tudor Gothic porch of the same date, also the bays to the S front. C18 staircase with columnar newels, otherwise remodelled inside.

Flint, brick, cob and thatch are in much evidence in the village street. THE EAGLE, a model pub, E side, is dated 1865 (picked out in grey brick in the gable-end of adjacent outbuilding). THE SCHOOL HOUSE, opposite, has one end rebuilt in the early C19 as a pretty Tudor *cottage orné*. N is TASKER'S COTTAGE, *c.* 1800, occupied by the blacksmith Robert Tasker soon after his arrival in the village (*see* Anna Valley). NE of the church, PENNYMARSH, a C15 cruck-built hall house.

ALDERSHOT*

8050

Aldershot has two faces: the Military Town to the N, established in 1854 on open heathland and stretching up to Farnborough, and the civilian town that grew up to the S in order to service it, engulfing the old village. The army's part is in turn divided by the Basingstoke Canal into South Camp and North Camp. Not much of its C19 architecture survived the 1960s replanning and reconstruction, which turned 'miles of great dreariness' (Pevsner) into something like a New Town crossed with a vast low-rise university campus. The results no longer suit the army's needs, however, and South Camp in particular is changing rapidly (*see* p. 113), while reconstruction of the 1960s–70s sectors of the civilian town is also under discussion. So the following account is partly an advance obituary for post-war Aldershot.

The civilian town is described first, then the military. The division runs W–E along Wellington Avenue, High Street, and the railway. Some former military buildings now lie in the civilian part.

THE CIVILIAN TOWN

The Victorian town conjured into being by the army lies to the N, under the scarp of the South Camp. To the S is the old village centre with church and manor, to the NW the early C20

* Town and secular buildings revised by Simon Bradley.

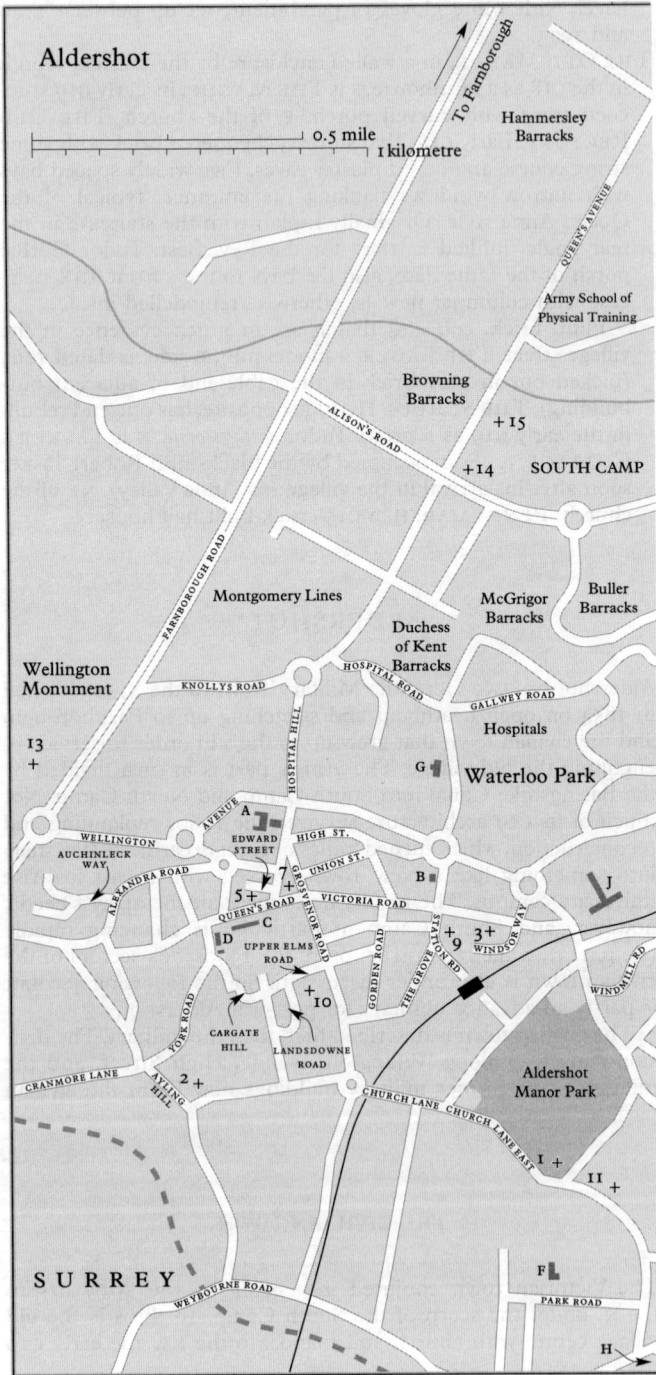

Aldershot

0.5 mile
1 kilometre

To Farnborough

Hammersley
Barracks

Army School of
Physical Training

QUEEN'S AVENUE

Browning
Barracks

+ 15

ALISON'S ROAD

+14 SOUTH CAMP

FARNBOROUGH ROAD

Montgomery Lines

McGrigor
Barracks

Buller
Barracks

Duchess
of Kent
Barracks

HOSPITAL ROAD

Wellington
Monument

KNOLLYS ROAD

GALLWEY ROAD

Hospitals

13
+

THE TUPALDITH

G

Waterloo Park

AVENUE

A

WELLINGTON

AUCHINLECK
WAY

EDWARD
STREET

HIGH ST.

B

J

UNION ST.

ALEXANDRA ROAD

5 +

7
+

QUEEN'S ROAD

VICTORIA ROAD

3 +

C

GROVENOR ROAD

GORDEN ROAD

THE GROVE

9

WINDSOR WAY

WINDMILL RD

D

UPPER ELMS
ROAD

STATION RD

WINDMILL RD

YORK ROAD

+
10

AYLING HILL

CARGATE
HILL

LANDSDOWNE
ROAD

Aldershot
Manor Park

CRANMORE LANE

2 +

CHURCH LANE CHURCH LANE EAST

I +

II
+

SURREY

F

WEYBOURNE ROAD

PARK ROAD

H

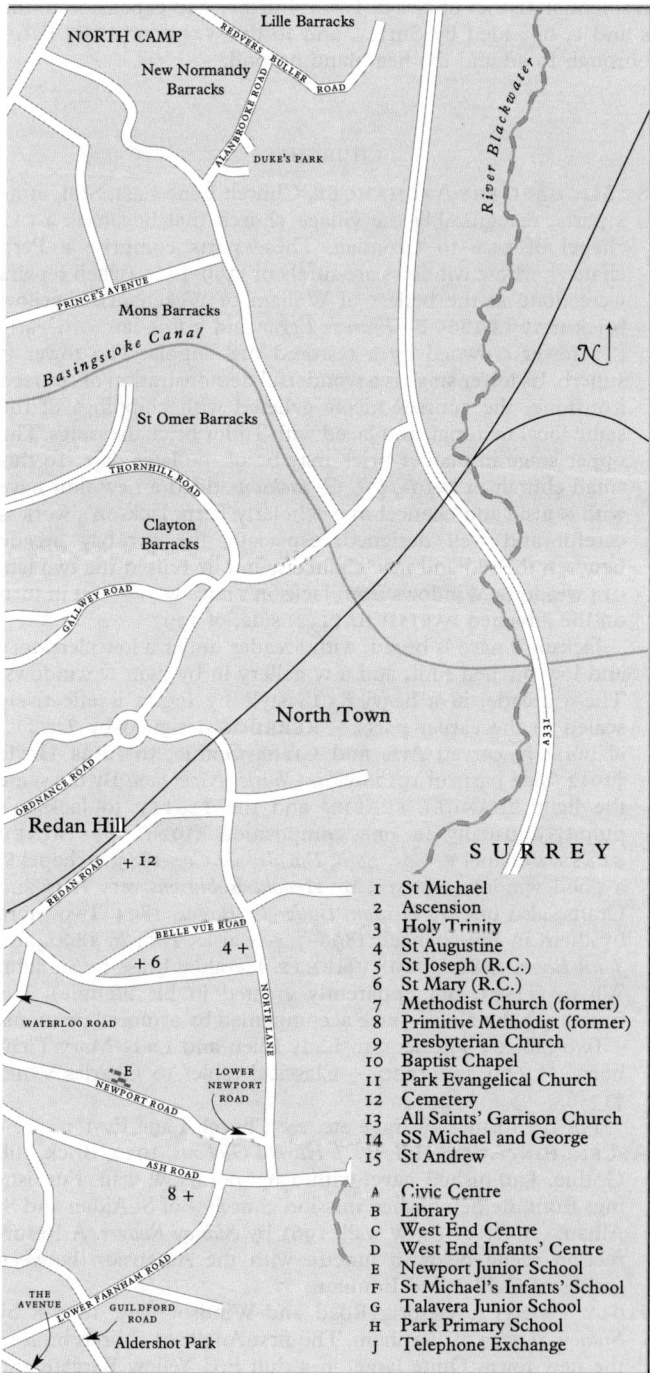

NORTH CAMP

Lille Barracks

REDVERS BULLER ROAD

New Normandy
Barracks

ALANBROOKE ROAD

DUKE'S PARK

River Blackwater

PRINCE'S AVENUE

Mons Barracks

Basingstoke Canal

N

St Omer Barracks

THORNHILL ROAD

Clayton
Barracks

GALLWEY ROAD

North Town

A331

ORDNANCE ROAD

Redan Hill

REDAN ROAD

+ 12

S U R R E Y

BELLE VUE ROAD

+ 6   4 +

WATERLOO ROAD

NORTH LANE

E

LOWER
NEWPORT
ROAD

NEWPORT ROAD

ASH ROAD

8 +

THE
AVENUE

LOWER FARNHAM ROAD

GUILDFORD
ROAD

Aldershot Park

1	St Michael
2	Ascension
3	Holy Trinity
4	St Augustine
5	St Joseph (R.C.)
6	St Mary (R.C.)
7	Methodist Church (former)
8	Primitive Methodist (former)
9	Presbyterian Church
10	Baptist Chapel
11	Park Evangelical Church
12	Cemetery
13	All Saints' Garrison Church
14	SS Michael and George
15	St Andrew

A	Civic Centre
B	Library
C	West End Centre
D	West End Infants' Centre
E	Newport Junior School
F	St Michael's Infants' School
G	Talavera Junior School
H	Park Primary School
J	Telephone Exchange

residential district of North Town. Further C20 expansion to the
S and E, bounded by Surrey, and to the W, bounded by Farnborough Road and the heathland beyond.

CHURCHES

ST MICHAEL THE ARCHANGEL, Church Lane East. Still, in its
S parts, recognizably the village church that began as a C12
chapel of ease to Crondall. These parts comprise a Perp
chancel, whose windows are surely of 1399–1400 (when repairs
were done at the behest of William of Wykeham), a yellow
brick nave of 1865 by *Francis Eggar* and a fine late C16–early
C17 tower crowned by a restored C18 cupola. The tower is
superb. Its lower stage is a wonderful demonstration of coursed
ironstone, the courses nicely galleted with chippings of the
same local material, and laced with Tudor brick dressings. The
upper stage in plainer brick may be of the later date. To this
small church in 1910–11 *T. G. Jackson* added a new flint nave
with N aisle and chancel in a scholarly Perp. Jackson's work is
careful and well designed, especially the two-bay arcade
between the old and new chancels, and he reused the two late
C14 windows. Windows from Jackson's nave were re-set in turn
on the attached PARISH HALL, N side, of 1997.

Jackson's nave is broad, with arcades under a low clerestory
and low-pitched roof, and a W gallery lit by twin W windows.
The S arcade, in a heavier C14 style by *Eggar*, is effectively
scaled to the earlier parts. – REREDOS designed by *Jackson*,
elaborately carved Arts and Crafts Gothic, to Anna Hoyle
†1912. Side parts of 1917 by *Sir Charles Nicholson*. By the same
the light CHANCEL SCREEN and the TESTER to Jackson's
pulpit, unusually in one composition (1926). – STAINED
GLASS. S chapel E, *Cox, Sons, Buckley & Co.*, 1885. S chapel S,
a good window of 1918, by *Arnold Robinson*; very Arts and
Crafts; also one by *Heaton, Butler & Bayne*, 1894. Two more
by them in the chancel, 1896–7. – S aisle, *Powells*, 1890, and
John Blyth, 1981. – MONUMENTS. Heraldic brass to Sir John
Whyte (†1573, but apparently erected in his lifetime). His
funerary helm above, once accompanied by armorial pennons.
– Two tablets, 'kneelers' to Lady Ellen and Lady Mary Tichborne, †1609 and 1620. – Classical tablet to Charles Vyner
†1756.

For the former vicarage etc. *see* Church Lane East, p. 110.

ASCENSION, Ayling Hill. By *J. Harold Gibbons*, 1939. Brick, still
Gothic. Unfinished nave, with a temporary W wall. Furnishings from the demolished mission churches of St Aidan and St
Alban. – PAINTING, W wall. 1961 by *Sidney Rodger*. A Resurrection scene below a lunette with the Ascension between
scenes of Galilee and Emmaus.

HOLY TRINITY, Victoria Road and Windsor Way. 1875–8 by
Sidney Stapley of Farnham. The first Anglican church built in
the new town. Quite large, in a dull E.E. Yellow Bargate and

Bath stone. No tower. Clerestoried nave with N and W porches in a more muscular Gothic than the rest. NE vestry added 1890. Dignified, dull interior. Five-bay arcades with varied foliate capitals. The W end partly screened off by *Norman Davey*, *c.* 1980s, who reused the former reredos and Decalogue on the screen.

Elaborately furnished chancel: fine TILES on the sanctuary floor, 1878; wooden Gothic ALTAR and COMMUNION RAILS of 1918 by *Jones & Willis*; REREDOS and canopied SEDILIA, 1904, of wood, in similar style; STALLS, minimally Gothic, 1893 by *E. P. Warren.* – STAINED GLASS. One extraordinary N aisle window, an extreme Aesthetic Movement piece of *c.* 1882 by *J. G. Sowerby* (*Gateshead Stained Glass Co.*). Females symbolizing Faith, Hope and Charity designed by *Arthur Hardwick Marsh*, in foliate surrounds by *T. R. Spence* (cf. his windows at St George, Jesmond, Newcastle upon Tyne). Lime greens and pinks. – Ambitious E window by *Powell Bros*, Leeds, another firm seldom encountered in the south. Christ and archangels over small scenes. Good traceries with emblems and Evangelists. – W window, *F. G. Christmas*, 1919. Christ in Majesty. – Two by *W. Glasby*, 1928 and 1931, S aisle.

ST AUGUSTINE, North Lane, North Town. In a largely Edwardian residential district. By *T. G. Jackson*, 1906–8. A cheap church in red brick, with a timber-framed porch and dormers. W window with Dec tracery freely treated. The E end finished, alas not from Jackson's designs, in 1964. More timber framing inside with enormous piers and bracing of Oregon pine. – STAINED GLASS. E window, a colourful roundel of 1964 by *Margaret Traherne*. Abstract, symbolizing the Work of the Holy Spirit, in varying shades of red, orange, blue and pale grey. – Large CHURCH HALL of 1914–15, W, in keeping.

ST JOSEPH (R.C.), Queen's Road. 1911–13 by *George Drysdale*, 112 Leonard Stokes's former pupil and future partner, as a result of limited competition.* One of the most impressive churches of its date, brilliantly planned on a narrow triangular site, steeply sloping down to the central belfry and the apse on the apex. This ingenious and inventive design makes fullest use of the restricted space. The narrow apse has a sacristy below the raised sanctuary. At the W end, a baptistery is flanked by apsidal chapels, in a narthex to the nave. This is of four bays between windowless aisles which taper sharply inwards to the choir and apse, where the vestries are reached down steps. Even at the W end an extra aisle tapers from N to S. After such virtuosity the detailing is ordinary polychrome Italian-basilican. Outside, the bold Butterfieldian striping of scarlet and dark red on the windowless drum contrasts strangely with the Lutyens-esque grey and dark red brick of the clerestory. MOSAIC over the S doorway, style of *Gabriel Pippet*. Fine

* *H.R. & B.A. Poulter* of Camberley produced a more ambitious design in the same Romanesque style.

contemporary furnishings, especially the ROOD (carved, painted and gilt ebony) by *J. H. Bonnor*. – Late C19 PRESBYTERY, W, from the previous, temporary church.

ST MARY (R.C.), BelleVue Road. 1961–3 by *H. Bingham Towner*. Old-school longitudinal plan, with a tower. Round-arched windows, low arcades with shallow segmental arches.

METHODIST CHURCH (former), Queen's Road and Grosvenor Road. Of 1875–8, by *Thomas Wonnacott*. Fully Gothic, with an asymmetrically placed SW tower, surmounted by Aldershot's only prominent steeple. Rich, overwrought detail, e.g. the swirling tracery of the S transept rose window. The church goes with WESLEY HOUSE, N, a former soldiers' home that turns the corner into Upper Union Street, and WESLEY HALL, W, with a French tourelle. All restored and reconstructed 1992 by *Ambergrange Design*: the church and hall for offices, with inserted floors, the soldiers' home for housing, replacing inserted shopfronts with new Gothic detail.

Further W, visible from Edward Street, is a five-bay hall: a fragment of Miss Daniell's Soldiers' Home (Methodist) of 1863, by *W. W. Pocock*. Also in a rather gritty rubble-stone Gothic. It was the first such British foundation designed for soldiers' welfare.

PRIMITIVE METHODIST CHAPEL, Ash Road. 1885. Modest, with a baby rose window. Sunday School behind. Disused.

PRESBYTERIAN CHAPEL (former), Victoria Road. 1863–9 by *G. B. Musselwhite* of Basingstoke. Yellow brick, round arches. Two short square towers, and a graduated five-light window between.

BAPTIST CHAPEL, Upper Elms Road. Of 1883–6. Paired lancets and Y-tracery.

PARK EVANGELICAL CHURCH, Church Lane East. Formerly St Saviour (R.C.), 1960. A persistence of the interwar type with a broad blockish W tower, *à la* Cachemaille-Day.

CEMETERY, Redan Road. Twin CHAPELS joined by a deep covered carriageway, dated 1861. Dec tracery. By *Thomas Goodchild*.

PUBLIC BUILDINGS

CIVIC CENTRE, Wellington Avenue and Princes Way (future uncertain). By the *Building Design Partnership*, opened 1970–3, part of the masterplan of 1965 for the civilian town (cf. p. 112). The affinity with the practice's military work is obvious, and – for a civic commission – dispiriting. A low U-shaped complex linked by a first-floor deck. Aggregate-faced concrete and boxy shapes. N part for magistrates' courts and police station, car-park decks to the S, terraced into the slope. A smaller block between, housing a health centre, was demolished in 2009. To the E, PRINCE'S HALL, a performance venue. Only the big external staircase hints at the different function. Pedestrian approach landscaped by *Geoffrey Clarke*, featuring his twisting aluminium SCULPTURE, The Pillar. Also two carved PLAQUES from the gateway to the East Cavalry (Warburg) Barracks of 1856–9 here (dem. 1964), one of the three C19 cavalry barracks in Aldershot.

LIBRARY, High Street. Bland brick of 1953–4 (*F. W. Taylor*, Borough Surveyor); top storey 1963. Jolly mosaic MURAL on the S wall, a *Freeform Arts Trust* project, 1990.

SCHOOLS. In Queen's Road, Aldershot's first Board School, 1873 (now WEST END CENTRE). Broad shallow E-plan. Polychrome brick Gothic with chamfered bargeboards. Further W, the WEST END INFANTS' of 1898 is looser, with a little Baroque terracotta trim. NEWPORT JUNIOR, Newport Road, 1905 by *F. C. Uren*, another E-plan, makes a great show of its many plain gables. ST MICHAEL'S INFANTS' off Park Road, drab brick of 1939–48, is tempered by late C20 blue-and-yellow-detailed additions. TALAVERA JUNIOR, Gun Hill – actually in the military area – is typical four-square Hants County Council of 1963–4 (County Architect *H. B. Ansell*).

PARK PRIMARY SCHOOL, off Lower Farnham Road. Of 1994–5, another expressive and intelligent job by the *Hampshire Architects* (project architect *Joe Collins*). A broad brick drum faces the W approach, with staggered monopitch roofs resting on brick cross walls receding to its r. These walls and roofs carry on beyond the glazed ends of the classrooms, forming small sheltered play areas. The glazing continues as a clerestory up to each roof, running unbroken across the spine corridor that takes a slanting course through the cross walls within. The drum, housing the dining hall, is lit by a window band around the top. An angular music room balances it at the opposite, E end.

RAILWAY STATION, Station Road. 1870. A late example of the London & South Western's white brick Italianate. Moulded-arched openings.

TELEPHONE EXCHANGE, High Street. Vast and intimidating. Brick-ended slab of *c.* 1960, r. At right angles, a larger extension of 1971–3 by *Austin-Smith:Lord*. Bands of cladding faced in stack-bonded white tiles, big concrete uprights advancing forward.

For other public buildings *see* Perambulation.

PERAMBULATION

There is no central focus. A good starting place is in VICTORIA ROAD where it joins Wellington Street, N, and Gordon Road, S. Here the BANKS cluster. Clockwise from the NE: NatWest (dated 1896), one of *William Campbell-Jones*'s London and County Bank branches, cheery in banded stone and brick; Lloyds TSB (formerly Capital and Counties), all brick and more subdued, 1881 by *Frederick Mew*; former National Provincial, a Neoclassical-revival box with rocky rusticated quoins, 1925 by *Palmer & Holden*. On the NW corner the former George pub, modest 1850s stucco. To the w, Victoria Road is similarly unassuming mid-C19 on the s side, but the N side is cowed by the WELLINGTON CENTRE. Projected as part of the 1965 town plan, but not built until 1975–8; architects the *J. Seymour Harris Partnership*. Heavy office tower angled to the street, rising from a lower block for shopping; long multi-storey-car-park slab, w. Much chamfering and chunkiness, in forbiddingly tough materials: hard brown brick, white tile, white-rendered concrete. E EXTENSION of 1988–92 by *Michael Haskoll Associates*, linked by covered bridge across Wellington Street. Coloured brick Lego-style facing, but a cooler aesthetic of steel, glass and pale wood within, from remodelling as THE GALLERIES in 1999. To its s, i.e. facing Victoria Road, THE ARCADE for smaller shops, a poor replacement by the *Seymour Harris Partnership*, *c*. 1991, of the L-shaped predecessor of 1898. Further E the lanceted hulk of a former Baptist chapel of 1862. At the next crossing, NW corner, the ALDERSHOT INSTITUTE, 1886–7. Spartan, and missing its corner tourelle. It faces the POST OFFICE, 1902 by *W. T. Oldrieve* (Office of Works). Flemish and unusually festive, with a low sorting-office wing, N, doubtless for the vast mail generated by the army.

Victoria Road continues E with the former Presbyterian and Holy Trinity churches (*see* pp. 104, 106), and No. 49, an entertainingly pretentious stucco villa dated 1897. To the N in STATION ROAD, past the Post Office, the town's first CINEMA (1913), E side. Broad low French-accented front, characteristic of 1910s picture houses. On the w side a former MASONIC LODGE of 1899–1901, well-crafted gabled brick, by *Coggin & Wallis*. To its N, a curtain-walled office block on a podium, 1964 by *Carl Fisher & Associates*.

Then up to the NAAFI Roundabout, with the Library on the l. (p. 107), and w into HIGH STREET, which here forms the interface to the Military Town to the N. The other entrance to The Galleries appears on the s side, reworked in 1999 as a tall steel-and-glass gable. Opposite, a long tall outlier of the *Haskoll* retail scheme of 1988–92, housing multi-storey car park and market hall. Back on the s side, the old market building, 1859 by *Thomas Goodchild*. Three broad upper bays with big Venetian windows, lighting a former assembly room. The N side beyond, where the pioneer military surveyors put up their huts in 1854, was cleared after 1928, and two giant CINEMAS built. The Ritz, a brick streamliner by *Frank Verity & S. Beverley*, 1937, originally had its own variety stage. At the former Empire, w, of 1930 by *Harold S. Scott*, the motif is giant oversized pilasters. Both are under threat of demolition. To the w are public gardens, remodelled in 1994 with *Jill Tweed*'s small memorial STATUE of a leaping horse. High Street finishes with the QUEEN HOTEL, another Italianate 1850s survivor, overlooking the Civic Centre (p. 106) to its NW. To the SW a new mixed-use quarter is planned, to be called WESTGATE.

GROSVENOR ROAD leads s from High Street. Much ordinary commercial architecture of *c*. 1855–65 here, and along Union

Street off to the E. For the former Methodist church cluster *see* p. 106. Further down on this side, the modest former TOWN HALL, by *C. E. Hutchinson*. In a relaxed, quite attractive Free Style very typical of its date: 1904. The accompanying fire station has gone. To the S, MUNICIPAL GARDENS also of 1904, with a fountain with pebble pictures, 2000 (*Hampshire Sculpture Trust*). WAR MEMORIAL of 1925 behind, a blunt Cornish granite obelisk. Opposite the gates, BIRCHETT ROAD runs off E. On its N side, stretching up Frederick Street, the façade of a trim Italianate terrace of 1860, masking offices of 1981. The approach steps have gone, so the paired doorways now give onto nothing. At the corner with The Grove (S side), bulky private housing of *c.* 1991 in Neo-Early Victorian dress. The Wellington Press (Gale & Polden) works of 1893–1915, printers to the army, stood here until 1987.

BUILDINGS TO THE EAST, SOUTH AND WEST

ALDERSHOT MANOR. Set back in its own park S of the High Street, near the parish church. The effect is as of *c.* 1720–30, though a date of 1670 is recorded; some brickwork, and clashing window heights and sill bands behind, support the older origin. Seven sashed front bays, three storeys, tall panelled parapet. The last hides a five-part roof of C18 outline. C19 porch with moulded brick parapet and stepped gable, i.e. mid-C17 style. The r. flank is a refacing of *c.* 1976. In the entrance hall elongated Ionic pilasters from a blocked doorcase, and a partly renewed open-well stair. STABLES to the l., early C18, substantially reworked as offices in 1984 by *Howarth, King & Partners*. They opened up the giant round windows (a later C18 insertion?), and made a big but tactful rear addition.

Behind the house, an unusual war memorial or HEROES' SHRINE, 1950. Designer *F. W. Taylor*, Borough Surveyor. A baldacchino, sheltering an over-life-size statue of Christ stilling the storm by *Josefina de Vasconcellos* (carved by 1946), rather in the Eric Gill manner. All Portland stone. In front were rockeries with fifty-six fragments from notable blitzed buildings, mostly removed *c.* 1998 in favour of inscribed wall panels.

ALDERSHOT PARK. The domain of a mansion of 1842, demolished *c.* 1960. Its landscaped grounds and reshaped lake survive, as does a LIDO of 1930 to the NW. Other parts built up with municipal housing from 1920, after plans by *James Neave*, Town Surveyor. The earliest and best phases are in THE AVENUE (the former house approach) and along LOWER FARNHAM ROAD. Rendered, with big shared gables. Pairs, and symmetrical ranges of four.

ALEXANDRA ROAD. The leavings of BEAUMONT BARRACKS can be followed from the E end. Built 1854–9 as the southernmost of three identically planned cavalry barracks (*Capt. Robert Laffan*, R.E.); mostly demolished in the 1970s for council housing.

BEAUMONT VILLAGE, a retirement complex of 2003–5 by *Sidell Gibson*, incorporates two offset STABLE ranges. Long and low, with multiple doors sheltered by thin iron colonnades. Inside, roof-hooks remain for slinging up sick horses (the stables became part of a veterinary hospital *c.* 1910). New blocks rendered, or detailed after the C19 work.

Continuing s and then w, the perimeter WALL rises to some 40 ft (12 metres) as the land falls: the former frontier with civvy street, now reduced to a topographical curiosity. Before this slope steepens, AUCHINLECK WAY runs w, between re-set chunks of a big carved pediment. Beyond is the mighty RIDING SCHOOL. Fifteen bays plus two more for the E porch, its pediment echoed on the wider main part. All-over banded rustication, with big voussoirs to the side arcading, done almost entirely in brick. The training here left the young Winston Churchill 'shaken and sore'. Further w on Farnborough Road, the former GATEWAY with flanking guardrooms (restored 1984), also rusticated brick. Set in more of the perimeter wall, which accommodates the long slope in endless curving steps.

ASH ROAD. The old road E into Surrey. On the s side the RED LION pub, well-made Neo-Tudor of *c.* 1925. Further E, No. 233, a neat Neo-Georgian former pub by *G. Maxwell Aylwin* of Farnham, 1939.

CARGATE HILL. A landmark: steel WATER TOWER of 1907 (Mid-Southern Utility Co.), raised on high legs, like an H. G. Wells Martian.*

CHURCH LANE EAST. s of St Michael, the handsome former VICARAGE (No. 116) by *Charles Spooner*, 1901. Arts and Crafts of Old English ancestry. To the w, also of *c.* 1900–5 and more or less in sympathy, the ark-like former church hall; Glebe House, white and sub-Voysey; and the big tile-hung No. 104. Some way E on the N side, ALDERSHOT LODGE. Late C17, reworked in the late C18 with mostly Venetian windows in the outer bays, keeping the irregular spacing. Suburban-looking rear addition, *c.* 1910.

CRANMORE LANE. Nos. 20–22, ALMSHOUSES of 1922–3. Small, but lavishly done, with thick timber framing. Plaster portrait of the founder, J. O. Salter, on the gable. At the crossing where the lane ends, E, WEST END FARM (N side), C17, behind mid-C19 Neo-Jacobean elevations.

FARNBOROUGH ROAD, s part. Facing the old Beaumont Barracks gate (*see* Alexandra Road, above), the remarkable LODGE of the former Royal Pavilion of 1855–6 (dem. *c.* 1962). Its colonial-looking motifs – weatherboarded walls, deep eaves (here with a veranda), plain hipped roof – echo those of the Pavilion itself, a commission by *Prince Albert* for royal use during troop inspections. Its timber-built austerity was deliberately in keeping with the soldiers' own hutted

---

* Its counterpart to the E, the amazing 200-ft (62-metre) tall GASHOLDER of 1926–7 off Ash Road, was dismantled *c.* 2003.

accommodation. The design seems to have been shared between the Prince, *Sir Frederick Smith* of the Royal Engineers, and the builder, *George Myers*. The drive now leads to COMPUTER SCIENCES CORPORATION'S headquarters complex, an executive idyll by *RTKL*, 2002. Four curtain-walled blocks radiate out into woodland from a semicircular terracotta-faced linking corridor. Entry is through a long stone-clad spur projecting into the central corral. The group replaces the QARANC (nursing corps) training school of 1963–6, an outlier of the *Building Design Partnership*'s barracks of the Military Town (*see* p. 115–16).

Much further S, ANGLESEY HOUSE, built *c.* 1858 for the Commanding Officer, Cavalry Brigade. Yellow brick, tall, almost styleless, or at least neither classic nor Gothic.

LANSDOWNE ROAD. No. 23, *c.* 1910 by *Dan Gibson* of Windermere. Voysey-esque austerity amidst the fancy late C19 domiciles.

LOWER NEWPORT ROAD. Engulfed on the W side, HERRETT'S FARMHOUSE. C16–C17, the older, N part with thicker framing. To the N in HERRETTS GARDENS, a cluster of three linked dwellings; the S-facing with a mid-C19 elevation, the N-facing visibly timber-framed. In NEWPORT ROAD to the W, Nos. 132–136, a mid-C19 oddity with a rounded windowless end, the square-ended roof sailing over it on cusped struts.

WATERLOO ROAD, running through to Windmill Road. A nice pocket of local authority housing of *c.* 1965–70, making use of the hill slope. Mostly low, with split-pitch roofs and some tile-hanging.

WEYBOURNE ROAD, Nos. 47–59. A charming C17–C18 run in two adjacent builds, given a Picturesque helping hand in the C20, e.g. the square chimneystack, r., and the cross-wing's gable-end.

THE MILITARY TOWN

Military Aldershot owes its existence to the military reforms of the 1850s, after the Duke of Wellington's death. Existing barracks were then chiefly urban, and often situated to prevent civil disorder. A training barracks near open land suitable for large-scale exercises, a type increasingly fashionable abroad, was an obvious requirement. And so in 1853 Prince Albert and the new Commander-in-Chief Lord Hardinge selected the empty heath between Aldershot and Farnborough as a location. 8,000 acres were bought the following year, and work began. The plan was by the architect *Henry Clutton*, with buildings designed by the *Royal Engineers*; the contractor *George Myers* did much of the work. Several elements of the 1850s plan have endured, including the one-and-a-half-mile spine road of Queen's Avenue and the parade ground to its W.

The first BARRACKS were of two kinds. North Camp and most of South Camp had endless defiles of wooden huts of 1854–6. On the lower ground to the S and SW were three cavalry and three infantry barracks of 1854–9 (later designated the Wellington Lines), for which brick, stone and a measure of pomp were used. Very soon after came permanent churches, institutes and a library given by Prince Albert, who retained a close interest. Other, independent foundations for soldiers' welfare were built in Aldershot town, or in Farnborough; military hospitals were grouped on the scarp in the SE corner of South Camp. Then in the 1880s–90s the hutted barracks were rebuilt with larger brick blocks, as the Marlborough Lines (North Camp) and Stanhope Lines (South Camp). This completed what was the spiritual home of the British Army at its late C19 and C20 zenith.

Imperial retreat in the 1950s, coupled with the end of National Service, made REBUILDING inevitable. In the same decade the Royal Engineers' architectural responsibilities were transferred to the *War Office Directorate of Works*, headed from 1958 by the architect *(Sir) Donald Gibson*, best known for his replanning of post-war Coventry. In 1960 the War Office appointed *George Grenfell Baines* to the Aldershot project. Baines's practice, the *Building Design Partnership*, shared much of the ensuing design work (partner in charge *Peter Renninson*, also *J. Wilkinson* and *R. K. Dewhirst*), and also drew up a ten-year MASTERPLAN, published in 1965 along with an associated plan for the civilian town. By that time much had already been built, including areas of housing designed by the *Ministry of Public Building and Works* or by private practices.

The masterplan aimed to create a kind of military New Town for up to 26,000, including 2,000 service families. The new architecture indeed has more in common with Welfare State educational buildings than with older military traditions. System building was used for the new barracks (*Intergrid*, *Tracoba* and G80 types), with a fondness for semi-formal right-angled groupings, and for abstract-patterned concrete and murals, here by the busy firm of *W. G. Mitchell & Associates*. Users' needs were carefully analysed: barracks were broken into working and living areas, with an emphasis on the company unit; married quarters were grouped on the N and S fringes, to be close to the civilian towns. Specialist barracks were included for mechanized regiments, catering, etc. Landscaping and planting were treated with care, most impressively in South Camp, with its artificial hill and informal lake. A few late C19 blocks and interwar buildings were spared, and the early cavalry barracks have also left substantial traces, mostly in areas ceded after 1965 to the civilian town (*see* p. 109).

The 1960s plan, never completed in full, fell from favour in its turn. Rebuilding was first proposed as early as 1985. The present plans ('Project Allenby/Connaught') derive from the Strategic Defence Review of 1998, and extend to certain defence estates outside Hants. The Aldershot garrison is shrinking by 30 per cent, and some 340 acres of South Camp are to be relinquished for civilian housing. The remaining barracks have been or are to be rebuilt, this time with individual rooms for the men. The Defence Estates' MASTERPLAN for South Camp, published in 2004, includes a grand formal accent in the shape of a double avenue running at right angles E from Farnborough Road, echoing the C19 Stanhope Lines. A selection of historic buildings is also set to remain. Even so, the present military atmosphere of South Camp seems unlikely to survive.

South Camp

ALL SAINTS ROYAL GARRISON CHURCH, W of Farnborough Road, on rising ground at the head of Wellington Avenue. By *P. C. Hardwick*, 1863, for £16,000. 'The Cathedral of the Army'. Large and spreading, with bar tracery and a prominent NE tower, carefully grouped for the main view from the E. Red brick and Bath stone. The tower has a steep pyramid roof with lucarnes. Wide nave and aisles, wooden arch-braced roof with dormers (Hardwick's intended nave clerestory was unrealized). The capacious interior, pewed for 1,250, has an array of memorial furnishings and monuments. – Square FONT of 1863 with Evangelists' emblems in mastic. – REREDOS, 1923, elaborately Perp. – SE chapel enclosure, also 1923, also Perp. – STAINED GLASS. A full set, earliest at the E end. Colourful E window of 1864 by *O'Connor*. Old Testament scenes with Christ and angels in the tracery. Military insignia introduced in the predella. Intricate details throughout, worth a special look. Chancel N, †1869, and S transept window of c. 1868–9, *Heaton, Butler & Bayne*. Others by *Clayton & Bell*, including the W windows, N to S: 1885, 1872, 1886. N aisle, first and second from E, *Powells*, 1886–7, designer *Henry Holiday*. S aisle, one by *Reginald Bell*, 1947. – MONUMENTS. General Sir James Yorke Scarlett †1871, W end. A fine piece by *Sir J. E. Boehm*, of white marble. Bust and two standing soldiers, a dragoon and a hussar, showing great verisimilitude in military dress. Boehm's design follows an early C19 pattern. – Lt-Gen. Sir Charles Craufurd Fraser VC, †1884, unfortunately 'lofted' in the S chapel. Bust in arched recess between bronze panels of battle scenes. The Italian Renaissance composition crowned by a small equestrian figure. Very accomplished. By whom? – 1st Division, S porch. A giant, blackened, baleful crucifix made of timber from shelled buildings. Set up on the Somme 1917, moved here 1939. GATES 1st and 2nd Infantry Divisions.

ST MICHAEL AND ST GEORGE, Queen's Avenue. By *Major Pitt & Lt Michie*, built 1892; R.C. since 1973. Large, reasonable North German Early Gothic in brick, like a chapel for the Prussian Guard. Commanding W porch-tower with slated spire. Lancets throughout in groups of three. Carved stone tympanum of St George and the Dragon over the W doorway. Long-drawn interior, the brick exposed, noble and impressive for sheer size. The E end of the nave reordered with marble

altar and reading desk. Original chancel furnishings, outstandingly the REREDOS with a mosaic Last Supper made by
Powells to designs by *Heaton, Butler & Bayne*. By the latter
also most of the STAINED GLASS. The exceptions: S chapel
by *Kempe* (two of 1894) or *Kempe & Co.* (†1907); N aisle
third from E, *Kempe & Co.*, 1912; S aisle easternmost by *Morris
& Co.*, 1908 (by *J. H. Dearle*), to early army balloonists,
drowned in 1907. Also N aisle W by *Mary Lowndes* and *Isobel
Gloag*, 1909. Two elongated angels below cherubim. Bold and
strongly coloured, perhaps more Art Nouveau than Arts and
Crafts.

ST ANDREW (Scottish Presbyterian). Next to the former.
1926–7, extended W in 1939, both times to *Sir Robert Lorimer*'s
design. Much affinity with Lutyens. Blue and red brick, with
round-arched windows. Aisles and an apse. The 1920s church
tower, taken down in the enlargement, was not replaced. –
STATUE of St Andrew by the entrance, signed *J. G. Bubb*
(1782–1853), brought from elsewhere. – STAINED GLASS. E
window of 1934 in memory of Earl Haig, by *Walker* and *J. R.
Cook* of Edinburgh. The four medallions below the Crucifixion with war scenes like book illustrations. S transept, 1930,
and W, 1935, by the same.

PERAMBULATION. A walk out and back from the Royal Garrison Church takes in the key sites and monuments (public
access permitting). Structures due to be demolished for civilian housing under the 2004 masterplan are marked with a
dagger. First to the NW, where the WELLINGTON MONU-
MENT stands on a bluff. A titanic equestrian statue by *Matthew
Cotes Wyatt*, 1838–46. Made for the top of Constitution Arch
in Westminster, opposite the unwilling Duke's own house, it
aimed to be the biggest bronze statue in the world. Much
scoffed at once *in situ*, it was taken down when the arch was
moved in 1883, and brought here two years later. Now it shows
to better advantage, on a high pink Corsehill stone base ringed
by half-buried gun barrels. The horse stands still, the Duke
half-raises his baton, and his hat is much in prominence.

Returning E to FARNBOROUGH ROAD, the former GATE of
1856 to the Willems or West Cavalry Barracks appears opposite (cf. Beaumont Barracks gateway, S, p. 110). Now a screen
to a motel, behind which is *Lyons & Sleeman & Hoare*'s big
TESCO. Both of striped brick, both *c.* 1995. The C19 barracks
gave way to system-built military housing of 1965–7, since sup-
planted by conventional houses to the N and E.

Further N, KNOLLYS ROAD turns off Farnborough Road.
The PRINCE CONSORT LIBRARY here is of 1859–60 by *Capt.
Francis Fowke* R.E., built and stocked at Albert's initiative and
expense. A brick hall, pragmatic and not pretty. Top-lit inside,
with a timber gallery on thin supports. Lecture hall added
1911, N. In the grounds beyond, a PEDIMENT SCULPTURE
with royal arms, from the officers' mess block at Willems
Barracks, *c.* 1857. The 1960s OFFICERS' MESS type appears
through the trees to its N, part of the 1960s barracks cluster

called Montgomery Lines (*see* also below).[†] The design, published 1961, was by *Grenfell Baines & Hargreaves*, i.e. the forerunners of the *Building Design Partnership*, with *Donald Gibson* of the War Office (job architect *Robert Smart*). A strongly modelled concrete square, with kitchens and cloakrooms below, main rooms on the first floor, a boxed-out accommodation storey over it, and a rooftop penthouse for a senior officer. Later versions are coarser. Further w along Knollys Road, a white-painted group of 1907, formerly a school, hall and Catholic Soldiers' Club.[†] By *W. Bevan*, former Chief Government Architect, Transvaal. Knollys Road ends in a roundabout on the edge of the ridge, with commanding views over the Military Town to the N. On the sw side the 2nd Division WAR MEMORIAL, 1923, designed by *Capt. J. B. Scott* M.C., a slim Gothic cross. (To the se a large HEALTH CENTRE by *SR Architects*, 2005–8.) Then s down HOSPITAL HILL to the enigmatic gabled red brick complex on the w side. Begun *c.* 1630 as a house of Sir Richard Tichborne, it became a workhouse after 1782, a pauper school in 1849, a military hospital in 1854 and offices in 1879. Workhouse additions were made in 1838–40, and the s range was in its present five-gabled form by 1860. Matching reconstruction after a fire in 1907 makes dating difficult, but the low outer parts and porch at least are plainly C19. The centre, identifiable with the C17 house, has flush blue bricks in vertical, horizontal and diagonal lines, as if imitating half-timbering. Long L-shaped rear wing, with flint and ironstone passages in the walls: further domestic survivals, or a separate, workhouse phase? To the E, recent military housing replaces 1960s patio blocks. Back at the roundabout, NE side, the former SMITH-DORRIEN METHODIST SOLDIERS' HOME, tall and Tudor, with an odd double-turreted front. By *Robert Curwen*, 1908. To its N in QUEEN'S AVENUE, the MAIDA GYMNASIUM, very large, the walls pushed back between deep buttresses. A survivor from the Stanhope Lines rebuilding of 1890–5 (*see* p. 112).

The w side of Queen's Avenue gives a good view of the MONTGOMERY LINES, built for the Parachute Brigade in 1962–5.[†] Four barrack clusters, mostly of textured concrete or with blue spandrels. Then on the E side, along Steele's Road, the former SOUTH-EAST DISTRICT HEADQUARTERS BUILDING, 1894–5, long and badly proportioned, with a pedimented centre and Doric porch. At the corner, the 8th Division WAR MEMORIAL, 1924 (designer *Arthur C. Martin*), a lion-topped stone pylon, and further on a little circular OBSERVATORY of 1906.

Queen's Avenue carries straight on past the garrison churches and into North Camp (*see* pp. 113–14, 117). A turn l. into Alison's Road, and BROWNING BARRACKS appear on the N side.[†] Built 1964–8 (*Building Design Partnership*) as the

[†] Demolition proposed.

Parachute Regiment's training depot. The facing is blue-grey
mosaic. On the s side of Alison's Road, the regiment's
motor transport depot, 1965–6.[†] Broad pitched-roofed sheds,
curtain-walled above a low skirt of brick.

Now back w along Alison's Road, which becomes Thornhill
Road. Post-1960s barracks on the N side: PROVOST, brown
1980s brick with corrugated gable-ends overhanging, and
GALE, striped brick with blue details, 1990s, the gable-ends
with blue and white chevrons. On the s side, BULLER BAR-
RACKS (Royal Army Service Corps), 1965–70, another by the
Building Design Partnership with blue-grey mosaic cladding.[†]
(Within, another sculpted 1850s PEDIMENT.) The N side then
has the *Building Design Partnership*'s most impressive single
work, the POWER STATION of 1964–6. Not large, it has a row
of six oblong concrete stacks and an all-glazed cabin, l., on a
massive substructure of rough bush-hammered concrete. The
ribbed-concrete-clad group in front, by the same, was built as
a training ABATTOIR, 1966–7, with the involvement of the
Ministry of Agriculture. It goes with the practice's ST OMER
BARRACKS to the e, the army catering school, 1965–71
(rebuilding in progress 2009). The centrepiece was a square
fourteen-storey tower with visor-like windows. Where the road
turns s, a war memorial PAVILION and recreation hall for the
Catering Corps, 1955–6 by *E. T. Dowling* (modified from a
design by Messrs *Henry Tanner*, published 1948). Brick, mild,
with a flat-topped corner tower housing a shrine. Brick figure
relief on the tower. CLAYTON BARRACKS, w side, 1926–8 (also
Service Corps), has municipal-looking parallel blocks.[†]

The next junction is with Government Road, which runs e
to the canal; here a much-restored LOCK COTTAGE of *c.* 1795.
The military route is uphill along GALLWEY ROAD, which
climbs the scarp to the w. The MILITARY CEMETERY, s side,
has a basic polychromatic CHAPEL of 1879. On the N side an
artificial SKI RUN, one of England's earliest (1969; *Major Bruce
John* R.E.).

The road becomes HOSPITAL ROAD, with former military
HOSPITALS in defile and overlooking the town to the s. First
the THORNHILL ISOLATION HOSPITAL of 1894–6, long
symmetrical red brick with spur wings to the N. The LOUISE
MARGARET HOSPITAL of 1897, next, was for soldiers' wives
and children: the army's largest of this unusual 'family' type.
Shapeless, in yellow brick, with a matching NW extension dated
1926. Also a big Neo-Wren nurses' home of *c.* 1938, NE. The
C19 details derive from the mighty CAMBRIDGE MILITARY
HOSPITAL to the e, of 1875–9 (closed 1996). It has a classical
and conservative central unit, like one of the vanished C19 officers' mess blocks except for its giant ungainly central tower.
Square plan, turning octagonal and with an octagonal leaded
dome, then square again for the ogee-topped clock turret.

[†] Demolition proposed.

Behind is a lateral E–W spine corridor 800 ft (246 metres) long, from which pavilion blocks extend to N and S, after the 'reformed' model introduced at the Herbert Hospital, Woolwich (1861–5). No fewer than nine of these pavilions on the S side. The central one housed a dining room and library, the rest were wards. The outermost two, added 1893, are angled outwards. Bay windows with superimposed half-columns on their ends. Auxiliary buildings to the W include a late C19 water tower and another Neo-Wren nurses' home (*c.* 1908, extended 1938). On the lower land S of the hospital, WATERLOO PARK, married quarters of *c.* 1958–64 by the *Ministry of Public Building and Works*. Orthodox houses in short informal terraces.

Over the road to the N, three parallel other-ranks blocks remain of the MCGRIGOR BARRACKS (Army Medical Corps), more survivors of the Stanhope Lines rebuilding of 1890–5.[†] At the corner of Hospital Road and Gun Hill, the BOER WAR MEMORIAL of the Royal Army Medical Corps, 1905. An obelisk in an exedra, designed by *R. W. Schultz Weir*, with *Sir W. Goscombe John*'s bronze group of two soldiers and an orderly. Continuing W, on the S side is the SEBASTOPOL BELL, a Crimean trophy formerly in the hospital tower. To the N across open land is the DUCHESS OF KENT BARRACKS (Women's Royal Army Corps), opened 1969, with blue-grey tile facing.[†] The Hospital Hill roundabout is regained ahead.

REDAN HILL, to the SE. Restored as a park in 1990 (*Broadway Malyan Landscape Ltd*). The hilltop redan – an earth-and-timber fortification – echoes one made here *c.* 1856, modelled on Crimean examples.

North Camp

Less interesting architecturally and topographically; no perambulation.

ALDERSHOT MILITARY MUSEUM, Queen's Avenue. Housed since 1985 in two accommodation blocks from the old Oudenarde Barracks (Marlborough Lines), as rebuilt 1894–6. Single-storeyed, as was the norm in the late C19 rebuilding of North Camp. Patent ventilators on the roof ridge. Also a weatherboarded BARRACK HUT of *c.* 1938, moved from Queen Elizabeth Barracks, Church Crookham, and the MONTGOMERY GALLERY, moved in 1996 from Viscount Montgomery of Alamein's house at Isington Mill (q.v.). Built *c.* 1948 in vernacular fashion by *Robert Bostock* (*Unsworth & Bostock*) to enshrine Monty's three famous field caravans. Like the house conversion, the shelter uses superior materials donated by the Dominions. Weatherboarding; hipped and shingled roof of angled queen-strut pattern.

[†] Demolition proposed.

MARLBOROUGH INFANTS' SCHOOL, Redvers Buller Road. Of
c. 1897, for soldiers' children. To the E, the former junior
school, an unusual, blunt composition: twin house-like blocks
lettered for BOYS and GIRLS, entered via a single-storey linking
range. The style Neo-Wren. On the corner with Queen's
Avenue, W, the former infants' block, with a clock turret.
Further S in Queen's Avenue, past the museum, WAVELL
HOUSE, one of the more ambitious, two-storey headquarters
blocks of the 1890s (here, of the Second Division; cf. South
Camp, *see* above).

ARMY SCHOOL OF PHYSICAL TRAINING, further S on Queen's
Avenue. Late C19 initiatives to improve the physique of the soldiery have left two impressive red brick installations. FOX'S
GYMNASIUM, 1894, N, has stepped corbelling on the gable-
end, and a light metal truss roof. The SWIMMING BATHS, S,
by *J. S. Smith* FRIBA, have on the answering end slim battered buttresses and the prominent date 1900. Ottoman-
looking dome over the entrance. In 2009 disused.

BARRACKS. HAMMERSLEY BARRACKS, Queen's Avenue. The
first post-war barracks to be completed (1961–4; *War Office
Directorate of Works*), for the Army School of Physical Training.
Gentler in plan and expression than the South Camp barracks,
with much brown brick showing as well as concrete. Also some
retained interwar blocks.

LILLE BARRACKS, Redvers Buller Road. Now of 1959–64 and
c. 1987. The OFFICERS' MESS of the 1890–5 barracks (Marlborough Lines) was spared. A standard design, very long, with
numerous spur wings behind, visible from Lynchford Road
(Farnborough).* To the S, the NEW NORMANDY BARRACKS
retains a smaller 1890s officers' mess block, formerly of
Tournay Barracks, visible from Alanbrooke Road. Villa-like,
with a pedimented break-front.

MONS BARRACKS, Prince's Avenue. 2000–2 by *Kier Build*,
replacing 1920s buildings. Budget three-storey brick blocks,
and a clock turret for form's sake.

MARRIED QUARTERS, to the NW and NE. Mostly conventional
1960s houses, though DUKE'S PARK, NE, has two-storey
ranges of staggered plan, including some flats with upper
and lower entrances nicely juxtaposed. The CONNAUGHT
CENTRE to their N, 1990 by *PSA Projects*, combines NAAFI
stores and community facilities. Banded brick, formal top-lit
entrance.

HOUSES. Just W of FARNBOROUGH ROAD is VINE COTTAGE,
pre-1850s, with an over-scaled lean-to conservatory: the home
in the C19 of the Senior Royal Engineer Officer for Aldershot.
(Further N, GOVERNMENT HOUSE, a Queen Anne mansion
of 1883. Until 1939 the residence of Aldershot's General
Officer Commanding.)

---

* Aldershot's military prison stood to the W (1870, dem. 1958). The cell block had
a top-glazed central well of standard mid-C19 penal plan, hence the famous nick-
name, THE GLASSHOUSE.

ALRESFORD *see* OLD ALRESFORD
and NEW ALRESFORD

ALTON

7030

A thoroughfare town on the London to Winchester road where it crosses the River Wey. There were two medieval manors, East-brook and Westbrook, the former including the parish church and the latter containing the market established in the C13, both away from the main street to the NW. On the edge of the town to the SW is The Butts, a triangular green traditionally associated with

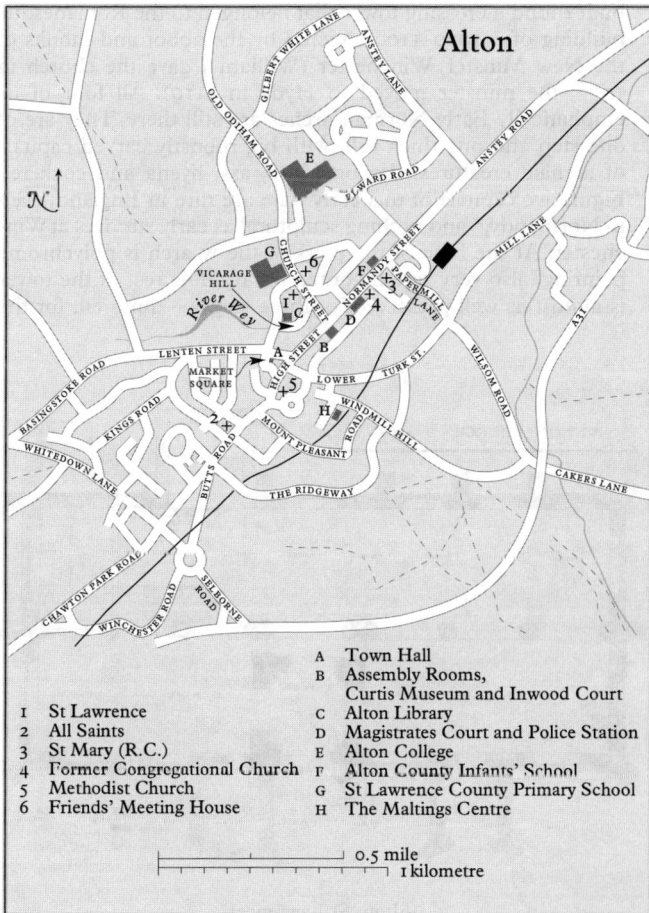

Alton

		A	Town Hall
		B	Assembly Rooms, Curtis Museum and Inwood Court
1	St Lawrence	C	Alton Library
2	All Saints	D	Magistrates Court and Police Station
3	St Mary (R.C.)	E	Alton College
4	Former Congregational Church	F	Alton County Infants' School
5	Methodist Church	G	St Lawrence County Primary School
6	Friends' Meeting House	H	The Maltings Centre

0.5 mile
1 kilometre

archery. Industries included tanning, cloth working and paper making. Brewing was particularly important from the C18. To provide water for milling and industry, ponds were formed by damming the Wey, one of which, King's Pond, survives. Although the railway arrived in 1852, the town did not begin to grow substantially until the very end of the C19. Most of this and subsequent development has been to the N and w.

CHURCHES

ST LAWRENCE, Church Street. An essentially Perp town church, built round a crossing tower that belonged to the Romanesque building of c. 1070–1100, erected by the abbot and monks of the New Minster, Winchester (William I gave the church in 1072; the minster moved to Hyde in 1110). All four of its emphatically Early Norman arches are still there. They are of one step and one thick roll, with big robustly carved capitals of archaic creatures: dragon, dove, ass, hyena and cockerel. Figurative capitals of this early date are rare in England, even in Normandy,* and nothing sculptural as early survives at Winchester. At the base of the piers of the w arch is polychrome painting, also very rare if contemporary. The rest of the tower is almost as well preserved, of three stages – quite tall for the

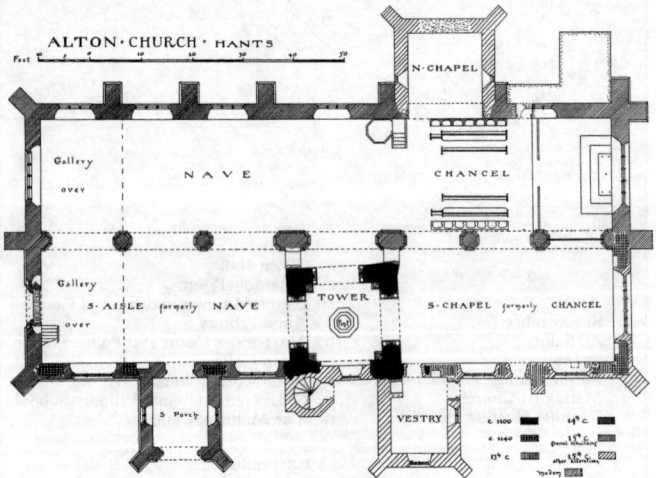

Alton, St Lawrence.
Plan

* Figured capitals of earlier date are found at Ste Trinité, Caen (crypt, c. 1062–72).

ALTON: CHURCHES 121

date, and perhaps modelled on the tower of Winchester's
New Minster but now with a C15 splay-foot spire (originally
leaded, shingled in 1874). The tower now stands in the s aisle;
for in the C15 a new nave and chancel were built to the N of
the previous church (both parts now under one roof of 1724–7)
and at the same time a new s vestry and N chapel were added.
This was probably shortly after 1400 on the evidence of a
corbel bust of Henry IV supporting the chancel roof inside and
the design of its large E window, which is identical to Farnham,
Surrey (probably by *William Wynford*, complete by 1399). This
is of five lights, reinstated in Selborne stone during the restoration of 1867–8 by *Ewan Christian*. s chapel E window with Perp
tracery of rare pattern, especially in the outer lights. This may
have been paid for by Hyde Abbey, Winchester, whose impro-
priation is marked by sculptured croziers inside in the E and
W walls. The former nave was also mostly rebuilt but inside the
s wall are traces of an arcade added *c.* 1140, i.e. remains of pier
imposts, unusually oblong with a band of ornament (cf. Winchester Cathedral Treasury of Henry of Blois, *c.* 1150–60). The
new nave and chancel are pedestrian, rather uniform Perp.
Three-light windows with panel tracery under segmental
arches. W windows of four lights; below that in the s aisle a
(blocked) door with C14 mouldings. s porch of *c.* 1520. The
church is essentially double-aisled, the s aisle as wide as the
nave. One arcade of seven bays the same all the way; octagonal piers, hollow chamfered arches. *Ewan Christian* re-fur-
nished the interior, as usual removing the galleries and box
pews. The nave W gallery remained until the C20.

– FONT. C11, a plain tub (cf. Crondall). Its successor of 1867
by the *Rev. Octavius Hodgson*: under the tower. – ALTAR of 1680
by *Thomas Challoner, Jun.*, lengthened in 1953. – REREDOS. By
Sir Arthur Blomfield, 1895, carved by *T. Nicholls*. It masks the
Minton tile reredos of 1867–9. – COMMUNION RAILS by *Robert
Potter*, 1970, of balusters from a staircase at No. 2 The Close,
Winchester (dem.). – CHOIR STALLS. C15. Commodious, with
seven plain misericords to the seats at the back (only the N
ones seem original). The rest mostly of 1880 by *G. H. Kitchin*
reusing parts of the C15 screen. – PARCLOSE SCREENS between
chancel and s chapel. Only the upper part of that in the E bay
is original C15. Conventional with cinquefoil-headed openings,
those in two W bays by *Kitchin*, 1918. – PULPIT. Outstandingly
fine Late Jacobean, of *c.* 1625, the panels as usual with simple
geometrical arrangements, but in addition detached ornamented columns carrying arches. The canopy, painted underneath by *Joseph Leach*, 1716, is in the tower. – CANDELABRUM.
Under the tower, but originally in the nave. Presented in 1780
by Thomas Baverstock, a brewer. – WALL PAINTINGS (discovered in 1839). On the N face of the second pier from the W,
of *c.* 1500: St Cornelius, C3 papal saint, Henry VI, and an
unidentified archbishop, possibly part of a large scheme. –
ROYAL ARMS of George III (s porch). Bought in 1811. Are they
Coade stone? – STAINED GLASS. Chancel E window, pre-1870

by *Capronnier*. Ascension scene of which the figures alone are preserved in a glaring clear setting of 1952. Tower window, †1857 by *J. Bell* of Bristol. Nave easternmost. By *Heaton, Butler & Bayne*, 1873. Figures of Three Holy Women, light in delicately patterned draperies, against a hedge of dense foliage. In a more pictorial idiom their S chapel E window, 1884, Christ healing at the sea of Galilee. – Chancel N by *Powell & Sons* to the brewer Henry Hall †1899: 'catalogue commercial'. – MONUMENTS. A few small brasses on pillars at the W end, one to a lady of *c.* 1510, effigy 1 ft 6 in. (45 cm.) long, another to three daughters of *c.* 1510. – Richard Clarke †1485, and daughter Margery †1523, wife of Richard Fylder †1534. – Christopher Walaston †1563, Keeper of Royal Goshawks to four Tudor monarchs. Nice Gothic lettered inscription, dated by Cave to 1560. – Several C17–early C19 mural tablets: Hawkins, with a large unfurled scroll. By *M. W. Johnson*, erected 1841. Also by him, a Neo-Tudor tablet to Richard Marshall †1843. – Maria Hall †1906. Inscription and panels in *opus sectile* of virtues, by *Powells* and related to their Henry Hall window. – Edward Hall †1917. Neo-C17 wooden plaque. Can it be Kitchin?

ALL SAINTS, Butts Road. 1873–4 by *F. C. Dyer* of London (contractor, *William Dyer* of Alton). E.E. of Selborne stone with black flints in the buttresses. With a SW porch-tower and spire of 1881. Chancel roof painted by *Hardman*, 1886. Elaborate chancel furnishings: wooden REREDOS by *Reginald Crowley*, 1892, with mosaic by *Ada Currey*, made by *Powells*. – SCREEN, wrought iron, by *Hart, Son & Peard*, 1894. – SCULPTURE at the W end, a stone relief by *Harry Hems*. – STAINED GLASS. In the chancel by *Hardman*, of 1874, to Samuel Wilberforce, bishop of Winchester †1873. In the nave, three S windows, by *Clayton & Bell* (E) and *Hardman* (†1872 and †1890).

Next to the church, the Register Office, built as the SCHOOL in 1876, also by *F. C. Dyer*.

ST MARY (R.C.), Normandy Street. 1966 by *Justin Alleyn* and *P. Durling*. Yellow brick. Low and spreading, with polygonal roof rising in stages to a lantern over the centrally planned interior. – STAINED GLASS. Deep-coloured *dalles-de-verre* by *Fr Charles Norris* of Buckfast Abbey.

FORMER CONGREGATIONAL CHURCH, Normandy Street. 1834–5, by *James Fenton* of Chelmsford. Thin stuccoed Tudor Gothic.

METHODIST CHURCH, Draymans Way. 1979–80 by *John Pantlin*, of brown brick with a steep pyramidal tile roof. Successor to the Wesleyan chapel of 1846 on the High Street, its site occupied by a supermarket.

FRIENDS' MEETING HOUSE. Church Street. The second oldest in England, built in 1672 for £204. Humble, low and long, with a single C18 sash window. Two attached cottages, the N one C18. The meeting room, lined as ashlar inside, has a flat ceiling, with pilaster supporting beams looking C19. Combined oak SCREEN, boldly panelled, and balustraded GALLERY of 1690, introduced to meet expansion soon after the 1689 Act of Toleration. Originally one of a pair (the s gallery removed). Secluded garden BURIAL GROUND at the rear, possibly formed in 1672 (Thomas Bullock, earliest occupant of the older cottage, 'weeded and kept the burial place in order').

PUBLIC BUILDINGS

TOWN HALL, Market Square. A handsome free-standing build-ing of 1813, enlarged in 1840, with an arcaded ground floor (now infilled with shops). Quoins, deep bracketed eaves and clock turret, added as part of its restoration in 1984 by *Richard Ashby Architects*.

ASSEMBLY ROOMS, CURTIS MUSEUM AND INWOOD COURT, Crown Hill (High Street). 1879–80 by *Charles E. Barry*, and a brave attempt to create a civic centre for the town. Buildings are set on three sides of a square open to the High Street, a successful composition, but the style a rather weak High Vic-torian Gothic in red and gault brick with some banded poly-chromy. On the r. the ASSEMBLY ROOMS with a tall window between a pair of square towers with steep pyramidal roofs topped by spired cupolas. The tower parapets, and a Dutch gable between, have been removed. Opposite is the CURTIS MUSEUM, founded by William Curtis, as the Museum, Mechanics Institute and Library, and completing the square the former COTTAGE HOSPITAL (now Inwood Court) with a slender flèche. At the open side of the square, the WAR MEMO-RIAL of 1919 by *B. D. Cancellor*, a beehive-shaped cairn of granite rubble.

ALTON LIBRARY, Vicarage Hill. Opened 2004. By *Hampshire County Architects* (project architect *Martin Hallum*). An intelli-gent design, of tall barn-like form in brick with a steep tiled roof; front elevation pierced by six tall openings with oak louvres, lighting the two principal floors. Low windows under the eaves light the offices.

MAGISTRATES' COURTS AND POLICE STATION, Normandy Street/Orchard Lane. 1976–8 by the *County Architect's Depart-ment*. A complex of low two-storey buildings, in a Late Bru-talist style.

ALTON COLLEGE, Old Odiham Road. The original buildings, of 1978 by the *County Architect's Department* (project architect *Peter Liddiard*), extended in 1984, are built around a series of courtyards. Low-pitched roofs with horizontal boarding to the eaves and clerestories. What impresses, however, is the group to the E set around a quad, of 1989–91 by the *County Archi-tect's Department* (project architects *Colin Stansfield-Smith* and *Peter Hayne*), of white steel frames and white brickwork with curved profiled aluminium roofing. The STEVENS BUILDING (E side), has two parallel low pavilions for teaching and offices, either side of a central open-sided corridor on what was

intended to be a new E–W axis. Covered colonnades link to the
FORUM BUILDING, S, which has a central multi-purpose hall
at right angles to the quad and flanking low wings. Good landscaping, by *Jakobsen Landscape Architects & Urban Designers*,
of tree-lined lawn in the quad and banks enclosing a lower
court to the S. On the W side of the square, a LIBRARY and
I.T. CENTRE, built 2002, in a watered-down version of the
earlier style, by *Baker Consulting Services* of Hartley Wintney,
who also completed a sports hall in the same year. New
entrance and reception to the 1970s buildings, by *Format
Milton Architects*, 1999. Good recent buildings by *Macallan
Penfold Architects* are the Beacon Science Centre 2005, Michael
Gray Building 2006, Berkoff Building 2008 and the Austen
Building 2008. Horizontal boarding, blockwork and curved
metal roofs are prominent.

ALTON COUNTY INFANTS' SCHOOL, Normandy Street.
Former British School of 1866. Gabled, in red and gault brick,
with Gothic windows. Girls' school added *c.* 1877.

ST LAWRENCE COUNTY PRIMARY SCHOOL, Church Street.
Pretty Tudor Gothic National School, of 1840 by *William Dyer*,
extended 1857–8, by *J. Colson*, and later, all in a matching style.

ALTON COMMUNITY HOSPITAL, Chawton Park Road. Site
of the Lord Mayor Treloar Cripples Hospital and College,
founded 1907. The octagonal MUSEUM, built *c.* 1912 by
patients, survives among new housing. In the Millennium
Garden a relocated bust of William Treloar by *Albert Toft*, 1926.

PERAMBULATIONS

The tour begins near the S end of CHURCH STREET with
GEALES' ALMSHOUSES, founded in 1653 by Thomas Geale
J.P., 'a Captain in Cromwell's Army'. A block of four with
doorways grouped in pairs, brick, two-storeyed with restored
mullioned windows. The HIGH STREET starts handsomely
with No. 1 on the S side. Early C18, remodelled *c.* 1770, with
elegant Adamish porch and staircase with scrollwork
balustrade (identical to stair at Will Hall Farm, q.v.). On the
N side, opposite the Assembly Rooms etc. (*see* above), a good
group on a raised pavement. The outstanding houses are No.
4, a mid-C18 remodelling of an older building, of plum-
coloured and red brick, with pedimented doorcase, and the
quite stately early C18 CROWN HOUSE (No. 6). Vitrified and
red brick with string courses and segmental-arched sashes.
Central open-pedimented doorcase with flanking, possibly
later, Venetian windows. Pair of partly tile-hung half-hipped
rear wings. Good interior with much C18 joinery including
square-well staircase with turned balusters and columnar
newels. From here there is a fine view of the street's sinuous
course as it descends to the Wey and rises up the other side.

Alton, former Old George Inn, reconstruction.
Drawing, 2003

The buildings are the usual Hampshire mixture of C18 and C19 brick and stucco with a significant mid-C20 Neo-Georgian contribution and some late C20 redevelopment, much of poor quality. On the r. THE WEY BRIDGE, good infill by *Format Milton Architects*, *c.* 2002. Large brick panel floats over colonnade. An alleyway beside the BAKER'S ARMS (C17 timber frame revealed on its side) leads to KINGDONS YARD, an inventive housing scheme for Downland Housing Society by *Format Architects* of 1994, clearly influenced by C18 industrial buildings and incorporating a surviving building of 1840. The same firm also refurbished and extended Nos. 17–19 High Street in 1995; see the rear wing with serpentine wall, pierced by tall vertical windows and supported on pilotis at the far end. Behind No. 23 High Street is a rare survival, the lodging range of the former Old George Inn, dated to 1501, built by Lord Ormonde. Two-storey and timber-framed with long curved braces, originally with jettied gallery on the courtyard side. There is evidence of former garderobes projecting over the River Wey, which flows along its rear.

The only old inn on the High Street now is the SWAN HOTEL, C18 with mid-C19 addition and alterations of *c.* 1900, the latter including the entrance hall with Neo-Jacobean screen and imperial staircase. Opposite, Nos. 36–42 provide an interesting comparative study of early C20 Banker's Georgian, although No. 40 is essentially the real thing, an early C18 house, remodelled for Lloyds Bank in 1923. As the street narrows again and climbs gently, there are more good C18 houses; first No. 74, *c.* 1740 with a central pediment, its tympanum with plaster cartouche and festoons, and Tuscan doorcase. Then the finest Georgian house in the town, WESTBROOKE HOUSE, also mid-C18, with later additions. Three storeys, red brick and unadorned; the projecting centre marked by a pedimented Ionic doorcase. The interior is particularly distinguished: the staircase has carved brackets, alternating fluted and twisted balusters, and columnar newels; above a fine decorative plaster ceiling. Of special interest are re-set sections of triglyph frieze, [78] in the entrance passage and stair hall, whose metopes depict military trophies and carcasses, a form of incendiary mortar – a motif known elsewhere only from the Great Storehouse at the Tower of London (1688–91 by *Sir Thomas Fitch* and *John Fitch*, burnt down in 1841). Are they part of the fabric said to have been brought here from Hartley Mauditt House (dem. *c.* 1789)? Large early C19 rear wing, probably added when the house became a lunatic asylum. The gardens were made into public gardens; two carved stone female busts are probably early C18 but of uncertain origin; the drinking fountain of *c.* 1880 was removed from in front of the civic buildings in Crown Hill (*see* Public Buildings).

MARKET STREET climbs W to MARKET SQUARE and the Town Hall. CROSS AND PILLORY LANE runs SW back to High Street. On the corner No. 8 with C16 cusped bargeboards and an adjoining timber-framed range with long curved braces. Further on CROSS AND PILLORY HOUSE, 1982 by *Patrick Garnett* of *CGB International*, is a fortress-like development of shops and offices. In the other direction from the square, AMERY STREET runs back down towards the river, past No. 1, late C17 brick with moulded eaves cornice and pedimented doorway. At the bottom of the hill near the headwaters of the Wey a group of C19 workers' cottages, some in rat-trap bond, particularly good Nos. 23–25, with pretty pedimented doors. Finally along LENTEN STREET, which begins at the corner with the former Adlam's Bakery, of *c.* 1900 by *R. A. Crowley* in the Old English style associated with Norman Shaw and extended 1926, by *M. G. Pechell*, in similar style. Further on, WILLIAM CURTIS HOUSE built for Nicholas Gate, a clothier, in 1702. The original five-bay front, with some cross-windows, is now the side elevation, and disfigured by an early C20 addition. Street front extended and remodelled in the late C18 with sashes and a central pedimented doorcase. Original staircase with simple plasterwork ceiling. William Curtis, the botanist, was born here in 1746.

The area S of the High Street has less of interest, although in TURK STREET Nos. 8–9 are cottages formed in the C18 from a hall house of *c.* 1450, of rural rather than urban form, with a fan truss in gable-end. Across the inner ring road is THE MALTINGS CENTRE, a mid-C19 maltings, low and wide with an unusually complex roof structure, converted to a church and community centre 2004–5 by *Format Milton Architects*. Lastly on the r. before the railway bridge, the former SAINT MARY'S HOME, one of the houses of the Anglican Community of Saint Mary the Virgin. The chapel, now offices, is by *W. D. Caröe*, 1913. Perp windows, but an overall cottagey feel with a 'quiet unostentatious beauty'. Simple plastered interior dominated by wide transverse arches supporting the bellcote. Chancel with square-headed sedilia, piscina and aumbry and panelled ceiling with carved bosses. Back to LOWER TURK STREET and the MANOR PARK BREWERY. Established as Hall's Brewery in 1841, one of the town's principal breweries.

Large mid-C19 malthouse on the S side of the road but the brewery rebuilt in 1962. Despite its size, its low-lying location means it is not unduly dominant.

Finally the rest of the town's main street NE of Church Street which begins as NORMANDY STREET. Nos. 7–7a, originally NORMANDY HOUSE, built c. 1840 for Abraham Crowley, brewer, with stucco detail, including a giant order of pilasters flanking the five-bay elevation. Further along, the Neo-Tudor NORMANDY COTTAGE, built in 1869 as almshouses, by Marianna Crowley. Red brick with diaper-work and two steep gables. Frederick Crowley, of the same family, also paid for the National School, now the Infants' School (*see* Public Buildings). Beyond is the ALTON HOUSE HOTEL, a stuccoed early C19 house (converted in 1932, with late C20 additions), with tripartite curved bay windows and a veranda on cast-iron columns. Inside, a groin-vaulted entrance corridor and a late medieval carved fireplace beam reused at the rear. Mid-C19 rusticated stone gatepiers, one with a cast-iron milestone by the *Tasker* foundry of Anna Valley (q.v.). Down PAPER MILL LANE, just before the railway bridge, is ROCK COTTAGE, a C19 single-storey rustic cottage faced in rough malmstone boulders. If Ledoux had built bungalows for the salt workers of Arc-et-Senans they might have looked like this.

The main street continues as ANSTEY ROAD. On the r. the TELEPHONE EXCHANGE, competent Neo-Georgian by the *Office of Works* 1936, and then, some way beyond, set well back and approached by a tree-lined path, is ADAMS HOUSE, the former workhouse of 1793. Brick with a mansard roof and a long front of thirteen bays, the central three breaking forward with pediment and inscribed oval panel. Lastly on the SE side, and once quite remote, are the buildings of EGGAR'S OLD SCHOOL, founded by John Eggar, who left money in his will in 1641 for 'finishing the free schoole', opened in 1642. The original building is brick, of symmetrical lobby-entry plan, the former master's house to the r. and the schoolroom to the l. Mullioned-and-transomed windows with hoodmoulds, and two large gables. C18 and C19 additions including a large wing in matching style to the l. of 1879–80 with a porch at the rear dated 1911. The site has been redeveloped as JOHN EGGAR'S SQUARE, housing by *Format Milton Architects*, completed in 2002.

WILL HALL FARM, 1½ m. W on the Basingstoke Road. Farmstead group centred on a fine c.1770 double-pile HOUSE, the centre marked by a triangular pediment with an *œil de bœuf* window and entrance with pedimented hood. Largely unaltered interior, the staircase with wooden balustrade successfully imitating Rococo ironwork (cf. No. 1 High Street). Impressive range of four early C19 HOP KILNS (converted to housing c. 2005) at the rear, with steeply pitched pyramidal slate roofs. FARM BUILDINGS include a C16 timber-framed aisled BARN (now offices) with curved braces and an early C18 GRANARY on staddle-stones.

ALTON ABBEY *see* BEECH

AMPORT

St Mary. Something almost unique in Hampshire: a Dec church, built *c.* 1320–30, perhaps by the Dean and Canons of Chichester, holders of the advowson from 1217 (by gift of William de St John, son of Adam de Port). The church is cruciform, with long chancel, N vestry – always a sign of consequence – low central tower, transepts and aisleless nave. Much is due to *Slater & Carpenter*'s conscientious and tactful restoration of 1866–7. The N transept and vestry were rebuilt and the nave (much repaired in 1671), almost reinstated and lengthened W by 12 ft (3.7 metres). Good chancel windows, with 30 excellent and unusual Kentish tracery (also occurring in the s transept) of mouchette wheels. Two small, typically Dec, two-light belfry windows and ballflower cornice on the central tower. Crossing arches of two chamfers dying into the imposts. In the chancel, fine SEDILIA and PISCINA, in good order.

Furnishings mostly of 1866–7, especially the elaborate FONT and FONT COVER. – PULPIT by *W. H. Randoll Blacking* and *Robert Potter*, 1951. Gothic, of carved oak, in the Comper tradition. – SCULPTURE. C15 alabaster panel of familiar subjects, heads of St John the Baptist and St Peter (l.), St Katherine and St William of York (r.), Christ rising from the tomb below, two angels above. No structural divisions at all. Little original colour. The panel was discovered in East Cholderton in the blocked chimney of a cottage. – Much STAINED GLASS. Chancel E window *c.* 1866. By whom? Medallions with Nativity, Crucifixion, Ascension scenes in patternwork. – N. Possibly by *Gibbs*, *c.* 1878. – SE. Commemorative date 1878. By *Clayton & Bell*. Rare subject of Jesus and the Pharisees. – By *James Powell & Sons*, the SW chancel †1860, S transept, quarries with C18 continental panels, and Paulet achievement, the N transept N and nave N and S mostly 1867 and 1880 by several designers, *Henry Casolani* (Noli me tangere, Woman at the Well, etc.) and *Henry Holiday* (Christ in the home of Martha and Mary, and Christ with St Mary Magdalene) to Mary, Marchioness of Winchester †1868. – MONUMENTS. Good architectural tablets – John Parke †1753, and John and Mary Duke †1754, both signed by *Leversuch*. – 15th Marquess of Winchester †1899. Large limpid white alabaster tablet by *Sir W. Goscombe John*, 1904. Outside, by the N porch, large railed tomb for the Rev. Thomas Sheppard †1812, founder of the village school.

E is the village green lined with many nice cottages and at the SW corner, the SCHOOL AND ALMSHOUSES erected in 1815 under the will of Rev. Thomas Sheppard. The school, with central open pediment and cupola, is to the fore with the main entrance set in an arch recess in the gable-end to the road. Almshouses above and behind, clearly considered as part of a formal composition with it. Two-storeyed of eight bays with a pediment. THE FIRS, ¼ m. W at the gate of Amport House, has a very fine rear wing of *c.* 1700. This was formerly the main house, reduced from five bays to two in the early C19. Inside, a room with bolection-moulded panelling. Late C18 wing, at right angles. Second floor added 1845 (rainwater head).

AMPORT HOUSE (now Combined Forces Chaplaincy Centre). 1855–7, by *William Burn* in his typical Elizabethan, for John Paulet, 14th Marquess of Winchester. 'Nothing special', was Pevsner's rather harsh verdict. Yellow brick. Symmetrical S front. Two gables and canted bay windows for the end bays, with strapwork crests. Centre with cross-windows and dormers. Asymmetrical E front, the entrance in the short gabled wing to the l., round-arched doorway and Tuscan columned porch with strapwork, and to the r. a large mullioned-and-transomed window. Both this and the W front have four-storey gabled towers at the N end, added in 1902. Compact service courtyard at the rear with two-storey ranges on three sides. Large Lutyensesque wing to the N, of 1998–9, by *Ferguson Mann Architects*. It includes a chapel with the Army Chaplain Memorial, formerly at Bagshot Park, and stained glass by *Henry Haig*. Inside, the best surviving Burn feature is the staircase, its arcaded balustrade with tapered balusters and square newels with pierced scrolly finials. At the top, a delicate ribbed plaster ceiling. Windows with heraldic glass by *Powell & Sons*, 1902; of the same date the Neo-Jacobean-style billiard room. The principal rooms were handsomely remodelled in Neo-Georgian style *c.* 1923, with some genuine C18 fittings introduced, possibly by *Lutyens* who was then at work on the garden. In the entrance hall, eight gorgeous early C18 bird paintings, two at least by *Tobias Stranover*, set in architectural frames and installed in 1928 (there are others in the dining room, possibly by the same artist).

The GARDENS, to the S, were laid out in 1923 by *Lutyens* with *Gertrude Jekyll* (who added the rock garden in 1927). A typically clever exercise in geometry and changing levels. Two broad terraces with an oval pool in the centre of the upper terrace with rills dropping down to the lower terrace and feeding a series of square pools. The E pool is raised above the lower ground level on this side of the garden and surrounded by a stone bench. The garden finishes in a raised walk above a ha-ha. Planned gazebos were never built. Parterre on the W front, with topiary crest and motto of the Marquess, probably 1850s. The entrance GATEPIERS are *Lutyens* too: 'If you don't want to believe that an architect can be monumental and whimsical at the same moment,' wrote Pevsner, 'here is proof, especially in the concave tapering-away bases of his piers. The vertical stone slabs up to the urns are curious too.' Neo-Tudor EAST LODGE of 1871.

Former STABLES, NE; the S range with centrepiece and stone cupola is by *Burn*, the others added later. Opposite the stables, Nos. 1–4 FURZEDOWN LANE by *Lutyens*.

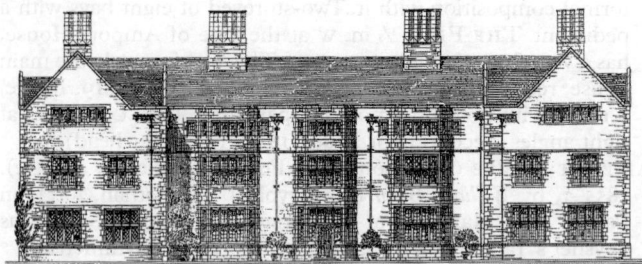

Amport, unbuilt design for Cholderton Lodge
by Gerald Horsley.
Engraving from *The Builder*, 1898

CHOLDERTON PARK HOUSE (formerly Cholderton Lodge),
4 m. wsw. Early c19, red brick with hipped slate roof. Two
storeys, five bays with stone Ionic porch. The rear wings are as
altered, with Neo-Tudor windows, *c.* 1885–90 for Henry
Charles 'Inky' Stephens (of Stephens' Inks), who developed
Cholderton as a model estate. At the E end a Neo-Tudor brick
and flint gun room, possibly by *A.C. Bothams* of Salisbury who
proposed additions in 1914. N, the extraordinary WALLED
GARDEN, probably by *Gerald Horsley*, who designed a number
of the estate buildings and published a scheme for replacing
the house (see *The Builder*, 1898). Of brick but with great buttresses of rubble stone and, as elsewhere on the estate,
uncoursed flint nodules like vermiculated rustication. Inside,
on the N side is a deeply recessed round archway of cyclopean
ashlar, set in a larger panel of rock-faced stonework, the irregular edges between the two emphasizing the massive and
elemental nature of the construction. On the S side the walls
taper towards a deep circular concrete-lined plunge pool,
surrounded by a series of small tanks, presumably for water
plants. SALISBURY LODGE and ANDOVER LODGE are *c.* 1900
by *Crickmay & Sons*, with mullioned windows, Gothic doorways and, at the rear, large roughcast dormers with chimneys
rising through them.

STABLES (Kingsettle Stud), ⅛ m. WNW of the house. Model buildings, *c.* 1900, probably by *Horsley*. The attached cottage, with its large tile-hung gables, soaring chimneys and oriels certainly recalls the Old English of his master Shaw.

At HOME FARM, the interest is in the model FARM BUILDINGS built *c.* 1894 by *Crickmay & Sons*. Showpiece flint N range with elaborately timber-framed entrance with brick-nogging.

ANDOVER*

3040

A small market town on the old Salisbury road, replanned and greatly swollen with London overspill after 1963.

Anglo-Saxon Andover, *Andeferas*, was royal property by the C10.** In 994 King Ethelred sponsored Olaf Tryggvason, first Christian king of Norway, at his confirmation by Bishop Alfege of Winchester in Andover church. The early centre was around this church, on a small hill E of the River Anton at the N end of the present High Street. After the Conquest the church became a priory, owned first by an abbey in Touraine, then after 1413 by Winchester College. A charter was granted by 1175, two hospitals were founded in the C13, and a merchant guild in 1415. Most of the settlement burnt down in 1435, and the oldest surviving buildings date from post-fire reconstruction. The chief industries into the C19 were cloth-based, but coaching and passing trade counted for more. The town centre shifted S from the church over the centuries, and when the London road was turnpiked after 1755 it followed the approach entering the High Street at its S end. But the railways extinguished coaching, and Andover grew comparatively little in the later C19 (4,748 in 1831, 6,509 in 1901).

A fresh chapter began in 1961, when Hampshire County Council and the London County Council became the dominant partners in a town expansion plan. The outline proposals dated from 1955, as part of the strategic decentralization of industry and employment from the capital. When the county subsequently rejected the LCC's New Town plan for Hook, the extension of Andover was a logical fall-back (q.v., and cf. Basingstoke). A Development Plan followed in 1963, by an *LCC* team headed by *John Craig*, working with *T. F. Thomson*, Hampshire County Planning Officer. It proposed a population increase from *c.* 16,000 to 46,000 over twenty years (in 2001 it was some 33,700). Most of the works date from after 1965, when the *Greater London Council* succeeded the LCC. London's architects designed the central precinct and peripheral public housing, Hampshire's the necessary new schools. Other areas were zoned for private houses or industrial estates, the latter on the E and W edges and served by

* Town and secular buildings revised by Simon Bradley.
** Earlier settlement is indicated by two C6–C7 cemeteries excavated E of the present town centre in the C20.

perimeter roads. The planning is compact without crowding, most of the new estates have lasted well, and the skyline of green hills girdling the town has been carefully protected. More destructive architecturally, especially to the E side of town, was the new inner ring road (the W section, following a former railway line, manages better). Redevelopment within this inner ring was concentrated in the NW quarter. Ambitious plans to redevelop areas on the fringes of the centre, including a new leisure and retail development to the NE, were under discussion in 2009.

CHURCHES

ST MARY, Marlborough Street, prominent at the N end of the High Street. A commanding Early Victorian church in the tradition of the greater Commissioners' Churches, set back in a medieval graveyard excellently placed a little above the town. The church stands partly on the site of a large CII–CI4 predecessor (formerly St Peter), which had a massive Early Norman central tower and a broad-aisled nave 76 ft (23 metres) wide. After a late CII grant to the Abbey of St Florent, Saumur, this served as both parish and priory church until the latter's suppression in 1413. Only the fine Norman former W doorway survives, possibly coeval with rebuilding after a fire in 1141, re-erected as a GATEWAY to the churchyard from the street.* Two orders of columns with decorated scallops. Zigzag in the arch, all at right angles to the wall.

The medieval church had become inconvenient by the early CI9. The arcades were altered with smaller columns in 1808 by *Ouzzell & Robinson*, but the nave remained overcrowded with pews. The present CHURCH, begun in 1840, is a remarkable building, quite unconventional in design and plan. It was built at the expense of Rev. William Stanley Goddard, who had retired to Andover from the headmastership of Winchester College in 1809. He died in 1845, aged eighty-eight, just before his church was finished. It opened in 1844 after remedial work following a partial collapse of the nave during construction, and was finally completed including the tower in 1846. The total cost was nearly £30,000, even without the intended spire. Goddard's architect was the little-known *Augustus Frederick Livesay* of Portsmouth (1807–79), the designer of Holy Trinity, Trowbridge, Wilts., and of Newtown church, Isle of Wight. After the structural problems the building was handed over to *Sydney Smirke*, but his creative input can only have been small.

Livesay's church is E.E., as was fashionable *c.* 1840. The difference here is the very close imitation of devices from Salisbury Cathedral, including trefoil-arched corbel courses, and multiple-stepped plinths and set-offs on the aisle buttresses.

* A smaller, Late Norman doorway was transported to Vernham Dean church (q.v.) during rebuilding.

Edward Garbett's church at Theale, Berks. (1820–32) and
G. P. Manners's St Michael, Bath (1834–7) also took their cue
from Salisbury, but most E.E. churches of the period are much
plainer and more economical. The whole is large-scaled and
extremely disciplined, of knapped flint and Caen stone. Tall w
tower, very sheer with no buttress set-offs, tall lancet bell-openings and blank lancets, and high pinnacles. Original clock
roundel; parapet and pinnacles correctly renewed in 1892 by
Ewan Christian. The rest of the church is more unusual: tall
aisles with paired lancets; clerestory; transepts, the N one with
three stepped lancets in the end wall, the S, facing the town
and much showier, with five equal lancets below a 'sham' rose
window in the gable. The triagonal apse appears externally to
be of the full height of the building. Its lower windows have
Geometrical tracery (three unfoiled circles). Small nave S
porch added in 1879, probably by *William White.*

The exterior is impressive enough, the interior is sensational.   99
Very high nave of five bays with an elegant plaster rib-vault.
Tall piers with six attached shafts with shaft-rings and rich
moulded capitals. Rib-vaults too in the aisles, transepts and
chancel chapels. The tower arch is high, but below is a strainer
arch, its lower part a normal arch, its upper part curving
upward. The E end is higher than the apse appears inside, and
most oddly has a stepped five-light window leading into the
space above the apse windows. What was the reason for this
unused space – is it merely a light chamber? The transepts are
only as high as the aisles: another idiosyncrasy. The wall-shafts
of aisles and transepts start from twisted or knotted corbels.
The apse – a stroke of genius – is separated by a screen of three
arches on immensely tall round shafts of cast iron, doubtless
made locally at *Taskers'* Anna Valley Ironworks. The apse itself
has double tracery, i.e. in two layers, the climax of this ingenious and fervent design. The whole interior has a satisfying
unity, with a strict geometrical symmetry, an excitingly uplifting space with a *sursum* recalling Salisbury.

The church was entirely refurnished by *W. White,* 1871. By
him the CHOIR STALLS, attached stone PULPIT of original
design without period precedent, and large marble FONT with
bold wooden COVER. – Nice ANGELS of 1887, designed by
White and carved by *Harry Hems* for the former chancel
screen; relocated successfully in the apse or on stall backs. –
MURAL over the chancel arch, Annunciation, 1891, by *C. G.
Gray.* – Later fittings in the N transept, forming a War Memorial Chapel of 1950 including a TRIPTYCH of Christ in Glory
and a SCREEN by *J. Wippell & Co.* (designer *F. Drury*). – BENE-
FACTIONS BOARDS, S transept. The earlier to Edmund
Wadham, 1692; another up to 1849.

STAINED GLASS. Chancel E windows *c.* 1843, probably by
Wailes. Effectively allied to the architecture. Decorative grisaille
patternwork. N and S chapels E windows *c.* 1850. S chapel S,
1874, good. By *Lavers & Westlake.* S transept E, 1934 by *Edward
Liddell Armitage.* Great S window, 1890 by *Mayer & Co.*

Ambitious and elaborate. N transept E, St Cecilia, 1953 by *Wippell* of Exeter, designer *Arthur F. Erridge*; to Agnes, Augusta and Arthur Bennett (organist and historian of the church). N transept N, c. 1883 by *Mayer & Co*. S aisle, E to W: first, 1876, High Victorian with intricate and colourful scenes in pattern-work; third, 1883 by *Charles Evans*, angels; fourth, 2002 by *Mel Howse*, adventurous: the Tree of Life and the Holy Spirit from Revelation 22. N aisle, E to W: c. 1886 by *Ward & Hughes*, 1884 by *Mayer*, 1923 by *Jones & Willis*, 2008–9 by *Deborah Lowe*, successfully architectonic.

MONUMENTS. Richard Kemys †1611, wife and family. Small figures. He seated frontally holding a skull, the others kneeling against a reredos with inscription and single shields in strapwork. Columns l. and r. – Nicholas Venables (†1598), merchant of London. Rare painted board of 1613, a simulated classical monument. – Richard Venables †1621 and wife. The usual kneelers facing one another. Large figures. Inscription between grotesque dragons. Armorial cartouche in typically Jacobean strapwork. Repainted 1969. – James Walter †1778 and Elizabeth Walter †1799, under the tower. Signed *Coade & Sealy*, 1800. Graceful female mourner by an urn. – S transept and W end, several monuments to Pollens, quite a Pollen count; e.g. Richard Pollen of Rodbourne, Wilts., †1838 (W). Large, austerely classical standing monument with long eulogy. Signed *Gibbs*. Pollen married a daughter of the architect S. P. Cockerell.

WAR MEMORIAL in the churchyard, S. Of 1920, signed *Herbert Cowley*, architect. Square, with Tuscan pilasters. Moved from in front of the Guildhall, 1956. To the NW an ugly CHURCH CENTRE of 1977.

ST MICHAEL, Colebrook Way, off Weyhill Road, 1 m. W. 1962–4 by *Roger Pinckney*. His first church, in a distressingly mundane setting. Brick, cruciform with a tall central spike over the crossing, sheathed in copper like the shallow-pitched roofs. Large-windowed E chapel, transepts and W end. Groups of four narrow windows in the nave. External SCULPTURE in low relief by *Arthur Morgan*, 2004, in panels beneath the E window. Unexpectedly impressive interior, with a strong folded concrete ceiling like a low spreading groin-vault on slender pilotis. Narrow aisles. Broad and spacious open sanctuary with a wide ALTAR, against a slate surround before a raised eastern chapel. Low WEST GALLERY. – Unusual E window of 2004: combined engraved and coloured GLASS with lettering.

ST JOHN BAPTIST (R.C.), Alexandra Road, off Weyhill Road, ½ m. W. 1957–8 by *Potter & Hare*. With slim shaped piers and an undulating timber-slatted ceiling. Completed at the W end by *A. G. Mackman*, 1989–90. – Excitable STAINED GLASS of the large E window by *Paul Jefferies*, with a dramatic Resurrection in deep intense colours, now darkened by trees. Baptistery window of the dedicatory saint. – The PRESBYTERY, r., occupies South Croye, a house of 1924 by *Edward Maufe*.

Tiled gambrel storey above, rendering below: a baby brother to his Andover Hospital (p. 136).

METHODIST CHURCH, Bridge Street. Undistinguished Perp of 1905–6 by *Gordon & Gunton*. Without a tower, but with a shallow but tall porch to the street. Inexpensive in flint, it cost £3,600 (Kelly).

UNITED REFORMED CHURCH (formerly Congregational), East Street. C18, enlarged in 1839 with a neat rendered classical façade set back from the street. Three bays, one-bay pediment, broad Doric doorway, and a Venetian window over. – CURIO-SUM. A miniature earthenware font, one of many models of the famous late C14 font of St Mary Magdalene, Oxford, prob-ably 1840s. – Outside, a mid-C19 TABLET to relations of the ironmaster Robert Tasker, with a simple pedimented frame.

BAPTIST CHURCH, Charlton Road, ½ m. NW. By *James & Kearns*, 1980. Barn-like, of brown brick. Perforated end wall displaying STAINED GLASS from the rose window of its High Street predecessor (1866 by *C.C. Searle*).

SALVATION ARMY (formerly Methodist), Winchester Street. A plain but handsome three-bay chapel of 1824. Tall round-headed windows in relieving arches.

CEMETERY, N of St Mary. Crisply detailed Gothic CHAPEL, in flint, mostly E.E.; disused. Built for Nonconformists, not long after 1869. By *William White*?

PUBLIC BUILDINGS

GUILDHALL, High Street. An excellent building of 1825–6, free-standing and overlooking the market place from the N. Designed by *John Langdon*, a London builder-architect (mason *William Gibbs*). Bath stone ashlar, five bays. Rusticated arches below in the Palladian way, but Greek Doric columns to the attached portico of the hall storey. Wreaths in the frieze. The weathervane above the pediment is from a clock turret, removed 1904.* Pilasters – more properly, antae – on the sides. Behind, a single-storey and pedimented projection, given back its odd-looking original form in *Brandt Potter*'s restoration of 1980–1. It houses twin swept-ended staircases up to a half-landing, from which a single flight ascends to the COUNCIL CHAMBER. Later C19 Tudorish plasterwork fills the Georgian anthemion border of the ceiling here. The ground floor was open for market use until 1846, as at the predecessor buildings (1724, 1583).

---

* A presentation drawing preserved inside shows three unexecuted classical reliefs below the S windows.

COUNCIL OFFICES, Weyhill Road, ⅔ m. w. By the *Cheshire Robbins Design Group*. Of 1989–92, i.e. near the zenith of anti-Modernism and anti-monumentality, with a corresponding tendency to over-compensate. Gables, and much visible roof-slope. Low square towers at the inner corners and flanking the portal. Materials include hand-made brick and tile, dark-framed panelling reminiscent of timbering, and varicoloured rendering. Circulation is by a glazed lean-to corridor around the courtyard. – SCULPTURE in the roadway in front, Tritree, 2003 by *David Booth*. Painted metal.

COURT HOUSE, CRICKLADE COLLEGE, and SPORTS CENTRE, N of West Street. A planned group within the town's NW quarter, by the *GLC Architects' Department*, 1972–6. The shared motif is yellow brick facing with vertical ridges. The college (N; future uncertain) was said to be the country's first purpose-built 'tertiary', combining sixth-form, technical and adult education. Nicely planned around small court-yards, with round-ended staircase enclosures protruding. The sports centre (SE), in two parts, has projections of smoked glass.

POLICE STATION, South Street. By *Simpson Low*, County Architect, 1958–9. Like a longhouse, with pantiles. Slightly twee for its purpose.

TELEPHONE EXCHANGE, Suffolk Road. 1939, yet still sincerely Lutyens-Wrenaissance. Brutalist extension, *c.* 1970.

LIBRARY, Chantry Centre. *See* p. 138.

MUSEUM, Church Close. *See* Perambulation 2, p. 141.

(HARROW WAY COMMUNITY SCHOOL, Harrow Way, 1 m. NW. Of 1966, the earliest new secondary school for the expanded town. By *Hampshire County Architects*.)

(JOHN HANSON COMMUNITY SCHOOL, Floral Way, 1½ m. SW. By *Hampshire Architects*, 2000–2. Brick-faced.)

ROOKWOOD SCHOOL, Weyhill Road, ⅔ m. w. In a small mid-C19 villa (No. 35) with non-balancing extensions. Framed by inward-looking lodges with Gothicky windows.

WINTON SECONDARY SCHOOL, London Road, ½ m. E. Its core is a girls' school of 1937–9, orthodox brick; by *A.L. Roberts*, County Architect. *Plincke, Leaman & Browning*'s wilder and brighter additions of 1987–91 include a sports hall with the framing of its huge pitched roof grounded like the guy-ropes of a tent.

PRIMARY SCHOOL (C. of E.), East Street. A well-preserved former National School group (girls, boys, infants, teachers' houses), 1859–60. By *William White*, and thoroughly Butterfieldian in its simple pointed openings and stratified polychrome brick. Extensions in similar brickwork: 1903 (NE), and late C20 (S, with twin glazed-gabled roofs).

ANDOVER HOSPITAL, Charlton Road, ¾ m. NW. A war memorial initiative of 1925–6, designed by *Edward Maufe & Leslie T. Moore*. White-rendered, low and domesticated. Steep bell-cast roof, swelling into a dormer storey on the main axis. Postwar additions, e.g. the little octagonal summerhouses in front.

Andover

K

CHARLTON ROAD

ARTISTS WAY

NORTHERN AVENUE

SHEPHERD'S SPRING LANE

NEW STREET

M

STATION APPROACH

JUNCTION ROAD

+ 6

River Anton

MARLBOROUGH STREET

CHURCH CL.

+ 8

1 +

WESTERN AVENUE

E

C

D

WEST STREET

CHANTRY STREET

PORTLAND GROVE

HIGH STREET

UNION ST.

EAST ST.

J

+ 5

L

+ 3

ALEXANDRA RD.

A

4 +

LONDON AVENUE

EASTERN AVENUE

2 +

H

WEYHILL ROAD

BRIDGE STREET

LONDON STREET

B

SALISBURY ROAD

G

F

7 +

WINCHESTER STREET

SUFFOLK ROAD

SOUTH STREET

WINCHESTER ROAD

N

A	Guildhall		
B	Council Offices		
C	Court House		
D	Sports Centre		
E	Cricklade College	1	St Mary
F	Police Station	2	St Michael
G	Telephone Exchange	3	St John Baptist (R.C.)
H	Rookwood School	4	Methodist Church
J	Primary School	5	United Reformed Church
K	Hospital	6	Baptist Church
L	Workhouse (former)	7	Salvation Army
M	Railway Station	8	Cemetery

0.5 mile

1 kilometre

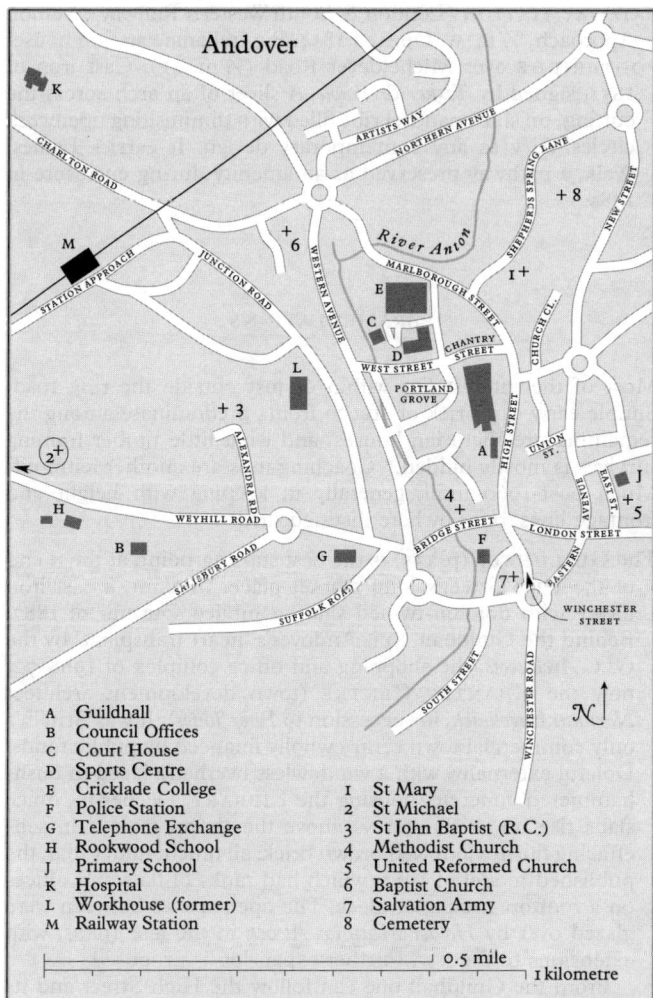

WORKHOUSE (former), now The Cloisters, Junction Road. ⅓ m.
w. Built in 1836 to one of *Sampson Kempthorne*'s standard
cruciform plans; converted for housing c. 1998. Central offices
of nine bays and two storeys, larger than at Kempthorne's
earliest workhouse designs (e.g. Hastings). Red brick, rendered
for the ground floor. Three-bay pedimental gable. Side ranges
for males (N) and females (S), taller but more rawly treated.
A transverse range behind, not quite touching these side
ranges. Rear wings that completed the cross-plan layout have
been demolished. The scandalous maltreatment of inmates
here ultimately led to the abolition in 1847 of the entire Poor
Law Commission. Later in hospital use; hence the block dated
1934, SW.

RAILWAY STATION (London & South Western Railway), Station
    Approach, ⅔ m. W. Opened 1854. Big Italianate station house.
FOOTBRIDGE over Micheldever Road (¾ m. SE). Cast iron of
    1851, signed by *Tasker & Fowle*. A sliver of an arch across the
    cutting, on slim spandrel ribs filled with diminishing openwork
    circles. Airy as any contemporary design. It carries Ladies'
    Walk, a pathway preserved as an amenity during enclosure in
    1785.

PERAMBULATIONS

Most of the interest lies within or just outside the ring road.
Simple early C19 brick or stucco fronts predominate among the
remaining pre-Victorian houses, and what little timber framing
survives is mostly hidden.* Coaching inns are another leitmotif.
Much post-1960 infill, generally in keeping with height and
frontage lines, but nowhere distinguished.

The GUILDHALL (p. 135) is the best starting-point, at the N end
    of the High Street's long market place. In front, a cast-iron
    LAMP with dolphin-twined shaft, a Jubilee souvenir of 1887.
    Behind the Guildhall, N, is Andover's 'heart transplant' by the
    GLC Architects, the shopping and office complex of 1968–72,
    now the CHANTRY CENTRE (town development architect
    Norman Engelback, in succession to *Peter Jones*). It was Britain's
    only commercial town centre wholly financed by public funds.
    Doleful externally, with a windowless overhang faced in bush-
    hammered concrete, housing the LIBRARY. Deeper in, office
    slabs rise up to six storeys above the shops, treated in self-
    effacing flush-windowed brown brick: all much milder than the
    published model of 1961, which had ranks of flats and offices
    on a rooftop circulation deck. The open spaces between were
    glazed over by *Holder Matthias Alcock* in the late 1980s, with
    extensions to the NW. Further expansion is proposed.
        From the Guildhall one can follow the High Street and its
    tributaries, S or N.

1. South of the Guildhall

The HIGH STREET, now pedestrianized, reflects the familiar
    medieval plan of narrow-fronted burgage plots with side alleys.
    The S part starts on the W side with No. 35, rectilinear early
    C19 brick. On the E side and also facing the Guildhall, No. 32,
    a solicitor's house refronted in the same period. Convex front,
    Gothick iron balcony. No. 26 has the stilted- or shouldered-
    arched windows of *c.* 1875; No. 24 is an early C19 front with
    the splay-sided surrounds sometimes taken for Egyptian.

*For more on the older houses *see* Diana K. Coldicott, *Elizabethan Andover* (2004).

LLOYDS BANK, No. 22, is a part-rebuild of 1919–21 by *Horace Field*: a five-bay stone front of Gibbsian-Palladian descent. Back on the W side, No. 23, THE GLOBE, Late Georgian in front with a neat first-floor bow. Through its carriage arch, a long rear range with stables, ending in a mid-C19 cross-range with another carriage arch. This housed a modest assembly room above, with a Venetian window, and a separate entrance on the l. At No. 19 a replica façade, *c.* 1970 (originally *c.* 1830): giant pilasters, wreaths in the frieze. Then on the E side an alley by No. 16 leads to the GEORGE HOTEL, a modest Georgian muddle. Part of the original timber-framed street range appears next to it. In the pavement in front, historical MOSAIC by *Alan Potter*, 1998. BARCLAYS BANK (No. 5, W side), originally Lloyds, is another Neo-Early Georgian essay, 1915 by *Horace Field & Simmons*, then No. 3, blazing High Victorian red brick. The humble No. 1, partly C16 but altered, has a nice later C19 shopfront curving round the S corner. At No. 6 (E side), C16 timber framing is exposed on the alley side. No. 2 is the DANEBURY HOTEL (formerly Star and Garter), a showpiece from the late stagecoach age. Spacious stuccoed frontage of *c.* 1830: five bays, three storeys, the end bays with shallow, wide, bowed oriels. Broad Greek Doric porch, not quite central. Its anthemion-pattern balcony carries on under the flanking windows. The rear wall indicates a mid-Georgian core.

Closing the S side of the High Street market place is BRIDGE STREET, here mid-Victorian or early C19. Going W, No. 6 (N side), also early C19, has first-floor windows under blind arcading. The front of the WHITE HART HOTEL at No. 12 looks *c.* 1840–50. Red brick, four bays, two-and-a-half storeys, with an encrusted Ionic doorcase and a sculpted hart on the parapet. Facing, BRIDGE HOUSE, stern Neo-Georgian municipal offices of 1935. The N side continues with the Methodist church (p. 135), by the River Anton. A path leads N here to the TOWN MILL, now a pub. A modest two-storey example, externally quite well preserved. Plaques tell of rebuilding: the house part, r., in 1753 (by the Hon. John Griffin Griffin; bailiff, John Pugh), the l. part, in line, 1764 (by *John Gibbs*, millwright), the N extension 1982. To the E, a small bronze SCULPTURE of goats by *Claire Norrington*, *c.* 2000. Looming up in the small park beyond is HAMBLEDEN HOUSE, the biggest office block to invade Andover's historic core. By *Syborn & Atkinson* for the Hospital Saving Association, built 1980–2. L-plan. Ribbed brick above mock-ironstone fibreglass panels.

Continuing W along Bridge Street, a red brick POST OFFICE next, no showpiece (1913). Nos. 34–40, early C19 with late C19 shopfronts rammed in, preserves two fat domestic bows on the r. flank. Beyond the ring road the STATION HOTEL: white and low, five bays, Tuscan porch. It was built alongside the basin of the long-lost Andover and Redbridge Canal, opened to Southampton in 1796 but infilled in 1858–65 for a now defunct railway. Flint-and-brick stable block behind.

Back to the s end of High Street. WINCHESTER STREET, running s alongside No. 1 Bridge Street, is early C19 on its w side (Nos. 4–12). Ahead, isolated by road widening and set about by late C20 office pavilions, the LAMB INN, late C16 or early C17 with timber framing exposed in the N wall, and the Salvation Army's chapel (p. 135). Then back N, to the E continuation of Bridge Street, LONDON STREET. On the s side the FORESTER'S ARMS, in origin C18 or earlier and nicely irregular. Nos. 31–33 (N side), red brick dated 1846, housed Messrs Heath, bankers and brewers. Off-centre doorway, showing Georgian symmetry dissolving. Over it a carved royal arms, and a sundial with the helpful reminder, '6 Min Faster for London Time'. The early C19 pair at No. 41 is extraordinarily sparsely windowed, with much plain wall: strangely like the later C20 Neo-Georgian of Raymond Erith. Pedimented doorcases. Set back on the s side, No. 10, a pub of c. 1983 replicating an early C19 building here. Two bows, curved porch, Venetian window over. Next door is the former SAVOY CINEMA, 1938 by F. Henshaw, of the blockish, non-jazz brick type. Nos. 14 and 16, r., simple early C19 stucco; a garden wall behind shows flint, brick and chalk cob. Just across the ring road, No. 22, the former King's Head pub, 1923 by B.D. Cancellor. A charming and thoughtful Arts and Crafts design, with an unexpected entrance loggia and timber-framed gables.

2. North of the Guildhall

The N part of the HIGH STREET seems to have little at first, but keeps more from the timber-framing centuries. The nondescript-fronted Nos. 64 and 66 frame BLACK SWAN YARD, with parts of the inn of that name. No. 66, N, formed a solar cross-wing to a now-lost hall part. It dates probably from soon after the town fire of 1435. No. 64 is more likely C16–C17. Nos. 74–80, early C19, in two groups. No. 84 retains a lower timber-framed rear wing, restored in 1987. Jettied, with large panel framing; probably mid-C16.

On the w side, Nos. 89–93 look late C18, red brick with a delicate cornice. The façade treatment continues across the ANGEL INN at No. 95, with a pedimental gable and Venetian window riding over its carriage entrance. To the r. a ground-floor Venetian window, with side recesses for sliding shutters. Much remains of the medieval inn behind, an exceptionally well-documented commission of 1445–53 for the Winchester College estate. Despite partial demolition, it is Hampshire's best surviving medieval inn. On the N side of the courtyard a lodging range, the square-panel framing exposed along its upper floor. The gatehouse is also original, in tile-hung disguise. To its s, the former hall part (with a scissor-braced roof of so-called jointed cruck type). The whole was of courtyard plan, from which a mid-C15 cellar survives under No. 89. The inn's contracting carpenters were *John Harding* and *Richard*

Holnerst or *Holnhurst*, who seems to have done the work, subject to advice from the king's carpenter at Eton. Also of the mid-C15 rebuilding, but masked by painted brick, No. 90 (E side). Three bays, parallel to the street. Next to it the reused arch to the churchyard. Minor houses follow, e.g. Nos. 94–96, early C19 brick. Also the reassembled Ford Cottage, a timber-framed C17 lobby-entry house moved from Chantry Street in 2009.

The E parts of the town are reached from the High Street via NEWBURY STREET, alongside No. 84. Boxy, austere Neoclassical houses at Nos. 4 and 6, s side. No. 8 (the Old Vicarage), detached and stuccoed, has a Greek Ionic porch to match No. 4, but the steep pediment and segment-headed windows mark it as Early Georgian. Expansive 2–5–2-bay composition; compact, curving Late Georgian staircase. It faces the original New Street, now by-passed and renamed CHURCH CLOSE. No. 4 here is C18 with a later C18 doorcase, No. 6 (now the MUSEUM) has a three-bay later C18 front of red brick and is larger behind. Between them the former Grammar School, tall, triple-gabled and artlessly plain. By *Alfred Purkess*, 1888. In 1986 reconstructed by *Burford, Marlow & Carden* as an Iron Age museum, including displays of finds from Danebury (q.v.). On the other side, late C18 GATEPIERS now give entry only to the little HARRIS HALL (Boys' Brigade), 1991, with a glazed roof ridge.

The E end of Newbury Street runs into EAST STREET, originally the back lane to the High Street, but here subsumed into the ring road. Older buildings survive on the E side, conspicuously the United Reformed church (p. 135). To its N the ACRE ALMSHOUSES, harshly rebuilt in 1869, a red brick slab with yellow quoins. To its s a run of older houses, beginning with No. 54, *c.* 1741. Four bays, chequer brick. Rubbed lintels, modillion frieze under the eaves. Finer is Nos. 36–38, a single early or mid-C18 house of six bays. Its ground floor has a moulded brick frieze, and the blind window over the original doorway has a raised brick surround. A wilderness of car parks opposite, where a *GLC* pedestrian shopping alley (UNION STREET), built in 1968 for traders displaced by other clearances, reaches out optimistically. Redevelopment is proposed here.

Now back to the N end of the High Street, and w into CHANTRY STREET. Nos. 11–15, timber-framed and jettied on curved brackets, is a subdivided mid-C15 house of Wealden type, i.e. with two-storey parlour and service ends. In the C16 a chimney was inserted in the hall between, making a hearth-passage plan. Later additions behind. Restored 1987–8 for the Hampshire Buildings Trust. (One moulded plaster ceiling with fleurs-de-lys, *c.* 1600.) No. 17, C17, has twin C18 shopfronts, nicely wonky. Chantry Street continues w with ANTON HOUSE, big yellow brick offices by the *Sawyer Partnership*. Designed 1983 for A.M.F. Legg, tobacco manufacturers. Canted details, as if to distinguish it from the Cricklade complex beyond (p. 136).

A large mixed-use development is intended to the w. Off West
Street, a little to the sw, PORTLAND GROVE, rebuilt as conventional municipal housing c. 1938.

Finally up MARLBOROUGH STREET, N of High Street and in
line with it. First THE LODGE, apparently once belonging with
the cemetery behind (p. 135). Small, taut, upright Gothic in
flint and stone with shouldered-arched windows, dated 1867.
Nos. 8–10, the former Pollen's School and master's house of
1872, take their cue from POLLEN'S ALMSHOUSES beyond,
radically restored in the same year. Flint with brick dressing
and lacing, with a dormer storey. Founded 1686, but only the
chimneys of the l. part remain visible of that time. They group
beautifully with the church tower. Beyond, No. 24, late C18
with a half-hipped roof. It goes with a former TANNERY
behind, one of the largest chalk cob buildings in Hampshire.
(Nine bays, defined by unusual internal buttresses supporting
the roof-truss ends.) Before that, SHEPHERDS SPRING LANE
leads off r. The surprise here is the INFORMATION PRO-
CESSING CENTRE of 1989 by *Leslie Jones*, an enigmatic High
Tech machine-building for the Trustee Savings Bank. A low,
largely windowless block clad in silvery metal panels, with
primary-coloured highlights – yellow and blue – or chrome
plating where the services are expressed. Porthole or round-
sided openings, set flush. The treatment is close to some early
works by Nicholas Grimshaw. To the w, masked by trees,
CHARLTON PLACE (LLOYDS TSB), a very large landscaped
office complex, c. 1990 onwards. Postmodern detailing under
broad, spreading Frank Lloyd Wright-ish roofs in a double-
deck configuration. Architects *Innerdale Hudson*.

HOUSING ESTATES

Public housing by the *London County Council Architects* and their
Greater London Council successors, to a total of 2,700 dwellings,
forms the N, E and SW districts of the expanded town. The estates
mostly have perimeter or spine roads, densely clustered two-
storey brick housing, and separate pedestrian pathways on the
Radburn principle. It is a similar recipe to the contemporary and
rather larger LCC and GLC estates in Basingstoke (cf. also Farnborough), but with greater variety of house and plan type. A more
developed sense of place resulted, since eroded a little by rebuilding here and there.

The earliest estate is FLORAL WAY, sw, completed 1964–5.
Slightly later are ADMIRALS WAY, E, and CRICKETERS WAY,
NE, completed 1968–9, now with pitched roofs added. Front
doors here face each other across rectangular pedestrian
streets. To the s of Cricketers Way are RIVER WAY (completed
1967, a variant of Floral Way) and PILGRIMS WAY, both with
original split-pitch roofs. The latter uses the panel-built Anglia

system, under which only conventional isolated blocks were possible. Further N is ROMAN WAY, designed from 1968 and built 1972–7. It shares with Pilgrims Way the motif of asbestos-slate-hung upper walls (partly stripped in the 1980s), but its plan is less conventional, with a green spine of trees and grass rambling N–S between the buildings. At KING ARTHUR'S WAY on the opposite, W side of Newbury Road, designed 1966–8 and completed 1972, the parking is more closely integrated: a retreat from the more expansive Radburn model. The densely planned core has deck-access flats rising from a D-shaped podium, with shops over underground garaging. Otherwise patio housing, also built out over garages. Across the River Anton to its SE is ARTISTS WAY, later, looser and less dog-matic, showing the informal landscaping to advantage.

OTHER OUTLYING BUILDINGS

Described clockwise, from E to W. For churches and public build-ings see pp. 132–8.

TWINING'S factory and warehouse, South Way, Walworth Industrial Estate, 1¼ m. E. Designed and built by *IDC Ltd* of Stratford-on-Avon, 1966–7. With a high slab glazed on one side, a rare upright accent in this low-rise town.

EASTFIELD HOUSE, Eastfield Close, N of London Road, ⅓ m. SE. A consequential stone-faced villa of *c.* 1860. Belvedere tower, round-arched porch.

WOLVERSDENE HOUSE, Dene Road and Love Lane, ⅓ m. S. A large and puzzling Late Georgian mansion, now a clubhouse. Is the big canted-ended E projection later than the main, N front?

ROOKSBURY MILL, Rooksbury Road, ¾ m. SW. First recorded in the mid C15. The present buildings C18, with a later tower. C18 GAZEBO.

ANTON ARMS, Salisbury Road, 1 m. SW. 1937, Modern Dutch brick, with a round-ended middle.

SCULPTURE, Weyhill Road, ½ m. W, corner with Salisbury Road. Walking Man, by *Claire Norrington*, 2000. He brandishes a gar-landed sundial.

DEFENCE LOGISTIC ORGANIZATION, Monxton Road, 2¼ m. W (just outside the town boundary). On the N side a large complex designed by *Capita Symonds*, 2000–2, one of the better Private Finance Initiative jobs. The office range long and low, three-storeyed, with storey bands of cream terracotta tiles broken three times by staircase projections faced in cedarwood strips. At the W end a big bulging module with zinc facing. Other blocks with flattened butterfly roofs. Dismal early 1990s blocks on the S side, also at least one interwar building left from the important RAF establishment here (1917–76).

HOCKNEY GREEN, ⅜ m. NNW, Artists Way. A short terrace of 'eco-housing' by *Zedfactory*, 2005–7, on the BedZED model developed by *Bill Dunster Architects*. The glazed full-height wall exploits solar gain. Wind cowls on the roof for natural ventilation. Other energy-saving features can be installed by individual householders: extra photovoltaic panels, boilers fired by wood pellets, etc.

6050

ANDWELL

ANDWELL PRIORY. Established early in the C12 after Adam de Port of Mapledurwell granted land to the Benedictine Abbey of Tiron. This was a prior's residence, rather than a monastery, with a chapel, hall, chamber and gatehouse. Sequestered by the crown in 1368 and acquired by William of Wykeham in 1391 to endow his new college at Winchester. Not much remains but the courtyard plan is still evident with fragments of flint walls on two sides. Of the chapel (dedicated to St John Baptist) on the N side, only sections of the S and W walls survive as garden walls. Before 1912 there was enough to see it was a simple two-cell structure of the C12, with inserted C13 and C14 windows. On the W side a C14 building (E and N walls), probably a chamber block, converted after 1391 into a hall. Two good chamfered-arched doorways and two small rectangular windows lighting the first floor. Corbels presumably supported a pentice. The smoke-blackened roof survives, of four-and-a-half bays, so probably truncated. It originally had arch-braced collars but was altered, presumably in the C17 when a first floor was reinserted. The W wall of this block was rebuilt in the early C19 and now forms part of the rear service wing of a brick farmhouse of that date. The pretty Gothic casements and porch are no doubt a concession to the antiquity of the site.

Wykeham's investment is evident in the quality of his farm buildings. These include a fine timber-framed STABLE range and aisled BARN. Both have queen-strut, clasped purlin roofs of *c.* 1450–1550 but with C17 additions and alterations.

3040

ANNA VALLEY
Upper Clatford

p. 65   The site of the famous iron works (later the Waterloo Ironworks) established in 1813 on the Pillhill Brook by Robert Tasker, the Abbotts Ann blacksmith, and his brother William. They had a wharf on the Andover Canal at Upper Clatford. Opposite the MONUMENT in Foundry Road, the former WORKMEN'S HALL, dated 1867, its porch with original cast-iron windows.

w is BROOKSIDE, built in 1834 for William Tasker, stuccoed and slated, informally fenestrated. Inside, a late C19 staircase with Old Testament verses painted on the elliptical arch at its foot. E is the so-called TASKER'S ARCH of 1836: a pair of single-storey lodges for school (l.) and schoolmistress's house (r.), flanking a segmental-arched entrance with a 'handsome room' above. Pretty Tudor-arched cast-iron casements with flint-vermiculated surrounds. The schoolroom doubled as a chapel on Sundays and the archway served the drive to Clatford Lodge (dem.), built 1834 by *Robert Tasker* for himself, and ST VINCENTS which he built for his successor George Fowle in 1836.

Nos. 1–14, WATERLOO TERRACE, ¼ m. E, are the last surviving early C19 workers' cottages, although altered. Thin pilaster strips with stone capitals.

APPLESHAW

ST PETER. At the N end of the long straggling village. 1830–1 by *T. M. Shurmer* of Andover, essentially a remodelling and enlargement of the medieval chapel. Stunted W tower (spire removed in the 1930s) with thin angle buttresses and pinnacles, large W window with intersecting tracery. Long aisleless nave and chancel in one. Lower transepts, probably of 1831. Attractive interior with plain segmental plaster tunnel-vault all along nave and chancel and pointed tunnel-vaults for the transepts. Restored in 1974–5 by *Kenneth Wiltshire*; ambones at the entrance to the chancel and W gallery rebuilt. – FONT. Arcaded E.E.; from Andover St Mary, no doubt by *Livesay*, 1844. – Painted ROYAL ARMS, 1831. – STAINED GLASS. Lurid decorative glazing of 1831 in the chancel and N transept N windows. – E window (Ascension) of 1952 by *G. B. Cooper Abbs* of *Wippell & Co.*

N is the MANOR HOUSE, in its own park. Early C19 stuccoed villa with bow windows. The front of its lodge is a half-octagon with a fish-scale slate roof supported on slender wooden posts.

Halfway down the W side of the long, narrow green is the OLD VICARAGE. C18, painted brick. Seven bays, the wider centre slightly projecting with a steep pediment (added *c.* 1865). Curved columned porch with Venetian window above. The rear belies the symmetry of the front: to the l. three large sashes, to the r. a Venetian stair window

HILL HOUSE, ¼ m. S. The pretty pilastered doorcase with Adamish decoration is late C18, the rest possibly earlier. Red brick with hipped roof, stuccoed string course and moulded eaves cornice. Five bays with a pediment over the slightly projecting three-bay centre. In it an oculus. Segmental-headed windows with stuccoed keystones. Service wing of *c.* 1830: square knapped flint with brick diapering. Cast-iron casements.

½ m. s towards Ragged Appleshaw, two other good late C18 houses: APPLESHAW HOUSE is of red brick, hipped roof. Two storeys, the windows arranged 2–1–2. Doorway with narrow sidelights and elliptical-arched fanlight. Curved porch with tall Tuscan columns. MEAD HOUSE, also of five bays, the centre slightly projecting, has header bond brickwork. Windows have stone segmental-arched heads with keystones. Tuscan doorcase with intersecting tracery in the overlight.

REDENHAM HOUSE, ⅝ m. WNW in a park. Stately, ashlar-faced house, built for Walter Holt in 1784. Two storeys. Five by seven bays. Parapet with pineapples at the corners and an entrance porch of paired Greek Ionic columns. Lower stuccoed service wing. Very good interior. Grand staircase, rising in one flight and returning in two; its stick balustrade replaced by *Colefax & Fowler*, *c.* 1969–70. Fine ceiling with mutule cornice, coffering, a band of Vitruvian scroll and a central wreath of scrolled plasterwork. The principal rooms with restrained Neoclassical ornament and good marble chimneypieces. One bedroom decorated with C18 prints, including Hogarth's Marriage à la Mode and various hunting scenes.

The EAST LODGE is late C19 but its conception – octagonal with a veranda and pyramidal roof with central chimney – is Picturesque in feeling and probably inspired by the rustic late C18 LODGE at PARK FARM, NW of the house. In the back garden, a late C19 octagonal brick DAIRY. N, the STABLES are 1913. Single-storey. The principal range brick and flint with central-pyramidal-roofed bellcote, the clock inscribed: 'Duty to God, Duty to Country and to King, Duty to Self, these will contentment bring.'

5040

ASHE

A tiny settlement, close to the source of the Test.

HOLY TRINITY AND ST ANDREW. 1877–8 by *G. G. Scott Jun.* Small, of flint and stone. Thin shingled bell-turret with tall pyramidal spire. Nave, lower chancel with N vestry. Timber s porch. Dec details throughout. The fine large E window with a large central quatrefoil (*c.* 1320–40, cf. Amport) is reused from the previous church. Harmonious interior, roofed and richly furnished in oak throughout; four timber posts support the belfry in typical rustic Hampshire fashion. Romanesque PILLAR PISCINA, of *c.* 1120. Small parts of the chancel screen are evidently Perp. ALTAR with an elaborate front of interlacing tracery by *Kempe*. – PULPIT, with brass candleholders. Full set of PEWS, the foremost with angel finials carving by *Farmer & Brindley*. – WALL PAINTING, over the font, of 1887 by *C. Godfrey Gray* (lower half restored 1981). Of his diaper pattern scheme in the chancel, only Gothic lettering survives. – STAINED GLASS. A rare complete uniform scheme of 1878 by *Kempe*. Only the E window is pictorial, the rest mostly grisaille. Inappropriate nave S window of 1919 by *Heaton, Butler & Bayne*. – MONUMENT. The Rev. Isaac P. G. Lefroy †1806, rector, with his wife, a friend of Jane Austen. Austere Neoclassical tablet by *Gibbs* of Basingstoke. – Sturdy timber LYCH-GATE by *Scott Jun.*

ASHE HOUSE, S of the church. Former rectory of *c.* 1780. Brick, of 2–1–2 bays with wooden dentil cornice and parapet. Central pediment and entrance with wide wreathed fanlight. ASHE COURT, NW, was its successor: by *B.D. Cancellor*, 1907.

(ASHE PARK, 1 m. S. Red brick with gault dressings. Built 1865 for Lt-Col. R. Portal, in the 'French Style' (Kelly). Roof removed after a fire in 1937, Georgianized post-war with 1960s wings and roof restored in 1990s. Nice Arts and Crafts coachhouse and cottage of *c.* 1900.)

BERRYDOWN. *See* p. 179.

ASHFORD HILL

5060

ST PAUL. 1844–5 by *Thomas Hellyer*; the NW tower with spire and lucarnes of 1860. Coursed knapped flint. Quite a large church. Big nave with five-bay arcades. High roof with hammerbeams. Varied Geometrical tracery. – Good FONT, probably of *c.* 1860. Chapel furnishings of *c.* 1970: ALTAR with a marble *mensa* nicely lettered by *David Wynne*. Original ceramic CROSS and CANDLESTICKS by *Aldermaston Pottery* (*Alan Caiger-Smith*). Arresting SCULPTURE of Christ in black marble by *Wynne*.

ASHFORD HILL SCHOOL, Ashford Hill Road. 1984 by the *Hampshire County Architect's Department*. A striking steel-framed and glazed box, incorporating the hall, surrounded by lower blocks in brick. A projecting wall leads the eye towards the recessed entrance. Extended 1994 (rear) and 2005 (front). Inside, mezzanine levels respond to the falling site.

ASHLEY

3030

On a commanding downland hilltop, with the wooded remains of GAINS CASTLE, a Norman ringwork. William Briwere was given licence to fortify in 1200. Traces of a rectangular flint building 107 ft (33 metres) long with an internal round tower were excavated in the NE corner in 1913.

ST MARY (Churches Conservation Trust) stands within the castle's outer bailey and probably pre-dates it. It is essentially Norman. Nave and narrower chancel of almost equal length.

The two round-headed openings l. and r. of the chancel arch are later. Brick s porch, 1701. Victorian bell-gable, with pointed double openings. Roofs (except four old tie-beams) and most of the furnishings of 1894. – FONT. Elemental, of Purbeck marble. – WALL PAINTING. In the jamb of a chancel s window, a young woman, possibly the Virgin, with a book under a gabled canopy. C13 or a little later. – ALMS BOX. Mid C17. An impressively rough job cut out of a post. – MONUMENTS. In the chancel. One provincial and robust, the other metropolitan and over-correct: Thomas Hobbes of Rookley Manor, royal surgeon †1698, with volutes and garlands l. and r. of the inscription; Abraham Weekes †1755. By *T. Baker* of London. Inscription, two columns, broken pediment.

Downhill is LITTLE THATCHES, a small cruck hall house dated *c.* 1451–83, of three bays, s part added *c.* 1600. Also the OLD MANOR, which incorporates at its s end the former parlour and hall of a yeoman's house dated to 1529–30. (Built with an open hall, possibly with a smoke hood. Floored *c.* 1605–6. Behind at right angles is a second timber-framed structure, dated to 1521 and interpreted as a detached kitchen. Edward Roberts.)

ASHLEY PARK, ½ m. SW. A country house of 2001–5 by *Robert Adam Architects*. Neoclassical with a balustrade and Grecian details, convincingly done. The principal part is square with symmetrical elevations of three bays, stone-faced with tall tripartite windows between pairs of giant pilasters with stylized caps. In the centre bay, a porch under a pedimented upper storey. E wing set back and distinguished from the rest by the use of pale brick for all except for its projecting domed tower.

ASHMANSWORTH

ST JAMES (formerly St Nicholas). Remote from the village. Essentially Norman nave and chancel although the brick E wall is dated 1745. Brick s porch of 1694 and low weatherboarded w bell-turret. The chancel has N lancets, restored in the C13 (see the lancet windows on the s). A more than usually sensitive restoration by *J. T. Micklethwaite* 1899–1900,* and nicely unrestored interior, with a genuinely antique patina. Narrow plain Norman chancel arch. To its l. and r. later squints and faded C13 WALL PAINTINGS (revealed in 1900). They are said to have represented in large medallions the Harrowing of Hell (l.) and the Resurrection (?) and the Pentecost (r.). The paintings above the chancel arch surrounding a former rood are C15. More in the chancel on the splays on the N window – a St Nicholas, and in the nave two consecration crosses, one either side of the s door. In the nave roof, one of two late medieval

---

* Fragments of Roman urns and pottery were discovered at this time.

tie-beams has a rare pendant boss with a rose and four suns (possibly an emblem of Edward IV). Both beams are said to have been brought in from Winchester (the church was held by the see until the early C19). – FONT. Norman, 'recut within memory' (VCH, 1911). – PULPIT, with tester, part of an C18 'three-decker'. Simple WEST GALLERY, bifurcated into two balconies under the bell-turret, part of a once complete gallery possibly for the Wallop family (Earls of Portsmouth). (MONUMENT. A. Beckett Terrell. Slate tablet by *Voysey*, 1919.) ENGRAVED GLASS. In the porch, a celebration of English music by *Lawrence Whistler*, 1976, to Gerald Finzi, composer, †1956. He is buried outside the porch under a simple grey slate headstone, simply lettered by *Reynolds Stone*. Inside the porch, a later plaque by *Tom Perkins*.

CHURCH FARMHOUSE, SW of the church. 1938–9 by *Peter Harland* for Gerald Finzi. Traditional, understated vernacular. Long garden front, relieved only by a gabled cross-wing to the l., which contained the composer's study; to the r. was a loggia, now hidden. Front porch with knapped flintwork.

A cluster of greens lie ¾ m. NW of the church. NE is ASHMANSWORTH MANOR. Probably early C18, remodelled late C19. Brick with hipped roof and three-bay front facing SE. S, THE OLD VICARAGE. Neo-Georgian of 1907 by *Granville Streatfeild*. Built in part of the garden to the S is HALLAM by *Richard Cutler* of *Cutler Architects*, of 1998–9 with rather exaggerated features derived from the southern English vernacular. Opposite, the former METHODIST CHAPEL of 1888 with terracotta window ornament.

AVINGTON   5030

The village lies S and W of the house and church.

AVINGTON PARK. The manor was a possession of the Priory of   74
St Swithun, Winchester, until the dissolution and in 1547 was acquired by Edmund Clerk (†1578). The earliest surviving parts of the house probably date either from his time or that of Thomas Clerk (†1617). The W front is wide and low, of only two storeys. It has a deeply recessed centre of five bays, which with the first two bays of the wings probably represent the Clerks' U-plan house, but of this period externally there is only a pair of octagonal-shafted chimneys at the back. The rest is largely a rebuilding, probably carried out by George Brydges soon after inheriting in 1713 from his father George Rodney Brydges, who had obtained the estate in 1665. The material is red brick, of at least two subtly different shades, with some vitrified brick in the parapets. Broad giant pilasters to the fronts and inner sides of the wings, rubbed brick architrave, a deep frieze with raised rubbed brick panels and wooden cornice. The windows are segmental-headed, those to the first floor

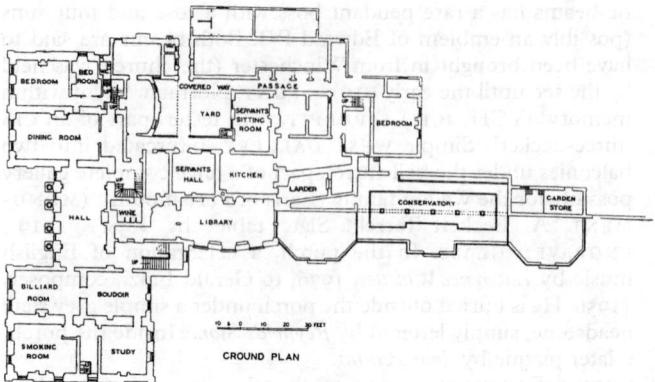

Avington Park.
Plan, 1922

with rubbed brick half-H aprons. The centre is almost entirely
filled by a giant Doric portico, the four mighty columns, stuccoed with stone bases and capitals, supporting an entablature
and pediment of wood. The design is strongly reminiscent of
the porticos of Wren's Royal Hospital, Chelsea (1682–91) and
Hawksmoor's Clarendon Building, Oxford (1712–13), which is
also crowned by figures: the three fine lead statues here,
however, are said to be mid-C18 possibly imported from
Cannons, Middlesex (dem. 1747), by James Brydges (later 3rd
Duke of Chandos) who came into the property in 1751 and for
whom *James Darley* made alterations *c.* 1787–9. He doubled
the width of the wings (the S wing incorporates an earlier, curiously slightly askew, addition at the SE corner. Was this early
C18?) and added the balustrade with urns. The fronts of his
additions to the wings carefully match, but the house's simpler
side elevations, with widely spaced bays and pediments, betray
their date and, in aspects of the design, perhaps Darley's inex-
perience as an architect (e.g. chimneys rising from the
pediments).

The early C18 architectural treatment continues on the E
front and the S front of the kitchen wing that extends E. In the
angle with the wing is a square projection with a round-arched
staircase window. It has been suggested that the 3rd Duke
intended to create a grand S-facing formal elevation on this
side of the house by remodelling the kitchen wing as the
entrance and building another wing to the E. But this was never
built. Instead, in front of the kitchen is the single storey late
C18 library, with its gently bowed front. Attached to the E is
the brick ORANGERY built *c.* 1850 for John Shelley, brother of
the poet, who bought the house in 1848. To l. and r. are fine
cast-iron and glass pavilions with curved roofs, from between
which the former linking section has been removed revealing

an open colonnade of Tuscan columns, allegedly reused from a C17 banqueting house. Burke's *Seats* (1853) adds '. . . fair flowers having succeeded to fair faces, and the quiet license of nature to the colours of the wine cup, and the shouts of midnight revelry'. Above, a high parapet with balustrade, concealing a remaining section of curved glass roof behind.

The principal INTERIORS were begun before 1789 and still 'not yet finished' in 1792 when the house was in the possession of Earl Temple (created Duke of Buckingham and Chandos in 1822). The ENTRANCE HALL occupies the centre behind the portico. It has screens of paired marbled wooden columns l. and r. and Neoclassical painted decoration including grotesque ornament, smoking altars, parrots and flying birds on the ceiling. Dog-leg staircase, SE, with wrought-iron honeysuckle-pattern balustrade. In the centre on the upper floor is the SALOON with delicate plasterwork and late C18 ceiling paintings of putti cavorting with garlands among clouds, and grisaille panels of Neoclassical figures. They are attributed to *Vicenzo Valdrè*, who worked for Earl Temple at Stowe in the 1770s and 80s. The quadrant panels are C17, perhaps reused: the Seasons, Astronomy and Music, possibly by *Verrio*. White marble chimneypiece with panels of Sèvres porcelain. The RED DRAWING ROOM (NW wing) has grotesque work made from red flock wallpaper, as well as painted scrollwork and festoons. In the narrow panels, C19 painted figures of Catherine of France, Sir Owen Tudor, Richard, Duke of York, Margaret of Anjou, the Empress Matilda and Geoffrey Plantagenet. Plasterwork frieze of wheat sheaves and sunflowers linked by festoons, and an elaborate enriched cornice. Simple veined marble chimneypiece with Sèvres porcelain panels in the reveals. The LIBRARY has round-arched recesses for shelves etc. In some, painted lunettes of Pegasus, centaurs and nymphs, with festoons of flowers beneath in Pompeian style. The ceiling was formerly painted in the same style.

The PLEASURE GROUNDS and extensive PARK are largely the creation of the 3rd Duke of Chandos who paid *James Darley* and *John Cox* over £4,000 for landscaping in 1787–8. They created the long, narrow lake on the park's N side, which widens at its W end in front of the house. N of the house, it is spanned by a graceful *c.* 1800 iron FOOTBRIDGE of three elliptical wrought-iron beams whose outer sides have pierced cast-iron panels with lion masks. Handsome parapet of circles splayed out to barley-sugar newels. Further E, an C18 brick BRIDGE with a pretty C19 wooden balustrade carries the Itchen Abbas road. The main entrance to the house and immediate grounds were created in the early C19, the date of the stuccoed LODGE, with scalloped valencing, and stuccoed GATEPIERS with ball finials. The gates, fine early C18 wrought iron, were moved here *c.* 1850. Opposite are early C19 gates, between stuccoed piers, to the lime avenue on the line of the drive. E of the house, a small former C18 DAIRY, its five-bay stuccoed front with Tuscan columns, the entablature breaking forward

83

over each and the pilasters at each end. The centre three bays open to a loggia, within which is a Doric door surround.

STABLES, SW of the house, with a show front (E), probably of the first half of the C18. Nine bays, with pediments over the ends and over the (blocked) central entrance. Each bay has a blind round arch with keystone and impost blocks; the sashes are later. The S range (coachhouse) has large round-arched doorways. N range of two dates, c. 1700 (E; with a stuccoed and rusticated carriage arch) and c. 1800 (W).

To the W, near where the road from Easton enters the park, is EASTON LODGE of c. 1800 with latticework loggia and by the lake to its NE of about the same date and similar form is NELL GWYNNE'S BATHING HOUSE. In poor condition, but a rare survival, with two rooms separated by a chimney. The bathing house (E) has round-arched doors to a terrace from which steps lead down to a pool fed from the lake.

ST MARY. A gem among Hampshire churches; perfect Georgian, the best in the county. 1768–71, essentially classical, by an unknown, possibly local architect. Built of brick for £2,500 defrayed by James, Duke of Chandos, yet the founder was his wife, as the inscription on her monument records. Embattled W tower, with its corner pilasters evidently to match those of the earlier Georgian parts of the great house. Three-bay body with decidedly Gothic battlements and with a Venetian E window. The other windows are arched. Doorways with stone rustication of alternating sizes. It all looks earlier than c. 1770. The interior is a delight and the furnishings are extremely well preserved. – Marble baluster FONT. – Three-decker PULPIT with domed tester. – BOX PEWS and FAMILY PEWS of mahogany. – HAT PEGS along the N wall. – The REREDOS with an open segmental pediment in the middle again looks decidedly earlier. Subtle polychrome painting in dull blue and red. – COMMUNION RAIL. Of metal. The chancel fittings are High Church for the date. – WEST GALLERY with the date 1771. On it a BARREL ORGAN, the case Gothick of 1830 by *Bishop* – CHANDELIER. Of brass; 1771. – HATCHMENT to Anna, daughter of the 3rd and last Duke of Chandos †1836. – MONUMENTS. George Bridges †1751. Yellow, grey, and pink marble. Two columns support a pediment. Sarcophagus and urn in the middle. – Margaret, Marchioness of Carnarvon †1768. It was she who had the church built. Cenotaph, pink and white marble with a long inscription, referring to her being religious without enthusiasm; an obelisk, and two urns. – Lady Anna Eliza Brydges, Duchess of Buckingham and Chandos †1836. Neo-Grecian tablet. – Elizabeth Peel (née Shelley) †1865 by *Nelson Brothers* of Carlisle. Paid for by the working men of Bury, Lancashire, for which her husband Sir Frederick was M.P. An angel carries her up – a Flaxman motif, but the treatment Victorian. – John Shelley †1866. Marble by *William Theed the Younger*. In the Renaissance style. Pilasters, pediment and bust.

SE of the church is the OLD RECTORY, possibly that designed by *Joseph Good* in 1828? Its Soanian stuccoed gateway certainly looks of that date. Nos. 1–7 THE ROW are C18 estate cottages with a pediment and, in front, a pretty, early C20 WELL HOUSE. Opposite, the WAR MEMORIAL of *c.* 1920, in the form of a wayside cross with superscribed Arts and Crafts lettering.

YAVINGTON MEAD, 1¼ m. E. Late C17 single-pile house, five bays. Restored mid C20 (sashes and doorcase). Brick with angle quoins, string course, wooden eaves cornice and hipped tile roof. Inside, nice dog-leg staircase with pierced lyre-shaped splat balusters.

BARTON STACEY

ALL SAINTS. The Late Anglo-Saxon stone church was connected with the de Pistes family in 1086. Llanthony Abbey, Gloucester, held the advowson from 1136 until 1541; Winchester Chapter held it thereafter. Inside, the greater part of the nave walls may survive. They are of a characteristically Saxon narrowness (2 ft, 61 cm.) and the arcades, as at Titchfield (South Hampshire) and Whitchurch (q.v.), are consequently slender. As so often, the certain visible architectural history starts with the N arcade. Its two W bays are of *c.* 1180–1200. Round pier, round abaci, capitals of flat, broad, upright leaves, pointed arches with one slight chamfer. The corresponding part of the S arcade has circular moulded capitals. Then followed *c.* 1220 the continuation E on both sides with octagonal piers and much dogtooth. The odd thing is that from the third pier not only the next arch springs to the E, but also the chancel arch, and arches across the aisles giving access to shallow transeptal chapels, a rare arrangement (cf. the Westcote Chapel, Binsted). So there is a chancel arch, but it has no structurally emphasized supports. Careful restorations of the chancel arch piers were done in 1894 by *Norman Nisbett*, and further structural repairs in 1900 superintended by *W.D. Caröe*. Externally a few mid-C13 windows are original (the largest of the chancel and chapels under a 'blind' containing arch), but most of the exterior is as restored by *Colson*, 1877. Later Perp, the fine, sturdy W tower, which is built into the nave, with higher SW stair-turret and, surprisingly, pinnacles like Winchester College Chapel. The typically Early Tudor W doorway and straight-headed uncusped bell-openings indicate an early C16 date. Inside, the big arch into the nave has dying mouldings. – ALTAR made up with elaborate early C17 Flemish-style figures of Faith, Charity and Hope. – Handsome Neo-Georgian REREDOS and PANELLING of 1916. – CREDENCE SHELF. A reused medieval corbel with a small head. – TILES on the sanctuary floor, with nicely varied patterns; are they mid-C13 and *in situ*? – FONT. Late Norman. Square, of Purbeck marble. Each side has eight of the usual flat narrow blank arches. – FONT COVER. A flat board made up of nine quatrefoils from a screen of Longparish church. – STAINED GLASS in the chancel by *Ward & Hughes*, the E window (Crucifixion) of 1877 and S window of 1886. Bad. – MONUMENTS. Inscription on the outer sill of mid-C15 S aisle window: HIC IACET HUMATUS/IHON PANN CIVELLIA NATUS. ('Here lies buried John Pann, born in Civellia') – Mary Harwood. C18 classical tablet of pink and white marble. – Michael and Maurice Hodgson of Gavelacre †1915, with a rounded pediment. Much nicer Arts and Crafts tablet below to Robert Hodgson †1924. War memorial. Like an Early Tudor Easter Sepulchre with linenfold panelling.

On the churchyard wall, the re-set base of a medieval churchyard CROSS. – In the churchyard several good C18 table tombs.

THE OLD VICARAGE, S end of the main street. C18, enlarged and remodelled 1841–3 by *George Forder*. Neat COACHHOUSE of 1877 by *Thomas Waldron* in up-to-date Queen Anne Revival.

CHURCH FARMHOUSE, ¼ m. NNE. A five-bay timber-framed hall house, probably *c.* 1541 when ownership was transferred from Llanthony Abbey to the Dean and Chapter of Winchester Cathedral. Two-bay hall with an arch-braced truss. Now floored, there is evidence that it was originally crossed by a gallery against the W wall linking the first-floor chambers (cf. Shillingbury Cottage, Micheldever). Grand two-bay solar, the parlour beneath with moulded joists. In its N side a pair of Tudor-arched doorways lead in to a wing rebuilt in the C18.

LONG BARROW, ⅓ m. E of Moody's Down Farm 1 m. S. The mound is 220 ft (68 metres) long, 75 ft (23 metres) wide and 4 ft (1.2 metres) high. The quarry ditch, 27 ft (8 metres) wide, can be clearly seen. A single sherd of Windmill Hill pottery was found on the surface of the mound.

LONG BARROW, 1 m. W of Moody's Down Farm and just S of the road to Wherwell. The barrow has been considerably spread by ploughing and now presents the appearance of a low oval mound, 125 ft (38 metres) long, 90 ft (28 metres) wide, and 4 ft (1.2 metres) high. No ditches are visible.

LONG BARROW, 2 m. SW of Chilbolton and ¼ m. SW of Middle-barn Farm. This barrow has been considerably reduced by ploughing and is now 150 ft (46 metres) long and 90 ft (28 metres) wide. It has a maximum height of 4 ft (1.2 metres). No ditches are visible.

BASINGSTOKE*

*The account of the town and its secular buildings revised by Charles O'Brien.

INTRODUCTION

The largest town in North Hampshire but much of it no older
than 1963 when it was subject to 'accelerated expansion' to
absorb new industries and businesses from London. Already a
market town in the C11, one of the earliest in the county, and
highly prosperous by the early C16, as the church attests, from
textiles and brewing. Trading connections with London were
improved by the opening of the Basingstoke Canal in 1787–94 to
the Wey at West Byfleet. The arrival of the railways in the mid
C19 was accompanied by the growth of other industries, notably
engineering and clothing, made famous by the raincoat manufactory founded by Thomas Burberry, a local draper. The town
grew from 2,519 people (1801) to 14,000 (1931) to 26,000 (1961)
and now over 152,000. The mid-C20 rise was the consequence of
new industries settling in the town, notably the fork-lift truck
manufacturer Lansing Bagnall (now Linde) from 1949, and
planned expansion after 1952 by the Borough Council. But this
was modest by comparison with what followed the 1963 plan by
the Basingstoke Development Group, a joint venture by the
London County Council (later Greater London Council),
Hampshire County Council and the town, which aimed to
increase the population to 80,000 by 1978. Priority was given to
new housing for workers in industries moving from central
London and for whom a series of industrial estates were developed. Plans were prepared under *Alan G. McCulloch* and executed in the initial phases by his successor, *R. A. Stevens*, group
architect. This activity was matched by several developments of
private housing and private industrial estates. After 1970 the
emphasis was on office building, previously discouraged by
central government, and as housing densities were lowered so the
area covered by the town expanded outwards, a trend which has
continued up to the present day. Pevsner's judgement of the town
in 1966 was of a place 'singularly devoid of architectural
pleasures', and that view has not been significantly altered by
buildings since that date. Half the town centre was cleared after
1967 for the brutish shopping centre and there is little of special
note in the housing areas where planning followed a standard
pattern, based on Radburn principles of pedestrian and traffic

segregation, and each with its own shops, community halls, churches and pubs. The inner area is encompassed by a ring road (The Ringway), which is crossed by a spine road (Churchill Way). Housing, industry and offices are mostly served by the ring road, so the role of the car was confirmed from the outset and remains essential to the visitor. Roads also made the town attractive as a distribution centre, with (in time) access to the M3 and M4 motorways also encouraging the development of business and retail parks.

TOWN CENTRE AND INNER BASINGSTOKE

CHURCHES

ST MICHAEL, Church Street. The Norman church was dependent on Basing (i.e. Old Basing, q.v.). The flint chancel and s chapel are earliest, the latter incorporating Norman masonry but the former remodelled in 1464–5 by Selborne Priory, who held the advowson. Nave, aisles and w tower built *c.* 1510–25
p. 24   to form a large Perp town church, financed by the local populace under the aegis of Bishop Fox of Winchester and, perhaps, William Lord Sandys and other landowners. Nave and aisles are remarkably tall, with interestingly varied stones except the showy s aisle, facing the medieval town, which has finely dressed limestone ashlar. It is of five bays with large, tall, typically Late Perp s windows of four lights and intricate tracery. Identical windows in the less opulent N aisle. Fine Tudor Perp NW doorway, similar to that at Lechlade (Glos.), the manor of which was given to Catherine of Aragon by Henry VIII: his portrait appears here in a corbel of the N parapet. The w tower, embraced by the aisles, was apparently left unfinished. It is of a Thames Valley type, with polygonal buttresses, pinnacles (added by *T. H. Wyatt* in 1879), a higher NW stair-turret and a Perp w doorway (now blocked). The composition is similar to that of the lower stages of the chapel tower at Magdalen College, Oxford (patron from 1486), but the details are conservative and the smaller windows, all of two lights, derive from Wynford at Winchester College (cf. Old Basing's nave). Two-storey s porch, under construction as late as 1539, in a more domestic Tudor Perp. Above the outer doorway, a small niche with a coeval fragment of stone carving, now almost lost. Contemporary stoup inside. Continuing the N aisle E is a remarkably sensitive addition for a War Memorial Chapel by *Sir Charles Nicholson*, 1919–20, in neat flint and stone chequer. He exposed the ashlar walls of the the nave and aisles.

51   The interior of the nave is very tall. Tower arch and impressive arcades of four bays, in clunch. Piers on high bases with four shafts and four diagonal hollows. Two-centred arches. The clerestory windows are of three lights under four-centred arches. Major restoration in 1840–1 by *J. B. Clacy.* He added

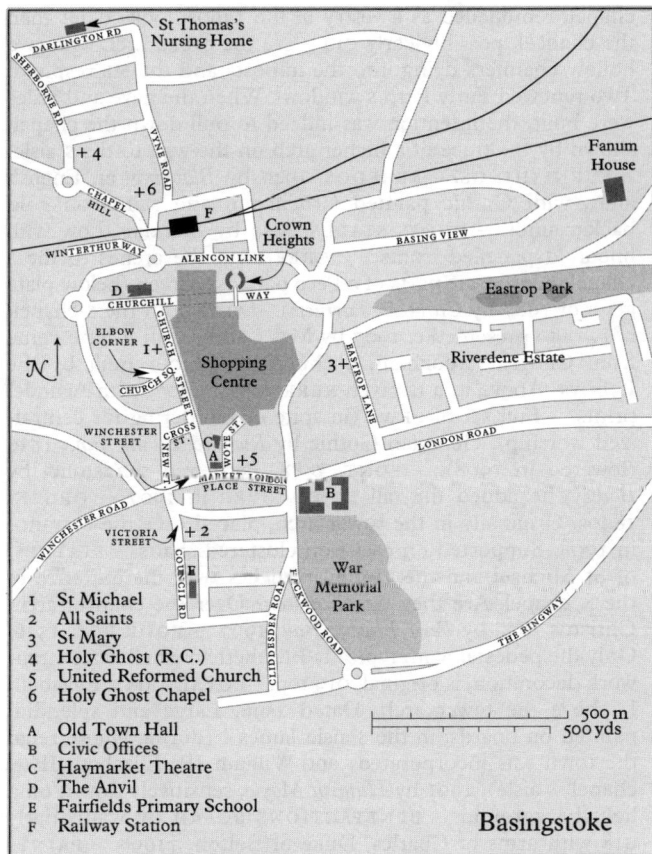

Basingstoke

1 St Michael
2 All Saints
3 St Mary
4 Holy Ghost (R.C.)
5 United Reformed Church
6 Holy Ghost Chapel

A Old Town Hall
B Civic Offices
C Haymarket Theatre
D The Anvil
E Fairfields Primary School
F Railway Station

galleries N and S of the tower (originally on three sides of the
nave but cut back in 1908 and the gallery fronts reused as panelling) and reconstructed the handsome roof on angel corbels,
with achievements of bishops Fox, Sandys, Wallop and others
(painted by *Thomas Palmer* of Basingstoke). Aisle roofs of
flatter pitch, that of the N aisle possibly original; the S aisle
renewed in 1939 after a fire. Chancel arch restored by *Wyatt*,
with headstops of Queen Victoria and Bishop Fox.

The chancel remains essentially as reconstructed in 1464–5,
with a fine roof: moulded beams, braced ties and two tiers of
wind-braces. Large five-light E window with tracery rebuilt by
W. H. Randoll Blacking after war damage. In the N wall, the
original Perp three-light windows and dainty priest's doorway,
dated 1525 in Arabic numerals on the N face, and an arch of
1920 to the War Memorial Chapel. This has a three-bay arcade
and narrow S aisle. E window modelled on the medieval N aisle
E window which is retained as a screen to the nave. The S

chapel, remodelled as a vestry in the 1460s, looks older than the chancel, possibly early C14 – see the broad arch with two hollow chamfers dying into the imposts and the NE respond. Two renewed Early Perp S windows. When the nave and aisles were built, the intention was indeed to pull down the chapel, shown by the trace of a higher arch on the wall to the S aisle.

FURNISHINGS. – REREDOS. 1947 by *Blacking*, an English altar, with Gothic painted Crucifixion and saints on gold backgrounds. – CHOIR STALLS. Also by *Blacking*. Low with linenfold panelled fronts. – SCREENS in the arches to the S chapel incorporate parts of a Perp parclose screen (below plate glass of 1987 by *Caroe & Partners*). – ALTAR. In the S chapel, of *c.* 1840 presented *c.* 1907 by Mrs Lefroy. Can it have come from Church Crookham, a church of 1840–1 built by the Lefroys? Above it, a triptych REREDOS of 1907, with Arundel prints. – Full set of PEWS (in spite of reordering for centralized worship). Georgian Gothic by *Richard Billing Jun.*, 1836 (lowered in 1908). – FONT. 1888. Perp, red sandstone, by *Bodley*; he added the tall FONT COVER in 1907. – ORGAN. 1840s. Originally in the tower arch, placed over the entrance in 1908. Supported on cast-iron clustered shafts. – STATUES, of St Michael and the Virgin, in niches over the entrance to the N chapel. Are they by *Nicholson*? Over the chancel arch, Christus Rex, by *Peter Eugene Ball*, 1997. – POOR BOX. 1576. Only the pedestal, with typically Elizabethan small-scale strapwork decoration, is original. C19 top. – ROYAL ARMS: Elizabeth I, above the tower arch. Dated 1596. Large and splendid, painted on boards; in the S aisle James I (during whose reign the town was incorporated) and William III; Elizabeth II (N chapel, S aisle), 1991 by *Hamish Moyle*, sensitively drawn on a light background. – BENEFACTIONS BOARD (W wall). Early C18 with arms of Charles, Duke of Bolton, †1698. – PAINTING. N chapel. A depiction of the nave E wall in 1850, showing the lost Decalogue (painted *c.* 1537–47). – STAINED GLASS. In the S chapel and aisle NE and SE, patterns of broken early C16 Renaissance glass from the Holy Ghost Chapel. – STAINED GLASS. In the S chapel and aisle NE and SE, patterns of broken early C16 Renaissance glass from the Chapel of the Holy Ghost (from where it was taken intact to Mottisfont Abbey and subsequently brought here but damaged by bombing in the Second World War). War Memorial Chapel, N, roundel of royal arms (Charles I), dated 1632, from the former rectory. Several windows by *Christopher Webb*: chancel E 1949, War Memorial Chapel E windows, 1950. – N aisle NW by *Lavers, Barraud & Westlake*, 1867. Old Testament Prophets. The corresponding window in the S aisle has tracery lights surviving from a window by the same firm, lost in 1940. – MONUMENTS. Small Jacobean brasses in the chancel. Robert Stocker †1606. John Hilliard †1621. Also several LEDGER STONES, the best to Thomas Wharton †1748, Professor of Poetry at Oxford, 1738–48. S chapel: hanging tablet to William Russell †1718 and wife †1725. Lively pear-shaped cartouche.

HOLY GHOST CHAPEL. *See* Cemetery.

ALL SAINTS, Victoria Street. 1915–17, by *Temple Moore*. A swan-song of Late Gothic Revival and an austerely beautiful and noble building, the exterior of smooth, neatly dressed ashlar facing with a prominent SE flanking tower, carrying a shingled bell-turret with a nice spire behind the battlements. Crisp, scholarly, mostly Dec detail throughout, kept simple, except for the tall W window, and the large E window with a display of curvilinear tracery. Much bare wall. Inside, an airy light-some aisled nave and chancel divided by a thin chancel arch. Arcades with mouldings dying into the piers without any capitals and giant 'blind' arches embracing the clerestory. Nave arcades of four bays, the chancel arcades lower and the upper windows much larger. Pretty painted barrel ceilings, that over the chancel with Gothic lettering in alternate bands of red and white panels. Good contemporary chancel furnishings: STALLS, low wooden SCREEN and richly traceried READING STAND. – ORGAN GALLERY, below the tower, a projecting balcony and intricate organ screen. – ROOD BEAM, with nice carved brackets of censing angels and ROOD, replete with winged seraphim. – REREDOS, 1917, painted by *Charles Head*, to designs by *Mary Temple Moore*, with demi-figures of Christ and His apostles, on a star-spangled red ground. – War Memorial Chapel. Simple furnishings by *Temple Moore*, 1920: plain stone ALTAR and tall, elaborately Perp REREDOS with Crucifix. – SCULPTURE. Over the font in the nave, a bronze head of Christ, by *Elizabeth Frink*, 1982 (installed 1993). – PAINTING. S aisle. The Harrowing of Hell by *Elisabeth Reyntiens*, c. 1986. – STAINED GLASS. Outstanding E window of 1917, possibly by *Burlison & Grylls*, an important example of early C20 medievalism with five tiers of scenes from Christ's life, effectively allied to the architecture. The firm's other windows (e.g. the Lady Chapel E window) are lower voltage. W windows by the mystic painter *Cecil Collins*; his only works in stained glass, made by *Patrick Reyntiens* in 1985 (aisles, with angels, electric, glaringly golden) and 1988 (nave, in golds and grisaille, with a central head, and circling angels, in a celestial firmament, all symbolic of the Holy Spirit and an affirmation of mystic love).

ST MARY, Eastrop Lane. 1993–4 by *Plincke, Leaman & Browning*. Brick and square, with a steep pyramidal roof with a lantern and inside tiers of bench seating facing the free-standing altar. It is linked to the diminutive old church. This has a flint chancel with Georgian brick E end but a higher stone nave of 1886 by *Raynbird & Sons*, extended with shingled bell-turret in 1911–12 by *T. G. Jackson*. – STAINED GLASS. In the wood-framed E window, rare and unusual Georgian painted glass of 1744, perhaps presented by Peter Serle, then holder of the advowson. Chancel lancet of 1897–8 by *John Jennings* in memory of his son, killed at Basingstoke Wharf by a brewer's dray horse. Unusual subject – Christ raising St Peter out of the water. Also by Jennings the nave S window, 1897. – Former VICARAGE (now offices). 1969 by *Michael Manser Associates*.

HOLY GHOST (R.C.), Sherborne Road. 1902–3 by *Canon A. J. C. Scoles*, the parish priest. Flint, late C13 style. Nave, N transept, polygonal apse, and slender octagonal SE bell-turret with copper spirelet. Ugly W gallery inside but fine scheme of original decoration, including the painted ceiling by *Westlake*, who also painted the figures of Old Testament prophets in the apse. The apse in addition has pairs of niches, marble wall-shafts and panels of intensely coloured and gilded decorative stencilling. – HIGH ALTAR and EXPOSITION THRONE, under a soaring crocketed canopy. Alabaster. – LAMPS on Gothic brass brackets. – LADY CHAPEL ALTAR and REREDOS of 1908, of the Virgin and saints, all in a rather eerie Gothic and of a weird marble and alabaster, like frozen aspic. – STATIONS OF THE CROSS, nave S wall, dark figures on gilt backgrounds, *c.* 1930. – STAINED GLASS, almost all by *Lavers & Westlake*. The N windows grisaille patternwork. In a S window, below the W gallery, a few small medieval fragments, including two good heads, from the Holy Ghost Chapel (*see* below). W window. 1992 by *Andrew Taylor*. – MONUMENT. Canon Scoles †1920. Large tablet in the Lady Chapel. Outside is his tomb with a sculptured crucifixion.

Red brick PRESBYTERY, attached to the SE corner, by *Scoles*, 1901. The mission church of 1878, by *John Crawley*, survives at the NE corner.

UNITED REFORMED CHURCH, London Street. Former Congregational. The sides (red and blue brick) are 1800–1, enlarged at the street end in 1854, and the façade, of five bays with pediment over the central three and giant columns in antis, added 1860 by *G. B. Musselwhite*. Interior remodelled 1882: horseshoe gallery with decorative cast-iron fronts and columns. Sanctuary arch with big keystone. Restored 1994–6 when adjoining schoolrooms were demolished and glazed extension added for café and bookshop.

CEMETERY, Chapel Hill. Opened in the early C13. Now as laid out in 1856–8 (lodge of that date; the chapels by *Poulton & Woodman* have gone). Of principal interest is the ruined HOLY GHOST CHAPEL, the earliest parts of which were complete by 1244. No more survives than part of the W wall of the W tower with C15 doorway and window, the rest marked out in the grass, showing that it later had a half-hexagonal apse. S of its chancel is the remains of the GUILD CHAPEL OF HOLY TRINITY, erected by Lord Sandys of The Vyne as his family burial place.* This was done in 1524, shortly after the main chapel had been reconstructed. Built of brick, originally faced inside and out with finely dressed malmstone. The surviving parts are the S wall and part of the half-hexagonal apse, with

---

*An earlier chapel dedicated to the Trinity may have existed at Basingstoke (1462 valuation of Selborne Priory).

Basingstoke, C17 view.
Engraving, C19

large windows, once of three lights, with four-centred heads
and tabernacles. The W end was also half-hexagonal: against it
stands the shell of a hexagonal SW turret. This has angle tabernacles for statues, with Tudor Gothic, Italianate arabesque and
Flemish elements in the Renaissance ornament of their
canopies and capitals. Motifs include the achievement and
emblem of Sir Reginald Bray, Sandys's father-in-law. Inside
the turret, finely laid brick with evidence of a spiral stair for a
lost W gallery or family chapel chamber (cf. the chapel gallery
at The Vyne) from which the rood loft across the other, earlier,
chapel was also reached.* A doorway on the S side retains
traces of a window above, evidently lighting the gallery.

The interior was famed for its painted roof showing
Prophets, Apostles and Disciples of Christ, noted in the early
C17 by Peter Heylin. Fragments of the large scheme of stained
glass commissioned by Sandys for both parts of the chapel
survive relocated at The Vyne (q.v.) and in Basingstoke at
St Michael and the Holy Ghost (R.C.). A little more is at
Woolbeding church, West Sussex. – MONUMENTS: Lord
Sandys's tomb of 1536, just a side bearing his achievement and
badges, and that of his wife. Commissioned from *Arnold
Hermanzone* (fl. 1536 at Aire-en-Artois). The Trinity Chapel
continued in use as a funerary chapel after the suppression of
the Chantry Guild in 1546, the rest as a school. But the roofs
were stripped of lead by Cromwellian soldiery in 1644–6 and
by 1742 three of the stained glass windows had been removed,
and the ruin was almost in the state of today.

---

* Evidence of a rood screen is provided by an account of 'payntinge of the roode'
in *Book of Accounts . . . of the Holy Ghost in Basingstoke 1557–1654* (1882).

CEMETERY, Worting Road. Opened 1914. Knapped flint LODGE.
CHAPEL with chequerboard flushwork and elongated octagonal bellcote with spirelet. Cross of Sacrifice by *Reginald Blomfield, c.* 1918. GATES by *Richard Bent,* 1995, brightly coloured
with twisting ironwork foliage.

PUBLIC BUILDINGS

OLD TOWN HALL, High Street. Now WILLIS MUSEUM. 1832–4
by *Lewis Wyatt,* and opened by Lord Bolton of Hackwood Park
(q.v.). Five bays, rendered, classical going Italianate originally
with an open ground floor. Façade altered 1864–5 when the
ground was enclosed and a porch added. A clock tower (rebuilt
1887 in a most curious elongated form) was taken down in
1961. Converted for its present use, 1981–4. The staircase hall
has original wrought-iron stair rails, decidedly Grecian, and
an extravagant, gilded gasolier, with dolphins and lights supported on volutes. The former Council Chamber, now subdivided by a mezzanine floor, retains a fine ceiling with generous
plasterwork roundels, acanthus leaf cornice and egg-and-dart
moulding.

BASINGSTOKE CIVIC OFFICES, London Road. Two phases:
DEANE, *c.* 1974–6 by *Eric Almond,* Borough Architect, and
PARKLAND, 1990–2 by *Casson, Conder Partnership.* Between
the two is GOLDINGS (Registry Office), a much-enlarged
Georgian mansion which grew *c.* 1765 from a small early C17
house. Facing London Road (N) four bays with Venetian
windows flanking the doorcase. Its neighbour (No. 3) has a
gable-end of panel framing and brick nogging. The present
appearance is of *c.* 1800, crisply finished in pale yellow brick.
E (entrance) elevation has a recessed centre with low Doric
colonnade between outer wings. Generous bow on the S front
and a stone band of rosettes around the parapet. The matching work W of the bow is of 1979. Inside, the NE room has fittings of *c.* 1765: fielded panelling, two glazed cabinets,
round-arched with keystones and grisaille panel paintings of
Italianate style, one very architectural and two others after
Giorgione – one with a naked woman with a towel, seated
beside putti within an idealized woody landscape. Chimneypieces of *c.* 1800 in several rooms.

In front of the offices the WAR MEMORIAL by *J. Arthur
Smith,* 1922–3, in a Baroque style with curved pediments on
four sides; Victory by *L.F. Roslyn.* It was previously within the
WAR MEMORIAL PARK, the former C18 parkland of
Goldings. A former summerhouse, hexagonal with a conical
roof, still serves as an eyecatcher in the informal, undulating
landscape of wooded belts and curving walks. Close to the
Hackwood Road entrance, a large Victorian bandstand,
restored in the 1990s.

HAYMARKET THEATRE, Wote Street. Former Corn Exchange, built 1864–5 by *Salter & Wyatt* (*Matthew Wyatt*). Italianate, of seven bays, with big arched windows above a deep basement. Tall keystones and thin central entrance bay with keystone pediment. Cast-iron interior largely destroyed by fire in 1925, after which the building became a theatre, now with a stylish, steel-framed auditorium of 1992–3 by *RHWL Partnership*. Traditional proscenium arch, moveable apron stage and gallery. Discreet zinc-clad fly tower.

The theatre incorporates the former LESSER MARKET (now café and box office). Opened 1835, by *William Yates Gibbs*, but remodelled 1884, the date of the surviving ground-floor frontage with surrounds of stucco-moulded fruit. Plain brick upper storey added *c.* 1985 by *Andrews Kalik Associates*. Entrance with stained-glass canopy by *Alan Dawson* and *Sasha Ward*, 1992–3.

THE ANVIL, Churchill Way/Alençon Link. 1993–4 by *RHWL Partnership* (project architects *Nicholas Thompson*, *Norman Bragg* and *Nicola Cowper*). Contemporary with refurbishment of the Haymarket Theatre (*see* above) and designed to complement it as a space for performing arts, within a 1,400-seat concert hall and smaller hall. The metallic-clad exterior tapers to a sharp point at its w end (cf. RHWL's Bridgewater Hall, Manchester, 1993–6) which opens to reveal a stair and balconies. Behind this, the main auditorium rises out of yellow brick flanks of varying planes. Drum-like entrance to the dashing interior spaces, with foyers on two levels and bar descending to a terrace, the underside of the concert hall projecting into the foyer. Colourful fittings by *Clare Ferraby*, and artwork including a mural by *Elroy Ashmore*. Steel trusses span the main auditorium, which has seating in the round but is also designed for flexible use. – Linking The Anvil to Church Street is a steel FOOTBRIDGE across Churchill Way, cantilevered from a beam, which provides a bold red slash of colour against the faceless flank of the shopping centre. By *RHWL* with *Whitby & Bird*, engineers, 1994.

FAIRFIELDS PRIMARY SCHOOL, Council Road. By *Charles Bell*, 1887–8, for the Basingstoke School Board. Hampshire palate of knapped flint and moulded red brick. Main building two storeys and of an urban scale. Extraordinary brick tower at the rear with an octagonal top stage with waterspouts. Single-storey infants' school, s, now FAIRFIELD ARTS CENTRE.

STATION, N of Alençon Link. 1903–4. Neo-Tudor in rich red brick. It replaced the station of 1839 (by *Sir William Tite* for the London & South Western Railway). In front, a SCULPTURE, Sailing by Stars by *Sarah Tombs*, 1990. Of the separate station to the N for the GWR line to Reading, there survives only the hotel; Italianate.

PERAMBULATIONS

1. The town centre: a circular tour

A tour of the town centre can begin at the station (*see* above).
First impressions are not good, formed by the SHOPPING
CENTRE (1968–72 by *Llewelyn-Davies, Weeks & Partners* with
Ian Fraser & Associates) covering over 500,000 sq. ft with
shops, sports centre etc. set on a large deck spanning the low
river valley and passing over the town's spine road. Unfriendly
dark brick exterior, not as Pevsner hoped in 1967 'something
worth looking at'. Closest to the station are THE MALLS,
a semi-enclosed precinct with an open square (Castle
Square) surrounded by shops. The S end of the centre was
completely remodelled inside and partly rebuilt to the E (*see*
below) as FESTIVAL PLACE in 1999–2002 by *Lyons & Sleeman
& Hoare*.

The shopping centre's relationship with the earlier buildings
around it is one of indifference. Particularly ill-served is St
Michael (*see* Churches, above) and a few old houses within a
hundred yards of it on CHURCH SQUARE. The best of these
is CHURCH COTTAGE, W of the church, a timber-framed
house built in several phases. The N end (the School Room) is
earliest, tree-ring dated to 1527. It may have been the service
wing of a hall to the S; this part rebuilt to a hearth-passage plan
in 1541–2 and with a jetty, projecting mullioned window, good
timber doorway, close studding and brick-nogging. Inside the
hall (now Chapter Room) has a splendid, wide Tudor fireplace
with Renaissance decoration. Second doorway (blocked)
perhaps originally serving the parlour. Extending behind the N
end, an aisled BARN, of nine bays, is a precious survival, dated
to 1747–8. Adjoining the cottage's S end is CHURCH COTTAGE
HOUSE (formerly Elbow Corner House), originally a separate
property with a mid-C18 frontage of Venetian window and
centre under an open pediment. The rest was cleared in 1867
for ELBOW CORNER, a close of flint and stone terrace cottages, which survive to illustrate the modest scale of C19
housing. Much of Church Square was destroyed by bombing.
N of the church, Nos. 81–83 LOWER CHURCH STREET is a
really enjoyable early C17 house – what one calls Artisan Mannerism. Plain brick to the street but its N façade has brick giant
pilasters and brick Ionic capitals and a big moulded brick
frieze. Raised brick window surrounds, and in the gable a very
odd flat aedicule with broken pediment. A little further N
CHUTE HOUSE, Brook Street, the former rectory, built 1763.
Handsome and solid, a double pile in red brick, originally of
five bays and two storeys with a steep attic with dormers and
big chimneys. Later additions, mostly *c.* 1890.

Now S along Church Street towards the 'Top of the Town'.
CROSS STREET, off to the r., has a small collection of two-
storey early houses on its N side. The corner building is C16,
with a jettied gable on Church Street, but extensively restored,
much like its neighbours. The group concludes with a nice

Georgian pair, with fanlights, pilastered doorcases and canted bays. w is QUEENS COURT, Art Deco flats above shops, contemporary with New Street, built as the by-pass in 1929–32. Just uphill, a 1930s former Post Office, in the recognizable Neo-Georgian of the *Office of Works*. Opposite, Nos. 3 and 4 are older, Georgian, two-storey with a pair of bows.

Now uphill along Church Street to MARKET PLACE on the old London–Winchester road (pedestrianized since 1976). Presiding over the N side is the former Town Hall (*see* Public Buildings, above) and, as one might expect of a market area and coaching stop, many inns and banks: lively English Baroque for LLOYDS TSB by *Musselwhite & Son* of Basingstoke, 1925–8. Almost opposite, on WINCHESTER STREET, the MAIDENHEAD INN was probably built as the Hampshire Bank *c.* 1894 and has a big Neo-Tudor gable with finial and the town badge. Attractively carved surround to the shopfront. Opposite, the former National Provincial Bank, 1931, has Ionic giant attached columns, an arched centre window, and inside, an oval roof-light with a late C17-style plaster surround. Next the former Burberry's Emporium, a long frontage of 1905 by *Cooper & Howell* of Reading. Cast-iron colonnade (unfortunately infilled) and some painted stucco details to the upper storey. Thomas Burberry founded his store in Basingstoke in 1856, with a factory in New Street from 1868 (*Howell* also designed premises for the company in Reading and London). Finally two bits of Late Georgian survival, both with stuccoed upper storeys: The Litten Tree pub (S) and the curved block with New Street.

w of New Street, a few good outliers: WINTON HOUSE, a Late Georgian town house of five bays with a porch of pairs of Tuscan columns, and MANOR HOUSE, Queen Anne Revival of 1897; good Jacobean-style staircase. By *Cooper & Howell* of Reading (extended by *Howell* in 1909), for John Mares, raincoat manufacturer, whose factory stood on New Street (dem.). Opposite, a few minor earlier Georgian and Victorian houses.

LONDON STREET, E of the Market Place, has few highlights apart from NATWEST by *Frederic Chancellor*, 1865 for the London & County Bank: three storeys, of yellow brick, in the palazzo style, with some characterful carving to pilaster capitals and expressive tall chimneys. Aside from the United Reformed church (*see* above), the rest of the street is without architectural incident (although several frontages mask older fabric) until the DEANE ALMSHOUSES, set back on the S side behind gardens. Founded by Sir James Deane (†1608), a merchant adventurer, the details of his foundation inscribed on a plaque. Row of eight with plastered fronts, lattice windows, panelled doorways in pairs and a centre with steep pedimental gable. Pretty backs with long sloping roofs with dormers. Diagonally opposite on the corner with New Road are the PAGE ALMSHOUSES, 1930 by *J. Arthur Smith*, a low and pretty rebuilding in C17 style of a small group erected in 1802 by Joseph Page. Before that, London Street is brought to a close by a GATEWAY by *Peter Parkinson*, 1992, of forged steel uprights with bronze panels depicting the town's history. LONDON ROAD continues the line of the street E. EASTLANDS (N side, now offices), *c.* 1800 with Doric porch, is one of the few early houses on the periphery of the town centre, including GOLD-INGS, opposite, for which *see* Civic Offices (Public Buildings, above).

The tour now returns to Market Place and N along WOTE STREET, winding downhill. The former Corn Exchange (*see* Haymarket Theatre) is the most prominent building. Of the rest, LAARSEN'S (E side, formerly The Feathers) was evidently a courtyard inn and has parts of a C16 timber-framed jettied construction, but heavily restored. Downhill the street re-enters FESTIVAL PLACE shopping centre (*see* above), but our tour skirts its W edge where an effort has been made to grant an architectural presence to the town centre's skyline by placing circular towers in key positions, with upper storeys of glazing for internal illumination. A small public square on this side is partly sheltered by three canvas canopies on tubular steel stanchions and leads to the CINEMA, which is advertised on the approach road to the town by a whizzy pagoda in Art Deco style.

N of this is the Bus Station, built on the site of the infilled Basingstoke Canal Wharf. Above to the N, are CROWN HEIGHTS, flats of 2001–2 by *Acanthus Holden Architects*, part of a growing number of high-density residential buildings within the town centre – a telling contrast to the planning prin-ciples of 1968, which reserved this space for offices (one of which to the E has been re-clad as apartments in 2008–9). Four quadrant blocks with curved façades, stepped and curved roof-lines, and colourfully rendered walls. W of the station along WINTERTHUR WAY, more flats of 2005–6, in a clichéd palette of steel and red tiled cladding.

2. The town within The Ringway

Basingstoke's expansion from its historic core began in the C19. A still attractive enclave exists S of the centre around All Saints church (*see* above). E of the centre, EASTROP was a manorial enclave, with its own chapel from an early date, expanded in the C19 to serve a small parish of new houses (*see* St Mary's, above). Its character was transformed by building N of London Road, notably the RIVERDENE ESTATE, a private develop-ment of 1964–6 by *Roy Chamberlain* for two-storey housing with flat roofs, weatherboarded fronts and brick cross walls. Terraces spill downhill with an attractive tightness of cluster and entrances opening onto courtyards, with car parking kept separate. Downhill is EASTROP PARK, created in 1972, whose lake, with tented bandstand, closely follows the line of the old Basingstoke Canal. A continuous green link leads back to the town centre but a bridge also crosses CHURCHILL WAY to the area developed from *c.* 1970 as the Eastrop business area around BASING VIEW. First, on the EASTROP ROUNDABOUT, is CHURCHILL PLAZA by *Hamilton Associates*, 1985–7, a flashy welcome to the town. Splayed plan of two high blocks, up to fifteen storeys, clad in blue-tinted mirror glass. Octagonal service core and a roof-line descending in steps to outer stair-towers. Facing it from the NE, with its entrance on BASING VIEW, is the cooler MATRIX HOUSE (Sun Life of Canada). 1983–7 by *EPR*. Two blocks of different heights linked by a sloping-roofed atrium. Full-height mirrored curtain glass and aluminium-clad stair-towers with rounded corners. Furthest E is a significant group, beginning with MOUNTBATTEN HOUSE of 1974–6 by *Arup Associates* (project architects, *Peter Foggo* and *Hans Siedenopf*), originally for Wiggins Teape. Modular design with dark, bronzed cladding. L-plan, facing SE, and descending from five storeys to two in layers of flat-roofed terraces covered by hanging gardens, designed by *James Russell*. The lowest terrace, filling the inner angle, opens in the centre to a sunken courtyard garden, visible only from the offices within. Similar openings in the plan enabled maximum exploitation of natural lighting for the office spaces. Its smaller neighbour, BELVEDERE (also by *Foggo*, 1981–2), took this further by incorporating a naturally ventilated atrium at its centre, still a relative novelty in British office design and repeated soon after on a grander scale by Foggo at Finsbury Avenue, London. The structure is a skeletal High-Tech steel frame, criss-crossed by walkways between offices and with wall-climber lifts. The block also has an external frame, another Arup trademark. FANUM HOUSE fulfilled the planners' requirement for a tower to bring the business area to a 'full-stop'. 1970–3 by *Farmer & Dark* for the Automobile Association, one of several big companies relocating from London at this time: Basingstoke was considered appropriately car-oriented and the tower is rightly the icon of the town for the passing motorist. Set above a podium with rooftop car parking and an open courtyard, it rises 240 ft (74 metres) with eighteen storeys of offices concealed behind a screen of tightly spaced vertical aluminium fins, laid flat against the bevelled corners. Rooftop viewing platform under a glass roof.

Streets N of the station and Chapel Hill were built up in the late C19 and early C20. ST THOMAS' NURSING HOME, Darlington Road, preceded the suburban development and was built as the Diocesan Penitentiary for Friendless and Fallen Women, 1874–8 by *A.R. Barker*. Handsome asymmetrical group to the road for infirmary and staff residences, broadly Arts and Crafts style. Large open quad behind, originally with a cloister linking five two-storey cottages for the inhabitants, a large laundry for them to work in (N side, destroyed by fire 1907) and associated buildings completing the E range. Small CHAPEL, 1884–5 by *Henry Woodyer*, with pressed terracotta tiles outside and bare red brick inside with black brick detailing. Tiny W gallery and screen. STAINED GLASS by *Lavers & Westlake*; the large gilded Gothic REREDOS is probably by *Westlake*,

1893, when he is credited with decoration of the E end in memory of Chaloner W. Chute of The Vyne.

OAKRIDGE, ¼ m N., was developed in phases 1964–8 by the Development Group, with two-storey terraces. Many are of the widely used prefabricated timber 'Vic Hallam' system with brick gable-ends and weatherboarded and tile-clad fronts. The later phase, begun 1967, provided a gloomy twelve-storey tower block and church. Deck-access flats have been removed in an impressive reworking of the centre as OAKRIDGE VILLAGE in 2004–6 by *HTA Architects*. Attractively varied, with two- and three-storey houses, with slate roofs, rendered façades and steel details. The feeling is pleasantly urban. Private and rented houses are intermingled in each group and the plan-forms flexibly designed for additions. The focus is a public square (landscaping by *Hyland Edgar Driver*) terminated at its N end by the large OAKRIDGE HALL, timber-clad with broad, downward-swooping roof.

HOUNDMILLS INDUSTRIAL ESTATE, provided under the development plan, has grown into a sea of warehouses and factories around Houndmills Road. The earliest are of 1963–4: the best of which remains MACMILLAN publishers by *Charles Pike & Partners*, with a single-storey warehouse block from which an office tower rises in a remarkably successful combination of deep concrete framing and timber cladding; and its imposing neighbour SAINSBURYS by *Scott, Brownrigg & Turner, c.* 1967, with canteen block raised to first-floor level, against a backcloth of giant sheds for the food-processing and distribution departments. Downhill along Kingsclere Road towards the town is ELI LILLY, an earlier industrial arrival with an all-white Art Deco range of 1939 by *A. G. Porri* for pharmaceutical laboratories and offices. Plain concrete with some cast detail of stylized classical motifs and a regular disposition of windows.

OUTER BASINGSTOKE

North: Popley, Merton Rise and Park Prewett

POPLEY, W of Reading Road, was built up from the early 1960s N and S of Popley Way, with low-density housing of a standard Development Group type with weatherboarded fronts and coloured panels. Off Shakespeare Road, S, CHINEHAM HOUSE is C18 and once handsome. Three bays, red brick, with advanced centre under an open pediment with semicircular opening. Also early are CHINEHAM FARM COTTAGES, a row of four with brick fronts but timber-framed rears.

ST BEDE (R.C.), Popley Way. 2005–7 by *JKBS Architects* with *Robert Maguire*. Steel-framed pyramid with glazed top, replacing a mission church of *c.* 1968. – STAINED GLASS by *Graham Jones*. Cloister, meeting rooms etc. adjoining.

EVEREST COMMUNITY COLLEGE, Merton Rise, off Popley
Way. 2006–7 by *Hampshire County Architects*. In scale, highly
typical of the enormous English secondary schools being built
in the early C21 but well detailed and impressive. Full-height
glazed façade, with external shade on columns. An internal
street runs along the front of the building, which contains the
communal spaces (café, offices, gym etc.). Three classroom
blocks in fingers behind and in between these excellently landscaped courtyards. Public square in front, shared with the
Youth Service Building.

POPLEY FIELDS COMMUNITY CENTRE, Carpenters Down.
1996 by *Feilden Clegg Architects*. Spacious, in brick, under long,
sloping roofs kept low to the edges of the plan and broken in
the centre by taller, monopitch sections of glazing, lighting the
principal hall and café.

NORTH HAMPSHIRE HOSPITAL, Aldermaston Road, on a large
parkland site at the edge of the town. Mostly of 1967–74 by
George Trew Dunn Beckles Willson Bowes. Several blocks, the
tallest of five storeys, in white brick with concrete bands and
powerful use of fluted concrete for stair-towers and services.

LIMES PARK, NE of the hospital. Housing of 2007–9 on the site
of the Park Prewett Asylum of 1912–16 by *G. T. Hine*. It was
laid out to the usual echelon plan of detached or semi-
detached patients' residences spreading out from a Late
Baroque-style administrative block. This is preserved along
with a few other ward buildings and the water tower with open
pediments in its upper storey.

East and North-East: Daneshill and Chineham

The expansion of Basingstoke has encroached upon the parish
of Old Basing (q.v.) and in particular Daneshill, originally rural
but now engulfed by industrial estates and suburban housing.
Its important building is DANESHILL HOUSE, Lutyens Close,
of 1903 by *Lutyens* for Walter Hoare. It is built with the thin
'Tudor' red bricks produced at his nearby works; Lutyens
designed the special moulded brick mullions and other details.
Conventional Surrey Style, with gabled wings and an arched
entrance, but good details, especially fireplaces with quirky
tiling and a stair with timber screen. DANESHILL COTTAGE
and THE OLD LODGE, E on Daneshill Drive, are both by
Lutyens, the latter especially complete with broad leaded
windows and tile-hanging. The brickworks stood downhill,
within sight of the house. On Bilton Road are its OFFICES
(now in the DANESHILL INDUSTRIAL ESTATE), also by
Lutyens, c. 1903, making great use of moulded brick for lively
details including two splendid chimneys. Nearby, on Wade
Road, INTEC BUSINESS CENTRE, by *Gebler Associates* (consultant architects, *Brian Taggart Associates*), c. 1984, is the only
distinctive development of its date in Basingstoke: a High-Tech
scheme of five flat-roofed office blocks of mixed heights, with

lightweight cladding of coloured panels. Two of the blocks are divided into quarters by pedestrian malls with functional steel frameworks and exposed services inside. NE is GREAT BIN-FIELDS PRIMARY SCHOOL, Binfield Farms Lane. 2002 by *Hampshire County Architect's Dept.* Horseshoe plan with mono-pitch-roofed classrooms on the inner curve and an outer corridor which at the entrance slices between the large wedge-shaped hall and admin block. Brick, shingle and a structural frame of reconstituted timber – one of several uses of recycled materials.

CHINEHAM, a hamlet absorbed by Basingstoke in 1972, continues NE from Daneshill without interruption. The feeling is consciously more rural with bands of woodland penetrating the housing areas.

CHRIST CHURCH, Reading Road. Ecumenical church of 1987, adapted and extended in 2001–4 by *Daniel Lelliott Krauze*.

FOUR LANES PRIMARY SCHOOL, off Hanmore Road in a broad open space with woodland backdrop. 1982–4 by *Hampshire County Architect's Dept* (design team, *Ian Templeton* and *Stephen Harte*) with later Infants' Building and Nursery. Roofs in the shape of marquees with colourful patterned glazed tiles and bright interior spaces. Inside classrooms group around a hall and central space.

CHINEHAM BUSINESS PARK, off Crockford Roundabout (SCULPTURE of cut-out figures Chineham Wave by *Ray Smith*, 2000). Expansive offices including several of *c.* 2005 on Crockford Lane and Lime Tree Way, mostly by *Dennis Lister Associates* and *Scott Brownrigg*, with rustic names (Ashwood, Oakwood, Maplewood etc.) belying the planar Modernism of their designs. On Lime Tree Way, SHIRE Pharmaceuticals, Postmodern offices by *RMJM*, 1989–91, conceived as the flagship of the new HAMPSHIRE INTERNATIONAL BUSINESS PARK. In brick with big slated roofs, forming two wings in a splayed plan opening to the main forecourt. Formalized classical entrance.

South: Cliddesden and Viables

QUEEN MARY'S COLLEGE, Cliddesden Road. Established in the 1950s, on land given by the Burberry family, and expanded as the sixth-form college for the developing town. Extended 1987–8 by *Kit Allsop Architects*, who created a new entrance and teaching block, conceived as a corridor between the earlier buildings with a central open grassy courtyard surrounded by covered walkways. Blockwork and light steel cladding. CENTRAL STUDIO, for theatre and performance arts, by *Hampshire County Architects c.* 1999, with vivid white cladding, curved flanks and oversailing roof on columns. Enamelled glass screen inside by *Martin Donlin*. The neighbouring REFECTORY, with crinkly roofed portico, is part of refurbishment and extension since 2001 by *Macallan Penfold Architects*.

A tiny group of older, rural buildings survive amongst numerous industrial estates and indifferent housing. VIABLES COTTAGE, Jays Lane, is thatched and timber-framed. Nearby in Cliddesden Road, FOYLE'S LODGE is early C19, stuccoed and picturesque.

South-west: Kempshott, Hatch Warren and Brighton Hill

CHRIST THE KING, Sullivan Road, Brighton Hill. By *Maguire & Murray*, 1974–7. Brick, with pantiled roof and stubby tower over the sanctuary.

ST MARK, Homesteads Road, Kempshott. 1986–7 by *Plincke, Leaman & Browning*. Brick, low with slate-capped bell-tower. FURNISHINGS by *Richard La-Trobe Bateman* and *Royal College of Art, Dept. of Furniture Design*.

ST MARK AND IMMANUEL ECUMENICAL CHURCH and C. of E. PRIMARY SCHOOL, Danebury Road. 1996–2004. Curving plan with brick monopitch classroom blocks and a square centre with pyramidal roof, the form repeated for the church at the S end. The classrooms open to gardens.

HATCH WARREN PRIMARY SCHOOL, Gershwin Road, off Brighton Way. Begun 1984 by *Hampshire County Architects' Dept* (project architect, *Stephen Harte*). A sloping site with a tiered arrangement in which infants and juniors were separated by the central hall. The addition of 1988–91 (Junior School, project architect *Joe Collins*), unfurls from a round-house-like hall with conical roof into a serpentine classroom block.

DOWN GRANGE FARM, Winchester Road. C18, the large bows to front and sides added in the early C19 when it belonged to the Terrys, friends of the Austens. Perhaps the date is 1818, inscribed on one of the brick outbuildings.

West: Winklebury, West Ham and South Ham

WINKLEBURY has Development Group housing of 1964–6 (cf. Popley) and LCC-designed single-aspect brick houses, arranged in varied groups and terraces, of a type used e.g. at Haverhill, Suffolk. Planned around the site of WINKLEBURY CAMP, an Iron Age hill-fort, some 19 acres in extent. The rampart is now much degraded but is still recognizable especially on the S. Excavations in 1959 showed that the fortification began as a palisaded enclosure in the C6 B.C. and was occupied until the C1 B.C. (in the Willis Museum is a mighty, roughly hewn Roman coffin, discovered in 1964). In its midst FORT HILL COMMUNITY SCHOOL of 1976–8 by *Hampshire County Architects Dept*, one of the county's first departures from the flat-roofed SCOLA building system and a return to traditional materials. Deep-plan blocks under big tiled roofs, descending low to broad overhanging eaves, arranged around a central courtyard.

s is the LEISURE PARK and the MILESTONES MUSEUM OF
LIVING HISTORY by *Hampshire County Architects' Dept.*,
1996–8 (project architect, *David Morris*). A graceful structure,
partly submerged into the landscape with a shallow curved roof
carried by tubular trusses spanning a 180-ft (55-metre)-wide
and 23-ft (7-metre)-deep concrete arena. 8,000 sq. metres in
area. Glazed walls at either end. Inside, detailed re-creations
of Hampshire streets and buildings. To the s of that WEST
HAM, one of the largest areas of Development Group housing.
The terraces in West Ham Close (1965–6) are characteristic,
built on the Hallam system, in blue brick and white weatherboard; garages are banished to the rear.

SOUTH HAM has public housing similar to Winklebury but
also much private housing. Good use is made of the undulating topography, with some of the terraces staggered in an
attractive way. ST PETER, Pinkerton Road, of 1964–5 by
Ronald Sims of Bournemouth is quite eyecatching. Octagonal
with roof jerked into a vertical triangular sail over the sanctuary. ST ANDREW'S METHODIST CHURCH, Western Way, is
1964–5 by *C. G. Lelliott.* Dull.

5050   BAUGHURST

A dispersed settlement of farms and cottages within a network
of lanes, formerly with small greens, now enclosed.

ST STEPHEN. 1845–6 by *Ferrey*, and for that date remarkably
'archaeological', i.e. tending to historical accuracy in the
Second Pointed (lancets and plate tracery), satisfyingly solid,
and no longer fanciful or of the papery Commissioners' kind.
Ferrey was a fellow pupil of Pugin in Pugin's father's office.
Flint and stone, crisply detailed throughout. Nave and lower
chancel, thin s porch-tower with octagonal bell-stage and stone
spire. The porch is rib-vaulted. The blocked w doorway is
genuine Transitional work re-set from the medieval church.
One order of thin shafts. The date may be about 1210. Inside,
good roofs (cf. Dogmersfield). Some of the furnishings modified in 1966, the choir stalls lowered and their ornate ends
removed. – FONT. Octagonal, Perp, with quatrefoils. –
SCREEN. Perp. Given by Archbishop Warham, *c.* 1520. One-
light divisions. Only parts are old, and some old tracery has
been reused in the STALLS on the N side. – STAINED GLASS.
E window by *Mayer & Co.* of Munich and 'Holles St. 10'. Pictorial Nativity-Crucifixion-Resurrection scenes, below a wheel
of angels. Nave SE by *Clayton & Bell.* NE by *Powell & Sons.* –
MONUMENT. H. Randell †1831. Austere tablet by *Jackson* of
Reading.

BAUGHURST HOUSE, ¾ m. SSW. 1698, for John Harris and Mary Potter. Enlarged in the C18 and remodelled and further enlarged in a late C17 vernacular style in 1847. Brick. Shallow E-plan. Left-hand gabled wing late C17, the rest of the front apparently mid-C19. Two-storey porch with Tudor-arched entrance. Gables with dentilled verges, the outer pair with raised panels. Entrance hall with late C19 Rococo-style plasterwork and a pair of Greek Doric columns screening the C18 staircase, which is lit by an arched window in the rear wall. Billiard room of *c.* 1900 in single-storey wing at rear. Simple Queen Anne Revival outside, Neo-Jacobean inside. Dais at one end with balustraded triple-arched Ionic screen and elaborate chimneypiece.

At HAUGHURST HILL, N, are several interesting houses among woods on the Berkshire border. The best is NEWBIES, Brimpton Road, 1902 by *Ernest Newton*. In his roughcast cottagey manner with leaded casements. Asymmetrical entrance front with a projecting gabled service wing to the r. and a pair of smaller gables to the l. Typical segmental-arched lattice wooden porch. Long garden front with six gabled dormers; gabled wing to the r. Simple interior, with a well staircase behind a screen. In Stokes Lane, Nos. 1–8 HIGHWORTH COTTAGES, 1953 by *Eric Chick* (consulting architects, *Powell & Moya*) for Kingsclere Rural District Council. Based on prototypes built for Highworth District Council (Wiltshire) in 1951 and intended to provide cheap housing for construction by local builders. Originally all weatherboarded. The living rooms run the full depth, with the front window at high level. *See* also Bishop's Green, Ecchinswell.

HILL MEADOW HOUSE, Haughurst Hill. 1907–8 by *Mervyn Macartney*. Free Georgian. Informal entrance front. The glazed porch was formerly of two storeys (upper stage removed *c.* 2000), and has a *serliana*, with Tuscan columns, echoed by the Venetian window in the single-storey r. wing. The garden front is more satisfying: stuccoed with a pair of full-height flat-roofed canted bays and asymmetrically placed chimneys and dormers. Neo-Georgian inside. Contemporary landscaping with sunken garden.

BEACON HILL *see* OLD BURGHCLERE

BEDALES *see* STEEP

BEECH

6030

Originally a hamlet with a cluster of houses on the wooded slopes W of Alton, much developed in the early C20 with smallholdings (cf. South Wonston and Four Marks). A few of the boarded and corrugated-iron-clad bungalows (e.g. Norton Bavant, a particularly large example of *c.* 1903) survive with ST PETER'S, also corrugated-iron of 1902 (enlarged 1904 and 1908).

ALTON ABBEY, 1 m. SW. Of the Anglican Benedictine Order of St Paul, founded 1889 by the Rev. Charles Hopkins for the welfare of retired merchant seamen. Moved to Beech in 1895. The earliest permanent buildings, including the church, are by *Percy Green.* They are of flint and yellow brick, and these are also the materials of the CHURCH (Our Lady and St John), begun in 1896 and continued in 1905–7 but left incomplete at the E end: a chancel was intended. The style is early C13 and very restrained. The interior, essentially an aisled clerestoried nave of six bays, of plain pointed brick arches, is determinedly divided by a big flint pulpitum. Behind it rises the low crossing tower (now a chapel) with three high E lancets and crowned by a bold tile-caped pyramidal roof designed *c.* 1930 by *Sir Charles Nicholson.* He also designed the SEAMEN'S HOME adjoining (1929–36), and his firm (*Nicholson & Rushton*) a further addition of 1955–6. A pleasantly easy, undogmatic design.

WYARDS FARMHOUSE, ½ m. ENE. 1691, for Robert Kercher. A very satisfying single-pile house of red brick with some vitrified headers and modillion eaves cornice to hipped roof. Six irregularly spaced bays with cross-windows, the entrance bay slightly forward with C18 Doric doorcase. C18 panelling in hall and staircase with turned balusters in tower at rear. Contemporary farm buildings.

THEDDEN GRANGE, ½ m. NW of the church. 1809, for Vice-Admiral Lawrence Halstead. Stuccoed and very plain. Pilastered porch with two doorways flanking a blind arch, cornices to ground-floor side windows and pilastered square bay to garden front. Extended 1835 for John Wood, a Bradford mill owner, with Tuscan porch to garden side, and further enlarged *c.* 1870 and later. Stables and coachhouse of 1809; central pedimented pavilion with cupola.

BENTLEY

ST MARY. The church stands away to the N of the village, almost on its own. The exterior, except the brick top of the W tower, appears mostly over-restored by *Henry Woodyer,* 1889–90. First recorded in 1129 as one of four chapels dependent on Farnham church (Surrey) held by the bishop of Winchester. The oldest fabric in the chancel must be coeval with that date: see the round-arched piscina with chevron moulding and an inner rolled edge. Already in the mid C12 a N chapel was added, with a two-bay arcade of round chalk piers, multi-scalloped capitals, and square abaci. The malmstone arches are C13 and die into the vertical pieces above the abaci. The S chapel followed in the C13. Round pier, round abaci, double-chamfered arches.

The strong Transitional tower arch is of *c.* 1190–1200. Pointed with two slight chamfers. Some Dec windows reused in N aisle. The final stage of medieval building was reached in 1400 with the remodelling of the chancel and new roofs to the chapels and nave (see the stone weather-moulding of the earlier roof above the tower arch). The chancel, unusually clerestoried, has a fine typically Early Perp E window of local type, three lights and tracery with large quatrefoil still agreeably un-restored.

FONT. Late Norman of common table type, Purbeck marble, each side with four flat round arches. The base with four detached shafts, and Neo-Norman FONT COVER of odd crowstepped outline, are Woodyer's of 1889. – COMMUNION RAILS. A composite work with stubby fat Jacobean balusters, formerly part of a W gallery and shortened when reused by Woodyer. The group of balusters is divided by rectangular stiles ornamented on both sides with guilloche and eight-petalled flowers in each ring. – CHEST. Made *c.* 1540 especially for the Parish registers. Woodyer's furnishings are complete, especially in the chancel: simple stone and alabaster REREDOS. – *Minton* TILES on the floor, to a pattern organized by Woodyer. – CHOIR STALLS, and low stone screen. Circular stone PULPIT and full set of PEWS in the nave. – WALL PAINTINGS. Traces of C12 decorative scrolly foliage on the soffit of an arch in the chancel N arcade. – STAINED GLASS. In one chancel S window many C15 fragments, relocated from the nave in 1890. More rewarding fragments in the E window, of 1400, *in situ*, especially Our Lady Annunciate with an angel censing, together with parts of canopies. The rest of 1889 by *Hardman & Co.* Also by them, five other windows: S chapel E and S, of 1900 and 1912, S aisle S of 1890 and 1901, and N aisle E of 1915. – MONUMENTS. S chapel. Margarita, wife of George Windsor, †1631. Portraits of the couple incised above an inscription (cf. the Hanbury tablet, Buriton). – War memorial by *Edward Ware*, completed 1949. St George within a round-arched niche.

JENKYN PLACE (formerly Bentley House), ⅛ m. SW of the church. Built 1687. Altered in 1963–7 for Gerald and Patricia Coke by *Trenwith Wills & Wills*, who had earlier laid out the gardens. L-plan, of brick with moulded eaves cornice to hipped roof, the main front of ten bays with some original crosswindows to the l. and the entrance bay slightly projecting with columned porch. A pretty FOOTBRIDGE spans the lane to the village.

BENTLEY MEMORIAL HALL. ½ m. S of the church on the main road by the crossroads. 1923. Brick and tile-hung with cupola. Immediately NW is SOMERSET'S COTTAGE, with a cruck hall range of 1311–12 (tree ring date), the earliest dated crucks in Hampshire, and gabled cross wing, refaced and extended in the C18. Further W a number of largish houses ending with CROCKS, a handsome late C18 farmhouse of three bays with a rear wing (inside an elaborate Queen Anne style inglenook of 1882). In the angle an elegant top-lit early C19 staircase. Also, some of the last working C19 HOP KILNS in the area.

COLDREY, ¾ m. W of the village. The earliest part appears to be
the projecting timber-framed solar wing on the SW front. This
is *c*. 1450, partly lowered but still with close studding and herringbone nogging. A second phase is attested by a tall chimneystack dated 1538, which is attached to the long N–S range
of *c*. 1640, with tile-hung jettied first floor and a pair of gabled
rear wings, one containing the stair. The S end of this range
was rebuilt in brick *c*. 1680 with Artisan Mannerist details,
cross-windows and a pair of tile-hung half-hipped gables.
There was probably originally a baffle entrance (present
doorway and porch of 1936). In the angle of the wing at the
rear is a *c*. 1680 stair-tower with a tall round-arched late C18
sash with Gothic glazing. The cross-wing projecting to the E at
the rear of the S end has a *c*. 1640 core (large multi-shafted
chimney) but is now as remodelled and extended in dressed
malmstone in the late C18, when the principal S elevation was
built in brick. This is of eight bays with a high panelled parapet
and a subtle play of shallow recession and progression. Fine
interior, only partly confused by 1930s restoration. The *c*. 1640
range has moulded door frames with carved vase stops. The
former kitchen at the N end has a large inglenook with shallow
Tudor brick arch and greensand jambs, and the bedroom
above has a carved stone fireplace and a sumptuous C17 panelled chimneypiece with colonnettes, probably a 1930s introduction. Main staircase of the 1680s with turned balusters
around a square well, smaller 1640s staircase of similar form.
S cross-wing largely early C19 in its details but with a fine mid-
C17 polygonal-arched carved stone fireplace on ground floor.
Also a brick barrel-vaulted cellar with formerly external Tudor-
arched doorway at E end. Farmyard to the S with C18 brick
STABLES and C17 aisled BARN.

WELCHES, ½ m. SE. Compact house of 1831. Roman cement
with ashlar dressings, the front asymmetrical with a full-height
bow to the r. and porch to the l. with paired panelled pilasters
(the pediment with cartouche looks *c*. 1900). Nice contemporary STABLES.

MARELANDS, ¾ m. SE, above the Wey. Front range C17,
refronted early C18; leaded casements and a pretty Chinese
Chippendale porch. Mid-C18 back range with mansard and
central three-storey canted bay. Austere double-pile SW block
added in the late C18, at which time the ground-floor rooms
were re-fitted: fine marble chimneypiece in the dining room
with a profile of Medusa's head. Staircase and upper rooms of
the mid C18. C17 aisled BARN.

MARSH HOUSE, 1 m. E. 1910 by *Ernest Emerson*. Neo-Georgian,
roughcast with bold cornice. Two-bay wings and five-bay
centre with full-height canted entrance bay. Shell-hooded
porch. Remodelled early C19 rear wing. Fine contemporary
interior in early C18 style with panelling and modelled plasterwork by the *Bromsgrove Guild* and light fittings by *Donnison,
Sillem & Co.* Gabled roughcast LODGE of the same date. Good
brick courtyard STABLES of 1873, incorporating a C17 timber-
framed barn.

NORTHBROOK, 1½ m. E. Early C19. Five bays with a pediment to the shallow projecting three-bay centre and two-storey canted bays. Good contemporary STABLES and LODGE.

BENTWORTH

ST MARY. Essentially late C12–early C13,* though the flint exterior appears Victorian with most windows renewed in restorations of 1849 and 1879–80 by *Carpenter & Ingelow.* Elaborately Perp timber W belfry and shingled spire by *Aston Webb,* 1890–1, when the low C13 W tower was buttressed. Genuine details in the E.E. chancel: the E window of three graduated lancets under a single arch (cf. Bishops Sutton and Newton Valence) and the priest's doorway with one order of shafts. The C14 S aisle E window has a label with good headstops of a king and queen. N aisle rebuilt 1879. The most consistent impression is inside, where the four-bay arcades, just as at Binsted and Selborne, look so much earlier than the late C12. They have thick round piers with multi-scalloped capitals and square abaci, i.e. a mid-C12 form, but pointed arches with a slight chamfer and a hoodmould of C13 moulding. The chancel arch also has a slight chamfer. After the forceful Transitional nave, the internal details of the chancel are a different story: demonstratively E.E. and of a quality due to the ownership of advowson and manor by the archbishops of Rouen (Odon Rigaud, archbishop, visited Bentworth in 1248, when the chancel may have been new). Good E window with fine shafts, moulded capitals and arched head with dogtooth. Fine contemporary trefoil-headed PISCINA in the E wall with yet more dogtooth. Plainer N and S lancets. S aisle rebuilt in the C14. Good S doorway with continuous mouldings. Tower arch of 1891. Handsome wrought-iron COMMUNION RAILS of 1849. – FONT. Of table type, probably C13 (are the cusped arches along the sides early C16?). Rustic pyramidal FONT COVER dated 1605. – REREDOS of 1868. High Victorian E.E. The designer had the temerity to outdo the genuine features that surround it. ROYAL ARMS of 1830. – STAINED GLASS. Colourful E window by *Heaton, Butler & Bayne,* 1868. Crucifixion, with Passion emblems roundels. – MONUMENTS. Nicholas Holdip †1606. Small kneeler, mutilated, once coloured and gilt. – Robert Hunt †1671. Very naïve cartouche. – Rev. John Calland †1800, known to Jane Austen. Standard tablet, signed *C. Regnart,* sculptor. In the nave, a series of simple classical tablets to the Battin and Coulthard families. Latest commemoration 1856. They look a century earlier. – Arthur Jeffreys †1906. Effusively Neo-Jacobean with a swagger achievement. By *Powell & Sons.* – LYCHGATE, dated 1938. By *Cancellor & Sawyer.*

* Norman architectural fragments loose in the N aisle are evidence of earlier fabric surviving in the nave; see also SE external quoin.

HALL PLACE, Holt End Lane. Formerly the house of a sub-manor of Bentworth, possibly built initially for William de Bentworth. Rendered flint with ashlar dressings. Hall, formerly aisled, of *c.* 1300 with projecting cross-wings, the W solar wing of *c.* 1480 and the E service wing of *c.* 1520. Two-storey porch also *c.* 1300 with moulded inner and outer arched doorways. Some medieval windows survive. Picturesque N front with four unequal gables, the largest early C17 marking the position of the hall. It was added in 1604 when the hall was floored and the roof replaced, presumably by the Hunt family, whose coat of arms is displayed inside. Partial survival of a shafted C14 arched doorway from the hall to the solar wing. This has two first-floor chambers; in the N room a four-centred arched fireplace and remains of painted decoration consisting of C15 imitation of striped hangings, overlaid with strapwork and inscriptions of *c.* 1600. The early C16 E service wing, which incorporated the kitchen at the rear, was remodelled in the C18. Very close to the NW corner is the former CHAPEL, possibly built soon after 1333 when Matilda de Bentworth was granted a right to a private chapel. Re-roofed and its W end truncated in the C19. The E end with trefoil-headed lancet, but the storey is confused by later alterations. Early C19 brick double BARN adjoining to N.

SE of the green on the N side of Village Street is the accomplished if externally severe MULBERRY HOUSE (formerly the rectory) of 1818, its architect unknown. Stuccoed, of three bays; handsome porch with two Doric columns *in antis*. Arched staircase window at rear with balcony; above it a surprisingly naïve motif of square panel with Vitruvian scrollwork, architrave and segmental pediment. Well-planned interior with a square entrance lobby leading to an oval hall beyond in which is the staircase, flanked by the apsidal-ended drawing room and dining room. Delicately detailed plasterwork.

OAKLANDS (formerly Loom Field), ½ m. NE on the Lasham Road. By *Gore, Gibberd & Saunders*, 1961–3. Single-storey, of brick, with the then-fashionable motif of full-height windows (lower parts now boarded) with brick piers between, carried up a little higher, just to break the evenness of the roof-line. The living room is emphasized by a wooden roof cantilevered above a glazed clerestory.

BENTWORTH HALL, ¾ m. S. Built *c.* 1830. A conventional symmetrical villa but with Tudor Gothic detail, in beautifully squared and coursed knapped flint. One LODGE, of *c.* 1850, is Italianate; two others Neo-Georgian of 1950 by *Hugh Vaux*, in brick and flint.

VALE FARM, ¾ m. NW. 1991–2, by *Stevenson & Thomas* (job architect *John Davidson*). Gault brick and shallow hipped slate roof with deeply overhanging eaves supported by timber columns at the angles. Recessed corner windows. On a falling site, the principal accommodation on the ground floor with dining room and kitchen below and a split-level galleried central space lit by full-height glazing to front and back.

BERRYDOWN
⅝ m. SW of Ashe

1897–8 by *Lutyens* but little known and rarely published. It is one
of his houses, between the early Surrey vernacular and later
classicism, in which the influence of Art Nouveau and the more
avant-garde English architects, such as E.S. Prior, may be identified. Designed for Archibald Grove, editor of the *New Review*
and M.P.; Lutyens and his wife were family friends and often
stayed here. The site was merely fields on an exposed hilltop,
and Lutyens used the existing field boundaries to structure his
design. Highly characteristic are the high walls to the main
road, roughcast with a tile capping and silent about what lies
behind. They curve in to a GATEHOUSE range, long and low
with a half-hipped tile roof. To the r., the LODGE, indicated by
chimneys, a dormer and just one window, tucked under the
eaves. Steps up to an arched doorway with voussoirs of tile
creasing. l., the STABLES, with a high loft dormer and an
oculus. In the middle, the entrance is flanked by low rounded
turrets, almost pushing themselves out of the walls, with tiny
square windows under the eaves and conical roofs finishing in
lead spikes. Above is a gabled dormer with a clock, and a
weathervane. The composition is a vernacular version of
Lutyens's Georgian gatehouse at The Salutation of 1911.

From here there is an axial entrance sequence to the front
door. First, an outer walled courtyard with formal planting,
and then a smaller inner courtyard enclosed by high walls.
Either side of the opening into this the curved ends of the tile
capping shelter small lanterns, and to l. and r. the walls are
pierced by round arches. The front of the house is quite simple,
also roughcast, with a hipped tile roof and central two-storey
gabled porch, not unlike Baillie Scott. This is womb-like inside,
barrel-vaulted with a splendid two-panelled door, the upper
panel glazed with exaggerated Mannerist lugging. It is flanked
by small square windows on the ground floor and larger
windows above, a strip to light bedrooms on the l. and a
deeper, mullioned-and-transomed, window marking the stair-
case to the r. The garden side is in complete contrast, restless   115
and disjointed, with apparently no order. The relationship
between the built forms and the internal spaces, particularly
on the ground floor, is tenuous. In the middle, a large M-
shaped tile-hung gable, the eaves sweeping down to the
ground-floor window height on each side. Large ground- and
first-floor leaded windows and attic windows in the pair of
small upper gables. l. and r., loggias supported on paired brick
piers and long wooden brackets with the flat bolection curve
that, as Gradidge points out, is so typical of Art Nouveau. To
the l., and quite separate, another two-storey element, its roof
hipped to the l. and returning around the side, but with a gable
end to the r., as though part of it had been shorn off. Full-
width mullioned-and-transomed window to the ground floor,
returning around the corners, and a pair of smaller windows

wrapping around the corners of the tile-hung first floor. As built, that was it, but *c*. 1926 a KITCHEN WING was added to the r., creating a third element to this extraordinary composition. The architect is unknown, but it is a creditable essay in Lutyens's language with a two-storey bay window under a projecting tile-hung gable.

The planning is simple: the porch leads to a lobby, then into a hall with windows under the rear loggia. The drawing room is r., the dining room l. The staircase rises from the back of the hall. Lutyens's interiors were plain – plastered walls, flush skirtings etc. – but the rooms had already received a Neo-Georgian overlay *c*. 1905. Lobby, hall and staircase have 1920s panelling. The staircase is Lutyens and an uncharacteristically historicist piece, in the style of the late C17 with bulbous turned balusters and square newels with finials. A remarkable Mannerist stone chimneypiece (cf. Overstrand Hall, Norfolk) was removed in 1926, but reconstructed to Lutyens's design in 2005. Also, discovered in the hall were mural drawings by Lutyens, in the form of fictive panelling with birds and figures, including a baby, reputedly his eldest daughter Barbara.

Little of the original GARDEN planting by *William Robinson* survives, apart from some formal yews. NW of the house is the large chalk-cob walled garden with a triple-gabled bothy in one corner. In the sequence of outdoor rooms created by the forecourts and walled garden Lutyens anticipates his Greywalls, Lothian (1900).

BIGHTON

The church, manor house and rectory are grouped together above and away from the rest of the village.

ALL SAINTS. Plain chancel, Late Saxon or Early Norman, see the N lancet (discovered in 1965) and S lancet. More powerful are the typically Hampshire, sturdy late C12 two-bay arcades of Binsted stone. Both with short round piers, spurs on the bases, square abaci (their upper parts possibly 'improved' during restoration in 1836) but pointed arches of one slight chamfer. The S, a little lower than the other, has a column with multi-scalloped capitals. The N arcade has a more elaborate capital with trumpet scallops developing into a wavy fringe, i.e. a little later, *c*. 1180–90. Each aisle opens into an E chapel of the same date as the arcades, see the plain pointed arches to both aisles and chancel. The S chapel was lengthened later. In the N chapel, the E window has two pointed trefoiled lights (blocked by the vestry) and a fine trefoiled PISCINA, each of *c*. 1300. Of the same date, or a little later, the big chancel E window with engaged angle shafts. Disappointing early C19 intersecting tracery. Lancets are mostly C19. Low W tower, attractively weatherboarded, the upper part with a late medieval frame re-set from the nave on the stone base of 1836. Simple groined plaster ceiling of that date inside. Small s porch and NW vestry of 1836 still have a Late Georgian Gothic air. – PILLAR PISCINA. The leaf capital goes well with the N arcade. – FONT. Of Purbeck marble, late C12 table type, but the sides slightly tapered. Four blank arches to each side. Corner columns are lost, as the base suggests. – COMMUNION RAIL, PANELLING and REREDOS. In a finicky Gothic, by *Thomas Garrett*, 1904. Pretty SCREEN in green, red and gold, of 1899 by *J.N. Comper*, who in 1904 designed the detached ROOD BEAM with filigree Gothic fretwork as a 'surround' for an intended rood and provided the prettily painted panelled ROOFS, attractively barrel-ceiled over nave and chancel. – PULPIT of *c.* 1955 by *Sebastian Comper*. – ROYAL ARMS. 1707, over the tower arch. – STAINED GLASS. E window by *O'Connor*, 1856. – S aisle E by *Burlison & Grylls*, 1904, and W by *J. N. Comper*, 1924. – MONUMENTS. Two fine cartouche tablets. Mary Hopkins †1695, attributed to *William Woodman the elder* (GF). Good, though of a rather heartless competence. – Grace Hawkins †1735, with bunched drapery. – Rev. John Harrison †1811 and wife †1816. Grecian tablet by *W. Behnes* (signed), commissioned by their daughter Esther North (cf. Old Alresford). – Brass to Richard Deane †1855 at Sebastopol. Inscription by *Waller*. In the churchyard wall, superbly lettered tablet to Margaret Sargent †1960 by *Reynolds Stone*.

BIGHTON MANOR, W of the church. *c.* 1675, but much altered at the rear *c.* 1950 and later. The best thing is the façade: five bays, brick with raised brick quoins and architraves to the windows. Central one-bay projection with some stone detail, including the door surround with open triangular pediment. Round-arched window above with a row of dumpy balusters and square surround. Flanking l. and r., vertically set *œils de bœuf*, a typical motif of the date. The shaped gable above, with a keyed oculus, looks like a later rebuilding.

THE OLD RECTORY, SE of the church. Double pile of *c.* 1732. Front of five bays with moulded string course and eaves cornice. Central doorway with lugged architrave, pulvinated frieze and cornice, but an additional entrance seems always to have been in the l. gable-end (good C20 pedimented porch). Adjoining the r. gable-end, nice eary C20 one-storey weatherboarded addition with large Venetian window. Inside, good staircase with column-on-vase balusters. C18 panelled rooms.

BIGHTON HOUSE, 1¼ m. NE on top of a hill. Built 1844 for the Rev. John Thomas Maine, at a cost of £10,000. The architect is unknown. Two storeys, very cubic in gault brick with a partly balustraded parapet. Five bays on two sides, three bays to the front which has a Grecian porch with Doric columns *in antis*. The motifs include angle pilasters, tall round-arched panels and plain and lugged window architraves with a play of alternating straight cornices and segmental and triangular pediments. Nice interior: square lobby with rich modillion cornice of a type repeated in the staircase hall which has a lantern with rounded ends and scrolly plasterwork.

Small COACHHOUSE with a pedimented gable and circular, columned, domed bellcote. At the end of this range a WELL-HOUSE with wooden donkey wheel. INNER LODGE, ¼ m. SE, is an early C19 flint *cottage orné* with a tea-cosy thatched roof and rustic veranda. 1 m. SE at the entrance is an early C19 cottage with KENNEL. Brick and flint with thatched roof, extending over curved end, open with wooden posts.

BINSTED

A large parish with many small settlements. The village is situated on a spur above the scarp that winds NE–SW through the parish, with hangars dropping away to the Weald. Hop kilns are a prominent feature of the locality.

HOLY CROSS. One of the largest and most interesting medieval churches in North-East Hampshire, with an especially fine interior. Remarkably capacious, it was the mother church of several small chapels in the royal forest of Alice Holt, and yet itself remained for centuries a dependent chapel of Alton (under ownership of Winchester Abbey from 1110 until the Dissolution). It became independent in 1854. The exterior, now mostly heavily rendered, looks C13 to C14, with a proliferation of lancets on the nave and W tower. But the phasing is of longer range, from *c.* 1140 to *c.* 1430. Of the first date the big nave (54 ft (17 metres) long) and the chancel's W half. To this low N and S nave aisles were added, possibly with the low gruff W tower, dated to 1180–95 by W. G. Horseman. The N aisle was begun a little earlier than its counterpart, as we shall see inside. At the same time, most unusually, large two-bay chancel chapels with pitched roofs were added. In the early C13, the church was brought to its present length (120 ft, 37 metres) by extension of the chancel, and the nave given its clerestory of four small lancets (cf. Crondall). Restoration of the S chancel chapel followed *c.* 1300 (see the priest's doorway). Finally the big N transept was erected a little before 1331–2, when Richard de la Bere (or de Westcote) was granted a licence for a chantry chapel then newly built. However, it has pointed-trefoiled window lights and bar tracery, which one would call 1300. It extends over the site of the former N chapel and retains its late C12 two-bay arcade. Below is a low crypt – a bone-hole: see the low arched entry, now blocked in the N wall. Later additions include the Perp E windows of chancel and S chapel, the small C15 N vestry, and the spire, perhaps C18 and unusually for Hampshire placed behind the plain parapet of the tower. Rare bellcote, low down on the E face, with medieval angelus bell. The major restoration of 1863–4 by *Ewan Christian* was destructive: the original low, Transitional pointed chancel arch was replaced with the present taller opening, and the roofs replaced. Until then, nave and aisles were covered by a huge sweeping roof obscuring the clerestory (shown in a drawing of 1682). The aisle roofs are now clad in Horsham stone slabs. Gentler restoration of the tower in 1900, when the parapet was built and the s and w faces were renewed in clunch by *Gilbert Ogilvy*.

The interior is impressive. The nave is wide (19 ft, 6 metres) and has noble but simple arcades of four bays l. and r. which Pevsner dated to 1160 at the latest. They are of clunch, with short, sturdy round piers, multi-scallop capitals (and parts of two with stylized leaves). On the piers are pointed arches with a thin angle roll. The N aisle and all clerestory windows are lancets. The E lancets are genuine early C13, under a foil, restored, probably correctly, in 1863–4. They form a rare composition for a nave E wall and may have lit a rood (cf. Tenterden, Kent, and unusual in SE England). The chancel chapel arcades of two bays are Transitional with round piers and round abaci and now round arches of one step and one hollow chamfer. One capital has decorated trumpet scallops. One a nice variation on the trumpet motif. The tower arch may be a little later. It is pointed and has one step and one chamfer. Above it is a restored round-arched opening, possibly representing a Norman w window. Inside the tower a dramatic timber framework of indeterminate, possibly C13, date for the support of a medieval bell-frame (removed 1958). The sturdy criss-crossing beams, N and S, make an impressive composition.

The N chapel has two piscinas. – ALTAR. Early Jacobean with baluster legs. – REREDOS. Perp, of wood, by *G. H. Kitchin*, 1930. – (TILES. A few medieval tiles beneath the altar.) – CHOIR STALLS of 1863–4. The fronts made up of parts of C15 parclose screens from the chancel arcades. – PULPIT by *Christian*. A plain stone tube. – FONT of 1896. Alabaster, replacing a transitional Norman font. – STANDARD. Banner of Lord Montgomery of Alamein †1976, nicely displayed at the w end. – STAINED GLASS. Small achievement of Sir Henry Wallop †1599. Quartered with the arms of Valoins, dated 1578, in s aisle. Nave E windows of 1863–4. *Powell*'s grisaille patterns. – Chancel E window. By *Capronnier*, 1875. The Deposition. – MONUMENTS. In the s chapel, a low tomb-recess of *c.* 1300 with a simple slab incised with a cross. In the transept, another low recess with fine mouldings has a fine cross-legged Knight, Richard de la Bere (de Westcote) †1333, with two angels by his pillow, originally very good but damaged when the transept was used as a schoolroom. The inscription, in Norman French, is still partly readable. – William Wickham Ogilvy †1918. A nice Arts and Crafts early C17-style mural tablet above the N arcade signed by *C. J. Pibworth*, 1921. Skew-set achievement in the rounded pediment.

s of the church an attractive row including the Old English style former King's Arms pub (now KINGS BOUNTY and KINGS LEIGH) of *c.* 1895–6, built for the Wickhams of Wyke Place possibly by *Gilbert Ogilvy*, who also designed the Voyseyish WICKHAM INSTITUTE in 1900 and restored the church at the same date.

TELEGRAPH HOUSE, about 1 m. E. Built 1828–9 as the River Hill Station on the Admiralty's uncompleted semaphore line from Chatley Heath (Surrey) to Plymouth. Stuccoed three-storey square tower with single-storey wings (raised in the mid C20). One of a series of standard designs (*see* also Four Marks), either by the Admiralty's architect, *Edward Holl* or his successor *G. L. Taylor*.

SOUTH HAY HOUSE, ¾ m. S. *c.* 1600 timber-framed range on a sloping site, extended downhill *c.* 1700 over a high basement of malmstone and brick. Restored and enlarged in an Arts and Crafts manner in the 1920s. Linked to this is a C19 hop kiln, converted in 1936 to a library/study for *H. V. Morton*, to his own Neo-Tudor designs. Pseudo-hammerbeam roof and leaded oriel windows.

WYKE PLACE, 2¼ m. S on the edge of the scarp. At its core an C18 hipped-roofed malmstone box, altered and extended for Sir William Wickham in the C19. Gabled, thinly Neo-Tudor S wing of 1866 (top-lit staircase hall inside of this date) and late C19 square N tower with conically roofed circular corner stair-turret. W porch of 1895. Cottagey LODGE and STABLES/COACHHOUSE (converted) of *c.* 1866; brick and tile-hung with diamond chimneyshafts.

WEST COURT FARMHOUSE, ½ m. W. Built *c.* 1315, probably for Richard de Westcote. Two-bay base-cruck hall with crown-post roof. Glass link to extension of traditional form by the *Haddow Partnership c.* 2008. Four-bay aisled BARN of *c.* 1300 with evidence for passing braces; roof reconstructed, probably in the C17.

MILL COURT, 1 m. WNW by the Wey, has a remarkable malmstone BARN and attached STABLES with lodgings over, built *c.* 1600, probably for Nicholas Wheeler. The barn has tall vertical vents and queen-strut roof. The stables/lodgings are of two storeys and attic. The principal S front has three-light mullioned stone windows with hoodmoulds, a central large stone dormer and Tudor-arched entrance (restored). Simpler rear with two-light first-floor windows and two (blocked) doorways, one formerly to the lodging staircase. Inside, the lodgings have fireplaces, chamfered door frames etc. For whom was this high-quality accommodation intended?

BISHOPS SUTTON

6030

A manor of the Bishops of Winchester from 1136 and the location of a large palace built by Henry of Blois. Nothing survives among the meadows and watercress beds.

ST NICHOLAS. Plain exterior with shingled W bell-turret. Flint, unrendered since light restoration of 1891–3 by *G. C. Awdry*. Norman nave of the rebuilding *c.* 1150 by Bishop Henry de Blois, see the two doorways, both with beakheads (the N doorway's left uncut) and nook-shafts well preserved. Some Norman N and S windows. Internally the nave is remarkably wide. The timbers of the bell-turret, four sturdy C14 chamfered posts, stand at the W end framing the W window. The chancel arch is again Norman and also very wide with nook-shafts and a low-flighted plain pointed arch, remarkably early for *c.* 1150. The chancel is of the early C13, see the N lancet with pointed-trefoiled head and the E window with three stepped lancets externally under one blind retaining arch (cf. Bentworth and Newton Valence). Originally there was a N chapel (an anchorite's cell?) – see the early C14 squint. Nave W window of *c.* 1300 or a little later. C17 and C18 brick S porch with basket-arched doorway. The chancel is left nicely uncluttered, after a good restoration of 1961–2 by *Potter & Hare*. – PISCINA. C13, unusually with three drains. – FONT. A large, rather ungainly C18 stone baluster. – COMMUNION RAIL. Of slim, vertically symmetrical balusters. Probably *c.* 1630. – PRIEST'S STALL, LECTERN and PULPIT of 1969 by *Robert Thompson* of Kilburn with his mouse trade mark. The pulpit timidly Gothic with a top frieze of quatrefoils. – S DOOR. Probably C18 with earlier hinges and lock. – WALL PAINTING. Two C14 consecration crosses l. and r. of the E window. – ROYAL ARMS of William III, dated 1700. Rustic quality. – MONUMENTS. Brass. Knight and Lady, 17½-in. (44.5-cm.) figures, *c.* 1500 (chancel floor). – William Cowper †1709, the anatomist and surgeon, Fellow of the Royal Society (1696). Plain ledger with inscription hung under the chancel arch. – John Waight †1776. Large classical tablet, erected in his lifetime (the faculty is dated 1771). – In the churchyard, several late C18–early C19 TABLE TOMBS by Winchester masons: Gillum (earlier date of 1827), possibly by *Kellow*, and Collis, a stone sarcophagus with a surmounting urn by *White*.

SUTTON MANOR, W of the church. Brick front of about 1700. Five bays, two storeys, hipped roof. The central bay broader than the rest, marked by a doorway with Doric doorcase and a Venetian window pushing up into a wide, open pediment, supported on short sections of triglyph frieze. At the rear, three gables; C17 to the l. the others *c.* 1700.

The triangular core of the small village is bounded by Church Lane, School Lane and Ship Hill. OLD SHIP COTTAGE is a late medieval timber-framed house, with prominently displayed curved braces; diagonally opposite, THE SHIP INN, modest C18 vernacular. Two interesting later C20 houses by *Chris Hughes*: PILGRIMS, School Lane, is *c.* 1970. Two storeys of white-painted brick with a flat roof. Steeply battered ground floor and at the front a long strip window with wooden fins separating the lights. The rear openings are punched in the brickwork. Extended E in matching style in 1978. DELL HOUSE, at the W end of the village, of 1972–3, is more conventional but showing the same interest in geometric forms. White-painted brick, pitched roof and black square oriels. On the main road out to the E a series of good-sized houses, C18 and later.

THE MILL HOUSE, ¼ m. NW. Handsome late C18 front range. Brick with hipped roofs behind parapet. Five widely spaced bays, the centre marked by a pilastered doorcase with open pediment. Older parts to the rear. Early C19 MILL.

7030

BLACKMOOR

The village is the creation of Sir Roundell Palmer, barrister, M.P., Attorney-General 1863–6 and later Lord Chancellor, who was made 1st Earl of Selborne in 1872. Between 1865 and 1869 he purchased land in the area and set about creating a model Victorian country estate with his architect, *Alfred Waterhouse*.

ST MATTHEW. 1867–70 by *Waterhouse*. Quite large and self-confident in clunch with Bath stone dressings. Positive Geometrical Gothic. Nave and chancel and a large W tower with steep pyramid roof and an attached SE stair-turret with its own spirelet. In the chancel ambitious bar tracery. That in the nave is less archaeologically convincing. Plate tracery. Tiny triangular lucarnes in the tiled roof. Large aisleless interior of ashlar. Coeval coloured dado of *Godwin*'s tiles. Good massively framed muscular Gothic roofs. Well-preserved furnishings especially in the chancel. – CHOIR STALLS (with wrought-iron candleholders). – ORGAN CASE and the iron gates of the low screen. – Elaborate PANELLING by *F. L. Pearson*, 1905, and the wooden REREDOS by *Herbert Baker*, 1917. In the nave: FONT, PULPIT and LECTERN by *Farmer & Brindley*. – STAINED GLASS. Several of the windows still have *Waterhouse*'s characteristic abstract glass in mauve and grey by *Odell*. Chancel s window by *Heaton, Butler & Bayne*, 1868, with good figure panels by *Henry Holiday* in light surrounds of geometric patternwork. Also by them, the E window tracery lights. Angel roundels below by *H. Hendrie* c. 1920 in a distinctly Arts and Crafts style influenced by Whall. – Nave. Again by *Hendrie*. Second from E by *Powells*, 1929. W window by *Heaton, Butler & Bayne*, 1889, to Laura, Countess of Selborne. – MONUMENTS. Tablet to the founder under the chancel arch. By *Powells*, 1895. In the churchyard, table tomb to the 2nd Earl †1942. Cyril Eastaugh †1988, Bishop of Peterborough. Headstone by *Timothy Lees*. Simple with mitre and staff. – Timber LYCHGATE by *F. L. Pearson*, 1899. Elaborately Perp with traceried bargeboards and a good carved crucifixion group over the W entrance.

Immediately NE, the WAR MEMORIAL CLOISTER of *c.* 1920 by *Herbert Baker* at his most Arts and Crafts (cf. Winchester College). Oak-framed, open to a garden with a well-detailed memorial cross. Next to it the nicely informal VILLAGE HALL (former school), of 1870 by *Waterhouse*. Gothic, but not slavishly so. Sensitive additions at the rear of 1999 by *Robert Denning*. The following are also by Waterhouse: in The Drift, two rows of COTTAGES of 1866–8; attached to the rear of No. 21 is the Gothic SCHOOL ROOM (reading room after 1870); in Drift Road, the unpretentious former VICARAGE (Aldworth House and Aldworth End) of 1867–8. In uncoursed malmstone. Central gabled wing with recessed corner porch. (Its stables have been converted as the present vicarage.)

BLACKMOOR HOUSE, ½ m. S. 1868–73, by *Waterhouse* for Palmer, with additions of 1882–3. Built around the core of Blackmoor Farmhouse, which was initially enlarged and improved in 1865. At £16,675, one of Waterhouse's grander domestic commissions. Now flats.

The first design, produced in 1866–7, was more assertively Gothic, but as built is tempered by elements of Norman Shaw's Old English manner with Aesthetic Movement motifs in the decoration and fittings. Uncoursed malmstone with Bath stone dressings, the carving by *Farmer & Brindley*, steep roofs of banded patterned tiles and tall stone chimneys, some with circular shafts. The entrance front has a Gothic porch, a large buttressed gabled wing to the r. and to its r. a lower gable with a large Geometrical Gothic window lighting the staircase. The garden front is roughly symmetrical: continuous penticeroofed veranda to the ground floor and three gabled dormers; flanking gabled wings, that to the l. with pent roofs over the windows and that to the r. with a full-height canted bay, replicated in the addition to its r. of 1882–3. Low gabled service wing to the W with a water tower, its tile-hung gabled upper stage set back behind the parapet with a hipped-roofed stair-turret on the E side. This, and the tile-hung gabled porch to the servants' hall at its base, with its wrought-iron sunflower finial, strongly displays the influence of Shaw, particularly of the latter's contemporary Leyswood. However the arrangement of the circular stone chimneyshafts, stepped like organ pipes, is distinctly Waterhouse. Covered way with central gabled archway screening the entrance from the service court and linking to the STABLE COURT, the entrance marked by a pyramid-roofed clock tower with gabled stone oriels to front and back.

Inside, the beamed HALL has an inglenook with wooden seats, stone fireplace with ceramic tile frieze and panelled overmantel. Separated from it by an arcade, the barrel-vaulted grand STAIRCASE with bobbin balusters. Its landing is lit by the great three-light window with fine heraldic stained glass by *Heaton, Butler & Bayne*. Other stained glass by them includes a depiction of William of Wykeham in the garden door of the former dining room. Other rooms have ribbed ceilings and doors with shafted surrounds; ceramic tiles in fireplaces by *W. Godwin, Heaton, Butler & Bayne* and *W. B. Simpson*, e.g. those in the former STUDY depicting scenes from Aesop's

Fables. Also good ironwork by *Robert Jones* and *Hart Son & Peard & Co.*

Mid-C19 Tudor Gothic NORTH LODGE and charming SOUTH LODGE of 1870–1 in full-blown Shaw/Nesfield style.

BLACKWATER *see* HAWLEY AND BLACKWATER

7030

BORDON

Begun as an army camp on the edge of Woolmer Forest but with all the characteristics of a permanent settlement by 1905. Its civilian population has swelled to 15,000 and housing now encompasses Whitehill to the S. Some early C20 commercial development on Chalet Hill and the High Street, and a poorly detailed SHOPPING CENTRE in Pinehill Road of 1982–3. Nearby ST MARK (1982 by *Gerald Goalen*). Best is the LIBRARY by *Robert Adam*, 1985–6, a rather surprising reinter-pretation of an early Christian basilica. Double-height centre with lunettes in the gables front and back and lean-to aisles all round. Roman-tiled roof.

Former ARMY FIRE STATION, Camp Road. 1906. Its Post-modern successor, on Condé Way, is of *c.* 1987, by *Cecil Denny Highton.*

Former POST OFFICE, Camp Road. An attractive Arts and Crafts-influenced design of the early C20.

WOODLEA PRIMARY SCHOOL, Atholl Road. 1990–1, by *Hamp-shire County Architect's Dept* (job architects *Neville Churcher* and *Sally Daniels*). A magical building on a sloping wooded site, with the crescent-shaped school wrapping around three sides of a grassy bowl. Mostly timber-framed with dark weather-boarding and a complex roof-line of opposed shingle-covered monopitches. In the centre, at the highest level, is the hall; at a lower level, at the front, is the library raised above the sloping ground. Lower again, projecting diagonally to the r., is the infants' wing and diagonally to the l. is the cranked primary wing, slightly larger in scale. Small flat-roofed addition to the infants' wing, 2005. Inside, open-plan classrooms loosely linked to shared spaces.

THE GARRISON. The first hutted camps, now demolished, were built E and W of Camp Road in 1901–5. LOUISBURG BARRACKS, Station Road, is of 1906–7, with red brick build-ings of standard type for their date and slightly grander house for the commanding officer, 1904. Contemporary GARRISON CHURCH (St George) built as the Royal Artillery Institute but converted 1983. Fittings are from the old church of 1921 (many originally from the depot at the Curragh, Ireland); also a large painting of Christ on the Battlefield, 1964 by *David Shepherd.*

PRINCE PHILIP BARRACKS (formerly Havannah Barracks),
Budds Lane, has one massive Neo-Georgian block of 1939
with wings and a cupola. More interesting are buildings by
Westwood, Piet, Pool & Smart, 1977–9, whose leitmotif is the
square pavilion with pyramidal roof, grouped in informal clusters, e.g. Physical and Recreational Training Centre and also
the HAVANNAH OFFICERS' MESS, in an attractive wooded
setting by Station Road.

BOSSINGTON

3030

Little more than a country house estate since the clearance of
the medieval village in 1829.

ST JAMES. 1839–40, built for J. M. Elwes of Bossington House.
Small, of flint, nave and short chancel, and a gabled stone bellcote on the E end of the nave. – COMMUNION TABLE. Jacobean
with a nice scrolly front. – STAINED GLASS. S window (W. H.
Deverell †1920) by *Christopher Whall*, two others by *Veronica
Whall*, E (†1928) a striking design with a lighthouse, and W
(†1930). LEDGER STONES. Fragments only for John Kelsey of
Pittleworth Manor †1682 and his son.
BOSSINGTON HOUSE. 1834 for J. M. Elwes by *John Davies*; on
the site of an earlier house. Pale yellow brick with shaped
gables in Jacobean taste. Symmetrical main and rear façades.
Two-storey front porch. Many tall diamond chimneystacks and
mullioned windows. Picturesque flint entrance LODGE. – By
the Test, a FISHING LODGE. Early Victorian thatched octagon
with cast-iron Gothic windows (cf. Bossington Mill).
BOSSINGTON MILL, ¼ m. NE. Properly Houghton Mill. Now a
house. Rebuilt 1764, after a fire. Three storeys, very red brick,
many small hoodmoulded windows with cast-iron Gothic casements. Smart five-bay front with three-bay pediment and
windows in the outer bays under four-centred super-arches.
Rear porch (C20) with reused cast-iron columns. F. M.
Halford, late C19 pioneer of dry fly fishing, conducted his early
experiments on the Test from rooms at the mill.
PITTLEWORTH MANOR HOUSE, 1 m. SW. C18 brick casing a C16
timber frame with later C17 cross-wings. In one room an early
C16 fireplace and WALL PAINTINGS, revealed in 1922 behind   64
Jacobean panelling. On one wall one of the familiar large scale
damask or brocade motifs in dark red, say *c.* 1540; on another
a gay and naïve depiction, dated 1580, of the parable of Dives
and Lazarus, with scenes of feasting and figures in extravagant
costumes above a dado of geometric designs. The story is
related in verse along the top. In the frieze, the initials IK and
MK, possibly for John and Margaret Kelsey who owned the
house after 1600.

6040

BRADLEY

A small downland village, with the church standing almost alone on higher ground to the NE at the end of a lane once lined with cottages.

ALL SAINTS. Virtually rebuilt in 1875–7 by *J. Colson*. Nave and chancel and small wooden bell-turret. Windows with pointed-trefoiled heads, in the chancel possibly replicating early C13 originals. Low three-bay arcade of clunch, early C14. Octagonal piers and double-chamfered arches dying into vertical pieces above the abaci. – PULPIT. A delightful amateur piece by *J. Bowley*, 1921 (acquired in 1931), with tree trunks at the angles and stories between them. The style is still derived from 1900. – STAINED GLASS. E window. 1869 by *Bell & Almond*, re-set in the new window of 1877. A crisp Crucifixion, with Christ in Majesty above. Evidently by the same firm the S aisle E window, 1868. Nave N lancet *c.* 1882 by *Lavers & Westlake*. Nave W, 1877 by *Mayer & Co.*

UPPER FARMHOUSE, NE. C17 lobby-entry hall range, rebuilt in brick in the early C18. C16 gabled cross-wing (Tudor-arched fireplace inside); its front rebuilt in brick in the mid C17 and extended r. C18 stair-tower at the rear.

The village, to the SW, is clustered around a pond. W of the pond the early C19 MANOR FARMHOUSE. To its E, on the site of the farmyard, OAKMOOR COTTAGES by *Robert Adam* of *Winchester Design*, 1985–6. Neo-Victorian Gothic villas, originally intended to be low-cost housing. Of the same date is *Adam*'s BRADLEY LODGE, by the pond, where the inspiration appears to be the more conservative mid-C19 villa. Sea-horse brackets supporting the flat door hood are a witty touch.

6020

BRAMDEAN

ST SIMON AND ST JUDE. Small and rather plain, with Early Norman nave and chancel. The former with a simple N doorway; the latter with external outlines of two single-light E windows. Chancel and nave lancets renewed or C19. Brick N porch of 1733–4. Big flint S transept of 1853, extended by *Charles Parish*, 1868. SE vestry and organ chamber of 1910 by *J. H. Ball*; the two-bay nave arcade is contemporary. Robust Transitional chancel arch, unrestored, of two orders with capitals still decidedly Norman and a low-flighted pointed arch with two slight chamfers. Original nave roof; the chancel was heavily restored and re-roofed in 1863. – FONT. High Victorian E.E., with plentiful stiff-leaf ornament. – CREDENCE TABLE made up with parts of the former C17 communion rails. – PULPIT. From St Barnabas, Silvertown (E London); introduced 1972. – SCULPTURE. Small oval panel above the arcade.

Italian, of indeterminate date. A head of Christ. – STAINED
GLASS. W window. Two heraldic panels from Hinton Ampner,
with the achievements of Augustus and Honora Legge. 1828
by *J. Edwards*. Chancel windows of 1863 by *O'Connor*. S
transept W, 1877 by *Hardman*. Nave NE by *Ward & Hughes*,
1861, and NW, 1875. Upper W window of 1863 by *O'Connor*,
The Baptism.

In the churchyard, to the S, a big Grecian stone sarcophagus
to Henry Lomax Walsh †1831 and wife †1834. By *U. Warren*.

CHURCH IN THE WOOD, Bramdean Common. Charming 'tin
tabernacle' built for £75 in 1883 for the Romanies who lived
on the common. Spired bellcote and Gothic windows.

BRAMDEAN MANOR HOUSE, by the parish church. Georgian.
Two storeys with high basement and attic. Dormers behind
C20 balustrades in the parapet. N entrance front with deep, full-
height bays apparently added after 1842. C18 doorway with
Corinthian columns and open pediment.

The village is strung out along the Winchester–Petersfield road
about ¼ m. NE of the church and manor house and has several
good houses, the best of the C18 and early C19. BRAMDEAN
HOUSE is possibly as late as 1784 (the date on a rainwater
head), of 2 1 2 bays extended r. in the early C19 with a single-
storey wing, and l. *c.* 1900 by *E. Arden Minty* of Petersfield. His
are the oversized semicircular hood on carved consoles, the
curved stone steps with wrought-iron railings, and the charmingly eclectic interior. Fine gates of *c.* 1900 in front and to the
C18 brick walled garden; The SUMMERHOUSE is an early C20
confection reusing some old materials.

WOODCOTE MANOR, ½ m. E. Built of brick. W front dated 1630
(rainwater head). Originally three gables, the gabled porch
between the second and third. The fourth (r.) dated 1677. The
windows sashed except in the gables which have their mullioned casements. Around the corner to the l. later C17 additions at the rear of the 1630 range. But at the back is a C15
wing. Restored and SE wing added in 1911 by *Reginald
Blomfield* for the artist Edwin Abbey. The style Georgian.
Blomfield also added the Dutch gabled archway linking the
entrance front to the C17 STABLES, which have three blind
gables and an octagonal domed wooden bellcote at the N end.
Blomfield's entrance hall has *c.* 1700 bolection-moulded panelling and a plaster ceiling in late C17 style. The room at the S
end of the W range has carved bolection-moulded door and
chimney surrounds and a coved plaster cornice with scrolly
ornament. It all looks late C17. The two middle rooms of this
range have been combined – C18 panelling and chimneypiece
– but in the N room is a sumptuous early C17 wooden chimneypiece, with Corinthian colonnettes and a carved scene in
the centre (has this been introduced?). Early C17 square-well
staircase on the E side, and on the first floor of the C15 wing,
a two-bay great chamber, the centre tie with solid curved spandrel braces. Also a fine four-centred arched doorway, possibly
ex situ.

Blomfield redesigned the gardens (planting scheme prepared by *Jekyll*) and some of the estate buildings must also be his (e.g. GARDENER'S COTTAGE and WOODCOTE MANOR COTTAGES).

BROCKWOOD PARK (Krishnamurti school), 1¼ m. SE. Rambling stuccoed house begun in 1769 for Richard Smith but with many later additions, including a billiard room of 1903 by *E. A. Gruning*. Most of the interiors, in Jacobean and Adam Revival styles, appear to be of around the same date or possibly by *J. B. S. Abercrombie* of Paisley who made alterations before 1914. These would have been for Daniel Coats, of the Paisley cotton thread manufacturers, who was the owner when the tall battlemented Neo-Tudor WATER TOWER was built in 1912. It is similar to that at the Dower House, Crawley (q.v.) designed by *Fryers & Penman* for Otto Philippi, Coats's foreign sales manager. Early C19 Greek Revival LODGE.

Additions for the school since 1969 include the understated CLOISTER of 1971, N of the C18 walled garden, for bedrooms around a courtyard. An octagonal assembly hall, in the form of an early C19 pavilion, reuses old sashes. The ART BARN by *Jon Allen* & *Keith Critchlow*, 1990s, is of traditional construction with Arts and Crafts-influenced details (cf. Krishnamurti Study Centre).

KRISHNAMURTI STUDY CENTRE, S of Brockwood Park. 1986–7, by *Keith Critchlow* and *Triad Architects* (project architect, *Jon Allen*) for the Krishnamurti Foundation. Around a courtyard, Neo-vernacular, strongly influenced by Arts and Crafts ideas.

TETRALITHION, 1¼ m. ESE, by the side of the main road. The partially collapsed remains of a stone circle, about 25 ft (8 metres) across, built in 1861 by Col. George Greenwood of Brockwood Park to mark the grave of his horse.

ROMAN VILLA. ¼ m. NE of Woodcote Manor. A site of more than ¾ acre in extent, partly excavated in 1823 and since reburied. It seems to have been of courtyard type, with most of its rooms floored with plain red tesserae. Two, however, contained fine polychrome mosaics: one had a central panel showing a fight between Hercules and Antaeus surrounded by four panels containing heads; the other bore a central Medusa head surrounded by pictures of the deities who presided over the days of the ancient week.

LONG BARROW. *See* Hinton Ampner.

BRAMLEY

ST JAMES. Quite plain outside with nave and chancel in one, originally of *c.* 1180, shown externally by one complete, one renewed and one fragmentary Norman window – they are all provided inside with a continuous roll. Other externally interesting features are the under-restored Perp E window, an Elizabethan window in the nave, brick W tower of 1636–40 with typically Gothic Survival W window and bell-openings. Humble brick S porch of 1806 and prominent S transept (Brocas Chapel) by *Soane* built on the site of the C13 S chapel in 1801–3. Big S window of 1889. Unusually sensitively restored 1877–8 by *G. G. Scott Jun.* and 1884–91 by *Temple Moore*, chiefly financed by the Rev. Charles Eddy. The nave has a plaster tunnel-vault pierced by dormers, but the chancel roof is ceiled with painted ribs and gilded bosses following alterations in 1966.

The BROCAS CHAPEL, entered through a low, plain, single-chamfered C13 arch, is a separate space with a marquee-like pointed rib-vault of plaster with crisp, exquisitely moulded ribs of Soane's invention, built up with the same standard applied plaster rolls seen in his classical buildings. Handsomely placed centrally is the important Neoclassical MONUMENT to Bernard Brocas †1777, almost certainly by *Thomas Carter Jun.* (cf. Chaloner Chute's monument at The Vyne). White marble, with Brocas, a fat stately man, expiring in the arms of a kneeling young woman, possibly his wife Harriet who erected the monument 'as a testimony of his merit and her affection' and rebuilt the chapel.* Completely detached figures, visible all round. On the large base fine reliefs on the short sides of Bellona defeating an enemy, and Fame writing down the events, and on the other Charity giving alms and grapes from a cornucopia with Justice and Fortitude. In the large S window early C16 Netherlandish STAINED GLASS panels and medallions, many of them purchased by Mrs Brocas from the Farebrother sale of 1802, the bidding organized by Soane, who designed the original setting (with assistance from *John Carter*) in *Coade* stone. Two donor figures have been identified as emanating from the former Charterhouse at Louvain (Hilary Wayment) and the larger panels may have been part of cloister glazing in North Brabant (Yvette Van den Bemden and Jill Kerr). The genteel starred quarries were probably introduced in 1889 when the glass was re-set by *Burlison & Grylls* as a memorial to Henry Welch-Thornton (his achievement at the head). Further reinstatement in 1930 by *Townshend & Howson*.

The FURNISHINGS are described topographically. In the chancel a PILLAR PISCINA probably early C13 but the pillar with shaft-ring looks highly suspicious. – COMMUNION RAIL. C17 from Hexham Abbey. Thin twisted balusters. – Neo-Tudor linenfold PANELLING, late C19 by *Thomas & Co.* – CHOIR STALLS. 1890 by *Temple Moore*. Scholarly Perp. – REREDOS, painted triptych by *Victor Milner*, 1885. Scenes on gilded surrounds, in a *c.* 1850 romantic style influenced by Schongauer or Dürer engravings. – The division between nave and chancel is marked by the ROOD SCREEN. One of the few Perp screens

90

*Her sister was married to Samuel Bosanquet for whom Soane had worked in 1786 and later designed the memorial at Leyton, E London.

to have survived in Hampshire, late C15 or early C16 in a conservative idiom, the basic formula of five-light divisions apparently genuine (cf. Winchester Cathedral Lady Chapel screen).
Its rood loft, documented to 1525, has been lost and the rood
beam is a replacement of 1880, with cross by *Temple Moore*,
carved by *Elwell* of Beverley, 1882. – In the nave, PULPIT. Plain
C18 altered in 1879. – PRIEST'S CHAIR and STALL by *Edward
Barnsley*, 1970. Beautifully crafted (cf. Hinton Ampner). –
BENCH-ENDS. Straight-headed with buttresses. Mentioned in
accounts for 1535–6, those of the N side mostly genuine, others
replicated in 1879. – WEST GALLERY of 1728 with elegant
fluted Ionic columns, added with the classical ORGAN CASE by
Temple Moore in 1884. Under the gallery a C12 FONT. Very battered Purbeck marble with fragmentary *Agnus Dei*, the four
supporting columns restored in 1892. – WALL PAINTINGS.
Painted over *c.* 1850 but revealed in the 1880s. In the chancel,
bold C13 masonry pattern with addorsed flowers on stalks (cf.
nearby Silchester). Also, N of the E window, large over-restored
and faded St James, and S, lower down, a shadowy Virgin.
Above her a quatrefoil. In the nave, confusing scenes on S side
with more than one scheme of painting including a well-
preserved C13 depiction of the murder of Becket, and other
events. More rewarding, a beautiful figure of a woman. Opposite the former nave S door a large, very elaborate late C15 St
Christopher in a flowing cloak with staff in hand. Revealed in
1874. – ROYAL ARMS. In the Brocas Chapel, the badge of
Charles, Prince of Wales (1612–25) against a painted perspec-
tival background; a rarity. – STAINED GLASS. E window, by
Victor Milner, 1887. In a nave N window, an interesting array
of medieval fragments, outstanding among them seven small,
partly original mid-C14 figures, especially St Catherine tri-
umphant over a royal persecutor. In the heads sunburst and
radiant suns – emblems of Edward IV – also crowns from a
window probably presented by a Brocas between 1461 and
1483. Lower down, heraldry from the former Brocas aisle
arranged in 1930 by *Townshend & Howson*. – BRASSES. William
Joye †1452 (18-in. (47-cm.) figure) under the tower and to
Gwen Shalford †1504 (29-in. (73-cm.) figure). Richard Carter
†1529 and wife (15-in. (39-cm.) figures) both in the Brocas
Chapel. – MONUMENT. Thomas Shaw †1751, the clergyman
explorer. Classical tablet. Plain pyramid with inscription by
James Ring of Reading.

NE is the CHURCH CENTRE of 1994 by *M. E. B. Partnership*, carefully related to the church and THE OLD SCHOOL
(now a house). The earliest part, of 1848, is very humble.
Schoolroom of 1909 with cast-iron lattice windows and pretty
timber bellcote. S of the church, GRAYS HOUSE (former
rectory), set behind pretty cast-iron Gothic railings. Mid-C19
Neo-Tudor front but the rear is earlier with a late C18 elliptical bow. Flanking bays, to the l. *c.* 1700, with segmental-headed
sashes, and to the r., mid-C19. Fine (re-set) late C18 pedimented stone doorcase.

In THE STREET are THE COTTAGE and EXON HOUSE, a pair
of semi-detached cottages, typifying the late C19 Beaurepaire
estate style of brick and tile-hanging with oriels, jetties, and
lozenge-pattern cast-iron windows. The MANOR HOUSE,   46
timber-framed with an impressive display of close studding to
both floors, is dated to c. 1545–6 (dendrochronology). H-plan
with a hearth passage, jettied hall range and gabled wings.
Originally with an integral open-hearth kitchen at the rear of
the service (r.) end. Restored by *Thomas Stopher c.* 1884–5. His
are the diamond-leaded oriel windows, the star chimneys and
scallop tile-hanging.

In the neighbourhood three interesting C17 houses: MIDDLE
FARMHOUSE, ¼ m. NE of the church, is a brick-nogged early
C17 timber-framed lobby-entry house with an end wall refaced
in brick in the mid C17 with Artisan Mannerist detailing.
MINCHINS HOUSE, 1 m. NE, is a seemingly thorough mid-C17
rebuilding in brick with giant pilaster strips and a nice
moulded and dentil brick eaves cornice, and enlivened by late
C19 lozenge-pattern cast-iron windows. BULLS DOWN FARM-
HOUSE, 1¼ m. E at Bramley Green, is an important Artisan
Mannerist brick house of *c.* 1670, again incorporating an earlier
timber frame. Double pile, two storeys and attic. Three-bay
front with two large gables flanking a central two-storey gabled
porch. Giant pilasters at the angles have moulded capitals.
Several moulded oval openings. The N side has a pair of gables
with prominent chimneystacks. Inside, a contemporary staircase with bulbous vase balusters.

BEAUREPAIRE HOUSE, ¾ m. SW. An attractive sight, set within
a square moat at the centre of a large park. The Tudor house
of the Brocas family was rebuilt probably *c.* 1750 but demolished after a fire in 1941. The present house is its early C19
service wing as reconstructed in 1964 by *T. A. Bird.* His is the
S end feature of two narrow rectangular battlemented towers
flanking a deep recess with diaper brickwork, a large staircase
window and lattice veranda. Partly cloistered rear court incorporating C18 service buildings and attractive classical alterations by *Hutton Nicholls c.* 1985.

The moat is crossed by C19 BRIDGES (the E bridge timber,
the SW one a suspension bridge with a fine C18 wrought-iron
gate and overthrow at one end). E GATEWAY with quite excellent early C18 wrought-iron gates with overthrow. At the NE
and SE corners of the moat, picturesque C19 octagonal
BASTIONS with steep pyramidal roofs. – STABLES, N, with battlemented Neo-Tudor brick SCREEN, *c.* 1980s; central archway
with cottage to the l. and sham cottage to the r. NE, FARM
BUILDINGS converted in the early C20 as part of a charming
Arts and Crafts yew-hedged sunken GARDEN with pagoda-like
SUMMERHOUSE. On the N side, C18 timber-framed barns,
altered to form open loggias. LODGES. Late C19. Irregular
polygonal plan with canted corners and steeply pitched roofs.

Particularly fine examples of estate work include BRAMLEY
CORNER HOUSE, N of the house, and the enchanting

BEAUREPAIRE MILL ½ m. E on the Bow Brook, which has a wonderfully exaggerated timber lucam on curved brackets. BEAUREPAIRE MILL BRIDGE is of 1831. Elliptically arched cast-iron beams with cusped piercings and delicate iron balustrade of cusped saltire crosses.

BULLSDOWN HILLFORT. See Sherfield-on-Loddon.

7050

BRAMSHILL HOUSE
(National Police Training College)

Bramshill was mostly built by Edward, 11th Lord Zouche of Harringworth (Northamptonshire). He began in 1605; the King visited in 1620 but work was still going on at Lord Zouche's death in 1625. He had been raised as a Ward of the Crown by William Cecil, Lord Burghley, and in his youth travelled in Germany and Italy, where he became friends with Sir Henry Wotton. It is one of the largest Jacobean 'prodigy' houses. What it has in common with the other grandest Jacobean houses – Hatfield and Holland House – is the concentration on a piece of really spectacular display with few decorative embellishments otherwise. It is also distinguished by a plan quite exceptional in an age of standard plans. Four ranges are built around a long, very narrow service courtyard, with the main entrances in the shorter N and S* sides rather than the longer sides as is more usual. Zouche appears to have remodelled an older courtyard house, of inward-facing type, whose gateway survives in the N range. But the unusual plan may also have been a response to the narrow site, a projecting spur of high ground above the valley of the River Hart. Zouche's heirs were forced to sell in 1638. The house was then acquired by Sir Robert Henley and remained in his family until 1695. In 1699 Sir John Cope bought Bramshill and made changes to the exterior; his Victorian descendant Sir William Cope (†1892) did much to restore the Jacobean character, with architectural advice from *James Fergusson*.

60 EXTERIOR. Zouche appears to have begun his remodelling with the S RANGE. This (and the whole of the house) is of brick. It is of two-and-a-half storeys in height and has mullioned-and-transomed windows – the C17 windows are of four lights with king mullions. Square bays project in the angles between centre and wings, that to the r. marking the dais end of the hall. This appears normal enough and would appear yet more so if the wings, which originally extended along each side of the forecourt (its extent marked by a surviving pair of domed, octagonal brick turrets) had not been cut short *c.* 1703. As remodelled, they have three-bay fronts, originally with wooden cross-windows, later replaced by stone mullions and transoms,

---

* The true orientation is NE and SW but for ease of description the cardinal points are used.

within simple C18 classical surrounds. The l. wing was largely rebuilt by Sir John Cope II *c.* 1820, at which date the C17 pierced parapet of the centre was carried around both wings. The grand display is the central frontispiece and its impact must have been even greater when it was seen at the end of the long forecourt. On the ground floor it is an arcade of three bays set in front of the façade, with rusticated details, the outer bays required to resolve the characteristic Jacobean problem of uniting a symmetrical façade with an asymmetrical entrance, which in this instance was originally set behind the l. bay, but moved to the centre in the mid C17. (These outer bays also awkwardly overlap the bays in the inner angles with the wings, suggesting they may have been an afterthought.) The centre part of this then rises to the top on the principle of such frontispieces as those of Burghley or Hatfield, but here the closest model is Northumberland House, London (*c.* 1605–12; dem 1874). *Richard Goodridge*, mason, is mentioned in connection with work at Bramshill in 1617 and 1621 and it is likely that he was responsible for its construction, if not for its design. The centre has three tiers of paired superimposed pilasters, all tapering and all decorated, each tier with a different pattern. The sources are clearly Vredeman de Vries and, particularly, Dietterlin. The capitals bulge out or curve in without rhyme or reason. It is among the most fanciful pieces of Jacobean design in the country. On the first floor in the middle is a bow-fronted oriel. The second floor has a pair of round-arched windows. The top, standing against the sky, is strapwork of a coarse kind.

Next in sequence is the two-storey E RANGE, which is the longest side of the house and provides the second show front. It is the only range which appears to be entirely Jacobean and is dated 1612 (rainwater heads). The long recessed part has four canted bays and, between each, two long, slender cross-windows, whose height at first floor emphasizes the position of the state rooms. As the S and N fronts are somewhat wider than the rest of the house, this side also has projecting wings of two bays. Set into their inner angles are loggias with decorated pillars, spandrels and arches, probably re-set from the fore-court wings. Such loggias were a fashion of the early C17 and in their original position must have resembled the similar arrangement at Holland House. Both have early C17 wooden benches with carved arched panels; the SW loggia also has small re-set Jacobean carved reliefs of animals, discovered in the cellar in the late C19. Between the loggias a terrace, its balustrade removed *c.* 1840, with at each end staircases.

The N RANGE, like the E, is also of two storeys in height, containing the long gallery at first floor, and is punctuated by three full-height canted bays. The middle bay is a porch, projecting further than the others and crowned by a rusticated shaped gable with an ogee top, a niche with a statue of Lord Zouche and flanking obelisks. The round archway leads to a C16 double-chamfered four-centred archway which must have been the entrance to the previous house (inner archways visible inside, leading to the courtyard, must go with it) but the door has fine C17 lozenge panels. Much of the brickwork also appears to be pre-C17.

The irregular W FRONT is the service side and presents a puzzle. It also of course has two projecting wings (the full-height canted bay of the N wing contains the C17 mezzanine floor between the ground floor and long gallery in the N range; the S wing is as rebuilt *c.* 1820). But the recessed centre, with four straight gables, appears to be C16. A brick plinth extends the full width and is contemporary with an early C16 doorway towards its N end. Windows are of three dates: the brick mullion-and-transomed openings of the top two storeys are earliest (C17?). The ground floor was evidently lit by high-level horizontal mullioned windows above the plinth (traces of which survive at the S end) but this part was later extensively altered by the early C18 insertion of a mezzanine, lit by small sash windows, and late C19 mullioned windows that have been cut into the plinth. On the rear face of this range are rows of Tudor chimneys towards the INNER COURTYARD. It is diffi-cult to believe that this narrow, 'rather unsightly' (Pevsner) space represents the shape of the courtyard before 1605, even before the (former) CHAPEL was squeezed into the S end in 1621 (tall Gothic Survival four-light window, divided horizon-tally by a band of diapered brickwork) and the two-storey cor-ridor added on the N side *c.* 1810. The E range is all Lord Zouche's work, so he may have demolished an earlier range that was set further out.

INTERIOR. The HALL, in the S range, is only single-storey and lit by an E window and the windows at the dais end. The stone doorway is a fine piece of classical design, inserted when the entrance was moved to its present position, probably in the 1670s. Bolection-moulded architrave, carved frieze with hunting scene and segmental pediment. The stone screen is of course Jacobean. Its principal decoration is a plethora of painted heraldic shields. Pilasters flank a pair of just-pointed arches with pendant keystones and the four Cardinal Virtues carved in the spandrels; they correspond with a pair of smaller rusticated arches on the cross-passage's W side. On the back of the screen a bust of an ecclesiastic has been attached, prob-ably from an early to mid C17 monument, and the passage has *trompe l'œil* panelling, probably early C18. The hall chimney-piece is not specially spectacular and cannot be in its original condition since its panelled overmantel covers an inscription on plaster dated 1630. The panelling was probably formerly half or three-quarter height. Beneath the hall, UNDERCROFT, probably C16, vaulted with stone ribs; C17 cellars below the E range with a pair of parallel shallow vaulted chambers divided by a wall pierced by Tudor-arched openings.

The GREAT STAIR, NE of the hall, is a mid-C19 Neo-Jacobean confection by William Cope. It has an alternation of twisted balusters with normal, vertically symmetrical balusters.

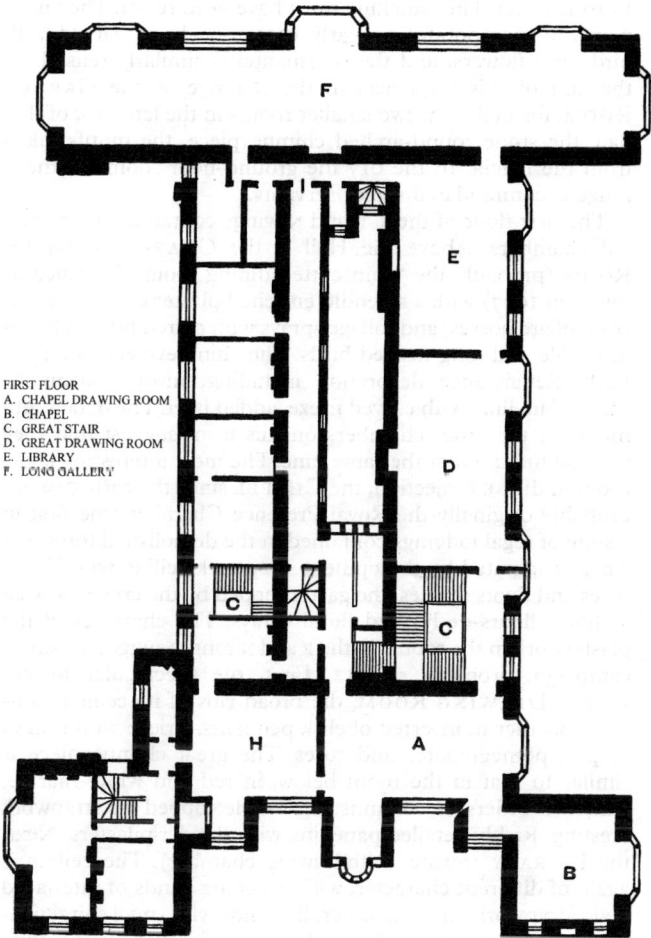

Bramshill House.
First-floor plan after Cope

It superseded an Early Georgian staircase, which itself replaced the early C17 original. Along the E front are the MORNING ROOM (the 'Great dining room belowe' in an inventory of 1634), with austere black-and-white marble chimneypiece, its overmantel with a polychromatic geometric design, apparently reflecting the formal patterns of early C17 gardens. The fireplace surround, with tapered Ionic pilasters, is probably late C18, the panelling, with Gibbons-style carved drops, probably late C17. Next is the BAR ROOM, originally the 'withdrawing room' and 'bedchamber beyond', combined in the 1930s for

Lord Brocket. The panelling must have been re-set. The chimneypiece incorporates an early C17 stone lintel carved with birds and flowers, and the overmantel is similarly reused. At the end of this sequence, in the N range, is the GARDEN ROOM, formed from two smaller rooms in the late C19; of that date the stone round-arched chimneypiece, the motifs taken from the loggia. In the C17 the ground-floor rooms of the N range accommodated senior servants.

The first floor of the S, E and N wings contained the principal chambers. Above the Hall is the CHAPEL DRAWING ROOM (probably the 'wainscotted dining room' described as 'niew' in 1607) with a splendid enriched plaster ceiling, of thin ribs, foliate bosses, and foliage sprays with paired human heads in profile and long-necked birds. The chimneypiece lintel has Early Renaissance decoration including, most charmingly, snails. Panelling with carved frieze, added later. The details and motifs in the other chambers on this front suggest that they were all fitted out at the same time. The most interesting is the room in the SE projection, the CHAPEL since the early C19 but probably originally the Royal Presence Chamber (the first in a suite of regal lodgings contained in the demolished forecourt wing), suggested by the opulent strapwork ceiling with Tudor roses and Scots thistles, the garter topped by the crown, as well as lions, fleurs-de-lys and floral sprays. The character of the plasterwork in the rooms in the E and N ranges suggests a single campaign, probably c. 1612. First, the spectacular former GREAT DRAWING ROOM, the broad ribs of its ceiling gathered together in inverted obelisk pendants. Frieze with trail of grapes, pomegranates and roses. The great chimneypiece is similar to that in the room below, in red and white marble, with two orders of columns, the whole topped by strapwork cresting. Richly detailed panelling with slender pilasters. Next, the LIBRARY (former withdrawing chamber). The ceiling is again of different character, with sweeping bands of interlaced plain strapwork finishing in scrolled ends with small spiral pendants. Also, larger gadrooned pendants. Rich frieze with foliage, strapwork and grotesque heads. Another splendid chimneypiece in black, white and brown marble, the overmantel with Ionic columns. The fireplace surround replaced in the early C19 but retaining flanking gryphon-like caryatids. Intricate panelling as before with slender fluted pilasters and strapwork details, clearly modelled on the wainscot at Lord Cecil's Theobalds, as recorded by John Smythson.

The LONG GALLERY, running the length of the N range, is the climax. Again a fine broad-ribbed plaster ceiling, enlivened by tiny pendants and lion masks. The fireplace in the S wall has a stone surround similar in style to that in the Chapel Drawing Room, its broad frieze beautifully carved with fruit and birds. The rest of the chimneypiece is wood, the most ambitious example in the house, with carved pilasters, arched and square panels and a deep carved frieze. The shallow arch into the central bay window has plaster shields and scrollwork in the spandrels. The square panelling is of the 1670s, painted in imitation of pollarded oak, and originally ran across the centre bay (removed in the late C19). It continues across the position of the former windows in the projecting ends of the s wall. The ground floor of the w range has the former kitchens and other service rooms. On its first floor is a run of C17 bedrooms, with panelling, chimneypieces and ribbed plaster ceilings. One has panels painted with plants, their source possibly a contemporary herbal. At the level of the early C18 mezzanine is a further suite of rooms, presumably to compensate for the loss of the forecourt wings. The staircase at the s end is contemporary: a fine piece with turned balusters, ramped handrail and a dog-gate at its foot. A second staircase in this range was removed when the corridors were inserted in the courtyard in the early C19.

SERVICE COURT, w of the house. Early C18. Gateways on three sides; those at each end have been widened. Brick piers with vitrified headers and large stone urn finials. Gateway in curved w wall with wrought-iron gates and overthrow. N is the STABLE COURT with quite modest early C18 STABLES.

On the main axis with the N entrance is the early C17 stone POSTERN GATE (restored in the late C19). Round archway flanked by pilasters supporting entablature and broken pediment with obelisk finials. Flanking lower arches under gables have C19 openwork balustrades. Between this and the house is the contemporary WALLED GARDEN which is divided N–S by a wall of 1675. Lord Zouche had a particular interest in gardening. He had a physic garden at his house in Hackney, supervised by Matthias de L'Obel, and corresponded with the French botanist, Charles de L'Escluse. He surely transferred this interest to Bramshill, but details of his gardens, which must have surrounded the house, are unknown. A couple of C18 plans show the Baroque gardens laid out by Sir John Cope, probably designed by *George Charles Deering c.* 1715. As well as formal layouts to the front and back of the house, there was a parterre in the angle of the E front and the TROCO TERRACE, for the croquet-like game of French origin, which is set at right angles to the NE corner of the house (a stone sphere with hollows for storing the Troco balls is in the N loggia). To its E was a trapezoidal Italian garden with three stone water basins.

PARK. In 1347 Sir Thomas Foxley had obtained a licence to enclose a 2,500-acre deer park at Bramshill. By 1699 this was crossed by formal avenues on the s and N axes of the house and by the early C18 was covered by a network of intersecting avenues. N of the house is a dammed LAKE, dug by Zouche, with a square island that probably originally had a fort or similar construction on it (cf. the C16 former crescent-shaped lake at Elvetham Hall). In the late C18 the area E of the house was landscaped and the parkland brought right up to the house. The Hart was also dammed to form the long serpentine BROAD WATER, now largely silted up. SW of the house is a canal, probably created in the early C18 from medieval fish

ponds; restored by Lord Brocket in the 1930s. W of the house
are White Pond and Dog Kennel Pond, the latter restored in
1949; of that date the ornamental balustraded BRIDGE at its
dammed end, designed by *Angela, Lady Brocket*. Between here
and the lake are the buildings of the TRAINING COLLEGE,
which took over the house in 1953. The first buildings are of
1958–60 by the *Ministry of Works*, the best Scandinavian-
influenced, of brick and tile. Of the later buildings the bunker-
like and moated FOXLEY HALL is of 1985–6 by *Ian Hunt
Associates*. A forbidding truncated tiled pyramid with sinister
strip windows at the corners. Most successful is the residential accommodation of 1992–5 by *Haverstock Associates*. Two
pairs of two-storey ranges at right angles, fully glazed on the S
side with a continuous first-floor terrace.

The drive, which in the early C17 descended from the forecourt on a great earth ramp, crosses the Hart over the mid-
C19 Jacobean HIGH BRIDGE. At the entrance is HAZELEY
LODGE, with three-storey brick towers with rendered quoins
and ogee roofs of *c.* 1820, the linking crenellated screen with
tripartite archways added after 1851.

MOOR PLACE FARMHOUSE, ¾ m. NW. Former manor house of
Great Bramshill. Early C17, incorporating a C16 cross-wing at
the lower end. Conservative plan, with hall and cross-passage,
but proving that such an arrangement was still associated with
high status even by this date (as at Bramshill House). Main
doorway to the r. has moulded surround with vase-stops; the
l. doorway probably an C18 insertion. Kitchen in cross-wing at
the rear of the lower end and stair-tower projecting from the
upper end of the hall with plain winder staircase. Three large
brick chimneys along the back, each with three diagonally set
shafts, and that at the upper end with a mullioned window to
a former garderobe. Inside, a Tudor-arched brick fireplace in
the hall, the finest in the house. The partition between hall and
passage is later, probably replacing a screen. The front wall of
the hall and the great chamber over have pairs of posts with
moulded capitals, which formerly framed bay windows. This
strongly suggests that the front of the house had a central projecting two-storey bay which, with the tall central chimney
above it, must have produced an imposing elevation.

BRAMSHOTT

A dispersed settlement among sunken lanes N of the Portsmouth
Road and E of the southern branch of the Wey.

ST MARY. The E parts, mostly in sandstone, survive from a small
cruciform church built around a low central tower. Its lower
stage may be the earliest fabric, for it is narrower than the
chancel of *c.* 1220 (see the typically E.E. lancets, a graduated
wide-spaced group of three in the E wall, and two in the N wall)

and the N and S transepts of *c.* 1400. There is a noticeable contrast in the sandstone of the transepts: coursed ashlar freestone
for the S transept (a chantry chapel of the de Bramshott family
of Bramshott Manor), and rougher rubble for the N transept.
Good Early Perp fenestration. The upper stage of the tower
and the shingled splay-foot spire are also of *c.* 1400, restored
and given a S-facing clock in 1910 by *H. Inigo Triggs*. Big
nave and aisles in C13 style of 1871–2 by *Sylvester C. Capes,* a
relation of the rector, replacing a Neo-Perp nave of 1834–6 by
James Harding of Farnham. The heavy, rather clumsy N and S
arches of the central tower are genuinely Perp, left unrestored.
The W and E arches are High Victorian E.E. and by Capes,
who scraped the transept walls, revealing two prominent
squints into the chancel. Good original roofs in both transepts,
each differing in detail (nice kingposts). Dull nave of four bays
with elaborate small rose window above a W porch. – FONT.
C13, with plain tapering octagonal base. Several other furnishings introduced in a reordering begun in 1932 for Canon
E. A. Beresford, masterminded by *W. H. Randoll Blacking*. By
him, the Neo-Tudor PULPIT of 1935, with linenfold panelled
back-board and crested tester. The ambitious canopied Neo-
Tudor PRIEST'S STALL and the fine LECTERN in a crisp
Renaissance of 1954. – STAINED GLASS. In a chancel N lancet,
medieval bits, including a tiny C15 group of figures and a few
heads, from 'many vestiges' extant in the early C19 (Bingley).
– More pieces in the porch presented in 1957. Plenty of Victorian and later glass, by different firms, the most impressive
N aisle W, by *Holiday*, 1895, with seated females representing
Virtues. Decidedly classical and clearly influenced by Burne-
Jones. Chancel E window of 1948 by *Martin Travers*, with good
heraldry in memory of Canadian troops who trained on
Bramshott Common. – CURIOSUM. Two C13 earthenware
bowls found embedded in the tower interior walls during
repairs in 1910. – BRASS. John Weston and wife, with long
scrolls upward from their mouths, *c.* 1430? The figures are 17½
in. (44 cm.) long. MONUMENTS. Sir James Macdonald †1832
and his son †1831 aged ten. By *Westmacott Jun.* Relief
of St James, as a pilgrim, and the little boy. Sentimental. –
H. Inigo Triggs †1923. Modest tablet. – LYCHGATE of 1925 by
G. H. Kitchin and good group of C18 stone TABLE TOMBS SE
of the church (earliest date 1765). WAR CEMETERY, SW, with
a classical gateway by *Triggs*.

BRAMSHOTT MANOR, SW of the church. An extraordinary
group of three medieval chamber blocks, which must have
been linked by a hall range, now lost. Each has a ground floor
of stone and tile-hung timber-framed upper floors. The earliest is mid to late C14 and has two-light ground-floor windows
with cusped ogee-headed lights under square heads. One pair
are set so closely that the hoodmoulds are clumsily joined in
the middle. Inside is a three-bay chamber with a stubby crown-
post roof with moulded capitals and bases (mouldings are rare
in Hampshire). It appears to have been originally unheated;

Bramshott Place, gatehouse.
Drawing by Charles E. Flower, 1903

the chimney is c16. The next block, also with a three-bay
chamber, adjoins at right angles at the NE corner. Jettied at its
E end and with a typical early c16 crown-post roof. The
chimneypiece has the initials of Sir Edmund Mervyn (†1553).
Its NW stair-tower is later, with a wide Tudor-arched doorway
with carved spandrels; a smaller doorway of the same style
links the two ranges inside. The third block, abutting the SE
corner, also with a crown-post roof and a possible former
garderobe alongside the lateral chimney, has ogee wall-braces,
suggesting a mid-c16 date, but can the fine windows with
cinquefoil-headed lights be that late?

In the area are several other good houses: Along Tunbridge Lane,
BRAMSHOTT VALE, ¼ m. w of the church. Built 1731–2 for
John Butler, a Wealden ironmaster. Principal elevations (s and
E) in red brick with vitrified headers, the rest in dressed sand-
stone. The front is now of 2–1–2 bays, but originally had the
typical very narrow early c18 windows l. and r. of the centre,

in a broad shallow projection. Later C18 Ionic porch with open pediment. The original doorcase, re-set on the S front, has the characteristic frieze coming up by curves to a point in the middle under a segmental pediment. On the W front, a tall arched staircase window in a pilastered surround. The interior lives up to the exterior – its staircase rising in three flights with fluted column-on-vase balusters and brackets carved with ears of wheat. Panelled rooms, mostly late C18 chimneypieces.

QUINCES, N of Bramshott Vale, is *c.* 1700 but picturesquely altered and enlarged *c.* 1926, by *Tubbs, Messer & Hambling*. Further N, COOPER'S BRIDGE by *Unsworth & Triggs*, 1911, in brick with much tile-hanging and sweeping tile roofs. BRAMSHOTT COURT, ¼ m. N again is *c.* 1700 and very striking, with a three-bay pediment and contrasting light and dark coloured stones with bright red brick dressings. Its wing of 1910–11, by *J. D. Coleridge*, is in a matching style and it forms an asymmetrical U-plan on the garden side. Good interiors of the later date.

BRAMSHOTT PLACE VILLAGE, Hewshott Lane, ½ m. SSE, across the A3. Early C21 housing on the site of the C16 manor house. All that remains is the miniature brick GATEHOUSE, probably built by Henry Mervyn or his son Edmund, who inherited in 1585. He was thrice M.P. for Petersfield. The angles have circular buttresses with moulded bases and ball finials, two with a trellis pattern, two encrusted with closely set blobs within a diagonal grid. On each face an ogee gable with a finial. The N gateway has a four-centred head, above it an oriel. Oriel to the E side too. Smaller arch on the S side, above which appears to be a former doorway. There is evidence that the gatehouse interrupted a brick wall, so it may have led either into a walled garden or courtyard to the house. Its first-floor chamber might have been a banqueting house or gazebo, perhaps reached by an external stair. The WALLED GARDEN is probably C18. Early C19 NORTH LODGE.

LUDSHOTT MANOR, ¾ m. N. Built as Woolmer Lodge in 1827–8 by *P. F. Robinson* for Sir James Macdonald. Neo-Tudor style. The N wing contains an older house, the W side of which Robinson refronted in stucco with gables and wooden windows. The S extension is much more robust in dressed greensand and with hoodmoulded windows. Its square SE tower contained the porch but the doorway was moved W by *G. H. Kitchin* in 1928. At the N end, a two-storey wing with polygonal end, added 1869–70, for Sir Archibald Macdonald, who created a Catholic chapel (by *P. P. Pugin*, dem. 1908). Converted to apartments in 2002 by *mbp Architects* and the interior restored, although the early C18 staircase, noted by Pevsner, had been sold. Early C17 former STABLES, a rare survival. One storey with a gabled projection in the centre. WALLED GARDEN also partly early C17, with moulded Tudor-arched doorways. Regrettably a terrace of four houses (by *Moxley Architects*) has been erected within this space. The pair of charming N and S LODGES, *cottages ornés*, must be *Robinson*'s.

HIGH HURLANDS, 1½ m. NNE. Vogue Regency of 1934 by *Curtis Green & Partners*. Y-plan with a central hexagonal tower and pantiled roofs.

WATERSIDE, 1 m. NW of the church. Farmhouse remodelled and enlarged in 1921–3 for George Anketell, a Member of the Stock Exchange. Possibly by *J. D. Coleridge* who worked at Bramshott Court nearby. In the Lutyens-influenced Arts and Crafts style typical of him. The principal addition is the so-called 'barn' at the E end which contains a great hall with open timber roof and minstrels' gallery and incorporating a magnificent Renaissance chimneypiece. C17 panelling and chimneypieces in the drawing room (from Swan Hall, Suffolk) and dining room (from Urishay Castle, Herefordshire). In the entrance hall a fine carved Renaissance panel with carved heads in roundels. Billiard room and swimming pool added by *Adrian Bird* in the 1990s. The gardens, on the banks of the Wey, include a Japanese garden, probably by *Jekyll*. Pretty stone WELL-HEAD.

CONFORD HOUSE. 1½ m. W. *c.* 1630. Now all stone, but the first floor originally timber-framed (cf. Black House Farm, Hinton Ampner). Three-bay S front with early C19 sashes. The householder occupied the two E bays (this part with chamfered plinth and evidence of mullioned windows with hoodmoulds) and his servants the bay W of the chimney. Separate doorways for each in the rear outshot.

BROUGHTON

A large village closely following the course of the Wallop Brook.

ST MARY. Quite large, of C12 origin* and an early dependant of Mottisfont held by the Archbishop of York. The big W tower, with angle buttresses, and other external motifs, is Perp but has a plain, castellated and rendered bell-stage of 1845 and a re-set early C13 doorway (with dogtooth in the arch). Nice C16 S porch, restored in 1924 by *G. H. Kitchin*. Chancel restored in 1886 by *A. R. Barker*, with E and N window in E.E. style. The two straight-headed S windows were probably inserted *c.* 1638 after a fire. The scarred N arcade is of, say, *c.* 1200. Three wide bays, round piers, multi-scallop capitals (cf. Nether and Over Wallop), round abaci, pointed arches with two chamfers. S arcade of *c.* 1210. The capitals are now moulded. Then the nave was extended W, see the one N and one S lancet (and the W doorway). Bland chancel arch of 1870. – OAK BENCHES of 1906 belong to the chancel reordering instigated by *E. Doran Webb*; he also added the vestry. – PILLAR PISCINA. Large and Perp like a miniature font (it served as

---

* The chancel may be Norman: see the chamfered SE quoin and the neat coursed flint S wall.

such until the mid C19). The capital is enchanting with little figures attached to the wall. – READING TABLE. With brass sconces. The possession of John Keble while vicar of Hursley (s Hampshire). – ALTAR TABLE. In the s aisle, a fine (domestic?) Jacobean piece, with a TRIPTYCH made up from a small, early C16 Netherlandish painting of The Lamentation, flanked by two C19 panels of saints. – PEWS. Assembled in 1853 from those of 1638 (dated on one pew). – STAINED GLASS. In the chancel of 1904: E window by *Kempe*, others by *Campbell & Christmas*. N aisle w attributed to *Clutterbuck*. 1876 but looking earlier, with Evangelist emblems. s aisle SE by *Clayton & Bell* to Dr Luther Owen Fox †1879, who appears as the Good Samaritan (also in his memory the nearby FONT, ugly C13 Gothic style). MONUMENT. Chancel s side, Margaret Hearst †1647. Tablet with shaped pediment and ball finials.

DOVECOTE, NE of the church. Brick, with a conical roof and a little lantern. Built 1684; inside 482 brick nesting boxes in tiers, serviced by a revolving central ladder (reconstructed in 1984). N of this the OLD RECTORY is early C18 brick encasing a C15 three-bay open hall; the medieval rectory was attached to the Treasurer of York Cathedral.

Several good timber-framed as well as Georgian brick houses in the village, especially nicely grouped around The Square. OLD CHURCH FARM, opposite St Mary, must be *c.* 1760 but pleasantly enlarged with tripartite windows, canted bays and a large wing by *Douglas Stewart* of Westminster, 1909. He also made alterations in 1919 to BROUGHTON HOUSE which lies across fields E of the church. Its centre is *c.* 1700 between C19 and C20 wings. At the N end of the High Street is the former BAPTIST CHAPEL, founded 1655, for one of the oldest rural Baptist communities in England, and rebuilt in 1816. Its present façade is *c.* 1926, in a C17 classical style with Doric columns, hoodmoulded windows and pediment. Just beyond is LINDEN HOUSE, early to mid Georgian of three bays. Its s chimney is dated 1777 but the graceful door surround with thin Tuscan columns carrying an open segmental pediment is of 1932.

GRANDFATHER'S, Rookery Lane. Late C17 features: brick with platband and five bays of cross-windows.* Clunch block walls at the rear, perhaps of 1732 when the back part is described in a diary as 'now building'. Stair-passage entry with central stack and rear staircase with spindle balusters. One room with C18 panelling. This was the childhood home of the hymn writer, Anne Steele (born 1717).

HILDON HOUSE, 2 m. s. *Aston Webb*'s mansion of 1898 for Sir Augustus Webster has been demolished. The former stables (converted as Hildon House *c.* 1990) are from the previous house of the 1870s. Towered centre with cupola on a pyramidal roof behind.

* Inventories for 1663 and 1680 appear to describe a medieval hall house.

Brown Candover, St Mary.
Brass of *c*. 1490.

ROUND BARROWS, 1 m. w, in Whiteshoot Plantation, on the
s edge of Broughton Down. The most conspicuous monument
is a fine bell barrow 60 ft (19 metres) in diameter and 6 ft

(1.8 metres) high with low saucer barrows to the E and W. The
large mound has a central depression suggestive of robbing.
LONG BARROW. *See* Nether Wallop.

BROWN CANDOVER   5030

ST MARY. 1844–5 by *T. H. Wyatt* for Lord Ashburton of The
Grange. Stolid Perp of coursed, knapped flint and freestone.
SW porch-tower with lead broach spire. Big nave and short
chancel. Depressingly uniform windows, but with lively foliate
label stops. Commodious open interior with impressive roof,
almost C17 Gothic in its bold simplicity. Good furnishings:
COMMUNION RAIL from the old church at Northington (q.v.).
Pierced panels of lush acanthus and, mixed up with them,
cherubs with Christian virtues. Late C17, probably Flemish.
Original FONT, given by the architect. Later C19 wooden
LECTERN and open-traceried PRIEST'S DESK, also from Northington, no doubt by *Butterfield*. Good STAINED GLASS E
window of 1845, probably by *Miller*, the London glass painter
favoured by Wyatt. – MONUMENT. Brass to a husband and
wife, c. 1490. They stand praying, but unusually arm in arm,
and are cut out of one brass plate. A flower grows behind and
between them. The figures are 19 in. (48 cm.) long.
CANDOVER HOUSE, ¼ m. S. C18. Brick. Nine bays, with slightly
projecting three-bay pedimented centre. Later brick porch.
Garden side similar with central bow.
ROBEYS FARMHOUSE, ⅓ m. SW. Late C17. Knapped flint and
brick with coved plaster eaves cornice. L-plan with two almost
identical five-bay fronts giving the appearance of a double-pile
house. C19 brick porch to SE.

BULLINGTON   4040

ST MICHAEL, Lower Bullington. Small, nave and chancel in one.
Distressingly over-restored by *Ewan Christian* in 1871 (chancel
E window, S porch and N vestry). Norman nave, see the blocked
N doorway and single W lancet windows. S doorway widened
1871. The chancel is E.E.; one S lancet, and a lancet re-set in
the vestry. Flint and brick W tower, pre-dating restoration, with
late C14 W window (the re-set E window). – STAINED GLASS.
E window by *Wailes*, 1871.
    Nearby CHURCH FARM, the farmhouse probably a frag-
ment of a larger timber-framed structure, much rebuilt in brick
in the C18. Behind, by the Dever, a C19 weatherboarded BARN
with attached water wheel. BULLINGTON MANOR is a modest
early C19 house with a top-lit galleried stair hall.

BURGHCLERE

Strictly speaking 'New' Burghclere, a scattered settlement 2 m.
N of Old Burghclere (q.v.) and now the centre of the parish.

CHURCH OF THE ASCENSION. 1836–8 by *George Guillaume* of
Southampton. The church, long and low with a plain W tower
and apse, was enlarged in a sensitive Perp, and generally
restored by *Norman Shaw* in 1874–5 for the Rev. G. R. Portal.
The chancel is Shaw's, but the oddly blunt tower top with
square-headed two-light mullioned windows is of 1838. Shaw's
tall impressive tiled spire of *c.* 1876 with long lucarnes was
taken down and the original parapet substituted by *Paul &*
Palmer in 1963 – a landmark loss. The aisleless earlier parts of
coursed flint have E.E. details. Broad interior with thin timberwork roofs. The furnishings richest in the Shavian part, which
is unaltered. – FONT. From Old Burghclere. C15 with quatrefoils. C17 font cover. In the chancel, a complete ensemble:
especially the DADO of *Maw* tiles and the carefully related
REREDOS to Portal †1886. Of mosaic and *opus sectile*. By
Powells, with a red cross and angels. – Elaborate wooden
CHANCEL SCREEN of 1914 by *Francis Bacon*, completed with
light Dec tracery *c.* 1919, over Shaw's low stone screen and
nice Gothic iron gates. – LECTERN. A big brass eagle of 1875.
– PULPIT, unusually of wrought iron. – STAINED GLASS in the
chancel by *Clayton & Bell*, except for one N window of 1905
by *Powells*. More later work by them in the nave. – N transept
E by *Wailes* of 1859 from the old chancel. – N transept N by
Martin Travers, *c.* 1944. The best MONUMENT is in the churchyard, a sarcophagus, SW of the tower, to Anna Villebois of
Beenham Park †1840, signed *C. Smith*. – LYCHGATES. Muscular Gothic of 1885, probably by *Bacon*.

PORTAL HALL, Church Lane. Domestic Revival of 1890.
Cottage attached at the rear is Shavian, with banded tile-
hanging, large gable with oriel and shafted chimney. Over the
road, the mid-C19 Tudor Gothic PRIMARY SCHOOL and the
WAR MEMORIAL, *Blomfield*'s 'Cross of Sacrifice'.

SANDHAM MEMORIAL CHAPEL (Oratory of All Souls), Harts
Lane. The first quarter of the C20 was the heroic age of
Modern painting. Today everything is possible and will find
enthusiastic journalists and a patron. The step from Impres-
sionism to Cubism, Expressionism, and abstraction was into
unknown and dangerous territory. France created Cubism,
Germany's strength was Expressionism, both reached abstraction. England was peripheral, and her contributions were
inspired by one or another Continental trend. An exception is
Stanley Spencer, whose style came to full fruition after the First
World War and is essentially original.

Spencer spent part of the war as an orderly in a Bristol hospital and later went to Macedonia. The idea for a series of war
paintings was in his mind from 1918 as a great 'opus' on private
commission, like Giotto in the Arena chapel at Padua. A failed

opportunity was first presented at Steep (q.v.) before Mr and
Mrs J. L. Behrend saw his sketches and commissioned the
cycle for the chapel. This was also to be a war memorial and
more specifically a memorial to Lieut. H. W. Sandham, Mrs
Behrend's brother, who had died in 1919 from an illness contracted in the war in Macedonia.

The chapel, built in 1926–7, was designed by *Lionel Pearson*.
It is an oblong block of brick with stone dressings, and l. and
r. of it low three-bay Neo-Georgian cottages. The chapel itself,
while not strictly imitative, suffers from the very convention-
ality that Stanley Spencer abhorred. All he wanted was a 'holy
box'. Spencer was thirty-six, and at the summit of his art, when
he started in the chapel in 1926. His work was finished in 1932.

There are nineteen paintings in the chapel, their scenes of   117
army life based directly on Spencer's own experiences at
Beaufort Hospital, Bristol; Tweseldown Camp, Aldershot; and
Macedonia. They are collectively the largest early achievement
of the greatest early C20 British painter and must be seen in
relation to his other works on the same theme in the Imperial
War Museum. As a cycle, they are unique, and in what they
represent without equal in England.

The arrangement is as follows:

E WALL

Resurrection of the dead soldiers

N WALL

Morning in the camp at Karasuli

The arrival of a convoy of wounded at the hospital	Hospital washroom	Kit inspection	Dug-out Salonika
Scrubbing the floor	Moving kit-bags	Sorting laundry	Filling tea-urns

S WALL

Soldiers in the river-bed at Todorovo

Shaving under mosquito nets	Convoy of wounded filling water-bottles	Officer and his men map-reading	Making a fire-belt
Ward with frostbitten soldier	Tea in the ward	Bed-making	Washing lockers

Pevsner's description needs no revision:

'In looking at the titles of the paintings the essential quality of Spencer's war recording is at once patent. There is no battle, no sword-rattling, no shining heroism. A war is not fought but undergone. It needs endurance day after day. The headline stuff is no business of other ranks.

The E wall is entirely filled by the Resurrection of the Dead, exactly as in Michelangelo's Sistine Chapel. But there is no Christ in Judgment. Christ is a small, white, distant figure, lovable and pathetic, and His role is not to elevate to Heaven and condemn to Hell. He is there just to receive the crosses which the soldiers hand in. In the foreground they rise, from under the thicket of tumbled crosses, shake hands, and clamber up in confusion. The pattern of all the crosses is disturbing. So is the pair of pink mules, large in the middle, with hieratically long necks turning l. and r. The men are not a variety of types, but mostly one and the same type, with flat, fat impassive faces and round limbs. We are looking at all this at an odd angle, as if from the air. This device to combat everyday normality was familiar to the Mannerists of the C16, and so was the device of placing the most important figure far away and high up, and also the stylizing of the human figures into enforced inertia. Yet no one in England in 1932, let alone 1919, knew about Mannerism. On the other hand there are also parallels with Casorati* and even de Chirico, and also the German Neue Sachlichkeit. On the N wall, bottom l., is a shell-shocked soldier scrubbing the hospital floor, violently prostrate, and alone in his tragedy with the others stepping by him and over him. This scene is exceptional in alluding so directly to tragedy. In the Moving of Kitbags, bottom two, the man on the l. shows particularly clearly how Spencer's figures are stylized into sacklike shapes so as to limit their freedom of action. Bruegel is the Mannerist who did that before, and Bruegel Spencer must have known and admired. Bottom three is a battle with laundry, and it is again typical how the r. hand soldier is nearly hidden by the geometrical shape of the towel – a sugar-loaf man. On the extreme r. is the only woman. Never is an episode told in a workaday way. Spencer intensifies and removes the stories from reality. At the bottom r. it is the huge tea-urns which provide the geometry.

The larger pictures of the second tier are upright and arched. In the Arrival of the Convoy Spencer's Mannerist trick of the view down at an angle is specially effective. The slings of the wounded are white triangles, the big hats are straight from Bruegel. Spencer's vegetation is dappled and flat. Background space must not be too true to nature and perspective either. In the washroom the soap-sud helmets are Bruegelish again, i.e. a lifting of the person out of what one would normally see about him. The soldier whose wound is being treated with iodine stands fat and inert. Kit inspection seems to move up

---

* Felice Casorati (1883–1963). Italian painter, one of the classicist figure painters of the interwar period.

a hill steeply. The gaiters must have pleased Spencer, converting human into insect legs. In the trench scene the principal figure, an exceptionally cool and courageous sergeant, is dressed up with fern to conceal him. The belts, taken off because the trench was so tight, form a pattern as unexpected as that of the crosses. The background is clouds of barbed wire. The top picture is not easily seen, and it spreads out in episodes. In front of one of the two rows of tents – dominant geometry again – stands the one really martial figure. But his sword is a stick to pick up litter, and his shield is a bag.

On the s side the first picture of the bottom row is a ward with soldiers in night-shirts and blankets all as baggy shapes, and the wire frame for the treatment of frostbite offering a view into a grotesque cave. There is horror, but also compassion in these hospital glimpses, and never sentimentality. Tea in the Ward: here in particular the identity of the mask-like faces is baffling. Number three has pin-ups on the wall, some of them private records of Stanley Spencer.* The man on the l. in his boulder of bed-clothes ought to be noted. He is sitting in a chair while his bed is being made. The Washing of Lockers is the most abstract picture of the series. The men play a minor part between curved baths and angular lockers.

Above, first l. is again full Mannerism, Tintoretto in the encasing of men in transparent abstract shapes and the others lining the margin. Only brushwork and modelling are of course utterly different from Tintoretto. The next scene could almost be a Mannerist painting of the c16, with the men in their ground-sheets converging and looking like strange angels in some incomprehensible glory. The topees also contribute to making the scene belong to a distant age. Large in the foreground two pink mules. In the map-reading scene the centre is the only officer, a lieutenant, in the whole cycle. That also is telling. He is sitting on a horse, but the map almost hides that. The men around form a radiating pattern. The view down at an angle is as before. So is the dappled leaf background, counteracting the funnelling foreshortening of the front parts. Making a fire-belt has connotations of Vulcan's Smithy. The ropes of the tent and the absurdly over-foreshortened long tube are worth looking for. Finally the top episode, looser than the rest, which was unavoidable in such a sprawling shape. The soldiers on the l. are playing housey-housey, in the middle they are washing clothes.

In the whole of the cycle there is no red, nor a strong blue or yellow. What one remembers is grey, browns, beiges, and silvery greens.

The chapel had already been dedicated in 1927. There was no special celebration for the finishing of the paintings. In fact one must be grateful to the church authorities for having tolerated a cycle as silent about organized religion as about the glories of a won war.'

---

* They are a poetic foretaste of the 1960s Pop Art of Peter Blake and admired by him.

BURGHCLERE HOUSE (originally Great Gravels), ¾ m. NE. Neo-Georgian of 1901–2, probably by *Francis Bacon.* Quite loose in its detailing and informally planned. Contemporary motor house. LITTLE EARLSTONE (originally Little Gravels) is by the same architect. Colour-washed brick and thatch, split level on a steeply sloping site.

ADBURY HOUSE, 1¼ m. NW. *c.* 1800. Stuccoed with moulded cornice. Front of three plus five bays, Greek Doric porch with unfluted columns. Nearby, ADBURY FARMHOUSE. Refaced in brick in the early C19 but probably early C17 with a C15 cross-wing. Late C17 staircase with twisted balusters in rear tower.

EARLSTONE MANOR, 1 m. SE. Early C17 lobby-entry house; the triple-gabled S front rebuilt in brick *c.* 1700, of five bays, re-windowed *c.* 1800. What makes it special is the remains of a chamber block, in line at the W end, which has a crown-strut roof of a type found in Kent in the 1320s. The hall to which it was formerly attached may have been on the site of the SW wing (*c.* 1800).

7020

BURITON

A pretty village dramatically sited under the steep wooded slopes of the South Downs near the Sussex border.

ST MARY. The church is of mixed flint and assorted sandstones with a plain W tower of 1714 in neatly coursed ironstone, probably on old foundations. It is a large church for Hampshire, with a wide sweeping roof in one over nave and aisles; perhaps of Saxon origin, it was the parent church of Petersfield (q.v.) and of small long-lost hamlet chapels. Externally the chancel of *c.* 1270 is the only noteworthy element. Bar tracery with an uncusped circle in the S windows. Also a priest's doorway. The interior is exceptionally fine. Nave of *c.* 1180–1200 with four-bay arcades of chalk. Round piers, multi-scalloped capitals, Greek-cross abaci (i.e. square with nicked corners), round, single step arches. The responds have waterholding bases and the capital (restored) of the NE respond also has water-lily leaves of *c.* 1180, of a rare form but also seen at Petersfield (nave arcade NW respond). Most of those on S side are renewed (evidence of H. Prosser's view of 1840) after C17(?) alteration. The noble early C13 tower arch is a great surprise. It has semi-circular responds of enormous heaviness, and they stand unusually on stone tables, projecting toward the centre so as to leave only a passage free. Can they represent the W wall of the previous church with its W doorway towards the village, or could they have supported a screen open in the middle? The feature is clearly C13. The finely proportioned chancel is sump-tuous with Caen stone detail in the continuous moulded string course, the N vestry door, and magnificent stepped triple

SEDILIA with crisp pointed trefoiled arches, and double
PISCINA. Large E window with nook-shafts and original headstops (one of a bishop) but the rest mostly renewed in the big
restoration of 1877–8 by *A. W. Blomfield* when Perp tracery
was removed, and the rest of the church re-roofed and refurnished. Few furnishings of interest. – FONT. C12 Purbeck
marble, of table type, on five supports. Badly preserved. –
TILES. A few of *c.* 1260 in the chancel. – WALL PAINTING. A
faded fragmentary early C14 throned Virgin and Child on
the E splay of the chancel SW window. – Traces of decorative
painting inside the sedilia. – STAINED GLASS. Chancel E
window a highly finished Ascension scene by *Powells*, 1886. By
them also the N aisle W window of 1916 to John Goodyer
(†1664, *see* Petersfield), the botanist, buried in the churchyard.
His achievement nicely done. S aisle centre by *Clayton & Bell*,
c. 1862. Not bad, with vivid reds and blues. – N aisle E, by
Morris & Co., 1928 and 1930. Belated Pre-Raphaelite angels:
Gabriel (by *J. H. Dearle*) and Michael (by *Burne-Jones*). –
MONUMENTS. Engraved polished black marble plate to
Thomas Hanbury †1617, Auditor of the Exchequer. Kneeling
family group with heraldry. – Thomas Bilson †1692. Marble-
topped tomb-chest. – Leonard Bilson †1695. Good wall tablet
attributed to *James Hardy* (GF). Inaccessible in the SW vestry.
In the churchyard are two good C18 tombstones (dates of 1757
and 1775) and a typically early C19 Tudor Gothic table tomb
to John Bonham-Carter †1838, who inherited the estate at
Buriton in the 1820s. Signed by *J. Browne*, London, 1839.
Another in plainer classical idiom to the infant George Portland †1839. – HALL. Transeptal addition to the N aisle, by *Terry
Roberts*, 1994.

MANOR HOUSE, N of the church. Acquired by Edward Gibbon,
grandfather of the historian, in 1719. He died in 1736 and
either he or his son rebuilt the E range (originally C17, see the
blocked mullioned window in the W wall). This is a singularly
felicitous composition of vitrified headers with red dressings,
stone platband, and moulded brick cornice to the parapet.
Three storeys and five bays to the garden, the centre three
breaking forward, keyed openings and central doorway with
moulded architrave. (Inside, an elegant C18 staircase with
column-on-vase balusters and good late C16 inlaid panelling
with perspective scene and arabesque ornament.) Round the
corner the house is part of the square farmyard. It has a big
canted bay window here and is continued by a lower C18
service range that incorporates earlier fabric and later porches
l. and r. This is of malmstone and brick like the beautifully
built large BARN, of *c.* 1700, opposite. It was clearly built for
some other use. Unfloored within but with two rows of
windows, those on the ground floor now largely blocked. The
gable-ends had oculi, cut into by the lower roof-line following
conversion in the later C18 when the rear was rebuilt in timber
with an aisle. The cart entrances, presumably added, have

basket-arched openings pushing up into the pedimented gables with blind *œils de bœuf* above. On the w side c18 STABLES, also malmstone and brick. Nine bays, the central three-bay break having a large pediment with *œil de bœuf* in the tympanum. c18 hexagonal brick DOVECOTE NE of house.

THE OLD RECTORY in the High Street has a late c13 stone-built hall block (blocked lancet in front wall and another re-set in the N gable) with an early c14 cross-wing to the l. (remains of traceried window in roof-space). Recast, however, in the early c16 and again *c.* 1800 when it was stuccoed and sashed and another projecting wing added r. The early c16 hall roof is of three bays with queen-strut trusses; vestigial cross-passage and remains of buttery and pantry doorways. In the rebuilt cross-wing two upper chambers and arch-braced collar-trusses.

BURITON HOUSE, ½ m. NE. 1912, by *J. H. Ball* for Lothian Bonham-Carter. Neo-Georgian, brick with modillion eaves cornice and hipped roofs. Attractively asymmetrical entrance front with two-storey porch and ogee-roofed tower, essentially symmetrical garden front with shallow wings.

NURSTED HOUSE, 1 m. NE. Dated 1767 inside, although probably a remodelling of a house of *c.* 1700. Malmstone ashlar, of nine bays with a pedimented three-bay projection. The windows have raised limestone ashlar surrounds with lugs, the angles raised brick quoins. Nice pedimented Doric doorcase. More informal rear, with later stucco wing to l. with ground-floor tripartite window (library) and first-floor Venetian window, both with Gothic-paned sashes. Billiard room to side, of 1928, in the same style. Interior mostly of 1767, the best rooms the entrance hall and stair hall with pretty Adamesque plasterwork, and the library with carved fittings, some probably reused. Malmstone and brick STABLES and COACHHOUSE of 1767. Ambitiously treated N gable with flanking square piers and blocked archway with Venetian window above.

82   OLD DITCHAM FARM, 1¼ m. E. The farm has a BARN that is truly amazing. It is of malm and brick and the exterior details point to a *c.*1700 date – round-arched openings with plain mullions and transoms and a pilaster strip surround – but inside is a series of enormous malmstone diaphragm arches, entirely unmoulded, carrying the roof instead of the normal timbers. For the late c17 it seems unbelievable. Can they be of 1757, the date carved on one of the arches? They look more like Lethaby or Prior than anything c18.

DITCHAM PARK, 1½ m. S, high up on the Downs. Now a school. Built 1886–7 for Lawrence Trent Cave by *A. W. Blomfield*; his clerk of works was *Walter Cave*. Immediately gutted by fire and rebuilt with modifications in 1888. Tall and compact Neo-Tudor, in a fiery red Rowlands Castle brick. Three gables to the front and polygonal SE stair-turret (the copper cap is post-war), which served the R.C. chapel. Panelled library and impressive galleried staircase rising through the centre of the house. The pretty timber-framed and tile-hung service wing is probably of the first build, like the charming Old English-style NORTH LODGE.

QUEEN ELIZABETH COUNTRY PARK, on the A3 1½ m. SE.
Opened 1976. Unremarkable VISITORS' CENTRE, by *Casson,
Conder & Associates*. The country park incorporates the great
flat-topped BUTSER HILL, 889 ft above sea level, on which are
a number of earthworks. On the spur called Ramsdean Down
are three BOWL BARROWS, each approximately 60 ft (19
metres) in diameter and 4 ft (1.2 metres) high. All have depressions in their centres suggesting previous examination. On the
flat top of the hill are two large round barrows set close
together. The S example is a BOWL BARROW, badly damaged
by rabbits; the N one is a great BELL BARROW, 135 ft (42
metres) in diameter and 8 ft (2.5 metres) high, which shows
signs of having been robbed. Across the ridge on the SW of the
hill which links it with an adjoining hill are three lines of BANKS
AND DITCHES which effectively block access to the hill at this
point. Finally on the S and SE slopes of the hill are a series of
CELTIC FIELDS. Romano-British pottery has been found in
this area, although the field systems may have been laid out in
the Iron Age.

CHARLTON

Andover

3040

ST THOMAS. 1908 by *H. C. Benson*. Small, minimally Perp, a successor to the medieval church at Foxcotte (q.v.), from which
the C15 (VCH) canopy of a niche in the N wall is taken. Low
polygonal W baptistery below the small tile-caped timber W
belfry (derived from the bell-turret of Bemerton, Wilts.)
Simple interior, with a fireplace at the W end of the N wall,
evidently always intended for flexible use. – STAINED GLASS.
E window. St Michael. 1917 by *Emily Ford* (Peter Cormack) to
Benson †1915 in Flanders.
UPPER CHARLTON HOUSE, SE. C18 with stuccoed front and tripartite sashes. Pretty group of cottages by the stream.

CHAWTON

7030

The village lies in the valley of the Lavant Stream on the former
London–Gosport road with the manor house and church quite
separate to the S.

ST NICHOLAS. Essentially by *A. W. Blomfield*, 1871–2. Old
masonry only in the chancel (which is noticeably skewed) surviving from the Norman church that Jane Austen knew, and
its few details, apart from the Perp E window, are mostly of the
restoration and enlargement in 1838 by *G. & W. Dyer* of
Alton. The rest of the church is flint, with a tall pinnacled SW
porch-tower, and a N aisle with three cross-gables, all with

Geometrical tracery looking 1850 rather than 1870. Rather
solid, but richly furnished. Chancel arch of 1838, unusually of
wood. – COMMUNION RAIL. Early C18; pretty. ORGAN CASE
and SCREEN with ROOD. By *Bodley*. Also by him, the REREDOS
of 1899 incorporating a panel painting of the Crucifixion,
attributed to the *Workshop of Frans Francken I* (1542–1616). –
STAINED GLASS. E window of 1914 by *Kempe & Co.* A delicately drawn Nativity scene. – Chancel S by *Bell* (of Bristol). –
Nave, SE and SW by *Daniel Bell, c.* 1877. The centre window,
†1886, highly finished by *Edward Frampton*. W window, by
Hardman, 1880, with scenes in large medallions. – N aisle
mostly by *Kempe*, the earliest two saints of 1896–7. – MONU-
MENTS. Sir Richard Knight †1679. Good standing marble
monument attributed to *Jasper Latham* (GF), crowding the
chancel, though set within a deep bay. Semi-reclining figure in
armour. Big back display with military trophies. The whole
remarkably Dutch. Sir Richard was an exile with Charles II in
Holland, and he lavished £500 on the monument, a sum
purposely set aside in his lifetime. – Several classical tablets
without figures, to Knights (e.g. William Knight, erected in
1723, ascribed to *Edward Stanton* (GF)). – Edward Knight,
†1879. Neo-Jacobean (cf. John Portal, Whitchurch, †1877). –
Cassandra Austen †1827, and Cassandra Elizabeth Austen
†1845 (Jane's mother and sister). Plain tablets in the former
organ chamber.

In the village cemetery, across the main road, a slender CROSS,
by *Bodley*, to Corporal Ernest White, †1901 in the Boer War.
A surprisingly ambitious memorial for one soldier, subscribed
by parishioners in 1903. The cross is 30 ft (9 metres) high.

CHAWTON HOUSE. Largely the creation of John Knight after he
inherited the manor in 1583, but with some significant mid-
C17 alterations by Richard Knight. C19 changes by Edward
Austen (Jane's brother, later Edward Knight) and his descendants included a covering of Roman cement and the replacement of the original stone mullioned and transomed windows,
although these were largely undone in the later C19 by Montague Knight, partly with advice from *Lutyens*. Pevsner thought
it 'so much restored that it is no longer a pleasure to look at';
a deficiency happily remedied 1993–2003 by Sandy Lerner
who has converted the house to a library of women's writing
1660–1830.

59   The house makes a fine sight against the rising ground of
the park. The W front has the hall and a broad projecting wing
coming out at the N end. Close to the S end is a malmstone
ashlar three-storey porch built *c.* 1590 after Knight seems to
have abandoned plans to continue this front S to form a symmetrical E-plan and instead opted for the more compact and
less showy arrangement now seen, with two brick wings at the
rear, the N wing containing the kitchens and the S one the
parlour range. This is of two storeys and attic with three gables,
the central bay apparently altered *c.* 1655, the date of the staircase behind. Of the same date the two-storey corridor range

along the E side of the house, which links the staircase and N wings, by-passing the hall and the chambers. It has two original brick mullioned-and-transomed windows. On the E side of the rear courtyard is a small office building, probably of the 1590s with an C18 upper floor.

The entrance was originally in line with the screens passage of the hall, but after *c.* 1590 the passage was moved to encroach on the hall and a small projecting bay added in line with this in the angle of the porch and hall. This was removed *c.* 1860, the entrance to the passage now through a square lobby with a pretty plaster vault. The screen, probably of the early 1580s, is plain with moulded stiles, muntins and rails. The HALL has a flat plaster ceiling and panelling, with fluted pilasters and a frieze with carved guilloche ornament. Elegant stone fireplace surround, probably 1580s, but its low wooden overmantel of distinctly early C17 character; three pairs of round-arched panels with strapwork and terms. N of the hall, the C16 STAIRCASE with turned balusters, altered when attics were inserted in this wing in the mid C17 and again in 1884. The small staircase at the NE corner of the hall has C18 panelling and evidence of a former dog-gate. The DINING ROOM in the N wing was fitted out in Jacobean style 1895–6: the sumptuous chimneypiece is by *Bodley*, executed by *Farmer & Brindley*. In the S wing, the STUDY (remodelled from the buttery). C16 stone fireplace and Jacobean overmantel, possibly relocated from elsewhere. The STAIRCASE HALL, although enlarged *c.* 1859, has the fine open-well staircase of *c.* 1655, with heavy turned balusters, moulded handrails, square newels with globe finials and pendants. In the N wall a relocated doorcase of the same date with fluted Ionic pilasters, gadrooned frieze and broken pediment. Panelling with fluted pilasters too and an early C18 round archway, with panelled antae and a deep moulded cornice above. LIBRARY at W end of S wing remodelled *c.* 1897 by *Lutyens*.

The GREAT GALLERY was created in 1880 by combining the landing and rear corridor. C17 fireplace with carved overmantel but much else has been introduced, e.g. the an elaborate C13 wrought-iron door-hinge, from Neatham Manor House, Holybourne (q.v.). The two rooms over the hall were created *c.* 1619 when the Great Chamber was divided. The fireplace in the N room, a Tudor arch with delicately carved leaves in its spandrels, presumably dates from the 1580s while that in the S room is an addition of *c.* 1619. The OAK ROOM, at the SW corner, was restored by *Lutyens* in 1897, including the stone Tudor-arched fireplace with flanking wooden Ionic columns. The overmantel probably incorporates C17 work.

Nice OUTBUILDINGS on the approach, the best thing being the former STABLES, built in 1593, of flint and malmstone with projecting gabled wings. Central Tudor-arched entrance. One- and two-light windows in the upper parts of the wings, the ground-floor fenestration altered (two blocked original small windows survive). To the E, the small, flint DOVECOTE, actually probably a falconry or kennels of *c.* 1600. Narrow ground-floor openings, two-light windows to attic. w side rebuilt in the late C20 with a two-storey gabled porch based on the glimpsed view of the building provided by a painting of *c.* 1740 by *Mellichamp*. The formal GARDENS at the W front were swept away at the end of the C18 to be replaced by sloping lawns with clumps of trees, a ha-ha to the S with a meadow beyond and a temple on the high ground to the SE, now gone. Parkland and WALLED GARDEN created 1819–20. *Lutyens* appears to have been involved in the design of the UPPER TERRACE (1901) and the LIBRARY TERRACE (1905–6), but neither are significant works.

The village has good cottages and houses of the C16 and later. Immediately opposite the church is the former rectory (now CHAWTON GLEBE and RECTORY COTTAGE), a stuccoed house of 1803 by *John Eads* of Headley. The main village street extends N of the junction with the former Winchester Road. On the W side is JANE AUSTEN'S HOUSE, a modest, two-storey house of *c.* 1700 provided for Jane, her mother and sister by Edward Austen who inherited the estate in 1794. It had been converted *c.* 1769 for a pub (The New Inn) and was divided into three after Cassandra Austen's death in 1845, but the interior restored in the mid C20 and opened as a museum. Five-bay front elevation, showing evidence of the various alterations. On the informal garden elevation an early C19 sash window with Gothick lights. At the rear, L-plan range of C18 brick and weatherboarded outbuildings, including bakehouse/washhouse, granary, stables etc.

BAIGENS, W, is a *c.* 1500 timber-framed hearth-passage house, re-clad in the C18, with the remains of a contemporary painted scheme on the hall, with IHS monogram over the fireplace and a frieze of scenes of the chase (hare, dog and deer) alternating with panels of debased classical ornament.

CHAWTON PARK FARMHOUSE, ¾ m. NW of church, on the old London–Winchester road. Late C17, five bays, red brick, with extensive alterations and additions inside and out by *Paul Paget*, 1939.

CHERITON

5020

Described by Cobbett as 'a little hard iron village where all seems to be as old as the hills that surround it'. It is haphazardly scattered, with a loose centre on both sides of the Itchen, with the church perched on an oval mound – a prehistoric long barrow – and houses by the village green. The best cottage groups are out of the picture, on the N edge.

ST MICHAEL. Essentially C13, large for this part of Hampshire, but the story begins with the Transitional tower arch (of *c.* 1129–1171) of two square orders, which opened to an earlier nave. The s porch entrance is C13, re-set. It prepares one for the fine three-bay arcades, with round piers, leaf base spurs (restored from the one original in the easternmost column of the N arcade), round abaci, and double-chamfered arches dying into rounded vertical pieces. Restored semicircular responds. The date must be *c.* 1230. The use of base spurs was by then old-fashioned (cf. Selborne arcades of *c.* 1180), but continued at St Cross, Winchester. The bishops of Winchester were Cheriton's patrons. Can Winchester masons have been employed? The broad chancel arch goes with the arcade. Its semicircular responds rest on 4-ft (1.2-metre)-high stubs of an original stone wall (cf. Ditchling, East Sussex), possibly representing the dado of a lost screen. The greater part of the long chancel is C13 too, with paired lancets at the w end (renewed in 1879). It was altered *c.* 1396 and enlarged eastward *c.* 1500, over the sloping mound. Re-set Early Perp four-light E window and good N and s windows of *c.* 1396, differing in design. C13 PISCINA (trefoiled top), re-set. Aesthetically, the most interesting features are the two mysterious blank spherical triangles with tracery l. and r. of the porch entrance. They must be early C14 and of the same date are two carved heads above the triangles. What can they have come from? The church was much altered after a fire in 1744 and the agreeable flint and brick mixture of the tower and parts of the aisles is robustly Georgian (especially the latticed w windows of the aisles). Restoration by *David Brandon*, 1879: new roofs and furnishings. N and s aisle windows are Perp of 1919 by *Martin Travers*.

ARCHITECTURAL FRAGMENT. A C12 chevron re-set on the N wall. – TILES under the altar. Early C14, including one with a head of Christ, another of the Virgin. Both excellent. – STAINED GLASS. E window by *Cox, Sons, Buckley & Co.*, 1881, Evangelists. – Four aisle windows by *Martin Travers*, 1919, to four nephews of Mary Egerton. She is depicted in heraldic robes in the s aisle E window of 1941, also by Travers. – MONUMENTS. C17 ledger stones on the tower floor from the chancel.

In Freeman's Lane, the former CONGREGATIONAL CHAPEL (now offices) of 1862 in Lancet style, and the SCHOOL of 1875. Minimally Gothic, with red and buff brick polychromy. OLD RECTORY, s of the church. *c.* 1700. Five bays, two storeys over a semi-basement, hipped roof. Raised brick quoins and, on the entrance side only, rubbed brick window surrounds with lugs. Some wooden cross-windows. On the garden side the windows are sashed. Door with radial fanlight and straight hood on consoles. Inside, dog-leg staircase with heavy turned balusters (originally separated from the entrance passage by a wall). The stair, with service stair beyond, occupied a quarter of the floor plan (cf. Dymoke House, Easton). On the w side of the main road RECTORY COTTAGES are an interesting C18 semi-detached pair in brick, flint and thatch; U-plan with doorways in the angles with the gabled wings. The centre was formerly a reading room. Beyond the church path, more cottages,

including the former Hampshire Hunt Inn (now H. H.
Cottage). Built 1894 after fire destroyed its predecessor opposite. Attractive original signage, including the Prince of Wales's
feathers (the Prince Regent rode with the hunt). At the NW
corner of the green, CHERITON COTTAGE, built c. 1700 but
remodelled on the front c. 1885 with full-height canted bays,
gabled porch and square oriels. The later addition of Neo-
Georgian glazing bars and pedimented doorcase lends it the
air of the Queen Anne Revival. Inside, a good staircase with
turned balusters and square newels with ball finials and
pendants.

CHERITON HOUSE. SE of the green, in substantial grounds. Mid
C18, but much enlarged in the late C19 (porch of this date).
The core is five bays, two storeys, of vitrified headers and red
dressings, including panels linking the windows vertically. The
centre bay has giant pilasters carrying an open pediment. A tall
round-arched window reaches up into it (cf. No. 5 East Street,
New Alresford).

COLSTONS, ½ m. SW. Attractive L-plan house around a garden
courtyard, built of brindled brown brick in 1967–8 by *Martyn
Harvey*, who had worked in Denmark. Originally single-storey
and flat-roofed, but bedrooms added over the dining/living
room wing in 1974. Porch in same style, early 1980s.

CHILBOLTON

ST MARY THE LESS. The church, held by Winchester Cathedral
Priory from King Athelstan's gift in the C10, started as an aisleless building (evidence of the nave walls, of Late Saxon width
with one coeval or Early Norman window 15 ft (4.5 metres)
above the S arcade). Disproportionately long early C13 chancel.
The aisles early C14 of two bays only and standard elements
in clunch, and good simple mostly two-light windows. The
broad chancel arch goes with the arcades rather than the
chancel lancets. The C13-style E window is of the restoration
of 1893–4 by *W. D. Caröe* (paid for by Edward Silva of Testcombe) who found the original openings and buttressed the E
wall. The low SW tower, of coursed flint, is of 1842 probably
by *Owen Browne Carter*. The small spired weatherboarded
bellcote was relocated from the nave. Caröe preserved old
internal plaster, reconstructed the C14 nave roof (retaining the
tie-beams) and added the N vestry. – SCREEN. Largely early
C15, with good tracery of elongated trefoils, carefully restored
in 1842. – DESKS, in the chancel, against the screen, with early
C16 linenfold panelled fronts. – REREDOS. A wooden tryptych
by *Caröe*, with a well-carved Crucifixion. – PULPIT. Fine Late
Elizabethan with guilloche decoration and brackets for the
book-board. Can it be of 1575–1609 when Michael Reniger was
rector (*see* Crawley)? – FONT. Elaborately panelled Perp of

1893. – SCULPTURE hanging above the screen. Armless Christ of 1998 by *David Begbie*. Original, of sculpted wire. – STAINED GLASS. The W window signed by *Wailes*, 1847, Crucifixion. E window of 1892 by *Powells*. Also by them, the S aisle SW window. – MONUMENTS. Small early C17, brass over the pulpit to Thomas Tutt. Affirmative inscription undated. – Edward Silva of Testcombe †1899. A modish Arts and Crafts plaque of beaten copper. Churchyard walls and gates also by *Caröe*.

NORTHWOOD HOUSE, NE of the church, was the rectory. A double pile of *c.* 1700, of five bays to the front, two storeys, chequer brick, coved plaster eaves and hipped roof. Narrower rear elevation, just four bays, with a C16 timber-framed range retained as a service wing to the l. Inside, bolection-moulded panelling and marble chimneypieces. The rear wall of its coachhouse dominates the village green. In Winchester Road, the old NATIONAL SCHOOL, Neo-Tudor of 1844. Further out, alone in the fields by the river, is the MANOR HOUSE. C18 brick possibly masking an earlier front. Five windows and pilastered doorcase behind a tented-roofed porch.

On the SE side of the village green is a picturesque row of whitewashed thatched cottages, including CHILBOLTON COTTAGE, formerly two separate cottages joined into one in 1921 by *Ernest Barrow*, for himself, by infilling in an accomplished Late Arts and Crafts manner, with a large gabled brick wing and porch with waney-edged weatherboarding and bracketed oriel. The old part set back to the l. is C15, of cruck construction. SW along the main street, ROOM COTTAGES are of 1893 for Edward Silva of Testcombe (*see* below) by *Caröe*. An attractive row, in an informal Queen Anne Revival. Caröe did much work for Silva in the village, including the modest village hall of 1891 (now demolished) and further SW, on the r., is his Neo-Georgian HAZEL HOUSE formed from two cottages in 1911. Also notable Nos. 1–3 Joys Lane, of 1975 by *Jennie Saunders Designs*. A discreet and exceptionally well-integrated development of three single-storey L-shaped houses, cleverly planned to provide private courtyard gardens.

TESTCOMBE, 1 m. SW. By *W. D. Caröe* for Edward Silva; built 1892–3 (dated rainwater heads) but designs were prepared as early as 1887. It incorporates an overblown mid-C19 *cottage orné* fishing lodge, which probably prompted adoption of a variant on the Olde English style i.e. close studding with brick-nogging over a brick ground floor, leaded windows and tall chimneys, although with stone slates instead of the original thatch. Inside, the best remaining feature is the Neo-Jacobean staircase with splat balusters and galleried landing, which breaks forward on posts which also form the newels of the stair. Magical setting, with lawns amongst the braided streams of the Test, part of which is formally canalized in front of the house. Rustic FISHING HUT of 1888 and a boarded BOATHOUSE with scissor-truss bargeboards, possibly mid-C19. SW, the former COACHHOUSE and WALLED GARDEN.

WATCH COTTAGE, ¼ m. NE. Also by *Caröe*, 1893, but with a
gault brick studio added in the 1950s for the artist and ento-
mologist, John Hull Grundy. At the rear, a carved stone relief
of Hull Grundy in profile, by *Mark Batten*.

CHILBOLTON OBSERVATORY, I m. S. On the site of a Second
World War airfield and dominated by the RADIO ANTENNA of
1964–7 by the *Ministry of Public Building and Works*. Base of
in situ cast concrete carrying the rotating steel platform for a
65-ft (25-metre) parabolic dish.

5020

CHILCOMB

ST ANDREW. Away from the village, under the downs. Early
Norman, see the windows in nave and chancel and their inner
appearance. Twin bell-openings in the nave E wall. See also the
two plain doorways. The strange double arch of the N doorway
requires explanation. Unmoulded chancel arch. On the
imposts incised zigzag. The lower part of the bell-turret is
exposed to the nave. – PILLAR PISCINA. Norman, with flat
leaves. – FONT. An octagonal pillar with a kind of shaft-ring.
It is Gothic in an approximate way and may be C18. Unusually placed on a medieval stone coffin lid. – SCREEN. Perhaps
late C14 with original doors. – TILES. In the chancel C15, nicely
patterned. – CRUCIFIX by *Peter Eugene Ball*, 1996, over the
chancel arch. – BISHOP'S CHAIR, by *John McFarlane*, 1996, in
the Arts and Crafts tradition. – STAINED GLASS. Chancel S
window, C15 bits. E window 1916, by *Kempe & Co.*

5040

CHILTON CANDOVER

A shrunken village, depopulated and destroyed by its landowner
between 1562 and 1595. The earthworks of former houses surround the church.

ST NICHOLAS. The mid-C12 church was demolished in 1878 but
its Early Norman CRYPT, mostly of flint, was rediscovered and
excavated in 1927. It consists of an apse and a rectangular,
tunnel-vaulted room, separated by an unmoulded arch. Its
original length was 32 ft (10 metres), much longer than now,
and it was not wholly sunk – small windows allowed some light.
Walls were added to the apse, perhaps in the C14, when the
chancel was greatly enlarged E. – FONT. Of Purbeck marble.
Possibly C12. Table-top type with six of the usual flat blank
arches per side. MONUMENTS. Large medieval stone coffin
and two Purbeck sepulchral slabs, one with a cross and inscription in Norman French along the side to John of Candover

(probably John d'Andeley, a descendant of Richard d'Andeley, holder of the manor in 1086).

SE on the main road is CHILTON HOUSE (formerly the rectory). 1760–70 may be a likely date. Painted. Of five widely spaced bays. Two storeys high. The centre bay has a pedimental gable into which rises a round-arched window. The end bays have Venetian windows on both floors. Unusually fine door surround with laurel frieze and pediment on carved brackets with eagle heads.

CHILTON MANOR, ¼ m. NW, is of 1937 by *J. A. Smith* (*Wallis & Smith* of Basingstoke). Neo-Georgian, a version of Lutyens's Middlefield (Cambs.), but otherwise without his touch. 1 m. SE is CHILTON DOWN, a pair of late C19 brick and flint cottages transformed into a Regency-style house by *Francis Johnson, c.* 1970. Farm buildings converted 1987, with copper cupola. Screen inside with Batty Langley-esque Gothick columns carved by *Dick Reid*.

CHURCH CROOKHAM

A southern suburb of Fleet.

CHRIST CHURCH, Galley Hill Road. Built 1840–1; the village became an ecclesiastical parish in 1842. Of brick, cruciform in the lancet style, by *James Harding* of Farnham. Chancel of 1876–7 in a more learned and solid E.E. by *Woodyer*. By him the nice brick W bellcote. Original roof in the earlier part, over the crossing with carved pendants and a central boss with the royal arms. By *Woodyer*, the SEDILIA and PISCINA and the arrangement of *Minton* floor tiles in the chancel. The FONT, FONT COVER (now adapted to a book-stand at the W end) and the STONE PULPIT are of 1893. Low brass SCREEN of 1890–1 with Art Nouveau details. Wooden SCREEN to the Lady Chapel by *G. A. Parsons* of 1932. SGRAFFITO decoration over the chancel arcades of 1893 by *Heywood Sumner* (cf. St Paul, Winchester), who also designed the outstanding STAINED GLASS of the W window in 1900, made by *Powells*. Two exquisite angels on light backgrounds, very progressive for the date. Powell's E window, 1879, is darker and denser – a dusky Crucifixion scene. Other windows in the transepts by *Gibbs* of 1871 and 1879, and in the nave, of after 1880 mostly by *Heaton, Butler & Bayne*.

108

In the churchyard, by the lychgate, a nice Arts and Crafts headstone to William Eggleton †1936. By *F. Martin*. A Gill-influenced cross and roundels with animals and foliage alluding to the seasons.

CHURCH CROOKHAM JUNIOR SCHOOL, Tweseldown Road. A SCOLA design of 1967 made special by refurbishment in 1987 by *Edward Cullinan Architects* (cf. Calthorpe School, Fleet) who re-clad the buildings with plywood sheets and battens and added sun-screens. The overall effect is very lively and

whimsical, and was more so before the original blue, yellow
and red colour scheme was replaced. Inside roof-lights were
added with pivoting crescent-shaped shutters operated by
handles in the shape of propellers. Window shutters fold back
to form pinboards (some removed). The block linking the two-
storey parts with the hall and kitchens was enlarged in 2003
by *John Alexander* of *Alexander Design*. Interesting steel-framed
WATER TOWER of 1967, with a fully glazed cube at the base.

TWESELDOWN RACECOURSE, Bourley Road. Established by
the army in 1855. Pretty late C19 buildings (grandstand, jockey
quarters and stables) of brick and tile with wooden verandas.

ST NICHOLAS'S SCHOOL, ¾ m. SW. Formerly Redfields House
of 1877–9 by *Alfred Eggar* of Farnham for George Atty, a barrister of the Middle Temple. Neo-Jacobean. Impressive square-
well staircase with Gothic-arched balustrade, lit by tall
three-light window and open to a high pyramidal roof with
coving and quatrefoil ornament.

BROOK HOUSE, in Crookham Village to the E. Fine Artisan Mannerist house of 1664. Baffle entry with a Dutch-gabled cross-
wing to the r. Richly decorated with pilaster strips, the lower
ones with convex mouldings, string courses with semicircular
dentils, and windows with architraves, those on the first floor
flanked by round-arched panels.

CLIDDESDEN

A long village with a small green at a staggered cross-roads.
The barrier of the M3 has saved it from engulfment by outer
Basingstoke.

ST LEONARD. Nave destructively restored in 1868–9 for the
Earl of Portsmouth, possibly by *Clark & Holland* (cf.
Hurstbourne Priors). A plain doorway of *c.* 1100–50 (blocked)
survives in the N wall, built of large flints laid in lines (cf.
Wield). Early Decorated-style windows, S porch and stone
gabled bellcote, although the original Perp w window was
faithfully restored (as an early C19 drawing shows). Attractive
six-bay late C15 nave roof with tie-beams and wind-braces
below the purlin. The E bay, marked off by a large timber arch
brace of 1869 on contemporary naturalistic carved stone capitals, formed part of a small chancel – an Early Norman
arrangement for smaller unaisled churches (cf. Martyr
Worthy). Chancel and N vestry in a more elaborate Late Dec
of 1888–90 by *W. S. Hicks* of Newcastle, paid for by
W. Bradshaw of Audleys Wood (*see* below). Contemporary
FURNISHINGS in richest Perp (cf. Hicks's furnishings at
Glandford, Norfolk) and especially fine TILES on the chancel
floor, – STAINED GLASS, by *Kempe* of 1890 (E window) and
after. W window of 1971 by *Barton, Kinder & Alderson* of

Brighton. – MONUMENT. A nicely lettered tablet to Louis de-Luze Simmonds †1916 and wife †1930. By *Frederick Etchells*, 1931.

Former METHODIST CHAPEL. Brought from Basingstoke in 1906 (Kelly's). Large and very urban with an ironstone front in Middle-Pointed Gothic.

CLIDDESDEN DOWN HOUSE, sw end of the village. Late C18 brick rectory. Curious dumb-bell plan with two hipped-roofed pavilions linked by a central arm. Five-bay front, the centre three marked by giant pilasters and pediment with oculus. The OLD SCHOOL HOUSE, nw on Cliddesden Road, is dated to 1656. Lobby-entry house of brick (now rendered) with stone plinth and string course. Windows with moulded brick surrounds survive in the gable end.

AUDLEYS WOOD, ¾ m. NE. Vernacular Revival of 1884 for W. Bradshaw, a relative of Sir George Bradshaw, publisher of the railway guides. Altered and enlarged *c.* 1900 for Henry Simonds, the Reading brewer, and substantially added to in 1986–9 during conversion for a hotel by *Peter Inston*. Two storey Gothic porte cochère, the traceried arches with wrought ironwork in the form of halberds and in the return a wooden oriel of 1892. Conservatory at the rear of *c.* 1900 in the form of Roman baths, with lunettes in gables and very un-Roman large curved mullioned-and-transomed bays. Former billiard room adjoining at right angles. Long matching flanking wings of *c.* 1989. The traceried nail-studded door is C15, and there are many reused fittings inside, e.g. elaborately carved C17 chimneypieces, panelling (some incorporating paintings) and an early C18 staircase. The rear hall is all late C19, with a barrel-vaulted plaster ceiling, minstrels' gallery and stained glass with the arms of the Simonds family.

In the grounds, the AUDLEY RESOURCE CENTRE for the disabled. 1996 by the *Hampshire County Architect's Dept.* A single-storey L-plan around a courtyard. Brick with monopitch roofs at different levels and clerestory lights.

COLEMORE

7030

A small and remote settlement in upland country with a cluster of buildings around the church.

ST PETER AD VINCULA (Churches Conservation Trust since 1973). Nave and chancel in one, originally an C11 cruciform plan. The main interest is the N transept. A small E window with a round-arched head of a single stone (of Liss sandstone) proves the date. Inside survives the arch which once separated it from a crossing. Plain typically Early Norman imposts and an unmoulded arch. In the transept w wall, a blocked Norman doorway, which is unusual. Was it a manorial entrance (the church was held in the late C11 by the Count of Mortain)?

s transept taken down in 1670 (the jambs of its arch still show outside). Timber bell-turret with splay-foot spire of 1975 by *Richard Sawyer* (succeeding the bellcote of 1866 by *Colson*). C14 diagonal buttresses (southern one renewed 1612). W window of 1845 by *Owen Browne Carter* over a blocked W doorway. Nice timber S porch probably also by him. Chalk Gothic doorway, C17(?). In the nave, on the N side, one original small C12 lancet. Chancel extensively rebuilt in hard E.E. by *Colson*, 1874–5. – FONT. Purbeck marble, Norman, of table type. Five supports (the corner shafts are Early Victorian). Two sides with ornament. – EASTER SEPULCHRE. A plain pointed-arched recess, probably early C16 (evidence of bare stone panel on E side). Chalk. Perhaps rebuilt with the N chancel wall in 1875. – CHANCEL SCREEN. Early C17 Gothic. Only the frame and the traceried head to the doorway are old, after repairs in 1845 and 1874. – PEWS of 1845. – PAINTING. Around the broad splays of the E window, by *Bell & Almond*.* – STAINED GLASS. E window 1876 by *Kempe*.

To the E, COLEMORE HOUSE, formerly the rectory. Mostly *c*. 1800 and stuccoed, the front with recessed centre. Tuscan porch of 1995 by *Anthony Jaggard*, who added the single-storey E extension and created a symmetrical rear elevation by duplicating the full-height canted NE bay (by *Dyer* of Alton *c*. 1835).

COVE

An extension of the Farnborough/Aldershot conurbation with only a few old houses surviving.

ST JOHN BAPTIST, St John's Road. 1842–4 by *G. Alexander*. Crisp Neo-Norman of dour heathstone with a low crossing tower, standing inside on four arches with semicircular responds and cushion capitals. SCREENS in the transepts, one with benches and the other still with its upholstered book-rests. – The REREDOS includes an earlier reredos of mosaic and *opus sectile* redecorated by *Emily Soames*, 1892; the decoration of the E wall is by *Ada Currey*, 1891–2. – STAINED GLASS. Almost all contemporary with the church, geometric patterns with etched panels especially in the E and W windows.

ST CHRISTOPHER, Cove Road, ¾ m. SE. 1934–5 by *W. Curtis Green*, one of only four churches by him. Brick, without a tower but with a very big roof in which on both sides a long continuous band of dormer windows appears as a clerestory inside. The interior timberwork is ingenious and original, with all timbers straight, nothing arched. Nave and narrow aisle passages. Chancel with tall unchamfered pointed arches framing a slightly narrower sanctuary, which is subtly lit by two

---

* Rev. Hervey, rector of Colemore, reported in 1876 the discovery of 'an ancient block pattern' upon the splay of the old Norman E window which had been covered by the jambs of an inserted E.E. window.

long lancets on either side. One long E lancet. Stone FONT,
COMMUNION RAILS, SANCTUARY CHAIRS, tiered CHOIR
STALLS, LECTERN and PULPIT, all by the architect's brother,
A. Romney Green. – Original metal light pendants with later
glass shades. – ORGAN CASE. Brought in from a house at Ash,
Surrey, but looking like an assemblage of C17 and early C18
woodwork. Unusual bare-breasted winged angels and a classical pediment, topped by a figure of Christ. The church has a
low W extension of *c.* 1985 by *Leslie Snell*.

SOUTHWOOD INFANTS' SCHOOL, Southwood Lane. 1991,
Hampshire County Architects' Dept. An elegant steel-framed
structure under a wave-form roof. Classrooms, separated by
low partitions, along the S side shaded by a brise-soleil, offices
under the low roof to the N.

SOUTHWOOD ESTATE. Developed from the mid 1980s on
former MoD land. VILLAGE CENTRE in Links Way, *c.* 1990,
has shops, pub and medical centre. Rather thin Neo-
vernacular with covered walkways on wooden posts that
project up through the eaves. Nearby the SOUTHWOOD
INFANTS' SCHOOL (*see* above) and the SUMMIT CENTRE in
Southwood Crescent, 1991 by *Norman & Dawbarn*, a quasi-
classical crescent of red brick offices with landscaped gardens
between the buildings and suspended iron bridges across a
vehicular moat. Also in Links Way, the HOLMES PLACE health
club, by *KSR Architects*, *c.* 1999–2001. A dramatic wedge
shape, the walls glazed, tile-clad and boarded. Full-height
glazed entrance wall with atrium behind. The swimming pool
has a wavy acoustic ceiling.

RAFBOROUGH, 2 m. SE. Begun for munitions workers at the
Royal Aircraft Factory in 1917–18 on the N edge of Farnborough Airfield; by *R. J. Allinson* and *G. J. T. Reavell* of the *Office
of Works*. 250 cottages were built (of a planned 1,084) in a semi-
formal layout inspired by the pre-war Garden Suburb, but
simpler and more cheaply built.

RANDELL HOUSE, Fernhill Road. *See* Hawley.

CRAWLEY   *4030*

Crawley was transformed into a model village by Otto Ernst
Philippi of Crawley Court, who bought the estate in 1900. He
was managing director of J. & P. Coats Ltd of Paisley, the cotton
thread manufacturers, and employed as his architects *Fryers &
Penman* of Largs where Philippi kept his Scottish home.

ST MARY. Of Norman origin. Flint. Nave and aisles under a continuous roof, chancel and a thin W tower with Perp top of 1901
by *S. Gambier Parry*. S porch by *Cancellor & Hill*. The earliest
evidence is inside: the wide chancel arch has mid-C12
responds, with nook-shafts and scalloped capitals and a C13
arch. On the E side of the arch bits of the zigzag of the original Norman arch. To the l. of the chancel arch a squint.

The C13 chancel was almost rebuilt during the major restoration of 1887 by *T. E. Williams* (cf. Littleton), closely to the original, e.g. the E window of three graduated trefoil-headed lancets (evidence of a drawing of before 1831). In the N vestry and organ chamber of 1887, parts of two lancets re-set. The nave and aisles are late C14, perhaps of the 1370s when the advowson was held by William of Wykeham, Bishop of Winchester (bishops held the manor in 1086) – see the Early Perp stone details of the N and S windows with good headstops; that to the S aisle SE window possibly Edward III (†1377). Inside, instead of arcades there are rough wooden posts with longitudinal arched braces, also tie-beams on arched braces, the timbers dated to 1347–79. – Nice Perp FONT of clunch, with the usual quatrefoils. The elaborately furnished chancel is a memorial to the Very Rev. John Mee (†1883) a former Dean of Grahamstown, South Africa, and rector of Westbourne, Sussex. E wall panelled in ashlar, carved by *Farmer & Brindley*. TILES by *Maw & Co.* – STAINED GLASS. In the chancel by *Hardman*. The E window of 1887 much the best, a splendid Te Deum with innumerable figures. – MONUMENTS. Brass inscription to Michael Reniger †1609, rector from 1559 and Archdeacon of Winchester from 1575. – John Jarrett †1809 with an inscription against drapery hung from a dart. By *Henry Westmacott* (signed). – John Ashton †1814. Signed *T. Franceys & Spence*, sculptors, Liverpool. Low modest NW extension by *David Trussler*, 1999.

The village consists of a single, curving main street climbing downhill from the church. THE DOWER HOUSE, opposite the church and at right angles to the street, is the former rectory. Its earliest part is the N end, with flint ground floor and mullioned windows, probably early C17. The late C17(?) brick first floor also has mullioned windows but these are of 1912 when the rest, including the *c.* 1700 S extension, was enlarged and radically transformed in Neo-Tudor style by *Fryers & Penman* for Philippi's daughter, Dora. The most prominent addition is the squat brick water tower with machicolated and battlemented parapet (cf. Brockwood Park, Bramdean). Beyond a series of older village houses and cottages is The VILLAGE HALL, another of Philippi's improvements converted from late C19 farm buildings. It contained reading room, billiards room and, latterly, a covered roller-skating rink. In the courtyard was a bowling green. Of the cottages the most entertaining are Oak Cottages (Old English), and ORCHARD COTTAGE and ORCHARD END, a small piece of Bavaria: stuccoed with a gambrel roof, at each end of which are pairs of steeply gabled dormers with fretted bargeboards and oval windows, and in the middle a balcony, via which a ladder once gave access to a dormitory for estate workers. Could the German-born Philippi have been its author? Then THE FOX AND HOUNDS, re-created as an Old English fantasy in 1907. Finally the village pond, prettily surrounded by thatched cottages and with the former FIRE HOUSE built *c.* 1900–10, like a Tudor Gothic gatehouse.

CROOKED PIGHTLE HOUSE, NW of the pond. 1988–9 by *Robert Adam* for himself. An impressive red brick classical house of villa form, drawing inspiration from mid-C17 English domestic architecture but with an Arts and Crafts sensibility, particularly in the use of materials. Two storeys, three-bay front, the broad centre projecting with implied angle pilasters. The doorcase is based on that of the Parthenon. The garden side is very satisfying, with a middle bay flanked by rusticated pilaster-strips. A doorcase is cleverly implied by brick piers, a stone architrave that also spans the flanking windows, a pulvinated frieze of knapped flintwork and a moulded stone cornice. Above this, a lunette. The outer bays have square bay windows. Symmetrically planned interior with an axial entrance passage leading to the double-height hall, a 20-ft (6-metre) cube flanked by rooms on each side on both floors. Stair in the style of *c.* 1700, the details matching the substantial gallery across the W side of the hall. The GARAGE has rusticated brick piers and a pyramidal roof with a tall segmental-pedimented dormer. At the rear, a terraced garden in the form of a Roman peristyle court. ¹¹⁹

ARQIVA HEADQUARTERS. W of the church, in the landscaped grounds of Crawley Court, built in 1877 by *F. P. Cockerell* for Adam Kennard, a banker, 'in an undisciplined free Elizabethan, large and grand, of flint, brick, and red terracotta' (Pevsner). It succeeded the old manor house closer to the church but was demolished 1970. The main gateway and walled garden survive. The present buildings were commissioned in 1969 and completed in 1973 by *The Ware Macgregor Partnership* as the I.B.A. headquarters. Two three-storey courtyard blocks, one originally for administration, the other for the technical department connected by a two-storey entrance block, reached by a bridge across a moat. A single-storey link at the rear connects to a two-storey building for hall, social centre etc. The courtyard blocks are striking, with cruciform columns standing forward of the fenestration creating elevations that are extremely sculptural. Contemporary landscaping in the open court.

NORTHWOOD PARK, 2 m. SE. The late C19 house has been demolished. THE CLOCK HOUSE is the former stables, converted 1972. Completely Georgian in feel. WINSLEY COTTAGES are a former sanatorium built for Clayesmore School in 1923 by *J. J. Joass*. A single-storey Y-plan, rendered with a hipped Roman tile roof.

CRONDALL

A large village that appears to have developed around a former green with the church at the SW corner, encroached onto from the C16 onwards, producing a grid street plan.

ALL SAINTS. One of the largest and most important medieval village churches in the county. It succeeded a Late Anglo-Saxon minster (flint foundations discovered in 1997 below the nave arcades), which was granted to St Swithun's Priory, Winchester, at an early but unknown date. This connection must explain the fine masons' work of the present building, which was begun *c.* 1170 and completed *c.* 1175. Crondall had four dependent chapels by *c.* 1200 – Aldershot, Farnborough, Long Sutton and Yateley.

66　　　　Externally its most prominent feature is the high and massive brick NE tower of four unequal stages, built in 1659, which stands against the chancel N wall and over the site of a possibly early C14 vestry (itself evidence of a high-status church). The Norman axial tower had endangered the walls of the church and was taken down in 1657, although its NE stair-turret remains, to which the present tower is connected by odd wooden galleries. The model for the new tower was old St Mary's Battersea (1639), which was visited by four Crondall vestrymen. Clasping buttresses and octagonal corner posts rising to a nicely finished parapet and brick pinnacles. The bell-openings, all neatly arched, are unusually framed in shallow panels. Those to E and N arranged in pairs, the others singly. All stages have crisp cornices of decorative mini-arcading of beautifully moulded brick. The W doorway with a slightly raised brick surround is Artisan Mannerist, but deadpan and sober. The cost was £428.

A walk round the outside of the church is confusing. It tells in odd places that this is a mostly Norman church and that Neo-Norman work was carried out to make it more Norman (in 1845–7 by *Benjamin Ferrey*). Chancel as well as clerestory and also some other details are E.E., or early C13. Best of these is the chancel N window (hidden below the gallery) with fine nook-shafts. Later C13 the large chancel S windows (with possibly C15 iron ferramenta). Norman features include a small blocked N aisle window, a fragmentarily preserved string course, also the S doorway (blocked) of *c.* 1200 with a roll moulding, and the larger ceremonial W doorway of *c.* 1200 with a richly moulded arch and head at the top. The N doorway is Late Norman, but restored in 1845–7. It is sheltered by an airy limewashed N porch mostly of brick with a depressed moulded stone outer arch and a mid-C16 brick crowstepped battle-mented gable. Much other mid-C16 work has been retained, especially the massive tile-capped buttresses at the W end and across the aisles.

17　　　　The outstanding interior, of *c.* 1170–1200, is much more consistent, showing the transition from Norman to Early English with unusual clarity. It is big-boned, and strongly detailed throughout. Nave and aisles, four-bay arcades, chancel. The E bay of the nave was unusually flanked by lower chapels which are well preserved with transverse arches opening into the aisles (that to the S aisle rebuilt *c.* 1790). The arches have two slight chamfers, and the details of the responds here and by the chancel arch are still entirely Norman, without Transitional elements. They are surely of the first phase of *c.* 1170. Massive semicircular responds, multi-scallop capitals, square abaci. The two W bays of the arcade follow. Same details, but one capital with waterleaf, typical of *c.* 1170–80 and the arches many-moulded. All in a fine limestone. The tall chancel arch with Norman-looking dogtooth responds was given new capitals in 1845–7 but the pointed arch is original and has side by side with zigzag also dogtooth. The clerestory windows are tall, pointed and shafted, i.e. after 1200. So is the chancel. Two exquisite bays, richly vaulted like the choir aisle of a cathedral, ribs with dogtooth. Crocket and stiff-leaf capitals. It must surely be the work of a mason influenced by the Canterbury choir of 1175–84 (the source for the boss over the altar space with the Lamb (*Agnus Dei*)). Only the E fenestration of two richly shafted lancets and a small quatrefoil are restored. They are essentially of 1871, by *Scott* who may have found their outer responds (the E window had already been twice replaced). At the same time, Scott raised the chancel floor (evidence of shortened priest's door). The stepped levels of the E end may be original.

Most of the fittings are of the C19 restorations. Exceptions are the FONT. Plain stone, a circular downward-tapering bowl of indeterminate, possibly Saxon, date, on a square chamfered base. (COMMUNION TABLE of 1550, a rare piece from the reign of Edward VI.) – CHEST. Quite small and strongly iron-bound with three locks. Bought second-hand in 1546 for two shillings (churchwarden's accounts) and probably of *c.* 1500. – BIER and CHILD'S BIER. Both of 1881 – CURIOSA. A rare Puritan font of the Interregnum. Acquired by the Rev. Humphrey Weaver, vicar, in 1647 for use inside the Saxon font. – HUDD, or shelter, of 1699 for use at funerals (cf. Odiham) – CHANDELIER. Of 1738–9 (Sherlock). – Most of the Victorian furnishings survive but Scott's reredos and clergy stalls in the chancel were removed in 1971. TILES of 1871 on the chancel floor – CHAIR in the sanctuary. An elemental Gothic piece. PULPIT and PEWS, probably of 1847 by Ferrey; of a heavy solidity.

STAINED GLASS. E window of 1890. Chancel SW by *Hugh Powell*, 1991. Jacob's Ladder. Overly intricate with much clear glass as background. S aisle SE, *c.* 1860, possibly by *O'Connor*, unusually showing Mrs Jeanette Lefroy and four children. – W window (Ferrey's former E window of 1856 relocated to the nave). Little figure groups in medallions and panels. – MONUMENTS. The best in the chancel. Brass to Nicholas de Kaerwent, rector 1361–81. A fine brass figure, 58 in. (147 cm.) long (chancel floor). Also in the chancel, two large C16 tombs: Sir George Paulet †1532, younger brother of William Paulet, 1st Marquis of Winchester (*see* Old Basing). Rather hard and heartless Early Tudor. Recess with depressed, straight-sided arch. Buttress-shaft. The tomb-chest under the arch may once have supported effigies of which two carved heads remain.

The quality not high with rather rudimentary carving. Some traces of colour in the heraldry. John Gyfford †1563. Very conservative Purbeck marble with depressed arch and cresting. Brass, against the back wall, with kneeling figure; the figures of his wife Lady Elizabeth, daughter of Sir George Throckmorton †1563 of Throckmorton Court, Warwickshire, and sons are missing. John Eggar †1641, founder of the grammar school at Alton in 1638. 'Imp' tablet with rare small brass plate of skeleton and shroud. One of only four in England. In the s aisle several C17–early C19 tablets. Dulcibella Rivers †1657. P. Nicholas Love, Sen. Warden of Winchester College, was her first husband. Their son, Nicholas Love Jun., the regicide, bought the manor and gave £70 towards the building of the tower in 1659. A characteristically mid-C17 piece. Alabaster with an inscription and cartouche in a broken pediment. Attributed to the workshop of *Edward* and *Joshua Marshall* (GF). – Peter Walraven †1737. Nice, especially lively cartouche with fruity swags between flaming urns. Below, cherubs in conversation between grisly winged skulls. – Deborah Maxwell †1789 and Henry Maxwell †1818 of Ewshot House and Ramsbury, Wiltshire, with a swagged urn. Signed upside down, *Lee*, Odiham.

One outstanding memorial in the CHURCHYARD, close to the s boundary: Paul Springman †1913. By *Hamo Thornycroft*. Youthful St Michael in finely stylized armour, on a granite pedestal with four rectangular bronze reliefs of the Good Samaritan, the finest of them excellent.

The CHURCH HALL in Croft Lane was an early C19 school, brick with pretty Gothic windows. Around the corner, CRONDALL LODGE is a mid-C19 double-pile house of C18 form, with pedimented centre, round-arched porch and hipped roof. Ironwork belvedere and rusticated brick chimneys of *c.* 1900, when it was a school; of this period also the two-storey canted bay of 1891, brick and stone with Neo-Tudor archway. Several good brick houses in Church Street, e.g. the C18 OLD VICARAGE with nice pedimented doorcase, and in The Borough, where there is the fine PLUME OF FEATHERS inn, with C17 hall range and a high-status solar cross-wing of *c.* 1500, jettied to the front and to its long side elevation. In Dippenhall Street, LIMETREES, a late C15 cruck-framed hall range with later tile-hung hipped-roofed cross-wings. Opposite, THE CLOSE, C17 with an early C18 brick front range; its row of small tile-hung gables is a motif that appears in other Crondall houses of *c.* 1700. Next door TUDOR HOUSE, a nice C17 hall and cross-wing.

CLARE PARK, 1 m. SE. Early C19, possibly a remodelling of an early C18 house. Three storeys. Stuccoed with five-bay front, the centre slightly projecting with elegant bowed porch on slim Tuscan columns. Well-detailed entrance hall and staircase.

DOWNSLAND HOUSE, 1 m. N. A William and Mary-style house of 1899. Brick and hipped roofed, with lower projecting wings and frontispiece with bracketed porch and segmental pediment.

CRUX EASTON

A remote hamlet high up on the Downs. The old manor house has gone but an avenue of limes survives to the NE. The nine daughters of Edward Lisle, Lord of the Manor, built a grotto that was celebrated in verse by Pope.

ST MICHAEL. Built in 1775 by Mrs Lisle. Small, of grey brick, with red dressings. Nave of three bays, narrower chancel and a semi-elliptical apse with one large arched window. Skimpy open bellcote, 1894. Low semi-elliptical chancel arch. Fine radial marble pavement in the apse and fine PANELLING round the altar with pilasters and oval paterae. – Of *c.* 1775 also the PULPIT, the LECTERN with a plump wooden eagle, the FONT, an apparently imported Italian marble bowl on a stone baluster carved in high relief with a religious scene (Continental too?) and the wrought-iron CHURCHYARD GATES.

CRUX EASTON HOUSE. S of the church. The former rectory, 'newly built' in 1765. Stuccoed N front with brick centrepiece. Matching S range by *Robert Adam Architects*, *c.* 2002. Both phases have canted bays on the W front flanking a Tuscan colonnade. Inside, an C18 octagonal room has a pretty plasterwork ceiling. NE, in a field, is a small brick MILL HOUSE of *c.* 1800 and its WIND ENGINE, of the 'Simplex' type of engines made by *John Wallis Titt*. Erected in 1891–2, its wheel has forty-eight canvas sails.

DANEBURY HILL FORT

Nether Wallop

Danebury Down has been the scene of extensive excavations (1969 88) during which more than half of the interior of the fort was excavated and the ramparts sectioned. Although all the trenches have been refilled the site continues to be dominated by its superbly preserved defensive earthworks. Three separate phases of enclosure can be traced. The INNER ENCLOSURE is the most dramatic with a substantial bank and ditch protecting the settlement of some 13 acres. The defences were built in the C6 or C5 B.C. with a timber-framed rampart pierced by two entrances, E and SW. Later in the C3 B.C. the fortification was enlarged in glacis form and at the same time the SW entrance was blocked. Subsequently the E entrance was elaborated with forward-projecting hornworks but the main gate was burnt *c.* 100 B.C. and the site largely abandoned. The MIDDLE ENCLOSURE attaches to the S side of the main hill-fort. Its ditch and bank are well preserved though slighter and it would seem that this was an ancillary enclosure perhaps to protect animals. The OUTER ENCLOSURE enclosing the entire hilltop is slighter still but can be traced throughout by the determined. It is the earliest feature now visible probably dating to the Late Bronze Age when the hilltop was first defended for human use. A linear boundary of the same date ran from the E side of the enclosure and can be seen sweeping across the valley past the Turret with its clump of trees to the E.

Excavation showed that the interior was heavily occupied from the C6 to the C1 B.C. Streets ran between circular timber-built houses and rows of granaries. Pits for grain storage were many and towards the centre were rectangular shrines – now it is tranquil parkland. Material from the excavations is well displayed in the Museum of the Iron Age in Andover.

LONG BARROWS, ½ m. NW of the fort. The W and larger of this pair of long barrows is 210 ft (65 metres) long and 72 ft (22 metres) wide at its broader E end, where it stands 6 ft (1.8 metres) high. The flanking quarry ditches, 27 ft (8 metres) wide, are still clearly visible. In a rabbit scrape in the ditch was found a single sherd of Late Neolithic Peterborough pottery. The E barrow is 170 ft (52 metres) long and 70 ft (22 metres) wide and, like its neighbour, is orientated E–W. The silted-up quarry ditches are visible here too. ½ m. NE is a third LONG BARROW, 85 ft (26 metres) long and 70 ft wide.

5050

DEANE

A small but pretty village, the view of the church and house one of the most pleasing in the county.

ALL SAINTS. The most complete and successful early C19 Gothic church in the county, rebuilt in 1818–20 by Wither Bramston of Oakley Hall as a thank-offering for the victory at Waterloo. The architect may have been *William Croggon* of the *Coade* manufactory in Lambeth, who supplied all the charming Gothic details. The original effect was altered by the removal of the prominent high battlements and pinnacles in 1976. W tower, nave and chancel, all rendered in 'Parker's Cement'. The once prettier S porch is attractively plaster-vaulted inside with a fine vine cornice of kind familiar from Perp screens. The interior is almost entirely preserved with a remarkable display of Coade details: the tower arch; a triple-arched chancel screen (designed by *Thomas Dubbin*); a pointed E wall with blind tracery and ogee window surround; tunnel-vault over the altar, ceiled with ribs; and the elaborate altar surround. Only the royal arms, originally above the chancel screen, have disappeared from this rare ensemble. The furnishings, alas, are later: FONT of *c.* 1875, replacing 'a loose basin . . . on a tottering moveable column' (Canon Millard, Visitation Notes 1876). CHANCEL PANELLING, CHOIR STALLS, PULPIT and the glazed TOWER SCREENS of 1895 are by *William White*. – A few TILES in the chancel. C14, with the usual stylized foliate patterns, fleurs-de-lys etc. (cf. St Cross Hospital, Winchester). –

STAINED GLASS. In the porch windows, pathetic fragments hugger mugger with only one early C16(?) figure. In the chancel and nave, a rare but slightly depleted scheme of *c.* 1820. In the E window a Crucifixus panel, possibly after *Van Dyck*, and said to be Belgian. Strong chiaroscuro, though rather monochrome, but the surround apparently Late Victorian. In the nave diapered stamped grisaille, with lurid borders and canopies. – MONUMENTS. Many C17–early C19 mural tablets, most of them from the former church. George Wither †1666, attributed to *Joshua Marshall* (GF). Oval inscription within a wreathed surround. Large achievement in a miniature broken pediment. Betty Harwood †1775. Urn with crossed torch and trumpet. Henrietta Maria Bramston †1771. Distinctive irregularly shaped scroll and draped urn against a pale russet-pink marble surround. – Wither Bramston †1832. Gothic tablet by *Croggon*, 1834.

The medieval village was removed in the C16 and the church now has a spacious park-like setting in front of DEANE HOUSE. This is brick, late C17, remodelled in the C18 when the parapet was probably added (downpipes dated 1789). To the S a five-bay front of two storeys with a square (early C20) porch. Doorway with lugged stone architrave, above it a window with moulded brick surround. Short projecting C18 wing to l. and five-bay E elevation with large mid-C20 Neo-Georgian wing. Good early C18 interior with much panelling, the staircase with carved brackets and turned balusters. Two reused early C17 overmantels with arched panels and paired colonnettes.

In the village, MANOR FARMHOUSE is C18, altered in the C19. S, near the main road, DEANE HILL HOUSE, the former rectory, is mid-C19 but still in the Georgian tradition. S of the main road THE OLD SCHOOL HOUSE. 1879, a good example of a small Victorian village school. Brick and flint with Gothic porch, the master's house with a bay window set diagonally at the corner.

DOGMERSFIELD   7050

The medieval village, including the church, was removed during the C18 as the park around the great house was developed and enlarged.

ALL SAINTS. 1842–3 by *Benjamin Ferrey* for the Rev. Charles Dyson, who had been John Keble's curate at Hursley (S Hampshire), and his sister. Of chalk, W tower, nave, and chancel. Not large. E.E. style. As often with Ferrey's smaller churches, the interior has good well-constructed roofs. 1840s FITTINGS little disturbed in the chancel. REREDOS. Elaborate carved Gothic of 1911, framing an outstanding PAINTING, attributed to *Van Dyck*, of the Burial of Christ. – STAINED GLASS. E window, a progressive highly finished piece of 1914.

N and s windows by *Willement*, 1843. – Nave, SE, two windows
with colourful medallions by *Hardman*, 1863. Nave SW by
Clayton & Bell, *c.* 1867. On the NE side by *Christopher Whall*,
1898. NW window, mid-C19. Two panels designed by *Lady
Charlotte Canning* of Jacob and the angel, re-set from W window
with new inscription, 2006. – MONUMENTS. An engaging
small brass to Anne Sutton †1590. Tablet with kneeling figure
(nave E). – Large tablet to Sir Henry St John Mildmay †1808.
By *Nollekens*. White, Neoclassical; no figures. – Charlotte
Mildmay †1810. Good. By *Benedetto Cacciatori*, of Milan, 1840.
Weeping young woman with a baby by an urn.

OLD CHURCH, Chalky Lane. 1803–4 by *John Eads*, a Headley
bricklayer, for Sir Henry St John Mildmay. A brick box with a
two-bay nave, no separate chancel and a battlemented W tower.
Gothic-arched wooden windows with Y-tracery. Lancets in the
E wall inserted *c.* 1980 on conversion to a house.

DOGMERSFIELD PARK (Four Seasons Hotel). The site is that of
a medieval palace of the Bishops of Bath and Wells and a C16
house of the Earls of Southampton, which was partly rebuilt
1728 for Martha Goodyer and her husband, Ellis St John.
Additions were made in the 1740s and later but there is little
to show for this history since a fire in 1981 left intact only the
E wing of the C18 U-plan house. Parapet with stone urns,
ramping down to a projecting pedimented three-bay centre,
which has a modest Tuscan doorcase (added by *William Burn*,
1861–2). In the penultimate bays are niches with classical
female figures and urns, both possibly of *Coade* stone. Two
first-floor windows were cut down in the early C19 and given
a pretty iron balcony. Converted for offices, by *Gebler, Tooth &
Partridge*, with S WING by *Robert Adam*, consultant architect,
completed 1986. This is powerful Hawksmoorian Baroque with
a central pavilion that has a giant order temple front with open
pediment and links to outer pavilions with recessed centres
with small pediments, Diocletian windows over and Tuscan
colonnades. Additions for the hotel, *c.* 2002–3 are extensive
and scandalously bad, barely Neo-Georgian.

Almost everything of significance in the interior, including
sumptuous C18 plaster ceilings and fireplaces, was lost in the
fire. The surviving rooms bear witness principally to C19 and
C20 changes. The grand Neo-Jacobean MAIN STAIRCASE with
lyre-shaped splat-balusters, in the angle of the wings, is by
Burn. Lit by a circular glass dome. Under the hall, however, is
a good C18 groin-vaulted CELLAR, lit by a C16/C17 stone-mullioned window (probably *ex situ*).

The former STABLES are similar to and almost as fine as
those at Hawley Park (q.v.). They look mid-C18 but could be
as late as the 1790s, when the park was redesigned. Single-
storey ranges around a courtyard. N front has a pedimented
entrance pavilion with round-arched entrance and square
cupola, the ends of the side ranges projecting as flanking pavilions. Side ranges with central pedimented breaks and former
coachhouses to the S with central two-storey pavilion. Copious
use of lunettes.

The formal GARDEN has a C16 or early C17 square, brick DOVE-
COTE with pyramidal roof, cleverly matched by *Robert Adam*'s
ELECTRICITY SUBSTATION of *c.* 1986. WALLED GARDEN with
a pretty GARDEN HOUSE of ashlar, round arches supported on
a central column and crude broken pediment with pinnacles.
What date is this? The unlearned classicism suggests the C17,
the masonry details the early C19, or is it part of the mid-C18
Rococo developments in the park? Inside, wooden benches and
C19 glazed tiling.

A remarkable Rococo PARK was created for Paulet St John
in the late 1730s or early 1740s. It was littered with fantastic
structures, including a belvedere, Gothick archway, obelisk
and, just possibly, a Palladian bridge. The Hunting Lodge (*see*
Odiham) in the SW corner is the only survival after remodelling of the park in the 1790s by *William Emes* in the manner
of Capability Brown. The park's extension forced the
Basingstoke Canal to take a wide detour to the N, saw the
removal of the medieval church and the remainder of
the village and the creation of the Tundry Pond from a formal
mid-C18 canal. Also of this date the pair of elegant triple-
arched brick BRIDGES over the lake on the N drive and the pair
of stuccoed LODGES on the Farnham road.

At PILCOT, ¼ m. NE of the church, old houses cluster around a
small triangular green. PILCOT MILL is C18 brick and timber
frame with half-hipped tile roof. C19 iron wheel. LORDS AND
LADIES was much rebuilt in the C18 but is originally a cruck
house of 1335–6 (tree-ring date), with a two-bay open hall and
floored bay to the E.

DUMMER   5040

ALL SAINTS. A delightfully modest church, first mentioned in
1198, of flint (rendered on the S side). Simple nave and
chancel, low W porch and bell-turret. The plain round-headed
S doorway of the nave, now blocked and fenestrated, may indicate Norman masonry. Perp windows and W porch, with rare
C15 arcaded panelling above the wall-plate (cf. Kingsclere).
The chancel is of *c.* 1200, see the typically early C13 priest's
doorway, unusually on the N side, and the wide-spaced trios of
lancets on either side, but re-roofed and restored. The E wall
was rebuilt in flint in 1893 by *J. P. St Aubyn*. Chancel arch of
c. 1200, with one slight chamfer, flanked on the N by an early
C14 niche for the reredos of a lay altar, and on the S by a round-
headed squint, opened out and restored in 2000. In the nave
N wall a low tomb-recess. Original roof of early to mid-C15
collar-purlin type (Richard Warmington) and massive wooden
bell-turret; the rare, timber ROOD CANOPY is possibly contemporary. Coved profile, placed on a cambered tie-beam formerly coloured. Four by two panels with big square bosses. –
COMMUNION RAILS. Late C17 with strong, twisted balusters.
– PULPIT. Of wood, *c.* 1380, with simple tracery at the top of

the panels. – Deep WEST GALLERY of *c.* 1660–85 extending
halfway down the nave. Nice balustraded front with ROYAL
ARMS of Charles II, dated 1672, of charmingly rustic quality.
– PEWS and low WAINSCOTING. – CURIOSUM. Rare C17
painted Ringer's Rules in crude blackletter on the belfry wall.
– STAINED GLASS. In the chancel by *Kempe* the E window
(1892), centre S (1898) and NE (*c.* 1907), and by *Lavers & Westlake*, the NW lancet of 1892. – BRASSES. A palimpsest to Allys
Magewick †1591, with reused inscription to Robert Clark
c. 1500. – William at Moore, alias Dummer, †1595, family
group only partly preserved, within a shallow round-arched
stone panel of a common London type.

DUMMER HOUSE, E of the church. Early Georgian, remodelled
and extended in the early C19. Stuccoed, of eleven bays in a
3–5–3 rhythm. Five-bay pediment and under it the five first-
floor windows all arched. In the pediment a big Palladian tripartite lunette window. Seven bays to the rear: only the four r.
bays are C18. Low entrance hall with ceiling of deep octagonal
coffers. Fine C18 square-well staircase with tapered square-
section balusters; band of Vitruvian scroll around the walls
with Doric pilasters above. Good staircase also in the early C19
addition On the first floor three early C17 arched panels with
painted scenes.

In Down Street, IVY and STABLE COTTAGES are C18, symmetrical with a central pedimented blind opening on the axis with
Up Street. Behind is MANOR FARMHOUSE, C17 with herringbone brick-nogging. THE NOOK, ¼ m. W on the same
side, is a nice three-bay cruck house of the early 1420s, the
one-bay hall with a well-preserved lower-end screen. THE OLD
RECTORY, in Up Street, is by *W. J. Donthorn*, 1850. Stone and
knapped flint, squared and coursed; Tudor style. Symmetrical
front with two gables and a smaller middle gable. Windows
with mullions and transoms and curiously carved label stops.
Decorated chimneys of moulded terracotta. Substantial rear
addition of 2003 in a matching style. Further on the l. a timber-
framed WELL HOUSE of 1879 with bold curved braces and
hipped roof with bands of fish-scale tiles. Inside is a large
wooden wheel.

DUMMER GRANGE, 1¼ m. S. E-plan with an early C17 hall
range, but what matters is the mid-C17 brick parlour cross-
wing with its Artisan Mannerist detailing (cf. Wyeford Farm,
Pamber). Giant Ionic angle pilasters with carved brick capitals, moulded string courses and remains of cartouche in the
apex of the gable. The central porch in matching style is by
G. H. Kitchin, 1921; probably also the r. wing. His alterations
inside include some nice C17-style overmantels. Altered C17
staircase with turned balusters. Attractive C18 outbuildings,
brick with flint bands, converted with an arcaded loggia.

KEMPSHOTT PARK, 1 m. NE. The C18 house, leased to the
Prince of Wales in 1789, was demolished in 1965. C18 brick
STABLES (now offices) with pediment and many lunettes.
Curious crinkle-crankle WALL adjoining at rear.

EAST MEON

A rewarding village, beautifully sited on the upper reaches of the
River Meon, in a bowl of the South Downs.

ALL SAINTS. One of the most thrilling village churches in
Hampshire, at the centre of a huge former estate of the Bishops
of Winchester, who held the advowson. They planned the
cruciform church c. 1080, and c. 1150 it was given its exceptionally splendid Norman central tower, a smaller version of
the cathedral tower. Although the church is mostly of flint, this
is of Quarr stone, ashlar-faced, and with nook-shafts at the
angles, and on each side three bell-openings richly shafted. The
capitals have several scallops, the arches much zigzag. A thin
zigzag frieze separates this stage from the top stage, which has
circular openings for a bell-chamber, perhaps formerly as at
Winchester. The lead-covered broach spire fits very well and
appears to be original (although repaired). If so, it may be the
earliest surviving timber-framed spire of its type in England
and Normandy. Norman also is the fine W doorway, also very
well preserved. Two orders of shafts, mostly of Quarr stone.
Fluted and primitive leaf capitals of Haselbury stone. The arch
with zigzag at right angles to the wall. The (re-set) S doorway,
of the same materials, is a little simpler than the W doorway
but goes with it in date. Externally otherwise there is one
Norman N window in the nave N wall, and there are two in the
S transept internally preserved by later works of enlargement.
The western one, now opening to the S aisle, shows that the
aisle came after the transept. The aisle windows are mid-C13
(simple plate tracery) but there is also a rare nook-shafted SW
quoin of Quarr stone. Either it was re-set from the corner of
the nave or it too is mid-C13, purposely carved to match the
nook-shafts of the tower. Other major C13 additions to the
Norman plan are best seen inside, and are described below.

Still outside are two curious windows, unique in Hampshire,
one in the nave N wall, the other in the S transept wall. Both
are of two lights with straight diagonals instead of an arch and
equally straightened Y-tracery, making an 'Anglo-Saxon
revival' head. They are perhaps of c. 1333–45, when Adam of
Orleton was Bishop of Winchester, and are reminiscent of the
strange contemporary Gothic of his native Herefordshire.
Inside, the nave window has sharply carved corbel heads of a
man and woman, apparently life-like, possibly representing the
bishop's steward and his wife, then resident at the Court
House. The large W window is shafted in an early C14 way but
the unusual design is mature for the date, looking forward to
Perp (cf. the later windows of Alton church in the S chapel).
Parts of the stonework are original and in place, but the rest
is C19, faithfully replicated during the major restoration of
1869–70 by *Ewan Christian*, when the roofs of the chancel and
transepts were raised and restored to their original pitch. The
even larger chancel E window also has shafting, but inside,

looking mid-C13, the shafts are replete with shaft-rings (cf. the
coeval E window of South Petherton church, Somerset, also
held then by the Bishop of Winchester). But the window itself
is in the Late Perp style by *Comper*, 1905–6, and undertaken
by *J. McCulloch*, 'architectural sculptors of London for Canon
Masters'. It replaced Christian's Geom-Dec window. Perp s
chapel E window – a typically Winchester window of five lights
with tracery under a segmental head. These alterations have
the arms of Bishop Langton (see his rebus in the adjacent
panel), so must date from 1493–1500. But the s chapel s
window must be earlier; it is of an Early Perp pattern familiar
in Hampshire. The trefoil-headed priest's doorway is Ewan
Christian's, replacing an apparently Early Norman doorway
relocated from the chancel.

Inside the church the interest is of course concentrated on
the crossing. The powerful E and W arches go with the tower,
but their details, typical of *c.* 1120, are noticeably simpler. Tripartite responds. Decorated scallop capitals. The N and S
arches are plain. Pevsner wondered if they had originally been
uncarved and then, much later, tidied up in a summary way,
but they were perhaps fashioned so discretely for economy.
(Inside the present belfry stage, the tower windows are of
ashlar, smoothly finished, and so evidently were intended to be
seen from below.) The chancel is separated from the s chapel
by a strong two-bay early C13 arcade. Sturdy round pier, round
capitals and abacus, big hollow chamfers in the arches – all in
a very similar language to the W tower arch at Buriton (q.v.),
possibly by the same mason. Low down on the central pier is
a crude, possibly medieval, graffiti shield, perhaps of de Clare,
Lords of Petersfield. The impressive, muscular s aisle arcade is
different, but in date only a little later. Very short octagonal
piers. The E respond with an extraordinary support, a bevelled
bracket. Arches with one chamfer and one thin roll. This may
match the window plate tracery. The aisle is connected with
the transept by a half-arch. Good Purbeck stone floors
throughout, some original C13, others restored by *Comper* to
their original level.

FONT. Originally in the nave, now in the s aisle. Almost cer-
tainly given by Henry of Blois, Bishop of Winchester. Of black
Tournai marble. Table-top type. Splendid bold, vigorous
carving of *c.* 1130–40 (cf. Winchester Cathedral and St Mary
Bourne), in its richness and quality comparable to the finest
Tournai fonts of NE France. On the N side Creation of Adam,
Creation of Eve, and Temptation. On the E side Expulsion from
Paradise and the Angel showing Adam how to dig. On the
other sides arcading and above this a frieze with affronted
dragons, birds and animals. On the top in the corners foliage
and affronted birds. Contemporary base of very different local
malmstone, left unrestored. – FONT. Small stone tub C12 and
FONT COVER (C17), a flat lid with bobbin handle. Both from
the chapel at Westbury (*see* below) – pulpit. Of 1706, from

Holy Trinity, Minories, London. With modest inlay. Most of
the furnishings are by *Comper*, 1905–12. Carefully coordinated
scheme of ENGLISH ALTAR, COMMUNION RAILS, CHOIR
STALLS (now in the N transept), an exquisite medievalizing
REREDOS in the Lady Chapel with carved alabaster panels,
delicately painted and gilt, PARCLOSE SCREENS with an
attached wrought-iron reading stand, and fantastical filigree
Gothic-traceried SCREENS between Chapel and S transept.
Simple nave ALTAR of 1995 by *Gary Seymour*, made by *David
Forest.* – LECTERN, a four-sided reading stand by *Comper*, 1905.
– Eccentrically triangular ORGAN in the nave's NE corner, in a
contemporary idiom of 1982 by *Brandt Potter & Partners*.
(ROYAL ARMS. James I. Dated 1613 (S. Watney).) – WALL
PAINTING. The faintest traces of a Crucifixion on the
stonework of the NE crossing piers. A former Doom, above the
W arch of the tower, has disappeared, together with a fine giant
St Christopher on the nave N wall, reported by the *Southamp-
ton Herald* in 1823 as 'well executed, especially the drapes'.
Traces of colour on the S arcade. – STAINED GLASS. Nave N,
Norman lancet by *Clayton & Bell*, 1870, presented by A. Smith
of Portsea, 'builder in the restoration of this church'. – S Chapel
S, attributable to *W. F. Dixon* (a Clayton & Bell pupil), of 1871.
– S chapel E, of 1907 by *Comper*. Medievalizing with the Annunciation between St Anne and St Agnes. Chancel E, of 1921–2,
a village war memorial, to designs of 1920 by *Comper*, and
typical of his later manner with deep coloured figures of Christ,
and patron saints of allied countries, including St Vladimir of
Russia, on clear, glaringly light backgrounds. Interesting heraldry. Also by him the chancel N (1926–7), and nave NE (1946).
– MONUMENTS. Stone tablet under a C17 label in the S
transept to four Parliamentarian soldiers killed in a skirmish
in 1644 and buried upright below the transept floor. Simply
inscribed 'Amens Plenty'. Identical tablet in the chancel
recording post-Commonwealth repairs *c.* 1660. Plenty of
C18–early C19 tablets in the S chapel: George Dickens †1708
and wife †1712 of Riplington, erected 1715 by their sons
Francis Dickens, Regius Professor of Law, University of Cambridge, and Ambrose Dickens, Sergeant Surgeon to Queen
Anne and George I. – John Bonham †1721 and Thomas
Bonham Smith †1742, erected *c.* 1764. – Ambrose Dickens
†1747 signed *Palmer* (probably *Benjamin Palmer*).

   CHURCHYARD. In the far NW corner, a square, rather
austere monument to Bonhams and Bonham Smiths (latest
commemoration date 1803), signed *Hay*, Portsmouth.
Pedimented on all four sides. – LYCHGATE. By *Comper*, 1905,
with hipped roof, unusually of Northamptonshire stone
slates. CHURCH ROOM. 2000 by *Gary Seymour*, nicely in
scale.
THE COURT HOUSE, E of the church. A lavish country residence
built for William of Wykeham, Bishop of Winchester, in 1395–7.
It was supervised, and probably designed, by his master

mason, *William Wynford*. It consists of a hall running N–S and at right angles to this a chamber block with attached garderobe block, both replacing earlier buildings serving these functions. The walls are of malmstone and flint rubble with sandstone dressings; the roofs steeply pitched and tiled, separately over chamber block and garderobe. Tall square-headed hall windows with pairs of cusped lights, smaller windows of similar form in the chamber block and garderobe. The upper (S) end of the hall was originally lit by an oriel but this has disappeared along with the S range that contained Wykeham's suite of state apartments, the existence of which can be inferred from the later masonry of the hall's skewed S wall.

29   A double-chamfered arched doorway leads into the HALL which has a fine, but typical for Hampshire, plain three-bay crown-post roof, the arch braces to the tie-beams springing from well-carved corbel heads of bishops and kings, probably representing Wykeham and either Richard II or Edward III, Wykeham's first patron. The small blocked doorway which led into the demolished S wing can still be seen. The hall now ends to the S with a fine mid-C15 stone chimneypiece with a quatrefoil frieze, set here in 1927 after its discovery by *P. Morley Horder* while restoring the house for himself. It may in the earlier C15 date from work by Cardinal Beaufort in the earlier C15. At the N end a pair of doorways lead to the former buttery and pantry in the ground floor of the CHAMBER BLOCK. The great chamber above, also with a crown-post roof, is approached by an original solid-tread wooden stair from an external doorway in the angle of the wing. The chamber probably served as the bishop's private accommodation complementing the apartments in the S range.

Episcopal residency had ceased by the C17 when a timber-framed farmhouse was attached at right angles to the E. *Morley Horder* remodelled the range of outbuildings which run N from this towards the road and added along their W side the flat-roofed corridor leading to a discreet entrance in a flint wall fronting a small forecourt. It also connects with a pretty early C18 thatched cottage on the road, which became the architect's office and workshop. He also designed the formal Arts and Crafts garden, with its terrace and clipped yew hedges. At the rear of the house is a fine C15 octagonal stone chimney with battlemented top, reused as a flowerpot. At the W entrance an C18 thatched aisled BARN.

Church Street has FORBES ALMSHOUSES (Nos. 5–6) of 1863, in the style of the late C17 with classical details. Opposite, more ALMSHOUSES (Nos. 6–7), in a cottagey Neo-Tudor, by *Comper*, 1905. In the pretty HIGH STREET, with the Meon running through it, are many good houses, notably GLEN-
72   THORNE of 1697 (cf. Hill Place, Empshott). Brick, in red and blue chequer. Five bays with a bold middle projection. In it the doorway with big pediment and lugged architrave with tiny volutes, the window also lugged with volutes. Oval windows to the sides. Raised brick quoins at the angles of the house. Two

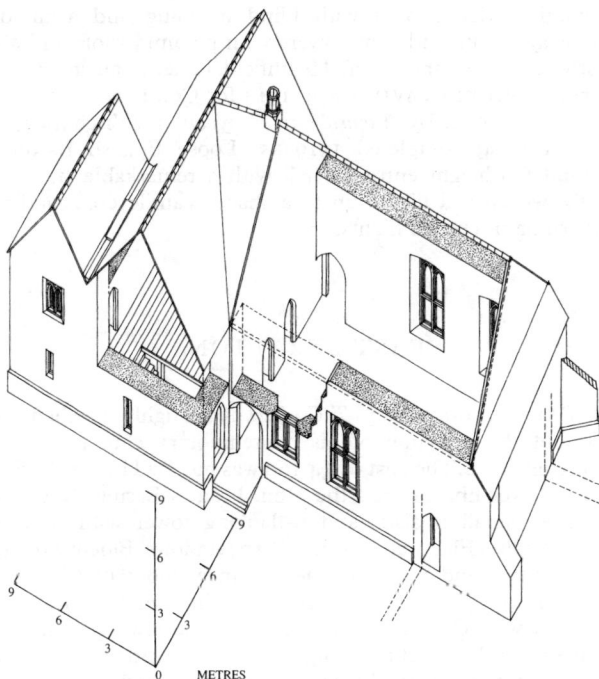

East Meon, The Court House.
Isometric by Jonathan Snowdon, 2003

houses at the street's W end are dated to *c.* 1350: FORGE
SOUND has a two-bay single-aisled hall, a rare survival.
RIVERSIDE also has an aisle but instead of an arcade it is
spanned by a base cruck. At the E end of the street in The
Square, is TUDOR HOUSE, much altered but containing a
remarkable truss dated to 1333, with cusped arch braces
beneath a steeply cranked collar. Fine C17 close-studded cross-
wing with flint-nogging.
EAST MEON HOUSE, WNW of the church. The former vicarage.
By *Crickmay*, *c.* 1870s, for William Nicholson of Basing Park.
Brick and flint, with Gothic details.
OXENBOURNE HOUSE, 1 m. SE. C17 with charming Arts and
Crafts additions of *c.* 1912, credited to *Geoffrey Lupton*.
WESTBURY HOUSE (Nursing Home), 1¾ m. NW. 1906 for Col.
Leroy Lewis. William and Mary style, clumsily handled. The
best room, the long library, has pedimented bookcases. In
front, across a canalized stream, is the ruin of the chapel of
ST NICHOLAS, probably late C13 (E.E. windows were still
extant *c.* 1900). A single cell of flint and stone, double bellcote
in W gable. *Charles Bridgeman* designed pleasure gardens for
Admiral Philip Cavendish in the 1720s, with bastioned walls.
Earthworks survive to the S. The former STABLES are also Early

Georgian. Seven bays with blind arcading and a middle archway, at the ends low towers with pyramid roofs and also with arches. To the N, off Heathfield Lane, is an impressive former CRICKET PAVILION of 1912 for Col. Lewis.

LEYDENE, 2 m. S. By *Auguste van Hooydonk* for Viscount Peel. Begun 1914; completed 1919–25. Loose English Baroque. Grand full-height entrance hall with a remarkable staircase, with two curved flights up to a shared cantilevered landing, returning in curved flights.

EAST STRATTON

5030

ALL SAINTS. 1887–8 by *T. G. Jackson*. Highly finished but without the ambition of his contemporary church at Northington (q.v.). The cost of £4,160 was met by Thomas Baring, Earl of Northbrook, and the Hon. Francis Baring. Nave and chancel, small N aisle, and N-flanking tower with shingled broach spire. Elaborate S porch. Perp windows. Finely wrought chancel arch and clunch arcades. Chancel floor with Greek key patterns. Original furnishings, Perp throughout: CHANCEL STALLS with evangelists' emblems on the low poppyheaded benches, and wrought-iron light-holders. – ORGAN CASE, over an elaborately traceried screen in the tower arch. Good brass LECTERN. – STAINED GLASS in the chancel by *Burlison & Grylls*, 1888. N window to William Russell †1683 and wife. The couple shown kneeling. Nave S of 1930 by *Clayton & Bell*. – MONUMENT. Large Arts and Crafts Perp tablet of 1906 to Earl of Northbrook †1904. Elaborate achievement with bear supporters, and angels representing Probity and Labour.

STRATTON PARK, ½ m. N. The house built in 1803–6 by *George Dance the Younger* for Sir Francis Baring (or rather remodelled from a Palladian mansion of 1731 by *John Sanderson* for the 4th Duke of Bedford) was demolished in 1960. Only the magnificent Paestum-inspired tetrastyle stone portico survives, with its mighty unfluted Doric columns and pediment, made wonderfully resourcefully into a piece of scenery for the house built in 1963–5 by *Stephen Gardiner & Christopher Knight*. The axis of the portico is continued in a long rectangular reflecting pool which passes beneath a double-height conservatory. This forms part of a larger block designed for entertaining, with to the E ground-floor guest bedrooms and a large first-floor drawing room. The ground floor is in a brown brick, the upper floor steel-framed. The cladding of this and the windows is in African mahogany. The upper frame extends beyond the conservatory to the E, over the main entrance on the N side. This is the link with the family wing, a two-storey block standing forward of the conservatory, and in contrast to it, continuously glazed on the ground floor (the pergola is not original)

93

and brick-clad above. Behind is a single-storey service range
and staff flat around a small courtyard. Originally the first view
the visitor obtained of the portico, with the parkland beyond,
was from the rear (N) entrance hall but this important element
of surprise has been lost by moving the approach to the E,
allowing a full and immediate view of the s front. Inside, the
principal space is the conservatory, leading off the hall,
spanned by three space frames and open to the upper drawing
room, which is reached by a staircase over the pool.

Former STABLES, NW of the house. By *Dance*. A two-storey
L-plan range, of painted brick and slate. Carriage arch through
the short wing, the longer wing with a clock turret. The upper
floor of this wing was removed in the 1960s but has been reinstated. A covered colonnade, also by Dance, linking the kitchen
with the brewhouse, washhouse and laundry, is now partly
enclosed as stores.

GARDENS and PARK. The house stands on a broad lawned
terrace with a HA-HA to the s. At each end GATEWAYS of
c. 1900: brick and stone with moulded caps and ball finials.
Flanking railings. About the same date is the border at the rear,
to the r. of the house, with a rubble-stone retaining wall
behind. It is interrupted by a flight of balustraded stone steps
and a small pergola with stone columns and seat. *Gertrude
Jekyll* provided a planting scheme in 1895. Nothing survives of
Dance's remarkable rock garden N of the house.

The PARK was probably first enclosed in the 1660s by Lord
John Russell, who removed part of the village to do so, and
further enlarged in the 1730s. In 1801 *Humphry Repton* made
a design for a new house and landscape. Some of his sugges-
tions for the latter seem to have been adopted, including the
moving the turnpike road on the W edge further away. At the
s end of the park the site of the old church (1810 by *Sir Francis
Baring**) is marked by a stone CROSS of 1890 by *T. G. Jackson*.
Nearby, THE OLD SCHOOLHOUSE, rebuilt after a fire in 1846,
in picturesque Neo-Tudor. THE BOTHY, to the w, is in the
same style.

LODGES: LONDON LODGE, 1⅛ m. NE by the M3. By *Dance*.
Two classical lodges, but in the centre a small castellated gatehouse with a round arch and polygonal corner turrets with
antefixae. Again in spite of this the parapet has a cresting of
Vitruvian scrolls and a central palmette-like motif. The turrets
originally had domed caps with waterleaf ornament and
kalasha finials, lending an Indian appearance. WINCHESTER
LODGE, ½ m. SW of the house, has as its principal feature a
miniature tetrastyle stone portico with unfluted Doric
columns. Could it be by *J. A. Repton*, who is known to have
assisted his father at East Stratton? Midway between the
two, PARKHILL LODGE, Tudor style of c. 1840, is on a drive
probably built for access to Micheldever Station (q.v.).

*Previously on the site was a Gothic church of 1677, built by William Russell to
succeed the medieval chapel dependent on Micheldever.

The VILLAGE lines a single street running s from the park. Clustered at the park gate, a pretty group of C17 and C18 thatched cottages. Also EAST STRATTON HOUSE, the former rectory, c. 1840, enlarged in the late C20. s, on the corner of Church Bank Road, EAST STRATTON FARM. Early to mid-C19 house, brick, of six bays, with three ground-floor tripartite sashes and later C19 porch. s are five pairs of MODEL ESTATE COTTAGES, 1806 by *Dance*, with thatched roofs, Yorkshire sashes and lean-to porches. At the far end, THE NORTH-BROOK ARMS. Early C19, originally three bays with a Tudor-arched central porch; addition to the r. with shopfront. Nice outbuildings at the rear including a wing dated 1842.

92

7030

EAST TISTED

ST JAMES THE GREAT. Largely rebuilt in 1846 by *James Winter Scott* of Rotherfield Park, assisted by his carpenter *William Puzey*. Flint-faced exterior. Of the medieval fabric, which was cruciform, the lower part of the w tower and the early C14 chancel arch remain. The upper stage of the tower has a stair-turret, an open parapet and pinnacles. All this is still pre-Eccle-siological Middle Pointed style, yet no longer as carefree as the Early Gothic Revival, or as matter-of-fact as the Commission-ers' type of Gothic church. The tower entrance with big ogee hoodmould is very Georgian Gothick. Correctly curvilinear tracery in the e window, but Late Georgian detail in the bat-tlemented aisles and inside even cherubs for the arch braces of the roof. Three-bay arcades with octagonal columns. Industrial materials are employed: cement for the arches, cast iron for the glazing and artificial stone for the pinnacles, all anathema to the Ecclesiologists. The FURNISHINGS are mostly by *Puzey*, except the Neo-Georgian COMMUNION RAILS by *A. Victor Heal*, 1931, PULPIT and READING STAND (now priest's stall). – REREDOS and STAINED GLASS window by *Powells*, 1911, replacing original of 1847 by *Anna Power*. – DECALOGUE in Gothic-framed stone panels, now in the s aisle. – MONU-MENTS. In the s aisle on the floor an early C14 slab with a cross in whose head is a sunk bust of a lady in low relief holding a heart. At the foot a dog. – Richard Norton †1536. Canopied altar tomb, erected c. 1530 as an Easter sepulchre in the old chancel. The tomb-chest already has Renaissance decoration round the shields, but above is the usual pre-Reformation recess with side pieces and depressed arch traceried inside and a straight cornice. Against the back wall kneeling figures looking from l. and r. to a Resurrection. Scrolls above the figures. Above the tomb a separate panel with arms supported by naked putti. – John Norton before †1564 and his wife Anne neé Puttenham. Early Elizabethan, of stone. Formerly with two small kneeling figures facing one another across a prayer-desk.

55

East Tisted, Rotherfield Park.
Engraving after G.F. Prosser, 1833

Oblong strapwork cartouche behind. Intricate strapwork and wreaths in the panels on the tomb-chest below. l. and r. Ionic columns. The top is a kind of flat-topped concave-sided gable. – Sir John Norton †1686. Large, with a very bad semi-reclining marble figure on a gadrooned sarcophagus. The style of *William Byrd* (C. Hussey). – Dame Dorothy Norton †1703. Black marble ledger in the chancel floor with the usual achievement. Richard and Dorothea Newlin †1725 and 1731. Finely inscribed tablet in the tower. – Busts of James Scott †1835 and James Winter Scott †1873; signed *E. C. Geflowski,* 1886.

ROTHERFIELD PARK. The house was built in 1815–24 by *J. Parkinson* for James Scott, son of William Scott, the London building contractor. It was Gothic in the sense that it was castellated and had four turrets including a big NE corner tower and a thinner, octagonal, SE turret. But the windows were normal sashes and the walls were stuccoed. This house survives only in outline as from *c.* 1850–60 onwards, starting with the S front, it was faced in ashlar and Elizabethanized. *George Devey* was employed from the late 1870s and to him can be ascribed the raising of the SE turret, with its ogee dome to his design of 1876. His work was continued after his death in 1886 by his nephew, *H. Devy-Brown* who added the gatehouse at the NW corner in 1891.

Inside an impressive central hall with cantilevered imperial staircase and coved ceiling to a square lantern; the balustrade and the lower flight were altered, and the stone newels added, in 1858 by *J. G. Crace.* He also inserted the fine pair of Gothic entrance doors and carried out the decorative scheme. The library at the NW corner, by *Devey* of 1876–7, has an inglenook in a curved bay with a stained glass window over the fireplace.

101

Mixed Tudor Gothic and C17 classical detailing. The decoration of the drawing room and dining room is a mixture, with doorcases and chimneypieces of the 1820s and rather flat late C19 Neo-Jacobean ceilings. The bold scagliola Corinthian pilasters flanking the bay in the dining room must be of the 1860s.

sw are the STABLES, early C19 Tudor Gothic, their proportionate cupola raised in 1887 as a tower to an excessive height. NW a mighty circular tower, with stair-turret and machicolations, probably of the 1860s, containing a lodge, linked to a lower square tower, formerly the meat larder. Nearby a slim conically roofed tower conceals the laundry and brewhouse chimney. – WALLED GARDEN with brick SUMMERHOUSE of 1889, with very Devey-esque pedimented gable, and fine GATEWAY of 1886–7, in the style of the late C18.

The position of Rotherfield Park is superb and the early C19 house and park represented the ideal of Picturesque theory. The C16 deerpark, associated with the manor house of the Nortons, had been landscaped in the C18, but it was further remodelled by *W. S. Gilpin*, who also extended it E of the Gosport road after 1818. Of this date the octagonal Gothic ROTHERFIELD PARK LODGE (in the village), with late C19 ashlar facing, and the Gothic BRIDGE, on the winding main drive, with splayed arch and oculi in the spandrels. At the N end of the park a further early C19 octagonal LODGE and a flint BARN, in its s gable a large blind Gothic arch as an eye-catcher.

In the village, many ESTATE COTTAGES, one row including the OLD SCHOOL HOUSE of 1837, with gabled wings and octagonal panes. Next door the CLUBROOM, 1873, with elaborate pierced bargeboards. At the N end TISTED HOUSE, the handsome former rectory, 1839–41 by *T. E. Owen*. Tudor Gothic, in malmstone, with steep gables and circular chimneyshafts. In STATION ROAD, a flint and stone mid-C19 WELL-HOUSE, with a chamfered arch and trefoiled openings in the side walls.

Former STATION (and stationmaster's house), ½ m. E. One of the neat series designed by *T. P. Figgis* for the Meon Valley Railway, built 1897–1903 (cf. Privett). Brick and stone with an Arts and Crafts feel.

EAST WOODHAY

Little more than the church, former rectory, a farm and a few cottages but many houses of interest in the scattered hamlets below the scarp of the Downs.

ST MARTIN. 1822–3 by *Richard Billing & Son* of Reading, as a tablet on the tower's w wall records. Brick. The tower with its pointed windows is still Georgian (a lead plate on the roof has the arms of the churchwardens (M. Millard)). Long nave with characteristically many and thin buttresses. Medieval chancel rebuilt in flint in 1849–50, possibly by *Richard Billing Jun.* N porch 1887 by *Francis Bacon.* Cast-iron window frames have been replaced by Geometrical tracery; five were done in 1931 by *Edwin Wait.* Inside, the nave is very typical of the 1820s, wide – almost 40 ft (12 metres) – and not high, with a complicated timber roof, essentially scissor-bracing but very stretched, and with plenty of curious cusping to enrich the effect. Quite daring for the date. The chancel is more Ecclesiological, with arcading below the large five-light geometrical E window. – ORGAN CASE of 1916. Boldly projecting, with ungainly effect. – LECTERN of 1887. A carved wooden eagle. – PULPIT. Richly panelled Perp of 1905. – PEWS. Of 1887 by *Bacon,* with candleholders of *c.* 1995. – ROYAL ARMS. Updated at the rebuilding to George IV. Larger supporters on a russet surround. – STAINED GLASS. E window. A highly finished Arts and Crafts piece of 1919 by *Louis Davis.* Nativity with St Christopher and the Child (l.) and St Michael (r.). Predella of angels. Yet more angels higher up. Chancel SE. No doubt the *O'Connor* glass mentioned in *Kelly's Directory* (1854). Chancel SW, designed by *Pugin* and made by *Hardman & Co.,* probably *c.* 1850. Two medallions, Noli me Tangere and the Holy Women at the Tomb. – MONUMENT. Edward Goddard †1724 and Elizabeth his wife †1732 of Stargrove House. The outstanding possession of East Woodhay. Large standing monument, with Baroque figures by *Francis Bird* of husband and wife in their everyday clothes, upright l. and r. of an urn. Reredos background with pilasters and broken pediment. The monument, left *in situ* at the rebuilding of the chancel, lacks swagger and flourishes. Is it meant to represent Goddard's 'sober life and conversation'?

N of the church, THE OLD RECTORY of 1828–9 by *Henry Harrison,* a Late Georgian box with Tudor Gothic trim.

STARGROVE, ½ m. SE towards East End, the principal old settlement. A bizarre castellated Neo-Tudor design with turrets and towers of French and Scots Baronial inspiration. Built for Sir Frederick Carden in 1879 and apparently enlarged from an C18 farmhouse. Inside is an impressive full-height entrance hall in a Neo-Jacobean/Early Georgian style, probably created soon after 1910 for Carden's son, also Frederick (*see* Copse Farm, below). A staircase with turned balusters leads to a gallery with seven elliptical arches supported on fluted square columns. Elsewhere in the house Adam Revival interiors. STABLES begun *c.* 1879 and expanded in 1894 in vigorous Domestic Revival style with some very original detailing.

NW of East End in a small park is MALVERLEYS, a quite large, yellow brick house of *c.* 1860–70 by *T. H. Wyatt* in unemphatic round-arched Italianate. Two storeys, all very horizontal. Entrance front with three-bay central and end pavilions, connected by recessed three-bay links (the l. pavilion might be later C19). On the garden side the centre is flanked by single-storey bows. Richly decorated interiors, most impressive the galleried entrance/staircase hall. Neo-Jacobean entrance LODGE of 1872. OLD MALVERLEYS, SW of the house, looks *c.* 1840 with Neo-Tudor details. Was it one of the 'handsome detached villas' developed in the area by the Rev. J. H. Ashworth (*see* also Burlyns, below) according to *Kelly's Directory* of 1848? The rear wall appears to have large blocked openings; was it converted as stables for the new house?

COPSE FARM, ¾ m. ENE of St Martin. An attractive model farm of *c.* 1862. The substantial farmhouse has much good introduced C18 woodwork, said to have come from Stargrove (*see* above) some time after 1910, e.g. the staircase with carved scroll brackets, column-on-vase balusters and fluted columnar newels. Set in front is an excellent DAIRY with eaves sweeping down over wooden verandas, and charming interior with slate shelves, glazed wall tiles with Greek key border and curious, Moorish plaster cornice. Striking landscaped GARDEN of the late C20, formal close to the house including a sequence of pools and rill with stone steps, statuary etc. Further out, less formal, including a Chinese bridge over a stream in the woods.

BURLYNS, 1 m. NE. Well sited overlooking a steep-sided narrow wooded valley with a lake. In 1848 the home of the Rev. Ashworth. Its five-bay core appears to be early C19 but remodelled in Tudor Gothic (reputedly in 1855) with a two-storey brick porch with diagonal buttresses and later extended in the same style.

ENBROOK HOUSE, 1¼ m. NE, at Ball Hill. Early C18, very pretty, of three bays and ambitious despite its size. Vitrified brick with rubbed red brick dressings, including giant order Doric pilasters at the angles.

HAZELBY HOUSE, 1¼ m. N. Mid-C19, Georgianized *c.* 1973–4. Important GARDEN by *Martin Lane Fox* in the Arts and Craft tradition. Terraces and a series of hedged spaces contrast with enclosed inward-looking and linear forms, including a sculpture walk, a lily pond, a columned pergola leading to a brick dovecote, and a classical pavilion facing on to another formal pond. It becomes progressively less formal until the open meadows merge into the surrounding woodland or run down to the lake.

EAST WORLDHAM

The village stands on the edge of an escarpment, with the small church very prominent in views from the E.

ST MARY. Early C13 all, but still with typically Late Norman proportions. Nave and chancel and, until probably the C14, an apse. Good Transitional and E.E. details throughout due to the Venuz family who held the advowson until 1254 when Sir John

Venuz granted the living to Selborne Priory. Lancet windows. In the w wall a group of three, widely spaced, shafted inside out. s and n doorways of two orders of colonnettes with water-leaf capitals, pointed, richly moulded arches, and dogtooth in the hoodmould (the s doorway with faint traces of medieval painting). The priest's doorway is contemporary too, though its stiff-leaf capitals have been lost and mauled by recent restoration, when the stonework was whitened. *David Brandon* did much in 1864–6: a more than usually sweeping restoration with new bellcote and roof. Good C14 iron HINGES on s door. – STAINED GLASS. E and W windows by *Hardman*, 1865. – Chancel S, 1865 – rare subject of Jacob's Dream. – (SCULPTURE. White marble copy of Thorwaldsen's tympanum of the Frue Church at Copenhagen.) – MONUMENTS. Lady, early C14, perhaps Margery de Venuz (John Harvey). Only the bust appears with delicate finely carved hands resting on the chest. The remainder of the slab is left flat and unworked. The effigy was discovered face down under the nave floor in 1865. – Heighes family. Several good late C17–early C18 tablets in the chancel. – William Dunce †1761 and Martha Dunce †1798. Separate tablets. Both with calligraphic winged hourglasses, more written than drawn. – LYCHGATE. By *T. D. Atkinson*, 1936.

Immediately s is EAST WORLDHAM HOUSE, formerly the rectory, *c.* 1800 of greensand ashlar with five-bay s front and Tuscan porch to the w. Good staircase hall. SE on the main road is THE OLD SCHOOL HOUSE of 1862–4 by *David Brandon*, extended 1897. Gothic, of uncoursed malmstone with planted timbers to gables.

s of the centre MANOR FARM has good late C19 brick model farm buildings, including a BARN of 1874 and HOP KILNS.

OLD HOUSE FARMHOUSE, ¼ m. w, has a *c.* 1625 hall range, refronted in the early C19. Cross-wing, *c.* 1600, timber-framed over brick ground floor with mullioned windows, lateral stack with sunk panels, and a rear staircase tower with scratch-moulded unshaped splat-balusters.

EASTON

5030

ST MARY. A rewarding church, in flint with stone dressings, entirely of *c.* 1170 and made more showily Norman in 1868–7 and 1872 by *Woodyer*. The low picturesquely outlandish stair-turreted W tower with its shingled top parts is his except for the lower parts, including inside the plain arch toward the nave, which takes us to *c.* 1170. Above it, an unusual feature, a round-arched doorway into the former nave roof. But the motifs will hardly be noticed, so strong is the impact of the chancel. It was almost certainly financed by the Bishop of

Winchester, who owned the advowson, and perhaps built by masons employed at St Cross. It consists of a rib-vaulted square bay and a semicircular rib-vaulted apse. Finely moulded ribs, simple foliate bosses. Between chancel and apse an arch of four orders of slender shafts, with typically late C12 capitals. Zigzag in the arch. The chancel has in addition a w arch. This has daintily shafted responds including some keeling and finely carved capitals with decorated waterleaf (cf. the late C12 crossing tower of Faringdon church, Berkshire, then connected with a prebend of Old Sarum Cathedral, Salisbury). The arch with keeled rolls. The windows are Woodyer's. Original floor levels, proved by the bases of the wall-shafts: those bases to the w are lower than those marking off the apse. Original string course which continues unusually at the same level in the nave. Genuine too, the C13 trefoil-arched PISCINA. The aumbry has polychrome decoration by *Harland & Fisher*, part of a lost scheme for Woodyer.

The nave, 50 ft by 21 ft (15 by 6.5 metres), is austerely simple by comparison, except for an unusually elaborate s doorway. This has ambitious Late Norman decoration (e.g. three shaft-rings around the shafts), but much renewed, the shafts faithfully, as evidenced from Buckler's drawing of 1836. Simple N doorway. The position of the doorways midway down the nave is perhaps unusual as late as *c.* 1170. Also two Norman N windows (the E most un-restored), small outside, but large and provided with continuous keel roll inside. Polygonal NE rood stair-turret, looking late C15, with two internal doorways, for access to the former rood loft and the chancel roof also evidenced at roof level of another, but truncated, Perp doorway. The nave roof is possibly late C15 too. It is of six bays with tie-beams to alternate bays, two purlins and two tiers of wind-braces. – COMMUNION RAILS. Made up, probably during a restoration of 1829–30, with parts of Jacobean Perp tracery from a screen. – PULPIT. Jacobean, with low-relief arabesque panels above panels with small double arches. Said to originate from a church in the City of London (Richard Sawyer) but looks provincial. Much over-cleaned. – Other furnishings mostly of the restoration, almost complete in the chancel: *Minton* TILES on the floor. – CHOIR STALLS, now only on s side, Perp with poppyheaded ends. – SCREEN, not perhaps a strict copy of the original as a glance at the fragments in the communion rails will show. – PRIEST S STALL incorporating a Jacobean back panel. – Brass READING STAND, with commemorative date of 1868, probably by *Hardman*. – SCREEN by *Woodyer*. – FONT. Appropriately Neo-Norman. – ROYAL ARMS. Probably William III, carved. – STAINED GLASS. In the chancel, of 1870 by *J. Hardman & Co.* The central E window of the Crucifixion fine in both colour and design. – W window of 1873 also by *Hardman*. – Nave N windows by *Kempe & Co.*, 1910. – MONUMENT. Agatha Barlow †1595 aged ninety, widow of William Barlow, bishop successively of St Asaph, St Davids, Bath & Wells, and

Chichester. He was the first Anglican bishop to marry after having been a monk. Small ogee-curved gable with date. A hanging tablet between two unfluted Ionic columns, briefly records their extraordinary family. Beneath this a brass plate from her grave in Latin reads:

> Barlow's wife, Agatha, doth here remain,
> Bishop, then exile, bishop again.
> So long she lived; so well her children sped,
> She saw five bishops her five daughters wed.

All repainted in the late C20. – Anna Coles †1661. Old-fashioned with an achievement, crudely repainted. – Rev. Algernon Wodehouse, †1882, rector, who largely financed the restoration. Small brass, perhaps by *Hardman*. Demi-portrait. – Harriett Dawson †1915. Carved panel in wood, nicely poly-chromed, possibly by *Kempe & Co.* Scenes of the Visitation and the Holy Family. – Harold Selwood Sawyer 1883–1951, architect. Modest tablet. Rev. Benjamin Pidcock †1899 by *Jones & Willis*. Airborne angel with inscription.

In the CHURCHYARD, by the E side of the path, several Germanic Gothic crosses, one to the Rev Wodehouse. Nice lych-gate of 1918 by *G. H. Kitchin*.

DYMOKE HOUSE, opposite the church and close to the site of the former manor house, is the former rectory of *c.* 1700. Brick front, the back and sides of reused limestone ashlar. Originally five bays, reduced to four in the early C19. Attractive pedimented porch of 1988, when a Victorian remodelling (perhaps by *Woodyer*) was reversed. The main staircase occupies almost one quarter of the plan (cf. the Old Rectory, Cheriton). Stubby column-on-vase balusters around an open well. Simpler service stair alongside. One room has bolection-moulded panelling and a late C18(?) painted overmantel of a Claudian landscape. NW, the picturesquely Tudor former SCHOOL of 1840 and beyond, the OLD RECTORY by *Colson* of 1852 but still Late Georgian in style. Its dining-room chimneypiece, a C19 concoction, incorporates a Tudor-arched stone fireplace with the initials ES possibly for Edmund Stuard, the mid-C16 rector. E from the church, EASTVIEW, a nice modest early C18 house of vitrified header brickwork with red brick dressings, mullioned-and-transomed windows. On the corner by the small triangular green, HOCKLEYS MEAD, of 1981 by *Robert Adam*, in the relaxed early Philip Webb tradition. Opposite, MANOR FARM HOUSE, late C18, red brick with a flush string course of vitrified headers, pilastered doorcase and later canted bays. Down the lane towards Martyr Worthy is the OLD MANOR HOUSE. *c.* 1700, and notable for a pair of large flint and stone buttresses in the gable-end (reused materials). Up the lane, on the corner into the Avington road, is THE CRICKETERS INN of 1905 by *A. J. Sawyer*, a charming model inn for the Lion Brewery, Winchester.

ECCHINSWELL

A small, uncannily pretty village scattered and straggling along a lane in still deep countryside s of Greenham Common.

St Lawrence. An excellent little church, satisfyingly simple; successor to the old church in the village. By *Bodley & Garner*, 1885–7, and recognizably theirs. Knapped flint; nave and chancel in one; sw porch-tower with weatherboarded belfry and steep pyramidal shingled spire. Ashlar-faced stair projection to the w. The windows mostly Dec. The e window is placed high up to allow for the reredos, as Bodley liked it. This gives an odd rhythm to the e wall, as the s chapel window is at a normal height. The s windows of the s chapel are small and straight-headed, of 3–3–2 lights. The interior strikes one as uncommonly high and yet peaceful. The arcades are of only two bays, and there is no chancel arch. Instead, a simple open screen, high and combined with the rood beam. Fine ceilure over the altar, i.e. a decorated canopy painted in red and dull green. – FONT. Perp with rosettes in quatrefoils. Small spired COVER by *Bodley & Garner*, 1893. – CHANCEL STALLS. Returned against the screen. – ORGAN CASE. Also by *Bodley*. – STAINED GLASS. Mostly by *Burlison & Grylls*. By them, the e (1886) and w (1933) windows. s Chapel se window by *Francis Skeat*, 1984. A dramatic ploughing scene. – LYCHGATE. By *Bodley & Garner*, 1895.

School, High Street. 1861 by *J. P. Harrison* of Oxford for William Kingsmill of Sydmonton Court. Complex, heavily picturesque Neo-Tudor in flint. The elaborate timber porch has ornamental details in the form of mill-rinds, alluding to the patron's heraldic charge. The brick OLD SCHOOL HOUSE to the r. has a playful tower-like porch with a spire and wooden bellcote topped by a steep conical roof.

The Old Vicarage, sw end of High Street, close to the site of the old church. 1853 by *Frederick Digweed* for the Rev. Lewis Rugg. Polychromatic red and gault brickwork with some grey bands. Many gabled with decorative bargeboards and chimneys with diagonally set square shafts. Gothic doorway with elaborate timber porch.

Bishop's Green, 2 m. N. A small early 1950s estate of innovative, modest and economical 'Highworth' houses by *Eric Chick* (consulting architects *Powell & Moya*) for Kingsclere Rural District Council following their experiment at Baughurst (q.v.). Terraces and semi-detached houses, including some bungalows. Buff brick load-bearing walls with painted weatherboarded lightweight panels between.

ELLISFIELD

6040

ST MARTIN. One of two churches in Ellisfield in the C14; All Saints was united with it in 1383. Of probably Norman origin but essentially of 1870. Flint with a Neo-Decorated w tower of 1884–5 by *J. S. Paull*. In the chancel a blocked C13 lancet, in the nave, the outline of its Norman s doorway. – COMMUNION RAILS. C17 with thin widely spaced balusters. – Plain octagonal E.E. FONT with nice Jacobean FONT COVER. – PEWS. From St James, Farnham (Surrey) of 1876 by *Woodyer*. – PULPIT. Finicky Gothic, *c.* 1917. – STAINED GLASS. Dominant E window (†1895) by *Clayton & Bell*. A Crucifixion scene against an aureole with airborne angels. – Chancel N and s by *Lavers & Co.* – WEATHERVANE. From *Sir Robert Taylor*'s demolished church at Thames Ditton, Surrey, of 1776.

THE OLD MANOR, s of the church. Mid to late C17 with hipped roof and modillion cornice. N front of four bays with angle pilasters, the E of three. The heavy segmental-pedimented doorcase is of 1922–3, when *H. S. Goodhart-Rendel* made alterations for the Countess of Portsmouth (cf. Farleigh House) in early Georgian manner. The s front was reworked and given a door with Gibbs surround in brick and a Venetian window. Stripy brick and flint addition to the l. of the same date. Further picturesque additions in similar manner beyond are post-war. Interior altered 1922–3 with panelling and fireplaces of the period. Good C17 dog-leg staircase with symmetrical double balusters. Garden also improved in 1922. Simple brick summerhouse.

(Former RECTORY, ¼ m. NW close to site of All Saints church. 1837, by *Edward Hellis* of Odiham. It cost £900.)

ELVETHAM

7050

ELVETHAM HALL (HOTEL). By *S. S. Teulon*, 1859–62, for the 4th Lord Calthorpe, replacing the Elizabethan house of the Seymour family. A major house of his but not one anybody would praise for its beauty. The style is Gothic, of course, extremely idiosyncratic, but faintly French with mansard roofs and tall hipped dormers, the composition as varied as possible in the grouping but not in the motifs. Red brick, very red, with a pattern of mainly horizontal painted black brick bands and stone details with stencilled red scroll ornament. The stone carving, inside and out, is by *Thomas Earp*, the iron- and metalwork by *Francis Skidmore*. Porch-tower on the front with a gabled square oriel with flanking figures, a pavilion roof topped by a decorative wrought-iron crown and a tourelle at one corner. Set back to the l. is the hall, with a two-storey bow. The porch was open until in 1901, in a deceivingly Teulonian

p. 258

103

Elvetham Hall.
Engraving from *The Builder*, 1860

style, a porte cochère was added by *Stanley Pool*. A yet later
addition by *Pool*, of 1910–13 and equally deceiving, to the r. of
the entrance for billiard room, with shaped gable-end, and
behind it, the library, marked by a bay window. The chapel, of
the same period, is almost invisible except for its hipped-roofed
clerestory with octagonal cupola. Pool also removed cast-iron
balconies from the two big polygonal bays projecting out on
the garden front, and added the domed cupola to the l. one.
A loggia with wide trefoil-headed arches continued around the
apsidal end of this range but was replaced by a conservatory
(the present conservatory is late C20).

Service ranges to the NW around a series of courtyards. The
main wing hinges on a prominent octagonal tower with an
extraordinary two-tiered Gothic cap.

The INTERIOR is a showpiece of mid-C19 applied art and
design (stained glass by *Lavers & Barraud*, paintings by
Harland & Fisher, tiles by *Blashfield*), the iconography assert-
ing the Calthorpes' ancient status and connection with the
history of Hampshire. The HALL has a heraldic frieze and panelled ceiling with carved bosses and Arthurian scenes, the
timber concealing, as elsewhere in the house, iron beams.
Grisaille glass with scenes from Hampshire history, the lancets
in the bow window with wild plants and poetic mottoes. In the
MORNING ROOM (originally library), the ceiling has portraits
of Tudor worthies, writers etc. Pedimented chimneypiece with
hawking scene. Next, the DRAWING ROOM, with characters
from Scott's *Kenilworth* and a very splendid chimneypiece with
wide cinquefoiled arch flanked by colonnettes and overmantel
with carved panel depicting Queen Elizabeth's visit to Edward
Seymour, Earl of Hertford, at Elvetham in 1591. Frieze with
good naturalistic carving of leaves, birds, squirrels etc., and

comical figures. Lastly on this side, the DINING ROOM, altered 1911, but retaining its chimneypiece. Like a C16 monument with a cusped opening flanked by demi-figures of Essex and Raleigh and an elaborate overmantel with colonnettes, culminating in a figure of Elizabeth I. The STAIRCASE has a balustrade with pierced trefoils and arcading with twisted balusters and horseshoe-shaped arches. The armorial figures on the newels were added in 1911. It rises within a polygonal apse lit by tall windows, the central one Gothic, with tracery of original form and glass depicting figures from the county's history. Painted frieze of shields below the panelled ceiling, the octagon over the apse with the Signs of the Zodiac and elsewhere the Seasons and Day and Night. Arcade to landing with clerestoried domed lantern, a *Pool* addition. Of Pool's additions, the best, in spite of the insertion of a floor, is the tall, apsidal-ended CHAPEL, with *trompe l'œil* wall hangings and ribbed and coved ceiling with an elaborate clerestoried lantern, the fine oak carving by *Herridge*.

STABLES, NE of house and matching it, by *Teulon*, E-plan with shaped gables but the central pyramidal-roofed cupola has been removed. Circular stair-towers with conical roofs. More carved stone panels by *Earp*, including at the rear a re-set trefoil-shaped relief, with a medieval scene of welcome, formerly on the porch.

GARDENER'S COTTAGE, W of house, also by *Teulon*, is more conventional than the house, but still individual, with trefoiled tile-hung tympana to the principal windows. Massive polychromatic Gothic WATER TOWER. FORMAL GARDENS lie SE of the house. Terrace, with pierced brick parapet and corner bastion, by *Teulon*. At NE end SUMMERHOUSE by *Pool*. Much of what survives, including the rose garden below the terrace, is the result of a 1911–12 redesign by *William Goldring*. A yew avenue runs SW from the garden's centre through pleasure grounds to another SUMMERHOUSE, of 1901. It has an oval panel carved with the goddess Flora, taken from above the former loggia on the SE side of the house. Large irregular shaped WALLED GARDEN W of the house, probably *c.* 1860 and later, with large ogival-arched gateways.

The PARK, of medieval origin, was in 1591 the site of the 1st Earl of Hertford's great entertainment for Queen Elizabeth. A crescent lake was cut in which were three islands, in the shape of a ship, a fort and a snail mount; on the high ground to the NE buildings were erected to house the Queen and her entourage. Little evidence for this survived landscaping by *William Emes* in the late C18. N of the house is a lake formed from fish ponds. BRIDGE and GATES of 1862 by *Teulon*.

ST MARY. Essentially of 1840–1 by *Henry Roberts*, in the briefly fashionable Neo-Norman style, for Lord Calthorpe. Nave and chancel under one slate roof. The stone spire, with its large showy angel statuettes, gargoyles and the Signs of the Evangelists on short shafts on the low broaches, may be by *Teulon* *c.* 1860. Converted in 1973 and all the furnishings removed.

A fine E.E. piscina has been covered over. – MONUMENTS. Reynolds Calthorpe †1714 and his wife. Twin monuments, moved to the w gallery from the e end in 1912. Nice busts. By *James Hardy*.

The village lies outside the park's SE gate. *Teulon* had already provided the 3rd Lord Calthorpe (†1851) with ESTATE BUILDINGS in a picturesque Tudor Gothic style, e.g. North Lodge and additions to the C17 South Lodge, both with Teulon's characteristic timber-framed porches; also two former schools, the modest boys' school of 1844 (Nos. 12–13 Street End) and the more ambitious Neo-Tudor girls' school (Old School House in Home Farm Lane) of 1847–8 of fierce orange brick. (The OLD RECTORY, 1857 by *Teulon*.)

EMPSHOTT

7030

A small and scattered village in pretty country of wooded hills and deep lanes.

HOLY ROOD (formerly St Lawrence). A complete early C13 church with evidence of Norman work in small lancets re-set in the w porch. The interior is a great surprise, with chalk arcades of astonishing richness (the advowson belonged to Southwick Priory, the manor to the Venuz family). They are of *c.* 1200, of four bays, their piers round, octagonal, round. The arches have two slight chamfers and are pointed. All have dogtooth hoodmoulds (much renewed). The capitals have trumpet scallops or are moulded on the s side, but have rich crockets on the N side. So s is probably older than N. The NE respond is tripartite, the NW respond, with a head, looks a little older than the rest. The chancel arch corresponds to the N arcade. The chancel had a one-bay N chapel and inside the blocked opening has a dogtooth hoodmould like the arcade. The aisles have small lancets, but the walls are far too close to the arcade to be possible as original C13 work. The VCH suggests that they were rebuilt so tightly in the C17, and that the w porch is C17 too. Externally much is of the major restoration of 1864 by *Puzey*, including the three stepped lancets of the chancel e wall and the nave roof. But pride of place must be given to the Victorian bell-turret with its glazed upper stage, below the spire of 1884. – FONT. Early C13. Of table type; Purbeck marble. Each side with five flat arches. – FONT COVER. 1626. With openwork ogee volutes and a decorated centre baluster. – SCREEN. 1624. From the chancel arch, now under the tower. The top of bold pierced strapwork with an armorial cartouche of the donor, James Metcalfe, who may have financed the C17 restoration. – PULPIT. Early C16, with linenfold. – BENCHES. With straight, moulded tops; early C15. – CHOIR STALLS. Early C17 on N side with attenuated poppyheads. – READING DESK. One Jacobean panel, probably from the pulpit. ALTAR and

frontal by *Comper*, 1911. – COMMUNION RAIL. Jacobean. –
STAINED GLASS. S aisle, SS Michael and George, 1900, and
chancel S, Sir Galahad, 1915; both by *Kempe & Co.* – MONU-
MENT. Captain John Butler †1876. Tablet by *J. Forsyth*, with
sword and pith helmet. Inscription upon a rolled scroll.

EMPSHOTT GRANGE, S, on the side of a hangar. Built *c.* 1860
as a dower house for Rotherfield Park (q.v.). Tudorbethan, the
garden front with gables and square bays, the whole stepping
up nicely from the E. Alterations of 1901 to porch and interior.

HILL PLACE, E of the church. Early C16 hall house floored in
the early C17. The great pleasure, however, is the work of
c. 1680, including the brick porch with large egg-and-dart-
enriched pediment and window above with lugged architrave
(cf. Glenthorne, East Meon). Inside, one room has a rich plasterwork ceiling of four round flower and fruit wreaths with styl-   79
ized motifs in the middle and spandrels of mixed Jacobean and
Restoration motifs. Later, probably late C18, are the plaster
enrichments to the beams. Rich C17 plaster cornice in the room
over the porch. All rustic work but very loveable.

LYTHANGER, ¼ m. S. A crazy mid-C19 *cottage orné* for the Rev.
Arthur Rickman. Possibly by *Thomas Rickman*, obscure cousin
of his famous namesake. Irregularly planned interior, the staircase with splat-balusters and barley-sugar newels.

ENHAM ALAMEIN   3040
Knights Enham

Established 1918 on part of the Enham estate by the Village
Centres Council for the rehabilitation of disabled ex-service-
men. They were accommodated in two late C19 houses
(Enham Place and Littlecote House) before COTTAGES, in
Garden Suburb style (some thatched), see e.g. Nos. 43–49
Newbury Road and Nos. 17–27 Anton Lane, and an INSTI-
TUTE and shops were erected in 1921–7, the designs by *W. H.
Thompson*. The centre is a triangular green. The thatched octagonal BUS SHELTER with ogee windows reuses materials from
an C18 lodge. ST GEORGE'S CHURCH (converted *c.* 1970) is
a pretty, late C19 former reading room of brick and tile, with
matching extension. Further developed after 1945 with the
'Alamein Village', the earliest houses rather good: semi-
detached, of yellow brick with white-painted tile-hanging and
tile roofs which sweep down over porches at each end.

FURNITURE FACTORY, Newbury Road. Built 1939 on the site
of Enham Place (dem. 1936 except for the C18 stables and N
lodge of c. 1900). Two-storey office block, brick with horizontal bands of windows, the parapet stepped up and the front
wall stepped out to a narrow central feature; steel-framed sheds
behind. Iron GATES given by the Egyptian government in
1945. The monstrous PHIPPS HOUSE was built in two stages

(1948–50 by *A. E. Mort* and 1978) as a hostel replacing the old house. Nearby, the superior RESOURCE CENTRE of 1990 by *Ken Scaddan Associates*. Horseshoe plan around an old cedar. Of brown brick with a low-pitched roof. Single-storey, but on sloping ground with flats in the basement on the down-hill side.

7060

EVERSLEY

A place of dispersed settlement amongst heaths and commons.

ST MARY. The handsome nave is of blue brick headers with red brick dressings. Arched windows. Date of 1724 over the S porch, the date 1735 on the sturdy W tower with brick battle-ments and pinnacles. This work is attributed to *John James*, who lived at Warbrook House, and certainly the tower might be his. At this time the old chancel (late medieval piscina inside) became the N chapel and the nave was rebuilt as the N aisle. The S chapel became the chancel and this is brick, built *c*. 1502, perhaps as a chantry chapel for Richard Pendilton (*see* below). It has a brick three-light mullioned S window with round-arched heads and inside a connecting arch. Early Perp E window, inserted in 1863–4 when the N chapel was recon-structed (good gothic leaden rainwater head), perhaps by *Bodley*. The N aisle was altered in 1875–6 as part of the major restoration by *Bodley & Garner* in memory of Charles Kings-ley, vicar from 1844 to 1875. Inside, surprisingly for Bodley, the N arcade was rebuilt in the same early Georgian as the original. Square piers with plain square abaci and unmoulded arches. The classical tower arch is also his. N extension 1996 by *Jackson, Greenan & Down*, linked to the N aisle by a small porch. – FONT COVER. Nice, plain, conical, with a big knob; early C17, in the vestry. – REREDOS. Neo-Jacobean, painted by *J. W. Sage*, 1864 – CHANCEL SCREEN. Classical of 1730 with three round-headed openings; the cross in strapwork (Bodley?) goes with the pretty painting on both sides of 1863 by *Charles Castell* of London. Lily panels on the inner side designed by *Charles Kingsley*. – WALL PAINTING above the low chancel arch. Of 1863, with angels holding a long scroll. – PULPIT. Plain, C18; formerly part of a three-decker. – SCULPTURE. In the N aisle oval bas relief, a copy of *Woolner*'s memorial to Kingsley in Westminster Abbey, a sensitive portrait. – STAINED GLASS. N chapel by *Clayton & Bell*. Chancel E by *Hardman*, 1863, designed by *John Hardman Powell*. N aisle N by *Holiday*, made by *Powells*, 1905. – MONUMENTS. Brass. Large, on the chancel floor, to Richard Pendilton †1502, servant to Giles Dawbeny, Chamberlain to King Henry VII, at Bramshill. A good example of a rare single-cross brass. – Two large architectural tablets in the chancel: Alexander Ross †1654 and Lady Henley, †1666. Both attributed to *Thomas Burman* (GF).

– Several smaller tablets in the nave. – Dame Marianne Cope
†1862. An exquisitely detailed alabaster effigy in contemporary
costume by *Redfern*, 1863. On a low altar tomb designed by
William Slater,* with achievements and inscriptions painted by
J. W. Sage. Brasses to the Rev. Sir William Cope †1892 with
cross and inscription, by *Hardman*, and Mary Kingsley †1900,
intrepid traveller, with palm fronds and text from the Koran,
by *Frank Smith & Co.*, London.

In the CHURCHYARD a stone cross to the Rev. Charles
Kingsley †1875. John James is buried on the w side in an
unmarked vault.

THE OLD RECTORY, SE of the church. C17 timber frame, remodelled and faced in brick in the early C18, but with no serious
attempt to hide its origins. Three-bay hall range, the centre
slightly projecting with Venetian window over the door, and
two-storey hipped-roofed bays to the flanking gabled wings.
The windows all casements. NE, THE OLD MANOR was also
remodelled in brick *c.* 1700 with angle pilasters and high
hipped roof. (Inside, a good stair of that date.) About ¼ m.
SE, BRICK HOUSE is mid-C17. Two storeys, the materials and
details suggesting a high status but just two rooms with a
central entrance leading into the larger one, and rear service
wing forming a T. Front with full-height canted bay to the l.,
formerly matched by one on the r., and a central hipped-roofed
porch; the door and frame with vase stops has been brought
forward. S again, HILL COTTAGE, 1906–7 by *R. Weir Schultz*.

CHARLES KINGSLEY PRIMARY SCHOOL ¼ m. N. 1853 by *J. B.
Clacy* of Reading for Kingsley. Black-and-white timber
framing, brick and tile-hanging. Hall with a large gabled
dormer braced by timber struts. The former schoolmaster's
house to the r. has a late C19 wing. Deferential addition of
c. 1900 to the l.

The principal settlement is ¾ m. NW with mainly C17 and C18
cottages and houses strung out along Eversley Street. In Warbrook Lane is a row of model workers' COTTAGES of 1902, the
best of a series built in the parish by Charles Kingsley's friend,
John Martineau. In the Port Sunlight tradition. The timbers
are carved with improving texts. Who was the architect? Others
include KINGSLEY COTTAGES, Eversley Cross, 1 m. NE, of
1896, which have a bust of Kingsley.

GLASTON HILL HOUSE, ¼ m. N. 1723. Vitrified headers with
red brick dressings. Five bays with parapet, three windows with
frilly brick arches. Neo-Georgian r. addition of *c.* 1920 when
the entrance was moved to the side, reinstated at the front
with Gothick doorcase in Batty Langley style by *Dick Reid*,
2002.

FIRGROVE MANOR, 1 ⅜ m. ESE. Now flats. The back with a big
hipped roof is *c.* 1700. Refronted, probably by *John James*, for
Wadham Wyndham who moved to Eversley in 1736. Nine bays,

---

* Slater and Redfern later collaborated on the reredos at Kilndown, Kent.

the three and three side bays are full height canted bay windows. They end in balustrades. The three-bay centre has a fine doorway with Ionic columns and is crowned by a pedimented attic storey. Early C19 additions to the l. and at the rear a 1930s L-shaped loggia with a re-set C18 classical marble relief. Fine entrance hall. The staircase with column-on-vase balusters and carved details, rising on three sides, and a gallery returning along the front wall. Former dining room to the r., panelled, with pedimented doorcases. At the rear the c. 1700 stair with barley-sugar balusters.

77 WARBROOK HOUSE, ½ m. NW. Built by *John James* for himself in 1724, as recorded on his monument in the church, no doubt as a country retreat from his duties as Joint Clerk of the Works with Hawksmoor at Greenwich. An impressive, remarkably individual house, originally extremely compact. The central block is a cube, of two storeys and attic over a raised basement (now concealed by terraces). Identical E and W façades of bright red rubbed brick, of three bays with full-width pediment that barely rises above a high parapet. On the end walls stately rows of chimneys, two pairs in the centre with arches between *à la* Vanbrugh flanking small pediments, and singly at the corners. The façades are treated as giant porticoes of broad raised rendered pilaster-strips, connected at the top by an equally flat band or frieze. Central doorways with simple surrounds and Venetian windows in the pediments. This block probably originally stood alone, like the very similar Iver Grove, the Buckinghamshire house of 1722–4 attributed to James, which had its kitchens and services in the basement and servants' rooms in the attic. So the flanking wings here, with one-bay links to two-bay pavilions with pediments, are probably late C18. Despite their inferior brickwork they relate well to the centre. Slight differences suggest that the roof over the N pavilion has been altered, probably in the early C19. The long Neo-Georgian N wing is of c. 1936 by *Wellesley & Wills*; its curved bay to the N has a swan-necked pedimented doorcase. Their two-storey pedimented S addition with a first-floor colonnaded sleeping porch has been removed.

Inside, the restrained panelled Entrance Hall, with plain stone chimneypiece and simple plaster ceiling, spans almost the full width of the E front. From its E end rises the fine dogleg staircase with alternating column and twisted balusters and carved tread-ends, their section continued as moulded undersides. Pedimented and lugged stucco wall panels flanked by drops suspended from lion masks, and panelled ceiling with putti at the corners and wreaths of fruit and flowers. Similar ceiling over the landing. On the W side the Garden Room, formed c. 1920 by *Richardson & Gill* from the drawing room (S) and dining room (N). The former has a pier glass with pedimented surround and the latter similar pedimented surrounds to recesses flanking the chimneypiece. Identical enriched plaster ceilings with broad bands of scrollwork and strapwork-like motifs at the corners. But what is James and what Richardson & Gill? Above, the principal Bedroom and Dressing Room. Running front to back across the house is a barrel-vaulted attic room, with smaller rooms off. Poorly lit and unheated, it was probably servants' accommodation rather than the architect's office as suggested to Pevsner. Elegant staircase in the link to the S pavilion by Richardson & Gill. In the N wing a groin-vaulted corridor, Library and New Dining Room. This forms the W side of the former service court NE of the house. The E range is still C18 but the stables to the S have been replaced by an undistinguished Neo-Georgian block of 1982.

Walled forecourt to the E with a charming Baroque SUNDIAL by *James*, a panelled circular pedestal with scrolls, and a brick HA-HA. Remains of impressive formal GARDEN W of the house, probably designed by *James*, who had translated d'Argenville's *The Theory and Practice of Gardening* in 1712. In the style of Le Nôtre, with a canal parallel to the house, with short returns to the E, and one on its axis, forming a T. Allées cut through groves of trees in the angles between, converging on the centre of the W front. Original approach on axis of E front, diverted to the N c. 1840, with mid-C19 LODGE.

EWHURST

5050

There is no village, just a house with the church tucked away behind.

ST MARY THE VIRGIN. Now a store. 1872–3 by *Charles Smith* of Reading. Small, of flint, with bellcote and transepts. C15 E window. – MONUMENT to Sir Robert Mackreth of Ewhurst Park †1789. He acquired the estate probably in the 1760s or 70s and 'much improved' the previous church and the house and park. He was the archetypal C18 self-made man, rising from a billiard marker at White's Club to become its owner, M.P. and notorious moneylender.

EWHURST HOUSE was partly demolished c. 1960 and the remains refronted with, in Pevsner's words, 'something neo-Georgian'. The garden elevation had been added as a wing to the previous house in the early C20. Impressive late C18 STABLES, N of the house, originally of three ranges around a courtyard, linked by pedimented archways at the corners, the middle one with coupled pilasters, steep pediment with blank lunette, and mansard roof, the surviving r. wing (the other regrettably demolished) with an arched window reaching up into the broken pediment. Fine fittings, including a central arcade of attenuated columns and shallow elliptical arches. Early C19 hexagonal GAME LARDER on cast-iron staddle-stones.

The PARK includes series of lakes. Two late C18 BRIDGES, one of five arches, the other of three. They have flint nodules for rusticated voussoirs and string courses.

HOLLY BUSH FARMHOUSE, 1 m. NE. Formerly the Red Lion
Inn. 1777. Three bays, the ground-floor windows set within an
arcade linked by a strong impost band and with flint nodules
around the arches (cf. Townsend Lodge, Wolverton; the two
estates were connected by the Pole family).

8040

EWSHOT

Originally a tiny settlement in wooded hills NW of Farnham,
much enlarged by C20 housing.

ST MARY. Small, of 1873. By *J. Oldrid Scott*. Bargate stone. Nave
and chancel under one roof-line externally. Stone gabled W
bellcote. Lancets and plate tracery. Inside, chancel arch and a
blocked two-bay arcade for an intended S aisle. Contemporary
fittings: FONT. Demonstratively E.E. with exuberant stiff-leaf.
– REREDOS. Finely carved by *Farmer & Brindley*. With a Crucifixion scene between medallions of the *Agnus Dei* and Pelican
in Piety. – Tile DADO of 1897 by *Powells*. – STAINED GLASS. In
the E window by *Clayton & Bell*, N and S lancets by *Powells*,
nave N by *Mary Lowndes*, 1920, W window by *Powell*.

3050

FACCOMBE

An extremely manicured village. In the medieval period the
parish church and principal manor were at Netherton 1 m. W
(q.v.).

ST BARNABAS. 1865–6 by *G. B. Musselwhite* of Basingstoke.
Small, of flint. W tower and nave. Conventional chancel
removed 1965 and the original E window re-set by *Sutton &
Gregory* of Newbury. Geometrical Dec, even to the bell-openings of the tower crisply detailed. – FONT. From Netherton.
Norman. Drum-shape, with tapering sides, one band of zigzag,
one of rope, one of two zigzags. – STAINED GLASS. Original
fleuron and cross patterns in most lateral windows – E window
by *Powells*, 1901. Christ the King between the dedicatory saints
of the old and new churches. – MONUMENTS from Netherton:
Anne Reade †1624. Incised slate panel, attributed to *Francis
Grigs*, and on it the kneeling lady with her kneeling children.
The interesting inscription refers to her parents (she was
descended from the Dymockes, Champions of England, of
Scrivelsby (Lincs.)). – Sir Berkeley Lucy †1759. Large architectural tablet.

FACCOMBE MANOR. Mostly Neo-Georgian of 1936–7 by *Floyd
& Robson* of Newbury but the quite swagger five-bay front is,
except for the Ionic doorcase, Early Georgian. Vitrified header
brickwork with extensive rubbed red dressings, including a

broad surround to the upper middle window, frilly lintels at ground floor and a string course which climbs over their keystones. The side of the C18 house is incorporated into the lively garden front as one of a pair of wings to a central pavilion. GATEWAYS contemporary with the remodelling.

FARLEIGH SCHOOL

1¼ m. s of Abbotts Ann

3040

Formerly Red Rice House. Traditionally, built *c.* 1740, see the plain six-bay SE elevation, possibly altered *c.* 1828, but rebuilt in a classical style in 1844–5 by *William Burn* for Rev. Best of Abbotts Ann. Further altered in 1883 by *J. Macvicar Anderson* and refaced in Clipsham stone by *R. F. G. Aylwin* in 1933. Long two-storey NE front with Burn's fine ashlar tetrastyle Tuscan porte cochère. The main part is of ten bays and suavely handled, the ground floor with French banded rustication and tall round-arched openings (some blind), and a bold cornice that stops short of the end of the façade beneath a parapet with ramped ends. Three-bay wing to the r., top floor added *c.* 1912. The rear elevation has canted and square bays, altered by Macvicar Anderson with the addition of Neo-Jacobean gables but re-Georgianized in 1933. The square INNER HALL is by *Burn* with balustraded gallery and shallow dome with glazed oculus, but much else was altered *c.* 1912 by *Richard Mauleverer Roe*. To the r. of the hall is his two-storey GREAT HALL (now the school chapel), replacing the 1840s dining room. Wide opening with Tuscan columns *in antis* and a coved ceiling with thick ribs and a band of enriched plasterwork. Bold C18 Kentian marble chimneypiece with well-carved drops of fruit etc. to the side scrolls, and the heads of winged putti in the middle of the deep frieze. The replacement DINING ROOM (in the former service wing) is Adam Revival with good plasterwork. Also Roe's is the stone STAIRCASE, with scrollwork and balusters in the wrought-iron balustrade. Throughout the house are several C18 and early C19 chimneypieces.

STABLE COURTYARD, NW, also by *Burn*, in brick and slate. Two storeys, except for the front range with pavilions flanking an archway under an open pediment, and cupola. Landscaped PARK. s, a WALLED GARDEN. C18, brick with tiled cap. Wrought-iron gates, part of mid-C19 alterations. Nearby, a large WATER TOWER of 1855, with arcaded brick base and cast-iron tank. N, a pair of LODGES, 1921–2 by *Leonard Stokes, Drysdale & Aylwin*. An accomplished design, in Stokes's Neo-Georgian, with steeply hipped tile roofs and tall central chimneys. Between the lodges, mid-C19 stone GATEPIERS, probably by *Burn* (whose Neo-Tudor lodge the pair replace), with wrought-iron gates.

Some good school buildings NW of the house by *Perkins Ogden* of Alresford: PRE-PREP KINDERGARTEN, 2000–1, with a row of six classrooms, in pairs, rendered with shallow monopitch roofs, linked by a lower corridor towards the playground; and the harder-edged ART/DESIGN & TECHNOLOGY building, which incorporates a late C19 estate outbuilding. Two brick pavilions connected by flat-roofed links and a glazed covered way around two sides of a courtyard.

FARLEIGH WALLOP

6040

ST ANDREW. The flint exterior looks deceptively Victorian (restorations of 1840, and 1871–2) but much of the fabric is of *c.* 1733 (Bingley) when the church was completely rebuilt in mixed Perp and classical styles by Viscount Lymington: a rare example of Early Georgian Gothic. He may have been his own architect; as Governor of the Isle of Wight, he rebuilt Carisbrooke Castle Chapel in 1734. Small W porch-tower of 1873. COMMUNION RAILS. Early C18, with twisted balusters, ennobled by large goats with wrought-iron heraldic pennants, made for the staircase at Hurstbourne Park by *Kempe*, brought here in 1938. – Elaborate REREDOS, and linenfold panelling of 1913, perhaps by *G. H. Kitchin*. – SETTLE in the chancel. A curious hybrid piece with tall linenfold panelled back. – OIL LAMPS in the nave. An unusual set mounted on delicate wrought-iron brackets. – SCULPTURE. On the W wall a very handsome Grinling Gibbons-style garland of wood, of course *ex situ*, as a 'surround' to a plain wooden tablet to the 8th Earl. – MONUMENTS. Quite a collection, mostly to the Wallops. The earliest in the chancel, a late C15 chest tomb with shields in quatrefoils including Wallop achievement. Purbeck marble top with indents for brasses. – Several fine C18 ledgers in the chancel floor with deeply carved heraldry. – Another in the nave to Mary Pyle (of Winchester) †1732, buried here for her 'sincere and constant friendship for the Lord Viscount Lymington and his family'. – 1st Earl (†1762) and Countess (†1738) of Portsmouth. Twin tablets, large with pilasters and pediments. The achievements with goat supporters are unusually in lead. Both identically designed. His must have been copied from hers. – 2nd Earl †1797. Signed *Coo[ke]*, London. Seated woman by an urn and weeping willow. Much smaller.

FARLEIGH HOUSE. A small country house built in 1731 by John Wallop, Viscount Lymington (1st Earl of Portsmouth from 1743) on the site of the great house of the Wallops (largely destroyed by fire in 1661) and perhaps intended as a place of resort from the principal seat at Hurstbourne Park (*see* p. 348). The architect is unknown. It consists of a single range, the S end of which incorporates a substantial part of a wing of the old house (masonry, mullioned windows and roof structure). The E, garden, front is of squared knapped flints with ashlar dressings, the ground-floor windows with keystones, cornices and aprons. In the centre a full-height canted bay in ashlar with a pyramidal roof, the ground-floor openings round-arched with Gibbs surrounds. Carved coat of arms over the door.* The entrance side was transformed by *H. S. Goodhart-Rendel* in 1936–7 for the 9th Earl, when this became the family seat. He removed minor late C19 additions and raised the existing C17 stair-tower, embellishing its tall arched staircase window with a Gibbs surround and adding a pediment against a high attic. Crowning this a *Coade* stone coat of arms, taken from a gateway at Hurstbourne Park. Flanking projecting hipped-roofed pavilions have ground-floor arched windows with Gibbs surrounds; between the wings and the centre, round-arched openings crossed by heavily keyed lintels.** Porch of the same date, its wide broken segmental pediment added 1989 by *Robert Adam*.

The staircase looks C18, but later than 1731, very elegant with attenuated column-on-vase balusters and ramped handrail. The OCTAGONAL SALOON is the best room. Fine doorcases and/with pulvinated friezes with oak-leaf decoration striking an appropriately rustic note. Chimneypiece with lugged architrave, scrolled to the centre with putto head set in shell. Next door, the PANELLED ROOM with small corner fireplace whose keystone is a vigorously carved head of the Green Man. In the kitchen, s end, an extremely interesting mid-C17 chimneypiece. The vertically halved pilasters carrying big lugs are as characteristic as the big, broadly decorated volutes in which the feet of the pilasters disappear. In *Goodhart-Rendel*'s dining room and drawing room, bold cornices and good stone chimneypieces (cf. The Old Manor, Ellisfield).

Former STABLES, to the N, apparently early C17 but remodelled *c.* 1731 with a good staircase at the E end. Most of the formal landscaping close to the house is of the late 1930s and the late 1980s (*John Phibbs* and *Georgia Langton*). The main W driveway was created by *Goodhart-Rendel*. GATEWAY with wrought-iron gates and stone and flint piers, topped by C20 copies of C18 *Coade* stone mermaids with mirrors and combs formerly at Hurstbourne Park.

HASSOCKS HOUSE, NE. The former home farmhouse. C17, flint and brick, with moulded string course and window surrounds. Fine five-bay aisled BARN of *c.* 1575–6 (dendrochronology).

FARNBOROUGH***

Farnborough is a NE Hants village that mushroomed in the C19 and C20 into a sprawling, traffic-dominated town, now part of

---

* Similar to an unattributed and undated design for a house for the Duke of Bolton at Abbotstone (Itchen Stoke).
** The motif taken from Lutyens's Homewood of 1901 (observation by Nick Carey-Thomas).
*** Churches and abbey revised by Rodney Hubbuck, Farnborough Hill, Farnborough Place and St Peter's Church House by Michael Bullen, other secular buildings by Simon Bradley.

the built-up area that stretches NE to Frimley and Camberley in Surrey. The London & South Western Railway main line came in 1838, followed sixteen years later by the army's settlement at Aldershot to the s (q.v.). From 1863 the area between village and army camp boundary was laid out with broad residential roads to a plan by *Henry Currey*, but these were slow to fill. Eugénie, the exiled and widowed French Empress, made her home in Farnborough in 1881. Her adopted house is on a hilltop E of the town, near which she founded an abbey and imperial mausoleum. These are the C19 highlights. In 1905 the fledgling air force established itself on open land SW of the town, later the primary research centre for British aviation. Some of its historic buildings remain, in an area now divided between continuing aviation and research uses and new business parks. Much land to the NW was taken for army barracks, since levelled. Later growth was abetted by the M3 motorway, opened in 1971 through the N edge of the town, and a planned estate for London overspill, built around the same time. All these developments have different centres of gravity, so the architectural interest of Farnborough is scattered. The aviation quarter is described at the end; the district of Cove, W of the town and running on from it, has its own entry (the boundary followed is that of the Cove Brook).

CHURCHES

ST PETER, Church Avenue. The village church of Farnborough, one of four medieval chapels dependent on Crondall, stands within a small, formerly circular churchyard (always a sign of early, possibly Saxon origin), on a low hill in leafy suburbia. As recently as 1900 it could only be approached through the park of neighbouring Farnborough Place (to the N; *see* p. 280), and lay aloof from scattered houses. The earliest surviving parts are Norman, specifically the N and W walls of the nave, and two typically Norman doorways. That on the s side, re-set in the s aisle of 1900–1 by *Sir Arthur Blomfield & Sons*, looks early C12, with billet in the (restored) hoodmould. The other, noticeably more ambitious, on the N side toward the former village, remains unrestored from *c.* 1200, with decorated trumpet-scallop capitals and a hoodmould with dogtooth. It is sheltered by a beautiful wooden Late Perp N porch: one of the best in southern England, with its refined detail quite a showpiece. Can it be of *c.* 1500–20, contemporary with the nave N windows? Low weatherboarded timber-framed W tower, probably of *c.* 1700 (evidence of plastered eaves cornice below the pyramid roof), but re-clad in 2003. The internal framing is evidently reused, possibly from a former medieval bell-turret of characteristically Hampshire 'four-poster' construction. The E parts are low and spreading: the chancel of 1886 by *A. Rowland*

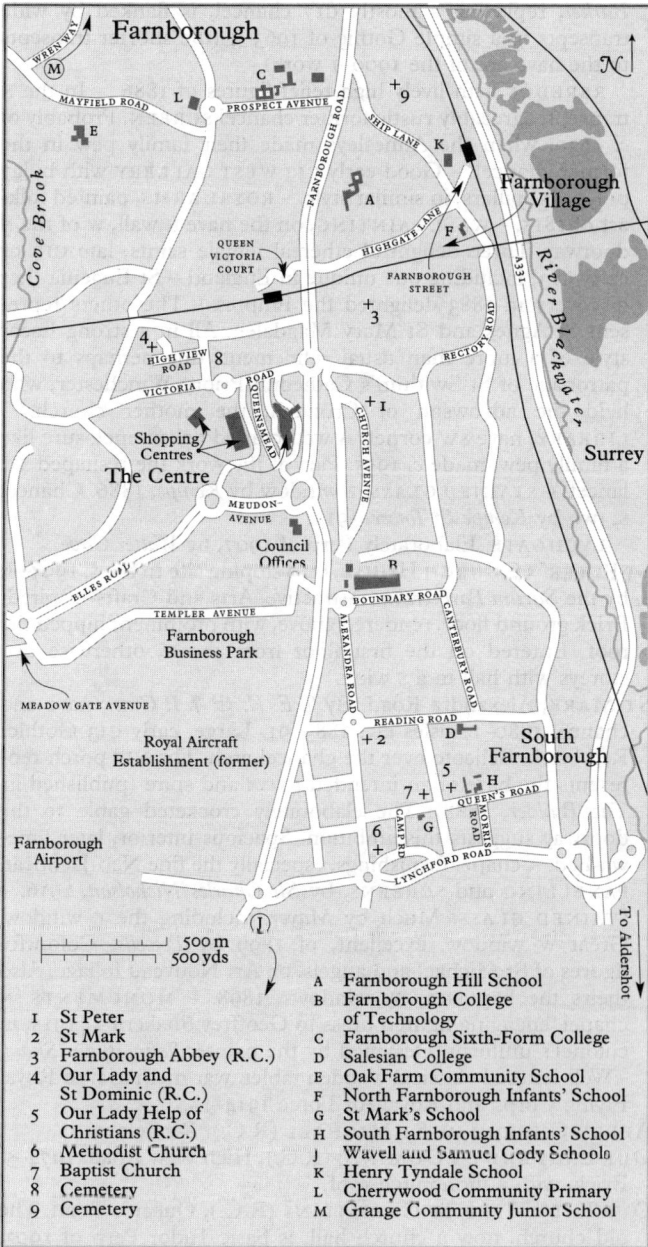

Farnborough

MAYFIELD ROAD

WRENWAY

Cove Brook

C
L
PROSPECT AVENUE
E

FARNBOROUGH ROAD

SHIP LANE

N

K

Farnborough
Village

A

HIGHGATE LANE

F

A331

River Blackwater

QUEEN
VICTORIA
COURT

FARNBOROUGH
STREET

+ 9

+ 3

4 +
HIGH VIEW
ROAD
8
VICTORIA

ROAD

QUEENSMEAD

+ I

CHURCH AVENUE

RECTORY ROAD

Surrey

Shopping
Centres
The Centre

MEUDON
AVENUE

Council
Offices

ELLES ROAD

TEMPLER AVENUE

Farnborough
Business Park

B

BOUNDARY ROAD

ALEXANDRA ROAD

CANTERBURY ROAD

MEADOW GATE AVENUE

Royal Aircraft
Establishment (former)

READING ROAD

+ 2

D

5
+

South
Farnborough

H

7 +

QUEEN'S ROAD

L

Farnborough
Airport

6
+

CAMP RD

G

MORRIS ROAD

LYNCHFORD ROAD

To Aldershot

500 m
500 yds

I   St Peter
2   St Mark
3   Farnborough Abbey (R.C.)
4   Our Lady and
    St Dominic (R.C.)
5   Our Lady Help of
    Christians (R.C.)
6   Methodist Church
7   Baptist Church
8   Cemetery
9   Cemetery

A   Farnborough Hill School
B   Farnborough College
    of Technology
C   Farnborough Sixth-Form College
D   Salesian College
E   Oak Farm Community School
F   North Farnborough Infants' School
G   St Mark's School
H   South Farnborough Infants' School
J   Wavell and Samuel Cody Schools
K   Henry Tyndale School
L   Cherrywood Community Primary
M   Grange Community Junior School

Barker, replacing a mostly C17 chancel, is flanked by wide transepts in a simple Gothic of 1963–4 (the shorter transepts to the nave are of the 1900–1 work).

REREDOS with lively high-relief figures of 1886. – In the N transept, agreeably rustic former chancel SCREEN. Probably of *c.* 1630, when the Annesleys made their family pew in the former chancel. – Good early C17 WEST GALLERY with bulgy polygonal pillars, in similar style. – ROYAL ARMS, painted folk-art of 1815. – WALL PAINTING, on the nave N wall, W of the N doorway. Three delightful ethereal female saints, late C12 or early C13, including one unique in England – St Eugenia (her discovery in 1883 delighted the Empress). The others represent St Agnes and St Mary Magdalen. All in a strong linear style of a more than usual refinement, due perhaps to the patronage of St Swithun's Cathedral Priory, Winchester, who held the advowson of Crondall, the mother church. – LIBRARY, nave SW corner. A well-crafted oaken enclosure like a family pew, made *c.* 1955. Part of the work the reshaped SW lancet. – STAINED GLASS. E window by *Kempe*, 1886. Chancel s, two by *Kempe & Tower*, 1915.

LYCHGATE. Elaborately Perp of 1907, by *Walter Cave*.

ST PETER'S CHURCH HOUSE, on a sloping site to the s. 1997–8, by the *Sarum Partnership*. Attractive, Arts and Crafts-inspired. Brick ground floor, rendered above, with prominent hipped tile roof. Entered on the first floor from the N, otherwise two storeys with hall in a s wing.

ST MARK, Alexandra Road. By *J. E. K. & J. P. Cutts*; nave and chancel 1880–1, aisles etc. 1889–91. Large, early C13 Gothic. Red brick. Bellcote over the chancel arch. The NW porch represents the base of an intended tower and spire (published in *The Builder*, 1888). The elaborately crocketed gable to the doorway suggests this ambition. Spacious interior, later lime-washed. N chapel furnishings, especially the fine Neo-Jacobean PANELLING and SCREENS, by *Sir Charles Nicholson*, 1916. – STAINED GLASS. Much by *Mayer*, including the E window. Great W window, excellent, of 1899 by *Powells*. Colourful figures of St Michael and angels, on Art Nouveau foliage. Also theirs the baptistery W windows, 1898. – MONUMENTS. N chapel, engaging figured brass to Geoffrey Shakerley †1915, in colonel's uniform. Designed by the painter *John Byam Shaw*. – Well-lettered classical wooden tablet, war memorial to Royal Flying Corps and Royal Air Force 1914–18.

ABBEY CHURCH OF ST MICHAEL (R.C.). *See* below.

OUR LADY AND ST DOMINIC (R.C.), High View Road. 1974–5. Brick, with a monopitch roof.

OUR LADY HELP OF CHRISTIANS (R.C.), Queen's Road. The old church, now a church hall, is basic Tudor Perp of 1903. Attached, N, its smaller successor of 2000, by *New Sarum Partnership*. Swept-back entrance section, then a rounded chapel wall of pale brick in header bond. The main interior white and calm. Natural light falls onto the altar platform and end wall from concealed sources in the tent-like roof.

METHODIST CHURCH, Lynchford Road. 1883. Red brick and lancets. Office wing of 1996 to the N.

BAPTIST CHURCH, Queen's Road. Dated 1905. Thin, fancy Dec tracery in the end window.

CEMETERY, Victoria Road, 1859. With a little CHAPEL by *Thomas Wilson*, Butterfield's assistant. Its black-diapered red brick and steepling roof echo his master's voice.

CEMETERY, Ship Lane, Farnborough Green. CHAPEL of 1932–3 by *E. H. Montague Ebbs*. A late case of archaeological Dec tracery.

ABBEY CHURCH OF ST MICHAEL

The secluded hilltop site was acquired in 1880 by the Empress Eugénie, to build a mausoleum and chantry for her husband (†1873) and her son (†1879 in Zululand), within sight of her home at Farnborough Hill (*see* p. 275). Her architect was *Gabriel Hippolyte-Alexandre Destailleur*, as at Farnborough Hill. Before the collapse of the Second Empire, Napoleon III and family had intended to be buried alongside the kings and queens of the *ancien régime* at Saint-Denis, where Viollet-le-Duc had created an imperial crypt (now destroyed). The Emperor and Prince Imperial were instead interred first at St Mary's R.C. church at Chislehurst, Kent, close to the place of the family's exile.

The abbey church was built in 1883–8. In his design ⟨107, 110⟩ Destailleur realized a building potent with Bonapartist iconography and, in its quotes from French medieval architecture,* symbolic of the claim to a place in French regal history. It is cruciform, of Bath stone, with a three-bay nave, broad crossing, shallow transepts and a short polygonal apse, raised above the crypt and enclosed by the sacristy, in the manner of a chevet. The style is French Flamboyant, partly inspired (inside and out) by Notre Dame des Marais at La Ferté-Bernard in the Loire, with elaborate chimaeras (by *Dousanny* of Paris) springing from the pinnacled buttresses, and rose windows, five in the apse, another singly in the weak W front. All quite convincing except for the dome, which is awkward over an ungainly octagon and concludes in a tall lantern with Renaissance details – fluted colonnettes at the base of the dome, round arches, pilasters and flaming urns – an elaboration of the early C16 W towers at Tours. The interior is more assured. It is impressively vaulted in stone throughout, the arches all with continuous mouldings that are intersected by the ribs of the vaults. The ribs form complicated patterns and pendants, again with small classical details, especially richly in the apse where they support a corona over the High Altar. Within the

---

* On these sources *see* A. Geraghty, 'Farnborough Abbey,' *Apollo* 143 (1996).

squinches below the dome, the imperial arms and regalia of Napoleon III and Eugénie. The w doorway has more exuberant naturalistic carving around the canopy. The painted polychromy of the apse and transepts, in mauve, purple and gold, is part of a scheme intended for the whole interior, designed by *J. Lachaise & L. Gourdet*, with the archangel in the central bay of the apse. Beautiful FLOOR of Corsican marble, highly coloured geometric patterns. – Of the original FURNISHINGS are the canopied STALLS in the apse, in character rather English, flanking the elaborate Gothic ORGAN CASE, installed in 1902 behind the High Altar (organ by the celebrated firm of *Cavaillé-Coll*). – MONASTIC STALLS, below PANELLING, in the N transept. – FONT. Appropriate Renaissance, the bowl with alternating Passion emblems and heraldic shields. – PAINTINGS in the transepts, from the Tuileries, copies of the side panels of Rubens's Descent from the Cross in Antwerp Cathedral. – The ALTARS are C19 from St Joseph's College, Mill Hill, introduced 2008. High Altar of Roman marble, by *Leonardi*. Delicate Early Renaissance detail with much colourful inlaid work. – St Mary altar (N), 1873. Frontal with Italian relief of the Flight into Egypt (early C19?) and large alabaster reredos with naturalistic flowers.* – St Joseph altar (S), 1874, by *Earp*. Dark red-brown Spanish marble, with a statue by *Coyers* of Louvain, under a rich Gothic canopy. – CHAIRS. A set of three, from Toledo. – STAINED GLASS. In the rose windows, naturalistic patterns *en grisaille*, effectively allied to the architecture.

Below the dome, reached from inside by capacious curved staircases and from outside by steps below the apse, is the CRYPT – the mausoleum proper. It is in a muscular Romanesque style, modelled on the crypt at Saint-Eutrope, Saintes, with heavy stone rib-vaults standing on short Early Gothic columns. The imperial TOMBS, three plain and impressive sarcophagi of polished red granite (by *Fraser & Co.* of Aberdeen) are identical, each with a simple recumbent cross atop. The colour recalls the porphyry tomb of Napoleon I at Les Invalides, a further reminder of which is the stellar pattern of the marble floor. They are separately placed: that of the Empress (†1920) within an arched recess above and behind the altar at the w end; facing each other in the transepts those of Napoleon III (N) and the Prince Imperial (s) given by Queen Victoria in 1888; the latter has a gilt-bronze palm. Above their tombs, fine BUSTS of Christ (from Schloss Arenenberg, by *Jean-Baptiste Clésinger*), and the Virgin, after Michelangelo's Pietà. Over the Emperor's tomb (N), bronze mural wreaths from the Italian nation, signed by *Diego Sarti* of Bologna, 1890, and *Munaretti* of Venice, 1909. – HIGH ALTAR with TABERNACLE, of stone, in a light Early Gothic. – In the ambulatory a wooden ALTAR (1880), the frontal with a seated Virgin and

---

* Its painting by *Soldadich*, noted in *The Buildings of England: London 4: North*, was stolen before the altar came to Farnborough.

Child between angels and saints, and REREDOS (1891) designed by *Medland*, carved by *Farmer & Brindley*, with Late Gothic scenes in high relief within an elaborated German Gothic framework. That of the Spies returning from Canaan is worth a special look. It came from St Katherine's Convent, Queen Square, London, in 1920. A second ALTAR from St Joseph's College, Mill Hill (*see* above): fine marble standing statue of St Peter flanked by good low-relief scenes from his life, dramatically rendered. – CHAIRS and PRIE-DIEU. From the imperial family's chapel at the Villa Eugénie, Biarritz. Sinuous interlace work on the backs.

The MONASTERY, s of the church, was established with an order of Premonstratensian canons but re-established from 1895 as a Benedictine community under Abbot Cabrol, former Prior of the abbey at Solesmes. The original part, of 1886–7 by *Destailleur*, is modest, red brick with gables. L-shaped, with a cloister on the inner (E) side and a big polygonal tower in the angle under a pyramidal roof with a picturesque Gothic turret (a Blois motif and a little like that at Farnborough Hill, *see* below). But to N and S are taller additions of 1902–12. The impressive s part is by *Benedict Williamson*, then a novice at Farnborough, in convincing French Romanesque style, faced in rough stone, with powerful buttressed corner tower, windows in arched recesses and corbel tables. It is only a small part of an ambitious plan (illustrated in *The Architect*, 1902) to build a complete set of claustral ranges copying the new monastery at Solesmes (by Dom J. M. Mellet, 1896–8). The N addition, for the noviciat, is by *George Goldie*, in the same spirit but with less verve.

SCHOOLS AND COLLEGES

FARNBOROUGH HILL SCHOOL. The Empress Eugénie bought the house in 1880 and lived here to her death in 1920. Set on a fine elevated site at the E edge of the town and N of the railway, it was built 1860–3 by *H. E. Kendall Jun.* for the publisher T. G. Longman, whose initials decorate a band of terracotta panels around the house. It is an outrageously oversized chalet, L-shaped, with big square entrance tower and a clock tower in the angle with the service wing, a lot of bargeboarding, carved timber framing, gables and Rhenish roofs. But many of the memorable details are of after 1881 and due to *G. H.-A. Destailleur*, architect of Waddesdon Manor for the Rothschilds.* He added a Winter Garden l. of the entrance, and altered the service wing. Initially he worked in the house's own style – see the tower on the entrance front of the wing,

* Commissioned only after Viollet-le-Duc had rejected an invitation to design the house.

raised higher under an outlandish two-tier octagonal top, and on the garden (w) side the gabled addition to the l. of the main elevation. But to the courtyard behind the character of the new work is decidedly French, including a stone tower with lucarnes and tourelles. Interior very nicely kept, the HALL much as Longman left it. Gothic style, with a fine stone chimneypiece with carved busts in roundels. Above, in place of Longman's arms, a profile of the Emperor by *Luigi Borro*. Wide central gallery behind with large staircase starting in one arm and returning in two. The former library (sw) and drawing room (s) were remodelled as a large DRAWING ROOM for the Empress, opening into a new Winter Garden on the E front. The former dining room (N of the hall) was recast as a GRAND SALON, extending w into a conservatory. Separating these rooms from the gallery are mirror-glazed walls and doors. The glass doors to the Dining Room, N of the salon, were recovered from the Tuileries: frames with Napoleon III's bee emblem. Reused C18 *boiseries* in the DINING ROOM itself, and a tremendous Neo-Baroque marble chimneypiece. Delicately painted cloud ceiling.

After the Empress died in 1920, the house was taken over for the convent SCHOOL she had founded at Hillside (for its old building *see* p. 279). Large additions were made by *Adrian Gilbert Scott*, 1931–2, in light brown brick. Continuing the w front N is the DINING HALL, of two storeys, with a cloister along its front. At right angles to this the CHAPEL, in a spare Gothic style with semicircular apse flanked by apsidal vestries and turrets with pointed caps, which recur at the w end. Here the treatment is severe, with chamfered corners. Simple but impressive interior with a barrel-vault, vaulting to the apse, and restrained furnishings. Scott's JUBILEE WING, NE of the main house, followed in 1939. Four-storey tower at the s end with the architect's characteristic stepping up from the porch. Colonnaded hall inside. At right angles to this, OUR LADY'S WING of 1952–3, the last work by Scott, recipe as before. Not undistinguished additions by *H. Cullerne Pratt*, 1964–5.

Formal GARDENS along the s front and, below the hill to the N, STABLES and COACHHOUSE of 1861, of the same strong meat as the house. WALLED GARDEN 1872, perhaps by *Devey*, who designed the NORTH LODGE *c.* 1870 in his extremely picturesque Domestic Revival style.

FARNBOROUGH COLLEGE OF TECHNOLOGY, Alexandra Road and Boundary Road. Routine post-war blocks at the w end, the older ones (1955–71) by *Hampshire County Architects' Dept*. Locking on at the E side is a large and low EXTENSION of 1983–6 by the same body, a major work from Hampshire's best period. The guiding concepts are familiar: a standard planning grid (here of 35 ft 10.8 metres), building services exposed and celebrated, energy-efficiency, and provision for changes in use. These are reconciled in a plan dominated by a broad central E–W street, with three lesser N–S glazed concourses around and between the teaching spaces and laboratories. The concourses show up externally as taller barrel-vaulted polycarbonate roofs rising above the glass walls, a quintessential mid-1980s motif whose echoes of the grid-planned Crystal Palace are nicely resonant here.* The framing is white-coated metal tubing. Within this frame, set back from the glazed outer skin behind circulation passages, are blockwork walls enclosing the rooms. These can be warmed using solar-heated air from the glazed areas, via fat white exposed ducts that snake about overhead. All this might be rather cerebral or clinical but for the generous planting along the concourse, and the inclusion of two garden courts, one glazed off, the other – with a big retained tree – open to the concourse along one side (interior designers *DEGW*, landscaping by *Jakobsen Landscape Architecture*; structural engineers *Anthony Hunt Associates*). A second extension, N of the older buildings, repeats the system. Both parts seem to be coping well a quarter-century of use.

FARNBOROUGH SIXTH-FORM COLLEGE, Prospect Avenue. At the core the former grammar school of 1936, flat-roofed brick, of an unusual T-plan. 1960s additions, and several large recent blocks. Theatre of 2000 (SE) with yellow-rendered walls, bright red service housings, and entrance canopy with a big circular opening to the sky. Arts, IT and Physics block by *Broadway Malyan*, 2009, with coloured glass to the entrance hall.

OTHER SECONDARY SCHOOLS. The SALESIAN COLLEGE (R.C.), Reading Road, has two expressive touches of *c.* 1960: a chapel block, E, with a cloister of catenary arches, and hall with a shallow-pitched butterfly roof, W. OAK FARM COMMUNITY SCHOOL off Mayfield Road, 1973, serves the Prospect Estate (*see* p. 281). It has white-painted timber cladding to the whole upper storey.

JUNIOR AND INFANTS' SCHOOLS. For St Peter's School *see* Farnborough Place, p. 280. The oldest purpose-built school is the original part of NORTH FARNBOROUGH INFANTS', Rectory Road, of 1868–9 and 1874 by *G. Devey*. Gothic and quite cheery, with black brick diapering. Attached, r., a gabled extension probably of 1888, a much bigger addition with the gable glazed (*Hampshire County Architects*, 1980), and a plainish gabled part built as an infants' school in 1910. ST MARK'S, Queen's Road, 1896–7 by *Charles Smith & Son* of Reading, shows the Anglican loyalty to Gothic. Further E on the same road, N side, SOUTH FARNBOROUGH SCHOOL, 1911, of the type with many-gabled classroom wings advancing from a central hall, here with a nice Baroque cupola. Of postwar schools, WAVELL JUNIOR (formerly Secondary), Lynchford Road, 1969, is centred on a four-storey block with a strong outline. To its S, SAMUEL CODY SCHOOL, a little later. Resourceful S addition designed in 1981 by *Ken Norrish*, then Portsmouth City Architect. Its side walls slope down to the centre, creating inward-facing clerestory lighting.

---

*The architects cited Hanne Kjaerholm's early 1980s Holstebro museum in Denmark as the immediate source.

GRANGE COMMUNITY JUNIOR SCHOOL, Wren Way, is by *Edward Cullinan*, 1987–90. Varied materials under curved metal roofs, to a Y-plan with a tall thin drum over the middle. Gawky, but memorable. HENRY TYNDALE SCHOOL off Ship Lane, 1999–2000, adopts a harder, right-angled Modernism: yellow-rendered walls, grey roofing, big metal entrance canopy on thin uprights. *Studio Four*'s work of 2002–3 at CHERRY-WOOD COMMUNITY PRIMARY, Mayfield Road, is gentler: four interlocking classroom units with monopitch roofs on a cranked plan, follow-my-leader style.

OTHER BUILDINGS

No easy perambulation suggests itself. The retail and civic centre is described first, then Farnborough Road to its N, then down to South Farnborough. The few village survivors to the NE come last, with other scattered buildings.

THE CENTRE, W of Farnborough Road. The main cluster is made of three shopping centres or precincts, each running N–S. Facing the road is the second in building order, KINGSMEAD, a dreary red brick complex by *Lister, Drew & Associates*, begun 1972. Five-storey office slab on top, multi-storey car park to the NE; shopping spaces remodelled by *BDP*, 1992, with a free-standing novelty CLOCK designed by *Marianne Forrest*. In 1984 *Arup Associates* finished off the S end with BRIARCLIFFE HOUSE, which shows more concern for the public realm. A half-doughnut plan, an elevated garden for the office workers filling the hole. The facing is a double skin of smoked glass, of which the outer one slants out canopy-wise over the pavement. Red ducting for the services is sandwiched in the service void between. Both double-skinned glazing and elevated gardens (cf. Mountbatten House, Basingstoke, p. 167) were favourite Arup motifs of the 1980s. Round the corner to the E is QUEENSMEAD, the earliest precinct, of 1958–60 by *George, Davies & Webb*. The usual 1950s model of a paved pedestrian street, with a pleasing, slightly winding plan. On each side are three-storey ranges of flats over shops, finished with panels of white and red tiles as well as brick. Much of the N part was demolished in 2007 under a redevelopment plan by *Benoy Architects*. Behind the W side of Queensmead is PRINCES MEAD, 1990s, dressed in the brick-and-coloured-bits fashion of the time.

CIVIC BUILDINGS are grouped to the S. N of Meudon Road a big drab RECREATION CENTRE (begun 1970), brick-faced, to its SE the LIBRARY (*c.* 1970), partly curtain-walled. More appealing are *Broadway & Malyan*'s RUSHMOOR COUNCIL OFFICES S of Meudon Road, built 1980–1 to a free plan of up to three storeys under shallow pyramid roofs. Much use of grooved timber finishes in the public areas, which are centred on a top-lit reception space. Commercial blocks in the vicinity include EMPRESS HOUSE, further W, overlooking the roundabout. 1987–9 by *Cecil Denny Highton*. Mixed-use (offices and light industry). The external framing and triangular lattice trusses reaching across the roof were calculated for internal flexibility.

FARNBOROUGH ROAD is the main N–S axis of the town. N of the commercial centre, large office blocks punctuate the route. First, W side, intersecting slabs on pilotis (formerly Kingsmead House), 1964–5 by *Alec Shickle* of *Campbell-Jones & Partners*. To the N, CLOCK HOUSE, a comic turn of *c.* 1895, with half-timbering and turret. Next on the E side, *Scott, Brownrigg & Turner*'s block of *c.* 1985, built with a slick mirrored skin like glossy graph paper. ABBEY HOUSE, six storeys, has the gritty pre-cast concrete finishes of the later 1960s (*Raymond Spratley & Partners*, 1968). On the W side, *T. P. Bennett Partnership*'s bulky brick-faced complex of 1989–90, all oriels and stumpy square towers, failed picturesque. FARNBOROUGH RAILWAY STATION beyond is a charming rebuild of 1904 (London & South Western Railway), with an elongated dormer in the roof. N of the railway bridge, Queen Victoria Court leads off W to THE LODGE, a stuccoed Neo-Tudor super-bungalow of *c.* 1820, with octagonal chimneys. Farnborough Road goes on N past Farnborough Hill.

SOUTH FARNBOROUGH can be approached from the centre along Farnborough Road. Soon, the E side shows the former HILLSIDE CONVENT, built for the Congregation of Christian Education under the patronage of the Empress Eugénie (*see* p. 270), then used for much of the C20 by the Royal Aircraft Establishment. Big, ambitious red brick buildings of 1892–5 by *J. S. Hansom*. Loosely Early French, with an underweight tower and an apse-ended chapel coming forward, r. Windows mostly in triplets or small dormers. Converted to offices in the late C20, with a projection to the S (meant to balance the chapel), amputation of the S wing of 1907, and big rear additions.

Facing the convent is the College of Technology (*see* p. 276), from in front of which ALEXANDRA ROAD runs due S. On the E side straight away is a six-bay stucco villa, of Early Victorian aspect but at least mid-1860s vintage. Nothing much before the next roundabout to the S, overlooked by St Mark's church (p. 272) on the E side. To its S, No. 107, a splendid Arts and Crafts house of *c.* 1890, with a big sheltering roof and such nice details as ornamented wrought-iron door-canopy stays. Facing it is a pilastered POST OFFICE, *c.* 1925 in the style of *c.* 1725. Set back to its r. is the former Town Hall of 1896–7, now offices called FERNEBERGA HOUSE. *George Sherrin*'s design has all the friendly littleness of the English 1890s, with exaggeratedly tapered pilasters, a round-arched ground floor and a small cupola. Converted in 1983 by *Sanders Norman*, who added a NW wing. Further down Alexandra Road, the E side has four stuccoed houses (originally Alpha Cottages) from South Farnborough's infancy, *c.* 1865. Facing at No. 18, a little cubic bank building of *c.* 1925, brick with a carved keystone.

The present HSBC branch at the corner with Lynchford Road is grander, dated 1899. Elaborate gable, intersecting chimney.

LYNCHFORD ROAD is a commercial street running E–W across the margin of the North Camp of Aldershot, with buildings mostly on one side only. Isolated by the junction with Alexandra Road is a former SCHOOL of *c.* 1910, perhaps by *F. C. Uren*. Quirky Neo-Georgian, with round first-floor windows and two-tone brick quoins.

From here one can turn W or E. Going W, PEEL COURT is a two-storey Postmodern terrace of 1986, by *R. Sharpe*, Borough Engineer and Surveyor. Nice garden behind, overlooked by a further, detached block, almshouse-fashion. Then on the S side RUSHMOOR FIRE STATION, 1994 by *Hampshire County Architects*. The best part is the Postmodern-classical E front, with its wiry steel perron stair under a pedimental gable made by bright red external framing. Behind, a PRACTICE TOWER of banded polychromatic blocks, distantly evocative of Lombardy. Next, by Queen's Roundabout, the QUEEN'S HOTEL of *c.* 1905 (now Holiday Inn), like a giant coarse-grained villa with a square central tower. On the roundabout island a singular WAR MEMORIAL of 1903, a kind of elevated miniature terrace with fountain basins above and below. This sinuous, decidedly Southern Baroque design is by *Clotilde Brewster*; donor and dedicatee remain undiscovered.

Going E, LLOYDS TSB BANK, *c.* 1890s, has a complicated Gothic ground floor. In CAMP ROAD, N, a former cinema of 1927 (now KINGDOM HALL) confronts a steep-roofed former YMCA hall of 1898. The cinema, by *R. A. Briggs*, has the characteristic French pilaster-piers, the other a fat rounded pediment. The next turning but one off Lynchford Road is MORRIS ROAD. On the E side, two-storey flats built in 1937 as married quarters for young soldiers, apparently on private initiative. Streamlined access balcony, shallow canted bays; a break from Army Neo-Georgian. Architects *Unsworth, Goulder & Bostock*.

FARNBOROUGH PLACE, now ST PETER'S SCHOOL, N of the parish church. The chief older residence of the village. Rebuilt (for the Earls of Anglesey) in the late C17, if the staircase, with its chunky turned balusters, is anything to go by. The form, a double pile with high hipped roof, is spot-on for the date too, but the house was remodelled *c.* 1800 for a Mr Wilmot. Of this time the stucco facing, porch, and some interior work. Seven bays, the centre three slightly projecting with round-arched windows flanking the entrance. ST MICHAEL'S MEWS, N, are the former stables, also of *c.* 1800. Quite grand, brick, of seven by three bays. On the long sides the central three bays slightly projecting. Round-arched ground-floor openings, originally blind except for lunettes. In the centre a doorway. The pediment and cupola at the end have been removed.

FARNBOROUGH VILLAGE. Most of the few pre-Victorian houses lie ¾ m. NE of the commercial centre, near Farnborough North railway station. At the SW corner of Highgate Lane and

Rectory Road, a former FARMHOUSE, of two storeys and two units (now subdivided), the C17 timber framing exposed. The NW corner is EMPRESS COTTAGES, an attractively plain Tudor-Gothic group of c. 1840. To the E in Farnborough Street, YEW TREE COTTAGE (No. 4), a neat sashed box of c. 1800; to the N in Ship Lane, Nos. 12 and 14, weighty Tudor-vernacular semis of 1910 by *H. R. & B. A. Poulter*. On the opposite, W side, No. 23 (ORIEL COTTAGE), genuinely timber-framed and of the C15 or C16, but masked by mid-C19 beautifications.

KNELLWOOD, No. 83 Canterbury Road, ⅔ m. SE of the town centre. Late 1860s. A big town Italianate villa by the builder *William Knell*. Eaves brackets and fancy bits. Now an old people's home.

PROSPECT ESTATE, I m. NNW of the commercial centre. London overspill of c. 1970, planned and designed by the *Greater London Council Architects' Department*. Mostly flat-roofed two-storey terraces grouped around shared spaces, following the Radburn principle of separated road and pedestrian access. Shops, a community hall and a four-storey slab are clustered in Mayfield Road. Some refurbishment of the houses by *Broadway Malyan* from 1986.

On PROSPECT ROAD, S of the estate, the THATCHED COTTAGE pub is C16, with some diagonal strutting.

THE ROYAL AIRCRAFT ESTABLISHMENT SITE

The Royal Engineers' balloon depot moved to Farnborough in 1905, after sojourns at Woolwich Arsenal, Chatham, and Aldershot (1890). In 1908 the army's first aeroplane was built here by an enterprising American, Captain Cody; in 1911 Farnborough became the headquarters of the Royal Engineers' airship battalion; in 1912 the Royal Flying Corps, forerunner of the RAF, was founded here. So the site was already pre-eminent before the First World War, which accelerated the technology of flight and confirmed the need for continuing research and development. Farnborough duly grew into the largest site of its kind in Europe, with huge and highly specialized structures in which both civil and military aircraft were housed and tested. In the 1990s the establishment relinquished much land, the research area (now part of DERA, the Defence Evaluation and Research Agency) having contracted into a smaller complex further W, opened in 1997. Redevelopment of the rest is being undertaken, with a civilian airport in the central enclave, business parks to its N, E and SE, and some new housing. A selection of the historic aviation buildings will remain.

FARNBOROUGH AIRPORT. A small but architecturally superior complex, won in competition by *Geoffrey Reid Associates* (later *Reid Architecture*; engineers *Buro Happold*), and built from 2001. Earlier proposals included the *Richard Rogers Partnership*'s project of 1989. The airport specializes in private business travel, for which the luxurious aluminium skins of the buildings have a nice affinity. As a whole it can stand comparison with the stylish, image-conscious pioneer airports of the late 1930s.

The CONTROL TOWER, 114 ft (35 metres) high and shaped like a giant Olympic torch, rises from a symmetrical fore-building with a swept roof. Shaft of elliptical section, clad with diamond-pattern aluminium shingles and cut by a glazed slit for the lift shaft. The control room has sixteen sides or facets. To its N, the HANGAR, undulating in three big humps each 302 ft (93 metres) wide. Concrete ties buried in the floor secure these arches without obstructing the space. Cladding is of the standing-seam type, i.e. without welds or rivets. A second hangar is proposed. E of the hangar, the low TERMINAL BUILDING, 2004–5: a taut, rounded and flattened shape cut off at the ends. The form reads like a section of a giant wing or aerofoil, which distances it from the arbitrariness of so many early C21 'blob' buildings.

FARNBOROUGH BUSINESS PARK, N and E of the airport. Developed from 1999 by Slough Estates to a masterplan by *Bruce Gilbreth Architects*, with *Julian Harrap Architects* as consultants for the historic core. Outside this area, at the NW angle off Elles Road, two notable office blocks of 2002–3. *Allies & Morrison*'s No. 1 Meadow Gate Avenue is an L-shape with aluminium brises-soleil, crisp and clean-lined. To its E, *Foster & Partners*' No. 25 Templer Avenue: sleek glazed walling, grey palette, very slim piers; the firm's house style of the latest C20. Lozenge or parallelogram plan, with a slanting entrance atrium.

The historic AVIATION BUILDINGS are clustered to the S. A bravely fought conservation campaign saved many of the best examples, whose full significance emerged only after the veil of military secrecy was lifted in the 1990s.* The wind-tunnel buildings in particular are as central to the history of C20 technology as the mills and factories of Lancashire and Derbyshire were to that of the C18–C19. Slough Estates' conversion of the site began in 2005. New office buildings are being slotted in, and an area to the NE has been given over to housing. The first office jobs to be completed have set a high standard for those still to come.

Coming W from Farnborough Road on FOWLER AVENUE, the first in line is R178 on the N side (Materials and Chemistry Building), a three-storey 1940s utility block now converted to flats. Next, the WIND-TUNNEL BUILDINGS: R52 and Q121 (S), and the conjoined R133 and R136 (N). The precision, size and ingenuity of these installations are decidedly at odds with their utilitarian housings, which were restored with impartial care by *Julian Harrap Architects* in 2006–7. R52, a twin-gabled complex in parti-coloured brick, is one of

* *See* the report by Adam Wilkinson for SAVE Britain's Heritage, 2001.

the world's earliest surviving wind-tunnel buildings (1916, extended later). In the much larger Q121, of 1934–5, full-size aircraft could be tested within a wind tunnel built of mass concrete, powered by a mahogany-bladed fan of 30-ft (9-metre) diameter. It is considered the most complete example of an open-return wind tunnel after that of 1929–31 at Langley, Virginia, USA. Steel-framed enclosure, the walls of grid pattern infilled with reinforced concrete, with a higher part including a clock tower. The s part has big doors where the aircraft were taken in. At R133 the specifications are: built 1939–42 as a variable-density high-speed 10-ft by 7-ft (3- by 2.1-metre) tunnel of return-flow type, modified 1951–6 as a transonic 8-ft by 6-ft (2.5- by 1.8-metre) tunnel. Enormous ducts, compressors and refrigerators were required for it: the wind-tunnel canister alone is 133 ft (41 metres) long. This appears externally as a flat-roofed (and blast-proof) concrete box 52 ft (16 metres) high. The w end has new facing after the demolition of attached structures. To the se by the road, R136, built in 1944 for wind-testing road vehicles. Some of these tunnels may be restored to use.

Further w, Q153 (Structural Test Building, 1942), N side, and the much larger Q134 (Weapons Test Department, *c.* 1938), s side, are more formally treated, each of three storeys and chiefly brick-clad. Next to Q153 is Q170, a blockish telephone exchange of *c.* 1957, now a nursery. Q134 has been converted for mixed uses by *Allies & Morrison*, with big bold glass-sided staircase housings on the s side. To the w and on the same alignment, two smart four-storey office blocks by the same architects (2005–6), faced in nicely graduated terracotta strips. These define the E edge of THE SQUARE, a formal planted space with a centrepiece of pure surrealist poetry: the skeleton of a demountable AIRSHIP HANGAR of 1910–11, put back together from parts that had been reused within two later RAE buildings. Splayed legs, curved top, W-braced lattice form; 70 ft high, 250 ft long (22 by 77 metres). *Julian Harrap*'s restoration strengthens the frame with additional slim grey purlins. The original skin was of canvas, which needed replacing every six months.

To the se on Farnborough Road, AVIATOR, a slick five-storey hotel by *Hamiltons*, 2008. A slab with the centre swelling outwards on both sides. Silvery finishes between dark window bands.

FARRINGDON

7030

ALL SAINTS, Upper Farringdon. An engaging exterior of unusual outline: low, rendered early C13 Sussex-like w tower with narrow lancets below and very distinctive later, possibly C19, bell-openings in the form of small pointed quatrefoils (cf. South Harting, West Sussex). Mid-C19 shingled broach spire.

The nave and N aisle, under a catslide roof, are Norman but in the s wall two good Early Perp windows, with rectilinear tracery of 1370–1400. The taller chancel in malmstone is of 1858 for the Rev. T. H. Massey, who became rector in 1857. He may have been his own architect. Nice brick s porch with a pedimented entrance of 1634 with C18 sides. Inside, a plain early C13 s doorway with contemporary DOOR: simple strap hinges.

The interior of the church is strong stuff, sensitively restored in 2001 by *Gary Seymour*. N arcade of three exceedingly wide bays with completely unmoulded round arches. The w bay, even higher and wider than the others, represents the first phase of a w enlargement of the Early Norman nave, when a transeptal NW chapel was built *c.* 1150. It consists of two Norman responds, semicircular with multi-scallop capitals and square abaci. The w respond has spurs on the base (evidence of high status: cf. Oakley). The E respond was a little later converted into a round pillar by adding a w respond for the next two bays which have plainly moulded capitals and round abaci. Small tower doorway with one continuous chamfer. The chancel, in a later C13 style, is High Victorian and *sui generis*, though modified in 1968 by the Puritan removal of wall paintings: pretty stencilled decoration of stars and tendrils on the roof survives. – ALTAR. With delicately painted front of small saints, and towering REREDOS of alabaster made in Florence with painted Nativity scene below a Crucifixion, in relief against a diapered gold ground under a gabled canopy. These look later than 1858, so too the double SEDILIA, CHOIR STALLS and ORGAN CASE (1869). – TILES. Exceptionally many of the C13 in the chancel floor in front of the altar. Several different foliate patterns (cf. Selborne). – FONT. Quite a puzzle for the antiquary. A composite piece of three different periods: The square base must be late C12, the stem, a strange later capital. Plain circular bowl. – FONT COVER. C17 with typically Jacobean scrolled top. – PULPIT. C18 from a 'three-decker'. PEWS, dated 1859 with trefoil-headed ends. – (WALL PAINT-INGS. Above the nave ceiling on the w wall, fragments of two medieval doom paintings discovered in 1986. The uppermost is *c.* 1380.) – STAINED GLASS. Of special note the E window by *Hardman c.* 1860. In the vestry, N window, abstract glass by *Hugh Powell.* – In the churchyard a tall Gothic CROSS and LYCHGATE. – Two Celtic cross grave markers to the Rev. T. H. Massey †1919, and his wife †1910.

MANOR HOUSE FARMHOUSE, NW of the church. Timber-framed hearth-passage house, possibly of *c.* 1546 when the manor of Episcopi passed from the Bishops of Exeter to the Earls of Southampton. Early C17 cross-wing and stair-tower, timber-framed on a malmstone ground floor. Front rebuilt in the C18, the porch is nice mid-C19 Gothic.

The buildings of Upper Farringdon are eclipsed by MASSEY'S FOLLY, a memorably fiery red brick and terracotta fantasy, so called because the Rev. Massey designed it and built it with

one bricklayer, one carpenter and one labourer. It was begun
in 1870 and kept him busy for thirty years. Its intended use is
unknown but after 1925 it became the village hall and school.
Long, rambling and eclectic, with strong Italian Romanesque
and Gothic elements, Dutch gables and French basket arches
to the windows. Three towers, the tallest marking the entrance
with round-arched openings and saddleback roof. The
moulded details and decorative panels are of the kind one
could buy from contemporary catalogues.

¼ m. SW is FARRINGDON PLACE, the former rectory, built
for Massey in 1860–1. Gothic, possibly his own design. The
interior includes a staircase with nailhead ornament and
Gothic architraves and fireplaces.

THE STREET represents the formerly separate Manor of
Popham, with two historic groups. At WEST CROSS are WEST
CROSS COTTAGE, a C17 baffle-entry plan with stair-tower and
mullioned window in outshot at rear, and JORDANS, C17
timber frame with herringbone brick-nogging over brick
ground floor, and a 1920s Late Arts and Crafts remodelling.
To the E at THE CROSS a pretty row includes C16 FOX
COTTAGE with massive timbers and curved braces and HALL
FARMHOUSE, a c. 1840 brick villa with windows set in shallow
arched recesses.

LOWER FARRINGDON, ½ m. W, is a later medieval settlement
that grew with the coming of the Gosport Turnpike. At its S
end is STREET FARMHOUSE. C16, encased in brick c. 1800.
Two-bay floored hall; great chamber with arched-braced
central truss: the chamber was divided in the C17 and one room
given a pretty moulded plasterwork ceiling with a band of
fleur-de-lys ornament in a square and other heraldic motifs
(identical motifs are also to be seen at Forge House and Little
Forge Cottage, a C17 hall-and-cross-wing house to the N). THE
FORGE itself retains its hearth, bellows and beam drill). At the
N end of the village is FARRINGDON HURST. An C18 double-
pile house with a stuccoed front and open pedimented porch,
Gothicized c. 1800, possibly by John Dyer of Alton (cf. his
refronting of Pelham Place, Newton Valence) by the addition
of three canted bays with Tudor-arched lights, panelling and
battlemented parapets.

LOWER WOODSIDE FARMHOUSE, 1 m. NW of Lower
Farringdon. Early C17 and remarkably complete. Brick
with moulded string courses, tile-hung timber-framed first
floor and end stacks with diamond shafts. L-plan with the
entrance in the side of the lower rear wing (cf. Black
House Farmhouse, Hinton Ampner). Procession of rooms
from the kitchen in the rear wing, into the dining room with
moulded beamed ceiling and arched fireplace, through the
stair lobby with vase-stopped door frames, and into the
parlour, which formerly had a fashionable flat plaster ceiling.
Elegant staircase with symmetrical double balusters and
soaring newel post.

FLEET

A sprawling town and administrative centre, a creation of the railway age, (of 'no shape nor character' was Pevsner's verdict in 1967). A station was opened in 1847 (close to Fleet Pond, a lake excavated in the C12 as a fishery for the Priory of St Swithun, Winchester) and was soon the destination of excursion trains. The settlement grew to the s, principally with villas along the main street and rapidly after the 1880s when a grid of streets was laid out to the SE. In 1871 the population was only 380 but by 1901 it was over 2,000. Expansion continued throughout the C20, the town merging with Church Crookham (q.v.) to the s. Development at Elvetham Heath since 1997 now takes the town N across the railway.

ALL SAINTS, Church Road. The town's best building. By *Burges*, 1860–2. Simple, somewhat Italianate First Pointed Gothic. Lengthened w by *Arthur J. Stedman*, 1934, vestry of the same date. Lady Chapel by *John Purser*, 1958. The original w end had an open narthex (cf. Burges's church at Lowfield Heath, Surrey, 1867); the wheel window has been re-set. Warm red brick inside and out with a terracotta cornice, and externally astonishingly restrained, perhaps due to the small budget. Good, steep-pitched bellcote over the E end of the nave. Lower apsidal chancel. Plain lancets and plate tracery all of rubbed brick. s door, formerly at the w end, with carved stone tympanum of Christ in Majesty, by *Thomas Nicholls*. Closely corresponding N doorway, by *Stedman* with the Transfiguration carved by *G. A. Parsons*. The interior is surprising, decidedly strong meat for the most avowed High Victorian fan to savour. It is impressive by the unexpected great height of the nave, so powerfully composed with the square brick pillars and the steep pointed transverse brick arches. Between them the vault is boarded. Throughout the nave much architectonic painted-on decoration of blue brick bands and ornamental motifs, but the original stencilled scheme of fictive masonry and other patterns in the chancel and apse were whitened over in 1949 to vapid effect. Nice vestry door with sculptured tympanum of a demi-angel holding a model of the church in 1861 state. The Burges floor restored in 2006. Several original FURNISHINGS (altar, pulpit and font) – STAINED GLASS. In the chancel, by *Clayton & Bell*, 1902. Disappointingly conventional. w window by *A. L. Moore*, 1906, overly elaborate. The original architectural glazing, appropriately C13 Italian style, survives. – MONUMENT. Charles Lefroy †1861, the donor of the church, and his wife Janet †1857, daughter of Alfred Burges's engineering partner. Originally on the chancel's N side. Recumbent effigies in their Victorian clothes, probably by *Nicholls;* he holds a model of Christ's tomb in the Church of the Holy Sepulchre, Jerusalem. The couple lie under an arch with carved angels. Watch for the two dogs by the feet of the effigies.

ST PHILIP AND ST JAMES, Kings Road. 1965–6 by *David Nye*. With an obligatory spike. Vertical boarded exterior. – Carving

106

of the Nativity by *G. A. Parsons,* 1920, from the previous iron church of 1900. – FONT of Corsham stone, by *Sidney Mardles,* 1901. – FONT COVER of 1966 by *Terence Randall,* carved by *Gordon Beningfield.* – WAR MEMORIAL, 1920, with lettering by *Parsons.*

OUR LADY (R.C.), Kings Road. Hexagonal, of 1966 by *Lanner Ltd* of Wakefield, centrally planned with four wooden arches meeting at a steel ring. Good contemporary FURNISHINGS by *Michael Murray* (of *Maguire & Murray*). – STATIONS OF THE CROSS. Bronze by *Rene Gourdon.* – MOSAIC. Madonna and Child by *J. G. Bajo.* The church has two predecessors. The first church, dedicated to the Holy Ghost was completed in 1908, probably by *Scoles & Raymond,* with lancet windows and a cinquefoil window in the liturgical E wall. It became the sanctuary to the second church, built in 1934 (later church hall) with a further addition in 1948.

CIVIC BUILDINGS, at the SW end of Fleet Road. These are unremarkable. HART DISTRICT COUNCIL OFFICES, Harlington Way. 1985–6, *Leslie Jones & Partners.* Rather lumpen, Brick with low hipped roofs. Facing across a courtyard the LIBRARY and HARLINGTON CENTRE of 1975. Gabled entrance lobby added on the SE side, 1994, after a fire.

CALTHORPE PARK SCHOOL, Hitches Lane. 1963, altered and extended 1984 by *Edward Cullinan Architects* (cf. Church Crookham), who encased it within a lightweight steel frame supporting a shallow-pitched steel roof with a generous overhang. Angled shades of blue corrugated plastic protect the windows of the lower floors. Two new blocks (maths and drama) flank the N end and are connected by a covered way. They have steel frames with glazed and solid panels, overlain by coloured wooden strips. They also have secondary external steel structures, but are more open in appearance. Entrance porch at the W end of the drama building.

ELVETHAM HEATH PRIMARY SCHOOL, The Key. 2003–4, by *Hampshire Property Services, Architecture and Design.* A cluster of simple, brick and tile buildings built right up to the pavement like a Victorian school. Entrance courtyard with hall on the l.; on its side wall a steel sculpture: The Tree of Life by *Paul Margetts.*

FLEET INFANTS' SCHOOL, Velmead Road. 1986 by *Michael Hopkins & Partners.* High-Tech, with an elegant lightweight steel frame. Top-lit spine separating main hall etc. (N) from classrooms (S), which have fully glazed walls shaded by delightful tent-like awnings; a relic of the original intention to have a stretched fabric membrane roof. Music Room pod (N side), added 1998 by the same architects.

HEATHERSIDE INFANT SCHOOL, Reading Road. 1980 by *Hampshire County Architect's Dept* (*Colin Stansfield-Smith* with *Trevor Harris* and *Alan Dyer*). A satisfying design of appropriately low, single-storey scale. Buff brick ranges around a square courtyard, with pantiled roofs extending over a glazed timber cloister. These ranges vary in width along their length and are staggered on the outside. Classrooms open off the cloister and on to the surrounding playground. Hall at the s corner. Hip-roofed LIBRARY of 1995, projecting into the landscaped courtyard.

PERAMBULATION. Along FLEET ROAD, some Edwardian commercial buildings, e.g. Nos. 140–148 (w side) by *H. J. & Stanley Pool*, 1913, built as their own premises. Neo-Georgian with Baroque touches. Prominent on the other side, at the corner with Upper Street, is THE EMPORIUM, 1880s, with an ogee-capped tile-hung octagonal cupola. Tucked behind the shops to the N on this side the HART SHOPPING CENTRE, by the *Fitzroy Robinson Partnership*, 1990, breaking through in two places with large Postmodern classical porches. It extends E with a Neo-vernacular frontage to Albert Street with polychromatic brickwork. Further N, by the railway, THE LINKS, built as the Station Hotel in 1893, by *F. H. Tulloch* for Thomas Kenward, the Hartley Wintney brewer. In the Olde English style.

Many substantial Late Victorian and Edwardian houses survive, e.g.: BEACON HOUSE, Victoria Hill Road, *c.* 1898, by *J. H. Ince*. Neo-Georgian. Columned porch in angle at rear and good interior with panelled inglenook; LADYBOWER (No. 47 Connaught Road), 1908, which has in its galleried entrance hall a Gothic chimneypiece with a faux-tiled roof; and No. 35 Church Road, Late Arts and Crafts by *W. H. Bidlake*. ORIEL LODGE, Dunmow Hill, has in its garden an arch from *T. H. Wyatt*'s Hyde Park Barracks (1878–80), with carved spandrels, possibly by *Earp*.

6030   FOUR MARKS

An early C20 plotland development. Of the original bungalows one of the best survivors is No. 71 Blackberry Lane, with reused early C19 curved sashes and columned porch.

GOOD SHEPHERD, Lymington Bottom. By *Felix Lander*, 1953–4. Brick, minimal Gothic, with a low porch-tower crowned by a tile-capped wooden belfry. Major extension and reordering of 1996–7. E window by *Mel Howse*.

SEMAPHORE HOUSE, Telegraph Lane. 1829. Of the same standard design as that at Binsted (q.v.).

3040   FOXCOTTE
                                      Andover

CHURCH. The site is of a small undedicated medieval chapel of C10 origin dependent on Andover. Rebuilt in 1853–4 but demolished in 1908 except for the lancet-style tower, from

which an 'ill proportioned' spire was taken down. Some fragments were taken to Charlton (q.v.). Modest addition for an
art gallery 1976 (now a house).

FOXCOTTE MANOR, opposite, is early C19. Brick and tile; three
bays with canopied doorway.

FREEFOLK

Laverstoke and Freefolk

4040

A small village, s of the River Test. The manor was acquired by
Joseph Portal in 1769 and combined with Laverstoke (q.v.) for
ecclesiastical purposes in 1872.

ST NICHOLAS (Churches Conservation Trust). Rendered nave
and chancel in one, with wee weatherboarded bell-turret. The
single-chamfered s doorway may indicate a C13 date. Single
lancet windows, all cinquefoil-headed, C15. Short brick buttresses and Perp E window added during the restoration of
1903 financed by Sir Wyndham Spencer Portal. Delightful
interior, little altered since remodelling in 1703 (the date on a
roundel over the s door), with well-preserved C13 roof, and surprisingly full of interesting furnishings: plain baluster COM-
MUNION RAILS. – Former REREDOS, now against the s wall.
Naïve painting of 1703 with a military Moses and a classical
Aaron holding the Commandment boards. Nice Creed and
Lord's Prayer panels *in situ* on the E wall, by the same, prob-
ably local, hand. – ROOD SCREEN. Perp, of single-light divi-
sions, relocated to the w end in 1703. Perhaps of this date, the
'Jacobean' CANDLESTICKS mounted on the cornice above. –
WALL PAINTINGS. St Christopher, partly overlapped by a
royal arms on the N wall. – HATCHMENTS, royal arms of
William III, dated 1701, and achievements of Pearse and Portal
families. – STAINED GLASS. E window, of 1910 by J. C. Bewsey.
Subdued in his sweetly medievalizing Perp (cf. Overton). –
MONUMENTS. Sir Richard Powlett of Herriard †1614. Large
standing monument against the N wall, but formerly N of the
altar (see the mural painting). He is represented stiffly recumbent but rolled on his side. On the tomb-chest strapwork but
also, kneeling in a recess, his two wives. Strapwork back panel,
and strapwork around his coat of arms. All stone and uncouth.
Above the monument his HELM. – Thomas Deane †1686.
The tablet's inscription is written on drapery which seems
pleated with a flat iron. The flowers below have accordingly a
herbarium look. – Thomas Pearse. Engraved brass dated 1743,
with inscription.

THE OLD RECTORY, E of the church. Built 1858 at the expense
of Melville Portal. Brick and flint, with tile-hung gables, a small
round turret, and altogether remarkably varied. Probably by
P. C. Hardwick, cf. the Gardener's Cottage, Laverstoke House

(q.v.). The staircase appears to reuse C17 newel posts and an C18 handrail.

FREEFOLK HOUSE, ½ m. S. By *Wilfrid Carpenter Turner, c.* 1960. Curved plan, enclosing a courtyard to the N and allowing panoramic views to the S: an Arts and Crafts idea in a Modernist idiom. Buff brick with a stone parapet to the flat roof. On the asymmetrical entrance side a projecting three-bay 'portico'. Some pattern-making on the garden side, including slate panels between the windows, incised work and projecting headers. Inside, the principal feature is the curved staircase, sweeping up to a curved balcony. One room has a conspicuous Neo-Palladian overmantel from Laverstoke House (q.v.), perhaps by *Seely & Paget*. – Landscaping by *Ian Mylles* and *Peter Coats*, including a stone terrace with a central pool overlooked by a reclining bronze female figure.

SPRING POND, ¾ m. S. C19 brick and flint farm buildings converted into a house, 1987–96, by *Francis Johnson*. Rich Neo-Georgian interiors including an C18 chimneypiece from Laverstoke House. Carving by *Dick Reid* and plasterwork by *W. J. Wilson*.

For buildings N of London Road *see* Laverstoke.

FROXFIELD

7020

ST PETER. 1887 by *A. W. Blomfield* for William Nicholson of Basing Park (Privett) on the site of the medieval church, demolished *c.* 1861, when the church was built at High Cross (q.v.). It had an axial tower. Small, but generously proportioned, E.E. in flint and stone. Nave and chancel in one with a wooden W bell-turret. Low domestic hipped-roofed S W vestry of 1932. E window, a graduated group of three lancets, apparently influenced by that of the old chancel. Austere interior with original furnishings, especially the gold mosaic REREDOS. Good STAINED GLASS by *Powells* in three windows, notably the W window of 1934, with crisply drawn figures and small groups. Several plain TABLETS, the earliest C17 to Dame Honor Neale (†1628) of Bordean House (Langrish), who 'lyved very vertously'. Barbara and Richard Love †1690 and †1696. Classical aedicule with floral carving on the pilasters.

In the churchyard, two fine C18 memorials, one by the r. of the path to the church, a richly Rococo gravestone to Baker, with two cherubs blowing the Last Trump, the other a classical table tomb to the Love family (Robert Love †1722), with metal inscription plaque. – Sturdy LYCHGATE of 1906 by *Blomfield*. In front of the gate the WAR MEMORIAL.

On the N side of the green, LOVE'S CHARITY, built in 1733–4 from a bequest left by Robert Love (†1722) of Basing Park (Privett) for a school for twenty boys. Like a smart five-bay house (which it has been since 1876), of two storeys, with

hipped roof and cross-windows. Façade hung with mathematical tiles in 1774. VENTHAMS FARM, just s, is one of the ambitiously scaled former model farms built for the Basing Park
estate from the 1860s. Very impressive large farmhouse with
Tudor stacks.

TREES COTTAGE, ½ m. N. Partial survival of a base-cruck hall,
dated to 1359–60. It must have had a third bay at the E end
(see the projecting arcade plates). Crown-post roof with at the
apex of the hall's central truss a beautifully crafted leaf boss,
evidently carved *in situ* and in a Dec style. The W end of the
house is dated to *c.* 1549–50 and after 1570 a floor and massive
chimneystack were inserted into the hall.

EDWARD BARNSLEY WORKSHOP, Cockshutt Lane, 1¾ m. ENE.
Originally built as house and workshop by and for Ernest
Gimson's pupil, *Geoffrey Lupton* in 1908–9. The modest but
robust handling is wholly characteristic of this designer: broad
oak floorboards in the main parlour and oak doors with beautifully handmade ironwork (possibly made on site; the workshops originally had a smithy). The newel stair has gargantuan
oak treads and under a hatch in the parlour floor is a concrete
bath. The WORKSHOPS, occupying a long, low, L-shaped
range, were taken over by *Edward Barnsley* in 1923.

Slightly downhill to the E is *Lupton*'s BEE HOUSE, originally
a tiny two-room outbuilding comprising a store and a study
for the poet Edward Thomas, later extended by *Barnsley* (this
part raised to two storeys by *Jon Barnsley* in the 1960s).
Thomas lived from 1909 to 1913 at THE RED HOUSE.
Designed by *Alfred Powell* and built by *Lupton*, it bears the hall-
marks of both builder and architect – notably Powell's favourite
gambrel roof form and the solid craftsmanship of the construction. Projecting N porch supported on roughly cut octagonal pillars. Massive chimneystacks with moulded brick tops
define the limits of the original house. Appended at the W end
is an extension for the water tank, accessed by a hand-carved
ladder with semicircular footholds. On the garden side, a
delightful seat tucked in beneath a projection containing the
kitchen's bread oven. Also of interest is COCKSHOTT by
W. F. Unsworth, 1908, with first-floor loggia (now glazed) and
LUPTON COTTAGE, built *c.* 1908 as two cottages and occupied by Charles Bray, Lupton's assistant.

See also High Cross.

FROYLE

ST MARY OF THE ASSUMPTION. A fine late C13 chancel, of local
malm, with characteristically E.E. chancel arch and windows
with pointed-trefoiled lights and bar tracery (e.g. a spherical
triangle). But the large E window is an ambitious replacement
of *c.* 1320 (see the contemporary heraldic glass below) and of

excellent quality. Five lights, reticulated tracery of the usual pattern, but uncommonly finely defined, framed by a continuous label extending downward to corbel heads of an early C14 couple (the bailiff and his wife, of the adjacent Grange of St Mary's Abbey, Winchester). Inside, the window has crisp moulded jambs, again with corbel heads. The SE window is Perp, internally combined with a cinquefoil-arched piscina. The nave is brick, with two-storey windows and lower projections N and S. It is of 1812, in a simple Tudor Gothic by *James Harding* of Farnham, paid for by the squirson the Rev. Sir T. Combe Miller. The lower N windows and wavy roof-line of the N porch are of 1993 by *R. Ashby*. Plain brick W tower of 1722 with segment-headed windows, corner pinnacles with vanes. The church was restored in 1847, 1888 and 1903, by *Bodley*, and is richly furnished, especially after the latter date, in advanced Anglo-Catholic taste. Baroque statuary in the chancel. – COMMUNION RAILS. Jacobean – FONT, originally C13, but re-cut and not improved in 1864. – PULPIT. *c.* 1876 by *A. W. Blomfield*. – CHANDELIER. Of brass, a gorgeous piece, one of a pair from Holy Trinity, Dorchester, dated 1716 (the other of 1709 is at Wolvesey, Winchester). – SCULPTURE. Large *della Robbia* lunette panel St Michael weighing souls. HATCHMENTS. Several in the nave, the latest of 2009 to Lt. Col. J. Willcocks of outstanding quality with exquisitely painted mantling. – STAINED GLASS of outstanding interest in the chancel, of two periods: late C13 grisaille patternwork in the N and S windows; and *c.* 1330 in the reticulation units of the E window, a colourful display of shields (Edward the Confessor, Edward I, Edward Prince of Wales, Humphrey de Bohun Earl of Hereford, Edward II, John de Warenne 6th Earl of Surrey, Edward III, Margaret of Anjou, Henry de Chatelon, and Edward the Black Prince). The rest below excellent glass by *Burlison & Grylls*, 1896. A Tree of Jesse. Many C14–C15 fragments in the nave N window. Much Victorian and early C20 glass: In the chancel, N and S windows by *Kempe*. The best in the SE window of 1878–9. Annunciation and Nativity scenes in light surrounds (others of 1877, 1878 and 1897). Nave windows by *Burlison & Grylls*, the SE as late as 1935, unusual with St John the Divine writing Revelations. – MONUMENTS. Low tomb-recess in the chancel. Segmental arch. – Brass. John Lighe (or Leigh) †1575. Small figure in clerical dress. From a raised tomb in the middle of the chancel removed in 1811 (according to *Collectanea Topographica*, 1843).

TRELOAR SCHOOL, SW of the church. Established in 1953 as a school for disabled children, previously in Alton (*see* p. 124). The core is FROYLE PLACE (Gaston House) a *c.* 1600 half-H-plan house built for the Jephson family, refaced in dressed malmstone with Portland stone dressings and refenestrated *c.* 1770 and further altered and enlarged in Neo-Jacobean style for Sir Charles Hayes Miller in 1866–7. The main front (NW) has a doorway with frieze and cornice on consoles, and three gables above with double-chamfered stone-mullioned windows. The SE garden front has gabled wings with large chimneystacks on their inner faces but dominant additions of 1866, with a full-height canted bay. Mostly late C18 inside with modest Neoclassical decoration. Neo-Jacobean hall of 1866 with at one end a triple-arched Neo-Gothic wooden screen with staircase beyond. In a curious plastered space in the chimneybreast behind the fireplace in the SE room is a pair of blocked late C17 oculi, not visible externally. C17 cellar with small shuttered windows and a reused moulded wooden door frame with fleur-de-lys stops.

Of the school buildings should be noted the DINING HALL on the S side of the service yard, 1953, by *W. Curtis Green, Son & Lloyd*, institutional Modernism of the pre-war kind, faced in stone, altered and enlarged 2002–3 by *Macallan Penfold Architects*; S, a large Neo-Georgian courtyard building, including BURNHAM and PIKE HOUSES, 1954 by *Christopher Green*; S and E, excellent Neo-vernacular boarding houses by *Macallan Penfold*: the HEYWOOD COMPLEX of 1995–7 and PIKE HOUSE of 2000.

Opposite the school, mid-C18 FROYLE COTTAGE has, like many others in the village, a statue of a saint, collected in Italy *c.* 1900 by Sir Hubert Miller of the Shrubbery House (*see* below). Further w, on the same side the severe stuccoed FROYLE HOUSE of *c.* 1820 for Thomas Burningham has fine cellars, of elegant shallow brick vaults with flat ribs on octagonal greensand piers. S is the MANOR HOUSE, built *c.* 1700. Irregular front, the narrow far r. windows lighting the service stair and the main stair marked by the arched window to the l. of the door. The staircase itself has barley-sugar balusters and, on the underside of the upper flight, three painted scenes of Arcadian landscapes. Screen of three round arches and fluted pilasters at the foot. Segmental-pedimented pilastered surround to the half-landing window. Attic stair with oval flower-painted panel and winder service stair with turned balusters. At the rear later C19 HOP KILNS with three pyramidal tiled roofs, converted for school use in 1990 by *Plincke, Leaman & Browning*.

NE of the church in the village street the usual attractive Hampshire mix. THE OLD SCHOOL, of 1867–8, is for once thoroughly Gothic in an Early Dec style with cusped lights and plate tracery. Pretty flèche for bell. BRECKLANDS, further N, is the former workhouse. *c.* 1800, with two large ground-floor rooms, presumably for dining and work, l. and r. of the entrance and central staircase to the dormitories. Attached at the r. two-storey master's accommodation.

At LOWER FROYLE, ⅞ m. N, are several good farms and cottages, many of them dated. SILVESTERS FARM is a complete C17 farmstead of timber framing and malmstone with brick dressings. A tile-hung gabled cross-wing to the front, the farmyard side also gabled with a wide mullioned ground-floor window to the former kitchen, the rear stone addition dated 1674. The stone hall range is set back to the l. with crosswindows; a second pile at the rear contains staircase and chamber, with mullioned windows and a blocked cross-window in the gable, of brick plastered to imitate stone. Rich interior including a fine dog-leg staircase with tall turned balusters, and a wide brick and stone inglenook. Excellent thatched farm buildings. HUSSEYS, N of the main street, is a C16 or C17 timber-framed hall-and-cross-wing house, rebuilt in the early C18. Brick with a high, hipped roof, the front sashed and the cross-wing to r. with low hipped roofs behind a parapet. Entrance now at the side with reused shell-hooded porch of c. 1900. To the N, THE OAST HOUSE, four circular late C18 hop kilns, converted to a dwelling in phases: 1950 by *Rachel Caro*, and 1973.

THE SHRUBBERY HOUSE, ¼ m. SE of St Mary on the A31. Small mid-C18 villa with a pair of full-height canted bays, enlarged to incorporate on the road side a pair of early C18 cottages with substantial Neo-Georgian additions of c. 1900 for Sir Hubert Miller. An Arts and Crafts-style billiard room is slightly later still. It has an open timber roof and inglenook with beaten copper hood. Also many reused fittings, no doubt imported by Miller, including a fine inlaid Doric doorcase and chimneypiece of 1601 and a late C19 Jacobethan staircase incorporating a genuine C17 newel post.

Further SW, THE HEN AND CHICKENS, an early C18 chaise-house with axially planned STABLES behind.

FYFIELD

ST NICHOLAS. Drastically restored in 1846–7 by *Owen Browne Carter*. Nave and chancel flint, the chancel rendered. Gabled bellcote, S porch and roofs are Carter's. Genuine Perp E window. The chancel S window probably C17. FONT and other furnishing all of the restoration. (The bowl of the medieval font is in the churchyard.) – STAINED GLASS. E window, probably by *Daniel Bell* (commemorative date 1863). Colourful with a Crucifixion above a little Pietà. W window by *Cox & Sons*, 1869. An even more excitable Ascension scene. Nave N, an oddity, of 1914, still with Virtues after Reynolds at New College, Oxford. – MONUMENT. Henry White †1788 (the naturalist's brother and grandfather of William White, architect), incumbent 1762–88. – WAR MEMORIAL. Large classical tablet by *Sir Ernest George*, made by *W. S. Frith*, 1920.

FYFIELD GRANGE, NE of the church. Home of the Rev. Henry White from 1770. The main range, at right angles to the road, appears to have been built or remodelled in 1774 (White's initials and the date appear on the sill of a rear window), with a striking high mansard. Inside is a large parlour with pretty plasterwork ceiling. Along the road a further addition of 1776 with a pair of brick gables with round-arched windows (the whole elevation was raised in the C19).

LITTLETON MANOR, ¼ m. NW. Externally early C19, but with a timber-framed hall range probably built by Sir John de St John who acquired the manor from Gloucester Abbey soon after 1545. Cross-wing built by his son *c.* 1578 (dendrochronology), with a jettied first floor to the front and close studding with ogee braces. Inside, sumptuously moulded beams in the ground-floor front chamber.

REDENHAM HOUSE. *See* Appleshaw.

GODSFIELD *see* OLD ALRESFORD

GOODWORTH CLATFORD

3040

ST PETER. A little above the village, with open country to the E. Deceptively simple exterior with nave and chancel under one roof. Lower N and S aisles. Solid sturdy W tower of coursed ashlar. Although the style is Dec, it was built *c.* 1540 of stone from Wherwell Priory (the medieval advowson holders; some carved Norman zigzag mouldings can be seen inside). Shingled spire of 1860 behind the plain parapet. The rest of the church is of flint. Partly timber S porch of 1872 (dated over the inner doorway). Internally there is much more interest (especially in the nave, where the story of gradual growth under the aegis of Wherwell Priory unfolds in phases). The arcades are by no means a homogeneous job. First come the three W bays of the four-bay S side. Round pier, square abacus, trumpet-scallop capitals with some decoration. Spurs on the base. Pointed arches with one slight chamfer (the third arch is enriched with dogtooth). That indicates *c.* 1190. Of the same time or perhaps a few years before is the transept arch, i.e. evidence of a cruciform church, planned (according to how one's dating goes) before, or at the same time as, the S aisle. Also early C13, the PISCINA in the S aisle, unusually with painted 'surround'. Only after that the N arcade: two bays plus the former transept. Round piers, octagonal abaci, arches with one chamfer and one hollow chamfer. The W respond and even more the E arch have good corbel heads of the early C14. Dec details also in the N aisle E wall. C15 roofs in chancel, nave and N aisle. – FONT. Late C12. Purbeck marble, of table type. Six flat arches on one side. Also other motifs. Original base. – PULPIT AND DESKS in plain Perp of 1860. – PAINTING. Christ and the Woman taken in Adultery. Large, English, *c.* 1800. – STAINED GLASS. In the chancel by *Wailes*, especially the E window of *c.* 1850 with tight figure groups in small medallions. – Neat MEETING ROOM of 1992–3 by *Sarum Partnership* abutting NW.

MANOR FARMHOUSE, SW. C18, brick, the front remodelled in
the mid C19 with stuccoed porch and pilastered window
surrounds. In the former farmyard NW of the church, ST
PETER'S CLOSE, a courtyard development of retirement
homes of 1998–9 by *Sidell Gibson Architects*. Well-detailed Neo-
vernacular. NE, attractive former PUMP HOUSE of 1937, a taste
of the American Mid-West with waney-edged boarding. The
main street, ¼ m. SW across the River Anton, has only a few
good houses. On the E side, the late medieval timber-framed
OLD STORES and MOLESEY COTTAGE; on the W side, the
early C17 QUEEN ANNE COTTAGE, timber-framed and
thatched with a pair of first-floor oriels, each on a single shaped
bracket. THE VILLAGE CLUB was given in 1923 by Sir Alfred
Yarrow of Green Meadow. Late Arts and Crafts style.
GREEN MEADOW, over the river at the N end of the village. Picturesque C18 mill and mill house, converted and enlarged in
1921–2 by *Davis & Emanuel & Henry Smart* for Sir Alfred
Yarrow, marine engineer and shipbuilder.

5030

THE GRANGE
1¼ m. SSW of Northington

'There is nothing like it this side of Arcadia', was Cockerell's
judgement on visiting The Grange in 1823, and even now, despite
the vicissitudes of the intervening years, we are still presented
with a convincing Arcadian vision: a Greek temple sited
assertively on rising ground, its great Doric portico facing E over
a lake, the whole set in a now decaying landscaped park.

The Grange.
Engraving after Prosser, 1833

THE GRANGE 297

Almost everything one sees was created for the banker Henry
Drummond by *William Wilkins c.* 1809–10, remodelling an
existing house, built 1664–73 by *William Samwell* for Sir Robert
Henley. Samwell's house was of brick, as shown by the w front   p. 48
(untouched by Wilkins and restored), with details of cut and
rubbed brick and some stone dressings. It was of two storeys
on a raised basement, with an attic and a garret, the latter in
a 'ponderous roof of great elevation' which was topped by a
cupola. The principal N and S fronts were of nine bays, the
centre three and those at each end slightly projecting. Wilkins
raised the ground level around the house, hiding the basement,
and removed the great roof, leaving only one storey of attic
rooms, largely unprovided with natural light. He clad the
exterior in Parker's Roman cement, reserving Portland stone
only for the bases and capitals of columns, the plinth and the
cornice. At the E end he added the magnificent pedimented
Doric portico, its order based on that of the Thesion in Athens.   94
Everything is bigger and better than the contemporary portico
at Stratton Park (q.v.): it is hexastyle rather than tetrastyle, the
columns are fluted rather than plain, and it is two columns
deep (an inner line of columns was planned but unexecuted).
It was one of the first credos of the coming Grecian mode,
highly exacting and far from domestic. Yet despite its grandeur
it does not mark the entrance, which remains in the centre of
the N side. The long elevations have giant pilasters and three-
bay anta porticoes, based on elements of the Choragic Monument of Thrasyllus as well as the Thesion. The whole is tied
together by the entablature of triglyphs and metope wreaths.
The windows have moulded architraves, those on the ground
floor tapering, and in stone.

In 1817 Drummond sold to Alexander Baring, second son
of Sir Francis Baring of Stratton Park (q.v.). Additions were
made at once by *Robert Smirke* for a single-storey range at the
W end; this was extended S at right angles in 1825 by *C. R.
Cockerell*, and raised by another storey, rather clumsily, in 1852
by *C. R. & F. P. Cockerell.* Tucked into the angle between this
and the W front was a dining room wing, of one storey and a
basement, also added 1825. These were lost to the orgy of
destruction before 1975, when the Barings stripped the house
of its fittings and commenced destruction before the Department of the Environment intervened to save what remained of
the roofless gutted shell. The remains of *C. R. Cockerell*'s CON-
SERVATORY to the S, completed in 1824, did survive. Like the
house, it is of temple form, stuccoed and pilastered with a full
entablature. The five-bay E front has an elegant tetrastyle Ionic
portico, a *sotto voce* restatement of Wilkins's, and like that is
also two columns deep. The columns are in Roman cement,
the capitals of *Coade* stone. S side of seven bays. It was built
with cast-iron glazing panels between the pilasters, but these
were removed and the openings blocked *c.* 1890 when it was
converted to a ballroom/picture gallery. A panelled ceiling of
this date is preserved inside but of the pre-fabricated cast-iron

structure of 1824, by *Jones & Clark* of Birmingham, nothing survives. Into this space in 2001–3 *Studio E. Architects* (job architect *David Lloyd Jones*) imaginatively inserted a 500-seat AUDITORIUM for Grange Park Opera. Its horseshoe-plan is based on Wilkins's Theatre Royal, Bury St Edmunds (1819) with two tiers of balconies. Externally the C21 additions are clad in horizontal oak boarding on a high plinth of knapped flintwork, and have a green roof. They are concealed from the gardens by a right-angled screen wall which re-establishes the link between the conservatory and the house and replicates the elevation of the demolished W wing. It stops short of the house's W front, as though decayed or partly demolished.

The stripped INTERIOR of the house is a shock* – the walls are bare brick and most of the floors and ceilings are missing – but the C17 structure is therefore revealed and it is clear, by comparison with an C18 plan of the house, that Samwell's plan is largely preserved. Governed by a strict system of proportion, its clarity is notable. The ground floor contained the family rooms, with the state apartments above. In the centre of the N front is the Entrance Hall, a 27-ft (8-metre) cube. It retains pairs of doorways, with oval panels over. Galleries were removed by Wilkins, who applied a giant order of Corinthian pilasters. On the S side a matching single-storey room of identical plan, formerly an eating parlour. Flanking rooms were bedchambers, 18 ft (5.5 metres) square, and in each corner were pairs of 9-ft (2.8-metre) square closets, now largely removed. On each floor was a central longitudinal spine corridor, still with C17 groin-vaulting at ground floor, with three arched openings into the hall at each level, the upper ones altered by Wilkins. The Staircase Hall at the W end is also a 27-ft cube, originally lit by a columned and domed cupola. The late C19 staircase (probably by *John Cox*, 1868–70, replacing Samwell's original but incorporating the C17 newels) was rescued by Donald Insall and reinstated in 2008–9. At the centre of the S front on the upper floor was the Saloon, another cube.** The basement is almost completely Samwell's, groin-vaulted and with much surviving C17 joinery, mainly door and window frames. Samwell's basement windows with their rusticated surrounds survive under Wilkins's terrace on the S side. Wilkins gutted the SE corner of the ground floor to form a new drawing room and raised the ceiling here and in the original dining room, introducing iron trusses to support the new floors. A serious loss during the 1970s demolitions was Cockerell's dining room, which was approached through an apsed lobby from the staircase landing (the doorcase was saved and has been reinstated). The room had six scagliola Bassae Ionic columns, with a shallow segmental coffered vault.

---

* Its late C19 grandeur is well illustrated by a series of 1870s photographs by Savage, the Winchester photographer.
** For analysis of plan and decoration before the C19 alterations see J. Geddes, *Furniture History*, v. XXII, 1986.

GARDENS AND PARK. The C18 plan of the C17 house shows elaborate courts and gardens on all sides. If any of this survived, or indeed was executed, Wilkins swept it away to create E and S terraces retained by massive, plain walls, with square plinths at the corners and flanking the flights of steps descending from the porticoes. A design of *c.* 1809 shows these with sarcophagi but there is no evidence that these were ever executed. There is a second grass-banked terrace below this. On the S side it is on the axis of the conservatory, from which steps descend, and on the E side it extends beyond the N front of the house and terminates in a semicircular stone seat, probably by *Cockerell*, flanked by a pair of truncated late C17 panelled stone gatepiers. S of the conservatory, a formal Italianate garden was laid out in 1825–6, one of the earliest examples of the revival in the country.

The lime avenue on the axis of the N front is probably a survival of the late C17 landscaping but in its present form the PARK dates from the late C18. The designer is unknown. Clumps of deciduous trees were planted and in the valley E of the house the Candover Stream was dammed to create a pair of narrow lakes (*Robert Adam* produced a design for a bridge in 1764). The park was further developed and enlarged after 1817; the rustic flint-built CASCADE between the lakes may be of this date. Also of the early C19 (certainly before 1833) is the CASTLE at the S end of the park, a battlemented flint tower, of two storeys, with an octagonal corner stair-turret. The paired round-arched windows look N, i.e. into the park, towards the house. Nearby an early C19 rustic flint two-arched BRIDGE. The best of the lodges is SWARRATON LODGE, an early C19 *cottage orné*, of flint with a rustic wooden veranda and leaded windows. Originally thatched. The last remnants of the old village of Swarraton, ½ m. NE of the house, were removed, apart from the church, which was demolished in 1849. Its site is marked by a stone CROSS (now in pieces), erected in 1858 within the old churchyard walls.

STABLES, ¼ m. N. of the house. *c.* 1870 by *John Cox* with a highly impressive gate-tower with a lead-covered pavilion roof and square cupola. GRANGE FARM, model farm of 1878, possibly by *Cox*, incorporating pioneering use of concrete blockwork.

LAKE HOUSE, ½ m. SSW of The Grange. Built 1971–6 by *Francis Pollen* for John Baring, later 7th Baron Ashburton, who had previously commissioned the new house at Stratton Park (East Stratton). Single-storey, built up against an early C19 garden wall which is punctuated by the doorway. This is flanked by *Coade* stone Ionic capitals, recovered from the window of Cockerell's dining room at The Grange. At the top of the wall a recessed gap, above which the flat roof appears to float but also combining to read as a frieze and cornice. Defining the forecourt a pair of hipped-roofed pavilions. Less formal garden side, lighter and more transparent, with large areas of glazing between vertical and horizontal cedar cladding. Drawing room in a projecting wing, glazed on three sides, with a wooden balcony extending over the lawn. Several fixtures were brought from The Grange, principally the drawing-room chimneypiece given to Alexander Baring by Napoleon I, with profile heads of the Bonaparte family in the frieze. Landscaping by *Geoffrey Jellicoe*, 1975–6, only partly executed.

GRATELEY

2040

A compact village with the church and manor house on an island site.

ST LEONARD. Of flint, and over-restored in 1851 by *Owen Browne Carter*. The eastern half of the nave is C12, with one N window and the plain S doorway. The N doorway is pointed, while the S doorway is round-headed, but in Hampshire that need not prove a difference of date. Broad stunted C13 W tower with small lancets and later, probably C15, angle buttresses.* C13 chancel with three stepped E lancets. Simple interior with original C13 trussed-rafter roof. No chancel arch. – FONT. A plain tub of indeterminate, possibly Late Saxon or Early Norman, date. Most of the other furnishings are Carter's, especially the typically Early Victorian Perp PULPIT. – ROOD. Of 1934 by *Gawthorp & Sons*. – TILES. Sixty in front of the communion rail. – HOURGLASS STAND. Against the nave N wall. – STAINED GLASS. In a S window a beautiful piece representing the Stoning of St Stephen. It comes from Salisbury Cathedral, and must according to style have been done for somewhere close to the E end, where work was ready for receiving glass from *c.* 1225 onwards. Also C13 glass, including the upper half of a small figure.

MANOR FARMHOUSE, E, C18 brick. Modest, with Tuscan porch. Fine early C18 five-bay BARN with tiled roof sweeping down over aisles. E again, the C17 timber-framed OLD RECTORY. Gabled stair-tower at rear. Cottagey Neo-Georgian additions of 1911 by *H. C. Benson*. SW, the attractive SCHOOL of 1845. Single-storey. Stuccoed, probably over chalk cob, with Tudor details.

GRATELEY HOUSE SCHOOL, S edge of the village. Early C19 villa, red brick, of three by three bays. S front altered mid C19 with ground-floor canted bays and pretty wooden veranda with lattice spandrels. E front still has a nice Ionic porch and a ground-floor window set in an arched recess to the l. Service wing of 1867–9 by *George Devey* for Emanuel Boutcher, in C17 Domestic Revival style of red brick with grey diapering.

---

* It had a spire removed in the C19.

GRAYSHOTT

In the wooded foothills of Hindhead (Surrey), much developed after the Enclosure Acts of 1859, when the attractions of the commons and wooded vales were discovered. Edward I'Anson and Edmund Woodthorpe were among the first to build houses for themselves (*see* also Headley). Notable local residents also included George Bernard Shaw,* who deplored the 'miserable eruption of ugly little brick boxes'. By 1898 a centre had been developed around a carrefour of five roads so there are hundreds of smallish houses and bungalows about, and larger houses hidden in the foliage.

ST LUKE. 1898–9 by *E. B. I'Anson*. E.E. of Bargate stone with a SE tower surmounted by an exaggeratedly broached shingled spire of 1910. Big clerestoried nave of five bays, with a large W window of five graduated lancets, short, uncomfortably low, chancel. Airy interior faced crazily with Headley sandstone. Old-fashioned furnishings, especially the FONT and PULPIT, looking twenty years earlier. – REREDOS and panelling by *Sir Charles Nicholson*, 1939. – STAINED GLASS. E window, an extraordinary and original piece by the little-known *Joseph Wilson Forster* of Bushey, 1918, to the architect (†1912) and his sister Catherine I'Anson. A pictorial resurrection scene, with a Raphaelesque figure over lilies and rosebush with pink doves, angels either side, their heads unnervingly photographic portraits, evidently from life. After this, the other windows (including a N aisle window by *Forster* of *c.* 1915, and four others, by *Jessie Bayes*) are disappointing.

ST JOSEPH (R.C.), ½ m. W. 1910–11 by *F. A. Walters*; paid for by Mrs Vertue. Perp, of Bargate stone, with a pert stone bell-turret over the E end of the nave effectively breaking the continuous roof-line. Presbytery attached to the W end. Inside the chancel, elaborate REREDOS of stone screenwork. – STAINED GLASS. E window by *Gladys Spawforth* (Peter Cormack) in a Late Arts and Crafts tradition.

SCHOOL, School Road. 1871 by *E. B. I'Anson*. Bargate stone.

WAR MEMORIAL, a Gothic stone cross set on a square base. Ogee-headed panels.

VILLAGE SIGN. 2000. Stainless steel with slender vertical rods supporting a crown with silhouette of buildings and trees.

In the village's long main street only a few buildings command attention. The Arts and Crafts-style FOX AND PELICAN by *Read & MacDonald*, 1899, was established as a reformed public house by the Grayshott & District Refreshments Association, which included G.B.S. in its number. At the front a large tile-hung gable with bands of windows over a colonnaded loggia, its unfluted columns with scrolly capitals. Original wide timber inglenook inside, but what has become of the original sign by

---

* Shaw lived at Blen-Cathra (now St Edmund's School) at Hindhead (Surrey). Grayshott Court, I'Anson's house, burnt in 1890.

Walter Crane? At the opposite end of the street is the Voysey-esque VILLAGE HALL of 1902–3, also by *Read & MacDonald*. Roughcast with leaded mullioned-and-transomed windows. Gabled front with low segmental-arched recessed porch, and to the r. a two-storey canted bay with witch's hat. Adjoining caretaker's house. Set back to the l., the matching former small hall (now the Library) of 1906 by the same architects. Gablet roof. Wide brick segmental-arched entrance. Between these landmarks are shops and businesses of *c.* 1900 and after, notably the handsome LLOYDS TSB BANK, Neo-Georgian of 1923.

GRAYSHOTT HALL, 1 m. w. The most ambitious of the many larger houses. 1886–7, by *J. H. Christian*, who lived nearby. Rather stodgy Surrey style but with an original three-storey stone tower over the entrance, with battlements, octagonal stair-turret and nicely detailed curved oriel. To its l. a large window lights the staircase. Wing added 1906–7, by *E. B. I'Anson*, with further minor work in 1939. Neo-Jacobean inte-riors of 1886–7 (e.g. the entrance hall, its staircase with lyre-shaped splat balusters, galleried landing and nice plaster ceiling and billiard room, with good chimneypiece and fittings) but the drawing room was altered 1939 and the dining room is of 1906–7 in a crisp Arts and Crafts Neo-Georgian. Stained-glass roundels with heads representing the Seasons, probably reused. To the E, the STABLES of 1888 in the same manner as the house. Attractive landscaped grounds, including ROCK GARDEN and rustic timber bowling green PAVILION. Entrance LODGE, 1880s by *Christian*. Pretty, in the style of the house, but handled more assuredly at this scale. The wooden GATE has a carved dragon's head on the curved end of the hanging stile.

GREATHAM

ST JOHN BAPTIST. Early Dec of 1874–5 by *H. & A. P. Fry* of Liverpool, cousins to the Fosters of Le Court, who financed the building; SE tower with shingled broach spire by *Frederic Chancellor*, 1897; NE vestry, 1994. Large and well-carved FONT. Marble and tile REREDOS, and tiled floor with strong pattern of chevron and fleur-de-lys. – CHOIR STALLS. With brass candle-stands. – CHANCEL SCREEN and PULPIT of 1891 by *James Fowler* of Louth. – SCULPTURE. St John Baptist by *Hew Lorimer, c.* 1960, still in the Gill tradition. – STAINED GLASS. In every window by *Clayton & Bell*, the earliest and best of 1875. E window, Scenes in the life of the dedicatory saint below the *Agnus Dei* and four small angels. Unusually large LYCH-GATE of 1907 by *Hems*. Perp.

OLD CHURCH (St John Baptist), s of the new. The chancel is roofed, the nave ruinous. Possibly mid C11; one blocked round-headed lancet survives in the s wall. Early C18 chancel arch (blocked) of the basket type. Original C14 sandstone w angle buttresses rebuilt in 1842. MONUMENT. Dame Margery Caryll †1632. Large, of alabaster and touch, relocated from the nave s wall. Tomb with recumbent effigy at prayer. Against the wall an aedicule with columns. Probably London work.

MANOR HOUSE, s of the old church. Of roughly coursed iron-stone. Probably late C18 but aggrandized for Frederick Coryton, 1898, in Neo-Tudor style.

GOLEIGH FARM HOUSE, ⅜ m. SE. Of two phases according to datestones – 1675 (E) and 1685 (W). Earlier part mostly iron-stone, with stone quoins, the later with horizontal stone, mul-lioned, windows to cellar and two rooms on the ground floor. Of 1685 also the gabled, broad staircase brick projection with plain mullioned opening; arched brick windows are perhaps contemporary. Double-pile plan, divided by a through passage. Large fireplace in one room with massive timber lintel.

GREATHAM MILL, Mill Lane, ½ m. w on the Rother. C18 miller's house, but of more than one phase between a former barn (s) and the mill itself (N) with two gables and weather-boarding. Machinery partly preserved. Cottage-style GARDEN, laid out from 1947 by *Frances Pumphrey*.

LONGMOOR CAMP, Woolmer Forest, ¾ m E. A permanent army camp was established in 1900–3 and shortly after connected to Bordon camp (q.v.) by a railway. Some early corrugated-iron clad huts are associated with Longmoor's subsequent expan-sion as the Army's Railway Training Centre. Fittings of the Garrison Church (dem. *c.* 2000) now at St Martin, Leconfield Barracks (Yorkshire East Riding).

GREYWELL   *7050*

ST MARY. Rendered nave of *c.* 1200, see the doorways, that to the N with a round arch and dogtooth (cf. Up Nately). The windows, only on s side, are later, one mid-C13 of two lancets, the other late C15 unrestored. The charming semicircular pro-jection for the rood stair in rough flint and stone chequerwork is of *c.* 1500 when the nave was restored and re-roofed. Low, much-patched w tower, essentially C17, after rebuilding (record of repairs in 1663) with big later buttresses, restored in 1895; Alma Tadema, Lord Leighton, Sir Henry Irving and Ellen Terry were among the subscribers as a document of 1896, framed under the tower in sprightly Arts and Crafts lettering by *Jessica Cave*, records. Of *c.* 1200 again the tower arch and the chancel arch, pointed arches on simple imposts. Good nave roof. The chancel, in a hard, flinty Perp, is of 1870–1 by *Ewan Christian*. – FONT. Octagonal, Perp, with quatrefoils. – SCREEN of *c.* 1500. Of veranda type, i.e. with a w front and a ceiling to carry the loft and cover the space between screen and chancel

arch. Single-light divisions. The ceiling nicely panelled with
rib-moulding. The screen was raised on a stone base in 1871,
when the rood loft stair was blocked. – ROYAL ARMS over the
screen. Dated 1768. – STAINED GLASS. E window by *Clayton
& Bell*, 1871. Nativity, Crucifixion and Resurrection.

The church is on its own by the River Whitewater. CHURCH
COTTAGE, at the end of the path to the village street, is C15.
In three parts with a jettied cross-wing (r.). In the l. range, a
massive stone fireplace with shafted and corbelled jambs, probably reused. Otherwise the best house is THE MALTHOUSE,
an early C16 hearth-passage house with cross-wing, fully jettied
to the front and close-studded with herringbone brick infill.
The central three bays are slightly earlier, possibly relocated
from elsewhere and originally not domestic, with a single first-
floor grand chamber. Was it a church house? Former malthouse
in rear wing. To the r. MALTHOUSE COTTAGE, the formerly
jettied C15 cross-wing with old scalloped bargeboards.

GREYWELL TUNNEL. ¼ m. N of the church. Built for the Basingstoke Canal, 1788–92. 1,230 yds long. Its curved and battered brick E portal has rusticated brick end piers and keyed
round arch with blind oculi in the spandrels. The roof collapsed in 1932.

GREYWELL HILL HOUSE, ½ m. NW. Remodelled *c.* 1786 for
Guy Carleton, 1st Earl of Dorchester and Governor General
of Quebec. A long and narrow stuccoed house on a falling site,
the principal E front with full-height canted hipped-roofed bays
at each end and a projecting centre, the three-bay S front with
central porch. Early C19 stuccoed LODGE with Tudor Gothic
details.

HACKWOOD PARK*

Hackwood Park was built in 1683–8 by Charles Paulet, 6th Marquess of Winchester (later 1st Duke of Bolton). It was, to judge
from illustrations, a plain hipped-roofed single-pile house of
thirteen bays with wings at right angles, joined to the main
block by quadrant colonnades, and a pedimented centre to N
and S fronts. This, essentially, is the arrangement still but with
alterations, principally by *John Vardy c.* 1761–3, who remodelled the S front, adding single-storey E and W wings with pyramidal roofs, and *Samuel Wyatt* after 1805. He gave the house
its present appearance by doubling the depth of the main block
on its N front, at the same time realigning the curved links to
the wings and heightening them to two storeys and extending
the wings N. Architect and client died in 1807 but remodelling
continued for the 2nd Lord Bolton by Samuel's nephew,

* The house and contents were sold in 1998. Access was refused to the revising
author.

Hackwood Park.
Engraving after Prosser, 1833

Lewis Wyatt. He is responsible for the appearance of the s front. The result is grand in scale and completely stuccoed, with architectural details in stone.

The N front is of nine bays, the outer pair set back, with a fine tetrastyle Ionic portico and a pediment. The capitals and the coat of arms in the pediment are of artificial stone and were modelled by *Francis Bernasconi*. In the middle of the three-bay quadrant links are porches with Tuscan columns *in antis*. The wings themselves are of five bays and terminate in Wyatt's flat-roofed extension with an elevation of triumphal arch form.

The centre block of the s front represents the late C17 house. Nine bays, with a (just) detached giant tetrastyle Ionic portico. No pediment, but an attic with panelled dies topped by urns (added later). The end bays have tripartite windows. Lewis Wyatt remodelled the ends of Vardy's wings, removing their attics and canted bays in favour of shallow hipped roofs and tripartite ground-floor windows under blank segmental arches. The single-storey links to the wings were also altered: reduced to two bays and raised to the same height as the wings. Only these retain C18 motifs of a blind round arch with a window inset. The E wing contains the former ballroom, whose principal elevation faces E and is of five bays articulated by an Ionic order of pilasters, and, in the three-bay pedimented centre, columns *in antis*. In the outer bays, niches. The N wall of the corresponding W wing faces onto a service yard, screened from the s by a wall, in front of which (on the site of an early C19 conservatory) is a Doric loggia of 1936 by *Francis Lorne* of *Burnet, Tait & Lorne* for William Berry, 1st Lord Camrose, who acquired the house in 1935.

(The dominant style of the INTERIOR is still late C17, created by original elements, probably from the house itself, certainly by materials reclaimed from the house at Abbotstone (q.v., demolished 1762) and, remarkably, by the revival of the style in the early C19 by *Lewis Wyatt*. Unfortunately much of the fine late C17 woodcarving, in the style of Gibbons, was removed to Bolton Hall, Yorkshire, in 1935. The ENTRANCE HALL is one of the earliest Caroline Revival interiors (cf. Wyatt's dining room at Lyme Park, Cheshire), with bolection-moulded oak panelling and a plaster frieze grained to match of 1808 by *Bernasconi*, like all the plasterwork in the house. Fireplaces in the end walls, their marble bolection-moulded surrounds probably late C17 with crested keystones by *Westmacott*, 1808. On the s wall, excellent carved drops representing the Seasons, which formerly flanked the chimneypieces, of 1815 by *Edward Wyatt*. The wide doorway in the hall's s wall leads into the SALOON. This was the hall of the late C17 house and went through both floors until *c.* 1760 when *Vardy* lowered the ceiling to create rooms at first floor, and introduced panelling from Abbotstone. Pair of bolection-moulded chimneypieces introduced 1968. E is the SOUTH LIBRARY (the C18 drawing room), the best of Wyatt's Caroline rooms, with an opulent enriched plaster ceiling and ducal coronet in a narrow carved wooden panel above the fireplace. The accompanying carved drops and swags around the overmantel have gone. A screen of green marble Corinthian columns separates it from the NORTH LIBRARY, also with a plaster ceiling in the Wren manner. The panel with two figures and a lace cravat is especially fine. In the SMALL DRAWING ROOM, w of the Saloon, a white marble chimneypiece, by *Richard Wyatt*, 1819, with a frieze representing the Four Seasons and with figures emblematic of Music and Drawing. The most radical Wyatt alteration to the existing house was the gutting of Vardy's single-storey E and w wings flanking the s front. In the E wing the former ducal suite was replaced by an apsidal BALLROOM and in the w wing a drawing room and servants' hall were amalgamated as a T-shaped DINING ROOM. The stem has a Neoclassical shallow barrel-vaulted plaster ceiling with thin ribs and corn and grape sprays, made by a *Mr Coffee* in 1811–12. At the w end it is domed over a shallow apse, and at the E an Ionic screen. Niches contained figures by *Westmacott*. The main STAIRCASE, w of the hall, is the only interior by *Samuel Wyatt*, but the cantilevered stone stair, with its delicate wrought-iron balustrade was executed by his nephew. The secondary stair, E of the library, was inserted by *Vardy*, but the twisted balusters must be reused late C17 fabric.

In the N forecourt, an equestrian STATUE of George I, in Roman dress, on a substantial stone pedestal. Made in 1725 by *John Nost II*. It stood originally in a prominent position in the formal gardens s of the house. Enclosing the forecourt a wrought-iron CLAIRVOIE, apparently C18 or early C19 but altered before 1910 by Lord Curzon, who moved it further out to embrace the statue. About ¼ m. N, a large oval stone BASIN is a further remnant of the formal landscaping on this side of

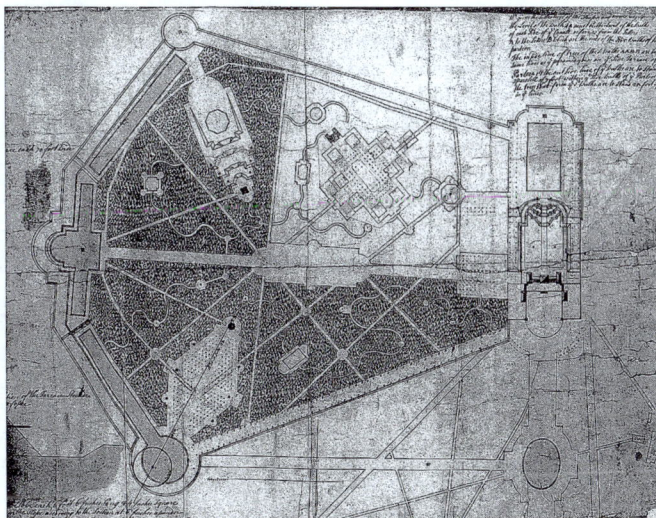

Hackwood Park, Spring Wood.
Plan, c18

the house. STABLES and RIDING SCHOOL, ¼ m. NW. 1818–19
by *Lewis Wyatt*, replacing stables and a riding house by *Vardy*.
Two storeys, stuccoed, with a pyramidal central pavilion and,
on the far side of the courtyard, the brick riding school with
octagonal pavilions at each end. The rear wall has blind arcading with lunettes.

The most important survival of the FORMAL GARDEN is
SPRING WOOD, E of the house. About eighty acres, created
from an existing area of woodland. Attributed to *Charles
Bridgeman*, its kite-shaped pattern was probably laid out for
the 3rd Duke in the 1720s and furnished with buildings by
James Gibbs (illustrated in his *Book of Architecture*, 1728). The
formal design, in the manner of Le Nôtre, consists of a series
of *allées* radiating from a central *rond-point*, the principal axis
being the BROAD WALK running E–W, aligned with the E front
of the house. At right angles is TWELVE O'CLOCK WALK.
Three canals were intended to run parallel with the W edge,
the central one on the main axis, as well as a raised terrace
around the garden's periphery, with circular bastions at the N
and S corners. Cathedral Avenue and the Mount appear to be
remains of such features. Within the segments between the
allées were various garden features, connected by further
straight rides and by sinuous paths cut through the woodland.
NE is the Amphitheatre, on the axis of the NE corner bastion.
A series of grass terraces survive and, at the SW end, eight stone
columns, the remains of *Gibbs*'s ROTUNDA. SW of the centre,
his MENAGERIE PAVILION of 1727. Stuccoed, it has a three-

bay Doric portico with unfluted columns *in antis* and a pediment. Windows l. and r. Animals were housed in (demolished) rear wings. The pavilion and the rectangular pool it faces were, or were intended to be, part of a complex parterre garden on the axis of the sw *allée*. THE CUBS, small wooden pavilions with seats, may also be by Gibbs. They are double-sided, with paired pilasters flanking a round arch and a pediment. N is the TEAHOUSE, another stuccoed temple-like pavilion. It may be later.

The circular BASIN in the sw corner of the garden was built in the early C19 to replace the large reservoir s of the house, as its chief water supply. The four metal dolphins supporting the fountain are of 1817, modelled by *Chantrey*. In one of the se segments was a French garden with the French House, a lost pavilion of Greek-cross plan with octagonal dome. Features introduced in the C20 include a STATUE of Ceres, at the centre of the radiating walks, the domed circular TEMPLE of 1980 in the pool at the e end of the Broadwalk, based on a design by *Vardy*, and the CHINESE PAVILION. At the w end of the Broadwalk, a pair of iron GATES, from *Lewis Wyatt*'s London Lodge (*see* below).

Large WALLED GARDEN, ENE of the house. Probably C18, altered in the early C19 and with C19 railed clairvoies in the centres of two of the walls. Piers with stone urns (some relocated to Spring Wood (q.v.) in the C20). Early C19 ORANGERY in the N wall, by *Lewis Wyatt*. Stuccoed with five-bay arcaded front and curved rear walls. Behind, THE BOTHY, C18 gardener's house, altered early C19. Nearby, KEEPERS COTTAGE, *c.* 1815, one of *Lewis Wyatt*'s estate houses. A neat design. Stuccoed with coved eaves to a low-pitched pyramidal roof. All the flues are gathered into a central chimney.

The PARK was first enclosed in 1226 and expanded over several centuries. Stretching as far e as Tunworth and by the C19 incorporating part of the old Basingstoke–Alton road as its principal N–S thoroughfare; the new road (A339) was moved further W. A lake was planned NE of the house in the early C19, but remained incomplete. Spanning this, an early C19 BRIDGE, probably by *Lewis Wyatt*. Stuccoed brick with three segmental arches; ashlar parapets, widening at each end and terminating in circular piers. At the park's NW entrance two LODGES. One is early C19 (contemporary gatepiers and railings) by *Lewis Wyatt*, replacing one by *Vardy*. Stuccoed, with coved eaves. Its pair is of 2003. NE of the house, DAISY and ROSE COTTAGES, an interesting miniature pair with all the *Wyatt* characteristics. Square plan, at each corner full-height canted bays.

LONDON LODGE. Cut off from the park, by the M3, on London Road, Old Basing (q.v.). By *Lewis Wyatt*, *c.* 1819–20 in the form of a monumental Greek Doric screen or triumphal arch, with widely spaced columns *in antis*, supporting a full entablature, but bereft of its blocking course and raised attic which formerly supported Lord Bolton's coat of arms (carved by *Richard Wyatt*). The boxy lodges flank and face inwards, each with a loggia divided by a central square pier, the motif drawn from the Choragic Monument of Thrasyllus.

HOME FARMHOUSE, NNE of the house. The best of *Lewis Wyatt*'s minor domestic designs for the estate, built *c.* 1820. Gault brick, but red on the farmyard (N) side. Pyramidal roof with central chimney. Farm buildings to the N, including a very long C18 brick BARN (now housing).

ROUNDTOWN, ¼ m. SW of the farm, is an interesting planned group of *c.* 1800. Semicircular plan, facing S. In the middle, a two-storey pavilion with pedimented gable, connected by quadrant link walls to a pair of flanking cottages. These are very small, of baffle-entry plan. The walled links have lean-to buildings in front. What was this built as? Converted to houses 2009 by *Robert Adam Architects*.

HANNINGTON

A large parish. In the centre, a hilltop village grouped around a large square green with the church on the W side.

ALL SAINTS. Victorian-looking, due to restoration by *Benjamin Ferrey* in 1855–6, when the flint walls were largely denuded of their original plaster, the church lengthened W and the shingled bell-turret put on, with its odd concave-sided piece below the spire. Good N porch of *c.* 1858. Not everybody will notice the characteristically Late Anglo-Saxon long-and-short work of the NE quoin of the nave nor some masonry in its N and E walls (a Saxon sundial was discovered in 1970). The next period is represented inside: the responds of the chancel arch may be Norman, and later, perhaps of *c.* 1180–90, are the two easternmost most bays of the sturdy S arcade of three bays. Round piers (only the E one, of chalk, and the E respond are old), square abaci, and trumpet-scallop capitals. But the double-chamfered arches are probably a remodelling of *c.* 1300, when the chancel arch was rebuilt and the S aisle received its E window of three lights and intersecting tracery. Also E.E., the N doorway, with C13 strap hinges on the door. At the same time, the chancel may have been rebuilt, to the width of the nave (evidence of the original chamfered rere-arch of the E window, restored in 1856) but its present appearance looks Perp with nicely traceried single-light C15 windows. The old roofs of the E parts of the nave and S aisle are possibly C14, the chancel roof of 1884 by *Baker* (probably *Arthur Baker*). Genuine ogee-headed PISCINA of *c.* 1300, unusually in the E wall. – PULPIT. Unusually attractive early C17. – WALL PAINTING. In the chancel, traces of possibly early C16 fictive brocade patternwork. – STAINED GLASS. In the E window, a luridly colourful Ascension scene (commemorative date †1863). More restful, the beautifully engraved glass in the chancel SE window, of 1988–9 by *Laurence Whistler*, with an exquisite foliate cross above a depiction of Stoney Hall. S aisle glass also by *Whistler*, 1979. – MONUMENT. Mary Webb †1825, signed *Gibbs*, B'stoke. With shallow fluted columns and a draped urn. In the churchyard, some closely clustered C18 and early C19 headstones. Sturdy timber LYCHGATE, 1897.

MANOR FARMHOUSE to the W is late C17, but still lobby-entry. Brick with moulded string course. Five bays with (restored) cross-windows. N, a large C17 five-bay aisled BARN. Fronting the green, the early C19 CHURCH COTTAGE (formerly a pair). Vitrified header-bond brickwork to the front, pretty bands of flint and brick at the rear. On the green, the timber-framed PUMP HOUSE of 1897. Square with Gothic arched sides and witch's hat roof. Just NE of the green is TAN-Y-BRYN, a four-bay cruck house of 1360. Two surviving trusses, that over the hall with elegant moulded arch bracing to the collar. Externally C18 brick and thatch. Several Late Georgian brick houses on the periphery. N, THE OLD RECTORY, of three irregular bays with tented canopy and side entrance, E, HANNINGTON HOUSE, four bays with string course of vitrified headers, and S, the largest, STONEY HALL, 1793, of five bays.

HAZELDENE MANOR, North Oakley, ¾ m. S. Substantial mid-C17 brick cross-wing with moulded string courses and evidence of possible former bay windows to front and back. Hipped roofed timber-framed stair-tower to the E, over a lower hall range. This is late C15 and timber-framed, but also faced in C17 brick. Nearby the mostly C18 MANOR FARMHOUSE; wavy splat-balusters in rear stair-tower. Impressive C18 thatched BARN. Six bays with aisles.

HARTFORD BRIDGE
Hartley Wintney

ALL SOULS. 1876 by *George Birch*. White weatherboard, with a bell-turret and no aisles. Fanciful lychgate.

ARLOTS FARMHOUSE. Tudor-Gothic trimmings, including a miniature timber-framed porch, almost certainly by *Teulon* for the Elvetham estate (q.v.)

THE HARTFORD BRIDGE (formerly the White Lion), on the A30. A nice irregular Georgian coaching inn with Venetian windows in the end wall.

HARTLEY MAUDITT

The church is on its own by a large pond, but until the C18 stood by the manor house and small village.

ST LEONARD. Nave and chancel and pertly pretty bell-turret (*B. Cancellor*, 1904) held up partly by an external buttress, partly by a stepped stone projection inside (both features date from the major restoration of 1854). The nave is largely of the foundation *c.* 1125 by William de Maudit, with Norman windows, no longer slits, and a sumptuous s doorway of clunch, *c.* 1190. The arch is pointed. The hoodmould has dogtooth, the main arch radially placed clasps or horseshoes. The nook-shafts are keeled – a sure instance of Transitional date. Later, in the c13, the nave was enlarged w (evidence of buttress and the trefoil-headed sw lancet). The plain chancel arch seems Earlier Norman. It is low and round and has a single-step arch with nook-shafts. Faint traces of medieval red decorative painting on the soffit. Chancel of *c.* 1300 or later; the e window of two lights with cusped Y-tracery is of *c.* 1350. – Elaborate Neo-Norman wooden ALTAR, and *Minton* tiled sanctuary floor and dado of 1854. Some early c13 TILES, in two strips. – FONT. Octagonal. Perp with quatrefoils and tracery panels, some with heraldry. – PULPIT. Gothic; of 1854? – STAINED GLASS. Nave s window by *Gerald Moira*, 1912 – MONUMENTS. In the chancel, those on the n wall with a riotous display of colourful heraldry. The tablet to Frances Steward (†1608) was erected in 1614 by Dr Nicholas Steward; the inscription completed after his death in 1633. Plenty of achievements. The larger and more elaborate monument is to his son, Sir Nicholas Steward (†1709/10), erected in his lifetime, perhaps *c.* 1690, and attributed to *William Stanton* (GF). Big open semicircular pediment, in the 'predella' a relief of a Crusader ancestor slaying a lion with a club. Between these Elizabeth Ady †1675, second daughter of Sir Nicholas, and wife of John Ady of Bekesbourne. A conventional *Stanton* workshop production, with achievement over a segmental pediment. Nice cherubs with swags below.

HARTLEY MAUDITT HOUSE, ¼ m. N. Formerly the rectory.* Mid-c17, hipped-roofed double pile. Remodelled and enlarged in 1821 when it was stuccoed and the entrance moved from w to n and marked by a Doric porch. The original plan survives inside, of entrance leading to a passage, separated from hall to its r. by an early c19 Ionic columned screen, with staircase at rear.

HARTLEY WESPALL   6050

St Mary. Flint-faced with a tile hung n tower, mostly due to c19 restorers, especially *G. G. Scott Jun.* in 1868–70. But it has one quite tremendous original feature, the huge timbers of the w wall, dated to *c.* 1330, at which time the manor and advowson were held by the Bishop of Bath and Wells. They are of extraordinary design, forming one enormous boldly cusped lozenge cut by a cusped middle post. Smaller cusped timbers in the gable. Can the church have been built by carpenters

28

---

*The late c17 Hartley Mauditt House w of the church was dem. *c.* 1798 and its fittings dispersed (*see* Westbrooke House, Alton).

employed by Ralph of Shrewsbury, diocesan from 1329 to 1263? Scott's N tower reuses the bell-stage rescued from the (C15?) W tower after it was taken down in 1865. It was low, X-framed, with a spire (cf. Yateley). Two bells were cast between 1439 and 1450 by *Robert Crouch* of London. Was the tower gifted by John Waspail †1448, patron of the church? Genuine also the rare timber N doorway, intact with its two-centred arch replete with rectangular frame, both parts having a label of the same section. Solid spandrels. Traces of red paint. The corresponding S doorway is only complete inside. Both doorways are part of a rare interior composition with the nave roof, a wagon roof with tie-beams on arched braces which rest on the timber wall-posts. The whole of three equal bays. The struts and principals in the upper part of the roof follow those in the exterior W wall. – FONT. Neo-Norman. Circular, with interlacing arcading. Presented by the rector, Dr Keate, in 1842. – PULPIT. Laudian i.e. 1630s. With wide panels having on the usual two short pilasters a twin instead of a single arch. The other furnishings are mostly by *Scott*, the notable exception being the beautiful Perp REREDOS of 1892–4 by *Temple Moore*. Crisply carved in alabaster. The *Agnus Dei* with two angels. SCREEN, well integrated with the early C14 wall-posts – in the place of the lost original screen. Richly traceried, with a central cross with Evangelists' emblems and a rood of *c.* 1920. – PEWS. Plain and solid in local C15–C16 Hampshire fashion. – ORGAN CASE of 1873–4 by *Scott* against the W end, with Perp fretwork at the top. – STAINED GLASS by *Burlison & Grylls*, of 1869–72 and later, under *Scott*'s careful supervision and consequently good to architectural effect. In the E window, a well-designed Crucifixion, and figures l. and r. in beautiful canopy-work. The other windows have mostly saints. – MONUMENTS. John Waspail †1448 and wife †1452. Large floor slab in the chancel with fragmentary brass inscription – Abigail, Lady Stawell †1692, 'relict' of Ralph, Lord Stawell, commemorated at Low Ham, Somerset. Large white and grey marble hanging tablet, in a decidedly individual style, perhaps by a West Country mason? Inscription between two standing putti l. and r. At the top, an oval medallion with bust in relief below a small achievement with fruity garland. At the foot a gruesomely pally demi-skeleton, leaning forward from a large acanthus bracket. – John Keate †1852, rector. Arched tomb-recess in the chancel, by *Scott*, 1868–70; brass signed *Waller*. Puginian Gothic cross, with central roundel of the *Agnus Dei*, with Evangelist emblems. Margaret Brown †1855. Black-letter brass inscription signed '*Waller* fecit', London.

HARTLEY COURT FARMHOUSE, W. Modest, late C18, brick, three bays with casements and canopied doorway. The large early C17 STABLE BLOCK served a now demolished great house. English bond with rows of vents, grouped in threes, to the upper floor. Some diaper-work. NW, a large moat encircles C17 MOAT COTTAGE. N, THE OLD RECTORY of *c.* 1842 (built to supersede Hartley House, *see* below). Neo-Tudor, brick, with mouldings in Roman cement. Two-storey porch.

PEMBROKE COTTAGE, ½ m. W in Hartley Lane. A pretty sight
with limewashed walls and long-straw thatch. A cruck house
of c. 1413. One-and-a-half-bay hall, with the cross-passage in
the half-bay, and a floored parlour end, the service bay rebuilt
in the C16. Four pairs of surviving crucks, the arch-braced hall
truss with low mantle beam.

HILL HOUSE FARMHOUSE, ½ m. ESE. A wonderfully isolated
site. An ambitious parlour cross-wing of brick, c. 1640 (the
windows and hipped roof are C18). Inside, on each floor are
high-quality Tudor-arched plastered brick fireplaces. Ground-
floor ceilings formerly plastered, with panelled spine beams.
The more modest timber-framed hall range cannot be much
earlier. Surely the intention was to rebuild it.

HARTLEY HOUSE, ½ m. N. Substantially enlarged for Dr John
Keate, c. 1833–4 (he resigned as Headmaster of Eton in the
latter year). Stuccoed with deep, bracketed eaves. Altered
c. 1900, porch added 1939. Brick STABLES with prominent
lunette.

HARTLEY WINTNEY

The medieval settlement was around the old parish church of St
Mary to the S of the present village, known as Hartley Row from
as early as the C17, which grew up on land claimed from greens
and commons that still provide the defining character. It
expanded in the late C18 and early C19 as a halt on the
London–Exeter coaching road, and is now the size of a small
town. On its periphery are a series of important houses, testament to the area's emergence as a centre for Hampshire's Arts
and Crafts Movement (cf. West Green). Weir Schultz and
Lethaby were residents (Lethaby at Albion, now Beech Cottage,
close to the Common) in the early C20, and Ernest Newton lived
nearby at Mattingley (q.v.).

ST JOHN THE EVANGELIST, Fleet Road. Quite large, of 1869–70
by *E. A. Lansdowne* of Newport, Gwent. Chancel altered 1897
by *A. R. Barker*. Red brick and stone. Broad and spreading in
a Frenchy C13 style with plate tracery. The composition is very
disjointed, the anticlimax being the starved polygonal NW
turret. Wide transepts, polygonal apse. Better interior, enriched
with much naturalistic carving, especially in the Bath stone
capitals of the six-bay arcades. Good recent reordering of
the chancel (sparing the well-designed CHOIR STALLS by *Sir
Charles Nicholson*, 1929) and the W end, the latter by *J. Lunn-
Rockliffe*, with an excellent resiting of the organ. – LECTERN.
A brass eagle to James Tennant Lyon the stained-glass designer
†1872. Panelling and war memorial screens in the S transept.
By *Sir Charles Nicholson*, 1919. – STAINED GLASS. In the
chancel by *Powells*, 1893; S transept windows by *Lavers, Barraud
& Westlake* of 1882 and W window of 1883. N transept windows

by *Margaret Rope*, 1937–9. Highly finished Arts and Crafts with scenes of St Francis of Assisi and St Nicholas. W extension planned in 2009.

St Mary (Churches Conservation Trust), Church Lane. In a still rural setting on a low hill with fine eastward views. Charming exterior. The tiny chancel partly of puddingstone rubble, disproportionately small in relation to the nave, is probably the earliest part: C11 or early C12 in its masonry (T. D. Powell in the early C19 referred to a 'Saxon' chancel arch now lost and Professor John Potter has found evidence of Anglo-Saxon quoins). The long nave has late C13 to early C14 details suggesting later enlargement or a rebuilding possibly for Hartley Wintney Priory, who owned the living from *c.* 1340. Tall brick transepts, in a debased Tudor Perp by *William Gover* of Winchester, of 1834, when the interior was renewed. Modest pinnacled W porch-tower in flint of 1843. Inside, the tower, a good original C13 W doorway. Also genuine are a few minor windows. One is of two lights with a spherical triangle in bar tracery, *c.* 1240. Inside, a niche in the nave E wall. The interior, left alone since the building of St John in 1870, has a hauntingly Late Georgian atmosphere. Brick-tiled floors, tall box pews, and three GALLERIES (one to each transept, the other at the W end) with Gothic panelled fronts bearing single HATCHMENTS (two to the Hawleys of West Green House, the other to General Sir Robert Sloper †1802). Nice ROYAL ARMS of 1705. DECALOGUE of 1834 over the chancel arch. The chancel fittings are earlier: PILLAR PISCINA. Late C12 with a plain foliage capital (VCH). – COMMUNION TABLE, dated 1636, with nice scrolly volutes. – COMMUNION RAILS, with twisted balusters; early C18. – WALL PAINTINGS. In the nave, on the N wall, traces of an early to mid-C14 scheme, found in 1977. Of these, the Seven Deadly Sins and part of a St Christopher are the best-preserved. An unidentified subject with horses has mystified experts. MONUMENT. Edith Lethaby †1927. Engaging small wooden mural tablet, with arched relief of a pigeon perched on an oak branch. Was it designed and carved by her husband *W. R. Lethaby*, †1931? Their grave marker in the churchyard is inscribed with Lethaby's maxim 'Love and Labour are All'.

s of the church several charming C18 headstones (e.g. John Taplyn †1730, a farmer, with fat bucolic cherubs by the s wall) and table tombs to Gibletts (dates of 1816 and 1826, the earlier tomb signed *Lee*, Odiham). *Robert Schultz Weir* †1951 and his wife. Carved wooden grave markers to his own design. By him also the LYCHGATE of 1927. In NE corner a large ledger to Lord Alanbrooke †1963, with the Field Marshal's achievement.

Baptist church, High Street. Simple classical of two phases: 1807 for the core with round-arched side windows, extended at the rear with a manse soon after. Front of *c.* 1830–40. Brick, with a pair of giant pilasters carrying an arch, which sticks into the broken pediment and frames an arched window. Large, plain round-arched stucco panels l. and r. Early C19 mural tablets on the rear.

METHODIST CHURCH, High Street. 1905, Perp style. S window
of 1919 by *George Farmiloe & Sons*.

VICTORIA HALL, West Green Road. 1898 by *T. E. Collcutt*. Arts
and Crafts Tudor Gothic village hall. Large roof sweeping
down over low buttressed aisles with glazing under the eaves,
the front with a large arched window flanked by circular stair-
towers. Triangular dormer and tall chimneystack on S side. At
the rear, EDWARD HALL, added *c.* 1910. Intelligent and well-
detailed extension of 1999–2000, by *Low Somorjay Talliss*.

PERAMBULATION. HIGH STREET has little earlier than the early
C18. On the NW side, facing the common, THE LIMES, a
c. 1800 villa distinguished by a pair of semi-elliptical bays with
tripartite sashes, each side of a porch with very thin columns.
Further E the street widens as it builds up on both sides.
ST KITTS HOUSE, early C19, was originally of three bays with
tripartite sashes and central doorcase with reeded pilasters and
open pediment, extended l. *c.* 1840 and given a large projecting shopfront, with pretty cast-iron Gothic railings. Further on,
the Neo Georgian LLOYDS BANK, 1927–8 by *Horace Field*,
which has sashes with oculi above (inspired by West Green
House?). On the SE side a good early C19 run ending with the
charming shop of A. W. PORTER & SON, watchmakers. Door
case with reeded pilasters and open pediment, and good Victorian shopfronts. HARES LANE forks N from High Street.
Further up, the early C17 OLD MANOR HOUSE, timber-
framed with a jetty and a pair of large tile-hung gables; much
restored and extended *c.* 1900? HARE'S FARMHOUSE, ¼ m.
N, is *c.* 1700, brick with modillion eaves cornice, and very
stately. Five widely spaced bays with cross-windows and
doorway with flat canopy on bold consoles. In BRACKLEY
AVENUE houses by *Schultz Weir* for the Fleet builders *Pool &
Son*, 1926.

CAUSEWAY FARMHOUSE, SE at Causeway Green. Mainly C18
brick, with a Neo-Jacobean remodelling of 1850, probably by
S. S. Teulon, then at work at Elvetham (q.v.). Good BARN of
three C16 bays, extended by a single bay at each end in the
C17. C18 lean-tos and porch.

HARTLEY GRANGE, Grange Lane, ¾ m. SW. Early C18, originally of 2–1–2 bays, the centre recessed with Venetian window
but extended, and rather unconvincingly remodelled in thin
Neo-Jacobean, in 1869 by *William Burn* for William Walkin-
shaw, a Scottish banker.

WEST GREEN HOUSE *see* WEST GREEN.

PHOENIX GREEN
½ m. SW

A fascinating group of buildings associated with *R. Weir Schultz*
who in 1899 (while working at West Green House) bought 26
acres of land with A. W. Pearce and Charles Read Seymour,
son of the rector of Winchfield (q.v.). One of a pair of old barns

on the site became the nucleus of Schultz's own home (now WEIR'S BARN) from *c.* 1901, with a wing added *c.* 1911–12 at the time of his marriage. He lived here until his death in 1951. Modest and cottagey with no attempt to retain the feel of a barn except in general outline. Elm weatherboarding and tile roofs with painted wooden casements. The front has that characteristic Arts and Crafts device of a row of three gables (e.g. Schultz's own Scalers Hill, Cobham), with under the r. one the entrance with bracketed flat hood and the inscription: PARVA DOMUS/MAGNA QUIES (small house, great peace). Gabled wing to the r. At the rear, an outshot over a continuous veranda, behind which are French casements with louvred shutters, and above which are three flat-topped dormers, the middle one dated 1911. Gabled wing to l. with full-height three-light mullioned window. Inside, galleried hall with ornamental plasterwork. Quintessential Arts and Crafts GARDEN also by Schultz consisting of a sequence of formal spaces with much yew topiary. At the front, a T-plan brick and timber PERGOLA and at the rear, a sunken garden with, on two sides, old open-fronted timber-framed SHEDS. The garden clearly extended further than it does now and included, to the N on Thackham's Lane, the very simple BARN COTTAGE, a gardener's cottage of brick with painted weatherboarded gable and Schultz's trademark glazed lozenge panel in the door.

s of Weir's Barn, Schultz built *c.* 1908 a pair of small brick houses on his land. Both are clever variations on a theme: MAYFIELD, with a pair of rendered gables, the l. one bisected by a chimneystack, and a pretty segmental-arched wooden porch, and ROSEMARY, with a large rendered gable to the r., a similar segmental-arched porch and a curious scatter of small flat-topped dormers.

(To the w, HARTLEY PLACE, formerly The Croft, by *Schultz* for Pearce, 1901–2. This has a more vertical emphasis and, originally, a tighter plan than one associates with Arts and Crafts houses. The striking SW front has a pair of large brick gables, the upper parts projecting as small weatherboarded gables over full-height canted plastered bays. Later additions.)

PARKER'S CLOSE, NW in Thackham's Lane, is by *Schultz* for the Misses Peebles, 1923. Beautifully proportioned and deceptively simple, with plastered ground floor, boarded first floor and hipped roof, carried down over outshots at each end. *See* also West Green and Mattingley.

HATHERDEN

CHRIST CHURCH. 1856–7 by *William White*, in his familiar muscular Gothic. Flint and brick bands. Nave and apse in one (cf. Smannell).★ Half-hipped double bellcote with chimney

---

★ Hatherden and Smannell were part of an independent district chapelry of Andover from 1858.

attached. It is supported by two buttresses with their set-offs in profile. Plate tracery. Incongruous metal roof, by *Richard Sawyer*, of the rebuilding 1976–7 following a fire. (FONT. By *Aldermaston Pottery*. Ceramic with hand-painted leaf decoration.) Fragment of STAINED GLASS by *Kempe*, 1885, reused.

HATHERDEN SCHOOL, NE of the church. Founded 1725 by the will of James Sambourn, an Andover wool merchant, and opened in 1727 as recorded, with writing-master's flourishes, in a pretty oval tablet above the door, with putti and flowers in the spandrels and crowned by a shield of arms. The house itself is C17, rebuilt in brick with a lobby-entry plan (cf. Old School, Sherfield-on-Loddon). Several C19 and C20 additions.

MICHAELMAS HOUSE, SW of the church. The former vicarage, *c.* 1865, almost certainly by *White*. Quietly domestic. Not Gothic. Good wooden staircase, typical of White.

HATHERDEN HOUSE, ¼ m. NE. C18. Painted brick. Five bays with stone-columned loggia, of 1938 by *A. J. Hardwick*. Flanking wings, the three-bay dining room to the r. of *c.* 1800, the upper storey added 1938. Small park.

HAUGHURST HILL *see* BAUGHURST

HAWKLEY

7020

ST PETER AND ST PAUL. 1864–5 by *S. S. Teulon*, for James Maberley of Hawkley Hurst. The site is of a small Norman chapel of ease perhaps inspiring the Neo-Norman, or rather mixed Continental Romanesque, style unfavoured among the High Victorians. Chalk, the walls in a crazy paving. Tall and impressively plain w tower with a Sompting top, i.e. Rhenish Romanesque. Tall w doorway with sculptured tympanum, with vine leaves around a central emblem, in low relief. The room inside is rib-vaulted. The E (chancel) arch is thickly Anglo-Norman with naturalistic capitals, imaginatively composed. The tall three-bay N and S arcades, with round piers on high bases, have very different capitals of decidedly Italian Romanesque form, with emblems of Christ and the Evangelists. Open timbered roof on corbels with scriptural foliage. The true Teulon comes through in the aisle roofs and fenestration. The windows are arranged symmetrically l. and r. of a gabled rose window with plate tracery. Anglo-Norman again, and richly appointed, is the entry from the N aisle to the N chapel, with two round-headed arches and an open roundel all with dogtooth. More luxuriant carving around the altar and the E windows in the chancel. – FONT, Late Norman of *c.* 1190. Purbeck marble, with crude painted text of 1845. – PISCINA, also from the earlier church, C13, with trefoil head. – TILES. On the sanctuary floor, possibly *Minton*, unusually white. –

104

ALTAR. In the N chapel. The former pulpit (by *Teulon*, 1877, but cut down when relocated in 1996), with nice decorative mosaic in grey and maroon, and a delightful crouching lion. – STAINED GLASS. E window, 1865 by *Ward & Hughes*. Chancel N, and N chapel windows (†1906), by *Powells*. N and S aisle 'roses', with central roundels possibly by *Lavers & Barraud*, 1865. N aisle w, by *T. F. Curtis, Ward & Hughes*, 1888. Tower window engraved by *Simon Whistler*, 2000. – LYCHGATE. Oddly Jacobean Gothic, dated 1859. *Teulon* provided sketch designs at this date for improving the earlier church.

HAWKLEY PLACE, SW beside Lower Green. Built around an earlier core *c.* 1880, in Norman Shaw's Old English style. Brick with timber-framed and tile-hung gables, on the entrance side a Gothic doorway and large gabled oriel lighting the staircase.

HAWKLEY HURST, I m. NNE. Of *Teulon*'s country house of 1860–1 for James Maberley, there survives only a circular stair-turret with characteristically crazy stonework, steep conical roof and lancets, incorporated in the service wing of the Neo-Elizabethan house of 1914 by *Granville S. Streatfeild*. Formal GARDEN by *Gertrude Jekyll*, 1914, partly preserved: E terrace, axial rustic pool with flanking steps below terrace wall, and pergola. Set into the terrace wall is stonework from Teulon's house.

HAWLEY AND BLACKWATER

Hawley was once a small settlement on the heathlands of the Hampshire–Surrey border, but engulfed by the C19 and C20 expansion of the larger village of Blackwater to the N and Fleet to the S. Even forty years ago it was part of the continuous Farn-borough–Camberley conurbation.

HOLY TRINITY, Hawley Road/Fernhill Road. Red brick, quite large, of accretive growth with a prominent embraced w steeple, all consistently in the style of *c.* 1300. Of the first build-ing of 1837–8 by *Robert Ebbels* for the Rev. John Randell, nothing remains visible. After the 1850s the church was Trac-tarian and remains Anglo-Catholic; the nave was rebuilt and the N aisle added in 1856–7 by *J. B. Clacy*. The S aisle and the more ambitious apsidal rib-vaulted chancel and chancel arch are of 1867–8 by *Charles Buckeridge*, with naturalistic carving by *Harriet Wyatt*, wife of the vicar. Bold polychromy of brick and stone, showing the influence of Street and Scott (Buckeridge's master). Later additions include the tall broach-spired steeple of 1882–3,* and the apsidal lancet-windowed N chapel of 1907–8 by *Arnold Hoole*. The church is more richly furnished than most in this part of Hampshire. In the chancel

---

* Buckeridge's design for the tower and spire, considered rather heavy, was modi-fied by *Arnold Hoole*.

an original scheme: REREDOS of Caen stone by *Redfern*, arcading on Connemara shafts, a central alabaster cross, and mosaics by *Daniel Bell*. Also by him, figures l. and r. in diapered backgrounds. – TILES, richest around the altar. By *Godwin*. – CHOIR STALLS. With open arcaded fronts and nicely shaped ends. In the nave, the elaborate PULPIT of stone dated 1857. No doubt by *Clacy*. – FONT, by *Buckeridge*, carved by *Harriet Wyatt*, on a floor of *Minton* tiles. – FONT COVER. By *Oskar Zwink* of Oberammergau. An unusual *tableau vivant* memorial to Field Marshal John Simmons †1903. – STAINED GLASS. Throughout of *c.* 1857–1908 by different makers, the earliest in the N chapel by *Wailes*, re-set from the former chancel. At the E end, a scheme by *Clayton & Bell*. Also by them, the colourful S chapel gable window *c.* 1868. In the N aisle much by *Ward & Hughes* and a composite W window, by *Hardman* and *Wailes*. N chapel lancets of 1908 by *Heaton, Butler & Bayne*. Good, with Christ and airborne angels.

The church stands at the NE corner of HAWLEY GREEN. On the W side, HENRY RANDELL'S ALMSHOUSES of 1857, a symmetrical composition of central two-storey gabled block with pretty gabled timber bellcote, linked by low wings to gabled pavilions. To the S, the timber-framed MEMORIAL HALL, Late Arts and Crafts of 1921 by *J. D. Coleridge* with pairs of tall Lutyens-esque hipped bays.

HAWLEY PARK, ½ m. S. A probably mid-C18 double-pile house, stuccoed in the early C19, with Neo-Georgian alterations of *c.* 1900 outside and in. Very fine mid-C18 STABLES (clock dated 1743), quite similar to those at Dogmersfield Park (q.v.). Three single-storey brick ranges with the show front to the house. Pairs of lunettes flanking a central pedimented pavilion with stone quoins and pedimented Tuscan doorcase. Above, a square bellcote with ogee lead cap.

RANDELL HOUSE, Fernhill Road, ¾ m. S. Originally All Saints Home for Girls, built 1881–2 at the expense of Charles Randell, cousin of the founder of Holy Trinity (q.v.), for children of the London slums. Interesting CHAPEL at the rear (later All Saints Church, superseded in 1976 by the church in Fernhill Road) by *Arnold Hoole*, 1882, in French C13 Gothic.

HEADBOURNE WORTHY
4030

A small dispersed settlement among water meadows, fish ponds and watercress beds, holding its own against the sprawl of Kings Worthy (q.v.). The church, placed close to the old pilgrim route to the shrine of St Swithun at Winchester, stands in a delightful woody churchyard encircled by streams of the Head Bourne, a modest tributary of the Itchen. The scattered, straggly village is at a distance to the W.

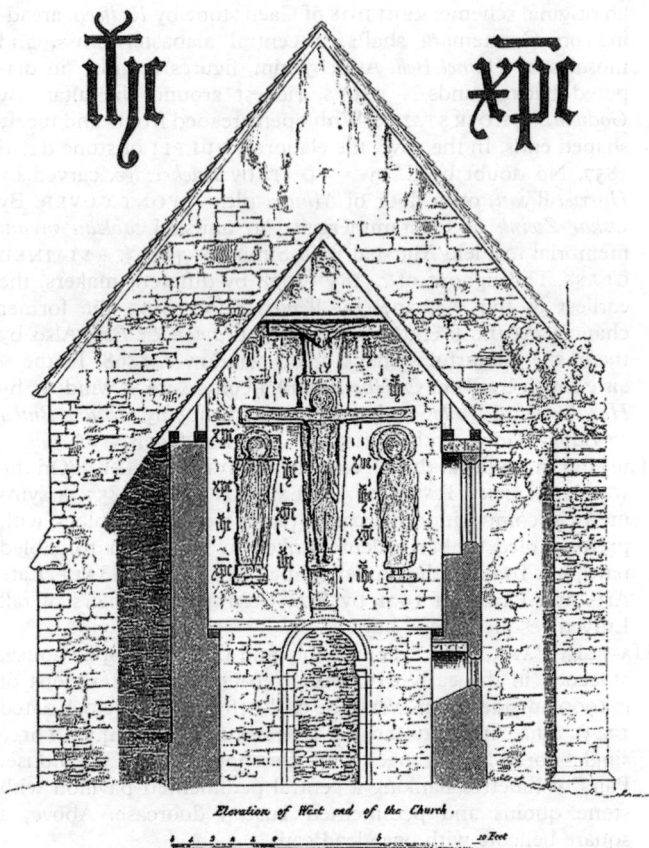

Elevation of West end of the Church.

Headbourne Worthy, St Swithun, elevation.
Engraving by Owen Browne Carter, C19

ST SWITHUN. A fascinating, essentially Late Saxon church of
  c. 1030 with one treasure of international value. Some original, typically Late Saxon features of Quarr stone in the
  chancel, especially the long-and-short quoins (presumably *in
  situ* because the chancel was extended E in the C13 and partly
  rebuilt during the major restoration by *G. E. Street*, 1865–6),
  and one lesene. In the nave, also long-and-short work (e.g. the
  well-preserved NE quoin) and three lesenes on the N side.
  Inside, the well-preserved W doorway is narrow and high, with
  pilasters on stepped bases and an arched band of the same
  width. This doorway opens into the unusual early C16 W
  annexe where, above the doorway (i.e. on the outer W wall) is
  an overwhelming ROOD in relief: Christ, the Virgin and St John.
  Unfortunately they were chiselled off in the mid C16 by ill-
  advised fanatics when Robert Horne, Bishop of Winchester,

prohibited all roods and crucifixes, so that only the silhouettes remain. But they show that these were well over life-size figures, that the grouping was the same as at Breamore (South Hampshire), and that Christ resembled the Christ of Romsey (South Hampshire), and that above him – and this one part is intact – is the Hand of God appearing out of a cloud, exactly as at Romsey. The Continent about the year 1000 has nothing that can compare with this monumental three-figure group, which may be due to St Swithun's Priory, Winchester, allegedly holders of the church in Saxon times. The rood may have been specially venerated as a focus of devotion, and the annexe may have been built not only as a shelter, but to contain an upper chapel, possibly with a small low altar: there is evidence of an Early Tudor piscina high up in the s wall and faint traces of contemporary WALL PAINTING (a repeat pattern of IHS motifs) on the E wall around the rood. There was more of similar design on the s wall (see Owen Carter's drawing of c. 1845).

The sw tower is early C13 but reduced in height and given a weatherboarded timber upper stage, probably in the later C18 (inside, a bell-frame, perhaps contemporary with two bells, dated 1420 (pers. comm. C. Dalton). The nave s wall was rebuilt c. 1239, see the typically E.E. s doorway (restored with a trefoil-headed arch in the 1860s, also the date of the s porch) and the pretty trefoil-arched PISCINA, formerly with a canopy. Concurrently the chancel was lengthened, and given a triple SEDILIA of noble simplicity and strikingly original design. The arches have segmental heads resulting in a broad sweeping design that late C19 Arts and Crafts church architects like J. D. Sedding admired and emulated. Good early C13 two-light sw lowside window, with transom (cf. the similar, but larger, lateral windows of the Great Hall of Winchester Castle, 1222). The nave has early C15 buttresses and characteristically Early Perp windows, N and s. Perp also, the ribbed, open barrel roof with restored bosses. The correctly E.E. chancel arch is Street's replacement of a straight-sided arch shown in drawings of 1844. *J. B. Colson* made further repairs and underpinned the nave in 1907.

FONT. Plain of Quarr stone. Is it C13, perhaps re-cut? – FONT COVER. Elaborately carved by the *Rev. J. H. Slessor*, rector 1861–1905, who also contributed the traceried backs of the CHOIR STALLS by *Street*, the Gothic framing of the ORGAN pipework and the READING STAND, with its two heads of Burgundian or German provenance. – DOORS. In the Saxon doorway, a C14 door (relocated from the coeval s door), and in the small Perp tower doorway an original door with strap hinges. – SCREEN. By *Harry Hems*, dated 1886. Three open-traceried gabled bays, clearly influenced by the early C14 Winchester Cathedral choir stall arcading. – WEST GALLERY. Utilitarian but well positioned. By *Stephens, Cox & Associates*, 1998. – STAINED GLASS. A small C15 angel in the w annexe's s window. Brought from Talaton church, Devon. Elsewhere, almost every window is by *Ward & Hughes c.* 1867–*c.* 1882, much the best the chancel sw (†1871) with four Evangelists seated writing in the lower half. – MONUMENT. Brass to John Kent †1434, a scholar of Winchester College as recorded in the lower inscription. A lettered scroll thrown up above his head, inscribed in Latin.

HEADBOURNE WORTHY GRANGE, School Lane, sw. Built as the rectory in 1853. Unemphatic Neo-Tudor. The large wing to the r. appears to be slightly later. On the w side of a small triangular green, ¼ m. NW, the MANOR HOUSE with simple C18 brick front, and on the s, the OLD RECTORY, a timber-framed hall and cross-wing, much refaced in the C18. This was the late medieval rectory, but is largely indistinguishable from a yeoman's house of the period.

HEADLEY

(near Grayshott)

A parish of wooded valleys and meadows on the Weald edge.

ALL SAINTS. Essentially late C14 but damaged by fire in 1836 and drastically restored by *T. M. Flockton* of Sheffield, 1857–9, when the chancel was added and the nave s wall refaced in neatly coursed sandstone ashlar (in the vestry a Norman former priest's door, relocated from the N wall). The unbuttressed w tower of local sandstone rubble is Perp of *c.* 1380 and, unusually, only half the width of the nave, allowing for a coeval three-light window of local type (cf. Bramshott) in the w wall. Characterful Gothic battlements and pinnacles of 1838. s porch with some C14 timbers. The window E of the porch is of a standard Perp pattern by Henry Yevele (cf. Westminster Hall) correctly replicated in 2000. Inside the nave, a remarkably fine late C14 roof, 26 ft (8 metres) wide. Five bays with half-bays to E and w. Crisply carved moulded wall-plates, crown-posts and struts. Contemporary tower arch. – REREDOS of 1882. Elaborately carved stone panels. – CHOIR STALLS, with effective panelled fronts of alternating linenfold and tracery. – SCREEN of 1892 by *Sir Robert Rowand Anderson* (a rare example of his work outside Scotland). – PULPIT. Open-traceried Perp of 1887. – PAINTINGS. Moses and Aaron, accomplished C18, relocated from the E end. – STAINED GLASS. In the chancel N window, brought in during the C19, is an exquisite, intensely colourful, oblong C13 panel, the greater part of a larger medallion showing the decapitation of a sainted queen. – Much C19–early C20 glass: E window, 1874, by *H. Hughes*; nave N easternmost of 1891, by *Heaton, Butler & Bayne*, to the architect Edward I'Anson (†1888) buried in the churchyard. s second from E. 1902 by *Powells*, to Edward Frineby Hubbuck. Standard archangels, SS Gabriel and Michael from clearly 'stock' designs also used at Alton (St Lawrence), Bentworth and East Lavant (Sussex). Two other

Headley, Benifold (formerly Pinehurst).
Engraving, 1900

windows by *Powells*, on N (dates of 1901 and 1917) W window
of 1894 by *A. L. Moore*, with elaborate scenes under canopies.
– MONUMENTS. Brass, by the font, to a couple of *c.* 1510. –
Three good tablets of the mid to late C18; especially that to
William Huggins, †1761, translator of Ariosto, whose grounds
at Heath House (now Headley Park) were laid out by him with
a classical temple to the poet. – In the churchyard, a good
headstone to Elizabeth Lee †1768 and John Lee †1769, by the
vestry. – Further W, an Italianate headstone to the architect
and surveyor Edmund Woodthorpe †1887. LYCHGATE, of
1954, supervised by *C. K. Johnson-Burt*.
WAR MEMORIAL, E of the church. Dignified design in Portland
stone with curved wall between square piers.
To the N in HIGH STREET is the mid-C18 RECTORY with greensand front. Five bays with boldly moulded string courses and
pedimented dormers behind a high panelled parapet. To the S
is SUTERS, a Wealden house possibly built in the early C16 as
a church house, the hall floored and the front rebuilt in stone
in the late C16. (Inside the parlour has a fine stone fireplace
with quatrefoil-carved spandrels and wall paintings with flower
and bird motifs.) E in Crabtree Lane, overlooking the green,
OLD HOLME SCHOOL and the OLD SCHOOL HOUSE, comprising the master's house of the free school founded 1755 by
the Rev. George Holme, of galleted greensand with string
course and hipped roof, and enlargements for the school of
1872 in a minimal Tudor Gothic with hipped porch and bellcote in the gable, and 1893–4, with tile-hanging etc.
ARFORD HOUSE ¼ m. NE in a steep-sided valley. Pretty early
C19 stuccoed Gothic villa with adjoining stable/coachhouse
wing at lower level. Tucked into the opposite side of the valley
to the E is HIGH BANK, of 1963 by *Murray, Ward & Partners*
(job architect: *George Buzak*). Wedge-shaped single-storey

pavilion, timber-clad timber frame on a horizontal steel base. Fully glazed end wall cantilevered out on steel posts. Enlarged with brick additions of the 1990s.

BENIFOLD (formerly Pinehurst), Headley Hill, ½ m. E on wooded slopes. By *A. C. Blomfield*, 1898–1900. Gabled front roughcast in Norman Shaw's manner, the rear Neo-Georgian (a late change of plan), brick with full-height canted bay and gables with oculi. Nearby, WINDRIDGE (formerly THE CHALET), of *c.* 1876 by *Edward I'Anson*, with odd semicircular shaped bargeboards and *œil de bœuf* windows.

HEADLEY GRANGE, Hurland Lane, ½ m. SE. Former workhouse of 1795, long and narrow, of stone with mansard roof (cf. Alton) with original walled yard at the rear, a rare survival. Remodelled *c.* 1870 as a house in a High Victorian Gothic style.

HEADLEY MILL and MILL HOUSE, ¾ m. SW on the Wey. An attractive C18 and early C19 group of the river's last working mill. Breast-shot wheel of 1927 and four pairs of stones. Nearby WEY HOUSE, timber and stone farmhouse, *c.* 1500 with later C16 and C17 additions. On the roadside a pretty pyramidal-roofed former hop kiln.

HEADLEY

(near Kingsclere)

A largely C19 settlement that grew up on the edge of Headley Common, close to the Berkshire border.

ST PETER. 1867–8 by *Edwin Dolby*, built for £456. A simple Street-like job in red brick, banded in blue with Bath stone details. Hipped-roofed SE vestry with tiny stone bellcote. STAINED GLASS. SW window, early C20. Two angels.

CHEAM SCHOOL, ½ m. S. Formerly Beenham Court. 1911–12 by *Blow & Billerey* in later C17 style, clearly inspired by Heale House, Wiltshire (restored by Blow in 1910). W front of five bays with tall stone cross-windows, the centre projecting as a two-storey porch, with pediment. It partly incorporates a house of *c.* 1880, whose brickwork is partly visible on the compromised S front and the E side. This is now the entrance front and has a single-storey addition by Blow with a large mullioned-and-transomed window, flanked by porches at the corners with open *serliana* to the front and sides. Two-storey CLASSROOM WING of 1934, by *Fox & Shearer* on the courtyard's N side. Very large mullioned-and-transomed stone windows. Adjoining late C20 extension by *Mervyn Orchard-Lisle*, of similar form.

The Edwardian INTERIORS are in a rich variety of C17 and C18 styles, notably the Saloon, which has bolection-moulded panelling and Mannerist style overmantel with lugged architrave around an early C18 female portrait, and Corinthian pilasters supporting an open pediment set within a wide

scrolled pediment. Impressive full-height Staircase Hall, its
upper part with giant Corinthian pilasters and a full entablature, above which is a lantern with an enriched plaster ceiling.
At the foot of the stairs three inventive Mannerist doorcases,
that to the Saloon with a floating segmental pediment within
a similarly floating triangular pediment, that to the Drawing
Room with an open scrolled pediment and to the rear hall an
archway with three-quarter Corinthian columns and a broad
open segmental pediment. What are the sources for these? The
former Billiard Room has an unusual marble chimneypiece
with fluted quadrant pilasters at the corners, an ogee curved
top leading to an integral glazed cabinet above. Formal sunken
GARDEN with rectangular pool and canal.

HILL HOUSE, Hillhouse Lane, 1 m. ESE. Designed c. 1969, built
1970–2, by *Denys Lasdun & Partners* for Timothy Sainsbury;
extended by the same firm c. 1984–5 and 1998–2001 by *John
Robertson Architects*. Of two storeys, long and low with a flat
roof, built of *in situ* reinforced concrete with concrete blockwork walling. A monumental building, in which the architect's
early interest in Le Corbusier and in particular the Villa Savoie
can be seen at once. Cruciform plan, its long NE–SW axis
aligned on the ridge of the hilltop site and centred around a
full-height staircase hall, which is flanked by private rooms on
the cross-axis. At the head of the cross (SW) is a full-height
drawing room and at the corresponding end, on the central
axis, is a porte cochère to the discreet entrance and a long
service wing which has garaging at ground floor and, at the far
end, the boiler house with distinctive shuttered circular
chimney. The EXTERIOR is characteristic of Lasdun's mature
period in the use of deep shuttered concrete beams at first-
floor and at roof level, where the transverse beams extend
above the flat roof and project, singly at the outer edges of the
side wings but paired at the centre and at the SW elevation.
This vertical counterpoint to the over-riding horizontality of
the design is reminiscent on a smaller scale of the National
Theatre. On the elevations of the side wings the top floor over-
sails, with floor-to-ceiling glazing at ground floor but just a
strip lighting the first floor (the windows were replaced in
1984). In the symmetrical SW elevation the walls to l. and r.
are blank at first floor except for two vertical slits but in the
centre projects the drawing room with an asymmetrical composition of full-height window with a pair of doors to its r.,
beneath a daringly cantilevered balcony. An early scheme had
a circular staircase descending from this.

The main Hall is a relative of the entrance hall at the Royal
College of Physicians (1961–4) with the staircase rising up the
r. side, its solid reinforced concrete balustrade with a metal
handrail, to a gallery on three sides. Clerestory lighting from
above in strips. A secondary staircase rises behind the l. wall
and is glimpsed through squints. From the hall, a glazed
doorway leads up steps into the full-height drawing room
beyond. From here a staircase rises up to a continuation of the

stair-hall gallery, which extends through the outer wall as the balcony seen outside. An island hearth with a white flue separates this double-height space from a small single-height area, which extends onto a covered NW terrace. The family rooms occupy the wings flanking the hall, those on the SE side for the children.

The extensions to the house follow its precedent in materials and details. SWIMMING POOL, NW of the house. Sunken with a barrel-vaulted roof, built *c.* 1984–5. Close to it is the wing 1998–2001, Lasdun's final work and developed from his outline plans by *John Robertson Architects*. This too is semi-sunken, screened from the garden by a concrete block wall, with a large circular window. Behind is a circular LIBRARY, with a curved concrete roof-light of semicircular plan that reads as a dome from the NW. The landscaping around the house is by *Michael Brown*, including a ha-ha.

HECKFIELD

ST MICHAEL. Well-preserved W tower of *c.* 1500. Coursed brown conglomerate in a Sarsen base with brick quoins, formerly rendered. Prominent higher SE stair-turret and battlements. Inside, a brick arch (now plastered) to the nave. Low stone doorway with windows with four-centred arches. Also early C16, the N chapel, with a brick window in the E gable: there is an inscription from the brass of John Cresswell †1518 who was 'lord of this towne at the tyme of the bylding of this stepyle and the new yle'. In 1876–7 *Butterfield* restored the chancel and nave and rebuilt the N aisle in a hard Dec; the renewed Perp chancel E window (inserted after 1383 when Winchester College took the advowson and of standard Wynford type) seems trustworthy. Inside, Butterfield removed a brick arcade with octagonal columns of *c.* 1500 for a four-bay stone arcade. Ribbed barrel ceiling in nave, canted in chancel and chapel.

FURNISHINGS. Mostly *Butterfield*'s, except the FONT of *c.* 1350, Purbeck marble, large octagonal bowl with tracery of diagonally set pointed quatrefoils. The rest, a typical Butterfield ensemble: in the chancel, a marble REREDOS, geometrical patterned dado and panels on the E wall. CHOIR STALLS and TILES. In the nave, a fine wooden PULPIT, brass eagle lectern (to Viscount Eversley, *see* below) and the more traditional Perp-style PEWS. – Brass CANDLE-STANDS throughout, a precious survival. – STAINED GLASS. Nave easternmost. Outstanding, of 1885 by *Morris & Co.* Graceful females of Charity and Faith by *Burne-Jones* on exquisite virile foliage. – Chancel E by *Clayton & Bell* of 1877. Ascension. – Chancel SE. 1884 probably by *Heaton, Butler & Bayne* to the Crimean General Sir William Codrington. Archangels.

MONUMENTS. Quite an array of early C16 to C20 tablets. Brass in the N chapel, John (†1514) and Elizabeth Hall. 15-in.

(38-cm.) figure of her, 'quorum sumptibus hec capella con-
structa' ('at whose expense this chapel was built'). In the
chancel several engaging small alabaster monuments with
kneelers facing one another, especially Thomas Creswell
†1607. – Anthony Sturt †1692, of a Dorset family seated at
Horton and More Crichel. Handsome early Dorset Baroque
hanging tablet erected 1724 in N chapel. Large and heavy with
long inscription above gadrooning and below an armorial cartouche. Possibly by *Thomas Cartwright* of Blandford. – General
Sir William Augustus Pitt, of another Dorset landed family
†1809 and his wife †1818, signed by *John Bacon Jun.* and
Samuel Manning. Large tablet of white marble. Big inscription.
Above it very big obelisk. At its foot a blank arch and in front
of it a disconsolate woman lying over two caskets. Flanking
panels of poppies. Quite moving. – Charles Shaw-Lefevre
†1823. By *J. Browne*, 1836. Marble tablet without figures, but
with cherub's heads in draperies as base supports. – Emma,
Viscountess Eversley †1857. A delicate Gothic lozenge-shaped
tablet by *Butterfield* at his most refined. – Neville Chamberlain
†1940, Prime Minister, who died at Highfield Park. A crisply
lettered stone tablet.

HIGHFIELD PARK (Conference Centre). Early C18 N front with
mid-C19 embellishments. L-shaped wing, once stuccoed, of
c. 1817, when it became the dower house for Stratfield Saye
(q.v.). Its nine-bay W front has full-height elliptical bows. The
centre of the S front slightly projects with a single-storey Ionic
portico, the end bays with blind openings, containing oculi and
round-headed niches. Austere Neo-Georgian residential addition on the site of the E service court, 1982–3 by *Robert Adam*.
Series of charming early C19 rooms inside, including oval room
behind one of the bows and top-lit oval staircase hall, the cantilevered sweeping staircase with wrought-iron balustrade.
Good original plasterwork and chimneypieces. Minor alterations in 1910 by *Horace Farquharson*. In the garden to the NE
an early C18 SUMMER SEAT, stone with Doric colonnade surmounted by cartouche. Inside, plaster casts of the Parthenon
frieze.

HECKFIELD MEMORIAL HALL and LADY EVERSLEY'S
ALMSHOUSES. 1863, by *Butterfield*. Attractive single-storey
courtyard group. Brick with diaper, stone dressings and timber
framing. Low wall on W side incorporates a charming pyramidal-roofed WELL-HOUSE.

HIGHFIELD FARM, ¼ m. NW. Pretty C18 house with pilasters
picked out in vitrified headers, coved plaster cornice and traceried Gothic windows.

HECKFIELD PLACE (Conference Centre), ¾ m. NE. *c.* 1780–90,
for John Lefevre. A three-storey double-pile brick box, five bays
to front and back. The two-storey wings in a matching style
are shown in Prosser's view of 1833 but the two-storey canted
bays on the garden side are mid-C19, like the opulent interiors.
Unremarkable residential additions of 1981–4 incorporate the
decent C18 brick STABLE BLOCK, with round-arched openings
and ogee-capped cupola. PARK and PLEASURE GROUNDS with

lakes, landscaped for Charles Shaw-Lefevre I *c.* 1818. The celebrated GARDENS were laid out for Charles Shaw-Lefevre II (from 1857 Viscount Eversley) by his head gardener *William Walker Wildsmith*; there remains the TERRACE with strapwork balustrade, extant by 1833, and a series of artificial stone flower baskets.

WELLINGTON COUNTRY PARK, ½ m. N. Created from parkland of the Stratfield Saye estate. VISITORS' CENTRE, 1975, by *Leonard Manasseh & Partners* (job architect: *John Thake*). An attractive low steel-framed building with a series of pyramidal roofs. To the E a restaurant pavilion.

6040   HERRIARD

Of the village only a few earthworks survive in the park of Herriard House, seat of the Jervoise family since 1601.

ST MARY. Sir Richard de Herriard (†1221) may have built the church *c.* 1200, yet the nave looks Norman with ashlar clasping buttresses and two small round-headed S lancets, of a typically C12 tradition dying late in Hampshire. The chancel is indeed early C13 with the lateral lancets enriched inside by their continuous roll mouldings. Late C14 Perp E window, possibly paid for by Hartley Wintney Priory, holders of the advowson from 1333. The fine wide chancel arch was much restored in 1876–7 by *J. Colson*, who left a heavy impression on the interior, but parts of the arch's rich mouldings and the hoodmould with dogtooth are original E.E. In date this goes with the tower S doorway, re-set from the nave S wall, and which has the same kind of hoodmould. The tower itself, and the N aisle, are by Colson. – (AUMBRY. Found in 1882, low down behind the altar, the usual place for relics in a smaller church.) – REREDOS of 1884, by *Harry Hems*. Dramatic Last Supper, in high relief and viewpoint. Figures of Christ (l. and r.). – *Minton* TILES on chancel floor. – CHOIR STALLS, artistically carved with Jervoise crest on the stall ends. – PULPIT and PEWS in the same Street-like Gothic style. – SCREEN, dated 1634, relocated from the Jervoise family pew. With basket arches and geometrical ornament in the frieze. – STAINED GLASS. A delightful small St Margaret, exquisitely drawn in outline. From a tracery light of the E window, alas crudely cropped, among other C14–C15 fragments in the chancel SW lowside window. C15 achievement of Popham. E window, commemorating the 1870s restoration. By *Ward & Hughes* (signed *H. Hughes*). Indifferent Nativity scene. Nave, S, easternmost. 1904 by *Powell*. 2nd from E, to Edwyn Jervoise †1955 'a lover of ancient bridges', with a glowing St Christopher and child, 1961 by *Hugh Powell*. Also by him: nave SW, N aisle NE (†1967) and the good tower window of 1968 with large Byzantine jewelled cross and Christ in majesty.

MANOR FARMHOUSE, SE of the church. Late C17. Brick with hipped-roofed wings. Splat-baluster staircase.

Former SCHOOL, ¼ m. SE on the main road. 1851. Attractive High Victorian Gothic composition in brick with lattice glazing. Master's house (l.) with buttressed arcaded porch.

HERRIARD HOUSE, ¼ m. E of the church. An unremarkable   p. 52 house of 1966 by *Sir Martyn Beckett*, incorporating a few architectural fragments from its predecessor of 1703–6 for Thomas Jervoise by *John James* – his earliest known commission. Some older buildings survive SW including former STABLES of 1798, enlarged *c.* 1825. Gault brick front with raised quoins. Seven bays with round-arched windows, the middle three breaking forward with open pediment and round archway with lunette above. Octagonal Gothic wooden cupola with ogee cap. Inside the courtyard is all red brick, with two-storey side ranges.

George London designed the GARDENS; drawings date from 1699. They appear to have consisted of a series of parterres on a terraced area S of the house and a long avenue linking it to Hackwood to the N. George Purefoy Jervoise made extensive changes, implementing designs of 1792–3 by *Repton* for park and pleasure grounds. The octagonal WALLED GARDEN SW of the house was built in 1796 and was originally surrounded by a circular shrubbery walk. George Jervoise's improvements are evident in the number of attractive brick-built early C19 model ESTATE COTTAGES.

HYDE FARMHOUSE, I m. SE at Southrope. Late C17. L-plan. Brick with flared headers, string course and modillion eaves cornice. Prominent catslide roof towards the road, the main front to the E, originally of five bays, with entrance in a shallow central break. Fenestration much altered. Both the side and the rear of the S wing have similar central breaks, the side with a lobby-entry too. Inside, a fine dog-leg staircase with pulvinated string and twisted balusters.

HIGH CROSS
Froxfield

7020

ST PETER. 1861–2 by *E. H. Martineau*, at the expense of Joseph Martineau of Basing Park (Privett) and superseding St Peter at Froxfield (q.v.). Quite large with a long nave, N aisle, disproportionately small chancel and SW porch-tower. Flint, the roofs slated and restored with original diaper pattern. Plate tracery and pointed-trefoiled lancets, a large group of five at the W end. Good ironwork on S door. Inside, the surprise comes with the five-bay N arcade: the three W bays are late C12, from St Peter. Round piers, trumpet-scallop capitals, and one with small pellets on a kind of shovel shape. Unmoulded round arches. The chancel arch was enlarged when the chancel was improved by *Sir Arthur Blomfield & Sons* in 1893. By them the

REREDOS with a cross flanked by two angels with Passion emblems on a gold foliated surround. Stone frame with richly carved vines. Further alteration in the chancel of 1913–14 by *Comper* (e.g. the COMMUNION BENCHES, and 'black and white' chequer floor). – STAINED GLASS. The earliest in the chancel s windows with bright colourful patternwork (dates of 1849). E window of 1871, perhaps by *Heaton, Butler & Bayne*. A Crucifixion with rich fruited trees. w window, in the same style, to the founder †1863. Life of St Peter. Two nave windows by *Kempe* of 1901 and 1909. – Arts and Crafts LYCHGATE. 1902. By *E. Arden Minty*.

SCHOOL, opposite, by *Blomfield*, built by *Gammon* of Petersfield, 1875–6. Tile-hung and gabled.

ALEXANDER'S FARM, 1½ m. NW. One of the late C19 Basing Park estate farms, with a U-plan of buildings around a central (formerly covered) cattle yard.

4060

HIGHCLERE

An estate of the Bishops of Winchester by 1208 and the site of a palace, rebuilt by William of Wykeham in the late C14, all trace of which has vanished. Dominated by the later house and park, the village has been pushed to the w edge of the parish and is strung out along the Newbury–Andover road.

ST MICHAEL. 1869–70 by *George Gilbert Scott* for the 4th Earl of Carnarvon. Flint and stone with a NE steeple carrying a shingled splay-foot spire. The style is of *c.* 1300. Lancets and plate tracery. N porch of 1935–6 by *T. D. Atkinson*, the hall of same date, enlarged 1974 by *Ernest H. Paul*. Low and dark interior, with a well-detailed three-bay s arcade and richly moulded chancel arch with naturalistic capitals. The chancel has a rose window in the E wall, and shafted N and s windows, the shafts being detached. The ALTAR composition is entirely part of it, with arcading framing panel PAINTINGS of 1892–4 by *Fairfax Murray*, a pupil of Burne-Jones. Effective figures on gold backgrounds, after Fra Angelico. LITANY DESK, now in the chancel. Elaborately carved in Scott's most sumptuous manner. In the nave, FONT and PULPIT by *Scott*, carved by *Farmer & Brindley*. – ORGAN CASE. Free Late Gothic by *F. E. Howard* (*The Warham Guild*), 1930. – STAINED GLASS. E and w windows by *Hardman*, 1872. Chancel sw by *Powell*, to the founder †1890. Musical scene with St Cecilia and a choir of angels. Chancel N and nave N windows by *Lavers & Westlake*. s aisle E by *Kempe* to the 3rd Countess of Carnarvon †1876. The best of the collection, with four angel musicians in elaborate draperies.

– MONUMENTS. Several of before 1870 transferred from the old church: Richard Kingsmill †1600. Late Elizabethan. By *Isaac James* and *Bartholomew Atye*. A long, standing monument. Recumbent effigy and to his l. two smaller kneeling figures, his daughter Constance and her husband Sir Thomas Lucy. Columns l. and r. Open top. Against the tomb-chest the kneeling children. – Sir Robert Sawyer, Speaker of the House of Commons †1692. A fine metropolitan standing monument, worthy of Gibbons, attributed to *James Hardy* (GF). Black and white marble. Reredos type. Draperies looped up to reveal a singularly small curved base and on it a skull with a laurel wreath. Top urn with garlands. – Several classical tablets, the best to Dr Thomas Milles, Chaplain to Thomas, Earl of Pembroke, Bishop of Waterford and Lismore †1740. Signed *Charles Frederick* invt. and *L. F. Roubiliac* sculpt. Sir Charles Frederick was Surveyor General of the Ordnance. Hanging monument with a big black basalt urn (a replica of the original) and to its l. a white genius extinguishing a torch. On the r. two books, one of them *Cyrilli Opera*, an edition of which Milles had published in 1703. Not one of Roubiliac's masterpieces, unfortunately divided in two. – William †1799 and Mary Coleman †1783. A pair of garlanded oval tablets with flaming urns. One at either end of the s aisle. Three attractive early C20 tablets – Gwendolin Herbert †1915. Of alabaster with two tiny cherubs beneath a broken pediment. By *Wratten & Godfrey*. Also by them, the WAR MEMORIAL *c.* 1919, also in sumptuous C17 style. – Winifred Herbert †1933. Neo-Jacobean cartouche.

SE of church the former SCHOOL of 1896. Woodyer-esque Gothic.

TOP FARMHOUSE, ¾ m. SW. Early C17 with a plaster royal coat of arms over a first-floor Tudor-arched fireplace.

VINNICKS, 1¼ m. SW. Formerly Hollington Farmhouse. Georgian, of brick. Three widely spaced bays. One-bay projection with pediment. This centre has blue headers and red dressings; the side parts are all red. In the side parts Venetian windows with segmental instead of semicircular arches.

FALKLAND FARM MILL 2¼ m. NE. *c.* 1800, tall with crow-stepped gable, seemingly intended as an eyecatcher.

HIGHCLERE CASTLE

The largest mansion in Hampshire, all but rebuilt by *Charles Barry*, 1838–48, for the 3rd Earl of Carnarvon. The house built in 1616 for the Lucys was 'much altered' by Robert Herbert in the early C18 into a big square classical mansion and further improved 1774–7 by Henry Herbert, who became 1st Earl of Carnarvon in 1793. His house was three storeys high, with a nine-bay N entrance front. His architect may have been *Capability Brown* who made 'many plans for the alteration of the house and offices' at the same time as his work on the park *c.* 1770–1. The 2nd Earl continued this tradition of tinkering until his death in 1833, employing *Thomas Hopper* to reface the

Highclere Castle, N front.
Engraving, C19

house in Bath stone, adding an applied giant portico to the
centre of the N front and paired pilasters at the angles. Of this
nothing is visible following *Barry*'s transformation. His work,
proposed following the rejection of other designs, is in the Elizabethan style; what he called 'Anglo-Italian'. A style of such
elaboration is still unexpected at this date, although it should
be remembered that for the competition to build the Houses
of Parliament in 1835 Elizabethan was explicitly permitted as
an alternative to Gothic. Barry's pattern was evidently Wollaton Hall (Notts.) but his design is far from imitative, the allusions restricted to the angle turrets and the great tower, which,
other than in views from the E, is not even strictly central. This
had not been Barry's intention; in an early design the tower
was to have stood above a full-height saloon. It is now placed
over the staircase, W of the centre.

The house is ashlar-faced, of three storeys with an additional
storey in the accentuated parts. These include the turrets, of
course, but also the central three bays of the N (entrance) front,
and the S front. The former is of eleven bays, i.e. the nine bays
of the C18 house plus the turrets. The windows are of the
mullion-and-transom type, their transoms higher up than in
genuine Elizabethan work, with carved panels beneath, and are
linked vertically. This, with the horizontal emphasis of the
string courses, establishes a strong grid pattern. At the top,
running all around the house, is a strapwork balustrade, with
emphasis over the windows and pinnacles to the turrets and
attic. The front is much flatter than an Elizabethan front would
be, and there is in fact very little decoration – just ornamented
pilasters on each floor in stressed places, i.e. the central three
bays and the turrets. Shallow porch with further pilasters at
the angles and a carved stone coat of arms with supporters

above. The S side, of thirteen bays, is flatter still and its undue length is due to Barry incorporating a private wing at the SW corner of the house.

The E front is the most opulent and the most Elizabethan in spirit. Eleven bays arranged in a most ingenious rhythm and with considerable movement, benefiting from the projection of the C18 outer wings on this side and from the corner turrets which extend forward by almost their own depth. There are further, smaller turrets at the inner angles of, and flush with, the wings. These smaller turrets are windowless, with arched niches instead, and frame the middle five bays, which are arranged in a 1–3–1 pattern. Here, and on the S side, there are three central doorways, the wooden lower panels of which were originally coloured to imitate stonework. Now, painted white, the illusion is lost.

Above all rises the great tower. Of three stages above the roof, this is the most highly ornamented part of the house. The ornament is quite grotesque, with griffins and what appear to be bats as capitals to the rows of pilasters. At each stage, in the centre of each face, are arched niches, and at each corner paired pilasters imply square turrets, which break the roof-line, producing a bold silhouette. Comparisons with Barry's Victoria Tower at the Palace of Westminster are difficult to avoid, and are reinforced by the liberal use of portcullises as ornament. On the N and S fronts especially, it is the evenness of the Georgian fenestration which most seriously destroys the Tudor illusion. And here also lies the difference between Highclere and a High Victorian descendant of Wollaton, the Rothschild mansion of Mentmore. There, the thick relief and boisterous decoration was much more in the spirit of the late C16 than Highclere, which eventually remains emphatically Early Victorian, i.e. closer to the Houses of Parliament, with its even window grid and its shallow all-over decoration, than to Wollaton.

The W side, the main front in the C17, is now the office side and clearly so being stuccoed (the private wing) and brick. Behind the NW turret is a short section of the side wall of the Georgian house, probably the 1820s remodelling, with a stone entablature. In the shadow of the house to the W side is the modest H-plan service range, originally of c. 1700 but entirely Tudorized in the mid C19 with gables and two ogee-capped turrets. It forms a courtyard to the W with the STABLES, also c. 1700, painted brick with hipped roofs.

Barry's remodelling of the INTERIOR seems to have begun in 1848 but remained unfinished when the 3rd Earl died the following year. It recommenced after 1860 under the direction of *Thomas Allom*, who was best known as an architectural illustrator and had produced perspectives of Barry's designs for Highclere in 1838 and 1840. The Gothic entrance VESTIBULE, of three by three bays with marble-shafted piers and thickly bossed ribbed vaulting, is by Barry, although the floor, with its pattern of coloured tiles, is 1863 by *Butterfield*. This leads into

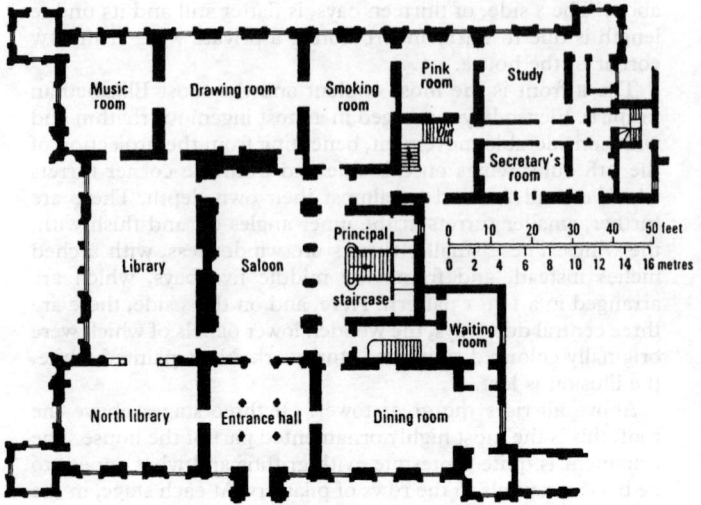

Highclere Castle.
Ground-floor plan

102   the full-height SALOON in the centre of the house, abandoned
as an idea when the tower was moved to its present position,
but revived in 1848. It is Gothic too, but only in its motifs, not
at all as an ensemble. In broad terms it is also by Barry, but
most of the detail, in stucco, is Allom's of the 1860s, by which
time it was a bit out of date. The details are mainly Perp, e.g.
the chimneypiece and door surrounds. An arcaded gallery runs
around at first-floor level, the openings with round-arched
balustrades and, below, panels with trophies and painted
shields. From here shafts rise, with elaborately modelled capitals, to the steeply pitched roof, with arch-braced trusses and
traceried glazed lights. The STAIRCASE, w at the base of the
tower, is 1861–2 by *Allom*. It rises around an open well to the
first floor, within an austere ashlar-walled space, the lower
flights rather tortuously designed to terminate on the central
cross-axis of the Saloon. The style is a mixture of Gothic and
Jacobean. It is lit by three tall Gothic windows in the w wall.
The other rooms are a bit of a mixed bag. On the E front the
LIBRARY, formerly the drawing room, and smaller NORTH
LIBRARY, separated by a screen of Ionic columns. Probably
by *Allom*, chocolate and gold with sumptuous chimneypieces
and overmantels in the style of William Kent with copious
carved ornament. On the other side of the entrance hall is the
less impressive DINING ROOM, in 'Stuart Revival' style appropriate to the setting of Herbert portraits copied from those at
Wilton. The panelled ceiling is probably Barry, but the carved
chimneypiece with barley-sugar columns must be later and the
Gibbons-like carved ornament may be a reused C17 work. The

MUSIC ROOM, at the E end of the S side, is a Baroque affair, with painted and gilded carved decoration and wall panels with C16 Italian embroideries. Its Pompeian painted decoration, and five ceiling paintings by *Richard Brompton* of 1776, are from the previous house. The Renaissance-style marble chimneypiece and door surrounds are by *Butterfield*, 1863, presumably dating the ensemble. The next three rooms (Drawing Room, Smoking Room, Boudoir) are creations of the 1890s in C18 styles. Bedrooms are rather plain, fitted out by Barry with simple ribbed panelled ceilings and reusing C18 chimneypieces.

Immediately NW of the house is the overgrown site of the medieval CHURCH, rebuilt by Sir Robert Sawyer in 1688. All that remains are a few courses of brickwork marking out the plan and the bases of the columns of the arcades. Both *Barry* and *Allom* produced unrealized schemes for rebuilding the church before it was succeeded by Scott's St Michael (*see* above). Further N on the drive, just beyond the Dairy Farm, however, is the MORTUARY CHAPEL of the 3rd Earl by *Allom*, 1855. Small, E.E. style. Big W doorway with five orders of shafts and elaborate gabled bellcote with carved dragons. Inside, the floor is a chequer pattern of gold and green glazed tiles. The fronts of the STALLS are copied from the marble altar rails of the Certosa di Pavia, Lombardy – STAINED GLASS. Renaissance-style glass in the W windows, probably by *Lavers & Westlake*, 1876. Single figures in the two E windows to the N and S, *c.* 1890s. – MONUMENTS. 3rd Earl of Carnarvon †1833. An ornate brass on the floor, depicting a Gothic aedicule, set in red marble. Outer border with symbols of the Evangelists.

PARK AND LANDSCAPE. The Bishops of Winchester had a deer-park and considerable lengths of pale survive. Milford Lake at the N end of the park appears to have begun as a series of fish ponds for the Bishop's estate. Otherwise the earliest known landscape feature, first mentioned in 1692 and surviving until the early C19, was the Long Walk, an avenue of beeches leading from the S front towards Sidown Hill. In the grounds the time of Robert Herbert comes to life. For him the areas to the S and E of the house were developed as Rococo pleasure grounds, including a wilderness. Principal among its surviving structures is the now roofless JACKDAW'S CASTLE, an eyecatcher in the form of a temple, raised on an earth mound about 250 yds from the castle on the axis of its E front. 'Lately erected' in 1743; Robert's brother, *Henry Herbert*, 9th Earl of Pembroke may have had a hand in the design. On each side, magnificent pedimented tetrastyle Corinthian *in antis* porticoes, whose stone columns were rescued from Berkeley House, Piccadilly (*Hugh May*, 1665) after a fire in 1733. Flanking niches above which are blind *œils de bœuf*. Skyline decorated with a plethora of ball finials. Inside, each end is apsed with niches. Of about the same date is the small Doric TEMPLE or SUMMER SEAT, in the former wilderness, SW of the house. It has a pair of widely spaced unfluted columns *in antis* between pairs of pilasters, with triglyph frieze and pediment. Inside is a modelled classical frieze. SE of the house is the trapezoidal-shaped MONK'S GARDEN, a mid-C18 walled garden. It has been opened up to the rest of the grounds by piercing an arcade in the W wall. At its SW corner a STATUE of Charlemagne, a stone bust set on a massive brick pedestal.

Detached from, but part of, the mid-C18 garden design is HEAVEN'S GATE, an impressive triumphal arch, high on the slopes of Sidown Hill ¾ m. S on the axis of the S front of the castle and the former Long Walk. Built in 1737, its exposed brick must have been, or intended to have been, stuccoed. The parapet curves up to a central pedimented attic and is decorated with stone urns. There were formerly rooms behind the small arches, in which Milles says 'the family sometimes drink tea'.

Henry Herbert inherited Highclere in 1769 and in 1770–71 *Capability Brown* provided a comprehensive design for alterations to the grounds. It seems likely that much of what he proposed was carried out, although it is clear that Herbert instituted his own modifications to the plantings as work progressed. It remains the best designed landscape in North Hampshire. Associated with this phase, although its date and architect are unknown, is the ROTUNDA, close to the drive 1 m. NE of the castle on a promontory above Dunsmere, a lake recommended by Brown and created in the 1790s. It is a circular peripteral Ionic temple, mainly of stuccoed brick, but with stone columns on a rusticated base. Built with concave-sided cella and hemispherical dome but substantially altered in 1838–9 by *Barry*, who reduced the cella to a cylinder, evenly spaced the columns and raised the dome higher on a drum. ¼ m. SSW, further down the drive, is LIVE ARCH BRIDGE. *c.* 1800 in gault and red brick. In Sidown Vale, ¾ m. SW of the castle, is DAN'S LODGE. Late C18 or early C19 Gothick, triangular with corner towers. Originally battlemented.

Some of the buildings at the entrance to the park are of significance. – CASTLE LODGE, 150 yds NE of the castle, is probably mid-C18, perhaps designed as an entrance to the pleasure gardens. Pedimented front with raised quoins, the central doorway (now blocked) with a Gibbs surround. GATEPIERS with wreathed-urn finials. On one a carved term, and on the other a herm. – LONDON LODGE, in the park's NE corner near the A30, was built in 1793, the year of Henry Herbert's creation as 1st Earl of Carnarvon. In the form of a Roman arch, with pairs of Greek Ionic pilasters, and crisp *Coade* stone enrichments. Above the arch stands an elaborate vase. One-storey ashlar-faced lodges l. and r., curving outwards, appear to be a little later. – Also *c.* 1793, BEACON HILL ARCH, marking the entrance from Winchester, ¾ m. SSE of the castle. A Gothic triumphal arch in gault brick, again with *Coade* ornament including a military trophy above the arch. – GROTTO LODGE, 1 m. SW of the castle, may be the 'Lodge at Crux Easton' by *Thomas Allom*, 'from an original design' by Henrietta, the 3rd Countess, *c.* 1849. Flint with stone dressings.

Large three-storey circular Gothic tower with a central battle-mented octagonal chimney, linked to a smaller stair-tower with pyramidal roof. Liberal scattering of lancet windows and cruciform arrow loops.

MILFORD LAKE HOUSE, 1½ m. NNE of the Castle by Milford Lake. A pleasure pavilion, probably built soon after 1743 for Robert Herbert, and perhaps by his brother, *Henry Herbert*, the 9th Earl of Pembroke. Remodelled for the 3rd Earl *c.* 1838 as a residence while the castle was building, possibly by his agent *Broome Pinniger*. 'The house faces the lake immediately, and if the modish term can ever be used meaningfully, is out of this world' (Pevsner). Single storeyed, with a higher centre and spreading out lower links and wings. The whole is humbly built of a pinky cream brick, but with an insistent diaper of plum-coloured and blue brick difficult to reconcile with an C18 date. Much brick rustication. The centre has a doorway with flanking arched windows, all of 1838. The parapet curves up to a central attic. The links are of three bays, with the original entrances, and the wings of one with a pediment. Inside, across the width of the centre, is the Dining Room, created *c.* 1838, although reusing fittings from Robert Herbert's Highclere, e.g. the oversized Ionic doorcase with segmental pediment and the chimneypiece with female terms, Ionic half columns and swan-necked pediment, flanked by shallow arched recesses, with crossed palmettes over, and drops with bunches of fruit. Above the doors are reliefs of eagles raising curtains in their beaks. Panelled ceiling with central oval, i.e. of 'Jonesian' form but the details distinctly mid C19. Alterations and additions of 1964 by *Sir Martyn Beckett* for Lord Porchester, later the 7th Earl.

HILL BROW

Liphook

7020

An area of Victorian, Edwardian and later development on a ridge of high ground on the border with West Sussex.

RAKE HOLT. 1936 by *Unsworth, Goulder & Bostock*. Plastered walls, green shutters and a hipped roof with red Roman tiles.

DURFORD COURT, SW off London Road. 1912 by *Unsworth, Son & Triggs* in their usual Sussex/Hampshire vernacular. It is L-plan, around an entrance court, with a two-storey porch and a staircase tower extruded from the corner. Charming dovecote on the forecourt wall (cf. Little Boarhunt, Liphook). On the garden side, jettied timber-framed wings, slightly asymmetrical. Inside, a large living hall open to the corridor, like many of the other rooms this is L-shaped with corner windows. Barrel-vaulted billiard room. Contemporary GARDEN, with a rill leading to a circular pool.

DURFORD WOOD, NE of Durford Court, is an estate of large houses developed by *Gerald Unsworth* in the 1920s.

Mainly Sussex vernacular, some others Neo-Georgian and
Moderne.

5020

HINTON AMPNER

ALL SAINTS. The small church looks Victorian but is partly
Saxon. The nave, originally a simple tall double cube (39½ ft
by 20½ ft, 12 by 6.3 metres) retains typically Saxon features in
the long-and-short NE quoin, the lesenes W of it and in the corresponding position on the S side. Also inside, in the doorway
into the N vestry – the former S doorway. This has straight
jambs too. The rest of the nave is as rebuilt and enlarged W in
1879–80 by *Capel N. Tripp.* Bland Victorian E.E., with heavy
roof and a small Butterfieldian W bellcote with a hipped, rather
French-looking top. But the chancel is partly genuine E.E.,
grossly over restored and externally refaced in neatly coursed
knapped flint of 1844 (White). Here the redone single lancets
represent C13 originals entirely renewed (those on the S side
are in place as shown by an C18 drawing). Also, the fine, but
alas equally over-restored, double PISCINA, with two trefoil-
headed openings, genuine early C13 work of high quality (cf.
the coeval piscina at South Hayling), no doubt due to St
Swithun's Cathedral Priory, who held Hinton Ampner. The
chancel was re-floored in stone, with some original C13 TILES
reused, and reordered in 1968–9 for Ralph Dutton by *Peter
Sawyer* to a satisfying simplicity. – COMMUNION RAILS. Late
C17, introduced in 1949. – PRIEST'S READING DESK and
CHAIR of 1969 by *Edward Barnsley.* – PANELLING. Behind the
altar, Jacobean, reused. – PULPIT. Essentially Jacobean. The
panels with geometrical fields. – VESTRY DOOR. Dated 1643,
presented by Nicholas Lacie (inscription). – STAINED GLASS.
In the E window of two lancets, by *Patrick Reyntiens,* 1969.
Colourful and rich, Pillars of Cloud and Fire (Exodus 13).
Commissioned by Ralph Dutton. – MONUMENTS. – Thomas
Stewkeley †1601 of Marstowne, Somerset, aged nine days.
Baby on his side, in a gold fringed crimson gown (an engaging piece; cf. Tichborne). – Thomas Stewkeley †1638, *gemmam
de stirpe Stewkleyana* ('the jewel of the Stewkley family'). The
monument, attributed to *Humphrey Moyer* (GF) gives no name
but refers to him as *florem...in primo vere decerptum* ('a flower
plucked in his first spring'). Small recumbent effigy. Columns
l. and r. At the top, angels in naïve clouds. – Sir Hugh Steweke-
ley †1642, largest of three small C17 brasses. This one, unusually signed *Thomas Brome.* Above this, the brass achievement,
with elaborate mantling and identical border, no doubt by the
same rare engraver. – Sir Hugh Stewkeley †1719. Fine cartouche tablet with inscription, and long drapes – a good copy
of John Stone's Bankes monument (1654) at Christ Church
Oxford (GF). – In the nave, two C17 monuments brought in

from Old St Mary, Laverstoke, in 1952: Sir John Trott †1672. Big conventional grey and white tablet attributed to *Joshua Marshall* (GF) with garlands. Broken pediment with cherubs – Katherine, Lady Stewkeley †1679. An interesting little-known Baroque piece, convincingly attributed to *John Bushnell.* Haughty bust in a recess, draped with curtains. Curiously shaped white urns l. and r. The feminist inscription makes interesting reading:

'She was equall to the Wisdom of the bravest of Men
Friendlie to the ignorance of the meanest of Women.
Yet She was not altogether exempt from the
Common Fate wch attends all Eminence of Parts
Of being in some things misunderstood.'

Henry B. Legge †1764. Fine large standing tablet with Ionic columns and a pediment. Trophy in the 'predella'. – Henry and Blanche Dutton †1946. Small Neo-Georgian tablet by *Trenwith Wills.* – Ralph Dutton, 8th and last Lord Sherborne, †1985. Simple ledger stone with achievement in the chancel floor.

HINTON AMPNER PLACE, N of the church. Early C18, built as the rectory. Two storeys and attic, double-pile plan. Plum-coloured brick with red brick dressings, hipped tile roof. Deep platband and wide rusticated quoin strips at the angles. 2–1–2 bays. Centre marked by a doorcase with rusticated pilasters and triglyph frieze. On the main road, ½ m. NE, THE OLD SCHOOL, founded by the will of William Blake in 1738. Brick and tile. Two storeys, one-room deep. 2–1–2 bays, wooden cross-windows with cast-iron casements. The central doorway with structural frame and bracketed flat hood is typical of the date. Extension of 1860.

HINTON AMPNER HOUSE. Of the plain Georgian box built in 1793 only cellars remain, it was first superseded by a large Victorian house, itself torn down (except for its service wing) and rebuilt in brick Neo-Georgian by *Wellesley & Wills* in 1937 for the connoisseur and collector, Ralph Dutton, later 8th Lord Sherborne. That house was severely damaged by fire in 1960 and immediately reconstructed by *Trenwith Wills & Wills* who took down the attic storey but otherwise left the exterior as it had been with its two symmetrically arranged bow windows on the S front. More special is the interior, decorated both before and after the fire by *Ronald Fleming* of *Mann & Fleming.* Four rooms along the S front; first the SITTING ROOM, simple Georgian with a good fireplace rescued pre-war from *Adam*'s Adelphi Terrace; next the DINING ROOM with another fortunate pre-fire survival: a copy of Adam's ceiling for the drawing room of Robert Child's house at No. 38 Berkeley Square, from which Dutton had salvaged the painted roundels before its demolition in 1939 (restored post-fire by *Elizabeth Biddulph*, in the style of Kauffman). The LIBRARY chimneypiece also survived: early C19, allegedly from St Cloud and with Napoleonic monograms. Elegant bookcases with painted porphyry Ionic pilasters designed by *Gerald Wellesley* and reconstructed to his design. The DRAWING ROOM in the 1930s house was at first preserved in a Victorian style but recast after 1960 in Neoclassical taste with a screen of Corinthian columns. Two beautiful late C18 white marble chimneypieces – one with figures – salvaged from Ashburnham Place, Sussex (also the source for the doorcases). Window casings derive from Adelphi Terrace.

The GARDENS are as much Dutton's personal achievement as the house, with formal planting of clipped yews on the s terraces giving way to small, informal compartments and dells and from there to open parkland.

BLACK HOUSE FARM, 1½ m. SE of the church. *c.* 1620. L-plan lobby-entry house. Fully framed kitchen wing but the hall and parlour range have a flint ground floor with brick dressings: one of the earliest known examples of such combined construction in a house of this status. First-floor oriel windows, each supported on a single shaped bracket.

LONG BARROW, 1 m. N of Hinton Ampner House and ¾ m. E of Cheriton. The mound is 200 ft (62 metres) long and 118 ft (36 metres) wide at its broader E end where it is 7 ft (2.1 metres) high. The site was partially excavated without result at the end of the C19 and again in 1932, when a small sherd of Late Neolithic Peterborough ware was found near the bottom of one of the flanking ditches.

HOLYBOURNE

Almost an E suburb of Alton but still with an individual identity.

HOLY ROOD. By the attractively overgrown source of the Holy Bourne on the edge of open country beside the Pilgrim's Way. Engaging exterior with agreeable textures on the S side. Flint W tower with C14 angle buttresses and a heavy shingled broach spire of 1902. Short nave, in its fabric C12 perhaps. Perp S windows, the westernmost re-set (in the 1880s?) from the C15 former N aisle, in the place of a doorway (now blocked; inside, possibly coeval with the doorway, a length of dogtooth moulding). The chancel is unusually both as long and wide as the nave. It is essentially E.E., of the early C13 (see single lancets N and S, and larger lateral SW and NE windows, both of paired trefoil-headed lights), but the E and SE windows are Perp. The former of *c.* 1400, renewed. Original E.E. piscina with cutting into the NW window for an unusually placed 'squint', possibly for passing pilgrims to view the altar. In it, a small fragment of a Norman capital (from the first chancel arch?). Broad C13 chancel arch, double-chamfered, dying into the piers. Unrestored Perp. N arcade of church, with octagonal piers and arches with two hollow chamfers. Good stone corbels of *c.* 1400 (one of them, over the pulpit, a Green Man) supporting contemporary nave roof tie-beams and framing. Restoration of 1878–9, by *Ewan Christian* with broad N aisle, of 'vertical crazy paving' externally, in Selborne stone. –

FONT. C13. Square, evidently renewed. – Unusually large
BENEFACTIONS BOARD dated 1784, under the tower, recording the charities of Thomas Andrews's will of 1719, including
the school, still in use. – STAINED GLASS. Mostly by *Alexander Gibbs*, especially the chancel, E window, of 1879 and the
more interesting NE window of 1906 with a dense Resurrection scene. N aisle, central N, 1918, by *Percy Bacon*, crisply
drawn females symbolizing Justice, Charity and Mercy.

In the churchyard extension to SW, a good typically Arts and
Crafts grave marker to Alexander Mackenzie Downie †1936,
with three cherubs, their upswept wings curling under the trefoiled head. Timber LYCHGATE dated 1899.

To the SE is CHURCH COTTAGE, a C15 hall house with C17 brick
wing, the latter with moulded string courses and, in the gable
to the road, terracotta panels. Further SW, THE BOURNE with
late medieval hall at the rear but mainly *c.* 1600, refronted in
the C18 with sashes and columned porch. In Howard's Lane
to the W, HOWARD'S FARMHOUSE, an early C17 timber-
framed baffle-entry plan house with to the side, and towering
above it, a brick addition of *c.* 1700 with gabled stair-tower at
the rear. Impressive C17 ten-bay BARN, now converted. THE
PRIORY, SW, is dated 1629. A hall-and-cross-wing plan house
of hybrid construction, originally timber-framed at the rear but
with a show front of squared and knapped flint with malmstone dressings.

On London Road, SW of Howards Lane, ANDREWS ENDOWED
PRIMARY SCHOOL. Founded 1719 in the will of Thomas
Andrews, built 1721–30. Brick with modillion cornice and
steep hipped roof. Five-bay front, originally for schoolmaster's
house, r., and schoolrooms, l., but this was remodelled in the
late C18 with tripartite sashes in the outer bays and pedimented
doorcase. Original cross-windows survive to side and rear.
Rear schoolroom, probably late C18, and an attached girls'
school of *c.* 1872. TRELOAR COLLEGE, to the N, was established as Florence Treloar School for disabled girls. Buildings
of 1963–5 by *J. M. Aylwin*, buff brick, in a thin Neo-Georgian
style set around two courts, the front marked by a central pavilion with pyramidal roof and the rear enclosed by a Tuscan
colonnade. The best of the later buildings are the TRAILL
CENTRE, of 1985–6 by *Plincke Leaman & Browning*; the
MUSIC STUDIO of 1998–9 and LEARNING RESOURCES
CENTRE of 1999–2000, both by *Macallan Penfold*. Furthest SW
is EGGAR'S SECONDARY SCHOOL a good example of the
system-built SCOLA schools of the early 1960s.

N of Howards Lane, the village WAR MEMORIAL by *Maurice
Adams*. Carved wood tablet, C18 style, with columns supporting a segmental pediment surrounded by putti heads, under a
tiled gable. At the NE end of the village, THE FORGE. A late
example of a baffle-entry-plan house: dated 1722. The segmental-arched opening to the former wheelwright's shop to the
r. must be later; attached to the rear is the former workshop.
At the front, the former blacksmith's shop, with an upright
furnace for metal tyres and a cast-iron tyre platform, both rare
survivals.

BONHAMS'S FARMHOUSE, London Road, ¾ m. NE of the
church. Built 1699 for Thomas Jeffery, yeoman. A half-H or
U-plan house, but at the end of the tradition and reversed so
that the wings enclose a very narrow rear service court (partly
infilled *c.* 1900) and the front has the appearance of a double-
pile house of six by six bays, with a high hipped roof and pedimented Doric porch. Some original cross-windows survive at
the rear and the entrance hall retains its staircase with vase-
shaped balusters (cf. Norton Manor, Wonston).
NEATHAM MANOR, ¾ m. SE. Late C15 Wealden house, altered
in the early C17 when the hall was floored and the upper bay
demolished. At the same time a wing was added at right angles,
with a pair of large gables to the front. Much C18 rebuilding
in brick with copious tile-hanging and leaded casements. Well
restored with minor alterations by *A. Y. Mayell*, 1919–21.
Inside, a C17 screen and staircase, both with turned balusters.
Good group of converted C18 and C19 MILL BUILDINGS, by
the Wey.

7050   # HOOK

Hook began as a collection of farms, at the crossing of the
London–Basingstoke and Reading–Alton roads. Later a coaching stop, it expanded after the opening of a station in 1883 and
required a permanent church by the 1930s. In the architectural
history of the later C20, its permanent – if unseen – importance
is as the site of the London County Council's abortive New Town
for 100,000 people, promoted in 1958 but unrealized following
local opposition. In 1960 it was agreed that the development of
Basingstoke, Andover and Tadley (qq.v.) should be accelerated
instead. In spite of this Hook grew considerably in the late C20,
with much housing and a business park at Bartley Heath, S of
the railway.

ST JOHN EVANGELIST, London Road. 1937–8 by *Sir Edward
Maufe,* in his unmistakably personal style, well crafted in
Daneshill brick and influenced by domestic early C17 vernac-
ular. Prominent NE flanking tower, with a recessed hipped
roof. Long and segment-arched windows with transoms.
Maufe's mannerisms are easily recognizable, especially in the
E and W windows, the former circular and high-set (as at
Guildford Cathedral), the latter recessed below a typical (Ost-
bergian) fancy arch. Lower extension along the S side 1990–2
by *Plincke, Leaman & Browning,* who also designed the bold
W gallery on red painted steel columns. Original furniture in
the chancel, especially the projecting organ gallery. – Chapel
furniture by *Richard La-Trobe Bateman,* 1991–2. – STAINED
GLASS. E window by *J. E. Nuttgens.*

Despite C20 expansion, the buildings of principal interest are
those close to the historic road junction, W of the church. THE
WHITE HART HOTEL, on the S side of London Road, is stuccoed Georgian but incorporating older fabric. Central carriage
arch under a canted bay carried on Tuscan columns. In the bay
(which is weatherboarded) a Venetian window pushing up into
an open pediment. The lower, three-bay part to the l., with
central pediment, is early C19. Tall shafted chimneystack at the
junction of the blocks. C18 staircase in hipped-roofed rear projection. C17 and C18 rear wing with at the end an accommodation range of 1986 in the style of a C17 galleried lodging,
in the context appropriate in scale and form. GEFFERY'S
HOUSE, ¼ m. E, sheltered housing of 1976, enlarged 1987, with
lead STATUE of Sir Robert Geffrye (†1703), by the *Nost* workshop, 1723, originally in a niche over the door of the Geffrye
Almshouses, Shoreditch. OLD RAVEN HOUSE, opposite, was
also an inn. Timber-framed with hall and gabled cross wings
and a continuously jettied first floor. Ogee braces, which
usually mean the early C16 in Hampshire. The herringbone
nogging dates from an early C20 restoration. Further out on this
side HOOK HOUSE HOTEL, C18 brick with hipped roof and an
asymmetrical 1–3 bay front with blind windows on the line of
the chimney, perhaps suggesting a rebuilding of an earlier
house. Doorway with pediment on consoles. ¼ m. E again is
THE CROOKED BILLET, an amusing butterfly-plan roadhouse
of 1934–5, and to its N the picturesque WHITEWATER MILL,
the house C17 and the mill C18, both timber-framed.
OAKLANDS, ½ m. SE of the White Hart. Accomplished early C19
villa with boldly projecting curved bays and Ionic doorcase
with segmental pediment.
BOROUGH COURT, 1¼ m. NE. An important house with a C15
timber-framed hall and an impressive late C16 brick chamber
block. Hall of four bays with arched-braced collar-trusses, the
principal central truss with arch-braced tie-beam too. Two tiers
of wind-braces. Floored probably in the C16, the S wall rebuilt
in brick in the late C17 and the N wall in the C18. The show
front is the N side, with the late C16 two-storey chamber block
to the l., presumably replacing medieval service rooms. This is
two-rooms deep, with an attic above the N rooms, and a pair
of excessively tall and showy chimneys on the E end, topped
by cut brick shafts; one with spiral decoration probably served
the principal chamber. Traces of mullioned-and-transomed
openings can be seen in the blocked square windows high up
to r. and l. on each floor. The ogee capped oriel window (N
side) is of *c.* 1900, the date of the house's restoration and
rebuilding of the W wing. Inside are a pair of C16 doorways
from the hall into the ground-floor chambers, with moulded
surrounds and vase stops, and a four-centred arched stone
chimneypiece in the principal chamber, also with vase stops
and carved initials IF AF, probably John and Ann Fielder. The
splendid Neo-Jacobean staircase with its hatstand-like post is
of *c.* 1900.

3030

HOUGHTON

On the w bank of the Test and famous for the fishing club (est. 1826, *see* Stockbridge) from which locals are excluded.

ALL SAINTS. Compact, rather low exterior, its Victorian look the result of restorations for the Rev. E. J. Boyce (rector 1865–97; he was the first Treasurer of the Cambridge Camden Society in 1839–40) by *G. G. Scott* in 1875 (chancel) and *J. Oldrid Scott* in 1882 (nave and aisles), when much was renewed in knapped flint. But the church is of Norman origin as worked stones re-set in the s aisle E wall attest. Big shingled w bell-turret, C15 in its framework (as can be seen inside) carrying a small broach spire of 1890. Nice timber s porch with cusped gable of 1882 and good cast-iron rainwater heads, signed *Potter & Sons*, South Molton Street, London. The chancel windows N and s are of *c.* 1325–50, correctly renewed, but the E window is of 1882 in matching style.

The interior reveals evolution from the early C12 to the C15. The sequence began with a simple aisleless nave and chancel. The round N arcade E arch followed first, the s arcade perhaps *c.* 1200. A further extension of late C13: see the w arch of the N arcade, divided from its companion by a piece of wall. Chancel arch of 1882 on plain responds, flanked by two squints, that to the s unusually cut through the centre of the E respond of the s arcade. Redundant stone brackets on the capitals of the s arcade (s side) for lost supports for a lower C13 roof. w belfry on C15 timber posts (contemporary bell-frame). C13 chancel piscina – l. and r. of the altar, parts of a C14(?) reredos. – FONT. Perp. Octagonal with quatrefoils on a C12 base. FONT COVER of 1886 by *Oldrid Scott*, as also most of the furnishings, especially the wooden COMMUNION RAILS with openwork Dec tracery of mouchette wheels, and the PULPIT of stone, effectively simple. – GRAFFITO. On the s arcade pier closest to the entrance a schematic depiction of the Trinity. – PAINTING. Ecce Homo, after *Albani* (1578–1660). – STAINED GLASS. E window. 1892 by *Burlison & Grylls*, Cruci-fixion. Much blue. – N aisle E *c.* 1892 by *Lavers & Westlake*. – MONUMENTS. N aisle. Maurice Bernard †1791. Large wreathed inscription on a proto-Gothic tablet, 'Legions of angels cannot confine him here'.

Outside, by the w wall, a sturdy timber-framed WELL-HOUSE by *Cancellor & Sawyer*, 1931. To Sir Lionel Wells of Houghton Lodge (†1929), Chief of the London Fire Brigade. s of the church, THE OLD RECTORY, a superior early to mid-C18 house, of two storeys raised on a basement. Five bays, the centre three under a pediment pierced by an oculus; two-bay s addition (late C19), concealing a flint and brick part at the rear of 1870. (Some interiors of the original date.) The rest of the village has the expected Test valley mix of timber-framed, thatched cottages intermingled with many later houses, among which should be noted Nos. 15–17 SOUTH END COTTAGES

and Nos. 19–25 High Street, estate cottages of 1881–2 by
George Devey for W. H. Deverell of Bossington House. In an
understated Arts and Crafts style of chequered brick with
jettied and pebbledashed upper storeys.

HOUGHTON LODGE.* A Gothick *cottage orné* probably built   91
c. 1786–90 (and certainly no later than 1799, when it was
advertised for sale in the *Morning Chronicle*) for Maurice and
Bridget Bernard (see his monument in the church). The architect, alas, is unknown. Could it have been *John Plaw*, living in
Southampton from *c.* 1795? The house has pointed windows,
small steeply gabled dormer windows, big cosy roofs that were
originally thatched, and high decorated brick chimneys. On the
E side there is a big bow with frieze of quatrefoil openings and
an iron veranda; this looks 1860s and might have replaced a
rustic canopy. A tree-trunk column survives in an outbuilding.
Some windows have cast-iron tracery in an Indo-Moorish
manner (cf. Sezincote, Gloucs.; 1805). Additions to N, mid-
C19, and S, mid-C20.

   Inside, much is still as described at its sale. The bow contains the circular 'rotunda', its domed ceiling painted as the
sky with swallows darting between clouds. Cupboards and
doors have sharply pointed-arches in reeded surrounds,
mirrors with coloured glass and a curious marble chimneypiece with ogee-topped frame in Blue John, based on a plate in
Batty Langley's *Gothick Architecture Improved*, 1747. A recur-
rent motif is an over-scaled trefoil-headed opening: either in
the form of arches e.g. to the staircase (spiral threaded balusters and Gothic panels) and the drawing room (with a Neoclassical chimneypiece – one of a number in the house) or as
a screen in the dining room. The N wing appears to be later
but has the same Gothic joinery in one room; it must have
been introduced from elsewhere in the house.

   The OUTBUILDINGS may incorporate the stables etc.
described in 1799; the two LODGES are also of that date and
match the house. The setting is exceptional with lawns running
down to the Test and informal plantings of trees. WALLED
GARDEN to the N. The S GATEWAY, an artificial Gothick ruin
of flint and rubble, marks the line of the village road before
the lodge was built.

HOUGHTON MILL. *See* Bossington.

HUNTON   4030

Small settlement on the N bank of the Dever, the church alone
in the water meadows but originally surrounded by houses, as
attested by earthworks in neighbouring fields.

---

*The dating of the house is the result of research by Michael B. Readhead.
See also his article in *The Georgian Group Journal* 18 (2010).

ST JAMES. A former chapel attached to Crawley until 1919 (1291 mention) but rebuilt in its present form c. 1500. Nave and small chancel. Bell-turret, altered in the early C20. The nave s wall is of C18 brick with random chequering. – MONUMENT. Of the same date as the rebuilding. Tomb-chest in a low arched recess. It is occupied, but not by Prior Hunton as previously believed.* The frieze of small panels with quatrefoils, leaves, the initials of the Virgin and Christ, etc., cannot have been part of a tomb-chest, but may have belonged to a cresting. – Outside, on NE corner of the nave a good cartouche wall tablet to Sarah Jeffery †1728, with putto and skull. In the churchyard, one good early C18 headstone against the s porch to Thomas Pitter †1735 with cherubs and flaming urn.

HUNTON MANOR, N of the church. Red brick, the early C18 centre of five bays and two storeys over a high basement; three-bay pediment. Added to this are projecting, two-bay wings (late C18?), originally single-storey but raised in the mid-C20, probably by *Ernest Barrow*. Their cupolas were added by *Raymond Erith*, 1961–4. He also reinstated the central doorway (it had been moved to the return of the r. wing by the early C20) and built the single-storey E wing. Inside, the early C18 front rooms form one large hall; chimneypieces presumably by Erith. The dining room has a re-set Baroque chimneypiece and panelling with a carved acanthus cornice. Fine early C18 staircase at the rear of the house. Small panelled room at the rear too, with arched niches. Erith's E wing has a gracefully curved second staircase with stick balusters and curious but effective stippled rustication to the tread-ends. Pretty lattice wooden SUMMER-HOUSE in the garden.

HUNTON DOWN HOUSE, opposite, is also by *Erith*, 1959. Beautifully restrained Neo-Georgian. with bow-fronted wings at the rear (one an addition of c. 1986). Behind is an impressive DOVECOTE. Probably early C17. Flint with stone dressings, pyramidal tiled roof. Low Tudor-arched doorway.

HURSTBOURNE PRIORS

Hurstbourne Priors was a possession of the Priory of St Swithun, Winchester, from the C13 until the dissolution and the prior had a substantial mansion here. In 1558 Robert Oxenbridge purchased the manor from the king, when 'there was in the park a lodge and a fayre manor house', and in 1636 it was sold to Sir Henry Wallop of Farleigh Wallop (q.v.). After Farleigh House was burned down in 1667, Hurstbourne became the chief residence of the Wallops, from 1748 the Earls of Portsmouth, who created most of the village and estate.

* See John Crook's article in *Hampshire Studies*, v.63 (2008).

St Andrew. Neo-Norman w tower of yellow brick and Neo-Perp nave of 1870, both very old-fashioned for the date, by *Clark & Holland*, architects to Isaac, 5th Earl of Portsmouth, who financed their building. But the fine w doorway is of *c.* 1130, re-set from the nave N wall. One order of colonnetes, two-scallop capitals. Arch with zigzag and rosettes in shallow relief. To the same predecessor building belongs the arch to the N chapel, originally the chancel arch. It has exactly the same ornamental motifs. Good, well-preserved early C13 chancel with two s lancets and fine priest's doorway with continuous roll moulding and Mass dial. The E end with a Perp E window of *c.* 1420 framed inside by a transitional pointed-arched recess. Below the springing of the arch are two small round-headed blind arcades, looking late C12, with carved capitals and moulded bases. The VCH suggests all are clearly a compote of old details. N chapel, Elizabethan, flint, with straight-headed windows (of five lights to E and W) but with arched lights. C18 s transeptal s chapel of brick, – REREDOS. 1920 by *Hardman.* Alabaster on a Portland stone shelf and corbels. – FONT. by *Marilyn Smith* 2008. – LECTERN. A splendid and unusual carved angel in wood, to 6th Earl of Portsmouth †1917. – BOX PEWS, as late as 1870. – STAINED GLASS. E window, 1920, by *J. Hardman & Co.* Lightsome and pale, Christ blessing between single angels. Quarry backgrounds. – Chancel s, 1903, by *J. Powell & Sons.* Angel with a harp. – MONUMENTS. Sir Robert Oxenbridge, †1574, Constable of the Tower of London. A fine Elizabethan monument between chancel and N chapel, and open to both, possibly by *Janssen* of Southwark. The arch and the jambs are patterned with the simplest geometrical motifs. Two recumbent effigies of stone, not good. Tomb-chest with kneeling children framed in guilloche moulding, on both sides. Also detached. Doric colonnettes at the angles. Above them, Ionic columns l. and r. of the arch for the effigies. Top achievement. The monument was repainted in 1705 (as an inscription records) and again in 1964 by *Miss Norholt.* Two HELMS are replicas of the originals consigned to the Tower of London.

In the village, THE LONG HOUSE is C18, of vitrified header brickwork with red dressings, linking the windows in vertical panels. Five bays, with additions at each end. s, towards the village's small triangular green, the former SCHOOL. Mid-C19, flint with gault brick dressings, cast-iron lattice windows and chimneys linked by an arch. Some modest C18 houses including MANOR FARMHOUSE, late C18, hipped roof, three bays with tripartite sashes.

APSLEY FARMHOUSE, 1½ m. NW. Early C18 with N addition of 1932 and gentrified in Arts and Crafts Georgian in 1936 by *A. S. G. Butler,* who added the chunky doorcase to the E front. This was of five bays but became three in the early C19. The N addition has a two-storey canted bay cutting through the eaves, its parapet with ball finials. s front of three steep gables, the l. one of 1936, with oculi. Butler inserted a hearth and a staircase in the original entrance passage, the latter with a pair of Solomonic columns at its foot. The weatherboarded and shingled FARM MANAGER'S HOUSE is of 1936, by *R. Hanbury Bateman*. Impressive large weatherboarded BARN of *c.* 1800 with a pair of hipped porches.

BOURNE WOOD, ¾ m. E. A (very) Late Arts and Crafts house of 1956, correctly described by its architect, *A. S. G. Butler*, as looking 'rather 1906'.

THE ISLAND, 1 m. NNE. A small brick house of 1756, notable for its elegant wooden loggia, with pairs of attenuated columns, by *Goodhart-Rendel*, 1922.

HURSTBOURNE VIADUCT, 1¾ m. NW. 1854 for the London & South Western Railway. Nine brick arches spanning the Bourne Valley. *Joseph Locke*, engineer.

HURSTBOURNE PARK
1 m. NE of St Andrew

HOUSE of 2003–5 by *Christopher Smallwood Architects*. Neo-Georgian, built on the site of the Palladian mansion designed by *James Wyatt* in 1778 for the 2nd Earl of Portsmouth. Its replacement, by *Beeston & Burmester* (1892–6), was largely demolished in 1965. Double pile, with a service courtyard to the W. Ashlar with some characterful carving. Two storeys, under a balustraded parapet, and of nine by three bays. The N front has the centre five bays set forward with a three-bay pediment against a raised attic. Tuscan porch. On the S (garden) front only the bays beneath the pediment project and have a wider portico with columns in pairs. W of the house are the former STABLES by *Wyatt*, *c.* 1780, partly remodelled *c.* 1850 when the central range was refaced. The wings are still largely

Hurstbourne Park.
Painting by John Griffier II, 1748

Wyatt: five bays with lunettes over blind, possibly blocked, doorways.

The sites of the medieval manor house and its Elizabethan successor were probably in the vicinity of the church. The early C18 house of John Wallop, which may have been designed by *Thomas Archer*, seems to have stood just to the E across the Bourne Rivulet and much of the LANDSCAPE appears to have been laid out around it. The park was extensively wooded at this time: in 1743 Jeremiah Milles describes a wood on top of the hill, cut through with vistas. Probably of the same period are the terraced walks and bastion cut into the sides of the spur of the hill which projects S between the valleys of the Test and the Bourne Rivulet and which in the C18 would have afforded views of the 1st Earl's house and its gardens. In front of the house was 'A very long canal . . . , at the upper end of which is a cascade which is ornamented with some rustick work built of flint'. These features are also shown in a view of 1748 by *John Griffier* with in addition a sham castle on the hillside beyond. A straight section of the Bourne Rivulet and a weir called the Cascades are probably remnants of this formal feature, and two other important structures also survive: ½ m. ESE of the present house, standing on an earth mound, is a wildly rustic MONUMENT, of tufa (or limestone aping tufa). The structure, which appears to be shown in the view of 1748, has four niches, lined with blackish-blue brick, and a domed top with a diminutive statue in Roman dress. The surrounding planting is mid-C19.

About 1 m. S of the house and ¼ m. E of the village i.e. close to the site of the 1st Earl's house, is the tower-like BEE HOUSE, probably built as a gazebo or garden pavilion but later converted to an estate lodge. Of grey brickwork with red brick dressings with tall arches, a segmental pediment on one side and a parapet with circular panels over which the top of the parapet rises. This curious detail appears to be echoed in the pavilions depicted by Griffier flanking the early C18 house. The first floor probably contained a single large chamber.

HURSTBOURNE TARRANT   3050

The village is one of the most picturesque in Hampshire.

ST PETER. Of flint, low, essentially early C13 and C14. In the C15 the shingled bell-turret was decided upon and in the C17 the clerestory. Restored 1849 (for the Ecclesiastical Commissioners, possibly by *Ewan Christian*), and 1889–90 by *William White* – his also the splay-foot spire of 1897. There was an earlier church, see the fine re-set Late Norman S doorway, perhaps of the 1180s when the advowson was held by King Henry III. Of Binstead stone but looking a composite piece, with one order of columns, their capitals just turning stiff-leaf, the arch pointed, with a slight chamfer and zigzag at right angles to the wall. At the start and end of the arch are monster heads, possibly an eagle and a lion, one of them a beakhead biting in the wrong direction. Next in order of time comes the chancel, though it looks all of 1849: heavily renewed lancets.

Original chancel arch of two chamfers, treated rather roughly. The arcades must be of about 1230. Three bays, round piers, round abaci, double-chamfered arches. The E respond of the S arcade has a corbel head below upright leaves. The aisle walls on the other hand look *c.* 1300. On the N side a fine three-light window with cusped intersected tracery. Early in the C14 the w bays were added to the arcades, and the w doorway (two continuous chamfers) was made. The bell-turret has a fine strong, remarkably tall, timber substructure (two painted C15 beams, reinforcing the belfry wall frames inside, are said to have been part of the lost rood screen; if so, they are a precious survival). Also Perp of *c.* 1450, the low-pitched nave roof and the large four-light chancel E window. – ALTAR, of 1890. – FONTS. The earlier, a rough stone bowl of pre-C13 date, the latter C13 with tile surround. – FONT COVER. Jacobean. – COMMUNION RAIL. Jacobean, brought in from Derbyshire, replacing the original communion rail of *c.* 1700, now in the nave and part of it used for the pulpit stairs. – WALL PAINT-INGS. In the N aisle, The Three Quick and the Three Dead, one of about thirty of this subject in Britain, sadly decayed. Also a very indistinct Wheel of the Seven Deadly Sins on masonry patterns. Better-preserved decorative chequerwork painting on the splays of the N aisle E window. – STAINED GLASS. N aisle E and N, both by *Lavers & Westlake*, the latter of 1882, a luxuriant Jesse Tree. N (commemorative date 1907) by *Jones & Willis*. – Chancel E, by *A. K. Nicholson*, 1934. Four single saints. Clear 'surrounds'. – S aisle S, 1919 by *William Morris & Co.*, Westminster. – N aisle NW, engraved glass of 2000 by *Tracey Sheppard*. – MONUMENTS. Several C18–early C19 tablets, e.g. Rev. Samuel Heskins †1732 in the S aisle. Local work, possibly by *Richard Leversuch* of Andover. – Sarah Debary †1823 and Anne, her sister †1834. Standing woman leaning against a Grecian sarcophagus. Signed by *W. Gibbs* of Basingstoke. The attitude is unhackneyed and shows the Flaxman influence on a provincial sculptor. See also his Neo-Tudor tablet for Rev. Debary †1841. He is also commemorated in the churchyard by a Neoclassical cylindrical column with an urn. – LYCHGATE of 1949, by *W. J. Court* of Andover.

CONGREGATIONAL CHAPEL (former). 1840, stuccoed Tudor Gothic with delicate cast-iron window tracery.

SE of the church, HURSTBOURNE HOUSE (former parsonage). Stuccoed early C19 front range of three bays, the centre recessed, with probably mid-C19 full-height canted bay to l. Flanking set-back mid-C19 wings. Inside, nice early C19 dining room with apsidal end and acanthus cornice. NW of the church, PARSONAGE FARM has fine brick GATEPIERS dated

1685 with moulded panels and stone caps with globe finials and a brick and flint wing of similar date with moulded string course to the otherwise early C19 house. Next, on the same side, DALTON HOUSE. Early C18 with later stucco. Hipped tile roof. Three wide bays, the centre slightly projecting, articulated by single and paired pilasters. The windows in the end bays are of the Venetian type, but with segmental arches; those on the ground floor with bold cornices. Single-storey wings. At the centre of the village BOURNE HOUSE is stately early C19 with a staircase that has a wrought-iron stick balustrade with panels of scrollwork, unusual in a Hampshire house of this size and date. SW is the C18 GEORGE & DRAGON inn. Stuccoed, the centre marked by pilaster strips and a first-floor tripartite sash with a painted blind tympanum pushing up into a gable. Large ground-floor flat-roofed square bay to r. Also a BRIDGE of 1831, a standard design by the County Surveyor: segmental arch, bold torus-moulded string course and parapet with rounded coping and circular end piers. Over the bridge, on the r., ROOKERY HOUSE of 1776. Carved in the front boundary wall is the date 1825 and the initials of William Cobbett, a friend of the occupant, Mr Blount.

WINDMILLS, ¾ m. WSW on Windmill Hill. A modest C19 villa, extended in 1920 by *S. Dexter* for H. W. Prosser, engineer. Charming former music room with a curious amalgam of Gothic panelling, a large inglenook and windows with Art Nouveau glass. Nice brick and flint GATEWAY, the piers with curious halberd finials. Nearby is IBTHORPE TOWER, the former water tower and workshops of *c.* 1903, converted by *Robert Adam.*

BOURNE PARK (formerly Doles), 1 m. SW. A compact Jaco-bethan house of *c.* 1861, but stuccoed in the 1980s, giving it a decidedly Early Victorian feel. Early C19 rustic lodge.

DOYLEY MANOR, 1¼ m. NNE. By *C. F. Short, c.* 1912. Neo-Tudor but with very incorrect hipped roofs. SSW, at Prosper-ous Farm, is one of three GATEWAYS built of coarse shuttered concrete but with elegant late C18 wrought-iron gates.

IBTHORPE
Hurstbourne Tarrant

3050

A very pretty hamlet of flint and thatched cottages and prosper-ous-looking early C18 farmsteads with grander brick houses e.g. YEW TREE FARMHOUSE of 1702 and IBTHORPE FARM-HOUSE, with a front of vitrified headers. IBTHORPE MANOR FARMHOUSE is also very handsome, red brick, of seven bays; doubled in size 2007 by *Robert Adam*. IBTHORPE HOUSE has chequer brickwork, five bays, a hipped roof and a dainty wooden dentil eaves cornice.

ISINGTON
Binsted

A collection of farms and cottages.

EGGARS COTTAGES is a very complete *c.* 1500 hall house with high hipped roof typical of the Weald edge. By the Wey is ISINGTON MILL. Mid-C18 and mid to late C19, converted in 1948 by *Robert Bostock* of *Unsworth & Bostock* as a house for Field Marshal Viscount Montgomery of Alamein (with garages in the hop kilns; some materials came from the Empire and Dominions). Much altered *c.* 1990. Pilastered octagonal GARDEN ROOM added by *Robert Adam Architects* (job architect *Hugh Petter*), 2000. BRIDGE, dated 1686, greensand ashlar and C18 brick parapet. Opposite the mill, THE MILLER'S HOUSE; C18, malmstone.

ITCHEN ABBAS

ST JOHN BAPTIST. Resolute Neo-Norman of 1861–3 by *William Coles* of Winchester. Cruciform. Gabled bellcote with roof far-projecting to the E. Genuine Early Norman doorway re-set as the outer entrance to the N transept: one order of columns with single-scallop capitals and heavy billets in the arch. According to Duthy, there were 'two fine Norman doorways opposite each other in the northern and southern walls' of the previous church (cf. Martyr Worthy). The chancel arch, of Binstead stone, is almost the same. Only one capital has flat leaves, and traces of original red decorative painting. Strange rounded roofs, complicated over the crossing. Aggressively Neo-Norman E window with elaborate zigzag. – FONT. Late C18 Gothic (cf. Chilcomb and Martyr Worthy). – Chancel reordered by *E. P. Warren*, 1905, see the COMMUNION RAIL, but his fittings removed for reordering in 2008–9 by *Gary Seymour.* – STAINED GLASS. All by *Lavers & Westlake* (especially fine the W windows and N transept windows, the latter with grisaille scenes of 1883). Nice clear glazed E window inserted 1905. – MONUMENT. Two small C17 cartouches in S transept. Are they from a discarded monument? – In the churchyard, stone grave marker to John Hughes, †1825, the last man in England to be hanged for horse stealing. Judith Lawrence †1991, the young woman shown reading a book. – LYCHGATE of 1933 by *W. Carpenter Turner.*

ITCHEN ABBAS MANOR, S of the church, is late C18, brick, three bays. Opposite, the C18 MILL HOUSE, and nearby a pair of C18 brick BRIDGES over the Itchen, with two and three segmental arches. N, on the main road, the VILLAGE HALL. 1999–2000, by *David Gregory*. Barn-like, but not slavishly so, with half-hipped tile roof, sweeping down low either side of the

N entrance and S side mostly glazed. MAYBLOSSOM HOUSE, NW, is a major enlargement *c.* 2000 of the roughcast former parish hall and men's reading room of 1903 by *Pink & Arnold* (women's library added 1906, the donor was Sir Edward Grey who kept his fishing cottage here). THE TROUT (formerly The Plough Inn) is by *Cancellor & Hill*, 1904.

BARN CLOSE HOUSE, Station Hill. 1910–11 by *Halsey Ricardo*. A compact, subtle and accomplished Arts and Crafts house with a strong vernacular tone. Clever contrast between the low homely front, which has a central brick break with low round-arched doorway and coved plaster eaves to a weatherboarded gable, and the tall, more spectacular garden side with its row of tile-hung gables on brackets and a rather seasidey two-storey curved bay with balustraded balcony overlooking the Itchen valley.

ABBEY HOUSE, Rectory Lane, ½ m. ENE. Formerly the rectory. Dated 1693, altered in the late C18 and in 1851 by *Colson*; he moved the entrance to the E side. Some original panelling, chimneypieces, and C18 staircase with turned balusters.

ITCHEN STOKE   *5030*

ST MARY (Churches Conservation Trust). Quite remarkable for its date, and one of the most uplifting Victorian churches in Hampshire. 1865–6 by *Henry Conybeare* of Westminster,[*] the cost was £7,000 paid for by his brother the Rev. Charles Conybeare. Tall nave and apsidal chancel in one. Bargate and grey limestone. Steep, originally patterned, slated roof, with restored iron gutterings and ridge. Slender gabled E bellcote. High plain lancets in groups of three along the four-bay sides, a distinctly English, rather than French, pattern. W wall with elaborately shafted doorway and a large wheel window over. Polygonal apse with cross-gables and large two-light windows with bar tracery. Low rib-vaulted W lobby with diapered walls and an inner doorway with marble and granite columns. The nave is decidedly high (40 ft, 12 metres) and unexpectedly impressive with a beautiful coloured boarded open timber roof, painted in Venetian red and stencilled with rosettes. All the walls are diapered below and, above, all the windows are shafted in the best Middle-Pointed fashion beloved of Scott. The W wall, just to be different, has blank arcading instead. More arcading around the apse, which is gracefully vaulted and decidedly French like Sainte Chapelle.

p. 73

Original furnishings of a strongly 'low church' scheme: especially the wooden HOLY TABLE, against glazed exotically gilded diaper patternwork in the arcading. – PAVEMENT. The apse

---

[*]Conybeare was a railway engineer but also published *Photographic Illustrations of the Proportions of Medieval Interiors* (1868).

floor of glazed green and brown tiles to a rare 'maze' pattern, on French models. – PULPIT (entered from vestry) and BENCH-ENDS, all with set-in cast-iron panels of repeat pattern scrollwork and foliage. – FONT. Of coloured enamel, gilt bronze and black Californian marble. This combination of materials was based on the tomb of Mary of Burgundy at Bourges (NT). – CREDENCE TABLE. An Arts and Crafts piece, probably of c. 1890, rather outré à la Mackmurdo. Tall, of wood, with carved vines and ears of corn, almost Art Nouveau. – STAINED GLASS throughout, a rare architectonic scheme, by *Gibbs*. Just excitably colourful geometrical patternwork. – MONUMENTS. Brass to Mrs Joan Batmanson †1518. Black-letter inscription (19 in., 48 cm.). Another brass to a lady, unknown, of c. 1500, kneeling afore a desk (11 in., 28 cm.), restored to the church in 1950.

ITCHEN STOKE HOUSE, s of the main road. Built in 1831 by Lord Ashburton for his brother, the rector. Was the architect *Edward Hunt* of Alresford who also rebuilt the previous church at this date? Stuccoed, entrance front with pretty lattice porch, the garden front with two tripartite sashes under elliptical arches. To the road an early C18 stone GATEWAY, of vermiculated rustication with a round arch reaching into a pedimented gable. There are designs for alterations to 'Itchenstoke House' made by the amateur architect *George Clarke*, and the gateway is similar to the rusticated door surround of his rectory at Kingston Bagpuize, Berks. (c. 1723).

By the small green, a pair of early C19 rustic COTTAGES (Old School House) with attached former schoolroom; uncoursed flint nodules, exceptionally large over the ground-floor windows. Down Water Lane to the water meadows, THE SHALLOWS, a C17 timber-framed house with oriel in the gable-end.

KILMESTON

ST ANDREW. Nave and chancel in one, basically C13 (chancel s lancet and piscina with octofoiled drain) but 'rebuilt in plain unpretending style' in 1772 (Duthy) and restored 1865 in simple E.E. Low s aisle of 1875 and bell-turret by *B. D. Cancellor*, 1911. Inside. – FONT. A stone baluster. Can it be of 1772? – FONT COVER. 1884, with crude scenes of the Baptism and Noah's Ark. – PULPIT and READING STAND by *Raymond Griffen*, 1985. – VESTRY SCREEN of 1936 by *Laverty*. – STAINED GLASS. w window, *Powell* grisaille quarries of 1865. E window. 1983 by *Hugh Powell*. s aisle lancets by *Veronica Whall*, 1937–8. – MONUMENTS. Thomas Ridge †1801. A few other plain tablets by Winchester masons (e.g. to Graemes †1823 and 1833, by *Kellow*). – Charles Gilbert Heathcote †1913. Nicely engraved small brass by *Culn, Gawthorpe & Sons*, London.

KILMESTON MANOR, N of the church, set back from the road. Quite large with an early C18 front of nine bays with two projecting wings. These are of two storeys but the centre is of two-and-a-half storeys; segment-headed windows with the original glazing bars, a one-bay central projection, and a doorway with Ionic pilasters. The floor levels express those of the C17 house behind, a hall and cross-wings still evident from the rear: the W (service) wing is early C17 and is timber-framed but faced in the same brick as the hall range and E (parlour) wing, which appear to have been rebuilt c. 1660. Good Artisan Mannerist details, especially to the E wing, in brick and red terracotta: two orders of pilasters, the lower plain, supporting an entablature with a pulvinated vine-trail frieze, and a moulded modillion cornice; above, short Ionic pilasters topped by discs, between them a short section of disconnected entablature, enriched with a guilloche frieze, repeated in the gable apex. On the inside face of this wing is a two-storey hipped roofed brick addition of c. 1700. In the centre, a large tile-hung gable marks the hall with, between the wings, a single-storey billiards room, Neo-Georgian, added 1902–3 by *B. D. Cancellor*. NE addition of c. 1936–8 by *Tatchell & Wilson* with an Ionic porch and Baroque gable with an oval window. Mixed interior with many early C18 fittings preserved, e.g. the fine staircase. The central hall was transformed in 1893 by *W. H. Veysey*, who made it double-height. Wooden gallery on four sides, in a curious mixture of Jacobean and Queen Anne, with elliptical arches on fluted square piers and a balustrade with barley-sugar balusters. In the early C18 E wing the rear room has a corner chimneypiece with reused C17 woodwork and painted overmantel of Europa and the bull.

In front an early C18 GATEWAY with panelled ashlar piers topped by later urns (signed *Coade & Sealy*). Gothick SUMMERHOUSE (E), and an early C18 brick PAVILION.

DEAN HOUSE, ¼ m. SE of church. Early C18 double-pile house with early and late C19 additions in Neo-Georgian style. Much C18 character inside. On the first floor is a painted overmantel, depicting a Venetian scene, flanked by arched recesses. NE of the house, a nicely detailed late C18 PAVILION, from the late C19 a billiard room etc. SE, late C19 STABLES of remarkable scale and deep plan more common to military stables. Surviving cast-iron fittings. C18 WALLED GARDEN, one section straddled by an octagonal POOL HOUSE, 2005, by *Barry Bohill*.

KIMPTON

ST PETER AND ST PAUL. The W tower is of 1837–9 by *Charles Parker*, a pupil of Wyattville, for G. S. Foyle of Kimpton Lodge and in a style designed to match the house (*see* below). It is of brick and flint, square, unfussy, and Gothick only in so far as it has a big high brick W lancet and lancets as bell-openings. Odd pediments with diamond-shaped panels to the parapet N and W. The rest is of *c.* 1220–1370. Flint nave and chancel under a continuous roof, a S aisle, and slightly lower transepts. Chancel essentially early C13, with lancet windows and priest's doorway – the two-light decorated E window renewed and SE window inserted in 1870. Early C14 N transept, with a tall N window left unrestored during renovations of 1901 by *B. D. Cancellor.* The S transept is slightly later, its two-light S window Dec, the small window below too, but re-set; for it cuts into the back wall of a tomb-recess. Original Perp NW window. The NE window imitates it, but must be post-Reformation. S porch, probably of 1702 when the S aisle was refaced. Striking S arcade, Early Dec with octagonal piers and double-chamfered arches dying into the imposts. Good trefoil-arch gabled PISCINA in the chancel. Also original early C14, the central tie-beam of the chancel roof with a foliate boss (cf. Overton), the rest of 1894. Other roofs renewed in 1896 (nave and S aisle) and 1899 (S transept). – ALTAR. A fine Elizabethan piece with elaborately carved balusters and typically late C16 carved rail at floor level. – STAINED GLASS. E window *c.* 1901 signed *Morris & Sons*, Kennington Road, London (not to be confused with Morris & Co.). – MONUMENTS. – Robert Thornburgh †1522. In the N transept, small Purbeck marble tomb-chest and, against the fragmentary back wall, brasses. Delightful kneeling figures of Robert (10 in., 25 cm. high), his first and second wives (with two children by the first and seven by the second) kneeling, all in the fashion of *c.* 1520, with Latin inscription issuing from the adults. Black-lettered inscription below already in English. – Foyle family †1658, unbelievably crude with rough lettering, skull and crossbones between hour-glass and pick and shovel. – Better early C17–early C19 tablets in the chancel, one severely classical. – Thomas Chalwell *c.* 1680 with oval inscription with fat cherubs in swags. – Edward Foyle †1732. Signed *Osmond*, with an urn. – Edward Foyle, of West Cholderton, thirty-four years rector †1781. Elegant Grecian manner. – George Soley Foyle †1839 and wife †1841, by *Osmond* of Salisbury.

Of KIMPTON LODGE, built *c.* 1835 and probably by *Parker*, there is only a fragment of the service wing and its former stables (now Coach House), with the same banded brick and flint walls and Dutch gables.

KIMPTON MANOR, NE of the church. A substantial fragment of the medieval rectory, comprising a long-jettied lodging range, built 1444–5 probably at the expense of John Lisle, Lord of the Manor. Close studding below the jetty of *c.* 1535, the date perhaps of the showy S wall of red brick and render in a che-querboard pattern; in the middle is a buttress and on the sides are further panels of diaper. Mullioned-and-transomed windows, restored in 2003–4 by *Robert Adam Architects*; the ground-floor oriel was reconstructed from evidence of oriels inserted in 1560. The original plan consisted of a central hallway with staircase, leading to chambers on both floors, two with inner rooms, all heated, and those on the first floor with garderobes too. Two good stone fireplaces survive, one C15 and one C16. The roof has unusual tapering unbraced crown-posts, found also in Cardinal Beaufort's lodgings at St Cross, Winchester (q.v.) Lisle was associated with the Duke of Somerset, a member of the Beaufort family, and served on a French expedition in the early 1440s financed by Cardinal Beaufort. The hall range appears to have projected at right angles at the rear, indicated by a four-centred arched doorway at the foot of the staircase. On its site a brick range, possibly added c. 1725 when alterations were carried out to the house. Staircase of about this date with turned balusters.

LITTLETON MANOR. *See* Fyfield.

KING'S SOMBORNE

A royal manor at Domesday, sold to William Briwere in 1190 (*see* Ashley) but returned into royal possession by the marriage of Blanche to John of Gaunt. 'John of Gaunt's Palace' stood s of the church but seems to have gone by the early C18 (Old Palace House, a very much altered C16 structure, may have been associated with its outbuildings). Between the village and Test stood the 400 acres of deerpark. C15 boundary banks with yews mark its extent.

ST PETER AND ST PAUL. Heavily restored by *J. Colson*, 1883–6. Long nave and chancel with the two aisles all under one roof. The w bell-turret with the stage below the bell-stage tapered and tile-hung is *Colson*'s. A few old windows, e.g. the reticulated E window, and the chancel s wall with external brick details of c. 1736, escaped attention. Part of the s arcade is early C13: round pier, round abacus, pointed arches of the same time. The one-bay N and s chancel chapels are early C14 (double-chamfered arches dying into the imposts). In the nave roof early C17 tie-beams with pendants. – FONT. Purbeck marble, of table type, octagonal. Unusually big. On each side two flat blank arches. – Former COMMUNION RAIL (s aisle). Jacobean. Charming, with alternating columnar and twisted balusters. It should be reinstated. – GRAFFITI on the E column of the s arcade, C13 Crucifixion and Virgin and Child. – STAINED GLASS. E window by *Ward & Hughes*, 1885. W window by *John Hayward*, 1996, to Sir Thomas Sopwith †1989. An aerial St Michael vanquishing Satan, with the artist's characteristically vigorous colouring. – MONUMENTS. Effigy of William de Brestowe, vicar 1305–27; very flat; under a Dec pointed-trefoiled canopy. – Brasses of two civilians (chancel floor), Tweedledum and Tweedledee, c. 1370–80. 29-in. (74-cm.) figures. Luke Stratton †1728. Old-fashioned cartouche with cherubs and a skull. Still C17 in style; by a local mason. – Needham family, 1736. Aedicule type with two columns and a broken segmental pediment. No figures.

N of the church on the green is the WAR MEMORIAL, *Lutyens*'s War Cross of 1921, paid for by Herbert Johnson of Marsh Court (q.v.), as at Stockbridge (q.v.). The Test valley vernacular is well represented in the village, including many high cob boundary walls, but the best house is the early C18 OLD VICARAGE, E of the church, with a handsome five-bay E front in header bond, raised on a substantial basement with flying stair and Doric porch. ('Interior almost completely unaltered, of great interest', DCMS.)

MANOR FARM HOUSE. ⅜ m. E at the edge of the village. Two parallel timber-framed ranges (now cased in flint and brick), built in 1504–8 by Magdalen College, Oxford. Inside, the W range has stop-chamfered mouldings to its doorways and evidence of two chambers, possibly originally served by a stair contained in the small projection at its NW corner. This accommodation was for the College's representative during visits (cf. Court House Farm, West Meon). The E range must have contained the hall of the farmhouse; it incorporates an even earlier cross-frame (tree-ring dated to 1301) with fragments of four-centred doorways, apparently leading to a lost service range.

COMPTON MANOR, 1¼ m. SW in its own park. Plain house of 1855, swankily embellished in 1890–1 by *Alfred Burr*. Brick DOVECOTE, 75 yds NW, dated 1726, with chalk nesting boxes. Unusually long weatherboarded BARN on over forty staddle-stones. KENNELS and other estate buildings of 1891 by *W. H. Mitchell, Son & Gutteridge* of Southampton.

At HORSEBRIDGE, ¾ m. N, the former STATION of 1865 (London & South Western Railway), nicely restored as a dwelling.

KINGS WORTHY

A large village, mainly suburban sprawl. Its historic centre lay on the King's Way to Winchester.

ST MARY. Largely Victorian as a result of three C19 enlargements. But the W half of the nave N wall and the plain unbuttressed W tower are medieval. The latter in three phases: the lower part perhaps early C13 (as Pevsner suggests) with a W doorway of two continuous nook rolls. The arch towards the nave on the other hand (two continuous chamfers dying into the imposts) looks rather *c.* 1300. The upper stage with straight-headed windows and a parapet is late C14. The S aisle is mostly of 1849 by *J. Colson* with a good low arcade. This was extended with the nave and a new chancel built in 1864, again by Colson, reusing C14 and C15 windows from the old chancel (one of the windows has elaborate Dec tracery, perhaps by a mason employed by Hyde Abbey who held the advowson). At the same time, the polygonal vestry, 'the only feature one may remember' (Pevsner), was added to the new chancel. S chapel by *W. O. Milne*, 1884, with two-bay arcade to the

chancel elaborately Perp but with original C15 chancel, s
windows re-set. Church Centre by *G. Swann*, 1999. – FONT.
C14. The bowl nicely panelled, including 'mouchette wheel'
tracery. Low C12 base of Purbeck marble. – LECTERN A good
brass eagle of 1842. – ROYAL ARMS of 1777, unusually with
curving ribbons with the churchwardens' names. – MONU-
MENTS. Fragment of a late C15 tomb-chest with four cusped
quatrefoils containing shields re-located in the chancel arcade
of 1884. In the churchyard, Lord Eversley and a classical urn.
– STAINED GLASS. s chapel sw, a small late C15 roundel of
SS Swithun and Birinus. Chancel E by *Ward & Hughes*, 1894.
s chapel E by *Powells*, *c.* 1885, with Cardinal Virtues represented
by female figures, from *Henry Holiday* designs. s chapel s and
s aisle w by *Alexander Gibbs*.

In LONDON ROAD, WISTERIA, an accomplished pair of early
C19 back-to-back cottages, occupied from 1812, and probably
designed, by the *Vokes* family of builders, carpenters and
wheelwrights. Two storeys, with three-bay fronts, in knapped
flint and brick with hipped tile roof. Ground-floor windows
with stepped voussoirs. Further on, the former READING
ROOM of 1885, in the Old English manner and behind it
former ALMSHOUSES of 1887; both must be by the same architect and were given by Richard Turnor of Kings Worthy House
(dem.).

KINGSWORTHY HOUSE, NW of the church, on the corner of
London Road and Church Lane. C18, with full-height bows
and porch, but refaced and remodelled in an Arts and Crafts
Neo-Georgian in 1905–6 by *H. J. Austin*, of *Paley & Austin*, for
himself. He first intended a more radical remodelling in a vernacular style, as seen in the character of the rear wings. They
are partly roughcast and tile-hung with some timberwork
under the eaves, and reuse old bricks. Set back between the
wings at the rear, a first-floor canted bay lighting the staircase,
tucked in under the jettied attic storey above. Wonderfully rich
interior, almost all Austin. Most striking, the series of fine
Neo-Georgian chimneypieces throughout the house, often
with exaggeratedly lugged architraves and old Delft tiles. Also
reused in attic rooms, a pair of painted C17 stone demi-figures
holding shields. In the grounds, an elegant OFFICE BUILDING,
1971 by *Sidney Kaye, Firmin & Partners* for Condor (Southern) Ltd, a steel construction company.

WORTHY PARK. *See* Abbots Worthy.

WORTHY DOWN CAMP. *See* South Wonston.

KINGSCLERE

5050

The town lies at the foot of the North Downs, at the junction of
roads to Newbury, Basingstoke and Winchester. Originally a
Saxon royal estate, Kingsclere was granted to the canons of St
Mary's, Rouen, in whose ownership it remained until 1335, when

it was transferred to the Archbishop of York, who passed it to his nephew, Sir William de Melton. It never achieved borough status but did have a market and the usual industries of milling, tanning and brewing. The town appears to have been moderately prosperous in the C18 but there was no major expansion (the railway never reached Kingsclere) until the C20.

ST MARY. At the centre of the town. Quite large, 130 ft (40 metres) long, impressive cruciform church, rebuilt shortly after 1130, when Henry I gave the advowson to the Augustinian Canons of St Mary's, Rouen. Of their church, the long nave, crossing tower and transepts survive, but the E end is mostly of c. 1270. The flint-faced exterior is the result of ferocious restoration by *Thomas Hellyer* of Ryde in 1848–9, apparently intending to return the Norman parts of the church closer to their pristine early C12 state. Old drawings show a very different exterior faced in Bembridge freestone (the northernmost use in the county), with a large Perp W window, and smaller windows to the originally battlemented tower. Many genuine Early Norman details remain *in situ* including several small windows high up in the nave walls, and best of all the well-preserved N doorway, with one order of columns and saltire crosses and zigzag in the arch evidently reddened by the major fire in 1402, after which Bishop William of Wykeham encouraged fund-raising for restoration. Also trustworthy, the small lower tier of single-light windows in the tower. They were l. and r. of the roofs and still open to the lantern space (21 ft, 6.5 metres square, like Old Basing) within – a feature of collegiate or monastic churches. The silly stone cap to the tower stair-turret is Hellyer's. Long chancel, with original but much rebuilt N vestry, and tall E window of three lights, heavily renewed externally with new cusps in 1848–9, but with apparently genuine internal angle shafts, moulded capitals and bases. The N windows of two lights are restored, retaining original stonework. The best-preserved part is the S chapel, originally of c. 1260 with a coeval SW doorway, but remodelled with typically Early Tudor windows of three lights c. 1502 (Dr G. H. Bull), possibly financed by the Prior and Canons of Bisham Priory, who then held the advowson. Both transepts have good Perp three-light windows, of characteristically early C15 pattern, in the style of Wynford and Yevele, no doubt inserted after 1402 (Dr G. H. Bull).

Inside, the powerful crossing arches set in ashlar walls are dominant. They are still impressive despite some partial pulling about and consequent restoration. The W arch toward the nave is mostly renewed but the elaborate patternwork below is genuine. – FONT. Norman, of Purbeck marble. Table-top type. The ornamental forms are the familiar blank arches, rosettes, arrows, roundels, and a four-petalled flower. Were parts re-carved in the C15? C19 base. – FONT COVER. Early C17. Typically Jacobean. – PULPIT. Carolean (?), with much carving.

In the main panels, a kind of Tree of Life. – CHANDELIER. Of brass, given in 1713. – ALTAR. In the crossing. Of the reordering, by *A. Cheek*, of 1966. – CHOIR STALLS. Of the restoration. – SCREENS. In the chancel arcade, also of 1848, modelled on late C13 parclose screens at St John Baptist, Winchester. (– TILES. Uncommonly many, of *c.* 1260 from the S chapel, now stored in the tower stair-turret.) – STAINED GLASS. In the chancel, by *Wailes*, all of 1848, especially the fine E window with geometrical grisaille patterns after early C13 work at Salisbury Cathedral. – S chapel E. A semi-abstract quilt-like landscape window of 1966 by *Lawrence Lee*. – SE. By *T. F. Curtis* of *Ward & Hughes*, 1902. The Marriage Feast at Cana. – SW of *c.* 1856 by *Wailes*. The Transfiguration. – N and S transepts, by *H. T. Bosdet*, 1901 and 1903. Dark, dense pictorial scenes. Another, N Transept W, of 1912 by *Bosdet*. – N transept E. By *Stanley North*, 1923, to John Porter, racehorse trainer. A shield shows the legendary Ormonde, greatest of his five Derby winners.

MONUMENTS. Quite a collection of small brasses and mural tablets in the S chapel, gathered from around the church. Brass to Cecily Gobard †1503. Small figure (15 in., 38 cm.). – Brass to William Estwood, vicar, †1519 (17 in., 43 cm.). – Smaller brass to John Bossewell †1580, author of the heraldic treatise *The Armoire of Arms* (1572). Inscription, appropriately with his own achievement! – Thomas Pryor †1780. The best of the tablets, with an urn held in a broken pediment. – Sir Henry and Lady Bridget Kingsmill †1625 and 1672 respectively. Evicted from the N chapel in 1965 (when railings were lost), now free-standing in the S transept. Large and impressive monument of white and black marble erected in 1670 by Lady Bridget who, at the same time, gave a large silver flagon to the church. Splendid, recumbent effigies of alabaster, unusually well carved, both in the faces and hands and in the draperies. Large tomb-chest with luscious armorial cartouches and swags at the ends. The inscription is followed by a signature, *W.S.* The style fits *William Stanton* (GF) but the details are old-fashioned for 1670.

In the CHURCHYARD, a large lidless C13 stone COFFIN of unusual form, perhaps the parish mortsafe, for holding corpses before burial.

ST PETER AND ST PAUL (R.C.), Swan Street. *See* PERAMBULATION.

The character of the town is prosperous Georgian, but this is largely skin-deep, with a significant survival of late medieval fabric behind. The church stands at the centre, since the C19 open on its N side to the former market place at the junction of the principal streets. On the W side of this is PRIORY HOUSE (No. 2, Newbury Road) and PRIORY COTTAGE (No. 1, North Street), Georgian fronts concealing a high-status late medieval house with two-bay hall, and cross-wing to the r. NW of the church, FALCONS has two rear wings, of which the E wing is a C15 three-bay timber-framed hall range, which was originally jettied on its E front with a two-bay cross-wing of similar date at the far end. Its projecting front has been shaved off, no doubt when this side was refaced. The other wing, along the road and defining the rear courtyard, is lower, with a jettied first floor at its W end. In North Street, off the market place, is another concealed medieval house (Nos. 3–5) with a first-floor trefoil-headed window, c. 1400, in the former cross-wing. Downhill along Newbury Road to the W is THE OLD HOUSE. 1684, brick, originally four bays, with segmental-headed first-floor windows. Extended one bay to the l. in the C18. Late C18 pedimented doorcase. Stair-tower at the rear. Close by to the S, in Fox's Lane, the OLD VICARAGE of 1850 by *Hellyer*. Brick and flint, an asymmetrical composition around a central gable with, to its r., a timber-framed porch and (truncated) chimney. It cost £1,407 to build. Hellyer's alternative Neo-Tudor design in diapered brickwork was no doubt too expensive.

GEORGE STREET leads E from the church. Built into the rear of PHOENIX HOUSE (No. 5) is a moulded archway of reused medieval stone, set in a surround of knobbly flintwork. Did it come from the church during its restoration? On the S side of George Street, No. 2 looks early C18, with panels of red and vitrified brickwork, but the chimney, with the remains of three octagonal stacks, is a clue to its earlier origins. Inside is a C16 timber-framed cross-wing, jettied to front and side, and, in a first-floor room, a fine Tudor-arched stone fireplace.

SWAN STREET, S from the centre, is the town's showpiece, with the best houses. After the church on the W side, and a vestigial piece of market place opposite, buildings are on both sides, including, on the r., Nos. 8–10, early C18 brick with vitrified headers, the arches of the upper windows cut in a wavy pattern. On the E side, THE SWAN HOTEL, which was acquired by Winchester College in 1485, and first recorded as the Swan Inn in 1533. In two parts, to the l. early C18, vitrified brick with red dressings, five bays, windows with cambered heads, and central doorway with flat hood. To the r. a similar, but unsymmetrical elevation. Behind this is a spectacular two-bay open hall, built 1448–9. The first floor, inserted 1533–6, has been removed, revealing the roof with its central jointed-cruck-truss and two tiers of purlins with curved wind-braces. Remains of a cross-wing to the r. Then, Nos. 21–23, and the same thing again. Externally a pair of nice early C18 three-bay houses, of vitrified headers with red brick dressings, but inside a substantial C15 framed house. In the centre a one-bay hall range and cross-passage; to the l. a two-bay jettied cross-wing, the upper chambers each with a central arch-braced truss; to the r. a further two bays, in line, also originally jettied, the bay closest to the hall with wall paintings: a trellis pattern with flowers. Also at this end, a good late C17 staircase with barley-sugar balusters. Next door, the ALBERT HALL (now St Peter and St Paul R.C. church), of 1886, by a '*Mr Doller*' (probably *Peter Dollar*). Brick, with a kind of Dutch gable and pilasters, culminating in a curved pediment. Opposite, No. 20, another hall-and-cross-wing house concealed behind an c18 brick façade. Of *c.* 1400, the central truss of the two-bay hall, originally arch-braced, has a carved boss of a head in a head-dress. Further along, SWAN HOUSE, the best early c18 house in Kingsclere. Of vitrified header brickwork with red dressings. Segmental-headed windows, those on the first floor with half-H aprons. Hipped roof. Neo-Georgian wing added 1928. Inside, staircase with ramped handrail, round-arched openings off hall and landing and a few chimneypieces.

GAILEY MILL, ⅜ m. S, in the open countryside. Early c19 MILL and MILL HOUSE with a contemporary five-bay timber-framed BARN and a GRANARY on cast-iron staddles. A nice unaltered group.

PARK HOUSE STABLES. ¾ m. S. Established in 1867 by Sir Joseph Hawley. His trainer, John Porter, influenced the design and bought the stables after Hawley's death in 1875, spending £20,000 on considerable additions and improvements. Red brick and tile ranges around two courtyards, solidly built with some terracotta ornament. The upper yard buildings bear the date 1897. Distinctive battlemented water tower in the lower yard.

KINGSLEY

7030

The site of a royal deerpark within Woolmer Forest and not recorded as a separate manor until the mid c15. It is an amorphous village, with a greatly reduced medieval core around the original parish church (St Nicholas) to the W and two post-medieval settlements on the N side of Kingsley Common to the E, around much-encroached-upon Upper and Lower Greens.

ALL SAINTS. 1875–6 by *J. H. & E. Dyer* of Alton. Nave and chancel; bellcote. Windows with plate tracery. Surprisingly violent High Victorian exposed brick interior with two shades of 'Fareham reds' and strident yellow diaper patterns. – TILES in the chancel by *Minton, Hollins & Co.* – STAINED GLASS. E window by *Ward & Hughe*s, 1876, with a restless Ascension scene. SW window. A c15 English roundel.

ST NICHOLAS, ¾ m. W. Brick nave and chancel in one; low with a small weatherboarded W bellcote. Mostly 1778 but the E and W ends are older and the E window (renewed) looks *c.* 1300, with two trefoil-headed lights and cinquefoil of odd shape. Decidedly domestic interior, with W gallery of 1800 by *Jason Harding*. – Plain stone tub FONT of indeterminate date and small c13 trefoil-headed PISCINA. – Painted paired inscriptions on E wall. DECALOGUE, probably c18, on the E wall. – STAINED GLASS. E window, by *Geoffrey Webb*, 1949.

Large C19 table tomb to William Bennett, with a conde-
scending inscription worth reading. Nice LYCHGATE of 1904.

LODE FARMHOUSE, ¼ m. W of St Nicholas, occupies the manorial site. Tile-hung C17 baffle-entry house, the ground floor
rebuilt in C18 brick. Earlier hall range at the rear. Prominent
early C19 farm buildings: seven-bay malmstone barn and pair
of weatherboarded granaries on staddles.

WESTERKIRK, ½ m. W on the N side of the main road. A modest
cottage of c. 1800 with an imposing four-window front, produced by an interesting plan of heated rooms placed either side
of the central entrance passage, and flanked in turn by small
unheated service rooms, repeated on the first floor.

OCKHAM HOUSE, SW on the common. Built in 1876 by *E. C.
Robins* for the Misses Lushington as the country's first co-
educational boarding school. Stuccoed Neo-Tudor, H-plan
with boarding houses in the wings and the headmistress's room
marked by a central canted bay with the hall and classrooms
in a wing behind. Converted to housing in 1980.

KNIGHTS ENHAM
Andover

Once a tiny village N of Andover, but the modern town has crept
up to meet it.

ST MICHAEL. Odd exterior with a small bell-turret and nave and
chancel in one. Early Norman in origin but in the chancel
lancet windows (E window by *A. R. Barker*, 1872); the nave
originally had a two-bay arcade, also C13, its blocked arches
exposed. Low C17 S porch. C15 nave roof with castellated wall-
plates (cf. Greywell). – COMMUNION RAILS. C17. – FONT.
Norman; defaced. Small, with tapering sides. Frieze of
stylized leaves. Perhaps of West Country Romanesque type.
Trellis below. – ROOD BEAM. Moulded, a rare survival. The
SCREEN looks post-Reformation. Can it be C17? – CHANDE-
LIER. Of brass, the Baroque type of body. Dated 1798. –
SCULPTURE. Outside, over the vestry N window, a C12 head,
probably from a rood. It could be earlier still. – STAINED
GLASS. E window. Quite good, signed *Alexander Gibbs*, 1876.
Three Archangels. Nave NE lancet. By *P. H Newman* (signed).
Poetic to a rector †1876. – MONUMENTS. Several C18 tablets.
The best to George Dewar †1786, signed by *Charles Harris* of
London.

OLD RECTORY, E. C18. Stuccoed. Five bays with pretty Chinese
Chippendale lattice porch. SE, MANOR FARMHOUSE. Late
C18. Brick. Three bays with segmental-arched tripartite sashes.
In the field to the N, earthworks and an avenue of limes.
Possibly the manorial site.

See also ENHAM ALAMEIN.

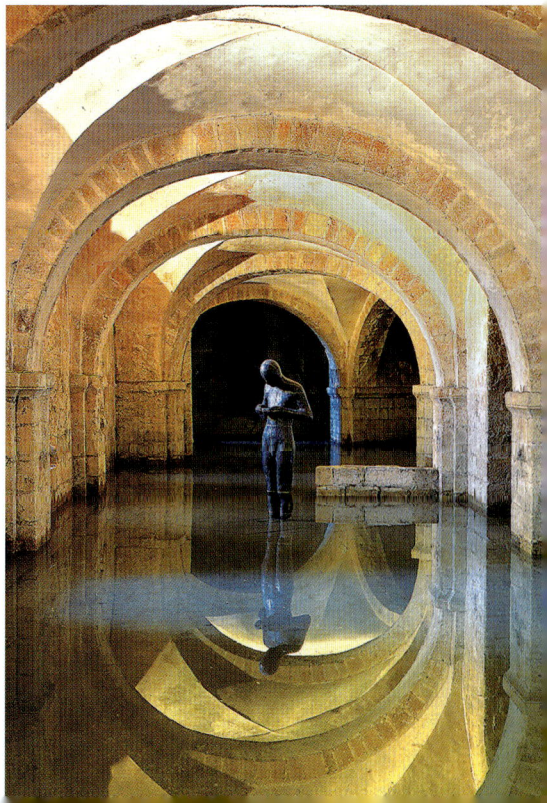

Winchester
Cathedral,
N transept interior,
begun 1079
(pp. 578–9)

East Meon,
All Saints, exterior,
with tower of *c.* 1150
(p. 241)

Winchester
Cathedral, crypt,
N aisle, C11, with
sculpture 'Sound II'
by Antony Gormley,
1986 (pp. 588–9)

19. Winchester, St Cross Hospital, church, capitals from the NE chapel, detail (p. 715)
20. Winchester, St Cross Hospital, church, exterior from the NW (p. 711)
21. Winchester, St Cross Hospital, church, crossing and S transept (p. 712)

7. Winchester Castle, Great Hall, interior looking W, 1222–36 (pp. 641–2)

8. Hartley Wespall, St Mary, W wall exterior, c. 1330 (p. 311)

9. East Meon, The Court House, hall interior looking N, by William Wynford, 1395–7 (pp. 244)

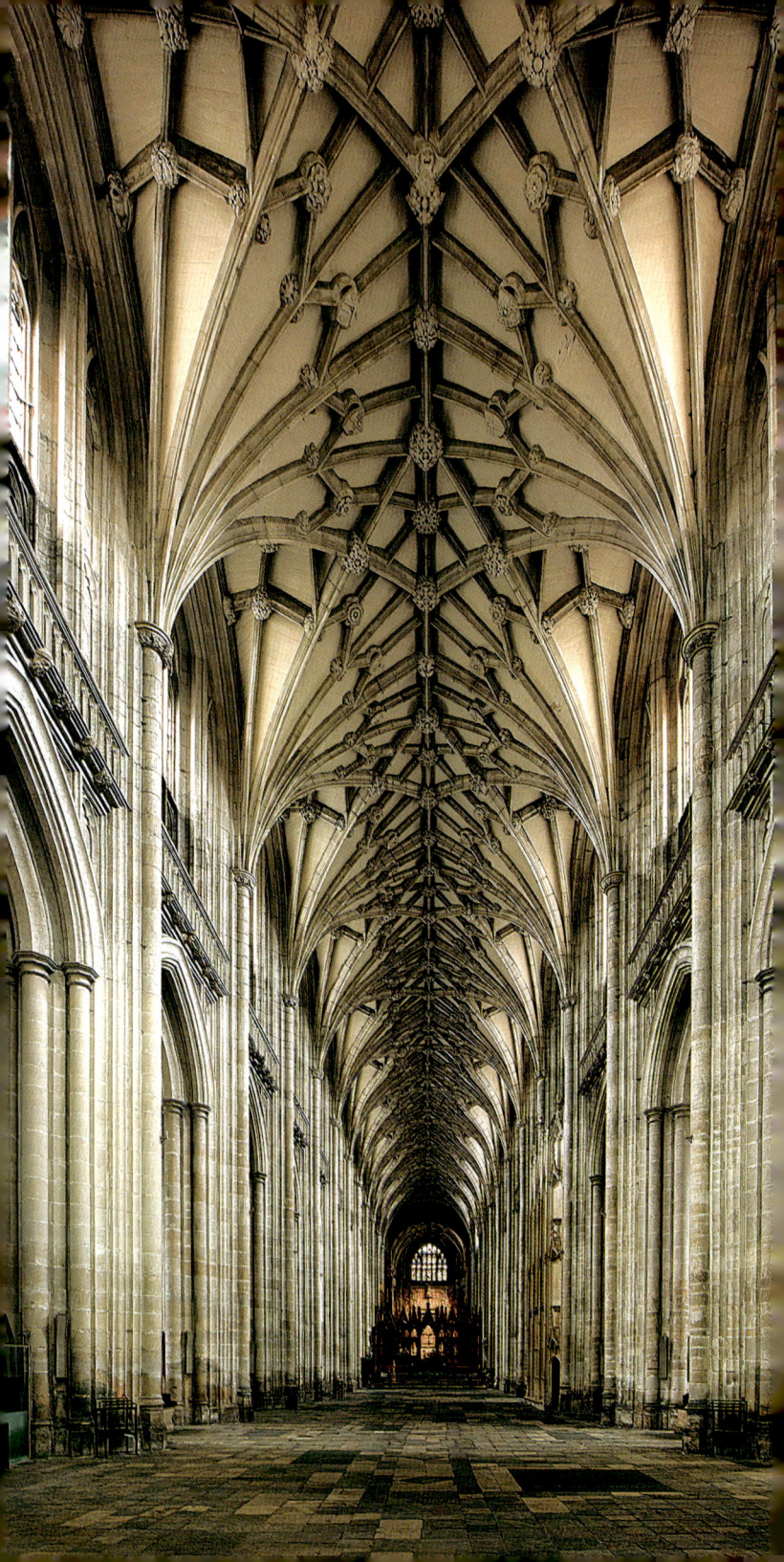

40. Winchester Cathedral, w front, c14 (pp. 575–6)
41. Winchester College, chapel from the NE, late c14, tower rebuilt by
    Butterfield, 1862–3 (p. 648)

42. Winchester College, Fromond's Chantry Chapel, probably by Robert Hulle, *c.* 1425–45 (p. 651)
43. Winchester College, stained glass, panel from the former E window, by Thomas of Oxford, *c.* 1393–1406 (p. 649)
44. Winchester College, statue of Virgin and Child above Outer Gate, *c.* 1395 (p. 646)
45. Winchester College, chapel, interior looking E, 1387–95 (pp. 648–9)

46. Bramley, Manor House, exterior, *c.* 1545–6 (p. 195)
47. Priors Dean, Goleigh Manor House, exterior from the E, *c.* 1464–6, hall rebuilt 1646 (p. 460)
48. Sherfield-on-Loddon, Breach Farm, barn, interior, *c.* 1391 (p. 477)
49. Old Basing, Grange Farm, Great Barn, interior, *c.* 1534–5 (p. 433)

56. The Vyne, Oak Gallery, linenfold panelling, *c.* 1525, (p. 538)
57. Old Basing, Basing House, carved stone bust of 'Roman Emperor', mid-C16 (p. 431)
58. The Vyne, chapel, interior with C16 fittings (p. 536)
59. Chawton House, exterior from SE, hall range and parlour wing *c.* 1583–4, porch and south range *c.* 1590 (p. 218)

66. Crondall, All Saints, tower, from the N E, c. 1659 (p. 232)

67. Kingsclere, St Mary, monument to Sir Henry and Lady Bridget Kingsmill †1625 and 1672, erected 1670 (p. 361)

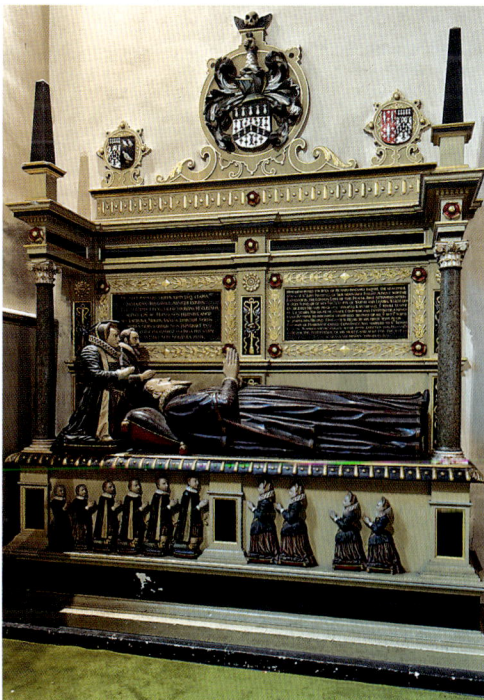

86. Avington, St Mary, interior, 1768–71 (p. 152)
87. Wolverton, St Catherine, exterior from the SE, showing nave and tower, 1717 (p. 728)
88. Mortimer West End Chapel, exterior, 1798 (p. 402)

93. East Stratton, Stratton Park, portico by George Dance the Younger, 1803–6 (p. 246)
94. The Grange, portico by William Wilkins, *c.* 1809–10 (p. 296)

95. Winchester Cathedral, monument to Joseph Warton †1800, by John Flaxman, 1801–4 (p. 617)

96. Highclere Castle, Rotunda, late C18, altered by Sir Charles Barry, 1838–9 (p. 336)

7. Micheldever, St Mary, by George Dance the Younger, interior of the nave looking E, 1806–8 (p. 394)
8. Deane, All Saints, interior looking E, with Coade stone chancel screen by Thomas Dubbin, 1818–20 (p. 236)
9. Andover, St Mary, interior, by Augustus Livesay, 1840–4 (p. 133)

100. Highclere Castle, exterior from the NE, remodelled by Sir Charles
Barry, 1838–48 (p. 331)
101. East Tisted, Rotherfield Park, staircase hall, by J. Parkinson, 1815–24,
altered and redecorated by J. G. Crace, 1858 (p. 249)
102. Highclere Castle, Saloon, by Sir Charles Barry, c. 1848, fitted out by
Thomas Allom, 1860s (p. 334)

103. Elvetham Hall, entrance front, by S.S. Teulon, 1859–60, altered and enlarged 1910–11, by Stanley Pool (p. 257)
104. Hawkley, St Peter and St Paul, tower, by Teulon, 1864–5 (p. 317)
105. Winchester, Guildhall, by Jeffery & Skiller, 1871–3 (p. 658)

106. Fleet, All Saints, by William Burges, 1861–2, interior (p. 286)

107. Farnborough Abbey, interior looking E, by Gabriel Hippolyte-Alexandre Destailleur, 1883–8 (p. 273)
108. Church Crookham, Christ Church, stained glass from the W window, by Powells, 1901, detail (p. 225)
109. Winchester Castle, Great Hall, statue of Queen Victoria, by Alfred Gilbert, 1887 (p. 642)
110. Farnborough Abbey, exterior, by Gabriel Hippolyte-Alexandre Destailleur, 1883–8 (p. 273)

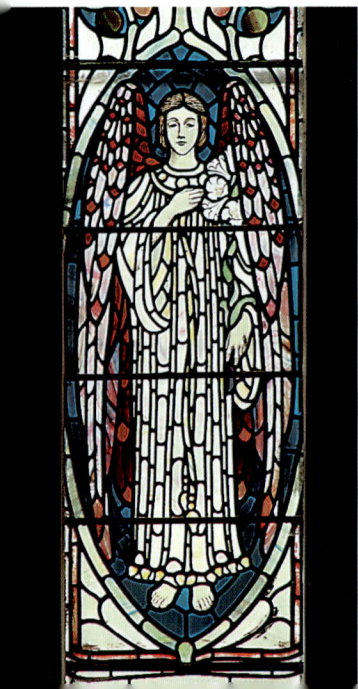

111. Basingstoke, All Saints, interior looking E, by Temple Moore, 1915–17 (p. 159)
112. Aldershot, St Joseph (R.C.), exterior, by George Drysdale, 1911–13 (p. 105)
113. Steep, Bedales School, Memorial Library, by Ernest Gimson, 1911, design revised and built 1918–21 (p. 496)

114. Marsh Court, s front, by Sir Edwin Lutyens, 1901–4, enlarged 1924–6 (p. 389)
115. Berrydown, by Sir Edwin Lutyens, 1897–8 (p. 179)
116. West Green, Four Acre House, by Ernest Newton, 1901–2 (p. 542)
117. Burghclere, Sandham Memorial Chapel, war paintings by Stanley Spencer, 1926–32 (p. 211)

118. Winchester, Elizabeth II Court (County Hall), by C. Cowles-Voysey, revised by John Brandon-Jones, 1956–9 (pp. 657–8)

119. Crawley, Crooked Pightle House, by Robert Adam, 1988–9 (p. 231)

120. Fleet Infants' School, by Michael Hopkins & Partners, 1986 (p. 287)
121. Winchester, County Record Office, by Colin Stansfield-Smith, 1992–3 (p. 662)

122. Farnborough Business Park, office blocks by Allies & Morrison, 2005–6, with the skeleton of a airship hangar, 1910–11 (p. 283)

LAINSTON

ST PETER, SW of Lainston House. In ruins, following the removal
of the lead from the roof in 1854 (the benefices of Lainston
and Sparsholt were united in 1850). Only the nave survives;
the E wall is wide open to the landscape. Probably early C12.
Flint with stone dressings, still partly rendered. Plain Norman
N and S doorways. By the N doorway a Tudor STOUP. Later
windows, the best-preserved the W window of three stepped
arched lights. It looks early C17 Gothic of a familiar type (e.g.
Folke and Leweston, Dorset).

LAINSTON HOUSE. A late C17 house given one beauty treatment
and then another. The older part is the garden (E) side which
was the entrance front. Two storeys with a hipped roof, a
moulded stone plinth, string course, stone quoins on the inner
angles of the two-bay wings, and windows with bolection-
moulded stone architraves. The centre has a three-bay pedimented break flanked by narrow bays, and basement windows
are mullioned. The entrance front is superficially similar, but
the windows have stuccoed lugged architraves, and it was probably altered *c.* 1700 (in 1714 Sir John Evelyn described the
house as '. . . very much improved by alterations and additions'). But what is the date of the single-storey porch filling
the width of the three-bay centre? Round the corners the
façades must be *c.* 1721 when John Merrill bought the estate:
five bays in a plum-coloured brick, the segment-headed
windows with lugged architraves of beautifully moulded
rubbed brick. Of similar quality, the brick quoins and moulded
platband, the latter taken around the entrance front. Of probably the same date also the handsome, brick, twelve-bay
arcaded LOGGIAS flanking the forecourt. Stout drum-like
GATEPIERS, with bands of brick rustication and spear-like
stone finials. Are they late C19? Nice wrought-iron gates,
reached by a bridge over a dry moat.

The T-shaped N wing is in matching style, added *c.* 1897
when Samuel Bostock bought and restored the house. The
interior is also mostly the same date, in the style of 1700. The
best thing, however, is the fine well STAIRCASE in the N wing;
its style suggests it must have been installed around 1721: four
flights, the upper flight curving out to a wider landing, with
pairs of slim twisted balusters, fluted columnar newels and a
ramped handrail with a pair of wreathed newels at the foot.
Matching panelled dado with fluted pilasters. Also at the foot,
a screen of Corinthian columns, and at the head an elliptical
archway.

Converted for hotel use (*c.* 1982 by *Green, Lloyd & Adams*),
with, to the N, a timber-framed building consisting of two parallel hip-roofed ranges. Beyond this is a nice early C18 octagonal DOVECOTE, with chequer brickwork and pyramidal tile
roof. Adjoining the walled garden, an C18 WELL-HOUSE, with
a horse engine inside. Remains of *c.* 1700 formal GARDENS.

LODGE, ¼ m. NE on the Stockbridge Road. By *Forbes & Tate*, 1922. Arts and Crafts Georgian. LAINSTON FARM, ½ m. WSW of the house. Arts and Crafts Tudor. Nearby, the model LAINSTON DAIRY (now a house), 1929 by *G. W. King Ltd*. Former cowhouses on three sides of a courtyard, with horizontal windows that have rather Baroque stuccoed lugged architraves. In the centre, the octagonal dairy, with pretty glazed tiles.

LAKE HOUSE *see* THE GRANGE

7020

LANGRISH

St JOHN EVANGELIST. 1869–71 by *Ewan Christian*. Freely treated E.E. Nave and chancel, lower N aisle. The small polygonal stone turret placed over a central buttress, between windows, is what one may remember. Three-bay arcade on low piers of polished Devonshire marble. Boarded pointed ceiling to the chancel. Open arch-braced roof to the nave. Contemporary FONT of Caen stone with inlaid marble and carved lilies in quatrefoils. STAINED GLASS. E window by *Heaton, Butler & Bayne* 1870. – Nave SE, possibly by *W. F. Dixon*. To John Waddington †1880, 'principal benefactor of the church'. MONUMENTS. War memorial. *c.* 1920 with sentinel sailor and soldier. A coloured wreath and crossed flags.

LANGRISH HOUSE, ½ m. S. Picturesque Neo-Tudor, for John Waddington, 1842.

LANGRISH MANOR FARM, ¼ m. NE above the village. Good C18 malmstone and brick farmstead group with simple farmhouse and aisled barn. Best is the square DOVECOTE with a wide gable to each face; converted to a hop store *c.* 1800, with inserted lancet openings.

BORDEAN HOUSE, ½ m. NW. Two-storey-and-attic main range with wings, probably built for Sir Roger Langrish in 1611; but brick quoins to the wings, sash windows, a single-storey stuccoed corridor between the wings and large Venetian staircase window at the rear are mid-C18 remodellings. The three-storey Northern Renaissance porch (reusing the C18 pedimented Ionic doorcase) and the canted bays of the wings are of 1879 for William Nicholson (*see* Basing House, Privett), while the Baroque dormers and the hipped roof are of 1911–13, contemporary with the very large service wing (now separate dwellings). Mainly good mid-C18 interiors except for the principal ground-floor rooms of *c.* 1911–13, e.g. pretty Arts and Crafts plaster ceiling in the drawing room. Stone stair with wrought-iron balustrade. Is it C18?

LASHAM

A compact village grouped around a large pond, with the church at a crossroads. Mostly C17 and C18 thatched cottages, timber-framed and brick.

ST MARY. 1866–7 by *Woodyer*. E.E. Coursed flint nave and lower chancel. Very tall single-lancet E window, massively shafted. Bell-turret with shingled broach spire. Excellent timber-framed S porch, beautifully carpentered. Tall pointed trefoil-arched inner S doorway. Inside, the E and S chancel windows all shafted. The vestry doorway has, hanging from one impost only, the most extraordinary drooping grapes of stiff-leaf. These are two personal touches. Original furnishings are almost all preserved. – Marble FONT. – REREDOS, with carved cross, grapes and wheat, effectively allied to the E windows which retain polychrome painting on the splays. Good chancel fittings. – TILES by *Minton*. – PULPIT replaced by *G. H. Kitchin*, 1933; Early Tudor style, with genuine Jacobean SOUNDING BOARD imported from St Mary, Herriard. – STAINED GLASS. By *Hardman*, especially good the E window with deep coloured medallions. – MONUMENTS. Tablets to Theobalds, †1910 and †1930, by the architect *Godfrey Pinkerton*, made by *Powells*.

LASHAM HOUSE, S, was the rectory. Mid-C18 in two phases, Five bays, brick, pedimented centre with lunette. Service wing added 1821 and later C19 alterations, e.g. doorcase.

MANOR FARMHOUSE, ¼ m. N. C17 timber frame with herringbone brick-nogging, much rebuilt in brick in the C18. Good farm buildings, including early C19 thatched GRANARY on staddles, mid-C19 brick STABLES/COACHHOUSE and good five-bay single-aisled barn dated 1810.

Former BENTWORTH AND LASHAM STATION, 1 m. SSW of the village. Corrugated-iron building of 1901, typical of the impecunious and short-lived Basingstoke & Alton Light Railway.

LAVERSTOKE

Laverstoke and Freefolk

Henry (or Henri) Portal, a French Huguenot, established a paper-making business at Bere Mill on the Test in 1712; in 1718 he took over Laverstoke Mill, around which the modern village has developed. The old village must have been to the E, close to the site of the partly Late Saxon church, SE of Laverstoke House.*

ST MARY. By *J. L. Pearson*, 1892–6, well detailed but not among his best; the cost of £10,000 was met by Melville and

---

*Restored and adapted as a mausoleum for the Portal family in 1876 by *Woodyer*, the church was dismantled in 1952. The monuments are at Hinton Ampner (q.v.).

Wyndham Spencer Portal. E.E., flint and brown stone. s flanking tower with shingled splay-foot spire. Five-bay nave, N aisle (both lancet-windowed throughout), chancel with plate tracery. No E window. Inside, nothing is vaulted, but everything is very highly finished. Especially elaborate, the detail in the chancel of Bath stone ashlar, with the one exciting feature of a wall passage or detached shafting and double tracery of the s windows. Exceptionally rich furnishings: luxuriant REREDOS, loosely modelled on Tilman Riemenschneider's Gothic altarpiece in St Jackob, Rothenburg-ob-der-Tauber, Bavaria. Central Crucifixion and saints, carved by *Moose*, the paintings by *Clayton & Bell*. – Stone PISCINA and SEDILIA combined in the SE window. – Patterned marble mosaic on chancel floor. Good ironwork on the vestry door by *Potter*, also above the organ screen. – ROOD SCREEN carved by *Luscombe* of Exeter. – ROOD with angels. – War Memorial Chapel of 1920 under the tower, with contemporary SCREEN and panelling by *Sir T. G. Jackson*, who at the same time provided dormer windows in the nave. – FONT. Elemental. Square, tapering to corner columns. – LIGHT FITTINGS of wrought iron. – STAINED GLASS. All by *Clayton & Bell*. Only the tower window, a Tree of Jesse, need be noticed. – LYCHGATE of c. 1896.

E of St Mary, the former SCHOOL and MASTER'S HOUSE of c. 1858 by *G. E. Street*, for Melville Portal. Flint with brick dressings, tile roofs. The school (l.) has a splendid timber porch with scissor truss in the gable and lattice glazing; r. the master's house, a cross-wing with half-hipped gable. Show front to the church with a large window, of three trefoil-headed lights and plate tracery. Flanking shields with Gothic monograms.

s of the church, MANOR COTTAGES, very extensive and entertaining model dwellings by *A. E. Mort* for Lord Portal. Late Arts and Crafts, with thatched roof and half-timbered gables, a style that Pevsner thought 'a little ridiculous' for 1939. At each end the row curves out with a loggia of paired brick columns. Landscaped garden and thatched well-head.

p. 82   LAVERSTOKE MILL, ¼ m. SE. Rebuilt in 1719 by Henry Portal; in 1724 he obtained the contract to manufacture banknote paper for the Bank of England. No early C18 buildings survive; the pedimented MILL HOUSE, outside the main factory, is c. 1800. The mill was largely rebuilt 1854–61 by *Thomas Hellyer* of Ryde to produce full-printed banknotes, see the protective three-storey GATEHOUSE, red brick with vitrified brick dressings. But within the courtyard are some workers' cottages (N side) of 1842, with cast-iron casements in paired Gothic lights, the two-storey glazing house of 1881 (E side) with a row of round-arched windows in the gable-end and re-set datestone recording the first house and mill, and beyond it the former wheel house of 1854, and on the N side the mid-C19 offices. On the W side a large and quite handsome free Neo-Georgian building of 1916 built to cope with wartime demand. It contained two cylinder moulding machines on the ground floor with a mould office above. The building is five bays deep with

a louvred ventilator. Production ceased *c.* 1963. Along the E
side of Laverstoke Lane, some workers' housing, e.g. No. 5,
Neo-Tudor of 1850. A plaque on No. 6 claims it was built for
the Bank's officer in 1785.

BERE MILL, ¾ m. SW of St Mary, on the Test. House and corn
mill of 1710, acquired by Henry Portal in 1712 for paper
making. The house brick, the mill weatherboarded, with a later
C18 range at right angles, of brick and flint but with weatherboarding at first floor on top of older, vertical boards laid so
one board can slide in front of another to allow ventilation.
A long brick rear wing, part thatched, presumably originally a
barn. Paper making ceased *c.* 1815 but in 1906 a turbine was
installed to supply electricity for the estate.

LAVERSTOKE HOUSE

The house, built in 1796–8 for Harry Portal, Henry's grandson,
is superbly sited in its landscaped park on the gently sloping
N side of the Test valley. It is by *Joseph Bonomi*, but quite
conventional and significantly different from the design he
exhibited at the Royal Academy in 1799, which has an *in antis*
portico and a semicircular service court. Yellow brick, the principal front of seven bays with a detached giant portico of very
slender unfluted Ionic columns with pronounced entasis and
Coade stone capitals supporting a triangular pediment with a
carved coat of arms. The entrances were in porches in the six-
bay side elevations. The E side now has the principal entrance,
and is marked by a stone porte cochère with paired Ionic
columns, probably of *c.* 1855 when alterations were made for
Melville Portal, almost certainly by *P. C. Hardwick*: he was
architect to the Bank of England, for whom the Portals' mills
supplied paper (*see* above). Of the same date, the oval carriage
sweep within a low balustrade, and probably the added canted
bay on the W front.

The C18 plan was of three rooms along the S front, with a
central staircase hall behind, reached by passages from the side
entrances. This is still legible in spite of mid-C19 changes and
remodelling and redecoration in 1932 by *Seely & Paget*. The
groin-vaulted E passage is possibly of the 1790s but the STAIR-
CASE HALL was enlarged in the mid C19 and the C18 stone
stair transformed into an impressive imperial pattern; the cast-
iron balustrade has Melville Portal's monogram. The 1790s
ornament was preserved, including the palmette frieze at first
floor, the cornice with alternating paterae and bucrania, and
the oval roof-light, with husk garlands and drops in its frieze.
The LIBRARY, at the SW corner, was combined with the
former W entrance corridor in the mid C19; and given a screen
of scagliola Ionic columns. The Adam Revival decoration of
the DINING ROOM (NE corner), including a screened alcove,
is of 1932 but with a good late C18 chimneypiece.

The rear service courtyard flanked by two-storey ranges was probably refaced, and closed off at the N end in the mid C19. The tower in the centre of this is a typical *Hardwick* feature. Further short wings project to form an outer court. NW ball-room wing of *c.* 1870, remodelled *c.* 1905 by *T.G. Jackson*, as a billiard room. He also built the single-storey linking corridor down the W side of the house; its interior is Baroque in feel and incorporates heraldic glass by *Powells*. The BILLIARD ROOM itself has good Arts and Crafts-inspired plasterwork and at one end a domed apse with curved benches and a chimneypiece with a mixture of Jacobean and Baroque motifs. Courtyard roofed over in *c.* 1998–2001 by *Robert Adam Architects*, taking over from, and adapting the design of, *Alan Bouverie*, and an atrium formed within, surrounded by a colon-nade on three sides and plain window openings to the upper two floors. Stripped classical internal elevations, with first-floor and attic openings framed by pilaster-strips. The S side is spanned at first floor by a glass gallery.

Adjoining to NW a large covered SWIMMING POOL AND GYMNASIUM, in the form of an C18 orangery, by *Robert Adam*. Around the same time a large walled court was created at the back of the house, incorporating the mid-C19 flint and brick STABLES. In the corridor to the swimming pool and gymna-sium are C18 grave-slabs to the Portals, presumably recovered from Old St Mary (dem.).

The impressive PARK, enclosed by thick belts of trees around the perimeter, was created in the early C19, probably with the removal of the main road to the S side of the Test. S of the house the lawn is separated from the park by a HA-HA, and below the W front are pleasure gardens with raised areas of rockery.

NW of the house, the brick WALLED GARDEN. In the centre of the E side is a mid-C19 gateway with wrought-iron gate on the axis of the GARDENER'S COTTAGE of *c.* 1854 by *Hard-wick*, in an elaborate Picturesque Gothic style. Flint and brick with a tile-hung first floor, banded tile roof with ornate barge-boards, and a chimney with a cluster of octagonal flues. To the garden is a projecting wing with an open Gothic arcade and a an oriel window on brackets. To its r., around the corner, a circular stair-turret which has lost its original steeply pitched conical roof (cf. The Old Rectory, Freefolk). At its foot is the Gothic timber porch with gableted roof. The other LODGES all share variations on this same style and materials and are prob-ably also by Hardwick although they range in date from 1848 to 1863.

ROUND BARROWS, ½ m. SW of Roundwood Farm. The group consists of two disc barrows, a bell barrow and a twin barrow – two mounds surrounded by a common ditch. The disc barrows have been almost obliterated by ploughing and are difficult to detect. The bell barrow, 70 ft (22 metres) in diameter and 9 ft (2.8 metres) high, was excavated in 1920 and

Laverstoke, Gardener's Cottage.
Design drawing by P.C. Hardwick, c. 1854

found to cover a central pit containing a cremated male burial. The twin barrow, which was excavated at the same time, proved to have been robbed.

LECKFORD

3030

ST NICHOLAS. Low, agreeably under-restored exterior. The identifiable external features are all Perp, but the chancel is Norman (round-arched priest's doorway) and the nave C13.

Timber s porch dated 1899. Blunt timber w bellcote of 1933–4
by *W. Ravenscroft*. Nice barrel-ceiled interior, well furnished.
Architecturally it is curious that the Late Perp chancel arch,
typically C15 with continuous mouldings, is off centre of the
nave. It is likely that a N aisle had existed and was at some time
thrown into the nave, perhaps *c.* 1500 indicated by N and S
windows with four-centred rere-arches on slender shafts and
by two Perp image niches in the E wall. – FONT. Late Norman
of Purbeck marble, square, with the familiar flat blank arches.
– ALTAR. Stone *mensa* brought up from the chancel floor and
set on stone columns by *Ernest Barrow* in 1921. – COMMU-
NION RAILS. Early C17, when the chancel was reordered and
repaired by the Thornborough family. – REREDOS. Introduced
in 1924. – PAINTINGS. Two panels of St Nicholas and St
Michael. – STALLS. Given in 1923 by Carroll Ansdell of Abbess
Grange. Seven and seven. They are Central or North Italian.
Allegedly from a convent. The back panels have fluted Doric
pilasters and finely designed panels. Frieze with cherubs'
heads. The date may be about 1650 (Charles Tracy). –
PRIEST'S STALL, or reading desk, incorporating traceries from
a dado panel of the C15 screen. – PULPIT. Plain Jacobean, but
the tester with little hanging arches. – SCREEN. Neo-Jacobean
of 1926 by *Ravenscroft & Cooke*. – BOX PEWS of 1821. –
STAINED GLASS. E window of 1875. The Three Maries. – MON-
UMENT. Sir John Thornborough †1630 and wife †1645. Small
tablet with rhymed inscription. LYCHGATE. Lightly framed by
G. H. Kitchin, 1918.

LECKFORD ABBAS (formerly Abbess Grange), ⅛ m. SSW.
A house of 1855–6, recast in Neo-Jacobean style in 1900–1 by
Banister Fletcher & Sons. Shaped gables l. and r., with Ipswich
windows on the ground floor. Central Ionic porch, with *in antis*
columns, their lower parts with blocks of rustication. Above, a
large mullioned-and-transomed staircase window. The single-
storey billiard room, added by Fletcher, is perhaps the most
successful part of his design: striking with a large
mullioned-and-transomed canted bay, a severe eaves line and
a hemispherical copper dome with round-arched dormers and
louvred cupola; inside it has crisp plasterwork decoration
with a composite Neo-Jacobean and Georgian chimneypiece
in an inglenook at the rear. The garden side is more severe,
asymmetrical with two full-height bays, square to the l. and
polygonal to the r., with Dutch gable above. Mixed interior
of Jacobean and Early Georgian styles, employed freely. The
house was acquired by the department store owner John
Spedan Lewis in 1929, the year he founded the John Lewis
Partnership (*see* also Longstock), which now owns the estate.
The drawing room and dining room have simple Art Deco
cornices; the drawing room with a green marble chimneypiece
too.

Halfway up the drive, the early C19 cob and thatch FISHING
COTTAGE built for Leckford Fishing Club, possibly by *William
Gover* of Winchester given its resemblance to Woodbury

House, Longparish, e.g. leaded casements with curved top and bottom corners, like extended portholes.

LINKENHOLT   *3050*

An estate village, and the highest in Hampshire. Its population in 1901 was only 88 and is probably no greater now.

ST PETER. 1870–1 by *William White*. Small, nave and chancel and splay-foot-spired bell-turret. Flint, banded in brick. Simple E.E., with bar tracery. One N window and the S doorway, *c.* 1200, are from the medieval church. The doorway has a round arch with one slight chamfer. Billet in the outer order. Some nice fossil decoration introduced by White over a window head. Neatly detailed interior, see especially the crisp niched CRE-DENCE SHELF. – FONT. C12. Of drum shape, with tapering sides, with bands of zigzag, rope and small raised triangles. – STAINED GLASS. E window by *Clayton & Bell*. Crucifixion. Prominent red background. – Chancel N. A dense design with Christ the Good Shepherd in foliate 'mosaic' patternwork. Can it be by *White c.* 1870? – Nave N. By *Burlison & Grylls* 1875, and typical. – Nave W and S by *Powells*, 1900 and 1901.

The tiny OLD SCHOOL, next to the church, is also of 1871, prob-ably by *White* (converted and enlarged *c.* 2008). Gothic, of large uncoursed flints with brick dressings and a tile roof with small wooden bellcote. E of the church the OLD RECTORY. Vernacular Revival style mixed with Queen Anne, probably by *Charles Watkins*, who designed the MANOR HOUSE, ¼ m. W, in 1905. This is like a large brick suburban villa. Tile-hung first floor, the tiles carrying down to pentice roofs. Impressive galleried entrance hall. Staircase with barley-sugar balusters. Original secondary glazing.

LIPHOOK   *8030*

Originally a small settlement with a coaching stop on the Portsmouth road (now by-passed) but greatly expanded follow-ing the coming of the railway in 1859, and throughout the C20. It is now almost a small town, much larger than Bramshott (q.v.) with which it shares a parish.

LIPHOOK CHURCH CENTRE, Portsmouth Road. A multi-purpose building of 1969–70 by *John Stammers* in brown brick, with a square lantern with a stressed timber shell roof and triangular areas of glazing.

IMMACULATE CONCEPTION (R.C.), Headley Road. 1908–11 by *Scoles & Raymond*. Small and loftily proportioned. Mixed Dec and Perp of rock-faced local sandstone; no tower but

an octagonal turret in the angle of the nave and lower s
transept. – Dominant ALTAR of Irish and Italian marbles, and
stone REREDOS within a plain arched recess. Old-fashioned
for the date. Much elaborate carving. – STAINED GLASS. In the
chancel, by *Lavers & Westlake*. Highly finished with saints in
canopy-work, *c.* 1911.

METHODIST CHURCH, London Road. 1931. Perp tracery.

VILLAGE HALL, Headley Road. Converted *c.* 1900 from an old
stone and brick barn; addition of 2004, by *Adrian Bird*.

LIBRARY, London Road. The former school, Gothic of 1872 by
E. B. I'Anson, with apse and a bellcote (converted 1976–7 and
extended 1993).

BOHUNT COMMUNITY SCHOOL, Longmoor Road. 1979–80 by
Hampshire County Architect's Dept. Brown brick with monopitch roofs, loosely grouped around a courtyard. Less coher-
ent rear additions.

STATION. Loudon-esque design of *c.* 1859. Late C19 shelter on
the down platform.

PERAMBULATION. The centre is The Square, with a prominent
reminder of its position on the old Portsmouth Road in the
ROYAL ANCHOR HOTEL. Early Georgian, altered *c.* 1800 with
two-storey canted bays on two fronts, one with Greek ornament, rather dominated by the addition in 1897 of the mansard
roof. Fine mid-C17 door inside, *ex situ*, with square-in-square
and lozenge-in-square panels and radial fluting at the top.

In Portsmouth Road running s two good houses: early C19
OSBORNES, stuccoed, of three bays with cast-iron veranda,
and HAILIE, the former rectory, of 1912, by *Unsworth, Son
& Triggs*, a highly attractive mixture of sandstone and tile-
hanging, with a high hipped roof, sweeping down over outshots
to each side, the l. of which has two porthole windows; the rear
is less formal, cosy even. The original garden layout includes
the low stone front wall with tile-capped piers and central lychgate, topiaried yew hedges and the sunken rose garden behind.

E of The Square, Haslemere Road curves past some nice C19
estate cottages and CHILTLEE MANOR, early C19, stuccoed
with porch of paired Ionic columns It is set well back with
some good 1970s terraced HOUSING flanking the lawn, stepping back in pairs, with raking dormers and porches. Part of
the same development is the rather self-consciously urban
ALLIANZ CORNHILL ASSURANCE offices, of 1972 by *Frank
Betts & Associates*, in reinforced concrete. About ¼ m. E, on
the same side, also surrounded by late C20 building is MALT-
HOUSE FARMHOUSE and COTTAGE. Formerly a single house:
C14/C15 hall range with crown-post roof; in the mid C17 the
hall floored and stair-tower added at rear. Staircase with turned
balusters and newel with polygonal finial. Wing added at high
end in the early C19, leaving older part as rear service wing.

Much later C20 expansion has spread s along MIDHURST
ROAD to the area around the station, e.g. SHIPLEY
COURT, 1960s high-density terraced housing, arranged around

a well-landscaped square. But most of the housing belongs to
the rebuilding since 1995 on the site of the Army's Ordnance
Supply Unit, in the manner of the Edwardian Domestic
Revival, and contemporary with SAINSBURYS supermarket,
of 1998–2000, which has corner pavilions with shallow pyramidal roofs. The eaves are supported by a thin pergola-like
loggia, in front of which, at intervals, are sandstone pylons.
Midhurst Road has been diverted to create a 'village green'
with bland MILLENNIUM HALL of 2000, by *John Bean*.

GOLDENFIELDS, Chiltley Lane, ½ m. SE. The core is of 1890–2
by *Philip Webb* for Mary Anne Robb, plantswoman and friend
of Gertrude Jekyll. Conceived as a cottage for her gardener, in
brick with a roughcast upper storey and hipped tile roof. Originally it had a timber-framed gatehouse adjoining which was
to have led to Robb's own house. This was never built* and
Webb amended his design by adding a two-storey hipped-
roofed bay to the side of the cottage, its upper part with an
elaborately timber-framed covered balcony. Further additions
after 1897, probably by *Owen Little*, for a two-storey gallery
range on the road side, and at the far end a two-storey wing
and angled range with a very distinctive pagoda-like tower
(similar to Pembridge bell tower, which *Webb* sketched in
1890). The two-storey library wing by *Inigo Triggs*, beyond, is
uncoursed sandstone with a two-storey canted tile-hung bay
window facing the garden. After 1910 the entrance range
replaced Webb's gatehouse: brick ground floor with corbelled
piers supporting a jettied tile-hung upper storey with a pair of
half-hipped gables. Several good rooms survive, one with a
Webb chimneypiece. Mrs Robb's garden has been built over,
destroying the setting.

LITTLE BOARHUNT, Portsmouth Road, ½ m. S. 1910–11, by
H. Inigo Triggs for himself. L-plan, incorporating an existing C18
farmhouse and barn which can still be made out on the long
entrance front. Tile-hung gabled wing, the eaves sweeping
down on one side over the porch. On the garden side, at the
far end, the roof sweeps down over a loggia, lit by a circular
window (cf. Hailie, above). The chief delight is the sunken
GARDEN with a narrow rill, widening at the centre into a rectangular dipping pool with a bronze cherub on a brick column,
brick paths in geometric patterns, a summerhouse with an
arched entrance and ogival roof and a stone wall extending
from the house's SE corner that terminates in a small square
brick dovecote (cf. Durford Court, Hill Brow). GATEHOUSE
built 1913–14.

FOLEY MANOR, 1 m. SW. A small mid-C19 vaguely Italianate
country house, with an orangery, and remains of Italianate
gardens. Two-storey STABLE BLOCK and LODGE, ½ m. ESE.
both *c.* 1870.

---

*This would have replaced Chiltley Farm House which was later added to for
Robb's son but demolished *c.* 1960 and its site built over.

¼ m. W of the house, a fine bronze equestrian STATUE of
Hugh Rose, Field Marshal Lord Strathnairn, suppressor of
the Indian Mutiny. 1891–5 by *E. Onslow Ford*, originally for
Knightsbridge, London, from where it was removed in 1931
and eventually given away by Westminster City Council in
1964. The pedestal is not the original, which bore scenes of
Strathnairn's battles.

LISS

The village has grown up in two parts: West Liss and East Liss.
The former includes the hamlet around St Peter's church, the
focus of the medieval manor of Liss Turney, and the settlement
around Upper Green, a post-medieval development. East Liss,
which grew up around the station following the coming of the
railway in 1859, is now by far the larger settlement but has fewer
buildings of interest.

ST PETER, Church Street. Engagingly rustic, in dark brown ironstone and honey-coloured sandstone. The W tower is early C13
with a later(?) weatherboarded top stage and probably
medieval timber-shingled spire. The chancel is also C13 though
over-restored in 1864 by *Ewan Christian*. Further renovation
by *E. Arden Minty* of Petersfield in 1903 when the S aisle wall
was rebuilt. The late C13 S doorway with filleted shafts and rolls
prepares one for the three-bay arcade whose double-chamfered
arches die into vertical pieces above the abaci. Typically Early
Decorated are the octagonal piers and capitals, the chancel
arch and the easternmost of the two nave N windows. The other
three-light N window is in a more conventional Perp. The lower
part of the red brick S porch is of Henry Haines's 1639
gift (dated inscription); its pretty cusped bargeboard
is C19. Inside, a medieval tie-beam evidently *in situ* from
an earlier porch. The S aisle W window is mullioned and
transomed and may be of 1655 (dated tie-beam in the nave
roof rebuilt in 1881). – FONT. Octagonal Perp with quatrefoils
and appropriate later FONT COVER with acorn finial.
– CANDELABRA. Two, of intricate wrought iron. From
Privett church. – STOVE. Cast iron, 1903. *C. Portway's Patent*
for 'slow-but-sure' combustion. – TABLETS. Several of the C18.
Edward Collins †1742. Unusually placed externally. – Charles
Cole †1752. Nice cherub in drapes below the inscription. –
Arabella Cole †1777. Garlanded oval inscription against
a grey surround. In the churchyard are four eroded medieval
stone grave-slabs and part of another. The church is
disused.

ST MARY, Station Road. 1890–2 by *Sir Arthur Blomfield & Sons*.
Dignified E.E. Clerestoried nave with crisply detailed stone
bellcote. Lower chancel and N organ chamber. W end completed with a SW porch and a commanding W tower, like the
rest of local Bargate stone, 1929–32 by *Sir Edward Maufe*, in a

freer and squarer Gothic. Dull whitened brick interior with
several original furnishings (e.g. the low SCREEN and PULPIT).
Flat, beamed tower ceiling prettily painted by *Maufe*. The
chancel has an English altar with a Baroque TRIPTYCH. All
by *Martin Travers*, 1927. The elaborate gilt triptych with a low
relief of the Virgin and Child. Classical COMMUNION RAILS.
– SCREENS to the S chapel by the *Rev. W. H. Thorold*, *c.* 1920,
former rector of Stainby, Lincolnshire, where he did much
carving. Elaborately Perp. – STAINED GLASS. Much by *Kempe*
in the chancel, especially the E window of 1901. Two small
windows in the N aisle by *Travers*, 1942. – SCULPTURE of the
child Christ by *Eric Gill*, 1932, brought in from the S porch
(replacement replica outside by *Gordon Bradshaw*). In the
churchyard, Gabbatt memorials also by *Gill*.

VILLAGE HALL, Hill Brow Road. 1897. Plum-coloured brick
with red dressings with Dutch-gabled porch.

JUNIOR SCHOOL, Hill Brow Road. *c.* 1995 by the *Hampshire
County Architect's Dept.* White-painted walls contrasted nicely
with a sedum-covered roof, supported on steel posts. Four
lanterns light the central corridor.

RAILWAY STATION, Station Road. A crisp *c.* 1970s steel-framed
glass box (project architect *R. Owen*) replacing the station of
1859. Attractive Victorian lattice iron FOOTBRIDGE and
wooden platform SHELTER.

BRIDGE, across the Rother between West and East Liss. Given in
1764, of stone with two segmental arches. Widened on its N
side.

The other buildings of principal interest are all close to St Peter's
church. SE, at the junction with Farnham Road, is SADDLERS.
Of two parallel ranges, that closest to the lane partly timber-
framed, perhaps *c.* 1600 with evidence of a former jettied
gable-end, altered in the C18, that behind an C18 addition with
a matching half-hipped gable. Next door, ALMSHOUSES of
1881, built for G. E. Coryton of Greatham 'chiefly for the
widows of agricultural labourers of the parish'. Gothic tracery
in the windows. Diagonally opposite is THE OLD RECTORY
of 1863, by *R. J. Withers* in Butterfieldian Gothic. N is BUR-
GATES, a late C19 farmhouse in an attractive Vernacular Revival
style. Probably by *Crickmay & Sons*.

LISS MILL, Mill Road, ⅓ m. NE of St Mary. *c.* 1900. Four
storeys, brick, with a splendid weatherboarded lucam on
wooden brackets. Now flats.

LYSS PLACE. ½ m. SW of St Peter. A neat brick house of
c. 1822–5 on the site of a medieval residence of St Mary's
Abbey, Winchester. Of this period, possibly C14, is part of the
service wing, built of malmstone with sandstone quoins and
with a re-set cinquefoil-headed window in its rear wall. It
appears to have been converted to a hall in 1542, the date of
its roof of arch-braced collar construction with butt purlins
and curved wind-braces. Four bays of this roof remain, smoke-
blackened and with evidence for a louvre, but it formerly
extended by one bay at least at each end. C17 mullioned
windows; the window high up in the gable-end suggests that

there was a floor before insertion of the first floor and attic in the early C19. The FARM BUILDINGS include a five-bay timber-framed barn incorporating reused timbers (two posts have been dated to 1542). Sites of medieval fish ponds.

THE WHITE TEMPLE, Brewells Lane, 1¾ m. E. 1974 by *Elidir Davies & Partners* for a theosophical sect. Like an Art Deco version of the Pantheon, comprising a circular drum with a low dome and portico. Flat-roofed aisles and wedge-shaped projection at the rear. Inside, the main space is top-lit by a band of glazing between the parapet and the dome. Low wing, r. of the entrance, added in 1985 by the same architects.

POPHOLE FARMHOUSE, Hill Brow Road. Timber-framed with a tile-hung first floor. The service wing is an older, three-bay house of *c.* 1500 retained when the rest was built *c.* 1600 in front and to the l. This part is of four bays and of extremely high quality. Close-studded ground floor with flint and herringbone brick-nogging. Above the r.-hand two bays is a large jettied gable, as though over a cross-wing, with curved-sided lozenges set in small square panels. The l.-hand gable-end is jettied on the first floor, denoting the importance of the two-bay upper chamber at this end. Inside, lobby-entry plan, with three Tudor-arched stone fireplaces and a mid-C17(?) staircase, in a rear tower, with turned balusters.

(STODHAM PARK, 1 m. S of St Mary. Stuccoed brick of 1827, for J. C. Hector, a Petersfield banker. Five-bay loggia on the garden side.)

WHEATHAM FARM, 1½ m. SW of St Peter. Mid-C17 house, of malmstone with ironstone dressings. Reused moulded stone plinth. Front refenestrated in the early C19, but mullioned stone windows survive at side and rear. Early C16 six-bay timber-framed BARN.

LITCHFIELD

4050

ST JAMES THE LESS. A small and now essentially C12 church of two phasings, with evidence of early C13 enlargement by N and S aisles, both later demolished, heavily overlaid by a major restoration of 1874–5 by *Henry Woodyer*. Simple exterior of flint. Nave and chancel in one below a continuous roof. The small shingle-spired wooden W bell-turret and the rebuilt N aisle are Woodyer's. Confusingly irregular windows outside suggest a complex interior. They include in the chancel three largish Norman ones not perhaps quite to be trusted, but faithfully restored in the late C20. Only the S window retains some original stonework. Again in the chancel, two small lancets, which are in order. The exterior also tells of a demolished S arcade, but not the whole story, which is best appreciated and fully understood inside. This S arcade (blocked) originally consisted of two bays with a round pier with a multi-scalloped capital, a square abacus, and steeply pointed arches with a slight chamfer, i.e. work of *c.* 1200. The N arcade is quite different. It has three bays with chamfered square piers, and single-chamfered arches. It was probably put in with its E bay when the rebuilding of the chancel had been completed. This is an interesting job of *c.* 1190. The arch rests on fluted corbels and in the four corners are corbels, three of them with excellent heads That means vaulting or the intention to vault. But it would have put the Norman windows out of operation – provided they are genuine and *in situ.* Was the S arcade bay built last, then, to link the old and the new? The trouble is that both these E bays, N and S, look older in their details than the rest. The VCH does not recognize this observation, but it makes another. The NE respond is set in front of a prior respond or jamb from which springs a segmental arch. This is clearly bonded with the chancel. What can have happened then? Was the connecting link of chancel and two-bay N arcade at first conceived to have a segmental arch? It seems too improbable. The problem of Litchfield is not yet solved; and it can here only be presented. The intended late C12 chancel vault may indicate a special importance (cf. Ripley, Surrey). Further evidence of something unusual is the remarkably large AUMBRY in the E wall – a segmental arched recess; the doors by Woodyer, for the reservation and exposition of holy relics. Can the vaulting have been intended as a canopy of honour for a specially sacred space? Timber framing at the W end.

FONT. A rough-hewn rugged monolith. – REREDOS. Typically *Woodyer* in E.E. style, of Bath stone and red Devonshire marble, with a central trefoil-arched gabled niche. – TILES. On the chancel floor. Strong geometric patterns. By *Minton*, of Woodyer's arrangement. – SCREEN. A commanding design, Romanesque rather than Jacobean, of timber. The upper part with a central red-painted cross, and open arcading inspired by the screen at Compton, Surrey, which church Woodyer had restored in 1859. – PULPIT. Plain, octagonal, of stone relieved at the top by a band of tiny arched openings with quatrefoiled circles. Woodyer at his most elemental. – STAINED GLASS. In the E window, perhaps by *O'Connor.* – MONUMENT to the S. A large, quite impressive Neoclassical piece to Sir Alfred Herbert †1957, the Coventry toolmaker, benefactor of Coventry Art Gallery. Large kneeling bronze angel. Very old-fashioned for the date.[*]

DUNLEY PARK, 1½ m. SW. By *William Bertram* of Bath, *c.* 1999. A large Neo-Georgian brick house constructed on organic principles without using steel or synthetic materials.

THE SEVEN BARROWS, Lower Woodcott Down, ¾ m. N along the A34. There are in fact ten Bronze Age round barrows in the cemetery. In addition to the group of seven W of the A34 there are two further sites on the E side between the road and the former railway line. A tenth barrow lies just E of the railway

---

[*] The SUNDIAL noted by Pevsner dated 1795 has been stolen. Its dial was signed *Holder*, Brixton.

cutting. Examples of bell and disc barrows as well as the ubiquitous bowl form occur in this group. All the barrows have been considerably reduced by ploughing, but the large bell barrow on the s is still 10 ft (3 metres) high and 150 ft (46 metres) in diameter.

IRON AGE HILL-FORT, Ladle Hill, 2 m. NE. Although the present apparently dilapidated condition of this small, 7-acre univallate fort might appear unattractive to the visitor, its very condition makes it a site of considerable interest and importance. Its appearance is not due entirely to the ravages of time, but to the unfinished state in which the Iron Age builders left it. Because of this it is possible to see some of the steps whereby this and presumably similar Iron Age hill-forts were constructed. The first phase consisted of the digging of a small marking-out ditch indicating the line of the later defence ditch. Traces of this small ditch can be seen on the ground in the NE part of the site. Elsewhere it has been largely obliterated by the work which was begun on the main ditch. The interrupted nature of the latter suggests that individual gangs of diggers were responsible for the cutting of each section. The topsoil and turf from the ditch were not piled immediately behind it on the projected line of the rampart, but were carried some distance inside the fort and there dumped – these topsoil dumps can still be seen as irregular mounds. Once the topsoil had been removed, the chalk rubble from the deeper levels in the ditch was dumped behind it to form a solid and stable core for the rampart. It was at this point that the whole work was abandoned. The final phase would have been the capping of this rubble core with the turf and topsoil from the dumps inside the earthwork.

Three Early Bronze Age ROUND BARROWS also occupy the hilltop. Just N of the fort is a fine DISC BARROW with a low mound 28 ft (9 metres) in diameter and 1 ft (0.3 metres) high surrounded by a ditch 12 ft (3.7 metres) wide and 76 ft (23 metres) in diameter and an outer bank. 600 yds SE is a BELL BARROW 56 ft (17 metres) in diameter and 5 ft (1.5 metres) high, the ditch of which cuts through the bank of an earlier SAUCER BARROW 47 ft (14.5 metres) in diameter and 1 ft high.

LITTLE SOMBORNE

A shrunken village in a remote downland setting.

ALL SAINTS (Churches Conservation Trust). A basic rectangle, with a tiny wooden bell-turret. Partly C11, when Little Somborne was a royal demesne, almost certainly one of two churches in Somborne mentioned at Domesday. Good Late Saxon features can be seen on the N side, e.g. the one lesene, and the smaller fragment of another on the s side, and a double-splayed window of rough rubble with quite wide splays.

Those inside retain a rebate for wooden shutters, and original plaster. Also, the w quoins, reused when the w end was curtailed and rebuilt in the C14, with long-and-short work. Nave extended E *c.* 1170 and a chancel added, although this was demolished in the early C17. Plain Late Norman s doorway with one slight continuous chamfer, square-headed N doorway (reopened in 1976–7) and several altered windows. These are square outside and round-arched inside. The blocked chancel arch is unusually low, with shafts and slender trumpet-scallop capitals and a slightly pointed head. The wall above must have been rebuilt in the early C17; it has two re-set early C13 narrow lancets. There is also evidence that the other walls were lowered. Inside, s of the chancel arch an image niche. In the N wall a blocked opening for a tiny mid-C13 annexe or anchorite's cell then associated with Peter de Rivalis, the 'Holy Man in the Wall' at Mottisfont Priory, whose prior and canons held the advowsons of the Somborne churches from 1209. Later it seems to have been used as an Easter sepulchre, see the footings marked on the ground outside. Bell-frame and bell of 1590 cast by *John Wallis* of Salisbury. SCULPTURE. A small Anglo-Saxon fragment beautifully carved. Discovered in 1976–7 (Edward Roberts).

SOMBORNE PARK, ¼ m. NE. Modest mid-C18 house. s front of 2–3–2 bays with central full-height canted bay. Substantially enlarged to N and W *c.* 1800, probably for William and Mary Paulet. The w wing has windows set within arches and inside a grand full-height entrance hall with a quadrant staircase in one corner and cantilevered gallery on one side: clearly a room for parade.

ROOKLEY FARMHOUSE, 1 m. E at Up Somborne. Cross-wing of 1388, probably built for Philip Aubyn III, a Winchester wool merchant. Jettied front with crown-post roof; two-bay chambers on each floor. Next door, its successor: ROOKLEY MANOR. Fine stuccoed Gothic front with pointed windows and battlements. Possibly of 1776–83, when the house was rented by the Duke of Cumberland, although some details look *c.* 1740–50. In the centre a taller broad canted bay, the entrance with reeded stone architrave. Around the corner to the l. a conventional late C18 five-bay stuccoed façade. Rear probably late C17, of the house built for Thomas Hobbes, royal surgeon (*see* Ashley), but with an C18 round-arched staircase window. Inside lots of early C18 details: good staircase with three fluted column-on-vase balusters per tread, columnar newels etc.

LITTLETON
Winchester

ST CATHERINE. The tall narrow proportions suggest *c.* 1100. Probably built by St Swithun's Priory, Winchester, whose guest master filled the rectory in its gift. Plaster removed 1885–6 by

T. E. Williams, who added the N aisle and vestry in tactful Perp; tracery of the E window possibly also of this date. Two arched bell-openings, restored in 1897. Inside, unusual chancel arch screen, the central arch on a Norman footing (original jamb stone near the ground), but altered, probably in the C17. Big rectangular openings l. and r. Massive nave roof, tree-ring dated to 1390 and 1412. Two bays. Crown-post with four-way arch braces. – FONT. The treasure of the church. Late Norman, of just before *c.* 1180 (when waterholding bases to columns were first introduced). Of table-top type; Purbeck marble. Simple patterns. – (REREDOS. 1903 by *Cancellor & Hill.*) – GALLERY. 1994 by *David Trussler.* – STAINED GLASS: E window *c.* 1885. Lightsome with Evangelists' emblems and *Agnus Dei* emblem.

MONK'S REST, E of the church. A small rectory of 1500–1. Three bays, the parlour end marked by an impressive brick chimney of flint and brick chequer, with an integral garderobe to one side, and close studding infilled with knapped flintwork. Otherwise much rebuilt in C18 brick. Inside, the former open hall with moulded dais beam and four-centred arched doorway to the parlour; this has a fine four-centred arched stone fireplace. W is LITTLETON MANOR built *c.* 1485 for John Smyth, farmer, who leased the manor from St Swithun's Priory. Timber-framed, with remains of original flint-knapped close studding in the gables, the rest of stuccoed C18 brick. Inside, the two-bay hall has arch-braced collar-truss and moulded dais beams at each end. Hall floored and stack inserted in the C17, the staircase with turned balusters of about the same time. S from the crossroads, THE WHITE HOUSE of *c.* 1500 has a one-bay hall and integral open-hearth kitchen at one end.

SIR JOHN MOORE BARRACKS (Army Training Regiment), Flowerdown, ¾ m. SE. 1983–6 by *DOE/Property Services Agency*. A campus-like complex of simple unfussy buildings with pitched roofs. The CHAPEL fittings are from the Peninsula Barracks, Winchester (q.v.). Most important is the miniature oak SCREEN, probably *c.* 1310 with two-light trefoil-headed openings, vigorous ogee tracery with pierced trefoils and quatrefoils and roundels with carved heads in the spandrels. First recorded at St Maurice's church, Winchester (rebuilt 1842, dem. 1954) but its quality strongly suggests it might have come from the cathedral. Was it part of a tomb-screen?

7040

LONG SUTTON

The village lane is a part of the Harrow Way, a branch of the medieval Pilgrim's Way.

ALL SAINTS. Formerly St Leonard, a medieval dependent chapel of Crondall. Plain rendered flint and rubble of early origin (the angle quoins stand on shaped Sarsen stones). Nave and chancel externally in one, the chancel with an Early Norman priest's doorway, revealed in the S wall, and early C13 lancet windows which at the E end are made to look Norman but have pointed rere-arches inside: an unusual Transitional arrangement. The composition of these windows in narrow but widely spaced pairs below a tiny circular gable window recalls the richer E.E. (restored) E window at Crondall. Capacious S chapel, perhaps built for pilgrims in the mid C13 (windows with pointed-trefoil heads) who would have had separate access through the W doorway. A double-chamfered arch with semi-circular responds to the nave. In the S chapel, ogee-headed PISCINA and Dec niche, and in the nave, one good N window of two lights of c. 1340 left unrestored. Simple Perp doorways, N and S. Rebuilt S porch, in the angle between nave and S chapel, unusually serving both. Inside, the bell-turret stands midway E of the nave W bay – an unusual position (cf. Thursley, Surrey), supported on four timber posts. Flat plaster ceiling. C19 chancel arch, apparently replacing a Tudor wooden screen (see *Collectanea Topographica*, 1843). Chancel restored in 1899, when the ceiling was raised. N vestry of 1960–1 by *Carpenter Turner & Burford*. – COMMUNION RAILS. Looking early C18 with twisted balusters. – FONT. A low, probably C12 ringed tub. – CHEST. A strong early type of c. 1200 with square framing at either end. – STAINED GLASS. W window, signed *O'Connor*, 1869. – Nave N window, by *William Aikman*, 1932. – MONUMENT. Nicholas Van Moppes †1979. Carrara marble tablet, finely lettered by *David Kindersley*.

Most of the village's best buildings are found in The Street. LONG SUTTON MANOR, NW of the church, is a substantial late C16 baffle-entry house with a roughly coeval rear service wing; this with an integral open hearth kitchen, a rare feature (now with a later inserted stack). C18 refronting and 1884 addition. E is THE OLD RECTORY, C17 and timber-framed, of hall-and-cross-wing plan with stair-tower at the rear and tall chimneys with diagonally set shafts. C18 brick W front with full-height pilasters flanking the entrance. Eastwards on the same side the C18 OLD CHAPEL, formerly of the Countess of Huntingdon's Connexion. Simple, of brick with hipped roof, the front with a pair of tall round-arched windows flanking a central door. The former manse to the r. is now a dwelling and altered. On the S side is a group associated with Lord Wandsworth College (*see* below) and by *Guy Dawber*. SAULGROVE HOUSE is a nice informal composition with door and stair window under a central gable and hipped wing to r.; HYDE CORNER and WHITELANDS are a semi-detached Neo-Georgian pair of 1925, with pedimented bracketed porches and tall chimneys. Further E, THE COURT, mid-C17 with Artisan Mannerist brick detailing, including string course with recessed cruciform panels, pilaster-strips and oriel windows on moulded brick corbels. S of The Street is the PRIMARY SCHOOL. Neo-Georgian. c. 1925 by *Guy Dawber*, the gift of Lord Wandsworth College.

SUMMERS FARM, ½ m. E. A grand early C17 lobby-entry house, formerly jettied but now with an C18 brick front. In the hall, *trompe-l'œil* panelling with brightly painted strapwork and the black-letter inscription: 'Looke well abowt thy house, in every degree, and as thy geting is, so let thy spending bee. Remember ye end eare ye begeene, think in death & feare to sinne. 1612'. Also a painted tulip of *c.* 1700. In the chamber over the hall the fireplace wall of exposed brickwork, painted with the joints picked out. Fine five-bay cruck BARN of 1441 with curved arch and wind-braces and one end bay formerly partitioned, possibly for stabling. Later box-framed sixth bay.

WELL COTTAGE, 1½ m. SE on the Crondall Road. Brick, with hipped roof, and dated 1686 in a pretty plasterwork panel consisting of an oval set in a square and with moulded ornament. A simple single-pile cottage with pilaster-strips flanking the front, casements and a central entrance leading into the main room, originally the only one heated.

LORD WANDSWORTH COLLEGE
¾ m. S.

Established with money left by Sydney James Stern, Baron Wandsworth, banker and Liberal M.P. (†1912), originally conceived as a model village for ex-servicemen and agricultural college for orphans from his Suffolk constituency. Designs were won in competition by *E. Guy Dawber*, 1914 and begun in 1915 but were abandoned after the war and developed on more conventional lines from 1925. The competition assessor was *Sir Reginald Blomfield* who seems to have retained a supervisory role, designing some buildings himself, e.g. the swaggering Neo-Baroque GATEWAY. Of Dawber's ambitious formal arrangement of buildings around three sides of a court, only the Neo-Georgian Administration and Engineering blocks were completed and in 1925–7 he replanned with the latter building on the main axis of the site and at the same time adding a Dining Hall and Library block, in matching style, and the impressive Y-plan School House. This is still Neo-Georgian, but more eclectic. SPORTS HALL (now Library) of the same period to the N. There are several nice Arts and Crafts COTTAGES by Dawber scattered across the site; the five pairs along the main drive, however, are by *H. P. G. Maule* of *Forsyth & Maule*, 1923, built after Dawber's original scheme had been abandoned. Dawber was called in to rectify their leaking roofs. Among the later additions the most significant are:

LABORATORIES of 1936 by *W. G. Newton*, brick and flat-roofed with a square cupola over the entrance, reminiscent of his laboratories at Marlborough College, Wiltshire.

GAVIN HALL. 1964–6 by *Robert Matthew Johnson-Marshall & Partners*. Square plan with low pyramidal copper roof, sunk glazing along the ridges and a steep lantern. Of the same date and by the same firm, HAZELVEARE and SUMMERFIELD, a

pair of linked cruciform three-storey boarding houses in buff
brick with copper roofs. The plan, with octagonal service cores
and radiating wings, is reminiscent of the panoptica of C19
workhouses and prisons.

JUNIOR HOUSE, ½ m. W. 1927–8 by *Dawber*, charming in a free
Neo-Georgian. H-plan with square staircase towers in the
angles of the wings, with low pyramidal roofs and tall canted
oriel windows with oculi over.

HYDE FARM. ⅛ m. NW. Remains of the college's Model Farm
of 1915, by *Blomfield*, alas bereft of its great covered yards. Neo-
Georgian front range with cupola over a central round archway
and short hipped-roofed wings to the front.

LONGPARISH

Appropriately named, actually three small settlements (former
tithings) running into each other for about 1½ m. along the NW
side of the River Test.

ST NICHOLAS. An interesting church of Norman origin. In the
chancel the priest's doorway has survived unaltered from the
C12. The nave either received its aisles or was put up with aisles
about 1210–25 when the church was held by Wherwell Priory.
Inside, the arcades are the most impressive feature. They are
of four bays and have round piers with waterholding bases,
octagonal abaci and capitals where the decoration of the
mouths of trumpet scallops creates a kind of running frieze.
One of the capitals is actually going stiff-leaf. Pointed arches
with two slight chamfers. The chancel arch, however, and the
details of the N and S doorway with rolls are full C13. Full C13
also the S doorway with rolls, fine for Hampshire, but capitals
and hoodmould much restored. Early Tudor Perp W tower, of
chequer flint and stone, built into the existing nave, probably
c. 1540, the materials possibly taken from Wherwell Priory (cf.
Goodworth Clatford). Thoroughly restored in 1833–43 for the
Rev. Henry Burnaby Greene and more drastically in 1851–2
by *Henry Woodyer*, i.e. the W doorway, inappropriately Dec W
window, the tracery of the belfry windows, and the bizarre
clock surround on the E face. – FONT. A fine classical piece of
c. 1700. A square, strongly moulded baluster on an oval basin-
like bowl with small cartouches, festoons and shells. – FONT
COVER. A portion of Woodyer's chancel reredos, removed in
1958 along with decoration and other furnishings in the
chancel. – Stone ALTAR, 1840. Is the painted decoration by
Woodyer? – CREDENCE SHELF. Elaborate projecting angel
bracket and nodding ogee-arched canopy. – TILES by *Minton*
on the sanctuary floor. – LECTERN. A strong wooden eagle of
1839. – PULPIT of panelled stone by *Woodyer*. – PEWS. A full
set of 1842 in traditional Perp. – STAINED GLASS. E window
by *Morris & Co.*, 1912, a Nativity scene, after *Burne-Jones*, used

earlier at Westerham, Kent. – Chancel N and S 1860–70 by
Clayton & Bell. – S aisle E, N aisle E (to the sporting diarist and
writer Lt-Colonel Peter Hawker of Longparish House †1853)
and central N windows, all by *Lavers & Barraud,* of *c.* 1860
and typical of them at that date, with vivid colours. – S aisle S
windows by *Hardman,* of *c.* 1881, 1906 and 1916. – N aisle NE.
1968 by *Francis Skeat* to the flying ace Lanoe George Hawker
V.C. †1916, shot down by the 'Red Baron' von Richthofen.
A powerful aerial St Michael the archangel above Bertangles
Airfield. – MONUMENTS. Large Elizabethan stone tablet on
the chancel S wall in place of a sedilia. Sadly bereft of identi-
fying inscription. Shields painted with C19 Passion emblems.

LYCHGATE of 1866 by *William White.* In the churchyard, one
very eroded early C18 headstone by the path with two large
angels, and cast-iron Gothic grave marker, NE of the vestry,
to Peter and Harriot Pricktoe (1832 and 1830) signed *David
Newington.*

NE of the church, the SCHOOL, with good additions of 2004–5
by *Hampshire Property Services, Architecture and Design.* Low,
brick and slate with overhanging eaves. N is WOODBURY
HOUSE of 1823, by *William Gover* of Winchester for the Rev.
Henry Burnaby Greene. Unusual leaded casements with
curved corners to the lights (cf. Fishing Cottage, Leckford).
In Southside Road, the former METHODIST CHAPEL of 1865
but looking earlier.

MIDDLETON HOUSE, ¼ m. W in parkland. Modest early C18
core, still discernible on the garden front but completely
remodelled on the entrance front in the early C19 with Doric
porch; two bay wings also of this date with elegant single-storey
bows with tented lead roofs at the back. The other wings projecting at right angles around the forecourt are later, one incorporating an existing pavilion. The NE wing added by *E. R.
Barrow,* 1921.

LONGPARISH HOUSE, at the far N end of the village. Largely
rebuilt for Peter Hawker *c.* 1700. Two-storeys, of shallow
E-plan. A five-bay centre with two-bay wings and central
two-storey pedimented porch with a squat Venetian window.
Given a rather agreeable, almost French, appearance by towers
appended to the wings, of unequal height with pavilion roofs.
The rear, facing the Test, has later C18 full-height canted bays
to the wings. Low service wing to SW. A corridor runs along
the entrance front with principal rooms along the garden side
and dog-leg staircases in the wings with closed string, turned
balusters and ramped handrail. Doorcases have pedimented
Palladian surrounds. Two rooms are curiously wainscoted, with
rosettes or bosses at the junctions of the panels. What date is
this?

The village road has been diverted around the park, the line
of the old road preserved as a majestic lime avenue. E of the
house, an C18 SUMMERHOUSE(?), incorporated in a brick
garden wall, with Venetian windows in the SE side. Altered in
the late C20.

UPPER MILL, ¼ m. E of Longparish House on the Test. Substantial working mill of *c.* 1870 with undershot wheel: three storeys, brick, partly weatherboarded. Brick and cob mill house, C18. The C18 LOWER MILL, ¼ m. S of Longparish House, was subsumed into an ambitious Arts and Crafts butterfly-plan house of 1922 by *E. R. Barrow* for Major W. T. Whiteley, formerly of Middleton House (q.v.). Its rear wing, spanning the mill race, incorporates a water wheel to generate electricity.

BUCKCLOSE HOUSE, ¾ m. SW at Forton. 1914 by *Brown & Barrow*. Rendered and tiled with cross-wings, the r. wing timber-framed with jettied first floor and oriel beneath a tile-hung gable. Large chimneystacks. Arts and Crafts garden, including hedged path to the front door.

Former STATION and STATIONMASTER'S HOUSE, 1¼ m. SW. Attractive brick and tile, in Queen Anne Revival of 1884–5 for the London & South Western Railway.

LONGSTOCK

A pretty village with many thatched cottages, interspersed with larger farmhouses, strung out along the W bank of the Test.

ST MARY. 1877–80 by *William White* with a Flemish-looking NW tower carrying a shingled splay-foot spire. In C13 style and on the plan of the C13 church: a reused lancet and two stone angels inside and the trefoil-headed S lancets in the chancel replicating originals. Muscular Gothic timber S porch The chancel is a climax, its roof with East Anglian angels and chancel arch, with lily and rose capitals, carved by *Harry Hems*. Rich furnishings. COMMUNION RAIL. C18 with fluted balusters. – Some thirty-six medieval TILES behind the altar. – CHANCEL SCREEN and REREDOS of 1902 and 1905 by *Harry Hems & Sons*. – Good wooden PULPIT and simple PEWS. – STAINED GLASS. E, chancel SE and nave S of *c.* 1882, all by *Mayer* of Munich. The E window much the best with a lively colourful Crucifixion scene with airborne angels. Some expressive force in the design. (MONUMENT. A Purbeck stone coffin lid.) – LYCHGATE. Elaborate Perp of 1907 by *Harry Hems*.

S of the church the humble former PRIMITIVE METHODIST CHAPEL, 1878. Classical in flint and brick. Opposite, the VILLAGE HALL. Neo-vernacular of 1991 by *Ashby Guion Associates*. Stained glass depicting local scenes, by *Suzanne Parker*. Beyond this, THE GRANGE, late C18, brick, with Gothic casements. Around 1800 the home of Longstock Fishing Club, the earliest on the Test. N of the church on the main street, the WAR MEMORIAL, a stone cross by *T. D. Atkinson*, *c.* 1920. Opposite, on a prominent corner site, THE PEAT SPADE, a good purpose-built pub of *c.* 1880, and next door LONG HOUSE, 2005 by *Place*. Very sleek with rendered ground floor and chestnut-clad upper parts, the walls curving seamlessly into the roof slope. SE at the river crossing is a rustic thatched FISHING HUT, a characteristic feature of the Test.

LONGSTOCK MILL, ¾ m S. C18, brick and tile, two storeys, of five bays, with doors, one above the other, beneath the central gable. Addition of 1893, originally four storeys, now two, with cast-iron casements.

LONGSTOCK HOUSE, 1¼ m. NNW. Stuccoed Neo-Georgian of c. 1914, probably incorporating an early C19 core. Opposite, an early C19 rustic Gothic PAVILION (probably a former fishing lodge) and, close to the entrance, the former GARAGE COTTAGES, c. 1914 in a Voysey-ish style. SE of the house, WATER GARDENS created by Reginald Beddington in the 1920s and greatly developed after 1946 by *John Spedan Lewis* (*see* Leckford) with the botanist, *Terry Jones*. THE BURROW, ⅓ m. S, was built for Lewis's retirement c. 1959. Quite conventional Neo-Georgian, in yellow brick and slate, by *Yorke Rosenberg & Mardall*. The garden, again by *Lewis*, is in the Jekyll tradition, with a terrace in front of the house and lower lawn surrounded by rockeried banks on two sides.

LOWER FROYLE *see* FROYLE

6050

MAPLEDURWELL

ST MARY. Rustic exterior distressingly over-restored in 1853 by *Benjamin Thorne*, who destroyed the C14 timber N porch. Nave and slightly lower chancel. Big, unusual weatherboarded W bell-turret, medieval or C17 timber-frame construction clad with originally C18 painted vertical boarding and with a low tiled cap. Plain single-chamfered Late Norman W doorway, perhaps the re-set N door. One small renewed Norman lancet in chancel N wall. Nice, probably C14, nave roof in unusual pointed barrel form, with plain tie-beams, braced collars and purlins. – ALTAR. Three painted panels by *M. Shuttleworth*. – FONT. Elaborate with crocketed ogee panels, presumably by Thorne, as also most of the chancel SCREEN (reusing a little late C15 work) and possibly the SCREEN below the tower. – DOOR. C15, with external battens, and square framing inside, the upper part of which renewed. – PULPIT. Heavily Neo-Jacobean with two brass candleholders. – BRASS. John Tanner and wife c. 1525 (John Barton). 14-in. (36-cm.) figures.

NW, RYE COTTAGE a cruck-framed hall house of c. 1487, a late example of that form of construction in the county, with a box-framed addition of c. 1526. Opposite, WEBBS FARMHOUSE, a showy early C17 lobby-entry house with large gables and much herringbone nogging. N again, the late C18 MAPLEDURWELL HOUSE, with three-bay garden front. The entrance side has reused c. 1700 cross-windows and a gabled Tudor-Gothic porch of c. 1840.

MARSH COURT
1¾ m. N of King's Somborne

114

Built for Herbert Johnson, a typically Edwardian 'adventurer,
stock jobber and sportsman', as Christopher Hussey put it.
The house was designed by *Lutyens* in 1901–4, with an addition by him of 1924–6. It has a splendid position above the Test
and is made visible for miles around by its walls of stark white
chalk ashlar (restored in 1995–6), finely jointed and patterned
with random bits of flint and tile: an amusing exaggeration of
the building traditions of the river valley, to the architect 'one
of God's kindest and gentle creations'. The N FRONT is in the
E-form suited to its basically Elizabethan fenestration and of
the type used by Lutyens elsewhere at this date (e.g. his modest
Daneshill, Basingstoke). The wings have mullioned-and-transomed windows, the recessed centre just low mullioned
windows, the upper ones almost as a continuous band below
the high hipped roof. A sketch appears to show that thatch was
considered. The porch has a gable, but inside a tunnel-vault
of stone and tile squares. Here the Lutyens of the unexpected
oddities and also the Lutyens of the classical future make their
appearance. The oddest thing is the skeleton arch of the porch
with stone tongues curving inward (reprised from Overstrand
Hall, Norfolk, of 1899–1901). That this front appears low is a
clever deception, achieved by building up the front courtyard
and surrounding it with a grassed moat.

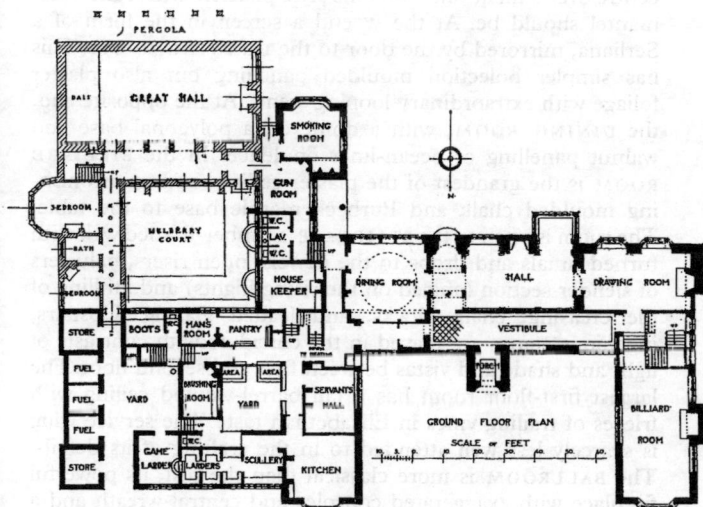

Marsh Court.
Plan

On the S FRONT, where the site drops downhill, the house is in the strongest contrast to the character as well as the motifs of the entrance side. It is as emphatically vertical as the other is horizontal (with a higher roof and basement storey at one end) and as emphatically broken up by bay windows, both straight-sided and canted, as the other is smooth. And it is as emphatically irregular as the other is symmetrical – with only the E wing projecting and answered instead by a sunken garden. The windows here also are all vertical and transomed. Punctuating the roof-line twisted cut brick chimneys sprout from the icy walling. In the angle with the wing, a vaulted loggia makes play with staggered patterns of chequered flush-work, and numerous other inventive details animate the display. Behind the wing is the BALLROOM added in 1924–6. It has tall windows with three transoms. Along the exposed sides they are smaller and placed high up, with oval niches below. Contemporary additions on the E front effect a clever transition from chalk to the brick service ranges of 1901–4. These are arranged around two secluded inner courts, the outer one set at higher level, all expertly crafted in brick and tile; windows and doors with robust pegged timber surrounds.

The interior is a primer in English architecture from Elizabeth to Queen Anne but with Lutyens' originality in the smallest of motifs. Long and low ENTRANCE HALL across the centre of the N front with geometric patterned Purbeck marble floor. Behind this, the LIBRARY is panelled floor to ceiling and has fluted Corinthian pilasters which rise from rusticated plinths. The ceiling, as in the other rooms is a rich piece of Wrenaissance. Handsome chalk fireplace with pedimented centre over a niche and Gibbons style pilasters where the over-mantel should be. At the W end a screen in the form of a Serliana, mirrored by the door to the DRAWING ROOM. This has simpler bolection moulded panelling but also plaster foliage with extraordinary looping stems. At the opposite end, the DINING ROOM, with a dome on a polygonal base and walnut panelling of ocean-liner opulence. In the BILLIARD ROOM is the grandest of the plaster ceilings and an astonish-ing moulded chalk and Purbeck marble base to the table. The room is open to the STAIRCASE a timber-framed well with turned finials and drops to the newels, open risers, balusters of slender section (angled on the rising flights) and infilling of tile creasing, chalk blocks, and leaded glazing. Upstairs, ingenious games are played in the corridors with contrasts of light and shade and vistas between first and second floor. The largest first-floor room has a tall barrel-vaulted ceiling with friezes of trailing vines in Elizabethan taste. The service wing is scarcely less well attended to in the crafting of its details. The BALLROOM is more classical than the rest, its powerful fireplace with exaggerated consoles and central wreath and a pedimented overmantel rising to the ceiling.

The GARDEN, arranged at a multitude of levels with each element linking to the next, was designed with *Gertrude Jekyll*.

It is full of Lutyens *faerie* from his magical romantic period but
formal and defined by yew hedging, stone balustrades, piers
with obelisks and walling of flint and ashlar. On the s front,
two terraces, a grass piazza descending to a sunken pool with
stepped sides and downhill, tucked against the lower terrace,
a loggia behind cut yews.

The LODGE and POWER HOUSE, formally composed on the
entrance approach are also of 1901–4 but in Lutyens'
picturesque Home Counties vernacular – tile roofs, flanks with
buttresses of tile-creasing, flushwork and weatherboarding.
The larger of the two incorporates a shed with rounded brick
columns.

MARSH COURT FARM, ½ m. E on the Stockbridge road. Also
by *Lutyens*, early C20. Large brick barn to the road with one
end on staddles. Cart sheds have brick columns like the lodge
at Marsh Court.

MARTYR WORTHY

5030

ST SWITHUN. The nave represents the church of *c.* 1140: see the
doorways of Binstead stone, of which the N has one order of
columns and zigzag at right angles to the wall, the s doorway
nutmeg. Perp windows, mostly renewed, hard Neo-Norman
apsidal chancel in flint of 1865 by *J. Colson*. Good partly tile-
hung timber bell-turret of 1871 and N vestry by *Henry Hill*,
1913. Inside, the E end of the nave roof has a late C14–early
C15 two-bay ceiling with carved bosses at the intersection and
moulded wall-plate. A fine feature, perhaps due to St Swithun's
Cathedral Priory who held the advowson from 1251. Unusually there is a separate roof above the original chancel. The rest
of the roof is of trussed rafters nicely braced by a pretty cast-
iron Gothic tie of the 1837. Of that date, the thick nail-studded
doors. FONT. One of a local multiple edition of *c.* 1830 (cf.
Chilcomb and Itchen Abbas). – STAINED GLASS. In the nave
by *Lavers & Westlake*, 1897. w window (tracery), 1994, St
Swithun. In the churchyard, a late C12 or early C13 ridged
sepulchral stone: the 'rich coped tomb' noted by J. H. Parker
in 1845, perhaps the earliest churchyard grave marker in
Hampshire.

A small village with buildings lining Church Lane, running
between the main road and the Itchen. E of the church, the
roughcast VILLAGE HALL, 1903 by *W. T. Rogers*, and the lively
Tudor Gothic former SCHOOL. MARTYR WORTHY PLACE,
NE of the crossroads, is at its core a modest C18 house but with
some interesting if rambling Neo-Georgian additions made
between 1905 and *c.* 1912 by *Cancellor & Hill*, especially the
entrance side with its attractive porch and to its r. a two-storey
frontage with quadrant corners to a recessed centre. Good
formal Arts and Crafts garden with gardener's cottage and
well-house, dated 1914.

7050
MATTINGLEY

Just the chapel in a delightful rural setting with a loose group of
farms and cottages alongside an open green. This tiny hamlet,
like Kingsclere and Overton (qq.v.), was a cloth-producing centre
by the C16.

CHURCH. Nave, with lower chancel and bell-turret. Timber-
framed throughout and late medieval. It was held by the
Bishop of Winchester from 1383, and there is a tradition of its
construction during the time of Bishop Waynflete (1447–87)
but the chancel E and W walls, infilled with brick-nogging, look
c. 1520. Straight-headed five-light E window without tracery.
The tall timber N porch was moved from the S side during
restoration in 1867–9 by *Butterfield* (SE vestry and aisles with
horizontal windows). Inside, the oak framing of the nave and
chancel is wonderfully preserved. Six-and-a-half bays, with
elaborately moulded bay posts, supporting a roof of arch-
braced, slightly chamfered tie-beams, side purlins and one tier
of wind-braces. Nice boarded panelled ceilings below the bellcote, and over the altar. Some small boxes. The arcade piers
are original on the inside. Their mouldings are Perp. FUR-
NISHINGS by *Butterfield*. DECALOGUE. Early C19? Round-
headed panels l. and r. of the E window. – PANELLING. In the
altar area; C17. – STAINED GLASS. In the chancel N window
some original bits including a damaged head, and cross-shaped
panels of pale flowered C15 quarries. E window, by *Hardman*,
1890, to Lord Eversley †1888 (*see* Heckfield). Restless figure
groups below canopies and Passion emblems. N aisle E, by
Lavers, Barraud & Westlake, †1875. A Renaissance Annunciation scene. Nave W. Possibly by *Gibbs*, c. 1869.

The CHURCHYARD has a nice C19 gate and low wall to the
green, both, no doubt, by *Butterfield*. Large early C20 Hiberno-
Romanesque CROSS to the Singleton family of Mell, Co. Louth
and Hazeley House.

HAZELEY HEATH COTTAGE, ¾ m. E. 1898 by *Ernest Newton*,
and his home until 1912. He incorporated a C16 farmhouse of
hall-and-cross-wing plan as the service range and added
another gabled cross-wing to the E. The old work is timber-
framed and C18 brick, Newton's additions similarly cottagey,
roughcast with folksy pargetted decoration including his family
tree. Entrance hall in the old house has a charming fireplace
with oak lintel and Delft-tiled reveals; elsewhere C18 chimneypieces. Contemporary formal garden with clipped yews.

MEDSTEAD

6030

ST ANDREW. Nave and chancel, with a short N aisle under a very low catslide roof, and Victorian N transept. The chancel lancets are late C14 or early C15, with low-flighted arched heads inside (like the former hall of St John's Hospital, Winchester; the Bishop of Winchester held the advowson). Weatherboarded tile-caped bell-turret over the W end, added during restoration in 1859–61, E window of the same date (renewed 1972). The interior is a surprise. Robust two-bay N arcade of *c.* 1160 i.e. during the episcopacy of Henry of Blois. Short round-pier, multi-scalloped capital, square abacus, and round, slightly chamfered arches. Hoodmould with a quarter-hollow. The collecting box stands on a fine later C13 stone tripartite corbel with leaf decoration, formerly an image bracket. – STAINED GLASS. In the chancel mostly by *Powells*. Indifferent E window by *Hardman*, 1875. Nave SE, of 1914, an early work of *A. K. Nicholson* with SS Elizabeth and Joan of Arc.

WAR MEMORIAL. SE of church. Granite, Celtic cross with crusader's cross in relief. 1920 by *Maile & Sons*.

CONVENT OF ST LUCY, ¼ m. NW. Formerly Medstead Manor. Mostly Neo-Georgian of 1905 by *W. G. Lower* of Guildford for Capt. Edmund Jervoise R.N., but its service wing is a brick and flint house of *c.* 1700, which has a dog-leg staircase and a re-set early C17 plank-and-muntin door with vase-stopped frame. Nice interior and Arts and Crafts garden. Simple Gothic brick CHAPEL of 1962 for the convent and residential building to the N, also 1960s.

SOUTHTOWN OLD FARMHOUSE, ½ m. S. Early C18, header bond with casements, bracketed porch and staircase with splat-balusters. Farm buildings include an early C19 weatherboarded well-house with donkey wheel and brick and flint outbuilding with lunettes and ogee-arched Gothic loft door.

MICHELDEVER

5030

A large village on the S bank of the River Dever at a staggered cross-roads.

ST MARY. The church is successor to a Saxon building first mentioned in 903 when granted to New Minster (after *c.* 1110 Hyde Abbey), Winchester, and later parent of four dependent chapels. The exterior is arresting, a shockingly odd and nakedly unadorned composition of three disparate parts, not a little strange in its rural setting. Its overwhelming unexpectedness is due to the major rebuilding of 1806–8 by *George Dance the Younger*, financed by Sir Francis Baring, his patron at Stratton Park (East Stratton) for £10,000 (White's Directory). Dance was ruthless, inserting a centre octagon in place of what had

p. 394

Micheldever, St Mary.
Section by George Dance the Younger, C19

been the C13 aisled nave of a normal medieval church. His octagon is of red brick, shown bluntly outside since the removal of its original details and plaster rendering during a restoration of 1881 by *J. Colson*. The walls are bare below – windows are only on the clerestory level, and they are just arch-heads without the original Gothic iron-framed glazing. The single windows of the shallow transepts with their curvilinear tracery are Colson's.

Of the medieval church, only the blunt w tower of 1544 (evidence of a will) remains standing. It is of flint and stone, evidently reused from Hyde Abbey, Winchester, and has a higher sw stair-turret and square-headed four-light bell-openings with a transom. The arches of the lights are uncusped. The tracery of the w bell-opening contains the rebus 'W. Overton'. Might this refer to a builder from neighbouring Overton?

The typically Tudor w doorway opens to an airy, lightsome INTERIOR, of a purity and simplicity characteristic of Dance's Gothic. The octagon is a thrill of rare delight, not least for its brilliant lucid planning and lighting. As mediation between the tower and the octagon, Dance retained the old nave's w bay of which the lateral walls are the beginning of the lost C13 arcades, and with the E arch (typically C13 dying mouldings) may have supported a small contemporary w tower. The interior of the octagon is derived from Dance's St Bartholomew-the-Less, Smithfield, London (1789), part of the uncommon Georgian tradition of centrally planned octagonal churches. This extreme evangelical form was perhaps dictated by Sir Francis Baring, whose grandfather, Franz Baring of Bremen, was a Lutheran pastor. Crisp detailing throughout: four shallow niches in the diagonals, two deeper ones in the transepts. All surrounds are of fine continuous mouldings. Plaster star-vault with chilly light blue colouring to the spandrels. This pristine effect is a little compromised by the chancel arch – clearly of 1881, with its foliate capitals on short circular marble shafts no doubt by Colson. The present chancel, unusually long for the auditory nave, is that of the medieval church, though slightly heightened and lengthened by Dance, who re-set the original Perp E window (replaced in 1866) in his new E wall and recast the rest, with plaster arches and a new roof. His work did not survive Colson's major remodelling. Elaborately traceried E window. But Dance's bare external plasterwork remains, no doubt masking medieval flint walls and several blocked lateral windows. No original furnishings.

FURNISHINGS. – Plain FONT and elaborate FONT COVER with crocketed ogee dome. *Dance?* – Brass eagle LECTERN by *Jones & Willis* of 1881. Stone PULPIT with elaborate foliate spandrel on low clustered columns. (A photograph of 1865 shows a complete scheme with double pulpits.) Awkwardly drunken CHOIR STALLS, oddly tipped rearwards. – Rich REREDOS of 1883 by *J. Colson & Son.* Alabaster carved by *Hems* of Exeter and mosaic with Evangelists' emblems. Dado of 1884 (dated) and chancel floor of marble mosaic by *Powell & Sons,* 1881. – COMMUNION RAIL of wrought iron with the usual brass roll top. – HATCHMENTS to Barings. – STAINED GLASS. E and W windows by *Clayton & Bell.* The former to the 1st Lord Northbrook, 1886, with a highly finished Crucifixion scene and the *Agnus Dei* and evangelists' emblems in the tracery. Vivid red backgrounds. Lower-voltage W window of 1881.

– MONUMENTS. A fine group in the chancel, especially the related trio to the Barings of The Grange and Stratton Park by *Flaxman,* on the theme of the Lord's Prayer. The commanding centre for Harriet Baring †1804, widow of Sir Francis, was erected in 1806 with a mildly Tudor Gothic surround designed by *Dance* to integrate with his chancel. It represents 'Thy Will be Done', a resignedly seated praying woman. The two smaller side pieces came from East Stratton old church (dem. *c.* 1890). Each has a square, surprisingly Baroque, panel: 'For Thine is the Kingdom', a mother and child carried heavenwards by a tangle of angels (replicated for Flaxman's memorial at St Giles-in-the-Fields, London), and 'Deliver Us From Evil', a figure battling devils and helped by angels. – Thomas Baring †1873. By *Sir J. E. Boehm,* in latest Tudor Gothic style to integrate with Lady Baring's monument. Two large graceful kneeling angels. Low pedestal, with decidedly proto-Art Nouveau incised foliate decoration. (It might be noted that the young *Alfred Gilbert* was employed as an 'improver' by Boehm at this time.) – Outside on chancel N wall, a mid-C18 oval tablet to Benjamin Whitaker †1751, Chief Justice of South Carolina, 1739–49 (his wife is commemorated in St Philip, Charleston, South Carolina).

The large CHURCHYARD has been cleared, most of the headstones removed (including that to the curiously named

Savage Bear †1813) or stacked lazily against the perimeter walls. Larger monuments remain, especially the fine group of large late C18–early C19 stone table tombs to the Kersley and Perry families (dates 1783 to 1843) alongside the church. – Charles Gundell †1809. Very Grecian, with acroterion at the corners, and strikingly similar to the cenotaph to Sir Joshua Reynolds in the garden at Dance's Coleorton Hall, Leicestershire (c. 1804–8).

N of the church is THE LIMES. H-shaped and externally largely C18 and C19 painted brick, but consisting of a two-bay hall of c. 1500 with a cross-wing at the lower S end and a C17 N cross-wing; this incorporates an earlier free-standing structure at its W end, possibly a former kitchen. To the r. at the front, a former baker's shop of c. 1900. Nice original shopfront with bowed windows. Opposite, on the E side of Church Street, the Gothic SCHOOL, 1845 with clock tower of 1870 by *Colson*. SE is a small triangular green with, on its S side, SHILLINGBURY COTTAGE, an example of that Hampshire peculiarity, the continuously jettied hall house. Late C15, of four bays originally with a two-bay hall. Hall truss of jointed cruck form, archbraced to a collar. At the front, the foot of the truss rests on what was an internal gallery, the width of the jetty. There was also an internal jetty at the upper end of the hall. Hall floored and a further jettied bay added at the r.-hand end c. 1600. E from the green, set back within a large garden, MICHELDEVER HOUSE. Early C19, stuccoed, of three bays, the outer bays projecting as wings, flanking a wrought-iron porch with tented roof. Gothic staircase window at rear. Opposite, FARDELLS, a four-bay house of 1572, timber-framed with curved braces at the front. It was built with a half-floored hall, i.e. a one-bay floored-over hall heated by a smoke-bay of the same size.

NORTHBROOK HOUSE, ½ m. N. Stuccoed. Five bays, the centre three probably late C18, the broader and quoined outer pair probably early C19. Single-storey wings with bows by *Pearce & Offer* of Bournemouth, 1898–9, for Lord Northbrook. Cob garden walls and early C19 octagonal rustic DAIRY, of chalk with leaded windows and a thatched roof supported on wooden posts.

NORSEBURY HOUSE. *See* STOKE CHARITY.

MICHELDEVER STATION
2¼ m. N of Micheldever

A small settlement which grew up around the STATION of 1840 on the London & Southampton Railway, a simple but elegant building by *William Tite* of squared and knapped flint with gault brick dressings, low hipped slate roof and canopy on cast-iron columns (from where the Hurstbourne Brass Band played 'a variety of pieces in a scientific manner' on opening day). POPHAM TUNNELS, ½ m. N, are part of *Joseph Locke*'s

impressive engineering on the railway (*Thomas Brassey*, contractor). Monumental brick portals, with battered pilaster-strips
flanking the opening, curved wing walls and a dentil cornice.

w of the station on the Andover Road, THE OLD STORES,
a pair of semi-detached cottages and former shop of 1897 by
Lutyens for the Earl of Northbrook. He plays games with the
cottages: first-floor oriels that one expects to see centrally
placed under the tile-hung gables are combined into one large
central oriel, apparently unsupported. Conversely, the ground-
floor windows have drifted to the outer corners.

WARREN FARMHOUSE, ¼ m. s. Dated 1775. Its curious stone
doorcase has pilasters supporting a moulded arch around the
fanlight, and floating above, interrupting the string course, a
segmental pediment on consoles.

MIDDLE WALLOP *see* NETHER WALLOP

MINLEY MANOR

8050

1858–62 by *Henry Clutton*, for Raikes Currie of Glyn & Co.,
bankers. One of the first English country houses inspired by
French Renaissance chateaux, principally Louis XII's *corps de
logis* at Blois.* Red brick, ashlar dressings with well-carved

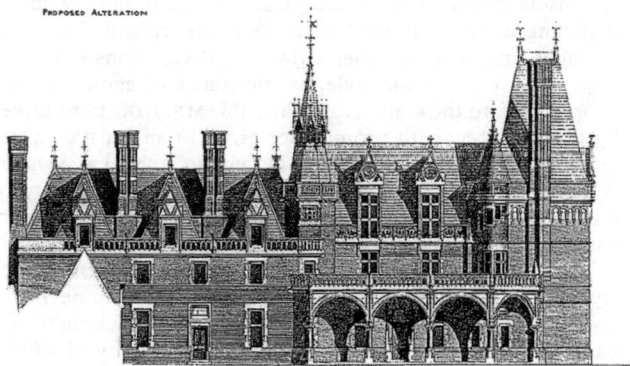

MINLEY MANOR
PROPOSED ALTERATION

Minley Manor, design for south wing.
Drawing by Henry Clutton, 1871

*Clutton published *Remarks with Illustrations on the Domestic Architecture of France
from the Accession of Charles VI to the Demise of Louis XII* (1853).

details and tall slate-covered pavilion roofs with correspondingly tall and thin gabled dormers and even taller chimneys. A
new domestic wing was added in 1870–1 after a fire. Currie's
son, Bertram, despaired of the house and in 1885–6 had it substantially altered and extended by *George Devey*; the work completed after Devey's death in 1886 by his chief draughtsman
Arthur Castings who made a further addition of his own in
1898. Devey commendably matched Clutton's style, his contributions often identifiable only by trademark brick diapering.
Inside, and elsewhere in the grounds, he is less constrained.
The Curries sold the house to the War Department in 1936
and it is now used by the Royal Engineers based at Gibraltar
Barracks to the NE.

The ENTRANCE (NE) FRONT of the house is extremely
varied and slightly confused by the later additions. The central
entrance block and the large square corner pavilion to the r.
are Clutton; the ground-floor addition with three-bay ashlar
porch and elaborately carved door surround is Devey, as is the
gabled clock tower and other alterations at high level. Of the
wing on the l. side of the forecourt, the ground floor is Devey's
but Castings added the substantial upper parts, terminating in
a large square pavilion to echo Clutton's. The tall octagonal
water tower in the angle is similarly work of two distinct phases.
A low brick wall encloses the forecourt. On the r. side of the
forecourt a screen wall by Devey with a gateway through to a
Gothic porch at the rear, itself part of a pent-roofed loggia with
carved wooden columns. The GARDEN ELEVATIONS remain
much less altered and are more originally Clutton, but on the
SE side is the dining-room wing by Devey, with in front a cloister, inside which are modelled plaster reliefs in blind windows
depicting scenes from the lives of SS Laurence and Catherine.
At right angles the former CHAPEL (R.C.), consecrated in
1890. In a C13 Gothic style, an elongated octagon with tall
copper roof. In the cloister, an admirable MEMORIAL to Devey
by *C. H. Mabey*, with prominence given to an artist's palette
over the architect's T-square, for Devey was trained as a water-
colourist by Cotman. Devey added the NE service courtyard
on the site of Clutton's stables NE of the house; the octagonal
game larder is probably of this date.

The INTERIOR appears to be by Devey, in a Renaissance
style. Cramped entrance hall with prominent chimneypiece,
above which is an arcaded gallery with wrought-iron
balustrade. In the inner hall, an equestrian relief by *M. Hiolle*,
1887, and heraldic stained glass by *Willement*, 1859–60. Fine
drawing room panelled in Spanish walnut with chimneypiece,
pilasters, much carving, and coffered ceiling. Dining room with
columned apses at each end. Panelled with chimneypiece and
thin-ribbed ceiling.

Also by Devey: ARCH COTTAGE, Neo-Elizabethan of 1887
with octagonal stair-tower, the fine STABLES, NW of the house,
of diapered brick with cross-windows under semicircular pediments and crocketed gables, the MAIN LODGE, and the

GATEWAY with diapered walls and pairs of piers, the outermost with carved stone griffons.

GARDENS AND PARK. Landscaping, with avenue of Wellingtonia etc., was by *James Veitch Jun.* but the gardens closest to the house due to Devey; the planting by *Robert T. Veitch* with his landscaper *F. W. Meyer.* The WINTER or DUTCH GARDEN, SW, has an especially fine ORANGERY, in Dutch C17 style. Further SW is the WOODLAND GARDEN, laid out by *Messrs Veitch* with, prominent on the crest of the hill, the magnificent brick WATER TOWER of 1896 by *Castings,* which has a steep pyramidal roof, an octagonal cupola and a conical-roofed turret. Incorporated at the base is a Gothic summerhouse, of ashlar and flint. Inside, a mosaic. 100 yds E of the house, a charming circular rustic SUMMERHOUSE, probably *c.* 1890s but looking early C19 with tall conical thatched roof with lunettes. An area of Hawley Common, ESE of the house, was laid out as PLEASURE GROUNDS from 1893 by *Messrs Veitch,* including a lake for water-lilies. There was a summerhouse and boathouse.

ST ANDREW, 250 yds E of the house. By *Clutton,* 1867–70, also for Raikes Currie. Small, of flint, in English mid-C14 style, unusual for Clutton who favoured a more muscular Early French Gothic (e.g. Woburn). Collegiate seating inside chapel and panelled roof, beautifully gilded and painted by *Crace & Son.* – FONT. By *Buckeridge.* – REREDOS. No doubt by *Clutton.* The lower part carved by *Ruddle* of Peterborough, below a Crucifixion, painted by *A. Gueffens* of Antwerp with dramatic shrouded mourning figures in the Nazarener tradition of fifty years earlier. – STAINED GLASS. Of *c.* 1870. The E window by *Morris & Co.* with foliate St Andrew's cross and Evangelists' symbols designed by *Philip Webb.* W window composite, with *Morris & Co.* figures (St Philip by *Morris,* St Andrew by *Madox Brown* and St John by *Burne-Jones*); smaller, more lightsome figures in the tracery by *H. E. Wooldridge.* By him, similar figures in nave N window by *Powells.* In the leafy graveyard, gravestone to Raikes Currie †1881. By *C. H. Mabey* (N. Taylor).

HOME FARM, ½ m. SE. 1899–1901 by *Arthur Castings.* A large and impressive model farm with buildings around two yards.

FLEET LODGE, 1 m. SW. 1899 by *Castings* in French Renaissance style. In the centre a sumptuous cut and rubbed brick archway with Corinthian columns and pediment, pavilions l. and r.

MONK SHERBORNE   6050

ALL SAINTS. Essentially Early Norman, almost perfectly preserved in plan. In its original state it must have been quite large – can it have been monastic, perhaps the parent church of Pamber Priory? Walling of *c.* 1100–30, see the herringbone flint-laying and one chancel window high up. Traces of two more are visible inside. A little later, *c.* 1140, the large N doorway with one order of columns, capitals of two decorated scallops, a roll and a zigzag order in the arch, and a plain tympanum with traces of incised lattice ornament. Above the doorway, a crowstepped moulding of distinctive and unusual form. Of the same time probably the wide chancel arch with a big semicircular single respond and a single subsidiary shaft to the W. The former (on N side) has a multi-scalloped capital with a flat face in the middle ending at the mouth, the latter reeded leaves. There is also evidence in the chancel E wall of an E arch with shafts and zigzag. It may have opened to a C12 apse. The present chancel has one blocked lancet, but the windows are of *c.* 1300 – the square-headed E window of *c.* 1340. Tile-hung timber bell-turret, probably of 1862; supported by sturdy C15(?) timberwork below. Perp W doorway and window. Very large medieval NW stair-turret. Was it for a lost or intended stone W tower? Next to it, big timber N porch of the C14, once a lychgate, the arch framed of two great baulks. – Old DOOR with iron hinges. – PILLAR PISCINA. Late C12 with broad leaves (vestry). – ALTAR with ALTAR FRONTAL by *Watts & Co.*, introduced with other good chancel furnishings during restoration of 1887–9 by *Bodley*. – LECTERN, a characteristically Bodley-like reading stand with traceried front. – FONT. An idiosyncratic C13 piece oddly with three supports of 1889, and three heads sticking out from the underside. Only one of them is original. – PULPIT. A rare Cromwellian piece, dated on the door, 1651, given by the rector: see his epitaph below. – PEWS, with the usual plain straight-headed ends. C15, restored in 1862. – COMMUNION RAILS. Jacobean. Now at the W end, with the relocated SCREEN. The C15 central parts of the screen are similar to that at Pamber, the rest by *Bodley*. – STAINED GLASS. Of the original scheme of 1862, much survives, especially the effective grisaille quarry glazing. Probably by *T. Wells* of Pimlico who signs a sweetly inept set in the vestry. Also by him perhaps, the boldly colourful W window with historical figures of King Edward III, Queen Philippa and Robert Geresford (commemorating the connection of the church with The Queen's College, Oxford, holder of the advowson by grant of King Edward IV). – E window of 1896 by *Lavers & Westlake*. Crucifixion with Renaissance tendencies in the canopies. – Nave N, easternmost, by *A. K. Nicholson*, 1915. SS John Baptist and Evangelist.

MONK SHERBORNE HOUSE, ¼ m. N. Arts and Crafts Neo-Georgian of 1911–13 for Harold Cowan by *R. Weir Schultz*; an interesting reworking of his earlier Inholmes Court (West Green, q.v.). Quite large, and revealing in its form and details a debt to Lethaby. Symmetrical elevations with flanking gabled two-bay wings that have diamond-shaped attic windows on the N side and much inventive brick and tile detailing to the garden side, which also has a chunky central oak veranda with balcony above (a late C20 replacement of the slightly shallower original). It originally had a dog-legged entrance (now axial) via a brick-vaulted lobby, leading to the large hall occupying the full width of the centre. Dog-leg staircase with alternating diamond-section and splat-balusters. *Schultz* also advised on the planting of the garden.

QUEENS MEADOW, ¾ m. N along Salters Heath Road, is a thatched late C14 three-bay cruck house. The dais canopy at the upper end of the hall is a rare survival in Hampshire.

MONXTON

3040

ST MARY. 1852–3 by *Woodyer*, replacing a larger Norman church held by the Abbey of Bec, Normandy, until 1441. Flint nave and chancel and somewhat overhanging shingled W bellcote with reused medieval bell-frame. Plate tracery. Big timber S porch. Inside, steep nave roof with collar-beams. Chancel-arch capitals, of the trumpet-scallop type of *c.* 1200 reused, together with the responds. – STAINED GLASS. Of 1853 by *Powells*, except the E window by *Kempe*, 1887. – BRASS. Alice Swayne and Arthur, her son, 1599. Engaging figures.

MONXTON MANOR, W of the church. An early C18 double-pile house with a central canted bay, containing an octagonal entrance hall and bedroom of the same shape above.

BEC HOUSE, E on the Amport road, was the rectory of *c.* 1796, probably designed and erected by *William Kimber* of Abbotts Ann, who had described its predecessor as 'in so ruinous and decayed [a] State as to be dangerous for any person to dwell any longer therein'. Two storeys, quite large, with a long seven-bay garden front of brick.

S of Andover Road is the OLD FARMHOUSE, a *c.* 1650 lobby-entry-plan house. Of two storeys and attic, this must be one of the earliest and largest vernacular cob houses in Hampshire.

MOORE PLACE FARM *see* BRAMSHILL HOUSE

MORTIMER WEST END

6060

A salient of Hampshire, until 1870 ecclesiastically part of Stratfield Mortimer, Berkshire.

ST SAVIOUR. 1855–6 by *Richard Armstrong* for Richard Benyon, of Englefield House, Berkshire, later his patron at Stratfield Mortimer and elsewhere.* In a less than perfectly correct Early

---

* As a marble tablet of 1896 inside relates. Benyon also employed *Armstrong* in Essex to work on the churches at North Ockenden (1858), South Ockenden (1865–6) and Cranham (1873).

Dec. Flint. Nave and chancel, polygonal vestry, bellcote. Low
w vestry with frilly Arts and Crafts detail of 1902 by *Hoare &
Wheeler* of Reading. – STAINED GLASS. E window, by *Horwood
c.* 1856, after Dürer's Crucifixion. The background of 1938. –
Two nave windows, one N, one S, of 1942 by *E. Liddell Armitage*.
– w window of 1953 by *Christopher Webb*. Above average for its
date, one has to say. – MONUMENT. Walter Roalfe Cox. By
Henry Pegram, 1928. Copper relief showing Christ healing the
sick.

THE OLD VICARAGE, N of the church. Neo-Tudor of 1855. Big,
with chequer brickwork. A good design. Is it by *Armstrong*?

88 MORTIMER WEST END CHAPEL, Chapel Lane. Now Countess of Huntingdon Connexion (since 1826). Built 1798 and
enlarged 1805. Chequer brick with the typical Late Georgian
segment-headed windows, wider than high. The chapel has a
three-bay front like a cottage; its aisled interior completely preserved (restored 1993 by *Gary Seymour*). Manse of four bays
and two storeys attached.

MOUNDSMERE MANOR

6040

½ m. NE of Preston Candover

1908–9 by *Reginald Blomfield*; one of his six great country houses.
The client was Wilfred Buckley, a lawyer and an authority on old
glass and dairy farming. Still the pattern of the sumptuous
Edwardian mansion, despite its later reduction, and one of the
best examples of the 'Wrenaissance' style in vogue before the
First World War. The model for the style was Hampton Court.

Two storeys and attic. Red brick with ample Portland stone
dressings including giant pilasters, a bold frieze and cornice
and a parapet topped by urns. N entrance front of seven bays
with two-bay wings, which before the 1970s projected far out
around a deep entrance court. Pilastered three-bay centre with
balustraded parapet. Some carved details, including swags in
the stone panels between the windows reused from the demolished w wing. Rusticated stone porch with segmental-
pedimented doorway. The symmetry is thrown by the taller
staircase window to the r. of the centre. The garden front is the
show side, also seven bays. It has a similarly embellished three-
bay centre with, in the attic, Wren's *œils de bœuf* windows with
swagged surrounds. The side elevation was originally seven
bays with a pilastered five-bay centre, reduced to four bays with
the shortening of the wing. Service court to the NE.

Equally sumptuous INTERIOR, in an early C18 style. The
enriched plasterwork and carved woodwork are by *George
Jackson & Sons*. Generous panelled entrance hall with copious
swags and drops. Fine chimneypiece with, in the overmantel,
the American eagle gathering the surrounding festoons, and an
enriched plaster ceiling. Beyond the Ionic screen to the r., the
cantilevered staircase, with delicate wrought-iron balustrade.

The principal reception rooms are along the S side. In the centre, offset from the hall because the front and back of the house are not on the same axis, is the drawing room, with elaborate chimneypiece and doorcases with scrolled pediments. Flanking this, to the r. the dining room, with bolection-moulded panelling and well-carved chimneypiece with Corinthian pilasters, and to the r., the library. Mrs Buckley is said to have influenced the planning of the bedrooms in the American manner, in pairs separated by walk-in closets and shared bathrooms.

Formal GARDENS demonstrate *Blomfield*'s expertise in garden design. N, a yew-hedged forecourt. S, a sunken rose garden with reflecting pool and flanking yew walks. Beyond these, herbaceous borders backed by clipped yew hedges and divided into compartments by projecting sections of hedge in the shape of scrolled 'buttresses'. To the S, ha-ha with terrace, breaking forward, with a semicircular viewing platform. A pair of SUMMERHOUSES with *in antis* Tuscan columns. E the WALLED GARDEN, with stone piers and small SUMMER-HOUSE, at the end of an axial walk, in the E side. Along the N side a long lean-to GREENHOUSE with a short projecting central arm. Elegantly curved roof. Neo-Georgian GAR-DENER'S COTTAGE behind. Brick with diapering and a hipped roof with a pair of chimneys linked by a arch. Further E, the STABLES/MOTOR HOUSE by Blomfield. Neo-Georgian, around a courtyard. Brick with diaper-work and hipped roofs. Nearby, a row of 1930s Neo-Georgian COTTAGES by *L. W. Franklyn Sterling*.

MOUNDSMERE FARM. The model dairy farm established by Buckley in 1907 to provide clean milk for his diabetic wife (he was founder and chairman of the National Clean Milk Society from 1915). Most of the buildings, apart from the milking barn and milk room (now converted), date from after a fire in 1915 and are simple Neo-Georgian structures, in brick and tile (they include the Queen Mary Barn, for housing dry cattle, a sleeping barn, a granary and food barn, a hospital and a pair of attractive timber-framed covered yards). C18 FARM-HOUSE, with an attached Neo-Georgian former generator house by *Blomfield*, and a C19 brick and flint stable range.

MOUNDSMERE LODGES, 1 m. SW. Interwar Neo-Georgian pair, quite accomplished. One storey and attic. Brick with steep hipped tile roofs. Dentil string courses and doorways set in raised brick surrounds. Gatepiers with pineapple finials.

NATELY SCURES

ST SWITHUN. A seemingly complete miniature Norman church, with only a C17 farmhouse and weatherboarded C18 barn for company. Simplest single-cell plan, with apsidal chancel and nave in one. The stone double bellcote is of *Salvin*'s major

restoration of 1864–6, paid for by Colonel D. W. Carleton and
the Rev. Richard Carleton. Large Perp windows were taken out
and genuine Norman windows renewed. The nice N doorway
is a showpiece looking *c.* 1130–60. Possibly one of the earliest
of its type: with a depressed trefoiled head with two big cusps.
Arch with zigzag, one capital with a mermaid (a mid-C20
replica of the original; a rarity in Romanesque sculpture). C19
W gallery on a roll-moulded beam from a gallery of 1591, a
very early Post-Reformation example, necessary in this tiny
space. The best of the other fittings are Salvin's, eccentrically
Neo-Norman. – MONUMENTS. Among the many a Gothic
brass to General Thomas Carleton (†1817), Governor of the
Province of New Brunswick from its foundation in 1784 until
his death. By *R. H. Green & Son*, St John, New Brunswick
(erected by the legislature of New Brunswick). Others include
a curious series of tablets looking like diamonds, hearts and
clubs.

3050

NETHERTON

No more than a hamlet in a remote, secluded valley. The old
parish church was largely demolished *c.* 1866 when it was superseded by St Barnabas, Faccombe 1 m. E (q.v.).

NETHERTON HOUSE, E of the old graveyard. Very fine rectory
of *c.* 1720. Brick, vitrified headers and red dressings. Smooth
entrance side with cut-in windows without surrounds. Five
bays, two-and-a-half storeys, only the top windows segmental-
headed. One-bay pediment with a blind lunette. Doric doorcase. Six bays on the garden side, the middle two with
mezzanine windows representing the staircase, segmental-
headed except for the tall round-arched top windows. Three-
bay side elevations. S extension of 1966–7 by *Raymond Erith*: a
timber-clad canted bay with Ionic pilasters to the door, supporting a full entablature. The interior has quite a number of
the arches characteristic of Queen Anne houses. The staircase
has three slim balusters to each step. Contemporary STABLES.
Brick and flint with round-arched windows and doors.
NETHERTON COTTAGE is probably medieval, converted to
lobby-entry plan *c.* 1600, refronted in C18 brick and flint. Over
the road, NETHERTON FARM has a splendid C18 BARN.
Timber-framed with long-straw thatched roof. Eleven bays
with aisles.

3030

NETHER WALLOP

Locally important before the Conquest as a royal demesne manor
in the possession of Countess Gueda of Earl Godwin, which may
account for the early work in the church.

ST ANDREW. Perched on the shoulder of a hill, shelving steeply
to the E and N. Low, flint W tower of 1704 by *Thomas Muspratt*,
mason (inscribed on the exterior). The exterior is not very
rewarding. The chancel was rebuilt in 1845 by *F. R. Fisher* of
Salisbury and much of the N aisle is brick of 1752. Otherwise
the medieval features are Perp, except for the Norman N
doorway with one order of columns and a simple arch, re-set
when the N aisle was added in the early C13. The cushion capitals have unusual hanging drapery, however, which might
suggest a Late Saxon date (cf. chancel arch capital at
Stoughton, West Sussex; both were owned by Earl Godwin).
The core of the church is indeed Saxon, of the early C11 on
the evidence of its unique wall painting (*see* below), and its
original form was probably aisleless but appears to have had
transepts and a small chancel. The church was granted by
Henry I to York Minster in 1133 and about 1200 it was given
a S aisle of three bays. The arcade has the usual round piers
and round abaci, with capitals of flat, broad, simple leaves.
Pointed arches with one step and one slight chamfer. Also of
about this time is the chancel arch (its predecessor must have
been extraordinarily low to accommodate the painting above)
with semicircular responds with square moulded and scalloped
capitals.

The remains of the original chancel now forms a 'crossing'
but that this was a chancel *c.* 1200 is shown by the W respond
of the S arch which was part of the arch into a S chancel chapel.
The N nave arcade was built very soon after (i.e. early C13,
traces of fictive masonry survive of this date). The capitals are
now moulded, and the arches have two slight chamfers. The
fourth bay of the S arcade is contemporary; the wall thickness
between the third and fourth bays of both arcades indicate the
position of the former transepts, the last traces of which were
removed with the later widening of both aisles. The N arcade
was once continued by at least one bay to the E as the N chancel
chapel; an octagonal pier survives but in its present form the
N chapel is clearly mid to late C14: square-headed N window
and two niches with nodding ogee canopies. Also early C13 is
the tower arch, though the responds have two chamfered
orders and half-round shafts to the inner order with moulded
and scalloped capitals, and so they may be reused from somewhere else. The present chancel is Neo-Norman of 1845, a
rebuilding of a Perp extension.

WALL PAINTINGS. On the nave E wall, over the chancel arch,
are two flying angels, all that survives of a depiction of either
Christ in Majesty or the Ascension (a popular subject in
the first millennium). Dated to the early C11 and in style
closely paralleled by contemporary illumination and sculpture.
Uncovered in 1971, these are the earliest known *in situ*
mural paintings in England and attributed to an artist of the

*R. Gem and P. Tudor Craig, *Anglo Saxon England* vol. 9 (1981), 115–36.

Winchester School.* A horizontal line above suggests that a second tier may have existed originally. Others are of *c.* 1430. On the s nave wall St George and the Dragon, tower on the r. with a king and queen looking down. To its l., a large figure of Christ with trade emblems, as a warning to Sabbath Breakers. In reveal of the s aisle E window, St Nicholas. Over the tower arch a large painted bell. – Post-Reformation PEWS in the aisles, C17. – STAINED GLASS. In the chancel by *Clayton & Bell*, dull stuff, the E window of 1868. N chapel, N and E windows by *Burlison & Grylls*, 1909. Pictorial and livelier. s aisle s by *Clayton & Bell*, 1909. N aisle by *V. M. Barnewall*, 1938, SS Cuthbert and Margaret with Celtic symbols. – MONUMENTS. Nave aisle, brass to Dame Mary Gore, Prioress of Amesbury, Wilts. (Henry II gave the manor of Wallop to Amesbury Abbey in 1177), †1436. A 22½-in. (57-cm.) figure with damaged inscription over her head. Brasses to prioresses are rare. – *Ex situ* C14 ledger stone in the N aisle for a brass to a bishop.

Large ashlar PYRAMID with a fine flaming finial, set uncomfortably close to the w tower. Originally railed. It was built in 1748 by *John Blake* of Winchester for Dr Francis Douce †1760 who was evidently as fearful of bodysnatchers as he was fascinated by Egyptian burial rites; his body is sealed within a vaulted chamber.*

In the village, a pair of COTTAGES, dated 1861, built to designs by *Henry Roberts* for the Society for Improving the Condition of the Labouring Classes.

WALLOP HOUSE, ½ m. WNW of the church. Former rectory of 1838 by *Owen Browne Carter*. In the Tudor style. Red brick with diapering of knapped flint. Façade with four steep gables: the w gable added 1896 at the same time as the single-storey ballroom at rear. Porch with polygonal buttress-shafts and Yorkist sun emblem over, the badge of York (the rector was appointed by York Minster from *c.* 1460 until the late C20).

GARLOGS, ½ m. s in parkland, where the Wallop washes into an ornamental lake. 1841, replacing an earlier house destroyed by fire (retained panelling inside has the date 1636 and initials G.W.E.). Three storeys and three bays square, stuccoed, with later C19 embellishments: shutters, cornices, blind boxes etc. Some Neo-Tudor ribbed ceilings inside and cast-iron staircase in Grecian taste.

BERRY COURT FARM, ½ m. SSW. The BARN is quite exceptional, dated to 1580 (dendrochronology). Built by the brother of William Paulet, 3rd Marquess of Winchester. Low flint walls with ashlar quoins, one mighty hipped roof over all and a cart entrance to the yard. Inside, aisles, tie-beams on crown-posts, supporting queenposts, collars and four tiers of wind-braces. The hipped sides of the roof have their wind-braces too. The large mansion house with which it was associated was demolished *c.* 1700.

---

* The remarkable story behind this monument is told by Matthew Craske in *Church Monuments* XV (2000).

FIFEHEAD MANOR, Middle Wallop. Now flats. A fine C17 centre range, rendered with stone mullioned windows and diamond chimneystacks (carved fireplaces with four-centred arches in the ground floor), book-ended by a tall C18 double-pile house and early C19 domestic range.

DANEBURY HOUSE. 1 m. E on Danebury Down. Built after 1832 by Lord George Bentinck. The courtyard's E range with clock turret was the entrance to the enormous STABLES built by him and Lord Sherborne for the trainer John Day. 500 yds E is the site of STOCKBRIDGE RACECOURSE (active from c. 1735, closed in 1898). Overgrown, ruinous GRANDSTAND, erected by the Bibury Racing Club who took over in 1832.

LONG BARROW, E on Houghton Down, ¼ m. N of Chattis Hill House (A30). This is a much denuded long barrow now only 1 ft (30 cm.) high and having a length of 170 ft, (52 metres). The side ditches can still be traced on the ground. Part of the barrow was excavated in the C19, when a number of crouched inhumation burials without grave goods were found.

See also DANEBURY HILL FORT.

NEW ALRESFORD

5030

New as against old, because this is a made little town, founded by Bishop de Lucy of Winchester and laid out by 1200 when the 'Novum Forum' was awarded its market charter. As with Overton and, less successfully, Newtown (qq.v.), it was planted in one of the Bishop's manors (*see* Old Alresford) and done at about the same time as the Bishop created the grand reservoir, Old Alresford Pond, to its NE by damming the River Arle with the Great Weir, over which runs the road between the old and new parts of Alresford. The reason for the town's founding was to generate income from rents charged for building plots. It has one wide sloping market street (Broad Street) running N–S with the church behind the streets (East and West Street) that cross at the top. This T-shaped plan invites comparisons with Overton (q.v.) but is misleading, as the medieval route through the town was actually from Old Alresford to the N then up Broad Street before turning W to Winchester. East Street only became important after the creation of the turnpike in 1753. Medieval fabric is little in evidence in the town's buildings, having suffered a series of conflagrations in the C17 and C18, most seriously in 1689, when a 'Sudden and most Dreadful Fire' laid waste to most of the town, destroying the market house and damaging the church. The town's major medieval industries were cloth making and tanning, and by the C19 the growing of watercress had become an important local activity, no doubt boosted by the coming of the Alton to Winchester railway line in 1865. The town grew little in the C19 but there was substantial C20 development to the S of the railway.

CHURCHES AND PUBLIC BUILDINGS

ST JOHN BAPTIST. Held by the Bishops of Winchester, but surprisingly disappointing. The fire of 1689 left only the flint lower
stages of the W tower and the outer walls of the aisles. Rebuilding, completed in 1694, was extensive (old photos show a nave
with boarded timber posts) and major restoration in 1896–8
by *Sir Arthur Blomfield* is in a crisp hard Perp, including the
chancel. But two medieval doorways and several windows are
in place. The oldest window, a C13 lancet at the W end of the
S aisle, may have been part of an addition to an earlier church,
of which no other traces remain. Next in date, a little later in
the C13, come small fragments of shafting of the former
chancel E window, relocated in the C19 E window of the N
chapel; the typically Late E.E. roll-moulded bases of the nook-
shaft r. are genuine. The blocked S doorway is early C14, as are
the lower stages of the W tower, of neatly knapped flint, with
two small single lancets N and S, unusually with cusped ogee
heads, looking early C14. Restored later C14 arch inside. Above
it, the original weather-mould of the former medieval roof.
Plain brick top, probably of *c.* 1694, with a big clock dial of
1811 toward the town. Fine N doorway (blocked), in the late
C14 Court style of Yevele and Wynford (cf. Hursley, South
Hampshire) with arch and quatrefoiled spandrels, worthy of a
bishop's mason. Reordering of 2000–1 by *The Sarum Partnership*: new fittings at the E end of the nave in the mode of the
1960s liturgical movement. – COMMUNION RAILS. Early C18.
– REREDOS, unusually combined with E window, with the Last
Supper in *opus sectile* of 1900 by *Powells*, who also designed the
fine glass. – MURAL TILES of unusual pattern in the altar area
(cf. Petersfield). – ARCHITECTURAL FRAGMENTS. Found
during the rebuilding. They include a small portion of a circular Norman font of oolitic limestone with pelleted chevron
ornament (cf. Overton, where the church also pre-dates the
C13 new town). – SCULPTURE. Outside, on the W wall of the
tower, fairly high up, a Crucifixus of indeterminate post-
Conquest date, possibly C13 (E. Coatsworth): small figure on
a larger cross, but the whole quite small. Clearly re-set, but
where from? – STAINED GLASS. E window, *see* above. N chapel
E window by *Ward & Hughes*, 1879. S aisle SW by *Chris Ainslie*,
2007. – MONUMENTS. Three cartouche tablets in the style of
1690, but dated 1759, 1762 and 1763, all possibly by the same
hand. Two hanging tablets in the Neoclassical style of *c.* 1800,
dated 1789 (Woolls) and 1798 (Harris).
    Low CHURCH HALL of 1967–8 by *K. G. Brooks* to SE. The
churchyard has been partly cleared, but several C18–C19 table
tombs survive, with, SW of the tower, headstones to French
prisoners of war, held between 1808 and 1814.
ST GREGORY (R.C.), Grange Road. 1967–8 by *Melhuish Wright
& Evans* and quite an adventurous, not to say outré, design
for its date for a small country town. Square, with the strong

pyramidal roof set back behind broad eaves, dramatically broken by a sheer N-facing skylight. Direct timber-lined centrally planned interior, with simply ordered furnishings: freestanding stone ALTAR and FONT. Low bench seating on three sides. – Contemporary STATIONS OF THE CROSS by *Lynn Constable Maxwell*.

ALRESFORD AND DISTRICT COMMUNITY CENTRE, West Street. The former Market House, built in 1865–6 by *William Hunt*. Pevsner thought it 'dreary' and 'ought to be rendered'; instead its yellow brick with red and black brick has been painted over, not an improvement. Three bays with a pediment, tall round-arched windows to the assembly room above stilted segmental arches to the former market hall. Entrance to the l. under a cartouche and swags.

FIRE STATION, The Mount. A neat, very well-detailed, one-storey design in brick of 1939–40 by *A. Simpson Low*, the County Architect.

PERIN'S SCHOOL, The Mount. 1909–10, succeeding the school in West Street. Late C17 domestic style. Small octagonal cupola. Of the later buildings, the most interesting is THE HUB, a drama centre, of 2002. Brick, steep tile roofs with flat tops. At the corner the entrance and a large flat roofed dormer. Otherwise windowless.

RAILWAY STATION, Station Road. Built *c.* 1865 as the largest, and best, station on the Mid-Hants Railway (restored as the Watercress Line between Alresford and Alton). Red brick with gault polychromy to the round-arched windows. Central booking hall with flanking gabled wings. The platform side (cement-rendered) has a canopy on cast-iron brackets. Altered inside in 1893. At the E end is a boarded building with valenced canopies: salvaged from Lyme Regis station. The down platform waiting room looks *c.* 1890. – SIGNAL BOX. A standard London & South Western Railway type I design, with brick base and timber-framed cabin, but its distinctive saltire bracing boarded over. Cast-iron FOOTBRIDGE made by *H. Young & Co.*; formerly at Uckfield, re-erected here 1995. N is a tall former WAREHOUSE of 1873, by *William Hunt*. Yellow brick. Three storeys and loft with loading doors on the front. Cast-iron windows (with stone sills and lintels) and cast-iron columns inside.

PERAMBULATION

BROAD STREET, sloping gently downhill, is one of the best streets in Hampshire, and broad indeed since the demolition of the market hall and shambles which occupied its middle until the early C19. It now has two rows of trees. The houses l. and r. are agreeable without exception: all post-date the 1689 fire, and many façades have been remodelled in the late C18 and early C19. So there is plenty of brick but also lots of stucco and much of it coloured with attractive variety. The doorcases, here and in the other streets, deserve a study of their own and even the later shopfronts do not detract, see e.g. the fancy cast-iron colonnade for a former butcher's shop on the w side. Nos. 1–5 at the corner with West Street, of brick with moulded string course, modillion eaves cornice and steeply hipped roof. Five bays to Broad Street and three to West Street, the centre bays slightly projecting, on the E side with a broad (later) doorcase with fluted Doric pilasters and metope frieze. Inside, a staircase with barley-sugar balusters. The showpiece, however, is No. 47, which must have been built almost immediately after the fire. Red brick with burnt headers, moulded rubbed brick string course and modillion eaves cornice, with five slightly irregularly spaced bays, cross-windows and early C19 doorcase with bracketed flat hood. The E side has no houses of comparable quality but some later buildings of appealing character, e.g. tiny OLD FIRE STATION, 1881 by *William Hunt,* and some clever late C20 classical infill (Nos. 36a–b) by *Robert Adam* capturing the spirit of the street, without resorting to copyism: brick and stucco with chunky doorcases and garage doors tied together by a continuous entablature. Further up, Nos. 16–20 are the former George Inn of *c.* 1690. Owned by Winchester College and once the doyen of the town's inns and impressively large. Of course the stucco and fenestration are all later alterations, but the modillion cornice and the staircase with column-on-vase balusters are original features. Finally the HORSE AND GROOM, whose late C19 planted timber framing almost convinces, but what is good is the curved wrought-iron sign over the former carriage arch.

In EAST STREET, No. 6 (s side) is a handsome early C18 house, of five bays, the front remodelled in the late C18, stuccoed with bracketed cornice and charming central doorcase with a touch of Chinoiserie in the fanlight pushing up into an open pediment with concave sides. Inside, the dining room is panelled with a late C18 decorative scheme of Pompeian red and black, and has a late C18 marble chimneypiece. Diagonally opposite NatWEST, an early C18 house, grey headers and red dressings, five bays with the centre framed by giant pilasters and topped by an open pediment. The tall arched window reaches into it. The design is very similar to Cheriton House (q.v.). After this the street continues with rows of very pleasing late C18 and early C19 houses and modest cottages, mostly highly coloured stucco or painted brick, and several nice old shopfronts. No. 22, late C18, has a standard repertoire of Georgian motifs – bows, pilasters with consoles etc. – used in an extraordinary way. CARDEW HOUSE also stands out, a large C18 double pile, with a front of mathematical tiles. (In the neighbouring field Robert Dennet Rodney laid out a private miniature railway *c.* 1843, surely one of the earliest of its kind.)

Now downhill along WEST STREET, past the unobtrusive Market House (*see* above). The largest buildings are the inns on both sides: first THE SWAN HOTEL, C18 but now with a late

C19 appearance of stucco with quoins and lugged window architraves. In the late C18 rear wing, the former assembly room and a long elliptically arched barrel-vaulted cellar. Almost facing The Swan, THE BELL HOTEL, formerly the Market Inn, of 1767. Stuccoed front of four widely spaced bays, a pilastered surround to the former carriage arch. A few more good Georgian buildings on both sides. The most striking is No. 36 (N side), with a pair of shallow full-height bows, altered in 1868 by its owner, *William Hunt* (see his initials in the stuccoed surround of the doorcase). Finally, at the bottom of the hill is No. 60, also with a full-height bow and doorway with an open segmental pediment on consoles. These belong to an early C19 remodelling of the master's house of Perin's School, whose schoolroom adjoined to the r. (converted to shops *c.* 1910, when the school moved to The Mount, *see* Public Buildings above). Founded by the will of Dr Henry Perrin in 1697, the buildings are essentially of that date. Late C17 window openings are still visible at the rear. Then starts POUND HILL with the former CONGREGATIONAL CHAPEL. 1825, but datestone re-set, the front part of a *c.* 1840 enlargement. Three bays with pediment. Doorway with pilastered doorcase. Then No. 20, a nice early C18 house, three storeys, five bays. Vitrified header brickwork with red dressings, including rubbed brick string course and moulded eaves cornice. Finally, the area close to the foot of Broad Street, where the road swings to the r. into the narrower SOKE towards the weir over Old Alresford Pond (*see* p. 426). The BRIDGE spanning the pond's s outlet is late C14, of ashlar with a double-chamfered Gothic arch, widened on the upstream side in the C18 in brick, the downstream parapet also rebuilt but reusing the old stone coping.

MILL HILL leads downhill from the NW corner of Broad Street and contains some of the few buildings to escape the great fire, particularly Nos. 3–7 on the l., a mid-C14 base-cruck hall of two bays with cross-wings, the r.-hand one of *c.* 1500, formerly jettied. Downhill to the r., the former TOWN MILL, 1893 by *William Hunt*. Replacing an earlier mill, it was designed to contain rollers rather than stones. Tall, four storeys, of brick, with pilaster-strips with an ungainly mansard roof of 1973. A short walk along the riverside is the OLD FULLING MILL, a C17 timber-framed thatched building, with the miller's cottage on the N bank and, attached to it, the former mill astride the river. Converted to a house in 1950. Preposterously picturesque. About ¼ m. further on, an early C19 EEL HOUSE, a simple red brick and tile structure, built on arches over one branch of the river. A rare survival.

ARLEBURY PARK, ½ m. W on The Avenue (N side). Stuccoed Italianate house with a three-storey tower, begun in the mid C19. Its long elevation has two pediments: that to the r. must have been central originally, the l. part added some time after 1870. Large columned porch in the centre. The site was first occupied by a house of 1774 for William Harris. Its park was extended the full length of The Avenue in the late C19. Nearby, THE ROUNDHOUSE, a former toll house of *c.* 1753.

LANGTON'S, East Street. A fine house of *c.* 1770 set in large grounds. Two full storeys with attic. Vitrified header brickwork with red dressings linking the windows vertically. Five bays, with a central first-floor Venetian window. Additions *c.* 2005 by *Robert Adam Architects* (job architect: *George Saumarez Smith*), including rebuilding wings to create symmetrical elevations. Also a POOL HOUSE in the form of an C18 orangery. Brick with Doric pilasters.

BELL HOUSE, Tichborne Down, ¾ m. s on the edge of the town. The former workhouse, now flats, of 1835–6 by *Edward Hunt*. A standard panopticon plan, the w wing demolished after a fire in 1907 and reconstruction carried out 1907–8 by *Cancellor & Hill*. The former infirmary block behind, also of this date.

NEWNHAM

7050

ST NICHOLAS. A hard Neo-Norman remodelling of 1846–7 with a NW tower carrying a crude sort of Rhenish helm by *Benjamin Thorne*, financed by the Earl of Dorchester (cf. Mapledurwell). But parts remain of the Early Norman church (mentioned in a Charter of Henry de Port to West Sherborne Priory of *c.* 1130). Re-set s doorway in the tower with a roll moulding and plain capitals, and the nave w doorway, also re-set, with ornamented capitals. Inside, a good chancel arch of *c.* 1125 under-restored with jamb shafts, a curious zigzag of 45 degrees only, chip-carved, also with traces of decorative painting on the soffit. Nave roof, looking *c.* 1500. Three bays, with tie-beams and wind-braces. – COMMUNION RAILS. Nice Early Georgian, possibly of 1731, when the E window was glazed with painted glass by *John Rowell* (removed 1847). Chancel paving probably of the same date. – STAINED GLASS. E window of 1891 by *A. O. Hemming*. An intricate Ascension scene. – MONUMENT. Chancel N wall, re-set early C14 gravestone with the bust of a priest, possibly a prior of Andwell, incised in outline below a trefoiled arch.

The village lies NE, with old cottages and farmhouses surrounding the large green. On the sw side is NEW HOUSE, of 1969–70 by *Ian Fraser & Associates*, quite startling in this context. COR-TEN steel frame, with brick cladding and flat roof. Two storeys, the N front with semicircular staircase projection and recessed porch, the impressive garden side fully glazed. Inside, central full-height space with the living room and main bedroom on the first floor.

NEWTON VALENCE

7030

ST MARY. Built *c.* 1250 and essentially E.E., with an unusually short nave and longer chancel in one and a w tower with Perp

W door (blocked) and pinnacled brick top of 1812 by *Thomas Chawner*. Flint with Selborne stone dressings, the strongly Victorian character due to a big restoration by *Blomfield* in 1871–2. Small W lancet in the tower, another in the rebuilt nave S wall, and more in the chancel, also the E window (of three stepped lancets very close together under one arch (like Bentworth) and the priest's doorway with inner segmental arch and two Mass dials (now opening into the vestry of 1871). Inside, the chancel has a fine original roll string, rising round the later reredos. The wide N chapel of *c.* 1300 Single arch springing from a corbel on the E, and a respond on the W. It is now transeptal but shown in a drawing of 1846 as a lean-to aisle. Inside, Blomfield's work is dominant, e.g. the continuous roof with a thin arch brace, and a boarded ceiling to the chancel. – PISCINA with a pointed-trefoil head, above the nice C12 PILLAR PISCINA. – REREDOS. Just three arched recesses of *c.* 1500, now without statuary. – URNS on small pedestals, l. and r. of the altar, probably of *Coade* stone and perhaps from the Manor House. (A *Coade* stone FONT has also been discovered.) – STAINED GLASS. Chancel E window. Poor, by *Ward & Hughes*, 1872. – Other chancel windows (lancets), two S, of 1919, and three N, of 1907 and 1909, all by *Bryans & Webb*. Also by them, the N aisle W window of *c.* 1906. St Francis in a golden landscape. – MONUMENTS. A variety of minor C18–mid-C19 tablets. – Robert Boyle Nicholas †1780, captain of HMS *Thunderer* of 74 guns . . . 'lost in a hurricane off the island of Hispaniola'. Neoclassical. – Audley Lempriere †1855 at Sebastopol. Military trophies and names of Crimean battles. Signed *W. Theed*, sc. London.

In the churchyard, NE, William Thomas Paleologus †1873 '*de Stirpe Imperatorum*', descendant of the last of the medieval Christian emperors of Byzantium.

The former MANOR HOUSE is of two phases. The earliest part (now The Old Manor) is *c.* 1700 but incorporating early C17 fabric, of dressed malmstone and brick with hipped roof and sashes with Gothic-arched lights. Blocked C17 elliptical arched doorway in rubble-stone rear wall and C18 rear wing with parapet. Inside a relocated early C17 plank and muntin screen. Extended NE (now The Manor House) *c.* 1812 for Henry Chawner, the London goldsmith, probably by his cousin *Thomas Chawner* (*see* St Mary). Gault brick, T-plan, with a single-pile range for the principal rooms and the entrance wing (enlarged to r.) with inset curved corners. The garden front, of five bays, has a canted bay at the NW end, originally with *Coade* stone embellishments. Later C19 gault brick addition to the r. of the entrance. Entrance hall has a curved wall facing three doorways set in round-arched recesses with panelled architraves, lion masks at the corners and shelf-like cornices.

Among the village houses is THE BARNS, strikingly converted in 1982–3 from the remains of a C15 aisled timber-framed barn with dressed malmstone outer walls of *c.* 1700. Fire destroyed its centre in 1915; the ends have been preserved as hipped-roofed pavilions separated by a courtyard garden. Inside massive framing with arch bracing.

NEWTON VALENCE PLACE, ¼ m. N. 1913–14 by *Henry Hill* of Winchester for Captain Edmund Jervoise R.N. (*see* also Medstead Manor). Competent Neo-Georgian. Two reused C18 chimneypieces inside. Arts and Crafts garden.

LONGHOPE, ¼ m. SE. The early C18 former rectory, H-plan, much altered and re-fitted inside in the early C19 with a new addition and two-storey porch. One room inside has an early C18 arched bed recess.

PELHAM PLACE, 1½ m. WNW, on the Gosport Road. A stuccoed Tudor Gothic villa of 1839–41 by *J. T. Knowles* for Admiral Lempriere, encasing the three-storey house built in 1781–3 for Admiral Dumaresq by *William Dawes*, an Alton carpenter. Symmetrical front, with three full-height canted bays; two of these were features of the earlier house but had already been rebuilt in Gothic style in 1803 by *John Dyer* of Alton with Tudor-arched lights, panelling and battlements (cf. Farringdon Hurst, Farringdon). The larger outer gables added by Knowles have ogee hoodmoulds to the windows and were originally adorned with pinnacles, also lost from a ground-floor stone loggia with four-centred heads to its arches. The S front similarly gabled with small oriels in the outer pair, but otherwise simpler. Entrance in N end with large battlemented porte cochère and small oriel in gable above. Inside, Gothic staircase with wrought-iron balustrade but the landing ceiling with three large octagonal coffers and much Greek-key and palmette ornament. The drawing-room ceiling has quatrefoils in soffit band and central saucer-shaped coffer with mouchette panels and pendant.

Of the same remodelling, the battlemented ARCHWAY and STABLES.

KITCOMBE HOUSE, 1½ m. NW, on the Gosport Road. Late C18. Five bays, two storeys with parapet. Striking plum-coloured header bond with bright red dressings and ashlar string and cornice. Restrained interior with delicate enriched plaster cornices, doorcase and chimneypieces. Stick-baluster staircase with mahogany treads and veneered and inlaid handrail. The STABLES have vitrified brick detailing, segmental-arched openings and central gable.

NEWTOWN
Burghclere

Established as the borough of Newtown in 1218 by Bishop Lucy of Winchester on part of his manor of Burghclere and described as 'de Novo Burgo de Clere'. It had significantly declined by the mid-C17 and is now a small village.

ST MARY AND ST JOHN BAPTIST. On the site of the medieval
chapel of ease to Burghclere. 1864–5 by *Woodyer*, paid for by
the Arbuthnots of Newtown House. Flint with N porch-tower
with shingled broach spire, the details vaguely in the style of
c. 1300. The E window tracery is fanciful. Richly appointed
interior, with much elaborate carving by *T. Nicholls* including
the N arcade of round piers, the round capitals decorated with
sprays of wild flowers, including ferns and buttercup; the
equally exuberant chancel arch with emblems of the Passion
and REREDOS with vividly carved medallion of Gethsemane.
– STAINED GLASS, in almost every window: by *Hardman*, the
E and W windows of 1865, the latter a good example of the
firm's work. Chancel NW by *Clayton & Bell*, among others of
varying quality. Window in the N aisle by *Kempe & Co.*, 1923.
The best of the older buildings is the SWAN INN, a good-quality
lobby-entry house of *c.* 1600, heavily restored. Close-studded
timber framing and an ovolo-moulded door frame. Inside a
richly moulded spine beam in the parlour. Contemporary stair-
tower at the rear.

NEWTOWN HOUSE. Early C18 five-bay brick centre, with early
C19 gabled wings; all stuccoed. Good staircase inside with
twisted column-on-vase balusters and carved brackets. Much
of the town may have been cleared for its park.

NEWTOWN GRANGE, Newtown Common, ½ m. SW. Late C19
brick house with well-detailed Arts and Crafts alterations and
additions of *c.* 1900–10. Inventive fenestration, a slender gabled
staircase tower and single-storey rear wing with large mullioned-and-transomed window. Inside this is an open hall with
arch-braced collar roof trusses, an inglenook and gallery.

NORTH WALTHAM

An attractive village on a gentle hillside with the church at the
top. Much late C20 infilling.

ST MICHAEL. Enlarged and almost rebuilt in 1865–6 by
J. Colson. Nave and chancel and neat bell-turret with shingled
spire. The window details *c.* 1300; the chancel N window
genuine early C13, and inside, a N arcade which has enough
work of *c.* 1200 to be regarded as authentic. Round piers,
square, chamfered abaci, single-chamfered pointed arches.
Medieval also the PISCINA, with its crocketed gable. This is of
course Dec, perhaps due to the advowson ownership of Hyde
Abbey. – FONT. Octagonal, Perp, with quatrefoils. From
Popham church. – REREDOS. By *Cox & Sons*, *c.* 1865, with
pretty diaper patterning. – STAINED GLASS. In the chancel,
1865 by *Thomas Baillie*; terrible E window.

PRIMARY SCHOOL, W of church. Muscular Gothic of 1873
by *H. F. Yelfe*, and interesting rear courtyard addition by
Keith Walker of *Hampshire County Architect's Dept*, early 1980s.

The triangular village green is bounded by nice cottages. At its
SE end in Popham Lane, BATCHELORS, a three-bay hall house
of *c.* 1500. Thatched with an internal jetty at the high end.
WHEATSHEAF INN, ¾ m. SE. On the A30. C18. Front of five bays
and two storeys, brick with panels of diaper (ground floor
altered in the mid C20). The interesting feature is the W elevation that has windows set in five giant arches which instead
of capitals and abaci have a raised block of flint. Also flint
keystones.

NORTH WARNBOROUGH

The village was a dependent chapelry of Odiham and has no
parish church. Although much developed, it retains its separate identity with an attractive group of vernacular buildings.
Some are of more than local interest, in particular CRUCK
COTTAGE in North Warnborough Street, a thatched hall house
of the early 1380s. To its r., a box-framed house (OAKHOLME
and SHEPHERDS COTTAGE), *c.* 1400, with a two-bay hall with
arch-braced collars and ties, the service end rebuilt as a cross-
wing in the C17. Further along TUDOR COTTAGE, a C15 hall
house, has *c.* 1500 wall paintings depicting horsemen in head-
dresses (possibly the Magi) and an early C17 plaster frieze with
terms and vines. SPRINGFIELD HOUSE (formerly Red House,
at the corner with Tunnel Lane), of 1717, incorporates an
earlier cross-wing at its l. end. Five bays with cross-windows
and coved cornice to hipped roof. C18 arched gateway in front
and late C18 extension to the rear of the r.-hand end creating
a three-bay NE front with pedimented doorcase.

N across the Basingstoke Canal, on the E side are CASTLE
BRIDGE COTTAGES, a startlingly long range of jettied houses,
with nine bays tree-ring dated to the late 1470s and a further
seven of the early 1530s. Surprisingly, only one bay was
originally heated. Edward Roberts has suggested that this was
the owner's dwelling with the remainder for artisans' cottages,
possibly connected with cloth making. Last is STRETE FARM-
HOUSE, whose solar cross-wing on the road side has been
dated to 1448. It was formerly jettied but refronted in brick in
the C18; the jettied-and-floored hall range at right angles to the
rear is a rebuilding of *c.* 1505.

ODIHAM CASTLE, ½ m. NW, on a bend in the River Whitewater
and with one corner of the site cut off by the Basingstoke
Canal. Built for King John on land taken from the royal
hunting park N of Odiham. The first phase of 1207–14 comprised moats, banks, palisades and stone buildings, including
a '*domus regis*' (King's house). The keep, or tower, is all that
remains, probably dating from soon after the French siege of
1216, when the castle was granted to John's daughter, Eleanor.
Originally of three storeys with large round-arched openings

and diagonal buttresses, it is now an eminently picturesque object of flint, most of its ashlar facing having been robbed. Little architectural detail survives. By the C15 the castle was in decline, and was described as a ruin in 1605.

LODGE FARMHOUSE, ¾ m. NE. A rare documented survival of a royal park lodge, rebuilt with a hall and cross-wing for Edward III's parker, William Prest. The cross-wing is almost as built in 1368–9, although refaced mid-C17 in brick with a Dutch gable. Two bays with a gableted hipped roof and great curved tension braces exposed at the rear. The first-floor solar has arch braces, tie-beam and crown-post roof, the service end beneath originally divided. The hall of 1375 is more altered, the chimney inserted in the 1540s and the outside wall rebuilt in brick in the C18, when the roof was reconstructed reusing the medieval rafters.

NORTHINGTON

5030

ST JOHN EVANGELIST. In a wonderful position set on a hillside with a broad view over the tiny village to open downland. 1887–90 by *T. G. Jackson* for the 4th Lord Ashburton of The Grange. A typical estate church proudly provided by the squire. Flint and stone chequer with a concrete core, unusual for the date. Also, flushwork. Big W tower of Somerset type. N aisle. Polygonal apse over a vaulted vestry cleverly making use of the rising ground. Perp windows. S porch curiously domestic. What looks like a rood stair-turret is access to the pulpit. Disappointing interior with fine furnishings; richest in the chancel. REREDOS with carved Last Supper scene by *Guillermin*. – CHOIR STALLS and ORGAN CASE. Splendid hanging CORONA – a crocketed wrought-iron hoop with candles. In the nave, a tall stone PULPIT, unusually with a stone canopy, and a fine set of PEWS with well-carved ends. – STAINED GLASS in the apse. By *Powells*, with apostles by *H. E. Wooldridge*. – Several MONUMENTS from the previous church. Robert Henley, 1st Earl of Northington †1770 and Robert Henley, 2nd Earl †1786, by *R. Hayward*. Large inscription plate. Above, crying putto in relief, and above him, an obelisk with two roundels with coats of arms and garlands. – Baring Family, 1848 by *Westmacott Jun.*, his magnum opus. Below, the entrance to the vault, complete with the door rendered in stone a Baroque to Canova motif. Above, two seated figures, one an angel with the key, the other seated on the ledge. Sentimental, but restrained. – Busts of the 4th Lord Ashburton and his wife, period pieces. Signed by *Sir J. E. Boehm*, 1879. – Claire, Lady Ashburton †1882. Neoclassical, signed *E. Fuchs*, 1899 with profile portrait.

Large, Granite CROSS, 100 yds NE. Erected 1865 in memory of the 2nd Lord Ashburton, on the site of the old church.

NORTHINGTON HILL HOUSE, N of the church. The former school, 1859–60 by *Butterfield* (he altered the old church in 1864). Large, impressive and typically Gothic more in spirit than detail. The schoolroom was contained in the cross-wing, which has a timber bellcote to the gable; between the tall windows (now divided horizontally) the Ashburton arms. ½ m. w, also by *Butterfield*, are some farm cottages of 1861, now NORTHINGTON DOWN HOUSE.

THE GRANGE. *See* p. 296.

LAKE HOUSE. *See* THE GRANGE.

6040

NUTLEY

Church (1845 by *Owen Browne Carter*) demolished in 1955.

NUTLEY MANOR. Dated 1814. Built for George Purefoy Jervoise of Herriard (cf. Manor Farmhouse, Preston Candover). Brick with flared headers. Pilaster-strips at the corners. Thoroughly gentrified and enlarged in the late C20.

AXFORD LODGE, ¾ m. S. Small, brick and flint house for the Purefoy Fitzgeralds. Probably begun in the late 1870s, see the s front in the Nesfield/Shaw manner, with later w addition, and Neo-Georgian E wing, 1920s by *H. H. Jewell*. On the corner of Berrydown Lane, a pretty Arts and Crafts SHELTER of 1929, circular, timber-framed with brick-nogging and conical tile roof.

MOUNDSMERE MANOR. *See* p. 402.

7030

OAKHANGER

A hamlet on the Oakhanger Stream between the hangers and the heaths w of Bordon. Looming over all on three separate sites are the golf-ball radomes of RAF OAKHANGER.

ST MARY MAGDALENE. Hard red brick chapel of 1873, by *M. Moreton Glover*. – (REREDOS from Blackmoor church, no doubt by *Waterhouse*.) – STAINED GLASS. E window by *Gibbs & Moore*.

5050

OAKLEY

The village has two historic foci: Church Oakley, centred on the church, and East Oakley, ⅓ m. SSE, clustered around a green. The latter has grown towards Basingstoke as a suburban area.

St Leonard, Church Oakley. A more than usually expensive restoration of 1868–70 by *T. H. Wyatt*, his plans of 1865 carried out under *John Clarke*. The cost was *c.* £5,000. W tower with much higher, spired NW stair-turret; nave, aisles and lower chancel. Perp style. Still *in situ* several items from the predecessor church: the Tudor Perp W doorway, parts of the C14 tower arch and, inside, the two-bay S arcade and Late Perp windows in the S aisle. The W bay of the S aisle has a semicircular respond of *c.* 1200 with a capital of very many small scallops and a base with spurs. The arch is pointed and has the usual two slight chamfers. The panelled arch of the E bay is also medieval, a rough version of the Sherborne Abbey arches (*c.* 1485–1520), and came from the Malshanger Chapel, which in the early C16 belonged to Archbishop Warham (*see* Malshanger House, below). He also rebuilt the tower (possibly *c.* 1510: the doorway's spandrels have the archbishop's arms, and a C12 carving is re-set in the central stage). The most memorable touch of Wyatt's is the internal appearance of the tower stair-turret, with its wild-flower corbel and incised floral decoration higher up. Good roof in the nave. – FONT. The base of a medieval cross(?), turned upside down. – Sumptuous furnishings of the restoration, especially the REREDOS and PULPIT. In the chancel, TILES by *Maw*. – STAINED GLASS, an early C16 figure of the archbishop (from Wootton St Lawrence) in a setting, probably *c.* 1869, by *Lavers, Barraud & Westlake*, who signed several windows. – MONUMENTS. Brass to Robert Warham †1487 and wife, the archbishop's parents. 20½-in. (52-cm.) figures. – Knight and Lady, *c.* 1520. Recumbent effigies of alabaster. At both their pillows pairs of tiny angels. Tomb-chest with shields in quatrefoils. – Tablet with guardsman's busby. By *Maile & Son*, 1915.

St John, East Oakley. Small Arts and Crafts chapel of 1913, of rendered concrete blocks.

Opposite St Leonard, the former SCHOOL (St Leonard's Centre) of the 1850s. Minimally Tudor Gothic, with house for the schoolmaster. SE is OAKLEY HOUSE, the mid-C19 rectory. Stuccoed, with Tuscan porch to the side. Is this the parsonage for which *Thomas Fulkes* produced a design for altering and enlarging in 1833? Then, SUNBEAM COTTAGE. 1825. Red brick with vitrified headers. Slated. Three bays, with ground-floor round-arched windows set in recessed arched panels. It makes an interesting ensemble with the contemporary octagonal pavilion to its l. said to have been a schoolroom.

Clustered around the green at East Oakley, pretty C17 and C18 cottages, the usual Hampshire mixture of timber framing, brick, flint, tile and thatch, but including a small METHODIST CHAPEL of 1866. Just to the NE, DEEP WELL COTTAGE (No. 16 Oakley Lane) is a thatched C15 cruck house. Three bays, with one-bay hall. Pair of surviving trusses.

Malshanger House, 1½ m. N. The house is Late Georgian, perhaps after 1806 when it was bought by Lord Thurlow. Stuccoed brick. Entrance (E) side of five bays and two-and-a-half storeys; refaced in 1957–8 by *Caroe & Partners* after removal of a large single-storey addition (made after 1862 for Wyndham Portal, probably by *T. H. Wyatt*). They added the curved porch with Venetian window above. Round the corner the main front has two big bows and in between another Venetian window with tripartite sash above. Interior altered in the C19 and C20 but the drawing room has a fine late C18 geometric plaster ceiling with circular panels representing the Seasons.

But what matters most is a slender octagonal brick TOWER at the E end of the stables, all that remains of the house built for William Warham, Archbishop of Canterbury, who was brought up at Malshanger and acquired it in 1504. The tower no doubt dates from soon after this time. It appears to have been a stair-tower in the re-entrant angle of two wings and has a number of arched doorways which must have led to chambers. The house was largely demolished in the early C18. The tower's battlemented upper parts are C19 restoration.

OAKLEY HALL, ⅝ m. SW, 'nearly completed' in 1792 but enlarged and thoroughly remodelled by *T. H. Wyatt* in 1860. Brick. Two-and-a-half storeys. Of the 1790s the nine-bay N front with two big three-bay bows l. and r. (as at Malshanger House). Wyatt provided the forecourt with low balustraded wall, bowed to the park, the elaborate stone porte cochère, most of the service wing and water tower. The space between the rear wings was also infilled. Typically eclectic interior of *c.* 1860, including a galleried saloon, Florentine Renaissance-style drawing room and Baroque-style Library with fitted bookcases with free-standing Corinthian columns and wooden ceiling with octagonal coffers. STABLES also *c.* 1860 but, remarkably, Early Georgian in style except for the characteristically mid-Victorian tower. The house stands in a small wooded PARK. Gardens were laid out in 1860 by *Edward Milner*.

ODIHAM

Odiham had two churches in Domesday Book and was an important royal manor after the Conquest with a deerpark to the N of the town, which is first mentioned in 1216. A royal presence ensured the town's prosperity in the medieval period and it remained an important local agricultural centre, with industries including brickmaking, brewing, tanning, and cloth making. Despite a superficially C18 appearance, many medieval and early post-medieval buildings survive. The medieval street plan is largely unchanged, with the broad High Street running a sinuous course from E to W (a free-standing market house and shambles were still extant in 1739), from the centre of which King Street runs S. In the SW quadrant is the church and The Bury, possibly the area of earliest settlement and a market place, with considerable later encroachment.

CHURCH AND PUBLIC BUILDINGS

ALL SAINTS. A large flint and rubble church, with a broad and spreading exterior. Rather harshly restored by *Woodyer* (1850–1) and *Colson, Farrow & Nisbett* (1897); external plaster was removed in 1902. The w tower, unusually embraced by the wide aisles, is the great feature of the exterior, rising from a very low C13 flint ground storey supported by ashlar buttresses to exceptionally fine brick upper stage (dated 1649, replacing the steeple that collapsed in 1647). English bond, with Artisan Mannerist Ionic angle pilasters and bell-openings surrounded by rustication flanked by pilasters with cut brick capitals; battlements. Stone-banded pinnacles, possibly later. Is the Perp w window early C17? Below it, a low Tudor Perp w doorway of 1897. The broad aisles (making up a rectangular plan 120 ft by 64 ft (37 by 20 metres) rather like Old Basing) have few windows, and mostly by Woodyer but three in the s aisle are 'Gothic Survival' from a restoration of 1634, with simple Perp Tracery (cf. Bishops' Waltham, South Hampshire). Shallow Perp N porch with outer doorway of continuous mouldings and a pretty Late Perp inner doorway of 1496 with nicely carved seaweedy foliage in the spandrels. Contemporary door.

The solemn interior shows a more varied history. Could the narrow walls of the nave suggest a Saxon date? In the nave w wall, the tower arch is early C13, see the imposts and the one slight chamfer, but decidedly rough and uncouth like Whitchurch. Above, the remains of a small Dec window for the bell-ringer – a rarity (cf. Winchester, St John the Baptist). Can it be C17, a late insertion (VCH)? The two-bay arcades to the chancel chapels are more impressively early C13 with round, short piers, octagonal abaci, single-chamfered arches. Aisled chancels are rare at this date and in this instance perhaps due to the Chancellor of Salisbury Cathedral to whom the advowson had been granted by Henry I in 1115. To the r. of the altar is a low segment-arched doorway (blocked but uncovered in the early C20) whose form is similar to the cloister doorway in the s transept (*c.* 1240s) of Salisbury Cathedral. It probably opened to a lost E vestry; that would be remarkably early in England but might have been built to serve the new and more elaborate liturgy of the Sarum Rite, first devised at Salisbury and popularized in the earlier C13 by Bishop Poore. The doorway's external face is covered by the Post-Reformation brick E wall. Chancel arch by *Woodyer*. Of late C13 form.

The nave arcades are surprising for Hampshire. They are high and Late Perp, but differ considerably; the three-bay N arcade is clearly earlier, perhaps contemporary with the N doorway, and characteristically Late Perp with plain octagonal piers, concave-sided capitals, and nearly round double-chamfered arches. The arches from the chancel chapels to the nave aisles are also probably late C15. The s arcade, looking earlier, surely must be a C17 reconstruction. It is of four bays, the slender piers of the often-seen Perp section of four shafts and four diagonal hollows. Moulded arches. They may have

replaced a C14 arcade damaged in 1647 when the S aisle S wall
was partly rebuilt incorporating octagonal fragments, perhaps
from the original columns. Reordering of the interior and S
extension planned in 2008, by *Michael Drury Architects*.

FURNISHINGS. PILLAR PISCINA in the chancel S wall, possibly relocated. Late C12, with a kind of thin crocket capital
typical of *c.* 1190 on a round shaft with base spurs. – COM-
MUNION RAIL. N chapel. C18. Is it from the chancel, whose
solid wooden COMMUNION RAIL and TILES on the chancel
floor are by *Woodyer*? – CHANCEL STALLS and VICAR'S STALL.
Mid C20. – FONT. Elegant and unusual of indeterminate date,
looking typical E.E. but probably C15 (VCH). Round, of chalk
with a black-letter inscription in the Anglo-Saxon tradition,
from the Vulgate version of Psalm 121: '*Auxilium meum a
domino*; *Qui fecit celum et terram*' ('My help is from the Lord
who made heaven and earth'). It has a bracket. What purpose
did it serve? – PULPIT. Well carved of 1634 (cf. Winchfield).
Arched upper panels with flower vases, rectangular lower strapwork parcels. Stone base of 1851. – LECTERN, A tall Neo-Car-
olean reading desk of 1952 by *C. Lovett Gill*, incorporating the
former door of the pulpit. – SCREENS. A nearly uniform set,
mostly 1908–12. – WEST GALLERIES. 1836, made up from the
bulgy columns of the balustrades and staircases of the former
nave W gallery of 1632. The inscription with names of donors
bifurcated into two parts is now confusing. – CHEST dated
1662 with four locks. – ROYAL ARMS, an interesting Caroline
design unusually with the motto 'Beati pacifici', but the date
1660. – STAINED GLASS. S chapel E window of 1858 by
Hardman, probably under *Woodyer*'s supervision. – N chapel
and chancel strikingly original works by *Patrick Reyntiens*,
1968–9. The former is a poetic Jesse Tree, dense colours on a
light background. The latter even more violently coloured in
an advanced semi-abstract idiom then still rare in England, but
firmly established in Germany, showing the Worship of the
Lamb and Evangelist emblems, the figure groups almost lost
in abstract colours. – N chapel N and S chapel S, 1892 by *Burlison & Grylls*. – S aisle S, 1895 and 1899 by *George Farmiloe &
Sons* with elaborate scenes (e.g. the Feeding of the Five Thousand). – RAF window. A bizarre historical glass screen of 1989
by *G. King & Sons*, Norwich, designed by *Penelope Douglas*.

– BRASSES. Quite a procession of mostly local people of
between 1480 and 1636. The earliest on the nave E wall a civilian and wife of the early C15 (19½-in., 49-cm. figures). – Mag.
William Goode †1498, priest, rector of Dogmersfield and vicar
of Ponteland, Northumberland (17½ in., 44 cm.). – Knight,
early C16 (23½ in., 60 cm. to below the knees). – Agnes
Chapman †1522 (18½ in., 47 cm.). – Elizabeth Haydock with
six daughters (the father figure lost) *c.* 1540 (19 in., 48 cm.). –
Margaretta Pye †1636. Rare and unusual. A baby in swaddling
clothes. Original setting on the S chapel floor. – Rev. William
Harriott †1847. Gothic brass by *Thomas Willement* with
achievement and black-lettered inscription. – MONUMENTS.

A few late C16 tablets, e.g. in the N chapel, on the S wall, part of an Elizabethan tablet with an ogee top. No figures, no inscriptions, just an achievement of Poynings. – Above it, tablet of Mary More (née Poynings) 1591, a grand-daughter of Sir Owen West of Wherwell (q.v.). – CURIOSUM. A shelter for the parson to be out of the rain at funeral services, in use between 1859 and 1891 (Jo Draper).

By the N wall of the church, headstones commemorating Pierre Feron †1810 and Pierre Jouneau †1809, French officers of the Napoleonic wars. Nearby a good classical table tomb to Robert May †1694, founder of the grammar school. Informative inscription. Of several early C19 table tombs S of the church some are attributable to the *Lee* family of local masons.

LIBRARY, Church Street. The former Bridewell, of 1743. Remarkably complete: two parallel ranges separated by a walled courtyard; the keeper's house at the front and rear range containing cells, brewhouse and prisoners' day room.

BURYFIELDS INFANT SCHOOL. Attractive original building of 1897 by *Colson, Farrow & Nisbett*.

MAYHILL JUNIOR SCHOOL, Buryfields. Founded as a Free School by Robert May in 1694. Lively Tudor style brick buildings of 1876 by *Edmund Woodthorpe*. Central tower with pyramidal cap, formerly with master's house to the r. and dormitories to the l.; furthest l. the dining hall is full-blown Dec.

WAR MEMORIAL, High Street. c. 1920 by *P. Morley Horder*. Portland stone cross with a carved St George and the Dragon in the head. Low brick flanking walls with inscribed panels. Extended after 1945 by *Charles Lovett Gill*.

PERAMBULATION

S of the church are single-storey ALMSHOUSES (The Old Court) founded in 1623 by Sir Edward More. And to the SW the PEST HOUSE, a tiny cottage 'lately erected' in 1622 for the sick poor of the parish. A very rare survival.

N of the church is THE BURY, irregularly shaped and surrounded by some good buildings, and the C18 STOCKS and a WHIPPING POST. From here CHURCH STREET leads NW towards the High Street with on the l. an early C19 attorney's office, with Grecian wreaths below the parapet, unfluted Doric columns *in antis*, and wrought-iron Gothick grilles over the windows. Further down, OLD CHURCH HOUSE, its C18 front concealing a solar block of c. 1366 with crown-post roof (presumably once attached to a hall). At the rear, re-set C14 wooden window with ogee-headed lights; that in the gable-end a reproduction. E of The Bury is KING STREET. At its S end on the brow of the hill, TUDOR COTTAGES, a continuously jettied four-bay hearth-passage-plan house of 1540, with a matching late C16 two-bay extension to the l. (its framing changing from curved to straight braces). Turning N back to the High Street, past a pair of C19 hop kilns is CHARLOTTE TERRACE, formerly the assembly rooms, probably designed by *Charles Smith* of Reading in 1865. Very old-fashioned for the date, with sashes set in full-height elliptical-arched panels.

The HIGH STREET is the showpiece with almost nothing that jars, and ought to be perambulated properly, starting towards the E end. On the N side THE WHITE HOUSE, built in 1812 for a local banker, John Grove Seymour. Stuccoed, of five bays, the centre projecting with a porch of Greek Doric cast-iron columns. The craftsmen were *John Lee* and *James Westbrook*. Good interior with delicate plasterwork and elegant curved staircase. Then THE OLD HOUSE, C18 with a pair of pedimented doorcases, and QUEEN ANNE HOUSE, with pilastered doorcase and ground-floor Venetian windows: both refrontings of a single early C16 jettied house. Oppsite, MARYCOURT of *c.* 1700, the most splendid house in Odiham. Brick, of five bays with a gorgeous shell-hood on carved brackets above the doorway. Staircase with barley-sugar balusters and nice panelled room. DIBRELL HOUSE, early C19, is stuccoed and quite imposing. Then on the corner of King Street, No. 65 with its exposed C16 framing, Nos. 67 and 69, the latter with a segmental pedimented doorcase matching No. 16. These formed the front range (dated to 1476–7) of a courtyard house; its E range facing King Street is dated to 1446–7 and has an upper chamber with an arch-braced collar-truss.

Back on the N side, THE GEORGE HOTEL, a late medieval courtyard inn behind an C18 front. The front hall range, of hearth-passage plan, is of 1486–7, floored from the start. The gabled E range is a high-status solar cross-wing of 1474. Inside, the hall range has a timber chimney, a carved C16 wooden chimneypiece and doorhood and in a first-floor chamber a remarkable wall painting of *c.* 1600 depicting the 'parliament of the fowls'. An even rarer early survival is found at MONK'S COTTAGE (No. 111 High Street, S side), which is a cross-wing of 1300 to a later medieval hall. The two-bay solar has a steeply cambered tie with a carved floral boss. Then another good run of C18 houses including KINGSTON HOUSE (N side) of brick, five bays, the centre three projecting with tripartite sashes and pedimented doorcase and KING'S BARN (S side), of 1790, brick, of three bays with pedimented doorcase, a fourth bay set back to the r. with arched service doorway. THE CLOSE is a five-bay late C17 L-plan house, altered *c.* 1800. Inside, a late C17 square-well staircase with barley-sugar balusters and acorn finials and panelling of the same date. Lastly on this side, charming WESTERN HOUSE, *c.* 1800 with tripartite sashes, the ground-floor openings with fanlights under elliptical arches. Full-height bay with set-back quadrant corners at the r.-hand end. Good interior.

PALACE GATE, N off High Street, is the site of Odiham Place, the manor house that stood close to the S entrance to the royal deerpark. The house, described in 1630 as having a 'faire gatehouse of bricke, cornered and windowed with stone', has gone but some interesting associated buildings survive among residential and office development of the 1990s. The CROSS BARN (now a community hall) of 1532, is the earliest dated brick barn in the county (cf. Grange Farm, Old Basing), unaisled with narrow ventilation slits, the seven-bay queen-strut roof with curved wind-braces. Equally remarkable still is SWALE HOUSE, a late C17 garden pavilion, later incorporated into the C18 farmhouse to the S (some of which probably also retains earlier fabric). It was probably intended to command views over a formal garden and deer park. Tall, of two storeys, brick with chamfered plaster quoins, the E and W fronts of three bays with projecting centres. It may have been a storey taller; the tiled roof is C18 when the windows were altered. Inside there are large chambers at the S end and a dog-leg NE staircase with turned balusters. Further W on High Street is THE OLD VICARAGE, a hall with cross-wings. Mostly C15 except the low-end wing with crown-post roof dated to 1395–6. Some close studding but much tile-hanging and later brick-work.

Lastly, THE PRIORY, the most interesting house in Odiham. Formerly the medieval rectory, when the rectors were the Chancellors of Salisbury Cathedral, hence its ambitious scale. It consists of three ranges, open to the N, but was probably originally a courtyard house. To the E, a large partly ruinous stone range, built 1448–9 during the chancellorship of Andrew Holes, with evidence for three first-floor chambers with arch-braced collar roof and windows with cusped lights. On its W side is a pair of doorways, which probably led from the service rooms into the missing N range containing a hall; a first-floor doorway perhaps gave access to a gallery above the screens passage. The S range is plain, sensible Queen Anne, seven bays, no ornament. This must be a rebuilding because late medieval timber framing survives at the W end, which has been cut through to give access to a miniature gabled brick porch, of two storeys, of c. 1530. This is entirely like such Norfolk buildings as Great Snoring and East Barsham. Polygonal buttress-shafts, four-centred archway, sweet little oriel. Short stubs of the W range.

THE HUNTING LODGE, Odiham Common, 1¼ m. NE in woods. An extraordinary eyecatcher for Dogmersfield Park (q.v.) and all that remains of the Rococo garden created for Paulet St John c. 1740–50 (see Dogmersfield). Early Georgian but with a pretended Gothic-cum-Jacobean front, i.e. ogee-headed lancets and a doorway, topped with three elongated shaped gables, the centre one larger, each with ogee-headed panel and urn finial. Restored from 1947 by *John Fowler* for himself. He also created the formal garden in front, a series of 'outdoor rooms' defined by hedges with a pair of Gothic PAVILIONS and a weatherboarded pyramid-roofed GARDEN ROOM. Beyond the garden is a lake, Wilks Water, with an OBELISK set

84

off the main axis of the garden. Fowler also added the pyramid-roofed entrance block to the house, with timber walls imitating rusticated masonry and a Doric doorcase.

LODGE FARMHOUSE. *See* North Warnborough.

ODIHAM CASTLE *see* NORTH WARNBOROUGH

OLD ALRESFORD

A manor of the Bishops of Winchester before Domesday. Part of the land s of the River Arle was taken by Bishop de Lucy *c.* 1200, when he founded New Alresford (q.v.), and built the GREAT WEIR, a dam (approximately 20–3 ft (6–7 metres) high and 1,300 ft (400 metres) long) across the river to create the expansive Old Alresford Pond, which supplied fish for his palaces at Bishops Sutton (q.v.) and elsewhere. The weir also carried the London to Winchester road, first mentioned as early as 1208–9.

ST MARY. Mostly rebuilt in 1753, when the long nave was reconstructed on the lines of its medieval predecessor, from which the disproportionately small chancel survives. The sturdy w tower, of 1769–70 is the finest feature. Built of brick reused from the Duke of Bolton's Abbotstone House (q.v., dem. 1762), it has a stone w doorway with crisp rustication of alternating sizes, twin-arched bell-openings, and a parapet sweeping up at the corners to ball finials. All this looks 1720 rather than 1770. The nave of the church was remodelled, the chancel restored, and a s transept added in 1858 by *J. Colson* for the Rev. George Sumner. By Colson, presumably, the flint and brick-banded external refacing of the nave. Dull interior. The nave roof is based on a C15(?) roof, parts of which remain *in situ*, against the w wall. Much heavy furnishing of 1870 by the local architect *W. H. Hunt*, again for the Rev. Sumner. – ALTAR TABLE. Dated 1620. Stout with heavy balusters. – BANNER by *Comper*. – STAINED GLASS. E window. *Powells* quarries of *c.* 1858. – Transept s, of *c.* 1870, to Henry Perin †1697 (founder of the school in West Street, New Alresford, q.v.), and George Wither †1688, poet. Good heraldry. – MONUMENTS. Margaret Needham †1693. Plain oval tablet with foliate frame, cartouche and roses. – Jane, 1st Lady Rodney †1757. A splendid large hanging monument of 1759, in richest Rococo, by *Sir Henry Cheere*. Adventurous use of white, pink, and black marble with many garlands etc. Two seated allegorical females representing Faith with a book, and Hope, with an anchor on the ledge on which the Rococo sarcophagus stands. Bust in circular recess at the top and above. Inscription added later to Lord Rodney †1792 who erected the monument. – Mrs Anne Davenport †1760, friend and housekeeper to Dr Hoadly, rector (did she inspire his play 'The Housekeeper', *c.* 1750?). Small oval, with a charming dog guarding the keys. – Esther North †1823. By *Behnes*. White marble. Large frontal angel with big wings and one arm raised. Below to his l. a pillar with profile bust. – Mary Sumner †1912, wife of the rector. Belated Arts and Crafts tablet of 1935 by *G. H. Kitchin*.

In the churchyard, by the chancel, good early C19 chest tombs to the Rodneys and on the s side by the nave to the Perins. – MAUSOLEUM. Designed 1931 by *J. B. S. Comper* for C. F. G. Schwerdt (†1939) of Old Alresford House. Ionic Temple front, a shallow four-columned portico with reused C17 capitals. Plain granite sides. In the marble-lined interior a large Italian marble relief of *c.* 1500, presumably acquired by Schwerdt. Seated Virgin suckling the child. Small angels above and in the predella (possibly in the Florentine Renaissance tradition of Lorenzo Ghiberti, cf. his casket of St Protus of 1428 in the Bargello museum). – LYCHGATE of 1893 by *W. H. Hunt* of Alresford. Frantically cusped timberwork.

OLD ALRESFORD PLACE, N of the church. (Now Diocesan Centre and Offices) Built as the rectory *c.* 1740, for Dr John Hoadly. Red brick, in header bond. Two-and-a-half storeys with a five-bay s front that has broad angle pilasters (with grey headers) and a dentil cornice beneath the high parapet. Slight middle projection, formerly the entrance bay, with elliptical arched heads to the windows: framed by pilasters at first floor. Entrance now on the w front of this part, with a Greek Doric stone porch, presumably of 1817 when the rectory was altered and enlarged to the N for Francis North (the date and his initials on the rainwater heads) in a remarkable imitation of the Early Georgian front. The two-storey E elevation more typically early C19. (Good interiors, including the large s room with a classical chimneypiece and a screen of two Ionic columns to a shallow bay, and the elegant cantilevered stone staircase with wrought-iron balustrade, lit by an octagonal lantern, no doubt of 1817.)

OLD ALRESFORD HOUSE, E of the church. 1749–51 by *William Jones* for Captain George Brydges Rodney, later Admiral the 1st Baron Rodney, who built it with his prize money from the War of the Austrian Succession. Rather austere. Red brick, two storeys over a semi-basement and high attic. Seven bays. Three-bay centre with a pediment. The flanking bays were brought forward in the late C18, including the boldly projecting stair 'towers' at each end. Columned porch with bucrania frieze, of *c.* 1760 but introduced after 1926 by C. F. G. Schwerdt, the art collector. Flanking the forecourt, single-storey Neo-Georgian wings of the 1880s (although the E wing incorporates an C18 barrel-vaulted cellar). Wrought-iron screen with gates between brick piers, introduced *c.* 1930. Unaltered garden front; it was hung with gault mathematical tiles in the late C18. Nine bays with a central three-bay projection. C19 wings remodelled *c.* 1993 and again *c.* 2009 by the *Haddow Partnership* with 'false' façades. In the centre of the s side a room with an excellent Rococo ceiling, including Jove's eagle discharging thunderbolts. Schwerdt introduced French *boiseries* and other objects. PARK between the house and Old Alresford Pond, designed by *Richard Woods*, 1764.

UPTON HOUSE, 400 yds NE. Five-bay house of 1764–8 for James Rodney, George's brother, but stuccoed and remodelled in the C19 (E wing *c.* 1890) and extended W 1986 by *Robert Adam*. In the dining room a good, introduced, C18 Palladian carved marble chimneypiece and wooden overmantel with swan-neck pediment.

In the village about ⅜ m. N is an interesting Neo-Tudor group of former SCHOOL (1846) and ONSLOW COTTAGES (*c.* 1852), both at right angles to the road, with WELL COTTAGES (probably later) set back between them. SOUTHDOWNS, 300 yds N on the rising ground at the village's edge, was the Industrial Home for Girls, 1838 (now much extended). Flint and brick centre range with later wings.

SWAN COTTAGE, ¼ m. S of the church by Old Alresford Pond. A pretty *cottage orné* of 1823 in unknapped flint with large central chimney. Hipped roof (originally thatched) sweeping over a rustic wooden veranda. A curved glass corridor cleverly links this to a weatherboarded, conical-roofed, circular tower, all by *Robert Adam*, 1992–4.

PINGLESTONE FARM, ½ m. SW. Fine timber-framed BARN of *c.* 1500, built when this belonged to the Bishop of Winchester. Seven bays, aisled, with curved braces and queen-strut trusses.

GODSFIELD FARM, 2¼ m. NE. The site of a preceptory of the Knights Hospitaller. The CHAPEL, with attached PRIEST'S HOUSE, survives. Built *c.* 1360, flint with ashlar dressings, under a continuous tile roof. Blocked E window, originally of three lights, single-chamfered N doorway, three single-light S windows with cinquefoil heads and hoodmoulds. Inside, image corbels flank the E window. The priest's house has one room up and down and a staircase lit by a slit window. The upper room has a S window with cinquefoiled head and square hood-mould but also a small window allowing a view of the altar. Attached on the W a garderobe. Both rooms have fireplaces. The roof of the priest's house has arch-braced collar-trusses and curved wind-braces; the chapel roof, apart from three couples of arch-braced collar rafters at the W end, is all early C19.

OLD BASING

A straggling village, on the S side of the upper reaches of the River Loddon. It was a Saxon Royal manor and the site of a minster church. 'Old' in relation to Basingstoke (q.v.), which was initially a dependent settlement but by Domesday had become the more important place, with a market. C20 Basingstoke encroached from the NW and much of the parish N of the river is now part of the town, in fact if not in name.

ST MARY. A big church, in appearance essentially Late Perp, ⁵⁰
with an airily capacious interior with a strongly Post-
Reformation atmosphere, heightened by limewashing during
restoration in 1989–97.* It is extensively of brick, most of it
originally lightly rendered, although most of the N chapel and
much of the nave and aisles are of flint. The exterior is just a
rectangle, three gables to the E, three gables to the W. The
centre of the building is the crossing tower and its lower flint
part is Norman, see the N and S arches inside. This belongs to
a church built c. 1120, perhaps by Hugh de Port, to succeed a
Saxon building (held, like Basingstoke, by the Abbot of Mont-
St-Michel). The tower, 21 ft (6.5 metres) square internally, and
of the same width as the nave, was flanked by much narrower
transepts; a characteristically Late Saxon plan (cf. Dover, St
Mary de Castro and (originally) Wimborne Minster, Dorset).
Of this building, an early C13 doorway also remains re-set in
the N aisle. Rebuilding probably commenced after 1428 when
John Paulet (†1435) married Constance Poynings, heir to the
manor. Nave and aisles came first. They are of three bays with
two-light windows N and S derived from Wynford's windows of
Hall at Winchester College (c. 1400). The stout octagonal piers
of the arcades (possibly brick, now rendered) look strengthened, and support clumsily moulded four-centred arches. Big
wide E and W tower arches. Next comes the four-light chancel
E window, late C15. An inscription inside over the E bay of the
N aisle refers to Sir John Paulet and the date of 1519, very probably for completion of the N chapel. The tracery of the side
windows is unusually of wood. More good figured corbels
inside of angels with heraldic shields. The S chapel was erected
by Sir William Paulet c. 1551–6, i.e. after he was created 1st
Marquess of Winchester and before the death of his first wife
whose monument it contains (the corbel heads on the S side
may be their portraits). Still in a typically Early Tudor Gothic
court style, in brick with three S windows. Of the same date
the nave W window, proved by the remarkable discovery and
identification (in 1997) of its tracery design inscribed inside on
the chapel's S wall. Reset above the W window at this time (i.e.
during the Marian Counter-Reformation), is a canopied
STATUE of a crowned Virgin and Child, no doubt originally
commissioned by Sir John Paulet (†1525) whose achievement
appears below. The brick upper stages of the tower are also
mid-C16, possibly replacing a lantern stage as at Kingsclere
(fragments of fictive medieval masonry patterns survive in the
windowless middle-stage chamber) but patched up during the
repairs of 1660–66 following damage by Cromwell's soldiery.
Flat, classical W doorway, also probably mid C17.

The N and S chapels are the most interesting parts of the
church. They are separated from the chancel by pairs of MONU-
MENTS in a noble architectural composition in Caen stone
consonant with the ashlar walls. They are open to N and S, each

* This description follows the analysis and dating by John Crook (J.B.A.A., v.154,
2002).

pair with a low doorway between. The monuments have panelled depressed arches. They are to Paulets as follows. N side:
Sir John †1492 and wife Eleanor and Sir John †1525 and wife,
Alice. No doubt both erected *c.* 1525 – see the Roman lettering towards the chapel like that of the Winchester Cathedral
presbytery screens. Dr Riall has identified other similar details
and attributes both works to *Thomas Bertie.* – S side: Sir
William, 1st Marquess of Winchester †1572 and wives (E) and,
probably, John, 2nd Marquess †1576 (W). These monuments
have Renaissance details. The former have not. Both sets were
carefully restored *c.* 1664–6, when some details damaged in
1645 were simplified (e.g. the inner canopies above the doorways and some heraldry with mantling renewed. (Roger
Harris). Over the S monuments runs a most remarkable and
unusual detail, a frieze or cresting comprising terms separated
by conventional acanthus foliage of possibly Spanish derivation. As Professor Colvin has shown these strange miniature
heads and skulls, alternately quick and dead, looking sadly at
each other, are a type of memorial unparalleled in English or
Continental Renaissance art.

The roofs over nave and aisles were much refashioned in
1873–4 by *T. H. Wyatt* but that to the nave is largely original
mid-C16 and of strikingly economical design with four centred
arches and combined scissor trusses. Two tiers of purlins and
arch-braces. Renewed aisle roofs of similar design. Nice carved
corbels throughout with angels bearing shields, mostly original. One mid-C16 corbel (nave NE) has a plain shield in Renaissance mantling.

FONT. Octagon of Purbeck marble. Late C15 Perp with quatrefoils. – HIGH ALTAR, of 1925 by *Harold Rogers.* An English
altar with frontal by *Watts & Co.* – PRIESTS' STALLS. The S
one dated 1918. Neo-Tudor with linenfold fronts. – PULPIT.
Brought from Basingstoke.* Made in 1622. Of a type used in
the villages around as well. Two tiers of panels, the upper ones
with flowers in vases under basket arches. The lower rectangular with strapwork. – PEWS. A full set of 1874 in the nave
and aisles. – DOOR. Probably C15 in the N doorway. – ROYAL
ARMS. Dated 1660. Naïvely painted with a black-and-white
perspective floor. – HELMS etc. in the N chapel. – Iron BRACK-
ETS for lost funerary helms and banners etc. in the N and S
chapels. – HATCHMENTS to Paulets, three in the S chapel, two
in the S aisle. – TILES. A few of the C13 or C14 in the N chapel.
– STAINED GLASS. E window of 1912 by *Powells.* Also by them,
the earlier nave W window, with flowered quarries. N aisle W,
by *Clayton & Bell* (commemorative date 1881). – S aisle W, by
John Hayward, 1971. An impressive Angel of Peace, rather
angular, and dramatic on a blue surround fading into white.
Powerful from near and afar. – MONUMENT. 6th Duke of
Bolton. 1794, by *Flaxman.* White marble, seated mourning
young woman in profile below a circular recess with bust.

* The gift in 1662 is recorded in the Churchwardens' Accounts.

BASING HOUSE

The manor of Basing was granted to Hugh de Port after the Conquest, and was the chief estate of the fifty-five he held in Hampshire. The original seat may have been the MOTTE AND BAILEY
at Oliver's Battery to the N, close to the Loddon, but this appears
to have been abandoned after one or two centuries and re-
established on the present site, where there are earthworks of a
RINGWORK AND BAILEY castle. The manor had gone by inher-
itance to the Paulets in 1498 and in 1531 Sir William Paulet,
holder of several important posts in the court of Henry VIII, was
granted a licence 'to build walls and towers within and around   p. 35
and to fortify the manor of Basyng'. This amounted to rebuilding the old castle in brick. It became known as the Citadel or
'Old House' after Paulet extended it NE, beyond the confines of
the medieval castle, with the even finer 'New House'. Paulet was
made Lord Treasurer in 1550, 1st Marquess of Winchester the
following year. A date 1562 survives on a stone in the museum
and building probably carried on until Paulet's death in 1572. An
account book for 1569 records modest works but names senior
men in the Office of the Queen's Works: *Lewys Stockett*, Surveyor,
Thomas Fowler, Comptroller, *Humphrey Lovell*, Master Mason
and *John Colbrand*, Master Carpenter. Illustrations show the
general appearance as decidedly Early Tudor and not Elizabethan. It is recorded that the 4th Marquess became so finan-
cially overstretched after the Queen's visit in 1601 that part of
the mansion had to be demolished. Thomas Fuller still described
it as 'the greatest of any subject's house in England' while resident during the famous siege by Parliamentary forces, from 1643
until its fall in 1645. One of the prisoners taken was Inigo Jones,
apparently 'carried away in a blanket, having lost his cloaths'. The
house was afterwards ravaged by fire and looted. At the Restoration, no attempt was made to rebuild and later the site was turned
over to gardens for the more modest house erected *c.* 1690 by
Charles Paulet, 1st Duke of Bolton (dem. *c.* 1740 after a fire).
Antiquarian interest grew during this period and by the late C18
the site of the ruins had been landscaped, although the Basingstoke Canal was cut across the site of the 'New House'. The
site has been subject to archaeological investigation since the
early C20 and is now in the care of the County Council. Among
the finds of stone sculpture is an impressive bust of a Roman   57
emperor within a tondo carved with Renaissance ornament, like
those made *c.* 1521 for Wolsey's Hampton Court. There are two
further carved stone heads, unframed, one probably of the
emperor Marcus Aurelius, the other possibly Hannibal.

The entrance is through the mid-C16 GARRISON GATE, brick
with a four-centred stone archway under a hoodmould. Above
the arch, probably re-set, the Paulet coat of arms. Figures with
coiled tails, supporting the open pediment, resemble those on
the overmantel of the hall fireplace at Longleat (*c.* 1575–80).
Mark Girouard has observed that two French mason carvers

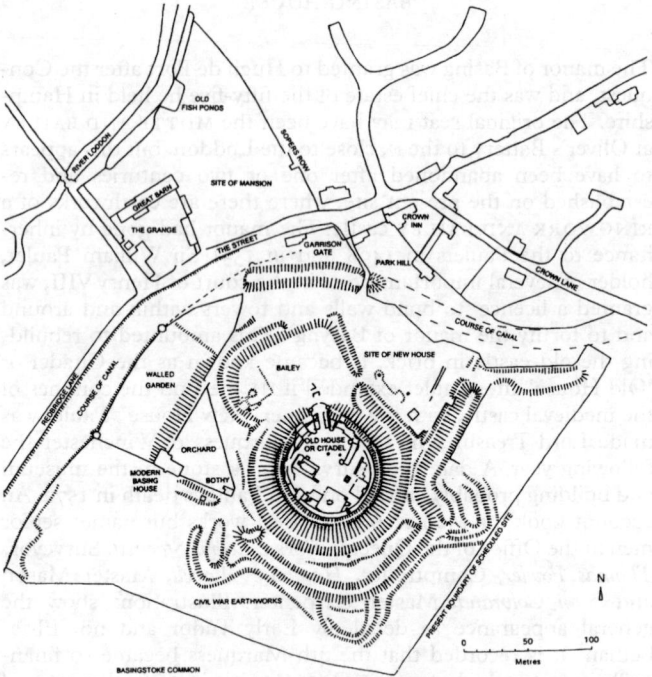

Old Basing, Basing House.
Plan

who worked at Longleat had very probably been employed at
Basing up to *c.* 1565. Was their source *du Cerceau*? The jagged
parapet is Victorian, an attempt to provide a suitably romantic ruined silhouette. Parts of the curtain wall survive to E and
w and partly incorporate village cottages in places. Behind
Turret Cottages, w of the gate, is a polygonal TOWER with
diaper-work. Inside the gateway, almost immediately, there is
a BRIDGE of the 1790s built over the Basingstoke Canal (now
infilled). From here the site opens out. s are the earthworks of
the motte and bailey. This has a large circular bank and ditch
about 300 ft (90 metres) in diameter, with the main entrance
from the bailey to the N. The surviving walls belong to the mid-
C16 'OLD HOUSE' or Citadel, which was tightly packed with
buildings around several courts. Visible are the cellar beneath
the hall and traces of the six-sided kitchen, with its four-
centred arched ovens built into the bank. Most impressive are
the footings of the great N gatehouse, shown in Hollar's view
of *c.* 1644 as a square structure of four storeys with octagonal
turrets at each corner. There was a similar, but smaller, gatehouse on the w side, also with octagonal corner towers. Even
less is visible of the 'NEW HOUSE' to the NE. It seems to have

been built around a courtyard, and have been entered through a gatehouse from the bailey of the Old Castle. The only uncovered remains are the footings of a stable in the NW range.

NW of the 'Old House' is the WALLED GARDEN, known as such since the C18, containing a re-created C16 garden. Bounding the NW side is a substantial length of C16 brick curtain wall with diaper patterning, punctuated by two octagonal interval towers, and evidence of a third, which were later converted to dovecotes. The N one is thatched, the other tiled. At the garden's SW corner is BASING HOUSE, apparently an early C19 Tudor Gothic cottage, altered and extended in the late C19 and the 1960s. Nearby is the cottage-like BOTHY, built by Lord Bolton in 1908 as a site museum, with rustic veranda and tile-hung half-hipped gable. It incorporates some early C19 fabric and is on the site of a building known as the 'banquetting house'. It stands on top of a high, mostly Tudor, wall, overlooking a triangular area that was an orchard in the C18. S of the Old House are EARTHWORKS, of C12 origin but in their present form dating from the Civil War.

Outside the walls of Basing House, on the N side of The Street, is a wall of (probably) reused Tudor brickwork, with GATEPIERS of rubbed bricks with moulded stone plinths. Behind was the site of the 1st Lord Bolton's house of c. 1690. Of about the same date is the farmhouse at GRANGE FARM to the SW. Brick, with a hipped roof. L-shaped, the entrance in the angle and the shorter wing housing the services. Wooden cross-windows. Inside, a couple of nice panelled rooms and a staircase with turned balusters. N is the excellent GREAT BARN, built c. 1534–5 (tree-ring dated) for Sir William Paulet. Brick, over 100 ft (36 metres) long. Six bays divided by buttresses, with four-centred arched cart entrances in the second and fifth bays on the S side. Smaller opposed doors on the N side. The roof is of ten bays, with two tiers of collars, the lower ones arch-braced, and two tiers of purlins with wind-bracing.

THE VILLAGE. The area immediately E of Basing House was razed in 1644 and concentrated here are several houses that appear to have benefited from the quarrying of brick and stone from the ruins of the Tudor house, e.g. Nos. 3 and 7 THE STREET, a pair of mid-C17 baffle-entry houses, and Nos. 10 and 12, also mid-C17, but humbler cottages with small leaded mullioned windows including a tiny pair in the centre. Opposite, Nos. 9–11 has a timber-framed upper storey with oriels on shaped brackets. STREET HOUSE, further E, is brick with a stone plinth and dripmould in the gable-end on the road, and alongside a converted C17 timber-framed and brick barn with a large door. Near the church, on the opposite side of the street, Nos. 45–47, a timber-framed hall and cross-wing; the latter refaced in brick in the mid C17 but at its side a large chimney dated 1593. From here the street funnels between two rows of C19 stuccoed cottages up to the high arch of the C19 RAILWAY BRIDGE. Curving around the churchyard is Church

Lane. WHYTEGATES has two chimneys with offsets on crow-steps. CHURCH LANE HOUSE looks mid C17. Brick, probably reused, originally lobby-entry plan with two later gables rising from toothed brick courses. Said to have been the workhouse. About ¼ m. N is OLD BASING HOUSE. Early C18, with the façade brought forward in the later C18. Stuccoed, of five bays, the centre three slightly projecting with pediment and arcaded loggia. Nicely fitted interior of surprising quality. For whom was it built? Also N again, incorporated into CAVALIER COTTAGE, a probably late C16 timber-framed WELL-HOUSE.

PARKERS FARMHOUSE, Crown Lane. Mid-C17(?), with a half-octagonal stair-turret in the middle of the front elevation. Next door a good C17 timber-framed aisled BARN. The aisle walls are of brick.

LYCHPIT FARM, Great Binfields Road, Little Basing, ½ m. NW. An exceptional mid-C17 farmstead group. The house is of reused C16 brick, with stone-capped plinth and string course, no doubt also reused. Large end chimneys. Stone mullioned windows. C18 addition. Excellent farm buildings, incorporated into the LYCHPIT CENTRE, with shops, pub, hall etc. by the *Hampshire County Architect*'s *Dept c.* 1986.

HUISH HOUSE, 1 m. SSE. Built 1909, in a rather ill-disciplined Vernacular Revival, for J. B. Westray, ship-owner. Very complete interior, including a Neo-Jacobean staircase with a strapwork balustrade.

LONDON LODGE, London Road. *See* HACKWOOD PARK.

4050

OLD BURGHCLERE
Burghclere

A former manor of the Bishop of Winchester. Rural, with church and former medieval rectory close together.

ALL SAINTS. Large, of flint, with a low tile-capped C19 W bell-turret. The hoary nave has two Norman doorways. The N doorway is Early Norman of *c.* 1120. One order of columns, plain capitals, with a volute. Billet in the arch. The narrower S doorway has a tympanum with fish-scale pattern of *c.* 1130. Lower C13 chancel with priest's doorway, unusually on the N side, and lancets, all over-restored for the Countess of Carnarvon in 1861. C13 also the fine W doorway, with two orders of shafts, stiff-leaf capitals, and several rolls in the arch. One of the orders of shafts has fillets. N transept, in stone-banded flint of *c.* 1280. The intersected tracery of the E and N windows all agreeably unrestored. The nave inside is long, plain and shapeless with a trussed rafter roof restored in 1861 and 1936–7 (by *Floyd & Robson* of Newbury, advised by *Walter E. Troke* of the SPAB). This is less impressive than the N transept roof, which has simple scissor-bracing to each couple – quite consistent with the date of the masonry. N transept arch dying into the imposts – again consonant with *c.* 1280. The chancel arch is

the same. The church is richly furnished. ALTAR TABLE. Dated
1716, when *John Stroude* was paid 8s. for a communion
table. – REREDOS of *c.* 1861. Charmingly painted, with an
orchestra of angels. – FONT of the restoration. High Victorian
and uncouth. – LECTERN, elaborately notched wood with brass
candleholders. – PEWS. Solid and sturdy, C16 or early C17. The
appropriately plain ends have moulded tops. – HATCHMENTS,
to Charles Herbert and wife (the latter †1818), and the 2nd
and 3rd Earls of Carnarvon, †1833 and †1849, placed above
the chancel arch where a medieval wall painting of the martyrdom of St Sebastian was found. – STAINED GLASS. E
window of 1861 by *Lavers & Barraud*. By them also the chancel
S window with portrait of the Countess of Carnarvon. –
SCULPTURE. Henry, 2nd Earl of Carnarvon †1833. White
marble by *Bartolini* of Rome (duplicate bust at Highclere
Castle). – MONUMENTS. Anne Eyre †1745, a tall standing
monument in the fashionable Cheere/Scheemakers tradition,
without figures. Strange section through an oddly blank sarcophagus. Inscription beneath a pediment. – Charlotte
Ambrose †1759. Classical tablet signed *Hicks*, Newbury. –
Herbert family of Highclere, tablet made up of golden tile
inscriptions (latest commemorative date 1862) in a red tile and
black marble frame in a horrid Gothic, less ugly than the
Herbert mausoleum of *c.* 1800–20 outside against the chancel
wall. – Edward H. C. Herbert, 1872. Large, Gothic almond-
shape, with dogtooth.

MANOR HOUSE, E of the church.* An important survival of a
medieval rectory. W front of vitrified brickwork, part of substantial alterations and additions of *c.* 1860, but the core is a
two-bay hall with a roof structure of raised aisle construction,
tree-ring dated to 1328–9. Large curved braces to tie-beam and
arcade plates and a crown-post roof, of typically simple Hampshire form. First floor inserted in the hall in the C16 and
removed 2008–9 as part of alterations by *Snell David Ltd Architects*. The cross-beam supporting the arcade posts was cut in
the C19. The rear (E) masonry wall survives with a pair of partly
reconstructed windows, each of two ogee-headed lights under
a square head. Corbel supporting wall-post carved as head of
King (possibly Edward III). Low end to N with C14 arched E
doorway and altered C16 porch. Also doorway to services,
leading to four-bay cross-wing of *c.* 1500. Arched E doorway
at high end too and four-bay chamber cross wing of *c.* 1500
with arch-braced and steeply cambered tie-beams, a three-bay
solar and a single-bay antechamber. C18 alterations including
staircase (rebuilt) of *c.* 1700 with vase-shaped balusters. At
MANOR FARM, N, is a fine eight-bay aisled BARN, built for the
Bishop of Winchester in 1451–52. Queen-strut trusses. The
tiled roof, timber cladding and side porches are original.

BEACON HILL, 2 m. SW. The hill-fort occupies a commanding
position (immediately W of the A34). It is of univallate construction with a well-preserved bank 7 ft (2 metres) high and
a ditch still 10 ft (3 metres) deep enclosing an area of 12 acres.

* This account relies heavily on investigation and research by John Crook.

The main entrance on the S is a complex one, with the bank and ditch inturned and additional outworks to provide further protection. There are traces of another entrance at the NW end which was blocked during the life of the fort. Within, numerous small circular grass-grown mounds mark the position of circular houses 20–30 ft (6–9 metres) in diameter. The site has never been excavated. At the W end is (appropriately) the grave of the 5th Earl of Carnarvon, sponsor of the Tutankhamun expedition.

OVER WALLOP

Like Nether Wallop, the village unfolds along the course of the Wallop Brook. Many good thatched cottages and cob-walled farmsteads, but also a high proportion of Georgian refrontings and a few Bolton estate cottages.

ST PETER. The special interest is in the thorough restoration by *J. L. Pearson*,* undertaken in 1865–7 (chancel) and 1874 (the rest including the plain W tower with saddleback roof). Of flint with brick quoins and stone dressings. The interior tells its earlier story with a minimum of authentic details. Two-bay N arcade of *c.* 1200: round pier, round abaci, capitals of flat, broad, smooth, upright leaves. Round arches of one step and one chamfer. Four-bay S arcade with moulded capitals (heavily restored), and pointed arches with two slight chamfers, i.e. early C13. Its taller E bay and the tower arch are later C13. The S aisle E window is authentic and Dec. N arcade third and fourth bays fully C13 or C14. The earlier part of the N arcade belongs with the re-set N aisle W doorway and the S doorway. Pearson's chancel is resolutely E.E. – SCREEN. Of wrought-iron. Good REREDOS with polychrome paintings by *Clayton & Bell*. – Muscular Gothic CHOIR STALLS and low stone screen with delicate wrought-iron PULPIT. – FONT. Big, Perp, octagonal. With quatrefoils. Nave roof by *Pearson*; braced tie-beams, crown-posts. – STAINED GLASS. E lancets, excellent *Clayton & Bell*. N aisle E window by *H. Stammers*, 1956. SCHOOL, NE of the church, now Church Room. Early 1860s.

WAR MEMORIAL, NE of the church. By *Gething & Co.* of Chilmark. Stone, octagonal shaft rising from a stepped base and with posts encircling, bearing names of the dead.

TOWNSEND MANOR, at the NW end of the village. Mid-C18 date, quite grand. Five bays, two storeys. Doorway with broken pediment on Doric pilasters. Early C19 service range and earlier core. Brick in header bond, old plain tile roof.

LONG BARROW, 3½ m. WNW. This is a small example of this class of monument, being only 100 ft (31 metres) long and 50

---

* Pearson's friend and patron Thomas Spyers lived at Wallop Lodge, which Pearson remodelled (dem. 1915).

ft (15.5 metres) wide at its broader E end, where it stands 5 ft
(1.5 metres) high. The side ditches are clearly visible.

OVERTON   5040

One of several new towns founded by Henry de Lucy, Bishop of
Winchester. A charter for a market was granted in 1218. It stands
on the S side of the Test, across the river from the church and
manor farm (cf. the relationship between Old and New Alresford). The plan, still evident, is an elementary grid of three N–S
streets and two E–W streets. The broad middle N–S street, Winchester Street, appears to have been the market street, and it is
here, and in High Street, the main E–W thoroughfare, that there
is a significant survival of early, mainly Tudor, buildings: testament to the town's prosperity in the early C16 (a second fair was
granted in 1519). In the C18 silk manufacture became an important industry. The town also became a staging post on the
Basingstoke–Andover road, turnpiked in 1754. In spite of this
there are no C18 houses of any ambition and the vernacular of
brick, render and tile is more generally characteristic for that
period and into the early C19. The most prominent buildings are
now Victorian and Edwardian intrusions.

ST MARY. Deceptively Victorian: the stonework of the flint nave
   and chancel faithfully renewed in 1850–4 by *Benjamin Ferrey*
   (S porch also rebuilt), 1897 (new N vestry and Perp E window
   by *E. P. Warren*) and 1905. The ashlar W tower, in a careful
   Neo-Perp with shingled spire, is of 1908 by *Cancellor & Hill*.
   Medieval features include the N aisle W lancet, re-set, a chancel
   N window with plate tracery, the chancel SW window, and parts
   of two minor doorways. Impressive three-bay N and S arcades
   of *c.* 1200. Round piers with waterholding bases, square but
   chamfered abaci, multi-scalloped capitals. Pointed, single-
   chamfered arches. The next element, in terms of chronology,
   is the chancel, of the same height and width as the nave: mid
   C13 according to the plate tracery. The single frame roofs of
   nave and chancel appear to be of *c.* 1300; the chancel roof has
   coupled rafters, with arch braces to the inner wall-plate joined
   to rafters with two short spurs. Two tie-beams with well-carved
   floral bosses (cf. Monk's Cottage, Odiham, of *c.* 1300). The
   nave roof with its simple arrangement of coupled rafters with
   soulaces and ashlar pieces is almost as well preserved. The SE
   arch of the arcade, with mouldings dying into the imposts, is
   perhaps of the same date. The western bays are Late Perp of
   malmstone with good moulded capitals. They were built to
   connect with the earlier W tower. This was erected in 1538 with
   stone reused from Titchfield Abbey (South Hampshire; a letter
   survives regarding a visit from the men of Overton 'to come
   and see the South aisle [transept] for the building of a tower
   for their bells. We do think it good to sell by grote [gross] and

let them take it down'), including the typical Early Decorated piers incorporated in the rebuilt tower arch – ARCHITEC-TURAL FRAGMENTS. W end of the S aisle. Three cushion capitals, pre-1120. Fragment of a font (cf. New Alresford), possibly Saxon or Early Norman, with exquisite interlaced fronds below the rim. Small battered C13 foliate capital. Two mid-C14 pinnacles, probably from a tomb. – CHANCEL STALLS. Early C20. Handsome, of oak, limed during re-ordering by *F. E. Howard*, 1933, see also the S Chapel REREDOS. – S DOOR. Probably of *c.* 1538, with original hinges, typically Tudor with fleurs-de-lys. The door is, unusually, double-leaved. – STAINED GLASS. E window of 1903 by *Kempe*. Christ the King and four saints. – S aisle E by *J. C. Bewsey*, 1916. The Annunciation. – Two other windows by *Christopher Webb*. – MONUMENTS. A funerary inscription on the inner sill of the chancel NE window: 'Hic iacet do. Willms Savage quondam rector istius ecclesie . . .' ('Here lies Master/Lord William Savage, former rector of this church') etc. – Thomas Streatwells †1812. Silk throwster, co-founder of Overton silk mill. Classical tablet in white and grey marble with a nicely draped urn. – Eric Carpenter-Turner †1916. By *Farmer & Brindley*.

Prominent rendered CHURCH ROOM, 1999 by *Winchester Design*, linked to the N aisle by a glazed corridor.

COURT FARM, W of the church. Early C18 brick over a timber frame of 1505–7. Built on the site of a minor episcopal palace. Two ranges (both of hearth-passage plan) forming a T. The S range, which contained accommodation for the Bishop's steward, now has a five-bay front with middle bay projecting, an open pediment and doorcase with octagonal columns. Staircase with vase-shaped balusters. BARN. Tree-ring dated to 1497–8. Timber-framed, aisled. Six bays survive of a probable nine.

Former RECTORY, Bridge Street, WSW of the church. Middle Pointed Gothic of 1851 by *Ferrey*, with later C19 additions in at least two phases.

The centre of Overton is the main cross-roads on the London Road, with THE WHITE HART INN, first built in the mid C15 and acquired by Corpus Christi College, Oxford, in the early C16, but transformed in the C17 and C18. Inside, one room has a Tudor-arched stone fireplace with carved spandrels. C17 stair rising around a timber frame, with finials at the top. Diagonally opposite, the former school of 1868, a typical design by *J. Colson* with a small spired cupola. WINCHESTER STREET, the town's wide and sloping main street, is not as impressive as Alresford and few of its buildings need singling out, although several modest Georgian frontages hide C16 jettied frames. HIGH STREET continues the London Road E. The buildings are much as Winchester Street, concealing some early structures, e.g. Nos. 7–11 (S side) incorporating an ambitious late C15 jettied building; No. 7 inside has a four-centred arched stone fireplace with carved spandrels, and alongside, an ogee-headed niche. Further out, on the corner of Red Lion Lane,

Nos. 31–35 hide a three-bay hearth-passage-plan house of 1541–2; it is jettied front and back, but not at the ends, a rare thing in the county. A further bay was added 1615, probably as a kitchen. In the back gardens of Nos. 20 and 26 on the N side are rustic Gothic SUMMERHOUSES of c. 1840; banded brick and flint with pilasters at the angles.

QUIDHAMPTON FARMHOUSE, ½ m. NE. SW of the house is a Norman chapel (disused by the C17). Plain rectangle of flint, laid herringbone-wise. The E wall is missing. Blocked S doorway. Traces of a S and a N window.

POLHAMPTON HOUSE, 1 m. ENE. An interesting mid-C17 double-pile brick house with Artisan Mannerist detailing including a deep, moulded string course and mullioned windows. The front was remodelled in the C18: three bays with wooden casements, central pediment with oculus. Panelled room to l. of entrance with enriched plaster frieze of double-headed eagles alternating with anthemion ornament. Panel over fireplace with three demi-figures set in foliage and flowers, possibly Green Men. At rear, dog-leg staircase with symmetrical double balusters and newels with finials.

OVINGTON

A compact and attractive village, with a few old cottages, between the lushest reaches of the upper Itchen and more open downland.

ST PETER. 1866–7 by *Colson*, paid for by Mrs Hewson of Ovington House. SW porch-tower with broach-spired wooden top. Aisleless, but with transepts, rather an early C19 taste. The windows are Early Dec. Colson's usual naturalistic carving inside and nice panelled chancel roof, prettily painted. – Brass eagle LECTERN from Itchen Stoke (q.v.); no doubt by *Henry Conybeare*. – STAINED GLASS. In the chancel and transepts by *Lavers & Barraud*, of 1867. W window by *Heaton, Butler & Bayne c.* 1878. – HATCHMENT. Sir Thomas Dyer †1838 with flags and military orders. His MONUMENT, NE of the church, is by *Owen Browne Carter*, made by *James Kellow* of Winchester, 1839. Still in the classical Late Georgian tradition. Stone sarcophagus on lion's paws surmounted by a draped urn. Contemporary railings, with appropriate halberds. Close by, a medieval doorway of the old church (Paul Jeffrey).

OVINGTON HOUSE, in walled grounds, S of the church. Mostly of c. 1790–1800 for James Standerwick, a London haberdasher. Originally Gothic, see e.g. the ogee-arched doorway etc. on the E front but encased and substantially extended c. 1919 for Harvey Hoare in a sedate Neo-Georgian. The NORTH LODGE is a *cottage orné* of 1837 for Sir Thomas Dyer. In the village DAIRY COTTAGE of 1838, brick and flint with matching STABLE range.

6050

PAMBER

A scattered settlement in country of wood and heath, in the medieval parish of Monk Sherborne.

PAMBER PRIORY (HOLY TRINITY, OUR LADY AND ST JOHN BAPTIST). Founded about 1120–30 by Henry de Port as a Benedictine cell of Cerisy-la-Fôret (Normandy) and consecrated, perhaps still incomplete, by William Giffard in 1129. The largest and second wealthiest of Hampshire's ten alien priories, it was dissolved in 1414 when the conventual buildings and most of the church were demolished. The estate later passed to The Queen's College, Oxford, and in 1475 religious life was revived (perhaps as an oratory or chantry in Monk Sherborne) with a resident chantry priest (cf. Selborne).

Pamber Priory.
Drawing by Jenny Wylie, 1911

The remains of the priory are exclusively of the CHURCH. The crossing tower dominates the scene. Largely Norman, it stands on its four arches (three blocked), but of details only the completely plain imposts and the roll mouldings of the W and E arches remain. The tower itself has inside on each side three tall blank arches with thin continuous rolls. The small windows are set in them. On the NW side there is an apparently contemporary square turret, with two small doorways (restored) in the S face, the lower one once opening to a passage for the lost N transept. The upper doorway was the entrance proper to the stair-turret, originally reached from the gallery over the pulpitum. The tower now has a pyramid roof, and probably always had one, though it is possible that it had one more storey. Of the transepts nothing survives, except a short stump of the SW wall with a small doorway into the cloister, and of the nave only the lower part of the S wall with traces of two doorways into the cloister, and a short stump of the N wall with one shafted jamb of an upper window. The place where the nave W wall was can still be deciphered. The wall continuing the S wall to the W must represent the N wall of the W range of the cloister.

Standing under the crossing one looks into the majestic and serene chancel, of c. 1220, preserved completely. It is very long and has first on the N and S depressed, blocked arches which represent the curiously low access to former chapels E of the transepts. Above them, high up, are two circular windows on either side. If Norman, they are unique in the northern county. Or are they of c. 1220? Then follow four lancets N and four S and the beautiful E wall of three widely spaced very long and slender stepped lancets. They have inside a continuous thin keeled roll moulding, oddly set on bases. Fine PISCINA with a trefoiled head. Traces of ornamental painting. Good roof, like a barrel vault. Can it be of the mid C13 when Henry III gave timber from the royal forest of Pamber for building?

The church was restored in 1847 by G. G. Scott, in 1936 by T. D. Atkinson, and again in 1989 (window stonework) with careful restraint. All paid for by The Queen's College. The present arrangement of FURNISHINGS is Atkinson's. He repaved the floors and removed stained glass of 1847 from the E and other windows. – FONT. Perp, probably late C15. Octagonal with the usual quatrefoils, – FONT COVER. Possibly late C17. Flat with a knob, shaped like an Elizabethan chalice. – SCREEN, across the open tower arch. Perp, but restored (cf. the C15 screen at Monk Sherborne). – PEWS. Of two dates, S side late C16 or early C17, the different ones of the N side possibly C17. – WALL PAINTINGS. C15 with a clear consecration cross and faded angels in red outlines. – MONUMENTS. An interesting and important collection mainly of late C12–early C13 COFFIN-LIDS, mostly of Purbeck marble. Their survival here must be due to statutory protection in 1475 by Act of Parliament. The finest is C12 with a foliated cross with big leaves also issuing from the shaft. Incised inscription interesting because so early a case of a familiar tag of the later Middle Ages: 'Si quis eris qui transieris, sta, perlege, plora † Sum quod eris, fueramque quod es; pro me precor ora' (whosoever passeth by, stop, read and weep. I am what thou shalt be, and I was what thou art; I beg thee pray for me). Small *Agnus Dei* at the foot. – Recumbent oaken effigy of a knight, possibly one of the St Johns of The Vyne, benefactors of the priory. Early C14. About 7 ft (2 metres) long, crossed legs, praying hands, feet against a lion.

PAMBER PLACE, ¼ m. NW. Substantial mid-C17 H-plan brick house with Artisan Mannerist detailing. Restored and extended in the early C20 in same style, see also the covered way to the front door. Two storeys and attic. Parlour wing (l.) of *c.* 1650 with moulded plinth, string course and pilaster-strips. The side is symmetrical with three-, one- and three-light windows on each floor (cf. Wyeford Farm). The r. wing is plainer, dated 1665.

WYEFORD FARM, ⅝ m. NW. An attractive ensemble, owing much to romantic restoration and enlargement of the house *c.* 1921. It stands in the corner of a large square moat with foot-bridges. Originally L-shaped. Fine mid-C17 brick parlour cross-wing with Artisan Mannerist detailing (cf. Dummer Grange). The angles have giant pilasters with brick Ionic capitals, and dentil cornice and verges. The windows have raised keyed surrounds; the mullions of the windows are of brick too, though they are cement-rendered. Its side elevation (l.) is of three bays; three-light windows in the outer bays and the narrow central bay with one-light windows flanked by pilasters. Hall range to the r. with C18 brick front, altered when the house was extended in matching style; the new wing has crow-stepped parapets and beyond is a timber-framed service wing with herringbone nogging. At the rear, in the angle of hall and cross-wing, C17 gabled stair-tower with pedimented mezzanine window. To its l., a large C20 gabled wing echoing the C17 original, with an outshot over a loggia. Inside, four-centred brick-arched fireplaces in the parlour wing and a fine square-well staircase, with lyre-shaped balusters and newel posts with finials and pendants.

PASSFIELD
Bramshott

A nice collection of timber-framed houses. The best is PASS-FIELD HOUSE, Headley Lane, an early C16 four-bay hall. First floor inserted in the larger of the hall bays *c.* 1550 leaving the cross-passage as a smoke-bay, in which a chimney was inserted *c.* 1600 creating a lobby entry. High end rebuilt as a two-bay cross-wing at about the same time. Refronted *c.* 1800, with

tripartite sashes, the r.-hand pair inserted *c.* 1950 and the original doorway reopened during restoration by *A. C. Fairclough*
and *D. R. Morris*. Beautifully restored HOP KILNS of local
sandstone rubble.

PASSFIELD BUSINESS CENTRE, Lynchborough Road. 1959–61
by the *Architects' Co-Partnership* as research laboratories, offices
and workshops for Metal Containers Ltd. The original offices
and laboratories, in white brick and black steel frame, are
grouped around a courtyard with a glazed link to a two-storey
former workshop. This is faced with cedar boarding. To the r.,
boiler house with circular chimney of engineering brick. The
design allowed for future expansion and these later parts are
in a matching style. Much of the original landscaping survives.

PENTON MEWSEY

3040

HOLY TRINITY. An essentially complete, if over-restored, small p. 444
manorial church of the mid C14 or a little later, perhaps built
shortly after 1367 by Edmund de Stonor of Oxfordshire, Lord
of the Manor, who held the advowson. Nave and chancel; bellcote. Flint and rough rubble stone, the s side flints finest-
knapped toward the manor house; good original stonework
details, especially the ashlar w bellcote with its two C14 bells,
each in a small gabled opening. Other genuine stone details,
not all of the restorations in 1844 and 1888 (by *Bodley &
Garner*), notably the nave SE window of two tall headed lights
and quatrefoil, and the s doorway with three continuous chamfers. Good contemporary hinges on the door. The even finer
two-light chancel N window, with rich curvilinear tracery, is in
place, having been temporarily relocated as the E window.
Small infillings in a reticulation unit typical of 1360–70. The
tall w window, with fine flowing tracery, is trustworthy too. The
chancel s doorway is of a sure Dec inventiveness, with a
pointed head in four cants – a 'Berkeley arch' – recorded in
this position by G. E. Street in 1840. The chancel arch (two
chamfers dying into the imposts), and the delightful small
ogee-trefoiled piscina with shelf, in the nave SE window, are
genuine too. The latter, no doubt, indicating the position of a
nave altar. The nave roof must be C14 too, with slightly canted
tie-beams, with kingposts with two tiers of rounded braces,
partly restored in 1889: all nicely contrasted by a plastered
ceiling. FONT. Octagonal, Dec, with two small ogee-headed
arches per side. – COMMUNION RAIL. Handsome, of twisted
balusters. C18. – (SACRING BELL. A small, decidedly secular
piece, dated 1555, probably Flemish, used here during the
Marian Counter-Reformation.) Furnishings mostly of 1888,
e.g. the simple combined CHOIR STALLS, PRIEST'S STALL and
the PULPIT with linenfold panels. – STAINED GLASS. In nave

South Elevation.

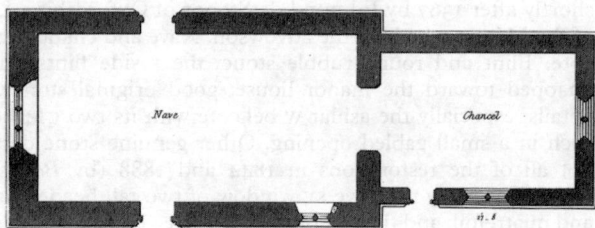

Nave   *Chancel*

Ground Plan

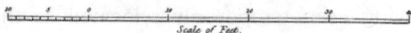

Scale of Feet.

G.E. Street, del.   J. Le K.

CHURCH AT PENTON MEWSEY, HANTS.
Ground Plan and S^th Elevation.

Penton Mewsley, Holy Trinity.
Ground plan and elevation

SE window, C14 foliate patterns and borders to the tracery light.
More coeval fragments hugger mugger below, from the w
window, now with colourful glass of 1869 by *Cox & Son*. A
busy Ascension with lively angels in the tracery. The larger
churchyard memorials include a sarcophagus to Mary Bour-
dillon †1817, and an obelisk of pink Peterhead granite to
William Cubitt †1863 (*see* Penton Lodge).

PENTON MANOR, SW of the church, is probably mainly *c.* 1700.
The N front stuccoed, with five bays divided by brick pilaster
strips. Neo-Tudor alterations and addition.

The village is grouped around a cross-roads. Most of the houses are in Chalkcroft Lane, beginning with the OLD RECTORY of 1833 by *Robert Wallace*. Neo-Tudor and very grand in squared and coursed knapped flint, typical of the date, with gault brick dressings and raised shields and crosses. In Newbury Hill are stables, of 1865–6, built for PENTON LODGE. This is to the S and is early C19 of three storeys, with lower flanking wings. *William Cubitt*, building contractor and M.P. for Andover, altered it for himself in 1852. The entrance moved from the N to the W front, which was remodelled in a stuccoed Italianate style, the kitchens moved to the basement and on the N side a sunken service courtyard created with an ice house tunnelled in to the bank (all these parts are vaulted with fireproof construction). The transformation was radical inside, creating a new top-lit staircase hall, with a deep coving and a guilloche-ornamented architrave to the roof-light. Cantilevered stone stair with cast-iron balustrade. The other significant interior is the former library (E wing) with a handsome marble chimneypiece and bold plaster cornice etc. Other rooms redone in Adam style in the late C19.

NEOLITHIC LONG BARROW, 300 yds NE of Nutbane Farm. The barrow now presents the appearance of a very low mound, 180 ft (55 metres) long and 110 ft (34 metres) broad. Excavation showed the surviving mound to be 170 ft (52 metres) long and 75 ft (23 metres) wide at its broader E end, tapering to 25 ft (8 metres) at the W. Beneath the E end was a complicated timber mortuary building showing several phases of construction and four crouched inhumation burials within a small mortuary enclosure. These wooden structures at the E end had been deliberately burnt down before the erection of the mound over them. The barrow has flanking quarry ditches, but these are no longer visible on the ground.

PETERSFIELD

Of the small market towns in Hampshire, Petersfield is perhaps the most fortunate in its setting, a lovely undulating vale between the whale-backed downland heights of Butser and Wardown Hills to the S, and the beautiful wooded hangers along the chalk escarpment to the N. The town was at first a holding in the estate of the royal manor of Mapledurham (the ancient neighbouring parish of Buriton) and the earliest parts are centred on the large Norman church. The emerging town received its first charter in the mid C12 and from that time forward its prosperity was in wool and cloth. As in so many other places, that trade declined in the C17, and the Petersfield we see now gives the impression of the affluent but not spectacularly rich C18 country town that it became on the back of the coaching trade along the main London–Portsmouth road. About 1700 it had nine inns. Its best houses are all Georgian, though significant numbers of earlier timber-framed houses also survive. Petersfield's expansion was encouraged by the arrival of the London & South Western Railway in 1859, which made possible commuter services between Portsmouth and London. In spite of this the town did not augment its medieval pattern with streets of shops and villas until the last decades of the C19. Further change was limited until the second half of the C20 but even the inevitable, sometimes baleful, effect of suburbanization has not spoiled the town's attractions and the by-passing of the main Portsmouth Road has even enhanced it.

CHURCHES

ST PETER. Here is one of the most interesting Norman churches in Hampshire, interesting especially because of the several phases it represents. It probably began *c.* 1120 and seems to have been intended as an extremely lavish, cruciform-plan church with a crossing lantern tower. Its progress seems to have been halted, probably by the Civil War that broke out in 1139 in which the founder, Robert, Earl of Gloucester, was deeply involved, but resumed before his death in 1147. His heir granted the advowson to the Benedictine nunnery of Eaton (Nun Eaton), Warwickshire. The church finally emerged as nave and aisles with a long narrow chancel and w tower. Despite its size it served as a chapel of ease to Buriton until 1886.

The E ends of the aisles have flints and sandstone 'cobbles' laid in herringbone patterns, and these are the remains of the early C12 transepts. The E wall of the s aisle also has an enigmatic small niche with traces of a carved surround. One Early Norman single-light window, re-set in the N aisle w of the porch; can this be even earlier than 1120? The low w tower was added before 1147, probably after the crossing-tower had been curtailed (the bases of the NW and SW corners of which were only removed in 1731). Its rubble lower stage has flat Norman buttressing. The top, of sandstone ashlar, may be mid-C12 and has corners with nook-shafts like East Meon church. Next, the N aisle was built w from the transept, unusually embracing the tower, and also with clasping buttresses. Late Norman N doorway with one order of nook-shafts (the r. shaft is original, of Binstead stone) and typically late C12 waterleaf capitals. The s aisle followed perhaps a little later, but again embracing the tower, and there is evidence that this formerly contained a separate w chamber, purpose-built as a feudal estate office, originally walled off from the church and only entered from the tower. Fine w wall, of coursed Sussex sandstone ashlar, with paired Late Norman windows and Late Transitional capitals. Contemporary sandstone s doorway, even more elaborately

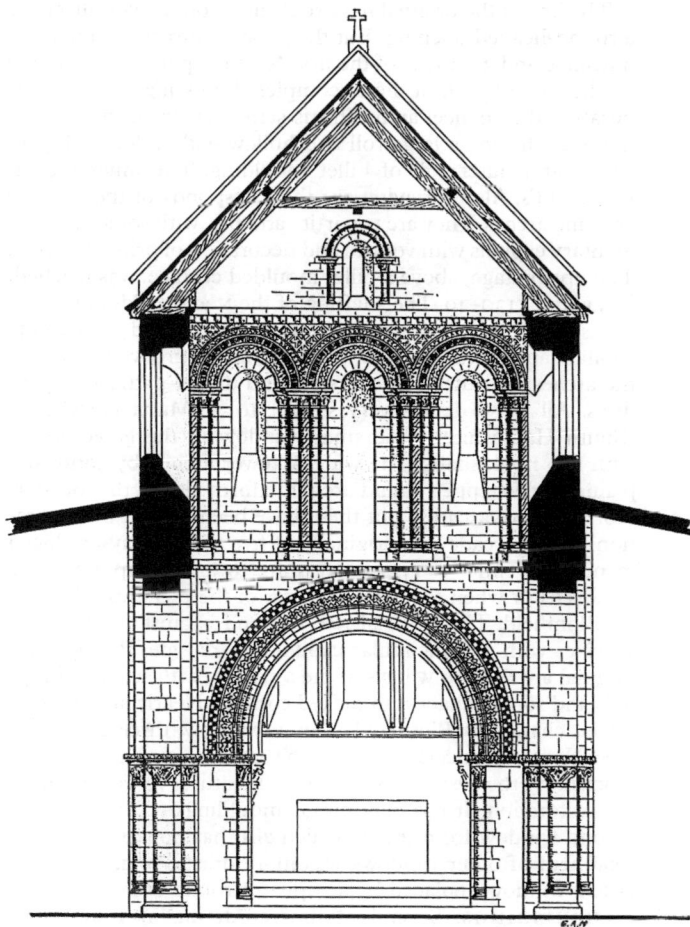

Petersfield, St Peter, elevation of chancel arch.
Drawing, C19

moulded, with two orders of columns and delicate waterleaf
capitals, now very eroded. The upper stage of the tower has
mostly renewed Perp windows (and battlements of *c.* 1960
replicating Early Tudor originals); one of the Perp windows of
the N aisle is of a type extensively used *c.* 1425 at Ewelme
church, Oxfordshire. Much else has been obscured by restoration in 1873–4 by *A. W. Blomfield*: chancel rebuilt, N vestry and
organ chamber added, clerestory created, W doorway reconstructed and battlements added, roofs renewed in good Neo-
Norman style for the the nave, Perp for the aisles. Projecting
N porch of 1887.

The line of the original nave roof shows on the w wall, above a round-headed opening. But the greatest surprise is the magnificence and grandeur of the first Norman phase, represented by the stone E wall of the uncompleted crossing tower, incorporating the chancel arch. This is semicircular, of two orders, the outer having a large roll and hollow with a double line of zigzag and outer roll of billet moulding. The inner arch is Blomfield's. Also surviving are the E responds of the N and S crossing arches. They are tripartite and big, with somewhat elementary capitals with volutes and decoration of primitive ferns. The upper stage, above a billet moulded cornice, was reached, say, about 1130–40. The shafting of the N and S sides only just starts but it has three E windows, thickly shafted with volute capitals and spiral ornament, more zigzag, grooved pieces in the arches, an outer order of stars and diaper-patterned spandrels. All these details very similar to St Mary, Portchester (South Hampshire). One small window in the gable above, with two nook-shafts. The wide W tower arch is by contrast a plain, single-stepped round arch, the form also of the four-bay Norman nave arcades, but these have been altered by restoration. The N arcade was originally of five narrow bays, reduced in number either c. 1731 (according to an inscription, since removed) or when the original order of the piers was changed by Blomfield. The original NW respond against the W tower survives with a semicircular capital of rare type. Perhaps also original are the two W bays of the S arcade, with scalloped capitals and square abaci with nicked corners. Nearly all the detail in the chancel is Blomfield's: his E window, three graduated Neo-Norman lancets, matches the genuine N window (now blocked by the vestry), one of several features revealed during the restoration. It has continuous mouldings (cf. the S aisle's second window from the W, which also has nook-shafts). The treatment of other windows was more drastic (e.g. the Dec S aisle E window, replaced by a triplet of round arches).

FURNISHINGS. Several of the reordering in 1999: altar, chairs and choir stalls by *Paul Velluet*. – FONT. Octagonal. Late C14, with Perp panelling. – REREDOS, 1903, with *opus sectile* work by *Powells*. – TILES by *Minton* and a rich glazed scheme to the walls surrounding the altar by *James Powell*, c. 1900. – STAINED GLASS. Chancel E by *Clayton & Bell*, 1875. – Nave E wall by the same firm but the gable window, 1958, by *H. Stammers*. – S aisle E, 1875, by *Lavers & Barraud*, perhaps the best with colourful medallions in 'mosaic' surrounds. – S aisle. Henry Stone of Castle House, †1879 by *Helmle & Merzweiler* of Freiburg, Germany, 1908. The Sower. – N aisle, 1888 by *Powell* (Christ between Elisha and St Luke). – MONUMENTS. N aisle. Crudely lettered tablet for the Worledge family, including John Worledge †1694, author of the pioneering *Systema Agriculturae* (1664). – Large arrays of C18–early C19 tablets were assembled at the W end in 1874, the best under the tower. Catherine Jolliffe †1731. By the little-known *Samuel Huskisson*. Large tablet. The interesting Latin inscription ought

read. – John Jolliffe †1771. Worthy of Sir Henry Cheere. Pink
and grey marble with an urn. – George Jolliffe †1799, a mid-
shipman killed at Aboukir Bay. Good Neoclassical tablet.
In the segmental top an allegorical figure with naval implements, at the bottom the battle scene in relief (cf. the identical memorial to Jolliffe at Merstham, Surrey). – John and
Elizabeth Sainsbury, 1801 by *Flaxman*. White marble. Two
standing mourners by an urn on a high pedestal. – Hylton Jolliffe †1843 by *Samuel Colecom* of Merstham, with attached
fluted Corinthian columns. – s aisle, w end. Edward Patrick
†1782, possibly by *T. Hews* (cf. his classical monument at Has-
combe, Surrey, to William Middlefield, *c.* 1785). The influence
of Adam on a local mason shows. – N aisle, w end. Mary Peryer
†1782. Nice, with floral ornament on pilasters, the top originally gilt.

ST LAURENCE (R.C.), Station Road. By *John Kelly* (formerly of
Kelly & Birchall) of Leeds. Begun 1890–1, completed 1909. A
handsome church, purely Italian, if it was not for the red brick,
and very restrained but for the copper octagonal dome with its
cupola, which provides one of the landmarks of the town. Nave
without aisles or chapels, transepts, and apsidal chancel with
square-ended chapels. Cool interior, the nave has a coffered
segmented vault, another bow to England. Open lantern below
the dome. Good coeval furnishings. FONT of assorted marbles.
– COMMUNION RAILS of alabaster with brass gates. –
FRONTAL of the High Altar. Fine intricately patterned C17
Italian Renaissance fabric. – PAINTING. Large lunette in the s
transept. A late C19 copy of Fra Filippo Lippi's St John the
Baptist and Seven Saints. – MONUMENT. Under the organ, a
Gothic brass by *Hardman* to Lawrence Trent Cave of Ditcham
Park (Buriton) †1899. He, with his sons, was the founder.

UNITED REFORMED CHURCH, College Street. By *J. B. Sulman*,
1882, succeeding a Congregationalist chapel of 1801. Gothic,
in crazy sandstone, all the details in *c.* 1260 style. The brick
rear wall in a starved E.E. Furnishings by *Edward Barnsley*, e.g.
chairs by the Holy Table. HALL, 2009, in matching style.

METHODIST CHURCH, Station Road. 1902–3 by *Josiah Gunton*,
of *Gordon & Gunton*. Quite showy in black flint, red brick and
stone but very conservative for the date. Prominent NE lantern
tower, with pinnacles and a shingled spire. Perp details. Elaborately traceried E window. Some dashing Art Nouveau glass
in the windows. Wide interior, with arch-braced roof and a
shallow apse. Reordered *c.* 2005 when the Church Hall was
linked to the church by a canted porch in sympathetic style.

Former WESLEYAN METHODIST CHURCH, Station Road. Now
Masonic Hall, 1903 by *T. E. Davidson*. Minimal Gothic. Later
Masonic glass in the lower part.

CEMETERY, off Ramshill. Finely landscaped setting, laid out
1857. Dec style chapels by *Colson*, with steep roofs, the Anglican one topped by a spirelet. N of the Nonconformist chapel
a headstone for Owen Outridge †1861. The design still Georgian, with urn and weeping willow in relief.

PUBLIC BUILDINGS

TOWN HALL (District Council Offices), Heath Road. 1935–6 by
Seely & Paget in a modern style for its date: flat-roofed with
generous fenestration and rounded corners. Rear extensions by
Kenneth Claxton, 1987.

POLICE STATION, St Peter's Road. 1858 by *Thomas Stopher*.
Local flint with red brick quoins.

INFANTS' SCHOOL, St Peter's Road and Hylton Road. 1894–5
by *H. T. Keates*, a former assistant to Butterfield. Street façade
boldly crowned by shaped gables and open turrets. Unattrac-
tively overlaid by glass and blockwork extensions of 1984–5 by
Plincke, Leaman & Browning but the rest of their enlargements,
to the S, done with aplomb. Further extended towards Hylton
Road in 2001–2 by *Robert Warren*, in smooth pale yellow brick,
the roof-line punctuated by cotton-reel vents.

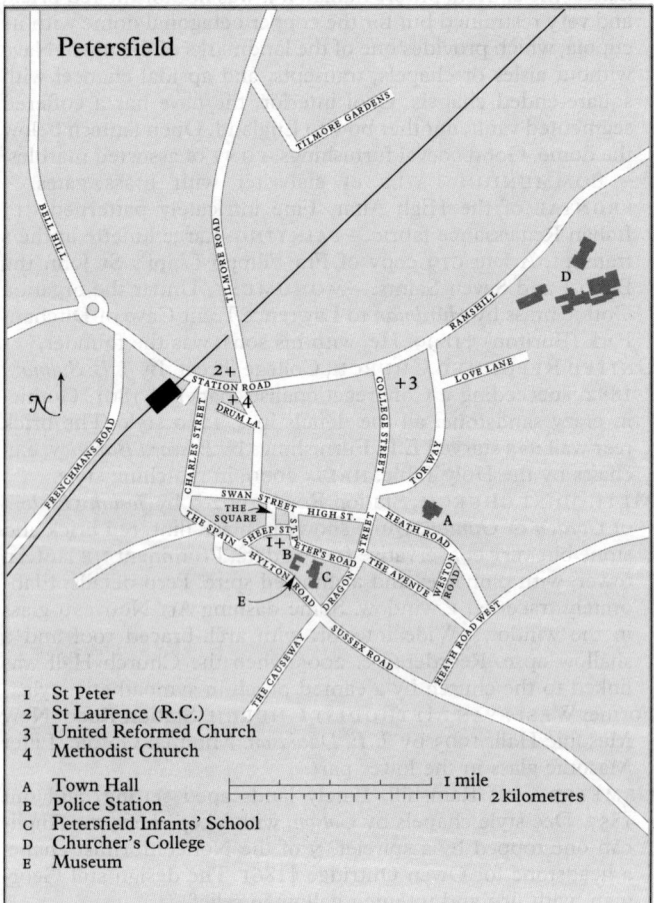

Petersfield

1	St Peter
2	St Laurence (R.C.)
3	United Reformed Church
4	Methodist Church

A	Town Hall
B	Police Station
C	Petersfield Infants' School
D	Churcher's College
E	Museum

1 mile
2 kilometres

CHURCHER'S COLLEGE, Ramshill. Successor to the school
founded in College Street (*see* p. 455). Design won in competition in 1877 by *G. R. Crickmay* of Weymouth; built 1879–81.
Butterfieldian Gothic, built of Bargate stone. A long, rambling
arrangement with the entrance under a tall tower with a steep-
sided pyramid roof. Headmaster's house E, taller boarding
house in the centre, classrooms and assembly hall (former
School Room) w, the latter like a chapel with a flèche and
wheel window. Good-mannered 1930s gabled Neo-Tudor
range on the s side and gymnasium (now pavilion) of the 1890s
with a veranda. Some graceless late C20 extensions but good
science laboratories by *Lewis & Hickey*, 1999–2000, in yellow
brick with up-and-down roof-line.
LEISURE CENTRE, Penn's Place, 1¼ m. E of the centre by the
District Council Offices. A lively design of *c.* 1992. Low and
spreading in dark brick with sweeping metal roofs.
MUSEUM. Between St Peter's Road and Hylton Road. The
former court house. Brick and flint palette similar to the Police
Station. One large room.
STATION. Neo-Tudor of 1859, probably by *Sir William Tite* and
E. N. Clifton (the design is nearly identical to Godalming,
Surrey).

PERAMBULATION

The perambulation of course starts in THE SQUARE, which faces
the N side of the church. It has an almost perfect form, with
streets leading off at all four corners, and its centre ennobled
by the beautiful equestrian lead STATUE of William III, origi-   89
nally gilded, made by *John Cheere* (possibly to a design by *Sir
Henry Cheere*). It was acquired with money from the estate of
Sir William Jolliffe (†1749), M.P., and set up in 1757 at the
entrance to Petersfield House; since 1812 it has been in The
Square. The King appears as a Roman, with a laurel wreath
and scroll, i.e. after Scheemakers's statue at Hull (1734). The
horse is not moving. Good stone pedestal with rounded ends.
Since 1898, when the Town Hall was demolished, The Square's
s side has been open to views of the church (the arcade of the
Town Hall's ground floor has been reused as the façade of a
café). Round The Square are several C18 fronts (e.g. Square
House, w of the church) which conceal earlier buildings, mixed
with neo-C18 buildings and one significant late C20 interloper,
the LIBRARY by *Hampshire County Architects*, 1982, in an overpowering Neo-vernacular with steeply ascending roofs. The
POST OFFICE, 1922, in creditable domestic Neo-Georgian by
the *Office of Works*, replaced a picturesque, creeper-clad C16
mansion, Castle House, built for the Mervyn family (*see*
Bramshott). Turning out of the NW corner of The Square is

HSBC (formerly the London, City & Midland Bank), handsome Baroque of 1918–20 by *T. B. Whinney* with a clock tower, composed as a *point-de-vue* from the E. Set back from the line of The Square's N side No. 1, a hearth-passage house whose timber frame is dated to 1532–3. Tall brick stack and a façade of closely set studs and crusty flint infill above an excellent castellated continuous jetty. Its moulded bressumer (restored) is a rare feature in Hampshire and further evidence of the house's status. Later attic floor, probably C17, but the dormers of the restoration *c.* 1918 by local artist *Flora Twort*. (Chamfered beams in the passage, a Tudor doorway and wide stone fireplace in the former hall.) LLOYDS TSB, a handsome red brick house, was probably built for John Sainsbury, attorney, resident here in 1759. Five bays, two-and-a-half storeys, with heavy modillion cornice and stone doorway with Tuscan columns and a triglyph frieze. Window above with elegant volutes and a pediment; all of a sophistication commensurate with the best houses in Winchester. A humbler eight-bay C18 front, in blue and red brick, masks at its E end (No. 12) a fragment of a large house erected *c.* 1590 for John Barlow, son of the Bishop of Chichester. Exceptional carved details inside. Restored as part of the sympathetic RAMS WALK development of 1992–3 by *Plincke, Leaman & Browning*.

Many of the buildings along HIGH STREET, running E, retain long, narrow burgage plots to the rear but it is primarily the prosperity of the late C18 which displays to the street. The most forceful accent on the N side, however, is NATWEST (former London & County Bank), a stately Italianate palazzo by *Frederic Chancellor*, 1865–7. Among its lower neighbours, the dwarfish No. 6 is a fragment of a much larger timber-framed house but with a delightful early C19 garden room with Gothick details. No. 12 is solid Regency, with two-storey canted bays and open pedimented doorcase with reeded pilasters (like No. 16 with its inserted consoled hood); its walled rear plot is the C17-style PHYSIC GARDEN, laid out in 1988. Then WINTON HOUSE, with Greek Doric doorcase, remodelled *c.* 1808 from half of the late C16 White Hart Inn. Winton House was originally joined to No. 20, within which the inn's late medieval structure is part preserved (including a Tudor stone fireplace). Between the two runs FOLLY LANE, a brick-paved alley which seems to have acted as a conduit for private coaching traffic from the inn to the London road (*see* College Street, below). More has been lost from High Street's s side. At No. 13, a big commercial development of 1915 by the local architect *E. Arden Minty*, in Queen Anne style with bay windows in the upper floors and pedimented dormers. Nos. 17–19 are the only buildings in the street to retain a pre-Georgian appearance. Described as 'new' in 1580 but presumably rebuilt in 1613, the date carved on pendants from its jetty which are also initialled NP, probably for Nicholas Page. Segmental coved hood over the door to No. 19, possibly

p. 39

c. 1733, when the property was divided; and an artlessly pretty early C19 Gothick shopfront to No. 17. At the lower end of the street the WAR MEMORIAL by *H. Inigo Triggs*, 1922. Urn finial and four sides with segmental-headed blind aedicules, learnedly derived from Michelangelo's Medici Chapel, Florence.

High Street is terminated by the old London Portsmouth road. From the late C17 it was lined by coaching inns, of which the RED LION HOTEL survives on the E side. Mid-C18 but its smart street front looks *c.* 1790: four bays, widely spaced, with dentilled cornice and pediment. Doorway with Roman Doric columns and little flanking bows. The taller (early C19?) extension contained the Assembly Room; behind this a former Masonic Lodge of 1826 by *L. W. Lloyd*, later altered for the Red Lion brewery. Now S along DRAGON STREET, beginning with WORCESTER HOUSE, a grand house with fluted Greek Doric doorpiece, Adamesque cast-iron fanlight and distinctive serpentine cornice. Altered ground floor for shops. The garden wall to its S is associated with a house (dem.) which was occupied in the C17 by the agrarian improver, John Worledge. Further down is DRAGON HOUSE, with a charming early C18 brick front of grey headers and thin red courses and dressings. But this is only a refronting, and the rear is Elizabethan and timber-framed with close studding and flint infill. Two gables with mullioned windows, dormers and substantial cruciform chimneys. The double-gabled rear is of the attractive Wealden type with tile-hanging. Long garden with a Georgian gazebo. Opposite, Nos. 9 and 11 have a slate-hung front, sadly overpainted, and a superb bowed Regency shopfront with clustered Gothick shafts to the doorcase. Further S, a house with a long jetty with unusual acorn carving.

S is The Causeway, the medieval crossing over the pastures to Buriton. In SUSSEX ROAD, 200 yds E, is HEATH LODGE, a handsome, white three-bay house of *c.* 1780–1800 with a segmental porch of Tuscan columns and l. and r. tripartite windows with segmental heads filled by an Adamish fan.

E of The Causeway is THE GRANGE surgery, formerly a coachhouse built within sight of the Jolliffes' Petersfield House (1739), which stood on the higher ground to the N across canalized streams and ornamental lakes. So the front is treated in a superior manner, in malmstone, of seven bays, with stone quoins, raised window surrounds with keystones and a doorway with Tuscan columns and pediment. Nicely restored *c.* 2001 after a fire. To the W is the TESCO supermarket, low and unobtrusive except for car parks.

The line of HYLTON ROAD, E of Dragon Street, was closed off by the Jolliffes and only reopened after Petersfield House was pulled down in the 1790s. On the N side, integrated with 1980s housing, the former schoolroom of the National School, by *J. Colson*, 1854, and then three enigmatic houses: Nos. 17 and 19, of five and three bays with painted brick fronts, are

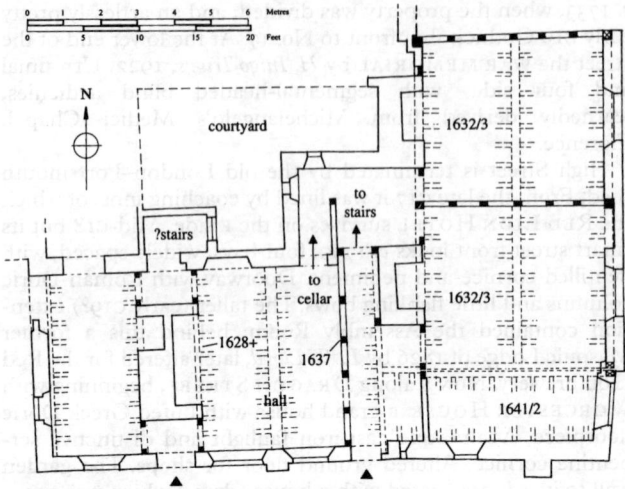

Petersfield, Goodyers.
Plan

outwardly Georgian but in their details, such as a coved cornice
and evidence of blocked windows, suggestive of an earlier
vintage. No. 21 has corner pilasters and traces of an earlier
roof-line.

Hylton Road debouches into THE SPAIN, which lay at the
edge of the medieval burgh and provided a second market
place for livestock. Houses are grouped around a triangular
green in a good mix of scale and character and include
GOODYERS, one of the best houses in the town. It is a three-
storey timber-framed gentry house built (or extensively remodelled) c. 1632–7 (tree-ring dating) by John Goodyer, the
botanist. Its engaging double-gabled façade of pink-washed
Georgian brick was added in 1784 by *John Marman* of Buriton,
who inserted sashes and placed the entrance at the front. The
original entrance on the s side, where there are still two doorways, indicates the segregated plan within: the l. door
(blocked) led to a lobby entry at the service end while the r.
opens into a passage between the hall (l.) and parlour range
(r.) and leading to the well stair at the rear, contained in a brick
turret. Both hall and parlour have timber-lintelled, limestone
fireplaces; the jambs of the smaller, parlour fireplace with scroll
stops. The SE corner of the parlour range was added in 1641–2,
indicated by a change in the sandstone walling on the s side.
Surprisingly, the house is only one of two L-plan ranges that
are connected around a central courtyard – an intriguingly
complex plan. The other range has straight mullions.

Goodyers's tile-hung and squatter neighbour (TULLY'S) is
rather altered but discernibly of Wealden type inside, the
timbers dated to 1441–2. Turning back to the centre of town

along The Spain's N side, No. 15 (dated to *c.* 1580) is shored up on the street side by brick buttresses. (Inside, an early example of a lobby-entry house, with the large fireplace heating its hall only.) Two good Georgian houses follow: the first, SHIPTON HOUSE, dated 1710, is low, with grey headers and red dressings; its neighbour is the handsome and high four-bay SPAIN HOUSE with a nice late C18 doorcase of plain columns and embellished cornice.

Now back to The Square along SHEEP STREET, past a timber-framed C16 row with narrowly spaced upright timbers and jettied upper storeys which acts as the prelude to the unbroken, picturesque sequence on this side of modest two-storey cottages, several refronted *c.* 1800, with simple bracketed hoods.

Finally, a short walk E of the church down ST PETER'S ROAD. The first part is the stub of the medieval Port Street (later Market Street), with several brick-fronted timber-frame cottages, including one with a robust chimney of distinctively local materials: dark ironstone rubble and russet brick. The street originally continued S but was truncated in 1740 when the 'New Way' was cut through the burgage plots S of High Street to give the Jolliffes access to Petersfield House. Their private steps to the churchyard survive on the W side. The opposite corner is dominated by the former BELL INN by *G. E. Smith* of Southsea, 1912, freely styled with curvy gables topped by aedicules. Some Art Nouveau glass. The Police Station and School (*see* Public Buildings) face ST PETER'S HALL, the former Methodist church of 1871 by *W. W. Pocock*. Suburban development between the town square and the station did not take hold until the 1880s, typified by the commercial buildings along CHAPEL STREET. Close to the S end of Chapel Street is SWAN STREET, with SWAN COURT, a Neo-Georgian office building by *Sir John Brown & Henson, c.* 1960, a real oddity (Pevsner called it 'deplorable') for its date and with tiers of oriels, a reference to Norman Shaw's Swan House, Chelsea. Downhill from the station along CHARLES STREET, at the corner with Swan Street, is a domestic Georgian group of cottages, 'given to the parish for a Poor House' by the Jolliffes in 1771. W of the railway line in FRENCHMAN'S ROAD, the PETERSFIELD & RELIANCE LAUNDERERS, 1905, unusually well preserved, with large washing halls under iron-truss roofs.

COLLEGE STREET (formerly Stoneham Street) was the main approach to the town from the N until it was by-passed in the C20, and the buildings at its N end originally belonged to the hamlet of Stoneham. On the W side, the United Reformed Church (*see* above) and the OLD COLLEGE (County Council Offices), built in 1729–30 with a bequest from John Churcher (†1723), a local apothecary with interests in the East India Company, 'to educate . . . local boys . . . so they could be apprenticed to masters of ships sailing in the East Indies'. Its appearance is that of a gentleman's town house and in its details wholly fashionable and up to date, although its architect is unknown.* Five bays and three storeys, all quite tightly grouped and tall, with an emphatic moulded cornice, rendered to look like stone, and panelled parapet. Red brick and blue brick chequer walls with angle pilasters in tiers and a projecting centre whose stone doorcase has a straight hood on modestly carved brackets. Sash windows to the street front but casements on the garden side. Double-pile plan with a fine staircase, centrally placed in a tight narrow compartment, with dainty columnar and twisted balusters. Two single-storey N and S wings; the N wing appears contemporary, the S extension perhaps added as a schoolroom in 1762. Restored by *Neville Churcher* for the County Council *c.* 1989.

Opposite is a small two-storey house, refronted in the C18 and clearly inspired by the façade of the college with a projecting centre and flat parapet. It conceals an older house (*c.* C14 crown-post roof parallel to the street and projecting chimney dated 1600. Edward Roberts). Parts are probably C16 and perhaps contemporary with Nos. 50–52, which are set back from the street. Also refronted in brick with ground-floor sliding sashes. Most unusual is the large cement-rendered doorcase to No. 50 with an Egyptian cornice. This range concludes nicely with a Late Victorian brick addition with terracotta and moulded decoration: probably for Gammon & Son, brick and tile manufacturers, see the monogram.

STATION ROAD leads E and crosses Tilmore Brook, beside which, S of the road, is TILBROOK HOUSE, strikingly sensitively designed offices of 1994–6 by *Neville Churcher*. Low, Dudokian brick front with flat-topped tower and balcony and a spreading monopitch roof at rear. On the N side, OAKLEA (No. 86), *c.* 1800, has excellent cast-iron railings with Gothick gatepiers made by *Cannings & Howell* of Finchdean (Rowland's Castle). Further E, on a rise in LOVE LANE, the former WORKHOUSE, begun by *Edward Hunt* of New Alresford, 1835. Truncated, red brick with low-pitched slate roofs now part of the housing. Later chapel, detached to NE.

The junction of Chapel Street and STATION ROAD has the nice contrast of styles between the Methodist and R.C. churches. Rows of attractive cottages, including No. 16, at the corner with Tilmore Road, converted and extended *c.* 1908 by *W. F. Unsworth* as his own office (extension with large windows). It typifies his Lutyens-esque manner. Uphill on TILMORE ROAD is LITTLE TILMORE, of *c.* 1910 by *Unsworth & Unsworth* in the same style. ½ m. N, HOLLY BRAKE by *R. Weir Schultz*, 1911, with gablets over canted bays with weatherboard fronts. In TILMORE GARDENS, housing of 1921–2 for the Petersfield Co-Partnership Housing and Land Society by *Unsworth & Triggs* in a most plain style with rendered and brick

---

* David W. Lloyd has suggested *Thomas Steel Jun.* of Chichester. Churcher came from a family at Funtington, near Chichester, where he is commemorated by a table tomb.

facings. For houses in Reservoir Lane *see* Sheet. To the w, off
BELL HILL, BUCKMORE HOUSE, a convincing imitation of
Voysey by *Walter Cave*, 1897.
On the heath are twenty-one ROUND BARROWS, the majority of
bowl type, but including two fine bell barrows, one disc and
four saucer barrows.

POPHAM   5040

A shrunken village. Its medieval church has disappeared, so too
its replacement of 1875–8.

POPHAM COURT. Mid-C18. Brick with vertical panels of flint
and hipped slate roof. A long narrow plan, one room deep with
a corridor on the E side. This side originally of seven bays with
a giant order of pilasters and a slightly projecting three-bay
centre, altered with a 1930s porch in the angle of an early C19
addition to the l. The garden side is a rustic version of the E
front of Farleigh House (Farleigh Wallop) – central full-height
canted bay, with, to l. and r., a pair of windows flanking
ground-floor niches and first-floor blind windows. Giant
pilasters at the angles. An entrance lobby leads into a central
octagonal room, the staircase squeezed in to the l. of the
entrance. Striking Gothic archway into the 1930s porch.
FLOWERPOT COTTAGES, ½ m. N on the A30, is a piece of C18
vernacular classicism.

PRESTON CANDOVER   6040

A long village with an unusually good selection of houses.

ST MARY. 1884–5 by *A. W. Blomfield*. Brick and unusually large
flints for deliberately rough effect with Bath stone details, especially the freely Geometrical tracery, in Early Dec style. Low
NW porch-tower with a slender shingled spire. All this is rather
coarse for Blomfield. Much smoother interior, with exposed
Fareham red brick facing and stone dressings. Boarded roofs,
nicely painted in chancel and N aisle. – REREDOS, with good
mosaics by *Powells*, and a corbelled CREDENCE SHELF with
dainty foliate decoration. – ORGAN CASE of 1999. – STAINED
GLASS. Good E window of 1885 by *Heaton, Butler & Bayne*
under *Blomfield*'s supervision. Crucifixion with kneeling
angels. Disciplined architectural grisaille surround. Other
windows by *Heaton, Butler & Bayne* and *Powells*.
ST MARY (Churches Conservation Trust), ⅛ m. SW. Only the
late C12 chancel survives, with small N lancet, after a fire in
1681 and subsequent rebuilding. Plain priest's doorway, now

blocked, and two-light Perp window in s wall. – COMMUNION
RAILS. perhaps *c.* 1681. – WALL PAINTINGS. Traces of C18
texts, some foliage and a pattern of fleur-de-lys and roses. –
MONUMENTS. Brass to Catherine Dabridgecourt †1607. –
Delightful tablets to John Soper †1729 and Patience Soper
†1731, perhaps by *James Hardy* (cf. Silchester). Armorial car-
touches with fringed drapes. – Thomas Baker †1794, of
Farnham. Neoclassical with urn against a pyramid. – Thomas
Hall †1812, signed *J. Bacon* and *S. Manning*, erected in 1820.
Long inscription between drapes.

NORTH HALL. w of the church, in a miniature park. Built in
1769, for *Thomas Hall the Younger*, who is described as its architect. Restored in 1959–60 by *Geoffrey F. Bateman*, who probably added the doorcase with segmental pediment on consoles.
Five-bay SE front, one-bay projection with lunette in an open
pediment. Of the later C20, the walled forecourt with reused
C18 stone busts on piers. One-bay projecting rear wings and
arched staircase windows in the recessed centre. Detached
service blocks flank the rear court, a very grand arrangement
for a house of this size. Inside, a delightful original staircase
with three twisted balusters to each step, and a number of panelled rooms.

MANOR FARMHOUSE, sw, of 1814, for George Purefoy Jervoise
of Herriard (cf. Nutley Manor). An original design. Five bays
with pilaster-strips at each end. Tripartite sashes alternating
with doorways, the latter with raised brick surrounds and
slightly cambered moulded cornices. Jervoise also built SOUTH
HALL, wsw of the parish church, in 1815. Like North Hall,
also five bays, also a one-bay projection, also an open pediment with lunette. Doric doorcase with pediment. Simpler
garden front, also with pedimented doorcase.

NNE of the church, SUMNER HOUSE, the former rectory. 1872–3
by *William Hunt* of Alresford, for the Rev. Sumner Wilson.
Gothic, brick and flint. Conventional but complete. Opposite
is KINGSMEAD of 1991 by *Robert Adam*. Small, just one storey
and an attic, but quirky and in a typically exaggerated manner
influenced by Artisan Mannerism (e.g., the lugged architrave
of its entrance derived from Thorpe Hall) and the Arts and
Crafts.

PRESTON HOUSE, ½ m. N. A modest country house but with a
complicated history. Built *c.* 1700, for Anthony Guidott, the
Duke and Duchess of Marlborough's lawyer. His was a hipped-
roofed brick double pile of seven by five bays, and of two
storeys over a basement, originally with a balustraded parapet
(removed 1961). The E front has giant pilasters at the angles
and flanking the central three-bay pedimented break but
regrettably stripped of their capitals etc. in 1979–80 by *Philip
Jebb*. The w front had two short wings added to it in the 1790s
and the entrance was moved to this side *c.* 1860, with a porch
and stair bay in a precocious Queen Anne style slotted in
between. It too has been remodelled, in 1961 by *Robert Bostock*,
who redesigned it to match the E front, with giant pilasters and

portico. In the former entrance hall, a nice early C18 stone chimneypiece with boldly scrolled lugged architrave and lion mask with swags. C18 back staircase. The offices were originally in the basement.

STABLES, SE of the house. Erected in the 1790s, for John Blackburn Sen. Two storeys with a fine square cupola with channelled rustication and columns set diagonally at the corners.* MILLENNIUM FOLLY, NW of the house, for Lord and Lady Sainsbury. Circular temple of British worthies, by *Robert Adam*, 2000. In the floor an inscribed spiral of slate by *Gary Breeze*.

FAWKNERS, ¾ m. N. 1911, by *J. B. Colson & Nisbett* in the Voysey manner.

PRESTON GRANGE, ½ m. S. 1913–14, by *Robert Atkinson* and *G. L. Alexander*. Arts and Crafts in a C17 style.

MOUNDSMERE MANOR. *See* p. 402.

PRIORS DEAN

A small village in a steeply sided downland valley.

CHURCH (dedication unknown). An enchanting tiny Early Norman church, probably of *c.* 1120–30 – N doorway of Liss sandstone with saltire crosses in the chalk abaci and billet on the hoodmould, also a round-headed piscina inside the skewed chancel. One C13 blocked lancet, and a trefoil-headed SW lowside window.** Spired bell-turret by *J. Colson*, 1857; he inserted the Neo-Norman lancets and distressingly dominant chancel arch inside and provided most of the furnishings. Open trussed rafter roofs, possibly C13. Four later, probably C16, timber supports for the bell-turret. – BENCH of *c.* 1400, of the same local design as Empshott and Selborne (qq.v.). – SEAT. Dated 1657. It can be adapted to form a table. – MONUMENTS. Surprisingly many for so remote a church. – Brass. John Compton †1605 and Jane Michelborne, his wife †1586. Elizabethan couple as in their salad days, with escutcheon on the chancel floor. – Four C17 tablets, mostly alabaster. Elizabeth Tichborne †1623, wife of Benjamin Tichborne, and eldest daughter of Sir John Compton. Small kneeler (cf. the Tichborne monuments at Aldershot, St Michael). – Bridget Stoughton †1631 attributed to *William Wright* of Charing Cross (GF). Matronly kneeling figure with four children, two of them infants in swaddling clothes (or shrouds). The latter, usually represented recumbent, are frontal and upright. – Sir John Compton †1653 and Dame Bridget, his wife †1634. Two rather flat busts in garlanded oval recesses. Attributed to the *Marshall*

---

*There is no evidence that it came from Southampton's audit house, as Pevsner claimed.
**Another blocked window found during repairs in 2009.

workshop. – Compton Tichborne †1657, also a bust in an oval recess, attributed to *Thomas Burman* (GF), but quite a lot more classical.

Immediately NE, the attractive MANOR FARMHOUSE, dated 1656 internally. Brick with moulded string courses and former central entrance, the probably originally gabled roof hipped in the C18 when the house was extended to the N. Restored 1930 by *Cundy Cooper* for himself, when the covered way was added.

47   GOLEIGH MANOR HOUSE, I m. N. Built by Winchester College in the mid 1460s for a lessee. A hall with gabled jettied cross-wings, all close-studded, the hall reconstructed with the addition of an attic in 1646 and the jetties probably underbuilt at the same time.

6020   PRIVETT

A remote upland village of scattered farms. It had a small chapel in the C13, dependent on West Meon.

HOLY TRINITY (Churches Conservation Trust). By *A. W. Blomfield*, 1876–8, for William Nicholson of Basing Park. It cost £22,000 and the building is indeed large and unusually elaborately detailed in the rather dry and correctly pedantic E.E. of Blomfield's maturity, no longer the bold Butterfieldian Gothic of his youth. Tall exterior in flint cobbles with stone dressings. W tower, with commanding stone broach spire, visible for miles around. Three tiers of lucarnes. The total height is 169 ft (52 metres). The interior seems even more impressively substantial and town-like, faced throughout in Ham Hill and Doulting stone, with bandings of Corsehill stone. Fine four-bay arcades of quatrefoil piers and button mouldings. Chancel arch with Purbeck marble shafts. Sumptuous chancel with short transepts. Magnificent nave roof, with castellated tie-beams, trefoil-braced principals and two tiers of purlins and wind-braces. Contemporary stone FURNISHINGS survive, richly carved by *Farmer & Brindley*, especially the REREDOS, with finely carved scene of the Supper at Emmaus, flanked by wall arcades with angels in mandorlas; the outer arches overlay the inner ones, an odd composition. (LECTERN of 1883 designed by *Blomfield*. Wrought-iron, with brass bookrest and most intricate. Made by *Hart, Son & Peard*, who provided all the other ironwork.) – STAINED GLASS of 1878, in the chancel and the tower window. By *Heaton, Butler & Bayne*, of their best. S transept S. By *Clayton & Bell*. E, of 1913, by *Burlison & Grylls*, coeval with their alabaster monument below to Sir Edward Bradford †1911, Chief Commissioner of the Metropolitan Police. MONUMENT. William Nicholson †1909 and his wife Isabella †1934. Good Neo-Georgian tablet. – LYCHGATE. No doubt of 1878 by *Blomfield*. Perp. Some of the timbers are from HMS *Hecla*, ship of the Arctic explorer

Rear-Admiral Parry. They had been employed in 1835 for columns in the old church.

Blomfield also provided the village SCHOOL (Privett Centre), W of the church, in 1869.

BASING HOUSE, 1 m. NNE. Convincing Neo-Regency of 1968–9 by *Claud Phillimore*, with segmental two-storey bows to the garden and splayed wings on the entrance front. It occupies the site of Basing Park, the fancy early C19 mansion ('considerably improved' by *Sydney Smirke*, *c.* 1830) that was acquired in 1863 by William Nicholson, the distiller. He was an energetic improver and HOME FARM, NW, built in 1865, is the largest exemplar of the many model farms erected on his large estate. E-plan, originally with covered yards between the buildings (barns, granaries, sawmill etc.). Also a symmetrical pair of Neo-Tudor cottages – one has a covered link to a small octagonal dairy with a lantern. The estate style, using knapped flint, is much in evidence throughout Privett.

OLD STATION HOUSE, Sages Lane. One of the sweet Arts and Crafts designs for the Meon Valley Railway by *T. P. Figgis* (1903, closed 1955; now a house). Platform and track preserved; the latter enters a tunnel beneath the Winchester Road.

QUARLEY

2040

ST MICHAEL. The nave is C11, mainly Saxon. The N wall shows herringbone laying of the flint, and the slate-like thin stones arranged ineffectually as voussoirs of the blocked S and N windows (the latter only visible inside) are typically Saxon. The splays are single, not double. The N doorway (blocked) has Saxon proportions. The upper W window is single-splayed but its voussoirs are Norman rather than Saxon. Some early roof beams inside. The church has no bell-turret or bellcote. Since the late C19 restoration (1878 and 1882, when the porch was added) the three bells hung from a wooden frame only a few feet high, standing on the ground N of the church. Two were stolen in 2006; an addition on the N side to include the bells is proposed 2010.

The E window is a completely different story. It is a Venetian window with square Ionic pillars to outside and inside, and it carries an inscription outside, GULIELMUS BENSON & HENRICUS HOARE A.F. A.D. 1723. Do the initials represent *architecti fecerunt*? The inscription repeats inside, with the names reversed. This is very interesting indeed. *William Benson*'s Wilbury House in Wiltshire is only a few miles away. He built it in 1710 and some people call it the first Palladian house in England. It is rather the first of the Inigo Jones–Webb Revival. But never mind; for Henry Hoare Sen., Benson's son-in-law, built Stourhead in 1721–3, and this is indeed among the earliest Palladian buildings in England. His architect was

Colen Campbell. Benson was his own architect. Henry Hoare Sen. acquired the manor of Quarley *c*. 1710. So he or his son clubbed together with Benson to produce this very early specimen of the Venetian window in England.

ALTAR. By *Richard Atkinson-Willes*, 2000, a strikingly original combination of the crown of an old yew tree, with a Purbeck marble *mensa*. – EASTER SEPULCHRE. Low roll-moulded arched recess, probably C14. – CHANCEL RAIL and PULPIT made up with balusters from the late C17 staircase of the earlier Amport House (q.v.). – FONT. Plain C12 tub with possibly C13 base of ring and roll-moulded columns. – STAINED GLASS. E (1899) and W (1898) windows, both possibly by *Gibbs*. – MONUMENTS. C14(?) coffin-lid with floriated cross. Caroline Cox †1793 and Richard Cox †1803, founder of Cox's Bank, paymaster to the army. Both tablets by the same sculptor, with inscriptions above cherubs. Richard Bethel Cox †1832. Grecian tablet signed *Osmond*, Sarum.

LONGMEAD HOUSE, opposite the church. The former rectory, built *c*. 1782–6 for £500, the cost met jointly by the incumbent, the Rev. Dr Sheppard, the banker Richard Cox, and the Hospital of St Katherine by the Tower, who held the advowson. A double-pile brick house of 2–1–2 bays, and two storeys and attic over basement with mullioned windows (reused?). Late C20 doorcase and on the N side a Venetian window (from Clatford Manor, dem. 1966). Stick baluster staircase with columnar newels and ramped handrail.

QUARLEY HILL. The most conspicuous feature on the hill today is the oval bank and ditch of the Iron Age HILL-FORT enclosing some 8 acres. The ramparts are broken by gaps on the N, S, NE and SW, the latter pair marking the original entrances. Excavations conducted on the site suggested that an earlier Iron Age palisaded enclosure stood on the hilltop before the earthwork was constructed. Earlier still are the Bronze Age BOUNDARY DITCHES which run beneath the rampart N and S of the NE entrance.

5050

RAMSDELL

An ecclesiastical parish since 1868. The village, with four roads meeting at a crossroads by the church and school, is clearly imposed on an earlier landscape. Substantial brick villas amid mature pines complete the mid-Victorian picture.

CHRIST CHURCH. 1866–7 by *J. Colson*; the SW steeple on a truncated base by *J. B. Colson*, 1889–90. Small, E.E., of flint with red brick and grey stone dressings. Tiled roofs. Nicely polychrome painted roofs and full set of elemental Gothic pews. – STAINED GLASS. E and W windows, 1867 by *Clayton & Bell*.

SKYERS FARM, ¼ m. SW. A possession of Magdalen College, Oxford. William Waynflete paid £100 for it in 1481; the BARN must have been built soon after. Timber-framed with curved tension braces. Five bays with later(?) gabled porch.

RED RICE HOUSE see FARLEIGH SCHOOL

ROPLEY

6030

St Peter. Flint exterior, restored and enlarged in 1847–8 and 1896–7, the last by *C. T. Miles* of Bournemouth, that in parts almost amounted to rebuilding. But in the timber s tower a re-set plain Early Norman doorway, associated with an aisle-less church held from 1115 by Merton Priory, Surrey. The tower itself (impressive timbers preserved inside) was deftly inserted within the walls of the Norman s transept in the c14 and the angle buttresses added. This is an unusual arrangement but like Stoughton, West Sussex. In the chancel a two-bay arcade to the s chapel of *c.* 1300, octagonal pier, double-chamfered arches dying into the vertical pieces above the abaci, all of chalk. In the chapel, traces of c13 e window and trefoil-headed piscina. Later medieval windows, especially the three-light Perp chancel e window and the late c15 Gothic s doorway, the latter unrestored with nice carved quatrefoils in the spandrels with a rose and a Green Man. Original stoup, unusually close to the e respond. Of 1847–8 the n chancel chapel (with arcade matching the s) and the e bay of the nave aisle. Then, the general restoration of 1896–7: the nave arcade, chancel arch, s porch, and roofs of *c.* 1700–14 replaced. – FONT. Octagonal, Perp; on the underside and the stem some bald decoration, rosettes and plain shields. – FONT COVER. Flat. Looking c18. Bead moulding around the edges. – REREDOS with shallow tester by *B. D. Cancellor*, 1923–4. – STAINED GLASS. Chancel e, 1911 by *Burlison & Grylls*. Nave s, 1930 by *Christopher Webb*. – MONUMENTS. A few minor late c18–early c19 tablets.

Church Street has a pretty row of cottages of the c16 and later, e.g. EXETER HOUSE, *c.* 1700, of plum and red brick with mullioned-and-transomed windows, and another good group in South Street, with the c17 baffle-entry OLD MANOR HOUSE and ROPLEY GROVE, its front apparently early c18 but embellished *c.* 1900 with segmental-pedimented dormers and rubbed brick Gibbs surround to doorway with putto head at apex and fruity carved brick swags.

ROPLEY HOUSE, ¾ m. w. Very fine early c18, of five bays, re-sashed late c18 and pedimented doorcase added. Parapet with urns at corners and shaped gable-ends to parallel roofs. BOUNTY HOUSE, ¼ m. NE at Gilbert Street, is also early c18, also five bays, also with shaped gable-ends. Plum and red brick with boldly moulded string course.

HAYS FIELD, ¾ m. s. 1975 by *Chris Hughes*. Brown brick. Upper
storey cantilevered front and back and slated at steep angle
with corner windows.

HARCOMBE, 1 m. SW in Park Lane. *c.* 1901, in Queen Anne
Revival style. Ionic porch and three large Dutch gables with
ogee-headed windows.

SOAMES PLACE, 1 m. SE in Soames Lane. Highly elaborate
framing, uncommon in the county, with close studding, ogee
braces and lozenges, and much flint-nogging. C16 with floored
hall, the lower end altered in the C17 to create a lobby-entry
plan.

ROTHERFIELD PARK *see* EAST TISTED

ROTHERWICK

Possibly an early medieval planned settlement with farmhouses
and cottages strung out along The Street, running approximately
E–W with wide grass verges.

CHURCH. The exterior is an agreeably mixed composition. The
flint chancel, mostly golden-hued with malmstone quoins,
looks C13 or early C14. E window (restored) of three graduated
lancets, and two cusped arched lancets on S side. Another, re-
set, in the N vestry. The nave, refaced in brick (S) and flint (N),
has much early C16 timberwork: the entire roof and both gables
survive. Contemporary W door, decidedly domestic, re-set
into the early C18 W tower – Flemish bond against the nave's
English bond – of a quite common Thames Valley type: brick
battlements, windows, basket arches. Flint N transept of the
major restoration by *T. H. Wyatt*, 1874–5; he was careful in his
repairing. The nave roof is of almost identical in form to Old
Basing (John Crook). It has remarkably fine, delicate timbers.
Five bays. Arched scissor-braces and two tiers of wind-braces.
The flat chancel arch goes with the timber-framed E wall, and
is original. Is the flint SE stair-turret of pre-early C16 date? –
FONT. Plain stone. Circular, of indeterminate date. –
BENCHES. Some C15. Sturdy, with straight, roll-moulded tops
(repaired by Wyatt). – STAINED GLASS. E window by *Lavers,
Barraud & Westlake*, 1874. Colourful, Angel of the Resurrection and the three Maries. N transept by *Geoffrey Robinson*, of
Joseph Bell & Son, Bristol, 1962. Good, with SS Nicholas and
Christopher. – MONUMENTS. Anthony More †1583. Hanging
tablet with achievement. Ogee gable with delightful painted
mermaid. Ann Tylney †1681. Marble ledger on the chancel
floor. Frederick Tylney of Tylney Hall †1725. Formerly on the
chancel N wall. A coolly classical metropolitan piece. Marble,
of reredos type, with Ionic columns and a pediment. Against
it, pyramid with inscription. Below, a small black sarcophagus,
heavily moulded. In front of the columns two urns. Erected,
as the inscription records, by his widow Anne, daughter of

George Pitt of Stratfield Saye.

VILLAGE HALL. 1932 by *Thomas Greenfield*. Surrey style, very
old-fashioned.

There is much work in and around the village by *R.Weir Schultz*,
1901–5 for Lionel Phillips of Tylney Hall (q.v.), e.g. Nos. 50–52
Wedmans Lane; the alterations to the C16 Old House and possibly also Poplars Farmhouse, 1 m. N, which has three gables
with dentil string course carried over the segmental relieving
arches of the windows, in the manner of Lethaby.

HADLEY DENE, 1 m. ESE on the Reading road. The former Hook
Brick and Tile Works, in production *c.* 1861–1900. Pair of
BOTTLE KILNS with house attached at right angles to the S.

TYLNEY HALL ¾ m. S. Now a hotel. The C18 house rebuilt in
1878 by *Edward Birchall* of Leeds but almost entirely reconstructed in 1899–1902 by *R. S.Wornum* for Lionel Phillips, the
South African gold and diamond millionaire and partner in
Wernher, Beit & Co. Interiors completed and much of the
garden works carried out 1901–5 by *RobertWeir Schultz*. Phillips
overspent himself on this 'gigantic blunder' and returned to
South Africa, *c.* 1918.

Jacobethan style, red brick with some diapering and Bath
stone dressings. Entrance front with far-projecting wings
enclosing forecourt. Porch with big Neo-Jacobean stone frontispiece with enchanting lanterns at the corners, by *Schultz*.
Varied large mullioned-and-transomed windows. The r. wing
has the ballroom with three large canted bay windows *à la*
Bramshill, repeated at its rear, where there is also, to the r., a
two-bay Ionic loggia (another motif from Bramshill), containing a very pretty polygonal stone stair-tower with polygonal
corner shafts, latticework and much flower carving, a miniature piece of Blois or Chambord, added by Schultz to give
access to his gallery inside (*see* below). Larger version of the
loggia on the long garden front, again with full-height canted
bays and shaped gables; to the r. a projecting winter garden
with dome behind a parapet.

Sumptuous and stylistically eclectic interior, with several
imported fittings, ranging from Neo-Jacobean (the Entrance
Hall with Italian Renaissance stone fireplace and woodcarving
by *Rogers*; the Morning Room and former Writing Room) to
Carolean in the Dining Room and Library and Rococo in the
Drawing Room (plaster ceiling by *Jackson & Sons*). But the
GREAT HALL (now Italian Lounge) has a C16 painted wooden
ceiling with octagonal coffers from the Palazzo Grimani,
Venice, and a stone chimneypiece possibly from the same
source, with strong guilloche carving to the boldly projecting
bracketed hood. Also some very fine marquetry panelling. The
climax is the panelled BALLROOM, its low pitched ceiling with
carved wooden ribs and pendants, and panels of good plasterwork by *George Bankart*. Charming gallery combined with a
full-height stone chimneypiece, its fireplace with Ionic
columns and strapwork overmantel, and slightly canted gallery
stage with three shuttered openings. The whole is a complete
Arts and Crafts composition.

Extensive STABLES adjoining to the SE, around two court-yards. The principal one has a gabled archway with paired Tuscan columns, pretty wooden cupolas with tented lead caps and Tuscan stone colonnades inside. At the W corner a colossal WATER TOWER, the top swaggeringly Baroque with leaded pavilion roof rising to a cupola. The GARDENS, pleasure grounds and park are excellent. NW of the house the ITALIAN GARDEN, by *Wornum*, stepping down to lawn with ogee-roofed summerhouses at the outer corners. Upper terrace laid out by Schultz with *Jekyll*. Wornum also designed the DUTCH GARDEN, between the house and the kitchen garden, the fantastic wrought-iron gates by Schultz, with whirling rose tendrils. In one of the walled kitchen gardens, SW of the house, an ORANGERY (reconstruction of Schultz's original) with a hint of Hawksmoor's orangery at Kensington Palace. Attached to the garden wall an ARCH with exaggerated brick and tile voussoirs and alongside a covered seat, octagonal with rustic wooden columns and bell-shaped shingled roof. SE, the WATER GARDEN (partly reworking an C18 canal for the upper pool), *c.* 1906 by Schultz, again with planting by Jekyll, but altered. At the far SW end of the further walled garden Schultz's mighty brick WATER TOWER, with an open-sided timber-framed upper stage, pyramidal cap and polygonal stair-turret on the side.

The best of the lodges is the Neo-Tudor NEWNHAM LODGE by *Wornum*, at the S end of the park, with prominent polygonal corner bay. TYLNEY HOUSE, E of Middle Lodge, is Voysey-esque by *Wornum*. He also designed some model FARM BUILDINGS but with a fine circular DOVECOTE whose details, especially the porch with battered brick piers and segmental arch, suggest *Schultz*.

ST CATHERINE'S HILL
Winchester

HILL-FORT. Established in the Early Iron Age (*c.* 400 B.C.). The fort is a roughly oval area of 23 acres defended by a single rampart and ditch with a slight counterscarp bank, still apparent. One entrance is known at the NE side, where the rampart ends are slightly inturned; excavations suggest that the entrance passage was originally revetted with timbers and had a double wooden gate with recesses behind for the gates to fold into. In a second phase, in the C3–C2 B.C., the gate was narrowed to a single passage. Like many hill-forts in the region St Catherine's hill-fort had probably been abandoned by the time the Romans arrived. Within the hill-fort stood the chapel of St Catherine, investigated in 1925–8. The excavators thought that the chancel was pre-Conquest, but that the rest dated from 1110–25. The chapel was suppressed by Wolsey in 1528–9 and sold to Thomas Wriothesley, who demolished it. Near the top of the hill, the 'miz-maze', a convoluted path (not really a labyrinth as there are no choices to be made), presumably a post-medieval folly—but the ingenious originator is unknown.

ST MARY BOURNE

4050

The centre of a large parish, at the crossing point of the Bourne Rivulet.

ST PETER. Originally a chapel of Hurstbourne Priors, held from the early C12 by Swithun's Cathedral Priory, Winchester. This explains the surprisingly fine interior, with its ambitious late C12 work in the nave. But it will not fall into place. Limestone arcades. The N arcade seems all of a piece from *c.* 1175. Square piers, with angle shafts, decorated trumpet-scallop capitals and capitals with upright leaves to the shafts, pointed arches with one slight chamfer. The piers resemble in form, if not detail, those of the slightly earlier round-arched arcades at Enford, Wiltshire (also held by St Swithun's) and Rainham, Essex, of *c.* 1178,* both influenced from examples in Normandy (e.g. Graville-Ste-Honorine Priory near Le Havre). The s arcade is not in line, and only one of its piers belongs evidently to the N arcade. This pier, second from the W, is in axis, not with the N arcade, but with the W wall of the (later) s chapel, and this wall is excessively thick. It probably represented a Norman s tower, earlier than the rest. If that is so, then that would explain the arch across from the s pier to the former tower (one slight chamfer), and the s pier would represent an otherwise altered arcade, whereas the N arcade was spaced from the start all the way from E to W. When the W tower was built in the early C15 it cut into an arch on the N side, a pier (not a respond) on the s side. The w bays of the s arcade are only a little later than the N arcade, perhaps *c.* 1180, the E bays to the fullness of E.E. (*c.* 1200–25) – cf. the bases and the fillets on the shafts.

The chancel arch, unusually wide and low in its proportions, is round and unmoulded and has small ornament of pellets. It can be compared with the tower arches at Portchester (South Hampshire) of *c.* 1133. Is it indeed so early? Pevsner thought that it had been radically interfered with. But the E bay of the N arcade has a respond different from all the others and also a different arch in that it is narrower and has a roll, and this seems *in situ.* Was the aisle started from the E, then, and the arch moulding changed almost at once? In that case the early chancel arch may well have been where it is now. But where did the enlarging of the earliest building start? By the NE bay, or by the s tower and the s pier? Stylistically one must vote for the former. Actually, if one takes the width of the NE arch and repeats it three times one comes to a position in line with the

---

* Rainham (London Borough of Havering) was built by Richard de Lucy, Grand Justiciary of England and father of Godfrey de Lucy, Bishop of Winchester 1189–1204.

s pier. Four such N bays would correspond to the present three-and-a-half. Several Dec contributions must now be mentioned: first and foremost the chancel of *c.* 1300. Quite dignified, of three bays with buttresses, priest's door, and two-light N and S windows with reticulated tracery. Large five-light E window with mostly original internal mouldings to the springing, but restored tracery of earlier geometrical pattern, obviously of the restoration of 1855 (when the roof was rebuilt). Inside, a good original PISCINA, richly moulded with an elaborately cusped ogee head. Next, the S aisle chapel – a part widening of the late C12 S aisle. Wide four-light E window with original flowing tracery, and inside, a contemporary tomb-recess with a big ogee arch. The plain flint W tower is in its lower half of *c.* 1420 with a typically Perp three-light W window. The battlemented upper stage is Elizabethan with typically late bell-openings. Also late C16, the low-pitched roofs of nave and S chapel. Good, intelligent restoration of 1905 and 1907 by *W. D. Caröe*. Organ chamber 1910 incorporating two C14 windows, by *Nevinson & Newton*.

FONT. *c.* 1150. One of the largest and most splendid of the English Tournai marble fonts. Square of table-top type, very large, acquired perhaps by Henry of Blois *c.* 1150. On the N and W sides low arches on coupled colonnettes. On the S and E sides two trees of life each with bunches of grapes and lilies, symbols of purity. On the top a round band of reeded leaves, and in the corners two leaf motifs and two of affronted birds drinking from a vase – an oriental motif. Around the circular bowl a frieze of leaves. Massive base of black marble, 1927. – COMMUNION RAILS. Early C17 with sturdy balusters. – CHOIR STALLS of 1910 by *Nevinson & Newton*. – LECTERN. Late C17. A fine piece with a gently tapering column supporting the four-sided book-rest (cf. Sherborne St John). – TILES. Some by the font. C14, from the S aisle. – WALL PAINTINGS. A fine black-letter text on the W wall of the S chapel introduced after the 1604 order of James I for 'godly texts from scripture'. Shadows of six others in the nave. – ROYAL ARMS of Charles II. – STAINED GLASS. Mostly by *Burlison & Grylls* (including the E window of 1928) except the poor S chapel E window of 1889 by *Mayer*. – MONUMENTS. In the savagely mutilated recess in the S chapel, a robust early C14 knight, with crossed legs, supposedly Sir Roger des Andeleys of Wyke Manor, who was killed in the crusade against the Albigensians in southern France (1209–17). In the churchyard, a fine set of C18 and early C19 TABLE TOMBS.

p. 29

PRIMITIVE METHODIST CHAPEL, at Swampton, ¼ m. NW. 1859. Beautifully simple, of whitewashed rendered cob and slate. Tiny bullseye window on the front. Small schoolroom alongside.

St Peter is in the best part of the long straggly village. Church Street curves S, picturesquely lined with cottages. Mainly C17 and C18, timber-framed, flint, brick and thatched, but a few more substantial early C19 houses. A little N of the churchyard in The Square is the chequer brick mid-C19 GEORGE INN and, on the s side, FOURWAYS, a good house of *c.* 1700. Bands of brick and knapped flint, five bays, the central doorway with original heavy oak frame and late C19 gabled porch. Lobby-entry plan, remarkable given its date and relatively high status. Many more good cottages in High Street, including two extra-ordinarily long cruck houses (Old Plough and then The Cottage etc.). Also, a row of four almshouses (Holdaway Cottages) of 1862. Gothic, brick and flint with gabled wings. 200 yds further on is the SPRINGHILL and its LODGE, the lodge with scalloped bargeboards and veranda around the polygonal end; the house itself with thin Neo-Tudor details. 100 yds s down a lane, BOURNE HOUSE, also mid-C19, is handsome with Late Georgian and Italianate features.

EGBURY HOUSE. 1¾ m. NE. Dated 1778. Brick. Five widely spaced bays. Doorcase with Doric pilasters and open pediment. NW, WADWICK HOUSE. Early C19, three bays, porch with slender Tuscan columns. Rusticated stone GATEPIERS with ball finials, joined to thatched cob garden wall incorporating small semicircular thatched garden house.

UPPER WYKE, 1½ m. W. A C16 house, remodelled in the early C18. Brick with hipped tile roof. Seven irregularly spaced bays. Of the late C19 the gabled vitrified brick porch and the gables to the four dormers. At the rear an outshot encases a tall C16 brick chimney with moulded plinth and four diagonally set shafts. Much C16 timber framing inside. In the hall a large four-centred arched brick fireplace, and in the principal chamber above a good Tudor-arched stone fireplace with the initials of Robert Oxenbridge, lord of the manor, in the spandrels. C18 staircase with turned balusters.

STOKE HOUSE, 1½ NW. Three bays with Ionic porch. In the main street, its former lodge (now Round House) is octagonal, of brick and thatch, with cast-iron lattice windows. Nearby, in Chapel Lane, THE OLD FARMHOUSE and URANIBORG, a late medieval hall and cross-wing with nice C17 bracketed oriels.

SELBORNE

A very pretty linear village situated below the hanger of Selborne Common, on the malmstone scarp between the chalk and the heaths. It was an important medieval centre developed by the Priors of Selborne.

ST MARY. One of the largest and most interesting churches in this part of Hampshire. By tradition built in 1049 on land given by Edith, queen of Edward the Confessor; she owned the manor. Radfred, a priest, is mentioned in Domesday Book. Quite broad and spreading with much good original C12–C13 detail inside spared during the thorough restorations in 1856, 1877 and 1883 (s aisle) by *William White*, great-nephew of the naturalist. Mostly the external details are his, excepting the w

tower, partly rebuilt and rendered in 1781, and the s aisle w
wall of 1730. The late c12 Norman arcades are of four bays.
Chalk round piers, square abaci, multi-scalloped capitals,
unmoulded pointed arches. It is a Hampshire problem. How
late are the square abaci, how early the pointed arches? The
chancel arch and the e wall and much else (especially the roofs
– excepting the chancel which may be c13 – and the stone wall
surfaces of the s aisle) were heavily but faithfully renewed by
White, although the the e window was originally of two wide-
spaced lancets. The s aisle was widened after the church had
been granted to Selborne Priory in 1234; unrestored tall s
doorway and s door with good ironwork. The n transept of
c. 1305 (restored n window with fine jamb shafts inside) was
the chantry chapel of Sir Adam de Gurdon. The tower arch is
possibly c14 with double-chamfered continuous mouldings. –
FONT. An impressively plain bowl. – COMMUNION RAIL. Rus-
tically Elizabethan, from St Juliot, Cornwall, after Thomas
Hardy's restoration of 1871–2. – ALTAR PAINTING. Outstandingly good Flemish triptych of c. 1520. Presented by Benjamin
White, the naturalist's brother, in 1793. In the centre the Adoration of the Magi, on the wings donors with St Andrew and
St George. The painting has been attributed to *Mostaert*. –
ALTAR, s aisle. 1998 by *Phillip Hussey*, made by *Peter Legg* from
timbers of the ancient yew noted by Pevsner. Deconstructivist
falling guttae below the table top. – READER'S DESK. Panels
from rustic bench-ends. They must be c15 (cf. Empshott). – N
chapel SCREEN. Neo-Georgian by *Caroe & Partners*, 1948. –
TILES. An impressive display in the s aisle floor. c13; most of
them from Selborne Priory, introduced in 1994. – SCULP-
TURE. Small relief of the Descent from the Cross; Flemish,
c. 1520. – STAINED GLASS. Four c16–c17 roundels in the n
transept window. In the s aisle two windows to Gilbert White.
The earlier of 1920 by *H. Hinckes* of *G. Gascoigne & Son*,
Nottingham. Fully in the Kempe tradition. St Francis
with 82 species of birds mentioned by White. The later by
J. Tarrant, 1993, with a large cross and large naturalistic
roundels. – MONUMENTS. Coffin slabs, one with a fine cross
for a Knight Templar. Gilbert White †1728. The naturalist's
grandfather. Cartouche with crisp writing master's inscription.
By *J. Lake*.

sw of the church is the former market place, now a green
(The Plestor), with attractive pitched ironstone paths and the
Tudor Gothic OLD VICARAGE of 1842. s on the High Street
is THE WAKES, home of the naturalist Rev. Gilbert White
(1720–93) but older than his time and much added to after his
death. A long rambling house, the core, containing the
entrance, is a c17 lobby-entry house (refronted) with a late c17
sw cross-wing on the garden side and stair-tower in the angle.
This is hidden on the street front by a taller wing, of brick with
malmstone sides, probably erected in 1794, after White's death,
incorporating a new dining room. At the n end of the house,
projecting into the garden, White added his Great Parlour in
1777, it was originally single-storey but it and the adjacent

library (added 1844), were raised to two storeys in the 1890s – on the garden front double-height square and polygonal bay windows. The final embellishments were the large NW wing, in Old English style, added soon after 1903, and the sensitive extension on the garden side by *Inigo Triggs*, 1910, carefully matching the C17 wing. In the yard to the SE are stables and brewhouse of 1764–5. White and his brothers developed the GARDEN and extended it to embrace the wider landscape, including the famous zigzag path up the hanger of 1752. SUNDIAL and HA-HA of 1761, the latter rebuilt in flint in the C19. Other structures reinstated in replica as part of the 2000 restoration, including an ALCOVE originally of 1762, the WINE PIPE of 1759, a revolving barrel containing a seat, and a *trompe l'œil* STATUE of Hercules of 1754. To the SE the FIELD STUDY CENTRE in a relocated and extended C18 barn opened 2002.

Opposite The Wakes, the C18 OLD BUTCHER'S SHOP, malmstone with barred windows, canopy and, in front, the limes planted by White to screen it from his windows. In the rest of the High Street to the SE, many attractive C17, C18 and C19 cottages, of stone and timber frame, thatch and tile. The same is true of Selborne Road to the N.

PRIORY. By Priory Farm, 1¼ m. ENE. An Augustinian house founded in 1233 by Bishop des Roches of Winchester and closed by Bishop Waynflete in 1486. There is nothing visible above ground but excavations in 1967–8 found the shape of the church, with aisleless nave, crossing, transepts and straight-ended chancel. The total length was 205 ft (62.5 metres). The church was of almost the same dimensions as that of the founder's other monastery, Titchfield Abbey (South Hampshire). Can both have been designed by the same master mason, either *Stephen le Mazun* or *Richard Cementarius* who worked for the Bishop elsewhere? There were chapels or other accessories on the E and W sides of the S transept. The cloister lay N of the nave. Among the individual finds (now in The Wakes museum) were vaulting-ribs and a boss belonging to the choir, and a pier with four detached shafts belonging to a screen 23 ft (7 metres) W of the E wall. PRIORY FARMHOUSE is early C18. Malmstone and brick, five bays with segmental-arched windows.

SELBORNE BRICKWORKS, 1¼ m. E. Late C19, with Hoffman kiln and chimney.

SHALDEN

A small village, sparsely developed, the lane bounded by flint walls for much of its length.

ST PETER AND ST PAUL. 1864–5 by *J. Colson*, largely paid for by John Wood, Bradford industrialist, of Thedden Grange (Beech). Flint. Nave and lower chancel. Open bell-turret. Lancets and plate tracery. The chancel arch with Colson's favourite naturalistic stiff-leaf capitals. FONT. Octagonal, Perp, with quatrefoils. From the Norman predecessor church. – LECTERN and PULPIT of 1915 by *Horace Field*. – REREDOS of 1871. – STAINED GLASS. All (except the E window) by *Hardman*, 1870s. The best with lively colours.

MANOR FARMHOUSE. A C16 timber-framed hall range with smoke-bay and C17 flint cross-wing with large lateral brick stack. Much tile-hanging. Interior with four-centred brick-arched hall fireplace, probably *ex situ* plank-and-muntin screen and reworked C18 staircase. Substantial additions by *Richard Ashby Architects* of 1991, in an Arts and Crafts style.

SHEET

The triangular green is the centre with houses nicely grouped on all sides.

ST MARY MAGDALEN. 1867–9 by *A. W. Blomfield*. Rock-faced sandstone, 1300 style, SE steeple completed at the expense of Bishop Wilberforce of Winchester, no aisles. N vestry by *Thomas Ford*. Adventurous detailing inside, especially in the E window with elaborate trefoil rere-arch and chancel arch with finely carved naturalistic lilies and passionflowers. Bold arch-braced roofs. – REREDOS and tile dado, of 1907 by *Powells*. – CHOIR STALLS, LECTERN and PULPIT by *Comper*, 1925 and 1927. His chancel screen has been removed. – STAINED GLASS. E window and two nave windows by *Powells*, 1893 and 1895.

VILLAGE HALL, facing the green. 1897 by *Paxton Watson*. Lutyens-esque with tile-hung front and canted bays under gables.

OLD SHEET HOUSE, 200 yds E of the green on London Road. The gatepiers proclaim it was 'built *c.* 1670' but the symmetrical brick front of two storeys above a basement is C18. Three bays with a raised centre under a small pediment with Diocletian window, flanked by pilasters supporting urns. C19 hoodmoulds.

ADHURST ST MARY, ⅜ m. NE in parkland. Large stone mansion of 1857–9 by *P. C. Hardwick* for J. Bonham-Carter. Gabled, with mullioned-and-transomed windows, essentially Tudor but with Gothic enrichments and some French Renaissance touches, e.g. the mansarded tower on the S front set at an angle. Plate-glass sash windows throughout, no doubt original from the start and an early use. W extension by *Horace Farquharson*, 1902–3 in matching style. A carriage arch connects the house with the former stables and coachhouse. Lodge and gates, dated 1861.

In Reservoir Lane, ⅝ m. SW, are a few Arts and Crafts houses by *Gerald Unsworth*: REDLYNCH of 1912 in Early Georgian style with three little gables and a Venetian window, and the less appealing Anglo-Dutch DOWNS HOUSE (now care home) of *c.* 1925. At the far end of the lane, THE PLATTS by *Unsworth, Son & Triggs*, 1907–8, constructed of neatly coursed Bargate stone, with lots of early Lutyens-style details. Gabled cross-wings on the garden front and close-studded jetty, with tall brick stacks and some tile-hanging. (Well stair with square newels ascending the full height and turned balusters, all by 'a craftsman of Ernest Gimson's office' according to Lawrence Weaver.) The formal gardens on s side were, of course, laid out by Triggs.

SHERBORNE ST JOHN   *6050*

ST ANDREW. Early Norman nave, *c.* 1150 (see the plain s doorway), and C13 chancel in one and a low w tower, the lower stage of which has late C14 angle buttresses. Belfry stage of 1834, paid for by Elizabeth Chute. Typical of that date with its windows and pinnacles, formerly in a more elaborate Perp, and with an uncommon copper spire. N aisle of 1854, but with three re-set C15 two-light square-headed windows. In the chancel s side, one Dec window with reticulation, probably the former E window, replaced by the present Early Perp E window. This might have been done *c.* 1395 in memory of Sir Bernard Brocas (its stained glass, recorded *c.* 1830 by T. D. Powell, included the achievements of Queen Anne of Bohemia (†1394) to whom Sir Bernard was Chamberlain). Brocas also left £700 for the Perp N chapel, built *c.* 1420–3 (much altered with Late Georgian brick). Its E window is Early Tudor with the initials of Ralph Pexall (*see* below) who inherited the Brocas estate. But the most interesting part of the church is the s porch of brick, dated by an inscription 1533. The entrance has a four-centred head, and in the spandrels is already Early Renaissance decoration. Over the s doorway inside one can see the donors of the porch kneeling, husband and wife. It was an unpedantic or perhaps simply unbookish age in which the donor could appear inside the porch as Iamys Spier and outside as Iames Spyre.

Interior much restored in 1854 and 1866–84 by *J. P. St Aubyn*; he raised the chancel floor, re-pewed the nave, and opened the arch between N aisle and the Brocas Chapel. Late C14 w tower doorway of continuous mouldings. Sturdy nave roof of the C15 with panelled ceilure over the rood beam. – FONT. Purbeck marble, of the table type, but with tapering sides. The sides carry the usual blank arcading, but the arches are not as flat as usual. – FONT COVER. Octagonal spire with a finial (possibly iron). Early C17. – COMMUNION RAILS. Late C17 with boldy twisted balusters. – REREDOS of 1886 by *Powells*. A Last Supper scene. Mosaic and tile. – PULPIT. 'Mad by *Henri Sly* 1634', coeval with a triple-arched wooden chancel screen lost in 1854. Characteristic familiar short blank arches, but this time diamond-studded. Back panel and tester. –

Sherborne St John, St Andrew.
Brass to Bernard Brocas †1488

LECTERN. Late C17, given by William Jackman, vicar 1652–89, with a three-sided reading surface for chained books – three volumes of Foxe's *Book of Martyrs*. – TILES. Medieval, in the N chapel. – SCULPTURE. In the N chapel bits from some Early Renaissance frieze with flowers and leaves. – STAINED GLASS. In the Brocas Chapel, E window, some early C16 and other later glass, nicely arranged for Mrs Brocas (cf. Bramley) *c.* 1804. One panel of St Lawrence dated 1638. The three panels of early C16 glass are Netherlandish, in an exuberant Early Renaissance style.

MONUMENTS. The principal monument is that to Ralph Pexall †*c.* 1535 and his wife Edith †1516, daughter of William Brocas of Beaurepaire. It is attributed to *Thomas Bertie*. Large opening between chancel and chapel, essentially Early Tudor Gothic but with Renaissance detail (cf. Thruxton, but less refined). Two recumbent stone effigies – his in armour, hers with a kennel headdress. Both are holding their hearts. The arch is baldly panelled, but there are dainty details above. The large tomb-chest also has some minimum Renaissance decoration including motifs seen also at East Tisted and Thruxton. The lettering no longer in black letter. Contemporary colouring, especially the heraldry (Keyser). HELM in the chapel. Many BRASSES also in the chapel, including the earliest in the county. – Raulin Brocas and Margaret, his wife, demi-figures at prayer, 7 in. (18 cm.) long. The inscription still in Norman French, *c.* 1360. – Bernard Brocas †1488. Kneeling figure of 20 in. (51 cm.) length in a tabard originally beside a cross replete with Evangelists' emblems. Below he is seen as a skeleton in a shroud. Inscription frame round the whole. – John Brocas †1492, kneeling, a 12½-in. (32-cm.) figure. Above, a shield and a panel of the Trinity. – William Brocas, †1540. – Richard Atkins †1635. Good hanging tablet. Alabaster pedestal bust (quite advanced for a commoner) in an oval recess of black slate. The top pediment is segmental, without a base but curled up at the ends. Two reclining putti on it. Finely detailed frame with exquisite foliage and hanging lamps. At the sides not pilasters but guilloche bands without bases or capitals. It is so similar in its details to Le Sueurs's monument to Sir Thomas Richardson (†1635) at Westminster Abbey that it has been attributed to *John Colt*, or his workshop. – George Beverly, dated 1678. Grey and white marble. A very restrained classical tablet. Garland at the foot. – William Chute †1824, and wife Elizabeth †1842. Two tablets by *Humphrey Hopper*. His still Grecian with a draped stele. Hers fully Gothic. No figures.

N, MANOR FARMHOUSE, *c.* 1830 Tudor, with railed forecourt. S, THE HAYE, C16, was evidently of high status. Three bays, formerly jettied on the N side (underbuilt 1836) and close-studded (rendered over) in the E gable but altered and extended *c.* 1900. Of that date the attractive glazed entrance corridor, with entrance set an angle facing a yew-hedged forecourt. Inside, a good mixture of both dates. E, in Vyne Road,

EDERNISH HOUSE is mid-to-late C18 in brick and tile. Originally of three bays but with its doorway placed off-centre, no doubt when its r. wing was added in the early C19 (the wing's upper floor is later). Behind the entrance a commodious entrance hall of that date. C18 staircase with column-on-vase balusters.

THE OLD RECTORY, ¼ m. WNW of St Andrew. Late C16 timber-framed hearth-passage house but its upper end has been demolished and the lower end substantially rebuilt c. 1700, of two bays with plinth, platband and higher eaves; the centre, also rebuilt in the C18, is simpler. Two fine rooms have raised and fielded panelling, bolection-moulded architraves etc.

SHERFIELD-ON-LODDON

ST LEONARD. Cruelly over-restored in 1865–76 by *W. Woodman* of Reading and the outsized s porch-tower with shingled broach spire added 1871–2 by *J. W. Hugall*. Medieval N doorway and some original windows, e.g. C14 E window. Disappointing interior. – ARCHITECTURAL FRAGMENTS. Early C16 spandrels with shields of the Puttenhams of Sherfield Court, and part of a figure. – STAINED GLASS. Nave SE, three early C16 achievements of the Puttenhams of Sherfield Court. Nave rose window, early C16 St George and Dragon panel. Several windows by *Clayton & Bell*, e.g. E window and a small chancel window (both 1866). Chancel SW by *Kempe & Co.*, 1918. Vestry, by *Burlison & Grylls* of c. 1870 in their best early manner. – BRASSES. Mary Palmes and children †1595 and Stephen Hadwall †1600.

BAPTIST CHAPEL, Breach Lane. 1923 by *Harry Hutt* of Reading.

SHERFIELD COURT, NE of the church, beside a moat. c. 1700 with a spacious seven-bay front. The middle window Venetian. High panelled parapet. Neo-Georgian porch and wings of c. 1922 by *Wellesley & Wills* (for Wellesley); the wings subsequently heightened and given bow fronts. The cottagey rear range also transformed with a loggia, courtyard and wings terminating in polygonal thatched pavilions. Interior of both phases, also with some imported C17 fabric. Bolection-moulded panelling in the dining room, the panels over the fireplace carved with laurel leaves, the central one with a painting of Neptune(?). The 1920s interiors are impressive, see the Panelled Room (S wing), with deeply coved plaster ceiling, and the Octagon Room (SW pavilion), with painted cupola and Baroque stone fireplace.

The main village is ¼ m. N. OLD SCHOOL HOUSE of 1737–8, founded and endowed by James Christmas (†1735). Lobby-entry plan with rear outshot, brick with hipped roof and casements. By the village pond, WHEELERS COURT, cottages by *Wade & Frankiss*, for the male servants of Sherfield Manor

(Sherfield School, *see* below). BREACH FARM, E of the A33,   48
has an impressive cruck BARN of *c.* 1391. Five bays, with arched
braces, the N end truss an C18 box-framed replacement.

LONGBRIDGE MILL, ¼ m. NE of the village by the Loddon. C16
cross-wing with curved braces to a mansarded C18 weatherboarded and brick main range. Late C19 undershot wheel.
Plain early C18 mill house. Restored after a fire and converted
into a restaurant, in 1997. Single-storey link with an octagonal
tower aping the form of a dovecote.

SHERFIELD SCHOOL (formerly Sherfield Manor), ⅝ m. ENE of
St Leonard. 1860s, thoroughly overhauled in 1898–9 by *Wade
& Frankiss* for James Taylor, South African mining financier
and friend of Sir Lionel Phillips of Tylney Hall (Rotherwick).
The contractors were *George Trollope & Sons*. In the typical
stripey Tudor-cum-Baroque of that time. Rich, eclectic
interior, at its best in the Staircase, a fine piece with conventional pierced strapwork balustrade but newels with curious
volute finials. Arts and Crafts naturalistic carving of flowers,
leaves etc. Also the hall with its bold stone chimneypiece, with
paired Corinthian columns and exaggerated carved voussoir.
Other rooms are in C18 taste; in the enclosed loggia, lovely
interwar Chinoiserie paintings. Gothic former STABLES, 1860s,
the courtyard glazed over for the school's art studio. CHAPEL/
ASSEMBLY HALL of 1963–4, by *Playne & Lacey*. Stained glass
by *Hugh Powell*.

In the WALLED GARDEN, an impressive timber- and iron-
framed PALM HOUSE by *Messenger & Co.* of Loughborough,
1898–9 (now a house).

SHERFIELD HALL, ½ m. SW of St Leonard. A rambling multi-
phase house. Core of 1775, brick with parapet and later stucco
dressings, three storeys and five bays. Later C18 additions and
attractive Queen Anne Revival style service wing terminating
in a gabled tower. Late C19 brick porch. Late C19 arcaded
entrance hall with a screen of barley-sugar balusters to the hall,
and library with Corinthian pilastered bookcases. Pretty flint-
rusticated late C18 summerhouse in the gardens.

BULLSDOWN HILLFORT, ½ m. W towards Bramley Green. This
is a small univallate earthwork of oval plan enclosing an area
of 10 acres. At no point do the ramparts stand more than 3 ft
high, and the silted-up ditch has a maximum depth of 5 ft.

SHIPTON BELLINGER   2040

A one-street village with a winter bourne flowing along the NE
side. Much late C19 and later infill.

ST PETER. Almost entirely rebuilt by *R. J. Withers* in 1877–9 but
still with some good C13 and early C14 details: S doorway with
continuous rolls and a hollow, and tracery in the nave NE
and SE windows; also priest's doorway and the two S lancets in

the chancel. Bold restored stone SCREEN between nave and chancel, apparently based on the existence of the arch springers against the imposts. Good nave roof, strictly based on the C14 original. – FONT. Outsize showy High Victorian E.E. By *Withers*, in top gear. – STAINED GLASS. E and W windows of 1878 by *Daniel Bell*. The latter especially good. Scenes in the life of St Peter. Nave SE by *A. L. Moore*, 1906, to W. H. Alexander †1905, the first financier of the National Portrait Gallery (*see* Snoddington Manor). Female Virtues of Faith and Hope.

Prominent next to the church is MANOR FARMHOUSE; probably early C19, with later C19 full-height canted bays and porch.

SNODDINGTON MANOR, ½ m. SE. *c.* 1885 for W. H. Alexander, with a much more interesting and dominating addition of 1907 by *T. P. Figgis*, for H. C. Formby, mostly in a free Arts and Crafts Georgian.

6060

SILCHESTER

The church and manor house lie just within the site of the Roman town, a little below its vanished E gate, and about 1 m. E of the main village by Silchester Common.

The Roman town of CALLEVA ATREBATUM originated as an *oppidum* of the Atrebates in the late C1 B.C. when a massive earthwork of polygonal plan was constructed enclosing 255 acres. Parts of the circuit can still be seen particularly to the SW in Rampier Copse where the bank rises 16 ft (5 metres) above the top of the silted-up ditch. Some time later, probably in the early C1 A.D., a new, smaller polygonal enclosure of 80 acres was built within the earlier system and a settlement of regular plan was laid out. The Roman town, which developed immediately after the invasion of A.D. 43, grew from this early beginning. By the late C2 the built-up area was enclosed with an earthen bank fronted by a ditch with the four gates built in stone. Later, probably in the late C3, the bank was fronted with a wall of flint rubble bonded at intervals with courses of horizontal limestone slabs. It still survives in places to a height of 10–15 ft (3–4.5 metres) and is the most impressive Roman town wall in Britain. It can be followed throughout its length.

The city within the defences was extensively excavated in a series of large-scale excavations beginning in 1864 and lasting until 1909, which has allowed a plan of the masonry buildings of the city and its grid of roads to be prepared. A new programme of work began in 1974 and is still in progress.

In the centre lay the Forum and Basilica, measuring 313 ft by 275 ft (96 by 85 metres). The Forum court was surrounded on the N, E and S sides by a continuous row of shops and offices, flanked inside and out by porticos of Bath stone Tuscan

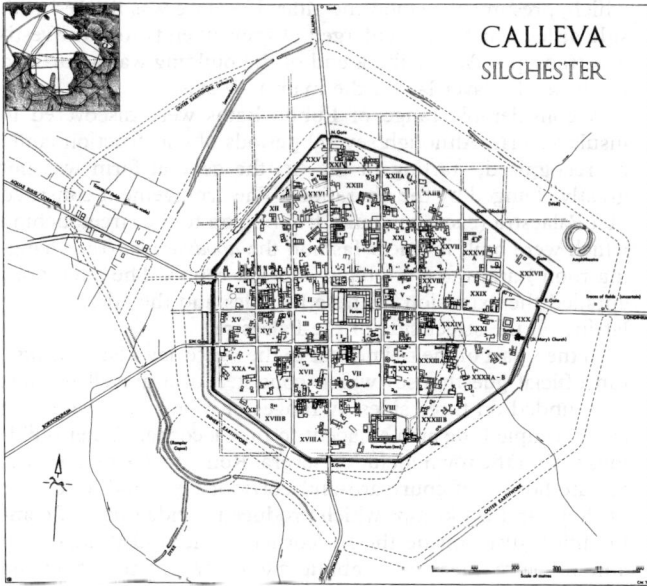

Silchester, Calleva Atrebatum.
Plan

columns; the main entrance was in the centre of the E side. Across the w side of the Forum court lay the Basilica – an aisled hall 234 ft (72 metres) long and 58 ft (18 metres) wide with tribunals at each end; it had been partly rebuilt and slightly modified during the latter part of the Roman period. The columns of the main order were Corinthian, standing about 27 ft (8 metres) high. The w side of the Basilica hall was flanked with a range of offices with an apsidal-ended curia in the centre. Fragments of marble from Purbeck and Italy were found in rubble layers within the Basilica, indicating a fine finish. The more recent programme of excavations showed that a masonry-built structure comprising a Forum and Basilica was constructed in the mid C2 to replace a timber building of much the same plan dating to about A.D. 85. This had been preceded by an earlier timber public building originally constructed c. A.D. 50. The sequence, so far unparalleled, is of great interest to the study of Roman Britain. Another notable discovery was that the great masonry Basilica served its public function as a place of assembly for a comparatively brief period before being taken over by metalworkers, using it as a workshop, in the mid C3.

SE of the Forum was a small Christian church, recently re-excavated and dated to the mid C4. It consists of a central nave about 10 ft (3 metres) wide and 30 ft (9 metres) long with an apse at the w end containing a small geometric mosaic on which, presumably, stood the altar. The nave was flanked with side aisles which were enlarged at their W ends to form vestigial transepts. Across the E end of the building was a narthex; the base of a laver lay on the main E–W axis.

A considerable range of Public Baths were discovered in insula XXXIII. Although several periods of construction could be recognized, starting in the CI, the general form was not greatly changed by the alterations. The arrangement consisted of a Palaestra (exercise court) fronting on to the street, behind which were built in linear fashion the *apodyterium* (the changing room) and the cold, tepid and hot rooms. The alterations entailed the extension of these facilities and the addition of a latrine on the street side of the Palaestra.

In the s part of the town, near to the s gate, lay a large *Mansio* (an official guesthouse) which consisted of a gravelled court surrounded on three sides by ranges of rooms; a private bath suite occupied the area adjacent to the SE corner. Other buildings within the town included several Romano–Celtic temples, private houses of courtyard-and-corridor type, and a number of shops and workshops which produced a wide range of commodities. Just outside the NE corner of the walled area is an amphitheatre measuring about 250 ft by 220 ft (77 by 68 metres) overall. Excavation has shown that the amphitheatre was first constructed in the period A.D. 50–70. The arena, elliptical in plan, was at this time enclosed by a timber revetment fronting a surrounding bank which supported the timber terracing for the spectators. In the C3 the amphitheatre was refurbished in masonry. The structure could have accommodated between 5,000 and 9,000 spectators. For the visitor today there is a small site museum ⅓ m. W. The Iron Age defences, the impressive girdle of Roman walls and the earthworks of the amphitheatre are well worth exploring. Of the city itself all is tranquil beneath its fields – apart from the annual archaeological excavations. The fine collection of finds from the excavations is housed in Reading Museum.

ST MARY. A length of ragged C3 Roman wall forms the E boundary of the churchyard. The church, now lightly rendered rubble with brick patchings, is agreeably unrestored. Short nave, aisles and chancel, and the usual shingled bell-turret. The story is one of accretive growth from an aisleless, possibly apsidal C12 fabric represented by the nave. The N arcade of two bays was added *c.* 1200. It has a round pier with a square chamfered abacus, trumpet-scallop capitals, and pointed arches with a slight chamfer that one would call 1210 at the latest. But the N aisle has not only a W lancet but a N doorway, unrestored, with a hoodmould decorated with dogtooth, which indicates a date of *c.* 1230, a date which would fit the s arcade better than the N arcade. The capitals here are moulded, and the arches have a proper chamfer. Again of the early C13 must be the chancel, see its lancet windows and priest's doorway – unusually on the N side (cf. Dummer). The s aisle with a s doorway of *c.* 1230 was much rebuilt about 1325–50 with windows with reticulated tracery (good coeval corbel heads inside including those of a man and a woman) and an ogee-headed tomb-recess with uncommonly big, rather crude cusps. Contemporary nave w window, externally renewed. The large E window is Late Perp, possibly after 1500, renewed in 1998, replacing lancets, their outer splays partly revealed internally. There is no chancel arch. The bell-turret is supported by four late C15 arch-braced timber posts. Careful restoration by *T. H. Wyatt* assisted by *Walter Spiers*, 1872 (chancel) and 1878 (nave and aisles), when the roofs were renewed. The nave roof, by *Abraham Ham*, retains late C15 wind-braces. – FONT. Octagonal, C14 probably, with a short moulded stem. – FONT CANOPY. A hanging corona in wrought iron by *Giuseppe Lund*, 1985. Adventurously Gothic but a little intricate. – PULPIT. A delightful and rare C17 piece, with panels looking mid-C17, and a fine domed canopy surmounted by a dove, dated 1639, the gift of James Hore. – SCREEN. Perp of *c.* 1508–33 (pomegranate emblem of Katharine of Aragon), of one-light divisions, with richly traceried heads, and a charming pierced top frieze of angels with spread wings. – SCULPTURE. A painted Christ, *c.* 2000 by *Peter Eugene Ball.* – WALL PAINTINGS, extensive, a once complete scheme, in the chancel, probably *c.* 1230, masonry patterns with the achievement of the Bluetts, lords of the manor. Restored in 1972 and 1998. – STAINED GLASS. E window, 1873 by *Clayton & Bell*, and typical of them at that date. Chancel N and S lancets by *Horwood* of Frome, 1878. The four Evangelists. – SW Lancet, 1922 by *Stuart Newnham-Davis*. – W window, with decorative quarries, *c.* 1878. – N aisle E. Original late C14 grisaille quarries with exquisitely small-scale foliate pattern borders in the tracery and towered canopies in the heads. – N aisle W lancet. By *Jon Callan*, 2005. Related mural inscription by *Gary Breeze*. Deep, densely glowing, with a shaft of light between dusky blues and mauves.

MONUMENTS. Outside by the S aisle of the church two excellent, possibly C13, COFFIN-LIDS. One has the busts of husband and wife (perhaps Bluetts) but below the busts just the lid with a foliated cross; the other has a man's head in a quatrefoil, and also a cross below. Now very weathered, can they have come from the chancel? Inside, in the tomb-recess, a beautiful effigy of a Lady, possibly Eleanor Barnard, one of two daughters of Sir John Bluett (†1316). She lies, flattened as if drowned, an essentially early C14 figure, very slender, with two angels by her pillow, a pet dog at her feet. Scant traces of original ground colour. More traces of a wall painting at the back of the tomb-recess were extant in 1845, showing the Lady at prayer, ascending heavenwards, carried by angels (G. C. Boon). – James Butler, 5th Viscount Ikerrin †1712, aged fourteen. By *James Hardy*. Cartouche with drapery and two putto heads, fine metropolitan standard. Erected by his grandfather, Viscount Blessington, lord of the manor. – John Paris, †1743, rector 1726–43, with a winged skull at the foot, and an open book atop.

32

THE OLD MANOR HOUSE, NE of the church, has a mid-C16
three-bay hall range with a curious plan: its ground floor was
apparently originally completely open and the principal first-
floor chamber, with an arch-braced collar-truss, occupies only
the centre bay. Both rooms are heated by a single external side
chimneystack. C17 cross-wing with a staircase with splat-
balusters, and at the junction of the two ranges a brick chimney
with arched panels, dated 1682. Good farmstead group
with C17–C19 buildings, including a C17 five-bay single-aisled

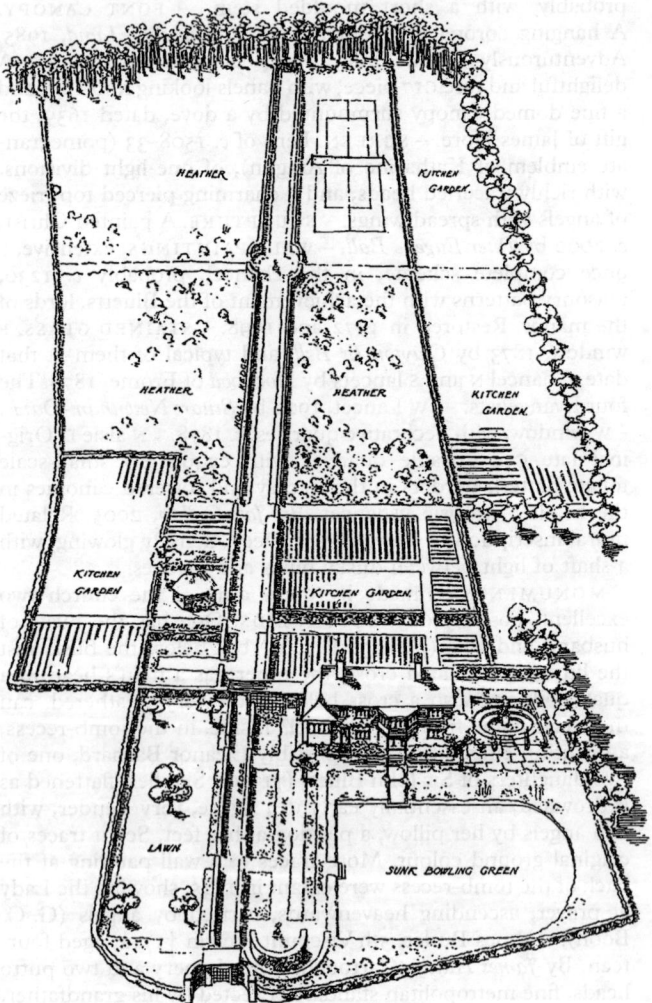

Silchester, Macartneys, bird's eye view.
Drawing, 1911

barn, a large staddle granary and five-bay cartshed. NE again, MANOR FARMHOUSE, 1865. Minimally Gothic. THE MOUNT, further NE, beyond the Roman amphitheatre (*see* above) is a cruck hall house of *c.* 1405.

METHODIST CHURCH, Pamber Road. 1926–7, by *H. K. Armitage*. Late Arts and Crafts Gothic. To the rear the former Primitive Methodist chapel of 1839 (church hall).

The centre of the village is the junction of Pamber Road and Little London Road at the edge of the common. Among the local vernacular some larger houses of distinction.

THE OLD HOUSE, *c.* 1700. Brick with hipped roof, five by five bays, except for the asymmetrical front of *c.* 1900 with canted bay and porch. Additions of *c.* 2008. 1 m. SW of this in Holly Lane, SILCHESTER HOUSE, *c.* 1840, Neo-Tudor and big, following alterations and extension *c.* 1913. This was done by *Norman Evill*, Lutyens's former assistant, who also designed ROMANS HOTEL (formerly New Timber), ⅛ m. W off Little London Road, in his master's Surrey style. Formally less assured but beautifully detailed, especially the massive chimneys of inventive form, the brick-vaulted porch and on the garden front the tile roof sweeping over a colonnaded loggia. Inside, surprisingly, Neo-Georgian but good. His also is THE GRANGE, ⅛ m. NNE off Kings Road, *c.* 1909, with a cranked plan and tile-hung front with row of gables stepping back, one in the centre one with an Ipswich window. On the garden side, with its pair of gabled wings, the close-studded framing is jettied out over square bays. ¼ m. W, close to the junction with Pamber Road, is MACARTNEYS, an idiosyncratic house of 1895 by *Mervyn Macartney*, designed as his holiday cottage. It incorporated an existing building. Enchantingly simple, in brick, tarred weatherboard and tile with a central polygonal bay window on posts. Prominent single-storey gabled addition to the l. for a drawing room, slightly later and raised up to view the excellent GARDEN. This has Macartney's typical synthesis of formality and informality, including a straight path through yew hedges, which led into the woodland beyond, a bowling green in front and sunken Italian garden to the E. LYCHGATE entrance, almost Chinese, with square brick piers, curved wing walls and mortarboard canopy.

SMANNELL

3040

CHRIST CHURCH. By *William White*, 1856–8. A small, quite original High Victorian church of many oddities. Flint, banded with brick lacings. Nave and apse in one; N aisle added by *White*, 1894. Brick S porch, but timber-framed roof with wood and metal inventively combined in the trusses. The W wall, with sturdy brick angle buttresses, carries the muscular bellcote which is in two stages, the lower one cross-gabled. The upper is all brick and not really a bellcote but a bell-turret squashed longitudinally so as to be broader than deep. Elsewhere the tracery is of the plate type but not archaeologically correct. The inside is brick-faced (yellow over a red dado, with red brick arcade and lacings). Very low piers, square and chamfered. Absurdly tall impost blocks in which the chamfer fades out so that their top is square. Unmoulded pointed arches. – STAINED GLASS. In the apse of 1887 by *P. H. Newman*. – W window by *A. L. Moore*, 1915. – N aisle N, 1979 by *J. N. Lawson* of *Goddard & Gibbs*. – NE millennium window by *Lilian Shaw*. A lively swirling design.

PRIMARY SCHOOL, N of the church, probably by *White*. Gothic. Before the church and school were erected the hamlet consisted of a few cottages and WOODHOUSE FARMHOUSE, S of the church, of 1746.

FINKLEY HOUSE, ½ m. SE. Neo-Jacobean, *c.* 1860, with Dutch gables. Contemporary stables with crow-stepped gable, and later C19 lodges.

SOUTH TIDWORTH

South Tidworth is two things: mansion and estate church, and the Edwardian part of Tidworth Camp, which was laid out after the War Department acquired the estate in 1897.* Outside the barracks to the E, a settlement grew up around the station. The camp was extended post-war into North Tidworth (Wiltshire) but much of the housing has been rebuilt, the first phase by *Shepheard Epstein* in 2000–5. The layout and traditional designs were directly influenced by Poundbury, Dorset.

ST MARY (Churches Conservation Trust). By the Salisbury Road. Built at the expense (£12,000) of Sir John Kelk of Ted-worth House. In the most elaborate and highly finished E.E. style, designed 1873–4 by *John Johnson* (†1879) but undertaken in 1879–80 by *G. H. Gordon*. Externally the church does not appear very large, but it packs a powerful punch. It is the interior that is sensational, in scale as in everything else. Externally it is rather a crotchety church, but the interior has absolutely nothing of that. It is the bell-tower that is so perverse and wilful, of a High Victorian fecundity of invention *a la* Burges. Round and thin with a round, extremely elongated spire. And this thin round beacon stands on a mighty, far-projecting mid-buttress. Otherwise the church is of small rock-faced Bargate stone and has lancets and plate tracery and quite some dog-tooth. The S transept is balanced on the N side by the vestry with two very high chimneys, one on the W, the other on the

* South Tidworth was united with North Tidworth in 1992 as a single parish in Wiltshire.

E wall. The impressive S porch prepares for the interior, with its size and its many-columned entrance, modelled on that of the C13 porch of Skelton (Yorkshire West Riding, North), with much stiff-leaf, and the blank arcading l. and r. with yet more stiff-leaf. The interior of finely dressed ashlar consists of a strikingly high, short, sumptuous nave of three bays and a yet more sumptuous chancel. The nave has tall quatrefoil piers of grey, veined marble, stiff-leaf capitals, and upper shafts with stiff-leaf to support the principals of the steeply pointed roof. The aisle bays are marked off one from the other by steep rising half-arches. The chancel arch goes all out with stiff-leaf and dogtooth, and the chancel is marble-shafted with more dogtooth. To the organ chamber and the S chapel are large three-light screens like very large windows. Their tracery is geometrical, but with just one touch of Dec. Surely a church like this is as valid a monument of architecture as any of the Middle Ages or the C17 or C18?

Much elaborate carving throughout by *Farmer & Brindley*, especially opulent furnishings. In the chancel, sanctuary floor of Italian mosaic, and pavement, again of mosaic, by *Bourke & Co.* – Triple-canopied REREDOS with dramatic superb high relief of the journey to Calvary, excellently carved with real feeling by *Farmer & Brindley*, and among the finest C19 ecclesiastical sculpture in England. – Low CHOIR STALLS and higher PRIEST'S STALLS. Over all the wonderfully painted chancel roof, with vesica panels above the altar area, and repeated patterns in quatrefoils elsewhere. By *Heaton, Butler & Bayne*. Robust round PULPIT of stone, richly carved, with short colonnettes of Breche-Violette and a naturalistic stone book-rest. – FONT with flat FONT COVER enriched with iron and scrollwork. The font stands forward of a canopied trefoil-arched niche in the W wall from which bells – 'a carillon of gongs' – are rung. – CANDLE STANDARDS, a set in the nave. Of brass, by *Hart & Peard*. – STAINED GLASS throughout. In the chancel, E window by *Heaton, Butler & Bayne*. Large Nativity, Crucifixion and Emmaus scenes. In the aisles, much by *Clayton & Bell*. More successful the W windows. Affective geometric grisaille by *Heaton, Butler & Bayne*, given by the Rev. Henry Radcliffe, rector (inscription).

MORTUARY CHAPEL, Church Lane, ⅜ m. ENE. Built in 1784 with materials from the demolished medieval church. Early C14 E window, very weathered. Low W porch and miniature gabled stone bellcote. (Simple oval tablet to Lieut. Thomas Assheton Smith †1806; he fought on *HMS Temeraire* at Trafalgar.)

TEDWORTH HOUSE (Officers' Mess). ¼ m. SW of St Mary. Built c. 1829–32 for *Thomas Assheton Smith III*, 'after his own plans' according to Prosser but its similarity to Spetchley Park, Worcerstershire (*John Tasker*, 1811), is striking. Remodelled 1878–80 to *John Johnson*'s design for the contractor Sir John Kelk (Johnson remodelled Kelk's former house, Bentley Priory, Harrow, and was architect for several of his projects, notably Alexandra Palace, London). The form of the early C19 house – two storeys, E side of seven bays and longer S side of nine bays, with projecting two-bay wings at each end – is preserved but faced in Portland stone and made very Baroque with typically florid mid-Victorian detailing and lots of rustication. S front with an attached tetrastyle portico of freely detailed Ionic columns, between this and the wings short Tuscan colonnades with blocked *in antis* columns. Single-storey conservatory to the W with Ionic colonnade, added for Assheton Smith. The E front also has a portico but without a pediment. On the N front a porte cochère, and to its l. a blank gault brick wall for a conservatory, built *c.* 1845 but altered. At the E end was a palm house (dem.). The W side of the courtyard has the plain early C19 service wing with handsome later frontispiece.

Interior also overlaid 1878–80. OUTER (N) HALL with grand chimneypiece, with a chimneypiece of coloured marbles and a more sober stone overmantel with a clock surrounded by carved festoons; wide open segmental pediment above. Pretty stained glass with birds, animals, flowers etc. Beyond is the cubic full-height and top-lit HALL, with entablatures at ground- and first-floor levels, and in the middle of each, superimposed orders of Tuscan and Ionic columns in pairs, the Ionic columns *in antis*. Theatrical STAIRCASE rising from the W side passing between the columns, within a deep rectangular well until the first landing. This space is lit by two circular glazed domes set on pendentives, the spandrels with delicate plaster decoration. Broad transverse arches with guilloche decoration, supported on brackets in the form of Corinthian capitals. In the arches on each side and at the ends, circular Neoclassical plaster plaques depicting angels etc.

STABLES, NW of the house on rising ground. Highly regarded when built in 1829, again by *Assheton Smith*. Plain, but of impressive size and generously appointed to accommodate Smith's hunters and racehorses along with rooms for coaches, grooms, tack and blacksmith's shop. Brick, partly painted, with slate roofs. Two-storey, apart from the S side, around a 150-ft (46-metre)-square courtyard. Cupola over archway. W is THE PLANTATION, laid out as pleasure grounds for Assheton Smith III. N of the house, the WALLED GARDEN, in its S side a GATEWAY, presumably by *Johnson*, but looking Edwardian Baroque. The house stands within a wooded PARK, with lime avenue extending NE to the early C19 White Lodge.

TIDWORTH CAMP
NW of Tedworth House on the edge of Salisbury Plain

The camp was built 1902–5 on the S and E sides of Clarendon Hill. The spacious layout was developed by the Design Branch of the War Office (head *Major E. H. Hemmings*), under the

Deputy Inspector General of Fortifications, *Colonel C. M. Watson*, with eight separate barracks for infantry and cavalry arranged in a cranked formation along the slope of the hill within a grid of streets and served by a branch line of the railway. Each had two parallel pairs of barrack blocks with combined cookhouse and washhouse and separate dining room between, forming a distinctive H-plan. Each also had its own guardhouse, quartermaster's store, officers' quarters and parade ground. Almost all have been demolished. At the bottom of the hill, facing The Mall, are the OFFICERS' MESSES, like large and austere Late Victorian classical villas but with distinctly Baroque details. Adjacent to each is the former COMMANDING OFFICER'S HOUSE and between the messes pairs of semi-detached houses for the regimental quartermasters. ¼ m. SE, in ARCOT ROAD, some Arts and Crafts-style houses built for senior officers, 1912. All the barracks, apart from Jellalabad, will be demolished as part of the MoD's redevelopment of barracks at Aldershot and around Salisbury Plain.

ST MICHAEL, St Michael's Avenue. 1911–12 by *E. Douglas Hoyland* of London. Large in a vaguely Arts and Crafts Perp, described by Pevsner as 'really terribly lifeless'. Buff coloured terracotta of smooth and untextured hollow blocks. Spired bell-turret over the crossing transepts. Capacious interior.

ST GEORGE AND ST PATRICK (R.C.), St Patrick's Avenue. 1912 by *G. L. W. Blount* of Salisbury, who also designed some of the commercial buildings along Station Road. Flint, with low-pitched slated roofs, low and long with a short pyramid-capped NE tower. The style is a minimal most basic Perp, with prominent clerestory windows in the exceedingly long nave. Simpler straight-headed windows of three lights in the aisles. Short chancel with bare windowless E wall. Pevsner found the interior, with its white walls and its complicated thin, black timber roof, reminiscent 'somehow of churches in Africa'.

YOUTH AND COMMUNITY CENTRE, Kohat Road. Former Wesleyan Soldiers' Home of 1907–8. An ambitious building in the Voysey manner, roughcast with tiled roofs; rubbed brick window details and some modest planted timberwork. Also a prominent two-storey octagonal corner turret with a wavy parapet and copper dome. Nearby, the handsome Neo-Georgian former POST OFFICE of around the same date, presumably by the *Office of Works*.

LLOYDS BANK, Station Road. Stuccoed Neo-Georgian of 1914–15, an early work of *Edward Maufe*, its roof altered.

SOUTH WARNBOROUGH

ST ANDREW. Nicely framed by tall trees. A once essentially Norman church. Nave and chancel, with a later timber bell-turret, but much restored by *Street* in 1869–70, when the s aisle was added, and the N porch rebuilt. The Norman N doorway is a fine piece for North Hampshire, with a continuous order of lozenges broken at an angle. Three small Norman windows in the nave, and fragments of a C12 carved capital possibly from a destroyed chancel arch. E.E. chancel with three closely set stepped E lancets, Dec single-light nave N window and Dec s aisle W window, the latter re-set from the former nave s wall. Late Perp three-light chancel N window of *c.* 1530 externally unusually above decorative quatrefoils, and internally framed, with early C13 nook-shafts reused from a larger earlier window. Can they have come from a destroyed C13 chapel, of the former manor house? Sturdy C14 timber framing below the bell-turret (cf. Stondon Massey, Essex). Original, probably early C13 trussed-rafter roofs over nave and chancel. No chancel arch, only a ROOD SCREEN, by *Street*, with part of the C14 ROOD LOFT, a rare survival. Glazed screens to the arcade by *Arthur Gomez*, 2006.

Good furnishings, several of the restoration, especially the FONT of Irish marble – said to be a copy of the old one, whose base survives – and the Caen stone PULPIT carved by *Earp*. – COMMUNION RAIL and LECTERN, of 1955 and 1960 respectively, by *John Skelton*. – BRACKET. A fascinating piece, perhaps mid-C16, on the E wall, with a Gothic foliage trail, castellated top and Renaissance cartouche with painted achievement of Whyte. Might it relate to John White, last Roman Catholic Bishop of Winchester (1556–9), who died here in 1560? It carries a Jacobean cartouche, again with Whyte heraldry, perhaps from a destroyed monument. – STAINED GLASS. s aisle E and south-easternmost windows, C16 heraldic glass, from the manor house arranged by *Clayton & Bell*. Also by them, the chancel E window of 1870. Good with colourful scenes, in the firm's small medallion format. – Chancel N by *Francis Spear*, 1946, with a predella of wartime London people and scenes. – Nave N. By *Ruth Taylor Jacobson*, 1992. A duskily glowing expressionist piece showing Christ healing a blind man. – MONUMENTS. Almost crowded in the chancel. The earliest, a big panelled tomb-chest, below the Perp window, with shields in quatrefoils. Late C15, possibly to Henry Whyte. – Against the E wall, behind it, brass to Robert Whyte, kneeling. He died 1512, and is shown wearing armour in a by then old-fashioned style. Above it, a C16 HELM with wooden Whyte crest. Against the N wall, Sir Thomas Whyte, †1570, and family. Large Tudor Perp recess of stone, of a type more usual in Purbeck marble. Against the back wall, small kneeling figures of Sir Thomas, his wife, and fourteen plus six children. No trace of the Renaissance. Decidedly old-fashioned, it is based on the strikingly similar monument of 1558 at Crondall to Sir George Paulet †1532, whose son was married to Sir Thomas's daughter, and probably by the same (London?) mason. – Above, two small Late Elizabethan tablets with kneelers. – Elizabeth Paulet, daughter of Sir Thomas Whyte and first wife of Lord Chideock Paulet. – Richard Paulet and his first wife, Ellen Kyrton (†1597), and their daughter, Ann Philpott. With achievements and crests of the Whyte and Kyrton families. – On the s wall, late c16 tablet with Whyte brothers, kneeling tweedledum and tweedledee, as if they were twins. – Thomas Newland †1768. Plain pedimental tablet with verbose inscription.

MANOR HOUSE, NE. Early c19 remodelling of an earlier hall-and-cross-wing house. Tall sashes and porch with Doric columns *in antis*. Brick stables of 1824. THE OLD RECTORY. 1862, brick, gabled. Is this the building, by *William Wilkinson*, advertised for tender in 1857? BLOUNCE HOUSE, 1 m. SSE, is a very attractive brick house, built for William Burch in 1699. Five bays with modillion eaves cornice to hipped roof, and pedimented porch.

SOUTH WONSTON
4030

A plotland development laid out on a grid-plan *c.* 1900 by Henry Brake, a local farmer. Its tin tabernacle (1909 by *Messrs Humphries* of Liverpool) is at the Weald and Downland Museum, West Sussex.

ST MARGARET CHURCH and SOUTH WONSTON SCHOOL. 1995–6 by the *Hampshire County Architect's Dept.* An entrance tower, partly hollow and pierced by openings, marks the junction of the school (s) and church (N). The church has its sanctuary within a continuous monopitch top-lit range; the worship space is in the low apsidal projection on the other side of the spine wall which divides the entire building; the school has a top-lit corridor between two monopitched ranges. The classroom range (E side) becomes two storeys with the fall of the site; its upper rooms reached from an internal gallery.

WORTHY DOWN CAMP (Royal Army Pay Corps), ½ m. S. In the c18, the site of Winchester Racecourse. Aerodrome established 1917. Circular CHURCH of 1966, with reused stained glass of 1866 by *M. & R. Silery*, Dublin.

SOUTHINGTON
0000
Overton

SOUTHINGTON HOUSE. Late c18. The service wing has a late c19 tile-hung upper storey and at the rear substantial additions, which must be part of the alterations by *Waterhouse* for William Wyndham Portal, *c.* 1880.

PARSONAGE FARMHOUSE. A high-status house at the centre of an ecclesiastical living, a sinecure in the gift of the Bishops of

Winchester. Stone rubble for the ground floor of both the hall range, dated to 1546, and the cross-wing of 1431–5.

SOUTHINGTON MILL, N across the Test. C18, with former weatherboarded mill and adjoining brick mill house, but altered in 1939–40 for Sir Thomas Dunhill by *Oliver Hill*, who rebuilt the adjacent granary as a living room.

4030

SPARSHOLT

On high ground NW of Winchester. Much good earlier C20 development for middle-class Wintonians.

ST STEPHEN. Perched above the road. Much of the church is by *Butterfield*, 1882–3. Typical of him, the boldly timber-framed upper part of the tower and the timber s porch. He extended the short chancel a little, and added a N aisle with vestry and organ chamber, making the N side resemble 'part of an Anglican convent or a rather rigid public school' (Pevsner). Most medieval details were kept, e.g. the simple C13 priest's doorway, probably re-set when the chancel was widened in the C15 to the width of the Norman nave. The lower parts of the tower are late C14. Big SW angle buttress. S doorway dated 1631. Classical, and very attractive. The DOOR with exceptionally fine strapwork in low relief. Unexpectedly spacious inside. Good transitional s arcade in chalk of *c.* 1200; round piers, round abaci, round arches with two slight chamfers; all handsome, on a small scale (cf. Steep, N arcade). The lofty and wide chancel arch of continuous mouldings looks late C15 of the type at Leckford and Thruxton. The tower arch also Perp. Reset in the s aisle a canopy, C15, from the replaced chancel E wall. Some of Butterfield's furnishings have survived reordering (including works of 1928–9 by *Sir Charles Nicholson*). – CHANCEL SCREEN of 1909 by *G. H. Kitchin*, made by *Thomas & Co.* with later painted decoration in coloured plaster. – CHAPEL SCREEN; classical, of wood, with circular columns. It is part of the former W gallery, presented in 1721 by John Merrill of Lainston House (q.v.). – LECTERN. A strange eagle of West Country provenance. – SCULPTURE. Three Netherlandish panels of the second quarter of the C16, or early C17, allegedly from Otterbourne old church (South Hampshire). The Temptation of Christ ought to be looked for. – SCREEN in the tower arch. By *W. H. Randoll Blacking*, 1957, with his favourite linenfold panelling. In the arch above the screen, painted ROYAL ARMS. By *Brian Thomas*, dated 1977. – STAINED GLASS. E window, 1883, in the style of *W. F. Dixon*. Elaborate, with the Risen Christ amid airborne angels in the centre. – s aisle E. By *Morris & Co.*, 1900. Belated Burne-Jones tradition. – s aisle W, †1885 by *Lavers & Westlake*. Also by them, the tower W window, to General Sir Herbert Stewart, †1885 commanding the relief column for General Gordon at Khartoum. Appropriately martial David and Goliath.

PRIMARY SCHOOL. Tudor Gothic of 1850–1 by *William Coles* of Winchester, enlarged 1876 and 1997 by *Hampshire County Architect's Dept*: in matching brick and flint.

s of the church the pretty CHURCH COTTAGE, *c.* 1850. *L. W. Barnard* of *Barnard & Carter* altered it for himself in 1921. Further s on the w side also JOLLERS by *Robert Bostock*, 1935 as the vicarage; *moderne* meets Neo-Georgian. NE of the church a nice brick WELL-HOUSE of 1897 designed by *B. Vaughan Johnson.* Further E, on the N side of the main street, TAYLORS MEAD of 1843–4, built as the vicarage; stuccoed, of three bays, the centre slightly recessed and with Tuscan porch. Then, on the r., MANOR COTTAGES of 1937 by *Unsworth, Goulder & Bostock* for Samuel Bostock of Lainston House. An attractive asymmetrical pair, a late example of the Unsworth Arts and Crafts Style. The dovecote in the garage gable is a playful touch.

SPARSHOLT MANOR, ⅛ m. E. Built for Samuel Bostock of Lainston House (q.v.) in 1922 by *H. Inigo Triggs* of *Unsworth & Triggs:* his last house and still in his full-blown Arts and Crafts style, taking the form of a hall with gabled cross-wings. Show front overlooking open country, more or less symmetrical with windows in strips, wrapping around the projecting wings, and to l. and r. small projecting hipped-roofed open-sided pavilions on circular barley-sugar twisted brick columns, the right-hand one returning along the side as a loggia. The GARDEN has all of *Triggs*'s characteristics: broad grass terrace, low rubble-stone retaining wall, fountain and stone-lined rill, semi-circular pools and a large circular basin, pergola, summerhouse etc.

SPARSHOLT COLLEGE, ¾ m. NW. Established as the County Farm School at Old Basing in 1899, before moving to Westley Farm in 1914. Y-plan Neo-Georgian MAIN BUILDING of 1926 by *R. F. Gutteridge*, rather unsatisfactory; the best of the rest is the LIBRARY AND RESOURCE CENTRE, 1993 by *Perkins Ogden Architects* with *Hampshire County Architect's Dept.* Glazed steel-framed rectangular box, standing on a high brick plinth over the falling ground to the w, with curved profiled-steel roof supported on laminated wooden beams with steel tension rods.

STEEP

Not a large village but with an unusually interesting group of early C20 houses, many associated with Bedales School and the local Arts and Crafts Movement.

ALL SAINTS. An essentially C12–C13 church thoroughly restored in 1875–6 by *R. W. Edis* when the dominating partly tile-hung timber-framed NW bell-turret replaced a medieval turret. The exterior, heavily rendered, hardly prepares one for the more interesting earlier features inside, though the small lancets in the N aisle wall and in the chancel s wall are all early C13 (some restored). Early C14 S doorway with corbel heads, and nave W window. Inside, the story starts with the low four-bay S aisle, still as narrow as it was when added to the earlier nave *c.* 1180. Circular piers, trumpet capitals, circular abaci. The two E arches have round single-chamfered arches but the two W arches are replacements: the third is C13, the fourth of 1875. That the nave is older, as the VCH suggests, and part of a possibly early C12 cruciform church, cannot be attested, as features have not survived. The capitals of the four-bay N arcade are moulded, and the arches have two slight chamfers. Edis introduced a larger chancel arch and E window but spared the early C13 chancel roof with its pointed-arched trusses. Later medieval timbers in the nave roof, with original crown-posts on new tie-beams, and N aisle roof. SW vestry of 1923 by *J. Cogswell*, tactfully enlarged in 1988–9. – FONT. Late C13, of Sussex sandstone, robust, hexagonal with big pointed trefoiled arches. – NORTH DOOR. A precious survival, one of the few C15 panelled doors in Hampshire with tracery in the head. – REREDOS. A small triptych of 1923 by *Cogswell* with a carved Crucifixion between St Martin and St Wilfred. – ORGAN CASE by *Wilfrid Carpenter Turner*, and ORGANIST'S SCREEN by *Edward Barnsley*, both 1954. – ALTAR CROSS (N aisle). Set free of a copper panel with a wild abstract relief. By *Tania Ashken*, 1962. – STAINED GLASS. E and W windows by *Clayton & Bell*, the former of 1876 in the firm's small figured medallion manner. Vibrant reds and blues. N aisle E of 1923 by *Sidney Meteyard*, made by *Martyn & Co.* of Cheltenham. Single saints with little scenes like engravings below. – ENGRAVED GLASS in the S aisle by *Laurence Whistler*, 1978, to Edward Thomas †1917 illustrating his haunting poem 'The New House'.* – MONUMENTS. A collection of C18–early C19 tablets under the bell-turret, probably by Petersfield masons, to the Baker and Clement families, especially a large marble, signed *Brewer*, on N wall. By him, an oval tablet on the N arcade to Martha Legg †1829, aged 105. Small brass to Ormelie Campbell Hannay †1900 at Paardeberg. Nicely lettered with achievement. By *Barkentin & Krall*. – War memorial placed between two lancets in the N aisle. A Perp canopied crucifix. By *Unsworth & Triggs* (*H. Inigo Triggs*), carved by *Hicks*.

STROUD CHURCH, Ridge Common Lane, 1 m. SW. Mission church built 1897. Brick and stone with timber lancets.

VILLAGE HALL, Church Road. *c.* 1920 (extended 1995). *Stanley Spencer* was commissioned by Sir Muirhead Bone to produce war memorial panels for the interior. Although abandoned, aspects of the design emerge later at Burghclere (q.v.).

PRIMARY SCHOOL, opposite the church. 1875 by *J. B. Colson* in his usual brick and flint. Two excellent extensions by *Tim Dyer* of the *County Architect's Dept*, 1995 and 2004, the latter a hall: vertical timber facing under a dominating roof with brown and red tiles in thick bands.

---

*Thomas moved to Steep in 1906 so that his children could attend Bedales. He lived first at Berryfield, near Ashford Chace, then Red House, Cockshutt Lane, Froxfield (q.v.).

E of the church is RESTALLS, L-plan C16 or C17 lobby-entry house (an inscription 'John Restall 1677' is preserved in a cupboard) which was transformed after 1905 by *W. F. Unsworth* for himself. Brick, tile-hung, with dormers 'but Unsworth's loving care has made it a Victorian fantasy' (Nicholas Taylor) in the local vernacular. Big Lutyens-esque square chimney in the SE angle. The service end (N), incorporating the main entrance, was also remodelled and extended with a double gable on the W front. Exquisitely designed fittings throughout, notable the sinuous wrought-iron window furniture – made by the Steep smithy. Unsworth's design for the garden is strongly formal in the upper part, where a principal N–S axis passes along a terrace between topiary yews and borders.

W along Church Road begins a sequence of the many smaller post-1900 houses, about thirty in all, the best of which have a connection with Bedales School (*see* below). First ROZEL, of 1907–8 by *Raymond Unwin*, for Lord John Russell, first headmaster of Bedales Junior School. Virtually unaltered. Three gables to the front, the porch recessed beneath the centre. Clay tile-hanging, nice tile creasing to the doorways and shutters with Voysey-esque heart motifs. Next door, PENNYFOLD, of 1905 by *Parker & Unwin*, with canted bays under a pentice and windows in projecting frames, then MERRIES, of 1925–6 by *Barry Parker*, not so special. Opposite the school gates, set well back, is LITTLE HAWSTED, an austere essay by Ernest Gimson's pupil, *Alfred Powell*, 1902. Built for his brother Oswald, co-founder and second master of Bedales. Of extremely simple but robust construction, inside and out. It looks like a Dutch barn. The thatched apple store is a picturesque delight. ROW COTTAGE, SW, was built by *Powell* for the gardener, with a mansard roof descending almost to the ground, so that the eaves are at hand-height. L-plan with the entrance in the angle. Interior crafted by *Geoffrey Lupton* (*see* Froxfield), who also built FIVE OAKS, slightly W, of 1913 by *Humphrey Gimson*, for Basil Gimson, second master at Bedales. Simple vernacular, with a nicely controlled short vista down the path to the porch. The large stack gives the impression of a lobby-entry house but inside the rooms radiate off the hall.

The lovely undulating spurs below the hanging woods N of the village hide a series of good houses, several of the larger ones almost invisible in trees. In MILL LANE, first MILL COTTAGE, by *Unsworth, Son & Triggs, c.* 1912, in the local vernacular nicely done with a big triangular tile-hung gable on the S side extending over the corner porch. Then 150 yds on, MILLPONDS, by *Kenneth Claxton*, 1964, on stilts, with one end resting on the edge of the mill pond. Originally nearly all glass-walled but since remodelled with pitched, boarded gables. Uphill, also by *Claxton* and also altered, is MILLFALL, *c.* 1972, bestraddling the mill stream and overlooking a small pond at the front. The top-lit living room has an ingenious sunken area with glazed sides overlooking the stream. (Further on, LITTLE LANGLEYS, of *c.* 1912 by *Horace Farquharson*, in expansive grounds.)

ASHFORD CHACE, ¾ m. N of the village above Mill Lane. By *Unsworth, Son & Triggs*, 1912, for the explorer and naturalist Aubyn Trevor-Battye. Retained from an earlier house is a brick and malmstone barn to the road, remodelled as a protective entrance range with stoutly framed carriage arch. Entrance front with splayed wings and polygonal stair-towers in the angles – the effect rather German. The garden side has a quite different, late C17 character with short projecting wings and cupola on the centre range. Formal GARDEN (evidently by *Triggs*), including a 'Moorish' sunken garden to the SE surrounded by pergola. The rest of the gardens were planted by Trevor-Battye and embellished further with rock gardens etc. by the next owner, Lord Horder.

Tucked below the house in a peerless woodland setting is a remarkable, but alas altered, single-storey STUDIO designed for Mervyn Horder by *Edward Cullinan*, 1958–60, and built by *Horace Knight*, the estate gardener. Much of the concrete was cast *in situ*, including the end walls with pivoting doors. Sloping glass front with aluminium mullions; this originally extended to provide a protective shelter to the entrance. Kitchen and two tiny bedrooms cantilevered at the ends. Roof-line of intersecting planes.

COLDHAYES, 1¼ m. NE. Built in two stages, 1869–73 and 1875–82, by *Alfred Waterhouse* for the Rev. George Horsley-Palmer, brother of Roundell Palmer (*see* Blackmoor). Oddly free and undisciplined. The motifs are partly English but mostly French. The latter, e.g., the basket arches to the window lights and the half-hipped dormers with exposed timbers to carry the eaves. Decorated Tudor brick chimneys. Perp staircase window. Asymmetrical entrance elevation with projecting three-storey porch. (The screen of black marble columns has gone from the entrance hall. The interior stone carving was by *Farmer & Brindley*, tiles by *W. B. Simpson & Sons*.) Service range reduced; the surviving STABLES are faced, like the house, in local stone. Angled entrance with trussed gable over the arch. GARDEN with apsidal-ended pond.

KETTLEBROOK MEADOWS, Steep Marsh, ¼ m. E. 1955 by *Eustace Salaman* of *Carter, Salaman, MacIver & Upfold* for his brother-in-law, the actor Alec Guinness. Quite large, flint-faced below, timber-clad above. The main cruciform part is joined by a bedroom wing to the projecting studio over the garage. Somewhat altered.

COLLYERS, ¾ m. SW off Ridge Common Lane. A peculiar house of 1883–4 by *Bateman & Keates* (*Robert Bateman* and Butterfield's pupil, *H. T. Keates* of Petersfield) for Lt-Col. Ughtred Shuttleworth – 'we have not for many a day seen so strange a design . . . it is so entirely original as to baffle criticism and must be judged by canons as yet unformulated' (*The Builder*, 1884). Of red brick, red sandstone and roughcast – an unusual combination in this area – but the oddities are all in the Free Renaissance decoration, especially on the entrance front.

STONERWOOD PARK, opposite Collyers. 1931 by *Baillie Scott & Beresford* for Alfred Boswell (a Swiss musician, formerly Buss-weiler) for whom Scott had designed The White Cottage, Harrow, in 1908. One of their rarer Neo-Georgian designs, with a canted central bay on the garden front. GARDENS of 1919–20 by *Unsworth & Triggs* in their familiar, and charming, Arts and Crafts style.

ISLAND, Stoner Hill, ⅝ m. WNW. William and Mary Revival of *c.* 1904. Quite convincing. Terraced gardens by *H. Inigo Triggs*, nicely restored and sympathetically extended, with outbuild-ings in Arts and Crafts style by *Jill Manson*.

TANKERDALE FARM, Tankerdale Lane, E of the A3. Dated to 1621–2 (dendrochronology), possibly built for Thomas Eames of Steep and of an unusually grand type for the area. Close-studded with stone infill and a tile-hung upper storey on the front. Lobby-entry plan with stair-tower in a rear outshot.

LYTHE FARM, Lythe Lane. Early to mid C18, with pretty ogee-headed windows and oval window in the centre of its front.

BEDALES SCHOOL

J. H. Badley founded Bedales School in 1893, near Lindfield in Sussex. Established on progressive lines, from 1898 it was one of the first co-educational boarding schools in England. Forced to move, Badley bought Steephurst, a late C19 villa, and reopened the school in 1900.

The MAIN BUILDING is by *E. P. Warren*, built in stages 1899–1907. Eclectic, in a Free Tudor style with William and Mary elements, brick and roughcast. Arranged around two sides of a courtyard (roofed over in 1907 and again in 1975, now in use as an auditorium), classrooms on the ground and first floors, linked by round-arched cloisters, and dormitories above. Hall at the SE corner and to the E the headmaster's wing with a smaller service yard at the rear. Three projecting wings on the S front with shaped gables; the largest for the hall, with a huge stone-mullioned canted bay window (marred by a late 1960s flat-roofed addition). *Warren* also extended STEEP-HURST by adding an arcaded service court to the E, the S side with cross-windows and dormers echoing the Main Building. It was further enlarged and remodelled in 1908 by *W. F. Unsworth* who completely encased it, adding an extra storey, in the style of an East Anglian Tudor manor house. The top of the prominent water tower has a gabled roof pierced by a square capped by a pyramid. E is STEEPCOT, also by *Unsworth* of the same date, for staff accommodation. In a Domestic Revival style with leaded casements and much tile-hanging. The two buildings are now linked by a curved range, 1966–70

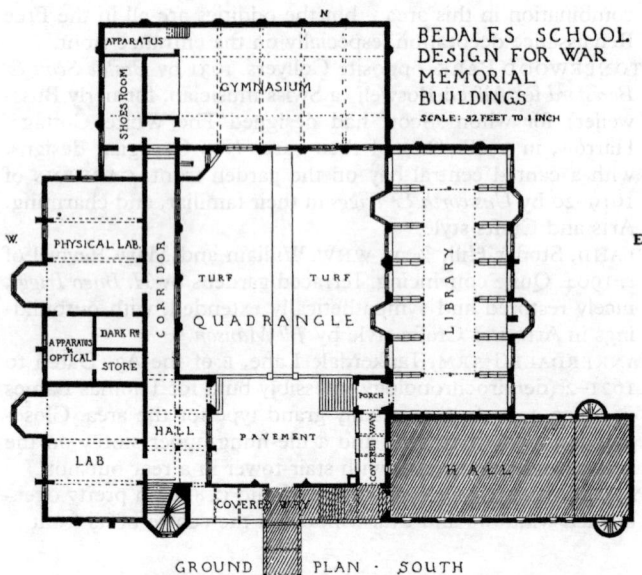

BEDALES SCHOOL
DESIGN FOR WAR
MEMORIAL
BUILDINGS
SCALE: 32 FEET TO 1 INCH

Steep, Bedales School,
War Memorial buildings.
Plan

by *Greville Rhodes*, with two tiers of windows in its long sloping roof. Nearby, an aisled barn (now DRAMA STUDIO). Also of 1908 by *Unsworth*, the former sanatorium (FAIRHAVEN) like a cottage hospital, rendered and tile-hung, with a central gabled block and flanking low wings linking to pavilions with gablet hipped roofs.

LUPTON HALL and MEMORIAL LIBRARY. N of the Main Building. By *Ernest Gimson*, and probably his chief architectural achievement, built in two phases, the Hall 1911, the Library 1919–21, after Gimson's death. The commission was made and largely paid for by Gimson's former apprentice, *Geoffrey Lupton*, a former pupil of the school (*see* Froxfield), who built both parts – for the library he was assisted by *Edward Barnsley* (another former pupil) and supervised by *Sydney Barnsley*. Gimson's design was for a quadrangle with Hall and Library forming an L-shaped group on the E side, laboratories to the W and a gymnasium to the N. The HALL is of cruck construction with five great oak trusses, the blades truncated at collar level with kingposts above, less dramatic externally, of local hand-made brick with large oculi in the gable-ends and transeptal timber gables at the E end. Semicircular stair-tower at the SE corner. The Hall is linked to the Main Building by an L-shaped covered way of massive oak construction, with barn-like hipped porches over the intersecting driveway, which originally continued to the Library. Gimson revised the

LIBRARY design in 1918 when it was decided to complete the
quadrangle as the school's war memorial (it remained uncompleted). Like the hall it is oak-framed internally, in the manner
of an aisled barn, of seven bays with a crown-post roof, and
planned like an Oxbridge college library with a central reading
space and bookshelves in the galleried aisles. Externally of
brick, rather in the Garden City style with Neo-Tudor details,
particularly the pairs of full-height canted bays with brick-
mullioned windows. The aisle galleries did not allow sweeping
roofs and are lit by dormers behind parapets. The ironwork is
by *Stevie Musto*, Gimson's blacksmith from Sapperton. Excellent furniture by *Gimson* and *Edward* and *Sydney Barnsley*.

HORSELY LABORATORIES, a minor work by *Sir Edwin
Cooper*, 1923, built by the school's staff, has been altered and
extended.

Post-war is the CENTRAL WELCOMING AREA, MASTER'S
FLAT AND BOYS' DORMITORIES (now COMMON ROOM),
alterations of 1989 by *Maguire & Murray* to the N range of the
Main Building. The SWIMMING POOL was rebuilt in 1984,
long and low with glazed ridge and full-height canted glazed
bay at the N end.

Of the 1990s the GEOGRAPHY BLOCK to the NE, 1994 by
Hampshire County Architects, is two storeys, of brick, with continuous ridge light. Six-bay front with brick buttresses and
window panels with diagonal boarding. This was part of a masterplan which also included ORCHARD FIELDS and QUAR-
RYSIDE, dormitory blocks to the SE of the Main Block. They
are picturesquely arranged around a courtyard on a falling site,
of brick with many details clearly taken from the Lupton Hall.
Conceived at the same time was the OLIVIER THEATRE, NW
of the main building. This is the best post-war building,
built 1994–6, by the *Oak Design Group* (*Feilden Clegg Architects,
Roderick James & Co.* and *Carpenter Oak & Woodland*) and
intended to demonstrate Arts and Crafts principles in its use
of simple natural materials from sustainable sources and
natural ventilation for the building. Square auditorium under
a pyramidal roof which extends over side verandas and is
topped by a square lantern; in front a foyer wing in the form
of a five-bay aisled structure with central gallery lit by a
clerestory and a glazed front wall. Both are oak-framed, with
the use of some stainless-steel flitch plates, fixings and tension
elements, but the rear backstage wing is of Douglas fir.
Cladding of horizontal boarding and roofs of zinc. Inside, the
auditorium is defined by four corner posts, connected at their
heads by trusses, from which the balcony fronts are suspended
by steel rods. At each corner, staircases.

Most recent is THE ORCHARD BUILDING, 2003–5 by
Walters & Cohen. In fact two buildings, for teaching and administration, linked by an entrance block at right angles. Timber-
clad, two storeys with a third in the steep steel-clad roofs with
clerestories along the ridge; its design indebted to Chipper-
field's Henley Rowing Museum. Small rooms in projecting

boxes along the s sides. The link is lower, flat-roofed and fully glazed. A third building for art, design and technology is planned (2009).

In the BARNYARD, E of the entrance, are a couple of relo-cated timber-framed buildings, re-erected with the help of staff and students. An C18 aisled BARN, now a WORKSHOP, from Sotherington near Selborne, with pantile roof and brick-nogging, re-erected 1981–3, and a smaller building from Holybourne, now a BAKERY, re-erected 1983. Nearby, an oak-framed CARPENTRY SHOP of 2003 and two granary-type buildings, one square with turf roof and the other octagonal.

DUNHURST, SW. The prep school. 1904–5, by *Percy Worthington* in an Arts and Crafts style. Mansard roof, the shallower upper pitch carried through to the gable-ends, the steeper lower pitch hipped. Three gabled dormers to the front and a pair of full-height canted bays. At the rear, DUNNANIE, the pre-prep school, with a long 1950s range, attractively remodelled by *Devereux & Partners* in 1990.

STEVENTON

A village with two centres: the small group of church and manor house on a spur of high ground to the s, and the mainly C18 and C19 settlement which largely replaced it in the valley to the NW. It is famous as the birthplace of Jane Austen, whose father, the Rev. George Austen, was the rector. Here she wrote *Pride and Prejudice* and *Northanger Abbey*.

ST NICHOLAS. Small, essentially early C13. Nave and chancel nicely rendered. The bell-turret with a spire is of a major restoration in 1835 for the Rev. William Austen. The early C13 former s doorway was re-set in a puzzling arrangement with new windows in a redesigned W front. Elsewhere the details (e.g. three nave windows) are E.E., of Binstead stone. The E window, replicated in 1975, and three others are Perp. Inside, the details are E.E., and more rewarding. The genuine lower part of the W tower is unusually embraced by bays. The arches around here all have just one slight chamfer. So has the chancel arch, flanked by the flat reredos niches for lay altars. In one of these are remains of C13 WALL PAINTING, especially a head-less ecclesiastic in a chasuble, and a decorative pattern. Early C13 double piscina in the chancel uncovered in 1988. The chancel vault must be of 1835. It is of plaster with wooden ribs and roundel bosses. – ALTAR. With painted front of the Good Shepherd and saints. – FONT. Dated 1868, of white marble that looks as if made of caster sugar. – FONT COVER of 1999 by *James Smyth*. – CHOIR STALLS (s side only) and PULPIT. Still Late Georgian Gothic of 1835. With foliate finials to the arm-rests. – SCREEN. Rather flimsy early C17, from the Manor House pew, now near the W end. Simple geometrical openwork patterns. – SCULPTURE. Saxon cross-shafts, assigned by Sir Thomas Kendrick to the late C9 and connected with Prior's Barton (Winchester) and Colerne in Wiltshire. One panel with two intertwined dragons, another with very wild interlace. – ARCHITECTURAL FRAGMENTS. Stone with a possibly C13 winged creature and a seated figure holding a head (St Denys?). – STAINED GLASS. E window by *Mayer & Co., c.* 1890. Gethsemenc. – Others in the nave by *C. G. Gray,* of Cambridge. – MONUMENTS. Anne Austen †1795, pleasant tablet. – Rev. James Austen †1819, the eldest brother of the author. Gothic, of stone, by *Humphrey Hopper.* – Jane Austen †1817. Simple tablet with crisp Roman lettering, of 1936, from a design by *F. Osborne & Co.,* erected, as the inscription relates, by her great grandniece, Emma Austen-Leigh.

STEVENTON MANOR, W of the church. Unremarkable Neo-Tudor house created *c.* 1990, incorporating a service wing of the 1880–2 house by *Alfred Waterhouse* (the rest destroyed by fire *c.* 1932). The house that Sir Richard Pexall was rebuilding at his death in 1571 was incorporated into a larger house in 1935, the whole demolished in 1970. Remains of a C19 fernery with some architectural fragments, including C16 fire surround. SE of the church the former walled garden, in which is THE GARDEN HOUSE of 1987–9 by *David Scull* of *QED Architects.* Neo-Georgian, in the form of an orangery.

STEVENTON HOUSE, ½ m. NNW, on high ground. Built 1826–7 for the Rev. William Knight to replace his grandfather's rectory in the valley below. Stuccoed with hipped slate roof. Quite informal, of three by three bays. C20 lattice porch. Lower service wing to the l., with behind the former STABLES. One storey but large. Brick. Pedimented centre with frieze, dentil cornice and oculus in tympanum.

ROUND BARROW CEMETERY, in the extreme S of the parish of Overton, just N of the A30 at its junction with a minor road to South Litchfield Grange. This is a linear cemetery of five barrows. The S site is a fine bell barrow 7 ft (2.1 metres) high and 130 ft (40 metres) in diameter. N of it are first a bowl barrow 118 ft (36 metres) in diameter and 6 ft (1.8 metres) high, and a saucer barrow partly cut through by the building of the former mound and by a second bell barrow. 40 ft N is a further bowl barrow, 90 ft (28 metres) in diameter and 6 ft high.

STOCKBRIDGE

3030

Stockbridge strikes one as a town, with its wide High Street and some of the buildings along it. What one does not realize is that there is nothing behind the street N or S except water meadows, whose multiple channels pass under High Street and form the boundaries of the long medieval burgage plots behind. The town lies on the old Winchester–Salisbury road where it crosses the Test between steep-sided hills. The earliest reference is in 1141; it was also known as White Somborne, no doubt to distinguish it from the large parish of King's Somborne (q.v.) from which it was formed and of which it remained a dependent chapelry until 1848. In 1200 Richard I granted a market to the lord of the manor, William Briwere, whose seat was at Ashley (q.v.). A fair was granted in 1221. The town never received a borough charter but in 1562–3 was granted the right to send members to Parliament – Stockbridge was a notorious 'rotten borough' until 1832. In 1795 Warner described it as 'a noted thoroughfare with some good inns . . . but a declining place'. The Andover Canal, from Redbridge to Andover, was opened in 1794 – the Town Hall and the rebuilding of several inns date from this period – but was unprofitable and was superseded by the London & South Western Railway from 1865 (closed 1967). The Victorian town became popular for horse racing which took place until 1898 on Danebury Down (*see* Nether Wallop), and as a centre for fishing on the Test, which it remains.

OLD ST PETER at the E end of the street. Only the chancel stands of a sizeable medieval church. The aisled nave, low W tower and S chapel were demolished in 1870 and the C13 chancel arch blocked. The chancel looks E.E., but there is inside, E of the S chapel arch, a round arch with a slight chamfer. This was probably connected with the SEDILIA and, if so, would date the masonry of the chancel to the late C12. Perp W doorway in the chancel. E window C14 of two lights re-set. Simple interior, lightly limewashed. – DOOR. Dated to 1354. – ALTAR. Dated 1696. – COMMUNION RAILS. Early with flat balusters three-sided, a now rare type. – COMMANDMENT BOARDS. C18 (restored 1992). – ROYAL ARMS of 1726, robustly painted with lively mantling. – WALL PAINTING. On the E wall, rare cipher of Queen Elizabeth I dated 1588. – MONUMENTS. A few mural tablets, inside, and more unusually outside on the walls. Among the best, l. and r. of the altar, two headstones of Welsh slate, brought in from the churchyard, to Nicholas Pyle of Marsh Court. The graveyard is bounded on two sides by low medieval walls with original C15 capping stones. By the path a GRAVESTONE to John Buckett †1804, landlord and election agent, with long punning inscription:

'And is alas poor Bucket gone?
Farewell, convivial honest John.
Oft at the well by fatal stroke
Buckets, like pitchers, must be broke.' Etc.

WAR MEMORIAL. *Lutyens*'s War Cross, commissioned by Herbert Johnson of Marsh Court (cf. King's Somborne). The plinth has a coved cornice forming a bench. In the town cemetery, ¼ m. E off Winton Hill, is a MEMORIAL CROSS to Violet Johnson, also by *Lutyens*, 1923.

St Peter. 1865–6 by *J. Colson*; the sw porch-steeple of 1887 by *J. B. Colson*. Flint exterior, conventional Early Dec. Some genuine c14 windows from the old church (*see* above) reused in the aisles and in the s transept e wall. The new windows are from plate tracery to Early Dec. High Victorian interior with Colson's favourite foliate carving. Lush n arcade. Tall round piers, free Dec naturalistic capitals and corbels here and in the transepts and the chancel. All by *Hems*. – FONT. Of the standard c12 Purbeck table type, much decayed and without a proper base. – PULPIT by *E. H. New*, 1940–1, made by *The Warham Guild*. – SCULPTURE. Small Crucifixus, c15(?), made up with new parts into a stone cross. Figural corbels in the vestry are c15. – STAINED GLASS. e window by *Clayton & Bell*, 1866. s transept e window of 1867, possibly by *O'Connor*. In the aisles, by *J. Powell & Sons*, 1904–29 better and more pictorial in treatment.

TOWN HALL. Built, it is said, in 1790, at the expense of Joseph Foster Barham, one of the town's M.P.s: 'very elementary and without graces', thought Pevsner, but a definite presence in the street. Classical with a pediment framed by the bracketed eaves of the roof. Gault brick. Three bays with giant order of pilaster-strips. Arched windows to front and sides. Oculi flanking the central blind window. Ground-floor arcade first infilled in 1810; also the date of the clock turret with its ogival lead cap and later fish-shaped weathercock. Matching entrance wing to l. of 2009 by *Guion & Brown*, in place of an addition of 1911.

HIGH STREET runs between the old church and the Test, punctuated midway along by the Grosvenor Hotel and the Town Hall (*see* above), and the vertical accent of the c19 church steeple. The rest is mainly architecturally modest if agreeable c18 and early c19 buildings on both sides, made attractive by an enthusiasm for brightly coloured frontages. The apparent absence of medieval fabric is surprising, perhaps the consequence of a reported desertion of the town in the c15, following an outbreak of plague. The earliest visible survivors are late c17, e.g. at the e end on the n side where KING'S HEAD HOUSE is brick with pilasters, wooden modillion eaves cornice and hipped tile roof. Next door OLD SAWN HOUSE is similar in form but late c19 in its details. On the other side of the road at this end, at the corner with Trafalgar Way, RAILWAY COTTAGE and CANAL COTTAGE are also late c17, with modest Artisan Mannerist surround to a window in the gable to the road. Also on this side, THE VINE INN, later c18, stands out by virtue of its height. Nothing special thereafter, until the BUTCHERS and OAKLANDS with late c18 octagonal window panes and shopfront, and one cottage further along which has late c17 timber framing exposed at its end.

The major event on the other side, apart from the church (*see* above) is the GROSVENOR HOTEL, the town's grandest coaching inn. Built *c.* 1820, presumably at the expense of Robert, 2nd Earl Grosvenor, who acquired property around this date as a means of gaining political influence in the town

– his cousin Thomas was M.P. in 1826–30. Gault brick, two-and-a-half storeys, five bays, the windows of the first and fifth set in giant arches. Far-projecting porch (clad in mathematical tiles) on unfluted Doric columns and a whole room projected with it (the meeting room of the Houghton Fishing Club, founded 1822). Entrance with fluted pilasters, sidelights and radial fanlight. The red brick part to the r. is the former market hall; its tile-hung first floor added for the hotel in 1897. Neo-Georgian rear additions of 1937 by *A. E. Mort*, including the round-arched staircase window. To its r., THE OLD RECTORY. Mid-C19, quite handsome; its E side wall has diaper patterning – a very late use. Opposite, TESTLEA, probably mid-C18, but typically modest. Originally 2–1–2 bays, but remodelled in the late C19, stuccoed with a moulded string course, and a full-height shallow half-hipped bay added to the r. Inside, an original staircase with pairs of barley-sugar twisted balusters and columnar newels. Back on the N side, set well back, the former BAPTIST CHAPEL of 1904, by *C. K. Fry*. Brick with stone dressings, Gothic but with a sprightly Neo-Jacobean gable. Next door the charming STOCKBRIDGE HOUSE, testament to the town's short-lived late C19 prosperity, with pretty first-floor veranda and valencing. At the w end of the street, close to the bridge (rebuilt 1963) is MULBERRY HOUSE (N), probably late C18, and the early C19 WHITE HOUSE (S) with slate roof, also five bays, with curiously narrow sashes, central arched staircase window and columned porch. Across the bridge is a cluster of houses around a cross-roads, e.g. CARBERRY GUEST HOUSE, early C19, with Gothic windows in the side wall, and DROVERS HOUSE on the Houghton road, with painted lettering on its C18 brick front promising Welsh drovers 'Gwair tymherus porfa flasus cwrw da a gwal cysurus' (seasoned hay, tasty pasture, good ale and a comfortable bed). On the Longstock Road, BRADFIELDS, a handsome early C19 brick house, of three storeys and three bays, with stone Doric porch. The latter's pierced balustrade and the flanking canted bays are later C19 additions.

At the opposite end of the High Street, the busy roundabout is the site of the station (dem. *c.* 1970). On its S side the WHITE HART INN has a memorable early C19 front, of two storeys with the upper floor carried out on thin wooden Tuscan columns. At the rear, a long range of C19 brick stables (now converted). Beyond, by the King's Somborne road, is the old church and to its S MANOR FARMHOUSE, a mid-C17 lobby-entry house, altered and extended *c.* 1700 but stuccoed and sashed in the early C19. Two early C18 staircases, one with splat and turned balusters. E, on the corner of Winton Hill, SEVEN GABLES, ungabled, 'recently built' in 1710. Staircase with turned balusters. Up hill, WINTON HOUSE, with the date 1771, and SHEPHERDS HOUSE, an early C19 villa with Doric porch. In Old London Road AVALON, a modestly polychromed Gothic villa of 1879, its angle porch with carved flowers, fish and birds, and timber-framed above with nogging.

GREEN PLACE, 1 m. ESE. 1906–7 by *M. H. Baillie Scott*. Built as a holiday cottage for Elen and Arthur Norman Hill, a Liverpool solicitor and notary. Single storey; roughcast with tile roofs, mullioned windows and elegant brick chimneys. Originally a U-plan, with the rooms in the rear wings (bedrooms and kitchen) linked by a timber-framed corridor, but extended with a new kitchen by Scott in 1913. Hall-like drawing room divided by a dramatic oak truss. Broad inglenook with oak beam and mantelshelf, lit by a small window. One bedroom has a sentimental inscription painted by Arthur Hill: 'And it fell . . . that they were in a green place . . . and they were near their friends . . . and they could see everyone and no one could see them'. Sweet chimneypiece with Delft tiles. In the grounds, a roughcast and tile garden shed by *M. H. Baillie Scott*, made into something special by a raking brick buttress at the front.

ROUND BARROW CEMETERY, 1 m. ESE, just N of the A272. The group consists of fifteen bowl barrows, 25–45 ft (8–14 metres) in diameter and 6 in.–3 ft (15–90 cm.) in height. One of the group was excavated in 1938. Beneath the centre of the mound was an oval grave containing a crouched inhumation accompanied by a bell beaker and a copper awl. Two cremations were found in the filling of this grave, and a third cremation in a collared urn had been inserted, presumably at a later date, on the periphery of the site. This latter burial was accompanied by a bronze awl and beads of shale, amber and faience.

WOOLBURY RING, 1¼ m. E. This univallate Iron Age hill-fort encloses an oval area of 20 acres. The rampart, some 10 ft (3 metres) high, can still be traced around most of the circuit but is ploughed out at the E. Excavation (1989) has shown that the defences date to the C5 B.C. but the site was not intensively occupied and may soon have been abandoned altogether. There was some limited reuse in the Roman period.

From the SE side of the fort a DITCH can be traced running along the N side of the open chalkland of Stockbridge Down. Pre-dating the hill-fort, it was probably constructed in the Late Bronze Age to separate a large area of Celtic fields to the N from contemporary pasture to the S – an area which, remarkably, seems to have remained as pasture ever since.

STOKE CHARITY   4030

A shrunken settlement with the church standing alone in a field. Earthworks SW indicate the site of the former manor house and its garden. NW, close to the River Dever, is the former manorial pond.

ST MARY AND ST MICHAEL. Picturesque but rather unprepossessing exterior, mostly of flint and brick: nave and lower chancel, N aisle, and N chapel; shingled bell-turret with short splay-foot spire (restored 1849, retaining parts of a C14 or C15 bell-frame). Interestingly varied windows, almost all medieval: C13 lancets (restored with the chancel in 1848–9) in the chancel, early C14 two-lighters in the nave and C15 Perp in the N chapel. Fine tall Perp chancel E window of c. 1480 with three lights with a transom and unrestored tracery. Is the brick E wall contemporary? Inside, the church (which is uncommonly well restored and kept) contains to one's surprise a mighty Early Norman N arcade of two bays. The pier is octagonal, but of monstrous girth, and has, like the responds, a capital of many biggish scallops. The arches are round and unmoulded. A small arch, which opens from the E end of the N aisle into the later N chapel, is Norman and related to a small two-cell church of c. 900 of which the nave is represented by the N aisle. Evidence of flint footings have been revealed below the N wall. It looks older than the so much more elaborate chancel arch with zigzag at right angles to the wall, a fine Late Norman piece. The chancel arch is round, and its section is just a single step. The capitals have reeded foliage. Also Norman the small outer doorway with zigzag. In a very unusual position, so possibly re-set. But where from? Small round-arched window head in the N chapel with original painting (*see* below). C13 chancel. The nave, originally C12, was extended W in the early C14: angle buttresses support the bell-turret. The S wall was rebuilt at the same time. Simple Dec S doorway. Simple ceiled nave roof with rounded arch braces, probably Jacobean, possibly 1612 (see date panel on the modern pulpit below). The N chapel is now essentially Perp, seemingly all of a piece. The roof is unusual, a rather robust and rustic work with an enormous wall-plate frieze of a type more common in Somerset (cf. High Ham, 1476). Perhaps provided shortly after the death of Isabella Hampton in 1475 (Edward Roberts). In the walls of nave and N chapel, late medieval entrances to the rood loft (taken down in 1562) which were discovered and exposed in 1991–5.

FURNISHINGS. – FONT. C12. Purchased in Winchester in 1542. – PILLAR PISCINA. N aisle. C12 square foliate capital. – PULPIT. 1934 by *T. D. Atkinson*, incorporating a lozenge date-plaque of 1612. – ARCHITECTURAL FRAGMENTS. N chapel, S wall. A re-set window head, not later than 1200 (Harvey) with contemporary decorative paintings that related to the fragmentary C12 arch-head above the later C15 arch to the chancel. – SCULPTURE. Mass of St Gregory, c. 1500. Found embedded in the nave wall in 1849, when it retained traces of painting. It is rare in England that a stone-carved scene of this kind remained undamaged. But that does not improve the artistic quality of the piece. – TILES. Late C14 attractively jumbled in the chapel floor. *Minton* tiles of 1849 on the chancel floor. – WALL PAINTING. Large late C12 or early C13 fragment on the N chapel S wall. One of St Gregory's miracles at the Mass. – STAINED GLASS. Little is old but some nice Perp fragments in the N chapel windows, including heads of St Margaret of Antioch, the Madonna and child in the NW window, 'sun

badges' of King Edward IV in the E window. An extensive collection of medieval fragments was mentioned by Bingley in the
C18. Glass connected with Sir Thomas Hampton (see the initials repeated in borders) is worked into the chancel E window
but the rest is by *Lavers, Westlake & Co.*, 1908, in a scholarly
evocation of a late C15 design 're-created' from a few original
fragments.

MONUMENTS. No other small Hampshire church has such
a full and richly varied medieval collection. In the chancel a
C12 tomb-lid with carved patonce cross (from the churchyard).
Under the E arch of the nave N arcade, large Purbeck marble
tomb-chest with shields in quatrefoils. Believed to be that of
John de Hampton (†c. 1350), first of the Hamptons to own the
manor. Next, in the arch between chancel and N chapel, a plain
tomb-chest with shields at the heads of plain recessed panels.
On the Purbeck marble lid brasses of Sir Thomas Hampton
†1483, his wife Isabella †1475, and children. The main figures
are 2 ft 8½ in. (82 cm.) long. He is in swagger armour. The
eight children on a panel below a panel of the Trinity at the
top. Also in the chapel, a fine Early Tudor Gothic monument
to John Waller †1527 and wife Johanna, daughter and heiress
of Sir Thomas Hampton. Tomb-chest with back wall and
shallow four-centred arch all panelled; canopied niche on the
E side (for Waller's patron saint?). Achievements and cresting
on top. The tomb-chest has unusually crude and badly
preserved paintings of St Thomas of Canterbury. Colouring
elsewhere cleaned in 1946 by *George Nutt.* – Again in the chapel
a Jacobean tomb-chest with heraldry in panels to Sir Thomas
Phelyppes, 1st baronet, †1626. – Nave S side. Plain chest tomb
in a recess with brass to Thomas Wayte †1482. The figure,
2 ft 2 in. (66 cm.) long in full plate armour, is almost identical
with Thomas Hampton. There was certainly no craving for
originality among suppliers of funerary monuments or their
customers about 1480. Panel of Christ rising from the tomb.
– N aisle, W end. Sir James Phelyppes †1652. Very elementary
shallow tomb-chest with achievement and back wall only partially preserved. No figures survive.

CHURCHYARD, simply fenced from the open field, has C18
headstones and table tombs, among them a marker to the Rev.
Joshua Reynolds, rector †1734, uncle of the painter.

MICHAELS, E, is a good three-bay C16 timber-framed house, and
S is the OLD RECTORY, externally mid-C19 Neo-Tudor, brick
with blue diaper and hoodmoulds and many gables, including
Dutch gable to staircase wing. But inside is a C15 timber frame
with Tudor-arched doorway to cross-passage and hall with
remains of an arched-braced truss. The hall, floored over in the
C17, has good early *c.* 1700 bolection panelling with carved
acanthus cornice. W, near the cross-roads, a group of old cottages, including the cruck-built OLD KEEPER'S COTTAGE.

NORSEBURY HOUSE, ¼ m. NNE. 1919 by *Ernest Newton*, a Neo-
Georgian encasing of a Victorian villa. Four-bay W front to W
with cross-windows and wide arched-canopied porch. Walled

forecourt with rusticated brick piers. The garden front has larger windows and projecting wings with raised brick quoins. Lower wing set back to r. with arcaded loggia. Beyond, a wing of *c.* 2001, in matching style by *Guion & Brown;* much of the design due to *Roderick Gradidge*. Newton's staircase survives inside. Formal garden of 1919 with brick terrace and perimeter walls. Many yew-hedged compartments, in one a swimming-pool pavilion of 1990–1 by *Perkins Ogden Architects*, with a canopy suspended from a substantial steel roof structure supported on two columns at each end; glazed front, brick rear.

STRATFIELD SAYE

STRATFIELD SAYE HOUSE. Chosen by the 1st Duke of Wellington, and paid for by a grateful nation in 1817. It was a choice dictated more by the excellent condition of the estate than by any special qualities of grandeur or beauty in the house. Indeed, he intended to demolish and build anew on a different site. There were a number of designs for lavish palaces for the Duke, by *C. H. Tatham* of 1812, *C. R. Cockerell* of 1815 and, also in 1815, the grandest, by *B. D. Wyatt*. Plans for a more modest house by *Wyatt*, formerly secretary to Arthur Wellesley in Dublin, were still being considered in 1818, but it was not to be and the Duke settled for making modest additions to the existing building.

70   The HOUSE is largely that built *c.* 1630, probably for Sir William Pitt (†1636), and altered in the mid C18 for George Pitt, later the 1st Lord Rivers. Much of this work was probably by his uncle and amateur architect *John Pitt, c.* 1755. It is brick with Artisan Mannerist detailing, but later stuccoed. Of two storeys, long and low, the plan a shallow H. The entrance front is thirteen bays wide, with two-bay wings projecting by two bays. In the middle the ground-floor windows have triple keystones, dropping down from the string course. Sitting on the string course are Tuscan pilasters, between the first-floor windows except for bays three and four and ten and eleven, which are combined and share a single window flanked by arched niches. Each pair of end bays is slightly set back and the centre bay projects slightly. Its first-floor window with an C18 lugged architrave, the flanking Ionic pilasters and the pediment must be C18 alterations, carried out when the roof was altered and the dentil cornice, tying the elevation together, added. The stone porch with baseless Doric columns *in antis* was added by *Benjamin Deane Wyatt* in 1838, and the tall copper-domed wooden cupola on the roof above was added *c.* 1965 by *Trenwith Wills*, the architect 7th Duke's erstwhile partner, in an attempt to counteract the excessive horizontality of the elevation. A cupola is known to have existed in the C17.

Stratfield Saye.
Plan

The wings are treated differently, with raised quoin strips
and architraves, and end in big Dutch gables. Were there more
gables along this front originally? There are also outer wings,
which project further, and are of two dates: the ground floors,
with blind arcading to the sides, are c. 1755; the upper parts,
replicating the C17 wings, were added for the 1st Duke in 1847
by *Philip Hardwick* and *P. C. Hardwick*. The E, garden, side is
equally strung out. The C17 wings are immediately identifiable.
Between them are eleven bays of c. 1755 infill, with a separate
hipped roof. However, the walls are treated in the same way as
the wings, with flat string course and architraves. In the
middle, a five-bay pediment with oculus and a pair of ground-
floor canted bays flanking a three-bay Tuscan porch. At the
r.-hand end, an addition of c. 1775 with a two-storey canted
bay, echoed at the l.-hand end by the canted bay of the single-
storey conservatory, added 1838 by *Wyatt*. With a seven-bay
side elevation, it is tucked in the angle of the C17 wing, almost
obscuring its C18 pediment, and the rear of the C18/C19 wing.
Largely C18 and early C19 offices around a courtyard at the N
end, with beyond a late C19 brick water tower. With the addition of the C18 infill on the garden side, the centre of the house
is double pile, with central axial passage.

The principal INTERIORS date from c. 1745–75. The ENTRANCE
HALL is a double-height space, created c. 1755 for George Pitt
with the removal of the rooms above (he also removed a pair
of single-storey bays either side of the door). Around the lower
part of the walls, attached Ionic columns, forming a screen to
the central passage along the back wall and supporting a
balustraded gallery. Simple Palladian chimneypieces and
Roman mosaics from Silchester, installed in the floor in 1866.
s of the hall, the LIBRARY. Also mid-C18, the enriched ceiling
of papier mâché based on a design from Robert Wood's *The
Ruins of Palmyra* (published 1753, illustrated by *G. B. Borra*),
with octagonal and smaller diamond-shaped panels. Is it by
Borra? Also a frieze with scroll ornament. At the s end a screen
of Ionic columns *in antis*, leading into the Music Room. The
segmental tympanum interrupts the enriched frieze, and it is

clearly later. Was it one of *Wyatt*'s early alterations for the Duke
(it appears in a drawing of 1821)? From the MUSIC ROOM
one reaches the CONSERVATORY, with its cast-iron roof structure. Against the w wall marble columns from Naples, brought
to England *c.* 1821 with a view to their use in the new house,
placed here by the 7th Duke. Also a *Coade* stone plaque and a
sculpture of Aphrodite, *c.* 1793 by *J. B. Locatelli*. At the s end
of the central passage, the C17 main STAIRCASE, rising around
a square well, with square-section tapering balusters, linked by
arches, and carved pendants. The ceiling has Rococo plasterwork, of *c.* 1760, as do the study and Lady Charles Room in
the same wing, both with fine Rococo chimneypieces too. The
lesser staircase at the N end, *c.* 1640, with symmetrical double
balusters. A door at the back of the hall leads into the GALLERY
in the centre of the garden front. Mid-C18, and old-fashioned
for its date, with a screen of Ionic columns at each end and
the walls decorated with prints in the 1790s. A pair of chimneypieces, looking not much later than *c.* 1740. S, the PRINT
ROOM, decorated by the 1st Duke. N, the Rococo DRAWING
ROOM has a pretty ceiling with garlands in the cove, chimneypiece and doorcases. Beyond, the DINING ROOM in the mid-
C18 wing has another ceiling based on Wood's *Palmyra*, with
linked octagonal panels around a large central circular panel
which has a border of Greek key ornament (cf. Flitcroft's state
bedroom at Woburn, *c.* 1756 and Adam's drawing room at
Osterley of the 1760s). If it is by *Borra* it cannot be much later
than 1755. Contemporary marble chimneypiece with Ionic
columns.

The approach to the house is the long NW avenue through the
park flanked by the STABLES (N side) and OFFICES (S). They
are C17, brick, with C18 stucco to the front. Two storeys.
Towards the house, five bays with pairs of Dutch gables, the
long elevations facing each other with five gables, the second
and fifth over elliptical arches supported on giant pilasters. At
the w end of the s range, a C17 BARN, timber-framed behind
the C18 stuccoed facing, and at the end of the N range, a single-
storey C18 COACHHOUSE. In front of the house, a spacious
forecourt with an uncompleted STATUE of St George and the
Dragon, by *Matthew Cotes Wyatt*. It was commissioned by
George IV for St George's Hall, Windsor Castle, but was unfinished at the King's death. It was exhibited at the Great Exhibition and eventually purchased by the 2nd Duke in 1865 for
the garden at Apsley House. It was erected here in 1950. NNW
of the house, in the walled garden, is the early C19 CAMEL-
LIA HOUSE with a single-storey cast-iron glasshouse.

The PARK was first mentioned in 1261. It owes its present
appearance to the 1st Lord Rivers and the 1st Duke of Wellington. E of the house, the River Loddon has been formed into a
lake. NE of the house, the river is crossed by an elegant late
C18 stone BRIDGE, with three elliptical arches and a
balustrade. SW of the house is a cast-iron BRIDGE, of 1802 by
Thomas Wilson. It consists of four segmental-arched ribs, each

made up of five sections, with diminishing circles in the spandrels. Delicate railings and curved stone abutments ending in
square piers with vase finials. N and S of the house are wooded
pleasure grounds. Close to the N boundary, a rustic
SUMMERHOUSE, built in 1846 to commemorate a visit by
Queen Victoria. In the form of a double-sided temple, each
face with a gable and three arches on octagonal columns.
Inside, sticks have been used to create naïve pictures, as well
as the royal crown and ducal coronet. 1 m. E of the house on
the A33 the granite and bronze WELLINGTON MONUMENT
of 1866, a giant Corinthian column with tall base and entablature carrying a statue of the 1st Duke by *Marochetti*. Also two
early C19 LODGES, stuccoed with blind round arches and
pediments to the front, their style copied for the NW LODGES
of 1974 by *Trenwith Wills*.

ST MARY, in the park, ¼ m. SW. Built in 1754–8 by *John Pitt*, for
his father, George Pitt, 1st Lord Rivers, replacing the previous
church which stood nearer the house. Minimal Palladian style,
of brick, now effectively whitened, on a Greek-cross plan, with
octagonal central copper dome. Arched windows and pediments in the arms. Four small windows in the drum of the
dome. The W side has a three-arched entrance loggia below
three circular windows echoing those of the dome. The E
window, correctly of the Venetian type, is of 1904, replacing a
circular window. Restored 1965–6 by *Peter Sawyer*. The interior, although beautifully refurbished closely to Pitt's design,
is disappointing, with a flat plaster ceiling similar to the original (which was replaced by *Scott*). Most of the furnishings are
of 1965, apart from the early C18 BOX PEWS in the S transept,
the two-decker PULPIT, the FONT of 1897, allegedly copied
from one by Wren, and the BARREL ORGAN with a Gothick
case. Presented by the 1st Duke in 1835. – HATCHMENT of the
Great Duke †1852. – STAINED GLASS. E window by *Powells*,
1904. The Risen Christ with angels. From Italy; cartoons for
All Saints, Bordighera, Italy (D. W. Hadley). – MONUMENTS.
Quite a variety. – Brass. George Dabridgecourt †1558. Black-
letter inscription. – John Howsman †1626. Niched kneeler in
Oxbridge gown. – Sir William Pitt †1636 and wife. Two semi-   68
reclining alabaster effigies, he above and a little behind her
between Corinthian columns, under an entablature and wide
segmental pediment, both broken for their arched achievement. Backplate with the inscription. Below in the sarcophagus two feigned grills behind which jumbled up feigned bones.
The monument is signed by *John & Matthias Christmas*, and
dated 1640. – Next, to l., Pitt family. Big tablet erected 1681,
with colourful heraldry: fourteen achievements, those of
Edward Pitt †1643, his children and alliances. Urn at the top
and garlands l. and r. The bottom part characteristically different: an addition for George Pitt †1734. Are the achievements
in the wall, either side of the marble, of the later date? – Anna
Maria Trapp †1762. Pretty tablet with oval inscription plate
hanging by a ribbon with dainty garlands. – George, Lord

Rivers †1803. Gracefully Grecian by *Flaxman* of 1804. Large with two tall standing figures in relief by an urn. Especially elegant draperies effectively contrasted by the grey marble surround. – The Hon. and Rev. Gerald Wellesley †1882. By *George G. Adams* of London, 1883. Bust, a fine portrait flattened and nearly in profile. Classical frame. – 2nd Duke of Wellington †1884. Again by *Adams* and lifelike bust, niched above trophies telling of the Duke's interests. – 3rd Duke †1900. Signed by *Conrad Dressler*. Bust, broader in treatment than the others and entirely classical. – Capt. Lord Richard Wellesley †1914. Long tablet by *Eric Gill*. Worth a special look, not only for the lettering but also the surmounting achievement with lively mantling. – 4th Duke †1934, by *Gerald Wellesley*, from Ewhurst church. – 5th Duke †1941. Conventional with a portrait. 1945 by *Percy Portsmouth*. – Gerald Wellesley, the architect 7th Duke †1972. Large tablet with an austere antique porphyry urn by his former partner *Trenwith Wills*.

In the porch a record of an amusing epitaph to John Baylie †1777, unofficial jester in the household of the 1st Lord Rivers: 'his only sin was a drop of gin'.

THE OLD RECTORY, by the church, was 'lately rebuilt' in 1765. With an attached Tuscan four-columned porch and a lunette over. Pediment above this. Taller addition to r., 1836.

VILLAGE, 1 m. W. Semi-detached MODEL COTTAGES of *c.* 1840 with mullioned windows and overhanging eaves. SCHOOLS of 1841 and 1843.

WELLINGTON COUNTRY PARK. *See* Heckfield.

STRATFIELD TURGIS

ALL SAINTS. Redundant since 1969. Nave and chancel and bell-turret, clearly always an impoverished building. At some time between 1282 and 1304, the parish was united with Lasham (q.v.). Nave of C13 origin in an agreeable mixture of chalk, flint and puddingstone. Original N doorway, *c.* 1300, partly blocked and converted to a window. Next to it a small coeval Y-tracery window with an un-restored ballflower hoodstop and the remains of another (Paul Jeffery). Brick chancel of 1792; the E window of 1877 and the timber bell-turret of 1899 by *Cancellor & Hill*. Homely interior, simply plastered with a plaster tympanum between nave and chancel.

Close by, TURGIS COURT, standing within a moat. A very satisfying double-pile house of *c.* 1700. Brick with big hipped roof. 1–3–1 bays, with later C18 sashes and pedimented doorcase.

THE WELLINGTON ARMS HOTEL, ½ m. NE, on the main road. C18, remodelled and extended in a heavy vernacular Grecian for the 1st Duke of Wellington. Stuccoed.

TURGIS GREEN, the principal settlement, has several good houses. On the W side, WHEELER'S FARMHOUSE, mid-C18, the three-bay front with vertical panels of red and grey brick and hipped dormers. E, WELLINGTON COTTAGE, C17 lobby entry, refronted in the C18 with a pair of full-height canted bays and central pedimented gable with blind lunette. S, the early C19 TURGIS HOUSE and THE CRICKETERS, the latter stuccoed with a pair of full-height bows.

SUTTON SCOTNEY
4030

Wonston

PRIMITIVE METHODIST CHAPEL. 1888, red brick with gault brick dressings and a mixture of Gothic and round-arched windows.

VICTORIA HALL, S end of the village. 1897. Roughcast and tile in the Voysey manner. The pretty clock tower was added in 1902. Substantially extended 2001 by *David Gregory*, in a sympathetic manner. Nearby, the WAR MEMORIAL, *c.* 1919 by *T. D. Atkinson* and an original design which has instead of a cross three small segmental-pedimented panels and an ogee finial.

Several old houses and thatched cottages centre on THE SQUARE at the junction of the London–Salisbury and Newbury–Winchester roads. It still has its inns: on the S side, the Georgian former White Horse Inn (now the WHITE HOUSE) and at the NE corner, the COACH AND HORSES, C17 and C18.

SUTTON MANOR (nursing home), SW edge of village. Fundamentally C18 but described as 'lately rebuilt' in 1908, see the porch with its broad open pediment. On the garden side three full-height bows. E, the former STABLES. Brick and timber-framed with herringbone nogging, gable over central archway. 1903 by *Cancellor & Hill*, who also designed the former water tower. In 1934 the film producer J. Arthur Rank acquired the estate and had the house altered by *P. J. Meredith*. Also for him the charming thatched ESTATE OFFICE of 1935, by *A. E. Mort* in his Late Arts and Crafts style. Mort also designed several groups of estate cottages in the village, e.g. Nos. 1–4 Old Stockbridge Road.

NAOMI HOUSE, W of Sutton Manor. A children's hospice. 1996–7 by *Wildblood Macdonald*, displaying strong Arts and Crafts influences, including a number of Lutyens quotations. Horseshoe plan, with lean-to ranges either side of a brick spine wall with tile capping, stepping down at each end (bedrooms on the inner side, corridor etc. on the outer). Four wings project outwards including, at the W end, the dovecote-like circular chapel. Inside, engraved glass by *Tracey Sheppard*. Additions 2009 by the same architects.

SYDMONTON

The village, which was probably grouped around a green to the
S of the church, has largely disappeared, possibly through the creation or extension of the park of Sydmonton Court in the C18.

SYDMONTON COURT. An original endowment of Romsey
Abbey, the manor was granted to Sir John Kingsmill (†1556)
in 1540 and the present house built *c.* 1545–65. A partial
remodelling by *Thomas Hopper*, 1832–7 for William Kingsmill,
was followed by further additions by *T. H. Wyatt*, *c.* 1880–2,
and 1994–5 by *Rod Hackney*.

The E-plan Tudor house, of brick with stone quoins, is still
clearly discernible on the S front. Two small crowstepped
gables in the recessed centre, both C16; the l. one marks a
polygonal corner staircase turret in the angle of the wing, and
this was probably matched originally by a similar turret in the
other angle incorporating an entrance into the cross-passage.
The other gable, flanked by tall chimneys, marks the position
of the hall in the centre. The wings have lateral chimneys on
their outer faces and the hall was probably heated by a chimney
on the N side, now gone. The bands of patterned roof tiles,
gabled dormers with cast-iron lozenge-pattern casements and
the pretty wooden bellcote all look mid-C19, by when other
changes had been made to the house. The W wing was
refronted *c.* 1700, in brick with stone dressings, including a
moulded plinth and regular, staff-moulded quoins. The
windows in its two-bay front, including the original cross-
windows on the ground floor, have raised brick surrounds
incorporating shallow flat arches. The ends of both wings were
no doubt hipped around the same time. The centre of the S
front also appears to have been infilled in the C18 with a
shallow two-storey flat-roofed block that incorporates the C16
angle stair-tower.* The ground floor of this addition was
removed in 2004 and a single-storey extension, with a large
canted bay, added by *Sturgis Associates* to provide a single large
reception room. The front of the E wing is still C16 brickwork,
although the details are all later, and it was doubled in width
by Hopper. His addition included a staircase hall, which is
marked on the W face by a slightly higher hipped roof and
lunette, on the axis of the entrance created in the middle of
the E front at this time. Hopper also appears to have faced the
house in 'Roman Cement' (now mostly removed), added or
rebuilt the parapet and inserted the present sashes. The N front
of seven widely spaced bays, like the E, retains stucco window
surrounds of the 1830s (the window openings, with slightly
segmental heads, may be part of an C18 refenestration), and at
each end has full-height canted stucco bays, which, like the
surviving string course, have Gothic mouldings. In the centre,
on the first floor, a carved stone royal arms, clearly relocated.

---

* This infill was covered over in the C19 but revealed once more in the 1950s.

In 1835 a 'Mr Fulkes', no doubt *Thomas Fulkes* of Reading, was paid for drawing the N front, presumably acting on Hopper's behalf.

The ground floor of the E front was extended forward by Wyatt and has in the centre a recessed three-bay porch with Tuscan columns *in antis* (late C20 pediment), leading into an enlarged entrance hall; to its r. a former conservatory of three by three bays, articulated by the Tuscan order carried around as pilasters, and to the l. the billiard room with canted bay windows to the front and side. A continuous cornice struggles to hold these disparate elements together.

At the W end of the house, facing onto the old service yard, is an addition of 1994–5 by Hackney: a two-storey porch with a remarkable carved stone frontispiece set between brick piers, the upper part of which consists of a two-light window pushing up into a gable. The head of this is a three-dimensional representation of a design by *Millais* (of 1853) for a window head with tracery formed from the figures of Blake-inspired angels. The tracery is pierced but the rest of the arch is blind except for doors to a stone balcony with wrought-iron balustrade, which is supported by a pair of fluted corbels, like fan-vaults, flanking the arched doorway. To the l. an ashlar-faced semicircular stair-turret with, in the clerestory light, stained glass of 1995 by *Joseph Nuttgens*, depicting freely treated pastoral scenes.

Despite the survival of the C16 plan, there is little to see of this period inside, apart from the circular wooden newel staircase with its pretty finial. Of the later work, the best thing is Hopper's Staircase Hall, Neoclassical in form but Neo-Tudor in detail and since the 1990s overlaid, like much of the interior, with a rich Neo-Victorian Gothic decoration: walls are picked out as masonry in red and ceiling painted blue with stars, 1997 by *Peter Stoff*. The imperial stair has turned balusters and octagonal newels with miniature buttresses, and rises within a cubic space covered by a handkerchief dome with moulded ribs and an octagonal lantern. Tudor-arched arcading to the upper parts of the walls, open to the landing. To the S, and extending into the end of the C16 wing, is Hopper's Drawing Room. The Dining Room, in the position of the C16 hall, is largely as remodelled by Hopper, with a moulded ribbed ceiling and linenfold-panelled doors. The Billiard Room/Library in Wyatt's extension is Neo-Tudor/Jacobean and has a stone fireplace with a wooden overmantel and bookcases incorporating old carved work. In the drawing room a fine marble chimneypiece of *c.* 1770–90, installed 2003, Doric with flanking figure groups of Cupid and Psyche and Bacchus and Ariadne and attributed to *Carlo Albacini*. Originally acquired in Rome by Frederick Hervey, the 4th Earl of Bristol and Bishop of Derry and until *c.* 1960 in No. 6 St James Square, the London home of the 1st Marquess, and then at the family seat, Ickworth House, Suffolk, where there remains an identical piece.

NW of the house, a large square DOVECOTE. Probably C17, rubble stone with pyramidal roof. W, the former STABLES. U-plan, the N range early C19, the rest mid-C19 and later. Brick and tile. Gabled central projection with hexagonal wooden cupola over. N wing, probably formerly stuccoed, with lunettes. PARK, with lakes formed from fish ponds in wooded valley to NE. Midway between the house and fish ponds an ICE HOUSE. Mid-C19 Neo-Tudor ENTRANCE LODGE on W side of park. Stuccoed, with diamond-leaded windows and highly decorative bargeboards. Pair of elaborate late C19 wrought-iron gates, introduced *c.* 1995, with much use of geometrical patterns.

Former ST MARY (now a private theatre), on the lawn in front of the house. Rebuilt in 1853 by *J. P. Harrison* of Oxford for William Kingsmill. Flint. Broad W tower with buttresses continued as detached angle pinnacles – the Somerset way. Nave and chancel. Dec details. However, the N and S doorways are genuinely Norman, from the earlier church held by Romsey Abbey, though sweepingly restored. In the arch chip carving and a band of small raised triangles. The chancel arch of this Norman church is now the tower arch. It has a broad band of leaf, represented by symmetrical volutes sprouting out of a central stem. Also an order with a big twisted rope. – PILLAR PISCINA. Norman; now outside the N doorway. – STAINED GLASS. Contemporary with the church. E and W windows by *W. Holland* of Warwick, part of a larger series now invisible within. In the N porch (former vestry) a fine imported panel by *Morris & Co.*, probably by *Burne-Jones.* A single figure of St Mary with a lily on a background of wild rose, oak and acorns below dense foliage with apples and pomegranates.

6060

TADLEY

Originally a scattered village around St Peter's church but then substantially developed on Tadley Common and much expanded after 1950 with housing to serve the Atomic Weapons Research Establishment at Aldermaston (Berkshire); its population nearly 12,000 by the early 1990s.

ST PETER, 1 m. SW of the town. Much restored in 1600 (F. G. Davidson, *History of Tadley*, 1913); the short brick W tower carries a stone inscribed by *Christopher Clifard* Bricklayer, 1685, but may have been rebuilt in the C18 and has a C20 roof. Nice brick S porch of 1689, with reused Tudor woodwork. The low, roughly chequered brick chancel must be Georgian. The S doorway is C15 with a curious look. Friendly interior, carefully restored in 1877–9 (nave roof) and 1890. Big WEST GALLERY with sturdy C17 balusters, the balusters alas half sawn off. Original balustered staircase in the tower. – COMMUNION RAILS and ALTAR TABLE. C17. – PULPIT. Dated 1650, hence a rarity of the Commonwealth. Very domestic, as if in a house,

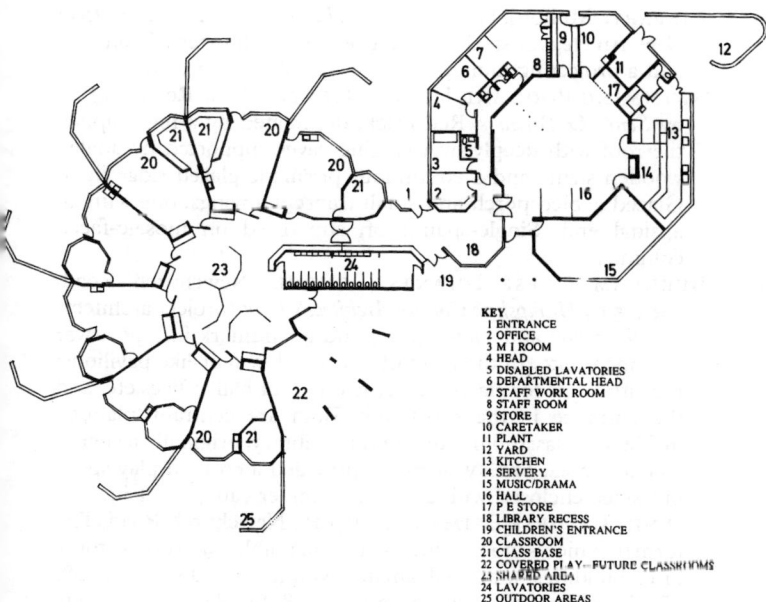

KEY
1 ENTRANCE
2 OFFICE
3 M I ROOM
4 HEAD
5 DISABLED LAVATORIES
6 DEPARTMENTAL HEAD
7 STAFF WORK ROOM
8 STAFF ROOM
9 STORE
10 CARETAKER
11 PLANT
12 YARD
13 KITCHEN
14 SERVERY
15 MUSIC/DRAMA
16 HALL
17 P E STORE
18 LIBRARY RECESS
19 CHILDREN'S ENTRANCE
20 CLASSROOM
21 CLASS BASE
22 COVERED PLAY
23 SHARED AREA
24 LAVATORIES
25 OUTDOOR AREAS
FUTURE CLASSROOMS

Tadley, former Burnham Copse Infants' School.
Plan

panelled throughout. Back panels round the corner, flat sounding-board. Nice little triangular seat in the angle for the
preacher, a thoughtful provision when long sermons were
mandatory. – BENCH-ENDS with moulded tops. Some Perp or
C17(?), some dated 1756. – STAINED GLASS. E window (commemorative date 1917). By *A. O. Hemming & Co.*

ST PAUL, The Green. 1965–6 by *Roger Pinckney*. Brick with
slim bell campanile. Steep pantile-roofed nave and apsidal
chancel in one with narrow internal aisles. Inside, concrete
diaphragm arches. Mostly contemporary FURNISHINGS and
lurid, abstract STAINED GLASS in *dalle-de-verre*. N chapel in
the link to the slender campanile.

UNITED REFORMED CHURCH (former OLD MEETING), Malthouse Lane. Successor to a meeting founded in 1662. Humble,
of brick, of two phases, with parallel roofs. The earlier part,
half-hipped with a rendered front, is of 1718–19 (C. P. Wagner)
though altered in the C19, when the doorway was made central
and windows repositioned. The rear part is early C19, when the
interior was remodelled, with wood-panelled galleries on iron
columns on three sides. Early C18 panelled pulpit with back-
board and balustered stair. Later pews. Still an atmospheric
meeting room. Later lower brick schoolroom, attached at right
angles.

LIBRARY, Mulford Hill. 1992 by *Hampshire County Architect's Dept.* An elegant steel-framed glass box with external columns and a projecting monopitch roof. Parallelogram plan.

SWIMMING POOL AND HEALTH CENTRE, New Road. 1997–8 by *Scurr & Partners.* Red brick, dominated by a high hipped tile roof with deeply overhanging eaves supported by angled wooden struts and a continuous prismatic glazed ridge light. Glazed gabled porch and small transeptal wings, one with an apsidal end. Single-span roof, supported on mosaic-faced columns.

p. 515 BURNHAM COPSE INFANTS' SCHOOL, Newchurch Road. 1983–5 by *Hampshire County Architect's Dept* (project architects *Ian Templeton* and *Steve Harte*) and a landmark in a post-war housing estate. In the form of a pair of low tent-like pavilions; the larger one for classrooms, the other for hall, offices etc. and the entrance in the short link. Both are centrally planned inside: the classrooms surround the library, originally a shared teaching area. The SW segment provided a covered play space but since enclosed with a separate timber canopy outside.

BURNHAM COPSE PRIMARY SCHOOL, Newchurch Road. The former junior school, with its unremarkable 1950s two-storey brick buildings, was amalgamated with the infant school 2008. The buildings were remodelled 2007–8, by *Hampshire County Council Architects* (project architect: *Nick Yarrow*) with the addition of an external first-floor walkway connecting the three blocks and a specialist teaching extension.

TADLEY PLACE, ¼ m. SW of St Peter. What remains is the parlour wing of a larger house. It is *c.* 1600. Brick with stone-mullioned windows. Two storeys and attic. It has two parallel ranges, with gables to the S front, which is articulated by giant pilaster-strips. The W range is noticeably grander with an impressive multi-shafted chimney and taller windows, while the E range is timber-framed at its rear. Was this range built first but refaced in brick *c.* 1600 and the W range added soon after, wholly in brick? (Inside the W range, a fine stone fireplace with Tudor arch and Ionic pilasters.) Good thatched C17 four-bay aisled BARN.

3050

TANGLEY

ST THOMAS. Much rebuilt in 1875 by *William White.* Nave and chancel and a low apse reconstructed on Norman foundations. Above the apse, in the chancel E wall, is a Norman twin window with a strong middle pillar. Is this *in situ*? It is an odd place to be in. The apse arch inside is partly original. It is pointed, with one slight chamfer. W steeple ashlar-faced, built in 1897–8, also by *White.* – FONT. Engagingly odd. Of lead, drum-shaped. It is decorated with roses, fleurs-de-lys, and thistles, i.e. must be Jacobean or could be early Charles I. It is a very handsome piece in its minor way. Perhaps it was paid for by the royalist Reades of Faccombe (q.v.) who held the advowson. Anne Reade (†1624) was daughter to a Clerk of the Signet to James I. – FONT COVER of typically Jacobean shape.

N of the church is the former school (Church View), of 1870, possibly by *White*. ½ m. W in the village is BELLS COTTAGE, a curiosity. Brick and flint with some grand stone details, including keystones to the ground-floor windows and an obelisk over the central door connecting to a blind *œil de bœuf* above. Is it C18, or a late C19 confection with reused stonework?

THRUXTON

2040

One of the most enchanting of the chalk-cob-built villages of North-West Hampshire. The church stands in trees next to the mysterious overgrown site of the large, once fossed and ramparted, manor house of the Cormeilles and Lisles. When Henry VIII stayed with Sir Thomas Lisle for five days in 1539, the house is thought to have equalled Stokesay Castle in extent.

ST PETER AND ST PAUL. Undistinguished low exterior, heavily refaced in flint during major restorations begun in 1843–4 with refurnishing the interior and continued in 1849 (nave, and N aisle added) and 1869 (chancel, with enormous 'whole flints') but with some genuine medieval details, e.g. the almost round-headed E window with three early C13 lights, the two late C14 nave S windows, one with good headstops, and also perhaps the two N aisle N windows, re-set from the nave N wall. Of greatest interest is the low stunted ashlar W tower, built in 1801–2 (the earlier tower fell in 1796). It is of finely dressed Chilmark stone, clearly reused from the Early Tudor chantry chapel for Sir John and Lady Lisle completed in 1527 (dated battlement), which stood on the N side of the chancel (*see* below). Nice W window and carved battlements with Early Renaissance decoration and a frieze of running foliage. On the E side are medallions held by griffins, with two portraits (Sir John and Lady Lisle?), and on the N side the initials of their successor Thomas Lisle. There was an earlier chapel (dem. 1800) on the S side of the chancel to Sir Nicholas Lisle †1506, whose tomb-recess survives within the chancel S wall. It is no later than 1515 (N. Riall) and received extraordinary attentions from the restorer of 1869. What he did was outrageous but full of pluck. The shape of the arch is repeated in an inserted four-centred window, its Perp details consonant with the tomb below, whose panelled S face is left oddly exposed and so appears to have been turned around. He wanted a priest's doorway as well, and so the doorway merrily cuts off about two-fifths of the arch. Moreover, a normal doorway would have been no fun and so for a canopy he introduced a copy of the C14 ogee-canopied priest's doorway at Bishopstone (near Salisbury).

Inside, little architectural interest (excepting C13 chancel roof and late C15 chancel arch of continuous mouldings), but much in the FURNISHINGS. In the chancel, stone ALTAR, of 1843 by *Osmond*, and REREDOS, with crisp Perp panelling, with small statues of SS Peter and Paul, all looking *c*. 1849. – ALTARPIECE of 1869 attributed to *George Daniels*, then working for *Clayton & Bell* (P. Cormack). Highly finished and rich, showing Christ the King, enthroned with angels. Other furnishings of 1843–4 in topographical order: – TILES. In the surrounding sanctuary by *Maw*. Elaborate C13 patterns. – CHOIR STALLS and PRIEST'S STALL, richly carved. In the nave, two-sided wooden desk LECTERN, and PULPIT, made by *John Francis*, village carpenter and wheelwright. – PEWS of 1844. The ends carved at Stamford in 1857. – FONT. By *Osmond*, presented by the Rev. William Grey, architect of Swanmore church, Isle of Wight. – FONT COVER. Richly crocketed, gilded and painted by *F. R. Fisher*.* Painted TEXTS in the nave, with Gothic letters. By *Willement*. In the N aisle, a stone ALTAR, of 1869, really a tomb-chest to Nanny Baynes. – STAINED GLASS throughout in every window (dates 1843 onward to 1869 by at least four different makers). The best in the E window of 1843 by *Willement* at his most antique. Early C14 style, Via Crucis, Crucifixion and Deposition scenes. – Chancel SE, in the tomb-recess, of *c*. 1869, probably by *Clayton & Bell*. – Chancel SW, of 1857. – Vestry N and nave SE windows of 1844 by *Willement*. – Nave SW, of 1857, by *David Evans*. Excitable, with highly finished figures of David and Aaron. N aisle W and N windows, again by *Evans*.

MONUMENTS. An interesting collection. In the tower, archaic effigy of a knight, perhaps Sir John Cormeilles †1200 since it has a primitive square 'bucket' helm of late C12 or very early C13 type. Purbeck marble, very defaced. Strictly frontal, in chain armour, full kite shield on breast. It is the earliest monumental effigy in Hampshire, and possibly the oldest military effigy in England (cf. the better-preserved early C13 Knight at Kirkstead, Lincolnshire). – Coffin slab. C13 with a floriated cross. – Large brass to Sir John Lisle †1407 (chancel floor), son of the earliest Lisle, lord of the manor of Thruxton. One of the biggest and best-preserved brasses in Hampshire. Conventional figure, nearly 5 ft (1.5 metres) long. The figure, one of the earliest in full plate armour, is conventional, but the triple canopy is splendid. – In the chancel S wall, the tomb-recess of Sir Nicholas Lisle †1506, a robust Early Tudor architectural piece. Conventional, elaborately panelled tomb-chest. The panelled arch with charming detail – a central lily with angels (Nicholas Riall has noted a similarity with angel corbels in the presbytery aisles at Winchester) carrying shields l. and

* Fisher restored the church at Allington, Wiltshire, for Rev. William Grey in 1848–51. Were they the restorers of Thruxton in the 1840s?

r. in the castellated cornice. Two more below. As we have seen, the arch opened to a s chapel.

On the N side of the chancel is the finely carved architectural front to the lost chapel created for Sir John Lisle †1524, and his wife Mary †1524. A remarkably advanced design, with Early Renaissance elements, in a typically Early Tudor Gothic composition very daring for the date. Her will specified 'a chapell or an ambulatory after the plott and bargayn made by my husbande wt my lorde of Wynchestre's mason', possibly referring to *Thomas Bertie*. Like the monument to Ralph Pexall at Sherborne St John (q.v.), it consisted of a large arch into the chapel (replaced by the vestry in 1839) and a smaller arch filled by the tomb-chest itself. Both are four-centred. The tomb-chest is two-faced, of two dates and two styles: the s side, of Purbeck marble and of the usual Late Gothic details, was erected for Sir John Lisle †1471 and has an inscription; the N side, however, is of Caen stone and of refined Renaissance details similar to those of *c.* 1525 to Bishop Pontoise in the presbytery screens attributed to Bertie at Winchester Cathedral, but here with achievements in lozenges (of Courtenay and Lisle). The contemporary effigies of Sir John and Lady Mary are carved in a fine-grained Caen limestone. His armour of Milanese fashion. Her mantle falls in beautiful folds around her feet. Plentiful Early Renaissance details, especially in the arches, friezes and crestings. – Lady Elizabeth Philpott (according to church guide and VCH) †1616. A very rare, but alas, sadly damaged oak effigy from a lost monument. The lady wearing a ruff and richly patterned dress. Good carved details in the pillow. Very late for the use of oak.

CHURCHYARD GATES of iron. By *Skidmore*, 1870.

THRUXTON MANOR, SW of the church. Late C18. Painted brick. Three bays. The stable and coachhouse, NW of the house, are particularly charming. Quite substantial. Cob with a hipped thatch roof. Arched openings with flint dressings. Original fittings. The OLD RECTORY to the E, of 1836–7. Gault brick. Five-bay garden front, the entrance side less formal with entrance in a re-entrant angle. In the village, the MEMORIAL HALL of 1817, built as the Methodist chapel. Red brick with modest stone details and two tiers of arched windows set in tall arched panels. Rear wing *c.* 1870 with blue diaper brick. Beyond the Memorial Hall on the other side of the road, GEORGE COTTAGE, a small C15 cruck house. Inside, the two-bay hall remains open to the roof. The chimney forming the lobby entry was probably a C17 addition and externally the walls have been rebuilt in brick.

ROMAN VILLA, ½ m. ENE. In 1823 a Roman villa of basilican type was discovered. One room contained a fine mosaic in the centre of which was a circular panel depicting Bacchus seated on his tiger. Surrounding this were squares containing heads. The mosaic is unusual in that on two sides were inscriptions: the one that can still be made out mentioned Quintus Natalius Natalinus and a group or family called Bodeni – a Celtic name. The second line, almost completely lost by the time of discovery, contained the word 'voto' indicating some kind of dedication. The mosaic was lifted in 1899 and is now on display in the Roman Britain gallery in the British Museum. Further excavation in 2002 showed that the villa had been a very modest establishment up to the late C4 when the mosaic was laid. One possible explanation is that at this time the old house was fitted out as a shrine for ancestors, the mosaic room providing the place for celebratory dining. Significantly a C1 burial immediately outside the building was enclosed within a fenced enclosure at this time – could he have been the ancestor revered?

TICHBORNE

A delightful village in the valley of the upper reaches of the Itchen. The church stands apart, on higher ground sw of the village.

St Andrew. Mostly of flint, with a sturdy Saxo-Norman chancel – cf. the still Saxon tradition of the double splays of the single windows, but the typically Norman flat buttresses. The tall nave, in its masonry coeval with the chancel, has two blank arches high up in the E wall. Were they bell-openings (cf. Chilcomb)? Plain w tower originally with vaned corner pinnacles of agreeably mixed brick, blue and red, and dated 1703. Contemporary s windows to the s aisle. Sympathetically repaired inside by *Colson & Nisbett*, 1909, and *T. D. Atkinson* in 1924. Rough two-bay nave arcades, probably late C12, when the aisles were added. The N arcade has as its pier a hardly treated chunk of wall and pointed arches with one slight chamfer. The s arcade has the same arches but a thick octagonal pier. The plain round-headed N doorway (now blocked) may be late C12, but the s doorway is C14. The chancel has an under-restored E window with reticulated tracery. The N chapel E window is renewed. A medieval chancel screen was lost in 1820 but the C15 door to the loft stair survives. – FONT. Norman, circular, turning at the top with a little bald decoration at the top. – FONT COVER. Probably C17, an ill-fitting pyramid, with an elegant finial. Original, of square plan to fit Post-Reformation form. – BOX PEWS in nave and s aisle, mostly Jacobean, the taller squire's pew with achievement no doubt made for Sir Benjamin Tichborne. PULPIT. Georgian Gothic (from Cheriton, made after the 1745 fire). Octagonal, with two tiers of open quatrefoils. – STAINED GLASS. In the tracery of the chancel E window, early C14 fragments of a St Andrew and exquisite foliage. – s aisle. 1998 by *Diana Snagge*, painted by *Trevor Whiffen*. Local scenes.

The N aisle is the Tichborne Chapel, divided from the rest by sturdy cast-iron RAILINGS of indeterminate (*c.* 1820?) date, with gilded crucifixes facing inwards. Built as a chantry chapel in 1338 by Sir Roger de Tichborne and still Roman Catholic, a rare anomaly within an Anglican church. The MONUMENTS are to members of the family. Richard †1619 aged eighteen months. Small hanging tablet, with the baby in red gown and booties lying on his side, below an alabaster arched frame. – Sir Benjamin †1629, and Dame Amphillis, his wife. An excellent standing alabaster monument of the Southwark school. Two recumbent effigies. Against the tomb-chest outstandingly fine kneeling children. Very good back wall with columns too. Sir Benjamin, High Sheriff of Hampshire, gained the friendship of James I and thereby ensured the survival of the family chapel in Roman Catholic use. – Sir Henry Joseph †1845. By *J. E. Carew*. Unfortunately placed close to the floor. Ethereal white relief of the deceased on his deathbed surrounded by his family. Two angels above embracing. – Henry Tichborne Doughty †1835. Against w wall, a Gothic canopied classical relief by *G. Canigia* (Peter Howell) with a boy and his guardian angel. – Edward Doughty †1835 of Upton House, near Poole, and his wife Katherine Arundell †1872. Elaborate tomb-chest.

CHURCH COTTAGE, down the lane towards the village, is dated 1729 in vitrified brickwork. This was the home of Tichborne's Catholic priest. (Inside, a C16 moulded brick fireplace, the beam above with Latin inscriptions and the date 1589.) GRANGE FARM, at the village's s end, is a well-preserved traditional farmstead, once a sub-manor of the Bishops of Winchester. Substantial C17 house, timber-framed, encased and extended in the C18, in brick and flint. Of the buildings around the yard, the most interesting is an L-shaped barn range incorporating part of a C16 timber-framed structure. This was probably a former sheephouse. These were substantial buildings: this was of at least seven bays, reduced to four-and-a-half. The walls were originally close-studded, infilled with wattle, with arch bracing. Its se side, towards the fields, was open with tie-beams cantilevered beyond the posts to carry an oversailing roof. There was a loft in at least two bays. The roof is of 'raised aisle' construction; the queenposts have jowls on their outer faces and support upper wall-plates and tie-beams, from which queen-struts rise to collars and conventional clasped purlins. But its conversion to a barn, perhaps in the C17, saw the addition of aisles and a further barn at right angles, incorporating two rebuilt bays of the truncated sheephouse.

TICHBORNE HOUSE, ¼ m. E. Built *c.* 1803, following the demolition of the old house of the Tichbornes, and designed, according to Baigent, by *Joseph Hodgkinson*, the estate steward. Two storeys. Painted brick (originally stuccoed). Seven-bay se front, the outer pairs slightly projecting with the ground-floor windows set in round-arched panels. Central raised section of blocking course with carved stone coat of arms. Very fine tetrastyle Greek Doric stone portico with unfluted columns and triglyph frieze, of one storey on a rusticated plinth. Five-bay sw front, the centre three slightly projecting. Curious plan:

a narrow rib-vaulted entrance passage passes between (but allows no access to) the front rooms and leads into the fine rear staircase hall. Staircase rising in three flights, with a delicate balustrade incorporating lattice panels, apparently wrought iron, but largely of timber.

In the sw range, the CHAPEL (St Margaret of Scotland, R.C.) has a coved cornice, a ceilure of pretty geometric Gothic ribs over the altar, and w gallery with panelled front. – REREDOS. C18. Corinthian pilasters and open segmental pediment with flaming urns. – ALTAR RAILS. 1683. Brought from Rome by Sir Henry Tichborne. Stubby symmetrical double balusters between wide bands of carved scrollwork. The dies with carved putti. – BENCHES. Late C19, the ends with scrolled sides and small pediments. – PAINTINGS. Flanking the altar, Our Lady by *Sassoferrata* and St Peter by *Guido Reni*. On the s wall, Crucifixion, school of *Dürer*. – STAINED GLASS. Late C19. Figures of SS Margaret and Henry set in Renaissance aedicules. The third window with the Tichborne arms.

NE, the STABLES, a late C19 model design with buildings around three sides of a courtyard.

SEVINGTON MANOR, ½ m. SE. Sevington was the home farm for a large estate of the Bishop of Winchester. Grand lobby-entry farmhouse (documented by 1606), with an early C19 stuccoed front. One room each side of the chimney, which has four diagonally set square stacks. Two storeys and attic, with mullioned windows in the end wall, which also has flint-nogged close studding exposed, also at the rear which has a substantial hipped-roofed stair-tower. Well appointed inside: hall to r. of chimney with a large brick four-centred arched fireplace and a doorway, its moulded frame with, alas mutilated, jewelled vase-stops, leading to the fine closed-well staircase. The parlour, l. of the chimney, has a panelled end wall, the frieze of which has inlaid arabesque ornament. The kitchen wing is C18 but incorporates late medieval timbers, possibly from an earlier hall range.

TUFTON

ST MARY. Austerely simple aisleless nave and chancel (restored 1887 with new buttresses, E window and roof) with a stunted C18 bell-turret and homely brick s porch. Two small Early Norman windows high up in the nave N wall (opened by *W. Carpenter Turner*, 1940). Another, on the s side, with a doorway, plain and very tall with a big lintel, an undecorated tympanum, and an arch with small saltire crosses and a billet hoodmould. The nave has also on either side a big domestic early C18 wooden cross-window. Inside, the unmoulded chancel arch is typically Early Norman. But the chancel is early C13 and has lancet windows, N and s, set internally in monumental robust three-bay arcading with proper columns and arches. Can this work be explained by the ownership of the church by Wherwell Priory then under the dynamic Abbess Euphemia?

WALL PAINTING, on the nave N wall, a faded but still fine, very large early C15 St Christopher with an ornamental frame but none of the genre details one sees so often. The compelling figure is incised with concentric circles. What is the mystic symbolism of this surely medieval graffiti? – Fragments of medieval painting with later texts over the chancel arch, cut off by the low C18 roofing. – FONT. A plain medieval tub. The only other furnishings that need be noticed are in the chancel, all of the 1960s reordering by *Colin Shewring*. Uncompromisingly of the Liturgical Movement. The altar free-standing on a hard-edged floor of industrial brick.

TUFTON MANOR. Mid-C19, stuccoed. Rented in the late 1930s and early 1940s by Wells Coates and friends, including the graphic designer, Ashley Havinden, and painter and cartoonist, Walter Goetz.

TUNWORTH

Hidden and secluded, only five miles from Basingstoke: it might as well be fifteen.

ALL SAINTS. A tiny church, of flint, nave 32 ft (9 metres) long, and chancel 15 ft (4.5 metres) long internally, with a bell-turret. Almost rebuilt in 1854 by *Woodyer*, keeping one small genuine Norman N window in the nave, one small C13 window in the chancel. The chancel arch is *c.* 1200, pointed with one slight chamfer, the nave S doorway of malmstone with two continuous chamfers probably *c.* 1300. Typical Woodyer, the timber S porch (restored in 1908), the E and W windows, and the large square-headed nave S window, and inside, the simple furnishings. – CHOIR STALLS. With griffin heads. – ALMS BOX. A curiosity, funny and engaging; probably Victorian in a folksy, rustic C17 idiom. – STAINED GLASS. E and W windows of 1854. Grisaille. – NAVE S by *Jane Gray*, 1992–3. Mostly heraldic. – Outside, large stone TABLE TOMB to the Rev. John Hewer †1845, yet still Late Georgian with original railings.

N of the church, MANOR FARMHOUSE, of the second half of the C15 with copious original herringbone brick-nogging. A two-bay hall with arched-braced collar-truss, converted to a lobby entry in the C17. E end refaced in brick in 1715 with good bolection-moulded panelled room inside. ¼ m. E at the crossroads are TRELAWNEY and MANOR FARM COTTAGES, estate cottages built for George Jervoise of Herriard in 1817 and 1828: unusual plan, formerly two semi-detached pairs with each pair sharing a lobby entry. BEECHCROFT is an interesting timber-framed lobby-entry house of *c.* 1602. Originally there was no brick chimney, only a smoke-bay divided lengthwise to form a hearth and a lobby, the latter with a gallery above connecting the upper chambers.

TUNWORTH HOUSE, ¾ m. NE. Neo-Georgian, c. 1910–20, possibly by *Robert Weir Schultz* who designed CHALK COTTAGES to the E for the same client in 1920–1.

7050

UP NATELY

A loose group of cottages and farmhouses around a road junction.

ST STEPHEN. Charmingly rustic pre-Ecclesiastical Tudor Gothic exterior largely of 1844. The N doorway, however, is Transitional, of c. 1200, round arch, a slight chamfer, and dogtooth (cf. Greywell) and left under-restored, as is the Perp nave SE window. Interior with a surprisingly Late Georgian 'feel' for 1844. The plain chancel arch looks Early Norman, with grooved and hollow-chamfered abaci. Nave roof early C16, with arch braces and scissor-braces above the collars, partly renewed in 1891. – COMMUNION RAIL. c. 1700, with twisted balusters. – POOR BOX. With an C18 back-board unusually with a painted cherub.

3040

UPPER CLATFORD

The church is in a placid pastoral setting between streams in water meadows, at a distance from the village amid a managed landscape recorded in a pictorial map of 1733 by John Reynolds. The main village street is to the W across the former Andover Canal. It has cottages and houses of modest character.

ALL SAINTS. The big nave roof is of such a broad spread it suggests an unusual interior. Its most peculiar and rare form is the result of a draconian reordering in the early C17. The nave is a wide space for preaching, divided by wooden posts on the S side, and the builder showed imagination in his extraordinary chancel arch, which is double. This arch is in fact a Late Norman two-bay piece, ingeniously re-set it seems from a former N aisle.* Round pier, round abacus, some nailheaded decoration. Of about the same time, the plain N doorway (also re-set). In the chancel S wall, a fragmentary Norman window too, said to come from the E wall. Blunt W tower, with C14 flint lower stage with angle buttresses and square top, of rendered brick with plain two-light square-headed windows, of 1578

---

* The late C12 church was held by the abbey of Lire, in Normandy.

(dated stone inscription inside). The stone tower arch is of the later date with good typically Elizabethan mouldings (its upper part restored in 1909). Also post-Reformation, the s porch of brick. Probably C17, but could be C18. Major restoration and enlargements by *J. E. K. & J. P. Cutts*, of 1890–1: chancel extension in a conventional Perp, smooth N arcade of three bays in Bath stone, N aisle with two C14 windows, W and north-easternmost, evidently re-set from the earlier aisle (incorporated in the early C17 nave). Big NE hall and vestry extension of 1996–8 by *Clive Spencer*. Rendered.

FURNISHINGS. – PILLAR PISCINA. With a decorated scallop capital of *c.* 1200, made up with fragments found in the tower in 1909. – FONT. Dated 1629. Octagonal baluster and semi-globular bowl. – Strange FONT COVER. – PULPIT. A well-preserved Jacobean piece, with back-board and tester, the latter with some decoration. Perhaps originally placed midway against the s wall. – S DOOR. Is it C17? The simple iron hinges look earlier still. Could they be C13? – The glazed outer DOORS of 2003–4, with excellent carved trout handles, by *Nick Barberton*. – (STAINED GLASS. Nave W window. 2006 by *Gabrielle Preedy*. Crucifixion. Much blue.) – MONUMENT. Rev. Edward Frowd, rector 1863, signed *T. Page*, Andover. Old-fashioned. – In the churchyard, two early C19 grave markers, James Guyatt †1818 and wife †1811, with nicely draped urns, each differently attired. 'His' and 'hers'.

CHURCH BRIDGE, spanning the River Anton, is of 1843 by *Tasker & Fowle* of Anna Valley (q.v.) and constructed completely of cast-iron components. Two spans formed from eight shallow-arched ribs with diminishing pierced roundels in the spandrels, supported on cast plates at the abutments. Delicate balustrade with slender columns.

At the N end of the village COPTHALL PLACE, a curious house, with giant pilaster strips with Corinthian capitals tucked under the eaves. The effect is charmingly naïve. The giant order suggests the early C18 but the other features look a century later.

THE OLD RECTORY, less than a ¼ m. s of the church. A rambling late C18 and early C19 house with early C19 cast-iron Gothic casements on the garden side. A small cast-iron FOOT-BRIDGE in the garden of 1835 by the *Taskers*. Two shallow elliptical arches with decorative scrollwork in the spandrels and a delicate balustrade with saltire-cross bracing and spindle-type balusters.

NORMAN COURT FARM, ¼ m. SE. A good early to mid-C18 house. Vitrified header brickwork with red brick dressings, which include the platband, cornice with moulded dentils and window surrounds with flush brick keystones. Seven bays, five bays forming a symmetrical front, its doorway with later pedimented doorcase, and two bays to the l., beyond a garden wall, presumably representing the service end. C18 aisled BARN.

BURY HILL-FORT, ½ m. W. A carefully hidden hill-fort overlooking the river valley. Two lines of defences are evident and sense has been made of them by two excavations in 1939 and

1990. The outermost earthwork enclosing 22 acres is the earlier and now stands to a height of 6 ft (1.8 metres) behind a ditch 11 ft (3.4 metres) wide and 5 ft (1.5 metres) deep. It was timber-fronted and dates to the C6 B.C. The site seems then to have been abandoned but at the end of the C2 B.C. it was redefined on a more massive scale with concentric ramparts over 8 ft (2.5 metres) high and a V-shaped ditch 20 ft (6 metres) wide and 10 ft (3 metres) deep in between. Excavation within showed there to have been circular timber-built houses and storage pits. By the mid C1 A.D. much of the interior had been abandoned but there were people still living around the entrance.

UPPER ELDON

Just a hilltop farmhouse with the church as a garden ornament.

St John the Baptist (Churches Conservation Trust). Late C12. Nave and chancel in one, although formerly longer at both ends. Two round-headed N windows with continuous rolls, plus one W, one S. Inside, the splayed openings are pointed, and there is evidence of three more. E wall rebuilt in brick (dated 1729 with initials W.H.; probably William Hussey, who held the advowson). Nine recesses for consecration crosses survive. Very early and a rare feature. Simple interior with a queen post roof.

(The FARMHOUSE has a C17 plaster overmantel with painted royal arms. In another room wall paintings in imitation of oak panelling.)

UPTON GREY

A pleasant village with several good houses, the main street climbing the hill with the church halfway up on the r.

St Mary. High, short nave, possibly curtailed at the W end, as we shall see inside, blunt axial tower, the upper parts of brick (dated 1690 on the E face) and disproportionately long chancel. In addition a fine, unusually wide, brick N aisle of 1715, built for John Limbrey of Hoddington House: *Henry Hore* of Odiham, mason, and *Thomas Marshall* of Upton Grey, carpenter. The bonding still English. In the W and E gables a blank oval – an old-fashioned motif, looking late C17. Nice W door of exquisite rubbed brick possibly c. 1900, and S vestry of 1909 by *Cancellor & Hill* on the site of a C13 S chapel, probably demolished in the C15, against the tower S wall.

The interior has plenty of puzzles. Worked into the internal SW quoin of the nave is an impost, possibly Saxon. The tall W crossing arch is Early Norman, possibly *c.* 1100–25, but evidently much pulled about, and probably heightened. It opened originally to a short C12 chancel over which the tower was raised in the C13. Arch of plain voussoirs with two rows of billet (some renewed in 1889 by *Colson & Son*). Inside the tower, much lower and more convincing E arch. E.E. single-chamfered (coeval fictive masonry patterns on the E face). The chancel, of the same width as the tower, is beautifully simple. E half is E.E., of *c.* 1230, probably financed by the Priory of West Sherborne as holder of the advowson. Lancets N and S, the easternmost on the S side carefully restored by *J. Oldrid Scott*, 1881–2 (good iron rainwater heads) when evidence of the C12 chancel at the W end was revealed. Lancet windows, and the finest feature, an E window, nicely composed of two lancets and quatrefoiled circle over. Plain E.E. S doorway. A S aisle has been demolished: the arcading of a two-bay or longer S arcade (blocked) is exposed in the S nave wall. It was Transitional and shows a W respond and a one-bay lengthening W beyond it. The central pier, of fine chalk freestone, chamfered. The robust, not to say clumsy, N arcade of three round-arched bays belongs to the N chapel, but is in its details much coarser. Tall octagonal piers, octagonal capitals. One would like to see Tuscan columns here. Nave roof with tie-beam dated 1608.

The FURNISHINGS are as motley as the building. – FONT. Small, Perp, octagonal, with quatrefoils. On the underside, more rewarding heads and flowers. – FONT COVER of *c.* 1660. – CHANDELIER. C18. – PULPIT STAND (one can hardly call it a proper pulpit) introduced some time after 1905. – PEWS. N aisle, early C18. In the nave, a set of 1908. – RAILING. Under the tower, the fine former balustrade from the destroyed W gallery of 1827, relocated as the belfry stair by *F. James*, of *James & Kearns, c.* 1990. Unusually mixed Late Georgian classical and Gothic elements. – WALL PAINTING. A tantalizing, almost indistinct fragment of a medieval inscription on the NE wall. Just twenty red Gothic letters, apparently in English, dated by J. C. Cox to the C13. An early use of English when Latin and/or Norman French were more common?

STAINED GLASS. In the chancel, of various dates, all by *Powells*, finest in the E window (commemorative date 1879) with Archangel Gabriel and Our Lady Annunciate in flowing drapes, *à la Henry Holiday*. – N aisle, E and W. Both again by *Powells*. – MONUMENTS. An instructive collection of mid-C17–early C20 hanging tablets. Lady Dorothy Eyre †1650. An important, typically mid-C17 piece, perhaps by *Joshua Marshall*, as strikingly similar to his coeval monument to Mrs Mary Brocas †1651 (of the Hampshire family of Beaurepaire perhaps?) in St Margaret's, Westminster. Flat frontal bust in a recess and a swag across. Two pediments inside pediments. Black marble and alabaster. Interesting inscription referring to her position as Maid of Honour to Queen Anne (James I's consort, Anne of Denmark). – John Matthew †1689, signed by *Richard Wood* of Oxford. A broad, gristly white Baroque cartouche, rather 1665 than 1685 in style. Oval inscription.

Upton Grey, Manor House.
Drawing by F.L. Griggs, 1925

Cherubs seated with the achievement, one with an expired
torch, the other with a trumpet. – Another tablet, metropolitan and up-to-date in style, to Barbara Opie †1657, erected
much later, possibly in the 1670s: it loosely resembles the tablet
to William †1672 and Esther Finch †1673 in St Helen's Bish-
opsgate, London (attributed to *William Stanton*). – Also in the
nave, James King †1766, with a circular garlanded inscription

on a veined red 'surround', and a smaller marble to Lt John
Beaufoy †1809, signed *P. Chenu*, London. Military trophies. –
John Hanbury Beaufoy †1836. Austere Neoclassical. Signed
Clark & Son, Reading.

Good memorials in the churchyard. Prominent w of the
church, a monument to Captain John Payne †1810 and wife,
signed *Coade & Sealy*, 1810. Very Grecian, with an urn. –
Charles Holme †1924. Very 'advanced', with arty lettering. A
quite extraordinarily outré proto-Art Deco piece in granite.

THE MANOR HOUSE, behind the church, is of interest for the
superb alterations and additions of 1907 by *Ernest Newton*, for
Charles Holme, editor of *The Studio* (although he always lived
at Upton Grey House). The old part consists of an early C15
hall range, altered and a cross-wing added in the early C17.
Newton formed this into an E-plan, with the addition of the
central timber-framed gabled porch and a service wing. The
Old English style, rather than Newton's customary Neo-
Georgian, is presumably used in deference. Simpler garden
side, but with another strong central accent added by Newton,
a tall timber-framed gabled bay. Is the later wing with loggia
his? Inside, impressive mid-C17 square-well staircase with
turned balusters and newels with finials and pendants.
Newton's panelling, fireplaces etc., are Neo-Tudor. Most
important are gorgeous enriched plaster ceilings by *George
Bankart* with naturalistic flowers and foliage. The drawing
room has broad bands of rose briars and square corner panels;
in the dining room these trail along the frieze and over a beam.
The low-walled forecourt has gatepiers with raised brick
diaper-work (cf. Four Acre House, West Green) and a
wrought-iron gate with a pretty early C19 elliptical overthrow
with radiating arrows. Otherwise the GARDEN is by *Gertrude
Jekyll*, 1908–9, well restored in the 1980s by *Rosamund
Wallinger*. At the front, a wild garden with pond alongside the
drive, at the rear a formal garden, terraced with rubble walls
of Bargate stone. A central pergola on the upper terrace leads
to steps down to a sunken rose garden, with further steps to
lower lawns.

(HODDINGTON HOUSE, ½ m. SE. A lovely double-pile brick
house with stone quoins and modillion eaves cornice. Five bays
with steep pediment over the projecting centre. The windows
have keystones with carved stylized faces, the centre one with
eared architrave and carved swags to top and sides. Probably
built for John Limbrey in the late C17 but enlarged 1886 and
altered 1888 by *J. B. Colson* for George Sclater, 1st Lord
Basing.)

VERNHAM DEAN   3050

A pretty, spacious village with many thatched houses. The church
is isolated in a deeply rural valley.

ST MARY. Embanked in a sloping churchyard. Nave and chancel
and w bellcote. Medieval flint masonry in the nave N wall. The
w doorway also is genuine, of Binstead stone, though it may
be re-set. It dates from *c.* 1220 – quite a showy Transitional
piece. Two orders of colonnettes, simple capitals, crockets,
stiff-leaf, and also turned-in leaves rather like oak. The arch is
still round and still has zigzag at right angles to the wall. But
the hoodmould is decorated with dogtooth. Restored in 1700,
but now essentially simple E.E. of 1851–2, either by *Arthur Ash-
pitel* (GR) or as *The Builder* says: 'The design of the curate, the
Rev. J. M. Rawlins'. Large E window of five slender graduated
lancets. Little altered inside. – STAINED GLASS. In the chancel,
of *c.* 1851. E window with elongated medallions – Annunciation, Holy Family, Crucifixion, the Holy Women and the risen
Christ. The lateral windows (commemorative dates of 1846
and 1848) with single medallions. All naïve, very lovable, and
with some deep blue.

THE OLD RECTORY, to the S. 1879. Gothic, of brick and flint,
with some polychromatic brickwork.

VERNHAM MANOR, ¾ m. E. Quite a grand house, in park-like
surroundings. Jacobean. Two storeys, brick and flint. Broad
symmetrical front, the centre of five bays flanked by gabled
wings; the r. wing incorporates a C15 timber frame. Original
bargeboards. C18 fenestration between the wings. Central nail-
studded panelled door. C18 corridor between the wings at the
rear; the central staircase tower is probably of this date. Inside,
early C17 panelling and hall screen with Ionic pilasters. Chamfered brick-arched fireplaces. Plaster barrel-vault in first floor
of r. wing. Nice, perhaps early C19, flint rusticated GATEPIERS.
In front, by the road, a C17 timber-framed BARN. Six bays with
curious cranked queen-struts, supporting both lower purlins
and collar.

UPTON MANOR, 1 m. SE. An early C18 farmhouse, with a five-
bay E front, the ground-floor windows with frilly heads and the
centre bay flanked by gauged brick pilasters. Gentrified in 1936
by *Wellesley & Wills*, who added the elaborate doorcase, with
Baroque double-curved pediment on heavy consoles, the bays
set back to l. and r., and the whole of the S front. On the N
side, onto a narrow service yard, one wing has Gothic
windows. Inside the library has bolection-moulded panelling
and a fine reused C18 alcove with fluted pilasters and ogee arch
with carved spandrels.

THE VYNE[*]
Sherborne St John

[65] The Vyne is one of the most rewarding houses in Hampshire,
both visually and historically. The house now represents four

[*] The entry for The Vyne has been revised by Charles O'Brien.

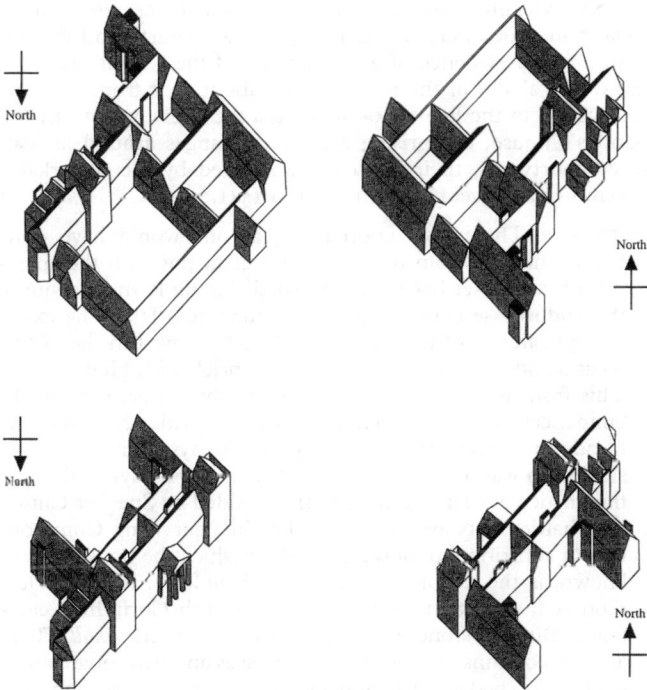

The Vyne, development 1530s–1660s.
Axonometric drawing, 2003

periods: the first is the period of William, Lord Sandys, who succeeded in 1496, received his title in 1523, became Lord Chamberlain in 1526, and died in 1540. Henry VIII visited The Vyne in 1510 but the bulk of the building work by Sandys must, according to dating of the roof timbers, have been done between 1524 and 1526. Chaloner Chute bought the estate from the 6th Lord Sandys in 1653 and reduced the extent of Sandys's mansion to a good-sized country house, employing *John Webb* for the purpose. Chute was a barrister, became Speaker of the House of Commons in 1659, and died in the same year. *John Chute*, amateur architect and friend of Horace Walpole, came into the property in 1754 and died in 1776, after making numerous important changes. Alterations were also made by William Lyde Wiggett Chute after 1837 and before his death in 1879, doing much to create the carefully layered historic character of the house today. That is the framework of dates. For the house they mean *c.* 1520–5, *c.* 1655, *c.* 1760–76 and the mid C19. The house was passed to The National Trust in 1956 on the death of Sir Charles Chute.

The Tudor house was much larger than the house is now and only that part containing the Great Hall, suites of apartments for the Sandys family and chapel survived the 1650s remodelling. Leland in about 1542 mentions a 'fair base court', and Wiggett Chute found evidence of a courtyard S of the S front, quite far away, and also N of the N front, only about 30 ft from the lake. Excavation in the late 1990s suggested the likely extent of Lord Sandys's house, comprising a series of ranges around at least three courtyards, their existence supported by the remarkable survival of an Inventory, compiled in 1541.*

EXTERIOR. The visitor approaches, as one would have done before the C18, from the NE, so a tour begins with the splendid N FRONT set back from a broad sloping lawn (the site of the Tudor base court) which runs down to a lake. The external appearance of the house was largely arrived in the 1650s. As it stands, it is of two storeys, red brick with blue diapers. This front is symmetrical with raised, three-storey tower-like eminences on the ends. They are two bays wide; the rest of the façade including the portico has eleven bays. This even, classical form was achieved in the 1650s, only the bays to the l. of the portico are Tudor, those to the r. added by Speaker Chute. The battlements are mid-C19. The chief surviving Commonwealth contribution, however, and for which the house is well-known, is the N portico. This is by *John Webb*. It is of brick, rendered, with giant columns carrying lush Corinthian capitals in Burford stone. The mason was *Edward Marshall*. There are two columns on Portland stone bases and two square angle pillars. The pediment is of wood. This is the earliest domestic portico in England, although Webb designed one for Durham House in London in 1649 (which was not executed), and the motif, derived from Palladio's Villa Barbaro at Maser, was no doubt among possibilities considered in the Inigo Jones office. The view from the portico to the lake is exquisite. The windows of this front, and all the elevations, have receding surrounds, all of Webb's time, though the sashing was done in the early C18. There are no Webb windows preserved at all. They no doubt had mullion-and-transom crosses. At the E end, as an appendix is the ante-chapel with Victorian windows in two tiers and the chapel with its polygonal apse and its blind, transomed windows with four-centred heads. The windows have uncusped arches below the transom, but cusped ones at the top. They are actually Victorian but repeat the original ones of the E apse. The battlements are again Wiggett Chute's but the chancel apse has original battlements with shields. To its l., i.e on the S side of the house, is a canted C18 bay, behind which is *John Chute*'s tomb-chamber. Behind this, facing S a two-storey Tudor survival with original windows with mullions and octagonal glazing bars.

The S FRONT became the main entrance to the house in the C18. It is E-plan with a recessed centre, central porch and two gabled wings with small square projections in the re-entrant

65

*The findings are detailed in *The Vyne: A Tudor House Revealed*, by Maurice Howard and Edward Wilson (2003).

angles of the wings. Though convincingly Tudor in precedent,
e.g. Barrington Court, Somerset, this is in fact a C17 creation.
The centre is of eleven bays but only the W part and SW wing
are part of the Tudor house, although the basement of the
rebuilt eastern part appears to have reused earlier windows.
The two-storey porch is C19. Just to its r. in the angle between
porch and wing are visible traces of an internal spiral stair,
which appears to have connected the cellars with the hall of
the Tudor house. The windows to the basement are original
Tudor fabric but probably re-set. They are of one and two
lights, with uncusped four-centred heads to the lights. In the
square angle projections are C17 side doorways. The wings start
to the inside with big chimney-breasts, but the stacks are mid-
C19, so too the canted bays in the end walls and straight gable
over the centre. A balustraded terrace runs along the s front,
bearing piers with stone eagles given by Horace Walpole to
John Chute in 1745. The weathered black-and-white paving
stones were originally in the Staircase Hall (removed in the
C19, they are almost certainly those laid by Edward Marshall
in the 1650s). The SW wing, which may have contained part of
the Royal Apartments of Lord Sandys's house, has evidence of
a two-storey canted bay window on its E side designed to light
the galleries which occupy each level of this wing. Remains of
a doorway have also been discovered and traces have also been
found of a stair-tower at the SW corner of this wing, suggesting separate access to this range during the C16.

INTERIOR. The tour of the house begins in the STAIRCASE   81
HALL which extends through the depth of the house from s
to N, including the N vestibule behind the portico along with
the upper adjoining rooms. The Great Hall of the Tudor house
may have occupied this space and evidence suggests that this
could pre-date the rebuilding of the 1520s. Webb must surely
have designed an appropriate hall to lie behind his portico –
Marshall was paid for black-and-white stone paving for the
staircase – but its appearance is unknown. *John Chute* reversed
the entrance to the house to the s side *c.* 1770 and the hall is
all his as far as design and detailing go. Its form was only
arrived at after nearly a decade of pondering, the affection for
Strawberry Hill Gothick eventually superseded by classical formality. Pevsner was struck by this choice – 'It has not a touch
of the Rococo, although its contemporary equivalents in
Central Europe are Rococo in every respect' – and considered
it 'the spatially most fascinating staircase composition of the
second half of the C18 in England'. The *Topographer* in 1789
called it 'theatric', and that it unquestionably is. The composition is hard to describe. The s porch enters into what is meant
as a tripartite room, though the l. third is stunted. On the r. is
a screen of fluted Roman Doric columns, set two deep and
connecting the room with an adjoining apartment, which
serves as a passage to the Saloon (the dining room in the C18).
The ceiling is coffered throughout between bands of guilloche.
The centre part is again divided in three. The l. and r. parts

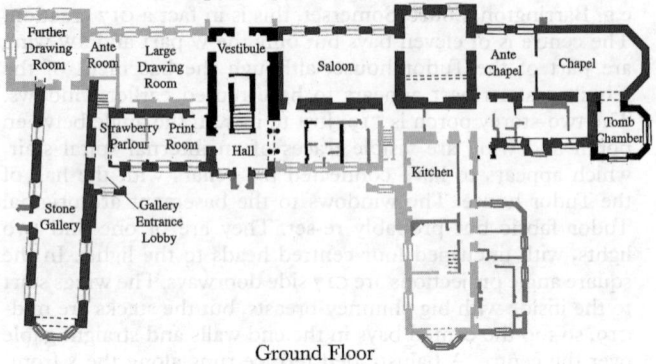

Ground Floor

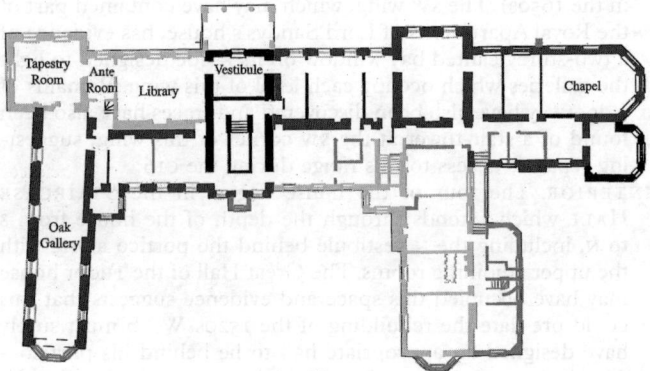

First Floor

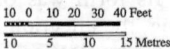

pre-1524–1526
1524–1526 building campaign
1654–1655 building campaign
18th-century work
19th-century work

10   0   10 20 30 40 Feet

10   5   10   15 Metres

The Vyne.
Ground- and first-floor plans

are low and connect with passages to the N vestibule. All ceilings are coffered again. The centrepiece is the staircase itself.
It is not wide, and rises first in the vestibule with balusters and
then between solid walls. After one straight flight it turns at 90
degrees and disappears out of sight. But this middle piece,
where the staircase goes up, is open to the ceiling (coffered of
course) of the first floor, and the ceiling at that level runs
through uninterrupted to the first-floor room above the portico

81

vestibule, which is visible from the foot of the stairs through a
screen of slender fluted Corinthian columns. There are also
upper columns on the r., and there again an upper room with
a coffered ceiling becomes visible. It is the most startling over-
ture to The Vyne.

w of the staircase hall are two rooms which were part of the
Tudor house of Sandys's time. The first is the PRINT ROOM,
refurbished in the c18 with a good chimneypiece. The walls
have been decorated with stuck-on prints since the early c19
(inspired by the print room at Stratfield Saye). In John Chute's
time this was known as THE STRAWBERRY PARLOUR, a reference to its use as the room for meetings of Walpole's Committee of Taste. The name is now applied to the adjoining
room, a small panelled chamber retaining its c16 panelling and
curious decoration of cusped arches over the fireplace. A small
service passage separates this from the STONE GALLERY in
the sw wing. This too belongs with Sandys's house but re-
created by Anthony Chute, John's elder brother, c. 1753 as his
Orangery and paved in black-and-white stones. Over the fireplace in the e wall is a terracotta medallion of the Emperor
Probus, who was credited with introducing vines to England.
It is so much like *Giovanni da Maiano's* at Hampton Court,
which were made in 1521, that it must be by the same (Florentine) sculptor and of about the same years. It has been suggested that John Chute acquired it after the demolition of the
Holbein Gate at Whitehall Palace, c. 1760.

The following sequence of rooms along the n side were
added to the house in the 1650s but now reflect the influence
and taste of John Chute, Horace Walpole and the Strawberry
Hill set. The FURTHER DRAWING ROOM, ANTE-ROOM and
LARGE DRAWING ROOM all have Rococo ceilings of the
1760s, executed in *carton pierre*. The Further Drawing Room
has at each corner a sunburst with Apollo's head. This room
and its neighbour also have crimson brocade hangings as a
backdrop to a display of Walpoliana that includes black-and-
gold picture frames executed to Chute's own designs. The
Large Drawing Room is similarly treated, its c18 uniformity
disrupted, however, by a wooden chimneypiece, with over-
large volutes l. and r., curling askew, and caryatids in relief
against the sides. This was created by Wiggett Chute from an
overmantel, originally coeval with a chimneypiece now in the
Library.* The curly style is mid-c17, very possibly by *Webb*.
John Chute had commissioned a chimneypiece for this room
from *Thomas Carter* but it was unfinished at his death. After
that follows the VESTIBULE behind the n portico, its minor
importance reflecting the reorientation of the main entrance
to the house to the s in the c18. Wall niches and Adam-style
pedestal.

On the e of the portico vestibule is the SALOON. It retains
plain Tudor panelling, although its form was probably arrived

* Originally placed in the first floor of the NE tower (the Tapestry Room, *see* below).

at in the 1650s, the date of the chimneypiece. This is one of ten new chimneypieces supplied by *Edward Marshall* and has termini Atlantes looking out of straitjackets of black blocks. Frieze with two heads and garlands. In the Tudor house this room appears to have been divided and incorporated a service stair in a compartment at its W end. The panels are studded with brass 'stars', a restoration of a scheme known to have been instigated by John Chute at Walpole's suggestion. Mid-C18 cornice and curious C19 ceiling with raised centre. Next is the DINING PARLOUR which, investigation has revealed, originally contained two rooms, one containing the main stair to the Sandys' private apartments at the E end of the house. Tudor floor tiles have also been discovered. The linenfold panelling which now covers the walls from floor to ceiling is genuine C16 but evidently re-set, probably in the C18 – the date of the plaster cornice and ceiling with quartered panels and light foliage – when it covered up a C17 doorway in the SE corner of the room communicating with the service wing behind.

The walls of the adjoining ANTE-CHAPEL are decorated with applied patterns of strips of wood. The style is John Chute-Gothick, apparently at Walpole's suggestion. The ribbed ceiling may be original i.e. of the 1520s. – In the windows heraldic STAINED GLASS from the Guild Chapel of the Holy Trinity at Basingstoke (q.v.), built by Lord Sandys (*see* p. 160). Inserted here in the early C20. – SCULPTURE. Excellent bearded bust, stone, early C16, 'as good as if it were from Champagne', thought Pevsner. Discovered in the C19 amongst other excavated relics of the Tudor house. The style is similar to sculpture at Winchester Cathedral.

The ante-chapel very probably formed a single space with the CHAPEL. Although altered in the C18 (e.g. panelling at the E end) and later, this is the best late medieval private chapel in England. It probably occupies the site of an earlier chantry chapel at The Vyne. The polygonal apse, already mentioned, has its counterpart in Lord Sandys's Chapel at Basingstoke. The ceiling is vaulted in a four-centred section and has wooden ribs in a pattern of overlapping octagons. Anthony Wells-Cole has pointed to Serlio as the source, and noted the similarity with Wolsey's Closet at Hampton Court, but it may be late C17 instead. In the manner typical of royal and major country house chapels, the family's access to the chapel was at first floor. There is still an opening into the GALLERY which served as Lord Sandys's 'Chamber over the chapel'. It has as its backdrop a fascinating, if simple, painted decoration (discovered in 1997) of black-and-white vertical stripes, clearly intended to reproduce the effect of hangings. An opening, presumably to Lady Sandys's 'closet next the chapel', was discovered in the S wall of the chapel in the 1990s.

The quality of the FURNISHINGS is outstanding. – STALLS. *c.* 1520s (cf. Lady Chapel, Winchester Cathedral). One tier and fronts. Ends with poppyheads, e.g. three putti, women and jugglers, also openwork decoration. The back panels have fine tracery tops in two tiers. Traceried fronts also. Horizontal canopy curving forward with heraldic bosses and frieze. The detail is entirely Gothic here as well, but the stress on the top horizontal with its classical ornament shows that England was ready for the Renaissance. A small doorway in the s stalls led into the vestry. – TILES. Mid-C16, probably Flemish, perhaps by Italian makers and in the style of vividly coloured Italian majolica with several portrait heads. First recorded here in the C18, they were re-laid in bands during the C19. The STAINED GLASS is the chapel's most celebrated feature and one of the most important ensembles in England for its date. Exquisitely coloured in reds, yellows and blues, the windows are of a quality matched only by royal commissions. Upper tier, from l. to r., Resurrection, Crucifixion, Christ carrying the Cross; below, Henry VIII, Catherine of Aragon, Margaret of Scotland with their patron saints, all in fantastic, typically Flemish settings although the architecture shows a clear awareness of Italy. The glass displays signs of having been cut down to fit the windows but the date of its insertion is uncertain. It may have been commissioned as part of a larger cycle of windows for the Holy Ghost Chapel at Basingstoke and removed from there in the C17. What is known is that in 1522 Lord Sandys engaged ten glaziers, including the Antwerp-trained *David Joris*, to travel to The Vyne. The design has been attributed to *Bernard van Orley*, court painter to the Regents of the Netherlands and Sandys is known to have shipped glass from Flanders in 1524. – PANELLING. Round the altar; late C17 or early C18. – PAINTINGS. Above the stall canopies, the only Gothick feature of John Chute's years, are a striking series of illusionistic paintings (restored and repaired in 1997). Perspective plays with fan-vaulting and Gothic tracery, and figures of the Evangelists in the spandrels. By the Greek painter *Spiridione Roma*, whose oil sketch is shown in the ante-chapel. Roma came to England about 1770 and shows himself inspired here by Italian stage design, most evident in the painted Baroque curtains which frame the opening to the gallery.

Opening off the chapel's SE corner is the TOMB CHAMBER designed by *John Chute c.* 1770 to house the memorial to Speaker Chaloner Chute (†1659). The panelling is poor Gothick, the ceiling also, created from papier mâché. The MONUMENT, completed after John's death, is one of the finest of its date in England and serves to show what quality could be achieved at that time. High tomb-chest with garlands, cartouches and fluted Ionic colonnettes, the four at the corners detached. Drawings show that this was designed by *Chute* but executed by *Thomas Carter*, who received payments between 1775–81. The Speaker looks younger than he was when he died, lying wonderfully at ease with his head propped up on his elbow. He seems to be musing and all alone. There is no playing to an audience as one finds so often in the funerary art of the Baroque and Rococo. He lies in Speaker's robes on the traditional straw mat, his large hat by his side. – STAINED

GLASS. Two English pieces, demonstrating John Chute's enthusiasm, like Walpole's, for contemporary stained glass. S wall: Adoration of the Shepherds attributed (by Michael Archer) to *William Price Jun.*, *c.* 1750, an oval frame set against blue and yellow diapering; E wall: the Adoration of the Shepherds, by the little-known *John Rowell* of Reading, after *Van Dyck*, and acquired by Chute from his widow *c.* 1732, i.e. long before inheriting The Vyne. Chute's designs for the Tomb Chamber show that he always intended it for this position.*

On the upper floor of the house, only the rooms W of the staircase are to be seen. First, along the N front, the Library and the Tapestry Room. In the LIBRARY is yet another mid-C17 chimneypiece, in stone. Two columns clothed by four tiers of upright leaves. Lintel with arms and palm fronds. Ceiling with ribs, probably C16, removed here from a room in the NE tower in the C19. In the TAPESTRY ROOM, bolection-moulded doorcase and large Jacobean chimneypiece of wood, moved here from the Chapel Parlour in the C19, with small figures of Justice and Faith. The most important room is the OAK GALLERY, occupying the whole SW wing and evidently part of a now destroyed sequence of royal apartments which, we must assume, must also have been accessed by other, lost ranges of the Tudor house. Though re-windowed in the C17, it is perfectly panelled still, the pattern being a specially intricate linenfold with devices not only of Lord Sandys and others but also the arms of Henry VIII and Katharine of Aragon who were separated in 1526, the year in which building is likely to have concluded. A doorway in the NE corner has an outstanding carved panel of the royal arms flanked by winged cherubs and Sandys crests in medallions, all in an Early Renaissance style. The chimneypiece is mid-C17, and plausibly by *Webb* for it is more classical than the others. It is white with just a dark green panel. Open broken pediment, and fat garlands and a cartouche in the centre. The furnishings are those of the C18 and C19 house including several items acquired by John Chute and Horace Walpole. A series of pedestals in imitation porphyry were designed by *Chute* to display antique busts acquired by him for his brother in the 1740s (now in the Stone Gallery). In the S window, STAINED GLASS panel by *William Price Jun.*, *c.* 1750, a colourful piece with a rustic maid carrying a basket of fruit, similar in style to the panel in the Tomb Chamber. Beyond the Oak Gallery is a suite of two small rooms. Though much altered, their position in relation to the Gallery supports the suggestion that they originally formed part of the King's Chamber in the Tudor house. Their precise function is unknown.

The rooms of the first floor in the E half of the house appear to have been the principal apartments in the C16 house, including 'the great dynyng chamber' (above the Saloon, its original ceiling still intact) and rooms for Lord and Lady Sandys, but these were plundered of much of their detail in the C19 for embellishment of the other rooms. The SE ROOM, above the

*The N window of the chapel gallery has further glass by *Rowell* and *Price*.

former vestry, was originally Lady Sandys's 'closet next the chapell' (*see* above) and 'The Study' in the C18. Its rib-pattern ceilings were removed in the C19 and reused in the Tapestry Room. In the N wall, a fine classical bookcase of Serlian form designed by *John Chute* before 1754, i.e. for his brother Anthony. Traces of linenfold panelling survive. Its form is similar to that in the Chapel Parlour (*see* above), suggesting Anthony Chute may have removed it for reuse there.

The outbuildings to the SE of the houses comprise the former LAUNDRY (C19 with gabled cross-wings) and BREW-HOUSE, C16 and later, which from the C17 formed a U-shaped group with the STABLES and a demolished barn. GATEPIERS. S entrance. Low, of stone, rusticated, with a niche. They are Jonesian in character, perhaps by *Webb*, but re-set.

GARDENS. The medieval park, never extensive, was reduced to its present extent in the C17. Formal gardens existed in the C16 and C17, probably on the N side of the lake, i.e. on either side of the main approach to Lord Sandys's house, but were swept away in accordance with prevailing fashion in the C18. The lake itself appears to have been formed into a single expanse from a group of smaller fish ponds. In the grounds, E of the house and close to the main road, is a SUMMERHOUSE, dated (tree-ring dating) to *c.* 1632. It was probably conceived as part of a formal garden layout immediately E of the then existing base court. It is of brick, perhaps originally stuccoed, and its form is remarkably novel for its date: two storeys and round, beneath a dome with a fish-scale pattern. Four projections, each with a round-headed doorway and a round-headed window over. The windows are flanked by brick pilasters. In the diagonals on the upper floor are two small niches, one above the other. The interior was originally floored and has surviving fragments of plasterwork around the base of the dome. John Harris has suggested the building was commissioned by Alathea, widow of the 4th Lord Sandys, whose connection with the circle of Inigo Jones might indicate an attribution to *Isaac de Caus*. An idealized perspective by J. H. Muntz, 1756, shows that a second, identical pavilion stood close to the lake. The same view shows an early to mid-C18 Chinese-style bridge over the water. WALLED GARDEN. Mid-C18. An ornamental canal running along its S side was originally contained within its walls. LODGES, on the Sherborne St John and Bramley roads E and W of the house. Mid-C19, but emulating the 1630s summerhouse. 62

WEST GREEN 7050
Hartley Wintney

WEST GREEN HOUSE. A delightful, if still puzzling, house whose modest core is said to be 1714 but encased and enlarged *c.* 1730–40 for Henry Hawley (General 'Hangman Hawley' of Culloden). 75

The entrance is on the N side. The centre five bays represent the original house – frilly window heads and panelled parapet – but in the middle is a two-storey polygonal bay, added by Hawley, with a battlemented parapet and entrance with a Gibbs surround and big iron lampholder above. Of the same date also one bay l. and one bay r. with on the ground floor a round recess (they held busts of the Dukes of Wellington and York). The modillion eaves cornice extending around the rest of the house is contemporary but the stone urns at the corners appear to be by *R. Weir Schultz* who made alterations in 1898–9 for Dr W. S. Playfair. Flanking arcaded forecourt walls, r. C18, l. largely Schultz. The W front showcases the quality of the mid-C18 changes. Five bays, hipped roof with dormers. Another Gibbs doorway but on the first floor are roundels with (original?) busts of Bacchus and Roman Emperors instead of windows (the height of the saloon within partly precludes upper rooms on this front). Flanking arcaded screen walls with rustication, the l. one the rear of the N forecourt wall. Schultz's remodelling of the S front was informal with a pair of Neo-Georgian full-height canted bays, both with his characteristic inset angles. To the l., a single-storey square bay with bust in circular recess above. Lots of good Arts and Crafts leadwork. The four-bay E front is the result of remodelling after 1974 by *Quinlan Terry*, its forecourt created *c.* 1980.

Inside, the early C18 entrance hall has raised and fielded panelling (prettily painted by *Adam Culkin c.* 1993) and a simple stone fireplace with a wind compass above, and to its E the small, similarly panelled drawing room. Their chimneys were of course external originally but beyond these are now small closets of *c.* 1730–40. That to the E incorporates the service staircase and that to the W has a pretty angle fireplace with a stepped and tiered mantelshelf. At the SW corner, lit by three windows on the S front, is the Neo-Palladian saloon, the most impressive room in the house, with plain dado and full Ionic entablature to high coved ceiling. Pedimented doorcases and chimneypiece. In the centre of the S side a small dining room, enlarged by Schultz. Panelling probably of that date but painted with flowers *c.* 1974. At the centre of the house is the top-lit staircase hall of Hawley's enlargements, with coved ceiling and panelled landing with round arches, but the staircase with stone treads and a wrought-iron balustrade with honeysuckle motifs in the style of *c.* 1770 is by Schultz. Behind the N front, early C18 attic staircase with carved tread-ends and square fluted balusters with carved Corinthian capitals, set askew following the ascent of the stairs: an original, if naïve, conception.

The GARDEN has been extensively restored since the 1990s by *Marylyn Abbott*. It is as enchanting as the house, with elements of the C18, C19 and early C20 layout preserved but as transformed *c.* 1975–90, by the Hon. Alistair McAlpine (later Lord McAlpine of West Green), with structures by *Terry* in the manner of William Kent. Its jocular tone is set by a COLUMN,

at the end of a lime avenue ¼ m. N of the house, with bands
of vermiculated rustication, bulbous finial and Latin inscription, 'This monument was built with a large sum of money,
which would have otherwise fallen, sooner or later, into the
hands of the tax-gatherers'. Beyond, a GATEWAY with piers of
lozenge-shaped plan, bands of flint and stone, topped by
stubby flint obelisks. The wide, hedged and terraced W lawn
has on its N side a simple brick ORANGERY with four tall
sashes, probably early C19, but restored. N of this lawn a
hedged walk leads to a rustic SUMMERHOUSE, with a tablet
of 1734 in memory of Hawley's spaniel, Monkey. Immediately
S of the house are two walled gardens with parterres, the
smaller with an C18 blackamoor SUNDIAL and a late C20 Chinoiserie FOWL HOUSE like a tent. Large C18 WALLED GARDEN
SW of the house. In the E part a relocated wrought-iron well-
head by *Schultz*. Also wooden latticed arbours and octagonal
timber fruit cages, all by *Oliver Ford*. Through a 'MOON GATE'
in the W wall is the main part of the 'philosophical garden'
created by McAlpine and Terry. A flight of brick steps flanked
by rills leads to a lawn terrace with a pair of formal pools. Into
this falls a short cascade, fed by the basins of the NYMPHAEUM
on the W edge of the garden, modelled on the fountain of Santa
Maria della Scala in the Via Garibaldi, Rome, and inscribed,
'A little learning is a dangerous thing, drink deep or taste not
the Pierian spring' (Pope). Pilastered with shell-headed niches
(originally holding statues), but with a *trompe l'œil* centre of a
pediment flanked by scrolls. Its back is a cowshed. S, at the end
of a long beech walk, is a small pedimented wooden SUMMER
SEAT and nearby a lake with a wooden CHINESE BRIDGE to
an island topped by an AVIARY with a frame of steel posts and
ogee top with pineapple finial. S of the lake, the DORIC LODGE
reproduces Laugier's primitive hut with tree-trunk columns on
two sides. E, a flint GROTTO with open pediment and round-
arched opening, the inside domed and apsed with a fountain
draining into a spiral stone rill in the floor. NE of the lake is a
stone OBELISK with a statue of Thomas Mann, gardener at
West Green 1946–86, leaning on its pedestal. Further N
another octagonal metal AVIARY and then a pair of wooden
Chinese PAVILIONS at the end of a beech avenue, square with
pyramidal pantiled roofs and openwork lanterns with tented
copper caps.

LAMBS COTTAGE, NE, *c.* 1899 by *Schultz*. Quite typical with
boarded and plastered gables and timber porch.

THE DUTCH HOUSE, West Green Road, ½ m. NE. probably
early C18. Three by three bays with giant pilaster-strips, a
mansard roof and a large central chimneystack that dominates
the interior. There were no sizeable rooms until the drawing
room was added at the rear in the C19, so it cannot have been
a gentleman's house. Late C20 staircase incorporating balusters identical to those in the attic stair at West Green House.

INHOLMES COURT, ¾ m. NE. A medium-sized Neo-Georgian
house of 1899–1901, by *R. Weir Schultz* for Charles Read

Seymour (*see* Phoenix Green, Hartley Wintney (q.v.)). Centre recessed between wings with shallow flat-roofed canted bays and white-boarded gables with keyed oculi. Rusticated door surround with carved coat of arms under a Lethaby-esque bracketed segmental hood. Service wing, set back to the r., in a different, more vernacular spirit. The other elevations are less formal, e.g. at the rear a garden door with tall canted oriel above; this lights the staircase, executed with Schultz's trademark simplicity. Single-storey billiard room, possibly an afterthought. Garden room with pyramidal roof added *c.* 2002 by *Richard Ashby.*

116   FOUR ACRE HOUSE, ½ m. E. 1901–2, for Dr William Wills by *Ernest Newton.* Possibly his masterpiece. Red brick and tile, in the same alluring cottagey Neo-Georgian of Newton's own house, Hazeley Heath Cottage (Mattingley), and as impeccably detailed. The principal, garden, elevation is roughly symmetrical. Flanking wings have shuttered segmental-headed sashes on the ground floor, leaded casements above and Wills's initials in raised brickwork in the gables. In the recessed centre rises the main chimney with grey diapering and three diagonally set shafts. Less formal entrance front with a diaperpattern string course stepping up over the entrance: it formerly had a lattice porch. Service wing, l., and further addition of 1914. Inside is a 'screens passage' with a beautiful oak screen, horizontally boarded with leaded lights flanking an ogee arch. In the hall a brick fireplace with chamfered oak lintel and the staircase, which retains its simple lattice balustrade to the landing. In the dining room another good fireplace with diaper-ornamented terracotta tiles and moulded stone surround with central panel of carved stylized foliage.

6020   # WEST MEON

A pretty village, whose ensemble of thatched, timber and brick cottages is memorable, the feeling prosperous.

ST JOHN EVANGELIST. 1843–6 by *G. G. Scott (Scott & Moffat)* for £12,000, amply financed by the Rev. Bailey. Remarkably large, of coursed cut flints and Caen stone dressings, with a prominent w tower. 'Second Pointed', i.e. with plate-and-bar tracery, the favourite idiom of the Ecclesiologists. Organ chamber of 1877 by *Scott* in a perfectly consonant E.E. Solemn interior with five-bay arcades and lofty nave roof with two tiers of wind-braces. Sparing carved decoration. Chancel reordered by *Sir Charles Nicholson,* 1923–4, and again more starkly in 1970, when late C19 wall paintings by *Heaton, Butler & Bayne* were removed. – REREDOS. Nice arcading by *Scott* effectively polychromed in the 1920s, with painting by *Claude Deverall.* –

CHOIR STALLS. 1893. – ORGAN SCREEN by *Nicholson*. – FONT, PULPIT and PEWS are still an effective Early Victorian ensemble. – ROYAL ARMS. Daintily carved, dated 1712, clearly designed to be seen from both sides, the back with putti and scrollwork. – STAINED GLASS. The chancel N, grisaille, and tower window, with heraldry, remain from the original architectural scheme by *Thomas Ward* of Soho. Chancel E by *A. K. Nicholson*, 1924; S aisle S by *Clayton & Bell*, 1896, N aisle E by *Hugh Easton*, 1955. – MONUMENTS. In the churchyard, Thomas Lord †1832, founder of Lord's Cricket Ground, erected over his grave in 1951 by the MCC.

Close by, the SCHOOL of 1852 by *J. Colson*. Of dark flint and Gothic, effectively allied to the church. Downhill is a triangular green, with a memorial CROSS of 1901 by *C. Harrison Townsend*, the cross-head densely covered with his trademark foliage, carved by *Farmer & Brindley*. Slightly S, behind the Queen Victoria Institute (1887), is GARDEN COTTAGE, a very early box-framed survival, its roof dated to 1441. Originally of three bays with the hall in the centre; extended in the C17 and later. Nearby, WEST MEON HOUSE, extensively reconstructed and enlarged in the mid C19 as the rectory, with kneelered gables and Neo-Tudor chimneys in clusters. Doric doorcase and shallow, two-storey bow projecting from the E front, probably *c.* 1920. NW of the church is COURT HOUSE (formerly Court Farm), formerly a rural residence of the Prior of St Swithun's. Three ranges form an approximate U-plan. The N range appears to be mid-C15 – arch-braced collar and fan truss visible in the roof – the other ranges mostly early C17 with C19 additions. The position of the entrance in the W range suggests a lobby-entry plan: the stair-tower to its l. is clearly *c.* 1900, when the S range was also enlarged. Garden front of flint rubble with stone quoins and Gothick casements and gablets. Large fireplace in the S room, presumably the former kitchen. The extent of the manorial complex is indicated by the superb group of large barns to the N (now housing).

HALL PLACE, ½ m. E. Late C17 centre of five bays, apparently begun by Isaac Foxcroft, who purchased the property in 1677 (see his cipher in the doorway with segmental pediment, pilasters carved with foxes and the fox-head keystones). Two-bay l. addition of *c.* 1720, with glazed headers and segmental-headed windows; the r. addition with its Neo-Wren W front is of *c.* 1900 – steep two-bay pediment containing a lunette. Some interior features also of this date, although the stair (with turned balusters) and other fittings are typical late C17. The rest altered by *E. R. Barrow* for the Hon. Mrs Ronald Cubitt *c.* 1936–7 and again *c.* 2000 by *Christopher Smallwood Architects*. GARDENS laid out by Mrs Cubitt, with advice after 1974 from *Lanning Roper*, and further improved in the late C20. Stunning avenue arranged axially with the W front. Attractive ORANGERY by *Jeremy Benson*, 1955, with ball finials.

WOODLANDS, 2 m. N. Former school, chapel and house of
1887–9 by *A. W. Blomfield* for William Nicholson, in his Basing
Park estate's usual brick and flint.

WEST STRATTON

5040

Hamlet of cob walls, timber-framed cottages and early C19 villas.

THE MOUNT. Bailiff's cottage for Lord Northbrook of 1880 by
Ernest Newton, still then under Shaw's influence.

WEST TISTED

6020

ST MARY MAGDALENE. The church stands inside the enclosure
of the demolished medieval manor house. Nave, essentially
Norman, with blocked S window and N doorway of *c.* 1100–20.
Later medieval windows, the two-light W window faithfully
replicated in 1962. Low weatherboarded bell-turret. Brick S
porch of 1750. The chancel largely rebuilt 1847–8 but the SE
window partly *c.* 1500 (re-set?). The inner frame of the N
doorway provides a backdrop for the FONT, a plain tapering
C13 stone tub. – C18 PANELLING in the sanctuary, Dutch;
nicely staged with the COMMUNION RAILS by *H. J. Stanley
Vaughan*. – STAINED GLASS. the E window by *Kempe*, 1892. –
MONUMENTS. Sir Benjamin Tichborne †1665. Plain oval
tablet of pink marble. War memorial in the porch by *E. Osborne
& Co.*, London, with a small bronze of Christ.
KNIGHTON, SE. The former vicarage of 1869, assertively Gothic
in brick and flint. Schoolroom attached to the w.

WEST WORLDHAM

7030

ST NICHOLAS. Nave and chancel in one. Granted to Hamble
Priory in the late C12 but held from 1414 by Winchester
College and restored for them from a roofless ruin by *C. R.
Pink*, 1888. Traditional early C13 S and N doorways (the latter
a faithful later C20 renewal). Of the same date, the jambs of
former lancets in the E wall (the present E window is Perp,
partly restored) with remains of a surmounting circular
window. Two small N lancets. N and S piscinas indicate the position of a screen to which altars were attached. – STAINED
GLASS. In the w window, two small enamelled panels (one
dated 1653), with birds and heraldry including the achievement

of the Mason family: they are from a window commissioned by the Rev. Nicholas Mason, ejected royalist vicar of Irchester (Northants), who conducted Anglican services here in 1650. SE window of 1888 by *Egan*.

MANOR FARMHOUSE, standing only feet away from the church, is an interesting triple-pile house of *c.* 1650, of brick with some diaper-work and high hipped roof around a central well. Originally with mullioned windows, replaced in the late C19. Central entrance passage with ovolo-moulded hall screen (cf. Chawton House) and similarly moulded hall fireplace with vase-stops and carved spandrels to a polygonal arch. Central staircase with symmetrical double balusters, handrail and square newels. Separate stair to (formerly heated) attic rooms. On the W elevation a change in brickwork probably marks the junction with an earlier house.

PULLENS, ¼ m. SE. C15 hall house with crown-post roof, remodelled as baffle-entry house in 1652 in dressed malmstone and brick.

THE ROUND HOUSE, ½ m. SE. Octagonal toll house, dated 1767.

BOWL BARROW, on the SW boundary of Littlewood Copse. The SW edge of the barrow has been ploughed out, the surviving monument being 75 ft (23 metres) in diameter and 6 ft (1.8 metres) high.

WESTON PATRICK

6040

The small twin villages of Weston Patrick and Weston Corbett lie either side of the main valley road.

ST LAWRENCE. E.E. style of 1866–8 by *T. H. Wyatt*, with spirelet bell-turret in a High Victorian rogue Gothic of his own. He became lord of the manor after inheriting Weston Corbett House. Flint; nave and chancel in one. The Norman N doorway of the earlier church remains in position. The S aisle, an addition, was paid for by Wyatt and his family. Dominant wooden chancel arch, with open-traceried spandrels on short marble shafts detached from the wall and naturalistic carved corbels.[*] Contemporary furnishings (e.g. the elaborate CREDENCE SHELF and choir stalls with brass candle-stands). – STAINED GLASS. E window, 1868 by *Lavers & Barraud*. Not bad. The Crucifixion, against an effective diapered dado and golden background. Chancel N by *C. Clutterbuck Sen.* W window by *Lavers & Westlake* of 1875 and 1880. The earlier glass was Wyatt's benefaction, the later his memorial.

The VILLAGE HALL is a weatherboarded C17 farm building, converted to the school in 1868. Motley collection of second-

---

[*] Contemporary ornamental stenciled wall decoration recently revealed in the chancel.

hand windows and, inside, C18 Commandment boards, presumably from the church. SW is THE CORNER HOUSE, *c.* 1884–6, by *Matthew Wyatt*, for himself, in Queen Anne Revival style. Opposite, set back from the road, the Gothic OLD RECTORY, *c.* 1868 by *T. H. Wyatt*. On the NE edge of the village, WESTON PATRICK HOUSE, a quiet and scholarly Neo-Regency villa of 1956–7 by *Sir Albert Richardson*, 'the professor at his best' (Nicholas Taylor). – Light brown brick. Chinese Chippendale porch, the garden side with tripartite sashes and central canted glazed bay. Stuccoed wing in the same style by *Michael Heber-Percy*, 2002.

WESTON CORBETT HOUSE, ¼ m. NW. Nice, brick, of 1720. Inherited in the mid C19 by T. H. Wyatt. Five bays, hipped roof, with late C19 pedimented dormers. Despite the showy front, originally single-pile with service rooms under a rear outshot, now with later gables. Kitchen formerly to r. of entrance; original fittings now at Sulgrave Manor (Northants).

THE DOWER HOUSE (formerly Weston Corbett Place), ¾ m. NNW. An accomplished small Neo-Georgian country house of 1936 by *Braddell, Deane & Bird*, with asymmetrical front and two-bay wings on the garden side. The best feature, inside, is a cantilevered stone staircase with Art Deco balustrade.

WEYHILL

Weyhill was famous in the past for its Michaelmas Sheep Fair, second only to that of Winchester. First referred to in the early C13, Piers Plowman knows it in the later C14, Defoe mentions it, Cobbett still writes of it in 1822, and Hardy fictionalizes it in *The Mayor of Casterbridge*.

ST MICHAEL. The parish church of Penton Grafton. Hard flint exterior, as restored in 1862–3 by *J. H. Hakewill*, when the chancel was carefully reconstructed. Odd spireleted timber W bell-turret of 1907 by *Cancellor*. Norman chancel arch of *c.* 1180, round with one slight chamfer. E.E. chancel with trustworthy side lancets, but heavily renewed E window. Good low-pitched nave roof, dateable to 1506 (from the audit account of Ramridge Manor for timber), with boldly moulded ties, purlins and rafters. S arcade, with scallop capitals of no period precedent, by *Hakewill*. Also by him, the arch to the N transept (built 1824) and most of the furnishings. – REREDOS of 1885, elaborately carved with central cross, in vines, between lilies and pomegranates. – STAINED GLASS. E window, 1864 by *Cox & Sons*. Above their usual standard, three archangels with vividly colourful wings. Chancel N and S by *Heaton, Butler & Bayne*, 1885. S aisle E (commemorative date 1899) designed by *Miss Steedman*, made by *Hardman*. By them, S aisle SE and W windows (dates of 1900 and 1903). S aisle centre, to

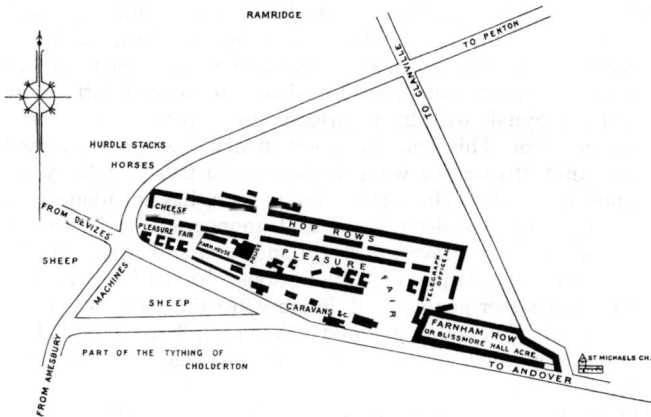

Weyhill, fair.
Plan of the main site

Frederick Tabor †1872 by *Clayton & Bell* and s w by *Comper*, 1947. – MONUMENTS. In the N vestry wall. Two possibly early CII sculptured stones, *c.*56 cm. by 36 cm. Re-set here in the C19 from the nave w wall. Described as a grave cover. The lower half a characteristically Saxon cross of *c.* 1000. – Quite an array of C18–C19 tablets. – Joseph Simpson, †1796. Oval inscription, with boldly shaped grey surround and a draped urn. – Christopher Bowerbank †1748. Plain, with a pediment unusually of two palms. – John Gawler of Ramridge House †1803. An excellent and moving piece by *Sir Richard Westmacott*. Two youths (his sons?) in contemplation of the broken-off capital of a column whose upper ending is now covered by a branch of weeping willow. – Henry Bosanquet †1817. Signed *Maddox*, Undertaker, Welbeck Street.

In the CHURCHYARD, a stone CROSS brought from Jerusalem in 1904. It stands over a fragment of a medieval cross (destroyed in the C16) whose base was then cut into by the widening of the road from Andover in 1626. The earlier cross was thought to have been erected to sanctify the fairground.

The FAIR was held on the downland NW of the church and had few permanent structures, but immediately w of the church is the exceptionally rare group of simple chalk, cob and slate BOOTHS erected in the early C19 for hop sellers, set against the high cob walls surrounding the tapering rectangular site. This is now the FAIRGROUND CRAFT CENTRE, converted 1999–2000 by *James Airy* for craft workshops and parish council offices. At the w end of the site, the VILLAGE HALL. 2000, extended 2003, by *Lyons, Sleeman & Hoare*. ¼ m. WNW, within an office development, is another FAIR BOOTH. Also early C19, but brick and slate with horizontally hinged shutters, the lower leaves of which drop down to form a counter.

RAMRIDGE HOUSE, ¾ m. NNW. John Gawler, attorney, built
the core of the present house *c.* 1779 (an earlier house is
shown on a 1741 map). Two storeys and attic over basement
offices, with an unadorned four-bay N front, with lofty Ionic
porch (capitals with husk garlands between the volutes) and
six-bay rear. This has two-storey flanking wings of *c.* 1858
and mid-C19 service wing. Converted to flats *c.* 1984–5, by
Anthony Stocken. The former dining room has an Adamesque
ceiling with Gawler's arms and monogram and circular
wreath with bay leaves, husk garlands and anthemion. In the
spandrels oval plaques with the Seasons. NORTH LODGE, early
C19, is a clever geometrical design consisting of a two-storey
stuccoed cube, with a pyramidal slate roof, flanked by slightly
projecting single-storey wings. (South Lodge is an interwar
copy.)

BLISSAMORE HALL, 1¼ m. N. Completely remodelled *c.* 1812
for Henry Bosanquet, whose monument is in the church. Stuccoed with rusticated ground floor and quoins, mansard roof
behind a parapet. Some late C19 additions, especially apparent
at the rear. Inside, the best feature is the early C19 cantilevered
stone staircase, which has a boldly curved wrought-iron
balustrade.

CLANVILLE HOUSE, 1½ m. N, close to the road. Early C18, in
header bond. 1–3–1 bays of segmental-arched windows with
keystones. Central pedimented porch, round-arched niche
above with gauged surround. Large late C18 addition in the
angle of the rear wing. Inside, early C18 fittings include the
staircase (reconstructed) and panelling with painted scenes,
including the grape harvest, in the dining room. Forecourt
walls terminate in piers with urn finials. Early C19 STABLE with
lunettes.

3040

WHERWELL

The Benedictine nunnery of Wherwell Priory was founded *c.* 986
by Elfrida, widow of King Edgar but 'Demolished By The Over
Acted Zeale Or Avarice Of King Henry...' after 1539. The
nunnery and its adjacent lands were granted to Sir Thomas West,
Lord de la Warr. The very pretty village lies NW of its site, between
the Test and the downs which form the steep edge of the valley.
Fragments of medieval carved stonework from the monastic
buildings appear throughout the village, re-set in the walls of cottages and houses.

ST PETER AND HOLY CROSS. The dedication is that of the
priory church (*see* below). Quite large, in flint and stone of
1854–8 by *Woodyer*. Mostly E.E. detail with a few original
quirks. Lively, rather Scandinavian wooden bell-turret with
spire over a W front with semicircular stair-turret. The nave
roof sweeps down with a break into the aisle roofs. The square-

headed window surrounds in the aisles are typically High Victorian, i.e. not archaeologically correct. Equally original inside
are the two slim stone piers supporting the bell-turret. They
are deliberately different to the arcade piers which are correctly
Transitional. The rest of the stern interior is straightforward,
except for the trefoil-headed arcade, with polished grey marble
in the free-standing shafts, between the chancel and the odd
diagonal passage to the vestry, a typical Woodyer touch. Mostly
coeval FURNISHINGS but REREDOS AND PANELLING by
W. D. Caröe. – STAINED GLASS. In the chancel by *Wailes*, the E
window of 1858. S aisle S. Engraved glass by *Tony Gilliam*. –
ARCHITECTURAL FRAGMENTS. An archaeologist's picnic in
the N aisle. Most, if not all, from the priory church, arranged
by *T. D. Atkinson* in 1932. They are tantalizingly incomplete but
varied. A Saxon cross-shaft with interlacing patterns part
reworked as a C13 corbel. Two late C13 carved stone reliefs, one
representing the Harrowing of Hell, the other an angel carrying a flower. A C15 worked stone inscribed Thomas Beow with
a Tudor rose. Can this have been a pier base re-cut into a credence shelf or pedestal for a statue? Fragment of a stone coffin
with a marginal inscription. More fragments in the gable wall
of an outbuilding behind the old vicarage. Cross, shaped from
parts of Perp windows. – MONUMENT. Nun, possibly Juliana
Overey, late C15, in an ample mantle, recumbent with a dog at
her feet. – Sir Owen West †1551. Austere Renaissance tomb-
chest, probably part of a large monument with reredos from
the earlier church, possibly from the chancel. The cartouches
in carved strapwork are quite advanced stylistically for the
date, yet the inscription is still in black letter.

   In the churchyard, the large Gothic ashlar MAUSOLEUM of
the Iremongers. 1858 by *Woodyer*. In C14 style, incorporating
fragments from the priory church (they had previously been
reused in the S aisle of the village church). Three Quarr stone
monster heads, C12, from the corbel table, stylistically related
to others at Romsey Abbey. Stone panelling on the N side with
seven original crocketed ogee arches with shields hanging by
straps. Small ballflower cornice, the date must be *c.* 1350–80.
The pieces no doubt formed part of a tomb. Two of the shields
have achievements, one for Segrave (T. D. Powell).

WHERWELL PRIORY, S of the church, on the site of the nunnery.
Probably early C18 or a bit before but remodelled and
extended, for the Iremonger family *c.* 1800 and again in 1914
(SW wing) by *J. W. O'Dell* for Sir Ernest Cassell, who gave it
to his niece. It was restored by *Sir Albert Richardson* in 1945
after a fire. Two storeys, stuccoed with hipped slate roofs
behind parapets and a square, domed cupola. Smart five-bay
E front with quoins; the central dining room marked by three
windows carried up through ground floor and first floor with
festoons above set in rectangular panels. Two-storey early C18
canted bays at each end, facing N and S. The W end of the N
front is probably *c.* 1800, the date of the Doric porch. Early
C20 canted bay to the W front. The SW wing is Neo-Regency;
beyond is a late C19 billiard room. Good early C18 main

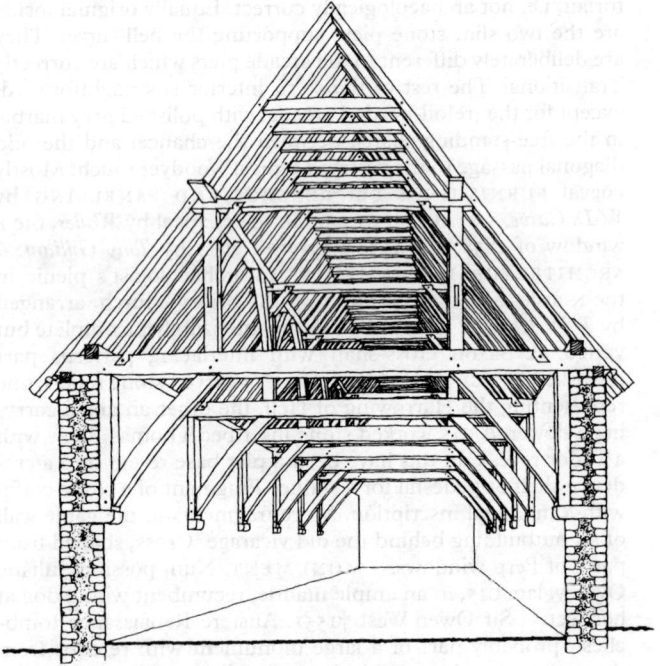

Wherwell Priory, stables.
Drawing by Jonathan Snowdon, 2003

staircase and, in the centre of the E side, impressive full-height dining room, of a cube and a half, with a coved ceiling above an enriched cornice. Wonderfully austere black marble chimneypiece with Doric columns, presumably late C18 or early C19. Four large paintings in bolection-moulded surrounds are copies *c.* 1990 of capricci, said to be by *Boucher*, brought from Brook House, Park Lane, London (dem. 1933). The late C18 chimneypiece with three-quarter Ionic columns in the drawing room came from the same source.

The house may occupy the site of the nunnery's reredorter and spans the water course which flowed N–S through the monastic site. Alongside this is the S (kitchen) wing, of brick, *c.* 1700, with cross-windows. Extending SW is another range of similar date (The Priory House), built over a fine brick-vaulted cellar.

The STABLES, S of the house, are outwardly early C18 but incorporate a substantial medieval timber frame, part of what was probably the monastic infirmary. There is old masonry in the walls, and inside six bays of a once more extensive roof of raised aisle construction, dated to 1250 and 1280, tallying with gifts of royal oaks from Henry III and Edward I. It seems to have been in use as a stable from at least the C17 – see chamfered posts with ogee stops and the segmental-arched wooden door frame in the front wall. The loft was inserted in the late C19.

The abbey church stood NW of the house and in its final form was cruciform with a nave, probably aisled, apsidal-ended chapels (or aisles) flanking the choir and apsidal E chapels to the transepts (like Romsey Abbey, where the E end was rebuilt in this form in the C12). The presbytery was rebuilt in the mid C13 by Abbess Euphemia, almost certainly with a square end (cf. Romsey). There was also a great W tower. Among the few monastic buildings assigned for retention after the Dissolution was the abbess's lodging which may have been part of a group of buildings, apparently ranged around a courtyard, which have been located immediately E of the house.

There is a small PARK, extending to the N and W. EAST LODGE, on the Winchester road, is early C18, an extended octagon in plan, of flint with brick bands and stone dressings, with nice ashlar gatepiers of c. 1700, panelled with moulded cornices and ball finials. Early C18 gatepiers also at ANDOVER LODGE, at the village entrance, which is a pretty, early C19 cottage orné.

At the junction of Church Street and Winchester Road is a small triangular green with a row of C16 timber-framed and thatched COTTAGES (thoroughly restored by *Wilfrid Carpenter Turner* in 1959) curving around the E side, and in its centre, the WAR MEMORIAL by *W. H. Ward*, 1920. Above the green's NW side, THE MOWLE HOUSE, 1972 by *James Brooks Fisher* of *The Architects Consortium* of Winchester, for himself. Traditional form – painted brick with a thatched roof – but with full-height glazing to the dining room (r.), and inside, a galleried first-floor living room, leading through an eyebrow dormer to the high-level rear garden.

Former STATION and STATION-MASTER'S HOUSE (Nos. 5 and 6 Chant Close). 1884 in Queen Anne style, cf. Longparish.

WHITCHURCH

4040

A small, quiet town on the Test. A possession of the Prior and Convent of St Swithun's, Winchester, by 1086. The market was established in 1241, the borough in 1248–9. From the C16 the principal industry was cloth manufacture, particularly of shalloons (closely woven woollen fabric) and, from the early C19, silks. The town's position made it an important coaching stop: the Andover–Basingstoke road was turnpiked in 1754, the Winchester–Newbury road in 1762. There are many good early and mid-C19 houses; the opening of a station in 1854 encouraged the spread of building in that direction. Modest C20 growth.

CHURCHES AND PUBLIC BUILDINGS

ALL HALLOWS, Church Street. Externally all of 1867–8 by *Ferrey*, except for the lower part of the W tower, which was restored in 1716 (dated). Prominent upper stage with a tall shingled splay-foot spire. Inside, the tower arch is probably early C13, slightly restored, with chamfered jambs and a rather irregular pointed arch. But the S arcade is genuine C13 work. Three bays, round piers, roll-moulded bases, round abaci, and single-chamfered arches. The N arcade is patently Perp. The piers have the four-shafts-and-four-hollows section and the arches three hollow chamfers. The high bases may indicate the height of lost late C15 pews. The E bays on both sides are of 1866 (when the aisles were widened, see the Perp roofs over the original), as is the chancel in a bold Early Dec style. Above the original bays of the nave arcades, a Perp roof with tie-beams, on braces and wall-posts. The tower has a rare surviving internal newel stair, also Perp with a half-octagonal wooden casing, with crenellated bands, pierced with small traceried openings and quatrefoils. – FONT. Octagonal. Late Perp with quatrefoils. – REREDOS. Elaborately carved, of 1892 by *Jones & Willis*, with colourful fabric panels of the 1990s. – PULPIT. By *Ferrey*. – ORGAN CASES. 1935 by *F. E. Howard*. – PAINTING. An enjoyable panel, 43½ by 48 in. (110 by 122 cm.) with the Ten Commandments surrounded by fourteen enjoyably naïve, but lively little paintings of appropriate scenes (e.g. punishment of wrongdoers). Dated 1602. It is like a broadsheet (cf. the Decalogue painting at Hedgerley, Buckinghamshire, of 1664). – STAINED GLASS. E window by *Ward & Hughes*, 1881, with their usual mauves, pinks and purples. Chancel S. An unusually dense intricate piece (†1854), with a single medallion lost in luxuriant patternwork. S aisle, by *Ward & Hughes* (of 1887) excepting westernmost by *Powells*, 1887. – MONU-MENTS. First of all an extremely interesting and important Anglo-Saxon gravestone or headstone (24 in. × 21 in. and 7 in. thick), found in 1867 in the former N aisle, originally perhaps in the churchyard or a lost *porticus*. Sir Thomas Kendrick dates it mid-C9 and Sir David Wilson has noted its stylistic links with metalwork of *c.* 800. The front is like that of a Roman gravestone of the legions (of the type recovered on Hadrian's Wall), and has an arched top and at the front an arched recess in which is the bold demi-figure of Christ. He is shown in high relief, one hand in blessing, the other holding the gospels. The inscription runs round the top in Roman letters: HIC CORPUS FRITHBURGAE REQUIESCIT IN PACE SEPULTUM (Here the body of Frithburh rests in peace). At the back, a lunette, in which an incised symmetrical plant scroll with terminal leaves, of 'delightful precision and Strength'. – Thomas Brooke †1612. Two recumbent stone effigies. Poor in execution. – Brass. Richard Brooke, first Governor of Mayland,

†1603. – Henry Portal †1747, the Huguenot founder of the paper makers (*see* Laverstoke). – John Portal and his wife †1877. A Neo-Jacobean tablet of alabaster, interesting for its date.

BAPTIST CHURCH, Newbury Street. 1836, an enlargement of a meeting house of 1777. Red brick with vitrified brick pilasters, paired at the angles. Schoolroom, s, added 1907. (Interior refitted 1901 but retains original s gallery on cast-iron columns.)

METHODIST (WESLEYAN) CHURCH, Winchester Street. 1812 but remodelled in 1903 with a Gothic front probably by *Gordon & Gunton*.

Former PRIMITIVE METHODIST CHURCH, London Street. 1902, in a sort of lively *Rundbogenstil*.

TOWN HALL, Newbury Street. 1786–7. Brick, of five bays with the middle three projecting and the centre under a pediment. Ground floor with arched openings, the upper floor with one monumental arched window in the centre. Hipped roof and domed cupola. Council Chamber, with moulded plaster panelling, cornice and pilastered aedicules.

GILL NETHERCOTT COMMUNITY HALL, Winchester Street. By *Macallan Penfold*, 2006–7. To the fore, a two-storey block with curved roof containing the hall and library, with a glass bridge over a stream to an oval pod containing meeting rooms etc.

Former COUNTY POLICE STATION, The Lynch. 1862 by *Thomas Stopher Jun.* Sturdy, of unknapped flint with generous brick dressings, including rusticated pilasters at the angles.

RAILWAY STATION, Station Approach. 1854 for the London & South Western Railway. Three bays, stuccoed, the entrance in a raised surround with curious quarter columns in the outer angles.

A PERAMBULATION can begin from the church. Opposite, to the sw, is KINGS LODGE, the former vicarage. Early C17 timber-framed core re-clad and extended in brick in the late C17 (now rendered), further enlarged in the same material in the late C19. Asymmetrical front with a central Tudor-arched doorway and stepped staircase window under a broad central gable. Distinctive chimneys, both late C17 and C19, with keyed-round-arched panels. N of the church, a series of early to mid-C19 houses which, like a number in the town of this date, are probably of chalk *pisé* construction behind the stucco: notably THE MOUNT, set back in a large garden behind a flint wall. Further up, THE HERMITAGE/THE COTTAGE, roughcast and tiled with a row of C19 dormers, but actually C15 of cruck construction, the first floor inserted in the hall as late as 1668. Curiously, the chimney, inserted at the same time, spans the crosspassage.

The centre of the town is the MARKET PLACE at the crossing of the roads to London, Andover, Newbury and Winchester. On the N side, the BEEHIVE. C18 front, with modest Georgian fenestration and a nice old pilastered shopfront, concealing a four-bay timber frame of *c.* 1500, jettied to the

front and r.-hand end. It may have had a civic function. Late
Victorian and Edwardian commercial architecture on the E
and W sides, e.g. the very characterful former International
Stores of 1896 between Church Street and Bell Street, but the
finest building is the WHITE HART HOTEL in the NW corner
between the London and Newbury roads, with a boldly
rounded corner and an Ionic porch of rather stocky
proportions, with a delicate wrought-iron balustrade with
anthemion motifs. That part facing Newbury Street has two
rooms, now pushed together, with splendidly rustic late C17
plaster ceilings. The bold friezes are particularly entertaining,
one room with strapwork, birds and female masks, the other
with scrollwork, festoons of fruit and lion masks. W, in BELL
STREET, No. 4, with a timber-framed jettied solar cross wing
of *c.* 1440, and the vestiges of a hall range of the same date.
Past THE LIMES, a stuccoed house of *c.* 1840 set back within
a walled garden, two more timber-framed survivals: No. 22 is
c. 1500, of two bays with a jettied first floor and on the other
side of Bell Yard, THE BELL INN, C17 with a C19 rendered
brick façade and substantial framed rear wing.

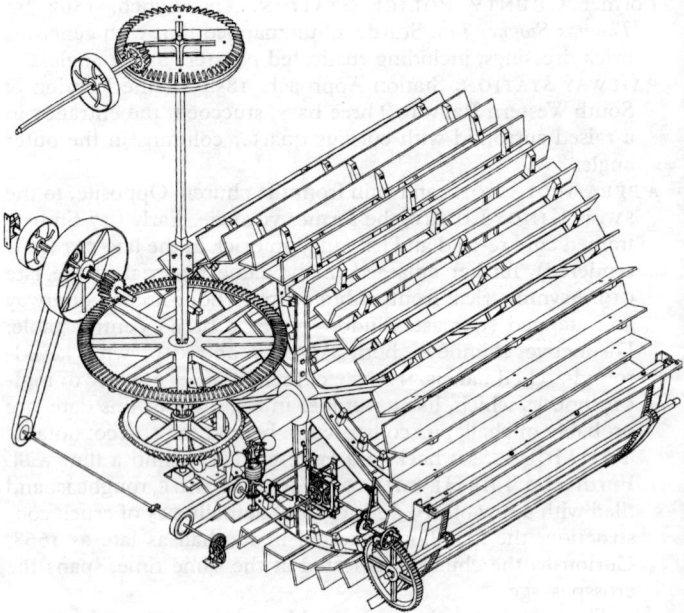

Whitchurch, The Silk Mill, waterwheel.
Isometric drawing by John Reynolds, 1970

s in WINCHESTER STREET is THE SILK MILL, on Frog Island,
between the Little and Great Town Bridges across the Test.
Built 1815 for William Hayter, 'iron founder, brush maker,
turner . . .', to make what is not clear* but acquired by the silk
manufacturer William Maddick in 1817 and altered to its
present form with the insertion of an extra floor and alterations
to the openings. Three storeys, faced in red brick. The N front   85
of five widely spaced bays, the centre widest with a steep plastered pediment on small wooden brackets. Above, a thin
cupola with ogival lead cap (cf. the Town Hall). Small-paned
cast-iron windows set in broad segment-arched openings.
Flanking symmetrical two-storey weatherboarded wings, to the
r. housing the waterwheel, to the l. offices. The s side is identical, minus the pediment. Repaired as a working mill by The
Hampshire Buildings Preservation Trust in 1985. Inside much
machinery, including a cast-iron breast-shot wheel installed
c. 1890. The earliest surviving powered looms are of about the
same date. NE, the single-storey visitor centre, c. 1960 (incorporating cast-iron windows from an early C19 building on the
site). On WINCHESTER STREET, No. 24 was the counting
house and is contemporary with the mill; beyond, a pair of
COTTAGES, converted in the 1880s from an 1840s weaving
shed. N of the centre, in NEWBURY STREET No. 31, of 1581–2,
gable-end to the road with a jettied first floor. Its narrow plot
was one of several leased out for building on the edge of the
town by the mayor and freeholders. On the corner of
OAKLAND ROAD, a c. 1925 Arts and Crafts house by F. G.
Weeks for himself, roughcast with sweeping tile roofs. Further
up, on the r., reached from KINGS WALK, is BEREHILL
HOUSE. Early C19 (porch with unfluted Doric columns) but
remodelled and enlarged c. 1895, and again c. 1908 with a
single-storey wing of Lutyens inspiration, e.g. the full-height
mullioned-and-transomed bay window in the gable-end.
Inside, massive arch-braced trusses. Formerly extensive
grounds have been built over but one early C19 lodge survives
as THE ROUND HOUSE (No. 113 London Road) with veranda
on rustic posts.

MANOR FARMHOUSE, Bloswood Lane, ¼ m. N. Rebuilt by the
Priory of St Swithun in 1497 (accounts); inside remains of a
timber-framed hall and cross-wing, outside stuccoed early C19.

THE GABLES, London Road. Built at some distance E of the
town as the workhouse in 1847–8 by S. O. Foden for c. £3,500.
Enlarged 1867 and c. 1900. Flint with brick dressings.
Symmetrical, with gabled centre and wings.

---

* Jeremy and Samuel Bentham were copyholders of the site. Samuel's connection
with the construction of the block mills in Portsmouth Dockyard might explain the
existence of such a sophisticated industrial building in rural central Hampshire.
Further research is required.

WIELD

ST JAMES. Nave and chancel, dated (by Professor Zarnecki) to
c. 1150, when Henry of Blois, Bishop of Winchester, held the
advowson. Of this date the S doorway, reopened in 1931 by
T. D. Atkinson, with one order of columns and single-stepped
arch; the chancel arch, with two slight chamfers; and the plain
priest's doorway. An even plainer N doorway was revealed in
1997. Four Perp windows of *c.* 1400. Tiny weatherboarded box
bellcote of 1812, over a charming domestic half-hipped W
gable. Minor restoration of 1884–5. E wall in flint with C14-
style window in place of the Georgian Gothick window shown
in an early C19 watercolour. – FONT. Late C12. Of table type.
Purbeck marble, with six flat arches to each side. Found in a
garden in The Close at Winchester, imported in 1900. – WALL
PAINTINGS. Two consecration crosses. Traces of a C13 scheme,
later overpainted, found in 1938 and now, in poor condition,
almost vanished. Scenes from the Life of Christ: the Visit of
the Magi (N wall), and Last Supper? (S wall). ROYAL ARMS.
Queen Anne, above the chancel arch. – MONUMENT. William
Wallope [*sic*] †1617, and his third wife Margery. Excellent
alabaster standing monument of the Southwark School, carefully restored in 1971. Two recumbent effigies, Sir William
behind and above his wife. Backplate with exquisite ribbons
and trophies. At the top a large coat of arms with two cherubs
with symbols of death. – Barbara Willys †1617, a relation of the
couple. Tablet with dainty garlands and achievements. Possibly from the same workshop.

Attractive group of typical Hampshire cottages to the SE of
the church, C16–C19, timber-framed, flint and brick, mostly
thatched. WIELD HOUSE FARMHOUSE, E of the church,
was built *c.* 1800 on the site of William Wallop's mansion
(*c.* 1580–5) and incorporates some reused material, including
a moulded stone plinth and carved coat of arms on the C19
Gothic porch. The impressive tile-capped flint garden walls are
C16 too.

WINCHESTER*

INTRODUCTION

Winchester, with not only its Cathedral but also the College, the [2]
Church and Hospital of St Cross, the Great Hall of the castle
and the episcopal palace at Wolvesey, is architecturally the richest
cathedral city in England. It lies in the narrowest part of the
Itchen valley, where a prehistoric E–W route over the chalk downs
forded the river, probably on the line of the present High Street.
There were several PREHISTORIC SETTLEMENTS in the valley,
and in the vicinity of the modern city there is not only the major
Early Iron Age hill-fort at St Catherine's Hill (*see* p. 466) but also
evidence of another settlement inside a D-shaped enclosure at
Winnall Down; a third was excavated in 1993 at Weeke. In the
Middle Iron Age a settlement was established on the E-facing

---

* The account of Winchester, except the parish churches, is rewritten by John
Crook.

spur of the chalk downland above the flood plain, centred around
the open space now called Oram's Arbour (Anglo-Saxon
'Erdburi'). By *c.* 100 B.C. this was enclosed by an earthwork ditch
(about 26 ft (8 metres) wide and 15 ft (4.5 metres) deep) and
bank, an area of about 50 acres (20 hectares) of roughly rectangular plan. Evidence for gateways, perhaps located at the point
where pre-existing trackways ran through the line of the defences,
has been discovered. One of these trackways seems to survive as
Romsey Road, leading towards Old Sarum. Another gateway was
later taken over by the Romans and continued in use in the
Middle Ages as the city's Northgate. There is some evidence that
the enclosure had been abandoned by the beginning of the C1
A.D. and was therefore uninhabited at the Roman invasion of A.D.
43.

The ROMANS in turn established their own settlement close
to and partly overlapping its predecessor. They called it *Venta Belgarum* ('trading place of the Belgæ'). Although Ptolemy first mentioned this name in the C2, it is unlikely that the Romans found
a thriving commercial centre when they arrived. They evidently
saw the strategic value of the river crossing, and their settlement
extended down the hill into the flood plain, where the river was
eventually diverted into its present course hard under St Giles
Hill. The town's DEFENCES, erected on three sides in the later
C1, comprised an earth bank and ditch on the three uphill sides
(the marshy valley bottom providing sufficient protection on the
E). The W side included an unexplained salient, perhaps related
to the Iron Age defences, or a Roman feature, which survives as
the site of the present castle. The fortifications were enlarged in
the late C2 with a new rampart and ditch completely encircling
the town, and by the early C3 had been further strengthened by
a massive masonry wall cut into the outside of the earthworks.
An excavated fragment of the E wall, running parallel with the
Itchen, is displayed S of City Bridge. The final area of the ROMAN
TOWN was 138 acres (56 hectares), the fifth largest in Britain.
Roads developed at an early date from the main gates towards
other major settlements: *Clausentum* (S, at the head of Southampton Water), *Sorviodunum* (Sarum) (W), Silchester (N) and
(branching from the latter, two miles N of *Venta*) Cirencester.

Roman Winchester may initially have been military in character, but by A.D. 100 had become a regional administrative centre
or *civitas*. Our knowledge of the city in Roman and Saxon times
comes mainly from archaeology, starting with the influential Winchester Excavations of the 1960s, directed by Martin Biddle, the
most extensive archaeological investigation of a British town.
Administrative buildings were centred around the forum, immediately N of the present cathedral. A regular street grid was completed in the early C3. Apart from the central axis of the High
Street linking the originally Roman E and W gates, the Roman
street pattern has vanished, though its alignment was similar to
today's. Other elements of its layout are gradually being discovered, but the Roman remains are deeply buried and in the E parts
of the city are mostly beneath the modern water table. Items in

the City Museum, such as the dolphin mosaic pavement from Little Minster Street, inscriptions and monumental fragments, give some idea of the splendour of the town in its heyday. In the mid C4, however, its character appears to have changed from a luxuriously spacious residential town to a more densely populated trading and industrial centre: the C4 *Notitia Dignitatum* mentions, for example, an Imperial weaving works, mostly probably located in *Venta*. Grave-goods in the extensive Late Roman cemeteries surrounding the town indicate the arrival of Germanic settlers. In the later C4 bastion towers were added to the defences, an indication of the uncertainties in Late Roman Britannia. A second wave of Germanic settlement occurred in the early C5, a date well before the traditional arrival of the Saxons in Wessex, by which time urban life in *Venta Belgarum* had come to an end. Martin Biddle and Birthe Kjølbye-Biddle argue, however, that the town continued to function as a focus of authority and lordship over the surrounding territory into the ANGLO-SAXON period, with clusters of extramural cemeteries and individual settlements within the walls from the later C5 to the C7.* According to the *Anglo-Saxon Chronicle* Cenwealh, king of Wessex, built a church here in 648 (later called Old Minster); it may originally have been a chapel to a royal palace (which certainly stood here by the C10). What is certain is that in the 660s the church became a cathedral, when the West Saxon see was transferred from Dorchester-on-Thames.

The present LAYOUT of the streets within the walls dates from the later C9, probably established by King Alfred in the early 880s (though possibly initiated by his elder brother Ethelred †871). The new street grid was set out, aligned to the Roman walls and evidently intended to provide access to the walls for defence (the Danes had ransacked the city in 860). The intramural streets, most obviously St Swithun Street and North Walls, together with the back streets parallel to the High Street, all date from this period. The town gates remained approximately in their earlier positions, although Southgate was rebuilt slightly further up the slope, W of its Roman predecessor. Kingsgate (Chingete) was probably also Roman in origin, but its name must reflect the fact that it led from the S directly towards the royal palace. In the late C9 the Lady Ealhswitha, King Alfred's wife (†902), founded Nunnaminster (subsequently 'St Mary's Abbey') on an urban estate that she owned in the SE quarter of the town. Its site is now Abbey Gardens. More securely dated is New Minster, founded by Edward the Elder in 901 on charter evidence, on a site immediately N of Old Minster. The body of King Alfred (†899), first buried in Old Minster, was soon moved into the new church.

The C10 MONASTIC REFORMS, which reached Winchester from Continental centres such as Ghent and Fleury, had considerable impact. Bishop Æthelwold expelled the secular canons

---

* Martin Biddle and Birthe Kjølbye-Biddle, 'Winchester: from *Venta* to *Wintancæster*', in *Pagans and Christians – from Antiquity to the Middle Ages*, ed. L. Gilmour, BAR International Ser. 1610 (2007), pp. 189–214.

of Old and New Minster in 964, replacing them with regular
Benedictine monks. The development of the cult of St Swithun,
a C9 bishop, was central to the reform of Old Minster, and following the elevation of his relics in 971 the cathedral was greatly
enlarged. Perhaps to rival these works, a great W tower was added
to New Minster. To accommodate the new monks domestic
buildings were constructed, and Æthelwold is remembered for
the monastic drainage system, the 'Lockburn', which served as
Winchester's town drain until 1875 and still survives. At the same
time King Edgar enclosed the three religious foundations within
a boundary wall, following the requisition and demolition of
many secular buildings within the area. The present boundaries
of the Inner Close (S of the cathedral) probably date from this
period. At about the same time the bishop's palace was constructed in the SE corner of the city at 'Wulf's Island', or
Wolvesey. Together the three monastic foundations and the episcopal palace occupied more than a quarter of the area of the
walled city.

The Conqueror's forces reached Winchester in November
1066, and work began by February 1067 on the construction of
a new castle, though his principal residence remained the palace
just W of Old Minster. The palace was enlarged c. 1070 over land
confiscated from New Minster, which in 1110 moved to a new
site, N of the walled city, and was subsequently known as Hyde
Abbey. At a time when English kings were peripatetic, MEDIEVAL
WINCHESTER has perhaps the best claim to be called a 'capital';
here was the royal treasury, famously seized by Henry I on the
death of William Rufus, and here in Henry's reign evolved the
exchequer. Winchester's mint, established at the end of Alfred's
reign, was retained near the Norman royal palace.

The Conquest had a major effect on Winchester's RELIGIOUS
ESTABLISHMENTS, and in 1079 work on a new cathedral began
under Bishop Walkelin, brought over from Rouen. By the later
C13 the city also possessed four friaries, whose existence is now
preserved only in place names. The Carmelite Friary was on the
E side of Kingsgate Street, and the site was acquired by Winchester College as an extension to Meads; the Augustinians were
housed on the E side of St Cross Road, just outside Southgate.
The Franciscans occupied a site between the N end of Middle
and Lower Brook Streets. The Dominicans (Black Friars) were
N of the E end of High Street, on the site later occupied by Eastgate House. Another important pre-Reformation ecclesiastical
institution was the College of St Elizabeth of Hungary, founded
in 1302 in the meadows S of Wolvesey. Several institutions, some
still in existence, made provision for healthcare. Henry of Blois
founded the leper hospital (dem. 1788) on the eastern downs,
which gave its name to Morn (Magdalen) Hill, and St Cross Hospital. St John's Hospital was certainly in existence by the early
C13. The Sustren Spital on the corner site between College and
Kingsgate Streets also ministered to the sick; maintained by nuns
and dependent upon St Swithun's Priory, it may date from as
early as 1110. Excavation on the site of the County Record Office

in Sussex Street revealed remains of the medieval royal hawk-house. By 1100 there were also about 1,300 houses (recorded in Henry I's survey), making Winchester second only to London. During this century the city gradually achieved a measure of independence, above all through the efforts of the Gild Merchant, forerunners of the City Council, to be allowed to pay their taxes directly to local officials rather than to the sheriff, an aim finally achieved by a charter of King John in 1215. Such royal charters to the city had begun with Henry II's in 1155; later, Henry III's charter of 1227 stated that the mint and exchange would remain in Winchester 'for ever' – its last coins were minted in 1243. The economy was based mainly on the weaving of wool; the Itchen provided the power for several fulling and tanning mills and at the beginning of the C13 there were at least nine water mills in Winchester, five on the Itchen (three at Durngate alone, two of which were rebuilt in 1429–30), and four serving the religious houses: in the Cathedral Priory precincts, at St Mary's Abbey, Hyde Abbey and St Cross. The population seems to have a reached a peak of about 16,000 by 1300, but the court had by then moved to Westminster, and Winchester ceased to be a royal residence in 1302 when the royal apartments at the castle were destroyed by fire. The Black Death of 1348–50 killed more than a third of Wintonians and also caused the steady decline of the wool trade, although the cloth-finishing industry remained the chief source of Winchester's wealth in the Late Middle Ages. A petition of 1440, however, stated that during the previous fifty years, seventeen churches, eleven streets and 987 messuages had fallen into ruin. There were fifty-four churches in 1300, just twenty-six in 1500 and twelve by 1600 (St Lawrence and St Swithun-upon-Kingsgate are now the only medieval churches within the ancient city limits). In the later C14 William of Wykeham's new college of 'St Mary nigh Winton' was a significant addition to the city.

The REFORMATION brought major changes to the cityscape. St Swithun's, Hyde, Nunnaminster and the smaller houses were all dissolved. Some of the conventual buildings were adapted for the cathedral, now staffed once more by secular canons, but of the other religious establishments only Hyde preserves a few vestiges of its monastic past. Stone from the dissolved houses was recycled throughout the city, and is particularly evident at Hyde.

The city walls were neglected from the C16 onwards – and additional openings were made, rendering the medieval gates redundant; in 1755 the upper floor of Northgate collapsed during a christening party and the gate was demolished in 1771, as was Southgate; Eastgate came down in 1791. Much of the circuit of city walls had been obliterated soon after 1800.

Economic crises in the 1620s and 30s put an end to the local textile industry, and the economy was further destabilized by the demands of Parliamentary troops in the early 1640s. The slighting of the castle in 1651 marked the demise of Winchester as a military stronghold. After 1660 some larger houses were constructed within the walled area of the city, such as Sir Robert

Mason's Eastgate House and Sir John Clobery's residence in
Parchment Street, and in the 1680s there was also much reconstruction in the Cathedral Close, almost all of it in brick. Had
Charles II's plans been fulfilled to build his new palace at Winchester, transforming the city into an English Versailles, it might
rapidly have regained its former status. But by the end of the
century it was, as Daniel Defoe wrote *c.* 1724, 'a place of no trade
... no manufacture ... no navigation', with a population of
fewer than 3,000. Nevertheless in the EIGHTEENTH CENTURY
Winchester settled down to a more modest prosperity as the
county town, with new public buildings of an appropriate character. Many large houses were built or rebuilt in up-to-date-styles
in the SW quarter of the town – notably along St Thomas Street
and in Kingsgate Street, one of the finest Georgian streets in
England – for the gentry and new bourgeoisie attracted by the
town's theatres and racecourse. Serle's House, by *Thomas Archer*,
dates from this period. Samuel and Nathaniel Buck's view from
St Giles Hill (1736) shows the extent of the city's development
by that time.

The population more than trebled between 1801 (6,194) and
1881 (18,467) with a particularly large increase in 1821–61 attributable to the coming of the railway. There ensued a frenzy of
activity in every sphere of building, initially within the medieval
city limits but later also breaking out to form suburbs in every
direction. Much of the work was in the hands of a small number
of LOCAL ARCHITECTS: *Owen Browne Carter*, whose most
notable pupil was *G. E. Street* (who assisted Carter in the alterations to the Great Hall of the Castle), *Thomas Stopher Sen.* and
Jun. of whom the younger married the daughter of another significant Winchester architect, *Henry Carey Brown*, was three times
mayor,* and recorded the city's evolution in his unpublished
'History of Winchester Streets' (started in 1895), a set of scrap-
books and other writings. The prolific *John Colson* from 1877 was
in partnership with his son *John Barnes Colson*. Both were
surveyors to the Chapter of Winchester. Some architects of
national repute were also busy in Winchester in the C19: *Butterfield* designed the new County Hospital and remodelled St Cross,
the latter work continued at the end of the century by *C. J. Blomfield*, then T. G. Jackson. It was at this time that the empty grazing
land of St Giles's Hill was landscaped and developed with fine
large houses. Then in the early C20 the comparative wealth of
Winchester attracted Arts and Crafts architects: Dawn House by
Ernest Newton is the finest example of the genre, but significant
contributions were made by *Robert Weir Schultz*, *E. C. Shearman*,
and *M. H. Baillie Scott*. In the 1920s the Stanmore Estate developed, with distinctive council housing designed by *William Curtis
Green*.

It is a regrettable irony that, although Winchester escaped
almost totally unscathed from bombing in the Second World War,
post-war 'improvements' led to the loss of some interesting architecture and streetscapes. Mainly C19 tenements in The Brooks

* Hereafter 'Stopher', when unqualified, always refers to Thomas Stopher Jun.

were condemned as slums but contained medieval elements. The motorcar was an equally destructive force, leading amongst other things to the demolition of the George Hotel and the unsympathetic widening of the s end of Jewry Street. The founding of the Winchester Preservation Trust in 1959 was one response to these threats. The following year the City Council engaged *Peter Shepheard* as consultant for overall development of the city. At around the same time S. J. Garton was commissioned by the Council to carry out a survey of Winchester's historic buildings. By 1963 he was evolving a scheme to redevelop the devastated area between Upper Brook and Eastgate Streets, which resembled a bomb site. Contemporary with these proposals were *Sir Hugh Casson*'s redevelopment of St George's Street N side and *Bernard Feilden*'s design for the future Wessex Hotel. They heralded an increasing awareness of the importance of Winchester's built environment. Some excellent projects have taken place recently, notably the sensitive development of the Peninsula Barracks site by *Huw Thomas*. The result of this long development is a city with architecture of unparalleled variety and buildings of outstanding quality and interest spanning more than nine centuries.

THE CATHEDRAL

Winchester Cathedral is still the city's most prominent landmark as one descends the hill from the E, but its relative squatness and, above all, the absence of a spire, means that from the nearby streets one enjoys only occasional glimpses of the building. Its exceptional length is best appreciated from Winchester College's playing fields to the s or from St Catherine's Hill, whose summit affords a fine view of the cathedral brooding in the valley bottom. The cathedral's length is indeed one of its most obvious features: as originally built it was 532 ft (162 metres) long externally; the C13 E arm increased this to 591 ft (180 metres), before the C14 demolition of the western massif reduced it to the present 554 ft (169 metres). The nave is 246 ft (75 metres) long internally, from the W end to the choir screen; 264 ft (80.5 metres) to the faces of the W tower piers. It was briefly the longest church N of the Alps, until outstripped by Abbot Hugh's Cluny III, begun in 1088. The importance of Winchester Cathedral as an example – indeed often as the cradle – of successive developments in English ecclesiastical architecture can scarcely be overstated. All major architectural periods are represented, from the Early Anglo-Norman crypt to the Late Gothic of the presbytery aisles; for the C13 there is the retrochoir; the early C14, the presbytery; and for the later C14 emergence of Perp, the remodelling of the nave. Almost every building scheme was abortive, ensuring an architectural diversity of unrivalled interest and charm that fortunately escaped the worst excesses of C18 'restorers', who might have been tempted to iron out some of the anomalies. No less interesting are the monuments and furnishings. The six purpose-built chantry chapels reflect English architectural developments in microcosm, and there are many other fine tombs and memorials. The C12 font, the C12 wall paintings of the Holy Sepulchre Chapel, and the C14 woodwork of the choir, are the finest surviving examples of English medieval craftsmanship, while the Early Renaissance is superbly represented by Bishop Gardiner's Chapel.

HISTORY

The first cathedral was OLD MINSTER, whose site lies N of the present building. Begun in the mid C7 by the recently converted Cenwealh, king of Wessex, as a small, cruciform church, it was much extended during the C10 monastic reforms by Bishop Æthelwold whose works included an impressive westwork, dedicated 980, over the grave of St Swithun. The empty grave, originally in an open forecourt between an entrance tower and the church, is now marked by a granite slab. The church's plan, known from the 1960s excavations, is marked out in red brick for the C7 church, grey for later extensions. In its final form it had a five-stage tower capped by a weathercock over the elevated High Altar, three other towers, and spectacular crypts. At the E end a spacious mausoleum was added to house the bodily remains of the Anglo-Danish royal house. Immediately N of Old Minster stood NEW MINSTER, a separate foundation begun in 901 as a mausoleum for King Alfred and his heirs and to serve the needs of the expanding city.

Winchester, Old and New Minsters, reconstruction.
Drawing by Simon Hayfield, 2005

Like Old Minster it became a Benedictine monastery in 964. It moved to Hyde in 1110. The 1960s excavations showed that the church was a transeptal basilica of virtually the same size and plan as Charlemagne's Saint-Denis,* and some of the conventual buildings (including the possible infirmary cloister) were also excavated.

Building commenced on the new CATHEDRAL in 1079, although planning probably began soon after the last Saxon bishop, the pluralist Archbishop Stigand, was deposed in 1070. He was replaced by Walkelin (1070–89), previously a canon of Rouen Cathedral during its mid-C11 reconstruction (dedicated in 1063), and the influence of Upper Normandy is evident in the surviving Romanesque parts at Winchester. The new cathedral's site, aligned to the street grid rather than true E–W, was carefully chosen so that Old Minster could continue to function until its replacement was usable. The *Annales Wintonienses* say the monks moved into their new church on 8 April 1093, i.e. just in time for Easter. By then those areas of the church that were needed for the liturgy had evidently been completed: the E arm, transepts and enough of the nave to support the crossing tower, together with the S nave aisle wall, which formed the rear wall of the cloister. St Swithun's reliquary was collected from Old Minster on 15 July 1093: Walkelin gave orders next day for the Saxon minster's demolition, permitting the completion of the nave which partially covers the Old Minster site. The cathedral's central tower collapsed in 1107. It was quickly rebuilt, and the quality of the early C12 masonry indicates greater care (or skill) in reconstruction. The nave was probably not finished until the late 1120s, delayed first by poor relations between bishop and king then by the collapse of the tower.

In 1202 Bishop Godfrey de Lucy (1189–1204) established a confraternity for the 'repair' of the cathedral. In fact a complete remodelling of the E arm ensued, with the addition of a spacious retrochoir. The original intention may have been to replace the entire E arm, but the project, advancing westwards, came to a halt on reaching the Norman choir apse. Work on the presbytery did not resume until the early C14, now in Dec style. This too seems to have proceeded by fits and starts during much of the century; meanwhile Bishop Edington (1345–66) began to remodel the W front, where the Norman W massif was demolished to make way for a triple porch. Building work was interrupted (perhaps by the Black Death), and resumed in a later phase that included rebuilding the W end of the nave aisle walls. Edington's works were taken up by his successor, William of Wykeham (1367–1404). In 1394 the remodelling of the nave began in earnest, work which perhaps could mostly be done in the dry, for the roof, tree-ring dated to 1249–50, was retained, side-purlins and queen-posts being added to strengthen it. Wykeham's will of 1403 shows how

* Information from Martin and Birthe Biddle: see *Winchester Studies* 4.i (forthcoming).

much had been achieved: remodelling the nave piers had begun but the main vault was probably not finished for two decades. At the end of the C15, Priors Hunton (1470–98) and Silkstede (1498–1524) rebuilt the E bay of the Lady Chapel. Bishop Richard Fox (1501–28) takes the credit for the final major works: rebuilding the presbytery's E gable and roof, remodelling the presbytery high vault and aisles (1503–9), adding his own chantry chapel (1513–18), and inserting screens between the C14 piers of the presbytery (1525), his later projects showing the first Renaissance influence in the cathedral. An indenture dated 1513 relating to the establishing of Corpus Christi College Oxford shows that Fox also planned to remodel the transepts and retrochoir, but the money ran out: the retrochoir vaults were simply repaired, and the transepts, fortunately, remained untouched.

The names of some of the MASONS and ARCHITECTS in charge of successive building projects are known. A *Willelmus cæmentarius* may have been the master mason for the Norman work; in the early C14 *Thomas of Witney* is credited with the initial stages of the remodelling of the presbytery, and after his departure for Exeter in 1316 the work may have been continued by *William Joy*. Late that century the remodelling of the nave under Wykeham's patronage was supervised by *William Wynford*. The close relationship between bishop and architect had begun *c.* 1360 when Wykeham was clerk of works at Windsor Castle and Wynford one of two wardens of masons working under John Sponlee. When Wykeham became Provost of Wells Cathedral in 1363 Wynford became master mason there two years later, remaining, however, in the King's service. In 1377–8 he was involved in the reconstruction of Wykeham's episcopal palace at Bishop's Waltham (South Hampshire), by which time he was considered master mason for all Wykeham's work, including New College, Oxford (1380–6), and Winchester College (from 1387). He worked for the royal castle and finally the cathedral. He died in 1405. The later stages of Bishop Fox's works in the cathedral, including the presbytery screens dated 1525, were perhaps undertaken by *Thomas Bertie* (or 'Bartewe') (†1555); in 1532–3 he was certainly employed by the priory, receiving an annuity in 1538 for his 'works and repairs' past and present. This architect later achieved renown as the designer of Cowes and Calshot Castles; possibly also Hurst Castle whose first captain he became in 1544. At his death he occupied living quarters at Hurst but also continued to hold property in Kingsgate Street, Winchester.

The REFORMATION brought about many changes. St Swithun's shrine was an early casualty (1538). Perhaps in the reign of Edward VI, images were removed from their niches, including those of the Great Screen, whose silver-gilt retable was eventually (1561) replaced by a board painted with the Ten Commandments. The High Altar became a plain wooden table *c.* 1550. The daily offices being reduced to Morning and Evening Prayer, and Holy Communion to Sundays and a reduced number of holy days, liturgical activity now focused on the choir and presbytery. All the minor altars (including those in the chantry chapels) were cleared away and the choir was fitted with extra stalls to accommodate the laity. Both the redundant Gothic rood loft and the pulpitum at the w end of the choir survived until 1638–9 when *Inigo Jones* formed a new choir screen to replace the pulpitum, with partial reuse of masonry from the rood loft. The fabric and fittings suffered further during the CIVIL WAR of the 1640s. Notably, in December 1642 Parliamentary troops allegedly ran amok, overturning the communion table and breaking the altar rail – carrying them to a nearby alehouse and setting them on fire; smashing the carved spandrel panels of the choir stall canopies, which depicted biblical scenes; destroying the organ; pulling down the mortuary chests and using the bones as missiles to break the windows; ransacking the reputed tomb of William Rufus (actually Bishop Henry of Blois); destroying the fittings of the chantry chapels and anything which suggested a royal or episcopal connection. Although the account, preserved in a Royalist pamphlet by *Mercurius Rusticus* (Bruno Ryves, later Dean of Windsor), is partisan, all the physical evidence suggests things happened as that author described. Another casualty was most of the medieval glass.

A few minor repairs were undertaken in the C18 before major alterations in the first quarter of the nineteenth century directed by *William Garbett*, surveyor to the Dean and Chapter. In 1821–2 he and *John Nash* (whom the Chapter had brought in as consultant) strengthened two piers at the e end of the s arcade, inserting cast-iron shafts coated in *Coade* stone. But the most important programme of work was the underpinning of the cathedral in 1905–12, directed by *T. G. Jackson* and *Francis Fox*, engineer. Most famous among their workmen was Diver William Walker, who, working some 13 ft under water, replaced a double layer of beech logs beneath the C13 walls of the retrochoir with bags of concrete to permit new foundations. The ends of the transepts and the entire nave, where the Romanesque builders had constructed the cathedral walls on thick medieval concrete foundations, supplemented in some areas by vertical oak piles, were similarly underpinned.

PLAN, ELEVATIONS AND MATERIALS

Much of the basic PLAN of Winchester Cathedral – the outer walls and the arcades – remains as conceived in the late 1070s; even in the e arm, completely rebuilt above pavement level between about 1200 and 1520, the original plan survives in the crypt. Many elements of the design of Walkelin's cathedral may be traced to churches in Normandy, such as Jumièges and Rouen Cathedral. It was cruciform, with transepts extending by three bays beyond the nave aisles, and a fourteen-bay nave, now reduced to twelve. The choir was located in the crossing, beneath a lantern tower, and extended as a platform by one bay into the nave. Beyond the crossing, the original E arm, raised above the crypt by 6 ft 6 in. (2 metres), comprised a presbytery of four straight bays terminating in an apse, around which the aisles continued as an ambulatory. Leading off the ambulatory was an unusually long axial chapel, also apsidal, flanked by square-ended chapels at the ends of the presbytery aisles. The transepts have aisles on both E and W sides: a feature of the great Continental pilgrimage churches going up at the same time, and one which Walkelin's brother Simeon soon adopted at Ely, where he was abbot from 1082. In addition the aisles continue around the ends of the transepts, as do the galleries, forming tribunes at the end of the transepts.* There may have been a similar tribune at the W end of the Romanesque nave, but all the evidence was removed in the C14 when work began on remodelling the W front. Excavation of the Norman foundations suggests that the original W massif had flanking towers (cf. La Trinité, Caen) rather than W transepts as at Ely. A portion of the SW tower survives as a boundary wall S of the cathedral forecourt. Numerous altars were needed for ordained monks to say daily mass: the E side of each transept (at ground and gallery levels) had six, and three more were at the E end. St Swithun's reliquary was originally on the high altar, but in the 1150s Bishop Henry of Blois inserted a 'Feretory platform' at the apex of the apse, beneath which the 'Holy Hole' allowed suppliants to crawl beneath a new shrine altar. The cult may also have determined the construction of Bishop de Lucy's retrochoir in the early C13 as a setting for pilgrim activity, though the shrine was not in fact moved there until 1476. The new E end used the footings of the old axial chapel for the foundations of its arcades. Despite the remodelling of the E arm, the High Altar and choir have remained in the same position. Changes to the presbytery in the C14, and its aisles in the early C16, scarcely affected the plan, the only change being the wider spacing of the presbytery piers, still supported on the Norman crypt arcade.

As for the main INTERNAL ELEVATIONS, Walkelin's design comprised the usual three storeys: main arcade, gallery and clerestory. In the nave and transepts these were of equal height (as at Saint-Étienne, Caen, and Cerisy-la-Forêt, both in Normandy); in the E arm, whose pavement is some 6 ft (1.8 metres) above that of nave and transept, the gallery sill was raised by a similar amount, giving a correspondingly shorter middle storey. The nave piers consisted entirely of compound piers (basically cruciform, with nook-shafts); evidence for the plan of the Romanesque plinths discovered in the 1960s (*see* p. 585) suggested that in the choir compound piers alternated

* In this account the middle storey of the Romanesque elevation is called the 'gallery storey', rather than 'triforium', a term better reserved for Gothic architecture; the platforms at the ends of the transepts are called 'tribunes'. The cathedral museum is infelicitously named the 'Triforium Gallery'.

with cylindrical columns; the surviving stump of one pier beneath the wooden stair in Bishop Gardiner's Chapel shows that the four supports in the C11 apse were all cylindrical.

The development of the C13 retrochoir involved many design changes. At one stage during its lengthy construction it seems to have been envisaged that it would be two-storeyed, with a clerestory (whose aborted access stairs survive at the E end) and a great east gable with lower chapels beyond, but the body of the retrochoir as eventually built is a 'hall church', the central vessel being roughly the same height as the aisles. The Lady Chapel was intended to have a clerestory illuminating the foiled openings in the apex of its vault; but here too there was a design change. Upper chambers were built over the side chapels, which meant that the clerestory openings of the Lady Chapel's w bay received no light and were never glazed. These changes meant that, perhaps in the C15, the whole retrochoir could be covered with a simple low-pitched roof, replacing what seems to have been a rather *ad hoc* system of roofing that included, for a time, transverse gables over the S retrochoir aisle, reminiscent of the original roof of the Great Hall. The main elevation of the C14 presbytery is two-storeyed (main arcade and clerestory), a scheme previously employed in the 1230s in more modest churches such as the E arm of Southwell Minster, at Netley Abbey (*c.* 1240), and in the transepts of Tintern Abbey (1270s), for the original scheme (subsequently altered) at Exeter (1280s), and – contemporary with Winchester – at Selby Abbey *c.* 1315–35. The main elevation of Winchester's remodelled nave, designed towards the end of the C14, has a shallow, balcony-like triforium stage between the main arcade and the clerestory.

Winchester Cathedral's architectural eclecticism is echoed in its diversity of BUILDING STONES, contributing to its striking textural and colour variations. The Norman church was constructed mainly of Quarr stone from the Isle of Wight, with its range of hues from green to purple, together with some use of a shelly, yellowish oolitic Limestone; later more of the same stone became available, salvaged from demolished Old Minster. Supplies of Quarr were nearly exhausted by the early C12 so the C13 builders employed reused blocks, together with some poor-quality Bembridge stone. Creamy Caen stone was increasingly chosen for fine carving, especially internally, together with contrasting, dark polished Purbeck marble for columns and decorative elements. A different fine-grained, white limestone, Beer stone (a variety of chalk), from the Devon–Dorset border, was used *c.* 1380–1420 for the remodelling of the nave. The last stone used for the medieval work (*c.* 1500) was an Oxfordshire limestone from Headington. The fashion for staring white Portland stone affected Winchester to a limited extent. The same stone was later used for repairs, and many other imported stones have also been used in this way, particularly from the mid C19 when they could be brought by rail. Bath stone was the first, then Ketton, Weldon,

Doulting, and Portland in the early C20; Portland and Ancaster in the mid century; French stones in the later C20, e.g. Lepine or Richemont, and now English stone again, with modern Beer replacing Caen and Beer and Clipsham in place of Quarr; some Caen stone is also available.

DESCRIPTION

A tour of the EXTERIOR begins with the TRANSEPTS, the oldest surviving parts. The squarish blocks of Quarr stone with wide joints are typical late C11. Each transept projects by three bays articulated by pilaster buttresses. Wider clasping pilasters at the E angles mark the position of corner turrets. Starting with the N TRANSEPT: on the W side the lowest tier of windows, lighting the aisle, retain their C12 openings – plain round-headed arches flanked by nook-shafts with cushion capitals or, in the case of the middle bay, early proto-scallops. The arches are surmounted by a double roll, a thin band of chip-carved saltire crosses, and a billet hoodmould. Tucked in the corner next to the aisle wall is the so-called 'Pilgrims' Door', a single-step doorway with one order of shafts carrying cushion capitals. Sculptural fragments recovered from the infill in 1886 showed that this doorway was blocked at the Reformation. Higher up, above a billet-moulded string, are the plain small windows of the gallery. The parapet is a rebuild; originally the roof over the gallery pitched steeply up to the sill of the clerestory windows. All the transept aisle roofs were eventually lowered to conform (more or less) with the adjacent aisle roofs of nave and presbytery: internally the roofs are supported in a very rough and ready way on stanchions probably of the early C16 which were perhaps temporary supports in preparation for Fox's anticipated remodelling of the transepts. The clerestory windows have been remodelled on the W side, with the insertion of Perp tracery perhaps of later C15 date. The gable-wall of the N transept is a symmetrical composition, with three wide pilaster buttresses: a central one, and two others between the central vessel and the aisles. From the gallery upwards the outer one on the E side contains a stair-vice now ending in a flat-roofed turret beside the central gable. The lowest tier of windows in the N wall were given Perp tracery but this was removed c. 1820 by *Garbett* and they now appear in their Norman form. The easternmost window was replaced in the early C14 by the existing one with cusped intersecting tracery within a pointed arch. The tall windows lighting the main vessel at gallery and clerestory level are also essentially Norman, with Perp tracery. In the gable is a rose window; its tracery (reconstructed 1982–3 by *Corinne Bennett*) is probably early C16 (contemporary with the transept roof) but is old-fashioned for the date. It may have been inspired by earlier exemplars in N France.

The windows at the ends of the E and W galleries are blocked, and this is to be associated with other anomalies at all four corners of the transept, but most evident externally at the NE corner. There, at clerestory level, a piece of blind arcading is visible in the N wall, just l. of the corner turret. This is a surviving fragment of one of four corner towers that were planned as an afterthought in the late CII but never completed owing to subsidence. Around the corner, in the E wall of the transept, the northernmost clerestory window is accommodated within a much larger Romanesque arch; had this corner tower been completed, the arch would have opened from the top storey of the tower into the body of the transept. These features were first analysed by the observant Professor Robert Willis in 1845. The C14 remodelling of the windows of the E aisle continues round the E side of the transept. From N to S are two windows (one tall, one short) with reticulated tracery, then a slightly earlier window of five lights with three curved triangles in the head, two of them set diagonally. The aisle windows were remodelled c. 1310–30 in order to light three chapels formerly located in the E aisle; as we shall see, the vault of the central chapel was renewed at the same time. The clerestory windows on this side are devoid of tracery, except for the northernmost, which has a central mullion, probably post-medieval. Above these windows is a corbel course of grotesque heads and moulded blocks (the corbel course on the W side of the transept was replaced in the C14 and has widely spaced square fleurons and grotesque heads). In the angle of the E arm and N transept, a 'utilities and flower room' by cathedral architect *Peter Bird* of *Caroe & Partners* (2010), replacing *T. G. Jackson*'s 1908 coke store.

As for the TOWER, rebuilt after the disaster of 1107, its treatment demonstrates developments in architectural decoration during the twenty years that had elapsed since the E arm and first tower were completed: the windows have chevron hoodmoulds and jambs, and chevrons also adorn the upper string course. The tower is roofed with a modern low double-pitch surmounted by a squat lantern: a remodelling of 1992 to carry the sound of the bells away from the canons' houses and over the city.

The W side of the S TRANSEPT is similar in many respects to the N, and here, too, the wide arch into the abortive tower survives, partially blocked and enclosing a Perp window. The S gable-wall leans dramatically, a sign of the subsidence that has so affected the cathedral over the centuries. Some abutment was provided even whilst the gable-wall was under construction, by infilling the space between the transept and the chapter house with two superimposed tunnels: the groin-vaulted slype at ground level and, above, a barrel-vaulted room perhaps originally used as the sacrist's offices, now the Cathedral Library (only the E half of this vault survives). As in the N transept, the big Norman windows are filled with Perp tracery. In the gable the central pilaster buttress continues to

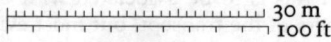

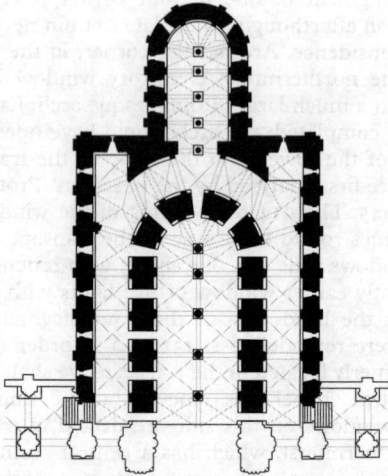

ROMANESQUE CRYPT

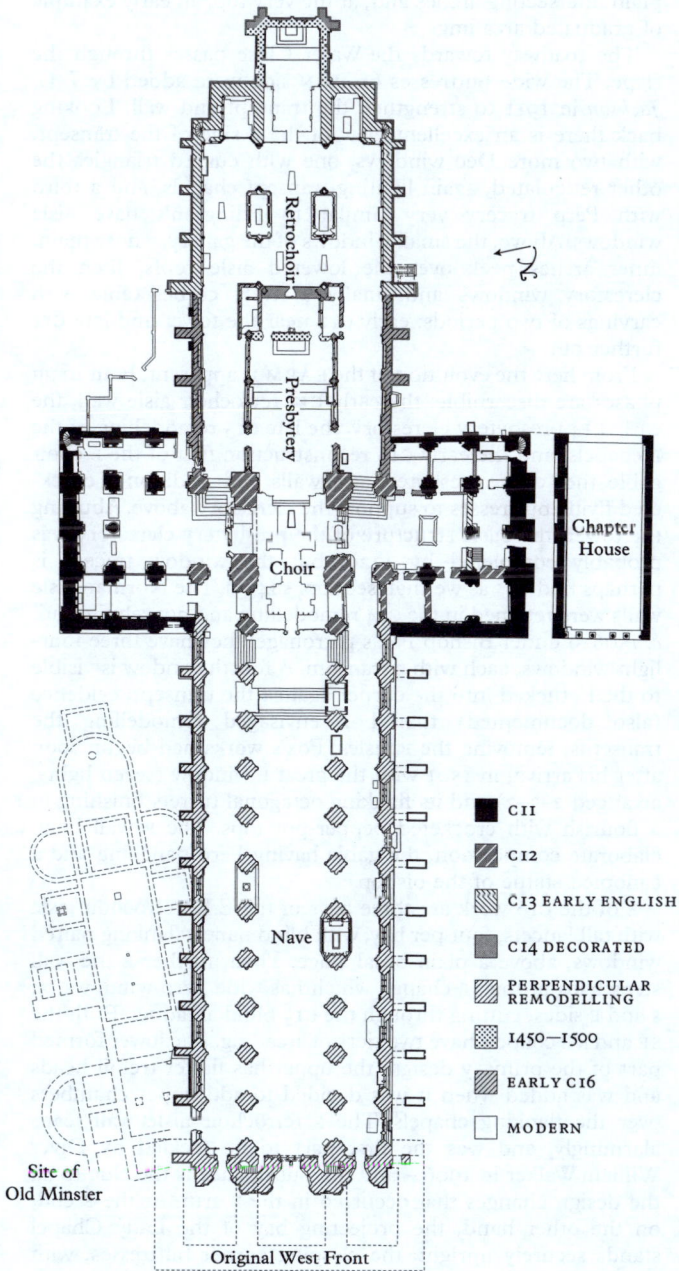

Retrochoir

Presbytery

Choir

Chapter House

Nave

CII

CI2

CI3 EARLY ENGLISH

CI4 DECORATED

PERPENDICULAR
REMODELLING

1450–1500

EARLY CI6

MODERN

Site of
Old Minster

Original West Front

Winchester Cathedral.
Phased plan (*above*) and plan of Romanesque Crypt (*left*)

rise in diminished form as far as the apex, and is flanked by plain intersecting arches and, at the very top, an early example of graduated arcading.

The roadway towards the Water Close passes through the slype. The wide buttresses on its N side were added by *T. G. Jackson* in 1911 to strengthen the transept end wall. Looking back there is an excellent view of the E side of the transept, with two more Dec windows, one with curved triangles the other reticulated, again lighting transept chapels, and a third with Perp tracery very similar to Edington's nave aisle windows. Above, the small windows of the gallery, whose main, inner arches peek over the lowered aisle roofs, then the clerestory windows and finally a lively corbel table with carvings of two periods: early C12 near the tower and late C11 further out.

From here the evolution of the E ARM is apparent. Four main phases are discernible: the early C13 retrochoir aisle wall, the early C14 presbytery clerestory, the late C15 remodelling of the E chapels, and the early C16 reconstruction first of the E choir gable, then of the presbytery aisle walls, with addition of crocketed flying buttresses to support the clerestory above. Abutting the tower, the basic structure of the presbytery clerestory was probably completed by 1320, but the window tracery is perhaps mid C15 as we shall see (pp. 584–5). The Norman aisle walls were retained in the C14 remodelling and not rebuilt until *c.* 1506–9 under Bishop Fox's patronage; they have three four-light windows, each with a transom. A fourth window is visible to the l., tucked into the corner against the transept, evidence (also documented) that Fox envisaged remodelling the transepts, removing the E aisles. Fox's works had begun soon after his arrival in 1501 with the great E window (seven lights, arranged 2–3–2) and its flanking octagonal turrets finishing in a flourish with crocketed pepper-pot tops. The E wall is an elaborate composition, the gable having Perp panelling and a canopied statue of the bishop.

E of the C16 work are three bays of the E.E. retrochoir aisle with tall lancets, four per bay, with blind panels flanking paired windows, above a plain basal stage. Then, further E the wall steps back at the SE chapel, which has wide Perp windows on S and E sides, cutting through the C13 blind arcading. Both the SE and NE chapels have two tiers of arcading. The lower formed part of the primary design; the upper has flatter trefoil heads and was added when it was decided to add upper chambers over the flanking chapels. The S retrochoir aisle wall leans alarmingly, and was the first part to be tackled by Diver William Walker in 1906 – and this subsidence is the clue to all the design changes that occurred in the E arm. At the E end, on the other hand, the projecting bay of the Lady Chapel stands securely upright; the clasping corner buttresses, with their crocketed ogees, form part of a C14 partial rebuild and were retained when this bay was reconstructed above crypt level starting in the 1490s. The latter phase is securely dated

by the heraldry of the corbels supporting the blind external
arcading on the s and e sides. The e, n and s windows have
two tiers of seven lights arranged 3–1–3, with a tight net of
panel-tracery lights; they could be contemporary with the presbytery aisle windows of 1506–9.

Now to the w end, to consider the external consequences of
the remodelling of the nave and the c14 refashioning of the
WEST FRONT. This replaced the Norman w massif, of which   40
only a fragment of the core of its s wall is upstanding, forming
an area of rough masonry in the boundary wall on the s side
of the forecourt, with pink mortar and bonding courses of
chalk (a plaque indicates its w extent). Pevsner rightly thought
the c14 façade disappointing, characterizing it as 'no more
than a section through the nave and aisles'. The three
entrances, in a screen wall set flat in front of the façade proper
and not reaching above the ground stage, are an example of
very Late Dec work under Bishop Edington (†1366). Debate
continues as to whether this phase was completed before the
Black Death: two to three years seems a short period in which
to demolish the Norman w massif and start its replacement.
The deep porches have panelled sides, lierne-vaults springing
elegantly from shaft-clusters, and four centred arches, those of
the aisles being straight-sided above the initial curve. The
central PORCH has twin doorways separated by a trumeau; the
doorways of the lateral porches are offset inwards so as to align
to the centre of the aisles. The centre is set forward, and to l.
and r. of the central porch has two tall image niches (the
statues, presumably of SS Peter and Paul, must have vanished
at the Reformation). Top balustrade. As for the façade proper
the aisle windows, set well back behind the porch balustrade,
have four-light (1–2–1) windows with foiled tracery, under
broad two-centred heads with deep casement mouldings. This
Early Perp design must belong to a second phase of work
at the end of Edington's episcopate,★ but it also shows the
consequence of the design change which occurred when
Wykeham's work started in earnest in the 1390s. The aisles
were vaulted at higher level than anticipated in the earlier
phase. Above the windows is an inclined balustrade identical
to that over the porch. Its foot corresponds with the level of
the planned aisle roof (visible internally), and the balustrade
must have originally been openwork but subsequently blocked
(and later rebuilt in that form) and the wall heightened above
it. A sloping cornice adorned with heads – a flourish contrasting with the austerity of the w window – marks the top of the
end wall of the roof space, after which is a plain parapet.
Similar windows, and later heightening of the walls, occur in
the first two bays of the nave n aisle and one bay on the s.

The great w WINDOW has mouldings similar to the aisle
windows and, like those, has blind panels and a balustrade
above so it is probably of the same phase; its glazing, dated

★ I have abandoned an idea, previously published, that this phase is attributable to
Wykeham c. 1371.

c. 1375 (*see* p. 613) provides an *ante quem* date. It is framed within deep jambs with wide casement mouldings and is nine lights wide, arranged 3–3–3, with two major mullions rising to the apex but also branching off in carving-knife profile to form the heads of the side parts. Transoms (five in the central division) subdivide the window into thirty-nine cinquefoil-headed lights plus tracery lights: an immense area of glass, occupying the whole upper cross-section of the nave within. Either side of the window are hexagonal stair-turrets which almost overlap the aisle windows; but the masonry of turrets and window courses together, so they are contemporary. The plain buttresses on the W side of the turrets are undoubtedly secondary (uncoursed with the turrets), though they resemble those at the outer corners of the aisles.

Above the W window, the triangular apex of the GABLE is decorated in a far more rectilinear pattern, and the tracery cusps lack fleurons, suggesting that it forms part of Wykeham's final phase and is therefore (as one would expect) contemporary with the vault and completed in the early C15. At the top of the gable a pinnacle contains a niche with a statue of a bishop (usually claimed to portray St Swithun) by *Mr Carter* of *Farmer & Brindley*, 1908.

Round the corner on the N side, in Edington's two remodelled aisle bays, a doorway of *c.* 1360 led to the chapel over St Swithun's grave, rebuilt at the same time. The remaining bays of the NAVE are all Wykeham's work. This is best appreciated on the S side, reached via 'Curle's Passage', cut through the SW buttress by Bishop Walter Curle in 1632, to which the casual *viator* was directed by pointing hands and Latin inscriptions on the W front. The idea was to stop him taking a short cut through the cathedral: only the *precator* should enter the church to pray. Another inscribed panel from the E end of the passage is now set in the wall halfway along. The buttresses along the S side of the nave were added by *T. G. Jackson* in 1911–12, for until the Reformation the N cloister walk abutted the aisle wall. The lower part of the wall here is rough, Romanesque masonry, with chases perhaps to house struts bracing the cloister roof. Wynford's aisle windows are taller than those of the previous phase at the W end, and are three lights wide, with a transom, and foiled shapes in the tracery lights, the whole rather strictly constrained by a four-centred arch; similar windows occur at clerestory level, where the remains of Norman pilaster buttresses may still be seen between them. Below the parapet is a charmingly varied frieze of square fleurons and grotesque heads, similar to those below the raised aisle parapets of the W front.

The S door, halfway along the N cloister walk, was inserted in 1818. Formerly access to the nave was through the blocked doorways at the N end of the E and W walks. The E doorway, copied for the 1818 replacement, is undoubtedly Wykeham's, whose heraldry it displays; the W doorway is a more modest affair, off-centre within the bay because the W wall of the cloister abutted the nave just to its l.; the removal of the cloister wall revealed the small fragment of Romanesque billet moulding from the previous doorhead. In 'Curle's Passage' are two further blocked openings. The taller one to the w goes with the later phase of Edington's work, and was an external door, perhaps leading to the graveyard; in the next bay to the E is a modest, unadorned doorway, which probably provided direct access into the nave from a room at the N end of the w cloister range. Its infill, and some of the *in situ* blocks of the surrounding wall, are adorned with interesting geometrical patterns and initials, apparently masons' doodles or trial pieces. Perhaps they had their lodge here for a time.

The INTERIOR is described in chronological order beginning with the Norman CRYPT. Its entrances were always, as still, on the N side, from the E aisle of the transepts, and vestiges of the CII entry tunnels and steps survive. There was also an external doorway, now a window, in the third bay of the N aisle.* But the present internal entry is an early C19 'Norman' door (by *Gurbett*), descending to a C14 inner doorway whose sill indicates the level to which the crypt floor had by then been raised to cope with the rising water table (the floor was restored to its CII level in 1886). Seen from the entry platform,** the N aisle of the crypt gives a fair idea of late CII architecture: squarish Quarr stone blocks with thick ribbon-pointing; groin-vaults separated by plain transverse arches resting on hollow-chamfered imposts; deep splayed windows sloping down from the higher ground level outside. The central vessel is an apsidal space echoing the form of the original choir above, though shortened at the w end where three bays were walled off after the collapse of the first tower in 1107. The thick, squat piers have very flat capitals, again supporting groin-vaults. The well next to the pier at the focus of the apse is immediately under the high altar, still in its CII position.

The ambulatory is partially blocked by a number of intrusive supports (C13 and C20) and is flanked by the square-ended chapels at the E ends of the aisles. There is another well in the SE chapel. Projecting E from the head of the ambulatory is a long axial crypt with a central row of five thinner columns with block capitals and terminating in an apse, now broken through. The blocks of masonry to r. and l., underpinned in brick in 1908, support the Beaufort and Waynflete chantry chapels above. The windows of this part of the crypt are blocked by the solid foundations of the C13 retrochoir which wraps around it. At the E end an entry has been broken through into a C13 crypt beneath the Lady Chapel, and in the passage on the s side, between the CII and C13 work are vestiges of a first, short-lived groin-vault: could there have been a C12 addition here, possibly represented by substantial amounts of finely decorated masonry reused in the retrochoir roof spaces? There

---

* In this account the bays are numbered working outwards from the crossing tower.
** For much of the year flooding prevents one getting any further.

are other anomalies: the C13 rib-vault of the Lady Chapel crypt may have been reconstructed, and its responds look C14. The two free-standing central columns are not a pair, and the change in floor level also hints at design modifications here.

The NORTH TRANSEPT is the least altered Romanesque space at main level. Aisles on three sides (as later at Ely), and round-headed blank arcading on the N and W aisle walls, much hacked about and subsequently reinstated. In the W aisle (now the Epiphany Chapel) many of the cushion capitals of this wall arcading were carved into human heads, probably in the early C14. Likewise, two of the paired respond shafts flanking that chapel's chancel were shortened and the stumps fashioned into head corbels (a king and a bishop); small Atlantids were later similarly carved on the adjacent responds. All four shafts were reinstated in poor-quality Bembridge limestone in the early C19 giving a very strange effect. Other C15 examples of the same treatment occur in the S transept. There is no arcading on the E walls of the transepts, where altars were placed, nor in the first bay of the return of the W aisle, where the so-called 'Pilgrims' Door' was located.

In the body of the transept the great triple elevation of Walkelin's interior rises cliff-like. Three storeys of almost equal height: a main arcade with arches of two plain orders; a gallery storey with similar outer arches enclosing pairs of inner arches; and a clerestory with the usual passage, fronted by an initially confusing arrangement of arches: tall in front of the windows, flanked by smaller ones. The bays are separated by half-shafts on square dosserets ('masts', Pevsner called them), two of which on each side rise full-height to the wall-head. The transept terminates in a tribune platform, supported on a thick round pier between two great plain arches, behind which the aisle continues around the transept end. At the springing level of the gallery arcade the 'masts' either side of the tribune parapet are truncated, and the clerestory design above the tribune appears very illogical with large and small arches of greatly varying proportions. The basic design in the clerestory was evidently for a tall, wide arch flanked by two smaller arches, but this neat scheme really only occurs in one bay.

The anomalies result from three factors: the belated decision to add corner towers to the transepts, their abandonment, and the collapse of the central tower in 1107. The evidence for the aborted corner towers is clear in the transept aisles. While the two outer faces of each tower would have been supported on the aisle walls, the tower walls facing into the cathedral had to bridge the aisles, demanding a good deal of extra support. The transverse arches which would have sustained the tower walls above the E and W aisles have clearly been widened, and so have the piers from which they spring, at the innermost corner of each tower. The responds on the E and W walls have likewise been widened; on the E side the original capital peeks through the additional masonry.

The decision to add corner towers was probably taken when construction had risen as far as the gallery capitals. The 'masts' flanking the front of the tribune were abandoned as incompatible with the new scheme. In their completed form the wide arches at clerestory level would have opened from the body of the transept into tower chambers; indeed, vestiges of the springing of the groin-vault beneath the NE tower are visible in the gallery of the N transept. This tower, for which we have noted the external evidence, was probably the only one to be nearly completed, the others not being so far advanced when the scheme was abandoned. The reason for the abandonment is not hard to see. The transept walls clearly settled during construction: the arcade walls slope inwards up to gallery floor level, but most of the settlement had taken place by the time the aisle vaults were completed and work resumed on the next stage of the elevation, whose walls are more vertical. The most dramatic settlement occurred in the gable wall of the S transept, which slopes outwards by more than 4 ft (1.2 metres).

With the abandonment of the corner towers, the clerestory was modified in a very rough-and-ready way. The clerestory arcade was completed, retaining the big internal openings to the tower, and introducing a kind of double-bay system of arcading in the outermost two bays (the same system seems subsequently to have been used in the post 1093 bays of the nave, where the 'masts' still visible above the vault occur only in alternate bays).

The changes caused by the collapse of the tower are less complicated. A clear contrast is seen between the rough-tooled C11 masonry with thick joints and the finely cut, diagonal-tooled, thin-jointed C12 work. The junction between the two builds is obvious, and shows that the reconstruction comprised not only the tower but the eight adjacent piers of transepts, nave and E arm. Everything was built on a larger footing (the builders were taking no chances), which means that the arches adjoining the tower are exaggeratedly stilted.

The C12 builders introduced an innovation: rib-vaults. The rebuilt bays of the transept aisles have these on the E side, and the masons were so pleased with the effect that they even added dummy ribs beneath the surviving C11 groins in two bays of the E aisle of the S transept, and possibly also in the W aisle of that transept, though the latter vaults (and also the NE corner of the N transept, where there is a shallow foliate boss at the intersection) might be total rebuilds. Other stylistic updating took place: even though the basic design of the transept elevations was retained, the capitals of the C12 work are more advanced. In place of Walkelin's simple cushions, we have scalloped types in the galleries, and the introduction of foliate motifs at clerestory level.

The E aisle of both transepts provided space for altars both at main and gallery level, but the aisle bays have been subject to alteration, particularly in the C14 when new windows were provided. In the N transept the third bay from the tower has been particularly remodelled, the shafts of the Norman piers either side having been cut back for ogee tabernacles, and C14 vaults inserted with filleted ribs and a foliate boss. The ribs spring from capitals sculpted with four delightful figures including angels and a monk with a chessboard. The transepts' appearance changed dramatically *c.* 1820, when flat painted ceilings were installed in the main vessels of each transept, to a design by the antiquarian *G. F. Nott*, prebendary of Winchester. Almost a century later the W aisle of the N transept was adapted as the Epiphany Chapel (with N-facing altar).

The crossing piers below the central TOWER were rebuilt on a larger footprint after the collapse of 1107. A tiny fragment of the original SW crossing pier's plinth is visible in the S transept, overlapped by the post-1107 pier base. One can see how the C12 piers were elongated E–W; consequently, the new N and S tower arches needed to be greatly stilted. The piers are decorated with engaged triple shafts: two narrow shafts flanking a fatter segmental one below the E and W arches (a design that Bridget Cherry suggests resulted from contacts with eastern England), and equal-sized below the N and S arches. This was originally a lantern tower, but floors were inserted (probably in the C15) to form the ringing chamber and bell-chamber, and in 1635 the wooden vault was placed beneath the ringing chamber floor.

The space beneath the N tower arch became the CHAPEL OF THE HOLY SEPULCHRE in the 1160s, remodelled in the early C13. Two bays, with an entrance at the W end. Of the first build are the two bays of blind arcading on the S wall; a pilaster-buttress between them has the remains of a multi-scallop capital. Both buttress and capital were widened slightly in a later C12 phase. The earlier capital is cut through by one supporting the C13 quadripartite vault, which survives only at the E end (the vault of the W bay was cut through by a stair to the organ in the C19). Single-chamfered ribs. The E boss with *Agnus Dei* looks like an insertion; more convincing is the foliate boss reinstated in the wooden vault skeleton of the W bay. The front of the chapel was completely remodelled in the C13 phase, including the doorway with one order of shafts with stiff-leaf caps, and the splayed masonry on the E side, including a cupboard to house the bell-chiming rope, was added *c.* 1820 by *Garbett*.

The SOUTH TRANSEPT AISLES have been completely transformed. In the mid C12 the W AISLE'S arcade was blocked to create the room identified as the treasury for precious objects given by Bishop Henry of Blois to his cathedral. The N bay has two pointed arches with right-angled chevron on fluted pilasters, decoration derived from Burgundy and perhaps inspired by Bishop Henry's links with Cluny, where he trained and later went into exile 1154–8. The treasury's entrance arch may be that reused below the S tower arch (*see* Furnishings, S transept, below). Next, the S end beneath the tribune platform was walled off to form the 'Calefactory'. The name reflects the fact that this part of the cathedral was heated (some archaeological evidence for braziers has been found): possibly the scriptorium was located here. This separation of the aisle was done perhaps *c.* 1200 on the evidence of the door, with portcullis frame and C-hinges with lobes and tendrils, which opened to the monks' stair (now represented by the C17 stair to the Library). The door was closed by a drawbar on the monastery side when the monks retired; anyone knocking for access could be glimpsed through the cross-shaped squint at the stair foot. (The service door from the slype dates only from *c.* 1820). Finally, in the C14, CHAPELS were formed within the E AISLE, separated by wooden screens on low masonry walls. The work is datable to *c.* 1315 from the discovery in these walls of inscribed blocks from the retaining wall of the Feretory platform, demolished when the apse was replaced by the Feretory screen as described below. The Venerable Chapel (N), has a good C14 stone entrance screen, with six tabernacles for statuary in the upper tier. Next to it, the Chapel of St John the Evangelist and the Fishermen Apostles: wall paintings (still visible in the C19) suggested that the original dedication was to SS Peter and Andrew. The N chapel was refurbished in the early C16 by Prior Silkstede (1498–1524), presumably as his chantry chapel, which is mentioned in several documents. He even added his name, 'ThoMAsS', on the cornice of the early C14 stone openwork screen with reticulated tracery between the chapel and the transept. This screen appears to have been salvaged from elsewhere (possibly from a chantry chapel, maybe that of Bishop Adam Orleton, now represented by a simple platform on the N side of the nave). The SW bay (now, disgracefully, WCs), was divided from the Calefactory by a stone wall in 1820.

Steps from the transepts lead up to the cathedral's E ARM, raised on the C11 crypt. Remodelling of this part began *c.* 1202, and the only Romanesque vestiges at main level are the remains of the W respond of the first arch of the choir arcade, the springing of the first clerestory arches, the base and a few courses of one of the four cylindrical columns of the apse hemicycle, and the FERETORY PLATFORM that Bishop Henry of Blois created in the apex of the Norman apse in 1158, probably as an enhanced setting for St Swithun's relics. Beneath the platform survives a short length of the 'Holy Hole', a tunnel probably intended to allow pilgrims to crawl westwards from the ambulatory so as to absorb the healing emanations from the saint's reliquary above. It therefore resembled the form and function of the central passage of a ring crypt; precisely the sort of arrangement one would associate with the cosmopolitan Bishop Henry. The platform appears to have been remodelled in the C13 on the evidence of stubs of flanking pillars; either then, or more probably in the C14, a relic cupboard was formed in the W side of the platform. The area remained a focus of veneration until the mid C15 when the Great Screen (*see* Furnishings) was erected across the presbytery, blocking the view of the reliquary; the relics were then moved into the retrochoir, where a huge new shrine was inaugurated in 1476. The 'Holy Hole' was 'stopped up' in 1542.

Bishop Godfrey de Lucy, patron of the C13 remodelling of the E arm, is entombed in the centre of his very beautiful RETROCHOIR. This enveloped the Norman E end, and the lower part of its walls could have been started without disturbing the earlier phase. Its body is rectangular, comprising three bays, with three aisles of almost equal width (the proportions were determined by the cut-down side walls of the axial Norman chapel, used as foundations for the arcades). The aisle walls are articulated with trefoil-headed arches resting on detached Purbeck marble shafts supported on a wall-bench; Purbeck is also elegantly used for the foiled shapes in the spandrels of the wall arcade (attachment holes suggest metal ornamental features such as stars or rosettes have been lost), and for the string course above and the quatrefoils in the frieze below window-sill level. Full-length Purbeck triple shaft clusters rise full height to support the quadripartite vault. The upper part of the outer wall – still technically a 'thick wall' as it encloses a passage – is lightened by wide double rere-arches with plain moulded capitals and free-standing central shafts standing in front of the pairs of lancet windows. In the S wall, towards the W end, is a delightful door at the head of the 'Bishop's Stair'; it is cinquefoil-headed, and has stiff-leaf sprays on the arch and hoodmould. Stylistically this looks mid rather than early C13; disjunctions in the surrounding masonry also suggest that the door is a subsequent insertion.

The arcade piers have crocket capitals at the E end, developing to early stiff-leaf towards the W. The piers develop, too: the E responds and the first free-standing pair have eight Purbeck shafts clustered around an appropriately shaped Purbeck core; a change occurs above the intermediate shaft-rings of the next pair, where the diagonal shafts form part of the core itself; the W responds follow this design from floor to capitals. So work proceeded slowly from E to W and in an experimental way. It is likely, furthermore, that a clerestory was originally envisaged (which would explain the abortive stair-turrets above the E chapels, perhaps intended to give access to an internal clerestory passage); the builders, alarmed by the subsidence that must have been apparent as the S wall was being built, compromised by raising the central vault slightly above those of the aisles, on short raised shafts. The vault seems then to have been finished off in a hurry, with plain-chamfered ribs, in contrast with the moulded profile of the aisle vaults. The result is something of a mess, especially the junction between the central vessel and the entrance arch to the Lady Chapel. Whatever the original intentions, the result was a 'hall church' with aisles of equal height. The initial impression of space is seriously compromised by the dominant chantry chapels inserted within the arcade on either side. The notable tile pavement (*see* pp. 592–3) was added about fifty years later.

As originally planned, the Lady Chapel and flanking chapels would have projected E of a great gable wall, a design soon adopted at Salisbury. Although the E bay of the LADY CHAPEL was rebuilt in the 1490s, enough of the chapel's C13 work survives to give an idea of the original appearance. There was a dado of blind arcading (partly concealed by C16 stalls), with a quatrefoil frieze above, exactly as in the retrochoir aisles, and above this a design consisting of three deeply moulded trefoil-headed arches, each enclosing a pair of pointed arches, also with deeply moulded heads, springing from Purbeck shaft clusters. The clustered shafts stand in front of a wall passage, at the rear of which four tall unmoulded pointed arches opened into the lateral chapels (the arches on the N side were blocked in the early C17 by the Earl of Portland's monument in the Guardian Angels' Chapel). This wall passage evidently continued right round the chapel and in front of the windows of the E bay. In the tympanum above the trefoil arches is a large quatrefoil, flanked by trefoils. These openings were designed to be glazed and to receive borrowed light from a closely set row of segmental headed openings on the other side of a whitewashed clerestory passage acting like a light-box (a system later adopted by *John de Campeden* to light the belfry windows at St Cross, *see* p. 713). But there was an early design change to this bay: the flanking chapels were extended upwards as upper chambers; the redundant segmental openings were blocked and the foiled lights never received their glazing. If there were similar openings in the demolished E part the effect must have been spectacular; and one must also envisage the brilliance of the contrasting green and red polychrome, whose faded remnants survive in the arch-moulding hollows. The C13 vault was presumably quadripartite.

The changes to the Lady Chapel, probably completed by 1501, are the work of Priors Thomas Hunton (1470–98) and Thomas Silkstede (1498–1524). As noted externally, heraldry shows that the walls up at least to window-sill level date from the 1490s, for they include the arms of Bishop Courtenay (†1492) and Hunton's rebus (TH plus a barrel or 'tun') – as well as the royal arms of Henry VII, Queen Elizabeth of York and Prince Arthur. Hunton is also commemorated by a T and a tun transfixed by the letter H in the spandrels of a doorway which led to a now demolished vestry on the N side. But by the time the chapel's intricate stellar lierne-vault was created – carried westwards over the E.E. bay – Silkstede was prior, and both his name (E end) and Hunton's (W end) are painted around the charming central roundels representing (W) the Virgin as Queen of Heaven, supported by angels, and (E) Christ in Glory. The other bosses are smaller.* Other heraldry in the vault includes the arms of earlier bishops: Beaufort and Waynflete. Three Late Perp windows, each with seven lights, arranged 3–1–3, with a transom. The E end of the Lady Chapel is notable for its polychrome decoration and wall paintings (*see* p. 589, below).

---

* The vault and bosses were conserved by *Tobit Curteis Associates*, 1995.

The NE chapel is known as the GUARDIAN ANGELS' CHAPEL from the paintings of angels in roundels within its quadripartite vault. Here the C13 lancets have been cleverly knocked together to form Perp windows of *c.* 1500, each of three lights. The SE CHAPEL was remodelled during the same period as a chantry chapel for Bishop Langton (†1501), whose rebus occurs several times in the vault: it was provided with new windows, and ceiled with a developed lierne-vault, tending towards a fan-vault, though the tas-de-charge are angular, lacking the roundness of fans, and the ridge ribs also cut into the proto-fans. The Perp windows are identical to those of the NE chapel.

Remodelling continued W with the PRESBYTERY but this phase of work, credited to *Thomas of Witney*, did not begin until the first decades of the C14. So, for about a century the retro-choir simply abutted the outside of the Norman apse until this was taken down *c.* 1310. What look like responds at the W end of the retrochoir arcade were originally intended to be free-standing piers, complete on all sides; as planned this arcade would have continued W by at least one bay, as far as the chord piers of the Norman apse. Joining the retrochoir arcades with the new ones of the presbytery was a challenge because the presbytery is wider than the retrochoir, its width determined by the supporting Romanesque walls and arcades of the crypt below. The E end of the presbytery therefore comprises a trape-zoidal bay at the apex with its arcade splayed out westwards. A pair of arches opens between the retrochoir and the presbytery (supporting the presbytery's E gable) and rise from the Dec screen erected *c.* 1310 (*see* Furnishings) with a new entrance to the 'Holy Hole' beneath the raised platform of the FERETORY (*see* above) which occupies the E bay of the pres-bytery, an area concealed since 1450–75 by the Great Screen.

The arch on the N side of the Feretory was constructed at the same time as the pair on top of the Feretory screen, and has comparable deep hollows and fillets. The C14 pier sup-porting the E side of this arch was independent of the adjacent C13 one, though they were later partly linked with inserted reused C12 masonry. So much was achieved by 1316 when Thomas of Witney moved to Exeter. The arch on the S side of the Feretory is to a different design, whose shallow mouldings display busy combinations of hollows, waves and bowtells. The arch was probably executed very shortly after Thomas's depar-ture and is in the style of *William Joy* (later master mason at Wells). The arch mouldings of the straight bays of the pres-bytery, W of the Great Screen, follow a similar design. They are supported on Dec piers in the form of eight clustered shafts of coursed Purbeck marble. These three straight bays replaced four Romanesque ones. Below window level is a balcony of openwork quatrefoils, perhaps as early as 1315–20, and this may be the date of the clerestory window embrasures, which have rere-arches with foliate capitals. The tracery (originally of Beer stone) however is of later date, and given that it contains

in situ glass of the mid C15 the windows were perhaps remodelled when the Great Screen was erected. The stubs of the C14
mullions survive showing that the original windows were also
four lights wide.

The E window of the presbytery and the gable in which it is
set were rebuilt by Bishop Fox soon after his translation to
Winchester in August 1501. The presbytery vault is a wooden
version of the C15 nave vault, and is datable by its heraldry to
1503–9. It is supported on ten stone corbels depicting angels
with heraldic shields: at the W end Fox's four successive sees
(Exeter, Bath & Wells, Durham, Winchester); at the centre the
arms of Henry VII opposite the letters H and K joined by a
cord, symbolizing the betrothal in 1503 of the future Henry
VIII and Katharine of Aragon; at the E, emblems of the Passion
(the Veronica, Five Wounds of Christ, Calvary, Spear &
Sponge). This heraldic scheme continues on the vault itself.
Here the shields are bolted over foliate bosses, and it is possible that they were added to mark Prince Henry's visit to Winchester in January 1506. Even so the heraldry may not have
been an afterthought (the same stylistic conceit of shields part-
covering foliage occurs in stone in the aisles). The high vault
is divided into three zones overlapping the four bay divisions.
The W third is devoted to Bishop Fox and his bishoprics; the
centre celebrates Fox's patron Henry VII flanked by the arms
of Prince Henry and Katharine of Aragon, again representing
their betrothal. At the E end, emblems of the Passion. The vault
was repaired and the bosses recoloured in 1949–50. The nave
vault and that of the presbytery are linked by the square vault
under the tower, also of wood, inserted in 1635. The central
roundel, with a painted emblem by *Jerome the Painter* based on
the familiar Trinity badge, is a removable bell-trap: around it
the red letters of the Latin chronogram provide the date. The
bosses include a charming portrait of Charles I and Henrietta
Maria.

More of Bishop Fox's work can be found in the PRES-
BYTERY AISLES, datable by heraldry to before Henry VIII's
accession in 1509; the vault bosses include Prince of Wales
feathers, Henry VII's arms, the Beaufort portcullis of Henry
Tudor's mother, as well as Fox's arms and badge and the *Arma
Christi*. The N aisle was repaved *c.* 1969 in replica C13 tiles. A
band of pavement next to the Dec arcade had been relaid in
the C14, but the outline of C13 tile impressions survived
beneath the C14 ones. The earlier pavement abutted the
Romanesque piers, every other one of which had a respond on
the aisle side, suggesting that cylindrical columns alternated
with compound piers. This evidence is marked out in the C20
pavement.* The Norman choir arcade must have come down
when the presbytery was remodelled, although the outer walls

---

* The outline of the piers marked on the floor of the N presbytery aisle is entirely
conjectural; the only certain elements being the plinth plans represented in stone.
The 'compound' piers might simply have comprised a circular core with attached
rectangular elements as on the nave side of the piers at Ely.

Winchester Cathedral, elevation of two bays from the nave,
showing transformation from Norman to Perp.
Engraving by Robert Willis, 1846

survived for around two centuries (meanwhile the aisle was
presumably covered by a makeshift wooden roof). Fox was also
responsible for inserting the screens between the piers of the
presbytery in 1525 (*see* Furnishings).

Finally, to the NAVE, the magnificent feat of architectural
remodelling by Bishop Wykeham's architect, *William Wynford*.
In 1845 Robert Willis showed how Wynford changed the
Norman elevations into Perp ones, by demolishing the gallery,
thereby raising the height of the aisles, and altering the moulding profiles of the nave PIERS. He noted that at first the
builders retained much of the Norman masonry, retooling its
pilasters and shafts into Perp profiles. Clearly, areas where

arches had been removed had to be refaced. Once one has got one's eye in, the difference between retooled Norman masonry (thin courses, thick joints) and Wynford's refacing (deep courses, narrow joints) is quite obvious. Retooling was evidently time-consuming. As work proceeded E only the first seven piers were consistently treated in this way; the others were almost completely refaced, apart from the great shafts facing the nave and running right up the elevation. These were retained and thus form a link between the Norman and Perp masonry. Dr John Hare has argued that the change in technique marks the hiatus between an early phase of remodelling the nave piers at the start of Wykeham's episcopate and the resumption in earnest in the 1390s.

The best place to appreciate how the Norman profiles were adapted is at the E end of the nave, particularly on the N side. In two bays fragments of the Norman piers survive unaltered up to the abaci of the main arcade; at the time of the remodelling they were masked by a chantry chapel (only its platform survives) and by the pulpitum. Some of this evidence was tidied by *Garbett* in the early C19, but as well as providing precious evidence for levels, the surviving C11 masonry also shows how much the Romanesque elevations had deformed by 1400. Similar clues on the S side were partly removed in the early C19 when the piers either side of Edington's chantry chapel were repaired. The columns on the diagonals are of cast iron covered in *Coade* stone. This reinforcement was finally designed by *John Nash* in 1821–2 though Garbett must take much of the credit (the Dean and Chapter doubted his competence in so great a matter and consulted a more famous architect). On the S wall of the nave aisle nearby a leaning Romanesque respond again bears witness to early subsidence problems.

The ELEVATIONS of Wynford's remodelling consist of two storeys: a tall main arcade, and a clerestory of large windows. These match those of the aisles, but below the transom of each window is blind panelling in front of the aisle roof-space, and the windows are flanked by cinquefoil-headed panels. Beneath the clerestory is a balcony, jettied out on a cornice with delightful square fleurons and grotesques. These get bigger in the third bay from the crossing, which Dr Hare takes as further evidence of a twenty-five-year-interruption in Wykeham's works. Through the pointed arches behind the balcony the outer order of the Norman gallery is in places just visible from the ground; in the roof spaces a substantial amount of Romanesque masonry is visible.

The main elevation is a bold statement of Perp simplicity, and remarkably successful given the constraints of the Norman masonry within. The 'masts' are entirely Norman; their square pilasters have been transformed into a wave moulding that rises uninterrupted to the very apex of the clerestory windows. The square arrises of the other Romanesque arch orders have been cut into hollow chamfers, and the nook-shafts removed.

Whatever the dates of the progress of the remodelling of the main arcade, the clerestory and VAULT must constitute a single phase which began at the foot of the balcony balustrade where there is a disjunction in the masonry. The vault is Wynford's supreme achievement at Winchester, not yet started when Wykeham wrote his will in July 1403. It is a stellar lierne design of considerable complexity. Transverse ribs cross the nave between each pair of capitals. Thick diagonals run obliquely, crossing over each other and meeting the ridge rib at the three-quarter points, where they are joined by thinner tiercerons rising from the nearer capitals. The largest bosses are found here, and at the intersection of the diagonals. The vault is articulated by liernes, four radiating from the central boss, the others linking the middle tier of heraldic bosses in zigzag fashion, creating a star-like array around the capitals. Finally a third group of tiercerons and liernes fills the vaults above the window embrasures. The bosses and corbels repay study through binoculars. The aisle vaults are a simplified version of the same elements: each bay is basically quadripartite with an interrupted ridge rib, and liernes.

At the w end of the n aisle one bay contains an inserted mezzanine floor, inserted into the first phase of the remodelling of the nave and formerly housing the bishop's Consistory Court, now the cathedral's TREASURY. The lierne-vault beneath is identical to the aisle vaults above and includes a boss with Wykeham's arms.

FURNISHINGS AND MONUMENTS

Few cathedrals are as rich in furnishings as Winchester. They will be described topographically, starting E and moving W, usually taking N before S. It should be noted that many of the smaller medieval monuments were moved in 1815–25 in a wide-ranging reorganization by Prebendary Nott and Dean Rennell; their earlier positions are known from Clarendon and Gale's *History* (1715).

The crypt

LADY CHAPEL CRYPT. Two over-life-size STATUES in Caen stone, successive occupants of the niche in the gable over the w front: one of the C14, very weathered, the other (against s wall) its short-lived replacement of 1860, by *Newman & Son* of Winchester to drawings by *F. J. Baigent* (some art historians have been fooled into supposing it is also C14). Also, at the w end, a large SARCOPHAGUS, excavated from the Old Minster site in the 1960s.

9   ROMANESQUE CRYPT. In the N aisle, lead SCULPTURE, Sound II, by *Antony Gormley* (1986): a life-size standing figure with cupped hands, designed to be seen partly immersed in the waters that often flood the crypt in winter. In the central

vessel, Sounding by *Tim Harrison* (1994) carved in a 'drill rhythm' from a piece of bog oak from Snowdonia. It lies on a bed of chips of its own substance.

East chapels

LADY CHAPEL. – ALTAR REREDOS. The Annunciation by *C. E. Kempe*, 1905, in memory of Charlotte Yonge †1901, the Hampshire novelist. The frontal, designed by *Beatrice Parsons* in embroidered silk on damask, was presented in 1912. – COMMUNION RAIL. Discovered in the transept gallery in the late C19. Laudian style – 'a typical and enjoyable piece of *c.* 1635', thought Pevsner – but probably a Restoration replacement of the High Altar rail (smashed in 1642). It is shown in an engraving of 1677 of the presbytery in Sandford's *Genealogical History*. Twelve panels, each with an oval, with roses in the spandrels and turned finials projecting towards the centre but not touching; there are tapered shafts between the panels, adorned with applied drops, terminating in foliate capitals. Two more panels have been reused in seats in the presbytery. – STALLS. The only set of pre-Reformation stalls to survive complete in a Lady Chapel, probably created *c.* 1415, during Thomas Silkstede's priorate. Bench seating, without misericords, and glorious traceried backs, with delightful carved figures preaching from miniature pulpits on the desk-end buttresses. The carvings were mostly reinstated *c.* 1894 by *Thomas & Kitchin* (later *Thomas & Co.*)* – ENTRANCE SCREEN at the W end. 1490s. Five-light pierced tracery arches over a panel-tracery dado, arranged in three bays either side of a wider doorway with an openwork light over it. On the W side of its loft is a balustrade of narrow, perhaps originally paired open-tracery lights with trefoil heads. The loft, reached via a narrow stair in the N wall of the chapel (the stair's lower door has been panelled over), is coved over the stalls, and the coving returns along the sides. It terminates in a foliate frieze with cresting above. – WALL PAINTINGS. Early C16, all muted grey and brown, but covered in 1934–7 with replicas painted on hinged boards by *Professor E. W. Tristram*. The scenes represent miracles of the Virgin, arranged in two tiers, and include a portrait of Prior Silkstede (†1524); the costume suggests a date of *c.* 1510–20. The originals, English but showing strong Flemish influence, seem to be inspired by a similar set painted at Eton College Chapel in the 1480s. – PIETÀ, 1900, by *Peter Eugene Ball*; a sombre piece, typical of Ball in its execution, in oak with burnished copper and verdigris. – STAINED GLASS. The medieval glass was admired by Lieutenant Hammond on a visit in 1635, who noted the Jesse Tree in the E window. Some late C15 fragments in the tracery lights, attributed by Mary Callé to the king's glazier *William Neve*, are survivors of the devastation of 1642,

* Several of the C19 carvings, stolen in 2009, are to be replaced yet again by *Hugh Harrison*.

but all three windows were reglazed in 1897–1900 to designs by *J. W. Lisle*, C. E. Kempe's chief designer. The E window, celebrating Queen Victoria's Diamond Jubilee (1897), features a Jesse Tree, branches of which were copied by Lisle from fragments of 1490 that Kempe retained in his studios.* – Three LEDGER STONES. Only the W one corresponds with the vault pockets in the crypt. The central stone is thought to mark the burial site of John White, Winchester's last Roman Catholic bishop (deposed by Queen Elizabeth in 1559, †Jan. 1560). A body was excavated from the vault in 1884; the ledger stone dates from 1919. The ledger stone close to the chancel step (moved slightly W of its original position) may mark the grave of Prior Hunton, initiator of the chapel's remodelling. The main floor was re-laid in 1900 (it had previously been re-laid *c.* 1705: the Purbeck paviors to N and S are the original surface). – Raised SANCTUARY PAVEMENT re-laid 1901 in polished Ashburton and Dove marble. Outside the chapel on the S side, a SHAFT perhaps to support a statue, with nailhead decoration and an important corbel of a man with doleful countenance, typical of the vogue for emotional expression in early C13 sculpture. Outside the Lady Chapel, STATUE of Joan of Arc, carved under supervision of *Ninian Comper*, 1923.

GUARDIAN ANGELS' (NE) CHAPEL. – ENTRANCE SCREEN in memory of Canon J. S. Utterton, dedicated 1892 (the earlier screen is in the S nave aisle, *see* p. 616). Created in 'old wood' by *Thomas & Kitchin*. Naturalistic foliage; the *arma Christi* on the door. – PAINTED VAULT of *c.* 1225–30, partially repainted *c.* 1260–80, of very high quality. Angels in roundels with secondary gilt attachments of stars and rosettes. – REREDOS. A recycled portion of an originally wider reredos, now comprising seven tall stone niches (lacking their statuary) and datable by heraldry to the mid C14. – ALTAR CROSS in blue glass, by *Justin Knowles* (2001). – STAINED GLASS. In the E window, three tall made-up panels inserted in 1938, comprising C15 grisaille from Salisbury Cathedral, surrounding C15 fragments discovered in a Shrewsbury summerhouse and perhaps originally from Winchester College. – MONUMENTS. Beneath the altar slab, a reused Purbeck panel from the early C14 TOMB-CHEST of Arnaud de Gaveston (†1302) originally in the N transept (the effigy is now in the retrochoir). Five crocketed cinquefoil arches enclosing heraldic shields shown suspended on foliage: l. to r. Gaveston, Earl of Cornwall (Arnaud's son Piers), England, France, Castile & Leon. – Richard Weston, Earl of Portland and Lord Treasurer, †1634/5.** Praised by Pevsner as 'The most progressive and one of the finest monuments of that time in England. Westminster Abbey has nothing to vie with it.' The monument, under way in 1632, is the work of *Isaac Besnier*,† but the

_____

* Mary Callé has traced these fragments to the Museum of Art and Archaeology, Caboolture, Queensland, Australia. A head, 'Goldilocks', in the W window is also one of the cathedral's few remaining fragments from the late C15 scheme.
** i.e. 13 March 1635 modern style.
† See R. Lightbown in *Art & Patronage in the Caroline Courts*, ed. D. Howarth (1993).

Winchester Cathedral, Richard Weston monument.
Engraving after Charles Woodfield, 1715

recumbent bronze effigy, traditionally attributed to *Le Sueur* (from whom Weston commissioned the equestrian statue of Charles I in 1629) is more probably by *Francesco Fanelli*: head on three folded pillows, a staff in one hand (now a wooden replica), his right leg slightly raised, a pose first found in Italian sculpture of the *cinquecento*. The sarcophagus is of coloured marbles, and the monument as a whole is entirely classical in style. The segmental-headed reredos, flanked by scrolls descending from rams' heads, has a broken pediment and at the top a large heraldic shield held by two *putti*. Beneath are four unmoulded niches divided by shallow term-shaped pilasters in the Late Mannerist style. They held busts, thought to be of the earl's sons, three of which (one albeit headless) survive in the cathedral's collections. – Bishop Peter Mews †1706, the Royalist officer who supported James II at Sedgemoor. Tablet with long inscription in an aedicule with marble shafts, topped by a broken pediment enclosing the bishop's arms.

LANGTON CHANTRY (SE) CHAPEL. – ENTRANCE SCREEN. c. 1500 as shown by Langton's arms. Single-light divisions, with a double door. It was moved slightly eastwards in 1818. Elaborate PANELLING also of c. 1500, amply cusped and with openwork cresting. – REREDOS. Of stone. Seven Perp cinquefoil niches, with slender crocketed canopies and remains of colour. – PAINTING. Triptych, on loan from St Michael's church, Basingstoke. The central panel c. 1541, by the studio of *Pieter Coecke van Aelst*, portrays the Holy Family Resting on the Flight into Egypt. The wings, showing the donor Ralph Fruytirs and his wife and children, were added in 1599. – FLOOR TILES. On the altar step, a re-set collection mainly of Otterbourne types of the late 1390s; some smaller earlier tiles next to the step. The remainder of the chapel paved in Purbeck marble. – STAINED GLASS. E window by *Kempe & Co.* (design by *Lisle*), 1899. – MONUMENT. Bishop Langton †1501. A tall Purbeck marble tomb-chest with indents of brasses on the lid, including shields encircled by the Garter. Three bays separated by paired buttresses on each of the long sides, with quatrefoils enclosing shields. Outside the chapel, a small half-length effigy of William Walker, the 'Winchester Diver', by *Glynn Williams*, 2001.

Retrochoir

PAVEMENT. – A 'monument of international significance' (Christopher Norton): the largest English medieval tile pavement to have survived within a building. Between c. 1240 and c. 1325 the whole of the E arm was paved by a succession of different tilers working in much the same idiom. The largest area is in the retrochoir, paved c. 1260–80. Here the pavement was divided into rectangular panels, running E–W in the central area and N–S in the aisles, within which groups of tiles were laid in sets of nine, four, or singly, divided by narrow, plain borders. The designs include lions, griffins, eagles, and foliate and geometrical patterns. A few special tiles with figurative designs, similar to exemplars dated c. 1250 from Chertsey Abbey, survive as fragments, but their original position is unknown. The pattern of medieval tiles is greatly disturbed at the E ends of the retrochoir aisles by burials, these being the only areas where it was possible to create graves in the C13 infill (under most of the retrochoir the crypt vault lies immediately under the pavement). Elsewhere, replica tiles by *Diana Hall* were inserted in 1993–6, to fill gaps caused by the introduction of service ducts and also the removal of monuments. This policy of replacement started in 1969 with the decayed tile pavement of the N presbytery aisle (the replica work by *Professor R. Baker*).

RETROCHOIR 'NAVE' – FERETORY SCREEN by *Thomas of Witney*, [31] *c.* 1310. The only example of really florid Dec in the cathedral. Nine niches with nodding crocketed ogee canopies still with some surviving green and red polychromy. Plain lower register with central entrance arch to the C12 'Holy Hole', flanked by Latin inscription referring to the 'saints' whose remains rested nearby, probably in the reliquary armoire inserted into the Feretory platform. The niches contained pairs of statuettes of pre-Conquest bishops and monarchs (identified by names on the cornice, some the same as the names on the mortuary chests (*see* p. 602)), together with the Virgin and Child in the central niche. But the niches now hold ICONS by *Sergei Fyodorov*, 1992–7. Two local saints (Birinus and Swithun) at the ends; then, working inwards, the cathedral's patrons, Peter and Paul, Archangels Michael and Gabriel, and a central group of Christ Pantocrator flanked by Mary and John the Baptist. – ST SWITHUN'S SHRINE by *Brian Thomas* and *Wilfrid Carpenter Turner*, 1962, stands on the site of the medieval monument of 1476 but is an unworthy memorial. A strangely thin, delicate catafalque, which Pevsner judged inspired by the Swedish style of the 1920s and lacking 'sympathy with the tougher idiom of the C20'. Steel painted black, silver and brass, with small brass relief panel at W end, the latter little better than a tourist souvenir. – MONUMENTS. – Bishop de Lucy †1204, axially placed in the retrochoir which he initiated. Purbeck marble raised coffin with plain lid incorporating holes for a cross-shaped array of tapers burnt at his annual commemoration unless these be for an actual metal cross. – C13 TOMB-CHEST of Prior Basing (†1295), moved to this position *c.* 1810. Capped by a rare survival of an early incised slab, with a foliate cross rising from a stepped Calvary, above which the head of the mitred prior is flanked by the keys of St Peter and the sword of St Paul. Latin inscription on two lines around the edge promises three years and 50 days' indulgence to those who pray for his soul. Another incised drawing of the crucifixion flanked by the Virgin and St John is still just visible on the W face of the chest; it was noted by Schnebbelie in 1788. – In front of the 'Holy Hole' an immense Purbeck TOMB-SLAB of great size (12 by 5 ft, 3.7 by 1.5 metres), lacking its original brass. Probably the tomb of William Westkarre, Prior of Mottesham and Bishop of Sidon (†1486). It was opened in 1797 by Henry Howard of Castle Corby, and other officers stationed near Winchester with the York militia, who expected to find the body of St Swithun. – Bishop Sumner (†1874) by *H. Weekes*, 1876. Recumbent Carrara marble effigy on an empty Caen stone tomb-chest.

CARDINAL BEAUFORT'S CHANTRY CHAPEL (S). He died in 1447. The lofty monument, built 1450–76, entirely fills the space between two C13 piers, its pinnacles soaring to the vault. Central bay entirely open at the sides, apart from a low balustrade; short end bays enclosed by half-height screens: to

N and S in the E bay, all round at the W. The W bay has four-centred N and S doorways with traceried openings above and the W end has big arched openings above a low wall; all designed to give maximum visibility towards the altar at the E end. The Purbeck marble detailing, such as the use of triple shaft clusters and tiny carved capitals, is very similar to that of the recently discovered fragments of St Swithun's shrine, and the monument was probably executed by the same marblers. A different team must have been responsible for the freestone work, such as the panels at the E end. Inside the chapel, the greatly restored reredos comprises three empty niches over a frieze of angels holding heraldic shields (now blank). The fan-vaulting is the earliest at Winchester: at the apex a high vault with an angel holding Beaufort's arms forms a canopy over the bishop's tomb-chest which occupies almost the entire chapel. It is deeply cut with cusped, almost openwork panels with gilded fields – astonishingly showy – and twisted column shafts. The effigy was destroyed in 1642, its coloured successor a clumsy later C17 effort, showing Beaufort wearing his cardinal's hat. Milner described the dilapidated state of the chapel in 1798 ('a horse-load [of pinnacles had] fallen, or been taken down . . .'); it was restored at the expense of the Duke of Beaufort in 1819.

North retrochoir aisle

BISHOP WAYNFLETE'S CHANTRY CHAPEL (N). Built before the bishop's death in 1486. The architectural scheme is similar to Beaufort's, but the monument is more enclosed, the lower part of the sides of the central bay being filled with three four-centred arches blocked with iron rails. More affinities with the Great Screen than Beaufort's chapel, and perhaps started by master mason *Robert Hulle*, then, after 1462, *William Graver* his successor. Tomb-chest much smaller than Beaufort's. Recumbent stone effigy. Above is a rather flat vault with criss-crossing bands of tiny liernes springing from fans in the corners. A central roundel, with Waynflete's arms, borne by an angel. The lower E and W vaults have a large, petalled central roundel resembling a rose window, set within a rectangular frame. Altogether a very busy design. Over the (original) N door a spandrel carved with delightful trailing roses, and a tiny snail: the same motifs are found on the E side of the N doorway of the 1470s Great Screen (*see* Presbytery, below). The chapel was 'restored' by *John Buckler Sen.* at the expense of Magdalen College, Oxford, in 1828, using Painswick and Farley Down stone, and again in 1928–32, when *Sir Ninian Comper* repainted the effigy and designed the textile hanging of the Crucifixion behind the altar.

MONUMENTS. All were relocated in the early C19. – Bishop Aymer de Lusignan (alias de Valence), half-brother to Henry III and Richard of Cornwall, †1260 in exile in Paris, where his body was buried. The monument was originally located near

the High Altar, with a cavity behind it containing the bishop's
heart, but was moved here in 1818. Superb, of Purbeck marble,
probably by a London sculptor. The bishop, clad in vestments
with crisply carved sharp-fold draperies, is shown half-length
in a mandorla with stiff-leaf sprays, beneath a crocketed
canopy supported on slightly curved columns. The top, lost by
1818, was rediscovered in 1911 having been buried 6 ft (1.8
metres) below the cloister; it incorporates the earliest royal
heraldry in the cathedral. – Thomas Mason, son of the Dean,
†1559 aged eighteen. The reconstituted remains of an elaborate tomb, also dismantled in 1818. Entirely Early Renaissance
in character, its two inscribed front panels framed by a very
elegant and individual double guilloche either side of a pair of
coloured coats of arms; and (at each end) a fan-like double-
guilloche panel and a narrow apsidal niche with a shell-hood.
Other parts (including vigorous statues of naked male and
female supporters originally flanking the main cartouche) are
displayed in the Triforium Gallery. – Bishop Peter des Roches
(†1238). Recumbent effigy with archaic-looking curly beard,
beneath a pointed trefoil canopy with plate tracery on the
sides, a book in his l. hand, his r. hand on his chest. Very stilted
treatment of the arms and neck. No crozier. Although he is
depicted lying on a flat cushion, the draperies hang vertically
as though he were standing. The style of the effigy suggests it
was commissioned before 1238. – Damaged, headless effigy of
a bishop (perhaps commissioned for John of Exeter (†1268) or
Nicholas of Ely (†1280), both eventually buried elsewhere, or
possibly a prior) holding a crozier, his right hand blessing.
Dressed in chasuble, stole, maniple, amice and alb. Flat, sharp-
fold style, probably c. 1265–90. – Tomb of a knight, usually
identified as Arnaud de Gaveston (†1302; see also the Guardian
Angels' Chapel). A late example of a Purbeck effigy (freestone
was increasingly used as effigies became painted). The whole
figure sways in a typically early C14 way. Clad in chain-mail
and, unusually for an effigy, wearing ailettes on his shoulders,
he holds a sword in his r. hand. Shield with carved quarterings
including the cows passant of the viscounty of Béarn and the
sheaves (garbs) of Gaveston. Two pillows supported by angels
under his head, a lion beneath his crossed legs (much
restored). – LEDGER STONES only at the E end of the aisle, as
explained above. The great and good of the city and county
from the late C17/early C18. The black slate slabs with finely
carved heraldry have survived well.

South retrochoir aisle

SCULPTURE. Female statue of c. 1230–5 identified as *Ecclesia*,   26
possibly from one of the empty niches of the Deanery porch
(the other niche might have held the corresponding figure of
Synagoga). Headless, but even so of a quality as good as anything in France, thought Pevsner, for whom 'the draperies
show to perfection that nobility could be expressed in the C13

in drapery'. The flow of the folds downwards and the distur-
bance when they meet the ground can be matched, as Pevsner
noted, by sculpture in the transept porches of Chartres but also
develop ideas already found at the w front of Wells. Holes show
she had metal adornments (brooch, belt and sword). –
STAINED GLASS. Clear glass in small diamond quarries, with
twenty-four small lozenge panels of reassembled C13 glass,
from Salisbury Cathedral, donated in 1937. – MONUMENT. Sir
John Clobery (†1687), who played a prominent part in the
Restoration of Charles II and built a large house in Parchment
Street. The Latin inscription praises 'a man pre-eminent in
every path of life . . . whose singular talents bore the polish of
such refined erudition that you would have thought he had
grown older in Athens rather than military camps'. Very stiff
alabaster statue by *Sir William Wilson*, 1691, of Sir John in theatrical pose: one arm stretches forward a baton, but the commanding attitude is softened by his other held akimbo with
hand on his hips. Interesting for its depiction of late C17 military dress (scorned by Lord Torrington in 1782 as 'the ridiculous, cumbersome habits of those days with . . . more sash than
any modern miss'). Black columns l. and r. under a wide segmental top, formerly adorned with 'warlike implements, such
as guns, pikes, flags and helmets'. – WALL MONUMENTS.
George Turner, †1797. Simple lettering under an urn. – Mrs
Catherine Fulham, a niece of John Evelyn, who died in child-
birth in 1699. Chubby-faced putti raise tasselled curtains to
reveal the swelling cartouche carved with her epitaph. –
LEDGER STONES. Outside the Langton Chapel, excellent slab
to Frances, Countess of Essex, †1663. Within an extravagant
frame of black-and-white paving slabs set lozenge-fashion.
Nearby, James Touchet †1700. Florid lettering and superbly
cut coat of arms.

North presbytery aisle

C14 ARMOIRE, at the top of the Pilgrims' Steps. A rare survival
  of medieval furniture, which Simon Jervis has called 'the most
  sophisticated surviving piece of its type in England'. Surely a
  better place can be found for it?
STAINED GLASS. Early C16 glass in the heads of the tracery lights
  with scenes depicting three of the 'Joys of Mary' (Coronation,
  Purification, and Adoration of the Magi) and female saints
  beneath, all within canopies similar to those originally found
  in the Holy Ghost Chapel, Basingstoke, *c.* 1524 and probably
  by the same glass painter (*see* St Michael, Basingstoke, and
  The Vyne). Medieval fragments assembled in cinquefoil heads
  of the lower lights include an angel head from the *c.* 1490 Lady
  Chapel glass.
MONUMENTS. Beneath the presbytery lateral screens, all dating
  from 1525. Harthacnut's tomb-plaque features an early C16
  ship in place of heraldry, and an inscription; next to it, Aymer

('Ethelmar') de Valence's plaque marks the site of his heart-burial (presumably the C13 monument in the N retrochoir aisle came from here). In the next bay to the E a plaque corresponding to the tomb of Bishop John of Pontoise (†1304) within the presbytery: candelabra and empty shields flank an inscription within a cartouche decorated with classical motifs.

BISHOP GARDINER'S CHAPEL. Not really a chantry chapel, as chantries were illegal when it was built, though still with a vestry for the priest. It commemorates the last of the medieval statesmen-bishops who, deprived of his see under Edward VI, was restored to the bishopric under Mary, dying in 1555. It was presumably erected before the accession of the Protestant Queen Elizabeth in 1558. To the architectural observer the chapel tells this in a most illuminating way. Pevsner characterized it as 'far from homogenous. It is Gothic in parts, Early Renaissance in parts and as early as anywhere in England High Renaissance in parts'. The basic structure comprises a three-bay 'cage' (two-bay chapel and E vestry) over a high substructure containing the burial chamber. The tracery of the Gothic four-light windows is a squatter version of that of the presbytery screens of thirty years earlier (*see* below), and the cusped square panels of the stone vaults inside are late medieval in style. It is extraordinary that, given the decorative idiom, the Gothic features were not felt to be painfully outdated, for, as Professor Martin Biddle has demonstrated, the decoration is High Renaissance in the Mannerist style, derived from Henry VIII's Nonsuch Palace.* The substructure is decorated with elongated scrollwork cartouches in rectangular frames, both at the E end and in the outer bays of the N front; between them is a recess containing the *transi* image of the bishop's decomposed corpse, head on his mitre – 'very late, but still earlier than Pilon's Henri II of France', commented Pevsner – with a shallow plain cartouche over it. Above all this is a fluted frieze, at which level the octagonal shafts of the buttresses change to fluted semi-octagonal shafts rising up to a gorgeous High Renaissance entablature, with triglyph frieze, and metopes alternating with bucrania and paterae. Yet above this full-blown Cinquecento frieze the vocabulary regresses to the Early Renaissance, the cage being crowned with balustrade-like cresting of strapwork, grotesque masks, and displays of the bishop's arms.

Inside, the dominant feature is the stone screen occupying the whole E wall. The modern altar is offset to the S, giving room for a narrow doorway to the vestry, with its tiny fan-vault. Behind the altar is a rectangular panel for the reredos, with double guilloche frame. Above, an entablature supports the upper half of the screen; the frieze bears a cheerful central cherub between two large console brackets, and the ensemble

52

---

* 'Early Renaissance at Winchester', in *Winchester Cathedral 900 Years*, ed. J. Crook (2003), 257–304.

is flanked by pairs of putti in low relief. All this serves as a base to the upper part of the screen, a composition of three round-headed niches. To l. and r. are figures of *Ecclesia* and blind *Synagoga*. The central niche (empty) is apsidal with a shell-hood; either side are Ionic colonettes (amongst the earliest examples in England) supporting an entablature whose frieze is decorated with a wave pattern – one of the details linking the chapel with the Mason tomb (*see* N retrochoir aisle, above). The whole screen fits rather tightly beneath the vault – still Gothic, as we have seen, but springing from Cinquecento cherubs. One might, with Pevsner, have expected a coffered tunnel-vault. In the chapel's vestry, PAINTING, Christ before the Judge by *Cecil Collins*, 1954–6.

South presbytery aisle

PAVING SLABS. Interesting C16 use of Purbeck marble paviors, set in long panels, some diagonally. – COPE CHEST, by *A. G. Mondey* to design by *Corinne Bennett*. Given by Bishop Falkner Allison, 1974. – The so-called 'PILGRIMS' GATES': a wrought-iron grille at the head of the stair between the presbytery aisle and the transept. Probably recycled from a late C12 screen, and moved here from the W end of the nave N aisle in 1925 – though that was certainly not the original position either. An out-standing piece of metalwork. Each panel has three vertical stems linked by bent collars, with C-scrolls branching out sym-metrically to l. and r. Jane Geddes links the design with that commonly found in late C12 Spain and suggests the grilles might have been imported.

STAINED GLASS. The E window has an early C16 Nativity (another 'Joy of Mary') in the tracery lights and Christ's ances-tors beneath. – The second window, showing standing archangels and apostles, is by *Powells*, commemorating Lt-Col. J. J. Collins of the 60th Royal Rifle Corps (†1880); the third, the South Africa memorial window, 1909 by *Kempe & Co.*, designed by *John Lisle*. Richly detailed, showing St George in the upper lights, and Fortitude and Patience below, flanked by St George and a rifleman, all against landscape backgrounds.

MONUMENTS. Beneath Fox's presbytery screens. A slab of *c.* 1200 incorporated in the (presumably C14) wall-bench marks the double tomb of Richard of Normandy (elder brother of William Rufus, also killed in a hunting accident in the New Forest) and Earl Bjorn, kinsman of the Conqueror. Their coffin, now encased within the bench, probably originally sat on the Romanesque stylobate and was moved only slightly when the arcade was rebuilt in the C14. Above the bench in this bay are two shallow, cusped Gothic arches, one over the tomb of Richard of Normandy, and the one to its W over the heart-burial of Bishop Nicholas of Ely (†1280). Above each, an inscription in early C16 'Romano-Gothic' capitals. –

Bishop Brownlow North (†1820). White marble effigy by *Sir Francis Chantrey*, 1825. Shown in profile, kneeling piously in front of an altar. The composition is almost identical with other episcopal effigies by Chantrey: Shute Barrington (Durham), Ryder (Lichfield), and Archbishop Stuart (Armagh). It was previously in the Lady Chapel, then near Waynflete's chantry, and deserves yet another more favourable relocation. On the w wall, tablet to Bishop William Wykeham II, †1595 after only ten weeks in office, installed by his descendant of the same name in 1888. Copper-gilt mural tablet by *Kempe* to the Rev. Edward Huntingford †1905, near the top of the steps.

Unusually large (11 by 4 ft, 33 by 1.3 metres) Purbeck marble LEDGER SLAB (*ex situ*, there being no grave beneath) of a mitred bishop or prior, *c.* 1490, formerly with brass inlaid canopy, shields, and marginal inscription with Evangelist symbols at the corners: Nigel Saul qualifies it as 'absolutely superlative'. But whose monument is it? For Jerome Bertram the best candidate is Thomas Hunton, but this conflicts with his documented burial in the Lady Chapel. It might have been Bishop Courtenay's (†1492), moved from the same chapel.

FOX CHANTRY CHAPEL (Bishop Richard Fox, †1528). Fox [53] planned the chapel from 1513 and it was 'newly built' by 1518, ten years before his death. Probably designed by *William Vertue*, the King's Master Mason from 1510, and, together with the carpenter Humphrey Coke, designer of Fox's Corpus Christi College, Oxford (from 1512). Christopher Wilson has, however, argued that Vertue's alleged design drawing of the chapel (in the BAL) is a post-Reformation record of the existing structure. Another 'cage' chapel, raised high above the aisle on a substructure; this basement was necessary because Fox (and Gardiner after him) were buried beneath the edges of the Feretory platform. Four bays. The w bay contains the door, a fine survival of early C16 woodwork. The chapel proper is of two bays. A niche in the substructure in the third bay from the w contains Bishop Fox's chillingly realistic cadaver effigy (inserted *c.* 1523, five years before his death), behind a contemporary iron grille. The e bay forms a vestry at main level, within which cut-back remains of niches at the s end of the C14 Feretory screen are visible above and within C19 cupboards. Above the external substructure is a row of niches for statuary, all replacements. The statues of SS Cuthbert and Richard of Chichester were designed by *C. A. Buckler* and carved by *T. Boulton* of Cheltenham, probably *c.* 1891; several of the remainder are by *Basil Gotto*, 1920–31. The lower part of one very damaged original statuette has been replaced in a niche at the e end; fragments of others survive in the cathedral's collections. The upper part of the monument consists of open four-centred arches with ogee tracery, and top cresting. The corners and buttresses terminate in turrets; between them are secondary finials showing Fox's favourite pelican vulning.

Inside the chapel, the main part is ceiled with a richly cusped lierne-vault. The panelled w wall incorporates the rear wall of the Great Screen. The design of the chapel is entirely in the Late Gothic tradition except for one feature: along the interior side walls, between the Gothic arcading, are small classical volutes. If original to the chapel they would be the earliest Renaissance elements in the cathedral but, as Wilson has pointed out, they are merely pegged to the cut-off original mouldings and could therefore be later than 1518. The reredos has a recess framed by three hanging arches. Perhaps it contained a painting. The three statuary niches at the head of the E wall are empty, above an angel frieze with the polychrome arms of the Passion: a very pretty bit of work.

Presbytery and choir

GREAT SCREEN of 1450–75. A lofty reredos of Caen stone, 'one of the most important monuments of the late middle ages' (Phillip Lindley), blocking off the presbytery's E bay (i.e. the Feretory). A triptych-like arrangement with three tiers of statues, all of 1885–91 when the screen was restored under the supervision of *J. D. Sedding* as a memorial to Archdeacon Jacob, a popular Winchester churchman.* But the medieval architectural scheme and much of the intricately carved fili-gree work of the bases and canopies survives in remarkable condition. The central third, as in the Middle Ages, comprises the Crucifixion with Christ (the figure was added, after some experiment, in 1897) flanked by full-size niches for SS Mary and John; a row of statuettes above. The 'wings' to the triptych are subdivided vertically into three, the outer bays of which project forward like buttresses to l. and r. of a recessed middle containing a door; the splays between are enlivened by smaller niches with statuettes. Now a dreary monochrome, the screen was originally highly coloured, with realistically painted statues and a figure of Christ gilded and adorned with precious stones; above the altar was a retable featuring 'imagis of sylver and gilt garnyshed with [precious] stones' (part of Cardinal Beaufort's bequest) and suspended from the spire at the head of the screen was a hanging pyx. All this was intended to enhance the High Altar area as a setting for the Eucharist, whose cele-bration became increasingly dramatic during the Middle Ages – for example, with the introduction of the Elevation of the Host. Inevitably the precious metals were pillaged at the Reformation and the statuary was smashed, with the excep-tion of the relief carvings of the Annunciation and Visitation (which also retain some polychrome) in the spandrels of the doors.** A Laudian canopy was erected over the high altar

---

* For the works – and the controversy – see Geoff Brandwood, ' "Unlucky Experi-ments in Statues": Restoring the Winchester Great Screen', *Ecclesiology Today*, 31 (May 2003), 3–13.
** Significant fragments survive in the Triforium Gallery (*see* below).

c. 1635; it appears to have been modified at the Restoration. It was removed in 1818: the canopy is now in the Triforium Gallery; other parts were incorporated into the library doors and turned into mirrors for the Deanery. The sanctuary was remodelled *c.* 1700 from Prebendary Harris's bequest, when classical urns were placed in the statuary niches (also removed 1818), and in 1781 a large painting of the Raising of Lazarus by *Benjamin West* was placed in the rectangle formerly occupied by the retable.* In its place is a Nativity with statues l. and r. Of the C19 statues, all the large saints (including Winchester's sainted bishops) and sixteen of the smaller figures are by *Richard L. Boulton* of Cheltenham; SS Mary and John by *Thomas Nicholls* of Wincott Street, London; the rest (including various Winchester worthies) by *E. C. Geflowski* (ten), *Mary Grant* of London (1831–1908) (two), and *Farmer & Brindley* (one). In 1886 the Dean's drawing room was 'full of [plaster models of] statues of angels, saints and martyrs . . . by all sorts of artists and in every variety of tone and feeling'.

– HIGH ALTAR CROSS by *Leslie Durbin*, 1966. Brass, made of numerous small brass rods mounted in a steel armature, so that the highlights oscillate according to the time of day. – STANDARD CANDLESTICKS in memory of Bishop Talbot, by *Sir Charles Nicholson*, 1921. Baroque style, natural wood and gilding, claw feet. – COMMUNION RAIL. Probably paid for out of Prebendary Harris's bequest in 1700 (the carving is similar to that of the tympana of the doors in the Great Screen which bear his arms) though it looks earlier (1680s) and might be by *Edward Pearce*. Openwork with swirls of fruit, flowers, leaves and putto heads. The rail was remodelled in the mid C19 when the panels from the gates were reused as the chancel's flanking prayer-desks, with added carved brackets supporting the book-rests. – Two PRIE-DIEU, incorporating panels from the Restoration altar rail (*see* Lady Chapel above). – Fragments of Flemish CHOIR STALLS, probably to be identified with the sedilia recorded as being made in 1889–90. Each incorporating four stalls, divided by scrolled arm-rests and supported on turned columns with twisty fillet decoration. They have vestigial misericords, and Baroque strapwork on ends. – Brass CHANDELIER, one of a pair given by Dean Cheyney in 1756 to light the choir (the other now in the s transept); a large Rococo creation with only one tier of fourteen branches and pineapple pendant terminal, attributed by Robert Sherlock to *William Alexander* of London. – PAVEMENT originally *c.* 1700 (again, the Harris bequest) but renewed 1891 with marble supplied by *Guido Murray Fabbricotti* of Carrara.

Stone SCREENS fill the three bays of the presbytery's N and s arcades. Securely dated to 1525 by their inscriptions and in 'the purest and most finished style of the Gothic' as John

---

* In 1899 the painting was sold by the Dean and Chapter to J. Pierpont Morgan for £1,500 (they asked for £2,500, having paid £300 for it in 1781). It is now at the Wadsworth Athenaeum, Hartford, Connecticut.

Milner called them in 1798. With four-light windows, set in square frames, later glazed with quarries, replaced by plate glass in 1849. Doorways in the E half of the W bays (the other half of these bays filled by the bishop's throne on the S side and blind panelling on the N). The N door is four-centred, under an embattled lintel beneath truncated window tracery. It is framed externally by half-octagonal shafts with battlemented and crocketed pinnacles. The outer spandrels bear the initials of Prior Henry Broke (1524–36). The S door, two-centred under a crocketed ogee head, must be C15 recycled from elsewhere, and the screen is higher and thicker to accommodate it. Into its finial are inserted the royal arms, presumably of Henry VIII, supported by two (restored C19) angels. Slender rectangular buttresses internally, terminating in crocketed pinnacles. The most interesting elements of the screens are the incomplete entablatures, consisting of an architrave, a frieze, but no cornice. The architrave bears Fox's motto, *Est Deo Gracia* and carries the bishop's arms and (N side) those of his steward, William Frost. The friezes are very different in character. The N frieze is sparsely decorated with Renaissance detail in bas relief: tall vases with flowers alternate with smaller ones sprouting stylized plants, all linked by foliate scrolls. One of Frost's favourite owls perches on one of the tall vases. The S frieze is more luxuriant, crowded with angel heads, urns and pelicans. It is possible that the master mason responsible for this wonderful Renaissance work was *Thomas Bertie*; Nicholas Riall has pointed out the similarities with, for example, the Lisle tomb at Thruxton, part of works executed by 'my lorde of Wynchestre's mason', *c.* 1524 (*see* p. 519), though the evidence that this was indeed Bertie remains circumstantial. – Sitting on the screens, and with a disquieting resemblance to railway locomotives immobilized on a viaduct, the wooden MORTUARY CHESTS of pre-Conquest monarchs and bishops are the last in a series of similar arrangements for the entombment of Winchester's early illustrious dead. They replaced earlier chests, themselves originally containing lead coffers provided in the mid C12 by Bishop Henry of Blois. Four survive of the original ten of *c.* 1525–30, plus two replacements (at the W end) of *c.* 1661 of those smashed by Parliamentarians in 1642. The first entirely Renaissance monuments in the cathedral, so perhaps post-dating Bishop Fox with his taste for the Gothic. The sides of each chest bear inscribed panels like tea-trays with handles, flanked by putti, lions or eagles as supporters; at the ends are turned half-balusters. A band of applied metalwork above. Crowns on the lids, and finials at the gables. They were possibly not made for this purpose: Prof. Biddle suggests they were 'obtained, probably on the London market . . . and adapted to contain the relics of the Saxon kings'. The C17 replicas are poor imitations, with plump, pink putti like under-done sausages. All the chests were repaired and their colours 'revived' in 1932–3.

– PULPIT. A very strange, over-decorated piece and crowded with ornament including the name of Prior Silkstede (1498–1524) and his rebus of a skein of silk. But would a monastic cathedral have had a pulpit at so early a date? It has four facets of an octagon (apparently all there ever was of the main 'drum'), resting on a circular plinth and rising up in two registers. It is uncertain whether the desk, supported on coving, is part of the original. The elaborate ogival tester can be seen in late C18 illustrations of the choir, but appears to have been renewed to the same design in 1848 when it and the curved stair were carved by *Messrs Gover* of Winchester, assisted by *James Thomas* (then of London), to designs by *O. B. Carter*. All the other obviously modern woodwork is secondary. Could the medieval elements have come from something completely different: perhaps a very narrow spiral stair up to the rood loft destroyed in the 1630s, or simply the casing of a pier? – BISHOP'S THRONE. Erected 1827, the design by *William Garbett* inspired by the canopies of the early C14 choir stalls. The *Gentleman's Magazine* described it as 'one of the most splendid and elegant compositions in wood-work of the present age'. It replaced the throne given by Bishop Trelawny (1707–21). Next to it, two C19 chairs in the Dec idiom by *O. B. Carter*, 1841. – CONGREGATIONAL DESKS in front of the free-standing seating at the E end of the presbytery, by *Thomas & Co.*, 1913.

– CHOIR STALLS. An outstanding survival. They are dated to *c.* 1308 on the evidence of a letter of that year written by Bishop Woodlock to the Bishop of Norwich, begging for *William of Lyngwood*, a Norfolk carpenter, to be excused attendance at the local manorial court because his presence was essential to complete 'a certain piece of work relating to his craft that he had begun in the choir of our cathedral'. Sixty-two of at least sixty-six rear stalls have survived. The others must have been destroyed in the truncation of the choir's w end, probably in 1638 when *Inigo Jones*'s classical choir screen replaced the medieval pulpitum. The front row of sub-stalls may by then have already perished; they are represented only by six seats at the W end and fifteen butchered stall-ends incorporated in later modifications.

Charles Tracy, who rightly calls the stalls 'the finest set of choir furniture in Europe of their date', regards the design as a belated attempt at translating the language of Rayonnant architecture into wood. The rear stalls are sheltered beneath an arcaded canopy, and the seat-backs comprise plain trefoil-headed panels, grouped in twos within wide two-centred arches each of which has a large cinquefoil roundel at the apex. In the spandrels between each pair of seats are the great joy of the stalls, the carvings of very close and intricate foliage. Much of it is still botanically recognizable (oak, hazel, hawthorn, vine, geranium and ivy) but already bossy and knobbly throughout and inhabited – and herein lies the greatest charm of all – with human figures (e.g. a falconer on the S side, nose to beak with his charge; a soldier represented as a Green Man with a sword and round shield) and animals, including a monkey playing a harp and a lion trampling a hound. Other fine carving is found in the MISERICORDS whose unusually large supporters provided additional scope for the craftsmen. The subject matter is non-biblical: some portraits, both on the supporters and the seat brackets, but mostly allusions to human weaknesses and vices – and celebrations of misogyny. The seat brackets include (N side) a cat holding a rat, a squirrel, a man playing a pipe, a tumbler, an owl, a mock-bishop, fools, a lion, a monkey, a woman wearing a wimple, a fox with a goose. On the S side: a dog, a ram, a man with a hunting horn, a hare, a boar, monsters, seated people, etc. In the lower row on the N side a fine laughing figure. The figure beneath the vice-dean's sub-stall has a wagging tongue (restored), one of three with mobile tongues. Two misericords, portraying a pelican and a lioness with her cubs, were created in 1988–9 to replace lost medieval originals, by *Susan Wraight*. Now lost are some sixty-two historiated panels recorded in 1635 by Lieutenant Hammond 'over the seats': presumably meaning the blank trefoil arched spaces above the cornice, in the head of the seat vaults. They featured 'a lively, wooddy Representation, Portraiets, and Images, from the Creation to the Passion' and were destroyed in 1642, after which *Mercurius Rusticus* deplored the destruction of 'the Stories of the Old and New Testament, curiously cut out in carved work, beautified with Colours, and set round about the top of the Stalls of the Quire'. At the Restoration the empty panels were coloured blue and gilt stars were affixed (a small area of blue paint has been allowed to remain at the W end of the N stalls, the remainder being removed during refurbishment works in 1968).

The design of the seat-backs is replicated in the canopy, where pairs of cinquefoil sub-arches with tiny heads to the cusps are enclosed in major arches adorned with a variety of openwork cinquefoils (and – perhaps because no earthly creation should rival the perfection of Heaven – one six-pointed star on the N side, in the double-triangle configuration later adopted as the 'Star of David'). Above rise steep crocketed gables, enclosing elongated cinquefoils; again, the number five predominates.

Originally the canopy was supported by thin wooden shafts, alternating with quatrefoil shaft-clusters, rising from the armrests. All the front bases, mid-rings and capitals were lathe-turned to identical profiles, those intended for the foiled clusters then being cut into appropriate segments and glued together. The arrangement proved inadequate and the major supports were soon reconfigured by removing the outermost shaft of each cluster to permit the insertion of large stanchions set on the diagonal. These rise from the floor and terminate in pinnacles (all now C17 replacements) which presumably formed no part of the original scheme.

The return stalls at the W end, five on each side, were modified when the Inigo Jones choir screen was installed and again for *Sir (George) Gilbert Scott*'s rather pedantic CHOIR SCREEN of 1875 (which itself replaced a short-lived Gothic screen of 1819–20 by *Garbett* in imitation of Edington's W porch). Hitherto the seat-backs were panelled like the lateral stalls; Scott turned them into openwork and applied decoration on the W side exactly matching the medieval work on the E. On either side of the entrance to the choir the single stalls of the prior (S side) and bishop (as titular abbot) are now separated by a boarded partition from the adjacent pairs of stalls.

The front stalls are of various dates and of most interest are the sixteen (eight on each side) E of those now used by the choir. They have panels, inserted immediately after the New Foundation of the cathedral in 1541, which while doubling as seat-backs to the sub-stalls, function as display fronts to the main stalls for the Dean, twelve canons, and (probably) the precentor, sacrist, and seneschal (chapter clerk). The panels include the arms of Henry VIII, Bishop Stephen Gardiner, and the New Foundation, together with cherubs, heads in medallions, grotesques, and the full repertoire of Renaissance motifs. Two carvers seem to have been involved, the style rather old-fashioned and looking back to Franco-Italian models of the 1520s.

PAVEMENT. The W end of the choir re-laid in 1764. White limestone slabs laid diagonally with black marble quarries at the corners. The pavement, including that of the dais on the W side of the choir screen, was extensively repaired in 1953–4. – LITURGICAL BOOKS displayed behind the high altar: a folio King James Bible printed by Thomas Buck and Roger Daniel, the Cambridge University printers, 1638, and the new prayer book of 1662, in matching bindings. – CHOIR LECTERN. A wooden eagle on a big baluster, C17. Choirboys love to rotate the head into quizzical attitudes. – Victorian GASOLIERS, adapted for electricity 1937, four years after the choir was first wired up. Trumpet-shaped with foliate openwork and glass finials. Restored 1976 when the choir stalls were conserved.

– STAINED GLASS. Bishop Fox's E window was restored in 1850–2 by *Edward Baillie*; it retains a significant amount of early C16 glazing. Surviving *in situ* at the top of the tracery lights are figures of the Virgin and John the Baptist, but the figure they now adore is a poor C19 replacement. The E pair of clerestory windows, beyond the Great Screen, contain much reassembled C15 glass in the upper lights, notably four very early C15 figures of saints (originally in the nave) in the NE window, which previously had been reglazed by Fox. These include a sensitive portrayal of St Fausta, with the saw of her martyrdom. The portrayal of St Vincent in the r. light of the adjacent window is also from the nave. The remaining survivals are predominantly mid-C15, perhaps when the tracery was replaced (*see* pp. 584–5) – more saints and prophets, and, in the tracery lights on the N side rows, seraphim, which Fox

copied when he reglazed the E pair of windows. – ORGAN. In
the N crossing arch, a Gothick case of 1825 by *Edward Blore*,
with motifs derived from the choir stalls. This housed the predecessor of the present organ, which comprises two-thirds of
the instrument built by *Henry Willis* for the 1851 Great Exhibition and installed at Winchester in 1854. Subsequently added
to, altered, and three times rebuilt, last in 1985–8 by *Harrison
& Harrison*. Of this date the case of a new division of the Great
Organ, in the first nave bay, designed by *Corinne Bennett*.

MONUMENTS. On the N side of the presbytery, the Renaissance stone tomb-chest of Bishop John of Pontoise (†1304).
Within a rectangular panel on the front are three blank cartouches separated by candelabra; the outer two armorial cartouches have leathery scrollwork (which Prof. Biddle calls
'advanced for 1525'), within a rectangular panel with candelabra. Candelabra panels at end. Surmounted by an early C14
Purbeck tomb-slab, presumably from the bishop's original
monument. – On the S side, Bishop Peter Courtenay (†1492).
Gothic tomb-chest, without effigy, constructed in 1887 under
the supervision of the Dean's architect son, *G. H. Kitchin*, by
the cathedral's masons and 'a clever and intelligent carver', *Mr
Whitley*, in order to prove their competence to tackle the Great
Screen. Courtenay's body had been discovered in a lead coffin
in the Lady Chapel crypt in 1886, concealed within a wall
between the central row of pillars. – Next to the bishop's
throne, stone wall tablet by *Simon Verity*, 1994–5, commemorating Bishop Lancelot Andrewes (1619–26).* It includes a tiny
sculpture of the bishop preaching. – Centre of the choir, the
C12 tomb of Bishop Henry of Blois (†1171). Limestone sarcophagus with a Purbeck *dos-d'âne* lid, moved here from the
retrochoir in 1886, having already been moved eighteen years
previously from its original position in the middle of the
presbytery. Long wrongly identified as the tomb of William
Rufus. The simplicity of the tomb perhaps reflects Bishop
Henry's penitential attitude in his latter years, when he gave
away his possessions and devoted himself to prayer.

North transept

13 CHAPEL OF THE HOLY SEPULCHRE. WALL PAINTINGS, dated
to the 1170s and the best of their date in England. On the E
wall, the remains of a wonderful Descent from the Cross
(Deposition) and Entombment, uncovered and conserved by
Eve Baker, 1963–7. Stylistically they are similar to the later
paintings of the Winchester Bible, though they are not by the
same hand. The upper register (the Deposition) is damaged by
the insertion of the C13 vault; evidently the C12 scheme rose
higher. The Entombment below shows strong Byzantinizing

---

* Wrongly given as 1618 on the monument. His appointment was confirmed in 1619
after which he could call himself Lancelot Winton.

influences, and indeed was modified during painting to include the eastern themes of the Virgin embracing Christ and St John kissing his hand (originally the figure in the broad-brimmed hat was shown anointing Christ's torso rather than his legs). After the C13 reconstruction of the chapel the scenes on the E wall were repainted; this version has been transferred to an artificial support on the W wall. In partial compensation for the loss of the top of the Deposition is the powerful Pantocrator in the vault above; stern, soul-searching, again strongly Byzantinizing and no later than *c.* 1230 (David Park). The fainter C13 scenes on the S wall include the Entry into Jerusalem and Raising of Lazarus in the upper lunette of the E bay, with the Harrowing of Hell and *Noli me Tangere* on the wall below, and the martyrdom of St Catherine in the W bay. – ALTAR FRONTAL by *Alice Kettle*, 1994, in a subdued palette related to the wall paintings. – MONUMENT. Under the E arch of the chapel, C13 Purbeck coffin, probably of a prior and still inhabited, its lid adorned with a foliated cross starting from a twist of stiff-leaf.

E AISLE. – STAINED GLASS. Panel of kaleidoscopic medieval and possibly early C17 fragments in the SE window. In the next bay, memorial window by *Christopher Whall* to Edward Bligh, killed at Gallipoli 1915. SS Michael, George and Hubert. The N window tracery contains flashed ruby glass of *c.* 1330, the oldest glass in the cathedral, apart from the imports from Salisbury. – MONUMENTS. Dean Charles Naylor †1739. Within confronting C14 nodding ogee tabernacles in the central arch of the E arcade of the transept. Inscribed plaque over an elegant oval bas relief with emblems of Death, Judgment, Time and Eternity. – Frederick McCombe Turner (†1856) by *Edwardes & Co.* of London, 1857. A roundel of an Indian landscape, with a broken column, palm trees and Hindu architecture against a black-brown obelisk. – On the E wall of this aisle, George Frederick Nott, †1841. A large Neo-Norman arched mural tablet with a lengthy inscription commemorating the canon's extensive works at the cathedral. – At the foot of the 'Pilgrims' Steps', plaque commemorating Samuel Sebastian Wesley (†1876), white in dark marble surround, with title of his well-known anthem 'Ascribe unto the Lord'. – Relegated to the N end of the aisle, a regrettable mid-C20 Annunciation group in oak by *Alan Durst*, given by public subscription in 1945 in memory of Canon B. K. Cunningham. Behind it, wall tablet, Sir Robert Pescod †1725, by *Richard Leversuch*. – Against the N wall, early C14 tomb-recess with ogee arch; part of the Dec remodelling of the transept aisles. On front face of the gallery, *Christus*, a Romanesque-inspired Crucifixion by *Peter Eugene Ball*, 1987.

N AISLE. – MONUMENTS. General Sir Redvers Buller †1908. Recumbent bronze effigy by *Sir Bertram Mackennal*, 1910, proud and moustachioed, head resting on his soldier's bed-roll, on a black marble sarcophagus. A stylish monument by a foremost Edwardian sculptor. – Canon Frederic Iremonger †1820.

Recumbent effigy of the philanthropic canon in repose, finely carved in Roche Abbey limestone by *Chantrey*, 1823–7. On s arcade, wall plaques to Dean Michael Stancliffe (†1986) by *John Skelton*, 1989, and Bishop John Taylor (†2001), by *Alec Peever*, 2004. At the s end of the transept, finely carved bas-relief head of cathedral organist Dr G. B. Arnold (†1902), against a shallow shell-headed niche below a broken pediment, by *S. P. Cockerell*.

EPIPHANY CHAPEL. Formed on the initiative of Canon A. S. Valpy in 1908 by screening off the w aisle. The altar is at the N end. Fine ENTRANCE SCREEN in mid-C15 idiom, and linen-fronted desks, designed by *T. G. Jackson* and executed by *Thompsons* of Peterborough. In memory of Valpy (†1909) four STAINED GLASS windows of 1909–10 by *Morris & Co.*, designed by *J. Henry Dearle* and painted by the workshop team: *Titcomb*, *Stokes*, *Knight*, *Howard*, and *Watson*. They depict the Annunciation, Visitation, Nativity, and Adoration of the Magi, a scheme based on Burne-Jones's cartoons for the chapel at Castle Howard (1874). The Visitation ('Salutation of St Eliza-beth') by Dearle has been substituted for Burne-Jones's Flight into Egypt. Dearle's facial expressions are intense, even joyless. Deep reds, greens, and blues predominate in all the scenes, which are set against wooded backgrounds. These narrative panels are surrounded by swirling foliate designs and a vine-leaf border in typical William Morris green. – ICON. Mace-donian or Bulgarian, dated 1752, showing Baptism of Christ. – ALTAR FRONTAL by *Margaret Kaye*, 1962, combining archi-tectural elements of the w front and the Greek letters Chi-Rho. – At the entrance to the chapel, ENGRAVED GLASS PANEL by *Tracey Sheppard*, 2000. – MONUMENTS. On the w wall, Canon Thomas Rivers †1731. Obelisk with six fine armorial shields and palm fronds. – Plaque erected by Dean Cheyney com-memorating his friend Jean Serres, a Huguenot from Mon-tauban who spent twenty-seven years as a Marseilles galley-slave until the Treaty of Utrecht allowed him to flee to England where he died in 1754 aged eighty-five after forty-one years' residence in Winchester. To the r. of the altar, STONE ROUNDEL of the *Agnus Dei* by *Eric Gill*, c. 1920.

South transept

E AISLE. – VENERABLE CHAPEL. Superb C14 ENTRANCE SCREEN, once highly coloured and populated internally with statuary. The chapel was taken over by the Eyre family as a private mausoleum in the C18. Wrought IRONWORK of this date in the lower part of the screen. Altar workwork by *Rachel Schwalm*. Altar in Jerusalem limestone, and oak furnishings by *Luke Hughes & Co.*, 2010. – HATCHMENT of Bishop Brown-low North †1820. – ICON, Russian work of the C19 presented 1989. The next chapel to the s, separated by a low wall and a C15 wooden screen, is the CHAPEL OF ST JOHN THE

EVANGELIST AND THE FISHERMEN APOSTLES. Formerly
the 'Silkstede Chapel'; its re-dedication in 1996 took account
of the wall-painting evidence (*see* above, p. 581). By happy
coincidence this is the burial place of Izaak Walton (†1683),
the 'Father of Angling',* who followed Bishop Morley to Winchester as his steward ending his days in the Cathedral Close.
– STAINED GLASS E window by *Powells*, 1914, with scenes of
Walton reading by the Itchen and with Charles Cotton in
Dovedale; donated in Walton's memory by fishermen of
England and America. – ALTAR by *Peter Eugene Ball*, 1995, a
big block of oak, coloured in Ball's usual bronze and verdigris,
and adorned with fish. Large candlesticks by the same artist.
Curved BENCHES by *Alison Crowther* (1996) continue the
rustic theme. – MONUMENT. Canon John Nicholas, Warden of
Winchester College †Feb. 1711/12. By *William Woodman Sen.*
of London. Large urn on a pedestal within a Doric arch supporting his arms which are flanked by sepulchral lamps.
Underneath is a scroll supported by winged skulls. Its authentic black border was unfortunately whitewashed *c.* 1994.

CENTRAL VESSEL. N SCREEN. Re-set, slightly pointed C12 arch,
Quarr limestone, with chevron, removed from the original
entrance to Henry of Blois's treasury in the SW corner of the
transept in 1816 by *Garbett*, who supported it on early C19
'Norman' responds and capitals.** Above it, foliate SWAGS in
wood in the style of Gibbons (perhaps by *Edward Pearce*); part
of decoration added in the late C17 to the Laudian canopy over
the High Altar (*see* Great Screen, above). – Wooden BENCH
probably early C13. Solid, architectural rather than artistic in
conception, and much altered; the limited decoration comprises carved finials and knobs to the arm-rests. – Votive
CANDLE-STAND by *Antony Robinson*, 1985 – Brass CHANDE-
LIER (*see* presbytery and choir, above). – IRON-BOUND CHEST,
perhaps the muniment chest mentioned in the 1544 statutes,
with its three locks (keys were held by the Dean, Vice-Dean
and Treasurer so all three had to be present to open it) – At
S end of transept and extending up the W side for one bay are
CANOPIED SEATS with linenfold panelling. The coved canopy
includes a frieze of framed panels with Early Renaissance ornament, such as horned dolphins confronting urns, and include
(W side) the initials of Prior Silkstede (1498–1524); the tall
panels on the S side are separated by pilasters with Renaissance
candelabra motifs. Nicholas Riall convincingly points out the
similarities of the frieze to that of Bishop Fox's stalls at St
Cross (*see* pp. 717–18) but argues that the workmanship indicates a less skilled team. The original work might have been
done *c.* 1515–20, but its present form and arrangement date
from 1816 (the date in the frieze panel above the S door with
the initials of Dean Thomas Rennell (1805–40) and his arms

* Fortuitously the choice of dedication may have been its original one.
** Blore (1820) was unimpressed by this 'composition made out of old materials
brought from the S end of the Transept completed with a considerable portion of
new work'.

on the doorposts) when it appears that the seats were converted from presses for choir vestments.

MONUMENTS. Below the C12 arch on the N side, Sir Isaac Townsend, Commissioner of Portsmouth Dockyard, †1731 and his widow †1735. Probably moved here in 1820. Freestanding oblong base with apsidal ends supporting a square pedestal topped by an urn and adorned with appropriate naval and military trophies. Smaller vases l. and r. A fine relief of a rigged ship on the E 'apse'. – Canon David Williams †1860. By *W. Theed*. White marble, with languid figures of Faith, Hope and Charity. – In the centre of the transept, Bishop Wilberforce (†1873). Effigy on a slab supported by six kneeling angels, the whole in a shrine-like building: a canopy on eight columns. The architectural style is E.E. Designed by *Sir (George) Gilbert Scott*, evidently based on Walter de Grey's quasi-shrine monument in York Minster, and typical of Scott's style at its most lavish. The effigy by *H. H. Armstead*, 1878.

WALL MONUMENTS. Beside the steps from the presbytery aisle, charming portrait of Dean Thomas Garnier (†1873), after a miniature by *Richard Cockle Lucas*, a Hampshire artist who specialized in cameos modelled in wax (the original is in the Deanery). – Guy Victor Baring †1916 in the Battle of the Somme, small marble aedicule with standing portrait in uniform of the Coldstream Guards. – Canon Peter Atkinson †1888, with bust. – Officers and soldiers of 7th Royal Fusiliers †1854–5. Kneeling angel below flags, signed *E. Richardson* 1857. Above, the colours that they took to the Crimea.

LEDGER STONES. Huge Purbeck marble slab outside the Venerable Chapel with remains of early C15 indents for a brass. – Small lozenge-shaped slab commemorating Humphrey Salwey, first headmaster of The Pilgrims' School (†1985). Good lettering, by *Quin Hollick*.

'CALEFACTORY'. – WALL PAINTING in the SE corner. Benedictine saint writing at a desk, *c.* 1270, perhaps again hinting that this was the scriptorium.

SONG SCHOOL. Carved SCREEN and OAK PRESSES in C15 Gothic style by *T. G. Jackson*, 1909–10, executed by *Farmer & Brindley* as a memorial to Canon Valpy (†1909).

Nave

38 EDINGTON CHANTRY CHAPEL. Very simple, compared with its showy successors, and very important in that it is predominantly late reticulated Dec, despite its apparent date (William of Edington died 1366, though his chapel might have been built as early as 1350). Six bays of two-light openings in two tiers, trefoil-headed at the top and cinquefoil below the transoms, over plain panels; the doorway in the fifth. The jambs of the S doorway curve forward as they descend from the top, a motif found in the S transept at Gloucester, where, as Pevsner wrote, 'it also still represented the loyalty to the Dec among the first

Perp designers'. Likewise the treatment of the four corners.
The chapel is open, terminating in a band of quatrefoils in
square panels, surmounted by cresting; there is no reason to
suppose that a vault was removed when the chapel was rebuilt
c. 1822, following the reinforcement of the flanking piers. The
design of the tomb is suggestive of a London workshop. The
chest is of Purbeck, with exquisitely formed hexafoils, again
rather retrospective; the sort of thing Henry Yevele might have
done; at the top, a hollow with a row of tiny fleurons, most
unusual. Recumbent effigy of alabaster, once coloured and the
mitre adorned with precious stones. The bishop's hand raised
in blessing, a fashion by then outdated at a time when effigies
usually gave the impression that the deceased lay on his
catafalque. – ALTAR TABLE by *Corinne Bennett*, 1974.

WYKEHAM CHANTRY CHAPEL. Here is the change from simplicity to show: from 1366 to 1404. The chapel reaches right
up to the balcony. It is of three bays and wider than the piers
are thick. It has therefore canted extensions to merge with the
piers. These extensions house statuary niches and, at the w
end, the two doorways. Jane Geddes dates the NW door to
1394–1403, pointing out that pierced plates like the ring-plate
came in only around 1400. The floor tiles also indicate a date
of c. 1398. Outside, the lower half is of three tiers, the lowest
being panelled, the others open. The top tier has the Perp
equivalent of the reticulation unit, i.e. a unit with straight sides
– so things have moved on since Edington's chapel. The upper
half is entirely open, a feature followed in Beaufort's chapel.
The tall canopy is supported on the thinnest of shafts. At the
top, three crocketed gables superimposed on trefoil panelling,
simple to read and distinct, unlike the thicket of Beaufort's pinnacles. The wider central gable encloses an unusual motif: a
trefoil under a round sub-arch. Inside, a cusped lierne-vault.
The w wall has fleurons to the cinquefoil panels, with niches
above. The plinth of the altar survives. Above it, the reredos
has two tiers of five niches each with high canopies. The design
of the tomb is suggestive of a London workshop. The statuettes
are by *Sir George Frampton*, installed in 1897 after a major
restoration of the chapel at Winchester College's expense. It
had previously been restored by *William Bird* of Oxford in
1664, and again in 1741 and 1797, on the last occasion by
William Cave. The chapel was conserved in 1996–7 and the
cleaned Caen stone forms a notable contrast with the grubby
Beer stone of the arcade. There are no immediate parallels for
Wykeham's monument, though for Nigel Saul the use of composite materials suggests a metropolitan workshop. It is not
mentioned in the bishop's will, and is probably posthumous as
the burial would have been beneath it. Raised on a Purbeck
step, the body of the tomb-chest is in alabaster, with seven side
and two end-bay panels enclosing an alternating array of the
bishop's coats of arms. The panels terminate in steep crocketed ogees with the enclosed trefoil motifs as we noted in the
chapel's canopy. So Wynford's influence extended to the tomb;
could he have been its designer? Above the body, a Purbeck

39

slab with brass chamfer inscription (later replaced by the
present one in red enamel). Finally, again in alabaster, the
recumbent effigy, with hands joined in prayer, crozier laid
against his left shoulder. The effigy was repainted in the C17
and C18 restorations when many missing elements were
restored. The identity of the figures at Wykeham's feet is much
discussed, but they are unlikely to have been his chantry monks
as their original garments were coloured, not black; their ton-
sured heads are replacements as are those of the angels at the
bishop's head.

LECTERN. Brass, by *Hart, Son & Peard*, given 1878 for use
at 'Soldiers' Services', the only regular services held in the nave
until 1962.

FONT. The most famous of the black Tournai fonts in
England. Square, the shape which the Purbeck fonts were to
imitate on a smaller scale. Difficult to date, but possibly commissioned by Henry of Blois on his return from exile in 1158.
On two sides stories of St Nicholas, including the earliest
known depiction of a boat with a stern-post rudder, on the
third three roundels with pairs of birds, on the fourth roundels
with a quadruped flanked by single birds. On the top in two
spandrels foliage, in the other two affronted birds drinking
from a vase.

PULPIT. Early C17 hexagon on a substantial pillar with Neo-
Jacobean decoration of the mid-1880s. Originally from New
College Chapel, Oxford, and presented to the cathedral as a
memorial to Jane Mayo †1886. Possibly by *William Harris* of
Holywell, Oxford, who made new desks and stalls for New
College c. 1638.

SCULPTURE. Against the W wall stand excellent bronze
statues of James I and Charles I. They are by *Le Sueur* and
were designed for *Inigo Jones*'s choir screen of c. 1638. During
the Commonwealth the statues were hidden on the Isle of
Wight but restored to the screen in 1660 and retained within
its early 1820s replacement by *William Garbett* from which
their pedestals derive.

BATIK BANNERS (displayed at major church festivals).
Sixteen large banners by *Thetis Blacker* powerfully depicting
the Old and New Creations: from W to E, those on the N side
illustrate the seven days of Creation then the Fall; on the S side,
the Incarnation through to St John's vision of the Holy City.
The influence of her studies in South East Asia is evident. They
are suspended from rods attached to the iron hooks which are
traditionally claimed to have been first used to support tapestries which adorned the nave for the marriage of Mary Tudor
and Philip of Spain in 1554. In fact it is uncertain that the
tapestries reached Winchester; the hooks might equally have
held banners for Prince Arthur's baptism.

PAVEMENT. The pavement of the nave and aisles is a price-
less resource, unusual in that it has not been relaid since the
C14. A wonderful interplay of textures, the background comprising plain limestone and Purbeck paviors into which many
interesting ledger stones have been inserted over the centuries.

The Entrance to the Choir, the Work of Inigo Jones.

To the Revᵈ the DEAN, & CHAPTER, of yᵉ Cathᵉˡ Church of Winton this Plate is most humbly Inscribed.

Winchester Cathedral, Inigo Jones's choir screen of *c.* 1638.
Engraving after Charles Woodfield, 1715

TABLETS against the W wall commemorating preservation of the cathedral, by *Norman Nisbett* 1912.

STAINED GLASS. The original great W window was finally smashed to pieces in the Civil War and now comprises a mosaic of medieval glass from all over the cathedral, padded out with more recent additions. Yet enough remains *in situ* for the original scheme, dated by Sarah Brown to *c.* 1375, to be worked out. Mary Callé has compared the iconographical arrangement of this credal window to a triptych: the centre panel containing scenes from the life of Christ was flanked by images of apostles and prophets standing in niches. It may be by *Thomas of Oxford.* The window was re-leaded by the *Chapel Studio*

(*Alfred Fisher*, succeeded by *Steve Clare*), 1993–5. – Clerestory windows. Fragments dated to the first quarter of C15 survive in tracery lights.

– MONUMENTS (E to W). Bishop Hoadly †1761. By *Joseph Wilton*. Grey and white marble. Lively profile in an oval medallion against ample, still entirely Baroque, drapery and accompanied by symbols of political liberty including the Phrygian cap and text from Magna Carta. A black marble background, added in 1774 was removed 1969. The monument is inserted on a flat surface formed by cutting away the lower part of the Romanesque shaft: one recalls that critics of Hoadly, a central figure in that heated theological battle, the 'Bangorian controversy', observed that 'no-one had undermined the foundations of the church more than he.' – Bishop Harold Browne, †1891. Recumbent alabaster effigy on an alabaster tomb-chest with statuettes, designed by *Bodley & Garner*, carved by *Farmer & Brindley*, 1895. The monument is protected by good ironwork.

There may have been a similar tribune at the W end of the Romanesque nave, but all the evidence was removed in the C14 when work began on remodelling the W front. Excavation of the Norman foundations suggests that the original W massif had flanking towers (cf. La Trinité, Caen) rather than W transepts as at Ely. A portion of the SW tower survives as a boundary wall S of the cathedral forecourt.

North nave aisle

STAINED GLASS. Medieval fragments occur in a number of window heads, dated by Le Couteur to the second quarter of the C15. This agrees tolerably well with the evidence of Wykeham's will: he directed in 1403 that after the S side had been glazed any remaining money was to be used in glazing the N aisle from W to E. – The remaining glass is C19 and C20. In the first bay of the aisle by *Betton & Evans* of Shrewsbury, 1851. Garish with few lead lines, Christ flanked by Peter and Paul, over Old Testament patriarchs. – Next, a memorial window to Frances Chamberlayne Macdonald, comprising early C15 glass attributed to *Thomas of Oxford*, re-set,* together with new glass, by *Alfred Fisher*, 1992. – Fifth bay, George VI Coronation Window by *Hugh Easton*, 1939, illustrating the sacrament of marriage. Above the kneeling king and queen, dressed in Garter and Order of the Thistle robes respectively, the Miracle at Cana is flanked by King Henry IV and Joan of Navarre (married in the cathedral in 1403). – Then in sequence: memorial window to Charles Mayo †1876 and his son, also Charles, †1877 by *Clayton & Bell*, whose curious juxtapositions include William of Wykeham and St Cecilia; Jane Austen memorial window, by *Kempe*, 1901; and *Clayton &*

---

* The figure of St Genevieve was originally in the second window from the E in the N nave clerestory.

Bell's window to Harriet, Countess of Guildford †1874. – In the penultimate bay Rifle Brigade window by *Kempe*, 1900, featuring soldier saints against a silvery background of canopied niches.

– CROZIER and MITRE of Bishop Morley (†1684). The bishop is buried beneath a large black LEDGER STONE bearing the lengthy Latin epitaph listing his achievements, which he composed, on a platform answering to the Edington Chantry Chapel opposite; perhaps this was the site of Bishop Adam Orleton's chantry chapel (†1345). On the pillar below Morley's crozier, a small (13 in. by 9 in., 33 by 24 cm.) but significant BRASS PLATE commemorating Richard Boles, killed with sixty Royalist fellow soldiers during the siege of Alton church in 1643 (the brass has 1641). 'Bring me my mourning scarf,' exclaimed the king on hearing the news. The densely worded inscription in cursive script was composed by a kinsman in 1689.

The aisles of Winchester Cathedral have almost as many MONUMENTS as those of Westminster Abbey. This selection goes from E to W beginning with the N WALL. Anne Morley †1787. White and pink marble. Urn under a weeping willow. – Matthew Combe †1748. Urn and garlands in front of an obelisk. – Frederic Preston Joy †1913. Pre-Raphaelite *opus sectile* angel with a harp, by *Powells*. – Edward Cole, a lawyer, thrice Mayor of Winchester, †1617. An imposing polychrome limestone aedicule supported on disturbing grotesque heads, enclosing a plain panel, with much bold strapwork. Below it, an inscription was added in 1886 by *G. H. Kitchin*. It is the only one of its kind in the cathedral. – Brig. Gen. R. C. Maclachlan †1917, inscription within wreath under his VC; above it, Brig. Gen. J. E. Gough †1915, both by *Eric Gill*. – Edward Montagu †1776. Seated allegorical figures either side of an urn. – Col. James Morgan †1808. By *John Bacon Jun*. Small kneeling female mourner; and exotic reminders of his military past peeking from behind a draped urn: a flag, cannon, and an elephant's head. The small pelican might be further local colour rather than a religious symbol. – Jane Austen (†1817): ledger stone and brass of 1872 by *Mr Wyatt*. – Above it, elaborate tablet dated 1622 with entertaining inscription commemorating 'a Union of Two Brothers from Avington', namely Thomas and Thomas Clerk, who led singularly parallel lives. – Sir Villiers Chernocke †1779. Grey and white marble (†1804), by *Samuel Walldin*, a local mason. A flourishing weeping willow overhangs allegorical figures of Charity and Justice either side of a large urn. – Dr John Littlehales †1810. By *John Bacon Jun.* and featuring the parable of the Good Samaritan in low relief. – At the W end, MEMORIAL TABLET by *Alec Peever*, 1995, with the names of major contributors to the cathedral restoration of the mid 1990s.

South nave aisle

SCREEN of *c.* 1450 to the 'Scob' behind the westernmost choir stalls. Six bays, cusped tracery over a dado of panels, and an off-centre door. It was moved here from the entrance to the Guardian Angels' Chapel in 1817. – Opposite it, six-seat BENCH, *c.* 1830, originally at E end of choir. Further W, curved MEDIEVAL WOODEN BENCH. The radius fits the Romanesque axial chapel (dem. *c.* 1202),* and if it was made for that location it is an amazing survival of a piece of Romanesque furniture. – Inner SOUTH DOORS dated 1824, originally the central entrance in *Garbett*'s choir screen. In the style of 1500 with lettered inscription derived from the screen to Langton's chapel. – Gothic CHEST, *c.* 1300, with front of three wide planks, adorned with four roundels. – STAINED GLASS. In the first aisle bay, by *Betton & Evans*, dated 1853 (cf. N aisle). In the fourth bay, Hampshire Regiment window by *Powells*, 1904, with *opus sectile* work in the wall panels below forming part of the same scheme. – Then the George V window by *Hugh Easton*, 1938, whose top lights feature the 'King of Kings' (inscribed on the horse's shoulder), flanked by Edward the Confessor and William the Conqueror (with anachronistic CII heraldry). – The seventh and eighth bays both by *Clayton & Bell*. – Next, the Philpot window by *Powells* (1917), including a depiction of the burning of the Protestant John Philpot in 1555 in the predella beneath St Stephen. – Medieval fragments (*c.* 1365) in the tracery heads of the window in the final bay feature naïve angels playing musical instruments, qualified by Le Couteur as 'provincial work'. – The W window of the S aisle by *Charles Alexander Gibbs*, installed 1857 as a memorial to the fallen in the Crimea of the 97th (Earl of Ulster's) Regiment, including two of the first VC's ever awarded. Brightly coloured martial saints and monarchs. Rather heavy leading.

MONUMENTS, working W. Capt. Melville Portal and Sir Gerald Portal †1893 and 1894. By the American sculptor and Roman resident *Thomas Waldo Story*, installed 1897. Pevsner characterized it thus: 'A sensuous genius with the curvaceous lines of the Paris Salon, her breasts not bared but much noticed, holds the two medallions. Venetian semicircular pediment with lush decoration.' – Sir George Prevost, †1816, by *Chantrey*, 1819. Female mourner seated in profile on a Grecian chair. On a scroll we read St Lucia Taken / Dominica Defended /Canada Preserved. – Head of the much-loved surgeon William John Wickham †1864, by *R. C. Lucas*; another sensitive example of this artist's ability in portraiture (cf. S transept, Garnier monument). – Bishop Richard Willis †1734. By *Sir Henry Cheere*. A portentous aedicule with Corinthian columns under a pediment. Supported by a pile of books, eyes turned heavenward in an expression of piety, the bishop sprawls semi-recumbent on his sarcophagus, with its monstrous claw feet. – Mural monument to the 1st Earl of Selborne, Gladstone's

---

* Info. from Lee Stone, who has computer modelled the bench.

Lord Chancellor (†1895), by *F. W. Pomeroy*. – On the diagonal faces of the Wykeham Chantry Chapel, facing the aisle: Prebendaries Christopher Eyre †1743 and William Harris †1700. Pleasant cartouches with good lettering. – Thomas Cheyney †1760, possibly by *Sir Henry Cheere*. Large, oval palm wreath and in it on pink the white figures of Hope and Truth flanking an urn. The main panel shows a sarcophagus being opened by Religion so as to liberate the soul of the deceased. A Phoenix, the emblem of immortality, rises. It is a florid design but pretty all the same. – Bishop Tomline †1827. By *Richard Westmacott Jun.*, 1831. Stone tomb-chest and by it a pensive white marble angel 'brooding over his coat of arms' (Blore). – Joseph Warton, headmaster of the College, †1800. A superb Neoclassical monument in white marble by *John Flaxman*, 1801–4, crowned by acroteria and a lyre emerging from acanthus foliage. Warton is enthroned on a dais, looking benign but searching. In front of him stand four eager and improbably pretty boys, modelled on the sons of Flaxman's friends the Hare-Naylors of Herstmonceux Place, East Sussex (the boys were nephews of Dean Jonathan Shipley, 1760–9). At the back Aristotle in precise profile, Homer precisely frontal – 'as neat as Piero della Francesca'. We might be privileged spectators of an intimate schoolroom scene. It is one of Flaxman's most successful funerary monuments, and it is scarcely surprising that he attempted to repeat the scheme in the simpler monument he did for John Lyon at Harrow. The monument was originally placed opposite Bishop Hoadly. – Henrietta Maria North †1796. Also by *Flaxman*. White marble. Two allegorical figures representing Faith and Domestic Piety weep over an urn.

Cathedral Library and Triforium Gallery

The STAIR is late C17 with flat, pierced balusters similar to those in the houses in Dome Alley (1662–5). It is on the remains of a masonry stair leading up to what was probably the monastic sacrist's office, constructed over the slype. – ENTRANCE DOORWAY incorporates lozenge-shaped panels from the 1660s adornments to the high altar. – BOOKCASES. Late C17. Claimed to be from Bishop Morley's library at Farnham Castle, given *c.* 1669 at the same time as his books. Decorative entablature with running vegetal frieze and spiky finials above. – GLOBES, celestial and terrestrial (the latter datable to 1645–6) by the Dutch cartographer *Willem Janszoon Blaeuw* (1571–1638), purchased by the Chapter in 1685 under the terms of Morley's will. They cost £23 11s. to purchase and £8 for carriage from Holland.

In the Williams Room, cupboards and display cases by *Wilfrid Carpenter Turner*, 1952. The latter house the WINCHESTER BIBLE, supreme product of the C12 Winchester school of calligraphers and illuminators.

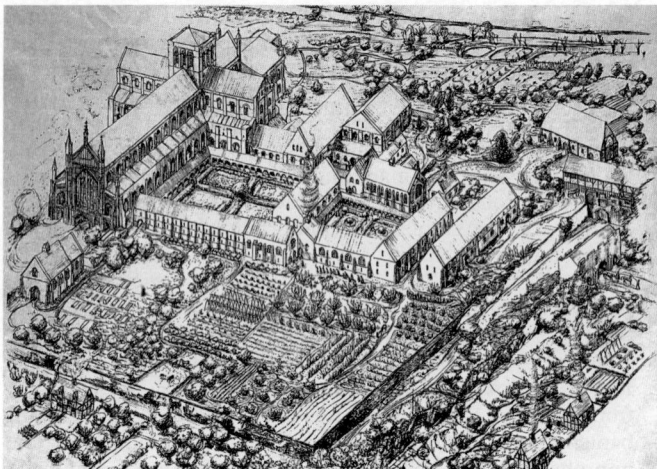

Winchester Cathedral, Close, reconstruction,
view from the south-east c. 1500.
Drawing by Judith Dobie, 1996

TRIFORIUM GALLERY. Designed by *Stanton Williams*, 1989.
Exhibits include superb C12 and C13 sculptural fragments, statuary from the Great Screen of *c.* 1470, the Lillebon Panel
(perhaps the lid of a reliquary chest given *c.* 1325–30), two
inner mortuary chests (of *c.* 1425 and *c.* 1500), the 'chair of
Mary Tudor', and much more besides.

THE CATHEDRAL CLOSE

The Inner Close

The INNER CLOSE was formed from the priory precincts at the
Reformation. The monastic buildings stood around a Great
Cloister and to the S of this was a 'little', or infirmary, cloister.
The refectory stood E–W between the two squares, with the
Infirmary Hall on the S side of its cloister. To the SE, entered
through the Close Gate, was the outer court, the more 'public'
part of the precincts. Each of these parts is now represented
by open grassy lawns.

Most of the Great Cloister was destroyed in the later C16,
although some vestiges still remain incorporated within the
present buildings. What remains visible is this. S of the transept
is the groin-vaulted SLYPE, or passage, under the former
Sacrist's offices (now the Cathedral Library). Then the
entrance to the CHAPTER HOUSE (dem. 1580). Pevsner called
it 'one of the mightiest pieces of Early Norman architecture in
the land'. Entrance and two bays of arcading l., two r. Huge

monolithic columns, three of oolitic limestone, presumably reused from a Saxon or even Roman building, with one (r.) of Quarr added to match. Big capitals of proto-scallops, i.e. of the 1090s, below abaci with an angle roll. There were steps to the chapter house itself, which seems to have been draughtily open to the cloister. To the r. there is evidence of a seat, perhaps for an official during chapter meetings. Inside, remains of blind arcading on cushion capitals along the N wall. The E wall is represented only by stubs at either end. A scar on the S wall of the transept suggests that the W end of the chapter house was oversailed at right angles by another early building; perhaps providing a link between the transept and the DORMITORY which stood S of the chapter house, and parallel with it, above a vaulted undercroft. Its site was laid out in 1994–5 as the Dean Garnier Garden. The arched entrance (also with a seat beside it) is now represented by a few voussoirs and infilled blind arcading which flanked it (such arcading probably ran all round the Norman cloister apart from the N side). The arch was blocked in the C13 when the doorway to its l. was inserted. This is of finely moulded Purbeck marble under a Caen stone tympanum, outer arch and hood. The upper part of the wall was extensively rebuilt in the C16 when the blind recesses were blocked. Inside, fragments of jamb plinths and moulded bases of two doorways with pellet enrichment indicate a remodelling of the S wall in the mid C12. The REREDORTER to the SE lies beneath a terrace in the Deanery lawn; part of its W wall was excavated in 2005. It was served by the Lockburn, the medieval culvert that was the city's only main drain until the 1870s.

S is THE DEANERY, the former Prior's House. During the Commonwealth it was held by the regicide Nicholas Love, who demolished much of the stone medieval dwelling. Like several other houses in the Close, it was then rebuilt in the 1660s in brick. Here the work was supervised by *Richard Frampton* of Kingsgate Street. The oldest visible part is the early C13 PORCH of four bays, three open and one enclosed. The open arches have continuous double chamfers and statue niches in the piers (one may have held the figure of *Ecclesia* now in the retrochoir). Behind the piers, and linked to them by small transverse shouldered lintels, are compound Purbeck piers, each of a core and four detached shafts, supporting a quadripartite vault with single-chamfered ribs. The ribs rest on Purbeck wall-shafts on the N side. On the E wall a motif of a big trefoil over paired arches (cf. the contemporary Lady Chapel). The prior's chapel was above. Vestiges of its E window survive but on the S front are late C15 windows of two and four lights, dating from the remodelling of this part as two storeys (for the audit house etc.). Fine clasped-purlin roof inside, possibly by the same carpenter as the roofs of the Priory stables and Porter's Lodge (*see* below). The timbers of the associated wall-plates and main joists are carefully moulded.

It is possible that the porch was built to give access to a pre-existing ground-floor hall on its N side and extending E. But the present stairs out of the porch are C19, leading up to the so-called PRIOR'S HALL, originally his great chamber. This was probably also C13 (remains of an internal wall arcade survive in a cellar at the SE corner) but was reconstructed *c.* 1459, when oaks from Manydown were provided. Within forty years the chamber seems to have taken on the functions of the old hall, which was probably demolished when the porch was modified. Of the late medieval great chamber, tall Perp windows survive, five on the W side, one on the E (blocked) between the scars of demolished buttresses. Two lights with mullions, the tracery lights blocked. The roof is arch-braced, in six bays, with two moulded purlins and three tiers of wind-braces, the uppermost tier inverted. Superb carved corbels depicting bishops, and spandrels decorated with roses within quatrefoils, and cusped daggers. There are remains of a louvre: it seems the chamber was warmed by a central hearth, by the C15 an old-fashioned arrangement. Of the later C17 alterations are the inserted second floor and the massive chimneystack dividing the first floor into a bedroom and 'Great Dining Room'; the panelling and chimneypiece of which are of 1666–7 by London joiners, *Whetstone*, *Lewis*, and *Oke*. Also, the well staircase, which has flat balusters, regrettably stripped of their painted ornament in the C20. But the staircase has also been altered, notably in 1807–8 when *William Garbett*, Surveyor to the Dean and Chapter, enlarged the entrance hall and added the wooden 'Romanesque' E porch. To the N of the E front is the LONG GALLERY added by Dean Clarke, *c.* 1673. It is of brick, laid in Flemish bond (the first use in the Close), with an open arcade along the S front of varied supports: brick piers, round-headed arches, then in the centre a composition of two pilasters with bulgy brick rustication. Above this is a Perp five-light window under a pediment, possibly original despite the jarring style, with stone cross-windows l. and r. The E window is a cruder timber imitation of 1807. In the gallery, an inserted Georgian chimneypiece and some fragmentary STAINED GLASS, including Flemish work of the C15 and later English glass. In the Deanery yard between the house and the dormi-tory site, concealed within a shed, are the remains of a doorway, which probably led into the dormitory undercroft. On the E side of the yard is the BAKEHOUSE, probably built as the Deanery washhouse after the destruction of the reredorter; it is faced in reused ashlar and until 2003 also held a fragment of a Purbeck niche from St Swithun's final shrine. Extended N and remodelled in 1663 (dendrochronology) and given a gallery at the S end. The older part, remodelled as the brew-house, remained open to the roof but was subsequently floored.

Next follows THE PILGRIMS' SCHOOL (No. 3), set well back to the SE of the Deanery on the E side of Mirabel Close, the former 'Outer Court'. Formerly a canonry house and externally predominantly brick of late C17 date but in fact older, incorporating the monastic guest hall and guestmaster's quarters. This was a six-bay range of two halls end to end, all covered by a single roof dated to *c.* 1310 (dendrochronology), probably therefore by *Thomas of Witney*, and highly significant as displaying all the variant forms of 'aisle-derivative' structure. The three-bay stone-built GUEST HALL is preserved as the so-called 'Pilgrims' Hall' at the N end, and possesses the earliest surviving hammerbeam roof in England. The hammerbeams terminate in heads including a probable representation of the young Edward II. At the apex of the roof scissor-bracing is supported on a central collar-purlin; the heavy sooting of the upper roof shows that the hall was heated by a central hearth; there was no louvre, but the smoke escaped through open gablets at either end of the entire roof. A post-medieval stable loft was removed in 1959 and the floor lowered to its original level, except at the stage end. The unfortunate proscenium, a pastiche of medieval timber framing, formed part of these works. The timber-framed two-bay guestmaster's hall (with a central base-cruck truss concealed within a cross-wall), and the service bay at its S end, are subsumed within the main building whose internal layout still betrays its medieval origins. This was first refaced in brick in the mid C17, see the rear, but the principal front with its dentilled cornice and chunky sash windows is mostly of 1685–6 (dated rainwater heads) for Canon John Nicholas, Warden of Winchester College. Of the same date, the fine staircase with barley-sugar-twist balusters, its coved ceiling with luxuriant swags of fruit and foliage enfolding the canon's arms and those of the diocese, and panelling in the 'parlour' and 'withdrawing room' by *Valentine Housman*, one of Wren's chief joiners, who created the panelling for Winchester College now in New Hall (*see* p. 653). One area of panelling has been transferred to the entrance hall, which also has an 1890s fireplace with the initials of Canon Valpy. He added the bay window to the library and, probably, the Doric porch. Bland s extension for the school, 1932. Around the rear quad, the Stancliffe Building of 1989 by *Radley House Associates* with unfluted Doric colonnade and gallery and a bold classroom block by *Barry Taylor Associates* of Warminster, again comprising classical elements, but with a modern hexagonal theatre-cum-recital room. To the E, single-storey pre-prep department by the same architects.

In Mirabel Close, between No. 3 and the Deanery, SCULP-TURE by *Barbara Hepworth*, 'Construction (Crucifixion), Homage to Mondrian', 1966.

Near the Priory Gate is the former PRIORY STABLING, a long ten-bay timber-framed range, with remains of close studding at ground floor with brick nogging, and a roof of clasped-purlin construction. It has been tree-ring dated to 1479. The stable occupied seven bays, with the entrance facing E to the stableyard. Its first floor, which had windows below the eaves, probably accommodated guests of modest station and has a fine surviving doorway at the head of the internal access stair. This passed through a two-storey apartment at the N end for

the horse-master: first-floor mullioned windows on the N and
w sides. The s bay had rooms, probably for the grooms, with
direct access to the stable. After the Dissolution the building
was subdivided into six individual stables with hay lofts over.
Drastically restored at the s end for The Pilgrims' School, 1939,
and with more restraint in 1957 (dormer windows).

Adjoining the stables to the w, and partly incorporating an
addition to them of 1643, are the highly picturesque CHEYNEY
COURT and PORTER'S LODGE, built against, and in parts penetrating, the massive city wall. Late C15; the principal part
served as the bishop's courthouse until 1835. It has three steep
gables running right across the house and appearing over the
Close wall to the s. They show that the roofs are of clasped-
purlin type (though the E gable is a rebuild). Good fretted
bargeboards to the w gable. There are C17 oriel windows under
gablets in two of the bays and the windows indicate the com-
plexities of the interior (three storeys in the l. bay, two in the
centre, four to the r.). At the core is a tall room, which originally formed part of the courthouse. The l. bay has a low jetty
and is reasonably intact; the other jetties are set higher, above
walls rebuilt in 1892 by *Colson & Son*, when the building was
remodelled as a dwelling. They inserted the large window and
moved the four-centred doorway to the l. bay. Inside, a C19
stair of late C17 flat-balustered type. Originally the porter occupied only the front room of the ground floor of the bay abutting the priory gate, but this is now divided into four low floors,
plus a gallery extending towards the gate. The PRIORY GATE
is late C15. Chequerwork masonry and flint, four-centred arch,
original doors with later wicket. On the w side, the royal arms
(last repainted 1996), which have hung here since at least the
C17.

Opposite The Pilgrims' School is THE JUDGES' LODGINGS
(No. 4), another large former canonry house. Externally the
1660s and 70s, concealing its origins as a medieval double-pile
house forming part of the Infirmary complex (the Infirmary
Hall probably stood to the NW; footings of a large C12 building were excavated here in 2003). The three-bay N frontispiece,
in brick over stone footings (perhaps earlier), has stone quoins
resembling half-pilasters. Chequer brick bays l. and r. with
wooden cross-windows on the E side. The staircase, E of the
entrance hall, has three twisted balusters to each tread. Regrettably dominant NE wing, added late C18 or early C19; and w
extension of the 1890s after the house had been converted for
the circuit judges. w of No. 4, the CATHEDRAL WORKSHOPS
by the cathedral architect, *Peter Bird*, 1992. A quiet brick building intended to blend into historic surroundings.

DOME ALLEY, running w, is a cul de sac, formerly known
as 'Dumb Alley'. It led to the 'Great Garden' in the sw corner
of the Close but now has an interesting planned layout of four
long houses (Nos. 5–8 The Close), two N, two s, laid out in the
1660s by the Cathedral Chapter after destruction during the
Commonwealth. They are of red brick (burnt in the Close by

Thomas Colly) on Purbeck footings, and each pair has eight triangular gables. The original cross-windows have mostly been
replaced by sashes. Both pairs face s, so whereas the N pair
has windows to the street, the others have the two main chimneystacks there. Nos. 7–8 (N side) are the best-preserved.
English bond still but treated quite crudely, like masonry,
except for some moulded brick decoration. The heavy modillioned cornice is cut through rather aggressively by the gable
bargeboards (the original design, never realized, was for curly
Dutch gables). Exceedingly fine leadwork, surprisingly with
Tudor motifs, e.g. a rose under a crown, vine leaves, pomegranates, which must mean the castings were made from
earlier matrices. Each house was L-plan, with the main rooms
in the principal range along the street and kitchens, etc. in a
wing projecting at the back. The plan of each house also
mirrored that of its neighbour, and seems to have been very
experimental in character. At ground floor, r. and l. of the
party wall, was a 'Great Parlour', then the entrance hall with
stair-turret behind, which could be accessed also from the
parlour. A corridor to the service wing also led to a 'Lesser
Parlour' (an early example of a purpose-built dining room) in
the angle between the main range and the service wing, with
an adjacent pantry taken out of a corner of the entrance hall.
Further along the passage was a service stair. Of the bedrooms,
that over the entrance hall also had a closet over the porch.
Small-square panelling in several ground-floor rooms of a type
decidedly old-fashioned for the 1660s. Also some early C17
chimneypieces. The hall of No. 7 boasts three, two probably
salvaged from Nos. 2 and 11 The Close, demolished in the mid
C19. The main stairs (replaced in No. 6, whose stair-turret has
vanished) had flat balusters similar to those leading to the
Cathedral Library. All had built-in presses and cupboards, of
which a few survive. Between the stair-turrets of the N pair is
an addition of 1683. Two of these rooms are traditionally associated with Izaak Walton, whose son-in-law, Canon Hawkins,
occupied No 8; Walton died here in 1683.

Contemporary with the houses in Dome Alley is No. 9 The
Close (Cathedral Office), also with three straight gables to
front and back. But it is of stone and was built for Canon
Lewis, who had lived in an earlier stone house on this site
before the Commonwealth. It is possible that parts of its w
front survived, for this side has mullion-and-transom windows
that look early C17. The other windows are C18 and much
refacing must have occurred; s wing probably early C19, late
C19 Portland stone porch. Inside, the staircase, with three
balusters to the tread, is C19 in the style of *c.* 1700.

The next house (No. 10a) was rebuilt in 1804–5 of recycled
stone, with tall first-floor sashes; further additions were made
on the N side in the 1820s and again *c.* 1918 (entrance pentice
by Norman Nisbett). But C13 features are apparent at the rear,
and inside are remains of the springing of a rib-vault, showing
that it had a vaulted undercroft. The medieval building was

adjacent to the Romanesque refectory on the s side of the cloister, and documentary and archaeological evidence suggests
that 10a originally housed the priory kitchen, unusually a first-
floor structure. Then the building line steps back; much more
medieval work survives in No. 10 (a single canonry house with
10a from 1539 to 1972). It too was refronted in 1804–5 but was
originally part of the cellarer's range along the w side of the
Great Cloister. It retains an undercroft of three bays and two
aisles, with single-chamfered ribs springing from half-round
wall-shafts and circular piers of coursed masonry; the moulding of their Purbeck abaci suggests a date of *c.* 1225–50. The
piers have suffered greatly from subsidence, the N pier having
sunk vertically by over a foot. In the undercroft, a pair of C13
carved STONE TRESTLES. Very unusual, they have probably
always been in this room. In the exterior s wall of No. 10 is the
head of a blocked C13 window, with a C15 cusped sexfoil light
above, introduced when the roof was rebuilt in 1435–6 (it was
rebuilt again at the Reformation). The first-floor room, originally open to the roof, was probably the Hordarian's chamber,
mentioned in several medieval documents. The Hordarian, in
charge of provisions for the kitchen, was one of the monastic
officials ('obedientiaries') who by the C13 were provided with
their own suites of rooms – far from the Benedictine ethic. His
chamber was accessed by an external stone stair on the E side
(demolished in 1797). A second floor was inserted into the
open chamber at the Reformation, and cutting across the
earlier window is an early C17 six-lighter, probably attributable
to Canon Barlow (1611–31), who introduced the fine panelling
and Jacobean overmantel to the room behind.

No. 11 lies further back at the NW corner of the cloister. It
was completed in 1665, again succeeding an earlier house. The
E façade was completely refaced in the C18. Central bay under
a segmental pediment, flanked by brick half-pilasters (cf. No.
4). Double-pile plan, originally with four rooms on each floor;
the N wing is early C18. The great delight is a staircase with
lush open foliate decoration. It is so similar in style to *Edward
Pearce*'s College Chapel communion rail (and that of the cathedral) that if it is mid-1660s it is early indeed.

Finally, No. 1, lying on its own near the E end of the cathedral, approached through the slype. From the w this appears
as a broad, U-shaped building of chequer brick, with hipped
roofs. The N wing is dated 1699 and was added to a pre-existing house, of which only the stone s wall survives, the rest being
replaced in 1727; the E façade with its pedimented centrepiece
and s wing are of this period. Between the wings, a porch of
the 1850s, when this became the entrance front. It was adorned
with sgraffito work by *Heywood Sumner* (son of Mary, who
founded the Mothers' Union and lived here with her husband,
the Archdeacon of Winchester) including a lurid depiction of
Judith and Holofernes. This was too much for subsequent
inhabitants, who had it whitewashed (cf. St Paul's church).

Less controversial, Sumner's *sgraffito* drawing of 'Flora', surviving in a conservatory on the N side of the house.

The Outer Close

The OUTER CLOSE lies N of the cathedral. This was the site of the Old and New Minsters (*see* pp. 564–5) to the N of the cathedral, and to the W side of the Outer Close was the site of the Anglo-Saxon and Norman palaces. The Outer Close served as the town cemetery until 1848. In 1885–6 Dean Kitchin landscaped it, reducing the ground beside the nave by several feet and removing many of the gravestones. The area is bounded by Great Minster Street (W), The Square (N), and Paternoster Row (E). The buildings in these streets are less closely or not at all connected with the cathedral and are described in the perambulations.

Outside the cathedral's W front, the VISITOR CENTRE offices and SHOP, formed in a C16/C17 coachhouse formerly belonging to No. 11 The Close (*see* above). Until the Reformation this had been the site of the charnel chapel of St Mary in the Cemetery. Originally Romanesque, but substantially rebuilt in the C14: part of the N wall survives above ground level; three bays defined by the scars of vanished buttresses, built in flint with Caen buttresses, quoins, and moulded plinth. Two-centred doorway in the central bay, leading down to the crypt, still partly preserved, which was lit by a low window in the W bay, beneath a deep hoodmould. Another blocked window in the E bay lit the chapel. Excavation of the crypt floor in 1991 revealed a Roman pavement 12 ft (3.7 metres) below the present ground level. Until *c.* 1300 the graveyard extended well to the s including the area partly covered by the cathedral REFECTORY of 1991–3 by *Plincke, Leaman & Browning*. A single-storey, bold, geometric design in steel and glass (engineers, *Anthony Ward Partnership*), with a triple-gabled roof projecting forward over the courtyard and supported inside by tree-like tubular stanchions. W extension in 1999 by *Architecture plb*, a transparent pavilion permitting views of the flint and rubble Close Wall behind.

In front of the cathedral, the county WAR MEMORIAL. Stone cross on a stone-flagged terrace by *Sir Herbert Baker*, 1921. Also the KING'S ROYAL RIFLE CORPS MEMORIAL by *John Tweed*, 1922, with a bronze soldier. A few GRAVESTONES survive, including the famous headstone (renewed 1966) of Thomas Thetcher †1764, a grenadier in the Hampshire Militia who died of fever contracted 'by drinking small beer when hot'; a verse admonition warns against his fate. – SCULPTURE. At the entrance to the Outer Close from The Square, interactive light column Luminous Motion by *Peter Freeman* (2002). The colour patterns may be changed by text message.

WOLVESEY
College Walk

Wolvesey ('Wulf's Island) is the site of the bishop's palace and
has been since the late C10. The site, 370 yds SE of the Saxon
cathedral, was bounded on the E and S by the Roman wall lines,
Æthelwold's new wall to the W, and a boundary with
Nunnaminster to the N. The medieval ruins lie N of the present
episcopal residence. Of the standing remains, which are
arranged around a grassy courtyard, the earliest is the so-called
'WEST HALL', probably of the time of Bishop Giffard
(1107–29), actually a suite of private apartments for the bishop
and his entourage, together with his treasury, exchequer, and
other offices. Its S end has been largely demolished but at its
full extent was one of the largest domestic buildings of its day,
entirely faced in narrowly jointed Quarr stone with fine diagonal tooling, comparable to that of the rebuilt cathedral tower.
The walls were articulated by broad pilaster-buttresses, visible
at the N end. The ground storey was at two levels: on the E side
the 'cellars' were originally ground-floor service rooms. (At the
S end, fictive archaeological stratigraphy gives an idea of the
amount of subsequent build-up.) The main rooms were raised
up on chalk infill laid between the grid of partition walls, either
as an expression of prestige or to guard against floods. At the
SE corner of this range Bishop Henry of Blois (1129–71) added
a CHAPEL (its substructure survives below the present chapel)
and a PORCH at the N end. The latter is now represented only
by excavated footings and a few courses of walling on the N
side, showing that it was entirely built of Caen stone; an exquisitely carved jamb and other sculptural fragments are now in
the City Museum.

The hall of the Anglo-Saxon palace (of which only vestiges
have been excavated) may have remained in use until Bishop
Henry built the EAST HALL in the mid 1130s on the opposite
side of the court. The *Winchester Annals* for 1138 describe a
'house resembling a palace'. It comprised an audience hall with
an integral chamber block at the S end, now represented only
by the footings of the internal partitions. A continuous gallery
ran along the W side. The N and S gable walls survive to their
full height and, like most of the later buildings, are of flint with
Quarr stone dressings (often replaced by tile, a device initiated
by *W. D. Caröe* and repeated in later conservation work). A
bull-nosed string course marks the point where Bishop Henry
subsequently added another storey, with a higher clerestory
and wall passage. At this stage a blind arcade supported on tall
shafts was added to the N (and presumably also the S) wall, in
order to support the thick wall of upper storey; some of the
carved decoration of the arches survives. Prof. Biddle dates
these changes to before Henry's exile in 1154–8.

At the start of the conflict between Stephen and Matilda,
i.e. *c.* 1138–41, the residence was fortified by construction of

a moat and curtain walls to N and S. Of this phase also is a
LATRINE BLOCK at the N end of the WEST HALL. Its design
betrays Bishop Henry's monastic background: this is a secular
version of a reredorter, served by a watercourse that Giffard
had first brought to the palace. Next was built the square, keep-
like tower on the E side of Bishop Henry's hall, perhaps
c. 1141–8. It was the palace kitchen, but lit by narrow splayed
loops, heightening the martial effect. Flint and rubble, including reused masonry perhaps from the old royal palace, with
stone dressings: on the exterior of the W wall is a band of stone
shafts used as walling. The SE TOWER (Wymond's Tower) had
its origins in a latrine, whose walls were greatly thickened. The
S curtain wall abutted the corner of this tower, providing a
small entrance court S of the E Hall. Finally, following his
return from exile at Cluny in 1158, Henry built WOODMAN'S
GATE, the main entrance to the palace, on the N side of the
court between the E and W halls. The E Hall was altered in the
C13 when its W wall was replaced by an arcade opening into
the former W gallery, forming a single-aisled hall. Extensive
renovations were done under William of Wykeham and his
successors, but the palace fell into decline after the most
spectacular event of the later Middle Ages, the marriage of
Mary Tudor and Philip of Spain in 1554.

WOLVESEY PALACE, to the S, is the new residence begun   71
for Bishop Morley (1662–84) after an attempt to renovate the
medieval buildings. The designer was not Wren, as implied in
that architect's grandson's *Parentalia*, but the leading London
master bricklayer *Sir Thomas Fitch*, and work continued on
the house into the early C18. Its principal front was to the S,
of eleven bays, with a projecting central three-bay frontispiece
under a triangular pediment. There were wings to E and W, set
back from the S front, but only the eleven-bay W wing survived
reconstruction in 1786 by *Sir Robert Taylor*, who demolished
the E wing and all but one bay of the S front. The house is faced
in ashlar, evidently reused, with rusticated quoins, tall wooden
cross-windows, each with a curved hood, hipped roofs, carved
modillions, and dormers: all strongly reminiscent of Felbrigg

W. Cave del. Winton   I. Taylor sculp.t

A View of the Episcopal Palace of Winchester

Winchester, Wolvesey Palace, south front.
Engraving after William Cave, 1773

Hall, Norfolk (*William Samwell*, 1675). The doorway on the w front has a segmental, almost semicircular broken pediment, on rather rustic Ionic pilasters with tall pulvinated capitals. The arms are of Sir Jonathan Trelawny (Bishop of Winchester, 1706–21), so it is probable that he completed this wing. On the e front there are five bays between the medieval chapel (*see* below), which Fitch retained, and the stump of the s front, whose new e wall incorporated reused windows from the demolished portions. Inside, the passage through the main range and the bishop's study both have fielded panels with bold 1680s mouldings, but most of the rooms have early c18 unfielded panels with simpler quadrant mouldings. Some bolection-moulded fireplaces may belong to the first phase. The two staircases are *c.* 1720, with broad handrails and slender turned balusters on a moulded string; that in the inner hall (possibly already remodelled in a new position) has been extended up to the attic in the same style. In the dining room, an elaborate carved overmantel (not necessarily designed as such), late c16 and therefore presumably reused, with biblical scenes: Adam and Eve, Abraham and Izaac, the Annunciation, Nativity, Resurrection. The interior was, however, extensively refurbished by *W. D. Caröe* in 1927–8, when the bishops of Winchester returned to the palace after a long absence at Farnham Castle.

The CHAPEL is probably mid-c15 but raised up on the infilled remains of a c12 lower room, perhaps originally a lower chapel. Five-light e window, three three-light s windows. The tracery is of a Perp design but with a notable absence of cusping and it must have been replaced in 1671–4, when Morley spent a considerable sum on the chapel, during his attempts to refurbish the medieval buildings. The entrance was at the w end until 1927–8 when Caröe extended the main range of the house N and created a passage in this position. He built the outshot on the s side of the chapel containing a stair to a new entrance (matching the original), and at the head of this stair is an excellent classical arch to a landing, which is lit by a two-light mullioned window with elegant internal brackets to the lintel (the other window to the stair is c17, recycled and shortened). All this detailing was designed by *John Summerson*, then a young architect in Caröe's practice. The chapel is a large and lofty room, the fittings mostly of 1671 including the black-and-white pavement. – W SCREEN, similar to that at Farnham Castle attributed to Webb, with a central pair of panelled doors (redundant since 1928) surrounded by a lugged architrave and triangular pediment; the entrance is flanked by pairs of round-headed lights separated by panelled pilasters. Above an entablature is the front of the gallery, also panelled with pilasters, terminating in a neatly carved cornice. – BOX STALLS with moulded unfielded panelling and simple benches. – ALTAR RAIL, 1680s, with chunky turned balusters and square, panelled newels. The CEILING is by *Caröe*, the decorative scheme of 1993–4, including sanctuary furniture by *Paul Watson*.

– SCULPTURE by *Peter Eugene Ball*, 2006. – CHANDELIER. A fine piece, dated 1709, by *Samuel Smith* of London (Robert Sherlock); originally from Holy Trinity, Dorchester. – STAINED GLASS. E window by *Christopher Webb*, 1933.

STABLES, SW of the house. By Bishop Trelawny, *c.* 1710. Strictly symmetrical façade in two storeys, reused ashlar facing, hipped tiled roof. The central bays, containing two coachhouse doors with *anse-de-panier* arches, project forward under a wide pediment containing an oculus. The bishop enjoys a private way to the cathedral via the Water Close. Over the door a datestone, 1670.

CHURCHES* AND CEMETERIES

ALL SAINTS, Petersfield Road, Highcliffe. By *J. L. Pearson*, designed 1885–9, built in stages 1889–97. All for £5,000. It is not among his memorable churches. Flint and brick. Four-bay nave with equal N aisle. Two W gables. Lancets (the nave W window a graduated group of five), plate and bar tracery. In the chancel high lancets; the E window a triplet, placed very high up. The SE tower was never built. Chancel arch and arcade of local clunch. Arch-braced collar roofs with tie-beams. – FONT. From St Peter Chesil, Late Norman, of the Purbeck table-top type. With shallow blank arches. – ROYAL ARMS of George II, of 1730 from the same source. – STAINED GLASS. Nave S, one good window by *Powells*, 1893, to the Rev. Barr †1891 who built the church. Successfully architectonic with panels of the Acts of Mercy in grisaille pattern surrounds.

CHRIST CHURCH, Christ Church Road. 1859–61 by *Ewan Christian*. Quite large and serious High Victorian E.E. Prominent SE tower and stone broach spire, completed in 1904, and polygonal apse. Wide interior, reordered in 1995–7. Low round piers of Devonshire marble with naturalistic capitals, cinquefoiled clerestory and large W window with plate tracery. – STAINED GLASS in the apse, colourful with symbols and geometric patterns. Possibly by *Heaton, Butler & Bayne*.

Large NE vestry, of 1906 by *Colson, Farrow & Nisbett*, and CHURCH CENTRE, extended with a top-lit ambulatory along the N side of the church by *Sawyer Architects*.

HOLY TRINITY, North Walls. 1851–4 by *Woodyer*, an important early work, i.e. Early Victorian rather than High Victorian and in the Early Dec style favoured by the Ecclesiologists. Flint and stone, the latter of reused architectural fragments dating from C12–C16, presumably from Hyde Abbey. Aisled and clerestoried nave and chancel in one. Slender flèche over the E end of the nave. Big E and W windows. Low W porch and SE vestry of 1894, the latter by *Woodyer*. Airy interior with continuous seven-bay arcades, whose arches die into broaches above the

*The church entries have been revised by Rodney Hubbuck.

CHILBOLTON AVENUE

N

STOCKBRIDGE ROAD

HATHERLEY ROAD

FAIRFIELD ROAD

CLERTON ROAD

O

ANDOVER ROAD

WORTHY LANE

HYDE STREET

4 +

HYDE CLOSE

KING ALFRED PLACE

9 +

H

14 +

CITY ROAD

MILVERTON ROAD

GREENHILL ROAD

WEST END TERRACE

ST PAUL'S HILL

CLIFTON TERRACE

UPPER HIGH

SUSSEX STREET

TOWER STREET

STAPLE GARDENS

G

11 +

JEWRY STREET

ST PETER STREET

Orams Arbour

STEP TER.

CLIFTON HILL

A

15 +

ST GEORGE'S

K

STREET

HIGH STREET

C

THE SQUARE

ROMSEY ROAD

D

E

TRAFALGAR ST.

ST CLEMENT ST.

SOUTHGATE STREET

ST THOMAS STREET

LITTLE MINSTER ST.

SYMONDS ST.

GT. MINSTER ST.

Castle Hall and Peninsula Square

13 +

F

ST JAMES' LANE

ST SWITHUN STREET

12 +

SPARKFORD ROAD

CANON STREET

2 +

L

ST MICHAEL'S ROAD

CLIFER ROAD

8 +

KINGSGATE STREET

ROMANS ROAD

SLEEPERS HILL

AIRLIE ROAD

CHRISTCHURCH ROAD

ST CROSS ROAD

NORMAN RD.

KINGSGATE ROAD

Ridding Meads

7 +

GREEN JACKET CLOSE

STANMORE LANE

GARNIER ROAD

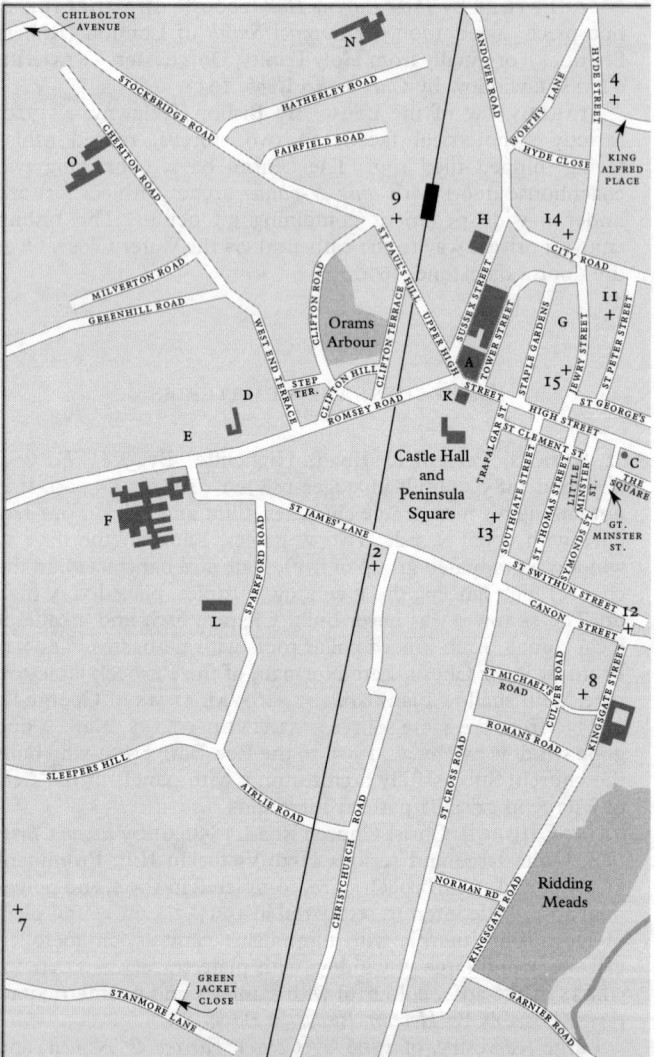

A   Elizabeth II Court (County Hall)
B   Guildhall (City Council)
C   Butter Cross
D   County Police Headquarters
E   Winchester Community Prison
F   Royal Hampshire County Hospital
G   Winchester Discovery Centre (library etc.)
H   County Record Office
J   City Museum
K   Westgate (museum)
L   University of Winchester
M   Winchester School of Art
N   Peter Symonds College
O   Westgate School

Winchester

River Itchen

North Walls
Recreation
Ground

N

M

NORTH WALLS
PARCHMENT ST.
UPPER BROOK ST.
MIDDLE BROOK ST.
LWR BROOK ST.
+ 3
FRIARSGATE

BLUE BALL ST.
5 +
ST PETER ST.
ST JOHN'S STREET
M°GDALEN HILL
ALRESFORD ROAD

ST.
HIGH STREET
+ 6
MARKET LA.
B
THE BROADWAY
ABBEY PASSAGE
EAS'GATE
BRIDGE ST.
CHESIL STREET
BARING ROAD
St Giles's
Hill

COLEBROOK STREET
J
Winchester
Cathedral
+ 10

STRATTON ROAD

Wolvesey
Palace
QUARRY ROAD

COLLEGE ST.
WHARF HILL
EAST HILL
CANUTE ROAD
+ 1

Winchester
College
COLLEGE WALK

St John's
Winchester Charity

1000 m
1000 yds

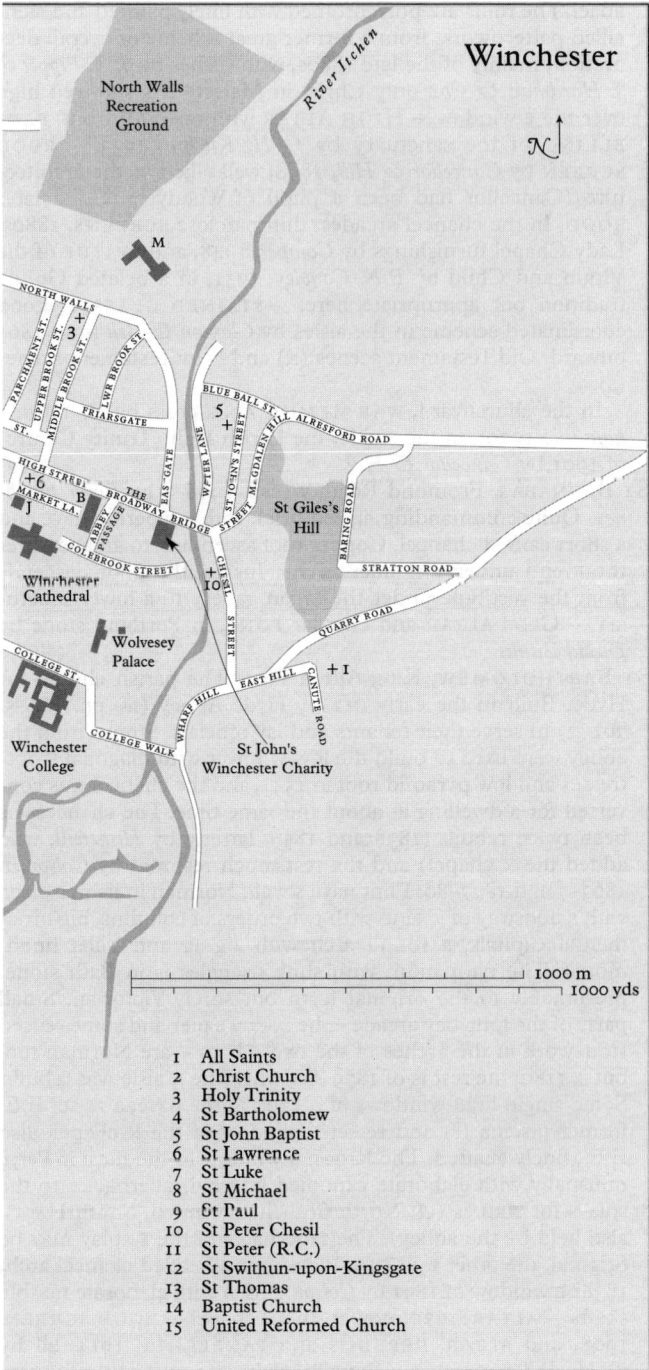

1   All Saints
2   Christ Church
3   Holy Trinity
4   St Bartholomew
5   St John Baptist
6   St Lawrence
7   St Luke
8   St Michael
9   St Paul
10 St Peter Chesil
11 St Peter (R.C.)
12 St Swithun-upon-Kingsgate
13 St Thomas
14 Baptist Church
15 United Reformed Church

abaci. The roofs are polychromed with finely painted and sten-
cilled patternwork, from a former great scheme of overall dec-
oration, mainly of the late 1880s, with scenes by *J. A. Pippet* of
J. Hardman & Co.: only Christ in Majesty has survived high
over the E window. – HIGH ALTAR with open (?) front. PAN-
ELLING of the sanctuary by *G. H. Kitchin*, 1933. – ROOD
SCREEN by *Cancellor & Hill*, 1898, well allied to the architecture (Cancellor had been a pupil of Woodyer). Good later
ROOD. In the chancel arcades, thin parclose SCREENS, 1880s.
Lady Chapel furnishings by *Comper*, 1948, and STATUE of the
Virgin and Child by *P. N. Conoley*, 1951, in a belated Gothic
tradition but appropriate here. – STAINED GLASS. A good
coordinated scheme in the aisles by *Clayton & Bell* from 1865
onward. Old Testament scenes (N) and New Testament scenes
(S).

In the churchyard, WAR MEMORIAL, a cross by *Paul Waterhouse*, c. 1920; on the S side, the Parish Hall (Trinity Centre)
of 1901 by *Cancellor & Hill*.

ST BARNABAS, Fromond Road, Weeke. 1966–7 by *Roger Pinckney*. Quite commanding, in red brick with a tapering nave and
a short canted chancel. Copper roof ascending to an apex over
the E end under a slender flèche. Inside, the floor descends
from the vestibule under the organ gallery to a lower sanctuary. – Good ALTAR and circular FONT, in Portland stone by
David Banks.

ST BARTHOLOMEW, King Alfred Place. The parish church for
Hyde. Built in the early C12 by Hyde Abbey (*see* pp. 564–5,
701–2) to serve their tenants and lay officials. Stones from the
abbey were used to build the low W tower with diagonal E buttresses and low pyramid roof in 1541, and the chancel was converted for a dwelling at about the same time. The chancel has
been twice rebuilt (1838 and 1859, latterly by *Hakewill*, who
added the N chapel) and the rest much restored by *Colson* in
1863–7 and 1877–80. Flint nave S wall, Norman in its masonry,
with S doorway of *c*. 1130 with two orders of columns, big ornamental capitals, a round arch with zigzag and billet hoodmould. The tympanum with sunk triangles is in Bath stone,
presumably to the original form but surely Victorian. Small
parts of the four-bay arcade – the *in-situ* E pier and some reused
stonework in the arches of the two E bays – are Norman too,
but *c*. 1180; the rest is of 1879–80, when the N aisle was rebuilt.
Some single-light windows of *c*. 1300 in the nave, a re-set E.E.
former piscina (?) and re-set E window of the N chapel, also
E.E., finely shafted. The largest S window of the nave is Perp,
unusually with elaborate canopied internal tabernacles to the
splays for statues (cf. North Stoneham church, South Hants,
also held by the abbey). The tabernacle of the E splay may be
original, the other mid-C19. Plain round-headed chancel arch,
1838? E window of 1891 by *Colson & Son* with elaborate marble
shafts. – ALTAR, 1620, now in the N chapel. – ROOD SCREEN,
1908, and ALTAR, REREDOS and PANELLING, 1914, all by
G. H. Fellowes-Prynne. Equally elaborate PULPIT of 1910.
LECTERN of 1946 by *T. D. Atkinson*, with carved foliate panels

on three sides of the book-rest. – ARCHITECTURAL FRAG-
MENTS from Hyde Abbey. They are to be dated *c.* 1130 and   II
come in all probability from the cloister. There are five capitals, the best those with animals or symmetrical foliage trails
in roundels. Other, possibly related, capitals to be relocated to
the City Museum. Also a springer stone with zigzag, leaf and
pellets. In the porch, a composite stoup, of a shaft and bowl
formed of an imported C12 capital. – STAINED GLASS. E
window by *Clayton & Bell*, 1894. Two tiers of scenes in the
firm's usual Perp canopy-work. Also by them, the larger Perp
window in the nave (†1873). N chapel E and N transept
windows, possibly by *A. Gibbs*. Typical of the 1860s with their
bright colours. – Nave S, third from E. By *J. E. Nuttgens*, 1948.
King Alfred, in a belated Arts and Crafts tradition.

ST JOHN THE BAPTIST, St John's Street. A church is mentioned
just before 1142, when Jocelin de Bohun, Archdeacon of
Winchester, gave the advowson with that of St Peter Chesil to
the prior and canons of St Denys's Priory near Southampton.
To this single cell N and S aisles were added *c.* 1179–89. There
are remains of a contemporary N aisle W window with traces
of fictive painted masonry on the splays. It is close to the arcade
and thus indicates the narrowness of the original aisle. The
arcades are of three bays with round piers, trumpet scallop
(just one) or its reverse, i.e. concave-fluted capital and pointed
arches. S arcade arches restored in 1884. The E view of the
church along the street is three-gabled. The N aisle had been
widened by the early C13: see the two narrow lancets, now
blocked (externally) in the N wall and the base of another
below the Perp W window, with excellent contemporary WALL
PAINTINGS on the splays of figures of St John, St Peter, St
Anthony and the Devil. The full scheme, recorded by Baigent,
was destroyed in 1854. The S aisle was also enlarged to the same
ambitions, possibly *c.* 1260 on the evidence of the spectacular
window of its S chapel. It is of four lights with bold Geometrical tracery, with three bar-tracery circles, two quatrefoil, the
large top one sept-foiled. Good mouldings inside. The other
windows are Early Perp, mostly three lights but of three different types. They are perhaps contemporary with the stout
battlemented SW tower. It originally doubled as a porch (see
the small Perp doorway inside with a fine corbel head of a
bearded king) and has a sturdy arch to the S aisle, with continuous mouldings of strong wavy profiles. These works are
possibly late C14, perhaps 1382–5 when the church was used
as a temporary chapel for the scholars of Bishop Wykeham's
College. Might *Wynford*, whose son was one of the first pupils,
have provided designs for the windows and arch? Also Perp,
the roofs with crown-posts. Next to the S window is the early
C16 rood stair-turret. Its entrance is from the E and doors
inside, now blocked, gave access to lofts on the existing
screens.

Interior reordered and restored in 2006 by *Daniel Forshaw*,
when the Perp N aisle N doorway was reopened (traces of a
contemporary painted line 'surround'), C19 pews removed and

floors re-paved. – FONT. Octagonal Perp with quatrefoils (cf.
Crawley). – NICHE, in the chancel, evidently mid-C16. Identical to that in St Swithun-upon-Kingsgate. Both with the
Diocesan armorial. – REREDOS (s chapel). 1876, relic of an
elaborate lost scheme of decoration in the chancel which
included the mosaic floor. – PULPIT. Perp of wood, with
cinquefoil-headed panels, and buttress-shafts at the angles.
The earlier door a reused C14 bench-end. – Between the
chancel and chapels, C14 PARCLOSE SCREENS. Slender shafts
with shaft-rings instead of muntins and cusped ogee arches
and cusped open spandrels. Some mid-C19 restoration of the
shafts. Unusually, the s screen retains a contemporary attached
stall-end. – ROOD SCREEN, extending across the church. Perp,
of one-light divisions with traceried heads, the centre with a
richly cusped arch and traceried panelling (restored by *G. H.
Kitchin*, 1925). The dado to the N aisle section has tiny quatrefoil openings, possibly spyholes for children at mass. ROOD.
Early C20. – BENCH-ENDS. Two poppyheads and tracery
worked in 1925 into the priests' stall by *G. H. Kitchin*, 1925. –
CHANDELIER. Brought in. *c.* 1700, attributed to *Robert
Rowland* of London, or his son (R. Sherlock). – SCULPTURE.
In the Perp canopied image niche outside, a figure of St John
the Baptist as a boy, after Donatello, by *Blackwell & Moody*,
1973. – STAINED GLASS. In the s aisle E window tracery lights,
attractively kaleidoscopic late C14 or C15 fragments. Chancel
E, s aisle E and N chapel N of *c.* 1885 by *Clayton & Bell*. Also
theirs, the s aisle s window appropriately in late C13 style successfully related to the tracery. – MONUMENTS. In the N
chapel, a panelled tomb-chest with shields bearing the
emblems of the passion. No doubt indicating a former Easter
sepulchre. Several minor C18 tablets, four of them from St
Martin, Winnall (dem. 1973). – Mary Stevens †1763, with
interesting reference to her husband Lewis Stevens, 'late of ye
Island of St Christopher', i.e. St Kitts in the West Indies. Was
Stevens a returnee sugar trader or plantation owner? – Robert
Leversuch †1776, mason. Simple classical tablet. – William
Moss †1790, with conventional inscription including 'religious
without enthusiasm'.

ST LAWRENCE, The Square/High Street. Probably of Norman
origin; the N wall may be part of the outer wall of the royal
palace of 1069–70. Little is visible outside except for the C15
W tower, for the church is closely confined by buildings on all
sides (part of a C13 N doorway can be seen inside a shop on
High Street). W doorway of continuous mouldings and two-
light window above with good tracery. The uppermost stage
looks later, rendered with ashlar battlements. Higher SW stair-
turret. Simple open interior, just an irregular rectangle, 32 ft
(10 metres) wide, under a broad roof (perhaps of *c.* 1662–72
when the church was restored, having been used as a school
during the Commonwealth). Perhaps the s wall formed part
of a lost s aisle to which the skewed w tower was later attached.
Five-light Perp E window of 1475. Restorations of 1847–8 by

J. Colson Sen., 1881 by *Stopher*, and 1979–80 by *Richard Sawyer*; the last, after a fire, has left a rather spruce and over-tidy impression. – Handsome Neo-Jacobean PANELLING against the s wall. – STAINED GLASS. E window by *O'Connor*, 1848, Good Shepherd amid grisaille quarries with two small panels added from the W window (also by *O'Connor*). – S window by *Powells*, 1898; four bishops of Winchester. MONUMENTS. A few small C18 tablets at the W end.

ST LUKE, Battery Hill and Mildmay Street, Stanmore. 1960–2 by *Cecil Evans*. Hard-edged minimalist Gothic. – FONT. A white marble baluster, of *c.* 1730–40, originally given to Stinsford church, Dorset (Thomas Hardy was baptized in it).

ST MATTHEW, Stockbridge Road, Weeke. The village church of Weeke, subsumed in leafy suburbia. Low rendered exterior with Early Norman nave (s doorway of *c.* 1100–25 and single-light N window), lower possibly E.E. chancel, weatherboarded bell-turret, and flint NE vestry by *Owen Browne Carter* (p. 562). Most windows are C17. Pointed chancel arch with slight chamfers, C13. The nave roof, two-and-a-half bays with wind-braces, is late C15, possibly *c.* 1493 when the church was re-dedicated and made parochial. – REREDOS with traceried panels carved by the *Rev. John Barton*. – TILES. A few, of the C14, below the chancel arch. – STAINED GLASS. C15 Fragments in the E window, mostly quarries, with much restoration by *Castell*. Of the Evangelist's emblems in roundels, only that of St Luke is old. Vestry windows by *O'Connor*. Colourful angels of the Resurrection. – BRASS. William Complyn †1498 and wife. No effigy, but a tiny St Christopher, 8½ in. (22 cm.) high above an inscription recording the gift of the great bell. – MONUMENTS. William Blake †1729. Accomplished classical tablet, also in memory of his wife, daughter of Sir Hugh Stewkely. Rev. Edward Nott †1842. A Dec recessed wall tomb in the vestry. No doubt by *Owen Browne Carter*.

ST MAURICE. *See* p. 675.

ST MICHAEL, St Michael's Passage off Kingsgate Street. A curious building of Saxon origin (see the pre-Conquest sundial in the s wall), first mentioned in the Winchester *Sacramentary* as one of the churches employed for funerals of monks of the Priory. Externally it is now nearly all *Butterfield*, 1879–82. But the low medieval W tower is fully preserved: its lower stage possibly C13 (W window of two lancets within a retaining arch), with C14 buttresses and an arch of two continuous chamfered orders inside. The upper stage is Perp, restored in 1582 (the date was recorded over the window in 1818) with a tiled cap, like St Bartholomew and St Peter Chesil. Butterfield found a church of nave with N aisle, but the Perp N arcade removed in 1822 to create the wide area the Late Georgian churchmen demanded. The tower thus was entirely out of true. Butterfield kept the wide area but had intended to rebuild the N arcade. In the event, only the E respond was built and the nave still retains the shallow coved plaster ceiling of *Henry Carey Brown*'s 1822 evangelical reordering. *Butterfield*'s chancel has a flint

and stone checkered E gable and, inside, a barrel ceiling with
cusped arch braces. – Tile REREDOS with a large cross. Chancel
floor of red and yellow tiles, low CHOIR STALLS. – PULPIT by
G. H. Kitchin, 1908, with central figure of St Michael. In the
nave, FONT, late C15. – STAINED GLASS. W window of 1822;
in the E window, intricate work by *Lavers, Barraud & Westlake*.
MONUMENTS. Quite an array of minor late C17–early C19
mural tablets. Beeston family, 1660–85, children of Henry
Beeston, Headmaster of Winchester College and, from 1679,
Warden of New College Oxford. Hanging tablet with an oval
cartouche and a row of small skulls, possibly by Oxford
masons. James Rivers †1807. By *Reeves & Son*, Bath.

ST PAUL, St Paul's Hill. By *J. Colson Sen*. the chancel (1872) nave
and transepts (1889); aisles of 1902 and 1910 by *Colson &
Nisbett*. All of flint, no tower. Broad nave and aisles. The S aisle
is very wide. The style is a correct, rather dry Middle Pointed.
Geometrical tracery. The chancel had sgraffito WALL PAINT-
INGS of 1903–4 by *Heywood Sumner*, disgracefully whitened
over in 1962, although a fragment is now revealed on the S wall.
– LECTERN. A large brass eagle from St Thomas. – PULPIT.
Probably of 1872. Elaborate Flamboyant Gothic traceried
panels (cf. St Matthew, Weeke, reredos carved by the *Rev. John
Barton*, incumbent of both churches). – STAINED GLASS. S
chapel S, of 1907 by *Powells*. Chancel E, of 1949, again by
Powells, and above average with a band of scenes in clear
settings.

ST PETER CHESIL, Chesil Street. Closed 1949 and converted to
a theatre in 1963. The church lies along the street between
houses but may originally have been free-standing in the
highway. It is first mentioned in the Winton Domesday (1148)
as procured by St Denys's Priory (near Southampton, cf. St
John). The nave and chancel in one is probably of early C12
origin, with a narrower S aisle of equal length of *c.* 1200–30,
and a low SE flanking tower also early C13, mostly in flint with
a tile-hung timber-framed bell-stage and pyramid roof. By the
C13, the church may have had two aisles, see the N doorway of
two chamfered orders. If so, the N aisle must have been taken
into the nave, which is unusually wide, or taken down to
provide room for the neighbouring house (The Soke), built
c. 1609; a new table and pulpit were also made for the church
in 1607. In the tower, an interesting two-light square-headed
E window with an external E.E. shaft. W windows both Dec,
that of the nave with reticulated tracery. Vestry added to the S
aisle in 1908. Adaptation of the church to its present use preserved the interior, despite partition of the S aisle. Prominent
three-bay S arcade of chalk (round piers, round abaci, arches
with two slight chamfers), and broad mid-C14 nave roof with
round-arched collar-braces, of a local type (cf. Owslebury,
South Hants). In the S aisle, a C13 roof with big cambered principals and strutted kingposts, very roughly repaired in 1895.
Wall-plates supported by good E.E. corbels. (In the tower,
massive C14 timber framework for the lost bells. The bracketed

lower stage visible from the floor.) At the E end of the aisle, two good canopied niches. The earlier one, N of the Perp E window, has exceptionally fine nodding ogee carving of *c.* 1350. The niche on the S wall is of *c.* 1400, clearly from the Wynford workshop, as of a similar pattern to earlier image niches in the gatehouse towers of Winchester College. Nice little lion at the base, alas damaged. Below it a small square PISCINA. In the chancel E wall, toward the S corner, another, much mutilated niche possibly early C16, with imported Renaissance details, possibly by *Thomas Bertie*.

ST PETER (R.C.), Jewry Street. 1924–6 by *F. A. Walters*, succeeding the R.C. chapel nearby (*see* Milner Hall, p. 683). In a richly detailed Late Dec, built of Bargate rubble with Bath stone dressings. Big NE tower with higher pinnacled stair-turret. 'All very reactionary for 1926', thought Pevsner. Set in the N wall, a fine Late Norman doorway of 1174, formerly the W doorway of the church of the Morn Hill leper hospital. Two orders of shafts, trumpet scallop capitals. Arch with rolls. Spacious interior with six-bay arcades. Outer N aisle. Chancel sensitively reordered in 1988 by *James Lunn-Rockliffe* of *Plincke, Leaman & Browning*. – Marble ALTAR, now brought forward, and elaborate stone REREDOS with saints under canopies, carved by *Earp & Hobbs*. – SCULPTURE. A fine C15 Flemish Virgin and Child. – STAINED GLASS. E window of 1926 by *Burlison & Grylls*. Colourful and highly furnished after Van Eyck's altarpiece at St Bavon, Ghent. Outer N aisle (Lady Chapel) by *Goddard & Gibbs*, a series of Catholic martyrs.

ST STEPHEN (R.C.), Oliver's Battery Road, Stanmore. 1969 by *Alan Stewart*. Octagonal with a spirelet.

ST SWITHUN-UPON-KINGSGATE. The church, which sits above the city gate (*see* p. 692), is first mentioned in 1264, held by the Cathedral Priory, and may have served the monastery servants. It now has small and domestic late C15 or early C16 windows and is reached by a charming timber-framed and tile-hung early C16 stairway, with a tiny hutch-like weatherboarded bellcote, as restored by *W. Carpenter Turner* in 1954. The upper doorway, facing into the church, looks of the same date. Simple interior, with a medieval single-framed roof, once divided by a wooden screen with altars on the W side, as shown by evidence of a piscina in the sill of the SE window. Battered minor Perp features: the E window with C14 frame and later tracery. Original niche in the E wall. Another in the N wall, of *c.* 1530–50 with the diocesan achievement. The E and W windows are of three lights, the latter probably renewed in the restoration of 1853 by *Colson*. – FONT. Perp with panelled bowl purposely sunk under a niche within the W wall to save space. – STAINED GLASS. In the E window, three small panels of C15 fragments from St Peter Chesil, one with the golden seraphim. W window of *c.* 1861 by *Powells*, with a central panel of St Mary Magdalen and the Angel of Resurrection. The rest delicate patternwork. Good angels in white draperies on red backgrounds in the tracery – MONUMENTS. On the W wall, from St Maurice.

Children of John Bond M.P. Tablet with inscription and an appropriately tiny brass (dated 1612). The four infants lie together in their shrouds, strangely viewed from a high perspective. – William Widmore †1756. Tapering with an achievement and laudatory inscription. – Nicholas Baconneau †1778. Nice, probably local mason's flat tablet obelisk with oval inscription hanging by gilded ribbons (cf. Cheriton). –William Henry Laverty †1917. Vaguely Arts and Crafts tablet, presumably executed by his father *Edwin Laverty*, from a design by *B. D. Cancellor*.

ST THOMAS AND ST CLEMENT, Southgate Street. Redundant since 1972; now offices. 1845–7 by *E. W. Elmslie* of Malvern, the commanding steeple completed to his design in 1856–7. The builders was *George Myers*, who had built many of Pugin's best buildings. St Thomas is the most ambitious Victorian church in Winchester – the cost was £8,152 with a further £1,800 for the steeple – and it is remarkable that it should be so early, for it is 'archaeological', i.e. no longer uninformed in its Gothic motifs, and their handling. Geometrical tracery, i.e. the Second Pointed which Pugin, Scott and Ferrey and of course the Ecclesiologists were bringing back in those very years. The church makes an impressive show to the street with its three gables of chancel flanked by pinnacled buttresses, and chancel aisles, and the commanding steeple, a s porch-tower with broach spire rising to 180 ft (55 metres). Pinnacles on the broaches; lucarnes. Tall nave with clerestory. The ensemble as well as the details excellent, especially convincing. The s doorway below the steeple has a trumeau loosely modelled on the early C13 w doorway of St Cross. Low SE vestry tactfully enlarged in 1891 by *Stopher*. (The interior was spacious, with much figurative and naturalistic carving. – STAINED GLASS. E window by *William Warrington*, 1857, in a manner that Pevsner would have called *altdeutscher*.) In the s chapel by *Powell*, 1858 (designed by *Lyon*) and 1861 (designed by *Moberley*).

BAPTIST CHURCH, City Road. 1864–5, from a classical design, completed by *Mr Briggs* of the Royal Engineers. Tall pilasters supporting entablatures l. and r. of a blind, round-arched centre. All-inclusive pediment. Lower, later, porch at the side. (Interior altered in 1978.)

UNITED REFORMED CHURCH, Jewry Street, incongruously set within the N parts of the former county gaol (*see* p. 681). 1852–3 by *W. F. Poulton* of Reading in a rather straitened E.E. with prominent lancets. Surprising interior, inventively and sympathetically subdivided horizontally at gallery level in 1989–91 by *Plincke, Leaman & Browning*. Elongated octagon with lanky arcades of steeply pointed arches and a powerful double-hammerbeam roof. – Original Gothic ORGAN CASES *in situ* on the w side. – STAINED GLASS. In the (ritual) E window by *J. Bell* of Bristol. E.E.-style grisaille.

Former PRIMITIVE METHODIST CHURCH, Parchment Street. Essentially of 1903. Thin, First Pointed façade to the street in brick with few redeeming details. The rest in a simpler classical style.

Former WESLEYAN METHODIST CHAPEL, St Peter Street. 1864 by *W. W Pocock*. Geometric Gothic. Quite large-scaled, in flint with stone dressings. The façade with two wide-spaced two-light windows with plate tracery and a surmounting rose window of a coarseness, looking as if stamped out of leather. Twin gabled porches projecting below. Tall, slightly detached pinnacles at the corners. The E wall, crowned by a low chimney, is an anticlimax after the side walls with their serried windows of two lights. (The interior, first converted to offices in 1978, was adapted for housing in 2007.)

SALVATION ARMY HALL, Parchment Street. 1995 by the *Bruce Oldfield Partnership*. Brick, in a friendly, decidedly domestic style.

CHRISTIAN SCIENCE CHURCH, Tower Street. The former St Thomas's National School of 1848 by *J. Colson*.

CITY CHURCH, Jewry Street. *See* Perambulation 3.

ST FAITH'S CEMETERY, Kingsgate Road. The last vestige of St Faith's church, dem. *c.* 1507.

ST JAMES' (R.C.) CEMETERY, Romsey Road. The site of St James' church, which provided a halt for medieval pilgrims passing through Winchester. The church is said to have closed in 1396. The burial ground was established in 1589, when the recusant Nicholas Tichborne was buried here after his death in the city gaol. Neat little four-square LODGE, brick under a slate roof, with mullioned windows, built in 1829 on the initiative of James Farquarson and other 'pious' (i.e. R.C.) citizens. Near the highest point is a small classical MAUSOLEUM to the Constable family. Rendered, rusticated quoins, plain pediment. Another in the NE corner, designed by *G. Garralt* and built in 1833 by Sir Oliver Grace of Mantua House, Co. Roscommon, for his wife Mary Frances (†1826 in Southampton). Rendered stone, with stone slab roof. To the SE, a very overgrown early C19 Neoclassical tomb in Grecian style supporting a plain sarcophagus. Another tomb surrounded by good iron railings has achievements on W side and a kneeling woman at prayer on the E. Near the entrance, John Henry King (†1965), Bishop of Portsmouth 1941–65. Plain, simply lettered, with carved crozier.

ST GILES HILL CEMETERY. On the Alresford Road. Derelict.

WEST HILL CEMETERY. Now redundant. Opened 1840, after burials ceased in the cathedral churchyard. Buildings by *O. B. Carter*; only the Tudor Gothic LODGE survives, with a very correct large Perp window with diamond-shaped label stops. The chapels were demolished in the 1930s.

CASTLE

(including County Council Offices and Law Courts)

The site of the castle, on the high ground at the W end of the city centre, is impressive for Victorian and post-Victorian rather than medieval reasons for, the C13 Great Hall aside, the castle itself is known only from archaeology and building accounts.

It was however the site of the Roman defences and of William the Conqueror's castle, begun early in 1067 when William FitzOsbern was left in charge of the garrison there, and also of a palace chapel (usable by 1072) whose long-and-short quoins suggest Anglo-Saxon builders, and then of an earth motte that was replaced by a square stone keep in the early C12. Of these a little was revealed by excavations in 1962–71. Only from the early C13 do we have a better idea of its layout and of the works undertaken during the minority of Henry III, born here in 1206. The castle was besieged and taken in 1216 by the Dauphin, the future Louis IX of France. Rebuilding was necessary after its recapture the following year. So between 1222 and 1258 the E defences were rebuilt, including the ROUND TOWER (of which remains can be seen) at the NE angle of the castle enclosure, near to the West Gate (*see* pp. 662–3). The Great Hall was also begun in 1222 and complete by 1236. At the same time the royal apartments were remodelled and extended, works in which *Elias of Dereham* may have been involved. The functions of the castle were essentially residential, the treasury and exchequer having settled at Westminster half a century previously. Henry died in 1272 and a fire in 1302 marked the end of royal residence. The Great Hall remained in use as a court and was retained as such by the city after the castle itself had been slighted in the Civil War and its site subsequently offered to Charles II for the building of his royal palace (*see* Barracks, pp. 690–1). The construction of further buildings in the late C19 emphasized the castle's symbolic significance as a centre for legal and county administration.

The approach is along CASTLE AVENUE created in 1895 to supersede Castle Hill, a narrow roadway which climbs steeply from the s side of the West Gate, just inside the line of the city wall. What one mainly sees are the COUNTY OFFICES on both sides. They are of a unified Neo-Tudor character, though differing in details. On the E side most of the Tudoresque long range (Castle Hill offices) is by *James Robinson*, County Surveyor, and *Sir Arthur Blomfield*, 1894. Huge bay window to the Council Chamber, octagonal stair-turret next to the main door. Oriel windows on the E side overlooking the city. At its s end, the corner with Castle Hill incorporates the former Hampshire Friendly Society offices, by *Stopher*, 1875. Opposite, the present Education Office, 1910 by *W. J. Taylor*, County Surveyor, with *T. G. Jackson*. Three storeys, flint and rubble faced, with mullioned-and-transomed windows with arched heads and leaded lights. The façade is framed between wide bays and there are steep gables over the central windows. The range's s end is of 1931–2 by *Sir Herbert Baker* and *A. L. Roberts*, County Architect, in a less exuberant reprise of Jackson's themes, with square-headed rather than arched windows, and gables without finials. The s end projects in a twin-gabled composition with rather small mullioned windows. Round the corner is the former GRAND JURY CHAMBER AND LAW LIBRARY, originally of 1774 by *Thomas*

Whitcombe, County Surveyor, but remodelled (and expanded) in Tudor Gothic by *O. B. Carter*, 1849–52, who refaced it in flint to match the Great Hall. Whitcombe's Grand Jury Room is oak-panelled to dado level, with coats of arms of successive chairmen of quarter sessions on the cornice.

The GREAT HALL, of 1222–36, is the finest (and largest) surviving medieval hall after Westminster. The master mason was called *Stephen*. Stone came from Selborne, the Isle of Wight, Haselbury (near Bath) and Caen. It is a double cube: 111 ft (34 metres) long by 55 ft (17 metres) wide and high, and aisled. Five bays with large two-light windows to N and S with a transom, trefoil-headed lights, and a quatrefoil in plate tracery. (Those of the N front are replicas reinstated in the remodelling of this side in 1843–5 by *O. B. Carter*, who removed Gothick sashes.) Above the windows were originally tall gables enclosing round lights. Probably in 1348–9, when much expenditure is recorded, this arrangement was changed. The gables were removed, the side walls raised, and the aisles re-roofed (introducing a change in pitch); the round lights were re-set as blind internal oculi lower down, between the windows. Evidence for the original design is discernible in the masonry of the S wall: one advantage of the otherwise distressing C19 internal repointing is the way the standing archaeology is so obvious. The central doorway, in the middle of the hall in a totally unmedieval way, dates from 1789 but was rebuilt in its present form in 1845, to a design by Carter's pupil *G. E. Street*. The original doorways were where one would expect to find them, in the (E) end bays at the lower end of the hall. Only the S door survives complete: inside it has one order of shafts, a depressed two-centred arch, and a hoodmould on stiff-leaf stops; externally there are three shafts (mostly replaced) and the arch mouldings are deeply undercut, with keel-moulded rolls to the outer orders. Foliate stops to the hoodmould. This door led to the king's apartments and was set within a porch, shown by external thickening of the wall. Over this was a room, reached from inside the hall by a vice, whose simple entrance, E of the S door, has roll mouldings to the arris and a moulded hood on stiff-leaf stops. Of the N doorway only the remains of the E jamb are visible inside (but straight joints outside show its extent). There is also evidence of smaller service doors at the E end. The dais (W) end has a fine doorway in the NW corner, with Purbeck marble shafts and reveals, and low two-centred Caen stone arch – it probably led to the queen's apartment.

The arcades are of beautiful tall Purbeck piers comprising a core of coursed marble drums with integral shafts on the diagonals, the other shafts detached with barely noticeable shaft-rings. Stout, round moulded plinths, and shallow waterholding bases for the shafts. The abaci are almost round, on bell capitals. Arches of one chamfered inner order, two thin rolls, another chamfer, and a hoodmould. The roof was reconstructed when the aisles were raised (probably 1348), but at the same height so the graduated lancets in the E and W gables were unaffected. The trusses consist of a slightly cambered tie-beam, wall-posts, and braces with tracery in the spandrels; these are the only elements to survive, the roof having been rebuilt in 1873 by *T. H. Wyatt* and his son *Matthew Wyatt III*. Each tie-beam has a badge identified by Biddle and Clayre as a wind-rose (wynde-rose), an anagram of Wyndesore (Windsor), where Edward III was founding the Order of the Garter the year the roof was probably rebuilt. The scissor-braced common rafters with lower collars, giving a five-canted profile, may have been Wyatt's design. He also formed the twin-arched opening in the E wall, leading to his new Assize Courts (*see* below); armorial bearings revealed on this wall after the stripping of plaster inspired the painted scheme of 1876–81 by *J. Hardman;* he also designed the heraldic glass in 1871–80. – GATES. Forged stainless steel by *Antony Robinson*, 1981, to commemorate the marriage of the Prince of Wales. Beneath the E end of the hall are brick vaults used as cells when the courts were located here.

The hall was originally brightly decorated, with a Wheel of Fortune behind the dais and a *Mappa Mundi* at the far end. Now on the W wall is the huge ROUND TABLE (moved here from the E wall in 1873). First recorded hanging on the wall in 1463 but indeed originally a real table, with twelve legs. It is dated to 1250–80 (tree-ring dating) and, Prof. Biddle argues, was commissioned by Edward I for the tournament and dynastic party of 1290. 18 ft (5.5 metres) diameter, built of oak in 'clasp-arm' technique (a central hub clasped by a square frame) and perhaps therefore by a wheelwright. It was first painted in 1522, when Henry VIII entertained the Emperor Charles V at Winchester, and redone by *William Cave*, 1789. It has a central Tudor rose, radiating quadrants of alternating green and white (the Tudor colours), the names of King Arthur's twenty-four knights on the outer ring and a portrait of a luxuriantly bearded Arthur (perhaps intended as a portrait of Henry VIII, though a poor likeness) with orb and sword.

109   The magnificent bronze STATUE of Queen Victoria by *Alfred Gilbert* was commissioned for the hall in 1887 by W. Ingham Whitaker, High Sheriff of Hampshire, for the Golden Jubilee. It is one of the best sculptures of its date and was to have been in marble but then cast in bronze so that it might be placed in Castle Yard. From 1894 to 1910 it stood in Abbey Gardens, where it was vandalized; the sculptor made repairs and set it up on a new, mightier, base before it returned to the hall in 1912. It is typical Gilbert, especially the fantastic gilded openwork crown suspended above the queen's head, the Roman Baroque inspiration for the throne peopled by numerous small allegorical figures, and the queen's capacious robes. Behind the hall, QUEEN ELEANOR'S GARDEN, designed as a c13 *herbarium* by *Sylvia Landsberg*, 1986 (advised by *John Harvey*).

Linked to the E end of the hall are the LAW COURTS (Winchester Combined Court Centre). Designed by *Louis de Soissons*, 1961, completed after his death by *Richard Fraser*. Constructed 1964–73. It was built on the site of *Wyatt*'s Assize Courts, which had been erected 1873–4, hurriedly abandoned in 1938 owing to deterioration of the external walls, especially the flintwork at upper levels. The courts moved back into the Great Hall for a time. The building is raised above the Great Courtyard (*see* below) and has a N front composed of full-height canted bays of Clipsham stone and recessed grey flint panels, alternating with windows in the recesses. At second floor the windows span between the projections and at third floor it is the bays which have openings, while the principal walls are blank brown brick: all clearly intended to evoke a fortified appearance. The effect is enhanced by the full-width bronze doors at the base of the three central projecting bays. The link to the Great Hall is a plain slab of brown brick, sadly unarticulated. Utilitarian S front, visible only from the Lower Barracks. Immense foyer inside, clad in polished travertine, with a MOSAIC, by *George Dereford*, of scenes from Winchester's history. By the same artist the coats of arms in each of the crown courts. To r. and l. wide stairs of polished Italian granite lead up to the public gallery which is panelled in afromosia.

The GREAT COURTYARD lies between the Law Courts and County Offices. To the SW, on the approach from Trafalgar Street, are wide flights of steps flanked by high granite walls, evoking an amphitheatre. The effect, while at odds with Winchester's compact architectural grain, provides an imposing architectural build-up on the steep slope towards the castle. In the centre, the outline Round Table is replicated in black-and-white flints and pink stone. Nearby, HAMPSHIRE JUBILEE SCULPTURE by *Rachel Fenner*, 2003, combining a hard French limestone and mosaic work influenced by medieval manuscripts. Beside it, a modern entrance leads into part of one of Henry III's sally-ports in the remains of the early C13 round tower.

WINCHESTER COLLEGE

We owe Winchester College to William of Wykeham, Bishop of Winchester (1366–1404), who within three years of his enthronement had bought land in Oxford for his New College (built 1380–6), and by then may have conceived the innovative system of tuition comprising a university college complemented by its feeder school at Winchester – the college of 'St Mary nigh Winton', whose foundation deed was finally sealed in 1382. Wykeham's two establishments, each on an unprecedented scale, were intended to create a body of clergy well educated in canon and civil law and suited for public office. The greater part of the

Winchester College site was acquired from St Swithun's Priory and the Bishop by royal licence: seven narrow tenement plots along the extramural way (now College Street) on the N side, and a large meadow (Meads) to its S. The school was to comprise a warden, ten fellows, a headmaster, a second master, three chaplains, three chapel clerks, seventy 'poor and needy scholars', sixteen quiristers, and up to ten fee-paying students, 'commoners', from wealthy or noble families. By the time of Wykeham's death in 1404 the population of the college numbered 115, not including lay servants.

Winchester College was equally innovative in its PLAN, which was carefully considered from the outset, rather than developing piecemeal. The architect for both Winchester and New College was *William Wynford*, who established in their designs the precedent for the Oxbridge colleges. Winchester's buildings are grouped around a central quadrangle, Chamber Court, where the original seventy scholars were housed. To the N is an irregular oblong entrance courtyard, containing various service buildings (those on the E side later replaced by the Warden's Lodgings). S of Chamber Court are Chapel and Hall.* They are built end to end, a device copied from *Sponlee*'s hall and chapel for the 1358 royal lodgings at Windsor Castle, where Wykeham had been clerk of works and Wynford warden of the masons. S of Chapel is Cloisters, angled slightly, perhaps as a response to a kink in the course of the Mill Stream ('Logie') which bounded the site to the E. The experience of the building of New College also led to several design improvements at Winchester (for example, placing Chapel E of Hall, allowing a great E window).

The first stone was laid on 26 March 1387, and within seven years the Warden and scholars could take possession of Chamber Court and the surrounding buildings. Chapel and Cloisters were consecrated in 1395. Work began on the outer gatehouse in 1394 and by Wykeham's death in 1404 Outer Court had also been completed. Many additions were made subsequently: Fromond's chantry chapel, in the centre of Cloisters, was completed by 1445; Thurbern's chantry was begun at the time of Warden Thurbern's death in 1450 but was mainly built, with a new tower over its W bay, in 1473–85 and consecrated three years later. The architect was probably *William Graver* (fl. 1465–93), chief mason at Wolvesey Palace and Winchester Cathedral during that period. Major additions in the C17 included the Sick House in Meads (1656–7), and the free-standing 'School' in 1683–7.

The College was considerably extended to the W after 1739 on the site of the former Sustren Spital (*see* p. 560), where Dr John Burton, headmaster, adapted an accretion of existing buildings grouped around a quadrangle to form Old Commoners, so that boys not in College could be accommodated in a single enclave rather than boarding in the town. This was replaced by *Repton*'s New Commoners further S, planned from 1839 for headmaster Moberly, whose house was built on the site of Old Commoners.

---

*The omission of the definite article is a feature of Wykehamist speech.

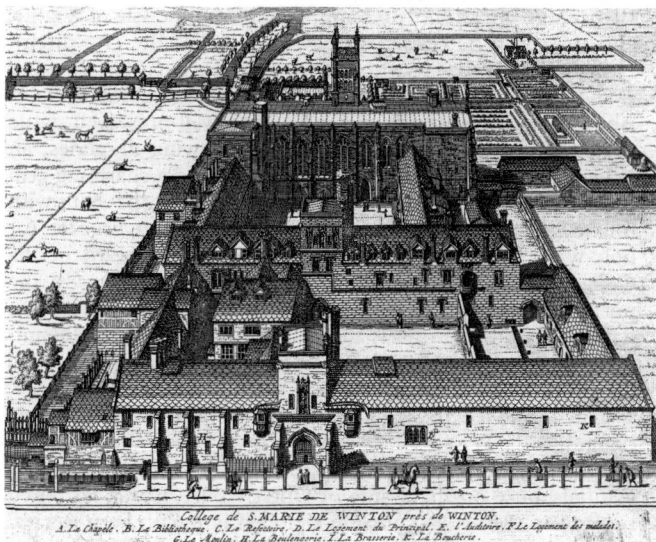

Collège de S. MARIE DE WINTON près de WINTON.
A. La Chapèle . B. La Bibliothèque . C. Le Refectoire . D. Le Logement du Principal . E. L'Auditoire . F. Le Logement des malades .
G. Le Moulin . H. La Boulangerie . I. La Brasserie . K. La Boucherie .

Winchester College.
Engraving by David Loggan, 1675

As the College continued to grow in the c19–c20, so its central buildings have been enlarged under many different architects in varied styles.

The buildings are described topographically, starting with the long, fortress-like range facing COLLEGE STREET. At the W end the first building to make the College's presence felt is the former HEADMASTER'S HOUSE, by *G. S. Repton*, 1839–42; the first stage of the replacement of Old Commoners. Forbidding c19 Gothic. Knapped and squared flint, three tall storeys, basically symmetrical, with a central battlemented Perp porch, but the wide bay window is balanced by a contrasting plain chimney-breast with soaring chimneys above. Windows straight-headed with pointed, cusped lights. The back of the house is still 'Georgian', though also Repton's work, and inside there is the same mix. Its service wing approximately follows the line of the cloister of Old Commoners. STAINED GLASS in a first-floor room a beautiful panel from the abbey of St Germain des Prés, Paris. An important fragment. Continuing E, after PARLIAMENT GATE, a Gothic link of *c.* 1930, comes the bleak rear of the late c14 range facing Outer Court (*see* below), including the porter's lodge by the main gate. Slit windows, high up and barred – defence may have been uppermost in the designer's mind in the years after the Peasants' Revolt. The larger windows are later insertions.

OUTER GATE was begun in 1394. Two storeys with a taller SW stair-turret, also flint but with Green Ventnor and

Bembridge 'Firestone' dressings (both from the Isle of Wight), and massively buttressed (the street overlies the city ditch). Four-centred gateway with hollow chamfer – typical *Wynford* – and sinuous curve to the innermost order. Original door. Above, windows l. and r., and in a niche a well-preserved statue of the Virgin and Child, with graceful flowing draperies, an enigmatic smile on the face of the mother and a charming grin on that of the baby. The gateway has a stellar lierne-vault with foliate bosses and one grotesque head. Cresset bracket (or holy-water stoup) just inside the door. The steward of the College's manors lived above the gate; the room over the porter's lodge has a good mid-C16 fireplace (graffiti of 1571–2), with nested lilies in the spandrels, sprouting from shields initialled P and R; possibly for *Philippus Rex*, so perhaps installed for the royal wedding of 1554, when Philip visited the College.

The E end of the College Street frontage, and the area behind, is the WARDEN'S LODGINGS. He lived above Middle Gate (*see* below) until Warden Bilson (1576–96) built a substantial house on the E side of Outer Court; it was refronted by *Repton*, 1832–3, in coursed, knapped flint with Perp Revival windows, prefiguring those of the Headmaster's House, lighting a Long Gallery. In 1597 Warden John Harmar (1576–1613) added a Great Chamber to the N. To College Street this has buttresses and originally an oriel window. The segmental-arched windows are of 1730, when a dining room was created on the first floor and a second floor added, the latter in brick with crisp modillion cornice. It followed remodelling of the garden wing around the corner, dated 1692, by Warden John Nicholas; with rubbed brick window heads and sunken panels between the windows. Inside the entrance vestibule, STAINED GLASS by *J. H. Russell* of Oxford, 1833, with a full-length portrait of an improbably portly Wykeham beneath a Gothic canopy. An interesting example of early revival glass painting. The principal rooms are on the first floor. 1690s staircase with barley-sugar balusters and a handsomely proportioned drawing room with bolection-moulded oak panelling by *Edward Pearce*. A second-floor room adjoining the gate-tower (Senior Poser) has oak panelling and chimneypiece with Warden Nicholas's arms, *c.* 1697, also attributed to *Pearce*. The room below (built by Warden Harmar as his study) had its floor lowered to accommodate a wonderful carved wooden chimneypiece adorned with terms resembling Native American Indians (those of the mantel posts are said to be 'Adam and Eve'), satyrs playing flutes, mythical beasts, and the College arms in the centre. It is dated 1615 and was created by *Mr Townesend* together with the wainscoting.

The W side of OUTER COURT is a screen of two arches ('Paradise Lost and Paradise Regained'), the larger (N) in four-centred brick, dated 1663. The court formerly continued on, with the late C14 N range containing the brewhouse (E) and slaughterhouse (W) and stables in the W range. The brewhouse is now MOBERLY LIBRARY, converted 1932–4 by *Sir Herbert*

Baker. Its eleven-bay roof is of two forms. The three E bays, where the building was full-height over the brewing vat, have arch braces springing from corbels down the wall and tenoned into the principal rafters and collars. Curved wind-braces. The rest is of collar-purlin type, later reinforced by an extra purlin. This part also had an upper floor from the outset and the posts which supported its massive spine beam can be seen in the ground-floor Eccles Room created at the E end of the library during alterations in 1994 by *Martin Caroe*. EMPIRE CLOCK, E wall, by *Baker*, 1936, with sun and moon emblems by *Sir Charles Wheeler*.

The STABLES were possibly built in two stages *c.* 1400. Roughly symmetrical E elevation with twin doors, two pairs of windows to right and left, and small openings to the hay loft. Four double-height trefoiled openings and one larger one on the W side. Collar-purlin roof similar to that of the E end of Brewery.

The S range of Outer Court has the three-storey MIDDLE GATE, its arch like that of Outer Gate, with original doors. Two storeys of flint, one of ashlar, originally with the Warden's Lodgings and Election Chamber in the tower. First-floor windows of two lights with a transom. Then three statue niches: the Virgin in the centre, with Archangel Gabriel of the Annunciation (l.),* and William of Wykeham kneeling (r.). Two one-light windows between. Stellar vault within. The S front has the same design except for a higher stair-turret at the SW angle, and all three statues survive, very weathered.

Flint-paved CHAMBER COURT is the main quadrangle, with Chapel and Hall on its S side, Kitchen at the S end of the W side. Outside Kitchen is a stone trough beneath a low arch; the remains of 'Conduit', a projecting bath house whose portico was built 1651 (removed 1837). The N end of the W range and the other two sides comprised accommodation. On the ground floor were six (numbered) chambers for the seventy scholars, including Sixth ('Thule') chamber in the NW corner, with cubicles ('toys') on the E wall and a painted frieze above by *Christopher Hawkes*, 1924. Doorways with Wynford's typical hollow chamfer and windows of one and two lights: these openings have hoodmould stops with engaging and original portraits, though weathered. The first floor was occupied (N side) by the headmaster, chaplains and second master (the latter's rooms retain a fine Jacobean overmantel); fellows occupied the first floor of the E wing above First, Second and Third Chambers, three to a room. In the middle of this side at the rear was a garderobe block, enlarged 1542 with two wings projecting over the stream. Three-storey extension by *Seymour & Bainbridge*, 2007. Flint walls, large frameless corner windows, copper roof.

The arrangement on the S side is this. Chapel and Hall, both of ashlar, divide the S range between them, Chapel on the

---

* A replica, of 1997, of the original in the City Museum.

ground floor, Hall to its w on the upper floor above the original schoolroom (now Seventh Chamber), i.e. all as at New College, though reversed so that Chapel has a seven-light E window. The other chapel windows, to s as well as N, are of three lights with a transom. Hall has large two-light windows with a transom, the former schoolroom below small two-light windows (one converted to a door). Attached to Chapel at its NE end, and originally entered only from the chancel, is MUNIMENT TOWER, built to fulfil the founder's instructions that all College documents should be retained. The first-floor muniment room has a stellar vault springing from corbels representing St Michael, a king, and either two bishops or a prior and a bishop. Original window shutters, Flemish tiles and chests of 1394; large chests of drawers added in the C16.

CHAPEL is entered from a w passage which originally led to Cloisters, now forming an ante-chapel. Above this is the dais end of Hall. Heavy cast alloy and plate glass doors by *Geoffrey Clarke*, 1966–8. Against its w wall is *Butterfield*'s CRIMEAN WAR MEMORIAL, 1857–8. Five-panelled blank arcade in an eclectic, quasi-Gothic style, with shafts, plinth and seat of Frosterley and other English marbles. Between the passage and Chapel, a stone SCREEN containing a tall doorway (the doors possibly incorporate original timbers including a small wicket), and four-light windows l. and r. Chapel was built 1387–95, although the glazing of the windows was not completed until 1406–7. It is of six bays, originally divided 4–2 by a rood screen whose position is evidenced by a high, blocked doorway. The roof and the fine timber vault were presumably designed by Wynford's carpenter, *Hugh Herland*, who later designed the roof of Westminster Hall. The cusped lierne-vault, rising 56 ft 9 in. (17.3 metres), is close to a fan-vault in appearance and therefore perhaps the earliest of its kind. Very thin ribs. The 'fans' spring from moulded and sculpted stone head corbels. The vault is painted white, with scarlet ribs, as originally (but repainted by *W. D. Caröe* during his restoration of 1913–21 and recoloured by *S. E. Dykes-Bower*, 1952). – REREDOS. Elements of the stone reredos of 1468–73, revealed during *Butterfield*'s restoration of 1864 and scrupulously restored by him in 1874–5. Fifteen niches, all with crocketed canopies, the taller middle three reconstructed by Butterfield but altered by Caröe in 1920 as a war memorial: Christ over the altar, flanked by a gas-masked soldier and a grieving mother, by *Ernest Gillick*; the other figures are by *Eardley* of Westminster, 1877. To uncover the reredos, Butterfield reluctantly removed the panelling of *c.* 1683 attributed to *Edward Pearce*. It was taken to Hursley Park (South Hampshire) but is now in New Hall; the ALTAR RAIL was also returned. It has, between the uprights with their foliate drops, four wide panels of chunky swirling foliage (cf. the cathedral's altar rail and the staircase of No. 11, The Close). – SEDILIA. Stone, with a panel of Laudian STUMPWORK depicting the Last Supper, from an altar cushion by *Mr Cheevers*, 1636. Eight years later he was paid to replace the image on the cushion with plain satin. – SERVERS' STALLS, chancel N side, 1903, with delightful detailing, especially the texturing of the carvings. – CHOIR STALLS. Rear stalls mostly late C14, apparently the rump of a larger group. The seat rail, seats, standards, and seat capping survive. Nine seats on the N side, nine plus the Warden's throne on the S, nearly all with misericords of remarkable quality: on the N side these include a dragon, a shepherd, a falcon with a mallard, a half-figure of a man; on the S, a cripple moving on hand- and foot-trestles, another dragon, a pelican, two goats confronting one another, a man with a dagger. – The front stalls, along with the lavish PANELLING, PEWS and WEST GALLERY, are *Caröe*'s; the stalls have geometrical detailing and carvings by his assistant, a First World War conscientious objector, the gallery in three bays, separated by small niches, supported by angels, containing metal statues. The overbearing ORGAN CASE is also his, 1908. Flowing Gothic and Renaissance motifs. The organ case on the N wall, more restrained, is by *Dykes-Bower*, 1948–9. In the vestry, cupboards and chest by *Edward Barnsley*, 1955. – STAINED GLASS. The famous Jesse tree E window was made 1393–1406 by *Thomas of Oxford*, probably designed by *Herebright of Cologne*. What is there now is by *Betton & Evans* of Shrewsbury, 1821–9. They were sent the original glass for cleaning and 'retouching' but instead replaced most of it. Their colours are lurid and the figures caricaturish, an effect even more noticeable in the side windows, 'restored' at the same time. At the foot of the Jesse tree, figures of Wynford, Simon Membury and a 'Carpentarius', who must be Hugh Herland, and r., Thomas of Oxford's own portrait. – BRASSES. Late C19 replicas of 1412–1560 originals (some now in Cloisters and Chantry) made from earlier rubbings by Edwin Freshfield and Richard Baigent. The largest, made in 1881, is after the original prepared by Warden John White (1542–54), showing him in a magnificent cope.

Added to the S side of the chapel is the landmark tower of the CHANTRY CHAPEL of Warden Thurbern (†1450). Building began 1473–4, the high tower above it was started 1476, and the structure was complete 1485. But it was pulled down and rebuilt by Butterfield in 1862–3 after the foundations failed. Bath stone (a regrettable economy; Butterfield wanted Purbeck) in four stages, with stepped buttresses, a yet higher stair-turret and tall pinnacles (entirely Butterfield's design). The chantry is of two bays separated by a panelled arch with a pier on the N side between two big arches into the main chapel. Butterfield salvaged the stellar lierne-vaults of 1484–5. Deeply carved bosses of heraldry, monograms and naturalistic motifs, perhaps by the carvers of the Oxford Divinity School (designed by *William Orchard*). Large PAINTING, the Annunciation by *Le Moyne*, 1727, purchased by the headmaster Dr Burton for the High Altar. – TAPESTRIES. Flemish. One large and two well-preserved pieces from another of *c.* 1500, the Tapestry of the Roses, said to have been woven for Prince

Arthur's christening in Winchester Cathedral. – STAINED
43   GLASS. In the w window recovered elements of Chapel's Jesse
window (reassembled by *Dennis King*, 1950–1) signed by
Thomas of Oxford. Drawing and colouring of superb quality.
Scenes include Richard II kneeling before his patron, and St
John Baptist. More of the original nave glass in the SW window.

HALL is approached via a broad flight of stairs in the SW
corner of Chamber Court. 62 ft (19 metres) long and 40 ft (12
metres) high, very lofty. It has a roof of low pitch in four bays,
with pierced spandrel pieces below uncambered tie-beams, a
design typical of *Hugh Herland* but apparently replicated in
1819–20 by *William Garbett* (boarded floor of the same date).
Until then Hall had an open hearth; in the remodelling the
louvre was omitted.* – Oak PANELLING of 1540, given by
William Fleshmonger, Dean of Chichester. Tall rectangles, rails
and stiles moulded all round. The second tier, with coved top,
above the E dais is of the 1660s. – TABLES and BENCHES, dated
to 1674, of robust design. Four of the tables have been
widened; one, perhaps the high table, has thicker boards and
is unaltered. Innocuous STAINED GLASS of 1926–8 by *R. M.
Y. Gleadowe*, the College drawing master, assisted by *Lady
Rachel de Montmorency*. At the W end is the SCREEN between
the hall and HALL-PASSAGE. The doors from the entrance stair
are original, with a stout timber drawbar, and in the passage's
W wall are the usual three doorways, also original but much
mended and modified. The larger r. one led to the staircase
from Kitchen, the others must have led to the pantry and
buttery (*see* below). All had hatches, the centre one with a
cat-hole for the college ratter (the panel has been turned
upside-down).

W of Hall is the four-storey EXCHEQUER TOWER of 1398–9,
faced in flint. On the ground floor, below the buttery and
pantry, is the beer cellar (now TREASURY, a museum with a
high lierne-vault supported on a single octagonal pier and big
corbels of grotesque heads in the side walls. On the tower's
second floor is AUDIT ROOM with a wooden screen and an
important spread of Wessex tiles, relaid after their discovery
beneath the floor of the chapel vestry in 1967. The top storey
is the former Cheese Room. KITCHEN lies in the W range and
has been much altered: square on plan, side-purlin roof. In the
kitchen lobby is the allegorical PAINTING of The Trusty
Servant, his virtues extolled in Latin and English verses by
John Hoskyns, College scholar, 1580. Repainted in its present
form by *William Cave* (probably Jun.), 1809, who adorned the
figure in Windsor livery to honour George III.

Wynford's CLOISTERS adjoins Chapel S tower almost
immediately. It is 132 ft (40 metres) square, but not on the
same orientation as the other buildings, being strictly aligned
to a change in angle of the E boundary. It has completely bare
stone walls to the outside, and as one enters it one is reminded,

---

*The iron stove which was introduced is now in the Science Museum.

as Pevsner was, of Italy, perhaps a kind of *Campo Santo*, an impression reinforced by the wagon roofs, like the Chichester Cathedral cloister. Three-light openings to the cloister garth, under two-centred arches. Some panel tracery. Within the cloister walks are interestingly varied MONUMENTS from the C15–C20 including some early BRASSES, the earliest being that of William Ball (†1492). Others are three-quarter or demi-figures. – John Erewaker †1514, an 18½ in. (407 mm) figure. – John Gylbert †1514, 15½ in. (397 mm). – John Taknell †1494, 12 in. (297 mm). – Edward Tacham †1493, 12½ in. (320 mm). – Among the later brasses, George Ridding, headmaster and later Bishop of Southwell, †1904, mural effigy by *Barkentin & Krall*. – WALL MONUMENTS: Audoen Phillips †1678, attributed to *William Stanton* (GF). – John Cobb *c.* 1724. A good, probably Metropolitan piece: look for the cherubs' heads holding draperies of refined quality. Charles Scott †1762. Charming relief in the predella featuring three putti with allegorical instruments and a profile medallion. – Warden Huntingford †1832, by *William Osmund* of Salisbury. Nearby, George Leigh-Mallory, who died 1924 attempting the ascent of Everest. A strange tablet in white and grey marble by *R. M. Y. Gleadowe* with a silhouette of the climber. Further along the N walk, Lord Wavell †1950, buried in the cloister garth nearby. STANDING MONUMENT – Humphry May (†1657, a relation of Hugh May) with a free-standing urn on a square base, perhaps by *Jasper Latham*. Among several LEDGER STONES, but evidently not *in situ*, is one to Thomas Welstead, scholar, †1676 aged eighteen, thus ending up 'in heaven instead of Oxford' (*in cælo pro Oxonio*).

FROMOND'S CHANTRY stands in the centre of Cloisters. John Fromond, steward of the College properties, made his bequest in 1420, the chantry was built *c.* 1425–45, probably by Wynford's successor *Robert Hulle* (fl. 1400–†1442), then employed on the cathedral nave. Two-storeyed with a stair-turret, largely of Green Ventnor stone. The chapel proper (now Junior Chapel) is on the ground floor; the lower room above (Chantry Room) may have been intended as a library (it was so used from 1629 to 1875). The roof, reconstructed *c.* 1818, rests on ten stone angel busts. Chapel windows of three lights N and S and five at the ends; the upper windows two or three lights with transoms under four-centred heads. Corbel course with heads, animals, monsters. The label stops of the main windows feature little figures of Fromond's officials. The W door cuts into the window. Beside the door, external stoup with miniature canted stellar vault hood. Inside, the vault is a complicated lierne-vault with bosses, coloured and gilded during restoration by *Martin Caroe*, 1991. Blank panels within the side window arches flank the three open lights, giving the same profile as the E and W windows. – REREDOS with PAINTINGS by *C. E. Buckeridge*, 1897–1900. l. and r. of the altar, figures of SS Gabriel and George by *George Frampton*, 1900. – STAINED GLASS. The E window was reglazed in 1978 to include five figures from the original E window of Chapel and two retrieved from Coleorton parish church, together with many C14–C16 fragments, probably including some from the original scheme of 1443–4 by *John Prudde*. The W window is a silvery composition by *R. M. Y. Gleadowe*, 1950. – C15 BRASS PLAQUE similar to those in Cloisters, commemorating the first chantry chaplain, William Clyff, †1433. – FURNITURE in Chantry Room by *Edward Barnsley*, 1951.

SCHOOL lies uncomfortably close to the W of Cloisters and s of Hall. Built 1683–7 for £2,600: Warden Nicholas paid more than half. Attributed without authority to *Wren* but closer in style to the City churches by Robert Hooke (e.g. St Benet's Paul's Wharf). Brick with Portland stone dressings, including quoins. Neat modillioned cornice. Hipped roof. Seven bays at the front, the central three projecting under a pediment, of big arched windows under straight hoods on brackets. Fine stone garlands above. In the three middle bays they have heads in the centres. The style suggests *Edward Pearce*. Large doorway with segmental pediment on brackets. Above, a niche with volutes and arched hood enriched by foliate frieze, containing a statue of Wykeham by *Caius Gabriel Cibber*, 1697. Plain rear, just two windows and pediment. The lead rainwater heads are large, modified and appear to have been introduced later. Were they, as Paul Holden has suggested, intended for Charles II's palace?* Spacious interior, 80 ft by 36 ft (25 by 11 metres). Remarkable plaster ceiling, with arms of benefactors, etc. on the deep coving, in a setting of branches and palm fronds. Huge scallop shells at the corners. Thickly garlanded, circular central panel between two simpler ovals. Bolection-moulded panelling and a s fireplace (added 1784) within a huge pilastered frontispiece under a wide segmental pediment, like a reredos. Some tiered seating remains; that for the boys along the W side has an upper row containing lockers. – PANELS. On the E wall, the school rules (*tabula legum*); on the W, the *aut disce* board, a Latin exhortation either to work hard and achieve public distinction (Wykeham's bishop's mitre) or leave and go into the law (an inkhorn), the army (a sword) or receive a flogging (cat o'nine tails). – BRASS CHANDELIER. Single tier of twelve branches, attributed to *William Gardner* (Robert Sherlock). One of a pair given to chapel in 1729 (the other is a reproduction). – TAPESTRIES. Two late C15 Flemish examples either side of the fireplace. – FURNITURE by *David Pye* (1960).

NW of School is NEW COMMONERS. This is by *Butterfield*, 1868–71, a remodelling, for classrooms and library, of Repton's job of 1839–42 (which replaced the slum-like Old Commoners but was itself condemned as 'a workhouse'). Mostly red brick (occasional blue headers) and Bath stone dressings. The N front, facing Moberly Court, is of nine bays and symmetri-

---

* 'The Lead-work at Winchester College School', *The Georgian Group Journal*. xii (2002), 238 ff.

cal with a central archway in C15 style with quatrefoils and cusped daggers, and a big canted bay window over. A tall diaper-patterned band above the first-floor windows. The first and last bays are higher than the rest, with stepped parapets. Along the w side of Moberly Court is Butterfield's continuation of Repton's work as far as the Headmaster's House. He also added the two wings, projecting s on each side of Flint Court and the Perp cloister between them. The w wing later extended s.

NEW HALL, SE of Cloisters, is by *Peter Shepheard*, 1958–61, with a copper roof, walls of brown brick except for the w end with startlingly chequered stone, and an entrance cloister which wraps along the N side. Its primary interest is as the setting for the superb WOODWORK of 1680–7, which was almost certainly designed for Chapel by *Edward Pearce* and executed by *Valentine Housman* but removed by Butterfield (*see* above). It is arranged as chancel, aisles and nave (although the hall is wider than the chapel) and consists of three tiers of fielded panels, the lower two with foliate surrounds. In the area corresponding to the former chancel the rhythm is tighter; the upper tier gives way to foliate garlands and swags cascading between larger panels. At the E end a broken pediment supported on pairs of fluted columns, with the Founder's arms between. At the w end, an entrance screen of openwork carving of great delicacy. All the light comes from a clerestory of splayed, nearly square windows. The ceiling, suspended from steel roof trusses, is coffered over the aisles, and over the nave is decorated with coloured geometrical panels in a style reminiscent of the Festival of Britain.

On the axis of the hall, the STEWART MEMORIAL GATEWAY of 1885 by *G. F. Bodley*, formerly the entrance to Cloisters, flanked by ironwork screens. A few yards s, next to College Mill, is NON-LICET GATE of 1402–9 (i.e. forbidden gate in the College slang or 'notions'), the College's SE gateway.

Now the buildings to the w running parallel with Kingsgate Street. The first is *Sir Herbert Baker*'s WAR CLOISTER of 1922–4. It is one of his best buildings but only part of a larger scheme for memorial buildings, including a new hall. To the outside the walls are as closed as those of the ancient cloister. 'Only Baker would not have been satisfied with as discreet an entrance as the ancient one,' thought Pevsner. His is larger, central with wrought-iron gates in a round-headed doorway, and a gable over with a Madonna and Child by *Sir Charles Wheeler*. Inside, the cloister itself is of Portland stone Tuscan columns, two deep, carrying arches and an open oak roof. Against the walls a long inscription in flushwork and many shields and emblems by *G. Kruger Gray*. Marble memorials. At each end of the E and W walks are shallow apses beneath finely jointed ashlar hemi-domes. Stones were quarried in the Dominions and Empire. Baker liked this sort of thing. In the w walk a BUST of Air Marshal Dowding glares through the

73

gateway to Meads. The GARDEN was designed by *Jekyll*, the memorial CROSS, with figures on an octagonal shaft, by *Alfred Turner*.

The W entrance to the cloister from Kingsgate Street is SOUTH AFRICA GATE ('Commoner Gate'), by *F. L. Pearson*, 1902–3. C15 pastiche. Crocketed ogival doorway in Doulting stone, with the Virgin in a niche above, flanking octagonal towers. Pearson also designed the adjacent ARMOURY, 1909, and Fives Courts. Adjoining the cloister's S corner is the OLD MUSEUM (and art school) by *Basil Champneys*, 1894–7. Rather ponderously Baroque, in brick with Bath stone dressings. The E front is of nine bays, of which seven form a recessed, open ground-floor arcade supported on paired Tuscan columns. Gibbs surrounds to the windows of the end bays. Above are large oriel windows, prominently bearing the motto *Manners Makyth Man*, interspaced with Baroque medallion portraits by *Lucchesi* of three Wykehamists: William Grocyn, Bishop Ken, Lord Seaton (distinguished infantry commander during the Napoleonic wars), plus Queen Victoria. In niches at the ends, statues of William of Wykeham and Queen Victoria yet again. Tower with Baroque cartouches at the N end (obscured by War Cloister); four convexly projecting balconies at the S. Inside, two adjacent halls on the ground floor were dedicated to Science and Art respectively, and there were a number of smaller working rooms on the ground floor. A broad stair with excellent ironwork leads to two large rooms on the first floor. A lofty and spacious gallery runs N–S with arcaded screens at either end, rising to a splendid coved and coffered ceiling with baluster-like queenposts to the exposed roof timbers.

Between Old Museum and Kingsgate Street, RACKETS COURT by *Butterfield* (1872). Utilitarian celebration of C19 physical masculinity. A second court was added in 1909. Butterfield's gymnasium of 1877–8 was converted into the QUEEN ELIZABETH II THEATRE by *Edward Cullinan Architects*, 1982.

Further S, SICK HOUSE, a building put up at a suitable distance from the rest in 1656–7. Charmingly simple, of small bricks with stone quoins and mullioned windows, two gables flanking a projecting middle porch under a smaller gable. Extended S in 1775 by *John Taylor*, Fellow of the College. The C19 sanatorium, S of Sick House, of 1884–93 by *William White*, now ARTS CENTRE. Two similar but originally independent blocks, each with conically roofed corner turrets and four bays of wide windows on the N side with stone pilasters and columns between. Connecting them a steel bridge of 1984–5 by *Cullinan* with chequerwork panels and a central gabled cupola. On either side of the link, a humorous tile mural featuring a permanent shadow, as if cast by the adjacent gable. Inside, good use of traditional and modern materials. Then follows SCIENCE SCHOOL by *Henry Hill*, 1903–4; the first major building dedicated to school science in Britain. Worthy exercise in Baroque Revival in red brick and finely carved Portland stone. Thirteen bays to the E, the corner and central bays projecting slightly. Rear wings by *T. D. Atkinson*, 1926–7 and 1930 and dull later additions including one fronting the street by *Ruthven O. Hall*, 1957–8.

At the sw corner of Meads, MEMORIAL GATE to George Ridding, reforming Headmaster 1867–84. Tile-coped wall stepped over a simple four-centred arch (possibly by *W. D. Caröe*, who designed Ridding's memorial in Southwell Minster).

Other buildings

MUSIC SCHOOL, Romans Road. By *E. S. Prior*, 1903–4, with 1995 additions by *Louis de Soissons Partnership*. An extraordinary composition, redolent of Turkish Baroque. The main performance room at the s end has three big round gables enclosing Diocletian windows, rising to a pyramidal roof with a cupola. Textured walls of flint boulders and rubble (for the basement) and Bath stone above, with careful raked pointing. It recalls the Billiard Room which Prior built for Harrow School in 1883. To the N, a large extension by *Nugent Vallis Brierley* of Frome (2004) in yellow brick with stone dressings and metal cladding.

PHYSICAL EDUCATION CENTRE, comprising swimming pool, and gymnasium in Kingsgate Road by *Louis de Soissons Partnership*, 1970 (partner in charge, *Kenneth Peacock*). Squash Courts by *Seymour & Bainbridge*, 2000.

BOARDING HOUSES lie in a fairly compact block E and W of St Cross Road and most are named after their first housemasterly incumbents. The first is DU BOULAY'S, Edgar Road, purpose-built in 1862–3; probably by *William White*. Victorian Gothic meets Arts and Crafts. U-shaped plan with master's house r. of the asymmetrical front elevation and two wings at rear. Red brick and flint panels, with a flamboyant gabled and hipped tiled roof. Splendid chimneys. Otherwise the houses of this period (Morshead's and Fearon's) have the fortress-like character which the Victorians deemed suitable. Better is SERGEANT'S, on Romans Road, by *G. E. Street*, 1868–70. A bold brick exterior with Gothic windows in varied groupings and levels. Steep pitched roofs, recesses with trefoil shapes. It is linked to BRAMSTON'S, also 1860s. Further up Romans Road, on l., CHERNOCKE HOUSE was erected in 1910–12 to a Tudoresque Arts and Crafts design by *Sir Charles Nicholson (Nicholson & Corlette)*: flint and Bath stone, beneath low-pitched slate roofs. The interior is largely intact.

ANTRIM HOUSE, St Cross Road. Built in 1883 by *Stopher* for W. D. Forder, subsequently taken over as the sanatorium (now flats and a medical centre). Two-storey red brick under slate roof with generous eaves, on brackets. The porch has Corinthian pilasters.

For other buildings associated with the College, *see* Perambulation 5.

ST JOHN'S WINCHESTER CHARITY
High Street/The Broadway

The former buildings of St John's Hospital, first referred to in
1219 but possibly established earlier as a civic institution for
housing the poor (tending the sick was secondary). Major
endowments were made in the 1290s, and again in the 1330s
when a chapel of St Mary was added by mayor John Devenish;
by the mid c14 the hospital housed the Fraternity of St John
the Baptist. Usual pattern of two parallel infirmaries, male and
female, each with a chapel at the E end. The surviving S
CHAPEL (The Broadway, N side), much remodelled in 1428,
served as a boys' school from the early c18, was re-consecrated
as a chapel c. 1836, and finally restored 1874 by *Street*. It has
an E window of three stepped lancets under a rere-arch (the
sexfoil window over may be c15) and lancets on the sides, two
on the N with hoodmoulds, six plainer ones on the S. The porch
is Perp, with a hollow chamfer and sinuous inner order; reminiscent of Wynford's work at the cathedral. The gable is c19
restoration. Inside is a vestibule formed from the S half of the
cross-passage, which divided the chapel from its infirmary.
Flanking the doorway to the chapel, small Perp two-light
windows gave patients a view of the altar. Much of the
medieval roof, including the great tie-beams, survived the c19
restoration. The roof is boarded over the chancel and at the W
end. – FONT, early c19, possibly *Coade* stone. PEWS with panelled ends, by *Street*; the other oak furnishings mostly of the
reordering in 1922 by *W. K. Shirley* of London. A tablet by *Eric
Gill* records a beautification of the chapel in 1908. – Wrought-
iron GATES at E end of chapel attributed to *P. C. Jewell* of Winchester, 1874. – PAINTING. Large mid-c19 copy of Raphael's
Madonna del divino amore. – STAINED GLASS. E window by
Powells, 1929, incorporating the arms of Devenish and Lamb
(*see* below) in the flanking lights. In the side windows early c16
coats of arms, given in 1955; from Horselunges, Sussex, where
they were probably originally installed by Sir Richard
Devenish.

To the W extended the hospital proper (ST JOHN'S HOUSE)
which was 'rebuilt and roofed with lead' in 1409–17 by *Nicholas
Portland*, master mason of Salisbury Cathedral. The greensand
plinth and quoins are typical of the date and to the street four
narrow Caen stone windows remain at ground floor with
cusped trefoil heads (deeply splayed internally). The N wall also
survives, with more trefoil-headed windows, but the rest was
rebuilt in brick in 1769 when it was converted into assembly
rooms. Apparently of three storeys and six bays to the front
but the second storey is the parapet concealing the roof with
painted windows (see the paint pot, a painter's joke). Inside,
the building was divided on the ground floor into two infirmaries. In the spine and outer walls are small aumbries, each
presumably corresponding to a bed. The two rooms may have
housed two dozen or so separate cubicles.

The hall, sensitively refurbished in 1993, is 62 ft in length, 38 ft in breadth, 28 ft in height (19 by 12 by 9 metres). The plasterwork is of 1769, white on pink, with festoons, drops and Rococo masks, like Wedgwood porcelain. Oval and rectangular frames, the latter originally containing portraits including one of Charles II by *Lely*, now in the Guildhall.

Six ALMSHOUSES were endowed by Ralph Lamb in 1558 but these were demolished and replaced in 1852–9 by new buildings behind the chapel (ST JOHN'S ALMSHOUSES NORTH) by *Henry Carey Brown*. Red brick with stucco dressings. Beyond the first block, a recessed court between the ends of two ranges with curly Flemish gables and elegant tall chimney stacks. Carey Brown, ruined by his building speculation at 76–8 High Street (see below), was later taken in by the hospital as an almsman, dying there in 1854. His design is respected in two additional terraces of cottages by *Stopher*, 1862 and 1864. On the opposite side of The Broadway is a larger group of almshouses (ST JOHN'S SOUTH) built in phases 1831–47, to designs by *William Garbett* (†1834), completed by his pupil and successor, *Owen Browne Carter*. Garbett's 1831 Neo-Tudor gate-tower has an oriel window on the N side, and the inner face is also very fine, with a large Dec style statue niche between the first-floor windows. In the boardroom above the gate is a late C16 oak chimneypiece from No. 1, St Thomas Street, brought here in 1922 by *Stopher*. Flanking the tower, the main front of two storeys is grey brick with red diaper-work. It was extended w in the 1840s. The surviving E and N ranges of almshouses around the court behind are Tudor Gothic, with gables and bargeboards, and impressive groups of tall, octagonal chimneys. Colonnaded walkway along the front of the two wings, and a matching gallery above. On the site of the s and w ranges, by Carter, flats by *Richard Sawyer*, 1974, adopting a similar form. On the w side of these, overlooking Abbey Gardens, a recycled Portland stone Baroque swag.

To the s, overlooking The Weirs, ST MARY MAGDALEN ALMSHOUSES by *Harold Sawyer*, 1929, superseding almshouses in Rosemary Close (*see* Perambulation 6), with Neo-vernacular additions of 1984 by *Manning Clamp & Partners*: two storeys (the second beneath the roof with low gables) over a brick colonnade of four-centred arches.

PUBLIC BUILDINGS

Civic buildings

ELIZABETH II COURT (County Hall), High Street. 1956–9 by *John Brandon-Jones* with *Robert Ashton* and *John Broadbent* (reconfiguring a design of the late 1930s by *C. Cowles-Voysey*). Pevsner was dismissive of its 'Neo-Georgian' design, but failed

118

to recognize the obvious inspiration of Philip Webb and C20 brick buildings in Holland. The design is arranged around a courtyard with a boldly rectilinear front range and a single E wing projecting forward to define a shallow entrance court-yard. The façade is commanding: three storeys, with a high roof and gables. Splendid brickwork: red, laid in Flemish bond, with brown brick quoins and segmental headed window sur-rounds. The tiling is also of high quality. Cast lead down-pipes, nicely decorated with stars on the junctions, and well-proportioned wooden-framed casement windows, with bronze furniture. The ensemble is topped by a clock tower with a sprocketed roof and a spire mocked by Pevsner as 'Colonial-looking' but really an example of the 'North European urban-ity' of which Gavin Stamp has written. Hampshire Hog weathervane by *Laurence Bradshaw*. Beneath the trees in front, SCULPTURE: Hampshire Hog, by *David Kemp*, 1989. Main entrance of three big carriage arches with wrought-iron gates adorned with roses leads via a groin-vaulted passage to the front courtyard. Above the flanking pedestrian openings bas-relief coats of arms carved in Portland stone by *Norman Pierce*, then head of sculpture at Winchester School of Art; more in the courtyard. The latter is paved in granite sets; at the centre, a former FOUNTAIN BASIN by *Darcie Rawlings*. Inside, an entrance lobby rising through two floors, overlooked by a balcony. Elegant plasterwork, again by *Darcie Rawlings*.

N of Elizabeth II Court is ASHBURTON COURT, originally of 1966 by the County Architect but remodelled 2007–9 by *Hampshire County Council Architects* (Head of Architecture *Steve Clow*) with *Bennetts Associates*, and incorporating six tall and impressive STAINED GLASS windows in flashed glass by *Alexander Beleschenko*, 1990, inspired by maps of medieval and Victorian Winchester. They were removed from MOTTISFONT COURT, downhill from Elizabeth II Court, an idiosyncratic design of 1990–1, by County Architect (*Sir*) *Colin Stansfield-Smith*, with a stark exterior relying for effect on its massing and textures provided by brickwork laid in double bands of soldier courses. The entrances are sheltered by stepped glazed canopies supported on slender concrete shafts; the top storey is lit by glazed round-headed gables inspired by those on St Paul's Studios, Talgarth Road, London, by Frederick Wheeler (1853–1931).

105   GUILDHALL (City Council). 1871–3; won in competition by *Jeffery & Skiller* of Hastings. French Gothic, symmetrical, with a middle clock tower and this as well as the angle pavilions provided with tourelles and pavilion roofs banded in purple and green slate. The inspiration is the great C13 Cloth Hall at Ypres, via Godwin's Northampton Town Hall (1861–4, for the extension of which in 1889–92 *Jeffery* was made joint archi-tect). But at Winchester there are also projecting wings at either end, culminating in tourelles. Wide perron to a triple-arched entrance with granite pillars and polychrome brickwork ribs to the deep, vaulted ceiling inside. The W wing, added 1876

by *Stopher* for the School of Art and Reading Room, is in E.E. style, of flint with Bath stone dressings and with big triplets of full-height glazed lancets to light the first-floor studios. The naturalistic capitals of their shafts were carved by Messrs *Boulton* of Cheltenham. A further modest extension of 1988 at the E end of the front range, in diapered brickwork.

Inside, the KING ALFRED HALL has galleries on three sides supported on brackets springing from stone corbels, and additionally supported by slender cast-iron Gothic pillars at the N end. The coved ceiling is in seven bays springing from crocketed shafts with foliate capitals. The stage was extended in 1892–3 by *J. B. Colson* using the Southampton builder and local speculator, *John Crook*; at the same time were added a smaller banqueting hall and service rooms (now the King Charles Suite). The hall is of five bays in a late C13 idiom, with an impressive roof with wide coving at the sides and a flat ceiling above a frieze which now serves as an artificial clerestory. Big square tie-beams, like Jacobean balusters on their side, supported by royal busts bearing armorial shields. Gallery at the S end. Above the entrance hall, the mayor's parlour, oak-panelled.

BUTTER CROSS, High Street. Early C15 market cross, allegedly commissioned by Cardinal Beaufort, Bishop of Winchester 1404–47, and paid for by the brethren of St Cross Hospital (*see* pp. 701–25). Sweepingly restored by *George Gilbert Scott* in 1865 and conserved in 1991. The stepped octagonal base supports a stout square central shaft, decorated with panelling, and four panelled angle shafts support crocketed ogee gables over the lierne-vault which roofs the lowest stage. The angle shafts continue upwards, terminating in pinnacles. The second stage has niches for full-size statues, and there are smaller statues in the top register. The whole monument ends in a high pinnacle, 43 ft (13 metres) from the ground. The central stem, the lower parts of the shafts, and the vault are probably original. One C15 statue (St John) survives on the sheltered S side, the others are late C19 replacements.

Institutions

LAW COURTS. *See* Castle, above.
COUNTY POLICE HEADQUARTERS, Romsey Road. 1962–6, by *H. Benson Ansell*, County Architect, and characteristic of his work. Concrete, with strict lattice of windows on the main façades and tall chequer flint panels on the ends, forming a prominent slab on the skyline of West Hill.
WINCHESTER POLICE DIVISION STATION, North Walls. By *H. Benson Ansell*, County Architect, opened 1962. Conservative two-storey brick building of sound design.
FIRE AND RESCUE STATION, North Walls. 1935 by *A. Simpson Low*, County Architect. Elegant appliance room in brick with hipped roof and modillion cornice. Excellent lettering on the

lintel over the triple portals. Attached offices, again attractive domestic Neo-Georgian.

WINCHESTER COMMUNITY PRISON, Romsey Road. Screened by a massive brick wall and earth bank. Built 1846–50, begun by *C. J. Peirce* of London, who was later dismissed in favour of *Thomas Stopher Sen.* Peirce had worked for Joshua Jebb at Pentonville, 1840–2, and the design for Winchester conforms to the principles of radial planning pioneered there (itself derived from the Eastern Penitentiary, Philadelphia, of 1829). Star-shaped plan, with five wings radiating from a prominent turret designed for central supervision, perhaps doubling as a vent for heating and ventilation. The main entrance comprises an outsize arch with rusticated voussoirs in a broad-eaved porch with rusticated quoins. Modern additions include a prefabricated visitors centre designed by *AEDAS*, 2004. More relevant to those within, on the E side of the site, is the shell of the treadwheel house by *Thomas Stopher Jun.*, 1862–3 – a rare survival. The gaol featured (as Wintoncester prison) in *Tess of the D'Urbervilles*.

Former WORKHOUSE, Clifton Terrace. Now part of a residential development by *PRP Architects* 1999–2000. Built 1836–7; designed by *William Coles*, the City Surveyor, following model plans drawn up by *Sampson Kempthorne*, architect to the Poor Law Commission. It had a radial Y-plan, typical for the date, of three wings for a boys' school and the men's and women's wards, all still preserved, originally surrounded by exercise yards and enclosed by an hexagonal outer range containing the entrance, casual wards, girls' school, washhouse and work-shops (stone-breaking shed). Substantial elements of this, in red brick under a low-pitched slate roof, are preserved despite partial demolition and extension in the later C19. To the W the former infirmary of 1845, arched over a roadway. Nearby, the tall tapering incinerator chimney has been retained as a land-mark, as has a nurses' home of 1912, S of the main buildings.

THE ROYAL HAMPSHIRE COUNTY HOSPITAL, Romsey Road. Founded in Colebrook Street in 1736 (*see* p. 675) before transferring to Parchment Street in 1759. Built on its present site in 1863–8 by *William Butterfield*. It consisted of a 255-foot (78-metre)-long E–W range, in red brick with black diaper bricks and bands and Bath stone strings, comprising a central block flanked by narrower wings. The slope permitted four storeys to the N, five to the S. The entrance hall, as now, was in the central block, together with administrative offices, a single operating theatre and staff accommodation. The design was commended by the ailing Florence Nightingale as 'a model hospital': i.e. it was well ventilated (1,500 square ft per person), with huge windows to the wards' balconies at each end and bathrooms and WCs in separate corner towers.

Much of the S façade is concealed by later accretions but its centre is still imposing, under a gambrel roof. The E wing has fared better, flanked by square corner towers, like pavilions, with pyramidal slate roofs. Conspicuous are the S and E windows of the chapel, which occupied the entire E wing at second- and third-floor level. The N front is largely as built: calculatedly asymmetrical, with irregular window spacing. Here the chapel windows have varied tracery and below are five bays of four-centred arches surrounding the ward windows, under a Lombardic frieze at second-floor level. At the centre the entrance wing juts forward in two steps, towering above the single-storey attached porter's lodge, which resembles a little Gothic cottage. The high-level conservatory at third-floor level is a later addition. The ASHLEY WING of 1906 was formerly independent.

The wonderful CHAPEL (partly adapted as offices in 1994 with mezzanine floor) was largely paid for by Butterfield and Mrs Keble as a memorial to her husband. The E wall is still glorious, although the altar has been removed (frontals, including one by Butterfield, are displayed in the Nightingale Wing); it was flanked by a dado, continued around the side walls, painted dark green with gilt lozenges enclosing trefoil motifs. Above are large painted panels of vine scrolls on a pale green ground, enclosing vesicas with painted angels. The roof survives for most of its original length: steep, four-canted, and boarded. The lower areas are plain light green like the side walls; the apex is decorated with a raised trellis pattern adorned with red Hampshire roses and, over the chancel, monograms of the Saviour. By *Clayton & Bell*, the E window of 1883 and SE window 1884. A few notable later additions including the Isolation Block of 1881 by *Cancellor & Hill*, 1939, and the Nightingale Wing (1986), external wall with painted mural sculpture by *David Annesley*, 1993.

Museums and libraries

WINCHESTER DISCOVERY CENTRE (library etc.), Jewry Street. Adapted from the former Corn Exchange of 1835–8 by *O. B. Carter*, which since *c.* 1900 has served variously as a roller-skating rink, theatre, cinema and library. The façade is a classical composition of three-bay centre and three-bay links to end pavilions. Perhaps based on the stables at Althorp, Northants (*c.* 1732 by Roger Morris) but with pronounced Italianate roofs, i.e. low pitches and deep eaves, and a bold portico (inspired by Inigo Jones's St Paul's church, Covent Garden) with four Tuscan columns and deep eaves to the pediment. Surmounting the central block is a high bell-turret. Carter chose fashionable light yellow Exbury brick with Portland stone dressings (as used at Osborne House), and for the end pavilions rusticated masonry up to the sills of the Diocletian windows. Behind the main block (originally containing the 'sample market', committee room, etc.), colonnaded wings project W, originally flanking a 'pitched market' between two concentric rings of columns supporting a low-pitched slate roof around a circular central court; this was completely roofed

over by *John Colson* in 1859, and again in 1907, with steel
trusses supporting a big skylight. Adaptation to its present use
in 2006–7, by *Alec Gillies* and *Martin Hallum* of *Hampshire
County Council Architects*, who removed C20 interventions and
extended the N wing, with glazed E elevation framed by stone
columns. Multi-purpose 180-seat hall behind. In front, a new
public place linking the Corn Exchange and Theatre Royal. In
the lending library, TEXTILE HANGING, Looking Forwards to
the Past, by *Alice Kettle* in a colour scheme based on the C12
Winchester Bible, including local themes.

COUNTY RECORD OFFICE, Sussex Street. 1992–3, by *(Sir)
Colin Stansfield-Smith*, County Architect. A triangular site at
the foot of the hill, with a massive brick-faced basement
(enclosing the archive store) and in appearance like a defensive city wall. On the E side the basement is pierced by ranks
of tiny openings, evocative of a castle keep, and at its S end
follows the descent of the internal staircase, visible through the
plate glass above. A more open and airy treatment on the upper
storeys, where a steel-framed superstructure supports a series
of pitched metal roofs with generous eaves sheltering external
balconies. These continue over the reading rooms as a pavilion-like structure in the Japanese idiom with large glazed
panels in a light steel framework. Wide balconies sheltered by
eaves and slatted awnings on the SW side, overlooking an
enclosed garden which continues the oriental theme, with long
water channels and a bronze SCULPTURE by *Glynn Williams*,
Sitting, Holding, Looking (Madonna and Child), 1990.

REGISTRY OFFICE, Station Hill. Pub of 1871, sympathetically
restored by *Hampshire County Architect's Dept*. Large canted E
bay window with STAINED GLASS by *John Patsalides*, 1995.

TOWER ARTS CENTRE, off Romsey Road, by King's School (*see*
below). Octagonal 40-ft (12-metre)-high former water tower of
1898. Red brick, well detailed, with clasping pilasters at the
angles, round-headed recesses on the faces, a substantial
cornice, and stepped parapet. The porch is dated 1928. Converted to a theatre, 1964–9; enlarged in 1995–6 by the *County
Architect's Department*, with multi-purpose studio.

CITY MUSEUM, The Square. Tudor style by *Colson, Farrow &
Nisbett*, 1902–3, on a site previously occupied by the Mechanics' Institute and Reading Room, and the Market Hall before
that. Three storeys, the attic storey raised higher in the 1990s.
Flint with white oolitic limestone dressings. The main front
looks W, with rounded corners.

WESTGATE (museum), High Street. The Westgate was the only
medieval city gate belonging to the mayor and burgesses. In
use until 1959 when the road to Romsey was realigned on its
N side, over the site of the ancient Plume of Feathers pub (dem.
1940). The earliest significant surviving fabric is at the NW
angle, of Anglo-Saxon character, built of large, irregularly
tooled blocks. A major rebuild occurred in the C12, and the E
façade was reconstructed in the C13, as shown by the trefoils
at the head of the niches in the buttresses; the W side was

remodelled in the late C14 as a response to the French threat, hence the machicolations, portcullis slot and inverted keyhole gun-ports for handguns, the earliest in the country. The lower string course shows the White Hart badge used by Richard II from 1390. The pedestrian passage on the N side, echoing a former, earlier one on the S, was inserted in 1791. On the gate's E face, a small Gothic DRINKING FOUNTAIN by the City Surveyor, *William Coles*, dated 1859.

On the S side of the gate the stair to the upper floor was originally accessed via the tall door in the main passage, but this was partly blocked in the C19 when an external entrance was formed. A lock-up at the foot of the stair remained in use until 1760 to house drunkards and prostitutes. The room over the gate was being used by the Mayor and bailiffs as a prison by *c.* 1340. French prisoners during the Napoleonic Wars left their initials and other graffiti, including a drawing of a three-masted ship. The room later served as the smoking room of the Plume of Feathers, then as the city archive from 1837. GLASS on the E side, transferred from the Old Guildhall in the late C19. Mostly C15, including the shields of three Winchester mayors, but also a C16 royal arms in the northernmost window. Late medieval chimneypiece. Splendid PAINTED CEILING, made by John White to adorn his Warden's Lodgings in anticipation of a visit to Winchester College in 1554 by Philip of Spain and Mary Tudor. It was discovered reused as wainscoting at the College in 1885. The design is in grisaille with black and brown shading on a white ground, in the Grotesque style of the early C16. Each section of the coffering encloses a medallion including a portrait head in either classical or C16 dress, alternating with roundels with John White's initials. The frieze has more roundels supported by putti, texts from Ecclesiastes, and the device *Vyve le Roy*.

Education and recreation

WINCHESTER COLLEGE. See pp. 643–55.
UNIVERSITY OF WINCHESTER, West Hill. Established as a university in 2005. KING ALFRED CAMPUS, Sparkford Road. At the heart of the main campus is the former Winchester Diocesan Training School (MAIN BUILDING), which later expanded as a higher education college, 1859–69 by *John Colson Sen.* It initially comprised two classrooms, a lecture hall, and a dining hall in an eclectic composition, faced in rough-hewn Purbeck stone with Bath dressings, predominantly Gothic in conception with mullioned-and-transomed windows but influenced by French Second Empire style, with patterned tile roof, flèches, outlandishly tall chimneys and a tower capped by a spirelet. The ostentation has alas been tamed by remodellings since the 1950s. The CHAPEL, added 1881 by *Colson & Colson*, was restored to its original use in 1997 by *Feilden Clegg Bradley*. Late Dec style, stone-faced, with a tower capped by a flèche.

Originally four bays, extended w as a war memorial in 1927. The roof has canted rafter trusses, with two moulded tie-beams, mostly open but panelled over the sanctuary. – REREDOS by *Powells*, 1905, restored 2003. Turquoise and brown matt tiles, including two *opus sectile* panels designed by *Henry Holiday*. They depict angels set on a background of gold. – STAINED GLASS. E window, 1886; others 1888–1905 attributed to *Lavers & Westlake* (R. Eberhard). – In the w addition, SS Michael and George in the style of Christopher Whall.

Much architecturally regrettable expansion in the 1960s but the best buildings belong to late C20 and early C21, beginning with the MARTIAL ROSE LIBRARY EXTENSION, by *Feilden Clegg Bradley*, 1998–2000, designed to set a new standard for the main campus. A strong design in three storeys, with brick and glass walls, sheltered by light shutters, under a zinc roof. It is linked to the parent building of 1977 (which it fortunately shields from the s) by a glass atrium including a 36-ft (11-metre)-high internally lit glass MURAL in the stairwell by *Sasha Ward*. This features 156 panels of screen-printed enamelled glass, predominantly cerulean, yellow and clear, illustrating local subjects such as the Winchester Bible and the King Alfred Jewel. A nondescript gymnasium of 1974 was converted into an imaginative multimedia performance space in 2002 by *Design Engine*, who also transformed the inadequate John Stripe Theatre of 1969 into THE NEW STRIPE (2004), comprising a large raked auditorium, two large lecture rooms and a meeting room. Entered via a memorably spacious double-height atrium. Their UNIVERSITY CENTRE of 2008, overlooking Sparkford Road, provides what the campus has hitherto lacked, a clearly defined main entrance, intended to celebrate Winchester's new status as a university city. Four storeys, partly cut into the natural slope, it incorporates the Student Union, food hall, shops, internet café and (at the SE corner, with stunning views over the city) the boardroom. White render over a dark brick podium; overhanging glass roof over the s-projecting terrace.

MEDECROFT, on the other side of Sparkford Road, was built 1868 for Dr J. N. Heale, later serving as St Swithun's Prep School. A spacious two-storey stucco villa under slate roof with a long arcaded veranda on the s side.

WEST DOWNS CAMPUS, N of Romsey Road. The WEST DOWNS CENTRE was built *c.* 1880 as the Winchester Modern School by *Stopher* at the expense of Lord Northbrook. Collegiate Gothic. The s front is a long two-storey-and-attic range faced in grey flint, with tall sash windows dressed in red brick zigzag surrounds. At the centre, an entrance in the form of a gatehouse with an oriel, rising to a crenellated parapet; this doubled as a water tower; at the l. end a curved Dutch gable. The two-storey HALL and CHAPEL were added at the w end of the range *c.* 1905 by (*Sir*) *John Simpson* in Arts and Crafts style: red brick with steep tile roof and an octagonal bell-turret. The first-floor chapel has an exposed timber roof with base-cruck trusses. Extensively refurbished 2001–2 by *Feilden Clegg Bradley*, with removal of numerous accretions and inspired addition of a spacious double-height link between the two rear wings. Lime-rendered façades.

At the front, overlooking Romsey Road, the former Masters' Lodge, an Arts and Crafts dwelling designed to house bachelor schoolmasters by *Simpson & Ayrton* (1906). Red brick ground floor with tile hanging above; big central bay under a gable with arched window in the attic storey. Successfully refurbished as a graduate research centre, 2006, by *James Lunn-Rockliffe* of Winchester.

In the grounds WEST DOWNS STUDENT VILLAGE, by *Feilden Clegg Design* built in three phases, 1995–8. The earliest and most successful part is a double terrace of brownish brick accommodation comprising linked alternating four- and five-storey blocks featuring cantilevered balconies and prominent open-tread steel stairs to the first floor. The trees are an important part of the design.

WINCHESTER SCHOOL OF ART (Southampton University), Park Avenue. The art school opened in 1870 at Wolvesey Palace; from 1876 it was at the Guildhall. The present site was developed for the school in 1962–6 by *H. Benson Ansell*, County Architect, but greatly expanded 1990–9 by *Architecture plb* (formerly *Plincke, Leaman & Browning*). The earliest part, now EAST SIDE, of 1962–6, is a bold design, aligned to the river and still impressive.* The pre-cast concrete frame of the three-storey structure breaks up what could have appeared overbearingly massive. Infill panels are of rendered flint aggregate. Attached by a bridge to its N end and rising from a reflecting pool is a twelve-sided structure (designed 1964), built as the library (now graphics department), with first floor cantilevered out from a central stem. Bookshelves radiated from a central stair. At the E end of the main building is a SCULPTURE AND TEXTILE DESIGN STUDIO, of 1993. Clerestory-lit studio. Curved steel roof above. Lightweight profiled metal cladding. Running s from the w end is the former assembly hall (now restaurant), ten bays, with concrete portal frames and dark brick walls over a continuously glazed ground floor.

WEST SIDE (1995–6) is a group of four identical buildings linked by a two-storey gallery beside Park Avenue. Spacious and steel-framed, clad in lightweight textured steel plates. Seminar rooms, photographic darkrooms, and offices on the ground floor; a lecture theatre; the studios over are jettied out with cantilevered corridors at the rear. Each wing has a low-pitched roof facing s, overhanging the ample fenestration; steeper-pitched glazed roof to N lighting the studios. An almost sculptural quality in the interpenetration of solids and voids. Attached to the s end the WINCHESTER GALLERY is glazed only at the N end; the s end is rendered and wavy on plan.

* The County Council stipulated that the main building should be adaptable as a hospital in the event of civil emergency.

Further N, STUDENTS' UNION (1996), with blank white rendered concrete walls to N and S, steel and glass at the ends.

The ADMINISTRATION BUILDING and the former TEXTILE CONSERVATION CENTRE (1999) were both designed by *Richard Rose-Casemore*, then practice director of *Architecture plb*: two long parallel buildings running E–W with single low-pitched roofs sloping outwards. The Administration wing, steel-framed and three-storeyed, is faced in glass and anodized steel. The first floor has a spacious glazed balcony on the N side; the S façade is jettied but blind. At the NW corner a glazed apse contains the open stair (steel and wooden treads). The interior is spacious and light. The building originally designed as the Textile Conservation Centre (its future undecided at the time of writing) is the most ambitious development on the site, the design directly responsive to the demands of the conservators. Concrete frame. An open-tread stair leads up to the first-floor reception, with has a central corridor providing a view down into the double-height laboratories on the N side. These workshops require less natural light, whereas perforated aluminium and steel light-shelves and shuttering control the light levels in the conservation rooms on the S side. Public and teaching spaces on first and second floors. Despite the stringent functional demands the building is extremely satisfying visually.

PETER SYMONDS COLLEGE, Owens Road. Opened in Southgate Street in 1897 as a boys' school. The parent building on the present site is of 1899 by *B. D. Cancellor*, with a symmetrical Tudoresque S façade (plus slightly set-back caretaker's lodge at E end) in brown brick with Bath stone dressings, with two wide, gabled end wings and a smaller central entrance wing. Generous eaves are corbelled out at the angles, which are surmounted by ball finials. Further classrooms (1913) at rear; the building was designed for progressive expansion. School House (1908) was the first boarding house; further acquisition of houses in Bereweeke Road followed (1928 Wyke Lodge, 1947 Kelso). NORTHBROOK HALL (a library since 1973) was inserted between the classrooms in 1911. It has a spindly hammerbeam roof and a neatly detailed large four-centred twelve-light window at the N end. One of the glazed partitions within the wide arches into the classrooms survives. Cancellor's MEMORIAL LIBRARY was added at the W end of the old building (1922); woodwork by *Austin Laverty*. Principal rafter roof with closed arch braces; Tudor fireplace at E end. Despite gradual expansion, all new buildings have been constrained to a restricted footprint. The FREEMAN BUILDING is a two-phase addition of 1930–2, enlarged 1983–4 by *Peter Liddiard* for the *County Architect's Dept*, with long E–W corridor containing carrel-like study areas and new classrooms. All decorated in chevron red and green boarding, an effective scheme also employed in Lydiard's tall, generously lit ART BLOCK nearby. Big expansion in 1960–1 demanded the construction of VARLEY BUILDING (*County Architect's Dept*) with projecting hall added 1962. W of Northbrook, the RECEPTION

AND COLLEGE CENTRE, 1976 by *Liddiard*, then further additions cut into slope to avoid intrusion into playing-field area:
PAUL WOODHOUSE CENTRE, the students' common room,
by *TKL Architects* (1997–8); MERCER SPORTS HALL
(2001–2), by *Rainey Petrie Johns* with over-hanging light-shelf;
and FALKLAND LODGE (1997–8) by *Radley House Partnership*,
pavilion-like with low-pitched tile roof and deep eaves.
Between Northbrook and Varley, the JOHN SHEILDS
BUILDING (2004), by *TKL Architects*, dominant, in bright
red engineering brick, with stair-tower in SW angle.

At the NE corner of the campus, SCIENCE CENTRE of
1994–5, by *David Mansfield Associates*. Self-effacing two-storey
brick building under a low-pitched slate roof, with two-storey
glazed atrium on the corner. Opposite is ASHURST, a learning
resource centre and teaching block (2006–7) by *Harding, Neill
& Watson*. Steel frame, glass and anodized steel, with timber
cladding on E side.

ST SWITHUN'S SCHOOL, Alresford Road. 1931–4 by *Mitchell &
Bridgewater*, but not built to their original design of buildings
grouped around lawns and formal gardens and connected by
a cloister. Only the main teaching block and one boarding
house were completed in the first phase. The main block (now
senior school) is 250 ft (77 metres) wide, scholastic Late Neo-
Georgian, two-and-a-half storeys, in sienna orange brick,
darker quoins, and Bath stone plinth and platbands. Round-
headed windows to the ground floor with radial tracery and
festoons; rectangular sashes to the upper floors. Central
portico (rebuilt 2006 in synthetic materials), surmounted by
a balcony with opulent bay window beneath a moulded
tympanum. Plaque of St Swithun by *F. I. Sayers*. Pyramidal
roof topped by a tall cupola. Inside, a fine double staircase
leading from the entrance hall, flanked by short flights down
to the former 'Great Hall', converted to other use by *Solway
Brown Partnership*, 2007. Linked to the W is the BOARDING
HOUSE, E-shaped on plan with the end wings projecting
forward with a first-floor balcony between them. Round-
headed French doors below, with the same tracery as the main
wing. The upper-storey windows are paired, reflecting the
internal division into small individual cubicles. There ends the
original design. The SCIENCE BLOCK was added at the E end
of the main wing 1983 by *Barry Kenyon*. Half-hipped at the
end, barn-like, in rough Michelmersh brick with large
windows; a curious contrast.

By far the school's best post-war building is the PERFORM-
ING ARTS CENTRE, a 600-seat theatre/concert hall by
Solway Brown Partnership, 2003. Variegated brick with bands of
red brick. The main front faces W, with a flight of stairs, rows
of oculi. A long tiled roof, including shallow dormers with
oculi, comes right down to ground level along the N side,
projecting over a covered walkway and supported on stout
steel piers. Balconies at rear (N side). Carefully studied
acoustics and lighting in main theatre, the stage area clad in
pale wood.

KING'S SCHOOL, Romsey Road. A large comprehensive school formed in 1984–5 by the amalgamation of earlier schools (starting in 1953) on a large suburban site. The traditional brick building at its core (1958) has expanded in the same style; the other, free-standing buildings include a 1970 teaching block on the *County Architect's Department*'s usual SCOLA system and a sports hall (1993). More recent investment in building, landscape and infrastructure works have created a more civilizing environment for the educational campus.

HENRY BEAUFORT SCHOOL, off Bereweeke Road. Opened 1972, the city's first comprehensive school. Comprises central block surrounded by separate or loosely linked buildings on the SCOLA system, all by the *County Architect's Dept.*

WESTGATE SCHOOL, Cheriton Road. Former Winchester County High School for Girls. Principal parts 1910 by *W. J. Taylor*, County Surveyor, completed in 1931. Scholastic Neo-Queen Anne. More interesting is the STEPHEN HAWKING BUILDING (maths and science), 1993–4 by *Michael Wright* for *Hampshire County Architect's Dept.* Ogival in section, with bands of brick and stone at the ends, the tubular steel external frame extending downwards on the E side as a colonnade.

ALL SAINTS' PRIMARY SCHOOL, St Catherine's Road, Highcliffe. Earlier part by *Norman Nisbett*, 1892.

ST BEDE'S PRIMARY SCHOOL, Gordon Road. Formerly Danemark Elementary School, 1911–12 by *A. Haynes Johnson*; refurbished 2003. The school house, brick with large round-headed window at the N end and a rusticated porch on the W side, now contains Kingsmead Day Nursery and a house.

ST FAITH'S PRIMARY SCHOOL. The core buildings probably by *Colson & Colson c.* 1887. Flint with brick dressings. Extended towards St Faith's Road *c.* 2000 in a series of stepped wings.

STANMORE PRIMARY AND JUNIOR SCHOOL, Stanmore Lane. By *Cancellor & Sawyer*, 1927–8. Planned on three sides of a square open to the S and with access to the classrooms from a veranda, a characteristic plan for its date. Brick walls with red brick facings. Each classroom lit by entire walls of paned windows to SE and NW.

CARROLL YOUTH CENTRE, Stanmore. By *Graeme Stevenson* 1992–4. Distinctive build-up of low-pitched roofs nestling into the hill, housing main hall, various activities areas, offices and a quiet room.

LANTERNS CHILDREN'S CENTRE. Discreetly concealed behind earth banks, on the N side of Bereweeke Avenue. For pre-school children half of whom have special needs. Designed 2005 by *Colin Jackson* for *Hampshire County Council Architects.* T-shaped, quasi-vernacular style. Behind a deep full-length loggia the main wing, S-facing, has four big square playrooms each with a pyramidal roof terminating in a lantern; low perimeter ceilings give a more intimate feel nearer the walls. The cross-bar of the T contains entrance, offices, parents' room, etc. Most exterior walls are faced in red cedar, with some Michelmersh red brick; handmade clay tiles to the roofs.

OSBORNE SCHOOL, between Andover Road and Lankhills. Formerly Lankhills School. Mixed secondary special needs school by *Hampshire County Council Architecture and Design*, 2002–4. In the central atrium, Drawing in the Built Form by *Mitchell Bould* (*Trish Bould* and *Belinda Mitchell*), 2004: twenty-four glass panels illustrating the construction of the school.

INTECH, off the Alresford Road, on the E side of Morn Hill. Science and technology centre of 2002–4 by *Ian Templeton*, for *Hampshire County Council Architects*. 52-ft (16-metre)-high pyramid containing lecture theatre, classrooms and exhibition space. Big raking buttresses, glazed sides and a low tent-like aluminium roof. Inside, all the services, pipes, cables etc. are displayed: the building itself is intended to be an exhibit. The gleaming metal roofs, giant satellite dish, and the planetarium are inescapable features on the descent from Cheesefoot Head.

RECREATION CENTRE, North Walls. By *Scott, Brownrigg & Turner*. 1971–4. Massive and functional.

SPORTS CLUB AND LIDO, Worthy Lane. A rather impressive Palladian design with wings and pedimented centre. Designed 1934, by Sebastian Comper for its donor *C. F. G. Schwerdt*. The porch is late C18 with Adam-style festoons; Venetian window over. The swimming pool was in the present entrance courtyard.

RAILWAY STATION. 1838–9 by *Sir William Tite* for the London & South-West Railway's line from London to Southampton, opposition to which came from the Dean and Chapter and Winchester College. The entrance façade has a two-storey rendered central block flanked by single-storey wings. Shallow-pitched hipped slate roofs. Glazed roof over the pavement in front, supported on a file of thin cast-iron columns; nicely cut wood-plan fringe overhangs the front.

WATERWORKS, Romsey Road. The Winchester Waterworks Co. was founded 1849 to supply the developing suburb of West Hill by William White, local entrepreneur and patron of Owen Browne Carter. Now just an extraction plant just S of the R.C. Cemetery, but the manager's house survives on Romsey Road, as does one of the beam-engine houses (1870s) and an employee's cottage, both now developed (with additions) into housing.

PUMPING STATION, Garnier Road. Built 1878–80 to pump sewage to the treatment works behind St Catherine's Hill. By *James Lemon*, City Engineer. Named after Dean Garnier who supported the campaign for improved drainage in Winchester. Red brick with bands of contrasting blue brick. Steep roof with dormers and a tiled ridge; it originally had an unashamedly virile chimney. The station housed two beam engines, superseded in 1959. W extension of 1904 by *Walter V. Anderson* for a triple expansion engine. Refurbished for offices in 2002.

The first four perambulations begin in the High Street and cover the streets within the area formerly enclosed by the city wall. The remaining walks cover the extramural suburbs of the inner city.

CITY CENTRE

1. The High Street E to the river – a circular tour

The HIGH STREET, the *decumanus* of Roman Winchester, is still the spine of the town, although pedestrianized for much of its length. In the views E and W from the Butter Cross (*see* Public Buildings) the limits of the medieval city are apparent, defined uphill by the Westgate and to the E by the wooded slopes of St Giles Hill rising above the Itchen.

The medieval houses forming the backdrop to the Butter Cross on High Street's S side incorporate, just W of the cross, a covered passage which may preserve the site of a gateway. It now leads to the cathedral's outer close. The building on the W side, tree-ring dated to 1508, has on the first floor a big double chimneystack serving two rooms; the N room retains much C17 oak small-square panelling, and a splendid late C16 fireplace whose low four-centred arch has foliate daggers and the initials 'PA' in the spandrels; the overmantel is decorated with Renaissance painted cartouches of fictive leather strap-work and gemstones, and a coat of arms. The next-door neighbour stands behind the Butter Cross, indeed almost rests against it, and has a four-storey gabled front with a double jetty projecting so much that posts have been introduced to support the first floor. The building has been tree-ring dated to 1316–52 (its cellar is of similar date) and on the E side has an original three-light second-floor window with wooden ogee tracery; a similar fragment is preserved in the restored window at the front. Inside, a late C16 chimneypiece on the first floor. In the later Middle Ages this tenement was known as 'Hevene' ('*le Taverne de Paradys*' in 1380); the adjacent property (No. 41) was called 'Helle' and between the two, now infilled, was an entrance to St Lawrence's church, whose tower rises behind the houses. No. 41 is also the beginning of THE PENTICE, the picturesque colonnade which extends along this side of the High Street. It probably results from piecemeal encroachment on to the street since the late C13 (several tenements extended over the walkway by the 1330s) and was a continuous walkway by the mid C15, but the columns supporting No. 41 are cast iron (1862) and none of the others can be older than the early C18. The house itself is probably mid-C16, although externally brick Georgian and extensively renovated inside, and the exposed timbers over the Pentice include a dragon beam that shows the walkway once returned along the W side of the house. There is also an undercroft extending beneath the street. The next house to the E was rebuilt by *Stopher* in 1873. Red brick with grey diaper-work, stone dressings.

Two massive mock-Tudor frontages follow, both now occupied by BOOTS. They built the E half, designed in 1905 by their usual architect, *M. V. Treleaven*, in the black-and-white style that became the firm's trademark and with a Winchester stamp provided by wooden statues of Bishops Æthelwold, Walkelin, Wykeham, and Fox. The W half, built for International Stores, 1909–10, is less exuberant. Nos. 35–36 (also Boots), might be dismissed as another medieval pastiche but contains the two-bay hall of the earliest known Wealden house in England, tree-ring dated to 1340. It was set parallel to the street, with its long wall on the line of the present shopfronts, showing that there cannot have been a continuous covered walkway here in the mid C14. The E wing of the Wealden was subsequently replaced by No. 34, one of a pair of late medieval shops (Nos. 33–34) set perpendicular to the street, with galleried halls, tree-ring dated to 1463–4 (only No. 33 retains much of its hall roof).* The position of chamfer stops on the joists above the walkway shows that the deep jetties of their N gable-walls were supported on timber posts set further back than the modern colonnade. It was probably at this date that the hall of the Wealden was also jettied out over the walkway as an upper-storey forebuilding. Such were the beginnings of the continuous walkway here. Nos. 33–34 have matching bargeboards of continuous trefoil heads, perhaps originating in the C16. No. 33 has a pleasant Georgian bow; No. 34 was refurbished in the C17 with a panelled upper room and inserted fireplace. The startling composition next door (No. 32), a tall yellow brick house, was rebuilt by *Stopher c.* 1871, who complained that his client prevented him from reinstating a gable similar to those on either side. No. 31 has remains of bargeboards like those of Nos. 33–34, so it is even possible that Nos. 30–34 were all originally of the same design.

Opposite The Pentice, on the W corner with Parchment Street, is W. H. SMITH, by *G. L. Blount* (of *Blount & Williamson*) and *F. C. Bayliss*. A satisfying design of 1927, still very much in the Arts and Crafts style and sensitive to its setting. The first floor at the front is stone with a wide bay window on brackets; along the side, masonry gives way to timber framing with large casements above shallow ground-floor bow windows. Then at its N end, stone once more for the taller storage and office cross wing. Excellent lead rainwater heads including a ship motif, the WHS monogram, and the date. On the first floor is the former tearoom/dance hall, conceived as a late C14 timber-framed hall, with a false hammer-beam roof and appropriate decoration of colourful plaster low reliefs including King Arthur and the Round Table, King

---

*No. 34 lost its roof in the C17. Its late C19 tobacconist's shop fittings are preserved in the City Museum.

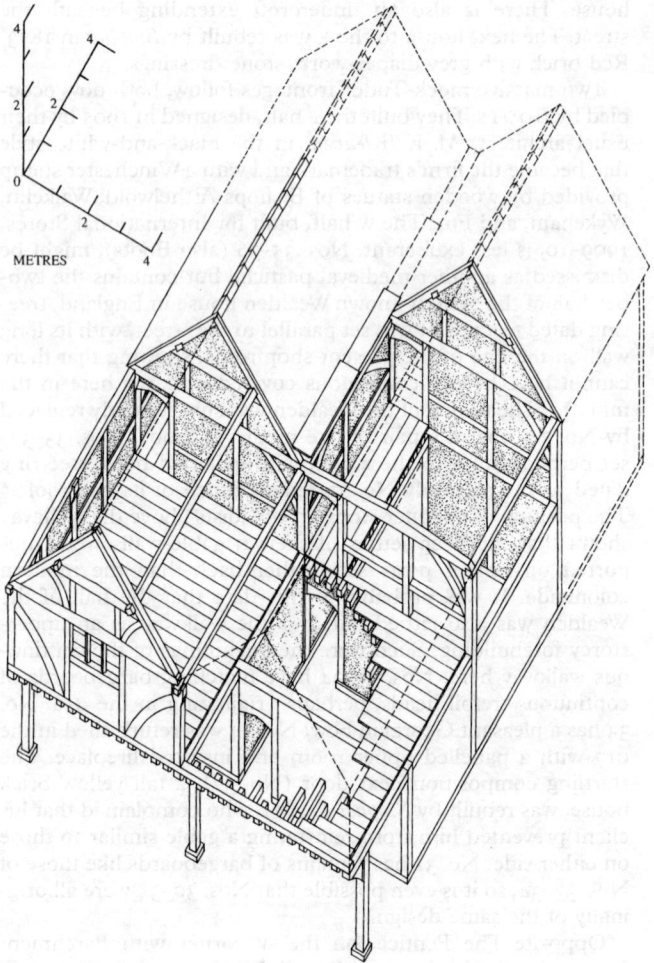

Winchester, Nos. 33–34 High Street, reconstruction.
Isometric drawing by Jonathan Snowdon, 2003

Alfred burning the cakes, and Bishop William of Wykeham laying the foundation stone of Winchester College. Some modest c19 fronts follow to the E but including a narrow stuccoed early c19 elevation of a former chapel, with a large arched window framed by Doric pilasters in Italian Renaissance style, and a wide triangular pediment across.

Back on the S side, Nos. 28–29 are probably on the site of one of the pre-Conquest gates into New Minster, later repositioned (as Thomasesgate) on what is now MARKET STREET. At the corner of Market Street is the Grecian former MARKET HOUSE in mellow Bath stone, a welcome relief from the mainly painted brick façades. Built in 1857 by the City Engineer *William Coles*. Doric columns and wreaths in the frieze, but with decidedly un-Greek arches on the w side, some of them originally open. Modified in 1896 by *Stopher*, who removed a tower from the front, and reconstructed as shops by *Tuffin, Ferraby & Taylor* in 1958. Attic storey of that date. Lower down the High Street some mid-c20 commercial frontages, e.g. the e part of MARKS & SPENCER, Neo-Georgian of 1934, and on the opposite side DEBENHAMS (1958), which extends into the adjoining buildings. Last on this side are two good designs by *Stopher*: the former City Arms Inn of 1873, in his favourite cream brick, flint, and Bath stone, with Tudoresque chimneys. This was a temperance hotel and its owners commissioned Stopher in 1898–9 to complete the charming refronting of the adjoining building as the 'Winchester Soldiers' Home and Mission' (now WELCOME GOSPEL HALL), in yellow brick with flint panels, castellated towards the High Street. Projecting first-floor window over the corner doorway. Across the street, the only items of interest are the medieval long jetty visible in CROSS KEYS PASSAGE, and the BUS STATION, with its Modernist archway by *Geoffrey Denham*, 1938.*

Now we are at the Guildhall (*see* Public Buildings), dominating the spacious e end of High Street. On the Guildhall's e side, down ABBEY PASSAGE, can be seen a small excavated area of the late c11 nave of the church of St Mary's Abbey, and the marked outline of its Saxon predecessor, Nunnaminster, founded for the convent of nuns established in the late c9/early c10 by the Lady Ealhswitha, King Alfred's wife. The abbey was dissolved in 1539 and the site granted to the Mayor, Bailiffs and Commonalty of Winchester in 1554 at the time of Queen Mary's marriage to Philip of Spain. The w end of the church must lie beneath the Guildhall, where remains of foundations were discovered during 1871–2 (the sw corner of the cloister has also been located).

The e end of the High Street has been known as THE BROADWAY since the demolition in 1798 of a block of houses which formerly ran down its middle. This was done by Thomas Weld of ABBEY HOUSE, which stands e of the Guildhall. Its street front is castellated Gothick with octagonal corner turrets, probably of 1794 when Weld, of Lulworth Castle, Dorset, had the house adapted as a nunnery. The architect was possibly *John Tasker*, who remodelled parts of Weld's Dorset properties in this manner. The toy fort character is reinforced by a bridge crossing a stream in front, like a moat. Either side of the entrance forecourt, two large volutes, possibly saved from Mildmay House (dem. *c.* 1847, *see* p. 698). The house incorporates part of a large c17 dwelling (a first-floor room contains apparently *in situ* panelling of the 1680s–90s); the w-facing wing was probably built in the early c18 by William Pescod, lawyer. The red brick s wing is later Georgian, of five

*The bus station site is due to be subsumed in the redevelopment of Silver Hill.

bays facing the gardens with a three-bay pediment over. Later ground-floor windows. Inside, the main stair, with swept-up handrail and slender turned and fluted balusters, looks no later than 1725; much plain deal panelling at the front of the house.

Pescod also created the gardens (now ABBEY GARDENS) from part of the former abbey precinct. He built summerhouses and diverted the abbey's mill stream, while also erecting the neat Roman Doric temple on the s side in 1751 to conceal the view of the Abbey Mill (*see* below). The urn on top may come from the cathedral's Great Screen (*see* p. 601). The High Victorian iron railings on the street frontage are of 1890, when the gardens and house were acquired by the City as the Mayor's residence.

Concluding the Broadway is *Hamo Thornycroft*'s heroic bronze STATUE of King Alfred, 1901, raising his sword with one arm. He stands on a pedestal of two Cornish granite monoliths weighing 103 tons, brought by rail from Penryn. On both sides of the street are the buildings of ST JOHN'S HOSPITAL (*see* pp. 656–7).

Now s along COLEBROOK STREET, parallel with the river. On the w side, No. 108 is of five wide bays, probably late C18; it was named 'Rustic Cottage' in 1870. The outer bays have wide blank elliptical arches of vermiculated rusticated stone, with keystone heads and another grotesque keystone leering down from the first floor. Adam-style doorcase with dentil pediment, fanlight and panelled reveals. The second storey in chequer brick was added by *Stopher*. Further on the street turns sharply w, tracing the line of the boundary of the medieval nunnery. The houses on the s side have their gardens backing on to the wall of Wolvesey (*see* pp. 626–30). The FRIENDS' MEETING HOUSE (No. 16) is a fine Georgian dwelling (formerly St Maurice's Rectory), perpendicular to the street, with a five-bay façade and a splendid doorcase with open pediment over a wavy fanlight. Then comes a pleasing row of C19 cottages opposite Abbey Gardens (*see* above), and PRESTON HOUSE with a front of *c.* 1800, when the house was extended E and w. The central feature is a giant arch under a stepped parapet, enclosing a tall arched window. COLEBROOK HOUSE, further on, stands on part of a site that belonged to Southwick Priory. It is at right angles to the street, its main elevation facing w: three storeys, dated 1720 on its rainwater heads but concealing remnants of a lower, timber-framed building, probably of *c.* 1586 when the tenant, Simon Trippe, Gent., apothecary and physician was licensed to erect a new 'frame'. Inside, much C17 and C18 panelling, a plethora of Elizabethan fireplaces, some perhaps imported, and an early C18 stair with barley-sugar-twist balusters. (the drawing room has early C16 linen-fold panelling, possibly brought in later.) The s-facing C18 entrance gateway, with its neat pediment, was brought from Winchester College by George Ridding, Headmaster, who lived here 1881–9. Opposite Preston House is ABBEY MILL, a sprawling agglomeration erected (or adapted?) as a silk mill in 1793; the mid-C18 MILL HOUSE has a rendered NE front and gabled end clad in large slates. Back on the s side No. 34, standing alone since flanking rows of cottages were demolished in the 1960s (the site of one group, beside the path to the cathedral's Water Close, forms an enclosed water garden for Colebrook House), is a very elegant villa built, or more probably remodelled, for himself by *Henry Holland c. 1790*. Plain Portland tympanum enclosing the fanlight over the recessed doorway (Roman Doric with free-standing columns and entablature), and large stone fans over the flanking windows. Then a length of the Close wall.

Colebrook Street now turns N back to High Street (the first County Hospital stood here); on the l. 1970s flats behind the retained façade of PATERNOSTER HOUSE, built as a bakery in 1888 by Stopher's pupil *Maurice Sherry*. PATERNOSTER ROW, a pathway w of these houses, must be a corruption of 'Postern', taking its name from the medieval GATEWAY within the Outer Close (*see* p. 625) which survives on the w side of the terrace. Now to the WESSEX HOTEL, by *Feilden & Mawson*, 1961–3; Pevsner considered it a 'triumph' for its use of the 'C20 idiom' – namely Modernism – 'without compromise and proves that it can stand up to the idioms of the past and even to a cathedral', an opinion that seems harder to accept today. It is in two blocks: one part is elevated over a car park on fat columns of grey brick, the red brick upper floors cantilevered on segmental concrete arches, while the main wing is a horizontal composition in two registers, the ground floor traditional but the upper storey all glass and stone and slate cladding. In the reception, STAINED GLASS panels designed by *John Piper* and made by *Patrick Reyntiens* and *David Gillespie*. Semi-abstract faces based on the Green Man, in square panels; ground ranging from dark blue to black. w of the hotel, staying on the Close side, one gets a sudden and unexpected glimpse of the C12 tower of ST MAURICE (dem. 1958), which has a Norman doorway with one order of shafts with block capitals and zigzag in the arch. In front, PUBLIC CONVENIENCES by *Richard Rose-Casemore*, 1998, a good design in red brick with a big window featuring a display of sanitary ware through the centuries.

From here we continue w past MORLEY COLLEGE, founded by the bishop in 1672 for clergy widows but rebuilt 1880 by *John Colson & Son* in a C17 style and retaining the dedicatory tablet. The building is aligned to the street to the w called, confusingly, THE SQUARE. On the s side, No. 3 faces Janus-like both the street and the cathedral, presenting to the latter a five-bay, two-storey early C18 town house, predominantly red brick with grey headers between the windows. The doorcase has Ionic columns and a reeded frieze with urns at the ends. The sash windows preserve their original thick glazing bars. Some nice shopfronts, better preserved than those in the High Street. Otherwise the principal building of interest is the ECLIPSE INN on the N side. This was St Lawrence's rectory until the 1850s and has a late C16 timber frame (although the framing exposed and mostly replaced in 1925), with a shallow-jettied gable facing the street. Opposite is the City Museum (*see* p. 662). The Square has a short continuation N back to High Street. Houses on its E side look C18 but several conceal C15 timber-framed buildings, and in No. 17 is a vaulted structure (perhaps part of a medieval cellar). Opposite, Nos. 15–16, apparently late C18, have mathematical tile cladding and rusticated timber quoins. In the other direction, i.e. along the W side of the cathedral churchyard, is GREAT MINSTER STREET, one of the most attractive rows in Winchester; charmingly varied with mainly Georgian façades concealing earlier fabric (the tenement history of the street may be traced back to the C12). THE OLD VINE pub, which presents to the street an attractive C19 Gothic window with five pointed arches on slender colonettes, has beneath it an early C14 cellar documented as having then belonged to Walter att Crouche, Taverner; it is perhaps the best example of how, before the Black Death, a tavern was normally established in an undercroft, not on the ground floor. This undercroft has remains of five lancet windows in the front wall and a service hatch where, as was usual, customers collected their wine. Doorways survive to a barrel-vaulted wine store at the rear. The row closes with MINSTER HOUSE, built by the Waller family in 1787 as a bank, possibly on the site of the tenement of Robert Hulle, master mason to St Swithun's Priory (fl. 1400–died 1442). Five bays, red and grey brickwork. The central first-floor window has a brick architrave; the others are almost flush. The round-headed recessed door is set behind a handsome doorcase with broken pediment supported on Tuscan columns and panelled reveals. Overlooking the cathedral churchyard is CONSTABULARY BUILDINGS (1725). S of this is a C19 GAS LAMP, a rare example of *Joseph Webb*'s patent sewer gas destructor. It burns continuously and was connected to the sewer beneath – it now runs on natural gas.

2. The W end of High Street

W of the Butter Cross the High Street continues its increasingly steep ascent towards the West Gate. Facing the Cross on High Street's N side is a dominant composition of 1912 by *L. S. Youngman* of Bournemouth, in the style of the 1730s. The house to its r. is more modest but dignified Late Georgian with an attractive pair of shallow bows to the upper floors, very typical of Winchester, which originally continued as bow-fronted shopfronts. Uphill, above Little Minster Street on the S side is a nice shopfront with big console brackets, then the urbane Neoclassical cream (Exbury or Beaulieu) brick façade of 1806 by *George Moneypenny* of the former White Hart Hotel (closed 1857). Large two-storey window in the centre with Ionic columns *in antis* and, above an entablature, a big glazed tympanum. Vestiges of a first-floor saloon survive inside.

The buildings on the N side of the High Street are on an equally grand scale, beginning with an attractive, three-storey, seven-bay Georgian façade of 1772 in red brick with rubbed details (now NatWest, rebuilt behind in the late C20). The ground floor, which originally contained an apothecary's shop, is articulated by narrow pilasters supporting a shallow entablature, adorned with medallions of bas-relief fountains. A flat canopy (probably an addition), with well-crafted C20 leadwork, runs full-width over the windows. Next to this a tall and forbidding yellow brick building of French Empire inspiration, dated 1881 on its segmental pediment. Further up, the principal eyecatcher on the S side is the Old Guildhall (LLOYDS TSB). On this site from the mid C14 (some medieval timber framing is reported), but refronted 1712–13 and from 1835 the meeting place of the City Council. At the W end of the roof is a square cupola with four-sided domed roof from which the curfew bell (cast by *Clement Tosier*, 1702) is still tolled. The tall ground floor was remodelled for the bank in 1915 by *Stopher* who suppressed a low mezzanine and inserted four depressed arches of rusticated Portland stone between the Doric columns, which had previously stood free of the façade (a detail in the margins of Godson's 1750 map suggests that the mezzanine was at an earlier date set back even further with a low-pitched roof over shops on the ground floor). The window tracery within the arches has lovely Georgian Revival pear-drop detailing, probably by Stopher. Above the entablature, red brick upper storey of six windows with stone surrounds. In a central niche, a lead STATUE of Queen Anne, attributed to *Francis Bird*. It was presented by George Bridges M.P. in 1713 to celebrate the Treaty of Utrecht, together with a clock by the Huguenot clockmaker *David Compigné*, who settled in Winchester from his native city of Caen. The present clock is dated 1812, supported by a wonderful foliate carved bracket by *Edwin Laverty*, 1916, copying an early C19 version by *W. Gover*, carpenter. Much of Stopher's interior survives. Further interior alterations were carried out in the 1990s, when the adjoining building was incorporated (late C18, originally part of the White Hart and subsequently a shop).

The block opposite the Old Guildhall, bounded by narrow passages, comprises the ancient liberty of God Begot, an intramural estate given to St Swithun's Priory by Queen Emma, who had been granted it by Ethelred 'the Unready' in 1012. Its medieval name 'Aelfrice's Goddebegeaton' seems to refer to the 'good bargain' obtained by an early lessee of a major part of the property. The site, which included the early C11 church of St Peter-in-Macellis (outline marked out on the N side), remained a 'liberty' until the Reformation, free of all service to the city, and the main building belonged to the Chapter of Winchester until 1866. The Tudoresque W half of the High Street frontage is of no great age; its tall façade, with twin gables jutting over polygonal bay windows, is by *B. D. Cancellor*, 1908 (at the expense of J. Pierpont Morgan, the

American tycoon) but this pastiche, and the adjoining frontage (rebuilt by *Douglass, Mathews & Partners* in 1962–3), conceal a genuine medieval mostly timber-framed building, with two long wings extending N from the ends of the High Street frontage. The W wing retains a queenpost clasped-purlin roof datable to the late C16. The double jetty in the passage on the W side is of this period, as is the entire rear façade overlooking St George's Street; the small-square oak panelling in the front first-floor room was probably fitted at the same time. The E wing has been subject to more alterations, but the jetty is still evident. At the rear of the ground floor is a fine, re-set C17 moulded ceiling, saved from the part rebuilt in the 1960s.

God Begot is dwarfed by four-storey commercial buildings (Nos. 98–100) uphill of Royal Oak Passage, built by *Stopher* in 1891–2 for the former mayor Cornelius John Drew. All are of red brick alternating with Portland bands. Canted bays to upper storeys, topped by curly, Flemish-looking gables nicely decorated with moulded terracotta work, and a balustrade between them; urn-like finials. No. 99 retains its shopfront. Stopher was also responsible in 1883 for the typically animated reconstruction of the former DOLPHIN INN, on the S side of the street, which incorporates its neighbour in St Thomas Street. Red brick and warm Bath stone, with tall rectangular bay windows rising through the upper floors, steep dormers, and a glazed corner turret bracketed over the door on the corner. The land was owned by St John's Hospital (indicated by bas reliefs of the Lamb and Flag, which also serve as a rebus for the benefactor Ralph Lamb who donated the property); the hospital imaginatively converted the buildings in 1982–3 (architects, *Plincke, Leaman & Browning*) for shops, offices and flats. The development pivots around an octagonal stair-turret leading up from St Clement Yard, and includes a small first-storey roof garden. Good detailing, including stone carving and clay roof finials by *David Ballantyne*.

Nos. 53–54 High Street are solid Early Victorian with twin bays, also rebuilt for St John's Hospital by *William Coles*, the City Engineer, replacing what Stopher called 'two of the quaintest old houses, with gables and curious bay windows'. Nos. 55–56 were remodelled as a cinema *c.* 1912 by *Greenwood* of Southampton, and adapted in 1936 as a department store. Tudoresque façade with projecting bay at upper levels, leaded lights, Art Nouveau lead decoration at the third floor, some exposed timbers in the gable. Beyond Hammond's Passage, however, is a relic of the lower scale of the late C18 High Street: two storeys and an attic, with a rare pair of shallow bow windows beneath a curvaceous fascia, flanking the entrance. The offices of the Hampshire Chronicle from 1813 to 2004; *Stopher* recorded the discovery of Roman foundations and paving when the printing offices were built at the rear in 1894. Next, a considerably taller, stuccoed Italianate frontage of *c.* 1855 by *Henry Carey Brown*, remodelled at ground floor for the Midland Bank (now HSBC) in 1915. More of the lower

Georgian scale thereafter, including No. 64 which has an under-croft of *c.* 1500, and concluding with HAYWARD'S CORNER, a distinguished and lofty curved elevation erected *c.* 1835 as the County Savings Bank. It is attributed to *O. B. Carter* and has first-floor windows in tapered stucco architraves (perhaps inspired by his travels in Egypt), under triangular pediments.

On the opposite corner with Southgate Street the BLACK SWAN BUILDINGS of 1935, bland but for a lively carving of a swan by *Austin Laverty*, 1945. The earlier Black Swan Hotel on this site was where Conan Doyle imagined that Sherlock Holmes stayed during his adventure 'The Copper Beeches' (1892). Between here and the West Gate is a less consistent mix beginning with economical infill (Royal Bank of Scotland) of 1965 by *Cruickshank & Seward* of Manchester, and little of interest until the wide corner frontage of No. 73, with its early C19 circular bow. This was the home of the Cave family of Winchester artists. Three late C18 oval wall paintings of rustic scenes by *William Cave Sen.* survived in a first-floor back room until 1958 (two are now in the care of the City Museum). No. 73 was enlarged in 1976 by *Evans, Roberts & Partners* on the side facing TRAFALGAR STREET (formerly Gar Street), which was remodelled at this time as a broad approach towards the new Law Courts and Great Courtyard (*see* p. 643).

A neglected raised garden, originally created for the sake of a luxuriant holm oak (replaced by limes) and to screen the approach to the courts, features the ubiquitous statue Horse and Rider by *Elisabeth Frink* (1974). The garden is part of a major civic redevelopment of this area by *Donald Insall & Associates*, 1972–6 for the City and County Councils, including TRAFALGAR HOUSE, on the s side of the Great Courtyard, which sensitively subsumes the shell of an C18 house into new offices. Six-panel door with panelled reveals, surround with reeded entablature, paterae and pediments. Less appealing is ATHELSTAN HOUSE, diagonally opposite, built in 1977 by *H. Greentree & Partners*, in uncompromising concrete and stainless steel on the ground floor, textured bricks in stretcher bond above (more stainless steel window frames). Insall's then-novel policy of retaining historic fabric within a contemporary envelope was pursued even more successfully in THREE MINSTERS HOUSE, whose rear overlooks the Great Court-yard's E side and acts as a counterpoint to the Law Courts with an interesting variation in roof-lines, harmonizing detail and varied textures of brick, concrete and lead. But to High Street the new build book-ends the frontages of a series of early C19 houses, apparently built by *H. Carey Brown*; the earliest is No. 76 (the rusticated ground floor is 1970s) and to its l. is a tall, elegant Regency house, the two bays of its upper storeys articulated by pilasters. The shopfront, with round arcaded windows on the slenderest of wooden Gothic colonnettes, was designed by *Thomas Stopher Jun.* who married Carey Brown's daughter. No. 77 (1847–8) is again enlivened by pilasters and retains the interior of its front first-floor room, with fine plaster decoration typical of Carey Brown. His own house, built next door at the same time, was demolished *c.* 1973. Then comes the WEST GATE (*see* pp. 662–3), marking the line of the city wall. It has been a mere pedestrian through-way since the diversion of High Street around its N side (where the Plume of Feathers Inn stood until 1940) and is now dwarfed by Elizabeth II Court (*see* Public Buildings). Adjoining its NW (i.e. outer) corner was the C12 church of St Mary in the Ditch, its Norman chancel arch still visible in the early C19. Uphill is the entrance to the Castle (*see* pp. 639–43) and the former Barracks (*see* pp. 691–2).

Now back down the N side of High Street. Set back from it is WALCOTE CHAMBERS, a substantial Georgian house, refronted in the mid C19. Its open forecourt (Walcote Place) was remodelled by *Plincke, Leaman & Browning* in 1986–90, when shops were added. On the corner No. 82 was built as the Capital & Counties (later Hampshire) Bank *c.* 1863 to a design by *Robert Critchlow* of Southampton, the earlier frontage being brought forward. Italianate, with two large projecting rectangular stone bays on the ground floor with a big window and the entrance door set in rusticated masonry under round heads. Deep eaves brackets. It is on the corner with STAPLE GARDENS, which retains on its W side the N half of a late C18 terrace of two-storey houses. The street took its name from the wool-staple established in the street in 1326. A little way up on the r. is the former Hampshire Observer printing works by *Cancellor & Hill*, *c.* 1899, two storeys with typical terracotta and gauged brickwork detailing. Between Staple Gardens and Jewry Street is a tranquil maze of small courts and narrow passages and a mix of old and new build. Up to the corner of High Street and Jewry Street a few other notable buildings: the former Talbot Inn (Nos. 83–84) of 1885 by *Stopher*, who reported discovering several Iron Age or Early Saxon burials when excavating the cellars; Stopher also designed the lovely shopfront for WARRENS THE STATIONERS, articulated by fine Corinthian pilasters supporting a confident entablature. A little further down is the former London & County Bank (No. 91) of 1863–4, almost certainly by *Frederic Chancellor*, with an exaggerated cornice resembling machicolations.

3. Jewry Street to The Brooks

JEWRY STREET follows the main N–S axis of the historic city centre. In the C13 this was home to Winchester's prosperous Jewish community, but is now a regrettable demonstration of late C20 subservience to the motorist. Remodelling for traffic in 1956 robbed its S end of several fine buildings, chief among them the George Hotel (rebuilt 1763), whose extensive site is now partly occupied by the massive, Neo-Georgian BARCLAYS BANK by *W. Curtis Green, Son & Lloyd*, 1957. This has a wide central bay beneath a pediment enclosing an oculus. The main doorway is dwarfed by two big flanking sash windows rising through two storeys; each has a pulvinated frieze and an entablature supported on consoles. Crowning the roof is a cupola like a little tetrastyle tempietto. Pevsner decried it as 'one of the last historicist buildings in England' but the detailing is excellent and inside is a very attractive double-height banking hall with a simple arcade behind the counter and a cornice of scallop shells and palm fronds.

The redevelopment of the opposite side of the street dates from C19 road widening so here are several big Victorian developments of commercial properties and housing, before we come to the curious remains of the COUNTY GAOL, probably on this site from the early C13 (certainly from the early C14), but rebuilt in 1788 and again c. 1805 by *George Moneypenny*. Originally symmetrical with projecting wings, but only the pedimented, five-bay central frontispiece and N wing remain and they are oddly separated by the Congregational church (*see* Churches) erected after the gaol moved to its present site in Romsey Road in 1850. The surviving parts of the three-storey building are still forbidding, with rusticated and vermiculated stone quoins that recall Dance's Newgate Prison, London (1770). The central part (now The Old Gaolhouse pub), housed the City Museum from 1850 to 1873; then the house was sold to the banker Mr Bulpett, who put in a new shopfront to *Stopher*'s design in 1876. This ground storey was further remodelled c. 1920. To l. and r. of the Congregational church doorways, now blocked, formerly the boys' and girls' entrances to the British and Foreign School (the inscription to the girls' entrance alone survives, the other lintel being a replacement). Then Nos. 12–13, solid brick of late C19, followed by Nos. 14–15 with entrance dated 1903 on the keystone; the flanking shopfronts, with slender columns with foliate columns, look like *Stopher*'s work, very likely as the N housed the ironmongery business of his brother, William.

On the other side of the street, N of the wide mouth of St George's Street, are C20 commercial premises, then, a little further along, SHERIDAN HOUSE, shops and offices of 1982–4 by *Robert Adam* of *Evans, Roberts & Partners*; an early work but already indicative of his traditionalist inspiration in its evocation of a Venetian palazzo. Its N end, red brick with a Venetian window, replicates a fragment which survived of the previous building on the site (a theatre of 1785) but collapsed during the building works. Back on the W side, No. 18 includes the remains of the upper storey of a C15 timber-framed building set parallel to the street, the N end of a row of cottages belonging to St John's Hospital. There is no evidence for its claim that this was the house of mayor 'Nicholas Waller, 1509'. Three bays, with later oriels. The roof has clasped purlins and queenposts. On the ground floor, two C16 fireplaces might be in their original position. The frontage to its l. (No. 17) is a good pastiche of c. 1930. Opposite, Nos. 31–33 were built for Mrs Frampton, oil and paint merchant, in 1923–4, designed by her brother-in-law *Alfred Frampton* and *Geoffrey Denham*. Gables have windows up to the apex; the ground floor has been remodelled. Next door, CENTURY HOUSE (Nos. 30–31, now City Church) was designed for the Hampshire & General Friendly Society by *T. D. Atkinson* in 1925, a text-book example of Classical Revival, with Tuscan pillars and pilasters on the ground floor. A little further on comes the wide frontage of THE OLD PRESBYTERY, handsome red-brick Georgian of *c.* 1820 (restored by *Paul Masser Architects*, 1998), comprising two storeys separated by a stucco string course, and an attic behind a parapet. Six bays of well-proportioned sash windows (still flush with the wall face), an arched doorcase with an open pediment above Corinthian pilasters. The house's extensive gardens originally fronted the street, site of St Peter's church since 1925.

At this point the road widens and veers l. towards the site of the Northgate, a late C18 deviation from the original Saxon alignment which is, however, preserved in property bound-aries. On the w side, No. 20 was by *John Colson & Son*, 1895, as was probably also No. 20a, a low, late C19 red brick shopfront characterized by two *anse-de-panier* arches in vous-soirs of alternating brick and Portland stone. This façade was retained in front of a large mixed commercial development by *Huw Thomas Architects*, 2006–7, on the site of a jumble of build-ings including a pub, a carriage manufactory and remnants of the town gas works. Well-built Postmodern interpretation in yellow brick and pale stone of traditional motifs including a colonnade with an arcaded clairvoie above and, on the corner, an Italianate tower, clearly intended to sympathize with Jewry Street's most prominent building which it faces, the OLD CORN EXCHANGE (*see* Winchester Discovery Centre, pp. 661–2), beyond which lies the THEATRE ROYAL. This was erected by Henry Vaughan, a speculative builder, as the Market Hotel to serve the local cattle market; given its resemblance to Clifton Terrace (*see* p. 699–700) it was probably designed by *O. B. Carter*. Plain ground floor; the first floor articulated by paired Ionic pilasters between which are well-proportioned sash windows with elaborately moulded surrounds; foliage swags beneath the cornice. First adapted and extended as a theatre-cum-music hall in 1912–14 by *F. G. M. Chancellor*; the character of his auditorium is largely preserved with its segmental barrel-vault and moulded Baroque plasterwork panels to the circle balcony. Renovated as a theatre in 1974 and by *Burrell Foley Fischer*, 1998–2001, who incorporated two adja-cent shops (as the box office and entrance). Of this date an artwork in the circle balcony: Reformation by *Sue Kennington* (2001), a series of 300 hand-painted tesserae inspired by the cathedral's w window. Opposite the theatre are the romantic DE LUNN BUILDINGS by *Stopher*, 1884, comprising five bays of stone shopfronts and red brick flats over, all on a curve. An idiosyncratic design with its profusion of shallow balconies behind a continuous cast-iron railing, each surmounted by a steep tile-hung gable.

Jewry Street ends in a cross-roads. To the l. is CITY ROAD, laid out *c.* 1800 by the Pavement Commissioners, whose surveyor *Henry Newman* also built the three splendid mid-Victorian villas on its s side in C13 Gothic idiom; similar villas follow but compromised by later shopfronts. Opposite is the Baptist church (*see* Churches, above) and at the corner with Hyde Street, a pair of semi-detached houses, now divided into flats, designed 1895 by *John Colson Sen.*, probably his last work.

The junction with HYDE STREET was the site of the Northgate, ultimately of pre-Roman origin and marking the start of the Roman road to Silchester. The gate is said to have collapsed on a christening party in 1755 and was demolished. Just N of its site, beneath the street, are the remains of a late medieval bridge (rebuilt as late as the C18) over the city ditch. On the r., the WHITE SWAN, a much frequented inn in the 1860s. Beyond are remains of the former Hyde Brewery, now redeveloped for housing. All that survives are the former COUNTING HOUSE and brewery offices (*Stopher*, 1907) in red brick, rusticated brick quoins, a big pediment over the entrance door, the latter round-headed, with Art Nouveau grilles, and flanked by round-headed windows with good engraved glass. For the rest of Hyde *see* Perambulation 8.

NORTH WALLS is a busy rat-run for motorists. Near the top on the s side is the former Winchester High School for Girls (later St Swithun's School, *see* p. 667) built *c.* 1886. *Stopher* added a school hall in 1890, and a colonnade known as 'the cloister' formed part of further enlargements in the late 1890s. Forbidding N frontage; the E front is more attractive, with canted bay windows.

ST PETER STREET, returning s, begins unpromisingly between C19 and late C20 apartment blocks. From the 1660s this was the centre of Roman Catholicism in Winchester. St Peter's church (*see* Churches, above) stands on the site of the Peterhouse (constructed in 1694 for Catholic priests) and just beyond is the entrance to MILNER HALL. This was built as a p. 59 chapel in 1792 by *John Carter* for John Milner, later Bishop of the Midlands. It was the first Roman Catholic chapel to be consecrated in England since 1558 and among the earliest examples of the Gothic Revival in ecclesiastical building – Milner was pleased that visitors commented on 'pleasing and awful sensations' on entering it, although its character has since been altered. Six-and-a-half bays in rendered brick, Perp tracery in the window heads, a crenellated parapet (a modification of the original design) and slender buttresses (originally terminating in tall pinnacles with gilt crosses). Inside, Carter's elaborate fan-vaulted timber roof has given way to thin-ribbed sexpartite plaster vaulting, with ogee hoodmoulds springing from cherub corbels over the blank fictive windows on the w side. The porch on St Peter Street originally incorporated the C12 w door of the Morn Hill leper hospital (dem. 1788), and the finely jointed Quarr stone masonry surround is probably from the same source. The door was moved to St Peter's

Winchester, Milner Hall, chapel interior.
Engraving, 1798

church in 1925 (*see* Churches). Further along is AVEBURY
HOUSE built 1692 for Charles II's mistress Louise de
Kéroualle, whom he had created Duchess of Portsmouth in
1673. The central part is set back from the road; the narrow
flanking wings extending to the pavement line were added
c. 1740. All is in red brick with grey headers, under a hipped,
tiled roof with a neat modillion eaves cornice. The elegant
doorcase is late C18, with Tuscan columns supporting a shallow
pediment and a fluted frieze. Inside is a fine late C17 stair with
barley-sugar balusters.

Across the road, the ROYAL HOTEL is on the site of the
house of Lady Mary West, a notable local recusant in the late
C16. It became the Roman Catholic 'bishop's house' in 1692,
and a convent from 1795 to 1857 when it was converted into
a hotel by the local entrepreneur, Charles Whitman Benny. He
must have built the present entrance wing at the N end, comprising three storeys in rendered brick with rusticated quoins;
older elements survive behind, and the octagonal chimneys
must derive from the C16 rebuild for Lady West. The C18 S
range, flanking a carriage entrance, housed William Shenton's
silk mill until it moved to Abbey Mill in 1793: the upper-storey
openings and lifting beams are visible from the car park. Then
No. 22, a C19 façade, conceals remains of a timber-framed hall

house with a narrow wing projecting E from the rear, dated to
the late C15. No. 23 (Trussell House), red brick with Portland
string course, is of two storeys plus an attic. Wide doorway
under a pediment on the W side, between two canted bays. On
the other side, No. 4 is a rather four-square C18 dwelling, brick
but rendered on two sides, with fictive joints in the stucco, a
good modillioned cornice, and a well-carved doorcase.

This brings us to ST GEORGE'S STREET, originally one of
the medieval service streets (cf. The Square and St Clement's
Street). A little way down, on the S side of this busy through-
way, is the former MASONIC LODGE, converted from a Wesleyan chapel by *Stopher* in 1866–7 and sensitively adapted for
W. H. Smith in 1991–2 by *Grayston, Alan & Durtnell*. From
here a short diversion up PARCHMENT STREET leads to
No. 9, on the l., a fine Queen Anne house (red brick, chequered
on first floor only), whose doorcase has a half-dome hood
raised on brackets, and fielded panels to the jambs and the
door itself. The sash windows are nicely proportioned, with
original glazing bars. An C18 wing adjoins to the N, formerly
the shop attached to this impressive merchant's house.

Now back to St George's Street, whose N side was entirely
redeveloped in 1963 as a rather bleak colonnade of shops and
offices by *Casson, Conder & Partners*. Pre-cast concrete frame
infilled in blue brick panels, the first floor carried over the
walkway (inspired by the Pentice on the High Street) on
spartan concrete piers. The original windows have been
replaced and the setting – an important element in Casson's
scheme – has not been treated kindly.

E of here are the parallel streets of Upper, Middle, and Lower
Brook Streets, named after the C9 water courses that flow
beneath them (they were open streams in the middle of the
road until the late C19). Before 1953 this area of the city was
a maze of small dwellings and industrial premises, mostly of
the later C19 but including medieval remains. Then, following
an ill-conceived town plan, about half the area between Upper
and Lower Brooks and extending NE towards the corner of the
walled city was cleared and Friarsgate thrust through the
middle. Excavation revealed a succession of Roman town
houses and the house in Upper Brook Street of John de Tytyng,
a late C13 merchant. Only a few buildings miraculously survived the devastation, e.g. the house (now HAMPSHIRE
CHRONICLE offices) of *c.* 1700 in UPPER BROOK STREET,
with a front of chequered Flemish bond brickwork on a plinth
of recycled medieval ashlars. The sides and rear are of ashlar
blocks and flint; one wall also has carved Norman and Saxon
stones. Inside, some original panelling survives. Next to it the
E end of the 1960s development, two storeys with Georgian
proportioned windows, topped by an entirely glazed attic
storey. No. 5 (Winchester Heritage Centre) is also early C18
incorporating medieval flint and stone walling. Further out
there is also a long terrace of small brick cottages erected in
1882–3. In MIDDLE BROOK STREET, No. 36 is a late C15

timber-framed dwelling whose gable, facing the street, shows the roof to be of clasped-purlin type. It has a shallow jetty over a rebuilt brick ground floor. On the first floor, remains of original wall paintings in a foliate and floral scroll pattern on a white background. Further along Middle Brook Street is the vicarage built by *Henry Woodyer* for Holy Trinity church *c.* 1865. But occupying the s half of the cleared area now is the BROOKS SHOPPING CENTRE by *BDP Architects*, 1987–90. Three floors of shops around a glazed atrium, with two storeys of parking below. Neo-Vernacular with a bell-tower. Further developments for housing and shops are planned for the area to the s, called Silver Hill.

4. s of High Street

4a. St Thomas Street, Symonds Street and Little Minster Street

ST THOMAS STREET is residential with large houses with extensive gardens intermingled with small cottages. It takes its name from the church, dem. 1845 and rebuilt on a new site on Southgate Street (*see* Churches). Beginning from High Street, after The Dolphin Inn and St Clement Yard (*see* Perambulation 2), the first important house is No. 24 (w side). This was the private residence of several mayors of Winchester since the medieval period, and behind the early C18 façade, with its late C18 pedimented doorcase with Doric columns and a fluted frieze, is mainly C17. But a rear wing also retains a C12 vaulted undercroft, in two groined bays separated by a transverse arch. The wing was rebuilt in the C15, then its first floor was again remodelled in the late C16 by mayor Richard Burton, including a fine stone fireplace. The small-square oak panelling in the large upper room probably dates from this phase.

Over the road the early C19 front of St Thomas' House conceals remains of a late C15 two-storey timber-framed building, refurbished in the C18 or later, when small-square oak panelling was reused in the hall and a turned baluster stair was inserted. Next door, the Gothic gable of the former St Thomas's National School for Girls' and Infants' School by *W. Westmacott*, 1846, now offices. Back on the w side, No. 23 also has extensive brick-vaulted cellars; the property belonged to St John's Hospital from the mid C16 until 1971. Next, Nos. 21–22, set well back behind a delightful garden which was St Thomas's churchyard; a few gravestones remain against the boundary wall. No. 22 still has late C17 cross-windows but No. 21 is early C18, red brick with vitrified grey headers between its segmental-headed sashes; red brick dressings and prominent stepped platband. Opposite is PENARTH PLACE, a terrace of 1882–3. Tall, forbidding street frontage in red brick barely relieved by yellow brick dressings and single-course string courses. Most curious are the paired round-headed arches to steep, narrow, covered steps up to the entrances.

Then, s of Minster Lane, MULBERRY HOUSE. Pleasing long and low proportions but a rather plain late C18 front in two storeys of red brick and mostly blue headers in Flemish bond, with rubbed red brick window arches. Unusual large sliding louvred shutters, very well restored and handsome doorcase, with Doric columns and a fluted frieze. Opposite are its former stables, late C18, redeveloped as MASON'S YARD, a group of four town houses by *Masons Builders*, 1972–4. Three semi-elliptical arches, the central one leading into the stable yard. The flanking wings have pediments with oval windows. Further along on the l., WICKHAM HOUSE (No. 12) is a scholarly design of the late C18, whose studied classical elements continue in the flanking boundary walls, with their blind, pedimented aedicules. The symmetry of the composition was spoiled by a C19 N extension. Three storeys, five bays, in red brick, with string courses at the upper-floor levels in flush grey brickwork. Above the cornice is a parapet. The fine doorcase has a fanlight under an open pediment and Roman Ionic engaged columns, with steps and railings. All windows in the s half of the street frontage are blind; the rooms behind were lit from the five-bay s front. s of No. 12 the long garden wall contains much reused Romanesque Quarr ashlar and some Caen.

Set back on the w side, another large C18 house of five bays and three storeys (formerly known as CHERNOCKE HOUSE). Perhaps built for Dr Matthew Coombs, who lived here 1722–51. In the mid C19 this housed Winchester College's first Commoner boarders. The varied brick with darker rubbed brick window arches is well shown off by repointing in the 1990s in the whitest of lime mortars. The mathematical tiling of the s elevation was renewed at the same time. Handsome though austere doorway with segmental pediment on consoles. Inside, a fine staircase with thin fluted balusters, two to a tread, typical of the 1720s. Finally on the E side WELL HOUSE, a large late C18 block of five bays; rather monotonous red brick again with blue brick bands, reeded doorcase. The E front is more attractive with a curved bay at the NE corner and a tall round-headed window through two floors lighting the wide cantilevered staircase. The two-storey C19 addition at the s end forms a good visual transition to the agreeable late C17 houses which continue to the end of the street, one of them with a datestone of 1695 and the initials BTS.

ST SWITHUN STREET ran parallel with the city wall and dates from the late C9 strengthening of the city defences. Nos. 26–27, facing down St Thomas Street, is the grandest house and was built in 1730 on the narrow space between the street and the city wall (whose footings it overlapped).* It is shown on the Buck Brothers' *East Prospect* as of five bays, in

---

*Thus disqualifying the myth that Charles II built the property for James, Duke of York; an idea which seems to have been first advanced in *Winchester: its History, Buildings and People*, by the Winchester College Archaeological Society, 1st edn. (1913), p. 100.

two storeys, flanked by tall, narrow, tower-like wings (then topped by cupolas). These are built on stone plinths, perhaps vestiges of an earlier phase. The doorway was originally central, but in 1790 the house was divided in two (the doorcases of that date mask the original window arches) and in the centre is now an unfortunate late C19 bay window with heavy terracotta ornament. The other windows are segmental-headed, except for the central one which is round-arched with the moulded eaves cornice arching over it. A little downhill is WAYNFLETE HOUSE (No. 25), set back from the road, with a pretty late C18 doorcase, almost identical with Well House (*see* above). For the E end of St Swithun Street, *see* Perambulation 5.

The tour now turns back along SYMONDS STREET, skirting the wall of the Cathedral Close. CHRISTES HOSPITALL (Peter Symonds' Almshouses) is of 1605–7 by *Thomas Paice* (weathered inscription on one of the quoins). The benefaction in 1586 of Peter Symonds, a London mercer and twice mayor of Winchester, was for 'six old men, one matron, and four boys'. Mostly red brick with grey diaper-work, although the Corporation purchased 100 loads of freestone from the ruins of Hyde Abbey for the project. The two-storey range comprised six self-contained dwellings grouped in pairs either side of three common stairs, each with a ground-floor room and a chamber above. The N end was soon extended by one bay and the central gable rebuilt in 1871 to a design by *Thomas Stopher Sen.* The W wing (visible from St Swithun Street) contained the matron's apartment and accommodation for the boys (from 1896 at Peter Symonds College, *see* pp. 666–7). Further N up Symonds Street, SYMONDS HOUSE was built for his own use in 1842–3 by Dr William Wickham at the E end of the garden of No. 12 St Thomas Street.* The main feature on the street front is a ponderous portico on Tuscan columns. Adam-style stuccoed elevations, deep eaves, shallow hipped slate roof.

LITTLE MINSTER STREET is the continuation of the line of Symonds Street back to High Street. The doorcase of No. 38 (W side) looks as though it has been salvaged (and heightened) from a late C17 interior, with well-carved acanthus and egg-and-dart decoration, a panel with an urn and more foliage, and a bold entablature over. But the rest of the street was much redeveloped in the late C20 and early C21 with a mixed development of offices and housing by *Plincke, Leaman & Browning, c.* 1984, between here and St Thomas Street to the W, an area formerly occupied by a brewery, chocolate factory, church hall and Mechanics' Institute. A more controversial addition to the townscape is MOZZETTA, by *Huw Thomas* (2005–6); a tall development of apartments, clad in brick at ground floor and rendered above, with beetling upper-storey triangular balconies in grey metal with face-mounted glass panes, surmounted by aggressively jutting roof elements.

* Research by Mrs Jane Hurst.

4b. Southgate Street and the former Barracks

SOUTHGATE STREET is characterized by some fine, large dwellings, increasingly converted for office or commercial use at the High Street end. It is the tall fronts of the Early Georgian houses that make the greatest impression, notably on the W side, beginning with No. 12, with its imposing Corinthian doorcase under a segmental pediment, and later wing projecting to the r. Also HOTEL DU VIN, dated 1715 on rainwater heads. Three storeys, red brick, with (originally) central Doric porch, above which the first-floor window is framed by brick pilasters and a segmental pediment. Tactfully extended by *Cancellor & Sawyer*, 1935.

Next, set back and dug into the hill, SERLE'S HOUSE (Royal Hampshire Regimental Museum), the best individual house in the street and a splendid Baroque design. Built *c.* 1730 for the recusant William Sheldon, probably to a design by *Thomas Archer* (cf. Archer's Chettle House, Dorset). It lies well back from the street in its gardens, and this front is theatrical in its impact: seven bays, low ground floor, tall *piano nobile*, and an attic, in red brick with blue brick dressings. The front projects by means of quadrant curves and is flanked by giant Doric red and blue brick pilasters with stuccoed swellings, rising to a curved pediment with a wavy parapet above it. Similar pilasters clasp the angles of the main wings, supporting a deep entablature. The windows are segmental-headed with painted keystones. Comparison with Godson's drawing shows that in 1750 the parapet only went around the projecting frontispiece, which was then capped by a gable. Peter Serle, of the South Hampshire Militia, sold the house to the government in 1796 for the militia's headquarters; hopper heads date successive changes in 1810 (at the rear, probably including the stout tetrastyle porch to the original entrance) and 1901. The fine Doric E porch was reinstated 1952. Innovative internal plan, notably the D-plan staircase hall. The wonderful stair, with extravagantly ramped handrails, fluted newels, and pairs of slender balusters to each tread, starts as a single flight up to a landing at the higher level of the W porch then doubles back in two curved flights leading via a vestibule to the first-floor saloon. The latter has a flamboyant inner doorcase with scrolled pediment, between two shell-headed niches.

S of Serle's House, at the corner of Archery Lane, is the former GUARD HOUSE to the Lower Barracks (*see* below); of 1901–5, followed by St Thomas's church (*see* Churches) and then the former GARRISON CHAPEL AND SCHOOLROOM of 1851 (converted to THE SCREEN cinema by *Fletcher Priest Architects*, 1996). Eleven bays of segmental-headed brick arches enclosing knapped flint panels, pedimented S front with cross finial. The apse, transepts and porches are additions of 1891–2. Original roof trusses inside. Close to the N end is the former schoolmaster's house of 1851.

On the other side of the street, again on an impressive scale, the former Hampshire Club (No. 32) by *Cancellor & Hill*, built after 1899 in hot red Rowlands Castle brick, with fine rubbed and carved details. Rather earlier, Italianate, in stucco with cream-coloured brick dressings, two big sections of terrace (Nos. 33–39 and 41–47) which together comprise CHERNOCKE PLACE, built, probably 1837–40, by *O. B. Carter* for William White, local entrepreneur (*see* the Waterworks p. 669). Inside No. 35, traces of Carter's Egyptian studies in plasterwork survive. On the site of the former mews between the two subtly different groups of terraces, like a Franciscan friar between smart Carmelites, are brown brick offices (Anglo-St. James House, formerly Meadow House) by *Evans, Roberts, & Partners*, 1975. Finally, on the corner of St Swithun Street, THE GREEN MAN pub, rebuilt in 1881 by *Stopher*, with his usual agreeable mix of local materials and exaggeratedly tall dormers surmounted by finials.

Southgate Street now becomes ST CROSS ROAD; the Roman s gate was located at this junction; its medieval successor was demolished in 1771 when the line of the street was altered. On the l. the painted stucco rusticated ground floor of No. 1 has a triplet of low segmental arches; the upper floors are of cream Exbury brick, with three bays of tall first-floor windows, the central one with a pediment. Formerly known as 25, Southgate Street this was the dwelling of Owen Browne Carter from *c.* 1835–56. Further along, No. 7 looks to be by the same architect, though it is not certain that this was Carter himself. CANON STREET to the s was built in the city ditch. At its corner QUEENS LODGE, a C17 L-shaped house with irregular brick elevations, is associated with Catherine of Braganza.

Here the perambulation turns w uphill along ST JAMES'S LANE, past ST JAMES'S VILLAS, a group of twelve pretty semi-detached cottages, a speculative build of the 1840s, and CHRIST CHURCH ROAD to the N, associated with mid-C19 suburban development to the s. On the corner, No. 2 Christ Church Road was enlarged by *Stopher* in 1884; he may have been the original architect too. The street crosses the railway line, the cutting for which was dug in 1837–8 and its spoil used to create the Barracks' parade ground by filling the medieval castle ditch. Raised above the w side of the cutting is ST JAMES'S TERRACE, which belongs with the Early Victorian development of West Hill (*see* Perambulation 8). It provides a view of the former BARRACKS to the E, which has its entrance on ROMSEY ROAD. This is the site of the medieval Castle (*see* pp. 639–43), which was slighted by order of Parliament during the Commonwealth. The site was then offered to Charles II for his grand Baroque palace. *Wren* was commissioned in 1683 to build a rival to Le Vau's Versailles (completed 1665); his design also owed much to Le Vau's Collège des Quatre Nations (now the Institut de France), with buildings around three sides of an open court, the side wings stepping inwards towards a

centre block at the w end comprising a giant portico with a
large octagonal cupola above. At the point where the lateral
wings stepped inwards were chapels – Anglican for the king,
Roman Catholic for Catherine of Braganza – behind colonnaded pavilions. There was to have been a park behind on West
Hill, and to the e the axis of the palace was to have continued
in a grand avenue flanked by housing for courtiers, descending as far as the cathedral's w front. Only the main block was
nearly complete when work ceased on the King's death in 1685.
It became a barracks in 1796, was destroyed by fire in 1894
and replaced 1899–1905, with new buildings by *E. Ingress Bell*
(with *Major F. S. Leslie*, R.E.). His are the gateway, with rusticated stone gate piers surmounted by lanterns, and GUARD
HOUSE (now a museum) on the r., modelled on that at Sand-
hurst Royal Military Academy. On the l., the w end of the
former infectious diseases hospital (Mons Block), parallel with
Romsey Road, built 1856, with appropriate advice from Florence Nightingale. Beyond the Guard House is the LIGHT
INFANTRY AND ROYAL GREEN JACKETS MUSEUM, formerly
the Militia Stores. Slightly projecting central entrance with
pediment over. Platband at first-floor level. Rusticated Portland quoins, moulded Portland eaves cornice, slate roof,
gabled ends with oculi. In the courtyard between the old stores
and QUEENS COURT (an addition of the late 1990s), a STATUE
of Field Marshal Lord Seaton (†1863) by *George Gammon
Adams*, 1866, originally at Seaton Barracks, Devon.

Now PENINSULA SQUARE comes into view, the former
parade ground re-landscaped in the 1990s as formal gardens,
in late C17 style, with gravel walks, raised parterres, pyramidal
yews and water features. Grouped on three sides are the former
buildings of Ingress Bell's UPPER BARRACKS of 1899–1905,
imaginatively adapted as housing by *Huw Thomas*, 1995–8:
Long Block (w; on the site of the King's House), Short Block
(N), and the Junior Ranks Club (E; later the Sergeants' Mess).
They replicate elements of Wren's design, in bright red
brick (from *Blanchard & Co.* at Bishops Waltham), with Portland dressings and grey slate roofs. LONG BLOCK is four
storeys and twenty-five bays with a central giant portico of
engaged Corinthian columns supporting a deep entablature
above which the columns continue as pilasters up to the pediment enclosing the royal arms of George III (recycled from
the King's House). To l. and r are tall openings with pairs of
giant columns *in antis*. Four other slightly projecting bays
beneath pediments enclosing oculi articulate the long wings.
SHORT BLOCK is similar but consists of three linked cross-
wings. The s front of the central wing resembles the frontispiece of Long Block. Between this and the block on the
square's E side, the former barracks GYMNASIUM, of contemporary date and with the characteristic red brick and Portland
stone dressings, rusticated around the main entrance.
Originally single-storey. Facing Long Block, the former
JUNIOR RANKS CLUB (Wren House), fifteen bays and two

storeys, with a slightly projecting pedimented central bay surmounted by a cupola. S of it is the weapons instruction shed
of 1901 (now called UPPER WARD); adapted with large plate-
glass windows behind the original colonnade of ten thin cast-
iron columns. Even this fairly utilitarian building is adorned
by Portland stone coped gables enclosing oculi. The quadrangle is closed at the S end by CASTLE KEEP, built in the 1990s
(on the site of the 1850s Officers' Mess) and replicating the
Edwardian buildings.

Downhill to the E is LOWER BARRACKS, also largely rebuilt
in 1901–5 but now with HOUSING of the 1990s, set around
Beaumond Square, with interesting concentric plantings. The
houses are red brick, enlivened by bold blind arcading in
yellow brick, a motif presumably derived from the former
lecture room (Old School House) on the N side of the square
(dated 1890), with the elegant boiler house (1900) to its E. N
of this square is the grassy former parade ground, St Thomas'
Place, enclosed by the Edwardian Short Block barracks (Clock
House) and the larger, Neo-Georgian Main Barracks building.
This is flanked by a 1990s replica of the earlier Dining Room
and cookhouse and, to the N, the former quartermaster's stores
of 1854 (Hussar House). The N side of the square is closed by
the stark rear elevations of the Law Courts. Just S of the SE
angle of Hussar House the old armourer's workshops of 1850
have also been converted into cottages called The Armoury.
From here a flight of steps leads back to Southgate Street.

INNER WINCHESTER

5. South: St Michael's parish and the environs of the College

The perambulation begins outside the Close Gate at the lower,
W, end of ST SWITHUN STREET. It ran between the wall of
the Cathedral Close and the city wall, vestiges of which still
survive in the gardens of the houses on the S side. Access
through the city wall was by the remarkable KINGSGATE (the
name first recorded in 1148), the entrance to the royal palace
before the Close was enclosed in the C10. It is on, or close to,
the site of one of the Roman gates. The present gateway is
probably late C14, and includes much Green Ventnor (Upper
Greensand), a stone also used in the 1390s in Wykeham's Winchester College. The main arch, with surviving pintles for its
gates (long gone) is divided from the flanking walkways by low
walls supporting four-centred timber arches adorned with
circles and daggers, perhaps C16 (their supporting brick walls
must be later still, and there is much brickwork in the gateway
generally). The lateral pedestrian walkways are C18. The gate
has two pedestrian entrances, the E one originally C18, the W
one, introduced in 1846, made consonant with the others in
1958 by *W. Carpenter Turner*, who also restored the delightful
little bow-fronted shop on the E side. In the upper floor of the

gate, the church of St Swithun (*see* p. 637). The gate abuts an
early C19 house of two-and-a-half storeys in three bays, with
fine Art Nouveau coloured glass over the front door.

Through the gate, on the r. are a pair of three-storey
dwellings by *Bridgwater, Shepheard & Epstein* (*c.* 1965); jettied
upper storeys in dark multicoloured brick, with polygonal
bows. Straight ahead are Late Georgian fronts along the s side
of COLLEGE STREET: Nos. 13–17 conceal a late medieval
timber-framed building; a dragon beam in No. 17 shows that
the jetty once continued round the corner into Kingsgate
Street. No. 12, late C18, has shutters that fold back to form
pilasters beneath an appropriately profiled entablature. No. 11
(WELLS BOOKSHOP), is *c.* 1790, altered and enlarged in
1891 by *John Colson & Son*, with a most agreeable panelled
shopfront: inside are the original late C19 shop fittings. Then,
up to the College itself, more C18 houses, including No. 8
where Jane Austen died on 8 July 1817.

Around the corner Kingsgate Street begins, but first a detour
into the delightful and narrow CANON STREET. It began as a
pathway on the outer lip of the city ditch, called 'Pallardes-
twichene' (i.e. Beggars' Alley) but was renamed in the C18,
reflecting the fact that many of the plots belonged to the cathedral. Several of the dwellings are on a village scale and the
fronts on the l. belie the age of the buildings behind: the long
row of late C17/early C18 façades (Nos. 58–62) with nicely variegated red stretchers and blue headers conceal at least one
C15 hall house formerly open to the rafters. Several original
mullion-and-cross casements survive on the first floor. On the
r. No. 54 is small but well designed and of first-class workmanship, apart from the replacement doorhood. Brownish red
bricks, rubbed brick window arches with big slightly dropped
keystones. The only house above two storeys is HAMILTON
HOUSE, large and plain C18 in header bond. This is allegedly
where Lady Hamilton, Nelson's mistress, stayed. A little
further uphill are remnants of ST MICHAEL'S SCHOOLS, by
John Colson Sen., 1856–7 (added to buildings of 1848) in
knapped flint and brick and including the schoolmaster's
house at right angles to the street, with flowing bargeboards.

KINGSGATE STREET was once a major approach to Winchester from the s and is surely one of the finest Georgian
streets in England. Much of it is owned by Winchester College
who *c.* 1538 acquired land on the E side previously occupied
by a Carmelite friary (founded 1278). A marvellous vista
begins with the WYKEHAM ARMS, mostly C18, with its nice
curved, corner entrance. Next to the pub, No. 74 is Arts and
Crafts Georgian of *c.* 1900. Red brick (badly weathered) with
limestone bands and dressings. Above, a heavily modillioned
wood cornice and central pedimented gable. No. 73 is late C17,
with first-floor mullion-and-cross wooden casements, and
good staircase inside. Opposite, No. 4, early C19 (now a shop),
has a wide tripartite doorway beneath a segmental arch of
dark rubbed brick enclosing a rather heavy fanlight. No. 5 is a

three-storey house of *c.* 1700, built of checker brick, brick platband, modillioned cornice and stone parapet over. The windows have lugged surrounds built in finely jointed bright red brickwork. The upper storey windows at the r. end were always blocked, and appear truncated by adjacent No. 6; one of the second-floor windows, also blocked, is painted with fictive black panes in a white frame. Of about the same date Nos. 8–9a, with raised brick surrounds to some first-floor windows, moulded brick strings, and a parapet. They were formerly three separate houses, now two, but brought into one composition with a charming bow window at the centre. The doorcases of No. 8 are pretty, and the front door retains a lantern in the fanlight. No. 9a was the house of Samuel Sebastian Wesley, organist of the cathedral and College (1849–65). It has an early C19 doorcase with Doric entablature on fluted pilasters. Opposite, No. 70, *c.* 1775, has elegant shallow ground-floor bow windows with small panes, a wavy fascia board over, and a C19 bow window over the door. It is one of the most important Georgian house fronts in Winchester.

MOBERLYS (No. 69) is in three parts. The oldest at the s end, dated 1571, is of red brick in English bond with grey diaper-work: two bays under steep gables under a tiled roof. One wide, low five-light stone-mullioned window survives on the ground floor, and there are original two-light windows in the gables. It was considerably extended in the C18 and later as a college boarding house. The centre is C18, has chequered brickwork and stone-framed sash windows. The N end is dull C19, with Bath stone surrounds to the windows of a type introduced into the C16 part at the same time. The doorway and Tuscan columned porch that straddles the C16 and C18 join was probably relocated from the C18 part. Inside, some good C17 panelling. Nos. 67–68 are essentially late medieval, with jettied first floor, unfortunately pebble-dashed, with C19 sashes. Inside, an arch-brace roof truss. The building was 'improved' during the Strawberry Hill period to make it more Gothick. So we have coving beneath the jetty, a cornice of round-headed arches springing from quarter-cut corbels, and a most unfortunate and possibly later gable with crude fake timber framing. Then Nos. 63–64 comprise QUIRISTERS' SCHOOL (for the singing-boys of Winchester College chapel): designed by *Stopher* 1882–3 on the site of the Crown Inn. In the style of Norman Shaw, in heavy late C19 red brick with use of ceramic 'specials' for the brackets under windows etc. The boys' side is distinguished by larger windows in two bays, with shallow gables over.

Back on the E side, No. 12 has a rebuilt façade with central frontispiece with rusticated quoins. No. 15 is good plain late C18, with a symmetrical façade despite the blocking of the r.-hand windows on all three floors. This feature and the design in general is identical to No. 12 St Thomas Street (*see* Perambulation 4b) and the two houses are perhaps by the same architect.

A short, agreeable detour should at this point be made up
ST MICHAEL'S PASSAGE, beside Quiristers' School, past the
church into ST MICHAEL'S ROAD. For the College's Music
School and boarding houses *see* p. 655. Further up is a
successful mid-1990s group of Neo-Regency houses with basement garages and canopied balconies to the main floor. Then,
set back from the road, FRIARY HOUSE, a Gothick *cottage orné*
of the 1840s, with steep gables adorned with rather heavy,
decorative bargeboards, Gothic lights to the first floor, and a
delightful veranda.

s of Romans Road, Kingsgate Street becomes KINGSGATE
ROAD. KINGSGATE HOUSE, on the corner, appears to have
been built *c.* 1845 but was bought by the College in 1904 and
much extended in the mid C20. It looks s over its garden, with
a bold Ionic tetrastyle portico between two projecting wings.
In the dining room, deal panelling from Mildmay House,
dem. 1847 (*see* p. 698). Thereafter the street has a more open
feel, with C17, C18 and C19 houses of smaller scale. Especially
nice rows of Arts and Crafts cottages (Nos. 38–39 and 34–37)
designed for College employees. Both have jettied fronts with
stout bressumers and beam-ends; the N pair has ingeniously
contrived ground-floor bay windows beneath the jetty. Furthest s, beyond Norman Road, are MEDE VILLAS, two pairs
of neat residences designed by *Stopher* in 1887 for a prominent
local businessman, James Cooper. A little further along is the
huge former St Swithun's Rectory by *John Colson Sen.*, 1873.
Off Kingsgate Road in GARNIER ROAD is PRIOR'S BARTON
HOUSE. Late Georgian. L-shaped, the rusticity of the rear with
its half-hipped roofs balanced by an urbane N façade, which
has two large bows with tall sash windows, flanking a doorway
with recessed Tuscan columns, with a round-arched window
above.

6. The Soke, Chesil Street and Wharf Hill

A tour can start at CITY BRIDGE, spanning the Itchen at the
foot of St Giles Hill, at the E entrance to the city. Single-arch,
rebuilt by *George Forder* in Portland stone in 1813. Handsomely
balustraded parapet, with remnants of wrought-iron lamp
standards at the W end. N of the bridge is the CITY MILL,
which belonged to the nuns of Wherwell from 989 to 1538.
Rebuilt in 1743–4 for John Cooke, a tanner, in red brick in
Flemish bond. The staggered butt-purlin roof in the main
building may be reused C15. It terminates in a tile-hung gable
to the s; to the N the brickwork continues to the apex. Given
to the National Trust in 1928, who have restored the machinery to working order. Beside the mill is a pleasant C18 house
overlooking the mill race. E of the bridge the road winds uphill.
On the r. THE RISING SUN, substantially late medieval in
spite of rebuilding by *Stopher* in the late C19. The front part
dates from *c.* 1600, and beneath is a stone barrel-vaulted cellar,

Winchester, Chesil Street, looking E.
Engraving by Owen Browne Carter, *c.* 1839

claimed to be the bishop's prison for the Soke, that part of the
Winchester S and E suburbs owned by the bishop in the Late
Saxon period, which remained under episcopal jurisdiction
until 1851.*

CHESIL STREET turns S, parallel with the river. The first
building is the OLD CHESIL RECTORY. It claims to date from
1450, and was perhaps built as a merchant's house. Timber-
framed, with a horseshoe-arched doorway, two large jettied
front gables and heavy curved diagonal bracing, revealed in
1892 during restoration by *Thomas & Co.* (i.e. *J. T. Laverty* and
G. H. Kitchin). Further restored 1960–1. Inside are remains of
original timber partition walls formed of horizontal edge-to-
edge planking. Rising behind, in Old Station Approach, is
a sensitively composed multi-storey CAR PARK, in Neo-
vernacular style, of 1985 by *Innerdale Hudson.* Built on the site
of Chesil station (Didcot, Newbury & Southampton Junction
Railway, opened 1885 closed 1960; a tunnel and obvious
railway cutting survive).

Further on, on the W side, come larger Georgian fronts, e.g.
THE SOKE (No. 12), whose five-bay front, in red brick with
flush grey platbands, is late C18. The pedimented doorcase,
flanked by engaged Tuscan columns, reeded capitals and frieze,
is particularly charming. But the house is shown as timber-
framed in the Bucks' panorama (1736), and at the back (visible
from the river) are C17 chimney-breasts of chequer stone and
flint supporting brick stacks set diagonally, and casements of
similar date. A plank-and-muntin partition around the stair

---

* Godson's map, on the other hand, shows the Soke Prison on the S side of nearby
St John's Street.

retains a bold foliate and floral wall painting on the first floor
dated 1609. The building seems to be a typically Elizabethan
E-plan town house, probably built *c.* 1585 the City Recorder,
Sir Thomas Fleming, who presided over the trial of the
Gunpowder Plot conspirators in 1605–6. He died in 1613 after
throwing a party for his tenants (his fine tomb is in North
Stoneham church, South Hants). Next is the redundant
church of St Peter Chesil (*see* Churches), which projects
forward into the street. Hereafter the houses on both sides of
the street are small-scale, concluding on the E side with the
former ST PETER'S CHURCH SCHOOLS, by *Filer & Son*, 1841;
knapped flint with flint dressings, a rebuilt bellcote, and a neat
schoolmaster's house behind (1844–5). Among the C18 and
C19 façades the unpromising frontage of Nos. 40–42 conceals
three surviving bays of a medieval hall house, with a single aisle
at the rear. The major timbers, many of which survive, have
been tree-ring dated to 1292–3, making it the earliest surviving medieval house in the city. The kingpost roof, with notched
lap joints, is remarkably complete. KINGSLAND HOUSE,
further along, is an imposing wholly Georgian dwelling; mainly
C18 with C19 additions. Two storeys plus basement and attic.
The basement is in rusticated stucco, as are the quoins. Tuscan
columns to the front door; either side are narrow windows. All
windows have curved shouldered architraves. The fine C18
wrought-iron front gates, with delicate scrolls and leaves, probably came from Eastgate House, demolished *c.* 1847 (*see* p. 698).

After the junction with East Hill, start of the old Petersfield
Road, the 1880s estate of Highcliffe towers above (*see* p. 705).
But our perambulation continues W down WHARF HILL, a
tranquil and verdant contrast, with buildings around a green
created by clearance of buildings in 1937. At the foot of the
hill, spanning the Itchen, is the imposing, four-storey WHARF
MILL (previously Segrim's Mill) of 1885, sympathetically converted into flats in 1970 by *Underdown & Brealey*, when a low
wing was added on the E side. Now back toward City Bridge
along THE WEIRS, the river path, with the City Wall on the l.
delimiting the grounds of Wolvesey Palace (*see* pp. 626–9), then
the buildings of St John's Hospital South (*see* p. 657). Over the
river, the backs of the houses in Chesil Street are visible; several
are timber-framed, showing that the façades on the street side
are later refronting. About 75 yds before City Bridge a flight of
steps up to the Scott Garden crosses the ROMAN WALL, a
fragment of which is visible behind a grille.

Back at the bridge, the perambulation can continue N of
Bridge Street uphill to explore the extramural parish of St
John. ST JOHN'S STREET, climbing gently up Magdalen Hill,
still shows clearly the narrow form of the medieval suburban
plots. A good deal of rebuilding took place in the C19, so the
first house of interest is halfway up: TUDOR HOUSE, which
has a jettied timber frame on a plinth of flint and, most importantly, reused ashlar, some of the stones Romanesque and
showing signs of burning – could they have come from Hyde

Abbey? Above the recycled Caen stone moulding at the top of the plinth, knapped flint and very small stones continue up to the level of the timber sill: possibly resulting from some post-medieval intervention. The house was more drastically restored in 1933–4 by *C. P. Carter*, and converted to flats, at which time the wide leaded casements were inserted, plus the oriel to the living room and two others in the second storey.

On the W side of the hill is the church (*see* Churches, above), facing its Hall, which was built as the National School in 1856–7 by *Colson Sen.* Four gabled bays with wonderful curly Baroque bargeboards. At the top of the hill, the street opens to a triangular green, site of a medieval monument known as Bubb's Cross and a splendid viewpoint over the city. On the N side, ST JOHN'S CROFT, a large Georgian house with a façade of mathematical tiles, so the trapezoidal window heads are not formed of rubbed brick but are of timber (painted white). The house is of six bays, but over the later, Adam-style porch the first-floor windows are interrupted. To the r. is an early C19 extension with tile roof, and then a barn. To the l., No. 35 Beggars' Lane perches on an earlier boundary wall of massive reused ashlar blocks; the house is Georgian but the mansard roof must be a later modification. A little way down Beggars' Lane on the l., ST JOHN'S MEAD, now three houses, comprises a big property built (or rebuilt) *c.* 1825 and extended S at the end of the century. The tall 1890s addition retains its Art Nouveau windows.

BLUE BALL HILL (originally Blue Boar Hill) is a rapid descent down the cliff to the Itchen. At the corner, the OLD BLUE BOAR, a jettied C14 hall house, drastically rebuilt by *Wilfrid Carpenter Turner* after it was nearly demolished by a runaway crane in 1968. Inside is a service bay with cross-passage, a hall and a parlour bay. The external continuous jetty is balanced by an internal gallery along the E side of the hall; less convincing W gallery introduced during reconstruction. To the r., set back high up the bank, are the former Magdalen Almshouses (now ROSEMARY CLOSE), a delightful higgledy-piggledy brick row incorporating material from the medieval Morn Hill leper hospital, demolished in 1788.

WATER LANE, at the bottom of the hill, along the E side of the Itchen, traces the line of the medieval drinking-water conduit to St Swithun's Priory, running parallel with the river. A little upstream the Itchen parts around an island, site of Durngate Mill (dem. 1966), named after the medieval NE gate of the walled city. The millstream successively powered St Mary's Abbey, St Swithun's Priory's Floodstock Mill, and College Mill.

Across the Itchen, one is in the race-track of EASTGATE STREET. The medieval E gate was demolished in 1791 and the present street laid out following the demolition in 1847 of Mildmay House.* This stood beside the river, surrounded by

---

* Its contents were auctioned but fittings survive throughout Winchester. The oak staircase was taken to Abbotts Barton House (Worthy Road), built by William Barrow Simonds *c.* 1855, and salvaged when that house was demolished in 1999.

11.5 acres of grounds, and had been built, as Eastgate House, in 1665 for Sir Robert Mason. The terrace on the W side, painted in a pleasing variety of pale colourwash, is contemporary with the development of the new estate, most of which was undertaken by *Mr Newlyn*, using chalk from St Giles's Hill. Two storeys, the first floor marked by the narrowest of string courses, which meanders up and down, being arched over the doors and dropped as a rectangular key over the wall panels between the windows and doors. The doorways are unmoulded and unusually narrow; at first floor level over each door is a moulded, blind recess. The eaves project, with a thin egg-and-dart moulding beneath. The roofs are of grey slate and at the rear the elevations are surprisingly more glass than masonry. Further S, the fronts of Nos. 10–19 have even narrower doors N, with eaves that jut out even further. The windows all have their glazing bars. Then come Nos. 4–8, a splendid range of stuccoed houses of *c*. 1845, with swelling bay windows separated at first floor by neat railed balconies, all superimposed on a curved façade to give a pleasant undulation.

7. West Hill, Romsey Road and Oram's Arbour

The city's Early Victorian suburb developed over the high, sloping ground to the W of the centre and N and S of Romsey Road. It is separated from the city centre by the cutting made for the railway in 1838–9, and there was little or no building in the area before that date: Thomas Stopher recalled that when his father was at work on the Prison (1846–50) there was only one house in Romsey Road.

One can start at the Westgate at the W end of High Street close to the entrance to the former Barracks and the Castle at the junction of Romsey Road and Upper High Street. UPPER HIGH STREET was the old road NW to Stockbridge but it was diverted to form Newburgh Street and Station Road with the arrival of the railway. In the angle with Romsey Road is the curved front of the WESTGATE HOTEL, setting the mid-C19 tone of the area with stuccoed walls and Italianate details. A little way uphill is the PLAGUE MONUMENT, a plain stone obelisk of 1821 (replacing that erected in 1759) commemorating the Society of Natives founded in 1669 to help the families of victims of the final outbreak of plague in 1666; the market was temporarily relocated here during the pestilence.

ROMSEY ROAD begins excellently W of the railway, with fine Early Victorian developments on both sides. First, on the N side, CLIFTON TERRACE, an exceptionally handsome design, equal to the Regency terraces of Bristol, Bath or Cheltenham. Building started with the central group of six in 1841; the rest was under way by 1851. The architect is almost certainly *Owen Browne Carter*, who was active in the suburb at this time. Upper floors of yellow brick on a rusticated oolitic limestone basement (except at the top of the hill), tall round-headed doorways, and softly contrasting oolite dressings. The later parts are more elaborately decorated; their window entablatures have acanthus modillions and decorated friezes, and the bay divisions are marked by giant stone pilasters. Nice cast-iron balconies, taken from L. N. Cottingham's *Smith and Founders' Director* (reissued 1840). Contrastingly rustic rear elevations, with flint panelling between brickwork. The s end makes an elegant curve to Romsey Road and corresponds with the elevation of CLIFTON LODGE at the corner with Clifton Road to the w. Also mid-C19, stuccoed with façades articulated by giant Corinthian pilasters. Extended (as flats) in 1933–4 by *J. B. S. Comper* for the art collector and local benefactor, C. F. G. Schwerdt (*see* Old Alresford House); Neo-Georgian to Clifton Road, with a niche containing a medieval statue of the Virgin and Child, dated 1543, acquired in France by Schwerdt (the Virgin's head is a C20 replacement). More typically 1930s modern at the rear.

Now the area to the n. Up Clifton Terrace, at the corner with Clifton Hill, is CLIFTON HOUSE, the finest villa in the neighbourhood, *c.* 1851, attributed to *Owen Browne Carter* and with much of his characteristic florid decoration. Yellow brick front on a coursed flint plinth, two storeys, with a full-height curved central bow. Wavy moulding to the first-floor string. Above it the cornice becomes a proper entablature, stepping up and gaining a deep frieze with floral swags and acanthus modillions to the actual cornice. Stucco sides. Inside, again typical of the architect, fine polished grey marble fireplaces, together with much original moulded woodwork and plasterwork.

n lies the open plateau of ORAM'S ARBOUR, site of the Iron Age settlement (a round-house, 42 ft (13 metres) in diameter, was excavated within the enclosure in 2001–2), now preserved as a park. Although part of the ground had been taken by the Workhouse (*see* p. 660) in the 1830s, the elevated setting with its extravagant e prospect of the Downs was a gift to the developers of the spacious C19 and C20 villas along CLIFTON ROAD skirting the w side of the park. Nos. 8–9, yellow brick, are paired under a single pediment, with flanking pilasters jostling for space in the centre. LITTON LODGE, adjoining to the r., is a nice, wide two-storey stuccoed Italianate villa with deep cornices to the windows, on big scroll brackets. Further n, fourteen gabled houses of 1884 by the speculative builder *Edward Haskell*. Another entrepreneur, Henry S. Frampton, built the three smaller terraced villas just below them; they were perhaps designed by his brother *Alfred Frampton*.

The perambulation continues up narrow STEP TERRACE, which reveals the massive gables and wavy bargeboards of a pair of big semi-detached houses, EAST VIEW (16 Clifton Hill and 3–5 Clifton Road) built *c.* 1850 of chalk pisé, possibly quarried from the railway cutting. The houses were linked and extended in 1908 by *Stopher*. In WEST END TERRACE, stuccoed three-storey dwellings of *c.* 1840 at Nos. 19–22 followed by simpler two-storey ones to the N. All are built of rammed chalk on a foundation (visible in cellars) of fist-sized chalk lumps.*

Now S back to ROMSEY ROAD. On the S side is the site of the waterworks, built to serve the emerging suburb in 1849 (*see* Waterworks, p. 669). Nos. 39–41 was the manager's house, amongst the earliest dwellings on Romsey Road. Stuccoed façade with rusticated quoins and a Doric porch with low, segmental pediment. To the W is St James' R.C. Cemetery on the l., and a steep bank on the r.; we are clearly on the line of a prehistoric hollow way. The major event, however, is the entrance to the Prison on the N side of the road (*see* Public Buildings). To its W is ILEX TERRACE, erected as workers' housing by Sir Harold Hillier; part of his once extensive market garden survives beyond.

The last part of the walk descends the hill sloping S of Romsey Road along ST JAMES'S LANE on the E side of the sprawling County Hospital. At the top of the Lane, perched above a terrace and facing S, is MARLFIELD HOUSE (now a Dental Centre) by *H. G. Courtney*, 1914, for himself. Early C18 revival, in brown brick with rusticated red brick dressings. Two wings with ground-floor bows, flanking a loggia. On the roof a charming glazed turret. Inside, an elegantly panelled drawing room, with bolection-moulded fireplace. Further downhill, more charming 1840s villas overlook West Hill Cemetery. First and best is PAGODA HOUSE, built 1844 for Richard Andrews, a wealthy Southampton businessman and five times mayor of that city. Possibly designed by *William Hinves* of Southampton, and originally in a Chinese style by then long outdated. It seems to have incorporated a single-storey lodge of flint and brick, see the ground floor. Deprived of much of its oriental character in 1874 and much enlarged thereafter, with veranda etc. Excellent front railing with two tiers of spearheads by *Lankesters* of Southampton, dated 1844, punctuated by charming brick and flint pillars. Then THE CRESCENT, large Regency-style houses built *c.* 1841 by James Robbins, the College bookseller and publisher, as part of his ruinous speculation in this part of the city (*see* also St James's Villas at the S end of the lane in Perambulation 4b). Robbins also developed the neat ST JAMES'S TERRACE, which runs parallel with the railway line back to Romsey Road (*see* p. 699) where this walk began.

8. Hyde

The city's N extramural suburb on the old road to Silchester (evidence for the Roman road was found in 2003). It owes its development to the establishment in 1110 of HYDE ABBEY, formerly the New Minster (*see* pp. 564–5). It was dissolved in May 1539; much of its masonry is reused in the local buildings.

*This information kindly supplied by Gordon Pearson.

The REMAINS of the abbey can be seen in KING ALFRED PLACE, off the E side of Hyde Street close to the church, which stood in the abbey's forecourt. The principal survival is the truncated GATEHOUSE (originally two storeys, now one under a hipped roof), which was probably built soon after the fire of 1445 that damaged parts of the abbey. It stood between the forecourt and outer court. Main front of varied ashlar. Four-centred moulded arch, with decayed headstops. The arch on the S side is plain-chamfered, and the elevation mostly flint with stone quoins. In the E half a chamber with two cinquefoil lights in the N wall, with rectangular external frames and deep internal embrasures. The big opening on the S side is post-medieval. Privy formerly adjoining E wall. Between the chamber and the gatehouse proper was a porter's lodge, and in the SE corner was a vice to the upper storey, with narrow external door. W of the gatehouse, parallel with the street, is a long range. The far end of its N wall has narrow window splays, apparently surviving from a building noted in 1769 by the anti-quary Richard Gough; he identified it as the almoner's hall.* To the SE of the gatehouse stood the guesthouse, whose E end had a latrine over the Abbey stream; a fragment of the arch in its S wall survives. Further S is a well-preserved BRIDGE, leading from the outer to the inner court; another bridge to the N led from the forecourt directly towards the W front of the abbey church. The footings of the nave lie under King Alfred Place and the plan of its chevet (excavated 1997–9) is marked out in the planting and paving of HYDE ABBEY GARDEN, designed by *Kim Wilkie*, 2003, at the E end of the street. The original chevet was of apse-and-ambulatory plan, with apsidal terminations to two chapels projecting from the E end of each aisle, and an apsidal axial chapel (cf. the abbey church of Fleury (Saint-Benoît-sur-Loire), with its two radial chapels). This was later replaced by a rectangular, buttressed chapel, perhaps after the abbey was destroyed in the 1141 fire (*see* Introduction). At the entrance to the garden, GLASS PANEL by *Tracey Sheppard* (2004) depicting the internal appearance of the chevet. Beyond is NORTH WALLS RECRE-ATION GROUND, on part of the abbey site which was taken for the building of the Bridewell in 1797.

The most important post-Dissolution buildings are in HYDE STREET, beginning with the remains of HYDE HOUSE (No. 75, E side), built for Richard Bethell in the late C16 on the site of the abbey's inner court (the C15 gatehouse was retained as the entrance to his property). It was later the residence of Sir John Paulet (†1632). Only the C16 service wing survives, at right angles to Hyde Street. The N and E wall is of reused stone and its roof, recycled from a substantial, presumably monas-tic, building incorporates a fragment of a C15 wooden church screen. The S and W walls are, however, brick-faced; the details suggesting a date in the late 1660s: big Dutch-style gable to

---

* It appears in an engraving by S. Hooper published in 1783.

the street containing a horizontal oval window and on the ground floor a blocked doorway with Doric pilasters and a moulded entablature. The main wing of the house, dem. *c.* 1769, stood to the SE; on its site, a former MALTHOUSE built mainly of recycled ashlar, again no doubt from the abbey. This was converted in 1981 by *Donald W. Insall & Associates* for the City Museum.

Almost opposite, HYDE ABBEY HOUSE is outwardly a large and elegant late C17 work, in chequered brick, of seven bays and two storeys with a dormered attic above a thick modillion cornice. But there are clearly two phases, the s end probably late 1680s, with flush sash windows (and, inside, the main staircase with twisty balusters) to which the N end was presumably added in the early C18, accompanied by re-roofing. In the first part, doorcase of *c.* 1800, particularly fine. Inside are earlier C17 fittings, clearly re-set but their original provenance uncertain. The most important is a splendid moulded plaster ceiling of *c.* 1620, in a first-floor room, with birds and foliage forming a representation of the Five Senses. The room includes small-square Jacobean oak panelling, also recycled; further panelling of *c.* 1600, once painted, in the front hall.* In the garden, statuary FRAGMENTS: female figures in paired round-headed niches with shell-hoods, a second pair of empty niches with flatter shell-hoods, and a gateway assembled of architectural elements. These might have come from Hyde House but could equally have been acquired from elsewhere by the Rev. Dr Charles Richards,** who from 1779 ran a school here founded by his father-in-law, *c.* 1760. Associated with this is the remarkable former schoolroom in HYDE CLOSE to the rear, erected 1795 to a design by *Soane*. Its elegance has been compromised by neglect, reuse, and intrusive neighbouring structures. Five-bay E elevation of red brick, with segmental-headed windows set within round-headed recesses; the central window has been converted into a door. Cornice punctuated by paired vertical traits like attenuated triglyphs. There was a stair-turret at the W end. Little remains of the original internal fittings.

Now for the later buildings in the street, among which are several minor but distinguished three-bay C18 houses of roughly similar design. N of Hyde Abbey House a High Victorian Tudor Gothic terrace (Nos. 27–30) of flint and brick paired cottages designed for W. Barrow Simonds, owner of Hyde Brewery (*see* p. 683) by *Stopher*, 1872, and excellently detailed. His cottages at Nos. 35–42 are contemporary, but far plainer. Stopher also designed EXETER HOUSE, in 1875, and further altered it in 1912.

CLARENDON HOUSE (No. 33), with grey brick flush platband, doorcase with open pediment and a flamboyant fanlight,

---

*One section, found 'under the stairs' *c.* 1930, is now in the Victoria & Albert Museum, London.

**As demonstrated by Claire Gapper, Karen Parker and Edward Roberts, 'Elizabethan and Jacobean decorative features at Hyde, Winchester', *Hampshire Studies* 57 (2002), 59–80.

is one of a number of attractive early C19 houses in the street
of roughly similar design at Nos. 58–60. N of King Alfred's
Place, the charming HYDE PARISH HALL, with a brick and
pebbledash front of 1903, dated on down-pipes and by cun-
ningly concealed numerals hidden in the florid decoration of
the paired doors. It conceals an older house, with a flat Tudor
chimneypiece in the basement served by a massive stack. A
datestone at the rear claims 'William Wickham built this stone
house Ano Domyni 1586'. In its garden, the spacious hall of
1898, built for St Bartholomew by Lutyens's pupil, *Ralph
Nevill*. Big arch-braced trusses, scissor-braced rafters above
(now, alas, concealed), and tall S windows.

Set back from the street is the VICARAGE (No. 54), of 1835
by *C. H. Tatham*. Yellow brick with projecting wings that have
scalloped bargeboards. At the S end, a wing added 1878 by
Colson & Colson as the earlier parish hall. The hall was on the
first floor, jettied over an undercroft. Timber-framed S elevation with decorative pargetting.

Finally, opposite the end of Hyde Street, HYDE LODGE on
Worthy Road. Built *c.* 1834–6 in stuccoed brickwork. E front
has 1–3–1 bays with centre three windows on a two-storey bow.
Corner pilasters etc. Inside, a fine geometrical staircase with
stick balusters, moulded mahogany handrail. For the rest of
Worthy Road *see* Outer Winchester (p. 706).

OUTER WINCHESTER

9. *East: St Giles Hill, Highcliffe, Morn Hill and Winnall*

ST GILES HILL, the truncated chalk spur above the Itchen, provides the classic view of the city from the E. The hill belonged
to St Swithun's Priory and at the summit was held the famous
annual St Giles Fair. First granted by the Conqueror in 1096
as a three-day event, by 1200 it was a major international fair
lasting over two weeks and the site functioned as an extramural
town, with streets occupied exclusively by traders from various
nations: Flemings, Genoese and French. The lines of the
streets were still preserved in field boundaries into the C19 but
the fair died out *c.* 1860. Its site is now represented by the
recreation ground laid out after the corporation purchased part
of the hill in 1878. The tree planting, diagonal paths and steps
up the W slope are of this date, by Mr Milner, probably *H. E.
Milner*, son of the better-known landscape gardener Edward
Milner. The bishop's holdings on the hill were later held by the
Earl of Northbrook, who also owned the quarry on the E slope,
and from 1894 much private housing was laid out; building
on the quarry site began after 1898. The large Victorian and
Edwardian houses have been increasingly hemmed in by
groups of smaller developments.

Amongst the first individuals to purchase property was
Thomas Stopher Jun., who built FAIR LEA, towards the W end

of Stratton Road, in 1883–4. Now divided, but retaining a good staircase in a vaguely Jacobean idiom and, in the hall, an early C17 fireplace in carved chalk adorned with rows of strapwork and cabochons, taken from No. 40 High Street, rebuilt by Stopher in 1873. He also salvaged another fine wooden Jacobean overmantel from the Dolphin Inn in the High Street (rebuilt in 1883, *see* p. 678) but this is now at CHILCOMB CHINE, next door, which Stopher built for himself in 1916. The dining room has a coffered wooden ceiling featuring the initials TS (in a similar style to the cartouche at the entrance to the Dolphin Inn), the city arms, the squares and compass (representing Stopher's Masonic interests), and grotesque heads.

At the summit of the hill, EARLSDOWN (originally High House) was built in 1895 by Lord Northbrook and leased to the Winchester High School for Girls (later St Swithun's, *see* p. 667). On the site of its tennis court, at the corner of Baring and Stratton Roads, is THE PARK HOUSE, an exciting (but at the time of construction controversial) design of 1984 by *John Bulford* of *Plincke, Leaman & Browning*. Square on plan, with mirror-glass cladding and stone buttresses. Pyramidal roof of dark blue slate, terminating in a central stack which carries all the internal service ducts and flues. Inside, bedrooms on the ground floor; the living area on the upper floor, with a studio perched immediately below the roof.

At the NW corner of the green, ST GILES' HOUSE (originally Coytbury), by *Alfred Frampton c.* 1906 for his brother. An exuberant design, in red brick with strong horizontal articulation provided by white limestone bands forming the window lintels, each topped by moulded string courses, tiled roof, diagonally set stacks. Wide bay window facing W over the terraced garden, under a Dutch gable; a pair of similar gables at the rear. At the NW angle, an octagonal stone tower. Also of note WYCHBURY in Quarry Road, by *H. Dare Bryan, c.* 1901, in Arts and Crafts style. The main building has alas suffered from alterations and additions but the pagoda-like coachhouse (a separate cottage since 1924) has fared better. It has a broad round-headed entrance doorway to the stableyard, flanked by the ventilated muck store with charming swept-up roof. In 2006 a matching garage was added nearby.

SE of St Giles Hill is HIGHCLIFFE, an estate of closely packed terraces laid out in 1881–91: Pearson's All Saints (*see* Churches) and its school were built shortly afterwards. The E side of CANUTE ROAD has an interesting group of small red brick dwellings, with paired porches under finialled gables and deep flint platbands at first-floor level; slightly grander versions of the same design are found in St Catherine's Road. Highcliffe expanded E with council housing in 1926–7 and has continued to grow since.

WINNALL, N of the Alresford Road, was a medieval village but now a sprawl of council houses (beginning with a new estate of 400 houses planned in 1953), industrial estate and student housing. Few buildings of special note. St Martin's parish church (rebuilt by *William Coles* in 1858) was demolished in the 1960s.

10. North: Worthy Road to Abbotts Barton

Busy WORTHY ROAD runs parallel to and N of the Itchen, just above the flood plain. Most housing dates from after the expansion of Winchester in the mid C19, some being replaced by more tightly packed late C20 developments. On the junction of Worthy Road and Northlands Drive (formerly Abbey Hill), SALCOT LODGE, a late C19 house in flint and brick with steep gables, curly bargeboards, and two extravagant chimneys, corbelled out at the top like Lombardic belfries; much of the fine detailing is as restored in 2003–5. Further out, BEECH-WOOD was designed for himself by *John Colson* in 1874. He died there in 1895. It resembles a small parsonage, with dog-tooth ornament over some of the ground-floor windows, his trademark curly bargeboards to the gables and deeply sprock-eted eaves. Just up Park Road, STAPEN HILL (formerly Byrnelmscote) was built in 1899 by *E. C. Shearman*, for his mother, and his own home from 1908. The main (E) front has shallow polygonal ground-floor bays extending right up to the low eaves; prominent gables in the long roof slope. Rear kitchen wing with cellar beneath. Awkward plan inside: the stair is tucked away at the rear of the hall, a door from the narrow central library provides the only entrance to the garden, and the bedrooms are accessed by extra flights of steps from the first-floor landing. Surrounded by suburban development.

E of Worthy Road is ABBOTTS BARTON FARMHOUSE in Chaundler Road. Its name (attested as early as 1272) shows that the site was originally the home farm of Hyde Abbey (*see* pp. 701–2). The core is a four-bay timber-framed house, jettied to front and rear. Roof of major trusses with queen-struts and clasped purlins and minor ones with arch-braced collars, tree-ring dated to 1491. This was of two storeys from the outset; the first floor was open to the roof, but was divided into two-bay chambers over the hall and parlour. Stone-built rear wing (now called Dairy Cottage) added after the Dissolution (with fine late C16 fireplace), the staircase block also rebuilt, the earliest framed staircase in the county (mid-C16 door inside) and oriel window added in the parlour (dated to 1560). SE front refaced in brick in the early C18: seven bays, in two storeys, with stone platband and quoins. The mullion-and-transom casements on the ground floor have flat brick arches over and ashlar keystones. The central porch is a C19 or later addition, with a round-headed stone panel above it. In the grounds is a DOVECOTE rebuilt on earlier footings in 1811 by the brewer Mr Barrow Simonds.

11. North-west: Fulflood, Weeke, Harestock and Teg Down

The NW suburbs lie between the Andover, Stockbridge and Romsey roads. Closest to the centre, FULFLOOD developed in the 1890s and has many serried ranks of Late Victorian terraces, e.g. at the E end of FAIRFIELD ROAD, designed by *Stopher* in 1893–5. At W end of HATHERLEY ROAD, contrasting with the respectable Edwardian semi-detached villas, a notable house by *Richard Rose-Casemore*, 2000: front of huge full-height reflective glass panels in a black steel framework beneath a low-pitched metal roof. Like a miniature version of his School of Art buildings of the same date. To the E in ANDOVER ROAD, just N of the railway bridge, RED HATCH (now Four Chimneys Family Centre), an Arts and Crafts house of 1913 by *R. F. Gutteridge* (of *Mitchell, Son & Gutteridge* of Southampton). Red brick with random black-burnt headers and some black diaper decoration. T-plan, with a steep tiled roof descending low so that the first-floor windows protrude through the eaves in low gables.

Bounding Fulflood to the NW is CHILBOLTON AVENUE, laid out through former market gardens and allotments *c.* 1908. It boasts a number of big dwellings set well back from the road. The earliest include at least two designs by *R. Weir Schultz*: on the corner with Stockbridge Road, PIPER'S FIELD, 1907–9. Symmetrical SW front with three gables, the outer ones over full-height polygonal bays. Diagonal stacks. Ruined by plastic windows throughout. Further along the road, SE side, *Weir Schultz*'s spacious KIRTLING HOUSE of 1910–11, was demolished in 2009 to make room for a development of ten two-bedroom apartments and three four-bedroom houses by Banner Homes. White pebbledashed two-storey L-shaped under slate roof, with wide bay windows on the W-facing garden front (the important side for Arts and Crafts architects). Others (ASHTON HOUSE, No. 32 Chilbolton Avenue; and TEGFIELD HOUSE, No. 24) may be by the same architect. On the other side, LANG HOUSE (No. 27) is by *Henry L. G. Hill* of Winchester, in whitewashed pebbledash with multiple wings of varying height and projection, steep sprocketed gables over each, and wide but very shallow casements. Hill also built the picturesquely asymmetrical BUTTS CLOSE HOUSE (off Stockbridge Road just beyond the Chilbolton Avenue junction) for himself in 1900. Pretty rounded stair-turret topped by a conical roof with lead finial. Original panelled interiors and excellent stained glass in the porch.

On the sloping hillside SE of Chilbolton Avenue, between GREENHILL and MILVERTON ROADS, is a compact development of well-built social housing erected in 1912 by the Winchester Working Men's Housing Society. Groups of 5–6 two storey attached cottages, brick and stucco under tiled roofs with first-floor windows rising above the generous eaves. SW, at the junction of Romsey Road and Sarum Road, WEST HAYES, a red brick house of the 1890s, converted into a school in 1911 and extended E by *Henry L. G. Hill* in a mixture of brown brick and well-cut Bath stone. Nicely detailed, with moulded string courses and some stone-mullioned windows, two-storey polygonal bay on w side with cinquefoil lights under ogee heads on the ground floor.

Furthest out, on Stockbridge Road, at the centre of a housing development is WEEKE MANOR, perhaps built for Mr Hinxman, described in 1792 as the principal inhabitant of Weeke and a very opulent farmer. Box-like three-storey E front, in red brick, the s face better, with chequer brick and flush sash windows and a single-storey porch with a segmental plan a little like the front of Serle's House (*see* p. 689). Semicircular porch on the N side. Long two-storey w wing adapted for housing in 2000.

12. South-west: Sleepers' Hill

SLEEPERS' HILL, whose C19 name presumably derives from Arthurian legend, is a private road winding downhill SE of Romsey Road through woodland. Many large Edwardian curtileges have been turned into small densely packed closes but at the top is DAWN HOUSE of 1907 by *Ernest Newton*, perhaps Winchester's finest early C20 home, showing his characteristic skill in designing buildings for their sites. The house, built up a brick terrace, is of two storeys plus an attic. William and Mary style built of Chichester bricks with deep red dressings and tiled roof. The garden front is pleasingly asymmetrical, with a projecting E service bay set back; the hipped roof covers the whole extent. The central tetrastyle Tuscan porch is roofed by a domed hood; either side of the porch are canted bays with big glazed gables over. Inside, the main stair has ramped handrails on slender turned balusters. Sensitively restored by *HGP Architects* (*Michael Underwood*) in 1997–8.

400 yds downhill on the r., THE DAY HOUSE by *Cancellor & Hill*, 1909–10 (just before their partnership was dissolved): striking Arts and Crafts with Art Nouveau influences, e.g. the battered brick corner buttresses. Rough-cast elevations with interrupted quoins of thin red brick; similar gauged bricks form the window arches. Jettied upper floor facing road, under steep tile-hung and timber-framed gables. Further down, on the l., LANDSEER, by *Architecture plb*, 1995, is Arts and Crafts Revival on a large scale. Red brick, tiled roof descending to deep eaves just above the first-floor windows, with projecting bay containing a big arched loggia and glazed balcony above. Prominent chimneystack, nicely detailed. Entrance up double stair on the E side; at the rear the N wing contains garages and rooms above. Then, perched up on a bank, massive WAVER-LEY, by *F. A. Walters*, built in 1882–3 for Mr Gudgeon, owner of the George Hotel. L-shaped, with brick ground floor, tile-hung above, and broad black-and-white framed gables. Tudoresque four-light window in main (SE) façade, and porch in similar style at the rear. (Gothic stair inside.) Near the foot

of the hill a drive leads to MILNTHORPE, hidden in woodland. It is the earliest house in this area, built 1856 for Dr J. N. Heale (who subsequently built Medecroft, *see* p. 664). Two storeys, red brick with black diaper, stone dressings. Three great cross-wings with steep slate roofs. The last house of significance is the roughcast PYOTTS COTTAGE, at the bottom of the hill in AIRLIE ROAD. It was built in 1907 by *M. H. Baillie Scott* for Rose Douglas and Florence Firmstone, renowned local champion of women's rights and Winchester's first woman councillor (elected 1919). L-plan with service wing, enclosing a little front court still laid out as designed. Elegant S front, with a loggia to the garden (Baillie Scott wanted his clients to employ Gertrude Jekyll; they didn't, but the layout is still Jekyll-inspired). Excellent fittings, as one would expect. Large drawing room with wide inglenook. Wooden stair of C17 inspiration with turned balusters and pyramidal finials to newels.

The STANMORE ESTATE begins to the W. The city's first experiment with public housing on a large scale, laid out in the early 1920s on 110 acres between Sleepers' Hill and Stanmore. The layout, by *William Dunn*, is of the Unwinian garden suburb type, with wide streets radiating from a long crescent, generous grassy areas, and individual gardens to the houses. 556 houses, ranging from single detached cottages to terraces of six, had been completed by 1923, together with eight shops; the designs by *W. Curtis Green*, with much pleasing variety in the Arts and Crafts idiom – a village street atmosphere was his aim – but regrettably altered by plastic windows and re-roofing. Off Stanmore Lane, GREEN JACKET CLOSE contains four pairs of semi-detached cottages (some subdivided) built in 1904 by *Cancellor & Hill* for riflemen disabled in the South African War. Remarkably complete (apart from modernization of windows and loss of some stacks), in red brick with good decorative tile-hanging to the first floor, twin gables over the projecting front wings; dormers rising above the rear eaves.

13. St Cross

The principal building is of course the Hospital (*see* below), founded in the episcopal *vill* of Sparkford, 2 m. S of Winchester. The village retained this name until the C19 but from 1850 much development occurred. Most of the surviving older houses are in BACK STREET, including OLD FARM HOUSE at the N end. The earliest part, probably built in the 1440s when Beaufort was enlarging the hospital, faces Cripstead Lane: a single-bay open hall (later floored over) with in-line wing (originally floored) at the E end – both covered by the same roof with purlins, large curved braces, and crown-strut roof – and a two-bay cross-wing with open two-bay solar at the W. The cross-wing was then extended towards the S and re-roofed with a queenpost roof whose profile is seen in the NW gable. This extension may probably be identified with recorded building works in 1541–2, and the stone chimney-breast, including reused ashlar, may have employed stone from recently demolished religious buildings. The w side of the street is dominated by BEAUFORT VILLA, early C19 and set at right angles to the street. Red brick with flush platband characteristic of the period, and a tiled roof. At the end, BROOK-SIDE is apparently late C18, with Greek Doric portico with panelled reveals and five-panelled door, but the Georgian brickwork conceals earlier timber framing at the rear.

THE HOSPITAL OF ST CROSS

Founded by Bishop Henry of Blois, between 1129 and 1137 (when his donation of the hospital to the first Master was confirmed by Pope Innocent II). But of that time nothing is left of church or hospital except the sacristy at the end of the s transept; the civil wars delayed construction (or, perhaps, reconstruction) of the church until the 1160s and progress was slow (in 1151 control of the foundation was given to the Knights Hospitaller, who drained its resources). Professor Kusaba★ suggests the following dates: choir by Bishop Henry's death in 1171; transept arms and E bay of nave by c. 1200; remainder of nave c. 1225–50. Extensive remodelling and refur-

W. Cave del. Winton.   I. Taylor sculp.

A View of the Hospital of St Cross.

Winchester, Hospital of St Cross.
Engraving after William Cave, 1773

★ Y. L. Kusaba, *Architectural History of . . . St Cross*, unpubl. PhD thesis, Indiana University, 1983.

bishment of the church, and possibly the hospital buildings, took place during the masterships of William of Edington (1335–45), Nicholas Wykeham (1374–82) and John de Campeden (1382–1410), some chronicled in the so-called *St Cross Register*. Of the hospital accommodation, the surviving buildings were mostly erected by Cardinal Beaufort in the early 1440s for the 'almshouse of Noble Poverty', which existed in parallel with the hospital, using the same church, and under the same master. Beaufort was acquiring land to finance the foundation in 1439, the statutes were drawn up in 1445–6; the buildings were probably complete by his death in 1447. The new foundation ran into difficulties immediately after Beaufort's death, its endowments being appropriated by the powerful Neville faction, and thereafter the two foundations effectively merged, the poor men of the original foundation moving into the new accommodation. The old hospital buildings were presumably demolished at that time. When William Waynflete re-founded it in 1486 there were only two 'red brothers' and a chaplain. The chaotic finances and misappropriation of funds in the early C19, satirized in Trollope's Barchester novels, were exposed by a series of Chancery suits between 1848 and 1853, when the two foundations were placed in the care of a board of Trustees. The church was substantially restored in 1864–5 by *Butterfield*, who also reconfigured the brethren's quarters; further changes were made to some of these by *C. J. Blomfield* in 1904, then *T. G. Jackson*.

THE CHURCH,* dedicated to the Holy Cross, is cruciform, with a short nave (surely originally intended to be longer) and stubby two-bay transepts. It immediately impresses by its height and is important as an example of Transitional architecture, with its rich interplay of Romanesque and emerging Gothic elements. The EXTERIOR is predominantly flint and   20
Caen stone rubble, with Caen dressings – presumably supplies of Quarr stone were exhausted by the time of building, though a small amount, perhaps recycled, is found in the N transept vaulting ribs.

The CHOIR came first and for that reason looks wholly Norman. The flat three-stage E façade has round-headed windows: two unchamfered orders to the ground floor and clerestory, the latter having nook-shafts with waterleaf capitals. The gable is pierced by two oculi, chevron-decorated but evidently restored, either side of a central pilaster buttress which runs up the entire elevation. The corner buttresses develop into solid square corner turrets. These are decorated with two tiers (the upper one now truncated) of narrow blind arches separated by thin engaged shafts with scallop capitals. The N and S aisles had roofs running up to the clerestory sills but these were lowered in 1383–5 (and the aisle walls raised), so revealing the triforium openings, which were modified as windows.

---

* The church is also the parish church of St Faith, whose original church was demolished in 1507.

Their pointed form results from matching the profile of inter-secting arcading on the inside. Above them the clerestory windows on the S side are of two unchamfered orders with nook-shafts and waterleaf capitals. The N side of the choir, facing the outside world, is more richly adorned than the S, with displays of chevron on the two aisle windows and those of the clerestory. No two chevron windows are exactly the same; sometimes the chevrons follow the window plane, some-times they project outwards. All is exciting variety, typified by the blocked doorway in the angle between transept and choir, opening into the choir aisle. It is surmounted by a broad chevron arch; the Purbeck marble nook-shafts have lovely foliate capitals: criss-crossing knots of foliage (l.), and palmate leaf forms (r.). On the S side, a weathering course above squat round-headed aisle windows (again with two unchamfered orders) provides evidence for a cloister which, judging from the SE angle, projected further E, implying that the C12 broth-ers' quarters were in this area: excavations in 2009 revealed foundations beneath the bowling green E of the church.

The S TRANSEPT walls also formed part of the first phase and evidence for the cloister is again seen on its E side. The triforium level of the transept E wall has no windows, but the clerestory has round-headed windows, whose two orders have chamfers on the arrises but no shafts. In the angle with the S aisle is a blocked doorway, which led from the cloister into the transept. In order to clear the pilaster buttress between two transept bays the opening intrudes into the wall of the aisle. A blind recess was formed there, which together with the doorway forms St Cross's famous 'triple arch'. The C12 arch mouldings are in superb condition in this sheltered spot: chevrons with pellets, surmounted by a moulded label com-prising cable decoration with pellets and mini-chevrons above that.[*]

The transept gable has a single window to the clerestory (two chamfered orders like the side walls), with an additional round-headed window above to the roof space. At the SW corner wider pilasters denote the stair-turret. The ground-level windows have plain chamfers. The general impression of the W side of the transept is one of plainness – there is not even the bull-nose string course below window-sill level which runs around the other late C12 parts of the church, merely a cham-fered offset. The S transept cuts off the N end of the SACRISTY, which survives from Henry's work of the 1130s, perhaps the undercroft of a domestic building (see p. 716). It has the remains of an arched opening on the E side and formerly continued S. Scars on the transept gable show the roof-line has been twice modified (probably both in the post-medieval period): it was first raised (cutting across the flanking quad-rant-headed windows at triforium level, which were then

---

[*] The surface irregularities in St Cross Park S of the precinct appear to derive from garden features rather than an Anglo-Saxon monastery as is occasionally suggested.

blocked), then finally (perhaps in the C19) it was lowered to its present pitch. Originally a doorway led from the transept's triforium into the roof space. The sacristy's present roof is probably C19 reusing old timber. Also visible are the ends of tie-rods inserted by *T. G. Jackson* in 1911.

In the first bay of the N TRANSEPT's E side a plain window is tucked into the corner, but the one in the second bay has broad chevron very like the E window of the N choir aisle and is clearly of the same phase. But the upper half of the N transept is evidently later, both in its fabric (small flints) and its taller, pointed windows; this was the last part of the E half of the church to be completed, after a pause. A blocked doorway in the angle between transept and choir opened into the choir aisle. The clumsy junction between transept and aisle walls looks like a compromise between two design schemes, but the common coursing in the angle proves that both walls rose together. The transept's N wall is partly obscured by the abutting ambulatory (*see* below), but both lower windows have chevron. The windows at this level in the W wall are plainer, with a different C12 repertoire of rolls and hollow chamfers.

The TOWER is well examined from this viewpoint: it is squat, built in flint rubble, with slightly chamfered Caen dressings on the angles. The upper part has clearly been reconstructed, part of a documented rebuilding of the tower in 1383–5 by John de Campeden. This operation followed the reroofing of the E arm and transepts, as is clear from the redundant roof creases visible on the faces of the tower. Then de Campeden formed eight tall windows as close as possible to the new, lower roof slopes. Each has two trefoil-headed lights in double-chamfer surrounds with Perp tracery heads. Next comes a string course and thereafter a well integrated design. Originally it was to have been an arcade of unglazed openings, five of them on each face, in front of an enclosed passage formed within the wall thickness. The arcade would have given plenty of borrowed light to the splayed windows in the tower's thicker inner wall, illuminating the bell chamber (the bells were presumably rung from ground level). There are just four of these inner openings, one at the centre of each face, with cinquefoil heads and grooves that never received their glazing – so the blocking of all but four of the twenty exterior arches must have occurred almost as soon as they were completed. The central arches of each face, opposite the internal windows were left open; Y-tracery was rather crudely inserted into them and they were glazed.

The NAVE clerestory is the documented work of William of Edington (Master, 1335–45), who replaced a lower, thatched, roof. The raising of the walls is apparent from a change in colour of the flintwork. The window tracery is curvilinear. The first bay has an open sexfoil; this feature is subdivided vertically into two narrower foiled shapes in bays two and three on the N side. The W window must be of the same date, for it has the same foiled vesicas. But the rest is the continuation of the story watched so far. The aisles still start Norman but then turn completely E.E. In the first bay the N window has a chevron arch supported on shafts with convex trumpet scallops to the capitals, on the S just a chamfer like the transept windows. Then on the same side another late C12 round-headed window with hoodmould and nook-shafts with bell capitals, but in this bay on the N side an early C13 keel-moulded arch supported on engaged shafts with caps with concave fluting. The window of the third bay of the N side is plain C13 while the S side's is slightly pointed, again with bell caps and nook-shafts, and a hoodmould with grotesque heads as label stops. Offset below the latter is the redundant nave S door, which has a roll-and-fillet-moulded outer arch on engaged shafts with bell capitals. The W door has double trefoil-headed doors separated by a trumeau, and a quatrefoil in the spandrel above. The innermost order has delightful openwork dogtooth; the hoodmould is supported on labels in the form of heads. The N PORCH, two-storey, with a chamber accessible from inside the church, is mature E.E., although the Greensand corner buttresses are clearly late C14. Quadripartite vault with chamfer-and-quirk ribs and a large foliate keystone: early stiff-leaf almost. Beautiful inner door arch with two orders of moulded arches on engaged shafts, retaining red paint; the outer arch, much restored, comprises one big chamfered order on large shafts with bell caps. Above, a single plate-tracery window with a quatrefoil in the spandrel. The porch's pavement has been re-laid, with a mixture of 1390s Otterbourne tiles surrounded by a border of Wessex tiles of *c.* 1270.

The story of the INTERIOR is much more intricate. The first impression is of loftiness, especially as the nave is so short. We begin again in the CHOIR. Three-storey elevation in two bays, with pointed arches into the side chapels (originally mere aisles) to N and S. The free-standing pillars between each pair of arches are square, with corner shafts. These are *Butterfield*'s approximate restoration of the original C12 design (soon after their construction the original Purbeck shaft cluster on the N side had been encased in Caen stone as a cylindrical pier, a design that was used from the outset on the S side, and in 1387–8 both piers were further encased to an octagonal form). So the nook-shafts are of Derbyshire marble rather than Purbeck; and Butterfield similarly restored the other shafts in the N and S arcades. The lower half of an original Purbeck shaft survives in the NW corner. The abrupt corbelling-off of the triple respond shafts in the spandrels between the N and S arches is an original feature, found also in the side chapels and the E end of the nave arcade. The window embrasures of the lower stage of the E wall, with varied chevron (the N one has chevrons projecting at right angles from the wall) were reopened by Butterfield, who also removed the reredos and lowered the floor (the windows had been blocked since the installation of a reredos by John de Campeden, who had raised the floor by 2 ft (600 mm)). The triforium level of the choir's

E elevation is formed of three low segmental-headed arches, whose intersections form pointed openings in front of the windows. To r. and l. similar openings originally opened into the aisle roof-spaces; as noted above, in 1383–5 John de Campeden modified the openings as sixteen external windows with downward-sloping sills and external splays, compensating for his blocking of the lower E windows. The major pilasters of the triforium stage of the E wall are keeled, flanked by chevron, and all the pilasters at this level in the choir have foliate capitals including innovative waterleaf, and further rows of protruding chevrons – the latter rather overloaded. At clerestory level we are back to round-headed arches, with chevron or deeply cut late C13 mouldings. The same mixture of decorative motifs is found in the vault ribs. The vault is basically quadripartite but with an extra rib in the E bay rising from the compound shaft which bisects the E wall from triforium sill level. The vaulting web is in the French style, the courses ending up parallel at the apex, rather than meeting at an angle. A marvellous display of Transitional workmanship at its best, perhaps dating from as late as 1175.

19

The low AISLES were at least partly screened off from the choir in the first half of the C13 (on wall-painting evidence – *see* below) to form two-bay chapels. They are similar in design, being lit at the E end and from the outer walls by round-headed windows with chevron. The side windows of the S chapel are of course shorter because of the former cloister outside; as if in compensation, the decoration of this chapel is even more exuberant. The vaulting, with chevron ribs, is an overpowering feature in such a small volume – quite overdone – but being low down one can admire the repertoire of capitals to the vaulting responds, with the caveat that those of the central piers are Butterfield's. Horizontal articulation is provided by a string course at window-sill level, which returns over the shafts as rings.

The CROSSING ARCHES rise to the apex of the main vaults, in two undecorated orders. The crossing was also intended to be vaulted, as shown by the clusters of stone shafts on the diagonal. Again, these have shaft-rings. What one now sees above one's head is tall C14 arches (part of de Campeden's reconstruction of the tower), then his belfry floor, also 1383–5, supported on grotesque stone head corbels, with some original polychrome.

21

The S TRANSEPT was completed before the N, as noted outside. A mainly two-storey elevation: the triforium of the choir returns into the transept by only two narrow, pointed arches, though access passages continue behind the blank mid-stage walls. A completion date at the end of the C12 seems likely in view of the scallop decoration of the capitals to the vaulting responds, which start halfway up the side walls. Quadripartite vaulting with moulded ribs. At ground level on the E side is a blocked doorway beneath a joggled straight lintel with a Greek key motif around the arch above. The doorway has been narrowed to include cupboards (a post-medieval modification with later, mid-C19 doors); originally full-width, it opened into the triple arch in the corner of the cloister. S of it, a wide round-headed recess, with flaking remnants of a once splendid C13 wall painting, evidently contained an altar. The larger of two small rooms in the 1130s SACRISTY at the S end is a rib-vaulted chamber, the ribs rising from floor level in the SE and SW corners; they have the profile of the post-1107 ribs in the cathedral, i.e. a demi-roll and two half-hollows. The vault was truncated by the subsequent construction of the transept wall. The fact that the capitals are so low down suggests that this was originally an undercroft, perhaps one of the domestic buildings of Bishop Henry's hospital.

The N TRANSEPT is still Transitional, but the design is two-storey, with a much taller clerestory. The E arm triforium returns by just one light, and the choir and nave clerestory passages end in mid-air in the S pair of window embrasures. The lower windows are part of the first campaign: the SE window is skewed, to give more light, like its counterpart in the S transept, both being so close to the external choir wall; the NE window has delightful eagles at the apex of each chevron. Two chevron windows in the N wall. The clerestory windows are pointed and unadorned. The tas-de-charge of the quadripartite vault are lower than in the S transept and the ribs come right down to the corbels. But the ribs still have chevron, and we are right at the end of the C12. Interestingly the ribs change from Quarr to Caen stone halfway up, perhaps when supplies of the former stone ran out. The vault web is of chalk rubble, plastered and painted in red ochre with fictive joints in the same French style as the E arm and S transept vaults.

In the NAVE, the E bay is contemporary with the lower parts of the E arm as one would expect; this bay was needed to buttress the tower. This work includes the first, stocky piers, which have busy scallop capitals with shallow scoops like those in the S transept vault responds. Above them the junction where work later continued is clear to see, made even more obvious by a change in the string course. The arches from the crossing into the aisles have fluted or scalloped capitals. The N aisle vault has chevron ribs; those of the S aisle are moulded. Bays two and three are C13, including the aisles which have foliate keystones, almost stiff-leaf. The massive round piers have increasingly large spur-bases, a motif first introduced quite subtly in the crossing piers. The nave triforium comprises simple arched openings at the centre of the two W bays. There were no such openings in the E bay, but on the S side are remains of a narrow C12 doorway perhaps giving access to a rood screen. The clerestory passage goes with the windows of 1335–45. If William of Edington envisaged vaulting the nave, the work must have been interrupted and taken up only in 1407–8 by John de Campeden, for the boss in the central bay of the vault has his badge, the emblems of the Passion or *arma Christi*. The arms of Wykeham (†1404) and Beaufort (bishop during the works) also feature in the bosses to W and E. The corbels at the vault springing are earnest-looking early C15 angels. The W window occupies much of the W wall. Its rere-arch has foliate capitals, and a walkway in front of the window links the stair-turrets flanking the W front.

FURNISHINGS. CHOIR. REREDOS and DADO by *Butterfield*, the latter with a design inspired by the medieval painting of the choir vault and featuring sparse foliate scrolls in slate embedded in white limestone slabs set lozenge fashion and separated by bands of blue and red ceramic with small *Minton* tiles at the intersections. Behind the altar was a quatrefoil frieze. Matching COMMUNION RAIL, of wrought iron, with thin scrollwork by *Hart & Son*. – TILES. According to the *St Cross Register* the church, including its chapels and aisles, was repaved in 1389–90. The majority of the tiles are by *William Tyler* of Otterbourne (late C14) but others are Wessex tiles of 1260–80. All were shuffled around by Butterfield when he took up the floors and created a ventilated space beneath. He re-set the band of Wessex tiles on the sanctuary step and more flank the W end of the choir but otherwise the tiles are by *Minton*. Several have a monogram ZO, commemorating an anonymous donor most probably Edward, Prince of Wales who contributed generously towards the restoration, subject to certain conditions (*see* below). – ALTAR. By *Butterfield* but the *mensa* is a Purbeck marble ALTAR SLAB added in 1929–30 by *Sir Charles Nicholson* who designed the riddell posts and curtains. The slab was discovered in 1861 in the E wall of the choir and subsequently set into the floor below the altar: it may be the *mensa* of the alabaster altar that, according to the *St Cross Register*, was provided by John de Campeden in 1385. Nicholson also removed Butterfield's decorative scheme, shadowy traces of which remain visible on walls and vault. – Standing iron CANDELABRA by *Butterfield*, 1865, brightly painted like tin-plate toys. – In the W bay Butterfield re-set fragments of early C16 CHOIR STALLS provided by Bishop Fox. The enclosed choir formerly extended beneath the crossing (nothing remains of the earlier stalls given by John de Campeden). Each fragment consists of two long seats with coved canopies and rather shorter prayer-desks.* The seat-ends, almost concealed, have linenfold panelling. The panelling behind the seats has *battant* cross-over of the mouldings producing little squares at the corners of the panels: a very French trait found in all the other fragments of stall-work dispersed throughout the church. The tall friezes of openwork panels, six per side corresponding to the individual seats, were originally fixed to the coving but have been incongruously re-set above. Some panels bear Bishop Fox's pelican badge and the diocesan arms, but most feature large medallions with human heads in profile. They are separated by pilasters with excellent

---

* Baigent's drawings of 1864 show superb medieval wall paintings on the wall behind the stalls, which Tobit Curteis notes have partially survived. S side, St Anne teaching Our Lady to read; N side, a crowned king, enthroned beneath a canopy, flanked by male and female figures, perhaps donors.

Renaissance foliate drops, and these continue below the mid-rail as pendant posts terminating in corbel figurines of sibyls and allegorical figures – reminiscent of Northern French work (for example, the stalls at Amiens Cathedral). The desk fronts have linenfold panelling, and the ends had dolphins but only their tongues remain. The N desk has abundant graffiti, some C16. The nationality of the craftsman is a matter of scholarly debate: for Nicholas Riall the stalls are influenced by Cardinal Georges d'Amboises' Château de Gaillon and date from around 1517; for Charles Tracy they were executed under direct Italian influence *c.* 1525, perhaps by Flemish craftsmen. – SCREENS. Between the E bays and the chapel, probably *ex situ*. Stone, Perp, with steep crocketed gables. Both retain traces of polychromy. The more elaborate N screen is said to have come from St Faith (dem. *c.* 1509). It is in three stages: lower open, the second with shallow panels, perhaps for painting rather than sculpture, the third open canopies. The S screen also incorporates an unusual SHELF, like a short Perp tomb-chest. Arcaded sides with ball-like terminals to the trefoil cusps; at the W end, an eagle carrying a scroll (presumably for St John). The edges of the shelf form a frieze of small quatre-foils. A canopy above it has clearly been hacked back flush with the face of the screen. – STAINED GLASS. In the larger E windows, four complete saints (St Swithun, St Katherine of Alexandria, the Virgin, St John Evangelist), in a distinctive later C15 style, against contemporary flowered quarries. Formerly at the W end of the nave clerestory, moved here by Nicholson. The first two clearly came from a Crucifixion scene; the Swithun figure includes fragments in the background. The middle tier of four windows fulfils 'ZO's' requirements, with (l.) monograms of the bishop of Winchester (CW for *Carolus Winton*, i.e. Bishop Charles Richard Sumner), in the two centre lights VR and AP (*Victoria Regina* and *Albertus Princeps*) also CR over a small V; and (r.) LMH for the master, Lewis Mac-naughtan Humbert. – MONUMENTS. COFFIN SLAB. N of the altar. C12 or early C13 with a cross in low relief and lettering. – BRASSES. – Richard Hawbard †1493. 2 ft (0.6 metres). – John de Campeden †1410. Fine, nearly 6 ft (1.8 metres) long with inscription. – Thomas Lawne †1518. 3 ft 2 in. (96 cm.) In the choir, well lettered and carved LEDGER STONES.

NE CHAPEL. C19 screen. – PILLAR PISCINA. It has a C12 spur-base but the top, with macabre animal grotesques around the capital, must be late C15. Also, two pretty brackets crudely inserted into the pillar. Perp with two heads as supporters. – ALTAR and REREDOS by *Sir T. G. Jackson*; his WAR MEMORIAL (1918) has a bold figure of St George by *Sir George Frampton* in a shallow shell-headed niche. – ALTAR RAILS. To Francis Jervoise Causton, Master 1909–27, with elegant open-work panels. – WALL PAINTINGS. Surviving C12 red and yellow scrollwork around a central roundel in the N and E quadrants of the vault of the W bay. This is the earliest poly-chrome in the church. On the N wall are remains of a painted consecration cross, and incised lines and fragmentary areas of red ochre survive from a C13 painted arcade; much more of the same scheme survives on the inserted S wall, where the arcades enclose figures of bishops wearing green and black robes. The C13 work was overpainted in the early C14 by double-red-line masonry, each fictive block decorated with a stencilled central motif with red tendrils projecting towards the corners, ending in green buds with black tips. Figurative painting on the E wall, probably C13, notably a bearded figure with a halo, possibly St John the Baptist holding the *Agnus Dei*. On the N splay of the E window, another saint, identified by Francis Baigent (who recorded all the paintings in 1864) as St John the Evangelist. – TILES. Two groups: a first scheme of Wessex tiles of *c.* 1300, complemented by Otterbourne tiles of the 1390s. – STAINED GLASS. Three windows by *Powells* of 1911 and 1917. Highly finished.

SE CHAPEL. SCREEN. Probably the former entrance to the C16 choir, inserted here in the late C19. Elaborate crocketed finial in broken tracery above the doorway, and a leafy cornice. Prayer-desks formed from a single desk cut in half; the ends are adorned with dolphins. Attached to the S wall, more open-work panels from the stall cresting. The carvings *all'antiqua* include cornucopias, winged cherubs emerging from urns, and some more delightful figurines. The Tiburtine Sibyl holding the pillar of the Flagellation of Christ has been stolen; she was wearing the turban-style headdress fashionable in the 1520s. – COMMUNION RAILS. Early C17, in an ingenious pattern, not of balusters, but of openwork cruciform shapes interlocking. – PISCINA. A probably C13 double piscina with trefoil heads, the drain formed of a small waterleaf capital. – WALL PAINTINGS. C14 masonry pattern (cf. NE chapel, but the S wall has black masonry lines and red tips to the buds). – PAINTING. Flemish triptych of *c.* 1520–5. The Rest on the Flight to Egypt, with half-length figures of St Catherine and St Barbara either side, cf. the Langton Chapel triptych in the cathedral – TILES. A group of 1260–80, re set by *Butterfield* and nicely contrasted with C18 ledger stones and the 'black-and-white' marble borders. – STAINED GLASS. E window by *Kempe & Co.*, 1907. – MONUMENT. Robert White, hospital steward †1755. Erected 1763. Aedicule tablet.

CROSSING. SCREEN to the N transept. Perp, *c.* 1500, of standard elements with an opening at the E end. – STALLS. By *Butterfield*, incorporating more elements of the Renaissance stalls. STAINED GLASS In the lantern. Geometric patternwork, *c.* 1863–5, perhaps by *Wailes*.

N TRANSEPT. PILLAR PISCINA. Older than the church, with a plain cushion capital. Another piscina in centre of E wall with image niche. – BENCH-ENDS. Early C16 with poppyheads. Fox's gift (diocesan arms and pelicans). – TILES. Mid-C15. Group of four incomplete tiles (the white slip infill is lacking) forming a square with a large roundel motif and the motto 'Have Mynde'. STAINED GLASS. SE window.

An incongruous assortment of late C15 fragments: below including important remains of a roundel comprising lilies and a knot of ribbons bearing the words 'Ave Maria'. – SE clerestory window by *Bell & Beckham*, 1889. Four other windows by *Powells*, 1908–12.

S TRANSEPT. ORGAN. 1862–3 by *J. W. Walker* of London, fitted up and decorated 1868, with elaborately polychrome pipes. Rebuilt and enlarged by the same firm 1907. WALL PAINTING. In the E recess, faded remains of *c.* 1275, including the martyrdom of Thomas Becket in the upper register, and a Passion cycle below. On the S wall, a wide view of Calvary, probably post-medieval. Almost invisible, known from Baigent's drawing of 1864. – STAINED GLASS. Clerestory NE. St Gregory. Remains of a painted inscription stating that it was given by Nicholas Bedford in 1480. Garish S window of the Crucifixion (1873), probably by *Wailes*.

NAVE AND AISLES. – FONT. Square C12 bowl from St Faith. Three sides with bold stylized foliage, the other with blind round arcading. Plain moulded C17 stone base of boldly concave profile. – OAK LECTERN. Subject of much folklore. Late C19, closely copied from a medieval one at Birtles church (Cheshire), and made in two parts like the exemplar. Its design, including the parrot-like eagle's head, ultimately goes back to latten exemplars in the Namur region. – PULPIT. By *Butterfield*, 1866. – PEWS. A full set by *Butterfield*. – ROOD BEAM with plain CROSS, both of 1909 by *C. J. Blomfield*, in place of the medieval beam which rested on the late C12 Romanesque corbels. – ARCHITECTURAL FRAGMENT by the font. A square capital with spreading waterleaves. – Butterfield regrouped the best medieval TILES in the aisles; those in the central aisle are *Minton* replicas. – STAINED GLASS. S aisle. Three windows in a 'medallion-and-mosaic' format, typical of the period, first from E †1875 by *Gibbs*, second possibly by the same, the third (related in subject to the font below) by *Wailes*, but designed by *Butterfield*, 1863, and noticeably better. W window *c.* 1873 by *Wailes*. N aisle, two windows by *Hugh Easton*, 1935 and 1938, the third by *Wailes*. Nave W window by *Wailes, Son & Strang*, 1873, with Old Testament prophets. – MONUMENTS. Large late C13 arched tomb-recess to Peter Seymour (de S. Mario), Master 1289–96. Quite impressive, the roll mouldings of the arch dying into vertical posts above the short columns. Charles Wolfran Cornwall, Speaker of the House of Commons, †1789 while staying at the Master's Lodgings. By *J. F. Moore*. Neoclassical, of coloured marbles. Pedimented sarcophagus with achievement, flanking lamps and an urn. Below it the Speaker's mace.

The HOSPITAL premises as they are now, NW of the church, were mostly put up in one build by Cardinal Beaufort (although incorporating an earlier hall and remains of an inner gate as we shall see). They consist of a quadrangle, reminiscent of an Oxbridge college, and a small entrance court to the N with the OUTER GATE. The latter has a moulded four-centred outer arch in Caen stone and a clasped purlin roof, with brick infill on the S side, possibly a later C15 modification following the refounding of the hospital in the 1440s. Inside, on the E and W are flint ranges, that on the E side on the site of the Hundred Menne's Hall, for the feeding of local poor men. The present building, adapted as the brewhouse in 1782, is probably mid C15, see the cinquefoil lights beneath stone labels and small four-centred doorway (blocked when the C19 carriage door was inserted at the N end). Linking it to the gate an addition dated 1675 with the initials inscribed of Henry Compton (Master, 1667–76). Original kingpost roof inside. Might this have housed an earlier porter's lodge? There were other buildings at the S end, taken down in the C19. The longer, two-storey W range contained the kitchen and meets the N range of Beaufort's quad, in a manner reminiscent of the College. The small rectangular windows are original; the larger one to the kitchen itself (and an identical one on its W front) is a C19 modification with Perp tracery and Bath stone dressings. Door to its l. of the same time. Pair of original doors near the N end.

The quadrangle is entered by a monumental GATE-TOWER. This, with its E wing (now Porter's Lodge*) which has a garderobe tower, contained the Master's lodgings. Its position, off-centre in the N range, seems to have been determined by the decision to retain the earlier hall to its W (*see* below); presumably the tower and wing replaced existing accommodation for the Master. On the outer face, the archway has a four-centred arch, with multiple continuous mouldings. In the spandrels are cusped daggers and octofoils enclosing the royal arms (l.) and Beaufort arms (r., differentiated by a 'bordure gobony'). Then a cornice with alternating heads and square fleurons and, above, a four-light mullioned-and-transomed window under a square label to the Master's chamber (later muniment room). Higher up three tall and slender niches with crocketed gables, in the r. one still the kneeling figure of Beaufort (wearing his cardinal's hat); the others must have contained the Virgin (centre) and another worshipper, as at Winchester College, and another person, adoring the Virgin, in the central niche. Over the passage beneath the tower is a fine lierne vault with bosses. The S face of the tower is superficially similar (though there is only one niche, with a C19 statue of the Virgin), but the arch, though with the same mouldings as the N arch, is wider, its four-centred arch is flatter, and the end-stops of the hoodmould have the Passion emblems of John de Campeden. This suggests that Beaufort remodelled an earlier gate-tower. The stair-turret at the SW corner certainly incorporates earlier elements, for inside the stair one sees that the neat small blocks of Caen stone that Beaufort used for his interior work have been clumsily bonded into large Greensand blocks forming the S half of the turret, and the Greensand step blocks of the newel stair are properly bonded with the Caen work but simply abut the Greensand masonry. So there are two phases and the actual stair has been

* The porter still provides the 'Wayfarer's Dole' to needy travellers.

rebuilt with greater care than its predecessor. The big buttress on the l. side of the gate-tower's S arch courses with the turret and must be of the same phase; likewise, presumably, the r. buttress and perhaps those on the N side. Presumably the first structure failed, or perhaps Beaufort wanted a higher tower than de Campeden's footings would bear.

34   The BRETHREN'S HALL, which Beaufort incorporated into his new buildings dates mainly from the 1360s as proved below. It is raised on an undercroft which originally comprised two slightly pointed tunnel vaults running the full length of the building; but the W half was remodelled in the mid C15 and replaced by a new four-centred vault with four quadripartite cells of plain chamfered ribs supported on an octagonal central shaft. Being a perfect square its E–W dimension no longer coincides with the earlier bay divisions. Fireplace on N side, unusual in a cellar. The entrances to the undercroft are of the same phase. The walls of the hall above are of flint and rubble, with Green Ventnor buttresses. There are three windows to the S, now two to the N (one was perhaps blocked up when the wing housing the kitchen was added in the C15). The E pair are taller and have window seats within; the one on the S side was shifted to the W to accommodate the first gatehouse stair-turret. All the windows have two two-centred lights with a transom, and at the top a quatrefoil in an oval. The tracery style, still slightly flowing, suggests the third quarter of the C14.

36   The porch with angle buttresses is an addition, see its lierne vault with a prominent display of Beaufort's arms and cardinal's hat at the key-stone. Inside are steps with seats on each side, and cleverly arranged beneath the porch is the access to Beaufort's undercroft. But the main door is of the C14 phase. Developed Perp: the jambs have double ogee mouldings with a fillet and a deep hollow – a small-scale version of mouldings found in Bishop Edington's remodelled aisle doors at the cathedral. The hood mould has end stops featuring an elderly king and his queen, which must represent Edward III and Queen Philippa (†1369); so the builder of the hall has to be John of Edington, the bishop's nephew, Master from 1349–66. The screens passage inside has original flat, four-centred doors at each end (the S one butchered). The N door, leading into the later kitchen range was external so opens inwards and has on the outside, broach stops, one half covered by the abutting passage wall. The screen is of several phases. The wings to l. and r. are earliest – C14? – and there may originally have been a free-standing 'standard' in the centre. Then, perhaps in the 1440s, it was made continuous, with doors and a big moulded bressumer running along the top (just visible in the passage). Next the passage was ceiled to form a gallery above – this covers the corbels of Beaufort's roof, showing it is later, and the door from within the hall to the gallery stair must have been formed at the same time. The coving on the hall side looks C17 and the parapet has also been altered, on the last occasion to create a central 'pulpit'.

In the hall's SE corner is a stone stair to the room above the gate. It is probably early C16, indicated by Bishop Fox's pelican emblem on the newel. It cuts across the SE window, making the window seats redundant. But the shadowy outline of an earlier doorway is just discernible in the side wall between the window and the corner; the opening is clearly visible within the stair-turret, and formed part of the first gate-tower. The scheme required the SE window to be shifted W as already noted. The doorway was probably accessed by eight or nine steps flat against the end wall, allowing the Master to retire to his chamber – and this arrangement was retained by Beaufort.

The great glory of the hall is the oak roof dendro dated to the 1440s. Four bays with arch-brace trusses, the braces almost entirely filling the spandrels and forming four-centred arches. Slightly curved collars. Two tiers of normal wind-braces and a further tier of inverted ones above the upper purlin. Angel corbels with alternation of Beaufort's and the royal arms. The corner corbels – angels playing musical instruments – are also C15, but there is one earlier corbel set slightly higher up in the SE corner, evidence for the earlier roof. – In the quatrefoils of the S windows and above the door, some C15 STAINED GLASS with Beaufort's arms or livery colours, against a background featuring his motto *A honor et lyesse*. The main lights were reglazed in the C19. Adjoining the W end of the hall, and separated from the kitchen passage by a timber-framed wall, is the buttery (now the bread room), accessed by an inserted door just E of the screens, with stairs up to accommodation and the hall gallery, and down to the undercroft – all part of the Beaufort kitchen wing on the W side of the outer court.

In the windows of the passage to the kitchen is some STAINED GLASS with initials of Robert Sherborne, his motto, and the date, in early Arabic numerals, 1497. Fragments of three other quarries in same window, one with the portcullis of Henry VII. The KITCHEN rises to a two-bay crown-post roof (ceiled at the level of the collars) of identical structure to that of the Brethren's Quarters (*see* below). Large fireplaces in the N wall with a range, supplied in 1860 by *Josiah Carter* of No. 65 High Street. It is a delightful tripartite design: on the l., a separate fire provided hot water; the main hearth has an ingenious way of altering the draught by winding the fire cheeks in and out, swivel gallows brackets to suspend pots, a smoke jack and trivets; to the r., a bread oven. At the S end of the kitchen, the MEAT ROOM. In the SE corner, steps down to the meat cellar. The N end of the wing was extended in a second C15 phase; it originally ended with the kitchen, as shown by the former external plinth, now within the building. Dr Hare has shown that this wing, later converted into stabling, comprised two storeys of heated guest accommodation with fireplaces. It has a garderobe tower at the NW corner.

THE BRETHREN'S QUARTERS ran continuously around the quad between the w end of the hall and the church. The s range was demolished in 1789, but see the blocked window in the one of the sw angle buttresses of the nave of the church to which it was joined (the buttresses also have much Green Ventnor sandstone). Built of flint and stone rubble, with dressings, doorways, and windows mainly of Green Ventnor. The apartments are grouped in fours, with a pair of 'quarters' on each floor either side of a staircase – the typical arrangement of an Oxford or Cambridge college – providing rooms for thirty-eight brothers. The original layout of each lodging has scarcely changed. A living room is heated by a big fireplace, hence the prominence on the main elevation of the projecting chimney-breasts with tall octagonal stone stacks, and has big mullioned windows with stone seats in the embrasures. A timber-framed partition with wattle and plaster infill separates this from two smaller rooms (bedroom and scullery, now kitchen) at the rear. They are also separated by a timber partition and although none of these partitions is original, this appears to have been the arrangement always, as the doors from the living room suggest. Each staircase has a garderobe turret with two privies to each floor (i.e. one for each apartment), each with its original doorway. The ground-floor closets were smaller, a chute behind serving those on the first floor. The only significant alterations have been in the NW corner of the quadrangle, where quarters were converted into the Master's House in 1696. *Charles Blomfield*, then *T. G. Jackson*, reinstated the rooms on the w side from 1904, when the Master's House was built (see below). The N range became the Trustees' Room, offices, etc. Late C17 panelling and a bolection-moulded fireplace survive in the Trustees' Room, together with early C17 STAINED GLASS (royal arms of James I etc.) and two C16 Flemish roundels (Christ before Pilate and Good Samaritan). In the ground-floor common room, relocated C16 PANELLING with cornice inscription including the motto of John Incent, Master 1524–45, later dean of St Paul's and founder of Berkhamsted School (same motto).

Finally the AMBULATORY linking the Master's House and N transept of the church. Rear wall of 1398, the rest by Robert Sherborne (Master, 1492–1508). He subsequently built a similar gallery at his palace at Chichester. Later changes have obscured the near symmetry of an open timber arcade articulated by two octagonal turrets of brick and checker flint (the s one mostly demolished) and a central brick oriel, the latter supported on twin brick arches and a central pier whose capital (replaced 1939) bears Sherborne's motto and initials. Later in the C16 the arcade between the N turret and the Master's House was rebuilt in brick, and a mainly stone porch was added on the s side of the turret; both parts castellated. Between the turrets extended a timber arcade of shallow four-centred arches (each 10ft wide) with cusped daggers and quatrefoils, supporting the bressumer of a slightly jettied timber-framed upper storey. The posts were supported on a low stylobate (checker brick and flint, greensand capping). Probably in the C17 the S turret was mostly demolished, the stylobate was raised higher, and the oriel was remodelled. An inscription 'Henry Compton *Episcopus*' dates these works to 1674–5 when Henry was concurrently Master and bishop of Oxford. In the C19 the S bay was bricked up to the soffit of the bressumer. The flimsy upper storey is mostly rebuilt, but Sherborne's original close studding and a window survive in the S bay next to the church. Behind the ambulatory is the Master's Garden, with low tile-capped stone wall. At the NE corner a semicircular projection was part of a dovecote.

N of the Outer Gate, the present MASTER'S HOUSE, Neo-Elizabethan by *C. J. Blomfield*, 1899. Flint, with gables and mullioned-and-transomed windows now divided into separate lodgings for master and chaplain.

A dispersed settlement with a group around the church, a more substantial settlement at Winchfield Hurst to the N and a further grouping which has grown up around the station to the N.

ST MARY. Much of the church is Norman, with sculptured detail of a singular ferocity; its richness must be explained by the ownership of church and manor by Chertsey Abbey. A date of 1150 is given for the completion, and that would agree with, if a little in advance of, Bishop Henry of Blois's project for the E end of St Cross. The original plan survives: nave and broad W tower of equal width with walls 5 ft (1.5 metres) thick with three original windows, N, S and W, and lower chancel. The tower's Neo-Norman upper part is obviously of the restoration of 1849–50 by *Woodyer*, when the N aisle was added and much renewing was done, especially to the chancel, e.g. the E window, evidently based on surviving Norman windows N and S, two of which are original and were left unrestored. Inside, the tower has a mighty, surprisingly large-scaled arch to the nave. The piers are triple-shafted with leaf capitals, also trumpet scallops and intersected flutes. Round arch with a slight chamfer and a roll. Sumptuous on both sides E and W. The simple N doorway has similar mouldings but a pointed arch. The S doorway, exceptionally finely preserved, is a big p. 18 hulking piece in clunch with extremely large, rude reeded leaves (that to the E pier a lotus leaf of Saracenic derivation), no two capitals alike – vertical zigzag projecting diagonally, and a round arch with much zigzag. The chancel arch, also of 16 clunch, remains as when carved, as a pre-1849 drawing shows. The character is exactly that of the S doorway. The main responds are keeled here. The innermost soffit of the arch has a most extraordinary profile of two hollows to one roll.

Actually the roll looks like sawn branches. Details inside the chancel are partly genuine. The s porch is an engaging mixture of periods, mostly Late Perp, with single C13 trefoil-headed windows reused from an earlier porch.

FURNISHINGS. – ALTAR STONE – a medieval *mensa*, buried in the chancel floor. – ALTAR CROSS and CANDLESTICKS of 1917. By *E. S. Prior*. – PILLAR PISCINA unusually integrated with the jamb of the SE window. – PISCINA. C14 with a trefoil head. In the E wall. – COMMUNION RAIL. Early C17, Laudian. – FONT. Late Norman. A plain Purbeck basin. – PULPIT. A Laudian piece, dated 1634 (cf. Odiham). Arched panels in two tiers. Pretty decoration, partly vegetable, partly strapwork in the panels. Restored by *Collcutt & Hamp*, 1908. – BENCHES. Two, on the s side of the nave, plain, probably C14. The ends with a curve down from back to arm. – DOOR. Convincingly Norman with strong ironwork. Presented by John Keble in 1849–50. – STAINED GLASS. In the chancel of 1849, perhaps by *O'Connor*. The s window, for Stella Charrington of Winchfield House †1978, has fantastical engraved glass by *Laurence Whistler*, with a Tree of Life rooted in her home. – N aisle w, *c.* 1910 by *Herbert Hendrie*. Excellent Arts and Crafts Annunciation. – MONUMENTS. In the N aisle, beyond the parclose screen, several ledger slabs, one to James Rudyerd †1687. A C17 transeptal Rudyerd family chapel stood here until 1849 (drawn by T. D. Powell). – Lady Margaret Beauclerk †1792. Elegant and understated with the inscription below an urn, together with draperies and ribbons within a shallow oval recess. – Rt. Hon. and Rev. Lord Frederick Beauclerk †1850, by *J. G. Lough*, 1851. Faith seated on the ground. White marble relief. Nothing special about the quality. – Charlotte Beauclerk †1866, wife. Separate tablet below, signed *J. G. Lough*. – Charles William Rawlinson †1910, a Master of the Supreme Court. Purbeck tablet by *E. S. Prior*, with a convex surface, chamfered edges, and lettering inlaid into panels of enamel. – War memorial tablet of 1919 by *Charles A. Nicholson*. – Charles Read Seymour †1934. Wood, by his architect *R. Weir Schultz* (*see* Inholmes, West Green) who probably also designed the good Arts and Crafts grave marker to Marion Seymour †1900.

To the w, THE OLD SCHOOL of 1860–1 by *William Burges*, with later alterations. Gothic, brick with patterned tile roof, the most striking feature the pair of bold full-height windows with open timberwork gables marking the former schoolroom. To the N the C18 COURT HOUSE, painted brick with Ionic pedimented doorcase. OLD RECTORY, ¼ m. SE, is C18 but thoroughly remodelled and enlarged by *Woodyer* in 1849–50 in badly handled High Victorian Gothic, the details of *c.* 1300. Two-storey porch. The good wrought-iron fingers of the outer door are C12 from the s doorway of the church. DAIRY COTTAGE, ¾ m. SW, has inside well-preserved C17 monochrome painted decoration, one room with the remains of an all-over scheme of flowers, leaves and fruits.

Winchfield Lodge.
Lithograph from *Building News*, 1883

WINCHFIELD COURT, 1 m. ENE at Winchfield Hurst. The former workhouse of 1871, by *Edmund Woodthorpe*. Handsome, in an Italianate style very old-fashioned for its date, with a square cupola. Former CHAPEL by *Ernest Newton*, 1911, with Arts and Crafts detailing.

WINCHFIELD LODGE, 1 m. NW off Old Potbridge Lane. 1885 by *T. E. Collcutt* for Spencer Charrington, lord of the manor. Old English style: a jettied timber-framed first floor, tile-hanging and plaster covings, leaded windows and tall shafted stacks. The E wing, bounding the entrance forecourt, is slightly later.

WINCHFIELD HOUSE, 1 m. NNW. A compact and severe Palladian villa of *c.* 1770, for Lady Margaret Beauclerk. Painted brick. Two storeys over basement, of square plan with central projecting canted bays to the drawing room (W) and dining room (E), and short pyramidally roofed towers, with *œils de bœuf*, in the centres of the N and S elevations. SW corner entrance with a segmental-pedimented doorcase. Of the same date the stables (now converted) and lodge.

WINNALL *see* WINCHESTER

WINSLADE

6040

In beautiful gently rolling downland scenery of beechwoods, copses and small fields in the remote-seeming country s of Hackwood Park (q.v.).

ST MARY THE VIRGIN. The fabric is medieval, recast and refenestrated in 1816 for Lord Bolton by *Lewis Wyatt*, his architect
at Hackwood. The details in Late Perp style are decidedly pre-
ecclesiological. Bleak w tower of yellow brick. (A possibly C14
window, now opening into the tower, survives inside. On the
E wall, a late C14 WALL PAINTING representing the Coronation of the Virgin inside an oval waved border. Uncovered in
1888; the roof timbers were exposed and restored at the same
date. – MONUMENT. William Pincke †1694. Cartouche with
flowers.)
(WINSLADE HOUSE. Originally the rectory. Early C19. Stuccoed
with shallow angular bays, a full-height arched recess and
wrought-iron balcony. Rear with ground-floor tripartite sashes
flanking an arched niche. Wrought-iron gates from the Priory,
Odiham (q.v.).)

5050   WOLVERTON

87   ST CATHERINE. In a fine, deeply rural position above parkland
in gently rolling landscape. Essentially a rebuilding of 1717, it
is the best Early Georgian work in Hampshire. Commanding,
very powerful, high and broad w tower of light red brick with
alternating raised stone angle quoins, a doorway with big rustication of alternating sizes, and a parapet upswept at the
angles in typically early C18 fashion. The body of the church
is decidedly artisan by comparison and if it appears disproportionately low in comparison, the reason is that the nave was
only a re-casing (as we shall see inside) in red brick with blue
brick dressings, a curious idiosyncratic combination. Curious
also, the decidedly Jacobean-shaped E gable and stepped gables
of the transepts, framing a niche. The silly brick mullions are
the worst effect of an otherwise relatively conservative restoration of 1871–2, by *Charles Smith* of Reading.
    The interior is dominated by the bold medieval timber nave
roof of four-and-a-half bays, with pointed-arched braces up to
the high collar-beams and the three tiers of wind-braces, two
of them forming themselves into circles (cf. Court Farm,
Overton, of 1505–7). The transepts are screened off from the
crossing (as it were) by a tripartite arrangement which is,
however, not at all straightforward. It consists of a narrow arch,
then a wide one, and then the second narrow one turned at 45
degrees so as to allow access to pulpit and reading desk
through them. Similarly inside the tower there are very long,
slim, blank-arched niches, and the upper floor is carried on
squinches. These arches with plain blocks instead of capitals
and abaci are typically Queen Anne and English Baroque, i.e.
Vanbrugh–Hawksmoor–Archer. Large, lofty arch to the tower,
filled until 1872 by a w gallery.
    The furnishings are an outstanding, almost architectural,
ensemble, integral with the building, especially the PULPIT

and READING DESK, either side of the chancel arch, a quin-
tessentially C17–early C19 Anglican arrangement, apparently
originating from George Herbert's early C17 scheme at
Leighton Bromswold (Hunts.). The chancel is wonderfully well
preserved. REREDOS, with good marquetry 'Glory'. – PAN-
ELLING. Also good, with Ionic pilasters. – COMMUNION
RAILS and parts of the original chancel screen, all of wrought
iron, effectively gilt. – CHANCEL FLOOR of inlaid marbles with
typically early C18 black lozenges. – BOX PEWS in nave and
transepts, with later brass candle-stands. Pendant OIL LAMPS,
adapted to electricity. FONT. A stone baluster. – Painted ROYAL
ARMS, dated 1846. Quite accomplished, nicely contrasted by a
dark sepia 'surround'. – STAINED GLASS. Quarries in several
windows, probably of 1872. The E window, with *Agnus Dei*
roundel in geometric 'mosaic' patternwork, probably by
Lavers, Westlake & Co. By them, the painted panel of the former
reredos, from Ewhurst (q.v.), brought in with other fittings
under the W tower in 1974.

WOLVERTON PARK. A rare thing in Hampshire, a Georgian
country house faced in ashlar; perhaps remodelled as late as
1837 after the Duke of Wellington purchased the estate. Seven
bays, two storeys, with a balustraded parapet and an Ionic
porch with coupled columns. Slightly lower wings, set back,
apparently early C19. C18 brick STABLES to the E. U-plan. One-
storey except for central two-storey pedimented pavilion with
octagonal domed cupola. Small landscaped PARK with lakes.

THE OLD HOUSE ½ m. SW. Formerly the rectory. Early C18,
refronted on the garden side in the later C18 and added to with
a wing of 1929–30 by *Elms & Jupp* (also the arched stone porch
on stubby columns). Nice group of outbuildings including C18
STABLE with early C19 Tudor Gothic alterations, probably
1833–41 when the house is known to have been improved.

TOWNSEND LODGE, Wolverton Townsend, ¾ m. E. Late C18.
Brick. Three bays with segmental-arched casements and
central pediment with lunette. More unusually, pilaster-strips,
frieze band and window surrounds of flint nodules (cf. Holly
Bush Farmhouse, Ewhurst).

WONSTON

4030

HOLY TRINITY. In a secluded position down a short lane at the
back of the former rectory, and facing fields away from the
village. This mostly rendered flint church may stand on the site
of a Saxon predecessor recorded in a charter of 901 and held
by New Minster. From 1086 it was held by St Swithun's Cathedral Priory.

The earliest visible fabric in the nave is late C12, but this is
not apparent outside unless the finely jointed chalk NE quoin
represents Norman work. Of about 1200, the Late Norman S

doorway of Quarr stone with its curiously imprecisely moulded round arch. But the finest early feature is the chancel arch, also of Quarr stone of a slightly later date, which is pointed. The responds are triple, and the carved capitals go from a design derived from trumpet scallops just going stiff-leaf proper, mostly of tripartite, fleur-de-lys-like leaves (transitional motifs, cf. Deerhurst church, Gloucs., nave arcades). The quality must be due to the Cathedral Priory. The chancel has four lateral lancets, all trefoil-headed *c.* 1235, and a large three-light Perp E window (restored tracery). The w tower is Late Perp of *c.* 1520. In the w doorway, a nice early C17 door with wicket entry. Inside the tower, a piscina, or STOUP. The church was damaged by fire and restored in 1714 (see the benefaction board recording John Wallop as 'best benefactor to this church') and enlarged with a N aisle in 1829. The windows and the elegant N arcade of three slender and finely continuous moulded piers and arches are of the restoration of 1871–2 by *G. E. Laing.* Much of his work in the chancel was lost in another fire in 1908. The chancel was restored in 1909 by *T. G. Jackson* and the chancel furnishings are mostly his. – FONT. 1871–2 by *Laing*, carved by *Farmer & Brindley.* Elaborately Neo-Perp with close foliate panels. – PULPIT. Of wood. E.E., also by *Laing*, in much the style of Sir G. G. Scott, with angle colonnettes, stiff-leaf and roundels. – LECTERN. A good brass eagle lectern dated 1909. – STAINED GLASS. In the chancel. Good, highly finished E window of 1909, by *Powells*, with fine groups of angels l. & r. of Christ in Majesty, above predella scenes of the Nativity, the Holy Family and Supper at Emmaus. Nice seraphim and emblems in the tracery. – Lateral windows – a coordinated set by *Morris & Co.*, 1909. Single saints on blue drapery. Morris foliage patterns, top and bottom. – N aisle by *Kempe* (commemorative date 1907) placed in 1932. Outside, close to the church, nicely carved C18 GRAVE MARKERS of interestingly varied designs. – LYCHGATE of 1903 by *Henry Hill.*

THE OLD HOUSE, w of the church. A substantial stone-built rectory of *c.* 1400, altered about 1740 for the Rev. Thomas Ridding (rector 1740–66). The medieval house consisted of a hall with gabled cross-wings, a further two-storey chamber block beyond the parlour wing, and a detached kitchen. This arrangement is still clearly seen in the E front. The hall is marked by a pair of tall early C19 sashes, to their l. a two-storey porch with a nice C18 pilastered stone doorcase. The kitchen block to the l. was largely rebuilt in brick in the C18 and is linked to the service wing by a later gabled range. The chamber block to the r. has a number of original single-light windows, including one with a cusped head, and a pair of external doorways, one above the other, which probably indicate the position of a former garderobe tower. The *c.* 1740 addition takes the form of a narrow two-storey range on the W side, evening up an irregular elevation and providing a corridor on each floor. A grand stuccoed frontage with stone dressings. Five bays with broad pilasters at each end, culminating in bold urns on the parapet. In the centre a two-storey porch with round-arched entrance and rusticated first floor. Inside, lots of mid-C18 details, including a fine square-well staircase with turned balusters. Also some good C16 linenfold panelling in the former cross-passage. The medieval roofs survive in parts.

The village street runs W from the church. At the very far end, ST OLAF's POND COTTAGE is a good mid-1530s hearth-passage house with a divided parlour and integral kitchen. Behind the houses on the S side of the street, UPTON HOUSE, of 1927 by *A. H. Johnson* of Winchester. Neo-Georgian with nice panelled rooms inside and a formal garden.

NORTON MANOR, 1 m. NW. Late C17 half-H plan house with rear wings, like Bonhams, Holybourne (q.v.). Hipped roof and stacks with arched panels. Giant angle pilasters with glazed tiles in the capitals. Early C20 alterations and additions for George Hampton, the estate agent, principally in 1912 by *Henry Tanner Jun.*, including infilling and extension at rear, loggia and domed conservatory with ogee cupola and Dutch-gabled porch. Inside, panelled entrance hall with painting of hunting scene in panel over fireplace and C17 staircase with turned balusters. Otherwise lavishly redecorated *c.* 1904 for Hampton by *Frayland Ltd* in a late C18 style. Large C17 aisled thatched BARN.

WOODCOTT

A scattered settlement of a few farms.

ST JAMES. In lonely isolation by a farm in remote downland S of Highclere. Built for the Earl of Carnarvon in 1853, possibly by *Thomas Allom* (Diana Brooks). Nave and chancel in one. Coursed knapped flint. E window with flowing tracery by *E.A. & H. W. Crickmay*, 1936. – The PULPIT and READING DESK incorporate angle posts with angels and C18 oval medallions vigorously carved with St Peter and St Paul and ribbons. This is certainly not English. Is it Netherlandish or French? It does not seem to be Italian.

WOODCOTT HOUSE, ½ m. SE on a fine site with views. 1909–10, by *Crickmay & Sons* for Richard Nicholson. Convincing William and Mary style, the garden front of eleven bays with projecting wings and central doorway with shell-hood on consoles. Good interior in early C18 style. The planting for the garden was devised by *Gertrude Jekyll* in 1911. Terrace with sunken rose garden below to the SE and lawn with Tuscan-columned timber summerhouse to the SW. This is linked to the walled garden W of the house by a path lined by beech hedges and fruit trees. The rubble-stone terraces and pergola on the edge of the SW lawn are alterations by Jekyll of 1924.

WOODMANCOTT

St James. 1854–6 by *J. Colson* at his simplest. Nave and chancel and bellcote. Flint. Consistently E.E.

WOOLTON HILL

An almost Surrey-like semi-rural enclave of large Victorian and Edwardian country houses deep in greenery between Highclere and the high downland of the Wiltshire border. The ecclesiastical parish was carved out of East Woodhay (q.v.) in 1850 and by then had similarly benefited from the local clerical developer, John Hervey Ashworth, who built several 'very handsome detached villas' (Kelly) hereabouts (e.g. Woolton House). Significant C20 development, however, has made it into an outlying leafy suburb of Newbury.

St Thomas. At a crossroads in the built-up area. 1849 by *Wyatt & Brandon,* but really not worthy of the architects of Wilton parish church. Early Dec in flint with a rather starved NE tower with stone broach spire. Like most churches of its date, with no concessions to local variations of style: there is Kentish plate tracery. Good w porch of 1919 by *G. H. Kitchin* and NE vestry of 1927 by *Sir Charles Nicholson.* Inside, the N aisle has alternately round and octagonal piers. The arches treated in exactly the same improbable way as by Hansom at Ryde (Isle of Wight, 1844–6): the arches proper are depressed on vertical pieces, but the hoodmoulds rise to form normal two-centred blank arches. Some original furnishings, especially the elaborately Gothic priest's seat built into the low sill of the chancel s window. Others mostly later: e.g. the font in a sumptuous E.E. with rich carving. Can it be by G. G. Scott, who worked locally (*see* Tile Barn)? – reredos, by *W. & C. A. Bassett Smith,* 1905, with an elaborate Last Supper scene in high relief within an arcaded frame; contemporary dado of alabaster. – stained glass. Much, but of the original scheme, in six windows, by *Clutterbuck,* the only survival is the w gable window, with a rare Early Victorian royal arms, still in the style of the first half of the C19. e window by *Kempe,* 1903. Standard with Christ crucified between David and the dedicatory saint. – Several early C20 windows by *Powells.*

In the churchyard, within an iron and timber enclosure, the Portland stone war memorial, with wreath around a cross. Contemporary with the church, the lychgate between stone piers, and the Neo-Tudor school by *Wyatt & Brandon,* 1850 (but much enlarged since, without aplomb in the C20).

Woolton Hill Junior School, ¼ m. e. 1977, by the *Hampshire County Architect's Dept* and a nice example of the period in dark brown brick. The classroom blocks have monopitch clerestories at the ridges and eaves projecting as porches, supported on short sections of tapering wall enclosing small paved terraces. Detached monopitch two-storey boiler house. Minor extension, 2001.

WELLBROOK HOUSE, ⅛ m. E. Formerly the rectory. 1875–7, by *G. G. Scott Jun.* for the Rev. Francis Moore in a remarkable early example of the Georgian Revival: a red brick box, relieved only by a string course and a few bands of vitrified brickwork. Hipped roof with small hipped dormers of typically Georgian design and tall, plain chimneys, asymmetrically disposed. In the entrance front, a central round archway to a recessed porch (with unfortunate late c20 Tuscan porch). A symmetrical elevation of five bays is implied, but because the rooms to the r. require no windows Scott left it blank, sticking to his Puginian principles, resisting the use of blind windows to articulate the façade in the c18 manner.

TILE BARN, ½ m. NE. A compact Gothic house of c. 1850–60, by *George Gilbert Scott* and one of his relatively few domestic commissions, for John Frederick Winterbottom. Altered and enlarged c. 1900 and subdivided in the mid c20 (now Tile Barn House, Tile Barn Holt and Tulip House). Two storeys and attic, the nearly symmetrical front with a pair of broad gabled wings flanking a slightly recessed four-bay centre. Vigorous use of structural polychromy. The windows have ashlar surrounds, those on the ground floor (and in the first floor of the r.-hand wing) having nook-shafts with foliate capitals, and stilted arches with hoodmoulds and allegorical majolica busts of the months set in roundels. Around the corner to the l. a lively asymmetrical elevation: on the r. a chimney-breast squeezes between two ground-floor windows and is corbelled out on the first floor to allow the flues to pass around a small trefoil-headed Gothic window. Rear wing of c. 1900 in a simple Neo-Jacobean by *Walter Cave*. At this date the interior was thoroughly re-done by *Cave* in the free Neo-Georgian style of Ernest Newton. The former hall and morning room were thrown together as a single large hall, the thick wall between the two rooms pierced by a wide *serliana*, with an elliptical arch (now blocked once more) supported on four square columns. Fine Neo-Jacobean chimneypiece in the former morning room. Staircase, behind an arcaded screen, with symmetrical double balusters, a ramped handrail and, as the half-landing newel, a short balustraded screen with lunette above. The attic staircase is more purely Arts and Crafts, with paired diamond-section stick balusters, which are used to form a lattice screen at the half-landing.

The setting of the house was lost to post-war housing development in the grounds. The former STABLES, N, also by *Scott*, were cruelly divided in the 1950s to create a pair of detached houses. Two lodges, probably by *Scott*, survive. The principal one, W of the house, is TILE BARN LODGE. Two storeys, of red brick, with minimal grey brick banding and Gothic windows with scalloped tile-hanging in the tympana. NEWBURY LODGE, E, is similar, but only one storey.

HOLLINGTON HOUSE, ½ m. SW. 1903–4, by *A. C. Blomfield*, for F. Festus Kelly, owner of Kelly's Directories. Large, Elizabethan style, of two storeys and attic, with tall brick chimneys. Snecked dressed stone, ashlar mullioned-and-transomed windows, brick plinth and rusticated brick pilaster-strips at the angles. The long service wing is partly timber-framed at first floor with roughcast gables above (cf. Blomfield's Ditcham Park, Buriton). At the far end a stocky square water tower looks very Baroque. Good interior all in the Elizabethan style, the stone and wood carving by *H. H. Martyn & Co.* of Cheltenham. Most impressive the panelled two-storey hall with a gallery and stained-glass roundels by *Campbell & Christmas* representing night and day, and the seasons. In the GARDEN the upper terrace, with arcaded stone balustrade and bowed projections at each end, is by *Blomfield*, but the rest laid out by *Gertrude Jekyll* in 1908.

WOOTTON ST LAWRENCE

A very small village, with one gently winding street of mostly Georgian cottages and houses.

ST LAWRENCE. Quite a commodious successor to a Late Saxon church first mentioned in 940 and long connected with Winchester: bishops until 1299, Prior and Convent and Dean and Chapter from 1540 to the present. But the story of its continuity has been confused by a more than usually devastating restoration of 1863–4 by *J. Colson* for the Rev. Walter Wither. Re-set in his harsh Dec s aisle, a solid Early Norman doorway of *c.* 1130 with one order of columns with cushion capitals having bead decoration. In the arch one order of zigzag and one of three bands of small triangles in relief. The massive N arcade of *c.* 1180 was rebuilt stone for stone on the foundations of an earlier wall. Three bays, stout circular piers with square abaci and trumpet-scallop capitals. Round arches with a slight chamfer. The respond capitals are supported by cones, a rare and apparently original detail (the E respond is restored). The narrower W bay was added later, probably to connect with a tower, or to relate to a timber bell-turret then in the W end of the nave. The chamfers to its responds have 'droplet' stops high up beneath the abaci (uncommon features but cf. Longparish, owned by Wherwell Priory). A few further genuine details in the chancel, virtually rebuilt in 1864, especially the NE and SW windows of Binstead stone. The former with good simple plate tracery of *c.* 1320. Another window, re-set in the N vestry of 1872 by *T. Chatfeild Clarke*. Also medieval is the plain W tower (but with a Neo-Tudor W doorway, and the incongruous 'Sussex cap' by Colson): see the two small, apparently Perp, single-light windows, one s, one w, and the contemporary cornice with carved heads. The latter inspired the passion for small heads so characteristic of Colson, and carved for him by *Thomas Plumley*. Even more elaborate carving in the naturalistic capitals of the s arcade.

ARCHITECTURAL FRAGMENTS. A damaged font bowl, still recognizably Perp with quatrefoils (Colson's font is a copy). Also part of a pillar piscina and a corbel head. Is it a Perp or Plumley? – PULPIT of 1863, demonstratively E.E. in wood with brass candleholders. – HATCHMENTS. Four to the Bigg-Wither family (*see* below), a fifth to Arthur Bates †1962. – ROYAL ARMS. Large, circular, painted on canvas. Perhaps the finest of George IV in the county. Now banished in the tower. – REREDOS. Neo-Perp in wood. By *G. H. Kitchin*. – ALTAR FRONTAL. Early C20, exquisitely embroidered with gold foliate motifs repeated on a light background. – STAINED GLASS. Mostly in the chancel. E window by *Ward & Hughes*, c. 1864, darkly dramatic in the firm's usual chiaroscuro. SE and s aisle E by *Wailes*. Both of 1864. N aisle N. By *G. E. R. Smith* of *A. K. Nicholson Studios*, 1953, to the Rev. Charles Butler, vicar 1600–47, author of *De Feminin Monarki* (1609), an early classic study of bees. – ENGRAVED GLASS. In the s aisle by *Laurence Whistler*, 1989–90. Light against an all too light view outside.

MONUMENTS. Unusually many ledger slabs, several to the Withers of Manydown.* They are C17–C18 and a delight to genealogists. – In the same artisan tradition, a tablet to Mrs Wither †1632. Oblong slate plate under a stone pediment with coat of arms and oddly stylized garlands. – Sir Thomas Hooke of Tangier House †1677. Convincingly attributed to *Abraham Storey* (GF) and probably among the best of his monuments, although it appears to have been reduced. The figure, within an arched recess, semi-reclining at perfect ease, though in armour, and so close to the altar. A beautiful piece of carving. Heraldic achievement with bold mantling below, detached from the rest. Back panel black-and-white marble, round arch, and a kind of Y-tracery division that looks like a later alteration. Still extant in the mid C20 was a wrought-iron bracket, of Jacobean pattern and inscribed 'T.H. 1677', no doubt for Hooke's funerary armour, helm, spurs, gauntlets and sword. – William Wither †1733. Good tablet with a long inscription and a bust on top in front of an obelisk. Almost certainly by *Roubiliac*** who began carving busts c. 1733; it is of identical date and design to the bust for Thomas Messing at Crofton (South Hampshire). The bust also has the same arrangement of drapery as the bust of Hawksmoor at All Souls College, Oxford, by Cheere, which was perhaps fashioned from a model by Roubiliac.

* Manydown House, a manor of the Priors of St Swithun and then the Dean and Chapter until 1649, was noted by Pevsner but has been demolished.
** Esdaile (1928) discovered a reference to Roubiliac in the parish records but misattributed the Hooke monument to him.

WOOTTON HOUSE, S, is the former vicarage. Queen Anne Revival, dated 1877.

TANGIER HOUSE, ¾ m. W. Built and named in 1662 by Sir Thomas Hooke after Charles II's marriage to Catherine of Braganza (said to be the subject of the bust on the NE garden front). Brick. H-plan. Two storeys and attic. SE front of three gables with a recessed centre. Raised brick quoins. The windows are now all sashed, with rendered architraves. Prosser (1833), however, shows the front with Dutch gables, cross-windows to the centre, and a balustrade below the central first-floor window. Central doorway with bolection-moulded architrave. Mid-C18 SW front of five bays with a three-bay pedimented gable. Of this date, panelling in a front room and the staircase, with column-on-vase balusters and exaggeratedly ramped handrail. Only the entrance hall with bolection-moulded panelling seems of 1662.

6050

WORTING

Still just about holding its own despite the proximity of Basingstoke to the E.

ST THOMAS OF CANTERBURY. Early Decorated of 1847–8 by *Woodyer*, rebuilt for the Rev. H. Bigg-Wither on the foundations of a Norman (and later) church. Flint. Nave and chancel with additional N aisle. Slender shingled bell-turret. Varied fancy Dec tracery. Inside, the bell-turret framing is strong with quirky trefoil braces against the walls. Pretty boarded chancel ceiling with original painted decoration. – FONT COVER of 1841, from the previous church. An elegant fish-scale-patterned ogee, with a later surmounting dove, of white marble, by *W. Warren*, 1881. – CHOIR STALLS. From St John, Kennington, London, and therefore possibly by *G. E. Street*. – ORGAN CASE. Quite a showpiece by the *Rev. F. H. Sutton*, 1873. – CANDLEHOLDERS. A rare set of wrought-iron wall pendants. – STAINED GLASS. In the E and W windows by *Wailes*. The former of the Crucifixion, initialled and dated 1848, the latter geometric patternwork.

WORTING HOUSE, NW of the church, overlooks a small park. Early to mid-C18 brick centre of five bays and two-and-a-half storeys, raised over a basement, with a central Tuscan porch under a Venetian window. Simpler windows of this type, but also lunettes set in round-arched panels, in the late C18 two-storey wings. Late C18 former STABLES, now converted. Three first-floor lunettes and central break with elliptical archway, now blocked. Three good Georgian houses on the E side of Church Lane: THE OLD RECTORY of 1732 (remodelled in the early C19); HATCHETTS, also before 1750, also altered c. 1840 when it was stuccoed, and with most interesting and extensive brick cellars, including one very large chamber extending over

80 ft (25 metres) from the house to the road, with a shallow barrel-vault and a triple-arched lobby at the E end. What was its function? Lastly HILLSIDE, C18 and early C19. Brick with columned porch.

YATELEY

Now almost part of the Blackwater valley conurbation (*see* Hawley and Blackwater), Yateley is an amalgam of several small historic settlements. The principal one centres on the church, one of the few remnants of a scattered village now subsumed in sprawling post-war housing estates.

ST PETER. By a small triangular green on the S side of Reading Road. A former dependent chapel of Crondall, of C11 origins yet retaining Late Saxon fabric in its nave N wall. Damaged by arson in 1979 and insensitively restored by *Derek Wren* in 1981. Much that Pevsner noticed has been lost, although the good C13 chancel and the fine late C15 timber-framed W tower were repaired. A substantial length of the nave wall is C11; E of the porch its extent is marked by a large *in situ* Sarsen stone. There was a NE long-and-short quoin (now covered up), and a small Saxon window remains visible. The W end of the nave is Early Norman (contemporary round-arched window in the W gable, mentioned by Pevsner, no longer visible). Also C12, the mutilated N doorway in chalk, with billet and nailhead mouldings. The remaining nave windows on the N side are mixed. The chancel, now screened off as a side chapel, is a complete piece of *c.* 1200 with three stepped E lancets and two S and three N lancets. In the N wall traces of an anchorite's cell with doorway and squint, or was it a NE vestry? The most exciting part is the late C15 W tower. This is timber-framed and has a N, S and W aisle like the more famous Essex timber bell-towers. Posts carry the shingled bell-stage. Originally the three aisles were separated from the core by arched braces, but later straight scissor-bracing was added, resulting in a most impressive thicket of timbers. The tower arch is of stone and of the same time as the timberwork. The exterior timber framing was over-restored by *A. W. Blomfield* in 1878, when the original brick-nogging was entirely replaced. Nice timber-framed N porch, probably mid-C14, and originally open, with typical Dec cusped bargeboard (cf. Binfield church, Berks.). – TILES. A few around the font, from the anchorite's cell. C14, produced at Penn and Tyler's Green, Bucks., and rare in Hampshire. – STAINED GLASS. Only the W window in the tower escaped the fire. It is by *Powell*, of 1885 with figures by *Henry Holiday*, influenced by Morris. – (The chancel E window by *Morris & Co.* of 1876, with figures by *Burne-Jones*, was lost.) – MONUMENTS. (In the tower C16 BRASSES. William Lawerd †1517 and wife, 18 in. (46-cm.) figures; William Rugg †1532 and wife,

19 in. (48-cm.); Elizabeth Morflett †1558, 7 in. (18-cm.) demi-figure (repaired after the fire by *William Lack*, 1982–3). – Two ledger slabs. Sir Richard Ryves †1671* and Thomas Wyndham †1768 with the usual achievement in a shallow recessed roundel. Nicely done.

In the still comparatively countrified churchyard, several C18–early C19 headstones. Robert Dalzell †1821, with a draped urn, near the N porch, and a rare C18 multiple memorial to the Simmonds family, close to the chancel, unusually with five linked wooden headboards, all painted white. Earliest commemorative date 1768. – LYCHGATE with revolving gate. Originally C17; so restored as to be almost replicated.

ST BARNABAS, Brinns Lane, Darby Green. 1989 by *Alastair Watson*. Brick. All facilities under one roof, with worship area below meeting rooms.

ST SWITHUN (R.C.) Firgrove Road. 1968–9 by *Barton, Wilmore & Partners*. In the grounds of Yateley Hall. Lozenge-shape plan. Yellow brick with clerestory lighting.

VILLAGE HALL, Old School Lane. The school of 1865, by *W. Woodman* of Reading, Gothic in the manner of Street or William White. Gabled, stepped windows under arches with herringbone nogging in the tympana and a wooden arcade with pierced trefoils in the spandrels.

NEWLANDS PRIMARY SCHOOL, Dungells Lane. 1978–80. One of the first primary schools by *Hampshire County Architect's Dept* under *Colin Stansfield Smith*. Two parallel ranges under spreading low-pitched roofs with continuous glazing along the ridge (classrooms in one; the hall, music room, administration etc. in the other), linked by a conservatory serving as the entrance and library and additional teaching area. Walls mostly of white brick with minimal openings, which in places extend out to define external spaces. The classroom block faces an outdoor teaching area. Later C20 extension in the same form, the junction between the old and the new marked by a glazed strip across the building.

FROGMORE COMMUNITY COLLEGE, Potley Hill Road. Begun 1974, the county's last major use of the SCOLA system: standard flat-roofed blocks of grey brick and lightweight panels, grouped around courtyards. In the second phase, 1979–80 by *Hampshire County Architect's Dept* (*Colin Stansfield Smith*, County Architect), the approach was more individual. The courtyards were completed by sleek low blocks, adopting a similar vocabulary, with the same grey brick for the end walls, punctuated by circular openings, but fully glazed (double-skinned for environmental control) to front and back with steel columns exposed at the corners. Paired apsidal-ended brick pods contain the lavatories.

There are a few buildings of interest scattered among later development.**

---

* The associated monument, attributed to *Jasper Latham* (GF), was destroyed by the fire.

** Yateley Place, noted by Pevsner in 1967, has been demolished.

YATELEY HALL, Hall Lane, ⅜ m. SW. Now offices. An almost complete rebuilding of *c.* 1700 around a late C16 core (brick fireplace in the N wing and remains of roof with ogee braces in the S wing) with significant Queen Anne Revival additions of 1871–2 by *Richard Norman Shaw*, for Martin de Winton Corry. The W front is of five bays with a recessed centre and hipped roof; the single windows on the projecting wings have clearly replaced paired openings, probably in the late C18 when the entrance appears to have been moved from the centre to the S wing (boldly projecting columned porch of 1991). To the l. an early C18 addition, again refenestrated. Shaw wrapped the house's E and S sides in a tactful, if slightly over-scaled, manner. To the r. of the entrance are groups of three closely spaced sashes in a full-height square bay under a hipped roof. At the rear, close up against the canalized remains of the moat, he repeats this motif informally, in a large shallow bay to the dining room and at a higher level to light the staircase. The pedimented semi-dormer is a particularly nice touch. His conservatory was replaced in the late C20 by a Neo-Georgian wing to the S. Inside, much bolection-moulded panelling in the ground-floor rooms of the old part. At the rear of the entrance hall a late C18 Doric screen leads to Shaw's staircase, a grand piece with pulvinated string, turned balusters and heavy panelled newel posts. To the landing a screen of three shallow arches on square columns. Also by Shaw, at the SE corner, the very pretty dining room, with white-painted bolection panelling partly covering the walls, a dentil cornice, and fireplace with delicate Delft tiles. Remains of a *c.* 1700 staircase at upper level. NE the former C18 STABLES. Central coachhouse with flanking projecting wings, a high screen wall to the w with central gable. Many lunettes.

MONTEAGLE HOUSE, Monteagle Lane, 1 m. SW of St Peter. A nice example of an early C17 (1619) baffle-entry house. Still timber-framed but with brick creeping in for the (now rendered) high-status two-storey gabled porch.

SAMSUNG ELECTRONICS QUALITY ASSURANCE LABORATORY, Blackbushe Business Park, ¾ m. SSW. 1996–7 by *RMJM* (project architect, *Ray Briant*). A smart, if unremarkable, corrugated-clad shed, containing two anechoic (echoless) steel testing chambers, their walls and ceilings covered with 8-ft (2.4-metre)-long cones, designed to absorb electromagnetic radiation. The internal effect is strangely Art Deco.

BARCLAY HOUSE, Vicarage Road, ¼ m. WNW of St Peter. A dashing villa of *c.* 1820. Stuccoed with deeply projecting eaves, the ground floor with French casements alternating with niches and a loggia on attenuated columns flanked by aedicular pavilions.

THRIFTSWOOD, ¾ m. SE in Stevens Hill. Lovely Late Arts and Crafts house by *A. C. Martin*, dated 1929 on a bay at the rear. Can it be that late? Plum brick with red dressings and diaper. Front with central arched entrance and shaped gable, with tall chimneys in the angles of low projecting wings.

The asymmetrical full-height bay and the small window in the front of the l.-hand chimney are playful touches. More conventional rear with a pair of gabled wings linked by the first-floor canted bay with the date.

At DARBY GREEN, 1 m. SE, a few buildings survive relatively unmolested by development, e.g. CLARK's FARMHOUSE, N of Reading Road. C17 lobby-entry house, refronted in red brick with panels of vitrified headers in the C18. In a rear tower a C17 stair, the remarkable half-landing newel with a finial in the form of a globe with pierced crest, but in two dimensions rather than turned. Further SE, on Yateley Common, is DARBY GREEN HOUSE, designed for himself in 1911 by *J. D. Coleridge*, a former assistant of Lutyens, the influence of whose later style is evident. A rich red brick, hipped roofs with prominently sprocketed eaves, and heavy leaded timber casements, segmental-arched with tile voussoirs and tiles in the tympana. The garden front symmetrical, in a cottagey Neo-Georgian; long and low with hipped-roofed wings. The living rooms are on this side, lit by large windows, the service corridors running the length of the house on the N side, with smaller openings. The details, staircase, chimneypieces etc., Neo-Georgian, except for the brick fireplace in the drawing room, which must date from its later extension by Coleridge.

GLOSSARY

Numbers and letters refer to the illustrations (by John Sambrook)
on pp. 750–757.

ABACUS: flat slab forming the top of a capital (3a).

ACANTHUS: classical formalized leaf ornament (4b).

ACCUMULATOR TOWER: *see* Hydraulic power.

ACHIEVEMENT: a complete display of armorial bearings.

ACROTERION: plinth for a statue or ornament on the apex or ends of a pediment; more usually, both the plinth and what stands on it (4a).

AEDICULE (*lit.* little building): architectural surround, consisting usually of two columns or pilasters supporting a pediment.

AGGREGATE: *see* Concrete.

AISLE: subsidiary space alongside the body of a building, separated from it by columns, piers, or posts.

ALMONRY: a building from which alms are dispensed to the poor.

AMBULATORY (*lit.* walkway): aisle around the sanctuary (q.v.).

ANGLE ROLL: roll moulding in the angle between two planes (1a).

ANSE DE PANIER: *see* Arch.

ANTAE: simplified pilasters (4a), usually applied to the ends of the enclosing walls of a portico *in antis* (q.v.).

ANTEFIXAE: ornaments projecting at regular intervals above a Greek cornice, originally to conceal the ends of roof tiles (4a).

ANTHEMION: classical ornament like a honeysuckle flower (4b).

APRON: raised panel below a window or wall monument or tablet.

APSE: semicircular or polygonal end of an apartment, especially of a chancel or chapel. In classical architecture sometimes called an *exedra*.

ARABESQUE: non-figurative surface decoration consisting of flowing lines, foliage scrolls etc., based on geometrical patterns. Cf. Grotesque.

ARCADE: series of arches supported by piers or columns. *Blind arcade* or *arcading*: the same applied to the wall surface. *Wall arcade*: in medieval churches, a blind arcade forming a dado below windows. Also a covered shopping street.

ARCH: Shapes *see* 5c. *Basket arch* or *anse de panier* (basket handle): three-centred and depressed, or with a flat centre. *Nodding*: ogee arch curving forward from the wall face. *Parabolic*: shaped like a chain suspended from two level points, but inverted. Special purposes. *Chancel*: dividing chancel from nave or crossing. *Crossing*: spanning piers at a crossing (q.v.). *Relieving or discharging*: incorporated in a wall to relieve superimposed weight (5c). *Skew*: spanning responds not diametrically opposed. *Strainer*: inserted in an opening to resist inward pressure. *Transverse*: spanning a main axis (e.g. of a vaulted space). *See also* Jack arch, Triumphal arch.

ARCHITRAVE: formalized lintel, the lowest member of the classical entablature (3a). Also the moulded frame of a door or window (often borrowing the profile of a classical architrave). For *lugged* and *shouldered* architraves *see* 4b.

ARCUATED: dependent structurally on the arch principle. Cf. Trabeated.

ARK: chest or cupboard housing the

tables of Jewish law in a synagogue.

ARRIS: sharp edge where two surfaces meet at an angle (3a).

ASHLAR: masonry of large blocks wrought to even faces and square edges (6d).

ASTRAGAL: classical moulding of semicircular section (3f).

ASTYLAR: with no columns or similar vertical features.

ATLANTES: *see* Caryatids.

ATRIUM (plural: atria): inner court of a Roman or C20 house; in a multi-storey building, a toplit covered court rising through all storeys. Also an open court in front of a church.

ATTACHED COLUMN: *see* Engaged column.

ATTIC: small top storey within a roof. Also the storey above the main entablature of a classical façade.

AUMBRY: recess or cupboard to hold sacred vessels for the Mass.

BAILEY: *see* Motte-and-bailey.

BALANCE BEAM: *see* Canals.

BALDACCHINO: free-standing canopy, originally fabric, over an altar. Cf. Ciborium.

BALLFLOWER: globular flower of three petals enclosing a ball (1a). Typical of the Decorated style.

BALUSTER: pillar or pedestal of bellied form. *Balusters*: vertical supports of this or any other form, for a handrail or coping, the whole being called a *balustrade* (6c). *Blind balustrade*: the same applied to the wall surface.

BARBICAN: outwork defending the entrance to a castle.

BARGEBOARDS (corruption of 'vergeboards'): boards, often carved or fretted, fixed beneath the eaves of a gable to cover and protect the rafters.

BAROQUE: style originating in Rome *c.*1600 and current in England *c.*1680–1720, characterized by dramatic massing and silhouette and the use of the giant order.

BARROW: burial mound.

BARTIZAN: corbelled turret, square or round, frequently at an angle.

BASCULE: hinged part of a lifting (or bascule) bridge.

BASE: moulded foot of a column or pilaster. For *Attic* base *see* 3b.

BASEMENT: lowest, subordinate storey; hence the lowest part of a classical elevation, below the *piano nobile* (q.v.).

BASILICA: a Roman public hall; hence an aisled building with a clerestory.

BASTION: one of a series of defensive semicircular or polygonal projections from the main wall of a fortress or city.

BATTER: intentional inward inclination of a wall face.

BATTLEMENT: defensive parapet, composed of *merlons* (solid) and *crenels* (embrasures) through which archers could shoot; sometimes called *crenellation*. Also used decoratively.

BAY: division of an elevation or interior space as defined by regular vertical features such as arches, columns, windows etc.

BAY LEAF: classical ornament of overlapping bay leaves (3f).

BAY WINDOW: window of one or more storeys projecting from the face of a building. *Canted*: with a straight front and angled sides. *Bow window*: curved. *Oriel*: rests on corbels or brackets and starts above ground level; also the bay window at the dais end of a medieval great hall.

BEAD-AND-REEL: *see* Enrichments.

BEAKHEAD: Norman ornament with a row of beaked bird or beast heads usually biting into a roll moulding (1a).

BELFRY: chamber or stage in a tower where bells are hung.

BELL CAPITAL: *see* 1b.

BELLCOTE: small gabled or roofed housing for the bell(s).

BERM: level area separating a ditch from a bank on a hill-fort or barrow.

BILLET: Norman ornament of small half-cylindrical or rectangular blocks (1a).

BLIND: *see* Arcade, Baluster, Portico.

BLOCK CAPITAL: *see* 1a.

BLOCKED: columns, etc. interrupted by regular projecting

blocks (*blocking*), as on a Gibbs surround (4b).

BLOCKING COURSE: course of stones, or equivalent, on top of a cornice and crowning the wall.

BOLECTION MOULDING: covering the joint between two different planes (6b).

BOND: the pattern of long sides (*stretchers*) and short ends (*headers*) produced on the face of a wall by laying bricks in a particular way (6e).

BOSS: knob or projection, e.g. at the intersection of ribs in a vault (2c).

BOWTELL: a term in use by the C15 for a form of roll moulding, usually three-quarters of a circle in section (also called *edge roll*).

BOW WINDOW: *see* Bay window.

BOX FRAME: timber-framed construction in which vertical and horizontal wall members support the roof (7). Also concrete construction where the loads are taken on cross walls; also called *cross-wall construction*.

BRACE: subsidiary member of a structural frame, curved or straight. *Bracing* is often arranged decoratively e.g. quatrefoil, herringbone (7). *See also* Roofs.

BRATTISHING: ornamental crest, usually formed of leaves, Tudor flowers or miniature battlements.

BRESSUMER (*lit.* breast-beam): big horizontal beam supporting the wall above, especially in a jettied building (7).

BRICK: *see* Bond, Cogging, Engineering, Gauged, Tumbling.

BRIDGE: *Bowstring*: with arches rising above the roadway which is suspended from them. *Clapper*: one long stone forms the roadway. *Roving*: *see* Canal. *Suspension*: roadway suspended from cables or chains slung between towers or pylons. *Stay-suspension* or *stay-cantilever*: supported by diagonal stays from towers or pylons *See also* Bascule.

BRISES-SOLEIL: projecting fins or canopies which deflect direct sunlight from windows.

BROACH: *see* Spire and 1c.

BUCRANIUM: ox skull used decoratively in classical friezes.

BULL-NOSED SILL: sill displaying a pronounced convex upper moulding.

BULLSEYE WINDOW: small oval window, set horizontally (cf. Oculus). Also called *œil de bœuf*.

BUTTRESS: vertical member projecting from a wall to stabilize it or to resist the lateral thrust of an arch, roof, or vault (1c, 2c). A *flying buttress* transmits the thrust to a heavy abutment by means of an arch or half-arch (1c).

CABLE OR ROPE MOULDING: originally Norman, like twisted strands of a rope.

CAMES: *see* Quarries.

CAMPANILE: free-standing bell-tower.

CANALS: *Flash lock*: removable weir or similar device through which boats pass on a flush of water. Predecessor of the *pound lock*: chamber with gates at each end allowing boats to float from one level to another. *Tidal gates*: single pair of lock gates allowing vessels to pass when the tide makes a level. *Balance beam*: beam projecting horizontally for opening and closing lock gates. *Roving bridge*: carrying a towing path from one bank to the other.

CANTILEVER: horizontal projection (e.g. step, canopy) supported by a downward force behind the fulcrum.

CAPITAL: head or crowning feature of a column or pilaster; for classical types *see* 3; for medieval types *see* 1b.

CARREL: compartment designed for individual work or study.

CARTOUCHE: classical tablet with ornate frame (4b).

CARYATIDS: female figures supporting an entablature; their male counterparts are *Atlantes* (*lit.* Atlas figures).

CASEMATE: vaulted chamber, with embrasures for defence, within a castle wall or projecting from it.

CASEMENT: side-hinged window.

CASTELLATED: with battlements (q.v.).

CAST IRON: hard and brittle, cast in a mould to the required shape.

Wrought iron is ductile, strong in tension, forged into decorative patterns or forged and rolled into e.g. bars, joists, boiler plates; *mild steel* is its modern equivalent, similar but stronger.

CATSLIDE: *See* 8a.

CAVETTO: concave classical moulding of quarter-round section (3f).

CELURE OR CEILURE: enriched area of roof above rood or altar.

CEMENT: *see* Concrete.

CENOTAPH (*lit.* empty tomb): funerary monument which is not a burying place.

CENTRING: wooden support for the building of an arch or vault, removed after completion.

CHAMFER (*lit.* corner-break): surface formed by cutting off a square edge or corner. For types of chamfers and *chamfer stops see* 6a. *See also* Double chamfer.

CHANCEL: part of the E end of a church set apart for the use of the officiating clergy.

CHANTRY CHAPEL: often attached to or within a church, endowed for the celebration of Masses principally for the soul of the founder.

CHEVET (*lit.* head): French term for chancel with ambulatory and radiating chapels.

CHEVRON: V-shape used in series or double series (later) on a Norman moulding (1a). Also (especially when on a single plane) called *zigzag*.

CHOIR: the part of a cathedral, monastic or collegiate church where services are sung.

CIBORIUM: a fixed canopy over an altar, usually vaulted and supported on four columns; cf. Baldacchino. Also a canopied shrine for the reserved sacrament.

CINQUEFOIL: *see* Foil.

CIST: stone-lined or slab-built grave.

CLADDING: external covering or skin applied to a structure, especially a framed one.

CLERESTORY: uppermost storey of the nave of a church, pierced by windows. Also high-level windows in secular buildings.

CLOSER: a brick cut to complete a bond (6e).

CLUSTER BLOCK: *see* Multi-storey.

COADE STONE: ceramic artificial stone made in Lambeth 1769–c.1840 by Eleanor Coade (†1821) and her associates.

COB: walling material of clay mixed with straw. Also called *pisé*.

COFFERING: arrangement of sunken panels (coffers), square or polygonal, decorating a ceiling, vault, or arch.

COGGING: a decorative course of bricks laid diagonally (6e). Cf. Dentilation.

COLLAR: *see* Roofs and 7.

COLLEGIATE CHURCH: endowed for the support of a college of priests.

COLONNADE: range of columns supporting an entablature. Cf. Arcade.

COLONNETTE: small medieval column or shaft.

COLOSSAL ORDER: *see* Giant order.

COLUMBARIUM: shelved, niched structure to house multiple burials.

COLUMN: a classical, upright structural member of round section with a shaft, a capital, and usually a base (3a, 4a).

COLUMN FIGURE: carved figure attached to a medieval column or shaft, usually flanking a doorway.

COMMUNION TABLE: unconsecrated table used in Protestant churches for the celebration of Holy Communion.

COMPOSITE: *see* Orders.

COMPOUND PIER: grouped shafts (q.v.), or a solid core surrounded by shafts.

CONCRETE: composition of *cement* (calcined lime and clay), *aggregate* (small stones or rock chippings), sand and water. It can be poured into *formwork* or *shuttering* (temporary frame of timber or metal) on site (*in-situ* concrete), or *pre-cast* as components before construction. *Reinforced*: incorporating steel rods to take the tensile force. *Pre-stressed*: with tensioned steel rods. Finishes include the impression of boards left by formwork (*board-marked* or *shuttered*), and texturing with steel brushes (*brushed*) or hammers (*hammer-dressed*). *See also* Shell.

CONSOLE: bracket of curved outline (4b).

COPING: protective course of masonry or brickwork capping a wall (6d).

CORBEL: projecting block supporting something above. *Corbel course*: continuous course of projecting stones or bricks fulfilling the same function. *Corbel table*: series of corbels to carry a parapet or a wall-plate or wall-post (7). *Corbelling*: brick or masonry courses built out beyond one another to support a chimney-stack, window, etc.

CORINTHIAN: *see* Orders and 3d.

CORNICE: flat-topped ledge with moulded underside, projecting along the top of a building or feature, especially as the highest member of the classical entablature (3a). Also the decorative moulding in the angle between wall and ceiling.

CORPS-DE-LOGIS: the main building(s) as distinct from the wings or pavilions.

COTTAGE ORNÉ: an artfully rustic small house associated with the Picturesque movement.

COUNTERCHANGING: of joists on a ceiling divided by beams into compartments, when placed in opposite directions in alternate squares.

COUR D'HONNEUR: formal entrance court before a house in the French manner, usually with flanking wings and a screen wall or gates.

COURSE: continuous layer of stones, etc. in a wall (6e).

COVE: a broad concave moulding, e.g. to mask the eaves of a roof. *Coved ceiling*: with a pronounced cove joining the walls to a flat central panel smaller than the whole area of the ceiling.

CRADLE ROOF: *see* Wagon roof.

CREDENCE: a shelf within or beside a piscina (q.v.), or a table for the sacramental elements and vessels.

CRENELLATION: parapet with crenels (*see* Battlement).

CRINKLE-CRANKLE WALL: garden wall undulating in a series of serpentine curves.

CROCKETS: leafy hooks. *Crocketing* decorates the edges of Gothic features, such as pinnacles, canopies, etc. *Crocket capital*: *see* 1b.

CROSSING: central space at the junction of the nave, chancel, and transepts. *Crossing tower*: above a crossing.

CROSS-WINDOW: with one mullion and one transom (qq.v.).

CROWN-POST: *see* Roofs and 7.

CROWSTEPS: squared stones set like steps, e.g. on a gable (8a).

CRUCKS (*lit.* crooked): pairs of inclined timbers (*blades*), usually curved, set at bay-lengths; they support the roof timbers and, in timber buildings, also support the walls (8b). *Base*: blades rise from ground level to a tie- or collar-beam which supports the roof timbers. *Full*: blades rise from ground level to the apex of the roof, serving as the main members of a roof truss. *Jointed*: blades formed from more than one timber; the lower member may act as a wall-post; it is usually elbowed at wall-plate level and jointed just above. *Middle*: blades rise from half-way up the walls to a tie- or collar-beam. *Raised*: blades rise from half-way up the walls to the apex. *Upper*: blades supported on a tie-beam and rising to the apex.

CRYPT: underground or half-underground area, usually below the E end of a church. *Ring crypt*: corridor crypt surrounding the apse of an early medieval church, often associated with chambers for relics. Cf. Undercroft.

CUPOLA (*lit.* dome): especially a small dome on a circular or polygonal base crowning a larger dome, roof, or turret.

CURSUS: a long avenue defined by two parallel earthen banks with ditches outside.

CURTAIN WALL: a connecting wall between the towers of a castle. Also a non-load-bearing external wall applied to a C20 framed structure.

CUSP: *see* Tracery and 2b.

CYCLOPEAN MASONRY: large irregular polygonal stones, smooth and finely jointed.

CYMA RECTA and CYMA REVERSA: classical mouldings with double curves (3f). Cf. Ogee.

DADO: the finishing (often with panelling) of the lower part of a wall in a classical interior; in origin a formalized continuous pedestal. *Dado rail*: the moulding along the top of the dado.

DAGGER: *see* Tracery and 2b.

DALLE-DE-VERRE (*lit.* glass-slab): a late C20 stained-glass technique, setting large, thick pieces of cast glass into a frame of reinforced concrete or epoxy resin.

DEC (DECORATED): English Gothic architecture *c.* 1290 to *c.* 1350. The name is derived from the type of window tracery (q.v.) used during the period.

DEMI- or HALF-COLUMNS: engaged columns (q.v.) half of whose circumference projects from the wall.

DENTIL: small square block used in series in classical cornices (3c). *Dentilation* is produced by the projection of alternating headers along cornices or stringcourses.

DIAPER: repetitive surface decoration of lozenges or squares flat or in relief. Achieved in brickwork with bricks of two colours.

DIOCLETIAN OR THERMAL WINDOW: semicircular with two mullions, as used in the Baths of Diocletian, Rome (4b).

DISTYLE: having two columns (4a).

DOGTOOTH: E.E. ornament, consisting of a series of small pyramids formed by four stylized canine teeth meeting at a point (1a).

DORIC: *see* Orders and 3a, 3b.

DORMER: window projecting from the slope of a roof (8a).

DOUBLE CHAMFER: a chamfer applied to each of two recessed arches (1a).

DOUBLE PILE: *see* Pile.

DRAGON BEAM: *see* Jetty.

DRESSINGS: the stone or brickwork worked to a finished face about an angle, opening, or other feature.

DRIPSTONE: moulded stone projecting from a wall to protect the lower parts from water. Cf. Hoodmould, Weathering.

DRUM: circular or polygonal stage supporting a dome or cupola. Also one of the stones forming the shaft of a column (3a).

DUTCH or FLEMISH GABLE: *see* 8a.

EASTER SEPULCHRE: tomb-chest used for Easter ceremonial, within or against the N wall of a chancel.

EAVES: overhanging edge of a roof; hence *eaves cornice* in this position.

ECHINUS: ovolo moulding (q.v.) below the abacus of a Greek Doric capital (3a).

EDGE RAIL: *see* Railways.

E.E. (EARLY ENGLISH): English Gothic architecture *c.* 1190–1250.

EGG-AND-DART: *see* Enrichments and 3f.

ELEVATION: any face of a building or side of a room. In a drawing, the same or any part of it, represented in two dimensions.

EMBATTLED: with battlements.

EMBRASURE: small splayed opening in a wall or battlement (q.v.).

ENCAUSTIC TILES: earthenware tiles fired with a pattern and glaze.

EN DELIT: stone cut against the bed.

ENFILADE: reception rooms in a formal series, usually with all doorways on axis.

ENGAGED or ATTACHED COLUMN: one that partly merges into a wall or pier.

ENGINEERING BRICKS: dense bricks, originally used mostly for railway viaducts etc.

ENRICHMENTS: the carved decoration of certain classical mouldings, e.g. the ovolo (qq.v.) with *egg-and-dart*, the cyma reversa with *waterleaf*, the astragal with *bead-and-reel* (3f).

ENTABLATURE: in classical architecture, collective name for the three horizontal members (architrave, frieze, and cornice) carried by a wall or a column (3a).

ENTASIS: very slight convex deviation from a straight line, used to prevent an optical illusion of concavity.

EPITAPH: inscription on a tomb.

EXEDRA: *see* Apse.

EXTRADOS: outer curved face of an arch or vault.

EYECATCHER: decorative building terminating a vista.

FASCIA: plain horizontal band, e.g. in an architrave (3c, 3d) or on a shopfront.

FENESTRATION: the arrangement of windows in a façade.

FERETORY: site of the chief shrine of a church, behind the high altar.

FESTOON: ornamental garland, suspended from both ends. Cf. Swag.

FIBREGLASS, or glass-reinforced polyester (GRP): synthetic resin reinforced with glass fibre. GRC: glass-reinforced concrete.

FIELD: see Panelling and 6b.

FILLET: a narrow flat band running down a medieval shaft or along a roll moulding (1a). It separates larger curved mouldings in classical cornices, fluting or bases (3c).

FLAMBOYANT: the latest phase of French Gothic architecture, with flowing tracery.

FLASH LOCK: see Canals.

FLÈCHE or SPIRELET (*lit.* arrow): slender spire on the centre of a roof.

FLEURON: medieval carved flower or leaf, often rectilinear (1a).

FLUSHWORK: knapped flint used with dressed stone to form patterns.

FLUTING: series of concave grooves (flutes), their common edges sharp (arris) or blunt (fillet) (3).

FOIL (*lit.* leaf): lobe formed by the cusping of a circular or other shape in tracery (2b). *Trefoil* (three), *quatrefoil* (four), *cinquefoil* (five), and *multifoil* express the number of lobes in a shape.

FOLIATE: decorated with leaves.

FORMWORK: see Concrete.

FRAMED BUILDING: where the structure is carried by a framework – e.g. of steel, reinforced concrete, timber – instead of by load-bearing walls.

FREESTONE: stone that is cut, or can be cut, in all directions.

FRESCO: *al fresco*: painting on wet plaster. *Fresco secco*: painting on dry plaster.

FRIEZE: the middle member of the classical entablature, sometimes ornamented (3a). *Pulvinated frieze* (*lit.* cushioned): of bold convex profile (3c). Also a horizontal band of ornament.

FRONTISPIECE: in C16 and C17 buildings the central feature of doorway and windows above linked in one composition.

GABLE: For types see 8a. *Gablet*: small gable. *Pedimental gable*: treated like a pediment.

GADROONING: classical ribbed ornament like inverted fluting that flows into a lobed edge.

GALILEE: chapel or vestibule usually at the W end of a church enclosing the main portal(s).

GALLERY: a long room or passage; an upper storey above the aisle of a church, looking through arches to the nave; a balcony or mezzanine overlooking the main interior space of a building; or an external walkway.

GALLETING: small stones set in a mortar course.

GAMBREL ROOF: see 8a.

GARDEROBE: medieval privy.

GARGOYLE: projecting water spout often carved into human or animal shape.

GAUGED or RUBBED BRICKWORK: soft brick sawn roughly, then rubbed to a precise (gauged) surface. Mostly used for door or window openings (5c).

GAZEBO (jocular Latin, 'I shall gaze'): ornamental lookout tower or raised summer house.

GEOMETRIC: English Gothic architecture *c.* 1250–1310. See also Tracery. For another meaning, see Stairs.

GIANT or COLOSSAL ORDER: classical order (q.v.) whose height is that of two or more storeys of the building to which it is applied.

GIBBS SURROUND: C18 treatment of an opening (4b), seen particularly in the work of James Gibbs (1682–1754).

GIRDER: a large beam. *Box*: of hollow-box section. *Bowed*: with its top rising in a curve. *Plate*: of I-section, made from iron or steel plates. *Lattice*: with braced framework.

GLAZING BARS: wooden or sometimes metal bars separating and supporting window panes.

GRAFFITI: *see* Sgraffito.

GRANGE: farm owned and run by a religious order.

GRC: *see* Fibreglass.

GRISAILLE: monochrome painting on walls or glass.

GROIN: sharp edge at the meeting of two cells of a cross-vault; *see* Vault and 2c.

GROTESQUE (*lit.* grotto-esque): wall decoration adopted from Roman examples in the Renaissance. Its foliage scrolls incorporate figurative elements. Cf. Arabesque.

GROTTO: artificial cavern.

GRP: *see* Fibreglass.

GUILLOCHE: classical ornament of interlaced bands (4b).

GUNLOOP: opening for a firearm.

GUTTAE: stylized drops (3b).

HALF-TIMBERING: archaic term for timber-framing (q.v.). Sometimes used for non-structural decorative timberwork.

HALL CHURCH: medieval church with nave and aisles of approximately equal height.

HAMMERBEAM: *see* Roofs and 7.

HAMPER: in C20 architecture, a visually distinct topmost storey or storeys.

HEADER: *see* Bond and 6e.

HEADSTOP: stop (q.v.) carved with a head (5b).

HELM ROOF: *see* 1c.

HENGE: ritual earthwork.

HERM (*lit.* the god Hermes): male head or bust on a pedestal.

HERRINGBONE WORK: *see* 7ii. Cf. Pitched masonry.

HEXASTYLE: *see* Portico.

HILL-FORT: Iron Age earthwork enclosed by a ditch and bank system.

HIPPED ROOF: *see* 8a.

HOODMOULD: projecting moulding above an arch or lintel to throw off water (2b, 5b). When horizontal often called a *label*. For label stop *see* Stop.

HUSK GARLAND: festoon of stylized nutshells (4b).

HYDRAULIC POWER: use of water under high pressure to work machinery. *Accumulator tower*: houses a hydraulic accumulator which accommodates fluctuations in the flow through hydraulic mains.

HYPOCAUST (*lit.* underburning): Roman underfloor heating system.

IMPOST: horizontal moulding at the springing of an arch (5c).

IMPOST BLOCK: block between abacus and capital (1b).

IN ANTIS: *see* Antae, Portico and 4a.

INDENT: shape chiselled out of a stone to receive a brass.

INDUSTRIALIZED or SYSTEM BUILDING: system of manufactured units assembled on site.

INGLENOOK (*lit.* fire-corner): recess for a hearth with provision for seating.

INTERCOLUMNATION: interval between columns.

INTERLACE: decoration in relief simulating woven or entwined stems or bands.

INTRADOS: *see* Soffit.

IONIC: *see* Orders and 3c.

JACK ARCH: shallow segmental vault springing from beams, used for fireproof floors, bridge decks, etc.

JAMB (*lit.* leg): one of the vertical sides of an opening.

JETTY: in a timber-framed building, the projection of an upper storey beyond the storey below, made by the beams and joists of the lower storey oversailing the wall; on their outer ends is placed the sill of the walling for the storey above (7). Buildings can be jettied on several sides, in which case a *dragon beam* is set diagonally at the corner to carry the joists to either side.

JOGGLE: the joining of two stones to prevent them slipping by a notch in one and a projection in the other.

KEEL MOULDING: moulding used from the late C12, in section like the keel of a ship (1a).

KEEP: principal tower of a castle.

KENTISH CUSP: *see* Tracery and 2b.

KEY PATTERN: see 4b.

KEYSTONE: central stone in an arch or vault (4b, 5c).

KINGPOST: see Roofs and 7.

KNEELER: horizontal projecting stone at the base of each side of a gable to support the inclined coping stones (8a).

LABEL: see Hoodmould and 5b.

LABEL STOP: see Stop and 5b.

LACED BRICKWORK: vertical strips of brickwork, often in a contrasting colour, linking openings on different floors.

LACING COURSE: horizontal reinforcement in timber or brick to walls of flint, cobble, etc.

LADY CHAPEL: dedicated to the Virgin Mary (Our Lady).

LANCET: slender single-light, pointed-arched window (2a).

LANTERN: circular or polygonal windowed turret crowning a roof or a dome. Also the windowed stage of a crossing tower lighting the church interior.

LANTERN CROSS: churchyard cross with lantern-shaped top.

LAVATORIUM: in a religious house, a washing place adjacent to the refectory.

LEAN-TO: see Roofs.

LESENE (lit. a mean thing): pilaster without base or capital. Also called pilaster strip.

LIERNE: see Vault and 2c.

LIGHT: compartment of a window defined by the mullions.

LINENFOLD: Tudor panelling carved with simulations of folded linen. See also Parchemin.

LINTEL: horizontal beam or stone bridging an opening.

LOGGIA: gallery, usually arcaded or colonnaded; sometimes freestanding.

LONG-AND-SHORT WORK: quoins consisting of stones placed with the long side alternately upright and horizontal, especially in Saxon building.

LONGHOUSE: house and byre in the same range with internal access between them.

LOUVRE: roof opening, often protected by a raised timber structure, to allow the smoke from a central hearth to escape.

LOWSIDE WINDOW: set lower than the others in a chancel side wall, usually towards its W end.

LUCAM: projecting housing for hoist pulley on upper storey of warehouses, mills, etc., for raising goods to loading doors.

LUCARNE (lit. dormer): small gabled opening in a roof or spire.

LUGGED ARCHITRAVE: see 4b.

LUNETTE: semicircular window or blind panel.

LYCHGATE (lit. corpse-gate): roofed gateway entrance to a churchyard for the reception of a coffin.

LYNCHET: long terraced strip of soil on the downward side of prehistoric and medieval fields, accumulated because of continual ploughing along the contours.

MACHICOLATIONS (lit. mashing devices): series of openings between the corbels that support a projecting parapet through which missiles can be dropped. Used decoratively in post-medieval buildings.

MANOMETER or STANDPIPE TOWER: containing a column of water to regulate pressure in water mains.

MANSARD: see 8a.

MATHEMATICAL TILES: facing tiles with the appearance of brick, most often applied to timber-framed walls.

MAUSOLEUM: monumental building or chamber usually intended for the burial of members of one family.

MEGALITHIC TOMB: massive stone-built Neolithic burial chamber covered by an earth or stone mound.

MERLON: see Battlement.

METOPES: spaces between the triglyphs in a Doric frieze (3b).

MEZZANINE: low storey between two higher ones.

MILD STEEL: see Cast iron.

MISERICORD (lit. mercy): shelf on a carved bracket placed on the underside of a hinged choir stall seat to support an occupant when standing.

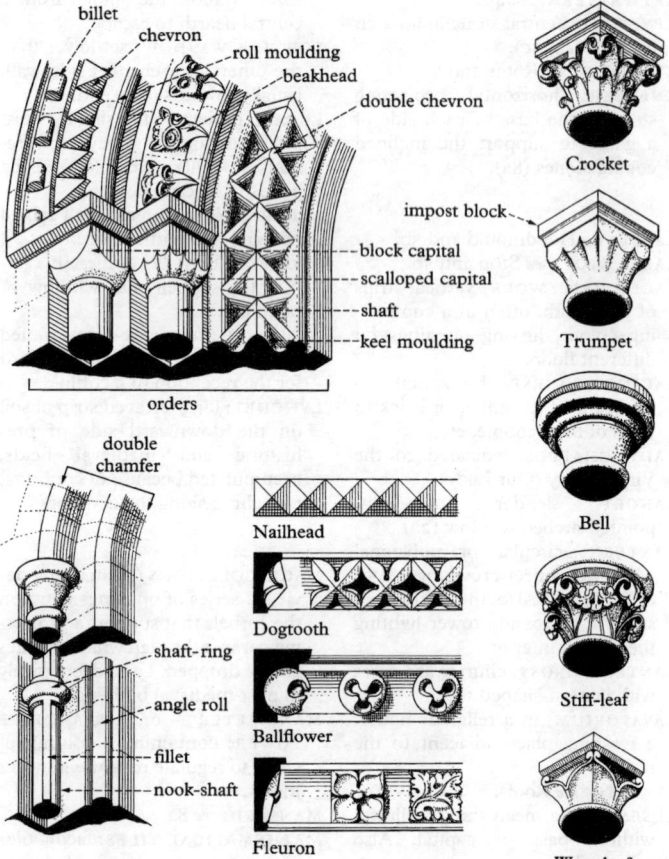

a) MOULDINGS AND ORNAMENT

Labels in figure:
billet, chevron, roll moulding, beakhead, double chevron, block capital, scalloped capital, shaft, keel moulding, orders

double chamfer, shaft-ring, angle roll, fillet, nook-shaft

Nailhead, Dogtooth, Ballflower, Fleuron

b) CAPITALS

Crocket, impost block, Trumpet, Bell, Stiff-leaf, Waterleaf

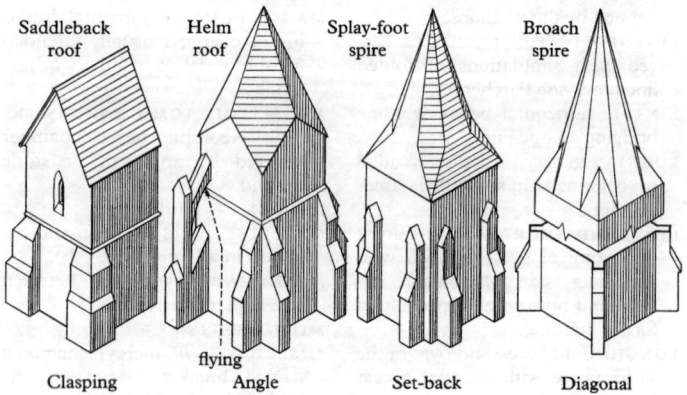

c) BUTTRESSES, ROOFS AND SPIRES

Saddleback roof, Helm roof, Splay-foot spire, Broach spire

Clasping, flying, Angle, Set-back, Diagonal

FIGURE 1: MEDIEVAL

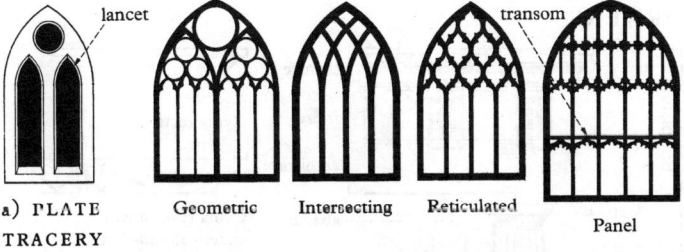

a) PLATE TRACERY

Geometric | Intersecting | Reticulated | Panel

Quatrefoil with Kentish cusps

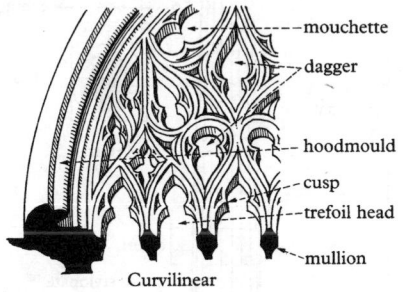

Curvilinear

b) BAR TRACERY

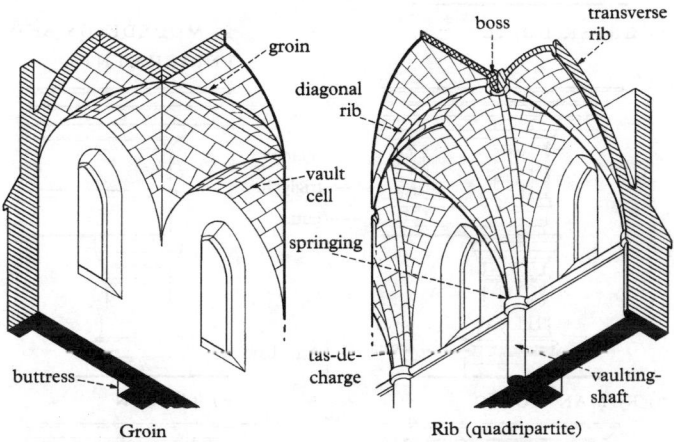

Groin

Rib (quadripartite)

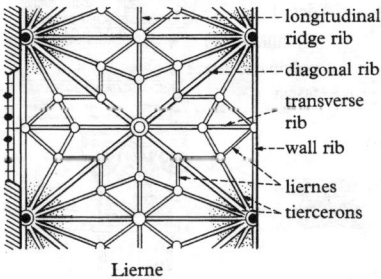

Lierne

Fan

c) VAULTS

FIGURE 2: MEDIEVAL

ORDERS

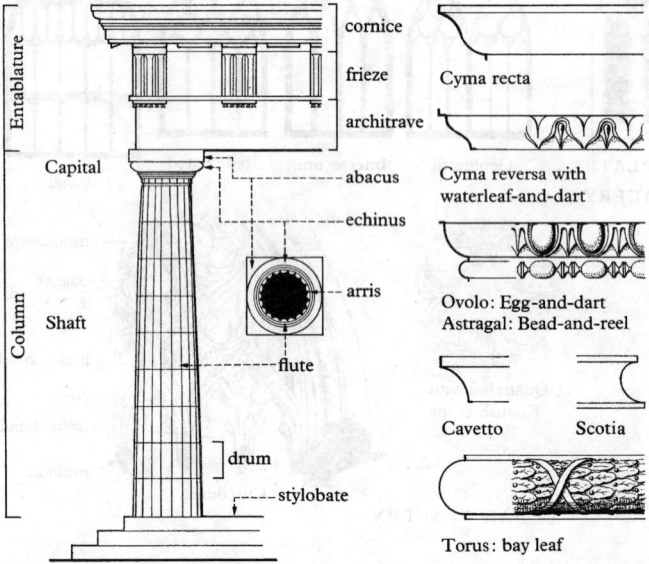

a) GREEK DORIC

cornice
frieze
architrave
abacus
echinus
arris
flute
drum
stylobate

Entablature
Capital
Column
Shaft

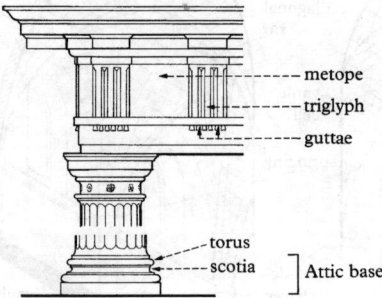

b) ROMAN DORIC

metope
triglyph
guttae
torus
scotia
Attic base

Cyma recta

Cyma reversa with
waterleaf-and-dart

Ovolo: Egg-and-dart
Astragal: Bead-and-reel

Cavetto   Scotia

Torus: bay leaf

f) MOULDINGS AND
ENRICHMENTS

e) TUSCAN

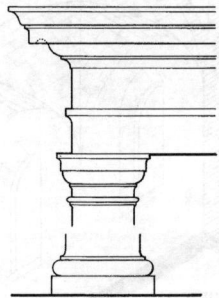

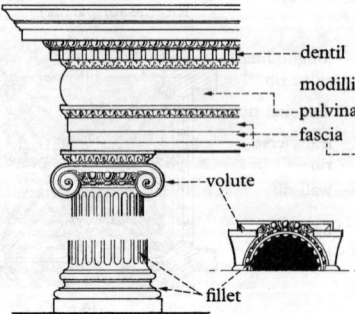

c) IONIC

dentil
modillion
pulvinated frieze
fascia
volute
fillet

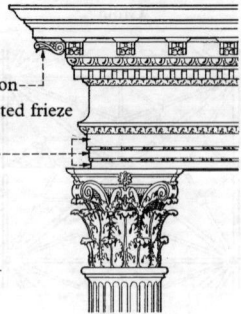

d) CORINTHIAN

FIGURE 3: CLASSICAL

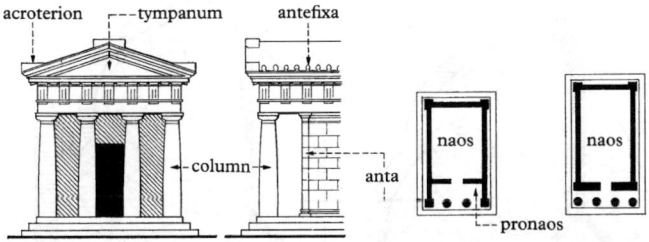

a) PORTICO

Distyle in antis   Prostyle

Anthemion & Palmette

Guilloche

Key pattern

Rinceau

Husk garland

Vitruvian scroll

Console

Diocletian window

Acanthus

Broken pediment

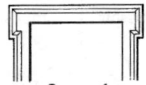

Lugged architrave

Segmental pediment

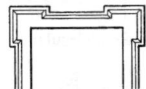

Shouldered architrave

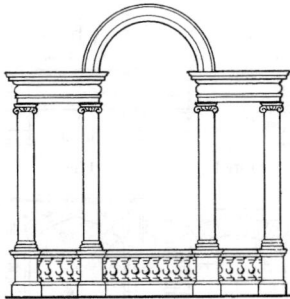

Venetian window

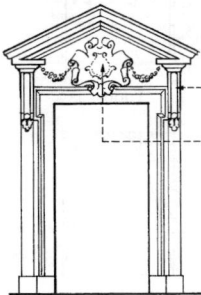

Open pediment

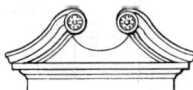

Swan-neck pediment

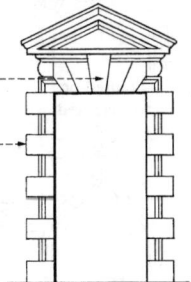

Gibbs surround

b) ORNAMENTS AND FEATURES

FIGURE 4: CLASSICAL

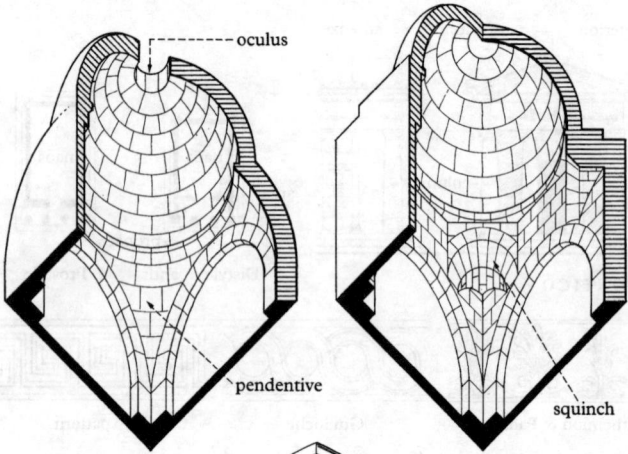

a) DOMES

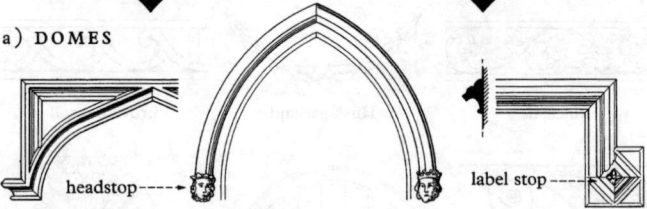

b) HOODMOULDS

Label

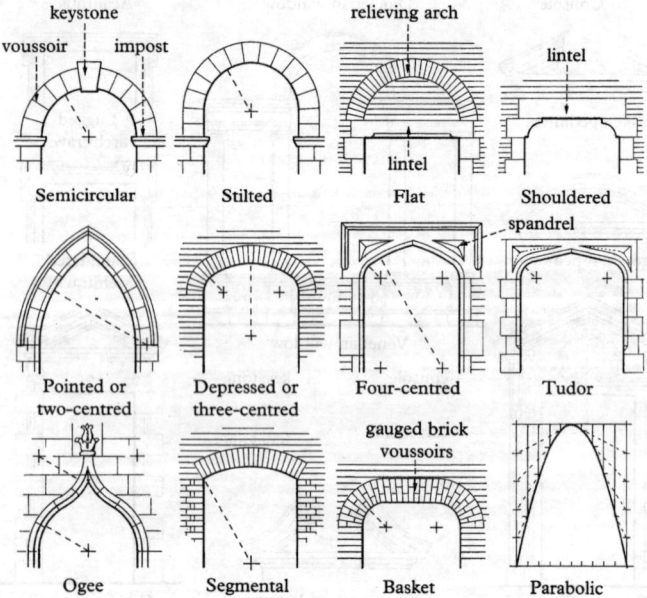

c) ARCHES

FIGURE 5: CONSTRUCTION

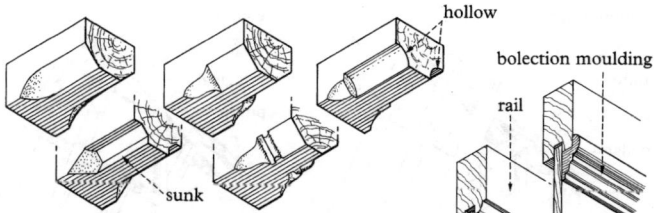

a) CHAMFERS AND CHAMFERSTOPS

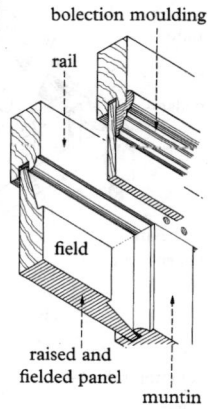

b) PANELLING

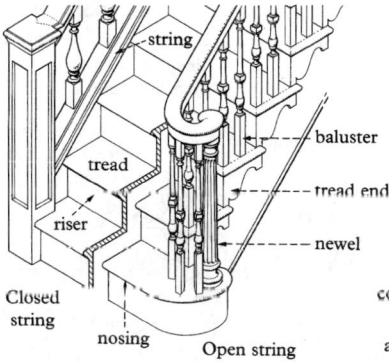

c) STAIRS

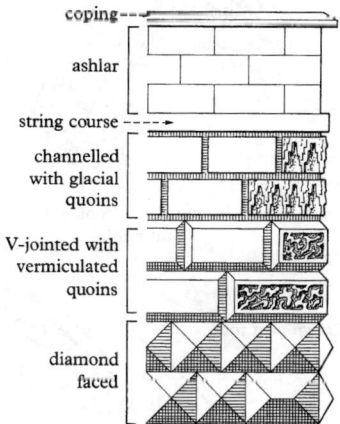

d) RUSTICATION

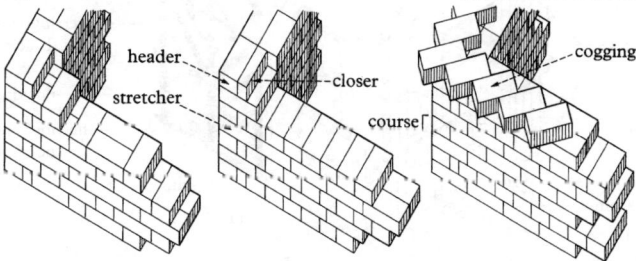

e) BRICK BONDS

FIGURE 6: CONSTRUCTION

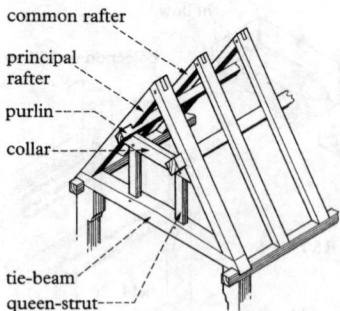

Queen-strut roof with clasped purlins

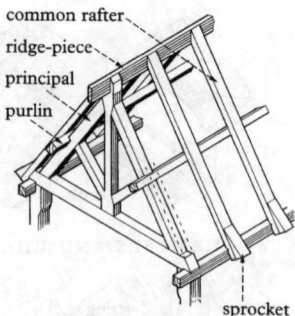

- common rafter
- principal rafter
- purlin
- collar
- tie-beam
- queen-strut

Kingpost roof with trenched purlins

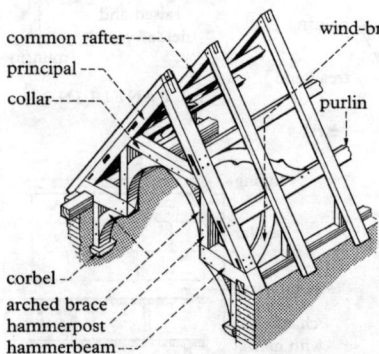

- common rafter
- ridge-piece
- principal
- purlin
- sprocket

Hammerbeam roof with butt purlins

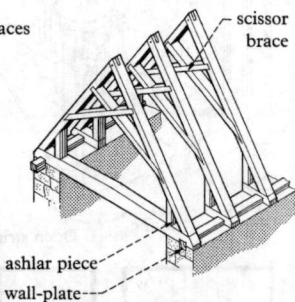

- common rafter
- principal
- collar
- wind-braces
- purlin
- corbel
- arched brace
- hammerpost
- hammerbeam

Scissor truss roof

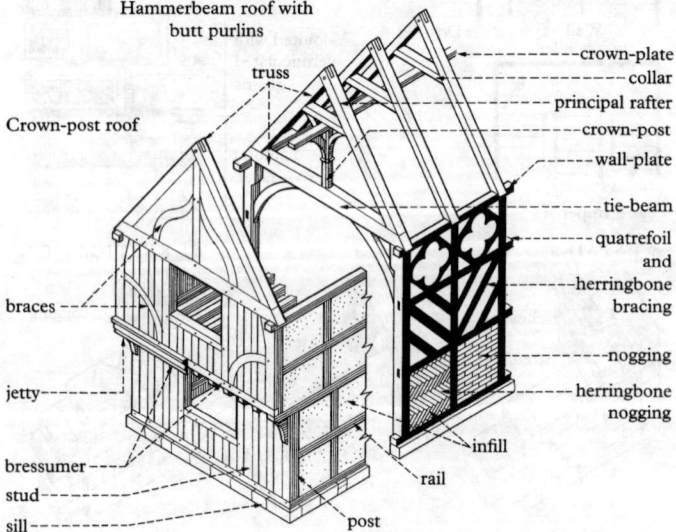

- scissor brace
- ashlar piece
- wall-plate

Crown-post roof

- truss
- crown-plate
- collar
- principal rafter
- crown-post
- wall-plate
- tie-beam
- quatrefoil and herringbone bracing
- nogging
- herringbone nogging
- braces
- jetty
- bressumer
- stud
- sill
- post
- infill
- rail

Box frame: i) Close studding   ii) Square panel

FIGURE 7: ROOFS AND TIMBER-FRAMING

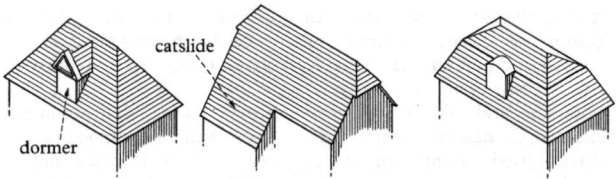

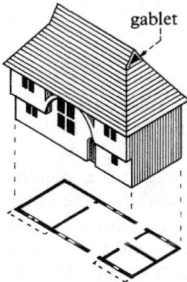

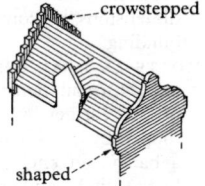

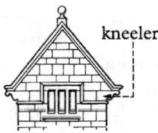

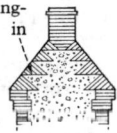

a) ROOF FORMS AND GABLES

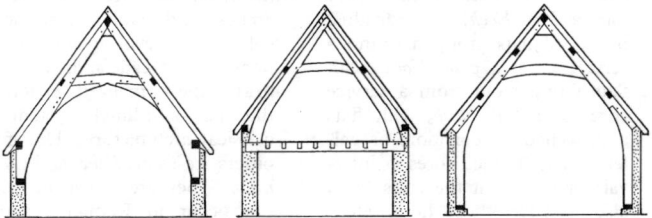

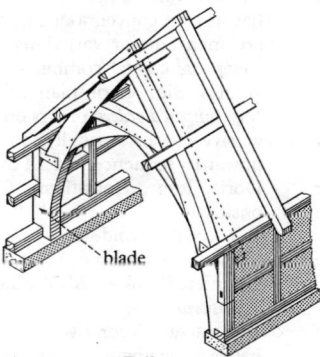

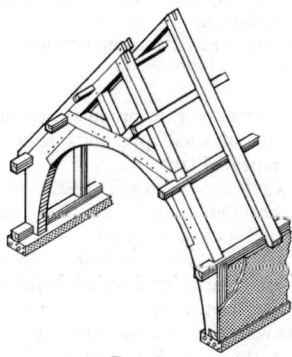

b) CRUCK FRAMES

FIGURE 8: ROOFS AND TIMBER-FRAMING

MIXER-COURTS: forecourts to groups of houses shared by vehicles and pedestrians.

MODILLIONS: small consoles (q.v.) along the underside of a Corinthian or Composite cornice (3d). Often used along an eaves cornice.

MODULE: a predetermined standard size for co-ordinating the dimensions of components of a building.

MOTTE-AND-BAILEY: post-Roman and Norman defence consisting of an earthen mound (motte) topped by a wooden tower within a bailey, an enclosure defended by a ditch and palisade, and also, sometimes, by an internal bank.

MOUCHETTE: see Tracery and 2b.

MOULDING: shaped ornamental strip of continuous section; see e.g. Cavetto, Cyma, Ovolo, Roll.

MULLION: vertical member between window lights (2b).

MULTI-STOREY: five or more storeys. Multi-storey flats may form a *cluster block*, with individual blocks of flats grouped round a service core; a *point block*, with flats fanning out from a service core; or a *slab block*, with flats approached by corridors or galleries from service cores at intervals or towers at the ends (plan also used for offices, hotels etc.). *Tower block* is a generic term for any very high multi-storey building.

MUNTIN: see Panelling and 6b.

NAILHEAD: E.E. ornament consisting of small pyramids regularly repeated (1a).

NARTHEX: enclosed vestibule or covered porch at the main entrance to a church.

NAVE: the body of a church W of the crossing or chancel often flanked by aisles (q.v.).

NEWEL: central or corner post of a staircase (6c). Newel stair: see Stairs.

NIGHT STAIR: stair by which religious entered the transept of their church from their dormitory to celebrate night services.

NOGGING: see Timber-framing (7).

NOOK-SHAFT: shaft set in the angle of a wall or opening (1a).

NORMAN: see Romanesque.

NOSING: projection of the tread of a step (6c).

NUTMEG: medieval ornament with a chain of tiny triangles placed obliquely.

OCULUS: circular opening.

ŒIL DE BŒUF: see Bullseye window.

OGEE: double curve, bending first one way and then the other, as in an *ogee* or *ogival arch* (5c). Cf. Cyma recta and Cyma reversa.

OPUS SECTILE: decorative mosaic-like facing.

OPUS SIGNINUM: composition flooring of Roman origin.

ORATORY: a private chapel in a church or a house. Also a church of the Oratorian Order.

ORDER: one of a series of recessed arches and jambs forming a splayed medieval opening, e.g. a doorway or arcade arch (1a).

ORDERS: the formalized versions of the post-and-lintel system in classical architecture. The main orders are *Doric*, *Ionic*, and *Corinthian*. They are Greek in origin but occur in Roman versions. Tuscan is a simple version of Roman Doric. Though each order has its own conventions (3), there are many minor variations. The *Composite* capital combines Ionic volutes with Corinthian foliage. *Superimposed orders*: orders on successive levels, usually in the upward sequence of Tuscan, Doric, Ionic, Corinthian, Composite.

ORIEL: see Bay window.

OVERDOOR: painting or relief above an internal door. Also called a *sopraporta*.

OVERTHROW: decorative fixed arch between two gatepiers or above a wrought-iron gate.

OVOLO: wide convex moulding (3f).

PALIMPSEST: of a brass: where a metal plate has been reused by turning over the engraving on the back; of a wall painting: where one overlaps and partly obscures an earlier one.

PALLADIAN: following the examples and principles of Andrea Palladio (1508–80).

PALMETTE: classical ornament like a palm shoot (4b).

PANELLING: wooden lining to interior walls, made up of vertical members (*muntins*) and horizontals (*rails*) framing panels: also called *wainscot*. *Raised and fielded*: with the central area of the panel (*field*) raised up (6b).

PANTILE: roof tile of S section.

PARAPET: wall for protection at any sudden drop, e.g. at the wall-head of a castle where it protects the *parapet walk* or wall-walk. Also used to conceal a roof.

PARCLOSE: *see* Screen.

PARGETTING (*lit.* plastering): exterior plaster decoration, either in relief or incised.

PARLOUR: in a religious house, a room where the religious could talk to visitors; in a medieval house, the semi-private living room below the solar (q.v.).

PARTERRE: level space in a garden laid out with low, formal beds.

PATERA (*lit.* plate): round or oval ornament in shallow relief.

PAVILION: ornamental building for occasional use; or projecting subdivision of a larger building, often at an angle or terminating a wing.

PEBBLEDASHING: *see* Rendering.

PEDESTAL: a tall block carrying a classical order, statue, vase, etc.

PEDIMENT: a formalized gable derived from that of a classical temple; also used over doors, windows, etc. For variations *see* 4b.

PENDENTIVE: spandrel between adjacent arches, supporting a drum, dome or vault and consequently formed as part of a hemisphere (5a).

PENTHOUSE: subsidiary structure with a lean-to roof. Also a separately roofed structure on top of a C20 multi-storey block.

PERIPTERAL: *see* Peristyle.

PERISTYLE: a colonnade all round the exterior of a classical building, as in a temple which is then said to be *peripteral*.

PERP (PERPENDICULAR): English Gothic architecture *c.* 1335–50 to *c.* 1530. The name is derived from the upright tracery panels then used (*see* Tracery and 2a).

PERRON: external stair to a doorway, usually of double-curved plan.

PEW: loosely, seating for the laity outside the chancel; strictly, an enclosed seat. *Box pew*: with equal high sides and a door.

PIANO NOBILE: principal floor of a classical building above a ground floor or basement and with a lesser storey overhead.

PIAZZA: formal urban open space surrounded by buildings.

PIER: large masonry or brick support, often for an arch. *See also* Compound pier.

PILASTER: flat representation of a classical column in shallow relief. *Pilaster strip*: *see* Lesene.

PILE: row of rooms. *Double pile*: two rows thick.

PILLAR: free-standing upright member of any section, not conforming to one of the orders (q.v.).

PILLAR PISCINA: *see* Piscina.

PILOTIS: C20 French term for pillars or stilts that support a building above an open ground floor.

PISCINA: basin for washing Mass vessels, provided with a drain; set in or against the wall to the S of an altar or free-standing (*pillar piscina*).

PISÉ: *see* Cob.

PITCHED MASONRY: laid on the diagonal, often alternately with opposing courses (*pitched and counterpitched* or *herringbone*).

PLATBAND: flat horizontal moulding between storeys. Cf. stringcourse.

PLATE RAIL: *see* Railways.

PLATEWAY: *see* Railways.

PLINTH: projecting courses at the

foot of a wall or column, generally chamfered or moulded at the top.

PODIUM: a continuous raised platform supporting a building; or a large block of two or three storeys beneath a multi-storey block of smaller area.

POINT BLOCK: *see* Multi-storey.

POINTING: exposed mortar jointing of masonry or brickwork. Types include *flush*, *recessed* and *tuck* (with a narrow channel filled with finer, whiter mortar).

POPPYHEAD: carved ornament of leaves and flowers as a finial for a bench end or stall.

PORTAL FRAME: C20 frame comprising two uprights rigidly connected to a beam or pair of rafters.

PORTCULLIS: gate constructed to rise and fall in vertical grooves at the entry to a castle.

PORTICO: a porch with the roof and frequently a pediment supported by a row of columns (4a). A portico *in antis* has columns on the same plane as the front of the building. A *prostyle* porch has columns standing free. Porticoes are described by the number of front columns, e.g. tetrastyle (four), hexastyle (six). The space within the temple is the *naos*, that within the portico the *pronaos*. *Blind portico*: the front features of a portico applied to a wall.

PORTICUS (plural: porticūs): subsidiary cell opening from the main body of a pre-Conquest church.

POST: upright support in a structure (7).

POSTERN: small gateway at the back of a building or to the side of a larger entrance door or gate.

POUND LOCK: *see* Canals.

PRESBYTERY: the part of a church lying E of the choir where the main altar is placed; or a priest's residence.

PRINCIPAL: *see* Roofs and 7.

PRONAOS: *see* Portico and 4a.

PROSTYLE: *see* Portico and 4a.

PULPIT: raised and enclosed platform for the preaching of sermons. *Three-decker*: with reading desk below and clerk's desk below that. *Two-decker*: as above, minus the clerk's desk.

PULPITUM: stone screen in a major church dividing choir from nave.

PULVINATED: *see* Frieze and 3c.

PURLIN: *see* Roofs and 7.

PUTHOLES or PUTLOG HOLES: in the wall to receive putlogs, the horizontal timbers which support scaffolding boards; sometimes not filled after construction is complete.

PUTTO (plural: putti): small naked boy.

QUARRIES: square (or diamond) panes of glass supported by lead strips (*cames*); square floor slabs or tiles.

QUATREFOIL: *see* Foil and 2b.

QUEEN-STRUT: *see* Roofs and 7.

QUIRK: sharp groove to one side of a convex medieval moulding.

QUOINS: dressed stones at the angles of a building (6d).

RADBURN SYSTEM: vehicle and pedestrian segregation in residential developments, based on that used at Radburn, New Jersey, USA, by Wright and Stein, 1928–30.

RADIATING CHAPELS: projecting radially from an ambulatory or an apse (*see* Chevet).

RAFTER: *see* Roofs and 7.

RAGGLE: groove cut in masonry, especially to receive the edge of a roof-covering.

RAGULY: ragged (in heraldry). Also applied to funerary sculpture, e.g. *cross raguly*: with a notched outline.

RAIL: *see* Panelling and 6b; also 7.

RAILWAYS: *Edge rail*: on which flanged wheels can run. *Plate rail*: L-section rail for plain unflanged wheels. *Plateway*: early railway using plate rails.

RAISED AND FIELDED: *see* Panelling and 6b.

RAKE: slope or pitch.

RAMPART: defensive outer wall of stone or earth. *Rampart walk*: path along the inner face.

REBATE: rectangular section cut out of a masonry edge to receive a shutter, door, window, etc.

REBUS: a heraldic pun, e.g. a fiery cock for Cockburn.

REEDING: series of convex mouldings, the reverse of fluting (q.v.). Cf. Gadrooning.

RENDERING: the covering of outside walls with a uniform surface or skin for protection from the weather. *Limewashing*: thin layer of lime plaster. *Pebbledashing*: where aggregate is thrown at the wet plastered wall for a textured effect. *Roughcast*: plaster mixed with a coarse aggregate such as gravel. *Stucco*: fine lime plaster worked to a smooth surface. *Cement rendering*: a cheaper substitute for stucco, usually with a grainy texture.

REPOUSSÉ: relief designs in metalwork, formed by beating it from the back.

REREDORTER (*lit.* behind the dormitory): latrines in a medieval religious house.

REREDOS: painted and/or sculptured screen behind and above an altar. Cf. Retable.

RESPOND: half-pier or half-column bonded into a wall and carrying one end of an arch. It usually terminates an arcade.

RETABLE: painted or carved panel standing on or at the back of an altar, usually attached to it.

RETROCHOIR: in a major church, the area between the high altar and E chapel.

REVEAL: the plane of a jamb, between the wall and the frame of a door or window.

RIB-VAULT: *see* Vault and 2c.

RINCEAU: classical ornament of leafy scrolls (4b).

RISER: vertical face of a step (6c).

ROACH: a rough-textured form of Portland stone, with small cavities and fossil shells.

ROCK-FACED: masonry cleft to produce a rugged appearance.

ROCOCO: style current *c.* 1720 and *c.* 1760, characterized by a serpentine line and playful, scrolled decoration.

ROLL MOULDING: medieval moulding of part-circular section (1a).

ROMANESQUE: style current in the C11 and C12. In England often called Norman. *See also* Saxo-Norman.

ROOD: crucifix flanked by the Virgin and St John, usually over the entry into the chancel, on a beam (*rood beam*) or painted on the wall. The *rood screen* below often had a walkway (*rood loft*) along the top, reached by a *rood stair* in the side wall.

ROOFS: Shape. For the main external shapes (hipped, mansard, etc.) *see* 8a. *Helm* and *Saddleback*: *see* 1c. *Lean-to*: single sloping roof built against a vertical wall; lean-to is also applied to the part of the building beneath. Construction. *See* 7. *Single-framed* roof: with no main trusses. The rafters may be fixed to the wall-plate or ridge, or longitudinal timber may be absent altogether. *Double-framed* roof: with longitudinal members, such as purlins, and usually divided into bays by principals and principal rafters. Other types are named after their main structural components, e.g. *hammerbeam*, *crown-post* (*see* Elements below and 7). Elements. *See* 7. *Ashlar piece*: a short vertical timber connecting inner wall-plate or timber pad to a rafter. *Braces*: subsidiary timbers set diagonally to strengthen the frame. *Arched braces*: curved pair forming an arch, connecting wall or post below with tie- or collarbeam above. *Passing braces*: long straight braces passing across other members of the truss. *Scissor braces*: pair crossing diagonally between pairs of rafters or principals. *Wind-braces*: short, usually curved braces connecting side purlins with principals; sometimes decorated with cusping. *Collar* or *collar-beam*: horizontal transverse timber connecting a pair of rafter or cruck blades (q.v.), set between apex and the wall-plate. *Crown-post*: a vertical timber set centrally on a tie-beam and supporting a collar purlin braced to it longitudinally. In an open truss lateral braces may rise to the collar-beam; in a closed truss they may descend to the tie-beam.

Hammerbeams: horizontal brackets projecting at wall-plate level like an interrupted tie-beam; the inner ends carry *hammerposts*, vertical timbers which support a purlin and are braced to a collar-beam above.

Kingpost: vertical timber set centrally on a tie- or collar-beam, rising to the apex of the roof to support a ridge-piece (cf. Strut).

Plate: longitudinal timber set square to the ground. *Wall-plate*: plate along the top of a wall which receives the ends of the rafters; cf. Purlin.

Principals: pair of inclined lateral timbers of a truss. Usually they support side purlins and mark the main bay divisions.

Purlin: horizontal longitudinal timber. *Collar purlin* or *crown plate*: central timber which carries collar-beams and is supported by crown-posts. *Side purlins*: pairs of timbers placed some way up the slope of the roof, which carry common rafters. *Butt* or *tenoned purlins* are tenoned into either side of the principals. *Through purlins* pass through or past the principal; they include *clasped purlins*, which rest on queenposts or are carried in the angle between principals and collar, and *trenched purlins* trenched into the backs of principals.

Queen-strut: paired vertical, or near-vertical, timbers placed symmetrically on a tie-beam to support side purlins.

Rafters: inclined lateral timbers supporting the roof covering. *Common rafters*: regularly spaced uniform rafters placed along the length of a roof or between principals. *Principal rafters*: rafters which also act as principals.

Ridge, ridge-piece: horizontal longitudinal timber at the apex of the roof supporting the ends of the rafters.

Sprocket: short timber placed on the back and at the foot of a rafter to form projecting eaves.

Strut: vertical or oblique timber between two members of a truss, not directly supporting longitudinal timbers.

Tie-beam: main horizontal transverse timber which carries the feet of the principals at wall level.

Truss: rigid framework of timbers at bay intervals, carrying the longitudinal roof timbers which support the common rafters. *Closed truss*: with the spaces between the timbers filled, to form an internal partition.

See also Cruck, Wagon roof.

ROPE MOULDING: *see* Cable moulding.

ROSE WINDOW: circular window with tracery radiating from the centre. Cf. Wheel window.

ROTUNDA: building or room circular in plan.

ROUGHCAST: *see* Rendering.

ROVING BRIDGE: *see* Canals.

RUBBED BRICKWORK: *see* Gauged brickwork.

RUBBLE: masonry whose stones are wholly or partly in a rough state. *Coursed*: coursed stones with rough faces. *Random*: uncoursed stones in a random pattern. *Snecked*: with courses broken by smaller stones (snecks).

RUSTICATION: *see* 6d. Exaggerated treatment of masonry to give an effect of strength. The joints are usually recessed by V-section chamfering or square-section channelling (*channelled rustication*). *Banded rustication* has only the horizontal joints emphasized. The faces may be flat, but can be *diamond-faced*, like shallow pyramids, *vermiculated*, with a stylized texture like worm-casts, and *glacial* (frost-work), like icicles or stalactites.

SACRISTY: room in a church for sacred vessels and vestments.

SADDLEBACK ROOF: *see* IC.

SALTIRE CROSS: with diagonal limbs.

SANCTUARY: area around the main altar of a church. Cf. Presbytery.

SANGHA: residence of Buddhist monks or nuns.

SARCOPHAGUS: coffin of stone or other durable material.

SAXO-NORMAN: transitional Romanesque style combining Anglo-Saxon and Norman features, current *c.* 1060–1100.

SCAGLIOLA: composition imitating marble.

SCALLOPED CAPITAL: *see* 1a.

SCOTIA: a hollow classical moulding, especially between tori (q.v.) on a column base (3b, 3f).

SCREEN: in a medieval church, usually at the entry to the chancel; *see* Rood (screen) and Pulpitum. A *parclose screen* separates a chapel from the rest of the church.

SCREENS or SCREENS PASSAGE: screened-off entrance passage between great hall and service rooms.

SECTION: two-dimensional representation of a building, moulding, etc., revealed by cutting across it.

SEDILIA (singular: sedile): seats for the priests (usually three) on the s side of the chancel.

SET-OFF: *see* Weathering.

SETTS: squared stones, usually of granite, used for paving or flooring.

SGRAFFITO: decoration scratched, often in plaster, to reveal a pattern in another colour beneath. *Graffiti*: scratched drawing or writing.

SHAFT: vertical member of round or polygonal section (1a, 3a). *Shaft-ring*: at the junction of shafts set *en delit* (q.v.) or attached to a pier or wall (1a).

SHEILA-NA-GIG: female fertility figure, usually with legs apart.

SHELL: thin, self-supporting roofing membrane of timber or concrete.

SHOULDERED ARCHITRAVE: *see* 4b.

SHUTTERING: *see* Concrete.

SILL: horizontal member at the bottom of a window or door frame; or at the base of a timber-framed wall into which posts and studs are tenoned (7).

SLAB BLOCK: *see* Multi-storey.

SLATE-HANGING: covering of overlapping slates on a wall. *Tile-hanging* is similar.

SLYPE: covered way or passage leading E from the cloisters between transept and chapter house.

SNECKED: *see* Rubble.

SOFFIT (*lit.* ceiling): underside of an arch (also called *intrados*), lintel, etc. *Soffit roll*: medieval roll moulding on a soffit.

SOLAR: private upper chamber in a medieval house, accessible from the high end of the great hall.

SOPRAPORTA: *see* Overdoor.

SOUNDING-BOARD: *see* Tester.

SPANDRELS: roughly triangular spaces between an arch and its containing rectangle, or between adjacent arches (5c). Also non-structural panels under the windows in a curtain-walled building.

SPERE: a fixed structure screening the lower end of the great hall from the screens passage. *Spere-truss*: roof truss incorporated in the spere.

SPIRE: tall pyramidal or conical feature crowning a tower or turret. *Broach*: starting from a square base, then carried into an octagonal section by means of triangular faces; and *splayed-foot*: variation of the broach form, found principally in the south-east, in which the four cardinal faces are splayed out near their base, to cover the corners, while oblique (or intermediate) faces taper away to a point (1c). *Needle spire*: thin spire rising from the centre of a tower roof, well inside the parapet: when of timber and lead often called a *spike*.

SPIRELET: *see* Flèche.

SPLAY: of an opening when it is wider on one face of a wall than the other.

SPRING or SPRINGING: level at which an arch or vault rises from its supports. *Springers*: the first stones of an arch or vaulting rib above the spring (2c).

SQUINCH: arch or series of arches thrown across an interior angle of a square or rectangular structure to support a circular or polygonal superstructure, especially a dome or spire (5a).

SQUINT: an aperture in a wall or through a pier usually to allow a view of an altar.

STAIRS: *see* 6c. *Dog-leg stair*: parallel flights rising alternately in opposite directions, without an open well. *Flying stair*: cantilevered from the walls of a stairwell, without newels; sometimes called a *Geometric* stair when the inner edge describes a curve. *Newel stair*: ascending round a central supporting newel (q.v.); called a *spiral stair* or *vice* when in a circular shaft, a *winder* when in a rectangular compartment. (Winder also applies to the steps on the turn.) *Well stair*: with flights round a square open well framed by newel posts. *See also* Perron.

STALL: fixed seat in the choir or chancel for the clergy or choir (cf. Pew). Usually with arm rests, and often framed together.

STANCHION: upright structural member, of iron, steel or reinforced concrete.

STANDPIPE TOWER: *see* Manometer.

STEAM ENGINES: *Atmospheric*: worked by the vacuum created when low-pressure steam is condensed in the cylinder, as developed by Thomas Newcomen. *Beam engine*: with a large pivoted beam moved in an oscillating fashion by the piston. It may drive a flywheel or be *non-rotative*. *Watt* and *Cornish*: single-cylinder; *compound*: two cylinders; *triple expansion*: three cylinders.

STEEPLE: tower together with a spire, lantern, or belfry.

STIFF-LEAF: type of E.E. foliage decoration. *Stiff-leaf capital see* 1b.

STOP: plain or decorated terminal to mouldings or chamfers, or at the end of hoodmoulds and labels (*label stop*), or stringcourses (5b, 6a); *see also* Headstop.

STOUP: vessel for holy water, usually near a door.

STRAINER: *see* Arch.

STRAPWORK: late C16 and C17 decoration, like interlaced leather straps.

STRETCHER: *see* Bond and 6e.

STRING: *see* 6c. Sloping member holding the ends of the treads and risers of a staircase. *Closed string*: a broad string covering the ends of the treads and risers. *Open string*: cut into the shape of the treads and risers.

STRINGCOURSE: horizontal course or moulding projecting from the surface of a wall (6d).

STUCCO: *see* Rendering.

STUDS: subsidiary vertical timbers of a timber-framed wall or partition (7).

STUPA: Buddhist shrine, circular in plan.

STYLOBATE: top of the solid platform on which a colonnade stands (3a).

SUSPENSION BRIDGE: *see* Bridge.

SWAG: like a festoon (q.v.), but representing cloth.

SYSTEM BUILDING: *see* Industrialized building.

TABERNACLE: canopied structure to contain the reserved sacrament or a relic; or architectural frame for an image or statue.

TABLE TOMB: memorial slab raised on free-standing legs.

TAS-DE-CHARGE: the lower courses of a vault or arch which are laid horizontally (2c).

TERM: pedestal or pilaster tapering downward, usually with the upper part of a human figure growing out of it.

TERRACOTTA: moulded and fired clay ornament or cladding.

TESSELLATED PAVEMENT: mosaic flooring, particularly Roman, made of *tesserae*, i.e. cubes of glass, stone, or brick.

TESTER: flat canopy over a tomb or pulpit, where it is also called a *sounding-board*.

TESTER TOMB: tomb-chest with effigies beneath a tester, either free-standing (tester with four or more columns), or attached to a wall (*half-tester*) with columns on one side only.

TETRASTYLE: *see* Portico.

THERMAL WINDOW: *see* Diocletian window.

THREE-DECKER PULPIT: *see* Pulpit.

TIDAL GATES: *see* Canals.

TIE-BEAM: *see* Roofs and 7.

TIERCERON: *see* Vault and 2c.

TILE-HANGING: *see* Slate-hanging.

TIMBER-FRAMING: *see* 7. Method of construction where the structural frame is built of interlocking timbers. The spaces are filled with non-structural material, e.g. *infill* of wattle and daub, lath and plaster, brickwork (known as *nogging*), etc. and may be covered by plaster, weatherboarding (q.v.), or tiles.

TOMB CHEST: chest-shaped tomb, usually of stone. Cf. Table tomb, Tester tomb.

TORUS (plural: tori): large convex moulding usually used on a column base (3b, 3f).

TOUCH: soft black marble quarried near Tournai.

TOURELLE: turret corbelled out from the wall.

TOWER BLOCK: *see* Multi-storey.

TRABEATED: depends structurally on the use of the post and lintel. Cf. Arcuated.

TRACERY: openwork pattern of masonry or timber in the upper part of an opening. *Blind tracery* is tracery applied to a solid wall.
Plate tracery, introduced *c.* 1200, is the earliest form, in which shapes are cut through solid masonry (2a).
Bar tracery was introduced into England *c.* 1250. The pattern is formed by intersecting moulded ribwork continued from the mullions. It was especially elaborate during the Decorated period (q.v.). Tracery shapes can include circles, *daggers* (elongated ogee-ended lozenges), *mouchettes* (like daggers but with curved sides) and upright rectangular *panels*. They often have *cusps*, projecting points defining lobes or *foils* (q.v.) within the main shape: *Kentish* or *split-cusps* are forked (2b).
Types of bar tracery (*see* 2b) include *geometric(al)*: *c.* 1250–1310, chiefly circles, often foiled; *Y-tracery*: *c.* 1300, with mullions branching into a Y-shape; *intersecting*: *c.* 1300, formed by interlocking mullions; *reticulated*: early C14, net-like pattern of ogee-ended lozenges; *curvilinear*: C14, with uninterrupted flowing curves; *panel*: Perp, with straight-sided panels, often cusped at the top and bottom.

TRANSEPT: transverse portion of a church.

TRANSITIONAL: generally used for the phase between Romanesque and Early English (*c.* 1175–*c.* 1200).

TRANSOM: horizontal member separating window lights (2b).

TREAD: horizontal part of a step. The *tread end* may be carved on a staircase (6c).

TREFOIL: *see* Foil.

TRIFORIUM: middle storey of a church treated as an arcaded wall passage or blind arcade, its height corresponding to that of the aisle roof.

TRIGLYPHS (*lit.* three-grooved tablets): stylized beam-ends in the Doric frieze, with metopes between (3b).

TRIUMPHAL ARCH: influential type of Imperial Roman monument.

TROPHY: sculptured or painted group of arms or armour.

TRUMEAU: central stone mullion supporting the tympanum of a wide doorway. *Trumeau figure*: carved figure attached to it (cf. Column figure).

TRUMPET CAPITAL: *see* 1b.

TRUSS: braced framework, spanning between supports. *See also* Roofs and 7.

TUMBLING or TUMBLING-IN: courses of brickwork laid at right-angles to a slope, e.g. of a gable, forming triangles by tapering into horizontal courses (8a).

TUSCAN: *see* Orders and 3e.

TWO-DECKER PULPIT: *see* Pulpit.

TYMPANUM: the surface between a lintel and the arch above it or within a pediment (4a).

UNDERCROFT: usually describes the vaulted room(s), beneath the main room(s) of a medieval house. Cf. Crypt.

VAULT: arched stone roof (sometimes imitated in timber or plaster). For types see 2c.
Tunnel or *barrel vault*: continuous semicircular or pointed arch, often of rubble masonry.

Groin-vault: tunnel vaults intersecting at right angles. *Groins* are the curved lines of the intersections.

Rib-vault: masonry framework of intersecting arches (ribs) supporting *vault cells*, used in Gothic architecture. *Wall rib* or *wall arch*: between wall and vault cell. *Transverse rib*: spans between two walls to divide a vault into bays. *Quadripartite* rib-vault: each bay has two pairs of diagonal ribs dividing the vault into four triangular cells. *Sexpartite* rib-vault: most often used over paired bays, has an extra pair of ribs springing from between the bays. More elaborate vaults may include *ridge ribs* along the crown of a vault or bisecting the bays; *tiercerons*: extra decorative ribs springing from the corners of a bay; and *liernes*: short decorative ribs in the crown of a vault, not linked to any springing point. A *stellar* or *star* vault has liernes in star formation.

Fan-vault: form of barrel vault used in the Perp period, made up of halved concave masonry cones decorated with blind tracery.

VAULTING SHAFT: shaft leading up to the spring or springing (q.v.) of a vault (2c).

VENETIAN or SERLIAN WINDOW: derived from Serlio (4b). The motif is used for other openings.

VERMICULATION: *see* Rustication and 6d.

VESICA: oval with pointed ends.

VICE: *see* Stair.

VILLA: originally a Roman country house or farm. The term was revived in England in the C18 under the influence of Palladio and used especially for smaller, compact country houses. In the later C19 it was debased to describe any suburban house.

VITRIFIED: bricks or tiles fired to a darkened glassy surface.

VITRUVIAN SCROLL: classical running ornament of curly waves (4b).

VOLUTES: spiral scrolls. They occur on Ionic capitals (3c). *Angle volute*: pair of volutes, turned outwards to meet at the corner of a capital.

VOUSSOIRS: wedge-shaped stones forming an arch (5c).

WAGON ROOF: with the appearance of the inside of a wagon tilt; often ceiled. Also called *cradle roof*.

WAINSCOT: *see* Panelling.

WALL MONUMENT: attached to the wall and often standing on the floor. *Wall tablets* are smaller with the inscription as the major element.

WALL-PLATE: *see* Roofs and 7.

WALL-WALK: *see* Parapet.

WARMING ROOM: room in a religious house where a fire burned for comfort.

WATERHOLDING BASE: early Gothic base with upper and lower mouldings separated by a deep hollow.

WATERLEAF: *see* Enrichments and 3f.

WATERLEAF CAPITAL: Late Romanesque and Transitional type of capital (1b).

WATER WHEELS: described by the way water is fed on to the wheel. *Breastshot*: mid-height, falling and passing beneath. *Overshot*: over the top. *Pitchback*: on the top but falling backwards. *Undershot*: turned by the momentum of the water passing beneath. In a *water turbine*, water is fed under pressure through a vaned wheel within a casing.

WEALDEN HOUSE: type of medieval timber-framed house with a central open hall flanked by bays of two storeys, roofed in line; the end bays are jettied to the front, but the eaves are continuous (8a).

WEATHERBOARDING: wall cladding of overlapping horizontal boards.

WEATHERING or SET-OFF: inclined, projecting surface to keep water away from the wall below.

WEEPERS: figures in niches along the sides of some medieval tombs. Also called mourners.

WHEEL WINDOW: circular, with radiating shafts like spokes. Cf. Rose window.

WROUGHT IRON: *see* Cast iron.

INDEX OF ARCHITECTS, ARTISTS, PATRONS AND RESIDENTS

Names of architects and artists working in the area covered by this volume are given in *italic*. Entries for partnerships and group practices are listed after entries for a single name.

Also indexed here are names/titles of families and individuals (not of bodies or commercial firms) recorded in this volume as having commissioned architectural work or owned or lived in properties in the area. The index includes monuments to members of such families and other individuals where they are of particular interest.

INDEX OF PLACES

Principal references are shown in **bold** type; demolished buildings are shown in *italic*.